Walter Scott (1770–1832) was born in Edinburgh. In his infancy he contracted a form of polio which left him lame in his right leg and led to him being sent to live for the next three years at his grandfather's farm in the Borders. Returning to Edinburgh, he was educated at the High School and Edinburgh University where, like his father before him, he studied law. He served an apprenticeship in the family practice and was called to the Bar as an advocate in 1792. In 1797 he married Charlotte Carpenter. His links with the Borders gave him an enduring interest in the history and the ballads of the region, a passion he pursued when he was appointed Sheriff-Depute for Selkirkshire in 1799, leading to the publication of his collection *The Minstrelsy of the Scottish Border* (1802–3). With an already developed interest in German literature, Scott was persuaded to try his hand at poetry of his own, leading to the long narrative poem *The Lay of the Last Minstrel* (1805) which proved a critical and financial success. This was followed by *Marmion* (1808) and, most successful of all, *The Lady of the Lake* (1810). By this time Scott had been appointed Clerk of the Court of Session in Edinburgh – a post he kept for the rest of his life – and had set up home at a little house in the Borders, which he was to develop over the years into nothing less than a baronial mansion which he called Abbotsford. The vogue for his long historical poems was passing and so he turned to prose fiction, with a manuscript he had started in 1805, subsequently published (anonymously) in 1814 as *Waverley*, a tale set during the 1745 rising. It was an immediate success and was followed by a series of historical novels produced in something of a creative explosion. These titles, later collected as The Waverley Novels ('by the author of Waverley'), included *Guy Mannering* (1815), *The Antiquary* and *Old Mortality* (1816), *Rob Roy* and *Heart of Midlothian* (1818), *The Bride of Lammermoor* and *A*

Legend of Montrose (1819), *Ivanhoe*, *The Abbot* and *The Monastery* (1820), *Redgauntlet* (1824), and many more. He also wrote biographical studies and the *Tales of a Grandfather* series which retold Scottish history for the common reader.

In effect Scott's fiction invented the historical novel – with its different perspectives on past and present values – while the Scottish texts played an enormously influential part in the popular discovery of the Highlands and in the construction of a romantic vision of Scotland which has survived until practically the present day. His books were equally famous in America and in Europe readers hailed him as one of the greatest writers of his age. Scott was made a Baronet in 1818 and supervised the elaborate celebrations to mark George IV's visit to Edinburgh in 1822. When his printer and his publisher, Ballantyne and Constable, suffered a financial crash in 1826 (also the year of his wife's death), Scott's intricate investments led him into insolvency as well, and he had to redouble his writing efforts to pay off his debts – a feat finally accomplished shortly before his death. These difficult years and his poor health are movingly recorded in his *Journal*, which also reveals a fascinating picture of the times, along with his talent for friendship and the breadth of his mind. He took a sea trip to the Mediterranean in 1831, in a frigate on government service, but his health continued to fail and he returned to Abbotsford where he died in 1832.

THE JOURNAL OF
SIR WALTER SCOTT

Edited and Introduced by
W. E. K. ANDERSON

CANONGATE

CLASSICS

87

First published in 1972 by Oxford University Press.
This edition first published as a Canongate Classic
in 1998 by Canongate Books, 14 High Street,
Edinburgh EHI ITE. Introduction and notes
copyright © W. E. K. Anderson 1972, 1998.

The publishers gratefully acknowledge general
subsidy from the Scottish Arts Council towards
the Canongate Classics series and a specific grant
towards the publication of this volume.

Set in 10pt Plantin by Hewer Text Limited,
Edinburgh. Printed and bound by Caledonian
International, Bishopbriggs, Scotland.

British Library Cataloguing-in-Publication Data
A catalogue record for this book is available on
request from the British Library.

ISBN 0 86241 828 3

Preface

Scott's daughter Sophia and her husband, John Gibson Lockhart, may be considered the first editors of Scott's *Journal*. Sophia wrote out a longhand version of the text which was then set up in type for her husband to read. Lockhart selected lengthy extracts for his *Life of Scott*, published in 1837, and added only a few notes, since his narrative provided what the reader was likely to want to know.

The next edition of the *Journal*, (the first in which is appeared as a work in its own right) was brought out by David Douglas in 1890. Again the task of establishing the text was not undertaken by the editor, but in this case by his friend Professor Hume Brown. No one who is familiar with the difficulty of reading Scott's handwriting in his later years will underestimate the problems he faced, and, as Victorian editions go, it is quite acceptable, even if it does not entirely merit Professor Masson's description of it in an early review as 'Sir Walter Scott's Journal in perfect form and with all requisite annotations'.[1] The text has a number of inaccuracies, corrections were made without any indication of the original readings, and passages were omitted without comment; but Douglas knew his Scott well, and his notes (especially to the new edition of 1927) are helpful.

The *Journal*'s next editor was John Guthrie Tait, who set out to revise the Hume Brown text from a photostat in the National Library of Scotland. Unfortunately the work was still incomplete at his death, but the last third was undertaken by W.M.Parker, who proved a better reader of Scott's hand than any of his predecessors. The result was a text superior to Douglas's, although the untimely death of Tait left it unsupported by adequate notes. It appeared in three volumes in 1939, 1941, and 1946, and was reprinted in one volume in 1950.

None of these editions seriously misrepresents Scott in major matters. Each of them, however, has its textual inaccuracies and omissions, and an index which leaves something to be desired. In the footnotes there is no systematic attempt to supply the reader with the information that he needs about the people and events of the *Journal*. It seemed that there was room for a new and more fully annotated

1. See David Masson, *Edinburgh Sketches and Memories*, 1892, p. 204.

text. That was what I was attempting to provide for the Clarendon Press in 1972. This present Canongate Press edition is in fact the paperback edition of that work, with some minor corrections and additions.

My aim has been to provide a complete and accurate version of what Scott actually wrote, with notes which in effect expand the work into a day-by-day biography of Scott's final years. As it happens, Scott's life at this time is exceptionally fully documented. A vast number of the letters he wrote survive, either published or still in manuscript; almost all the letters written to him during these years are preserved, along with dozens written about him by members of his family. We have the business letters and the diary of his publisher, and the minute-book of his trustees. Everyone who met him was likely to record the hours they spent in the company of so famous a man. On this wealth of published and unpublished biographical material, most of it in the great Scott collection of the National Library of Scotland, I have been able to draw freely for the notes.

In editing the *Journal* I have constantly had in mind the aim of producing a readable as well as an accurate edition. Some explanation of the editorial practices adopted may be helpful.

In order to keep the foot of the page as clear as possible of unimportant textual emendations, obvious slips of the pen have been corrected silently. All except repetitions like 'the the' have been listed in Appendix F. Mistakes which are of any interest for the light they throw on Scott's mind or, in some cases, on his pronunciation, have, however, been left in the text and corrected in a footnote.

The spelling and capitalization of the original have been retained, and the editorial punctuation kept as light as possible, in an attempt to retain something of the liveliness and spontaneity of the original that had been lost in previous editions. For reasons of readability or typographical consistency, however, the following alterations have been made:

A full stop has been supplied where, as is often the case, Scott omitted it before a following capital letter.

Brackets, inverted commas, and parentheses between dashes have been closed without comment where Scott forgot to close them. On a few occasions a capital letter has been supplied at the start of direct speech.

The dot after Dr., Mr., and Mrs., which Scott sometimes added, is supplied in every case, and the elevated letter occasionally used by Scott in these and other abbreviations has been brought down.

Ampersands, which Scott frequently but not invariably used, have been expanded.

'To-day' and 'tomorrow', which often appear as two words in the original, have been spelt throughout as they are here. Titles of books and names of ships, as well as quotations from foreign languages, have been set in italics. Scott occasionally underlined words in Latin or French but his practice was not consistent.

Titles of poems, songs, and pictures have been placed in editorial inverted commas and given the usual capital letters.

Date headings have been printed in the form most commonly used by Scott, as plain figures. Where the entry has been assigned to the wrong day in the original, the correct date is used and an explanation added in a footnote or in Appendix E.

Editorial punctuation, where the meaning would otherwise be in doubt or the sentence difficult to read, has been sparingly added. All but a few commas, semicolons, and question-marks are editorial. Colons and exclamation-marks are Scott's, as are dashes and all full stops except those mentioned above.

Emendation has been as sparing as possible. When we have Scott's warrant for it – 'a solecism in point of composition like a Scotch word in speaking is indifferent to me'[1] – I have not emended 'who' to 'who[m]' (p. 530), nor supplied a verb in such entries as 'This a morning of fidgetty nervous confusion' (p. 384), nor obscured Scotticisms like 'out the Bay' (p. 761) by inserting '[of]'. 'Max' has not been expanded to 'Max[popple]', nor 'the D. of B.' to 'the D[uke] of B[uccleuch]', since the flavour of the work depends so much on the hurried inconsequential jotting down of names and impressions. Obvious omissions have, however, been supplied. They appear in square brackets, thus [ ]. These additions have always been made reluctantly, but with least timidity when the omission occurs at the end of a line or page. Scott's mind moved faster than his hand, and it is at these places that syllables or whole words are most apt to be lost. 'Irritabi[lity]' (p. 68) and 'imagina[tion]' (p. 81), for instance, are the final words in their lines. Words which Scott should have omitted for the sake of the sense are enclosed in angular brackets, thus < >.

It was tempting to emend the last hundred pages of the text very considerably. I was reluctant, however, to obscure the 'hideous paralytick custom of *stuttering*'[2] which Scott's pen acquired in his later years, and decided to leave untouched, as far as possible, the mis-spellings and repetitions which so vividly illustrate the decline of his powers. The strangely garbled words of the final months are to be ascribed, therefore, to the confusion of Scott's mind, not to an inattentive reading of the proofs.

1. Entry for 22 April 1826.
2. Entry for 5 April 1831.

Deletions have not been retained. They are relatively few and for the most part without interest. Those of any importance are recorded in footnotes.

Mis-spellings, both Scott's habitual ones and those caused in his later years by confusion of mind, have been retained. The words for which Scott had his own personal spelling are 'accomodation', 'aflicted', 'astmha', 'embarassing', 'knowlege', 'plege' (for 'pledge'), 'segar', 'shufle', 'stopd' (for 'stopped'), 'untill', and 'wellcome'. In addition he usually, but not invariably, shortened the verb-ending 'ed' to plain 'd'.

Some of Scott's idiosyncrasies are worthy of notice. Certain omissions, for instance, occur so often that they probably reflect the way he spoke. He sometimes omitted the final letter of the present participle ('bein', p. 487; 'good-lookin', p. 521) and of the past participle ('look' for 'lookd', p. 117). In his last years the tendency to forget the final 't' in the perfect tense became more marked, and we have 'crep' (p. 652), 'wen' (p. 664), and 'lef' (p. 667). The 'd' sometimes disappears from 'and', as does in the last quarter of the *Journal* the final 'e' on a number of words. From the beginning, the adjective occasionally appears for the adverb and vice versa, and this confusion, connected perhaps with his by then slurred speech, is increasingly marked in the final hundred pages, where, for instance, 'exclusive' (p. 722), 'graduall' (p. 759), and 'splendid' (p. 770) appear instead of the corresponding adverbs.

Other mistakes and mis-spellings give an interesting indication of Scott's accent. He lived in the last age in which educated Edinburgh men spoke Scots rather than English, before increasing commerce of all kinds with England reduced the differences to insignificance. 'Scotch', he wrote to Constable in 1822, 'was a language which we have heard spoken by the learnd and the wise & witty & the accomplishd and which had not a trace of vulgarity in it but on the contrary sounded rather graceful and genteel. You remember how well Mrs. Murray Keith – the late Lady Dumfries – my poor mother & other ladies of that day spoke their native language – it was different from English as the Venetian is from the Tuscan dialect of Italy but it never occurd to any one that the Scotish any more than the Venetian was more vulgar than those who spoke the purer and more classical – But that is all gone & the remembrance will be drownd with us the elders of this existing generation.'[1] Scott was of the old school, and prided himself on his native accent and 'Berwickshire *burr*'.[2] The distinctive vowel sounds of his speaking voice survive for

1. *Letters*, vii. 83.
2. *Letters*, vii. 63.

us in words like 'Johnie' for 'Johnnie' (*passim*), and 'over' for 'offer' (p. 447); in 'debt' for 'date' and 'date' for 'debt' (pp. 444 and 574); and in 'a fear task' for 'a fair task' (p. 477). His *burr* accounts for a mistake like 'perils' for 'pearls' on p. 774.

A word should be added about Scott's quotations. The range of his reading was extraordinary and his memory unusually tenacious. He was able, therefore, to quote effortlessly not only from Shakespeare, the Bible and the Latin texts he had read at school but from ballads, popular collections of poetry, songs, plays and farces. In the novels, as Tom B. Haber showed in 1930,[1] Scott's practice was to invent some of the tags he needed, and to adapt – consciously or unconsciously – the lines he borrowed from other people. In the *Journal* almost every identifiable quotation is misquoted or freely altered, and no doubt many of those which have defied all attempts to ascertain their authorship are half-remembered adaptations of ballads and songs. The references at the foot of the page do not take notice of the correctness or otherwise of the quotation as it appears in the text, unless the link with the original version is so tenuous as to require explanation.

1. *P.M.L.A.*, vol. 45, 1930, pp. 1140–9.

Acknowledgements

My grateful thanks are due to the Pierpont Morgan Library, without whose generosity in making a photostat available the work of producing a new text would have been impossible; to Miss Tait for initiating and to the Abbotsford family for encouraging the project; to Professor William Beattie, until recently Librarian of the National Library of Scotland, for his fatherly guidance and shrewd advice; to the staff of that most friendly of great libraries, especially to Mr. William Park and Mr. Alan Bell; to Lord Clyde, Lord President of the Court of Session, and to Mr. David Edward, Treasurer of the Faculty of Advocates, who were my guides through the labyrinth of Scots Law; to Dr. John Cameron for allowing me to use his transcript of part of Cadell's Diary; to Dr. Donald Sultana for much expert advice on Scott in Malta; to Dr. John Pym of Dublin who identified for me Scott's Irishmen; to Mr. Robert Philp for his assistance with the classical quotations; and to the late Professor W. L. Renwick, to Professor A. F. Falconer, and Miss Mary Lascelles for their advice and encouragement. Mr. Bartle Frere kindly permitted me to quote from unpublished material in his possession. Professor C. P. Brand, Mr. K. W. Collier, Mr. David Fletcher, Mr. J. A. MacLeod, Lord Polwarth, Professor C. M. Robertson, Mr. Basil Skinner, Mr. A. W. Stupps and Mr. J. W. Willis-Fear were good enough to supply answers to some very troublesome questions. Mr. Andrew Burnett, Mr. Nicholas Burnett, Mr. Rory Lea, Mr. Patrick King, Mr. Neil Sanders and Mr. Gareth Pearce gave valuable assistance with the text and index, and Miss Charlotte Borthwick took on the very demanding task of typing the footnotes. Dr. J. C. Corson, with characteristic generosity, answered innumerable questions about matters of fact, and identified for me a great number of troublesome quotations. To him my debt is particularly great.

This edition of Sir Walter Scott's *Journal* owes much to the expert knowledge and advice on which I have fortunately been able to draw so freely. Its errors and deficiencies are of course my responsibility alone.

A special note of thanks to my wife. I am grateful to her not only for her hours of help with the text and the index, but also for submitting so uncomplainingly to the demands made by Sir Walter on the family over the past five years.

W. E. K. A.

Edinburgh, August 1971

FURTHER ACKNOWLEDGEMENTS

The revised edition has benefited from correspondents who were kind enough to supply me with comments and corrections. I am particularly grateful to Professor Frederick Pottle, to Professor Ian Campbell, to J. C. Trewin and to Timothy Strange (who supplied the extract from the manuscript diary of Lady Strange printed in Additional Note 7). As before, my principal debt is to Dr. James Corson, compiler of the *Index and Notes to the Letters of Sir Walter Scott*, who, until his death in 1988, continued to note for me anything relevant to the *Journal* which he came across in the course of his extraordinarily extensive reading.

W. E. K. A.

Lincoln College, Oxford, November 1998

In Memoriam J.C.C.

Contents

Abbreviations Used by Scott

1. Advocate, The   The Lord Advocate, Sir William Rae
2. C and Coy.   Constable and Company
3. Ch. Ba.   The Lord Chief Baron of the Exchequer Court, Sir Samuel Shepherd
4. Ch. Com.   The Lord Chief Commissioner of the Jury Court, the Rt. Hon. William Adam
5. Chief Baron   See 3 above
6. Chief Commissioner   See 4 above
7. H & R   Hurst, Robinson and Company
8. James
    James B   James Ballantyne
    J. B.
9. J. G. L.   John Gibson Lockhart
10. L. C. B.   See 3 above
11. L. C. C.   See 4 above
12. Lord Ch: Com.   See 4 above
13. L. J. C.   The Lord Justice-Clerk, the Rt. Hon. David Boyle
14. L. J. S.   Lady Jane Stuart
15. L. L. S.   Lady Louisa Stuart
16. Lord Register   The Principal Keeper of the Register of Sasines, the Rt. Hon. William Dundas
17. L. S.   Lady Scott
18. Missie   Miss Macdonald Buchanan
19. R. C.   Robert Cadell
20. Sir A. F.   Sir Adam Ferguson
21. Solicitor, The   The Solicitor-General, John Hope
22. S. W. S.   Sir Walter Scott
23. W. C.   Will Clerk
24. *W—k.*   *Woodstock*

Abbreviations Used in the Notes

Abbots.	Abbotsford Collection, Nat. Lib. Scot., MSS 1552–4.
A. L. C.	J. G. Cochrane, *Abbotsford Library Catalogue*, 1838.
Bannatyne Club Minutes	Nat. Lib. Scot., MS. 2046.
Bell's Dictionary and Digest	*Bell's Dictionary and Digest of the Law of Scotland*, ed. George Watson, 1882.
Blair-Adam Estate	William Adam, *Blair Adam Estate*, 1834.
Cadell Letters	Nat. Lib. Scot., MS. 1758 (vol. v of letters written by Scott to Cadell).
Cadell's Diary	Nat. Lib. Scot., MS. 5188.
Centenary Catalogue	*The Scott Centenary Exhibition Catalogue*, 1872.
Charles Scott's Journal	The Journal of Charles Scott, Nat. Lib. Scot., MS. 1614.
Cockburn's *Memorials*	*Memorials of his Time*, Henry Cockburn, 1856.
Cole's 'Memorial of a Tour'	Owen Blayney Cole, 'Memorial of a Tour to Italy', *Cornhill Magazine*, September 1923.
Croker Papers	*The Correspondence and Diaries of J. W. Croker*, ed. L. J. Jennings, 1885.
Dalgleish i, ii, iii.	'Memoirs of William Dalgleish, Butler to Sir Walter Scott', *Cornhill Magazine*, June, July, and August 1931.
Diaries of Helen Graham	*Diaries of Helen Graham*, ed. James Irvine, 1956.
Dibdin	J. C. Dibdin, *Annals of the Edinburgh Stage*, 1888.
Disc. i and ii	Discarded letters of Scott, collected by Grierson (but not printed in the *Letters*), Nat. Lib. Scot., MSS. 1752–3.
D. N. B.	*Dictionary of National Biography*

Douglas	*The Journal of Sir Walter Scott*, ed. David Douglas, new edition, 1927.
Edgar Johnson	Edgar Johnson's *Sir Walter Scott: The Great Unknown*, 1970.
Gell	*Reminiscences of Sir Walter Scott's Residence in Italy, 1832, by Sir William Gell*, ed. J. C. Corson, 1957.
Gibson's *Reminiscences*	John Gibson, *Reminiscences of Sir Walter Scott*, 1871.
Grierson	H. J. C. Grierson, *Sir Walter Scott, Bart.*, 1938.
Hall's *Fragments*	Basil Hall, *Fragments of Voyages*, Third Series, 1840.
Haydon's *Diary*	*The Diary of B. R. Haydon*, ed. W. B. Pope, 1960.
Herd	*Ancient and Modern Scottish Songs*, ed. David Herd, 1791.
Jamieson	Dr. John Jamieson, *Etymological Dictionary of the Scottish Language*, new edition, 1879.
J. G. L.	John Gibson Lockhart.
Lady Shelley's Diary	*The Diary of Frances, Lady Shelley, 1818–73*, ed. Richard Edgecumbe, 1912–13.
Letters	*The Letters of Sir Walter Scott*, ed. H. J. C. Grierson and others, 12 vols., 1932–7.
Letters from Scott's Family	*Letters from Members of Sir Walter Scott's Family*, ed. P. A. Wright-Henderson, 1905.
Letters to and from Scott	Nat. Lib. Scot., MS. 5317.
Letters to Laidlaw	Nat. Lib. Scot., MS. 860.
Letters to Scott	Nat. Lib. Scot., MS. 869.
Life	J. G. Lockhart, *Memoirs of the Life of Sir Walter Scott, Bart.*, second edition, 1851.
Life of Moscheles	Charlotte Moscheles, *The Life of Moscheles*, 1873.
Life of Napoleon	Sir Walter Scott, *The Life of Napoleon Buonaparte*, 1827.
Mackay's *Reminiscences*	MacIntosh Mackay, *Reminiscences*, no date.
Memoirs of Knighton	Lady D. Knighton, *Memoirs of Sir William Knighton*, 1838.

Memoirs of Mathews	Mrs. Mathews, *Memoirs of Charles Mathews*, 1839.
Memoirs of Moore	*Memoirs of Thomas Moore*, ed. Lord John Russell, 1853.
Memoirs of Mrs. Hemans	*Memoirs of Mrs. Hemans by her Sister*, 1839.
Misc. Prose Works	*The Miscellaneous Prose Works of Sir Walter Scott*, 1834–40.
Mrs. Davy's Journal	Mrs. Davy, 'Extracts from a Family Journal', Nat. Lib. Scot., MS. 3389.
Mrs. Hughes's Recollections	*Letters and Recollections of Sir Walter Scott by Mrs. Hughes*, ed. H. G. Hutchinson, 1904.
Nat. Lib. Scot.	The National Library of Scotland.
O. E. D.	*The Oxford English Dictionary*.
Omond	G. W. T. Omond, *The Lord Advocates of Scotland*, 1883.
Partington's *Letter-Books*	*The Private Letter-Books of Sir Walter Scott*, ed. Wilfred Partington, 1930.
P. M. L. A.	*Publications of the Modern Language Association*.
Royal Society Minutes	The Royal Society Minute-Book, MS. in possession of the Royal Society of Edinburgh.
Sederunt Book	The Sederunt Book of the Trustees of James Ballantyne & Co., Nat. Lib. Scot., MSS 112–14.
Shortreed Papers	Nat. Lib. Scot., MS. 8993.
Skene's Memories	*Memories of Sir Walter Scott by James Skene*, ed. Basil Thomson, 1909.
S. N. D.	*The Scottish National Dictionary*.
Susan Frere	Manuscript letters of Susan Frere, in the possession of Bartle Frere, Esq.
Tait	*The Journal of Sir Walter Scott*, ed. J. G. Tait, 1939–46.
Ticknor's Life	George S. Hillard, *Life, Letters and Journals of George Ticknor*, 1876.
Walpole	The Walpole Collection, Nat. Lib. Scot., MSS 3901–19. (Unless otherwise stated, Walpole letters are addressed to Scott.)
W.S.	Writer to the Signet
Youngson	A. J. Youngson, *The Making of Classical Edinburgh*, 1966.

Introduction

It is fortunate that Sir Walter Scott began his *Journal* when he did. He was already fifty-four, famous, and to all appearances wealthy. He was Laird of Abbotsford and a notable member of Edinburgh society; he numbered among his friends almost all the great men of his day; his public was the entire civilized world. As he wrote the first entry in November 1825 his fortunes were at their height. Yet within a few months the wheel had spun wildly and he had lost everything – his land, his money, and the wife he loved. The *Journal*, which would have been the informal record of a major writer's declining years, became instead the revelation of a great man's courage in adversity.

No one can fail to be impressed, like the early reviewer of Douglas's edition, by its account 'of indomitable manliness, and prodigious industry'.[1] He writes through days of pain and sickness; he writes down the depression of spirits which afflicted him more often than his friends or family were allowed to know; he writes day in and day out, weekday and Sunday, in Edinburgh and at Abbotsford, to pay the debts which he considered debts of honour. The *Journal* confirms, too, the opinion of those who knew Scott, that he was one of the pleasantest of great writers. His generosity is everywhere apparent – not merely the generosity which sends £10 to Haydon or £50 to Gillies, but a generosity of judgement, a willingness to be pleased by new acquaintances or new books. His evenness of temper, which only illness seems to have ruffled, is remarkable. He is pestered by coxcombs and eccentrics; his precious time is picked away by bores and foreigners and friends of friends. Scott does not claim the privilege of withdrawing himself, but does the honours of the house till they are gone, and settles again to his work.

The *Journal* is also to some extent a private diary of day-to-day events, although we have Lockhart's word for it that it was intended for publication. 'Scott clearly, and indeed avowedly, considered himself as writing what would one day be published', he told Croker in 1853. 'In his will he distinctly directs what shall be done with the money that his executors shall obtain in respect of this and other

1. David Masson, *Edinburgh Sketches and Memories*, 1892, p. 204.

manuscripts.'[1] No doubt Lockhart is right, although how far Scott's
bankruptcy and the need to turn every word he wrote to account may
have altered his original purpose is matter for speculation. Certainly
the internal evidence supports Lockhart's contention. A reference to
'those [who] may read my confessions'[2] is scarcely conclusive, as it
might refer only to his own family; but Scott's reticence throughout
the whole work seems to clinch the argument. He is much franker –
and ruder – in his correspondence than in his *Journal*. For the
character of Mrs. Jobson, or Mrs. Thomas Scott, or his cousin
Maxpopple, you have to go to the *Letters*; you can make no guess
at them from the *Journal*. Obviously he had one eye on future
publication, and had no wish to cause embarrassment to the people
he wrote about or to his own family. Nonetheless there are trivialities
that he would have expected to be excised, and much that was
obvious to himself and his contemporaries which the lapse of time
has made obscure. Some account of the world in which he lived is
therefore a necessary prelude to the *Journal* itself.

SCOTT'S EDINBURGH: THE CHANGING CITY

The Edinburgh of Sir Walter Scott was a city of astonishing
contrasts. Its centre was still the High Street running down the
hill from the Castle to Holyrood House, but its tenement buildings
and dirty wynds and closes were no longer the homes of the wealthy
and the well-connected. They had moved to what they called the
New Town, the severe and classical streets and squares which had
been built to the north of Princes Street Gardens, linked to the Old
Town by the steep slope of the Mound and the arches of the North
Bridge. Like generations of Edinburgh men before him, Scott was
born into the noisy, crowded squalor of the Old Town, although
the family moved three years later from the College Wynd to one of
a row of unpretentiously elegant houses in George Square, on the
south side of the city. At the time of his marriage Scott took one of
the new houses in Castle Street in the New Town, and there, but
for the financial disaster of 1826, he would have stayed until his
death.

   The New Town was largely created within Scott's lifetime. Craig's
plan was finally accepted, and the first feus (in St. Andrew Square)
were let only four years before he was born; when he married in 1797,
development had moved west only as far as Castle Street; by the time
of the *Journal* the town had grown considerably bigger, and there

1. *Croker Papers*, iii. 295.
2. *Journal*, Entry for 29 April 1829.

were complaints that the atmosphere was affected by the extent of the
expansion to the north. The great public buildings all belong to this
period. The Assembly Rooms in George Street were opened in 1787;
the old Parliament House, the seat of the Law Courts, was given a
classical façade between 1807 and 1810 and became a New Town
building at the heart of the Old Town. The Edinburgh Academy was
opened in 1824, the Royal Institution at the foot of the Mound in
1826, and the Royal High School in Regent Road in 1829.[1]

Every morning during the Session Scott passed from one world to
another as the Clerks' Coach trundled up the Mound to the Parliament
House on the High Street. The change of old ways into new, which is the
theme of *Waverley, Rob Roy*, and *Redgauntlet*, was visible around him in
substantial stone and lime. At the end of the day's work he returned from
the Scotland about which he wrote to the new Scotland in which he lived.
The New Town gave Scott and his generation an environment which
combined gracious living and intimacy to a degree that can scarcely have
been equalled anywhere else at any other time. Within half a mile of
Scott's house – in Princes Street, George Street, Heriot Row, Charlotte
Square, Shandwick Place – lived most of his Edinburgh friends, a
civilized, well-to-do, close-knit community, largely of advocates, many
of them known to each other from their school and college days. Scott
walked the mile home from Court in the afternoon, and he could go on
foot to the dinner parties and supper parties for which Edinburgh was
renowned. It was a far remove from the Edinburgh of the novels, from
Prince Charles leaving Holyrood for Prestonpans, from Covenanters
tried and tortured in the Laigh Hall, or Captain Porteous seized from the
Heart of Midlothian and lynched in the Grassmarket. That Edinburgh
survives in the novels. The *Journal* belongs to the New Town.

THE LAW

The most influential and frequently the most able men of Scott's time
in Edinburgh were lawyers. Whether or not he practised at the Bar, a
young man of good connections normally attended classes in law and
became a member of the Faculty of Advocates. Most of Scott's
friends in Edinburgh were therefore members of this 'noblesse of the
robe',[2] and references to the Parliament House and its Courts are so
frequent that some knowledge of the structure of the legal system in
Scott's time is necessary to a full understanding of the *Journal*.

The supreme civil court in Scotland (subject to a right of appeal to

1. For details of these and other buildings see A. J. Youngson's
   admirable *The Making of Classical Edinburgh*, 1966.
2. *Redgauntlet*, Letter II.

the House of Lords) is the Court of Session. The Judges are known as
the Lords of Session, and in 1825 there were fifteen of them. The
seven junior Lords of Session sat in the Outer House to hear cases at
first instance; the other eight sat in the Inner House in two Divisions
to hear appeals. The First Division was presided over by the Lord
President, the Second by the Lord Justice-Clerk. Scott sat as Clerk of
Session in the First Division.

The supreme criminal court, from which there is no appeal to the
House of Lords, is the High Court of Justiciary. In Scott's day the
Judges of this Court were the Lord Justice-Clerk and five Lords of
Session, known in this capacity as the Lords Commissioners of
Justiciary. Since this Court had its own Clerks of Justiciary, Scott
was professionally involved only in its sittings on Circuit at Jedburgh,
which he had to attend as Sheriff of Selkirkshire.

The Teind Court, which sat every second Wednesday during
session, performed administrative and judicial functions connected
with parish churches, manses, stipends, and 'teinds', or tithes. Its
Judges were the Lords of Session, but the Court had its own Clerks,
so Scott was free on a 'Teind Wednesday'.

The Jury Court, established in the teeth of heated opposition as
recently as 1815, introduced jury trials in civil causes to Scotland. The
Lord Chief Commissioner, who presided, was Scott's friend William
Adam of Blair-Adam. This Court had no original jurisdiction but
tried issues of fact remitted to it by, for instance, the Court of Session,
the Admiralty Court, or the House of Lords. Its existence as a
separate Court, which was appropriate while civil jury trial was an
innovation in Scotland, came to an end in 1830 when it was merged
with the Court of Session.

The Court of Exchequer concerned itself with such matters as
Customs and Excise, the approval of Sheriffs' accounts, and the
collection of Crown debts. The Lord Chief Baron of the Exchequer
Court (throughout most of the period of the *Journal* Scott's close
friend Sir Samuel Shepherd) was assisted by two Barons of Exchequer. The Court did very little, and Scott would not have refused a
Baron's gown had it been offered to him in 1826.[1]

The previous twenty years had been a period of upheaval and
reform. Between 1808 and 1830 the Court of Session, which
Cockburn described as 'a mob of fifteen judges, meeting without
previous consultation, and each impatient for independent eminence, and many of them liable to be called away and to return
irregularly in the course of the same day',[2] was reshaped in the

1. *Journal*, Entry for 4 March 1826.
2. Cockburn's *Memorials*, ch. 2.

manner described above. In 1825 the prize jurisdiction of the Admiralty Court was transferred to the High Court of Admiralty in England, and there was a far-reaching reorganization of the Sheriff Courts. To many of these changes Scott was opposed. The tendency in every case was towards a closer conformity with England, dictated not by reason but by 'Anglomania – a rage of imitating English forms and practices',[1] and Scott, whose poems and novels celebrated, as he said of *Waverley*, 'some traits of those characters and manners peculiar to Scotland the last remnants of which vanishd during my own youth',[2] saw Scots Law and the Scottish Church as the last bastions of national independence. He was not, however, opposed to all legal reforms. Indeed he acted as Secretary to the Parliamentary Commission which prepared the way for the reforms of 1808, and he voted with Jeffrey and other Whigs to reduce the number of judges in the Court of Session – a reform finally effected in 1830.

Scott did not practise long at the Bar. When the *Journal* opens he had held for more than twenty years two legal offices which brought him a decent salary and little danger of too much work. A Sheriff's duties were wide-ranging, but not particularly onerous – especially in Selkirkshire, which had a small, scattered, and, if poaching were left out of the question, a generally law-abiding population. Minor breaches of the law of all kinds came before his Court, and, as was inevitable in days of slow communications, frequent civil disorder, and no police force, he had considerable administrative and magisterial functions. It is clear from the *Journal* that Scott performed his duties conscientiously. He works on Sheriff Court processes, regularly transmits the county money to the Sheriff-Clerk, superintends elections to Parliament, creates a force of Special Constables during the unrest of 1830 and 1831, and conducts investigations into cases of assault and riotous behaviour; he attends the Circuit Court at Jedburgh, and occasionally presides himself in the Sheriff Court at Selkirk.

The Sheriff, who was paid £300 a year, was allowed to appoint a Sheriff-Substitute, resident in the county, to hear cases and conduct the day-to-day business on his behalf. During the years covered by the *Journal* Scott's deputy was his cousin William Scott of Maxpoffle, usually referred to as 'Max' or 'Maxpopple', who was neither very intelligent nor very efficient, but who badly needed the salary. From the letters which survive it would appear

1. *Substance of the Speeches delivered by some members of the Faculty of Advocates*, 1807, p. 33, Advocates Library C. 27. 3.
2. *Letters*, iii. 457.

that the real power lay in the hands of an admirable Sheriff-Clerk, Andrew Lang, grandfather of the man of letters.

During legal terms Scott was necessarily absent from his sheriffdom, by virtue of his other duties as one of the Principal Clerks to the Court of Session. The Clerks were not the mere scribes that their title suggests, but held a position roughly analogous to that of a Town Clerk or a Clerk of Parliament. They had charge of the papers connected with a case, and were responsible for ensuring that the correct legal procedures were followed. At the end of the debate they had to reduce the Judge's decision as delivered from the Bench to a concise written decree or 'interlocutor'. A Clerkship of Session was not a sinecure, but the salary of £1300 with which it was rewarded was handsome remuneration for the work involved. The Court sat from the 12th of November to the 24th of December, from the 15th of January to the 11th of March, and from the 12th of May to the 11th of July. Scott was not at the table before 10 a.m. and was often finished for the day by 1 p.m. If the sitting was prolonged beyond 2 p.m. he felt aggrieved enough to mention it in his *Journal*. Since cases were shared between three Clerks, there was often time during the day to write letters – although not novels, as he was at pains to make clear.[1] Saturday was a working day, but Monday was not, and Scott also had a clear day every second Wednesday, when there was a sitting of the Teind Court.

ABBOTSFORD

Because of his two official positions Scott divided his time between Edinburgh and Abbotsford. By 1825 the house, whose enlargement and embellishment had been one of his principal concerns for more than ten years, was at last complete. A great ball to celebrate his son's engagement to Jane Jobson was held in January of that year. He could look forward to spending his last years in the 'Conundrum Castle'[2] which he had created beside the Tweed, devoting himself to the care of his rising woods and plantations. Financially Abbotsford may have been the Dalilah who brought Scott to ruin,[3] but to see it, as so many commentators have done, as the embodiment of Scott's yearning for a feudal past, which he could relive as Laird of Abbotsford, is perverse. The plain facts are that an estate was the sensible investment for a man who was getting on in the

1. *Journal*, Entry for 21 March 1826 and note.
2. *Journal*, Entry for 6 January 1828.
3. *Journal*, Entry for 18 December 1825.

world, that the Sheriff of Selkirkshire was bound to live for some part of the year on Tweedside, and that Scott's was only one of 'the numerous families having independent fortunes that have chosen the neighbourhood for a place of residence, attracted', the *Statistical Account of Roxburghshire* suggested in 1841, 'by the amenity of the situation'.[1] Most of Scott's friends owned houses and estates in the country round Edinburgh or in the Borders; and by comparison with Arniston or Melville Castle, Mellerstain and Minto, Abbotsford is homely rather than grandiose. The public rooms are intimate, the upstairs more on the scale of a cottage than of a Gothic castle. For all the extravagance of its details, Abbotsford is a house for living in. It pleased Scott to return to the country from which his ancestors came, but he had other good reasons for building there.

Nonetheless he overreached himself. The house and its embellishments cost thousands of pounds that were always to be earned by the next novel or the next novel but one, and land was a constant temptation. As early as 1816, long before the house was built or money laid aside to pay for it, he had added Kaeside to Abbotsford; he bought Toftfield in 1817, and he carried as far as Italy the dream of buying the neighbouring estate of Faldonside from Nicol Milne.

In 1825 Abbotsford was finished, and, unless Scott lost the favour of the public, it would be paid for in a few years' time. But the financial storm-clouds were already gathering.

THE FINANCIAL CRASH

The country-wide financial crisis of 1825 had already brought down numerous banks and business houses when on 14 January 1826 Constable's London agents, Hurst, Robinson & Coy., stopped payment. Their fall brought down in turn Archibald Constable & Coy., Scott's publishers, and with them James Ballantyne & Coy., the firm which printed the Waverley Novels and in which Scott himself was a partner. As there was no limited liability in those days, Scott himself was held responsible not only for his private debts of £20,000, but also for the entire debts of the concern, which amounted to nearly £100,000.

This huge sum is largely accounted for by the incautious use of Accommodation Bills by Scott, Ballantyne, and Constable. An Accommodation Bill was a type of Bill of Exchange where one party lent his name in order to 'accommodate' another and enable

1. p. 63.

him to raise capital at a discount. In the case of an ordinary Bill of Exchange the party who signed as Acceptor intended to pay the sum due on the due date, but in the case of an Accommodation Bill the true intention was that the Drawer of the Bill would redeem or 'retire' it on or before the due date, thus relieving the Acceptor of his liability. If, however, the Drawer could not pay when the date came, the Acceptor was liable. The position of the Acceptor was therefore very much like that of a person guaranteeing an overdraft.

Archibald Constable & Coy. and James Ballantyne & Coy. were financed to a great extent by accommodating each other. Their system was to keep the amount guaranteed by each firm roughly equal and to adjust the balance from time to time. At the crash Archibald Constable & Coy. had accommodated James Ballantyne & Coy. to the extent of £29,088. 2s. 6d., and James Ballantyne & Coy. had accommodated Archibald & Coy. to the extent of £29,624. 2s. 9d., but neither firm had funds sufficient to repay the debts guaranteed by the other.

Scott, as a partner in James Ballantyne & Coy., was liable on both sets of Bills, since the partnership was the Drawer of one set and the Acceptor of the other. In addition he was liable on a further set of Bills which he had accepted in order to accommodate James Ballantyne & Coy. In the event, the liability of both firms was discharged by Scott, since the dividend of 2s. 9d. in the £ paid by Constable & Coy. was set off against interest.

The full extent of Scott's liability was not immediately recognized. The Trustees' first calculation of the claims against Scott and James Ballantyne & Coy., and of the funds available to meet them, was as follows:

	£	s.	d.
Amount of Claims	104,081	15	6
Funds	69,456	2	4
	34,625	13	2[1]

This was an underestimate. By the end of 1827, when the first dividend came to be paid, the claims were more accurately assessed at £120,899. 5s. 6d.[2] – and these figures did not include £10,000 raised on the estate a few days before the crash. The principal debts were:

1. Sederunt Book, i. 17.
2. Ibid., i. 333.

	£	s.	d.
Scott's private debts	20,066	19	9
J. B. & Coy.'s debts	12,615	6	7
Discounted bills granted by A. C. & Coy. to J. B. & Coy.	39,088	2	6
Discounted bills granted by J. B. & Coy. to A. C. & Coy.	29,624	2	9
Discounted bills granted by Scott to J. B. & Coy.	15,365	13	2
Debts for which Scott was liable, but which were proper debts of A. C. & Coy.	9,129	9	0[1]

The assets of Scott and Ballantyne, individually and as a company, totalled £48,494, of which Scott's share was almost exactly half. It was made up as follows:

	£	s.	d.
Life-rent of Abbotsford	8,491	10	0
Farm Stock	1,000	0	0
Library	5,000	0	0
Furniture	3,000	0	0
39 Castle Street	2,500	0	0
Coach House	200	0	0
Copyrights	4,600	0	0
	24,791	10	0[2]

Scott's assets were just sufficient to have met the private claims against him; they could not begin to pay off the debts of James Ballantyne & Coy. In any case it would not have been sensible to dispose of most of these assets for ready money, and the Trustees did not. On the understanding that Scott would write for their benefit, they left him Abbotsford to live in, along with his library and furniture, and since the copyrights were of infinitely greater value in their own hands they too were not sold. Their best hope was to trust in Scott's own resolve to write his way out of his difficulties. 'This right hand shall work it all off', he had said,[3] and work it off, with Cadell's help, he did.

1. Ibid., i. 4–9, and James Glen's account of Scott's affairs (which should be read) in *Letters*, i. lxxx–xcv.
2. Sederunt Book, i. 10–15.
3. Cockburn's *Memorials*, ch. 7.

When the crash came three possibilities were open to Scott: *Cessio*, Sequestration, or a Trust Deed. By the procedure known as *Cessio Bonorum* an insolvent debtor could, if his creditors agreed, put all his goods at the disposition of his creditors. He remained liable for the full amount of his debts, but could no longer be imprisoned for his failure to pay. At one point in the *Journal*[1] McCulloch of Ardwall avails himself of this procedure to procure his release from jail. For Scott, however, it was not the best solution, since it would have entailed the loss of his library, his furniture, and his life-rent of Abbotsford.

Sequestration was similar to modern procedures. It gave the debtor an absolute discharge, provided that four-fifths of the creditors, in number and value, concurred. It was available only to debtors engaged in trade. When harried by Abud in 1827 Scott was nearly forced to apply for Sequestration. Had he done so, it would have eased his burden and perhaps lengthened his life, but it would not have suited his creditors, who would have received some shillings in the pound instead of the full amount. None the less Sequestration was the course Scott himself would have recommended to a client in his position.[2] Why then did he not avail himself of it at the start? Firstly, because he was a gentleman. Sequestration was for debtors engaged in trade, and although Scott was legally entitled to it by virtue of his business interests, he could not take advantage of it without sinking himself for ever, in his own eyes and in the eyes of his friends, to the level of a shopkeeper. He might by this means have saved his library and bid his creditors defiance; but in doing so, he would, as he put it, in a court of honour deserve to lose his spurs.[2] Secondly, almost all the money he owned and much of the money he owed was sunk in the estate of Abbotsford, which he had effectively removed from the reach of his creditors by settling it on his son Walter at his marriage only a year before. If he had petitioned for Sequestration, he could have paid perhaps 7s. in the £; had he still owned Abbotsford, instead of merely the life-rent, he might have paid double. Evil tongues would not be lacking to whisper that he had foreseen the crash, and to protect Abbotsford had taken steps which although legal were scarcely honourable.

Instead, Scott took the third way that was open to him and signed a Trust Deed for his creditors. This had the advantage of allowing all parties to agree on the conditions that were to be observed. In this case the Trustees decided to sell 39 Castle Street,

1. Entry for 26 January 1831.
2. *Journal*, Entry for 24 January 1826.

but to leave Scott his official salary to live on, and the use of his library and furniture at Abbotsford. Scott in turn bound himself in these terms:

> I the said Sir Walter Scott have resolved to employ my time and talents on the production of such literary works as shall seem to me most likely to promote the ends I have in view, the sums arising from which works I am also desirous to devote to the payment of the debts owing by me as a Partner of the said Company [James Ballantyne & Coy.] and as an individual.[1]

Throughout the period of the *Journal* that is in effect what Scott did. Almost every moment when he is free from the Court is employed in the attempt to write off his debts. On Sundays, or on wet days at Abbotsford, he works harder than on ordinary days. As 1827 succeeds 1826 the number of Entries which record oir leaves completed in the day, instead of the original task of three, show that he is working twice as hard as before, and much harder than he ought. He has always written in the morning – that is, before breakfast – and in the forenoon at Abbotsford; now writing before dinner 'has become a habit',[2] and usually he works also in the evening. In 1829 he begins to fall asleep as he writes *Anne of Geierstein*. By 1831 the compulsion to write and keep writing, despite illness and disability, is so strong that Moore is told that 'The great object in sending him abroad is to disengage his mind from the strong wish to write by which he is haunted.'[3]

The result of Scott's unremitting labour was a staggering collection of titles. *Woodstock* was already begun at the time of the crash, and the first volume of the *Life of Napoleon* was finished. Between 1826 and 1831 Scott wrote five novels – *Woodstock, The Fair Maid of Perth, Anne of Geierstein, Count Robert of Paris,* and *Castle Dangerous*; one collection of short stories – *Chronicles of the Canongate*; one play – *Auchindrane*; the nine-volume *Life of Napoleon*; a two-volume *History of Scotland* for Dr. Lardner's *Cabinet Cyclopaedia*; four series of *Tales of a Grandfather*; Notes and Introduction to the Magnum edition of the novels; and two volumes of essays for the *Miscellaneous Prose Works*.

The numbers of each edition and the profits to the Trust were of this order:

1. Sederunt Book, i. 41.
2. *Journal*, Entry for 6 February 1827.
3. *Memoirs of Moore*, vi. 227.

	Copies	£
Woodstock	9850	6075
Napoleon	6000	
and	2000	9413
Chronicles of the Canongate	8750	2228
Fair Maid of Perth	8500	4200
Anne of Geierstein	8500	4200
Count Robert of Paris and		
Castle Dangerous	5000	1750[1]

In addition the small Collected Editions brought in £1950, and the Magnum Opus or Collected Edition, which was the means in the end of liquidating the debt, had contributed £18,000 by the time Scott went abroad. In less than six years he made nearly £50,000 for his creditors.

He also made some thousands for himself. It was not in his nature to pinch and scrape. 'Papa is a bad hand at economizing', Anne told Moore. 'All his great plans of retrenchment have ended in selling my horse.'[2] In truth no amount of retrenchment could have enabled him to live within his official income of less than £2000 a year, as long as he had Abbotsford, or as long as his fame drew every traveller of rank and eminence who visited Scotland to pass along Tweedside. His own generosity too made a mockery of his economies: £10 to save Haydon from his creditors; £5 to Laidlaw; £20 to Charles; £100 to Walter; £50 to Gillies and £50 again. 'I will grow hard-hearted and do no more',[3] Scott resolves in despair; but the next appeal always finds the same open hand.

Money had to be found from somewhere, and it came from the same unfailing source. In addition to the £50,000 for his creditors, Scott earned close on £6000 for himself. The four series of *Tales of a Grandfather* brought him more than £3000; there was £1500 from Dr. Lardner for his *History of Scotland*; £500 from Cadell for *Chronicles of the Canongate*; £100 or £50 for every lengthy review for the *Quarterly* or *Foreign Quarterly*. The Trustees were embarrassed to find that Scott was writing for his own profit as well as for theirs. The first case was *Chronicles of the Canongate*, which Scott intended to publish anonymously in a limited edition for a payment of £500. When he changed his mind and allowed Cadell to extend the impression to 8000, he told the Trustees about the work and stipulated that a further £2000 should be paid to them.[1] *Tales of a*

1. Sederunt Book, ii. 193–200.
2. *Memoirs of Moore*, v. 125.
3. *Journal*, Entry for 12 June 1829.

Grandfather posed them more of a problem. Scott kept the proceeds for himself, without a word to the Trustees, other than a remark 'in a jocular manner' to Gibson: 'Remember I do not mean to give you this little Book, I must keep it for myself to pay my current expenses and for my family.'[1] After anxious discussion they acted magnanimously:

> taking into view how largely the creditors have drawn and were continuing to draw from the treasures of his genius since his embarrassments came upon him, and the *high moral feeling* from which his great and productive exertions on their behalf spring, and how indispensably necessary it was both for his health and his spirits that he should continue to live in the same easy and comfortable style to which he had long been accustomed, the Trustees did not see it to be their duty to interfere with him in reference to the works in question.[2]

No claim was made either on his *History of Scotland* or his *Quarterly* money, and it was only when *Castle Dangerous* came to be written and they discovered that 'without communicating . . . with the Trustees Sir Walter had disposed of the First Edition of this new Book to Mr. Cadell and had applied the author's money to his own purposes',[3] that they had to make a stand. But by then Scott was too ill to be fully aware of what he was doing.

His contention that these works were written in his own time, 'in the hours snatched literally from rest and exercise',[1] is not to be taken as the whole truth, for the *Journal* Entries quite clearly show that, for instance, throughout the months of October 1827 and June 1828 he wrote nothing other than *Tales of a Grandfather*. The sums involved, however, can never have amounted to more than an eighth of what he was paying into the Trust, and ultimately it was in everyone's interest that he should be as free as possible from financial worries.

THE ARBITRATION

The Trustees of the two bankrupt companies – James Ballantyne & Coy., and Archibald Constable & Coy. – inevitably found themselves in dispute over a number of questions, and they agreed to submit their differences to the arbitration of Alexander Irving, who was raised to the Bench shortly afterwards as Lord Newton. Since the

1. Sederunt Book, ii. 214.
2. Ibid., ii. 214–15.
3. Ibid., ii. 251.

Journal's frequent references to the progress of the arbitration are confusing and in places apparently contradictory, it is worth setting out the individual points at issue.

Constable's Trustees laid claim to the *Life of Napoleon* and *Woodstock*, on the grounds that they had agreed with Scott to publish them. Scott's Trustees, in reply, argued that any agreement lapsed at the failure of Archibald Constable & Coy., for a company that no longer existed could not carry out its part of the bargain by publishing the works in question. While Lord Newton pondered, the works were completed and published, and by mutual agreement the profits were banked until the arbiter gave his judgement. When he declared in favour of Scott, on the grounds that the words 'had never been the subject of a completed bargain',[1] the Trustees were able at last to pay their first dividend.

At the time of the crash six volumes of *Miscellaneous Prose Works* were in preparation. Two volumes were already in Constable's possession, two volumes were in Ballantyne's printing office, and two volumes were as yet unfinished. Since in that state they were of no use to anyone, Scott proposed in July 1826 that he should supply the necessary copy, and that the whole work should be published as soon as possible, the profits to be laid aside until Lord Newton decided to whom they rightly belonged. The *Prose Works* were accordingly published jointly by Cadell in Edinburgh and Longman in London; but as Lord Newton decided in favour of Archibald Constable & Coy. ('altho' they had not paid the price', as the minutes of a meeting of Scott's Trustees complains, 'but had merely granted Bills which were dishonoured and now rank on Sir Walter Scott's Estate'),[2] the only profit to the Trust was £200 for reissuing and putting to press.

Scott also lost the copyrights of his earlier novels. These he had sold to Constable, but he argued that part of them remained his property as £3800 of the purchase price had never been paid. The arbiter declared otherwise; Constable's Trustees put them up for sale, and Cadell and Scott's Trustees had to buy them back for £8400.[3]

The final question to be settled was the ownership of the manuscripts of the novels. Scott had given these to Constable, but the condition on which the gift was made – that the secret of his authorship should be preserved – had been infringed, he said, by Constable. Lord Newton decided, however, that they remained the

1. Sederunt Book, ii. 134.
2. Ibid., ii. 200.
3. See the Entry for 20 December 1827.

property of Constable's creditors, as they were a gift of a remunera-
tory nature. They were sold at Evans's rooms in London in 1831 for
only a few hundred pounds. *Waverley* fetched £18, *Ivanhoe* £12, and
Rob Roy the top price of £50.[1]

On three out of the five main issues before him, Lord Newton
decided against Scott. Nonetheless 'the grand questions'.* of the
profits of *Woodstock* and the *Life of Napoleon* were settled in his
favour, and the loss of the copyrights, on which all hopes of paying off
the debt by the judicious management of further editions depended,
was not irreparable.

POLITICAL AFFAIRS

Scott followed politics with more than a spectator's interest. He was
the friend of Canning, Peel, and Wellington, and acquainted with
many other members of the Cabinet.[3] His link with London during
the turbulent years to which the *Journal* belongs was Lockhart, a
faithful and frequent correspondent on political affairs. By instinct
and long habit Scott was a high Tory, and on most of the important
issues he held the views that one would expect. On the Catholic
Question, however, his visit to Ireland in 1825 had made him change
his mind, and he gave a guarded welcome to the passage of the
Catholic 'Emancipation' Act in 1829, which threw open most civil
and military offices to Roman Catholics.

To Reform, however, he remained resolutely opposed. He did not
understand the forces that were at work, nor see that the new patterns
of production and employment forced on the country by the
industrial revolution and the needs of the war against Napoleon
had altered society beyond any possibility of going back. What he saw
was a prosperous and contented population of peasants and small
farmers turned in one generation into 'the stern sullen unwashd
artificers whom you see lounging sulkily along the streets of the towns
in Lancashire',[4] and unruly mobs filled with revolutionary ideas.

Reform of the franchise was, however, necessary as well as
inevitable. Omond, in his book *The Lord Advocates of Scotland*,
describes a state of affairs which cried out for action:

In Scotland the state of the representation was far worse than in
England. The population was, in round numbers, two millions

1. Cunningham, 19 August 1831, Abbots.
2. *Journal*, Entry for 27 October 1827.
3. For the Cabinets of the *Journal* years see Appendix D.
4. *Journal*, Entry for 24 November 1826.

three hundred and sixty thousand. The franchise was in the hands of about three thousand persons. The county franchise was the privilege of the freeholders. Of these fully one-half were Paper Barons, voters who possessed no property, but had voting qualifications. In Midlothian, out of one hundred and seventy-two electors, one hundred and forty-one were paper voters. . . . In Buteshire, out of twenty-one electors, twenty were paper voters. . . . The burgh franchise was in the hands of the self-elected Town Councils. Edinburgh, the population of which was upward of one hundred and sixty-two thousand, had thirty-three electors, the members of its Town Council; but the average number of voters in a Scottish burgh was nineteen, the average number of the corporations. The distribution of the burgh seats was, moreover, grossly absurd. Glasgow, with a population of one hundred and forty-seven thousand, had one-fourth of a member, whom it shared with Renfrew, Rutherglen, and Dumbarton, whose united populations came to a little more than ten thousand. Paisley with twenty-six thousand inhabitants, Greenock with twenty-two thousand, Kilmarnock with twelve thousand, Falkirk with eleven thousand, had no representation in Parliament. But five small burghs in Fife, the united populations of which amounted to only six thousand, returned a member.[1]

The reforms projected by Lord John Russell in March 1831 seem scarcely radical enough to make much impression on a situation as desperate as this. Only 60,000 new voters in Scotland were added by the new measures extending the franchise (i) to householders in the burghs rated at £10, and (ii) to all those in the counties who possessed real property to the value of £10, or were tenants on a long lease paying at least £50 in rent. But to Scott these proposals, as embodied in three successive Reform Bills,[2] were 'the most uncalld for attack upon a free constitution . . . which ever was ventured in my day'.[3] He campaigned against them with vigour, and urged his younger friends to adopt the same uncompromising principles. The news that the Third Reform Bill had finally received the Royal Assent in July 1832 was probably kept from him, but it would have consoled him a little, as he lay on his deathbed, to know that his young chief, the Duke of Buccleuch, as Scott had hoped he would, 'to the last protested against the bill'.[4]

1. Omond, pp. 309–10.
2. For the timetable of events see Appendix D, p. 825.
3. *Journal*, 'Interval', p. 743.
4. Omond, p. 328.

THE PEOPLE OF THE JOURNAL

Sir Walter Scott was fifty-four in 1825 and Lady Scott a year older. There is no clear description of her in the *Journal*, only the hint that she was not the person she had been. Other diarists were less reticent. 'Lady Scott was a little, made-up sort of personage in my time,' writes an Edinburgh lawyer, 'luxuriant, dark, and I should say not natural curls, shading a yellow face, blushing under a real or artificial bloom of crimson, a very little figure, and a *bustling* demeanour exhibited both a physical and moral manner in singular contrast to the manly plainness of her illustrious husband.'[1] Helen Graham was struck too by the 'complete contrast to her husband: she is a funny looking little bodie and very fond of showy dress, and completely foreign both in manner and appearance. She is said to be very variable towards her acquaintances. She was so kind, sweet and hospitable to us; nothing could exceed it.'[2] Lady Shelley found her in her younger days 'the greatest bore in Europe', speaking 'an almost unintelligible broken English',[3] and Mrs. Grant of Laggan thought her a snob. Scott's own testimony, however, should not be ignored. 'Whatever were her failings,' he wrote to Sophia after her death, 'they hurt only herself and arose out of bodily illness and must be weighd against one of the most sincere loyal and generous hearts that ever blood warmd.'[4]

His elder son Walter was twenty-four when the *Journal* opens. He was tall and bewhiskered, rode beautifully, and was seriously devoted to his army duties as a Captain in the 15th Hussars. Scott adored him. 'He has good sense and the most perfect good temper,' he writes to Lady Louisa Stuart, 'bel cavalier beau sabreur a very kind husband to his little wife.'[5] But he was also obstinate,[6] occasionally uncivil,[7] and, on the evidence of those who met him in Italy, 'rather an adept at the gaming-table'.[8]

His wife Jane, whom he had married in January 1825, was Sir Adam Ferguson's niece. 'Poor Jane's heart is so sincere and good that one must make considerable allowance for the narrowness of her

1. Hamilton Russell, W. S. See *Chambers Journal*, 6th series, vol. 5 (March 1902).
2. *Diaries of Helen Graham*, p. 37.
3. *Lady Shelley's Diary*, ii. 42.
4. *Letters*, x. 39.
5. *Letters*, x. 239.
6. See, for instance, *Letters*, x. 493 and 496.
7. *Letters*, xi. 190–1.
8. Cole's 'Memorial of a Tour', p. 261.

education',[1] Scott wrote to Walter, forgetting to mention the even greater allowances that should be made for the estate and fortune she brought with her. Mrs. Thomas Scott found her 'rather retired',[2] and such of her letters as survive reveal a humourless, insipid girl. To Scott's great grief she had no children. Neither the Lockharts nor Anne enjoyed her company,[3] but she was at least preferable to her widowed mother, 'the fat, vulgar Mrs. Jobson'. Mrs. Grant of Laggan says that she was not entirely happy at the match: 'her Jane might have looked higher; it was only a baronetcy, and quite a late creation'.[4] She was troublesome before the wedding – 'A perfect allegory on the banks of the Nile and all for nonsense of the first water'[5] – and no great favourite with her son-in-law after it.[6]

Scott's younger son Charles was 'a nice young man',[7] cleverer, more likeable, and more attached to his family than Walter. He was a little deaf and at times terribly afflicted by rheumatism. In 1825 he was still at Oxford; afterwards he was placed in the Foreign Office, and he died in 1841 of a fever caught while on a mission to Persia.

Sophia was Scott's favourite daughter, and 'much of her father's temper' was evident in 'her placidity of disposition'.[8] He loved to hear her sing Scots songs and was proud of her skill on the harp. Anne did not share his opinion: 'Sophia is rather too much with her harp,' she writes to Missie, 'I wish she would take example of old times and hang it up.' She was not strong, but she clearly made the most of her indispositions – much of her life was spent upon her sofa. Walter calls her 'a most established coddler'[9] and 'a croaker of the first magnitude',[10] and Scott was pleased when she found 'an anti-druggist' like Dr. Gooch to look after her in London.[11] She married John Gibson Lockhart in 1820. Their first child, Johnnie, who had a disease of the spine, was born in 1821. Walter and Charlotte were born during the *Journal* years, in 1826 and 1828.

John Lockhart, Scott's biographer, was by this time closer to him in

1. *Letters*, ix. 348.
2. 31 July 1827, Walpole.
3. Lockhart, 23 February 1826, Walpole; and Anne, 17 June 1826, Abbots.
4. Elizabeth Grant, *Memoirs of a Highland Lady*, ed. Andrew Tod, Edinburgh, 1992, ii. 74.
5. To Ballantyne, n.d. [1827], Letters to and from Scott.
6. See, for instance, Walter, 5 October 1829, Walpole.
7. *Letters*, x. 84.
8. Lockhart, 27 April 1826, Walpole.
9. 22 July 1830, Disc. i. 93.
10. 6 March 1831, Walpole.
11. *Journal*, Entry for 14 March 1826.

some ways than either of his sons. He was of the literary world and
Scott could discuss his work with him as with no one else. His
departure for London to become editor of the *Quarterly* was a loss
which was never made good, although it had the compensation of
quick and full access to events in the capital. Lockhart wrote
continually to Scott from London, two or three times a week if
political affairs were interesting, and though these letters have salt
enough to recall the satirist of the *Blackwood* days, they reveal a liking
for his father-in-law and a fundamental kindness with which he is not
always credited. To Scott he was 'the Hidalgo', prevented from
reaching the highest eminence only by a characteristically Scottish
mixture of pride and diffidence that made him reluctant to push
himself in society.

Scott's younger daughter Anne became the companion of his last
years. On the evidence of a young man who met her in Italy, 'she was
very pretty, with good eyes, clear colour, dark brown hair, and tall
figure',[1] and the truth of his description is attested by the fine portrait
of her which hangs at Abbotsford. He added that 'there was little or
nothing of the parental Doric in her accent'. Andrew Shortreed, who
met her in May 1827, found her 'clever – good looking – unaffected –
some what witty and rather arch',[2] and as a letter-writer she displays a
satirical and irreverent wit at times too cutting for the comfort of
those nearest to her. 'Miss Scott seems very satirical', was Helen
Graham's first impression of her. 'I fancy as Sir Walter's daughter,
she thinks she ought to be clever, which she is not, I am sure, and so
mistakes censure and satire for wit and cleverness. Scarcely a girl in
Edinburgh she had not something or other to say of, and unfavourable in general, which is a bad sign, I really think, particularly to a
person she never saw or knew before. I know I felt as if my turn would
come to be talked ill of to somebody else, when I myself was not
present.'[3] That she was also strong-minded and capable Scott himself
discovered only at the time of his wife's death, but Lockhart had
already discerned 'what a strong fund of good sense lies under the
disguize of her ladyship's persifflage'.[4] She was twenty-two when the
Journal opens, and she died unmarried in 1833.

Outside his immediate family the two men with whom Scott was
most concerned during these years were his printer and his publisher.
He first met James Ballantyne, usually referred to in the *Journal* as
'James' or 'J. B.', in the grammar school at Kelso. In 1802 Scott

1. Cole's 'Memorial of a Tour', p. 261.
2. 2–4 May 1827, Shortreed Papers.
3. *Diaries of Helen Graham*, pp. 37–8.
4. 23 February 1826, Walpole.

persuaded him to move his printing business to Edinburgh, and in 1805 became his partner in the firm which printed the Waverley Novels. He was indispensable to Scott. He carried out the elaborate arrangements of transcribing and double proofs by which his anonymity was preserved, and he was the representative of the popular taste to whose critical judgement Scott often deferred. Their correspondence at times bordered on acrimony, but Scott valued a man who knew his mind and was not afraid to speak it. The association remained unbroken by the crash, for the Trustees continued to employ Ballantyne as editor of the *Edinburgh Weekly Journal* and manager of the printing-house. His increasing melancholia, and growing addiction to religion of a fundamentalist kind, began to cool the friendship after 1829 and it did not survive Ballantyne's conversion to Reform.

With Robert Cadell, Constable's partner, Scott's affairs were inextricably linked. As 'a thorough man of business'[1] he was the first to see, after the crash, that the man who became Scott's publisher could pay off Scott's debts and make his own fortune; and Scott's publisher he duly became. A cautious man who yet took big risks successfully, he was a tireless worker, 'with whose activity and zeal' the Trustees declared themselves fully satisfied.[2] He was a Whig, and a philistine. He knew little about books as literature, but prided himself on his 'plain business way'[3] of looking at them 'as a Tradesman'.[4] As time went on he became Scott's confidential man of business, relieving him of petty worries, settling accounts for him, and lending him money without stint. The tone of his letters to Scott is deferential, but there is nothing to suggest that Scott was wrong in thinking that Cadell really liked him.

Behind these two men lurks a third man of business, the polite precise figure of John Gibson, junior. On the retirement of his partner Hay Donaldson only a short time before the crash he had become Scott's solicitor, and the creditors appointed him as one of the three Trustees. Naturally the main burden fell upon him, and he proved the ideal choice. His leading feature, according to Ballantyne, was caution – 'what [a] useful one!'[5] he adds feelingly – and his conduct of the Trust reveals a prudent, painstaking Edinburgh lawyer, who let nothing pass him by. He admired Scott immensely, and the letters written at the time, and his *Reminiscences*

1. *Letters*, xii. 28.
2. Sederunt Book, ii. 203.
3. 24 August 1827, Walpole.
4. 21 March 1828, Walpole.
5. 28 March 1826, Walpole.

written long afterwards, betray an awe of the great man that he never quite lost.

In Session time Scott's circle was centred on Parliament House and 'the society of my brethren excellent friendly men whom I prefer for general society to what they call a literary set'.[1] His daily companions were the Clerks of Session, a brotherhood within a brotherhood, who shared with him the duties of the green leather table below the bench: Sir Robert Dundas, Hector Macdonald Buchanan, and Colin Mackenzie. But he had also known for upwards of forty years the judges who were now at the top of the profession; and the dinner-parties recorded in the *Journal* are as often as not gatherings of these old school friends and fellow students.

Two later additions to Edinburgh society whom Scott particularly liked were William Adam of Blair-Adam (nephew of Robert Adam the architect), and the Lord Chief Baron, Sir Samuel Shepherd. From the first of these friendships sprang the 'Blair-Adam Antiquarian Club', whose annual meetings at Blair Adam, from Friday until Monday at the summer solstice, Scott never failed to attend from 1817 to 1830. The party was made up by Admiral Adam and Anstruther Thomson (Adam's son and son-in-law), Will Clerk, Sir Adam Ferguson, Thomas Thomson, and his brother the Revd. John Thomson of Duddingston, the artist.

At Abbotsford the society of lawyers gave way to an exchange of visits with the neighbouring big houses along Tweed and Ettrick. Within walking distance were the three Ferguson sisters at Huntly Burn on the Abbotsford estate, and until 1825 the Lockharts at Chiefswood. Scott's cousin Colonel Russell was at Ashestiel and a regular visitor at New Year. Scott did not share Anne's opinion that 'he is as great a bore as ever but it is a great advantage having the tweed between us for it is seldom fordable'.[2] On Christmas Day Scott's unvarying practice was to dine at Mertoun with Hugh Scott of Harden, whom he regarded as head of the family. As Appendix B at the end indicates, there was no lack of society. Apart from his visits to the chief of the clan (the Duke of Buccleuch), his time was passed for the most part among country gentlemen rather than the aristocracy.

It is clear from the *Journal* that he preferred to that of almost any other the company of Tom Purdie, his man of all work at Abbotsford. 'What a blessing there is in a man like Tom whom no familiarity can spoil', he writes in January 1826,[3] and two years later: 'I shall be glad to be at Abbotsford to get rid of this town where I have not in the

---

1. *Letters*, xi. 358.
2. To Sophia, 29 September 1826, Abbots.
3. *Journal*, Entry for 7 January.

proper and social sense of the word a single friend whose company pleases me. In the country I have always Tom Purdie.'[1] They first met when Tom was brought up before the Sheriff for poaching in 1804.[2] By the time of the *Journal* he accompanied Scott everywhere round the estate, and, improbably enough, also had the care of the library, in which he was, says Skene, 'remarkably fastidious'. He always referred to the Waverley Novels as '*our* books'. He carried on a mock war with Sir Adam Ferguson, 'whom he seemed to take a pleasure in assailing'.[3] He could be trusted, Scott is supposed to have said, with anything except a bottle of whisky.[4] He was, in short, a character.

Scott's three intimates at this time were Will Clerk, James Skene of Rubislaw, and Sir Adam Ferguson. William Clerk was a bachelor, the son of Lord Eldin, cultivated, fastidious, and a man of considerable talent; only his 'blameable diffidence',[5] thought William Adam, prevented him from making his mark in both the legal and the literary world. It was this old college friend whom Scott asked to be his second when a duel with Gourgaud seemed likely.

Scott first met James Skene of Rubislaw in the Edinburgh Light Dragoons, and the friendship thrived on their common interests in country life, German literature, and antiquities. Although not Scott's intellectual equal ('The early neglect of his education hangs by him in spite of his exertions',[6] Scott told Lockhart in 1830), Skene was an enthusiast, a traveller, and an artist. At the time of the *Journal* he was Curator of the Royal Society of Edinburgh and of the Society of Antiquaries, and Secretary of the Institution for the Encouragement of the Fine Arts. He was the brother-in-law both of Colin Mackenzie, Scott's fellow Clerk of Session, and of Sir William Forbes, Scott's old friend and rival, who was elected chairman of the creditors. On the day of their return to Edinburgh from Abbotsford it was the family custom to dine with the Skenes, and it was to Skene that Scott turned for sympathy on the day of the financial crash.

'The merry knight' Sir Adam Ferguson divided his time between Edinburgh, his estate in Dumfriesshire, and his sisters at Huntly Burn, where he had lived himself until his marriage in 1821. He was the son of Professor Adam Ferguson, at whose house Scott met Burns; he had served with distinction in the Peninsular Campaign and had been a prisoner of war; in 1818 he was appointed Keeper of

1. *Journal*, Entry for 4 March 1828.
2. *Life*, ii. 192.
3. *Skene's Memories*, p. 167.
4. Dalgleish, i. 742.
5. *Blair-Adam Estate*, Intro., p. xlii.
6. To Lockhart, 24 June 1830, Disc. ii. 81.

the Regalia of Scotland, and four years later was knighted during the King's visit. The familiarity of more than forty years had increased rather than diminished Scott's pleasure in the company of a man who never failed to be 'in good fooling'.

These people were closest to Scott during the *Journal* years. He had hundreds of other friends and a vast acquaintance. In the pages which follow, those who were of real importance to him are dealt with in a footnote on their first appearance; the remainder are briefly identified in the Index.

The Events of the Journal

1825		WORKS IN HAND
November	Reminiscences of Ireland, and of Moore and Byron – Visit of Mrs. Coutts – Lockhart's appointment as editor of the *Quarterly*.	*Life of Napoleon*, vol. i. *Woodstock*, vol. i.
December	Visits from R. P. Gillies – Departure of Lockhart and Sophia for London – Fears of Constable's failure – Christmas at Abbotsford – Attack of gallstones.	*Life of Napoleon*, vol. ii. 'Bonnie Dundee'. Introduction to *Memoirs of Mme La Rochejacquelin*. Review of Pepys for the *Quarterly*. Notes on Sheridan for Lockhart.

1826		
January	The Skenes, Knight, Mathews, and Scrope at Abbotsford – Scott returns to Edinburgh on the 16th and finds he is ruined – The creditors agree to a Trust.	*Woodstock*, vols i and ii.
February	Cadell flees to the Sanctuary – Scott refuses to consider a seat on the Bench – New Exhibition Room opened – 39 Castle Street put up for sale – Scott attacks the Government in the first two *Letters of Malachi*.	*Woodstock*: vol. ii finished 11 February; vol. iii. First and second *Letters of Malachi Malagrowther*.
March	Meetings of protest – A third *Letter of Malachi* – Quarrel with Lord Melville – Feelings of depression – Scott removes to Abbotsford on the 15th – Illness of Lady Scott – Letters from Croker, who has attacked *Malachi* – First news of the money in Chancery belonging to Lady Scott.	*Malachi Malagrowther*, Letter III. Notes for *Napoleon*. *Woodstock*: finished 26 March.

April	*Woodstock* sold for £8228 – Henry Scott of Harden to stand for Parliament – Lady Scott's illness continues – Birth of Scott's grandson, Walter, in Brighton – *Woodstock* succeeds in Edinburgh.	*Life of Napoleon*: vol. ii finished 12 April.
May	Anne Scott arrives from Cheltenham to help nurse Lady Scott – Scott returns to Edinburgh on the 11th, and lodges at 6 St. David Street – Success of *Malachi* – The Government measure dropped – Death and funeral of Lady Scott.	Review of Boaden's *Life of Kemble* and Kelly's *Reminiscences* for the *Quarterly*. *Chronicles of the Canongate* begun on the 27th: 'Introductory'. Notes on *The Omen* for *Blackwood's Magazine*.
June	Constable's claim to *Woodstock* and *Napoleon* – Hard work on *Napoleon* – Fear for the future of Scots Law – Short holidays at Abbotsford and Blair-Adam – *Chronicles of the Canongate* sold to Cadell.	*Life of Napoleon*: vol. iii finished 12 June; vol. iv begun 14 June. *Chronicles of the Canongate*: 'Introductory' and 'The Highland Widow'.
July	Davidoff at Abbotsford for the Selkirk election – End of the quarrel with Lord Melville – To Abbotsford on the 14th.	*Chronicles of the Canongate*: 'The Highland Widow' finished in mid-July. *Napoleon*, vol. iv. Corrections to *St. Ronan's Well*.
August	Niece Anne returns to Cheltenham – Walter and Jane arrive from Ireland – A great picnic at Cauldshiels Loch – Short visits to Drumlanrig and Blair-Adam.	*Life of Napoleon*: vol. iv finished 13 August; vol. v.
September	Walter and Charles go to Ireland – Anne takes 3 Walker Street for the winter – Sir John Sinclair proposes a match for Scott – Visits to Jedburgh for the Circuit Court, and to Melville Castle about the Universities Commission.	*Life of Napoleon*, vol. v.

October	Charles returns to Oxford – Scott goes to London by way of Rokeby – Meets many London friends and passes a day at Windsor – Works on the St. Helena papers at the Colonial Office – Reaches Paris on the 29th.	*Life of Napoleon*: vol v finished early in October.
November	In Paris until the 7th – In London early on the 10th – Wellington offers to assist with *Napoleon* – Scott returns to Abbotsford early on the 26th (by way of Oxford, Cheltenham, Birmingham, and Manchester), and to Edinburgh on the 27th.	
December	Scott suffers from a cold at the beginning of the month, diarrhoea throughout the month, and rheumatism at its end – To Abbotsford for Christmas – Walter and Jane.	*Life of Napoleon*, vol. vi.

1827

January	Rheumatism still severe throughout the month – Returns to Edinburgh on the 15th – Walter returns to Ireland – *Napoleon* to be extended to eight volumes.	*Life of Napoleon*, vols. vi and vii.
February	Hard work on *Napoleon* – Rheumatism – Edinburgh dinner-parties – Letter from Goethe – Scott confesses to the authorship of the Waverley Novels at the Theatrical Fund Dinner.	*Life of Napoleon*, vol. vii.
March	To Abbotsford on the 12th – Hard work on *Napoleon*.	*Life of Napoleon*, vol. viii. Review of *Home's Works*.
April	Fall of the Ministry – Circuit Court at Jedburgh – Hard work on *Napoleon*.	*Life of Napoleon*: vol. viii finished c. 14 April; vol. ix. Review of *Home's Works*. Criticism of Defoe for *Prose Works*.
May	To Edinburgh on the 14th – Decides to write *Tales of a Grandfather*.	Review of Hoffmann's *Works* for *Foreign Quarterly Review*. Criticism of Defoe. *Life of Napoleon*, vol. ix.

June	Oil Gas Coy. affairs – *Life of Napoleon* finished – *Tales of a Grandfather* sold to Cadell – Lockharts at Portobello – Scott at St. Andrews with the Blair-Adam Club.	*Life of Napoleon*: vol. ix finished 7 June. 'Culloden Papers', or 'Essay on Clanship', for *Prose Works*. *Chronicles of the Canongate*: 'Introduction' and 'Two Drovers'. *Tales of a Grandfather*.
July	Four days at Abbotsford before removing there for the vacation on the 11th – Visit to the Edinburgh Academy – Conversation with Lord Melville about politics – Emus offered to the King and the Duke of Buccleuch – Excursions to Yarrow and Minto – Death of Constable – Lord Newton arbitrates in Scott's favour.	'Culloden Papers'. *Chronicles of the Canongate*: 'Two Drovers' finished 15 July; 'Surgeon's Daughter' begun 27 July. *Tales of a Grandfather*: vol. i finished 26 July.
August	Visit from G. H. Gordon, who helps to arrange Scott's correspondence – Death of Canning – Possibility of a duel with General Gourgaud – Williams resigns as Rector of Edinburgh Academy – Excursions to Fleurs and Kelso.	*Chronicles of the Canongate*: 'Surgeon's Daughter'. Review of Monteath's *The Forester's Guide*.
September	To Glasgow with Lady Compton, by way of Melville Castle and Edinburgh; then to Blythswood, Corehouse, and Lanark.	Review continued. *Chronicles of the Canongate*: 'Surgeon's Daughter' finished 16 September. *Tales of a Grandfather* vol. ii begun 17 September.
October	Scott in Northumberland to see the Duke of Wellington – Letters from Lady Jane Stuart – Arbitration decided mainly in Scott's favour – Abud threatens the Trust.	*Tales of a Grandfather*: vol. iii half finished 16 October, two-thirds finished 20 October.
November	Scott returns to Edinburgh on the 4th – The Abud affair – Visits to Lady Jane Stuart – Prize Essay at the University – Plans to buy the copyrights – Union Scottish Assurance Coy. Meeting – A place in the Foreign Office promised to Charles.	'Ornamental Gardening' begun 7 November, finished 25 November. Last proof of *Tales of a Grandfather* corrected. 'My Aunt Margaret's Mirror' begun.

| December | Lord Newton decrees in Scott's favour – First dividend of 6s. in the £ declared – Further discussions of Abud, and of the copyrights – Cadell and Ballantyne dissatisfied with *Chronicles of the Canongate*; Scott fears the loss of his reputation – Meetings about the Advocates' Library, and the Oil Gas Coy. – Huntly Gordon asks for two sermons – Cadell buys the copyrights for £8400 – Scott returns by way of Arniston to Abbotsford. | 'My Aunt Margaret's Mirror' finished 3 December. *The Fair Maid of Perth* begun 5 December. Additions to *Tales of a Grandfather*. |

1828

| January | Birth of Charlotte Lockhart – Scott insists that Cadell employ Ballantyne as printer – Disagreements with Longman over 2nd edition of *Life of Napoleon* – To Edinburgh on the 13th – Retirement of Colin Mackenzie – Death of Glengarry – Visit of Mr. Moscheles – Abud's claim settled – Scott sits to Colvin Smith – Asked by Heath and Reynolds to edit *The Keepsake*. | Review of *Molière* for Gillies. Revision of *Tales of a Grandfather*. Corrections to *Life of Napoleon*. *Fair Maid of Perth*: vol. i two-thirds written on the 21st, nearly finished on the 30th. |

| February | Visit to Dalkeith – Negotiations on behalf of the Oil Gas Coy. – Feelings of *déjà-vu* – 'My Aunt Margaret's Mirror' offered to *The Keepsake* – Discussion on prisons – Ballantyne criticizes *The Fair Maid of Perth*. | *Fair Maid of Perth*: vol. i finished 5 February; vol. ii. |

| March | Fancy Dress Ball – Miss Stirling Grahame's personifications – Agreement with the Coal Gas Coy. – To Abbotsford on the 13th – The Yeomanry – Cadell's plans for the Magnum. | *Fair Maid of Perth*: vol. iii begun 5 March, finished 29 March. *Tales of a Grandfather* corrected for a 2nd edition. |

| April | Journey to London by way of Carlisle, Kenilworth, and Stratford – Terry's bankruptcy – Quarrel with Lord Minto – Scott rectifies the Road Bill threatening Darnick – Meets Wellington, Croker, Coleridge, Sotheby, Joanna Baillie, Morritt, Knighton, Lord Melville, and other London friends. | 'My Aunt Margaret's Mirror' revised for *The Keepsake*. Proofs of *The Fair Maid of Perth* finished. |

May	Dinners at the Literary Society, the Royal Academy, and the Roxburghe Club – The Chancery business – Scott sits to Haydon, Northcote, and Chantry – Breakfasts at Lincoln's Inn – Dines with the King, and with the Duchess of Kent – Visits the Lockharts in Brighton, and Walter at Hampton Court – Returns by Gill's Hill and Rokeby.	
June	Reaches Abbotsford on the 2nd, and Edinburgh on the 4th – Williams gives up his London chair – At Blair-Adam from the 27th to the 30th.	*Tales of a Grandfather*, 2nd series.

========

9 July–9 January 1829: No Entries.

========

1829

January	Scott returns to Edinburgh on the 13th – Dr. Knox's proposed paper on dissections – Thoughts on the anatomists – Visit to Milton-Lockhart and Allanton – Scott meets Greenshields and sits to Graham – Deaths of James Ferrier and Mary Ferguson – Execution of Burke – Cadell about to advertise the Magnum.	*Anne of Geierstein*, vol. ii.
February	Meeting of the Club – Sale of Stuart of Dunearn's pictures – Death of Mrs. Ballantyne – Skene assists with *Anne of Geierstein* – Stories of Waterloo – The Catholic Question.	*Anne of Geierstein*: vol. ii. finished 5 February; vol. iii.
March	The booksellers place large orders for the Magnum – Ballantyne condemns *Anne of Geierstein*, which is laid aside while the Catholic Question rages – Restoration of Mons Meg to Edinburgh Castle – Scott returns to Abbotsford on the 11th – Visit from Lord Dalhousie.	Notes for the Magnum and General Preface. Review of Tytler's *History of Scotland*. Notes on Boswell for Croker.
April	Visit from the Skenes – The Hunt meets at Abbotsford – Circuit Court – Death of Lord Buchan – *Doom of Devorgoil*.	Review of Ritson. Article for *Blackwood's*. *Anne of Geierstein*, vol. iii. Preface to *House of Aspen*. *History of Scotland* begun 18 April.

May	Scott returns to Edinburgh on the 11th – Dines at Dalhousie Castle – Walter's illness – Great expectations of the Magnum – The General Assembly of the Church of Scotland – Edward Irving – Farewell dinners to Dalhousie and Hay Drummond – Reflections on the Psalmody.	Review of *Le Duc de Guise à Naples*. *History of Scotland*. Notes for the Magnum.
June	Scott alarmed by passing blood – The Theatre given to Mrs. Siddons – Cadell plans to buy the poetry copyrights – Scott sits to Graham – To Abbotsford on the 13th for four days – Sophia, Charles, and the children arrive by steamboat – Meeting of the Blair-Adam Club and visit to Falkland.	*History of Scotland*, half-volume finished 1 June. *Tales of a Grandfather*, enlarged 3rd series.
July	His children and grandchildren go to Abbotsford, where Scott joins them on the 9th – The Stewart Papers – Death of Shortreed – Mrs. Hemans at Chiefswood.	*Tales of a Grandfather*. *History of Scotland*.

21 July–22 May 1830: No Entries.

1830

May	Death of Scott of Raeburn – New line proposed for the road – Scott intends to retire – The Lockharts arrive for the summer.	*Demonology*
June	Edinburgh, Abbotsford, and Blair-Adam – Visit to Culross – Fanny Kemble acts in Edinburgh – Visit to Prestonpans – William IV proclaimed King.	*Demonology*: one-third finished 2 June, two-thirds finished 16 June.
July	Dinners of the Club and the Bannatyne – Miss Doe Sinclair in love with Scott – Return to Abbotsford.	*Demonology*, seven-eighths finished 5 July.

19 July–19 December: One Entry only.

December	Second dividend of 3s. in the £ – Scott presented with his library and furniture – Retirement from the Court – Scott's two strokes – Political agitation – Scott stops a prisoner escaping from the Sheriff Court – Death of Bell Ferguson – New line for the road agreed.	*Count Robert of Paris*. Notes to *Woodstock*. Political article on Income Tax (unfinished).

1831

January	Scott 'Decidedly weaker in point of health' – Prepares to make his will – Discusses politics with Henry Scott – Sits to MacDonald the sculptor – Uses Laidlaw as amanuensis.	*Count Robert of Paris.*
February	Goes to Edinburgh to make his will – Acquires a brace for his lame leg – Delayed by snow.	*Count Robert of Paris,* vol. ii. Notes on *Redgauntlet* and *Tales of Crusaders.*
March	Reform meetings at Selkirk and Jedburgh – Scott refuses Cadell a half-share in the later copyrights – His typical day at this time – Reform Bill carried in the Commons – Scott sits to Grant.	Review of *The British Herald* (never published). Address on the Reform Bill (rejected). *Count Robert of Paris:* vol. iii begun 16 March.
April	Manuscripts adjudged to Constable – Foundation stone laid for Tweed bridge – Scott's third stroke on the 17th.	*Count Robert of Paris.*
May	The Lockharts arrive for the summer – J. B. and Cadell condemn vol. iii of *Count Robert* – Election at Jedburgh: 'Burke Sir Walter'.	*Count Robert of Paris* nearly finished, but laid aside on the 12th.

26 May–22 September: No Entries.

September	Yarrow visited with Wordsworth – Journey to London.	Notes to the Magnum. *Reliquiae Trotcosienses.*
October	London friends – Reform riots – Stories of magic, and of Garrick – Portsmouth – The *Barham* sails for Malta on the 29th.	
November	The voyage – Graham's Island – In quarantine at Malta until the 28th – Friends and sightseeing.	
December	Scott leaves Malta on the 13th, arrives at Naples on the 17th, and lands there on the 25th.	*Siege of Malta* (never finished). *Letters of the Seventeenth Century,* partly written by Lady Louisa Stuart.

SIR WALTER SCOTT BAR[T]

of

Abbotsford

HIS . GURNAL*

Vol. I.

As I walked by myself
I talkd to my self
  And thus my self said to me.

               Old Song.

A hard word so spelld on Authority of Miss Scott now
Mrs. Lockhart.

NOVEMBER

20 SUNDAY I have all my life regretted that I did not keep a regular [journal]. I have myself lost recollection of much that was interesting and I have deprived my family and the public of some curious information by not carrying this resolution into effect.

I have bethought me on seeing lately some volumes of Byron's notes that he probably had hit upon the right way of keeping such a memorandum-book by throwing aside all pretence to regularity and order and marking down events just as they occurd to recollection. I will try this plan and behold I have a handsome lockd volume such as might serve for a Lady's Album. *Nota Bene* John Lockhart and Anne[1] and I are to raise a society for the suppression of Albums. It is a most troublesome shape of mendicity – Sir, your autograph – a line of poetry – or a prose sentence among all the sprawling sonnets and blotted trumpery that dishonours these miscellanies – a man must have a good stomach that can swallow this botheration as a compliment.

I was in Ireland last summer and had a most delightful tour.[2] It cost me upwards of £500 including £100 left with Walter and Jane[1] for we travelld a large party and in stile.

There is much less exaggerated about the Irish than is to be expected. Their poverty is not exaggerated – it is on the extreme verge of human misery – their cottages would scarce serve for pigsties even in Scotland – and their rags seem the very refuse of a ragshop and are disposed on their bodies with such ingenious variety of

1. For the members of Scott's family, see Introduction, pp. xxxix—xli.
2. The main purpose of Scott's tour the previous July and August was to visit Walter and Jane, newly married, and quartered in Dublin. Lockhart and Anne were of the party. They went also to Maria Edgeworth at Edgeworthstown, and on the return journey passed some days at Storrs, on Lake Windermere, where Colonel Bolton was entertaining Canning. Wordsworth escorted them as far as Lowther Castle by way of Rydal Mount and Southey's house at Keswick. *Life*, viii. 1–52.

wretchedness that you would think nothing but some sort of perverted taste could have assembled so many shreds together. You are constantly fearful that some knot or loop will give and place the individual before you in all the primitive simplicity of Paradise. Then for their food they have only potatoes and too few of them. Yet the men look stout and healthy the women buxsome and well coloured.

Dined with us being Sunday Will. Clerk[1] and Chas. Kirkpatrick Sharpe. W. C. is the second son of the celebrated author of *Naval Tactics*.[2] I have known him intimately since our college days and to my thinking, never met a man of greater powers or more complete information on all desirable subjects. In youth he had strongly the Edinburgh *pruritus disputandi*[3] but habits of society have greatly mellowd it and though still anxious to gain your suffrage to his opinion he endeavours rather to conciliate your opinion than conquer it by force. Still there is enough of tenacity of sentiment to prevent in London Society, where all must go slack and easy, W. C. from rising to the very top of the tree as a Conversation man, who must not only wind the thread of his argument gracefully but also know when to let go. But I like the Scotch taste better: there is more matter, more information, above all more spirit in it. Clerk will I am afraid leave the world little more than the report of his fame. He is too indolent to finish any considerable work.

Chas. Kirkpatricke Sharpe[4] is another very remarkable man. He was bred a clergyman but did not take orders owing I believe to a peculiar effeminacy of voice which must have been unpleasant in reading prayers. Some family quarrels occasiond his being indifferently provided for by a small annuity from his elder brother extorted by an arbitral decree. He has infinite wit and a great turn for antiquarian lore as the publications of Kirkton[5] etc. bear witness. His drawings are the most fanciful and droll imaginable – a mixture between Hogarth and some of those foreign masters

1. See Introduction, p. xliv.
2. *An Essay on Naval Tactics, etc.*, by John Clerk, 1790, reputed to have inspired Nelson's tactics at Trafalgar.
3. 'Itch for argument'.
4. C. K. Sharpe (1781–1851), antiquary, artist, cynic, and dilettante, first met Scott in Oxford in 1802. He was living now at 93 Princes Street with his mother. Some of his characteristics are given to Sir Mungo Malagrowther in *The Fortunes of Nigel*.
5. *Secret and True History of the Church of Scotland from the Restoration to the year 1678*, 1817.

who painted temptations of Saint Antony and such grotesque subjects. As a poet he has not a very strong touch. Strange that his finger-ends can describe so well what he cannot bring out clearly and firmly in words. If he were to make drawing a resource it might raise him a large income. But though a lover of antiquities and therefore of expensive trifles C. K. S. is too aristocratic to use his art to assist his revenue. He is a very complete genealogist and has made many detections in Douglas[1] and other books on pedigree which our nobles would do well to suppress if they had an opportunity. Strange that a man should be curious after Scandal of centuries old. Not but Charles loves it fresh and fresh also for being very much a fashionable man he is always master of the reigning report and he tells the anecdote with such gusto that there is no helping sympathizing with him: the peculiarity of voice adding not a little to the general effect. My idea is that C. K. S. with his oddities tastes satire and high aristocratic feelings resembles Horace Walpole – perhaps in his person also in a general way. See Miss Aikin's anecdotes[2] for description of the author of *The Castle of Otranto*.

No other company at dinner except my cheerful and goodhumourd friend *Missie* MacDonald,[3] so calld in fondness – One bottle of Champagne with the ladies' assistance, 2 of claret. I observe that both these great Connoisseurs were very nearly if not quite agreed that there are *no* absolutely undoubted originals of Queen Mary. But how then should we be so very distinctly informd as to her features? What has become of all the originals which suggested these innumerable copies? Surely Mary must have been as unfortunate in this as in other particulars of her life.

21 MONDAY I am enamourd of my Journal. I wish the zeal may but last. Once more of Ireland – I said their poverty was not exaggerated. Neither is their wit – nor their goodhumour – nor their whimsical absurdity – nor their courage.

Wit. I gave a fellow a shilling on some occasion when sixpence was

---

1. Sir Robert Douglas's *Peerage of Scotland*, revised by John Philp Wood, 1813.
2. Laetitia Matilda Hawkins's *Anecdotes, Biographical Sketches, and Memoirs*, 1822, pp. 91–117.
3. Jemima, the tall, cheerful, noisy daughter of Hector Macdonald Buchanan, Scott's fellow Clerk of Session. She was a frequent visitor and Scott was fond of her although he thought the Buchanan girls 'accustomd to racket about a little too much'. *Letters*, x. 506.

the fee – 'Remember you owe me sixpence, Pat.' 'May your Honour live till I pay you.'[1] There was courtesy as well as wit in this and all the clothes on Pat's back would have been dearly bought by the sum in question.

Goodhumour. There is perpetual kindness in the Irish cabbin – butter milk – potatoes – a stool is offerd or a stone is rolld that your honour may sit down and be out of their smoke and those who beg everywhere else seem desirous to exercize free hospitality in their own houses. Their natural disposition is turned to gaiety and happiness. While a Scotchman is thinking about the term day, or if easy on that subject about Hell in the next world, while an English man is making a little hell of his own in the present because his muffin is not well roasted, Pat's mind is always turnd to fun and ridicule. They are terribly excitable to be sure and will murther you on slight suspicion and find out next day that it was all a mistake and that it was not yourself they meant to kill at all at all.

Absurdity. They were widening the road near Lord Claremont's seat[2] as we passd. A number of cars were drawn up together at a particular point where we also halted as we understood they were blowing a rock and the *shot* was expected presently to go off. After waiting two minutes or so a fellow calld out something and our carriage as a planet and the cars for satellites started all forward at once, the Irishmen whooping and crying and the horses galloping. Unable to learn the meaning of this I had only left to suppose that they had delayd firing the intended *shot* till we should pass and that we were passing quickly to make the delay as short as possible. No such thing. By dint of making great haste we got within ten yards of the rock when the blast took place throwing dust and gravel on our carriage and had our postillions brought us a little nearer (it was not for want of hollowing and flogging that he did not) we should have had a still more serious share of the explosion. The explanation I received from the drivers was that they had been told by the overseer that as the *mine* had been *so long* in going off he dared say we would have time to pass it. So we just waited long enough to make the danger imminent. I have only to add that two or three people got behind the carriage just for nothing but to see how our honours got passd.

---

1. This story goes the rounds as 'a good anecdote by Sir Walter Scott' and is heard in London three years later by Puckler Muskau. *A Regency Visitor*, ed. E. M. Butler, 1957, p. 289.
2. Clermont in Co. Louth.

Went to the Oil Gas Committee this morning of which concern I am president or Chairman.[1] It has amused me much by bringing me into company with a body of active business-loving money-making citizens of Edinburgh, chiefly Whigs by the way, whose sentiments and proceedings amuse me. The Stock is rather low in the market, 35/- premium instead of £5. 0. 0. It must rise however for the advantages of the Light are undeniable and folks will soon become accustom[d] to idle apprehensions or misapprehensions. From £20 to £25 should light a house capitally supposing you leave town in the vacation. The three last quarters cost me £10. 10. and the first, £8, was greatly over charged. We will see what this – the worst and darkest quarter costs.

Dined with Sir Robert Dundas[2] where we met Lord and Lady Melville.[3] My little *nieces* (*ex officio*) gave us some pretty musick. I do not know and cannot utter a note of music and complicated harmonies seem to me a babble of confused though pleasing sounds. Yet songs and simple melodies especially if connected with words and ideas have as much effect on me as on most people. But then I hate to hear a young person sing without feeling and expression suited to the song. I cannot bear a voice that has no more life in it than a pianoforte or a bugle horn. There is something about all the fine arts of soul and spirit which like the vital principle in Man defies the research of the most critical anatomist. You feel where it is not, yet you cannot describe what it is you want. Sir Joshua or some other great painter was looking at a painting on which much pains had been bestowd – 'Why yes' he said in a hesitating manner – 'it is very clever – very well done – can't find fault – but it wants some thing – it wants – it wants – damn me – it wants THAT' – throwing his hand over his head and snapping his fingers. Tom Moore's is the most exquisite warbling I ever heard.

1. The Edinburgh Oil Gas Light Coy., of which Scott had been chairman since 1823, was never commercially successful. It struggled until 1828, when it sold out to its older rival the Edinburgh Gas Light Coy. For some account of the affairs of the company see Note 1, pp. 805–6. Abbotsford was one of the first houses in Scotland to be lit by gas.
2. Sir Robert Dundas of Beechwood (1761–1836), Scott's fellow Clerk of Session, with whose family the Scotts had lived on terms of great intimacy.
3. Robert Saunders Dundas, second Viscount Melville (1771–1851), son of the great Lord Melville and a school friend of Scott's, was at this time First Lord of the Admiralty and a powerful source of patronage in Scotland.

Next to him David Macculloch[1] for Scots songs. The last when a boy at Dumfries was much admired by Burns who used to get him to try over the words which he composed to new melodies. He is brother of Macculloch of Ardwall.

22 TUESDAY *Moore*. I saw Moore[2] (for the first time I may say) this season. We had indeed met in public twenty years ago. There is a manly frankness and perfect ease and good breeding about him which is delightful. Not the least touch of the poet or the pedant. A little – very little man – less I think than Lewis[3] and somewhat like him in person, God knows not in conversation, for Matt though a clever fellow was a bore of the first description. Moreover he lookd always like a school boy. I remember a picture of him being handed about at Dalkeith House. It was a miniature I think by Saunders who had contrived to mufle Lewis's person in a cloak and placed some poniard or darklanthorn appurtenance (I think) in his hand so as to give the picture the cast of a Bravo. 'That like Matt Lewis' said Duke Henry[4] to whom it had passd in turn. 'Why that is like a MAN.' Imagine the effect. Lewis was at his elbow. Now Moore has none of this insignificance. To be sure his person is much stouter than that of M. G. L. His countenance is decidedly plain but the expression is so very animated especially in speaking or singing that it is far more interesting than the finest features could have renderd.

I was aware that Byron had often spoken both in private society and in his journal of Moore and myself in the same breath and with the same sort of regard.[5] So I was curious to see what there could be in common betwixt us, Moore having lived so much in the gay world I in the country and with people of business and sometimes with

1. David McCulloch, a Bengal merchant who had now retired to Cheltenham, and James McCulloch of Ardwall, near Gatehouse-of-Fleet in Kirkcudbrightshire, were brothers of Scott's sister-in-law, Mrs. Thomas Scott.
2. Thomas Moore (1779–1852), the Irish poet and biographer, whose visit to Abbotsford earlier in the autumn is described by Lockhart in his *Life*, viii. 65–72. Moore's *Life of Byron*, which appeared in 1830, was dedicated to Scott.
3. Matthew Lewis (1775–1818), author of *The Monk*, whom Scott first met in Edinburgh in 1798. Lewis was the first man of letters to show him some attention and Scott contributed to his *Tales of Wonder*, 1801.
4. Henry, third Duke of Buccleuch (1746–1812).
5. For an account of Scott's meetings with Byron in 1815 see Lockhart's *Life*, v. 38–45 and 88. Byron, who had attacked Scott in *English Bards and Scotch Reviewers*, made amends in *Don Juan*, where he called him. 'The Ariosto of the North'.

politicians, Moore a scholar – I none – He a musician and artist – I without knowledge of a note – He a democrat – I an aristocrat – with many other points of difference besides his being an Irishman, I a Scotchman, and both tolerably national. Yet there is a point of resemblance and a strong one. We are both goodhumoured fellows who rather seek to enjoy what is going forward than to maintain our dignity as Lions. And we have both seen the world too widely and too well not to contemn in our souls the imaginary consequence of literary people who walk with their noses in the air and remind me always of the fellow whom Johnson met in an ale-house and who calld himself 'the great Twalmly, Inventor of the flood-gate iron for smoothing linen.'[1] He also enjoys the *Mot pour rire* and so do I. Moore has I think been ill treated about Byron's Memoirs. He surrenderd them to the family (Ld. Byron's exors) and thus lost £2000 which he had raised upon them at a most distressing moment of his life. It is true they offerd and pressd the money on him afterwards but they ought to have settled it with the Booksellers and not put poor Tom's spirit in arms against his interest. I think at least it might have been so managed. At any rate there must be an authentic life of Byron by somebody. Why should they not give the benefit of their materials to Tom Moore whom Byron had made the depositary of his own Memoirs? But T. M. thinks that Cam Hobhouse[2] has the purpose of writing Byron's life himself. He and Moore were at sharp words during the negotiation and there was some explanation necessary before the affair ended. It was a pity that nothing save the total destruction of Byron's Memoirs would satisfy his Exors – But there was a reason – *Premet Nox alta*.[3]

It would be [a] delightful addition to life if T. M. had a cottage within two miles of one. We went to the theatre together and the House being luckily a good one received T. M. with rapture. I could have huggd them for it paid back the debt of the kind reception I met with in Ireland.[4]

1. Boswell's *Life of Johnson*, iv. 193.
2. John Cam Hobhouse (1786–1869), statesman and author, the early friend and travelling companion of Lord Byron, and his literary executor.
3. 'Deep night will cover it.' Horace's *Odes*, i. iv. 16.
4. At the Edinburgh Theatre there were 'shouts, cheers, bravo, and applause' when Scott, Moore, Lockhart, and Sophia entered in time to see *The Abbot*; and Moore, 'though modestly reluctant, at last yielded, and bowed, hand on heart, with graceful animation'. Dibdin, pp. 317–18.

   Scott's arrival in the theatre in Dublin the previous July had been greeted by 'a perfect cataract and thunder of roaring' which had brought the play to a standstill. *Life*, viii. 21.

Here is matter for a May morning.[1] But much fitter for a November one. The general distress in the city has affected H. and R.,[2] Constable's great agents. Should they *go* it is not likely that Constable can stand, and such an event would lead to great distress and perplexity on the part of J. B.[3] and myself. Thank God I have enough at worst to pay 40/- in the pound taking matters at the very worst. But much distress and inconvenience must be the consequence. I had a lesson in 1814 which should have done good upon me.[4] But success and abundance erazed it from my mind. But this is no time for journalizing or moralizing either. Necessity is like a sour-faced Cookmaid and I a turnspit whom she has flogged ere now till he mounted his wheel. If *W-st-k* can be out by 25 January it will do much and it is possible.[5]

Sir John Sinclair's son has saved his comrade on shipboard (young Hope) by throwing himself overboard and keeping the other afloat – a very gallant thing. But the *Gran Giag' Asso*[6] asks me to write a poem *on the Civic crown* of which he sends me a description quoted from Adam's *Antiquities*,[7] which mellifluous performance is to persuade the admiralty to give the young conservator promotion. Oh he is a rare Headpiece – an admirable Morion. I do not believe there is in nature such a full-acornd Boar.[8]

Could not write to purpose for thick coming fancies.[9] The wheel would not turn easily and cannot be forced.

> My spinning wheel is auld and stiff
> The rock o't winna stand Sir.

1. *Twelfth Night*, iii. 4.
2. Hurst, Robinson and Co., the London booksellers whose fall brought on the failure of Constable and ultimately Scott's ruin.
3. James Ballantyne.
4. The failure of his venture into publishing as John Ballantyne & Coy. *Life*, iv. 73–123.
5. To bolster confidence in Constable & Coy., Scott agreed with Cadell on this day to advertise that *Woodstock* would be published on 25 January. *Letters*, ix. 301. In fact it did not appear until the following April.
6. Scott's charity always fails him when he has to mention Sir John Sinclair of Ulbster (1754–1835). A Highland landowner, with advanced ideas on farming, he had been President of the Board of Agriculture and supervised *The Statistical Account of Scotland*. At this time he held the sinecure of Commissioner of Excise. For a later impertinence see the Entry for 13 September 1826.
7. Alexander Adam's *Roman Antiquities*, 1791. Adam had been Scott's headmaster.
8. An allusion to *Cymbeline*, ii. 4.
9. *Macbeth*, v. 3.

> To keep the temper-pin in tiff
> Employs aft my hand Sir.[1]

Went to dine at L— J— C—[2] as I thought by invitation but it was
for tuesday se'en night. Returnd very well pleased not being exactly in
the humour for company – and had a beefsteak. My appetite is surely
excepting in quantity that of a farmer, for, eating moderately of
anything, my epicurean pleasure is in the most simple diet. Wine I
seldom taste when alone and use instead a little spirits and water. I
have of late diminishd the quantity for fear of a weakness inductive to
a diabetes, a disease which broke up my father's health though one of
the most temperate men who ever lived. I smoke a couple of segars
instead which operates equally as a sedative –

> Just to drive the cold winter away
> And drown the fatigues of the day.[3]

I smoked a good deal about twenty years ago when at Ashestiel[4] but
coming down one morning to the parlour I found as the room was
small and confind that the smell was unpleasant and laid aside the use
of the *Nicotian weed* for many years, but was again led to use it by the
example of my son a Hussar officer, and my son-in-law an Oxford
Student. I could lay it aside tomorrow – I laugh at the dominion of
custom in this and many things.

> We make the giants first and then – *do not* kill them.[5]

23 WEDNESDAY On comparing notes with Moore I was confirmd in
one or two points which I had always laid down in considering poor
Byron's [peculiarities]. One was that like Rousseau he was apt to be
very suspicious, and a plain downright steadiness of manner was the
true mode to maintain his good opinion. Will: Rose[6] told me that

1. 'My Jo Janet' in Allan Ramsay's *Tea-Table Miscellany*.
2. The Lord Justice-Clerk, the Rt. Hon. David Boyle (1772–1853).
3. From 'Come, come, my Hearts of Gold' with and 'Every man take a
   glass in his hand'. *The Vocal Miscellany*, i. 163 and 103.
4. From 1804 to 1812, the year in which he moved to Abbotsford,
   Scott rented Ashestiel from his cousin Colonel Russell who was at
   that time in India.
5. Adapted from Fielding's *Tom Thumb the Great*, i. 5.
6. William Stewart Rose (1775–1843), poet and translator of Ariosto,
   who until 1824 was Reading-Clerk in the House of Lords. Scott first
   met him in London in 1803. He, as well as Lady Louisa Stuart,
   wrote introducing Morritt to Scott.

once while sitting with Byron he fixd insensibly his eyes on his feet, one of which it must be rememberd was deformd. Looking up suddenly he saw Byron regarding him with a look of concentrated and deep displeasure which wore off when he observed no consciousness or embarassment in the countenance of Rose. Murray[1] afterwards explaind this by telling Rose that Lord Byron was very jealous of having this personal imperfection noticed or attended to. In another point Moore confirmd my previous opinion. Namely that Byron loved mischiefmaking. Moore had written to him cautioning him against the project of establishing the paper called the *Liberal*[2] in communion with such men as P. B. Shelley and Hunt on whom he said the World had set its mark. Byron shewd this to the parties. Shelley wrote a modest and rather affecting expostulation to Moore.[3] These two peculiarities of extreme suspicion and love of mischief are both shades of the malady which certainly tinctured some part of the character of this mighty genius and, without some tendency towards which, genius – I mean that kind which depends on the imaginative power – perhaps cannot exist to great extent. The wheels of a machine to play rapidly must not fit with the utmost exactness else the attrition diminishes the Impetus.

Another of Byron's peculiarities was the love of mystifying which indeed may be referd to that of mischief. There was no knowing how much or how little to believe of his narratives. Instance. Mr. Bankes[4] expostulating with him upon a dedication which he had written in extravagant terms of praise to Cam Hobhouse, Byron told him that Cam had teased him into the dedication till he had said 'Well; it shall be so – providing you will write the dedication yourself' – and affirmd that Cam Hobhouse did write the high-colourd dedication accordingly. I mentiond this to Murray, having the report from Will Rose to whom Bankes had mentiond it. Murray in reply assured me that the dedication was written by Lord Byron himself and shewd it me in his own hand. I wrote to Rose to mention the thing to Bankes as it might have made mischief had the story got into the circle.

Byron was disposed to think all men of imagination were addicted

---

1. John Murray (1778–1843) of Albemarle Street. He was Constable's London agent until 1813 and publisher of the *Quarterly*. He introduced Scott to Byron.
2. A quarterly magazine of which only four numbers appeared, remembered chiefly for Byron's *Vision of Judgment* (1822) in the first number.
3. See Moore's *Life of Byron*, v. 313–21.
4. William John Bankes (d. 1855), the traveller, wit, and friend of Byron.

to mix fiction or poetry with their prose. He used to say he dared believe the celebrated courtezan of Venice about whom Rousseau makes so piquante a story was if one could see her a draggled taild wench enough. I believe that he embellishd his own amours considerably and that he was in many respects *Le fanfaron des vices qu'il n'avait pas.* He loved to be thought awful mysterious and gloomy and sometimes hinted at strange causes. I believe the whole to have been the creation and sport of a wild and powerful fancy. In the same manner he *cram'd* people as it is termd about duels and what [not] which never existed or were much exaggerated.

Constable has been here as lame as a duck upon his legs but his heart and courage as firm as a cock. He has convinced me we will do well to support the London House.[1] He has sent them about £5000 and proposes we should borrow on our joint security £5000 for their accomodation. J. B. and R. Cadell[2] present. I must be guided by them and hope for the best. Certainly to part company would be to incur an awful risqué.

What I liked about Byron besides his boundless genius was his generosity of Spirit as well as purse and his utter contempt of all the affectations of literature from the School-magisterial stile to the lackadaisical.

Byron's example has formed a sort of Upper House of poetry. There is Lord Leveson Gower a very clever young man. Lord Porchester too, nephew to Mrs Scott of Harden, a young man who lies on the carpet and looks poetical and dandyish – fine lad too – But

> There be many peers
> Ere such another Byron.[3]

Talking of Abbotsford it begins to be haunted by too much company of every kind. But especially foreigners. I do not like them. I hate fine waistcoats and breast pins upon dirty shirts. I detest the impudence that pays a stranger compliments and harangues about his works in the Author's house, which is usually ill breeding. Moreover they are seldom long of making it evident that they know nothing about what they are talking of excepting having seen the *Lady of the Lake* at the Opera.

Dined at Saint Catherine's with Lord Advocate,[4] with Lord and

---

1. Hurst, Robinson.
2. For Robert Cadell see Introduction, p. xlii.
3. An allusion to *Cymbeline*, iii. 1.
4. Sir William Rae, Bart. (1769–1842). His house of St. Catherine's lay three miles south of Princes Street.

Lady Mellville, Lord Justice Clerk, Sir Archd. Campbell of Succoth,[1] all class companions and acquainted well for more than 40 years. All excepting Lord J. C. were at Fraser's class High School. Boyle joined us at college. There are besides, Sir Adam Fergusson,[2] Colin Mackenzie,[3] James Hope, Dr. James Buchan, Claud Russell,[4] and perhaps two or three more of and about the same period. But

Rari apparent nantes in gurgite vasto.[5]

24 THURSDAY Talking of Strangers, London held some four or five years since one of those animals who are lions at first but by transmutation of two seasons become in regular course Boars. Ugo Foscolo[6] by name, a haunter of Murray's Shop and of literary parties. Ugly as a baboon and intolerably conceited, he splutterd blusterd and disputed without even knowing the principles upon which men of sense render a reason and screamd all the while like a pig when they cut his throat.

Another such Animalaccio is a brute of a Sicilian Marquis de Salvo[7] who wrote something about Byron. He inflicted two days on us at Abbotsford and they never know what to make of themselves in the forenoon; but sit tormenting the women to play at proverbs and such trash.

Foreigner of a different caste. Count Olonym (Olonyne that's it) son of the President of the Royal Society and a Capt. in the Imperial Guards. He is mean looking and sickly but has much sense, candour and general information.

There was at Abbotsford and is here for education just now a young Count Davidow with a tutor Mr. Colyar. He is a nephew of the famous

1. Raised to the bench as Lord Succoth in 1809.
2. See Introduction, pp. xliv–xlv.
3. Colin Mackenzie of Portmore, W. S. (1770–1830), a fellow Clerk of Session and a close friend.
4. Prominent in Edinburgh as Writer to the Signet, doctor, and accountant respectively.
5. Virgil's *Aeneid*, i. 118, with the first two words transposed: 'Here and there they appear swimming in the wide whirlpool.'
6. He came to London from Italy in 1816, 'a very singular man, uniting opposite qualities, and generally very pleasing in the early part of an acquaintance'. Redding's *Memoirs of Thomas Campbell*, i. 192. He stimulated the fashionable interest in Italian literature by his lectures and critical writings.
7. Carlo, Marchese di Salvo, author of *Lord Byron en Italie et en Grèce*, 1825, whom Scott refers to in a letter as 'a very accomplished and well informed man'. *Letters*, ix. 237.

Orlows. It is quite surprizing how much sense and sound thinking this youth has at the early age of sixteen without the least self-conceit or forwardness. On the contrary he seems kind, modest and ingenuous. Yet to questions which I askd about the state of Russia he answerd with the precision and accuracy of twice his years. He is but sixteen. I should be sorry the saying were verified in him

> So wise and young they say never live long.[1]

Saw also at Abbotsford two Frenchmen whom I liked, friends of Miss Dumergue.[2] One calld Le Noir[3] is the author of a tragedy which he had the grace never to quote and which I, though poked by some malicious persons, had *not* the grace even to hint at. They were disposed at first to be complimentary but I convinced them it was not the custom here and they took it well and were agreeable.

A little bilious this morning for the first time these six months. It cannot be the London matters which stick on my stomach for that is mending and may have good effects on myself and others.

Dined with Robert Cockburn.[4] Company Lord Melville and family, Sir John and Lady Hope, Lord and Ly. R. Kerr[5] and so furth. Combination of Coalliers general and coals up to double price. The men will not work *although* or rather *because* they can make from 30/- to 40/- per week. L. R. K. told us that he had a letter from Lord Forbes (son of Earl Granard, Ireland) that he was asleep in his house at Castle Forbes when awaked by a sense of suffocation which deprived him of the power of stirring a limb yet left him the consciousness that the house was on fire. At this moment and while his apartment was in flames his large dog jumpd on the bed, seized his shirt and dragd him to the stair-case where the fresh air restored his powers of exertion and of escape. This is very different from most cases of preservation of life by the canine race, when the animal

---

1. *Richard III*, iii. 1.
2. Lady Scott's friend. See the Entry for 18 October 1826 and note.
3. Pierre Lebrun, author of two tragedies (*Marie Stuart*, 1820, and *Le Cid d'Andalousie*, 1825). Scott made the same mistake about his name in Paris the following year, 'demandant par une erreur amusante "M. Lenoir" '. Margaret Bain's *Les Voyageurs français en Écosse*, 1931. It is probably Lebrun's visit which is described in *Mrs Hughes's Recollections*, p. 208.
4. Robert Cockburn, a wine-merchant who lived at 7 Atholl Crescent. He was a brother of Lord Cockburn and an old Yeomanry friend of Scott's.
5. Lord Robert Kerr was Assistant Adjutant-General of the forces in Scotland.

generally jumps into the water in which he has force and skill. That of fire is as hostile to him as to mankind.

25 FRIDAY Read Jeffrey's neat and well intended address to the Mechanics upon their combinations.[1] Will it do good? – Umph. It takes only the hand of a Liliputian to light a fire but would require the diuretic powers of Gulliver to extinguish it.[2] The Whigs will live and die in the heresy that the world is ruled by little pamphlets and speeches and that if you can sufficiently demonstrate that a line of conduct is most consistent with men's interest you have therefore and thereby demonstrate[d] that they will at length after a few speeches on the subject adopt it of course. In this case we would have [no] need of laws or churches for I am sure there is no difficulty of proving that moral, regular, steady habits conduce to Men's best interest and that vice is not sin merely but folly. But of these individuals each has passions and prejudices the gratification of which he prefers not only to the general weal but to that of himself as an individual. Under the action of these wayward impulses a man drinks to-day though he is sure of starving tomorrow – he murders tomorrow though [he] is sure to be hanged on Wednesday and people are so slow to believe that which makes against their own predominant passions that mechanics will combine to raise the price for one week though they destroy the manufacture for ever. The best remedy seems to be the probable supply of labourers from other trades. Jeffrey proposes each mechanic shall learn some other trade than his own and so have two strings to his bow. He does not consider the length of a double apprenticeship. To make a man a good weaver and a good tailor would require as much time as the patriarch served for his two wives. After all he would be but a poor workman at either craft. Each mechanic has indeed a second trade for he can dig and work rustic labour. Perhaps the best reason for breaking up the associations will prove to be the expenditure of the money which they have been simple enough to levy from the industrious to the support of the idle. How much provision for the sick and the aged, the widow and the orphan, have been expended in the attempt to get wages which the manufacturer cannot afford them at any profitable chance of selling his commodity.

I had a bad fall last night coming home: there were unfinishd houses at the east end of Athole place and as I was on foot I crossd the

1. Francis Jeffrey (1773–1850) was editor of the *Edinburgh Review* and a prominent Whig advocate. In 1829 he became Dean of the Faculty and in 1830 Lord Advocate. The pamphlet referred to is *Combinations of Workmen, etc.*, Constable, 1825.
2. Swift's *Gulliver's Travels*, pt. 1, ch. 5.

street to avoid the material which lay about. But deceived by the moonlight I slippd ancle deep into a sea of mud (honest earth and water thank God) and fell on my hands. Never was there such a representative of *Wall* in Pyramus and Thisbe. I was absolutely rough cast. Luckily Lady S. had retired when I came home so I enjoyd my tub of water without either remonstrance or condoleances. Cockburn's hospitality will get the benefit and renown of my downfall and yet has no claim to it. In future though I must take a coach at night. A controul on one's freedom but it must be submitted to.

I found a letter from R. C.[1] giving a cheering account of things in London. Their correspondent[2] is getting into his strength. Three days ago I would have been contented to buy this *consola*, as Judy says,[4] dearer than by a dozen falls in the mud – for had the great Constable fallen

N.B. Within eight weeks after recording this graceful act of submission I found I was unable to keep a carriage

> Ω my countrymen what a fall were there![5]

Mrs. Coutts[6] with the Duke of Saint Albans and Lady Charlotte Beauclerk[7] calld to take leave of us. When at Abbotsford his suit

1. Robert Cadell.
2. Robinson of Hurst, Robinson.
3. However, Lady Scott could not do without. 'We are to œconomize in order to keep the carriage', Scott writes to Sophia on 17 February 1826. 'Now this matter of the carriage is of great consequence as a daily drive about two is really essential to Mamas health and spirits.' *Letters*, ix. 427. It had always meant much to her. After the success of *Waverley*, 'Mrs. Scott set up a carriage, a Barouche landau built in London, and which from the time she got it she was seldom out of'. Mrs. Grant's *Memoirs of a Highland Lady*, ii. 72.
4. 'This alludes to a strange old woman, keeper of a public-house among the Wicklow mountains, who, among a world of oddities, cut short every word ending in *tion*, by the omission of the termination. *Consola* for consolation – *bothera* for botheration, etc. Lord Plunkett had taken care to parade Judy and all her peculiarities.' J. G. L. (This and the other notes by Lockhart are taken from the *Life*, in which much of the *Journal* was published for the first time.)
5. *Julius Caesar*, iii. 2.
6. Mrs. Coutts, described by Benson Hill as 'a fat, bare-"necked", downy-chinned, rouged, elderly dame, in velvet and ermine' (Dibdin, p. 317), had been an actress in her youth and was now the very wealthy widow of Thomas Coutts the banker, to whom Scott was distantly related. She married the Duke of St. Albans in 1827. 'I daresay the marriage will turn out very well,' Anne Scott writes to Miss Millar, 'for, though he is a great fool, yet he is very good-natured.' *Letters from Scott's Family*, p. 128.
7. His sister.

throve but coldly. She made me I believe her confident in sincerity. She had refused him twice and decidedly he was merely on the footing of friendship. I urged it was akin to Love. She allowd she might marry the Duke only she had at present the least intention that way. Is this frank admission more favourable for the Duke than an absolute protestation against the possibility of such a marriage? I think not. It is the fashion to attend Mrs. Coutts' parties and to abuse her.[1] I have always found her a kind friendly woman without either affectation or insolence in the display of her wealth and most willing to do good if the means be shewn to her. She can be very entertaining too as she speaks without scruple of her stage life. So much wealth can hardly be enjoyd without some ostentation but what then? If the Duke marries her he ensures an immense fortune. If she marries him she has the first rank. If he marries a woman older than himself by twenty years She marries a man younger in wit by twenty degrees. I do not think he will dilapidate her fortune – he seems quiet and gentle. I do not think that she will abuse his softness – of disposition shall I say or of heart – The disparity of ages concerns no one but themselves – So they have my consent to marry if they can get each other's. Just as this is written enter my Lord of Saint Albans and Lady Charlotte to beg I would recommend a book of sermons to Mrs. Coutts – much obliged for her good opinion – recommended Logan's[2] – One poet should always speak for another – The mission I suppose was a little display on the part of good Mrs. Coutts of authority over her high aristocratic Suitor. I do not suspect her of turning Dévote and retract my consent given as above unless she remains 'lively brisk and jolly.'

Dined quiet with Wife and daughter.

R. Cadell lookd in in the evening on business. I here register my purpose to practise oeconomies. I have little temptation to do otherwise. Abbotsford is all that I can make it and too large for the property so I resolve –

No more Building

No purchases of Land till times are quite safe

No buying books or expensive trifles – I mean to any extent. And Clearing off encumbrances with the returns of this year's labour:

1. Even her visit to Abbotsford was not passed without some incivility from Scott's other guests. See *Life*, viii. 72–6.
2. John Logan (1748–88), a versatile but unlucky man of letters, who was tutor to Sir John Sinclair and later minister of South Leith church. His poems were published in 1781, and two volumes of sermons posthumously.

Which resolutions with health and my habits of industry will make me 'Sleep in spite of thunder.'[1]

After all it is hard that the vagabond Stock-jobbing Jews should for their own purposes make such a shake of credit as now exists in London and menace the credit of men trading on sure funds like H. and R. It is just like a set of pickpockets who raise a mob in which honest folks are knocked down and plunderd that they may pillage safely in the midst of the confusion they have excited.

26 SATURDAY The court met late and sate till *one*.[2] Detaind from that hour till four o'clock being engaged in the perplexd affairs of Mr. James Stewart of Brugh. This young gentleman is heir to a property of better than £1000 a year in Orkney. His mother married very young and was wife mother and widow in the course of the first year. Being unfortunately under the direction of a careless perhaps an unfaithful agent She was unlucky enough to embarass her own affairs by money transactions with this person. I was askd to accept the situation of one of his curators and trust to clear out his affairs and hers – at least I will not fail for want of application. I have lent her £300 on a second (and therefore doubtful) security over her house in Newington[3] bought for £1000 and on which £600 is already secured. I have no connection with the family except that of compassion and [may] not be rewarded even by thanks when the young man comes of age. I have known my father often so treated by those whom he had labour'd to serve. But if we do not run some hazard in our attempts to do good where is the merit of them? So I will bring through my Orkney Laird if I can.

I was obliged to give this up in consequence of my own misfortunes.

Dined at home quiet with Lady S. and Anne.

27 SUNDAY Some time since John Murray enterd into a contract with my son in law John G. Lockhart giving him on certain ample conditions the Management and Editorship of the *Quarterly Review*[4]

1. *Macbeth*, iv. 1.
2. For Scott's duties as a Clerk of Session see Introduction, pp. xxvii–xxviii.
3. A fashionable southern suburb of Edinburgh, which began to be built in the 1820s. This loan was never recovered either by Scott or his Trustees, owing to the continued embarrassment of her affairs and the falling value of property. Sederunt Book, ii. 61.
4. Scott had been instrumental in founding the *Quarterly* in 1809. As its new editor Lockhart was to receive 'from £1250 to £1,500 per annum'. Lockhart, 27 November 1825, Abbots.

for which they could certainly scarcely find a fitter person both from talents and character. It seems that Barrow[1] and one or two stagers have taken alarm at Lockhart's character as a satirist and his supposed accession to some of the freaks in Blackwood's magazine[2] and down comes young D'Israeli[3] to Scotland imploring Lockhart to make interest with my friends in London to remove objections and so forth. I have no idea of telling all and sundry that my son in law is not a slanderer or a silly thoughtless lad although [he] was six or seven years ago engaged in some light satires. I only wrote to Heber[4] and to Southey[5] – the first upon the subject of the reports which had startled Murray (the most timorous as Byron calld him of all God's booksellers) and such a letter as he may show Barrow if he judges proper – To Southey I wrote more generally acquainting him of my son's appointment to the Editorship and mentioning his qualifications, touching at the same time on his very slight connection with *Blackwd Magazine* and his innocence as to those gambades which may have offended himself and Southey[6] and which I fear they may ascribe too truly to an eccentric neighbour of their own.[7] I also mentiond that I heard nothing of the affair untill the month of October. I am concernd that Southey should know this for having been at the Lakes in September[8] I would not have him suppose that I

1. John Barrow (1764–1848), the explorer and geographer, a self-made man who was at this time a Secretary at the Admiralty under Lord Melville. He was an indefatigable writer and contributed more than two hundred articles to the *Quarterly*.

2. Lockhart was one of the original contributors to the Tory *Blackwood's Magazine* founded in 1817, and was suspected of being part-author of the 'Chaldee Manuscript' which offended many Edinburgh notabilities.

3. Benjamin Disraeli was twenty-one at this time. He published *Vivian Grey* the following year, entered Parliament in 1837, and became Prime Minister in 1868.

4. Richard Heber (1773–1833), the book-collector and M. P. for Oxford University. He first met Scott in Constable's shop when he spent the winter of 1800 in Edinburgh, and he assisted him with the *Minstrelsy*. In 1826 he resigned his seat after a homosexual scandal.

5. Southey was a principal contributor to the *Quarterly* and a friend of John Taylor Coleridge, the previous editor. Scott was anxious to assure him that when they discussed the *Quarterly* in August he did not then know that Lockhart was to be offered the editorship. *Letters*, ix. 297.

6. A slip for 'Wordsworth'.

7. Professor John Wilson (1785–1854), better known as 'Christopher North', who lived at Elleray near Windermere.

8. A slip for 'August'.

had been using interest with Canning[1] or Ellis[2] to supersede young Mr. Coleridge[3] their Editor and place my Son [in] law in the situation. Indeed I was never more surprized than when this proposal came upon us. I suppose it had come from Canning originally as he was sounding Anne when at Colonel Bolton's[4] about Lockhart's views <he> etc. To me he never hinted anything on the Subject. Other views are held out to Lockhart which may turn to great advantage. Only one person (John Cay[5] of Charlton) knows their object and truly I wish it had not been confided to any one. Yesterday I had a letter from Murray in answer to one I had written in something a determined stile for I had no idea of permitting him to start from the course after my son giving up his situation and profession merely because a contributor or two chose to suppose gratuitously that Lockhart was too imprudent for the situation. My physic has wrought well for it brought a letter from Murray saying all was right,[6] that D'Israeli was sent to me not to Lockhart, and that I was only invited to write two confidential letters, and other incoherencies which intimate his fright has got into another quarter. It is interlined and franked by Barrow[7] which shows that all is well and that John's induction in to his office will be easy and pleasant. I have not the least fear of his success. His talents want only a worthy sphere of exertion. He must learn however to despize petty adversaries. No good sportsman ought to shoot at crows unless for some special purpose. To take notice of such men as Hazlitt and Hunt in the *Quarterly* would be to introduce them into a world which is scarce conscious of their existence. It is odd enough that many years since I had the principal share in erecting this Review which has been since

1. George Canning (1770–1827) had been a friend of Scott's since Ellis had introduced them in 1805, and they were associated in founding the *Quarterly*. At this time Canning was Foreign Secretary. He became Prime Minister a few months before his death in 1827.
2. Charles Ellis (1771–1845), M. P. for Seaford, cousin of Scott's friend George Ellis, and Canning's second in his duel with Castlereagh. He was created Baron Seaford in 1826.
3. Not the poet, but his nephew John Taylor Coleridge, who had edited the *Quarterly* since 1824.
4. At Storrs, Windermere, during the journey home from Ireland.
5. John Cay (1790–1865), of Charlton in Northumberland, at this time Sheriff of Linlithgow.
6. Scott enclosed Murray's letter in one written to Lockhart the previous day. Murray writes that 'There is nothing to apprehend'. *Letters*, ix. 302–3 and note.
7. The interlineation reads 'No one has any ill will against Mr. Lockhart!!!' *Letters*, ix. 303 n.

so prosperous and now it is placed under management of my Son in Law upon the most honourable principle of *detur digniori*.[1] Yet there are sad drawbacks so far as family comfort is concernd. To-day is Sunday when they always dined with us and generally met a family friend or two. But we are no longer to expect them – In the country where their little cottage was within a mile or two of Abbotsford we shall miss their society still more for Chiefswood was the perpetual object of our walks, rides and drives. Lockhart is such an excellent family man so fond of his wife and child that I hope all will go well.

A letter from Lockhart in the evening.[2] All safe as to his unanimous reception in London. His predecessor young [Coleridge] handsomely and like a gentleman offers his assistance as a contributor etc.

28 MONDAY I have the less dread or rather the less anxiety about the consequences of this migration that I repose much confidence in Sophia's tact and good sense. Her manners are good and have the appearance of being perfectly natural. She is quite conscious of the limited range of her musical talents and never makes them common or produces them out of place – a rare virtue – Moreover she is proud enough and will not be easily netted and patronized by any of that class of Ladies who may be calld Lion-providers for town and country. She is domestic besides and will not be disposed to gad about. Then she seems an oeconomist and on £3000, living quietly, there should be something to save.[3] Lockhart must be liked where his good qualities are known and where his fund of information has room to be displayd. But notwithstanding a handsome exterior and face I am not sure he will succeed in London Society. He sometimes reverses the proverb and gives the *volte strette e pensiere sciolti*[4] – withdraws his attention from the company or attaches himself to some individual, gets into a corner and seems to be quizzing the rest.

1. 'Let it be given to the more deserving.'
2. Scott replied at once, promising a review of Pepys for the *Quarterly* and inviting Lockhart to come the following Sunday to discuss 'the few ideas which occur to me about your new and important task'. *Letters*, ix. 308.
3. 'I am sure it will please you to hear', writes Sophia on 1 February 1826, 'we have been most prudent with regard to money matters since we came here . . . From the first I determined against a carriage till we see how we get on and pay our household servants every week.' Walpole.
4. In a letter Scott translates *Volto sciolto e pensiere stretti* as ' "An open countenance & close thoughts." There is no occasion to let anyone see what you exactly think of him.' *Letters*, v. 449–50.

This is the want of early habits of being in society and a life led much at College. Nothing is however so popular and so deservedly so as to take an interest in whatever is going forward in Society. A wise man always finds his account in it and will receive information and fresh views of life even in the Society of Fools. Abstain from society altogether when you are not able to play some part in it. This reserve and a sort of Hidalgo air joind to his character as a satirist have done the best humourd fellow in the world some injury in the opinion of Edinburgh folks.[1] In London it is of less consequence whether he please in general society or not since if he can establish himself as a genius it will only be calld 'pretty Fanny's way.'

People make me the oddest requests. It is not unusual for an Oxonian or Cantab who has out-run his allowance and of whom I know nothing to apply to me for the loan of £20–£50 or £100. A Captain of the Danish naval service wrote to me that being in distress for a sum of money by which he might transport himself to Columbia to offer his services in assisting to free that province he had dreamd I generously made him a present of it. I can tell him his dream by contraries. I begin to find like Joseph Surface that too good a character is inconvenient.[2] I don't know what I have done to gain so much credit for generosity but I suspect I owe it to being supposed, as Puff says, one of 'those whom Heaven has blessed with affluence.'[3] Not too much of that neither, my dear petitioners, though I may thank myself that your ideas are not correct.

Dined at Melville Castle whither I went through a snow storm. I was glad to find myself once more in a place connected with many happy days.[4] Met Sir R. Dundas and my old friend George now Lord Abercrombie[5] with his lady and a beautiful girl his daughter. He is what he always was, the best humourd man living, and our meetings now more rare than usual [this] was seasond with many a recollection of old frolics and old friends. I am entertaind to see him just the same he has always been, never yielding up his own opinion

1. In London, however, he 'really takes pains to make himself agreeable in society'. Sophia, 1 February 1826, Walpole
2. Sheridan's *School for Scandal*, ii. 2.
3. Sheridan's *Critic*, i. 2.
4. As the boyhood friend of the second Viscount Melville, Scott had been a frequent visitor in the days of the great Lord Melville.
5. George Abercromby (1770–1843), another boyhood friend, was married to Lord Melville's sister. He was the eldest son of General Sir Ralph Abercromby (1738–1801) and inherited the barony from his mother, who had been created Baroness Abercromby of Aboukir in recognition of her husband's victory against the French at Alexandria in 1801.

in fact and yet in words acquiescing in all that could be said against it. George was always like a willow; he never offerd resistance to the breath of argument but never moved from his rooted opinion, blow as it listed.

Exaggeration might make these peculiarities highly dramatic. Conceive a man who always seems to be acquiescing in your sentiments yet never changes his own and this with a sort of bonhommie which shows there is not a particle of deceit intended. He is only desirous to spare you the trouble of contradiction.

29 TUESDAY A letter from Southey, malcontent about Murray having accomplishd the change in the *Quarterly* without speaking to him and quoting the twaddle of some old woman, male or female, about Lockhart's earlier *jeux d'esprit* but concluding most kindly that in regard to my daughter and me he did not mean to withdraw. That he has done yeoman's service to the Review is certain – and his genius, his universal reading, his powers of regular industry and at the outset a name which though less generally popular than it deserves is still too respectable to be withdrawn without injury. I could not in reply point out to him what is the truth, that his rigid Toryism and high-church prejudices renderd him an unsafe counsellor in a matter where the spirit of the age must be consulted. But I pointed out to him what I am sure is true that Murray, apprehensive of his displeasure, had not ventured to write to him out of mere timidity and not from any [depreciatory feeling]. I treated his old woman's apprehensions and cautions and all that gossip about friends and enemies to which a splendid number or two will be a sufficient answer. And I accepted with due acknowlegment his proposal of continued support. I cannot say I was afraid of his withdrawing – Lockhart will have hard cards with him for great as Southey's powers are he has not the art to make them work popularly. He is often diffuse and frequently sets much value on minute and unimportant facts and useless pieces of abstruse knowlege. Living too exclusively in a circle where he is idolized both for his genius and the excellence of his disposition he has acquired strong prejudices, though all of an upright and honourable cast. He rides his high church hobby too hard and it will not do to run a tilt upon it against all the world. Gifford[1] used to crop his articles considerably and they bear marks of it being sometimes *décousues*. Southey said that Gifford cut out his *middle joints*. When

1. William Gifford (1756–1826), who edited the *Quarterly* from its inception until 1824, a little, bitter, deformed man, known as a translator and satirist as well as reviewer.

John comes to use the carving knife I fear Dr. Southey will not be so tractable. *Nous verrons.* I will not shew Southey's letter to J. Lockhart for there is to him personally no friendly tone and it would startle the Hidalgo's pride. It is to be wishd they may draw kindly together.[1] Southey says most truly that even those who most undervalue his reputation would were he to withdraw from the review exaggerate the loss it would thereby sustain. The bottom of all these feuds, though not named, is *Blackwood's Magazine*; all the squibs of which, which have sometimes exploded among the Lakers, Lockhart is renderd accountable for. He must now exert himself at once with spirit and prudence – He has good backing. Canning, Bishop Bloomfield,[2] Gifford, Wright,[3] Croker,[4] Will Rose, and is there not besides the Douglas? An excellent plot, excellent friends, and full of preparations.[5] It was no plot of my making I am sure. Yet men will say and believe that I, who never heard a word of the matter till first a hint from Wright and then the formal proposal of Murray to Lockhart announcd [it to me, was the maker of it]. I believe Canning and Charles Ellis were the prime movers. I will puzzle my brains no more about it.

Dined at Justice Clk's. The presidt,[6] Capt Smollet etcaetera. Our new Commander in Chief or Commanding in Chief Honble Sir Robert O'Callaghan,[7] brother to Earl of Lismore, a fine soldierly looking man with orders and badges. His brother an Agreeable and deserving the name whom I met at Lowther Castle[8] this season. He composes his own musick and sings his own poetry, has much

1. Sheridan's *Rivals*, i. 1.
2. Charles James Blomfield (1786–1857), Bishop of Chester (and later of London), contributor to the *Quarterly* on classical subjects.
3. William Wright of Lincoln's Inn.
4. John Wilson Croker (1780–1857), M. P. for Downpatrick and Secretary at the Admiralty, the friend of Wellington and Peel, and a frequent contributor to the *Quarterly*. His caustic tongue made him some enemies, but he retained Scott's friendship despite an attack on his *Letters of Malachi*. See the Entries for 17 and 28 March 1826.
5. An allusion to Hotspur's plot in *1 Henry IV*, ii. 3. 'The Douglas' is Scott himself.
6. The Lord President of the Court of Session, the Rt. Hon. Charles Hope of Granton (1763–1851), who had held the offices of Lord Advocate and Lord Justice-Clerk before becoming Lord President in 1811. He was the father of John Hope, the Solicitor-General.
7. Major-General the Hon. Sir Robert William O'Callaghan (1770–1840) commanded the forces at Edinburgh until 1830. Will Clerk describes him as 'a rich morceau when he becomes a little mellow'. 6 January 1829, Walpole.
8. During Scott's return journey from Ireland.

humour enhanced by a strong touch of national dialect which is always a rich sauce to an Irishman's good things. Dandyish but not offensively, and seems to have a warm feeling for the credit of his country rather inconsistent with the trifling and selfish quietude of a mere man of society.

30 WEDNESDAY I am come to the time when those who look out at the windows shall be darkend.[1] I must now wear spectacles constantly in reading and writing, though till this winter I have made a shift by using only their occasional assistance. Although my health cannot be better I feel my lameness becomes sometimes painful and often inconvenient. Walking on the pavement or causeway gives me trouble and I am glad when I have accomplishd my return on foot from the Parliament House to Castle Street[2] though I can (taking a competent time as old *Braxie*[3] said on another occasion) walk five or six miles in the country with pleasure. Well – such things must come and be received with cheerful submission. My early lameness[4] considerd, it was impossible for a man labouring under a bodily impediment to have been stronger or more active than I have been, and that for twenty or thirty years. Seams will slit and elbows will out quoth the tailor[5] – and as I was fifty four on 15 August last my mortal vestments are none of the newest. Then Walter, Charles and Lockhart are as active and handsome young fellows as you can see and while they enjoy strength and activity I can hardly be said to want it. I have perhaps all my life set an undue value on these gifts. Yet it does appear to me that high and independent feelings are naturally though not uniformly or inseparably connected with bodily advantages. Strong men are usually goodhumourd and active men often display the same elasticity of mind as of body. These are superiorities however that are often misused. But even for these things God shall call us to judgement.[6]

Some months since I joind with other literary folks in subscribing a

1. Ecclesiastes 12: 3.
2. A distance of just over half a mile.
3. Robert MacQueen, Lord Braxfield (1722–99), the legendary hanging judge whose coarse jocularity is well described by Cockburn in chapter 2 of his *Memorials*. Scott, who dedicated his thesis to the old man, liked to repeat the comment he is alleged to have made to a prisoner: 'Ye're a vera clever chiel', man, but ye wad be nane the waur o' a hanging.' *Life*, vi. 203.
4. An attack of polio at the age of eighteen months left Scott with a limp for the rest of his life.
5. Foote's *Maid of Bath*, i.1.
6. Ecclesiastes 11: 9.

petition for a pension to Mrs. G— of L—n[1] which we thought was a tribute merited by her works as an authoress and in my opinion much more by the firmness and elasticity of mind with which she had borne a succession of great domestic calamity. Unhappily there was only about £100 open on the pension list and this the ministers assigned in equal portions to Mrs. G— and a distressd Lady, grand daughter of a forfeited Scottish nobleman. Mrs. G—, proud as a Highland woman, vain as a poetess and absurd as a Blue Stocking, has taken this partition *in malam partem* and written to Lord Melville about her merits, and that her friends do not consider her claims as being fairly canvassd, with something like a demand that her petition be submitted to the King. This is not the way to make her *plack a bawbee*[2] and Lord M. a little *miffd* in turn sends the whole correspondence to me to know whether Mrs. G. will accept the £50 or not. Now hating to deal with ladies when they are in an unreasonable humour I have got the goodhumourd Man of Feeling[3] to find out the lady's mind and I take on myself the task of making her peace with Lord M— There is no great doubt how it will end for your scornful dog will always eat your dirty pudding. After all the poor lady is greatly to be pitied. Her sole remaining daughter, deep and far gone in a decline, has been seized with alienation of mind.

Dined with my cousin R. R.[4] being the first invitation since my uncle's death. Our Cousin Lt. Col. Russell[5] of Ashestiel with his sister Anne, the former newly returnd from India. A fine gallant fellow and distinguishd as a cavalry officer. He came overland from India and has observed a good deal. General L— of L—[6], in Logan's orthography a *fowl*,[7] Sir William Hamilton,[8] Miss Peggy

---

1. Mrs. Anne Grant, widow of the minister of Laggan, and author of *Letters from the Mountains, Superstitions of the Highlands,* and *Memoirs of a Highland Lady.* She was now seventy years old, very poor and very lame.
2. To make her farthing into a halfpenny.
3. Henry Mackenzie (1745–1831), the aged but still active author of *The Man of Feeling* (1771).
4. Robert Rutherford. W.S. (1790–1866).
5. Later Major-General Sir James Russell (1781–1859). Anne Scott considered him a bore, 'but it is a great advantage having the tweed between us for it is seldom fordable'. To Sophia, 29 September 1826, Abbots. Scott, however, enjoyed his company.
6. Baron Lynedoch of Lynedoch (1748–1843), at this time Governor of the garrison at Dumbarton Castle.
7. 'The *civilest* way of caa'ing a man a *guse.*' *Letters,* v. 128.
8. Sir William Hamilton (1788–1856), the Professor of Civil History at Edinburgh, a Balliol friend of Lockhart's and a foe to the phrenologists.

Swinton,[1] William Keith and others. Knight Marischal[2] not well so unable to attend this convocation of kith and kin.

1 THURSDAY   Colonel R. told me that the European government had discoverd an ingenious mode of diminishing the number of burnings of widows. It seems the Shaster[3] positively enjoins that the pile shall be so constructed that if the victim should repent even at the moment when it is set on fire she may still have the means of saving herself. The Bramins soon found it was necessary to assist the resolution of the sufferers by means of a little pit into which they contrive to let the poor widow sink so as to prevent her reaping any benefit from a late repentance. But the Government has brought them back to the rigour of their law and only permit the burning to go on when the pile is constructed with full opportunity of a *locus penitentiae*[4]. Yet the widow is so degraded if she dare to survive that the number of burnings is still great. The quantity of female children destroyed by the Rajahpout tribes Col. R. describes as very great indeed. They are strangled by the mother. The principle is the aristocratic pride of these high castes who breed up no more daughters than they can reasonably hope to find matches for in their own tribe. Singular how artificial systems of feeling can be made to overcome that love of offspring which seems instinctive in the females not of the human race only but of the lower animals. This is the reverse of our system of increasing game by shooting the old cock-birds. It is a system would aid Malthus rarely.[5]

Nota Bene the day before yesterday I signed the Bond for £5000 with Constable for relief of Robinson's House. I am to be secured by good bills.

I think this Journal will suit me well; if I can coax myself into an idea that is purely voluntary it may go on – *Nulla dies sine linea*.[6] But never a being from my infancy upwards hated task-work as I hate it –

1. Scott was connected with the Swintons through his maternal grandmother.
2. Sir Alexander Keith of Ravelston (1780–1833) had ridden as Knight Marischal in the procession during the King's visit in 1822. William Keith was one of his younger brothers. Scott was connected with the family through his mother.
3. 'Any one of the sacred writings of the Hindus'. *O. E. D.*
4. A phrase used in Scots Law meaning 'opportunity for change of intention'.
5. Scott sent to Lockhart on 17 February a short article on the burnings for publication in the *Representative. Letters*, ix. 427.
6. 'No day without a line', a proverb quoted by Pliny.

And yet I have done a great deal in my day. It is not that I am idle in my nature neither. But propose to me to do one thing and it is inconceivable the desire I have to do something else, not that it is more easy or more pleasant but just because it is escaping from an imposed task. I cannot trace this love of contradiction to any distinct source but [it] has haunted me all my life. I could almost suppose it was mechanical and that the imposition of a piece of duty-labour operated on me like the mace of a bad billiard player, which gives an impulse to the ball indeed but sends it off at a tangent different from the course designed by the player. Now if I expend such eccentrick movements on this journal it will be turning this wretched propensity to some tolerable account. If I had thus employd the hours and half hours which I have while'd away in putting off something that must needs be done at last, My Conscience,[1] I should have had a journal with a witness.

Sophia and Lockhart came to Edinr to-day and dined with us, meeting Hector Macdonald Buchanan,[2] his Lady and Missy (familiarly so called) – James Skene[3] and his Lady – Lockhart's friend Cay – etc.

They are lucky to be able to assemble so many real friends whose good wishes I am sure will follow them in their new undertaking.

2 FRIDAY Rather a blank day for the Gurnal.[4] Correcting proofs in the morning – Court from ½ past ten till two – poor dear Colin Mackenzie, one of the wisest kindest and best men of his time, in the country – I fear with very indifferent health[5] – from two till five transacting business with J. B. All seems to go smoothly.

Sophia dined with us alone, Lockhart being gone to the West to bid farewell to his father and brothers. Evening spent in talking with Sophia on their future prospects. God bless her, poor girl. She never gave me a moment's reason to complain of her. But O my God that

1. The catch-phrase of Bailie Nicol Jarvie in *Rob Roy*.
2. A Clerk of Session since 1805 and intimate family friend. His Highland prejudices endeared him to Scott. He was the brother of Staffa and a kinsman of Napoleon's Maréchal Macdonald. He adopted his wife's name on marriage.
3. See Introduction, p. xliv.
4. 'A hard word so spelld on Authority of Miss Scott Mrs. Lockhart'. Title-page of the *Journal*.
5. Scott wrote to him while the Court sat, urging him to rest until January: 'The business is very easy and you will really act very unwisely as well as unkindly if you do not leave us to manage it, but endanger your health so deservedly valued by your bretheren and many others.' *Letters*, ix. 313.

poor delicate child,[1] so clever, so animated, yet holding by this earth
with so fearfully slight a tenure – Never out of his mother's thoughts,
almost never out of his father's arms when he has but a single
moment to give to anything. *Deus providebit.*[2]

3 SATURDAY R. P. G.[3]came to call last night to excuse himself from
dining with Lockhart's friends to-day. I really fear he is near an actual
stand-still. He has been extremely improvident. When I first knew him
he had an excellent estate and now he is deprived I fear of the whole
reversion of the price. And this from no vice or extreme except a
wasteful mode of buying pictures and other costly trifles at high prices
and selling them again for nothing, besides an extravagant housekeeping and profuse hospitality. An excellent disposition with a
considerable fund of acquired knowledge would have renderd him
an agreeable companion had he not affected singularity and renderd
himself accordingly singularly affected. He was very near being a poet
but a miss is as good as a mile and he always fell short of the mark. I
knew him first many years ago when he was desirous of my acquaintance but he was too poetical for me or I was not poetical enough for
him so that we continued only ordinary acquaintance with goodwill on
either side, which R. P. G. really deserves as a more friendly generous
creature never lived. Lockhart hopes to get something done for him,
being sincerely attachd to him, but says he has no hopes till he is utterly
ruind. That point I fear is not far distant but what Lockhart can do for
him then I cannot guess. His last effort faild owing to a curious reason.
He had made some translations from the German which he does
extremely [well],[4] for give him ideas and he never wants choice of good
words, and Lockhart had got Constable to offer some sort of terms for
them. R. P. G. has always, though possessing a beautiful power of
handwriting, had some whim or other about imitating that of some
other person and has written for months in the imitation of one or

1. His grandson John Lockhart (1821–31), the 'Hugh Littlejohn' of
   Tales of a Grandfather. Scott dreaded the effect on him of London
   air: 'Poor little fellow he is most likely to suffer by this change of
   residence.' *Letters*, ix. 319.
2. 'God will provide.'
3. Robert Pearce Gillies (1788–1858), a nephew of Scott's friend the
   judge Lord Gillies. He was in dire financial straits as usual and
   about to remove to London, where he became the first editor of the
   Foreign Quarterly Review. In 1840 he fled to Boulogne to elude his
   creditors, and on his return was imprisoned for two years. His
   relatively worthless *Recollections of Sir Walter Scott* was published in
   1837.
4. Scott owned his translation of Hoffmann's *The Devil's Elixirs*, 1824.

other of his friends. Now at present he has renounced this amusement and chuses to write with a brush upon large cartridge paper somewhat in the Chinese fashion. So when his work which was only to extend to one or two volumes arrived on the shoulders of two porters in immense bales our jolly Bibliopolist backd out of the treaty and would have nothing more to do with R. P.[1] He is a creature that is or would be thought of imagination all compact[2] and is influenced by strange whims. But he is a kind, harmless, friendly soul and I fear has been cruelly plunderd of money which he now wants sadly.

Dined with Lockhart's friends, about fifty in number, who gave him a parting entertainment. John Hope Solicitor Genl.[3] in the chair and Robert Dundas[4] Croupier. The company most highly respectable and any man might be proud of such an indication of the interest they take in his progress in life. Tory principles rather too violently upheld by some speakers. I came home about ten. The party sate late.

4 SUNDAY Lockhart and Sophia with his brother William dined with us[5] and talkd over our separation and the mode of their settling in London[6] and other family topics.

5 MONDAY This morning Lockhart and Sophia left us early and without leave-taking. When I arose at eight o'clock they were *Gone*. This was very right. I hate red eyes and blowing of noses. *Agere et pati Romanum est.*[7] Of all schools commend me to the Stoicks. We cannot indeed overcome our affections nor ought we if we could, but we repress them within due bounds and avoid coaxing them to make fools of those who should be their masters. I have lost some of the

---

1. 'Mr. Gillies was, however, warmly welcomed by another publisher in Edinburgh, who paid him £100 for his bulky manuscripts, and issued the book in 1825 under the title of *The Magic Ring*, 3 vols. Its failure with the public prevented a repetition of the experiment!' Douglas.
2. An allusion to 'the lunatic, the lover, and the poet' in *A Midsummer Night's Dream*, v. 1.
3. John Hope (1794–1858), Solicitor-General for Scotland 1822–30: Dean of the Faculty of Advocates 1830, and later Lord Justice-Clerk. He was the eldest son of the Lord President, Charles Hope.
4. Robert Dundas of Arniston (1797–1838), son of the Lord Chief Baron.
5. 'Consuming little meat and much small beer.' *Letters*, ix. 321.
6. On the advice of Terry, Murray, and Disraeli, they decided 'to rent for 6 months a handsome & convenient *ready furnished* house in the best possible situation'. Terry, 16 November 1825, Abbots.
7. 'To do and to suffer is Roman.'

comforts to which I chiefly lookd for enjoyment – well – I must make the more of such as remain. God bless them.

And so I will unto my holy work again[1] which at present is the description of that *heilige Kleeblat* – that worshipful triumvirate Danton, Robespierre and Marat.[2]

I cannot conceive what possesses me over every person besides to mislay papers. I received a letter Saturday at *e'en* enclosing a bill for £750 *no deaf nuts* – well I read it and note the contents, and this day as if it had been a wind bill in the literal sense of the words I search every-where and lose three hours of my morning – turn over all my confusion in the writing desk – break open one or two letters lest I should have enclosed the sweet and quickly convertible document in them by mistake – send for a joiner and disorganize my scrutoire lest it should have fallen aside by mistake – I find it at last – the place where is of little consequence. But this trick must be amended.

Dined at the Royal Society Club where as usual was a pleasant meeting of from 20 of 25. It is a very good institution. We pay two guineas only for six dinners in the year present or absent. Dine at 5 or rather ½ past five at the Royal hotel where we have an excellent dinner with soups fish etc. and all in good order, port and Sherry till half past seven then coffee and we go to the Society.[3] This has great influence in keeping up the attendance, it being found that this preface of a good dinner to be paid for whether you partake or not brings out many a philosopher who might not otherwise have attended the Society.

Harry Mackenzie now in his eighty second or third year read part of an Essay on Dreams.[4]

Supd at Dr. Russell's usual party[5] – which shall serve for one while.

6 TUESDAY A rare thing this literature or love of fame or notoriety which accompanies it. Here is Mr. H. M.[6] on the very brink of human

1. A reminiscence of *Richard III*, iii. 7.
2. *Life of Napoleon*, vol. ii, ch. 9.
3. The Royal Society of Edinburgh, of which Scott was President. 1820–32.
4. 'A supplement to a Paper on Dreams formerly read to the Society.' Royal Society Minutes.
5. Dr. James Russell (1754–1836), Regius Professor of Clinical Surgery at Edinburgh University and Vice-president of the Royal Society, habitually held a supper party at 30 Abercromby Place after the fortnightly meetings of the Society.
6. Henry Mackenzie who, according to Lockhart, had been consulting Sir Walter about collecting his own juvenile poetry, and who apparently intended Scott to write his life. Disc. ii. 227.

dissolution as actively anxious about it as if the curtain must not soon be closed on that and every thing else. He calls me his literary confessor and I am sure I am glad to return the kindnesses which he shewd me long since in George's Square. No man is less known from his writings. We would suppose a retired, modest, somewhat affected man with a white handkerchief and a sigh ready for every sentiment. No such thing. H. M. is alert as a contracting tailor's needle in every sort of business, a politician and a sportsman, shoots and fishes in a sort even to this day, and is the life of the company with anecdote and fun. Sometimes his daughter tells me he is in low spirits at home but really I never see anything of it in Society.

There is a maxim almost universal in Scotland which I would like much to see contrould. Every youth of every temper and almost every description of character is sent either to study as a lawyer or to a Writer's office as an apprentice. The Scottish seem to conceive Themis the most powerful of Goddesses. Is a lad stupid the Law will sharpen him – Is he too mercurial the law will make him sedate. Has he an estate he may get a sherrifdom – is he poor the richest Lawyers have emerged from poverty – Is he a Tory – he may become a Depute Advocate. Is he a Whig he may with far better hope expect to become in reputation at least 'that rising counsel' Mr.— when in fact he only rises at tavern dinners. Upon some such wild views lawyers and writers multiply till there is no life for them and men give up the chase hopeless and exhausted and go into the army at five and twenty instead of eighteen with a turn for expence perhaps – almost certainly for profligacy and with a heart embitterd against the loving parents or friends who compelld them to lose six or seven years in dusting the rails of the stove with their black gowns or scribbling nonsense for twopence a page all day and laying out twice their earnings at night in whisky punch. Here is R. L.[1] now – four or five years ago from certain indications I assured his friends L— would never be a writer – goodnatured lad too when Bacchus is out the question but at other times so pugnacious that it was evident he could only be properly placed where fighting was to be a part of his duty regulated by time and place and paid for accordingly. Well – time money and instruction have been thrown away, and now after fighting two regular boxing matches and a duel with pistols in the course of one week, he tells them roundly he will be *no* writer, which common sense might have told them before. He has now perhaps acquired habits of insubordination unfitting him for the army where he might have been tamed at an earlier period. He is too old for the Navy and so he must go to India, a Guinea-pig on board a Chinaman

1. Robert Lockhart, brother of Scott's son-in-law.

– with what hope or view it is melancholy to guess. J. G. L. did all man could to get his friends to consent to his going into the army in time. The Lad has goodhumour, courage and most gentlemanlike feelings. But he is incurably dissipated I hear, so goes to die in youth in a foreign land.

Thank God I let Walter take his own way and I trust he will be a useful honourd soldier, being for his time high in the service, whereas at home he would probably have been a wine-bibbing, moorfowl shooting, fox hunting Fife Squire living at Lochore[1] without either aim or end – And well if he were no worse. Dined at home with L. S. and Anne. Wrote in the Evening.

7 WEDNESDAY Teind day[2] at home of course. Wrote answers to [one] or two letters which have [been] lying on my desk like snakes hissing at me for my dilatoriness. Bespoke a ton of Palm oil from Sir John Tobin.[3] Received a letter from Sir W. Knighton[4] mentioning that the King acquiesced in my proposal that Constable's *Miscellany* should be dedicated to him.[5] Enjoind however not to make this public till the drat. of dedication shall be approved. This letter tarried so long I thought some one had insinuated the proposal was *infra dig*. I don't think so. The purpose is to bring all the standard works both in sciences and the liberal arts within the reach of the lower classes and enable them thus to use with advantage the education which is given them at every hand. To make boys learn to read and then place no good books within their reach is to give men an appetite and leave nothing in the pantry save unwholesome and poisonous food which

1. His wife Jane's estate.
2. See Introduction, p. xxvi.
3. A Liverpool merchant who recommended it for making gas and sent Scott a trial cask in 1824. Walpole, 19 January 1824. He had been knighted in 1820 while Lord Mayor of Liverpool.
4. Sir William Knighton (1776–1836), physician and private secretary to George IV. Scott first met him during the royal visit to Scotland in 1822, and the friendship was kept in good repair by correspondence.
5. Scott had made the request in October. *Letters*, ix. 262. The Dedication, which was approved before 20 December, was in the following terms: 'To His Majesty KING GEORGE IV, The generous Patron even of the most humble attempts towards the advantage of his subjects, THE MISCELLANY, designed to extend Useful Knowledge and Elegant Literature, by placing Works of standard merit within the attainment every class of Readers, is most humbly inscribed by his Majesty's humble and devoted servant, ARCHIBALD CONSTABLE. *Letters*, ix. 327.

depend upon it they will eat rather than starve. Sir William it seems
has been in Germany.

Mighty dark this morning: it is past ten and I am using my lamp.
The vast number of houses built beneath us to the North[1] certainly
render our street darker during the days when frost or haze prevents
the smoke from rising. After all it may be my older eyes. I remember
two years ago when Ld. H—[2] began to fail somewhat in his limbs he
observed that Ld. S—[3] came to court at a more early hour than usual,
whereas it was he himself who took longer time to walk the usual
distance betwixt his house and the Parlt. Square. I suspect old
gentlemen often make such mistakes.

A letter from Southey[4] in a very pleasant strain as to Lockhart
and myself – of Murray he has perhaps ground to complain, as well
for consulting him late in the business as for the manner in which
he intimated [it] to young Coleridge who had no reason to think
himself handsomely treated though he has acquiesced in the
arrangement in a very gentleman like tone. With these matters
we of course have nothing to do, having no doubt that the situation
was vacant when M— offerd it as such. Southey says, in alteration
of Byron's phrase, that M. is the most timorous not of God's but of
the Devil's booksellers. The truth I take to be that Murray was
pushd in the change of editor (which was really become necessary)
probably by Gifford, Canning, Ellis etc. and when he had fixd with
Lockhart by their advice his constitutional nervousness made him
delay entering upon a full explanation with Coleridge. But it is all
settled now. I hope Lockhart will be able to mitigate their high-
church bigotry – it is not for the present day, savouring too much
of *Jure divino*.[5]

Dined quiet with Lady S. and Anne. Anne is practicing Scots songs
which I take as a kind compliment to my own taste as hers leads her
chiefly to foreign music. I think the good girl sees that I want and
must miss her sister's peculiar talent in singing the airs of our native
country which, imperfect as my musical ear is, make and always have

1. The development north of Queen Street as far as Royal Circus and
   Great King Street took place between 1803 and 1823.
2. George Fergusson of Hermand, who took the title of Lord
   Hermand when he succeeded Braxfield on the Bench in 1799. 'He
   was fond of the pleasures, and not least the liquid ones, of the table',
   says Cockburn (*Memorials*, ch. 2), and was a man of decided and
   outspoken views.
3. Sir Archibald Campbell, raised to the Bench in 1809 as Lord
   Succoth.
4. See *Letters*, ix. 309 n.
5. 'By divine right'.

made the most pleasing impression on me – and so if she puts a constraint on herself for my sake, I can only say in requital God Bless Her.

I have much to comfort me in the present aspect of my family. My eldest son independent in fortune united to an affectionate wife – and of good hopes in his profession. My second with a good deal of talent and in the way I trust of cultivating it to good purpose. Anne an honest downright good Scots lass in whom I would only wish to correct a spirit of satire – And Lockhart is Lockhart to whom I can most willingly confide the happiness [of the] daughter who chose him, and whom he has chosen.

My dear wife, the partner of early cares and successes, is I fear frail in health – though I trust and pray she may see me out. Indeed if this troublesome complaint goes on – it bodes no long existence – My brother[1] was affected with the same weakness which before he was fifty brought on mortal symptoms. The poor Major had been rather a free liver. But my father, the most abstemious of men save when the duties of hospitality required him to be very moderately free with his bottle and that was very seldom, had the same weakness of the powers of retention which now annoy me and he I think was not above seventy when cut off. Square the odds and goodnight Sir Walter about sixty. I care not, if I leave my name unstaind and my family properly settled. *Sat est vixisse.*[2]

8 THURSDAY Talking of the *Vixisse* it may not be impertinent to notice that Knox,[3] a young poet of considerable talent, died here a week or two since. His father was a respectable yeoman and he himself succeeding to good farms under the Duke of Buccleuch became too soon his own Master and plunged into dissipation and ruin. His poetical talent – a very fine one – then shewd itself in a fine strain of pensive poetry calld I think the *Lonely Hearth*, far superior to those of Michael Bruce,[4] whose *consumptition* by the way has been the life of his verses. But poetry, nay good poetry, is a drug in the present day. I am a wretched patron – I cannot go about with a subscription

1. Major John Scott.
2. 'It is enough to have lived.'
3. William Knox, from Lilliesleaf near Melrose, who had died on 12 November, aged thirty-six. Lockhart's note says: 'His publisher (Mr. Anderson junior, of Edinburgh) remembers that Sir Walter occasionally wrote to Knox and sent him money – £10 at a time.'
4. Michael Bruce (1746–67), the son of a Kinross-shire weaver. Scott probably had in mind his 'Elegy – Written in Spring', which is given added point by its author's untimely death.

paper like a pocket pistol about me and draw unawares on some honest country gentleman who has as much alarm as if I had used the phrase Stand and Deliver, and parts with his money with a grimace indicating some suspicion that the crown-piece thus levied goes ultimately into the Collector's own pocket. This I see daily done and I have seen such collectors when they have exhausted Papa and Mamma continue their trade among the Misses and conjure out of their pockets those little funds which should carry them to a play or an assembly. It is well people will go through this – it does some good I suppose and they have great merit who can sacrifice their pride so far as to attempt it in this way. For my part I am a bad promoter of subscriptions but I wishd to do what I could for this lad whose talent I really admired, and I am not addicted to admire heaven-born poets or poetry that is reckond very good *considering*. I had him, Knox, at Abbotsford about ten years ago but found him unfit for that sort of society. I tried to help him but there were temptations he could never resist. He scrambled on writing for the booksellers and magazines and living like the Otways and Savages and Chattertons of former days though I do not know that he was in actual want. His connection with me terminated in begging a subscription or a guinea now and then. His last works were Spiritual hymns and which he wrote very well. In his own line of Society he was said to exhibit infinite humour but all his works are grave and pensive a stile, perhaps like Master Stephen's melancholy affected for the nonce.[1]

Mrs. G. of L.[2] intimates that she will take her pudding – her pension I mean (See 30 November) – and is contrite as H. M.[3] vouches. I am glad the stout old girl is not foreclosed, faith. Cabbing a pension in these times is like hunting a pig with a soap'd tail, monstrous apt to slip through your fingers.

Dined at home with Lady S. and Anne.

9 FRIDAY Yesterday I read and wrote the whole day and evening. To-day I shall not be so happy having Gas Light Coy to attend at two. I must be brief in journalising.

The gay world has been kept in hot water lately by the impudent publication of the celebrated Harriet Wilson.[4] W—n from earliest possibility I suppose <who> lived with half the gay world at hack and manger; and now obliges such as will not pay hush-money with a history of whatever she knows or can invent about them. She must

1. An allusion to Ben Jonson's *Everyman in his Humour*, i. 2.
2. Mrs. Grant of Laggan.
3. Henry Mackenzie.
4. Harriet Wilson's *Memoirs*, 1825.

have been assisted in the stile spelling and diction though the attempt at wit is very poor – that at pathos sickening. But there is some good retailing of conversations in which the stile of the speakers so far as known to me is exactly imitated, and some things told as said by individuals of each other which will sound unpleasantly in each other's ears. I admire the address of L—d A—y,[1] himself very severely handled from time to time. Someone asked him if H. W. had been pretty correct on the whole – 'Why faith' he replied 'I believe so' – when, raising his eyes, he saw Quentin Dick whom the little jilt had treated atrociously. 'What concerns the present company always excepted you know' added ·Lord A—y with infinite presence of mind. As he was *in pari casu* with Q. D. no more could be said. After all H. W. beats Con Philips, Anne Bellamy and all former demireps out and out. I think I suppd once in her company more than twenty years since at Mat Lewis's in Argyle Street where the Company, as the Duke says to Lucio, chanced to be fairer than honest.[2] She was far from beautiful if it be the same *chiffonne* but a smart saucy girl with good eyes and dark hair and the manners of a wild schoolboy. I am glad this accidental meeting has escaped her memory – or perhaps is not accurately recorded in mine – for being a sort of French Faulkner who hawk at all they see[3] I might have had a distinction which I am far from deserving.

Dined at Sir John Hay's[4] – a large party. Skenes there – the Newenhams[5] and others, strangers. In the morning a meeting of O. Gas Committee. The concern lingers a little.

> It may do weel for ought it's done yet
> But only – it's no just begun yet.[6]

10 SATURDAY A stormy and rainy day – walkd from the court through the rain. I don't dislike this – Egad, I rather like it – for no man that ever stepd on heather has less dread than I of Le catch-cold and I seem to regain in buffetting with the wind a little of the

---

1. Lord Alvanley (1789–1849), the spendthrift wit to whom Brummel's famous remark about the Prince Regent was addressed: 'Alvanley, who's your fat friend?'
2. *Measure for Measure*, iv. 3.
3. *Hamlet*, ii. 2.
4. Sir John Hay of Haystoun near Peebles, a fellow Director of the Edinburgh Academy.
5. Probably the Newenhams of Coolmore near Cork to whom Mrs. Scott of Harden had introduced Walter and Jane. *Letters*, ix. 80. They had visited Scotland in 1823. *Diaries of Helen Graham*, pp. 29–31.
6. Burns's 'Dedication to Gavin Hamilton'.

high spirit with which in younger days I used to enjoy a Tam-of-Shanter ride through darkness wind and rain, the boughs groaning and cracking over my head, the good horse free to the road and impatient for home and feeling the weather as little as I did.

> The storm around might roar and rustle
> We didna mind the storm a whistle.[1]

Answerd two letters – One answer to a schoolboy who writes himself Captain of Giggleswick School (a most imposing title) entreating the youngster not to commence editor of a Magazine to be entitled the *Yorkshire Muffin* I think at seventeen years old. 2do. to a soldier of the 79th. shewing why I cannot oblige him by getting his discharge, and exhorting him rather to bear with the wickedness and profanity of the service than take the very precarious step of desertion.[2] This is the old receipt of Durandarte *Patience cousin and shufle the cards*[3] and I suppose the correspondents will think I have been too busy in offering my counsel where I was askd for assistance.

A third rogue writes to tell me, rather of the latest if the matter was of consequence, that he approves of the first three volumes of the *H. of Midlothian* but totally condemns the fourth.[4] Doubtless he thinks his opinion worth the sevenpence Sterling which his letter costs. However an author should be reasonably well pleased when three fourths of his works are acceptable to the reader. The Knave demands of me in a postscript to get back the sword of Sir W. Wallace from England where it was carried from Dunbarton Castle. I am not Mr. Genl of the Ordnance that I know. It was wrong however to take away that and Mons Meg. If I go to town this spring I will renew my negotiation with the Great Duke for recovery of Mons Megs.[5]

1. Burn's 'Tam o' Shanter', ll. 51–2.
2. It appears from the Walpole Collection that the schoolboy was called George Woods and wanted 'a few lines on any subject' for his 'Yorkshire Magazine and Provincial Repository', a more modest demand than that of the soldier, Joseph Wallace: 'All I request of you is to apply to the Commander in chief I dare to say that you may know him.' 5 and 11 December 1825, Walpole.
3. Cervantes' *Don Quixote*, pt. ii, ch. 23.
4. Since *The Heart of Mid-Lothian* was extended from three to four volumes, to fulfil the contract for a four-volume second series of *Tales of My Landlord* (see Grierson, p. 164), the correspondent was a shrewder literary critic than Scott allows.
5. The Great Duke is of course Wellington. Mons Meg, a huge fifteenth-century cannon, was returned to Edinburgh Castle in 1829 thanks to Scott's efforts. See the Entry for 9 March 1829.

There is no theme more awful than to attempt to cast a glance among the clouds and mists which hide the broken extremity of the celebrated Bridge of Mirza[1] – yet when every day brings us nearer that termination one would almost think that our views should become clearer as the regions we are approaching are brought nigher – Alas it is not so – there is a curtain to be withdrawn, a veil to be rent, before we shall see things as they really are. There are few I trust who disbelieve the existence of a God – nay I doubt if at all times and in all moods any single individual ever adopted that hideous creed though some have professd it. With the belief of a Deity that of the Immortality of the soul and of the State of future rewards and punishments is indissolubly linked. More we are not to know but neither are we prohibited from our attempts however vain to pierce the solemn sacred gloom. The expressions used in scripture are doubtless smoking metaphorical, for penal fires and heavenly melody are only applicable to bodies endowd with senses, and at least till the period of the resurrection of the body the spirits of men, whether entering into the perfection of the just or committed to the regions of punishment, are incorporeal. Neither is [it] to be supposed that the glorified bodies which shall arise on [the] last day will be capable of the same gross indulgences with which they are now solaced. That the idea of Mahomet's paradise is inconsistent with the purity of our heavenly religion will be readily granted, and see XII Mark 27 verse.[2] Harmony is obviously chosen as the least corporeal of all gratifications of the sense and as the type of love, unity and a state of peace and of perfect happiness. But they have a poor idea of the Deity and the rewards which are destined for the Just made perfect who can only adopt the literal sense of an eternal concert – a never-ending Birthday Ode. I rather suppose there should be understood some commission from the Highest, some duty to discharge with the applause of a satisfied conscience – that the Deity who himself must be supposed to feel love and affection for the beings he has calld into existence should delegate a portion of those powers I for one cannot conceive altogether so wrong a conjecture. We would then find reality in Milton's sublime machinery desired by Milton of the Guardian Saints or genii of Kingdoms. Nay, we would approach to the Catholic idea of the employment of Saints, though without approaching the absurdity of Saint-worship which degrades their religion. There would be, we must suppose, in these employments difficulties to be overcome and exertions to be made, for all which the Celestial beings employd would have certain appropriate powers. I

1. See Addison's *Spectator*, no. 159.
2. 'He is not the God of the dead but the God of the living.'

cannot help thinking that a life of active benevolence is more consistent with my ideas than an eternity of music. But it is all speculation and it is impossible even to guess what we shall [do] unless we could ascertain the equally difficult previous question what we are to be. But there is a God and a just God – a judgement and a future life – and all who own so much let them act according to the faith that is in them. I would [not] of course limit the range of my genii to this confined earth – There is the universe with all its endless extent of worlds.

Company at home Sir Adam Fergusson and his Lady. Colonel and Miss Russells, Count Davidoff and Mr. Collyar – By the bye I observe that all men whose name is obviously derived from some mechanical trade all endeavour to disguize and antiquate as it were their names by spelling them after some quaint manner or other. Thus we have Collyar – Smythe – Tailleure – as much as to say 'My ancestor was indeed a mechanic but it was a world of time ago when the word was spelld very unlike the modern' – then we had young Whitebank[1] and Will: Allan the artist,[2] a very agreeable, simple mannerd and pleasant man.

11 SUNDAY A touch of the *morbus eruditorum*[3] to which I am as little subject as most folks and have it less now than when young. It is a tremor of the heart the pulsation of which becomes painfully sensible – a disposition to causeless alarm – much lassitude – and decay of vigour of mind and activity of intellect. The reins feel weary and painful and the mind is apt to receive and encourage gloomy apprehensions and causeless fears. Fighting with this fiend is not always the best way to conquer him – I have always found exercize and the open air better than reasoning. But such weather as is now without doors does not encourage *La petite guerre* so we must give him battle in form; by letting both mind and body know that supposing one the House of Commons and the other the House of Peers, my will is Sovereign over both. There is a fine description of this species of mental weakness in the fine play of Beaumont and Fletcher calld *The Lover's Progress* where [a] man warnd that his death is approaching works himself into an agony of fear and calls for

1. Alexander Pringle junior, of Whytbank.
2. William Allan (1782–1850), a 'zealous cavalier & tory' (*Letters*, vii. 55) whose pictures on medieval and historical subjects Scott much admired. He became President of the Royal Scottish Academy in 1837, and was knighted in 1842.
3. 'The illness of the learned', that is, depression, or 'the Black Dog' as Scott calls it elsewhere.

assistance though there is no apparent danger. The apparition of the Innkeeper's ghost in the same play hovers between the ludicrous and [the uncanny]. To me the touches of the former quality which it contains seem to augment the effect of the latter – they seem to give reality to the supernatural as being circumstance[s] with which an inventor would hardly have garnishd his story.

Will Clerk says he has a theory on the vitrified forts.[1] I wonder if he and I agree. I think accidental conflagration is the cause.

12 MONDAY Hogg[2] came to breakfast this morning, having taken and brought for his companion the Galashiels bard David Thompson[3] as to a meeting of huzz Tividale poets. The honest grunter opines with a delightful naïveté that Moore's verses are far *owre* sweet – answerd by Thompson that Moore's ears or notes, I forget which, were finely strung. 'They are far owre finely strung' replied He of the forest 'for mine are just reeght' – It reminded me of Queen Bess when questioning Melville[4] sharply and closely whether Queen [Mary was] taller than her and extracting an answer in the affirmative she replied 'Then your Queen is too tall for I am just the proper height.'

Was engaged the whole day with Sheriff Court processes. There is something sickening in seeing poor devils drawn into great expence about trifles by interested attorneys. But too cheap access to litigation has its evils on the other hand, for the proneness of the lower class to gratify spite and revenge in this way would be a dreadful evil were they able to endure the expence. Very few cases come before the Sheriff Court of Selkirkshire that ought to come anywhere – wretched wranglings about a few pounds, begun in spleen and carried on from obstinacy, and at length from fear of the conclusion to the banquet of illhumour 'D—n—n of expences'[5] – I try to check it as well as I can. 'But so 'twill be when I am gone.'[6]

Dined at home and spent the evening in writing. Anne and Lady

1. 'A hill-fort of a type occurring in Scotland . . . the stones of which have been converted into a vitreous substance by the action of fire.' *O. E. D.*
2. James Hogg (1770–1835), the 'Ettrick Shepherd', poet, and contributor to *Blackwood's*. He was introduced to Scott by Laidlaw and assisted in the collection of ballads for the *Minstrelsy*. His personal vanity is well illustrated by his *Domestic Manners of Sir Walter Scott*, 1834.
3. David Thomson, a Galashiels weaver with a turn for poetry. *Life*, vii. 93.
4. Sir James Melville, whose *Memoirs* was published by the Bannatyne Club in 1827.
5. Burns's 'Address to the Unco Guid', l. 40.
6. Moore's 'Those evening Bells' in *National Airs* (1815).

Scott at the theatre to see Mathews[1] – A very clever man my friend Mathews but it is tiresome to be funny for a whole evening, so I was content and stupid at home.

An odd optical delusion has amused me these two last nights. I have been of late for the first time condemnd to the constant use of spectacles. Now when I have laid them aside to step into a room dimly lighted out of the strong light which I use for writing I have seen or seemd to see through the rims of the same spectacles which I have left behind me. At first the impression was so lively that I put my hand to my eyes believing I had the actual spectacles on at the moment. But what I saw was only the Eidolon or image of said useful servants. This fortifies some of Dr. Hibbert's positions about spectral appearances.[2]

13 TUESDAY Letter from Lady Stafford, kind and friendly after the wont of Banzu-Mohr-ar-chat.[3] That is wrong spelld I know. Her countenance is something for Sophia whose company should be, as Ladies are said to chuse their liquor, little and good – To be acquainted with persons of mere *ton* is a nuisance and a scrape – to be known to persons of real fashion and fortune is in London a very great advantage. She is besides sure of the hereditary and constant friendship of the Buccleuch ladies[4] as well as those of Montagu[5] and of the Harden family,[6] of the Marchss. of Northampton,[7] Lady Melville and others, also the Miss Ardens upon whose kind offices I have some claim[8] and would count upon them whether such claim existed or no. So she is well enough establishd among the Right Hand file[9] which is very necessary in London where second-rate fashion is like false jewels.

1. Charles Mathews (1776–1835) the comedian.
2. Dr. Samuel Hibbert's *Sketches of the Philosophy of Apparitions, or an Attempt to trace such Illusions to their Physical Causes*, 1824. The second edition (1825) was dedicated to Scott.
3. Banamhorar-Chat: Elizabeth, Lady Stafford (1765–1839) and Countess of Sutherland in her own right. Her Gaelic title means 'The Great Lady of the Cat'. She was a fellow resident of George Square in Scott's youth, and presented a set of colours to be carried in the 'bickers' described by Lockhart. *Life*, i. 135–9.
4. The Duke of Buccleuch's sisters.
5. The daughters of Baron Montagu, the Duke of Buccleuch's uncle.
6. See p. 91, n. 1.
7. Margaret, the daughter of Scott's old friend Mrs. Maclean Clephane.
8. Their mother, Lady Alvanley, died in Edinburgh, and the arrangements for the funeral and the erection of a suitable monument were made by Scott.
9. *Coriolanus*, ii. 1.

Went to the yearly Court of the Edinr. Assurance Company[1] to which I am one of those graceful and useless appendages calld Directors Extraordi[na]ry – an extraordinary director I should prove had they made me an ordinary one – there were there Moneyers and great Oneyers[2] – men of metal – Discounters and counters – Sharp grave prudential faces, eyes weak with cyphering by lamplight. Men who say to gold 'Be thou paper' and to paper 'Be thou turnd into fine gold' – Many a bustling sharp-faced keen eyed writer too – some perhaps speculating with their clients' property. My reverend seigniors[3] had expected a motion for printing their contract which I as a piece of light artillery was brought down and got into battery to oppose. I should certainly have done this on the general ground that while each partner could at any time obtain sight of the contract at a call on the Directors or Managers it would be absurd to print it for the use of the company, and that exposing it to the world at large was in all respects unnecessary and might teach rival companies to avail themselves of our rules and calculations, if false for the purpose of exposing our errors, if correct for the purpose of improving their own schemes on our model. But my eloquence was not required, no one renewing the motion under question. So off I came my ears still ringing with the sounds of thousands and tens of thousands and my eyes dazzled with the golden gleam effused by so many capitalists.

Walkd home with the Solicitor,[4] decidedly the most hopeful young man of his time. High connexion – great talent – spirited ambition – a ready and prompt elocution with a good voice and dignified manner, prompt and steady courage, vigilant and constant assiduity, popularity with the young men and the good opinion of the old, will if I mistake not carry him as [far as] any man who has been since the days of old Hal Dundas.[5] He is hot though and rather hasty. This should be amended – they who would play at single-stick must bear with patience a rap over the knuckles. Dined quietly with Lady Scott and Anne.

1. At this time eleven insurance companies had their head offices in Edinburgh. Scott was Governor of the Scottish Union, as well as Extraordinary Director of the Edinburgh Life Assurance Company of 24 George Street, referred to here.
2. An allusion to 1 *Henry*, ii. 1.
3. *Othello*, i.3.
4. The Solicitor-General, John Hope.
5. The first Viscount Melville (1742–1811), 'the uncrowned King of Scotland', whose rule by patronage stretched from 1783 until 1806. Throughout his tenure of different Cabinet posts he was, in effect, the arbiter on all Scottish affairs. Scott had been intimate with the family, through his friendship with the son, from an early age.

14 WEDNESDAY Affairs very bad in the money market in London. It must come here and I have far too many engagements not to feel it. To cut the matter at once I intend to borrow £10,000 with which my son's marriage contract allows me to charge my estate – At Whitsunday and Marts I will have enough to pay up the incumbrance of £3000 due to old Moss's daughter and £5000 to Misses Fergusson in whole or part.[1] This will enable us to dispense in a great measure with Bank assistance and sleep in spite of thunder.[2] I do not know whether it is this business which makes me a little bilious or rather the want of exercize during the season of late and change of the weather to too much heat. Thank God my circumstances are good, upon a fair balance which I have are <not> certainly not less than £40,000 or nearby £50,000 above the world. But the Sun and Moon shall dance on the green ere carelessness or hope of gain or facility of getting cash shall make me go too deep again, were it but for the disquiet of the thing.

Dined Ly. Scott and Anne quietly.

15 THURSDAY R. P. G. came *sicut mos est*[3] at five o'clock to make me confident of the extremities of his distress. It is clear all he has to do is to make the best agreement he can with his creditors. I remember many years since the poor fellow told me he thought there was something interesting in having difficulties – Poor lad he will have enough of them now. He talks about writing translations for the booksellers from the German to the amount of £500 and £600 but this is like a man proposing to run a whole day at top-speed. Yet if he had good subjects R. P. G. is one of the best translators I know, and something must be done for him certainly though I fear it will be necessary to go to the bottom of the ulcer – palliatives won't do. He is terribly imprudent, yet a worthy and benevolent creature – a great bore withal –

Dined alone with family. I am determined not to stand mine host to all Scotland and England as I have done. This shall be a saving since it must be a borrowing year – We heard from Sophia they are got safe to town but as Johnie had a little bag of meal with him to make his porridge on the road the whole Inn-yard assembled to see

1. Scott borrowed £10,000 from Mr. Farie of Farme, paid £3000 to John Moss's daughter, Mrs. Stevenson of Melrose, to clear off the mortgage on Kaeside, and sank the remaining £7000 in James Ballantyne & Coy. The money due to the Misses Ferguson was still unpaid when the crash came. Sederunt Book i. 71; ii. 127–8.
2. *Macbeth*, iv. 1.
3. 'As his custom is'. The point is that he arrives at or just before the dinner-hour.

the operation. Junor his maid was of opinion that England was an awfu' country to make parritch in. God bless the poor baby and restore his perfect health.

16 FRIDAY R. P. G. and his friend Robt. Wilson[1] came, the former at five as usual, the latter at three as appointed. R. W. frankly said that R. P. G.'s case was quite desperate – that he was insolvent and that any attempt to save him at present would be just so much cash thrown away. God knows at this moment I have none to throw away uselessly. For poor Gillies there was a melancholy mixture of pathos and affectation in his statement which really affected me while it told me that it would be useless to help him to money on such very empty plans. I endeavourd to persuade him to make a virtue of necessity, resign all to his creditors, and begin the world on a new leaf. I offerd him Chiefswood[2] for a temporary retirement. Lady Scott thinks I was wrong, and no body could less desire such a neighbour, all his affectations being caviare to me. But then the wife and children –

Went again to the Solicitor on a wrong night – being askd for tomorrow. Lady Scott undertakes to keep my engagements recorded in future. *Sed quis custodiat ipsam custodem?*[3]

17 SATURDAY Dined with the Solicitor, Ld Ch. Baron,[4] Sir William Boothby, nephew of old Sir Brooke the dandy poet. Annoyd with anxious presentiments which the night's post must dispel or confirm. All in London as bad as possible.

18 SUNDAY Ballantyne calld on me this morning. *Venit illa suprema dies.*[5] My extremity is come. Cadell has received letters from London which all but positively announce the failure of Hurst and Robinson so that Constable and Coy must follow and I must go with poor

---

1. Robert Sym Wilson, W.S., Secretary to the Royal Bank of Scotland.
2. As the Lockharts were now in London, Chiefswood, the small house on the Abbotsford estate which they used when in the country, was temporarily uninhabited. It was later let to Captain Hamilton.
3. 'But who is to guard the guardian herself?' – an adaptation of Juvenal's *Satires*, vi. 347.
4. Sir Samuel Shepherd (1760–1840). Before becoming Lord Chief Baron of the Court of Exchequer in Scotland he had been Attorney-General, and but for his deafness might have risen higher. He was a member of the Blair-Adam Club and a close, although not an early, friend of Scott's. Scott sketches his character in the Entry for 20 December 1825.
5. 'That final day has come' – a reminiscence of Virgil's *venit summa dies* in *Aeneid*, i. 118.

James Ballantyne for company. I suppose it will involve my all. But if they leave me £500 I can still make it £1000 or £1200 a year. And if they take my salaries of £1300 and £300[1] they cannot but give me something out of them. I have been rash in anticipating funds to buy land. But then I made from £5000 to £10,000 a year, and land was my temptation. I think no body can lose a penny, that is one comfort – Men will think pride has had a fall. Let them indulge their own pride in thinking that my fall makes them higher or seem so at least. I have the satisfaction to recollect that my prosperity has been of advantage to many and that some at least will forgive my transient wealth on account of the innocence of my intentions and my real wish to do good to the poor. This news will make sad hearts at Darnick[2] and in the cottages of Abbotsford which I do not nourish the least hope of preserving. It has been my Dalilah and so I have often termd it – and now – the recollection of the extensive woods I have planted and the walks I have formed from which strangers must derive both the pleasure and profit will excite feelings likely to sober my gayest moments. I have half resolved never to see the place again – how could I tread my hall with such a diminishd crest? How live a poor indebted man where I was once the wealthy – the honourd? My children are provided – thank God for that. I was to have gone there on Saturday in joy and prosperity to receive my friends – my dogs will wait for me in vain – it is foolish – but the thoughts of parting from these dumb creatures have moved me more than any of the painful reflections I have put down – poor things I must get them kind masters. There may be yet those who loving me may love my dog because it has been mine. I must end this or I shall lose the tone of mind with which men should meet distress. I find my dogs' feet on my knees – I hear them whining and seeking me everywhere – this is nonsense but it is what they would do could they know how things are – poor Will Laidlaw[3] – poor Tom Purdie[4] – this will be news to wring

1. As Clerk of Session and Sheriff of Selkirkshire respectively.
2. The village between Abbotsford and Melrose.
3. William Laidlaw (1780–1845), factor on the Abbotsford estate since 1816, and nephew of Scott's first Sheriff-Substitute, Charles Erskine. Scott met him in his ballad-collecting days, and the friendship ripened with the years. Kaeside, on the hill above Abbotsford, was the frequent object of Scott's walk, especially when there was politics to discuss, and the loss of Laidlaw was a cruel deprivation. Happily he was restored in 1829 when Purdie's death left the estate without a manager. Laidlaw wrote a little in prose and verse, and acted as Scott's amanuensis during his illness in 1819 and again in his declining months.
4. See Introduction, pp. xliii–xliv.

your heart and many a poor fellow's besides to whom my prosperity was daily bread.

Ballantyne behaves like himself and sinks his own ruin in contemplating mine. I tried to enrich him indeed and now all – all is gone. He will have the *Journal*[1] still, that is a comfort, for sure they cannot find a better Editor – *They* – alas who will *they* be? the *unbekanten Obern*[2] who are to dispose of my all as they will? Some hard-eyed banker – some of those men of millions whom I described.[3] Cadell shewd more kind and personal feeling to me than I thought he had possessd. He says there are some properties of works that will revert to me, the copy money not being paid. But it cannot be any very great matter I should think. Another person[4] did not afford me all the sympathy I expected, perhaps because I seemd to need little support – Yet that is not her nature which is generous and kind. She thinks I have been imprudent trusting men so far – perhaps so – but whatsoever I do I must sell my books to some one and these folks gave me the largest price. If they had kept their ground I could have brought myself round fast enough by the plan of 14 Decemr. I now view matters at the very worst and suppose that my all must go to supply the deficiencies of Constable. I fear it must be so. His connections with Hurst and Robinson have been so intimate that they must be largely involved. This is the worst of the concern; our own is comparatively plain sailing.

Poor Gillies calld yesterday to tell me he was in extremity. God knows I had every cause to have returnd him the same answer. I must think his situation worse than mine as through his incoherent miserable tale I could see that he had exhausted each access to credit, and yet fondly imagines that bereft of all his accustomd indulgences he can work with a literary zeal unknown to his happier days. I hope he may labour enough to gain the mere support of his family. For myself the magic wand of the Unknown is shiverd in his grasp. He must henceforth be termd the Too well Known.[5] The feast of fancy is over with the feeling of independence. I can no longer have the delight of waking in the morning with bright ideas in my mind,

1. *The Edinburgh Weekly Journal.* After the crash James Ballantyne continued to edit this paper and to manage the printing side of James Ballantyne and Coy.
2. 'Unknown superiors'.
3. In the Entry for 13 December.
4. Lady Scott.
5. Scott's authorship of the Waverley Novels was acknowledged at the meeting of his creditors a month later, although the better-known confession at the Theatrical Fund Dinner was not made until February 1827.

haste to commit them to paper, and count them monthly as the means of planting such groves and purchasing such wastes, replacing my dreams' fiction by other prospective visions of walks by

> ~~Fountain-heads and pathless groves~~
> Places which pale passion loves[1] –

This cannot be – But I may make substantial husbandry – write history and such substantial concerns. They will not be received with the same enthusiasm – at least I much doubt the general knowlege that an author must write for his bread, at least for improving his pittance, degrades him and his productions in the public eye. He falls into the secondrate rank of estimation.

Turn back to p. 41–42. I turnd the page accidentally and the partner of a Bankrupt concern ought not to waste two leaves of paper.

> While the harness sore galls and the spurs his sides goad
> The high mettled racer's a hack on the road.[2]

It is a bitter thought, but if tears start at it let them flow. I am so much of this mind that if any one would now offer to relieve all my embarassments on condition I would continue the exertions which brought it there, dear as the place is to me, I hardly think I could undertake the labour on which I enterd with my usual alacrity only this morning; though not without a boding feeling of my exertions proving useless. Yet to save Abbotsford I would attempt all that was possible. My heart clings to the place I have created. There is scarce a tree on it that does not owe its being to me and the pain of leaving it is greater than I can tell. I have about £10,000 of Constable's for which I am bound to give literary value. But if I am obliged to pay other debts for him I will take leave to retain this sum at his credit. We shall have made some *kittle* questions of literary property, amongst us.[3] Once more 'Patience cousin and shuffle the cards.'[4]

I have endeavourd at times to give vent to thoughts naturally so painful by writing these notices – partly to keep them at bay by busying myself with [the] history of the French Convention.[5] I thank God I can do both with reasonable composure. I wonder how Anne

1. Beaumont and Fletcher's *The Nice Valour*, iii. 3.
2. 'Ballad' in Charles Dibdin's *Liberty Hall*.
3. 'Kittle' means 'tricky'. Later events proved the truth of this prophecy. Constable's creditors laid claim to *Woodstock*, *The Life of Napoleon*, and the manuscripts of the novels.
4. *Don Quixote*, pt. ii, ch. 23.
5. *Life of Napoleon*, vol. ii, ch. 6.

will bear this afliction? She is passionate but stout-hearted and courageous in important matters though irritable in trifles. I am glad Lockhart and his wife are gone – Why? – I cannot tell but I *am* pleased to be left to my own regrets without being melted by condoleances though of the most sincere and affectionate kind.

Anne bears her misfortune gallantly and well with a natural feeling no doubt of the rank and consideration she is about to lose. Lady Scott is incredulous and persists in cherishing hope where there is no ground for hope. I wish it may not bring on the Gloom of Spirits which has given me such distress. If she were the active person she once was that would not be. Now I fear it more than what Constable or Cadell will tell me this evening – To that my mind is made up.

Oddly enough it happend. Mine honest friend Hector[1] came in before dinner to ask a copy of my seal of arms, with a sly kindliness of intimation that it was for some agreeable purpose.

Half past eight. I closed this book under the consciousness of impending ruin. I open it an hour after, thanks be to God!, with the strong hope that matters may be got over safely and honourably in a mercantile sense. Cadell came at eight to communicate a letter from Hurst and Robinson intimating they had stood the storm and, though clamourous for assistance from Scotland, saying they had prepared their strongholds without need of the Banks. This is all so far well. But I will not borrow any money on my estate till I see things reasonably safe. Stocks have risen from 42 to 46,[2] a strong proof that confidence is restored. But I will yield to no delusive hopes. And fall back fall edge my resolutions hold. Whitaker the rascally bookseller whose slip for £200,000 or thereabouts has brought ruin nearly on the trade kept seven hunters and be damnd to him. He must have ridden a fine weight to be sure with £200,000 of honest people's cash about him. I shall always think the better of Cadell for this – not merely because his feet are beautiful on the mountains who brings good tidings[3] but because he shewd feeling – deep feeling, poor fellow – he who I thought had no more than his numeration table and who if he had had his whole compting-house full of sensibility had yet his wife and children to bestow it upon. I will not forget this if I get through. I love the virtues of rough and round men. The others are apt to escape in salt rheum, sal volatile and a white pocket hand-kerchief. An odd thought strikes me. When I die will the journal of these day[s] be taken out of the Ebony cabinet at Abbotsford and read

1. Hector Macdonald Buchanan.
2. These figures are deleted in the original and 'This was a mistake' added in the margin.
3. An allusion to Isaiah 52: 7.

as the transient pout of a man worth £60,000 with wonder that the well seeming Baronet should ever have experienced such a hitch? Or will it be found in some obscure lodginghouse where the decayd son of chivalry has hung up his scutcheon for some 20/- a week and where one or two old friends will look grave and whisper to each other, 'poor gentleman' – 'a well meaning man' – 'nobody's enemy but his own' – 'thought his parts could never wear out' – 'family poorly left', 'pity he took that foolish title'? Who can answer this question?

What a life mine has been. Half educated, almost wholly neglected or left to myself – stuffing my head with most nonsensical trash and undervalued in society for a time by most of my companions – getting forward and held a bold and clever fellow, contrary to the opinion of all who thought me a mere dreamer – Broken-hearted for two years[1] – My heart handsomely pieced again[2] – but the crack will remain till my dying day – Rich and poor four or five times – Once at the verge of ruin yet opend new sources of wealth almost overflowing[3] – now taken in my pitch of pride and nearly winged (unless the good news hold) because London chuses to be in an uproar and in the tumult of bulls and bears a poor inoffensive lion like myself is pushd to the wall – And what is to be the end of it? God knows and so ends the chatechism.[4]

19 MONDAY Ballantyne here before breakfast. He looks on Caddel's last night's news with more confidence than I do. But I must go to work be my thoughts sober or lively. Constable came in and sate an hour. The old gentleman is firm as a rock and scorns the idea of Hurst and Robinson stopping. He talks of going up to London next week and making sales of our interest in *W—k* and *Boney* which would put a hedge round our finances. He is a very clever fellow and will I think bear us through.

Dined at Lord Chief Baron's – Ld. Justice Clerk, Lord President, Captn Scarlett, a gentlemanlike young man, the son of the great counsell[5] and a friend of my son Walter. Lady Charlotte Hope[6] and

1. Scott had unsuccessfully wooed Williamina Belsches, who in January 1797 married Sir William Forbes. See *Sir Walter Scott's Congé*, by Lord Sands, third edition, 1931.
2. By his marriage to Charlotte Carpenter on Christmas Eve 1797.
3. The failure of John Ballantyne & Coy., Scott's publishing house, was followed the next year by the success of *Waverley*, the first of his novels.
4. An allusion to Falstaff's soliloquy, *1 Henry IV*, v. i.
5. The 'great counsell' was James Scarlett (1769–1844), later Baron Abinger; his son was James Yorke Scarlett (1799–1871) who rose to the rank of major-general.
6. The Lord President's wife.

other woman kind.[1] R. Dundas, Arnistoun, and his pleasant and good-humourd little wife whose quick intelligent look pleases me more, though her face be very plain, than a hundred mechanical Beauties.

20 TUESDAY Smoke the New pen.[2] Oho-a-*Swift*. The ordinary Bramahs become execrable so the knave puts the extras upon us. I like Ch: Ba: Shepherd very much – as much I think as any man I have learnd to know of late years. There [is] a neatness and precision, a closeness and truth, in the tone of [his] conversation which shows what a lawyer he must have been. Perfect goodhumour and suavity of manner with a little warmth of temper on suitable occasions. His great deafness alone prevented him from being Lord Chief Justice. I never saw a man so patient under such a malady. He loves society and converses excellently yet is often obliged in a mixd company particularly to lay aside his trumpet, retire into himself and withdraw from the talk. He does this with an expression of patience on his countenance which touches one much. He has occasion for patience otherwise I should think, for Lady S. is fine and fidgetty and too anxious to have everything point device.

Constable's licence for the dedication[3] is come which will make him happy.

21 WEDNESDAY Dined with James Ballantyne and met my old friend Matthews the Comedian with his son,[4] now grown up a clever, rather forward lad who makes songs in the stile of John Smith[5] or Colman[6] and sings them with spirit. Rather lengthy though.

1. A phrase from Anthony à Wood, much used by Monkbarns in *The Antiquary* and by Scott himself.
2. A new make of pen from Joseph Bramah of Piccadilly, the inventor of patent locks and pens.
3. To his *Miscellany*. See the Entry for 7 December and note. Scott wrote at once to Constable with the good news. *Letters*, ix. 339.
4. Charles James Mathews (1803–78), later known as a comic actor and adapter of plays. 'On Tuesday we met the man of men – the great *Well-Known* – at James Ballantyne's. Charles was all hopes, all fears. Ballantyne, with great kindness, placed him next Sir Walter at dinner', wrote the elder Mathews to his wife. *Memoirs of Mathews*, iii. 511. Scott invited father and son to visit Abbotsford when they had finished their Scottish engagements. They arrived on 11 January.
5. A slip for James Smith (1775–1839), the wit, parodist and critic, joint-author with his brother Horace of *Rejected Addresses*. Some of his sketches were actually written for the elder Mathews.
6. George Colman the younger (1762–1836), dramatist and humorous poet.

There has been odd associations attending my two last meetings with Matthews. The last time I saw [him] before yesterday evening he dined with me in company with poor Sir Alexander Boswell who was killd within two or three months[1] – I never saw Sir Alex. more. The time before was in 1815 when John Scott of Gala and I were returning from France and passd through London when we brought Matthews down as far as Leamington. Poor Byron lunchd with us or rather made an early dinner at Long's and a most brilliant day we had of it. I never saw Byron so full of fun frolic wit and whim. He was as playful as a kitten – Well – I never saw him again – So this Man of mirth with his merry meetings has brought me no luck. I like better that he should throw in his talent of mimicry and humour into the present current tone of the Company than that he should be required to *give* this that or t'other *bitt* selected from his public recitations – They are good certainly – excellent – But then you *must* laugh and that is always severe to me. When I do laugh in sincerity the joke must be or seem unpremeditated. I could not help thinking in the midst of the glee what late gloom was over the minds of three of the company, Cadell, J. B., and the Journalist's. What a strange scene if the surge of conversation could suddenly ebb like the tide and [shew] us the state of people's real minds. Savary[2] might have been gay in such a party with all his forgeries in his heart.

> No eye the rocks discover
> Which lurk beneath the deep.[3]

Life could not be endured were it seen in reality.

Things are mending in town and H. and R. write with confidence and are it would seem strongly supported by wealthy friends. Cadell and Constable are confident of their making their way through the storm and the impression of their stability is general in London. I hear the same from Lockhart. Indeed I now believe that they wrote gloomy letters to Constable chiefly to get as much money out of them as they possibly could. But they had well nigh over done it. This being Teind Wednesday must be a day of leisure and labour.

Sophia has got a house, 25 Pall-Mall.

Dined at home with Lady Scott and Anne.

1. A slip for 'weeks'. For the duel in which Boswell was killed see the Entry for 14 December 1826 and note.
2. Henry Savary, a banker's son in Bristol, recently tried for forgery.
3. John Gay's *What d'ye call it*, sc. 8.

22 THURSDAY I wrote six of my close pages yesterd[ay] which is about twenty four pages in print. What is more I think it comes off twangingly. The story is so very interesting in itself that there is no fear of the book answering. Superficial it must be but I do not disown the charge. Better a superficial book which brings well and strikingly together the known and acknowleged facts than a dull boring narrative pausing to see further into a mill stone at every moment than the nature of the Mill stone admits. Nothing is so tiresome as walking through some beautiful scene with a minute philosopher, a botanist or pebble gatherer who is eternally calling your attention from the grand features of the natural scenery to look at grasses and chucky stones. Yet in their way they give useful information and so does the minute historian – Gad, I think that will look well in the preface.

My bile is quite gone. I really believe it arose from mere anxiety. What a wonderful connexion between the mind and body.

The air of 'Bonnie Dundee' running in my head to-day I [wrote] a few verses to it before dinner, taking the key-note from the story of Claverse leaving the Scottish Convention of Estates in 1688–9. I wonder if they are good – Ah poor Will: Erskine,[1] thou couldst and wouldst have told me. I must consult J. B. who is as honest as was W. E. But then though he has good taste too there is a little of *Big Bow-wow* about it. Can't say what made me take a frisk so uncommon of late years as to write verses of free will. I suppose the same impulse which makes birds sing when [a] storm seems blown over.

Dined at Lord Minto's.[2] There were Lord and Lady Ruthven, Will: Clerk and Tho. Thomson,[3] a right choice party. There was also my very old friend Mrs. Brydone,[4] the relict of the traveller and

1. William Erskine (1769–1822), the gentle, scholarly, retiring 'little man of feeble make' who had been one of Scott's most intimate friends from 1792. He was raised to the Bench in 1822 as Lord Kinnedder, and died a few months later, snuffed out by unfounded rumours of immorality. See *Life*, i. 279 and vi. 393.
2. Gilbert Elliot, second Earl of Minto (1782–1859). He was a Whig and later First Lord of the Admiralty.
3. Thomas Thomson (1768–1852) was the son of a clergyman and a brilliant graduate of Glasgow University. His bent for legal antiquarianism led him as Vice-president and later President of the Bannatyne Club to superintend the Club's publications, thirteen of which he edited himself. As Deputy Clerk-Register he brought some order into the records of Scotland, many of which he also published for the first time. He was a member of the Blair-Adam Club and a brother of the Revd. John Thomson of Duddingston.
4. Lord Minto's mother-in-law, the widow of Patrick Brydone, author of *A Tour through Sicily and Malta*, 1773.

daughter of Principal Robertson and really worthy of such a connection, Lady Minto who is also peculiarly agreeable and her sister Mrs. Admiral Adam[1] in the evening.

23 FRIDAY The present Lord Minto is a very agreeable, well-informd and sensible man but he possesses neither the high breeding, ease of manner or eloquence of his father the first Earl.[2] That Sir Gilbert was indeed a man among a thousand. I knew him very intimately in the beginning of the century and, which was very agreeable, was much at his house on very easy terms. He loved the Muses and worshipd them in secret and used to read some of [his] poetry which was but middling. One upon a walk with his lady which involved certain conclusions (most delicately couchd) but which it is not usual to allude [to]. Singu[l]ar that the wish to show what he thought and what perhaps was a clever thing was stronger than the feelings which induced to secrecy. Oh Vanity, where will you lead us poor authors. Tom Campbell[3] lived at Minto but it was in a state of dependence which he brookd very ill. He was kindly treated but would not see it in the right view and suspected slights and so on where no such thing was meant. There was a turn of Savage[4] about Tom though without his blackguardism – a kind of waywardness of mind and irritability that must have made a man of his genius truly unhappy.

Lord Minto, with the mildest manners, was very tenacious of his opinions although he changed them twice in the crises of politics. He was the early friend of Fox and made a figure towards the end of the Americain war or during the struggles betwixt Fox and Pitt. Then came the Revolution and he joined the Anti Gallican party so keenly that he declared against Addington's peace with France and was for a time I believe a Wyndamite. He was reconciled to the Whigs on the Fox and Grenville coalition but I have heard that Fox contrary to his wont retain such personal feelings as led him [to] object to Sir Gilbert Elliot having a seat in the Cabinet. So he was sent Governor General to India – a better thing I take it for his fortune. He died shortly after his return at Hatfield or Barnet on his way down to his native country. He was a most pleasing and amiable man: I was very

---

1. The daughter-in-law of Scott's great friend William Adam of Blair-Adam.
2. Gilbert, first Earl of Minto (1751–1814), Governor of Corsica 1794–6, an eyewitness of the Battle of St. Vincent, and Governor-General of India from 1807 to 1813. A triumphal welcome had been prepared for him in Hawick, but the Earl died of a chill on the way from London.
3. Thomas Campbell (1777–1844), the poet.
4. Richard Savage (1697–1743), the subject of Dr. Johnson's short *Life*.

sorry for his death though I do not know how we should have met, for the contested election in 1805[1] had placed some coldness betwixt the present Lord and me. I was certainly anxious for Sir Alexr. Don[2] both as friend of my most kind friend Charles Duke of Buccleuch[3] and on political accounts, and these thwartings are what men in public life do not like to endure. After a cessation of friendship for some years we have come about again – We never had the slightest personal dispute or disagreement. But politics are the blowpipe beneath whose influence the best cemented friendships too often disseve[r] and ours after all was only a very familiar acquaintance.

It is very odd that the common people at Minto and the neighbourhood will not believe at this hour that the first Earl is dead. They think he had done some thing in India which he could not answer for – that the house was rebuilt on a scale unusually large to give him a suite of secret apartments and that he often walks about the woods and crags of Minto at night with a white night-cap and long white beard. The circumstance of his having died on the road down to Scotland is the sole foundation of this absurd legend which shows how willing the vulgar are to gull themselves when they can find no one else to take the trouble. I have seen people who could read write and cypher shrug their shoulders and look mysterious when this subject was mentiond. One very absurd addition was made on occasion of a great ball at Minto House which it was said was given to draw all people away from the grounds that the conceald Earl might have leisure for his exercize. This was on the principle in the German play[4] where to hide their conspiracy the Associates join in a chorus song.

We dined at home. Mr. Davidoff and his tutor kept an engagement with us to dinner notwithstanding the death of the Emperor Alexander.[5] They went to the play with the women kind. I staid at home to write.

24 SATURDAY Wrote Walter and Jane[6] – and gave [the] former an accompt of how things had been borne through in the money market and of the loan of £10,000 – Constable has a scheme of publishing

1. A slip for '1812'.
2. Sir Alexander Don (1751–1815), fifth baronet, of Newton Don near Kelso, at this time M. P. for Roxburghshire.
3. The fourth Duke (1772–1819).
4. 'See Canning's *German Play*, in the Anti-Jacobin.' J. G. L.
5. He had died on 1 December. Scott met him in Paris in 1815.
6. He sent Jane a copy of 'Bonny Dundee' and received a characteristic reply: 'Many thanks for the beautiful song you sent me, I am quite delighted with it and shall try to sing it as well as I can, although you know I am not very fond of performing in that way.' 14 January 1826, Walpole. For the letter to Walter see *Letters*, ix. 345.

the works of the Author of W—y in a superior stile at £1. 1. volume.[1]
He says he will answer for making £20,000 of this and liberally offerd
me any share of the profit. I have no great claim to any as I have only
to contribute the Notes which are light work, yet a few thousands
coming in will be a good thing, besides the P. Office.[2] Constable,
though valetudinary and cross with his partner, is certainly as good a
pilot in these rough seas as ever man put faith in. His rally put me in
mind of the old song.

> The tailor raise and shook his duds
> He gar'd the *bills* flee aff in cluds
> And they that staid gat fearfu' thuds
> The Tailor proved a man O.[3]

We are for Abbotsford to-day with a light heart –

Abbotsford.

25 SUNDAY Arrived here last night at Seven. Our halls are silent
compared to last year but let us be thankful when we think how near
the chance appeard but a week since that these halls would have been
ours no longer – *Barbarus has segetes?*[4] – *Nullum numen abest si sit
prudentia.*[5] There shall be no lack of wisdom – But come – *il faut
cultiver notre jardin*[6] – Let us see – I will write out 'The bonnets of Bonny
Dundee'. I will sketch a preface to *La Rochejacquelin*[7] for Constable's
Miscellany and try about a specimen of notes for the W—y novels. If
together with letters and by-business it will be a good day's work.

> I make a vow
> And keep it true[8]

1. It is characteristic of Constable that his plan (abandoned because of
   his bankruptcy) should have been for a series 'in a Superior stile'
   and at double the usual price; equally characteristic of Cadell that
   the Magnum Opus which took its place should be a cheap edition
   for the mass market.
2. James Ballantyne's printing concern, in which Scott was a partner
   and for which a new edition would mean work and profit.
3. The Taylor Johnson's *Musical Museum*, no. 490.
4. '(Will) a stranger (reap) these crops?' Virgil's *Eclogues*, i. 71.
5. 'No divinity is lacking if we had prudence' – an adaptation of
   Juvenal's *Satires*, x. 365.
6. *Candide*, ch. 30.
7. *The Memoirs of La Rochejacquelein* was published as vol. v of
   Constable's *Miscellany*.
8. 'Gil Morrice', st. 7, in Percy's *Reliques*.

I will take no invitation excepting for dinner only save to Newton Don and Mertoun tomorrow instead of Christmas Day.[1] On this day of General Devotion I have a particular call for gratitude!!.

26 MONDAY My God! what poor creatures we are. After all my fair proposals yesterday I was seized with a most violent pain in the right kidney and parts adjacent which, joind to deadly sickness which it brought on, forced me instantly to go to bed and send for Clarkson.[2] He came and engineerd, pronouncing the complaint to be gravel augmented by bile – I was in great agony till about two o'clock but awaked with the pain gone. I got up, had a fire in my dressing closet, and had Dalgleish[3] to shave me – two trifles which I only mention because they [are] contrary to my hardy and independent personal habits. But although a man cannot be a heroe to his valet, his valet in sickness becomes of great use to him. I cannot expect that this first will be the last visit of this cruel complaint but shall we receive good at the hand of God and not receive evil?[4]

27 TUESDAY Slept twelve hours at a stretch being much exhausted with pain of last night and the action of the medicine. Totally without pain to-day but uncomfortable with the effects of calomel, which with me at least is like the assistance of an auxiliary army, just one degree more tolerable than the enemy it chases away. Calomel contemplations are not worth recording.

I wrote an introduction and a few notes to the *Memoirs of Made La Rochejacquelin*,[5] being all that I was equal to.

Sir Adam Fergusson came over[6] and tried to marry my verses to the tune of 'Bonnie Dundee.' They seem well adapted to each other.

Dined with Lady Scott and Anne.

Worked at Pepys in the evening with the purpose of review for

1. Christmas dinner at Mertoun, the seat of the Scotts of Harden, was 'an engagement of 150 years standing when we are all in the County'. *Letters*, xi. 448. With Christmas on a Sunday, however, the festivities this year were held on the 26th.
2. James Clarkson, the doctor from Melrose.
3. Scott's butler. He continued to serve Scott after the crash and, unknown to Scott, recorded some of his experiences. See, for instance, notes 2–6, pp. 806–9.
4. Job 2: 10.
5. These were urgently required by Constable, as a letter to Ballantyne of the same date makes clear. *Letters*, ix. 351.
6. From Huntly Burn, where he was spending Christmas with his sisters.

Lockhart.[1] Notwithstanding the depressing effects of the calomel I feel the pleasure of being alone and uninterrupted. Few men leading a quiet life and without any strong or highly varied change of circumstances have seen more variety of Society than I – few have enjoyd it more or been *bored* as it [is] calld less by the company of tiresome people. I have rarely if ever found any one out of whom I could not extract amusement or edification and were I obliged to account for hints afforded on such occasions I should make an ample deduction from my inventive powers. Still however, from the earliest time I can remember, I preferd the pleasures of being alone to waiting for visitors, and have often taken a bannock and a bit of cheese to the wood or hill to avoid dining with company. As I grew from boyhood to manhood I saw this would not do and that to gain a place in men's esteem I must mix and bustle with them. Pride and an excitation of spirits supplied the real pleasure which others seem to feel in society and certainly upon many occasions it was real. Still if the question was eternal company without the power of retiring within yourself or Solitary confinement for life I should say 'Turnkey, Lock the cell.' My life, though not without its fits of waking and strong exertion, has been a sort of dream spent in

> Chewing the cud of sweet and bitter fancy.[2]

I have worn a wishing cap the power of which has been to divert present griefs by a touch of the wand of imagination and gild over the future prospect by prospects more fair than can ever be realized. Somewhere it is said that this castle building – this wielding of the aerial trowel – is fatal to exertions in actual life. I cannot tell – I have not found it so – I cannot indeed say like Made. Genlis that in the imaginary scenes in which I have acted a part I ever prepared myself for anything which actually befell me. But I have certainly fashiond out much that made the present hour pass pleasantly away and much that has enabled me to contribute to the amusement of the public. Since I was five years old I cannot remember the time when I had not some ideal part to play for my own solitary amusement.

28 WEDNESDAY Some how I think the attack on Christmas day has been of a critical kind and having gone off so well may be productive

---

1. This too was urgent: it was to appear in the January *Quarterly*, as the first article of Lockhart's first number. Scott was working under the double handicap of his illness and of having left his copy of Pepys in Edinburgh. *Letters*, ix. 358.
2. *As You Like It*, iv. 3.

rather of health than continued indisposition. If one is to get a renewal of health in his fifty fourth year he must look to pay fine for it. Last night George Thompson[1] came to see how I was, poor fellow. He has talent, is well informd, and has an excellent heart, but there is an eccentricity about him that defies description. I wish to God I saw him provided in a country kirk. That with a rational wife, that is if there is such a thing to be gotten for him, would I think bring him to a steady temper. At present he is between the tyning[2] and the winning. If I could get him to set to any hard study he would do something clever.

How to make a critic – A sly rogue sheltering himself under the generick name of Mr. Campbell requested me through the penny post the loan of £50 for two years, having an impulse as he said to make this demand. As I felt no corresponding impulse I beggd to decline a demand which might have been as reasonably made by any Campbell on earth and another impulse has determined the Man of fifty pounds to send me anonymous abuse of my works and temper and selfish disposition. The severity of the joke lies in 14d. for postage,[3] to avoid which his next epistle shall go back to the clerks of the Post Office as not for S. W. S.[4] How the severe rogue would be disappointed if he knew I never lookd at more than the first and last line of his satirical effusions.

When I first saw that a literary profession was to be my fate I endeavour by all efforts of stoicism to divest myself of that irritable degree of sensibility – or to speak plainly of Vanity – which makes the poetical race miserable and ridiculous. The anxiety of a poet for praise and for compliments I have always endea[vourd to avoid].

1. The Revd. George Thomson, son of the minister in Melrose, the original of Dominie Sampson, and formerly tutor to Scott's sons. He had a wooden leg and an eccentric manner. 'I hope he will not go utterly mad till I can get some hapless congregation for him', wrote Scott in May 1826 (*Letters*, x. 26) but repeated efforts to recommend his 'very worthy friend George Thompson' (*Letters*, vii. 46), for whom he had a real regard, were in vain.
2. 'Losing'.
3. In Scott's day postage was paid by the recipient not the sender. The cost of a letter from London to Edinburgh was 13d. Scott says elsewhere that unsolicited packages cost him £100 a year. See the Entry for 6 January 1828.
4. This abbreviation of 'Sir Walter Scott' was coined by Tom Purdie, who took it upon himself, when Scott became a baronet, to change the markings on the Abbotsford sheep from 'WS' to 'SWS'. *Life*, ix. 32.

29 THURSDAY Base feeling this same Calomel gives one. Mean poor and abject – a wretch as Will Rose says.

> Fie fie on silly coward man
> That he should be the slave o't.[1]

Then it makes one sinfully dogged and snappish, as Dr. Rutt[y] the Quaker says in his *gurnal*.[2] Sent Lockhart four pages on Sheridan's plays[3] – not very good I think but the demand came sudden. Must go to *W—k* yet am vexd by that humour of contradiction which makes me incline to do anything else in presence. Commenced preface for New Edition novels.[4] The city of Cork send my freedom in a silver box.[5] I thought I was out of their grace for going to see Blarney rather than the cove[6] for which I was attackd and defended in the papers when in Ireland. I am sure they are so civil that I would have gone wherever they wishd me to go if I had had any one to have told me what I ought to be most inquisitive about

> For if I should as Lion come in strife
> Into such place 'twere pity of my life.[7]

30 FRIDAY Spent at home and in labour – with the weight of unpleasant news from Edinburgh. J. B. is like to be pinched next week unless the loan can be brought forward. I must and have endeavourd to supply him. At present the result of my attempts are uncertain. I am even more anxious about C. and Coy unless they can get assistance from their London friends to whom they gave much. All is in God's hands. The worst can only be what I have before anticipated. But I must I think renounce the Segars. They brought back (using two this evening) the irritation of which I had no feelings while abstaining from them.

---

1. Burns's 'O Poortith Cauld and Restless Love', ll. 11–12.
2. *A Spiritual Diary and Soliloquies*, by Dr. John Rutty (1698–1775).
3. To assist him with an article on Moore's *Life of Sheridan*.
   Lockhart had written on the 25th asking for 'what it wd cost you no trouble (certainly no reading) to throw off at once'. *Letters*, ix. 352n.
4. See the entry for 24 December and note.
5. Only the letter from Cork arrived on this day; the silver box came on 5 January.
6. Queenstown.
7. *A Midsummer Night's Dream*, v. 1.

Dined alone with Gordon,[1] Lady S. and Anne.

James Curle,[2] Melrose, has handsomely lent me £600. He has done kindly. I have served him before and will again if in my power.

31 SATURDAY Took a good sharp walk the first time since my illness and found myself the better in health and spirits. Being Hogmanae[3] there dined with us Colonel Russell and his sisters, Sir Adam Fergusson and Lady, Colonel Fergusson[4] with Mary and Margaret[5] – An auld-warld party who made themselves happy in the auld fashion. I felt so tired about eleven that I was forced to steal to Bed.

1. George Huntly Gordon was the son of Major Pryse Gordon, who showed Scott the field of Waterloo in 1815. Debarred by his deafness from becoming a minister of the Scottish Church as he had intended, he acted for many years as Scott's amanuensis, copying the manuscript for the press to preserve the author's anonymity and cataloguing his library. In 1826 Scott helped to procure him a post as assistant private secretary to the Secretary of the Treasury.
2. The lawyer who transacted most of Scott's local business. After the crash, the Trustees appointed him to supervise the day-to-day financial management of the estate.
3. New Year's Eve.
4. Sir Adam Ferguson's brother James.
5. The Misses Ferguson.

1826

1 SUNDAY A year has passd – another has commenced. These solemn divisions of time influence our feelings as they recur. Yet there is nothing in it – for every day in the year closes a twelve month as well as the 31st December. The latter is only the solemn pause as when a guide during a wild and mountainous road calls on a party to pause and look back at the scenes which they have just passd. To me this New Year opens sadly. There are these troublesome pecuniary difficulties which however I think this week should end. There is the absence of all my children, Anne excepted, from our little family festival. There is besides that ugly report of the 15 Hussars going to India. Walter I suppose will have some step in view and will go[1] and I fear Jane will not dissuade Him.

A hard frosty day – cold but dry and pleasant under foot. Walkd into the plantations with Anne and Anne Russell. A thought strikes me allied to this period of the year. People say that the whole human frame in all its parts and divisions is gradually in the act of decaying and renewing. What a curious time-piece it would be that could indicate to us the moment this gradual and insensible change had so completely taken place that no atom was left of the original person who had existed at a certain period but there existed in his stead another person having the same limbs thewes and sinews, the same face and lineaments, the same consciousness – a new ship built on an old plank – A pair of transmigrated stockings like those of Sir John Cutler all green silk without one thread of the original black silk left! Singular – to be at once another and the same.

2 MONDAY Weather[2] clearing up in Edinburgh once more and all will I believe do well. I am pressd to get on with *Woodstock* and must

---

1. The chance of buying promotion was greatest when a regiment was going on service overseas. Those who did not wish to go sold their commissions and retired to their country estates.
2. The financial storm-clouds.

try. I wish I could open a good vein of interest which would breathe freely. I must take my old way and write myself into goodhumour with my task. It is only when I dally with what I am about, look back and aside instead of keeping my eyes straight forward, that I feel these cold sinkings of the heart – All men I suppose do, less or more. They are like the sensation of a sailor when the ship is cleard for action and all are at their places – gloomy enough – but the first broadside puts all to rights.

Dined at Huntlyburn with the Fergussons en masse.

3 TUESDAY Promises a fair day and I think the progress of my labours will afford me a little exercize which I greatly need to help off the calomel feeling. Walkd with Colonel Russell from eleven till two, the first good day's exercise I have had since coming here. We went through all the Terrace, the Roman planting, over by the Stell and Haxellcleuch[1] and so by the Rhymer's glen to Chiefswood, which gave my heart a twinge so disconsolate it seemd. Yet all is for the best. Calld at Huntly Burn and shook hands with Sir Adam and his Lady just going off. When I returnd, signd the Bond for £10,000 which will disencumber me of all pressing claims.[2] When I get forwards *W—k* and *Nap.* there will be £12,000 and upwards, and I hope to add £3000 against this time next year or the devil must hold [the] dice.

J. B. writes me seriously on the carelessness of my style. I do not think I am more careless than usual but I dare say he is right. I will be more cautious.

4 WEDNESDAY Despatchd the deed yesterday executed. Yesterday Mr. and Mrs. Skene, my excellent friends, came to us from Edinburgh.[3] Skene, distinguishd for his attainments as a draughtsman and for his highly gentlemanlike feelings and character, is Laird of Rubislaw near Aberdeen. Having had an elder brother his education was somewhat neglected in early life, against which disadvantage he made a most gallant [fight] exerting himself much to obtain those accomplishments which [he] has since possessed. Admirable in all exercises there enterd a good deal of the cavalier into his early character. Of late he has given himself much to the study of antiquities. His wife, a most excellent person, was tenderly fond of Sophia. They bring so much oldfashioned kindness and good humour with them, besides the

---

1. The names of plantations on the Abbotsford Estate.
2. See the Entry for 14 December and note.
3. Skene 'had long been in the habit of passing Christmas with Sir Walter in the country'. *Skene's Memories*, p. 167.

recollections of other times, that they must be always wellcome guests. Letter from Mr. Scrope[1] announcing a visit.

5 THURSDAY Got the desired accomodation with Coutts which will put J. B. quite straight but am a little anxious still about Constable. He has immense stock to be sure and most valuable but he may have sacrifices to make to convert a large proportion of it into ready money. The accounts from London are most disastrous – many wealthy persons totally ruind and many many more have been obliged to purchase their safety at a price they will feel all their lives. I do not hear things are so bad in Edinburgh and J. B.'s business has been transacted by the Banks with liberality.[2]

Colonel Russell told us last night that the Last of the Moguls, a descendant of Kubla Khan though having no more power than his effigies at the back of a set of playing-cards, refused to meet Lord Hastings because the Governor General would not agree to remain standing in his presence. Pretty well for the blood of Timur in these degenerate days.

Much alarmed. I had walkd till twelve with Skene and Colonel Russell and then sate down to my work. To my horror and surprize I could neither write nor spell but put down one word for another and wrote nonsense.[3] I was much overpowerd at the same time and could not conceive the reason. I fell asleep however in my chair and slept for two hours. On waking my head was clearer and I began to recollect that last night I had taken the anodyne left for the purpose by Clarkson and being disturbd in the course of the night I had not slept it off.

Received from the Corporation of Corke a very handsome silver snuff box with my freedom of that ancient city – Obliged to give up writing to-day – read Pepys[4] instead.

1. William Scrope (1772–1852), from Lincolnshire, had leased the Pavilion, Lord Somerville's house on the other side of the Tweed from Abbotsford. He was a noted sportsman and painter, and the author of *The Art of Deer Stalking and Days* and *Nights of Salmon Fishing on the Tweed*.
2. They were liberal because they knew Scott was a partner and considered him wealthy enough to stand the storm. Gibson's *Reminiscences*, p. 12.
3. During his walk with Skene on 24 January Scott alluded to the fright that this gave him. 'You saw me under the apprehension of the decay of my mental faculties, and I confess that I was under mortal fear when I found myself writing one word for another, and misspelling every word.' *Skene's Memories*, p. 138.
4. The copy of Pepys which Ballantyne was asked to send (*Letters*, ix. 358) had evidently arrived.

The Scotts of Harden were to have dined but sent an apology storm coming on. Russells left us this morning to go to Haining.[1]

6 FRIDAY   This seems to be a feeding storm – coming on by little and little. Wrought all day and dined quiet. My disorder is wearing off and the quiet society of the Skenes suits with my present humour. I really thought I was in for some very bad illness. Curious expression of an Indian-born boy just come from Bengal, a son of my cousin George Swinton.[2] The child saw a hare run across the fields and exclaimd 'See there is a little tiger.'

7 SATURDAY   Sunday.[3] Knight,[4] a young artist, son of the performer, came to paint my picture at the request of Terry[5] – This is very far from being agreeable as I submitted to this distressing state of constraint last year[6] – to Newton[7] at request of Lockhart, Leslie[8] at request of my American friend,[9] Wilkie for his picture of the King's arrival at Holy Rood House[10] and some one beside. I am as tired of the operation as old Maida[11] who had been so often sketchd that he got up and went away with signs of Loathing whenever he saw an artist unfurl his paper and handle his brushes. But this young man is civil and modest and I have agreed he shall sit in the room while I

1. To visit John Pringle.
2. Secretary to the Council in Bengal.
3. See Appendix E, i, p. 827.
4. John Prescott Knight (1803–81).
5. Daniel Terry (?1780–1829), the gentleman-actor. Scott first met him through the Ballantynes in 1810, and their similar tastes for old plays drew them together. Terry idolized Scott even to the extent of talking like him and imitating his handwriting. He 'Terryfied' (that is, dramatized) some of the Waverley Novels, and helped to furnish Abbotsford. See *Life*, iii. 223 and, e.g., *Letters*, vii. 278.
6. Scott means 1824.
7. Gilbert Stewart Newton (1794–1835), an American.
8. C. R. Leslie, R. A., who painted Scott's portrait in October 1824.
9. George Ticknor (1791–1871), Professor of French and Spanish at Harvard, who had visited Edinburgh in 1819. The portrait was painted in 1824 and Scott 'with a tact and amiability very characteristic of him, selected the young American painter, then making himself known in England'. *Ticknor's Life*, i. 389.
10. The picture referred to, which now hangs in Holyrood, is a composite portrait, celebrating the visit of George IV to Edinburgh in 1822 when Scott himself arranged and managed the entire proceedings.
11. His favourite deerhound, which died in 1824.

work and take the best likeness he can without compelling me into forced attitudes or the yawning fatigues of an actual sitting. I think if he has talent he may do more my way than in the customary mode – at least I cannot have the hangdog look which the unfortunate Theseus has who is doomd to sit for what seems an eternity.[1]

I wrought till two o'clock, indeed till I was almost nervous with correcting and scribbling. I then walkd or rather was dragd through the snow by Tom Purdie while Skene accompanied. What a blessing there is in a man like Tom whom no familiarity can spoil, whom you may scold and praise and joke with, knowing the quality of the man is unalterable in his love and reverence to his master. Use an ordinary servant in the same way and he will be your master in a month.

We should thank God for the snow as well as summer-flowers. This brushing exercize has put all my nerves into tone again which were really jard with fatigue untill my very back-bone seemd breaking. This comes of trying to do too much.

J. B.'s news are as good as possible prudence – prudence and all will do excellently.

8 SUNDAY Frost and snow still. Wrote to excuse myself from attending the funeral of my aunt Mrs. Curl which takes place tomorrow at Kelso. She was a woman of the old Sandyknow breed with the strong sense, high principle and indifferent temper which belongd to my father's family. She lived with great credit on a moderate income and I believe gave away a great deal of it.[2]

9 MONDAY Matthews the Comedian and his son came to spend a day at Abbotsford.[3] The last is a clever young man with much of his father's talent for mimicry. Rather forward though.[4] Mr. Scrope also came out which fills our house.

1. An allusion to Virgil's *Aeneid*, vi. 617 quoted by Scott in the Entry for 14 June 1830.
2. Lockhart quotes Scott's letter to Mrs. Thomas Scott. 'Poor aunt Curle died like a Roman, or rather like one of the Sandy-Knowe bairns, the most stoical race I ever knew. She turned every one out of the room, and drew her last breath alone.' *Life*, viii. 192 n.
3. Mathews wrote to his wife the next day: 'Our reception was warm and kind after our cold and cheerless journey through a country covered with snow. Mr. Scrope, to my horror, took his own horses all the way, and we travelled about four miles an hour.' *Memoirs of Mathews*, iii. 551.
4. Douglas quotes the younger Mathews, *Memoirs* (1879), i. 284: 'I took particular notice of everything in the room (Sir Walter's sanctum), and *if he had left me there, should certainly have read all his notes.*'

10 TUESDAY Bodily Health, the mainspring of the microcosm, seems quite restored. No more flinching or nervous fits but the sound mind in the sound body. What poor things does a fever fit or an overflowing of the bile make of the master of creation.

The snow begins to fall thick this morning.

> The Landlord then aloud did say
> As how he wishd they would go away.[1]

To have our friends shut up here would be rather too much of a good thing.

The day cleard up and was very pleasant. Had a good walk and lookd at the curling. Mr. Matthews made himself very amusing in the evening. He has the goodnature to show his accomplishments without pressing and without the appearance of feeling pain. On the contrary I dare say he enjoys the pleasure he communicates.[2]

11 WEDNESDAY I got proof Sheets in which it seems I have repeated a whole passage of history which had been told before. James is in an awful stew and I cannot blame him. But then he should consider the hyasymus[3] which I was taking and the anxious botheration about the money market. However as Chaucer says

> There is na workeman
> That can bothe wirken wel and hastilie
> This must be done at leisure parfaitly.[4]

Matthews, his son, Scrope and the Skenes still our guests.

12 THURSDAY Mathews last night gave us a very perfect imitation of Old Cumberland who carried the poetic jealousy and irritabi[lity] further than any man I ever saw.[5] He was a great flatterer too, the old rogue. Will Erskine used to admire him. I think he wanted originality – a very high bred man in point of manners in Society.

My little artist Knight gets on better with his portrait – the features are however too pinchd I think.

---

1. 'Fal de sal tit', st. 4 in *The Charms of Melody*, Dublin, n.d., p. 100.
2. For an account of this evening or one like it, written by Scott's butler, see note 2, p. 806.
3. That is, 'hyoscyamus' or calomel.
4. *Merchant's Tale*, ll. 588–90.
5. Richard Cumberland (1732–1811), the dramatist, said to have been Sheridan's model for Sir Fretful Plagiary.

Upon the matter, the days pass pleasantly enough – work till one or two, then an hour or two hours' walk in the snow, then lighter work or reading. Late dinner[1] and singing or chat in the evening. Matthews has really all the will as well as the talent to be amusing. He confirms my idea of ventriloquism (which is an absurd word) as being merely the art of imitating sounds at a greater or less distance assisted by some little points of trick[ery] to influence the imagination of the audience. The vulgar idea of a peculiar organization (beyond fineness of ear and of utterance) is nonsense.

13 FRIDAY Our party are about to disperse.

> Like youthful steers unyoked east north and south.[2]

I am not sorry, being one of those whom too much mirth always inclines to sadness – the missing so many of my own family together with the serious inconveniences to which I have been exposed gave me at present a desire to be alone. The Skenes return to Edinburgh. So does Mr. Scrope – item the little artist – Matthews to New Castle, his son to Liverpool[3] – So *exeunt omnes*.

Mathews assures me that Sheridan was generally very dull in society and sate sullen and silent swallowing glass after glass rather a hindrance than a help. But there was a time when he broke out with a resumption of what had been going on done with great force and generally attacking some person in the company or some opinion which he had expressd. I never saw Sheridan but in large parties. He had a Bardolph countenance with heavy features but his eye possessd the most distinguishd brilliancy. Mathews says it is very simple in Tom Moore to admire how Sheridan came by the means of paying the price of Drury Lane Theatre when all the world knows he never paid it at all and that Lacy who sold it was reduced to want by his breach of faith.[4]

Dined quiet with Anne, Lady Scott, and Gordon.

1. In the country Scott often dined at half past four. 'Late dinner' suggests six o'clock.
2. *2 Henry IV*, iv. 2.
3. Mathews was returning to London; his son was bound for Wales. 'I was trundled into a cold post-chaise,' writes Mathews to his wife, 'to be conveyed into some road where coaches to Newcastle travel. Scott kindly sent Charlie in his own carriage to Selkirk, where he was to meet the Mail.' *Memoirs of Mathews*, iii. 552.
4. They were apparently discussing Moore's *Life of Sheridan*, which had just been published. For the matter referred to see p. 191 of the first volume.

14 SATURDAY An odd mysterious letter from Constable who is gone post to London to put something to rights which is wrong betwixt them, their banker and another monied friend. It strikes me to be that sort of letter which I have seen men write when they are desirous that their disagreeable intelligence should be rather apprehended than avowd. I thought he had been in London a fortnight ago disposing of property to meet this exigence and so I think he should. Well – I must have patience. But these tirrits and frights[1] are truly annoying. Luckily the funny people are gone and I will not have the task of grinning when I am serious enough.

Dined as yesterday.

A letter from J. B. mentioning Constable's journey but without expressing much if any apprehension. He knows C. well and saw him before his departure and makes no doubt of his being able easily to extricate whatever may be entangled. I will not therefore make myself more uneasy than I can help doing so surely if I will. At least I have given up segars since the year began and have now no wish to return to the habit as it is calld. I see no reason why one should not be able to vanquish with God's assistance these noxious thoughts which foretell evil but cannot remedy it.

15 SUNDAY Like yesterday a hard frost – thermometer at 10 yesterday was at 8½, to-day 12.[2] Water in my dressing room frozen to flint. Yet I had a fine walk yesterday, the sun shining delightfully on 'grim nature's visage hoar'.[3] Were it not the plague of being dragd along by another person I should like this weather as well as summer. But having Tom Purdie to do this office reconciles me to it – *I cannot cleik[4] with John* as old Mrs. Muir used to say. I mean that an ordinary Menial servant thus hookd to your side reminds me of the twin bodies mentiond by Pitscottie[5] being two trunks on the same waist and legs. One died before the other and remaind a dead burthen on the back of its companion. Such is the close union with a person whom you cannot well converse with and whose presence is yet indispensible to your getting on. An actual companion whether humble or your equal is still worse. But T. Purdie is just the thing, kneaded up between the

1. *2 Henry IV*, ii. 4.
2. In other words, at 10 a.m. the thermometer stood at 8½°F on the Saturday and at 12°F on the Sunday. (This reading of the sentence is confirmed by *Letters*, ix. 368.)
3. Burns's 'Vision', l. 215.
4. 'To link arms (with), walk arm in arm'. *S. N. D.*
5. Robert Lindsay of Pitscottie ed. Mackay (1899), *The Chronicles of Scotland*, i, 233–4.

friend and servant as well as Uncle Toby's Bowling Green[1] between sand and clay. You are certain he is proud as well as patient under his burthen and you are under no more constraint than with a pony. I must ride him to-day if the weather holds up. Meantime I will correct that curious fellow Pepys' *Diary*, I mean the article I have made of it for the *Quarterly*.[2]

16 MONDAY Came through cold roads to as cold news. Hurst and Robinson have sufferd a Bill of £1000 to come back on Constable which I suppose infers the ruin of both houses. We will soon see. Constable it seems, who was to have set off in the last week of December, dawdled here till in all human probability his going or staying became a matter of mighty little consequence. He could not be there till Monday night and his resources must have come too late. Dined with the Skenes.[3]

17 TUESDAY James Ballantyne this morning, good honest fellow, with a visage as black as the crook. He hopes no salvation, has indeed taken measures to stop. It is hard after having fought such a battle. Have apologised attending the R. Society Club who have a Gaudeamus on this day and seemd to count much on my being the Praeses –

My old acquaintance Miss Eliz. Clerk, sister of Willie, dead suddenly. I cannot chuse but wish it had been S. W. S. and yet the feeling is unmanly. I have Anne, my wife, and Charles to look

1. In *Tristram Shandy*, bk. vi. ch. 21.
2. Because of the next day's news it was, however, sent to Lockhart 'totally uncorrected'. *Letters*, ix. 367.
3. 'The family had been at Abbotsford, and it had long been their practice, the day they came to town, to take a family dinner at my house, which had accordingly been complied with upon the present occasion . . . and I never had seen Sir Walter in better spirits or more agreeable. The fatal intimation of his bankruptcy, however, awaited him at home, and next morning early I was surprised by a verbal message to come to him as soon as I had got up. Fearful that he had got a fresh attack of the complaint from which he had now for some years been free, or that he had been involved in some quarrel, I went to him by seven o'clock, and found him already seated by candle-light at his writing-table, surrounded by papers which he was examining. Holding out his hand to me as I entered, he said, "Skene, this is the hand of a beggar; Constable has failed, and I am ruined *du fond au comble*. It's a hard blow, but I must just bear up; the only thing which wrings me is poor Charlotte and the bairns." ' *Skene's Memories*, p. 135.

after. I felt rather sneaking as I came home from the P. House,[1] felt as if I were liable *Monstrari digito*[2] in no very pleasant way. But this must be born *cum caeteris*, and thank God however uncomfortable I do not feel despondent.

I have seen Cadell Ballantyne and Hogarth.[3] All advise me to execute a trust of my property for payment of my obligations. So does John Gibson[4] and so I resolve to do. My wife and daughter are gloomy but yet patient. I trust by my hold on the works to make it every man's interest to be very gentle with me. Cadell makes it plain that by patience they will in six months realize £20,000, which can be attainable by no effort of their own.

18 WEDNESDAY He that sleeps too long in the morning let him borrow the pillow of a debtor. So says the Spaniard and so say I. I had of course an indifferent night of it. I wish these two days were over. But the worst *is* over. The Bank of Scotland has behaved very well, expressing a resolution to serve Constable's house and me to the uttermost, but as no one can say to what extent Hurst and Robinson's failure may go borrowing would but linger it out.[5]

19 THURSDAY During yesterday I received several visits from friends. Skene, Colin McKenzie, who I am glad to see looks well, with every offer of Service. The Royal Bank also sent Sir John Hope and Sir H. Jardine[6] to offer to comply with my wishes. The advocate[7] came on the same errand. But I gave all the same answer that my intention was to put the whole into the hands of a trustee and to be contented with the event, and that all I had to ask was time to do so and to extricate my affairs. I was assured of every accomodation in this way. From all quarters I have had the same kindness. Letters from Constable and Robinson have arrived. The last persist in saying

1. Ballantyne's Printing House, not the Parliament House, which he attended, for the first time after the crash, on 24 January.
2. 'To be pointed out'. Persius's *Satires*, i. 28.
3. George Hogarth (1783–1870), brother-in-law and financial adviser of James Ballantyne. Later he became a music critic, wrote for the *Morning Chronicle*, and encouraged Dickens, who became his son-in-law in 1836.
4. John Gibson junior, Scott's man of business or law-agent since 1822. As the principal trustee in charge of Scott's affairs from this point onwards he is an important figure in the *Journal*. See Introduction, p. xlii.
5. For the butler's account of these days see note 3, p. 806.
6. Both were Ordinary Directors of the Royal Bank of Scotland.
7. Sir William Rae was an Extraordinary Director of the Bank.

they will pay all and every body. They say moreover in a postscript that had Constable been in town ten days sooner all would have been well. When I saw him on 24th December he proposed starting in three days, but dallied God knows why in a kind of infatuation I think till things had got irretrieveably wrong. There would have been no want of support here and his stock under his own management would have made a return immensely greater than it can under any other. *Now* I fear the loss must be great as his fall will involve many of the country dealers who traded with him.

I feel quite composed and determined to labour. There is no remedy. I guess (as Mathews makes his Yankees say) that we shall not be troubled with visitors and I *calculate* that I will not go out at all so what can I do better than labour? Even yesterday I went about making notes on *Waverley* according to Constable's plan.[1] It will do good one day. To-day when I lock this volume I go to *W—k*. Heigho –

Knight came to stare at me to complete his portrait. He must have read a tragic page comparative to what he saw at Abbotsford.

We dined of course at home, and before and after dinner I finish about 20 printed pages of *Woodstock* but to what effect others must judge. A painful scene after dinner and another after supper endeavouring to convince these poor dear creatures that they must not look for miracles but consider the misfortune as certain and only to be lessend by patience and labour.

20 FRIDAY Indifferent night – very bilious which may be want of exercize. A letter from Sir J. Sinclair whose absurd vanity leads him to thrust his finger into everyman's pie proposing that the Hurst and Robinson should sell their prints, of which he says they have a large collection, by way of lottery like Boydell.[2]

> In scenes like these which break our heart
> Comes Punch like you and lets a f—.[3]

Mais pourtant cultivons notre jardin.[4] The publick favour is my only lottery. I have long enjoyd the foremost prize and something in my breast tells me my Evil Genius will not overwhelm me if I stand by myself. Why should I not? I have no enemies – many attachd friends –

1. See the Entry for 24 December 1825.
2. John Boydell (1719–1804), engraver, printseller, Lord Mayor of London, and builder of the Shakespeare Gallery. Financial difficulties forced him to dispose of his property by means of a lottery.
3. Swift's 'Mad Mullinix and Timothy', ll. 111–12.
4. Voltaire's *Candide*, ch. 30.

the popular ascendancy which I have maintaind is of the kind which is rather improved by frequent appearances before the public. In fact Critics may say what they will but '*hain* your reputation and *tyne* your reputation'[1] is a true proverb.

Sir William Forbes[2] calld, the same kind honest friend as ever, with all offers of assistance etc. etc. etc. All anxious to serve me and careless about their own risk of loss – And these are the cold, hard, money making men whose questions and Controul I apprehended.

Lord Ch: Commissioner Adam[3] also came to see me and the meeting though pleasing was melancholy. It was the first time we have met since the *break-up* of his hopes in the death of his eldest son[4] on his return from India where [he] was Chief in Council and highly esteemd. Lord C. C. is not a very early friend of mine for I scarce knew him till his settlement in Scotland with his present office. But I have since lived much with him and taken kindly to him as one of the most pleasant, kind hearted, benevolent and pleasing men I have ever known. It is high treason among the Tories to express regard for him or respect for the Jury Court in which he prescribes. I was against that experiment as much as any one. But it is an experiment, and the establishment (which the fools will not perceive) is the onlything which I see likely to give some prospects of ambition to our bar which has been diminishd otherwise so much. As for the Chief Commissioner I dare say he jobs as all other people of consequence

1. 'Hoard your reputation and lose your reputation.'
2. Sir William Forbes of Pitsligo (1773–1828) was head of the private banking house which, ranking for more than £11,000, was Scott's largest creditor. Their friendship had survived their rivalry for the hand of Williamina Belsches, whom Sir William married in 1797. He had remained a widower since her death in 1810, an honest, amiable country gentleman, without the genius of his more successful father.
3. The Rt. Hon. William Adam (1751–1838), nephew of Robert and James Adam, the architects. When an Act of 1815 established a Jury Court to try civil cases with a jury (a new departure in Scotland) he returned from England as Lord Chief Commissioner. The Court tried its first case in January 1816 and was absorbed into the Court of Session in 1830. Each year, at midsummer, Adam played host to Scott and the other members of the Blair-Adam Club at the family seat of Blair-Adam. See the Entry for 24 June 1826, and Introduction, p. xliii. Lockhart calls Adam 'The only man I ever knew that rivalled Sir Walter Scott in uniform graciousness of *bonhommie* and gentleness of humour'. *Life*, vi. 258.
4. John Adam, who died on shipboard in June 1825 at the end of his second term of office as acting Governor-General in India.

do in elections and so forth. But he is the personal friend of the King and the decided enemy of whatever strikes at the constitutional rights of the Monarch. Besides I love him for the various changes which he has endured through life and which have been so great as to make him entitled to be regarded in one point of view as the most fortunate in the other the most unfortunate man in the world. He has gaind and lost two fortunes by the same good fortune and the same rash confidence which has raised and now threatens my *peculium*. And his quiet, noble and generous submission under circumstances more painful than mine, for the loss of world's wealth was aggravated by the death of his youngest and darling son in the West Indies, furnishd me at the time and now with a noble example – So the Tories and Whigs may go be damnd together as names that have distracted Old Scotland and torn asunder the most kindly feelings since the first day they were invented. Yet d—n them they are spells to rouse all our angry passions, and I dare say notwithstanding the opinion of my private and calm moments I will open on the cry again so soon as something occurs to chafe my mood. And yet God knows I would fight in honourable contest with word or blow for my political opinions but I cannot permit that strife to 'mix its waters with my daily meal',[1] those waters of bitterness which poison all mutual love and confidence betwixt the well disposed on each side, and prevent them if need were from making mutual concessions and balancing the constitution against the Ultras of both parties. The good man seems something broken by these aflictions.

21 SATURDAY Susannah in *Tristram Shandy* thinks Death is best met in bed.[2] I am sure trouble and vexation is not. The watches of the night pass wearily when disturbd by fruitless regrets and disagreeable anticipations. But let it pass.

> Well Goodman Time or blunt or keen
> Move thou quick or take thy leisure
> Longest day will have its een
> Weariest life but treads a measure.[3]

I have seen Caddell[4] who is very much downcast for the risque of their copy-rights being thrown away by a hasty sale. I suggested that if they went very cheap some means might be fallen on to keep up their

1. Wordsworth's *Poems on the Naming of Places*, v. 20.
2. Sterne's *Tristra— Shandy*, bk. v. ch. 10.
3. Joanna Baillie's *Rayner*, iii. 2.
4. Cadell came in response to a note from Scott: 'If you go out this morning I wish you would give me a call in passing. But do not interrupt any business as I have nothing to say beyond a wish to

value or purchase them in. I fear the split betwixt Constable and Caddell[1] will render impossible what might otherwise be hopeful enough. It is the Italian race-horses, I think, which instead of riders have spurs tied to their sides so as to prick them into a constant gallop. Caddell tells me their gross profit was sometimes £10,000 a year but much swallowd up with expences and his partner's draugh[t]s which came to £4000 yearly. What there is to show for this God knows. Constable's apparent expences were very much within bounds.

Colin McKenzie enterd and with his usual kindness engages to use his influence to recommend some moderate proceeding to Constable's crers which may permit him to go on and turn that species of property to account which no man alive can manage so well as he.[2]

Followd Mr. Gibson with a most melancholy tale. Things are so much worse with Constable than I apprehended that I shall neither save Abbotsford nor any thing else – Naked we enterd the world and naked we leave it. Blessed be the name of the Lord.[3]

22 SUNDAY I feel neither dishonourd nor broken down by the bad – miserably bad news I have received. I have walkd my last on the domains I have planted, sate the last time in the halls I have built. But death would have taken them from me if misfortune had spared them. My poor people whom I loved so well! ! There is just another dye to turn up against me in this run of ill luck – i.e. If I should break my magic wand in a fall from this elephant and lose my popularity with my fortune. Then *Woodstock* and *Boney* may both go to the

---

know how things go on.' *Letters*, ix. 373. The sale of the copyrights of Scott's works, although it could have raised an immediate few pennies in the pound for his creditors, would have put an end to any hope of eventually paying the debt off in full. Without the copyrights there could be no new editions and Cadell saw thus early that only clever management of the literary property which they held could raise the necessary sum. In the end the Trustees and Cadell acquired the complete copyrights between them. The collected editions which this made possible liquidated Scott's debts and made a fortune for Cadell, who was wise enough – or unscrupulous enough – to buy Scott's share of the copyrights from the family after Scott's death.

1. 'He and Constable are at daggers drawing and recriminate bitterly on each other.' *Letters*, ix. 384.
2. Colin Mackenzie also joined with Sir Robert Dundas and Hector Macdonald Buchanan to offer Scott a loan of £1000 to pay off private house accounts of £50 and under. Disc. i. 70.
3. Job 1: 21.

papermaker and I may take to smoking cigars and drinking grog or turn devotee and intoxicate the brain another way. In prospect of absolute ruin I wonder if they would let me leave the Court of Session. I should like methinks to go abroad

> And lay my banes far from the Tweed.[1]

But I find my eyes moistening and that will not do. I will not yield without a fight for it. It is odd, when I set myself to work *doggedly* as Dr. Johnson would say,[2] I am exactly the same man that I ever was – neither low spirited nor *distrait*. In prosperous times I have some-times felt my fancy and powers of language flag – but adversity is to me at least a tonic and bracer – the fountain is awakend from its inmost recesses as if the spirit of afliction had troubled it in his passage.

Poor Mr. Pole the harper sent to offer me £500 or £600, probably his all.[3] There is much good in the world after all. But I will involve no friend either rich or poor – My own right hand shall do it – Else will I be *done* in the slang language and *undone* in common parlance.

I am glad that beyond my own family, who are excepting L. S.[4] young and able to bear sorrow of which this is the first taste to some of them, most of the hearts are past aching which would have been inconsolable on this occasion. I do not mean that many will not seriously regret and some perhaps lament my misfortunes. But my dear mother, my almost sister Christy R—d,[5] – poor Will: Erskine – these would have been mourners indeed –

Well – exertion – exertion – O Invention rouze thyself. May man be kind – may God be propitious. The worst is I never quite know when I am right or wrong and Ballantyne, who does know in some degree, will fear to tell me. Lockhart would be worth gold just now but he too

---

1. The Marquis of Tweeddale's 'Tweedside', st. 1, in Herd *Ancient and Modern Scottish Songs*.
2. Boswell's *Life of Johnson*, v. 40.
3. 'Mr. Pole had long attended Sir Walter Scott's daughters as teacher of the harp. To the end, Scott always spoke of his conduct on this occasion as the most affecting circumstance that accompanied his disasters.' J. G. L. His letter said: 'I have five or six hundred pounds that I have no use for, as I am in debt to no soul, and if you can wait, I will dispose of all I have, and convert them into money. It is a duty I owe you; for it is by your kind countenance, as well as a share of good conduct, that I have been able to save a few hundred pounds, which are quite at your service.' *Life*, viii. 205.
4. Lady Scott.
5. Christian Rutherford, Scott's mother's half-sister.

would be too diffident to speak broad out. All my hope is in the continued indulgence of the public.

I have a funeral letter to the burial of the Chevalier Yelin, a foreigner of learning and talent, who has died at the Royal Hotel. He wishd to be introduced to me and was to have read a paper before the Royal Society when this introduction was to have taken place. I was not at the society that evening[1] and the poor gentleman was taken ill in the meeting and unable to proceed. He went to his bed and never arose again – and now his funeral will be the first public place that I shall appear at – he dead and I ruind. This is what you call a meeting.

23 MONDAY Slept ill not having been abroad these eight days. *Splendida bilis.*[2] Then a dead sleep in the morning and when the awakenings came a strong feeling how well I could dispence with it for once and for ever. This passes away however as better and more dutiful thoughts arise in my mind.

I know not if my imagination has flaggd – probably it has but at least my powers of labour have not diminishd during the last melancholy week. On Monday and tuesday my exertions were suspended. Since Wednesday inclusive I have written thirty eight of my close manuscript pages of which seventy make a volume of the usual novel size.

Wrote till twelve a.m. finishing half of what I call a good day's work, ten pages of print or rather twelve. Then walkd in the Princes Street pleasure grounds[3] with good Samaritan James Skene,[4] the only

1. On 21 November 1825.
2. A play on *bilis*. He is suffering from bile, and quotes the 'resplendent anger' of Horace's *Satires*, II. 141.
3. By an Act of 1816 the Princes Street Proprietors were allowed to lease the ground south of Princes Street 'for the purpose of laying out the same in whole or in part as a garden, nursery for trees, or pleasure ground or under grass, or otherwise embellishing and enclosing the same'. The Committee of Proprietors accepted Skene's proposed plan in January 1820 and he took over the task, in his own words, of 'laying out the grounds and superintending all the operations in the gardens towards transforming that subject from its original condition of a filthy and offensive bog to become one of the most beautiful and attractive objects of which this city can boast'. In 1821 the right of access was extended to suitable persons on payment of three guineas for a key. See Youngson, p. 276, and David Robertson's *The Princes Street Proprietors*, 1935, p. 20 and p. 40.
4. Skene printed Scott's note to him on this day: 'If you are disposed for a walk in your gardens any time this morning, I

one among my numerous friends who can properly be termd *amicus omnium horarum*,[1] others being too busy or too gay and several being estranged by habit. The walks have been conducted on the whole with much taste though Skene has undergone much criticism,[2] the usual reward of public exertions, on account of his plans. It is singular to walk close beneath the grim old Castle and think what scenes it must have seen and how many generations of three score and ten have risen and past away. It is a place to cure one of too much sensation over earthly subjects of mutation. My wife and girl's tongues are chatting in a lively manner in the drawing-room. It does me good to hear them.

24 TUESDAY Constable came yesterday and saw me for half an hour. He seemd irritable but kept his temper under command. Was a little shockd when I intimated that I was disposed to regard the present works in progress as my own. I think I saw two things – 1. That he is

---

would gladly accompany you for an hour, since keeping the house so long begins rather to hurt me, and you who supported the other day the weight of my body are perhaps best disposed to endure the gloom of my mind. – Yours ever, W. S. I will call when you please. All hours after twelve are the same to me.'

In the course of the walk, with all conversation returning inevitably to his misfortunes, Scott is reported by Skene to have said:

'Do you know I experience a sort of determined pleasure in confronting the very worst aspect of this sudden reverse – in standing, as it were, in the breach that has overthrown my fortunes, and saying, "Here I stand, at least an honest man", and God knows if I have enemies. This I may at least with truth say, that I have never wittingly given cause of enmity in the whole course of my life, for even the burnings of political hate seemed to find nothing in my nature to feed the flame. I am not conscious of ever having borne a grudge towards any man, and at this moment of my overthrow, so help me God, I wish well and feel kindly to every one. And if I thought that any of my works contained a sentence hurtful to any one's feelings, I would burn it. I think even my novels (for he did not disavow any of them) are free from that blame.' *Skene's Memories*, pp. 135, 137–8.

1. 'The friend of all hours'.
2. For instance from C. K. Sharpe, in a letter to Scott: 'He hath made a dismal spectacle here, his snip snap walks, and fiddlestick parterres entice the vulgar to pay for keys, so that is well – how in the name of Midas himself, that person could ever, even here, get the reputation of taste, I cannot guess.' Undated, but 1826, Walpole.

desirous to return in to the management of his own affairs without
Cadell if he can. 2. That he relies on my connexion as the way of
helping us out of the slough. Indeed he said he was ruind utterly
without my countenance. I certainly will befriend him if I can but
Constable without Cadell is like getting the clock without the
pendulum – the one having the ingenuity – the other the caution
of the business – I will see my way before making any bargain, and I
will help them I am sure if I can without endangering my last cast for
freedom. Workd out my task yesterday.

My kind friend Mrs. Coutts has got the cadetship for Pringle
Shortreed[1] in which I was peculiarly interested.

I went to the Court for the first time to-day and like the man with
the large nose thought everybody was thinking of me and my
mishaps. Many were undoubtedly and all rather regrettingly, some
obviously affected. It is singular to see [the] difference of men's
manner whilst they strive to be kind or civil in their way of addressing
me. Some smiled as they wishd me good day as if to say 'Think
nothing about it my lad; it is quite out of our thoughts – ' Others
greeted me with the affected gravity which one sees and despises at a
funeral. The best-bred, all I believe meaning equally well, just shook
hands and went on.[2]

A foolish puff in the papers calling on men and gods to assist a
popular author who having choused the public of many thousands
had not the sense to keep wealth when he had it.

If I am hard pressd and measures used against me I must use all
measures of legal defence and subscribe myself bankrupt in a petition
for sequestration. It is the course I would have advised a client to take
and would have the effect of saving my land, which is secured by my

1. Scott sent the news at once to the young man's father, Robert
   Shortreed, Sheriff-Substitute of Roxburghshire, enclosing Mrs.
   Coutts's letter. *Letters*, ix. 375. Pringle Shortreed was posted to
   the 58th Bengal Native Infantry, and rose to be a Colonel in the
   17th Native Infantry.
2. Lord Cockburn was among those present: 'Well do I remember his
   first appearance after this calamity was divulged, when he walked
   into Court one day in January 1826. There was no affectation, and
   no reality, of *facing it*; no look of indifference or defiance; but the
   manly and modest air of a gentleman conscious of some folly, but
   of perfect rectitude, and of most heroic and honourable resolutions.
   It was on that very day, I believe, that he said a very fine thing.
   Some of his friends offered him, or rather proposed to offer him,
   enough of money, as was supposed, to enable him to arrange with
   his creditors. He paused for a moment; and then, recollecting his
   powers, said proudly – "No! this right hand shall work it all off!" '
   Cockburn's *Memorials*, ch. 7.

son's contract of marriage. I might save my library etc. by assistance of friends and bid my creditors defiance. But for this I would in a court of Honour deserve to lose my spurs for – No, if they permit me, I will be their vassal for life and dig in the mine of my imagina[tion] to find diamonds (or what may sell for such) to make good my engagements, not to enrich myself. And this from no reluctance to allow myself to be calld the Insolvent which I probably am but because I will not put out of the [reach] of my creditors the resources mental or literary which yet remain to me.[1]

Went to the funeral of Chevalier Yelin, the literary foreigner mentiond on 22d. How many and how various are the ways of afliction. Here is this poor man dying at a distance from home, his friend[2] heart-broken, his wife and family anxiously expecting letters and doomd only to learn they have lost a husband and father for ever. He lies buried on the Calton hill[3] near learnd and scientific dust – the graves of David Hume[4] and John Playfair[5] being side by side.

25 WEDNESDAY Anne is ill this morning – May God help us; if it should prove serious as I have known it in such cases where am I to find courage or comfort?

A thought has struck me – can we do nothing for ourselves with the goblin drama calld the *Fortunes of Devorgoil*[6] – Could it not be added to *Woodstock* as a fourth volume? – Terry refused a gift of it but he was quite and entirely wrong – It is not good but it may be made so – Poor Will Erskine liked it much. Gave my wife her £12 allowance. £24 to last till Wednesday fort-night.   £24 J. B.

26 THURSDAY Spoke to J. B. last night about *Devorgoil* who does not seem to relish the proposal, alleging the comparative failure of *Halidon Hill*.[7] Aye, says Self conceit, but he has not read it – and when he does it is the sort of wild fanciful work betwixt heaven and earth which men of

1. For an explanation of bankruptcy proceedings in Scott's day see Introduction, pp. xxii–xxxvii. Scott clearly felt that to apply for a Sequestration, only a year after removing Abbotsford from the reach of his creditors by settling it on his son, would be dishonourable.
2. Baron d'Eichthal, with whom he was travelling.
3. The hill immediately to the east of Princes Street.
4. David Hume (1711–76), the philosopher and historian.
5. John Playfair (1748–1819), Professor of Mathematics and Natural Philosophy at Edinburgh University, and a noted geologist.
6. *The Doom of Devorgoil*, written in 1817–18, was eventually published early in 1830 along with *Auchindrane*.
7. A dramatic sketch published by Constable in 1822.

solid parts do not estimate. Pepys thought Shakespeare's *Midsummer's Night's Dream* the most silly play he had ever seen and Pepys was probably judging on the same grounds with J. B. though presumptuous enough to form conclusions against a very different work from any of mine. How if I send it to Lockhart by and bye?

I calld to-day at Constable's. Both partners seemd secure that Hurst and Robinson were to go on and pay. Strange that they should have stopd. Constable very anxious to have husbanding of the books. I told him the truth that I would be glad to have his assistance – and that he should have the benefit of the agency but that he was <not> to consider past transactions as no rule for settling those in future since I must needs make the most out of the labours I could: item, that I or whoever might act for me would of course after what has happend look especially to the security. He said if Hurst and Robinson were to go on bank notes would be laid down. I conceive indeed that they would take *W—k* and *Napoleon* almost at loss rather than break the connection in the public eye.

Sir William Arbuthnot and Mr. Kinnear[1] were very kind. But *cui bono*?[2] Received £6. 5. paid back of deposit for Wool stapling Stock Coy. Gave it to my wife with direction to repay Anne £1.1.

£6 5
1 1

Gibson comes with a joyful face announcing all the Creditors had unanimously agreed to a private trust.[3] This is handsome and

1. Two Directors of the Bank of Scotland, Scott's second largest creditor.
2. 'For whose gain?' Cicero's *Pro Milone*, xii. xxxii.
3. This was the solution Scott wanted: 'If they allow me to put my affairs into the hands of a private trustee, or trustees, and finish the literary engagements I have on hand, there is no great chance of their being ultimate losers. This is the course I should chuse. *Letters*, ix. 376. Gibson's account is as follows: 'At the request of the directors of the Bank of Scotland, and with Sir Walter's consent, I had a meeting with them, and explained that he was the sole author of the *Waverley Novels* – that he intended, if a trust was approved of, to devote his future works, as well as those then in progress, to the benefit of his creditors, *asking no discharge*, but merely indulgence in the meantime, and that it was wished the banks should name some one or more to be joined with me to represent them in the trust. *This was the first occasion on which the authorship was authoritatively announced*, although the more public admission was made by Sir Walter himself at a public dinner during the following year. The proposal of a trust being approved of, all the necessary arrangements were readily gone into. The late Mr. Alexander Monypenny, W. S., was named by the Bank of Scotland, and the late Mr. James Jollie, W. S., by Sir William Forbes and Company.' Gibson's *Reminiscences*, p. 16.

confidential and must warm my best efforts to get them out of the scrape. I will not doubt – to doubt is to lose. Sir William Forbes took the chair and behaved as he has ever done with the generosity of ancient faith and early friendship. They[1] are deeper concernd than most. In what scenes have Sir William and I not born share together – desperate and almost bloody affrays, rivalries – deep drinking matches, and finally with the kindest feelings on both sides somewhat separated by his retiring much within the bosom of his family and I moving little beyond mine. It is fated our planets should cross though and that at the period most interesting for me – Down – down – a hundred thoughts. – Jane Russel drank tea with us.

I hope I will sleep better to-night. If I do not I shall get ill and then I cannot keep my engagements. Is it not odd? I can command my eyes to be awake when toil and weariness sit on my eyelids but to draw the curtain of oblivion is beyond my power. I remember some of the wild Buccaneers in their impiety succeeded pretty well by shutting hatches and burning brimstone and assafœtida to make a tolerable imitation of *hell* but their *heaven* was a wretched affair – It is one of the worst things about this system of ours that it is a hundred times more easy to inflict pain than to create pleasure.

27 FRIDAY Slept better and less bilious owing doubtless to the fatigue of the preceding night and the more comfortable news.

I drew my salaries of various kinds amounting to £300 and upwards (£336 including cash due for su[r]- £136 plusages to county) and sent with John Gibson's consent £200 to pay off things at Abbotsford which must be paid. Wrote Laidlaw with the money directing him to make all preparations for reduction.[2]

Anne ill of Rheumatism – I believe caught cold by vexation and exposing herself to bad weather.

The Celtic Society present me with the most splendid broadsword I ever saw. A beautiful piece of art and a most noble weapon. Honble Mr. Stewart (2d son of the Earl of Moray) General Graham Stirling and MacDougal[3] attended as a committee to present it. This was very

---

1. Sir William Forbes, James Hunter & Coy., bankers.
2. See *Letters*, ix. 387.
3. General Graham Stirling and Captain John McDougall of McDougall were Vice-presidents of the Society, instituted in 1820 'to promote the general use of the ancient Highland dress in the Highlands of Scotland, and to encourage education in that part of the country'. Scott also was a Vice-president and occasionally attended the Society's meetings.

kind of my friends the Celts by whom I have had so many merry meetings. It will be a rare legacy to Walter; for myself, good lack, it is like Lady Dowager Don's prize in a lottery of hardware, she, being a venerable lady who always wore a haunch-hoop silk negligee and triple rufles at the elbow, having the luck to gain a pair of silver spurs and a whip to correspond.

28 SATURDAY Ballantyne and Cadell wish that Mr. Alexr. Cowan should be Constable's trustee instead of J. B.'s. Gibson is determined to hold by Cowan. I will not interpose although I think Cowan's services might do us more good as Constable's trustee than as our own.[1] But I will not begin with thwarting the managers of my affairs or even exerting strong influence. It is not fair. These last four or five days I have wrought little; to-day I set on the steam and ply my paddles.

29 SUNDAY The proofs of vol. I[2] came so thick in yesterday that much was not done. But I begin to be hard at work to-day and must not *gurnalize* much.

Mr. Jollie, who is to be my trustee in conjunction with Gibson, came to see me – a pleasant and goodhumourd man and has high reputation as a man of business.[3] I told him and I will keep my word that he would at least have no trouble by my interfering and thwarting their management[4] which is the not unfrequent case of trusters and trustees.

Constable's business seems unintelligible. No man thought the house worth less than £150,000 – Constable told me when he was making his will that he was worth £80,000. Great profits on almost all their adventures. No bad speculations yet neither stock nor debt to show. Constable might have eat up his share but Cadell was very frugal – No doubt trading almost entirely on accomodation is dreadfully expensive.

30 MONDAY *False delicacy.* Mr. Gibson, Mr. Cowan, and Mr. J. B., were with me last night to talk over important matters and suggest an

1. Alexander Cowan eventually became Constable's Trustee. See the Entry for 8 March 1826.
2. Of the *Life of Napoleon*.
3. Gibson says that Scott at first wanted him to be sole Trustee. He approved, however, of the choice made by the banks. Monypenny he knew slightly; Jollie he met for the first time on this day. Gibson's *Reminiscences*, pp. 15–16.
4. Scott kept his promise and 'in the management of this trust everything went on harmoniously'. Ibid., p. 16.

individual for a certain highly confidential situation. I was led to mention a person of whom I knew nothing but that he was an honest and intelligent man. All seemd to acquiesce and agreed to move the thing to the party concernd this morning and so Mr. G. and Mr. C. left me, when J. B. let out that it was their unanimous opinion that we should be in great trouble were the individual appointed from faults of temper etc. which would make it difficult to get on with him. With a hearty curse I hurried J. B. to let them know that I had no partiality for the man whatever and only named him because he had been proposed for a similar situation elsewhere. This is provoking enough that they would let me embarass my affairs with a bad man (an unfit one I mean) rather than contradict me. I dare say great men are often used so.

I labourd freely yesterday. The stream rose fast – if clearly is another question but there is bulk for it at least, about 30 printed pages.

And now again boys to the Oar.[1]

31 TUESDAY There being nothing in the Roll to-day I stay at home from the Court and add another day's perfect labour to *Woodstock* which is worth five days of snatched intervals when the current of thought and invention is broken in upon and the mind shaken and diverted from its purpose by a succession of petty interr-uptions. I have now no pecuniary provisions to embarass me, and I think now the shock of the discovery is past and over I am much better off on the whole. I am as if I had shaken off from my shoulders a great mass of garments rich indeed but cumbrous and always more a burthen than a comfort. I am free of an hundred petty public duties imposed on me as a man of consideration, of the expense of a great hospitality, and what is better of the great wast[e] of time connected with it. I have known in my day all kinds of society and can pretty well estimate how much or how little one loses by retiring from all but that which is very intimate. I sleep and eat and work as I am wont and, if I could see those about me as indifferent to the loss of rank as I am I should be completely happy. As it is time must salve that sore, to time I trust it.

Since the 16th of this month no guest has broken bread in my house save G. H. Gordon[2] one morning at Breakfast. This happend never before since I had a house of my own. But I have plaid Abou

1. Swift's 'The Country Life', l. 44.
2. 'Mr. Gordon . . . was at this time Scott's amanuensis; he *copied*, that is to say, the MS. for press.' J. G. L.

Hassan long enough and if the Caliph comes I would turn him back again.[1]

FEBRUARY

1 WEDNESDAY A most generous letter (though not more so than I expected) from Walter and Jane offering to interfere with their fortune etc.[2] God Almighty forbid – that were too unnatural in me to accept tho' dutiful and affectionate in them to offer. They talk of India still – with my damaged fortune I cannot help them to remain by exchange and so forth. He expects if they go to go out eldest Captain, when by staying two or three years he will get the step of Major.[3] His whole thoughts are with his profession and I understand that when you quit or exchange when a regiment goes on

1. Scott has played the great man long enough. Abou Hassan, in *The Arabian Nights*, was carried intoxicated to the palace and made to believe when he woke up that he was the Caliph. Scott found economies easier to write about than to make, however, as Dalgleish makes clear:

    'After the failure of Sir Walter he informed me to let the servants know that their allowance of ale was to be taken off, and if there was any of them that did not agree to his preposals, they could find themselves situations at first term. I assembled them together and informed them. They were all quite agreable.

    In about two months after this Sir Walter ast me how I was cuming on with my droothie servants. "No complaints amongst them."

    "Well, slip down to the brewers and order a cask of ale, and do give them a tasting, we must not let them gisen [shrivel] altogether." '

    A merry evening followed, and, notes Dalgleish, 'We had our allowance of ale after that, same as usual.' Dalgleish, ii. 81–2.

2. It was in origin Jane's fortune. Walter's letter reads: 'I rejoice *with grumbling* that it has given Jane and I an opportunity of showing you that we are not very ungratefull for all your kindness. I think there is a good deal of Jane's money vested in the funds she says to the amount of 14000 £ or more, now that money shall forthwith be sold out, and put into your hands, and you shall pay us the lawfull interest upon it, at such time as may best suit yourself. . . . I spoke to Jane about it and she is quite ready to do any thing that may be for the best.' 27 January 1826, Walpole. Like everybody else, Walter underestimated by more than £100,000 the extent of Scott's liabilities.

3. 'I shall get my next step myself if we are ordered to India. I beleive that I shall then be senior Captain as none of those above me think of going.' Ibid.

distant or disagreeable service you are not accounted as serious in your profession. God send what is for the best.

Remitted Charles a bill for £40. £35 advanced   Chs. Scott £40. at Christmas makes £75. He must be frugal.[1]

Attended the court and saw J. B. and Cadell as I returnd. Both very gloomy. Came home to work etc. about two.

2 THURSDAY An odd visit this morning from Miss Jane Bell of North Shields whose law suit with a Methodist parson of the name of Hill made some noise.[2] The worthy divine had in the basest manner interfered to prevent this lady's marriage by two anonymous letters in which he contrived to refer the lover to whom they were address[d] for further corroboration to *himself*. The whole imposture makes the subject of a little pamphlet publishd by Marshall of NewCastle. The Lady ventured for redress into the thicket of English law – lost one suit – gaind another with £300 damages and was ruind. The appearance and person of Miss Bell is prepossessing. She is about thirty years old, a brunette with regular and pleasing features markd with melancholy – an enthusiast in literature and probably in religion. She had been at Abbotsford to see me and made her way to me here in the vain hope that she could get her story workd up into a novel and certainly the thing is capable of interesting situations. It throws a curious light upon the aristocratic or rather Hierocratic influence exercised by the Methodist preachers within the Connexion as it is calld. Admirable food this would be [for] the *Quarterly* or any other reviewers who might desire to feed fat their grudge against this sept.[3] But there are two reasons against such a vindication. First it would do the poor sufferer no good. 2dly. It would hurt the Methodistic Connexion very much which I for one would not like to injure. They have their faults and are peculiarly liable to those of hypocrisy and spiritual ambition and priest-craft. On the other hand they do infinite good, carrying religion into classes in Society where it would scarce be found to penetrate did it rely merely upon proof of its

1. 'All you can help me in my dear boy is to be careful to keep your living within your income', Scott writes when enclosing the bill. *Letters*, ix. 398. But by 1 March Charles has run short again: see the Entry for 7 March 1826 and note. Scott did not warn him that he at first meditated saving £300 a year by removing him from Oxford at the end of his second year there. *Letters*, ix. 404 and 407.
2. See Thomas Hill's *Statement of the Cause, Progress and Termination of the Two Law Suits, in which Mr Thomas Hill has been engaged*, 1826.
3. A slip for 'sect'. A sept is a division of a clan.

doctrines upon calm reasons and upon rational argument. To these the Methodists add a powerful appeal to the feelings and passions and though I believe this is often exaggerated into absolute enthusiasm yet I consider upon the whole they do much to keep alive a sense of religion and the practice of morality necessarily connected with it. It is much to the discredit of the Methodist clergy that when the villainous calumniator was actually convicted of guilt morally worse than many men are hangd for they only degraded him from the *first* to the second class of their preachers, leaving a man, who from mere hatred at Miss Bell's brother who was a preacher like himself had proceeded in such a deep and infamous scheme to ruin the character and destroy the happiness of an innocent person, in possession of the pulpit and an authorized teacher of others. If they believed him innocent they did too much, if guilty far too little.

I wrote to my Nephew Walter[1] to-day cautioning him against a little disposition which he has to satire or *méchanceté* which may be a great stumbling block in his career in life – Otherwise I presage well of him. He is Lieutenant of Engineers with high character for mathematical science – is acute – very well mannerd and I think goodhearted. He has seen enough of the world too to regulate his own course through life better than most lads at his age.

3 FRIDAY This is the first morning since my troubles that I felt at awaking

> I had drunken deep
> Of all the blessedness of sleep.[2]

I made not the slightest pause nor dreamd a single dream nor even changed my side. This is a blessing to be grateful for. There is to be a meeting of the Creditors to-day but I care not for the issue. If they drag me into the Court *obtorto collo*[3] instead of going into this scheme of arrangement they will do themselves a great injury and perhaps eventually do me good though it would give me much pain.

J. B. is severely critical on what he calls imitations of Mrs.

---

1. Walter Scott (1807–76), the son of Scott's brother Thomas, who died at Quebec in 1823. He owed his education to Scott, and justified his uncle's hopes by rising finally to the rank of general. The letter referred to sounds similar to the one printed in *Letters*, ix. 269, which is dated 1 November 1825.
2. Coleridge's 'Christabel', pt. 2, ll. 375–6.
3. 'By the throat'.

Radcliffe in *Woodstock* – many will think with him – yet I am of opinion he is quite wrong or, as friend J. F.[1] says, *vrong*. In the first place I am to look on the mere fact of another author having treated a subject happily as a bird looks on a potatoe bogle[2] which scares it away from a field otherwise as free to its depredations as any one's else. In 2d place I have taken a wide difference – my object is not to excite fear of supernatural things in my reader but to show the effect of such fear upon the agents in the story – one a man of sense and firmness, one a man unhinged by remorse – one a stupid unin-quiring clown – one a learnd and worthy but superstitious divine. In 3d. place the book turns on this hinge and cannot want it. But I will try to insinuate the refutation of Aldiboronti's[3] exception into the prefatory matter.

From the 19 January to the 2d. february inclusive is exactly fifteen days during which time (with the intervention of some days' idleness to let imagination brood on the task a little) I have written a volume. I think for a bett I could have done it in ten days. Then I must have had no court of Session to take me up two or three hours every morning and dissipate my attention and powers of working for the rest of the day. A volume at cheapest is worth £1000. This is working at the rate of £24,000 a year, but then we must not bake bunns faster than people have appetite to eat them. They are not essential to the market like potatoes.

John Gibson came to tell me in the evening that a Meeting to-day had approved of the proposed trust. I know not why but the news gave me little concern. I heard it as a party indifferent. I remember hearing that Mandrin[4] testified some horror when he found himself bound alive on the wheel and saw an executioner approach with a bar of iron to break his limbs. After the second and third blow he fell a laughing and being askd the reason by his confessor said he laughd at his own folly which had anticipated increased agony at every blow when it was obvious that the *first* must have jarrd and confounded the system of the nerves so much as to render the succeeding blows of little consequence. I suppose it is so with the moral feeling – At least I

---

1. James Ferrier (1744–1829), a Clerk of Session and father of Susan Ferrier the novelist.
2. A scarecrow.
3. Short for 'Aldiborontiphoscophornio', Scott's nickname for James Ballantyne, taken from Henry Carey's play *Chronohotonthologos*. See *Life*, iii. 121 and 225 n.
4. Scott owned *The Authentic Memoirs of the Remarkable Life and surprising Exploits of Mandrin, Captain-General of the French Smugglers, who for the space of nine months resolutely stood in defiance of the whole Army of France, etc.*, 1755.

could not bring myself to be anxious whether these matters were settled one way or other.

4 SATURDAY Wrote to Mr. Laidlaw[1] to come to town on Monday and see the trustees. To farm or not to farm is the question.[2] With our careless habits it were best I think to risk as little as possible. Lady Scott will not exceed with ready money in her hand but calculating on the produce of a farm is different and neither she nor I are capable of that minute œconomy. Two cows should be all we should keep. But I find Lady S. inclines much for the farm. If she had her youthful activity and could manage it it would be well and would amuse her. But I fear it is too late a week.

Returnd from Court by Constable, and found Cadell has fled to the Sanctuary[3] being threatend with ultimate diligence by the B. of S.[4] about some £1900 drawn out of their Cash accot. the day before the stop. If this be a vindictive measure it is harsh useless bad[5] of them, and flight on the contrary seems no good sign on his part. I hope he won't prove his father or Grandfather at Prestonpans

> And Cadell dressd amang the rest
>   Wi gun and good claymore, man,
> On gelding grey he rode that day
>   Wi pistols set before, man.
> The cause was gude he'd spend his blude
>   Before that he would yield, man,
> But the night before he left the corps
>   And never faced the field, man.[6]

1. See *Letters*, ix. 404.
2. Scott's answer had been clear enough on 26 January: 'All our farming operations must, of course, be stopped so soon as they can with least possible loss, and stock, &c., disposed of.' *Letters*, ix. 377. But Laidlaw urged Scott to keep the farm, and Lady Scott was inclined to be difficult – 'but then she only sees the returns not the cost and outlay'. *Letters*, ix. 405. The Trustees' decision was 'to have as much of the estate as possible in grass, which might be let annually'. Sederunt Book, i. 33.
3. The area adjacent to Holyrood Abbey Church was Edinburgh's traditional Sanctuary.
4. The Bank of Scotland.
5. The words 'harsh and useless' were added in the margin as an afterthought, and 'bad' should probably have been deleted.
6. Skirving's 'Tranent Muir', ll. 83–90. Herd, i. 169.

Harden[1] and Mrs. Scott calld on mamma. I was abroad. Henry[2] calld on me.

Wrote only two pages (of manuscript) and a half to-day – As the boatswain said, one can't dance always nowther. But were we sure of the quality of the stuff what opportunities for labour does this same system of retreat afford us. I am convinced that in three years I could do more than in the last ten but for the mine being I fear exhausted. Give me my popularity, *an awful postulate*, and all my present difficulties shall be a joke in five years – and it is *not* lost yet at least.

5 SUNDAY Rose after a sound sleep and here am I without bile or any thing to perturb my inward man. It is just about three weeks since so great a change took place in my relations in society and already I am indifferent to it. But I have been always told my feelings of joy and sorrow, pleasure and pain, enjoyment and privation, are much colder than those of other people.

I think the Romans call it stoicism.[3]

Missie[4] was in the drawing room and over heard William Clerk and me laughing excessively at some foolery or other in the back room to her no small surprize which she did not keep to herself. But do people suppose that he was less sorry for his poor sister[5] or I for my lost fortune? If I have a very strong passion in the world it is *pride* and that never hinged upon world's gear which was always with me Light come Light go.

6 MONDAY Letters received yesterday from Lord Montagu, John Morritt, and Mrs. Hughes[6] – kind and dear friends all with solicitous

1. Hugh Scott of Harden (1758–1841), whom Scott regarded as 'chief' of the family. In 1835 he recovered the barony of Polwarth, to which he had a claim through his mother. His wife, Harriet, whom Scott particularly liked, was daughter to Count Bruhl, the Saxon Ambassador.
2. Henry Scott (1800–67), the eldest son of Hugh Scott of Harden, 'a real honest lad and my favourite of the young people'. *Letters*, ix. 348. He shared Scott's love of country pursuits and his political prejudices. In 1826 he was elected M.P. for Roxburghshire, and in 1841 succeeded his father as Baron Polwarth.
3. Addison's *Cato*, i. 4.
4. Miss Macdonald Buchanan.
5. Clerk's sister Elizabeth had died three weeks before. See the Entry for 17 January.
6. For Scott's replies, all dated 6 February, see *Letters*, ix. 406–13.

enquiries. But it is very tiresome to have to tell my story over again and I really hope I have [no] more friends intimate enough to ask me for it. I detest letter writing and envy the Old Hermit of Prague who never saw pen or ink[1] – What then! one must write; it is a part of the Law we live on. Talking of writing I finishd my six pages neat and handsome yesterday. N.B. At night I fell asleep and the oil dripd from the lamp upon my manuscript. Will this extreme unction make it go smoothly down with the public?

> Thus idly 'we profane the sacred time'[2]
> By silly pun, light jest, and lighter rhyme.

I have a song to write too and I am not thinking of it – I trust it will come upon me at once – A sort of catch it should be.[3] I walkd out feeling a little overwrought. Saw Constable and turnd over Clarendon.[4] Cadell not yet out of hiding. This is simple work.

Obliged to borrow £240 to be repaid in Spring from John Gibson to pay my Nephew's outfitt £240 to John Gibson. and passage to Bombay.[5] I wish I could have got this money otherwise but I must not let the orphan boy and such a clever fellow miscarry through my fault. His education etc. has been at my expense ever since he came from America.

7 TUESDAY Had letters yesterday from Lady Davy[6] and Lady Louisa Stuart.[7] Two very different persons. Lady Davy, daughter

1. *Twelfth Night*, lv. 2.
2. *2 Henry IV*, ii. 4.
3. The 'Glee for King Charles' in chapter 20 of *Woodstock*.
4. The Earl of Clarendon's *The True Historical Narrative of the Rebellion and Civil Wars in England*, 1702–4.
5. The money was enclosed in a letter to Sophia written this same day: Walter was to lodge with the Lockharts on his way through London. *Letters*, ix. 413 and 423. The debt was not repaid until 14 December 1827, Gibson apparently refusing to have it settled earlier.
6. Jane Davy (1780–1855), daughter of Charles Kerr of Kelso and wife of Sir Humphry Davy. Scott described her during his visit to the Inner Hebrides in 1810 as 'a fashionable little woman but who travels rather to *say she has seen* than to *see*' (*Letters*, ii. 368); and Lockhart, writing to Sophia on 4 July 1831, calls her 'finer than fine she, & more talkative than ever, & all very agreeable, much more so truly than correct'. Abbots.
7. Lady Louisa Stuart (1757–1851), the cultivated, intelligent daughter of the third Earl of Bute and grand-daughter of Lady Mary Wortley Montagu. Scott met her at Dalkeith and at Bothwell Castle, and from 1807 onwards they corresponded frequently. She was in the secret of the authorship of the novels.

an[d] coheiress of a wealthy Antigua Merchant, has been known to me all my life. Her father was a relation of ours of a Scotch calculation. He was of a good family, Kerr of Bloodielaws, but decayd. Miss Jane Kerr married first Mr. Apreece, Son of a Welch Baronet: The match was not happy. I had lossd all acquaintance with her for a long time when about twenty years ago we revived it in London. She was then a widow, gay, clever and most actively ambitious to play a distinguishd part in London society. Her fortune though handsome and easy was not large enough to make way by dint of showy entertainments and so forth so she took the *blue* line and by great tact and management actually establishd herself as a leader of literary fashion. Soon after, she resided in Edinburgh for a season or two and studied the Northern Lights. One of the best of them, poor Jack Playfair, was disposed 'to shoot madly from his sphere'[1] and I believe askd her – but he was a little too old. She found a fitter husband in every respect in Sir Humphrey Davy[2] to whom she gave a handsome fortune and whose splendid talents and situation as President of the Royal Society gave her naturally a distinguishd place in the literary society of the Metropolis. Now this is a very curious instance of an active minded woman forcing her way to the point from which she seemd furthest excluded – for though clever and even witty she had no peculiar accomplishment and certainly no great taste either for science or letters naturally. I was once in the Hebrides with her[3] and I admired to observe how amid sea-sickness, fatigue, some danger, and a good deal of indifference as to what she saw, she gallantly maintaind her determination to see everything. It markd her strength of character and she joind to it much tact and always addressd people on the right side. So she stands high and deservedly so, for to these active qualities more French I think than English and partaking of the Creole vivacity and suppleness of character, she adds I believe honourable principles and an excellent heart – As a lion-catcher I could pit her against the world – She flung her *lasso* (see Hall's *South America*)[4] over Byron himself. But then, poor soul, she is not happy. She has a temper and Davy has a temper and these tempers are not one temper but two tempers and they quarrell like cat and dog, which may be good for stirring up the stagnation of domestic life but they let the world see it and that is not so well. Now in all this I may be thought a little harsh on my friend but it is

1. *Midsummer Night's Dream*, ii. 2.
2. Sir Humphry Davy (1778–1829) had met Scott in Wordsworth's company in 1805 and paid a most successful visit to Abbotsford in 1820. *Life*, ii. 275 and vi. 239–46.
3. In 1810.
4. Captain Basil Hall's *Journal on the Coast of Chili, etc.*, 1820–2.

between my Gurnal and me, and moreover I would cry heartily if
anything were to ail my little cousin though she be addicted to rule
the cerulean atmospher[e]. Then I suspect the cares of this as well as
other empires overbalance its pleasures. There must be difficulty in being
always in the right humour to hold a court. There are usurpers to be
encounterd and insurrections to be put down – An incessant troop [of]
bien-seances to be discharge[d], a sort of etiquette which is the curse of all
courts – An old Lion cannot get ham-strung quietly at four hundred
miles distance but the Empress must send him her condoleance and a pot
of lip-salve. To be sure the monster is *consanguinean* as Sir Toby says.[1]

Lookd in at Constable's coming home. Cadell emerged from
Alsatia;[2] borrowd Clarendon.[3]

Home by ½ past 12. Much comfort in a stupid assistant. Sir R. D.
and R. H.[4] have two very clever men of business[5] whom the agents
like and carry their business to these two offices to favour the
Assistants. Mine, a good creature,[6] only accomplishes the character
of an Assistant so far as the three first letters go. So he gets fewer
pence and I less trouble.

My old friend Sir Peter Murray[7] calld to offer his own assistance,
Lord Justice-Clerk's and Abercromby's to negotiate for me a seat
upon the Bench instead of my Sheriffdom and Clerkship. I explaind
to him the use which I could make of my pen was not I thought
consistent with that situation, and that besides I had neglected the
law too long to permit me to think of that situation. But this was
kindly and honourably done. I can see people think me much worse
of[f] than I think myself. They may be right. But I will not be beat till
I have tried a rally and a bold one.

8 WEDNESDAY Slept ill, and rather bilious in the morning. Many of
the Bench now are my Juniors. I will not seek *ex elemosyna*[8] a place
which had I turnd my studies that way I might have aspired to long

1. *Twelfth Night*, ii. 3.
2. That is, the Sanctuary.
3. The book he had 'turned over' the day before. *Woodstock* is of
   course set in the period covered by Clarendon's *History*.
4. Sir Robert Dundas and Robert Hamilton, along with Scott the
   Principal Clerks of Session.
5. John Parker and John Hay, Assistant Clerks of Session.
6. W. Carmichael, Assistant Clerk of Session.
7. This is Sir Patrick Murray of Ochtertyre, whom Scott had
   known from their days together in the Civil Law Class at the
   University. He was now one of the Barons of Exchequer. In
   Scott's day 'Peter' and 'Patrick' were interchangeable.
8. 'By grace and favour' (rather than 'by merit').

ago *ex meritis*. My pen should do much better for me than the odd £1000 a year.[1] If it fails I will leave[2] on what they leave me. Another chance might be if it fails in the patronage which might after a year or two place me in Exchequer.[3] But I do not count on this unless indeed the D. of B.[4] when he comes of age should chuse to make play.

Got to my work again and wrote easier than the two last days. Gave Lady Scott her fortnight's allowance £24.0.0. The Laird of Harden made long visit. Spoke to Anne about a service for Dalgleish.[5] £24 Lad[y] Scott

Mr. Laidlaw came in from Abbotsford and dine[d] with us. We spent the evening in laying down plans for the farm[6] and deciding whom we should keep and whom dismiss among the people. This we did on the true negroe-driving principle of self-interest – the only principle I know which *never* swerves from its objects. We chose all the active young and powerful men, turning old age and infirmity adrift. I cannot help this for [one] guinea cannot do the work of five but I will contrive to make [it] easier to the sufferers.

9 THURSDAY A stormy morning lowering and blustering like our fortunes. *Mea virtute me involvo*[7] – But I must say to the Muse of fiction as the Earl of Pembroke said to the ejected Nun of Wilton 'Go spin, you jade, go spin' – Perhaps she has no *tow* on her *rock*.[8]

When I was at Kilkenny last year we went to see a Nunnery but could not converse with the sisters because they were in strict retreat. I was delighted with the red-nosed padre who shewd us the place with a sort of proud unctuous humiliation and apparent dereliction of the world that had to me the air of a complete Tartuffe – a strong sanguine

1. In fact only a few hundred pounds were involved. A Judge's salary was £2000 a year; as Clerk of Session Scott was paid £1300 and he had in addition £300 for his Sheriffdom, which he would have had to resign on being elevated to the Bench.
2. A slip for 'live'.
3. Scott would have preferred the Court of Exchequer, where the duties were much lighter, to the Court of Session. He had attempted to become a Baron of Exchequer as early as 1807 (see *Letters*, i. 394) and again in 1816, but refused to renew his application in 1819. *Life*, v. 191 and vi. 22.
4. The fifth Duke of Buccleuch (1806–84).
5. Dalgleish, however, refused to be turned away. See the Entry for 27 February.
6. See the Entry for 4 February and note.
7. 'I wrap myself up in my virtue.' Horace's *Odes*, iii. 29. 54.
8. 'Flax on her distaff'.

square shoulderd son of the Church whom a protestant would be apt to warrant against any sufferings he was like to sustain by privation. My purpose however just now was to talk of the strict retreat which did not prevent the Nuns from walking in their little garden breviary in hand, peeping at us and allowing us to peep at them. Well – now we are in *Strict Retreat* and if we had been so last year instead of gallivanting to Ireland this affair might not have befallen if literary labour could have prevented it. But who could have suspected Constable's timbers to have been rotten from the beginning?

Visited the Exhibition on my way home from the Court. The new rooms are most splendid, and several good pictures. The institution[1] has subsisted but five years and it is astonishing how much superior the worst of the present collection are to the tea-board looking things which first appeard. John Thomson of Duddingston[2] has far the finest picture in the Exhibitn. of a large size. Subject *Dunluce*, a ruinous ca[s]tle of the Antrim family near the Giant's causeway with one of those terrible seas and skies which only Thomson can paint. Found Scroop there improving a picture of his own, an Italian scene in Calabria. He is I think greatly improved and one of the very best amateur painters I ever saw – Sir George Beaumont[3] scarcely excepted. – Yet hang it I *do* except Sir George.

I would not write to-day after I came home – I will not say *could* not for it is not true. But I was lazy: felt the desire *far 'niente*[4] which is the sign of one's mind being at ease. I read *The English in Italy*[5] which is a clever book.

Byron used to kick and frisk more contemptuously against the literary gravity and slang than any one I ever knew who had climbed so high – then it is true I never knew any one climb so high, and

1. The Institution for the Encouragement of the Fine Arts was founded in 1819. Its first exhibition was of Old Masters lent by members, but thereafter the annual exhibition was of contemporary work. The new rooms mentioned here were rented from the Board of Manufacturers, who had built what is now known as the Royal Scottish Academy at the foot of the Mound.
2. The Revd. John Thomson (1778–1840), minister of Duddingston Church just outside Edinburgh, and one of the foremost Scottish landscape painters of his day. He was a younger brother of Thomas Thomson and a member of the Blair-Adam Club.
3. Sir George Beaumont (1753–1827), painter and patron of the arts. He was instrumental in founding the National Gallery and presented his own collection to it.
4. 'To do nothing'.
5. By Constantine Henry Phipps, Marquis of Normanby, 1825.

before you despise the eminence, carrying people along with you as convinced that you are not playing the fox and grapes, you must be at the top of the eminence. Moore told me two delightful stories of him.

One was that while they stood at the window of Byron's palazzo in Venice looking at a beautiful sun set Moore was naturally led to say something of its beauty when Byron answerd in a tone that I can easily conceive 'Ah come d—n me, Tom, don't be poetical.' Another time standing with Moore on the balcony of the same palazzo a gondola passd with two English gentlemen who were easily distinguishd by their appearance. They cast a careless look at the balcony and went on. Byron crossd his arms and half stooping over the balcony said 'Ah d—n ye if you had known what two fellows you were staring at you would have taken a longer look at us.' This was the man – quaint capricious and playful with all his immense genius – He wrote from impulse never from effort and therefore I have always reckond Burns and Byron the most genuine poetical geniuses of my time and a half a century before me. We have however many men of high poetical talent but none I think of that ever gushing and perennial fountain of natural water.

Mr. Laidlaw dined with us. Says Mr. G—n[1] told him he would despair of my affairs were it any but S. W. S. No doubt – so should I and am wellnigh doing so at any rate – But *fortuna juvante*[2] much may be achieved. At worst the prospect is not very discouraging to one who wants little.

Methinks I have been like Burns's poor labourer

> So constantly in Ruin's sight
> The view o't gives me little fright.[3]

10 FRIDAY Went through for a new day the task of buttoning which seems to me somehow to fill up more of my morning than usual, not certainly that such is really the case but that my mind attends to the process having so little left to hope or fear. The half-hour between waking and rising has all my life proved propitious to any task which was exercizing my invention. When I get over any knotty difficulty in a story or have had in former times to fill up a passage in a poem it was always when I first opend my eyes that the desired ideas throngd upon me. This is so much the case that I am in the habit of relying upon it and saying to myself when I am [at] a loss 'Never mind, we shall have it at seven o'clock tomorrow morning.' If I have forgot a circumstance or a

1. John Gibson.
2. 'If fortune favours me'.
3. Burns's 'Twa Dogs', ll. 115–16, slightly adapted.

name or a copy of verses it is the same thing. There is a passage about this sort of matutinal inspiration in the *Odyssey* which would make a handsome figure here if I could read or write Greek.[1] I will look into Pope for it who ten to one will not tell me the real translation.

I think the first hour of the morning is also favourable to the bodily strength. Among other feats when I was a young man I was able at times to lift a smith's anvil with one hand by what is called the *horn* or round projecting piece of iron on which things are beaten to turn them round. But I could only do this before breakfast and shortly after rising. It required my full strength undiminishd by the least exertion and those who choose to try will find the feat no easy one.

This morning I had some good ideas respecting *Woodstock* which will make the story better. The devil of a difficulty is that one puzzles the skean in order to excite curiosity and then cannot disentangle it for [the] satisfaction of the prying fiend they have raised.

A letter from Sir James McIntosh[2] of condoleance prettily expressd and which may be sung to the old tune of Wellcome wellcome, brother Debtor.[3] Another son of chivalry dismounted by mischance is sure to excite the compassion of one laid on the arena before him.

Yesterday I had an anecdote from old Sir James Stewart Denham[4] which is worth writing down. His uncle Lord Elcho was as is well known engaged in the affair of 1745. He was dissatisfied with the conduct of matters from beginning to end. But after the left wing of the Highlanders was repulsed and broken at Culloden Elcho rode up to the Chevalier and told him all was lost and that nothing remaind except to charge at the head of two thousand men who were still unbroken and either turn the fate of the day or die sword in hand as became his pretensions. The Chevalier gave him some evasive answer and turning his horse's head

---

1. Scott's brief skirmish with Greek came to an abrupt end when he wrote an essay for Professor Dalzell at Edinburgh University comparing Homer unfavourably with Ariosto. *Life*, i. 56–8. Douglas suggests that the passage referred to is *Odyssey*, vi. 20 or xix. 535.
2. Sir James Mackintosh (1765–1832), a Highlander who had made his career in India and England and was known as a philosopher, lawyer, historian, and conversationalist. He was a Whig and only slightly acquainted with Scott.
3. A song by Coffey in Ritson's *A select collection of English songs*, 1813, p. 122.
4. Sir James Steuart Denham of Coltness was a Colonel in the Scots Greys. His father, as well as his uncle, had fought for Prince Charles in 1745. The anecdote given here – and repeated by Scott in a note to *Waverley* and in chapter 83 of *Tales of a Grandfather* – appears in Elcho's *A Scort Account of the Affairs of Scotland*, Edinburgh, 1807, pp. 92–6..

rode off the field. Lord Elcho calld after him (I write the very words) 'There you go for a d—n cowardly b—g Italian' and never would see him again though he lost his property and remaind an exile in the cause. Lord Elcho left two copies of his memoirs, one with Sir James Stewart's family, one with Lord Wemyss.[1]

This is better evidence than the romance of Chevalier Johnstone.[2] And I have little doubt it is true. Yet it is no proof of the prince's cowardice though it shows him to have been no John of Gaunt.[3] Princes are constantly surrounded with people who hold up their own *life* and *safety* to them as by far the most important stake in any contest and this is a doctrine in which conviction is easily received. Such an eminent person finds every bodie's advice save here and there that of a desperate Elcho recommend obedience to the natural instinct of self preservation which very often men of inferior situations find it difficult to combat when all the world are crying to them to get on and be damnd instead of encouraging them to run away. At Preston-pans the Chevalier offerd to lead the van and he was with the Second line which during that brief affair followd the first very close. Johnstone's own account, carefully re[a]d, brings him within a pistol shot of the first line. At the same time Charles Edward had not a head or heart for great things notwithstanding his daring adventure, and the Irish officers by whom he was guided were poor creatures. Lord George Murray[4] was the soul of the undertaking.

11 SATURDAY Court sate till half past one. I had but a trifle to do so wrote to Miss Maclean Clephane[5] – and Nephew Walter. Sent the last £40 in addition to £240 sent on the 6th, making his full equipment £280.[6]

1. 'Lord Elcho' is the courtesy title of the eldest son of the Earl of Wemyss.
2. *Memoirs of the Rebellion of 1745*, 1820.
3. Like Falstaff, *1 Henry IV*, ii. 2.
4. Lord George Murray (1694–1760), son of the first Duke of Atholl and General of Prince Charles's army.
5. Printed in *Letters*, ix. 423. Anna Jane was the second daughter of Mrs. Maclean Clephane of Torloisk. Scott assisted the family in matters of business.
6. Of the first payment £220 was for his equipment and £20 to 'prevent him landing penniless in India'. Scott felt he had to economize – 'Had times been as they [were] wont to be I would have made it three hundred but as I really borrow the money I must not think of that' – but in the end his natural generosity overcame strict prudence, and he here makes the sum up to £280. *Letters*, ix. 415–16.

A man calling himself Charles Gray of Carse wrote to me expressing sympathy for my misfortunes and offering me half the profits of what he calls the anti radical Laika which, if I understand him right, is a patent medicine[1] to which I suppose he expects me to stand trumpeter. He endeavours to get over my objections to accepting his liberality (supposing me to entertain them) by assuring me his conduct is founded on a *sage selfishness*. This is diverting enough – I suppose the Commissioners of police will next send me a letter of condoleance begging my acceptance of a broom a shovel and a scavenger's great coat and assuring me that they had appointed me to all the emolument of a well frequented crossing – it would be doing more than they have done of late to the cleanliness of the streets which, witness my shoes, are in a piteous pickle. I thankd the Selfish Sage with due decorum for what purpose can anger serve? I remember once before a mad woman from about Alnwick, by [name] Latin or Laytoun,[2] baited me with letters and plans – first for charity to herself or some protegee – I gave my guinea – then she wanted to have half the profit of a novel which I was to publish under my name and auspices – She sent me the manuscript and a *moving* tale it was for some of the scenes lay in the *Cabinet a l'eau*. I declined the partnership. Lastly my fair correspondent insisted I was a lover of speculation and would be much profited by going shares in a patent medicine which she had invented for the benefit of little babies I believe. I declined to have anything to do with such a Herod-like affair and beggd to decline the honour of correspondence in future. I should have thought the thing a quiz but that the novel was real and substantial.

Anne goes to Ravelston[3] to-day to remain tomorrow.

Sir Alexr. Don calld and we had a good laugh together.

12 SUNDAY Having ended the Second Vol of *Woodstock* last night I have to begin the Third this morning. Now I have not the slightest idea how the story is to be wound up to a catastrophe. I am just in the same case as I used to be when I lost myself in former days in some country to which I was a stranger – I always pushd for the pleasantest road and either found or made it the nearest. It is the

---

1. Scott's joke. The *Anti-Radical* was to be a magazine. Gray, 11 February 1826, Walpole.
2. Jemima Layton, who sent Scott a novel in 1817 which he was to alter as he saw fit: 'If you will undertake the publication of the work I have no doubt it will prosper: the profit I will entirely relinquish to you.' Partington's *Letter-Books*, p. 227.
3. To visit the Keiths.

same in writing. I never could lay down a plan – or having laid it down I never could adhere to it; the action of composition always dilated some passages and abridged or omitted others and person-ages were renderd important or insignificant not according to their agency in the original conception of the plan but according to the success or otherwise with which I was able to bring them out. I only tried to make that which I was actually writing diverting and interesting, leaving the rest to fate. I have been often amused with the critics distinguishing some passages as particularly labourd when the pen passd over the whole as fast as it could move and the eye never again saw them excepting in proof. Verse I write twice and sometimes three times over. This may be calld in Spanish the *Der donde diere* mode of composition – in English *Hab nab at a venture*. It is a perilous stile I grant but I cannot help [it] – when I chain my mind to ideas which are purely imaginative – for argument is a different thing – it seems to me that the sun leaves the landscape, that I think away the whole vivacity and spirit of my original conception, and that the results are cold, tame and spiritless. It is the difference between a written oration and one bursting from the unpremed[it]ated exertions of the Speaker which have always something the air of enthusiasm and inspiration. I would not have young authors imitate my carelessness however – *consilium non currum cape* – [1]

Read a few page of Will D'Avenant who was fond of having it supposed that Shakespeare intrigued with his mother. I think the pretension can only be treated as Phaeton's was according to Fielding's farce.

> Besides by all the village boys I'm sham'd,
> You the Sun's son, you rascal? – you be damnd.

Egad I'll put that into *Woodstock*.[2] It might come well from the old admirer of Shakspeare –[3] then Fielding's lines were not written – what then it is an anachronism for some sly rogue to detect. Besides it

---

1. 'Take counsel, not a chariot' – adapted from Ovid's *Metamorphoses*, ii. 146.
2. The lines appear in *Woodstock*, ch. 25, with a characteristic apology: 'We observe this couplet in Fielding's farce of *Tumbledown Dick*, founded on the same classical story. As it was current in the time of the Commonwealth, it must have reached the author of *Tom Jones* by tradition – for no one will suspect the present author of making the anachronism.'
3. Sir Henry Lee.

is easy to swear they were written and that fielding adopted them from tradition.

Walked with Skene on the Calton Hill.[1]

13 MONDAY The Institution for the Encouragement of the Fine Arts opens to-day with a handsome entertainment in the Exhibition room as at Somerset House.[2] It strikes me that the direction given by amateurs and professors to their protégés and pupils who aspire to be artists is upon a pedantic and false principle. All the Fine Arts have it for their mightier and more legitimate end and purpose to affect the human passions or smooth and alleviate for a time the more unquiet feelings of the mind – to excite wonder or terror or pleasure or emotion of some kind or other. It often happens that in the very rise and origin of these arts, as in the instance of Homer, this principal object is obtain in a degree not equald by his successors. But there is [a] degree of execution which in more refind times the poet or musician begins to study which gives a value of its own to their productions of a different kind from the rude strength of their predecessors. Poetry becomes complicated in its rules, music learnd in its cadences and harmonies, Rhetoric subtle in its periods; there is more given to the labour of executing, less attaind by the effect produced. Still the nobler and popular End of these arts is not forgotten, and if we have some productions too learnd, too re-cherchés for public feeling, we have every now and then music that electrifies a whole assembly, eloquence which shakes the forum, and poetry which carries men up to the third heaven. But in painting it is different – it is all become a mystery the secret of which is lodged in a few Connoisseurs whose object is not to favour the productions of

1. The walk, *Skene's Memories* makes clear, was a regular event: 'Sir Walter withdrew himself almost altogether from society and was hard at work preparing for the press, and I was in the habit every day of unkennelling him from his study, when we walked for an hour and a half in Princes Street Gardens' (p. 139). Scott is led to mention it here perhaps because they had changed their ground. The Calton Hill, which is crowned by the Observatory, Nelson's Monument, and 'Edinburgh's Folly' (the half-completed imitation of the Parthenon), was laid out for walking, and its dramatic views of the city and the hills led visitors to compare it to the Pincio in Rome.

2. This dinner, presided over by Lord Elgin, marked the opening of the Institution's new rooms at the foot of the Mound. Previous exhibitions had been held in Waterloo Place. Somerset House had been the home of the Royal Academy in London since 1780.

such pictures as produce effect on mankind at large but to class them according to their proficiency in the inferior rules of the art, which though most necessary to be taught and learnd, should yet only be considerd as the *Gradus ad Parnassum*,[1] the steps by which the higher and ultimate object of a great popular effect is to be obtaind. They have all embraced the very stile of criticism which induced Michael Angelo to call some Pope a poor creature who turning his attention from the general effect of a noble statue his Holiness began to criticize the hem of the robe. This seems to me the cause of the decay of this delightful art, especially in history its noblest branch. As I speak to myself I may say that a painting should to be excellent have something to say to the mind of a man like myself, well educated and susceptible of those feelings of emotion which any thing strongly recalling natural emotion is likely to inspire. But how seldom do I see any thing that moves me much. Wilkie,[2] the far more than Teniers of Scotland, certainly gave many new ideas. So does Will Allan though over whelmd with their rebukes about colouring and grouping against which they are not willing to place his general and original merits. Landseer's dogs were the most magnificent things I ever saw, leaping and bounding and grinning on the canvas. Leslie has great powers and the scenes from Molière by [3] are excellent. Yet Painting wants a regenerator – some one who will sweep the cobwebs out of his head before he takes the pallet as Chantrey[4] has done in the sister art. At present we are painting pictures from the ancients as authors in the days of Louis Quatorze wrote epic poems according to the recipe of Made. Dacier and Coy. The poor reader or spectator has no remedy; the compositions are *secundam artem* and if he does not like them he is no judge – that's all.

14 TUESDAY I had a call from Glengarry[5] yesterday as kind and friendly as usual. This gentleman is a kind of Quixote in our age,

1. 'The ascent to Parnassus'.
2. Sir David Wilkie (1785–1841), notable for his lively treatment of scenes from humble life. He painted the Abbotsford family for Sir Adam Ferguson in 1817, and had been King's Limner in Scotland since 1823. He was knighted in 1836.
3. Gilbert Stuart Newton (1794–1835), from Nova Scotia. He painted a portrait of Scott for Sophia in 1824.
4. Francis Chantrey (1781–1842) the sculptor. Scott had sat to him in 1820 and was to do so again. See the Entry for 17 May 1828. He was knighted in 1835.
5. A splendid original, Colonel Alexander Ranaldson Macdonnell of Glengarry, who may have suggested features of Fergus MacIvor in *Waverley*. He married Isabella Forbes in 1802, and died in an accident in 1828. See the Entry for 21 January 1828.

having retaind in its full extent the whole feelings of Clanship and Chieftain ship elsewhere so long abandond. He seems to have lived a century too late and to exist in a state of complete law and order like a Glengarry of old whose will was law to his sept. Kindhearted, generous, friendly, he is beloved by those who know him and his efforts are unceasing to shew kindness to those of his clan who are disposed fully to admit his pretensions. To dispute them is to incur his resentment which has sometimes broken out in acts of violence which have brought him into collision with the law. To me he is a treasure as being full of information as to the history of his own clan and the manners and customs of the highlanders in general. Strong, active and muscular, he follows the chase of the deer for days and nights together sleeping in his plaid when darkness overtakes him in the forest. He was fortunate in marrying a daughter of Sir William Forbes who by yielding to his peculiar ideas in general possesses much deserved influence with him. The number of his singular exploits would fill a volume, for as his pretensions are high and not always willingly yielded he is every now and then giving rise to some rumour. He is on many of these occasions as much sind against as sinning for men knowing his temper sometimes provoke him conscious that Glengarry from his character for violence will always be put in the wrong by the public. I have seen him behave in a very manly manner when thus tempted. He has of late prosecuted a quarrel ridiculous enough in the present day to have himself admitted and recognized as Chief of the whole Clan Ronald or surname of MacDonald. The truth seems to be that the present Clanronald is not descended from a legitimate chieftain of the tribe, for having accomplishd a revolution in the 16th. century they adopted a Tanist or Captain, that is a chief not in the direct line of succession, a certain Ian Moidart or John of Moidart who took the title of Captains of Clanronald with all the powers of Chiefs, and even Glengarry's ancestor recognized them as Chiefs *de facto* if not *de jure*. The fact is that this elective power was in cases of minority imbecillity or the like exercized by the Celtic tribes, and though Ian Moidart was no Chief by birth yet by election he became so and transmitted his power to his descendants as would King William the III if he had had any. So it is absurd to set up the *Jus Sanguinis* now which Glengarry's ancestors did not or could [not] make good when it was a right worth combating for.

I wrought out my full task yesterday.

Saw Cadell as I returnd from the Court. He seems dejected, apprehensive of another trustee being preferd to Cowan, and gloomy about the extent of stock of Novels etc. on hand. He infected me with his want of spirits and I almost wish my wife had not asked

Mr. Scrope and Charles K. Sharpe for this day. But the former sent such lots of game that Lady Scott's gratitude became ungovernable. I have not seen a creature at dinner since the direful 17th. January except my own family and Mr. Laidlaw. The love of solitude increases by indulgence. I hope it will not diverge into misanthropy.

It does not mend the matter that this is the first day that a ticket for sale is on my House. Poor No. 39.[1] One gets accustomd even to stone walls and the place suited me very well – All our furniture too is for [sale][2] – a hundred little articles that seem to me connected with all the happier years of my life – It is a sorry business. But *sursum corda*.[3]

My two friends came as expected, also Missie, and staid half past ten. Promised Sharpe the set of Piranesi's views by Clérisseau in the dining parlour. They belongd to my uncle so I do not like to sell them.

15 WEDNESDAY Yesterday I did not write a line of *Wood—k*. Partly I was a little out of spirits – though that would not have hindered – partly I wanted to wait for some new ideas – a sort of collecting of straw to make bricks of – partly I was a little too far beyond the press. I cannot pull well in long traces [in] which the draught is too far behind me. I love to have the press thumping, clattering and banging in my rear – it creates the necessity [which] almost always makes me work best – needs must when the Devil drives – and drive he does even according to the letter. I must work to-day howere.

Attended a Meeting of the Faculty about our New Library.[4] I

1. 39 Castle Street, which had been Scott's Edinburgh home since 1802. It was not in fact sold until June. 'After repeated attempts at a public sale, at which no offer was made, the Trustees disposed of the house in North Castle Street to Miss Mary Macintosh, at the price of £2,300.' Sederunt Book, i. 182.
2. 'I wish it to be advertized as *the furniture in No 39 lately occupied* by Sir W. S. Your delicacy would I know boggle at this but mine does not', Scott writes to Gibson on 8 March. *Letters*, ix. 456.
3. 'Let us lift up our hearts', the introductory words of the Mass.
4. The Advocates' Library housed the most important collection of books in Scotland. The committee of management, of which Scott as a Curator was a member, resolved to move it from the rooms which now house the Signet Library into a new range of buildings stretching westwards from the south end of the Parliament House. These were opened for use in 1833. In 1925 the Advocates' Library, one of the copyright libraries, presented the bulk of its collection to form the National Library of Scotland.

spoke for the purpose of saying that I hoped we would now at length act upon a general plan and look forward to commencing upon such a scale as would secure us at least for a century against the petty and partial management which we have hitherto thought sufficient of fitting up one room after another disconnected and distant. [These] have always been costing large sums of money from time to time which is now in many respects thrown away. We are now to have space enough to have a very large range of buildings which we may execute in a plane and simple taste leaving Government to ornament them if they shall think proper – otherwise to be plain, modest and handsome, and capable of being executed by degrees an[d] in such portions as convenience may admit of.

Poor James Hogg the Ettrick Shepherd came to advise with me about his affairs – he is sinking under the times; having no assistance to give him, my advice I fear will be of little service. I am sorry for him if that would help him, especially as by his own account a couple of hundred pounds would carry him on.[1]

16 THURSDAY 'Misfortune's gowling bark'[2] comes louder and louder. By assigning my whole property to trustees for behoof of Creditors, and therewith two works in progress and nigh publication, with all my future literary labours, I conceived I was bringing into the field a large fund of payment which could not exist without my exertions and that therefore I was entitled to a corresponding degree of indulgence. I therefore supposed, on selling the house and various other property, and on receiving the price of *Woodstock* and *Napoleon*, that they would give me leisure to make other exertions and be content with the rents of Abbotsford without attempting a sale. This would have been the more reasonable as [the] very printing of these works must amount to a large sum of which they will reach the profits. In the course of this delay I supposed I was to have the chance of seeing some insight both into Constable's affairs and those of Hurst and Robinson. Nay employing these Houses, under precautions, to sell the works, the publisher's profit would have come in to pay part of their debts. But Gibson last night came in after dinner and gave me to understand that the Bank of Scotland saw this in a different point of view and considerd my contribution of the produce of passd present and future labours as compensated in

1. Hogg had taken the farm of Mount Benger on the Buccleuch estates, but, like Burns, proved a better poet than farmer. See also the Entries for 3 February and 27 December 1827.
2. Burns's 'Dedication to Gavin Hamilton', l. 96.

full by their accepting of the Trust deed instead of pursuing the mode of Sequestration and placing me in the *Gazette*. They therefore expected the Trustees instantly to commence a lawsuit to reduce the marriage settlement which settles the estate upon him[1], thus loading me with a most expensive suit, and I suppose selling library and whatever they could lay hold on.

Now this seems unequal measure and would besides of itself totally destroy any power of fancy or genius, if it deserved the name, which may remain to me. A man cannot write in the House of correction and this species of *Peine forte et dure* which is threatend would render it impossible for one to help himself or others. So I told Gibson I had my mind made up as far back as 24 January pp. 80–1 not to suffer myself to be harder pressd than Law would press me. If this great commercial Company through whose hands I have directed so many thousands think they are right in taking every advantage and giving none it must be my care to see that they take none but what Law gives them. If they take the sword of the Law I must lay hold of the shield if they are determined to consider me as an irretrieveable bankrupt they have no title to object to my settling upon the usual terms which the Statute requires. They probably are of opinion that I will be ashamd to do this by applying publickly for a sequestration. Now my feelings are different. I am ashamed to owe debts I cannot pay but I am not ashamed of being classd with those to whose rank I belong. The disgrace is in being an actual bankrupt not in being made a legal one.

I had like to have been too hasty in this matter. I must have a clear under[sta]nding that I am to be benefited or indulged in some way if I bring in two such funds as these works in progress worth certainly from £10,000 to £15,000.

Clerk came in last night and drank wine and water.

Slept ill, and bilious in the morning. N.B. I smoked a segar, the first for this present year, yesterday evening.

I have some apprehensions about Lockhart too.

17 FRIDAY Slept sound for Nature repays herself for the vexation the mind sometimes gives her. This morning put Interlocutors[2] on several Sheriff Court processes from Selkirkshire.

---

1. Scott's son Walter.
2. An 'interlocutor' was the expression in correct legal language of the judgment delivered in court. Writing interlocutors required considerable expertise, and it was a principal part of the duties of a Clerk of Session. Here, however, Scott is dealing with cases that have come before the Selkirk Sheriff Court.

Gibson came to-night to say that he had spoke at full length with Alexr. Monypenny, proposed as Trustee on the part of the Bank of Scotland, and found him decidedly in favour of the most moderate measures and taking burthen on himself for the Bank of Scotland proceeding with such lenity as might enable me to have some time and opportunity to clear these affairs out – I repose trust in Mr. M. entirely. His father old Colonel Monypenny was my early friend, kind and hospitable to me when I was a mere boy. He had much of old Withers about him as expressd in Pope's epitaph

> – O youth in arms approved
> O soft humanity in age beloved.[1]

His son David and a younger brother Frank, a soldier who perishd by drowning on a boating party from Gibraltar, were my school fellows, and with the survivor now Lord Pitmillie[2] I have always kept up a friendly intercourse. Of this gentleman on whom my fortunes are to depend I know little. He was Colin MacKenzie's partner in business[3] while my friend pursued it – and he speaks highly of him – that's a great deal. He is Secretary to the Pitt Club[4] and we have had all our lives the habit *idem sentire de republica*[5] – that's much too – Lastly he is a man of perfect honour and reputation and I have nothing to ask which such a man would not either grant or convince me was unreasonable. I have, to be sure, some of my constitutional and hereditary obstinacy. But it is in me a dormant quality. Convince my understanding and I am perfectly docile. Stir my passions by coldness or affronts and the Devil would not drive me from my purpose. Let me record I have striven against this besetting sin. When I was a boy and on foot-expeditions, as we had many, no creature could be so indifferent which way our course was directed and I acquiesced in what any one proposed. But if I was once driven to make a choice and felt piqued in honour to maintain my proposition I have broken off from the whole party rather than yield to any one. Time has soberd this pertinacity of mind but it still exists and I must be on my guard against it.

1. Pope's 'Epitaph on General Henry Withers'.
2. David Monypenny (1769–1850), who had been Solicitor-General and was now a judge in the Jury Court. He was a member of 'The Club'. *Life*, i. 208.
3. That is, they had been in partnership as solicitors. Mackenzie and Monypenny were both Writers to the Signet.
4. Scott was himself a councillor of this club of Edinburgh Tories.
5. 'To feel the same way about political matters'.

It is the same with me in politics – in general I care very little about the matter and from year's end to year's end have scarce a thought connected with them except to laugh at the fools who think to make themselves great men out of little by swaggering in the rear of a party. But either actually important events – or such as seemd so by their close neighbourhood to me – have always hurried me off my feet and made me, as I have sometimes afterwards regretted, more forward and more violent than those who had a regular jog-trot way of busying themselves in public matters. Good luck, for had I lived in troublesome times, and chanced to be on the unhappy side I had been hanged to a certainty. What I have always remarkd has been that many who have haloo'd me on at public meetings and so forth have quietly left me to the odium which a man known to the public always has more than his own share of – while on the other hand they were easily successful in pressing before me who never pressd forwards at all when there was any distribution of public favours or the like.

I am horribly tempted to interfere in this business of altering the system of Banks in Scotland[1] and yet I know that if I can attract any notice I will offend my English friends without propitiating one man in Scotland. I will think of it till tomorrow – It is making myself of too much importance after all.

18 SATURDAY I set about Malachi Malagrowther's letter on the late disposition to change every thing in Scotland to an English model but without resolving about the publication. They do treat us very provokingly.

1. Worried by the 'rash spirit of speculation which has pervaded the country for some time, supported, fostered, and encouraged, by the country banks', the Government proposed to stop them issuing notes below the value of £5, and the measure was to be extended to Scotland, although, in the Prime Minister's own words, 'these banks have stood firm amidst all the convulsions of the money-market in England'. *Annual Register for 1826*, pp. 57–8. In *Letters of Malachi*, after a general assault on the desire for uniformity which prompted many Government reforms in Scottish practice, Scott points out that Scotland's recent prosperity has been built on the credit made available by her banks, and that 'the nation which is too poor to retain a circulating medium of the precious metals, must be permitted to supply its place with paper credit'. The three letters were published first in Ballantyne's *Edinburgh Weekly Journal*, and then collected by Blackwood into a pamphlet. They can be found in vol. xxi of *Misc. Prose Works*.

> O Land of Cakes, said the Northern Bard,
> Though all the world betrays thee
> One faithful pen thy rights shall guard
> One faithful harp shall praise thee.[1]

Calld on the Lord Ch: Commissioner who understanding there was a hitch in our arrangements had kindly proposed to execute an arrangement for my relief. I could not I think have thought of it at any rate. But it is unnecessary.

19 SUNDAY Finishd my letter (Malach Malagrowther) this morning and sent it to J. B. who is to call with the result this forenoon. I am not very anxious to get on with *Woodstock*. I want to see what Constable's people mean to do when they have their Trustee.[2] For an unfinishd work they must treat with the author – it is the old story of the varnish spread over the picture which nothing but the artist's own hand could remove. A finishd work might be seized under some legal pretence.

Being troubled with thick-coming fancies[3] and a slight palpitation of the heart I have been reading the Chronicle of the Good Knight Messire Jacques de Lalain,[4] curious but dull from the constant repetition of the same species of combats in the same stile and phrase. It is like washing bushels of sand for a grain of gold. It passes the time however, especially in that listless mood when your mind is half on your book half on some thing else: you catch something to arrest the attention every now and then and what you miss is not worth going back upon. Idle man's studies in short.

Still things occur to one. Something might be made out of the Pass of fountain of Tears, a Tale of Chivalry; taken from the passage of arms which Jacques de Lalain maintaind for the first day of every month for a twelvemonth.[5] The first mention perhaps of red-hot balls appears in the siege of Oudenarde by the citizens of Ghent. *Chronique* p. 293. This would be light summer work.

J. B. came and sate an hour. I led him to talk of *Woodstock* and to say truth his approbation did me much good. I am aware it *may* nay

---

1. A parody of Moore's 'Minstrel Boy'.
2. As Scott expected them to do, they laid claim to *Woodstock* and the *Life of Napoleon*, on the grounds that they had agreed to publish them. A lengthy arbitration followed, and the money paid for both works was banked until Lord Newton decided in Scott's favour. See Introduction, pp. xxxv–xxxvii.
3. *Macbeth*, v. 3.
4. G. Chastellain's *Vie de Jaques de Lalaine* in *Chroniques nationales*, ed. J. A. Buchon, 1824–6. *A. L. C.*
5. 'This hint was taken up in *Count Robert of Paris*.' J. G. L., *Life*, viii. 265.

must be partial yet is he Tom Tell-truth and totally unable to disguize his real feelings. I think I make no habit of feeding on praise, and despise those whom I see greedy for it as much as I should an underbred fellow who after eating a cherry-tart proceeded to lick the plate. But when one is flagging, a little praise (if it can be had genuine and unadulterd by flattery which is as difficult to come by as the genuine Mountain dew) is a cordial after all – So now – *Vamos Caracco* – let us attone for the loss of the morning.

20 MONDAY Yesterday though late in beginning I nearly finishd my task which is six of my close pages, about 30 pages of print, to a full and uninterrupted day's work. To-day I have already written four and with some confidence. Thus does flattery – or praise – oil the wheels – It is but two o'clock.

Skene was here remonstrating against my taking apartments at the Albyn Club and recommending that I should rather stay with them.[1] I told him that was altogether impossible. I hoped to visit them often but for taking a permanent residence I was altogether the Country Mouse and voted for

> — A hollow tree
> A crust of bread and liberty.[2]

The chain of friendship however bright does not stand the attrition of constant close contact.

21 TUESDAY Corrected the proofs of *Malachi* this morning – it may fall dead and there will be a squib lost; it may chance to light on some ingredients of national feeling and set folk's beards in a blaze and so much the better if it does – I mean better for Scotland – not a whit for me –[3]

Attended the hearing in P. House till near four o'clock so I shall do little to-night for I am tired and sleepy. One person talking for a long

1. Skene proposed 'that for the next summer he should take up his quarters at my house, as my own family would be in the country, leaving a housekeeper to take care of my younger sons till vacation time, which would likewise be the termination of the Session'. *Skene's Memories*, p. 140. Scott's answer (*Letters*, ix. 382) was: 'I am a solitary monster by temper, and must necessarily couch in a den of my own.' In the end he decided against the Club at 54 Princes Street, 'where there are so many Dandies and confusion' (*Letters*, ix. 435), and took lodgings in North St. David Street.
2. Pope's *Imitations of Horace*, bk. ii, satire 6, ll. 220–1.
3. An allusion to *Richard III*, iii. 4.

time, whether in pulpit or at the bar or anywhere else, unless the interest be great and the eloquence of the highest character, always sets me to sleep. I impudently lean my head on my hand in the Court and take my nap without shame – The Lords may keep awake and mind their own affairs – *Quae supra nos nihil ad nos*.[1] These Clerks' stools are certainly as easy seats as are in Scotland, those of the Barons of Exchequer always excepted.[2]

22 WEDNESDAY Paid Lady Scott her fortnight's allowance £24. £24 Ly. Scott

Ballantyne breakfasted and is to negotiate about *Malachi* with Constable and Blackwood. It reads not amiss and if I can get a few guineas for it I shall not be ashamed to take them, for paying Lady Scott I have just left between £3 and £4 for any necessary occasion and my salary does not become due untill 20th March and the expence of removing etc. is to be provided for.

> But shall we go mourn for that, my dear?
> The cold moon shines by night
> And when we wander here and there
> We then do go most right.[3]

The mere scarcity of money (so that actual wants are provided) is not poverty. It is the bitter draught to owe money which we cannot pay.

Labourd fairly at *Woodstock* to-day but principally in revising and adding to *Malachi* of which an edition as pamphlet[4] is anxiously desired. I have lugd in my old friend Cardrona,[5] I hope it will not be thought unkindly. The Banks are anxious to have it published. They were lately exercizing lenity towards me and if I can benefit them it will be an instance of the 'King's errand lying in the Cadger's gate.'[6]

23 THURSDAY Corrected two sheets of *Woodstock* this morning. These are not the days of idleness. The fact is that the not seeing company gives me a command of my time which I possessd at no other

---

1. 'What is above us is nothing to do with us.'
2. Scott would have accepted one of those seats had it been offered. See the Entry for 4 March: 'The preferment would suit me well.'
3. *The Winter's Tale*, iv. 3.
4. Published by Blackwood.
5. Scott likened the Government to Mr. Williamson of Cardrona near Peebles, who, because he found a laxative pill necessary for himself, always insisted that his guests should take one too. *Malachi*, Letter I.
6. 'A case where the beggar can help the King.' A Scottish proverb.

period in my life – at least since I knew how to make some use of my leisure. There is a great pleasure in sitting down to write with the consciousness that nothing will occur during the day to break the spell.

Detaind in the Court till past three and came home just in time to escape a terrible squall. I am a good deal jaded and will not work till after dinner – there is a sort of drowsy vacillation of mind attends fatigue with me. I can command my pen as the School-Copy recommends but cannot equally command my thought and often write one word for another.

Read a little volume called the OMEN very well written, deep and powerfull language. *Aut Erasmus aut Diabolus* – it is Lockhart[1] or I am strangely deceived – it is passd for Wilson's though, but Wilson has more of the falsetto of assumed sentiment, less of the depth of gloomy and powerful feeling.

24 FRIDAY Went down to printing office after the court and corrected *Malachi* J B 's name is to be on the Imprint so he will subscribe the book. He reproaches me with having taken much more pains on this temporary pamphlet than on works which have a greater interest on my fortunes. I have certainly bestowd enough of revision and correction.

But the cases are different. In a novel or poem I run the course alone – here I am taking up the cudgels and may expect a drubbing in return. Besides I do feel that this [is] a public matter in which the country is deeply interested and therefore is far more important than any thing referring to my fame or fortune alone. The pamphlet will soon be out; meantime *Malachi* prospers and excites much attention. The Banks have bespoke 500 copies. The country is taking the alarm and I think the Ministers will not dare to press the measure. I should rejoice to see the old red lion ramp a little and the thistle again claim its *nemo me impune.*[2] I do believe Scotsmen will shew themselves unanimous at least where their cash is concernd. They shall not want backing. I incline to cry with Biron in *Love's Labour's Lost*

More Ates More Ates – stir them on.[3]

I suppose all imaginative people feel more or less of excitation from a scene of insurrection or tumult or of general expression of national

1. *The Omen* was of course by John Galt, not Lockhart. For Scott's review of the novel for *Blackwood's Magazine* see *Misc. Prose Works*, xviii. 333, or *Blackwood's Magazine*, no. 114.
2. Scotland's motto is *Nemo me impune lacessit,* or 'Wha daur meddle wi' me'.
3. Act v, sc. 2.

feeling. When I was a lad poor Davie Douglas[1] used to accuse me of being *cupidus novarum rerum*[2] and say that I loved the stimulus of a Broil. It might be so then and even still

> Even in our ashes glow their wonted fires.[3]

Whimsical enough that when I was trying to animate Scotland against the Currency bill John Gibson brought me the deed of Trust assigning my whole estate to be subscribed by me. So that I am turning patriot and taking charge of the affairs of the country on the very day I was proclaiming myself incapable of managing my own. What of that? The eminent politician Quidnunc[4] was in the same condition. Who would think of their own trumpery debts when they are taking the support of the whole system of Scottish Banking on their shoulders?

Odd enough too – On this, for the first time since the awful 17th. January, we entertain at dinner Lady Anna Maria Elliot,[5] W. Clerk, John A. Murray,[6] and Thomas Thomson, as if we gave a dinner on accompt of my *Cessio fori*.[7]

25 SATURDAY Our party yesterday went off very gaily – much laugh and fun and I think I enjoyd it more from the rarity of the event – I mean from having seen society at home so seldom of late. My head aches slightly though. Yet we were but a bottle of Champagne, one of port, one of old Sherry and two of claret among four gentlemen and three Ladies.

I have been led from this incident to think of taking Chambers near Clerk in Rose Court. Methinks the retired situation should suit me well. There a man and woman would be my whole

1. David Douglas (?1771–1819), later Lord Reston. He was a schoolfellow of Scott's and a member of 'The Club'.
2. 'Desirous of new things'.
3. Gray's 'Elegy in a Country Churchyard'.
4. In *The Upholsterer*, by Arthur Murphy.
5. The eldest daughter of the first Earl of Minto, she was clever, amusing, and a favourite of Scott's. In 1832, at the age of forty-seven, she married General Sir Rufane-Shawe Donkin. For Scott's opinion of her see the Entry for 10 August 1826.
6. John Archibald Murray (1778–1859), Clerk of the Pipe in the Court of Exchequer, and a contributor to the *Edinburgh Review*. Under the Whigs he became Lord Advocate and in 1839 a Lord of Session.
7. A Scottish legal phrase meaning 'cessation of business' or 'bankruptcy'.

establishment. My superfluous furniture might serve and I could ask a friend or two to dine as I have been accustomd to do. I will look at the place to-day.[1]

I will set now to a second *Epistle of Malachi to the Athenians*. If I can but get the sulky Scottish spirit set up the Devil won't turn them.

> Cock up your beaver and Cock it fu' sprush
> We'll over the border and give them a brush
> There's somebody there we'll teach better behaviour
> Hey, Johnie lad, cock up your beaver.[2]

26 SUNDAY Spent the morning and till dinner on *Malachi's Second Epistle to the Athenians*. It is difficult to steer betwixt the natural impulse of one's National feelings setting in one direction and the prudent regard to the interests of the empire and its internal peace and quiet recommending less vehement expression. I will endeavour to keep sight of both. But were my own interest alone concernd, d—n me but I wa'd give it them hot. Had some valuable communications from Colin MacKenzie and Lord Medwyn[3] which will supply my plentiful lack of facts.

Received an anonymous satire in doggrell which having read the first verse and last I committed to the flames.

Peter Murray,[4] son of the Clever Lord Elibank, calld – and sate half an hour – an old friend and who from the peculiarity and originality of his genius is one of the most entertaining companions I have ever known.

But I must finish *Malachi* –

27 MONDAY *Malachi* is getting on. I must finish him to-night. I dare say some of my London friends will be displeased. Canning perhaps for he is *engoué* of Huskisson.[5] Can't help it.

The place I lookd at won't do. But I must really get some lodging,

1. Scott did not in fact look at 'the small *titmouse* Houses about Saint Andrews Church', on the north side of George Street, until the following Monday, for he had not seen them when he wrote to Lockhart on the Sunday. *Letters*, ix. 435. They were not suitable, and he took lodgings instead in North St. David Street.
2. Rewritten by Burns for James Johnson's *Musical Museum*, no. 309.
3. John Hay Forbes (1776–1854), brother of Sir William Forbes and recently elevated to the Bench as Lord Medwyn.
4. Patrick Murray, natural son of the sixth Lord Elibank.
5. President of the Board of Trade at this time, and throughout his career particularly interested in finance.

for reason or none Dalgleish will not leave me and cries and makes a scene.[1] Now if I staid alone in a little set of chambers he would serve greatly for my accomodation. There are some nice places of the kind in the new buildings[2] but they are distant from the court and I cannot walk well on the pavement. It is odd enough that just when I had made a resolution to use my coach frequently I ceased to keep one[3] – in town at least.

28 TUESDAY Completed *Malachi* to-day – It is more serious than the first and in some places perhaps too peppery. Never mind – if you would have a horse kick make a crupper out of a whin-cow.[4] And I trust to see Scotland kick and fling to some purpose. *W—k* lies back for this but *quid non pro patria?*[5]

MARCH

1 WEDNESDAY *Malachi* is in the *Edinburgh Journal* to-day and reads like the work of an uncompromising right forward Scot of the Old School. Some of the cautious and pluckless instigators will be afraid of their confederate, for if a man of some energy and openness of character happens to be on the same side with these truckling jobbers they stand as much in awe of his vehemence as doth the inexperienced conjuror who evoked a fiend whom he cannot manage. –

Came home in a heavy shower with the Solicitor[6] – I tried him on the question but found him reserved and cautious. The future Lord Advocate must be cautious but I can tell my good friend John Hope that if he acts the part of a firm and resolute Scottish patriot both his own country and England will respect him the more. Ah, Hal Dundas.[7] There was no such truckling in thy day –

Lookd out a quantity of things to go to Abbotsford for we are flitting if you please. It is with a sense of pain that I leave behind a parcel of trumpery prints and little ornaments once the pride of Ldy. S—['s] heart but which she sees consigned with indifference to the

1. In order to stay he 'gives up poor devil £10 of his wages'. *Letters*, ix. 450.
2. To the north and west of the original New Town.
3. See the Entry for 25 November 1825.
4. 'A gorse bush.'
5. 'What [is] not [to be done] for our native land?'
6. The Solicitor-General, John Hope.
7. The first Lord Melville.

chance of an Auction. Things that have had their day of importance
with me I cannot forget though the merest trifles. But I am glad that
She with bad health and enough to vex her has not the same useless
mode of associating recollections with this unpleasant business. The
best part of it is the necessity of leaving behind, *Viz.* getting rid of, a
set of most wretched daubs of landscapes in great gilded frames of
which I have often been hea[r]tily ashamed. The history of them was
curious. An amateur artist, a Lady, happend to fall into misfortunes
upon which her landscapes, the character of which had been bouyed
up far beyond their proper level, sank even beneath it and it was low
enough. One most amiable and accomplishd old lady continued to
encourage her pencil and to order pictures after pictures which she
sent in presents to her friends. I suppose I have eight or ten of them
which I could [not] avoid accepting. There will be plenty of laughing
when they are to be sold. It would be a good joke enough to cause it
be circulated that they were performances of my own in early youth
and they would be look[d] on and bought up as curiosities – True it is
that I took lessons of oil painting in youth from a little Jew animalcule
– A Smouch called Burrell, a clever sensible creature though. But I
could make no progress either in painting or drawing. Nature denied
me correctness of eye and neatness of hand. Yet I was very desirous to
be a draughtsman at least and labourd harder to attain that point than
at any other in my recollection to which I did not make some
approaches. My oil paintings were to Miss —'s above commemor-
ated what hers are to Claude Lorraine. Yet Burrell was not useless to
me altogether neither. He was a Prussian and I got from him many a
long story of the battles of Frederick in whose armies his father had
been a commissary or perhaps a spy – I remember his picturesque
account of seeing a party of the Black Hussars bringing in some
forage carts which they had taken from a body of the Cossacks whom
he described as lying on the top of the carts of hay mortally wounded
and like the Dying gladiator eying their own blood as it ran down
through the straw, and I afterwards took lessons from Walker whom
we used to call Bluebeard. He was one of the most conceited persons
in the world but a good teacher – one of the ugliest countenances he
had than need be exhibited – enough as we say to spean weans.[1] The
poor man was always extremely precise in the quality of every thing
about him; his dress accomodations and every thing else. He became
insolvent, poor man, and for some reason or other I attended the
meeting of those concernd in his affairs. Instead of ordinary accomodations for writing each of the persons present was equipd with a
large sheet of drawing paper and a swan's quill – It was mournfully

1. 'To wean children'.

ridiculous enough. Skirving[1] made an admirable likeness of poor Walker; not a single scar or mark of the small-pox which seamd his countenance but the too accurate brother of the brush had faithfully laid it down in longitude and latitude. Poor Walker destroyd it (being in crayons) rather than let the caricatura of his ugliness appear at the sale of his effects.

I did learn myself to take some vile views from nature. When Will Clerk and I lived very much together I used sometimes to make them under his instruction. He to whom as to all his family art is a familiar attribute wonder[d] at me as a Newfoundland dog would a greyhound which shewd fear of the water.

Going down to Liddesdale once I drew the castle of Hermitage in my fashion and sketchd it so accurately that with a few verbal instructions Clerk put it into regular form, Williams (the Grecian)[2] copied over Clerk's and *his* drawing was engraved as the frontispiece of the 1st Edition[3] of the Kelso Editn. *Minstrelsy of the Scottish Border.*

Do you know why you have written all this down, Sir W? Because it pleases me to record that this thrice transmitted drawing, though taken originally from a sketch of mine, was extremely like Hermitage which neither of my colleagues in the task had ever seen. No – that is not the reason – You want to put off writing *Woodstock*, just as easily done as these memoranda – but which it happens your duty and your prudence recommends – and therefore you are loth to begin –

> Heigho
>   I can't say No
> But this piece of task work off I can stave O
> For Malachi is posting into an octavo
> To correct the proof-sheets only this night I have O
> So, Madam Conscience, you have gotten as good as you gave O
> But tomorrow's a new day and we'll better behave O
> So I lay down the pen and your pardon I crave O.

In the Evening Mr. Gibson calld and transacted business.

2 THURSDAY I have a letter from Colin McKenzie approving *Malachi.* 'Cold Men may say it is too strong but from the true

---

1. Archibald Skirving (1749–1819), the gifted but eccentric painter of 'the only good portrait of Burns'. *Letters,* iv. 243.
2. Hugh William Williams (1773–1829), who lived much of his life in Edinburgh. Scott reviewed his *Travels in Italy, Greece and the Ionian Islands* which was published in 1820.
3. A slip, Tait suggests, for 'volume'.

men of Scotland you are sure of the warmest gratitude' – I never have yet found nor do I expect it on this occasion that ill will dies in debt or what is called gratitude distresses herself by frequent payments. The one is like a ward-holding and pays its Reddendo in hard blows – the other a blanch tenure and is discharged for payment of a red-rose or a peppercorn. He that takes the forlorn hope in an attack is often deserted by those that should support him and who generally throw the blame of their own cowardice upon his rashness. We will see this will end in the same way. But I foresaw it from the beginning. The Bankers will be persuaded that it is a squib which may burn their own fingers and will curse the poor pyrotechnist that compounded it – if they do – they be d—d.

Slept indifferently and dreamd of Napoleon's last moments and last illness of which I was reading a medical account last night by Dr. Arnott.[1] Horrible death – a cancer on the pylorus – I would have given something to have lain still this morning and made up for lost time. But *Desidiae valedixi* [2] If you once turn on your side after the hour at which you ought to rise it is all over. Bolt up at once. Bad night last, the next is sure to be better.

> When the drum beats make ready
> When the fife plays march away
> To the roll-call To the roll-call To the roll-call
> Before the break of day.[3]

Dined with Chief: Com:, Admiral Adam, W. Clerk, Thomson and I. The excellent old man was cheerful at intervals – at times sad as was natural.[4] A good blunder he told us occurd in the Anandale case which was a question partly of domicile. It was proved that leaving Lochwood the Earl had given up his *kain* and *carriages*:[5] this an English Counsel contended was the best of all possible proofs that the Noble Earl designd an absolute change of residence since he laid aside his *walking-stick* and his *coach*.

First Epistle of Malachi is getting out of print: or rather is out of print already.

1. He had sent Scott his *Account of the last Illness, Decease, etc. of Napoleon Bonaparte*, 1822, on 20 February. Walpole.
2. 'I have said farewell to idleness.'
3. Unidentified.
4. He had just lost his eldest son. See p. 74.
5. 'Kain' is payment in kind and 'carriages' means services in driving.

3 FRIDAY Could not get the last sheets of *Malachi 2d Epistle* last night; so they must go out to the world uncorrected – a great loss – for the last touches are always most effectual and I expect misprints in the additional matter. We were especially obliged to have it out this morning that it may operate as a gentle preparative for the meeting of Inhabitants at two o'clock[1] – *Vogue la galère*[2] – we shall see if Scotsmen have any pluck left. If not they may kill the next Percy[3] – battle the next obnoxious measure – themselves.

It is ridiculous enough for me in a state of insolvency for the present to be battling about gold and paper currency – it is something like the humorous touch in Hogarth's 'Distressd Poet' where the poor Starveling of the muses is engaged when [in] the abyss of poverty in writing an Essay on payment of the National Debt and his wall is adorn[d] with a plan of the mines of Peru. Nevertheless even these fugitive attempts, from the success which they have had and the noise they are making, serve to shew the truth of the old proverb

> When House and Land are gone and spent
> Then Learning is most excellent.

On the whole I am glad of this bruilzie[4] as far as I am concernd; people will not dare talk of me as an object of pity – no more 'poor manning'. Who asks how many punds Scots the old champion had in his pocket when

> He set a bugle to his mouth
> And blew so loud and shrill
> The trees in greenwood shook thereat
> Sae loud rang ilka hill –[6]

This sounds conceited enough yet is not far from truth.

The meeting was very numerous, 500 or 600 at least, and unanimous saving one Mr. Howden who having been all his life as I have

1. A public meeting in the Waterloo Tavern attended by nearly six hundred people 'of the better and trading classes'. *Letters*, ix. 443.
2. 'Row the galley' (i.e. keep going), Le Sage's *Théâtre de la foire* (1721), Air 98.
3. *1 Henry IV*, v. 4.
4. 'Broil'.
5. 'The Child of Elle', ll. 145–8, or 'Hardyknute', ll. 61–4, slightly altered. Herd, i. 3 and 124.

been told in bitter opposition to ministers proposed on the present occasion that the whole contested measure should be trusted to their wisdom. I suppose he chose the opportunity of placing his own opinion in opposition, single opposition too, to one of a large assembly. The speaking was very moderate. Report had said that Jeffrey, John Murray, and other sages of the oeconomical school were to unbuckle their mails and give us their opinions. But no such great guns appeard. If they had, having the multitude on my side, I would [have] tried to break a lance with them. A few short but well expressd resolutions were adopted unanimously. These were proposed by Lord Rollo[1] and seconded by Sir James Fergusson, Bart. I was named one of a committee to encourage all sort of opposition to the measure. So I have already broken through two good and wise resolutions – one that I would not write on political controversy – another that I would not be named on public committees – If my good resolves go this way like *snaw aff a dyke*[2] the Lord help me.

4 SATURDAY Last night I had a letter from Lockhart who speaking of *Malachi* says 'The Ministers are sore beyond imagination at present and some of them I hear have felt this new whip on the raw to some purpose' – I conclude he means Canning is offended – I can't help it as I said before – *fiat justitia, ruat coelum*.[3] No cause in which I had the slightest personal interest should have made me use my pen 'gainst them, blunt or pointed as it may be. But as they are about to throw this country into distress and danger by a measure of useless and uncalld for experiment they must hear the opinion of the Scotsmen to whom it is of no other consequence than as a general measure affecting the country at large, and mine they *shall* hear. I had determined to lay down the pen – But now they shall have another of Malachi beginning with buffoonery and ending as seriously as I can write it – It is like a frenzy that they will agitate the upper and middling classes of society, so very friendly to them, with unnecessary and hazardous [measures].

> Oh thus it was they loved them dear
> And sought how to requite 'em
> And having no friends left but they
> They did resolve to fight them.[4]

1. A Director of the Commercial Bank of Scotland.
2. 'Snow off a wall'.
3. 'Let justice be done though the heavens fall.' William Watson's *Quodlibets of Religion and State*, 1601.
4. Swift's 'Duke upon Duke'.

The country is very high just now – but England may carry the measure if she will doubtless. But what will be the consequence of the distress ensuing God only can foretell.

Lockhart moreover enquires about my affairs anxiously and asks what he is to say about them. Says 'he has enquiries every day – kind most kind all, and among the most interested and anxious Sir William Knighton who told me the king was quite melancholy all the evening he heard of it.' *This* I can well believe for the king, educated as a Prince, has never the less as true and kind a heart as any subject in his dominions. He goes on 'I do think they would give you a Baron's gown[1] as soon as possible etc.' – I have written to him in answer shewing I have enough to carry me on and can dedicate my literary efforts to clear my land. The preferment would suit me well and the late Duke of Buccleuch[2] gave me his interest for it. I dare say the young Duke would do the same for the unvaried love I have born his house – and by and bye he will have a voice potential. But there is Sir William Rae in the mean time whose prevailing claim I would never place my own in opposition [to] were it possible by a *tour de force* such as L. points at to set it aside. Meantime I am building a barrier betwixt me and promotion – Any prospect of the kind is very distant and very uncertain – Come *time* come *Rath* as the German says.

In the mean while, now I am not pulld about for money etc. methinks I am happier without my wealth than with it. Everything is paid – I have no one wishing to make [up] a sum of money and writing for his accompt to be paid. Since 17 January I have not laid out a guinea out of my own hand save two or three in charity and six shillings for a pocket Book. But the cash with which I set out having run short for family expenses I drew on Blackwood through Ballantyne which was honourd for £25 to account of *Malachi's Letters* of which another edition of 1000 is orderd and gave it to Lady Scott because our removal will require that expence

Ldy S. £25 from Blackwood for *Malachi*.

in hand. This is for a fortnight succeeding Wednesday next being the 8th March current. On the 20 my quarter comes in and though I have something to pay out of it I shall be on velvet for expense – and

---

1. Judges in the Court of Exchequer were called Barons. That Scott thought wistfully of the £2000 a year with which their far from onerous duties were rewarded appears from the Entries for 8 and 21 February as well as from this day's letter to Lockhart: 'A Barons gown would be a very different thing and I should be glad to have it.' *Letters*, ix. 442.
2. The fourth Duke, who died in 1819.

regular I will be. Methinks all trifling objects of expenditure seem to grow light in my eyes: that I may regain independence I must be saving. But ambition awakes as love of quiet indulgence dies and is mortified within me – Dark Cuthullin will be renownd or dead – [1]

5 SUNDAY Something of toddy and Segar in that last quotation I think – Yet I only smoked two and liquified with one glass of spirits and water. I have sworn I will not blot out what I have once written here.

Malachi goes on but I am dubious about the commencement. It must be mended at least – reads prosy.

Had letters from Walter and Jane, the dears. All well. Regiment about to move from Dublin.

6 MONDAY Finished 3d *Malachi* which I don't much like. It respects the difficulty of find[ing] gold to replace the paper circulation. Now this [I] should have considerd first. The admitting that the measure may be imposed is yielding up the question. And Malachi is like a Commandant who should begin to fire from interior defences before his outworks were carried. If Ballantyne be of my own opinion I will suppress it. We are all in a bustle shifting things to Abbotsford and particularly a good cellar of wines etc. I believe we shall stay here till the beginning of next week. It is odd but I don't feel the impatience for the country which I have usually experiencd.

7 TUESDAY Detaind in the Court till *three* o'clock by a hearing. Then to the committee appointed at the meeting on friday to look after the small Note Business. A pack of old fainéants incapable of managing such a business and who will lose the day from mere coldness of heart. There are about a thousand names on the petition – they have added no designations – a great blunder – for *testimonia sunt ponderanda non numeranda*[3] should never be lost sight of. They are disconcerted and helpless, just as in the business of the King's

£20 Sent Charles to accompt of allowance.[2]

---

1. Macpherson's 'Ossian', *Fingal*, 1. 49–50.
2. In response to his letter of 1 March. 'I should not at present trouble you for money but I have been foolish enough not to have saved sufficient to pay my *battels* if you could therefore advance me 20 £ it would relieve me from my present embarassment. The best apology I can make is assuring you that it shall not occur again.' Walpole. However it does occur again – on 9 March 1827, when Scott has to send £50.
3. 'Testimonies must be weighed not counted.'

visit[1] when every body threw the weight on me for which I sufferd
much in my immediate labour and after bad health; it bringing on a
violent eruption on my skin which saved me from a fever at the time
but has been troublesome more or less ever since. In another time I
was so disgusted with seeing them sitting in ineffectual helplessness
spitting on the hot iron that lay before them and touching it with a
timid finger as if afraid of being scalded that I might have dashd in
and taken up the hammer, summond the deacons and other heads of
public bodies and by consulting them have carried them with me. But
I cannot waste my time health and spirits in fighting thankless battles.
I left them in a quarter of an hour and presage unless the country
make an alarm the cause is lost. The philosophical reviewers manage
their affairs better – hold off – avoid commit[ting] themselves but
throw their *vis inertiæ* into the opposite scale and neutralize the
feelings which they cannot combat. To force them to fight on
disadvantageous ground is our policy. But we have more sneakers
after ministerial favour than men who love their country and who
upon a liberal scale would serve their party. For to force the Whigs to
avow an unpopular doctrine in popular assemblies or to wrench the
government of such bodies from them would be a *coup de maître*. But
they are alike destitute of manly resolution and sound policy – D—n
the whole nest of them – I have corrected the last of *Malachi* and Let
the thing take its chance. I have made just enemies enough and
indisposed enough of friends.

8 WEDNESDAY At the Court though a teind day.[2] A foolish thing
happend while the Court were engaged with the teinds. I amused
myself with writing on a sheet of paper Notes on Frederick Maitland's account of the capture of Bonaparte[3] – and I have lost these
notes – shufled in perhaps among my own papers or those of the
Teind Clerks. What a curious document to be found in a process of
valuation.

Being jaded and sleepy I took up *Le Duc de Guise en Naples*.[4] I think
this, with the old *Memoires*[5] on the same subject which I have at

---

1. King George IV's visit to Scotland in August 1822. See *Life*, vii.
   47–84, and Robert Mudie's *Modern Athens*, 1825.
2. Usually a free day for Scott as the Court of Session did not sit.
   See Introduction, p. xxvi.
3. *The Surrender of Bonaparte*; see p. 128, n. 5.
4. *Le Duc de Guise à Naples etc. en 1647 et 1648*, by M. de Pastoret,
   1825.
5. *Mémoires relatifs à l'histoire de France*, second series No. 55, ed.
   M. Petitot, 1820.

Abbotsford, would enable me to make a pretty essay for the *Quarter-ly*.[1] We must take up *Woodstock* now in good earnest. Mr. Cowan, a good and able man, is chosen Trustee in Constable's affairs with full power –[2] From what I hear the poor man is not sensible of the nature of his own situation. For myself I have succeeded in putting the matters perfectly out of my mind since I cannot help them and have arrived at a flocci-pauci-nihili-pili-fication of money and I thank Shenstone for inventing that long word.[3]

They are removing the wine etc. to the carts and you will judge if our flitting is not making a noise in the world – or in the street at least.[4]

9 THURSDAY I foresaw justly

> When first I set this dangerous stone a rolling
> Twould fall upon myself –[5]

Sir Robert Dundas to-day put into my hands a letter of between thirty and forty pages in angry and bitter reprobation of *Malachi*, full of general averments and very untenable arguments, all written *at* me by name but of which I am to have no copy and which is to be shown to me *in extenso* and circulated to other special friends to whom it may be necessary to 'give the sign to hate.'[6] I got it at two o'clock and returnd with an answer five hours afterwards in which I have studied not to be tempted into either <into> sarcastic or harsh expressions:[7] A quarrel it is however in all the forms between my old friend and

1. In fact Scott's article appeared in the *Foreign Quarterly Review*, vol. iv, p. 355.
2. As Scott had hoped. See the Entry for 28 January 1826.
3. Shenstone's *Essays* (1765), p. 115.
4. For Dalgleish's account, see note 4, p. 808.
5. *Henry VIII*, v. 2.
6. Johnson's *Vanity of Human Wishes*.
7. Lord Melville's letter is printed in *Arniston Memoirs*, ed. Omond, 1888, pp. 316–22, and Scott's answer in *Letters*, ix. 457.
'Canning is the only one besides Lord Melville whom I care for', Scott had written to Lockhart on the 3rd (*Letters*, ix. 444) when discussing the effects of *Malachi*, and the tone of sorrow mixed with anger in the *Journal* Entry suggests how deeply he felt the disapproval of his old Colonel in the Yeomanry, the son of the patron through whom he had obtained his first appointment to the Sheriffdom of Selkirkshire, and 'the very early friend with whom I carried my satchel to school' (*Letters*, ix. 468). The breach, however, was not final. Within five months they met again and all was 'forgotten and forgiven'. See the Entry for 13 July 1826.

myself and His Lordship's reprimand is to be *read out in orders* to all our friends. They all know what I have said is true but that will be nothing to the purpose if they are desired to consider them as false. As for Lord Melville I do not wonder that he is angry though he has little reason for he, our *Watchman stented*,[1] has from time to time sufferd all manner of tampering to go on under his nose with the institutions and habits of Scotland. As for myself I was quite prepared for my share of displeasure. It is very curious that I should have foreseen all this so distinctly as far back as 17 february. Nobody at least can plague me for interest with Lord Melville as they use to do. By the way from the tone of his letter I think his Lordship will give up the measure and I will be the peace offering. All will agree to condemn me as too warm – too rash – and get rich on privileges which they would not have been able to save but for a little rousing of spirit which [will] not perhaps fall asleep again.

A Mr. Worsley, very gentleman-like but with distorted eyes, calld on the part of a Capt: to make enquiry about the Border Rutherfords. Not being very *cleever* as John Fraser used to say at these pedigree-matters referd him to Mrs. Dr. Russell[2] and Robt. Rutherford. The noble Captain conceits he has some title to honours of Lord Rutherford. Very odd – when there is a vacant or dormant title in a Scottish family or *name* every body and all connected with the clan conceive they have *quodam modo* a right to it. Not being engrossd by any individual it communicates part of [its] lustre to every individuall in the tribe as if it remaind in common stock for that purpose.

10 FRIDAY I am not made entirely on the same mould of passions like other people. Many men would deeply regret a breach with so old a friend as Lord Melville and many men would be in despair at losing the good graces of a minister of State for Scotland and all pretty visions about what might be done for myself and my sons, especially Charles. But I think my good Lord doth ill to be angry like the patriarch of old[3] and I have in my odd sans souciant character a good handful of meal from the grist of the Jolly Miller who

> — once
> Dwelld on the river dee
> I care for nobody no not I
> Since nobody cares for me.[4]

1. The phrase appears in stanza xv of Burns's 'The Author's Earnest Cry and Prayer' in the Kilmarnock Edition only.
2. Mrs. Russsell's mother was Jane Rutherford of Edgerstone.
3. Jonah, 4:9.
4. 'The Miller of dee', st. 1. Herd, ii. 185.

Breakfasted with me Mr. Francks,[1] a young Irishman from Dublin, who brought letters from Walter; and Captain Longmore of the Royal Staff.[2] He has written a book of poetry, *Tales of Chivalry and Romance*, far from bad yet wants spirit – He talks of publishing his recollections in the Peninsula which must be interesting for he has, I think, sense and reflection. Sandie Young[3] came in at breakfast-time with a Monsr. Brocque of Montpelier.

Saw Sir Robt. Dundas at court, who condemns Lord Melville and says he will not shew his letter to any one – in fact it would be exactly placarding me 'in a private and confidential' manner. He is to send my letter to Lord Melville. Colin McKenzie concurs in thinking Lord Melville quite wrong. '*He must cool in the skin he het in.*'[4]

On coming home from the court a good deal fatigued I took a nap in my easy chair. Then packd my books and committed the refuse to Jock Stevenson.

Left not a limb on which a Dane could triumph.[5]

Gave Mr. Gibson my father's cabinet which suits a man of business well.

Gave Jock Stevenson the picture of my old favourite Dog Camp mentiond in one of the introductions to *Marmion*[6] and a little crow quill drawing of Melrose Abbey by Nelson whom I used to call the Admiral. Poor fellow – He had some ingenuity and was in a moderate way a good pens-man and draughtsman. He left his situation of amanuensis to go into Lord Home's Militia regiment but his dissipated habits got the better of a strong constitution and he fell into bad habits and poverty and died I believe in the Hospital at Liverpool – Strange enough that Henry Weber who acted afterwards as my amanuensis for many years had also a melancholy fate ultimately. He was a man of very superior attainments, an excellent

1. Probably Thomas Harte Franks (1805–62), an Ensign in the 10th Regiment of Foot, whom Walter would have met at the home of his relative Mathew Franks of 28 Merrion Square. He must have been invited to breakfast when he delivered the letters some days before. *Letters*, ix. 451.
2. Captain George Longmore, author of *The War of the Isles*, 1826, which he no doubt presented to Scott at this meeting. It is listed in the *A. L. C.*
3. 'Alexander Young, Esq. of Harburn – a steady Whig of the old school, and a steady and highly esteemed friend of Sir Walter's.' J. G. L.
4. Allan Ramsay's *Proverbs* (1737), p. 44.
5. Henry Brooke's *Gustavus Vasa*, iii. 2.
6. The Introduction to Canto IV.

linguist and geographer and a remarkable antiquary. He publishd a collection of antient Romances superior I think to the elaborate Ritson.[1] He also publishd an edition of Beaumont and Fletcher[2] but too carelessly done to be reputable. He was a violent Jacobin which he thought he disguized from [me], while I who cared not a figg about the poor young man's politics used to amuse myself with teazing him. He was an excellent and affectionate creature but unhappily was aflicted with partial insanity especially if he used Strong liquors to which like others with that unhappy tendency he was occasionally addicted. In 1826[3] he became quite insane and at the risque of my life I had to disarm him of a pair of loaded pistols which I did by exerting the sort of authority which I believe gives an effectual controul in such cases. His friends, who were respectable, placed him in the York Asylum where he pined away and died I think in 1814 or 1815.[4] My patronage in this way has not been lucky to the parties protected. I hope poor G. Huntly Gordon will escape the influence of the Evil Star. He has no vice, poor fellow, but his total deafness makes him helpless.

11 SATURDAY This day the Court rose after a long and laborious Sederunt. I employd the remainder of the day in completing a set of notes on Capt. Maitland's manuscript Narrative of the reception of Napoleon Bonaparte on board the *Bellerophon*.[5] It had been presently in the hands of my friend Basil Hall[6] who had made many excellent corrections in point of stile. But he had been hypercritical in wishing – in so important a matter where every thing depends on accuracy – wishing this expression to be alterd for delicacy's sake, that to be

---

1. The works alluded to are Weber's *Metrical Romances*, 1810, and Ritson's *Ancient English Metrical Romances*, 1802.
2. This appeared in fourteen volumes in 1812.
3. A slip for 1814.
4. Weber died in 1818.
5. The manuscript (published in 1826 as *Narrative of the Surrender of Buonaparte*) had been lent to Scott by Basil Hall in October. *Letters*, ix. 246. Captain Frederick Maitland (1777–1839) received Napoleon's surrender on board H. M. S. *Bellerophon* in July 1815 and transported him to England. Scott makes considerable use of his reminiscences in his *Life of Napoleon*, vol. ix, ch. 2.
6. Basil Hall (1788–1844), traveller, author, and until 1823 a captain in the Royal Navy. He wrote several works on his voyages to Korea, South America, and elsewhere. Scott used his account of a visit to Napoleon on St. Helena in *Life of Napoleon*, vol. ix, ch. 7. It was he who arranged to have a warship put at Scott's disposal for the voyage to Malta and Naples in 1831.

omitted for fear of giving offence and that other to be abridged for fear of being tedious. The plain sailor's narrative for me, written on the spot and bearing in its minuteness the evidence of its notoriety.

Lord Elgin sent me some time since a curious account of his imprisonment in France and the attempts which were made to draw him into some intrigue which might authorize treating him with rigour.[1]

He calld today and communicated some curious circumstances on the authority of Fouché, Denon and others respecting Bonaparte and the empress Maria Louise whom Ld. Elgin had conver[s]d with on the subject in Italy.

His conduct towards her was something like that of Ethwald to Elburga in Joanna Baillie's fine tragedy,[2] making her postpone her high rank by birth to the authority which [he] had acquired by his talents. Dinner was usually announced for a particular hour and Napoleon's business often made him late. She was not permitted to sit down to table, an etiquette which was reasonable enough. But from the hour of dinner till the Emperor appeard she was to be in the act of sitting down: that is to say he was displeased if he found her engaged with a book, with work or with anything else. She was obliged to [be] in a state of absolute 'being about to sit down'. She seemed a good deal *gênée* by something of that kind though remembering with pride the have been Empress it might almost be said of the world. The rest for to-morrow.

12 SUNDAY Resumed *Woodstock* and wrote my task of six pages. I was interrupt[ed] by a slumberous feeling which made me obliged to stop once or twice. I shall soon have a remedy in the country which affords the pleasanter resource of a walk when such feelings come on – I hope I am not the reverse of the well known line

Sleepy myself to give my readers sleep.[3]

I cannot gurnalise at any rate having wrought my eyes nearly out.

13 MONDAY Wrote to the end of a chapter. And knowing no more than the Man in the moon what comes next I will put down a few of Lord Elgin's remembrances and something may occur to me in the meanwhile.

When M. Louise first saw Bon. she was in the carriage with his representative Genl. when she saw a horseman ride forward at the

1. Scott made use of this account in *Life of Napoleon*, v. 139–43.
2. *Ethwald*.
3. Pope's *Dunciad*, i. 94.

gallop passing and respassing the carriage in a manner which joined to the behaviour of her companion convinced her who it was especially as he endeavourd with a curiosity which would not have been tolerated in another to peep into the windows. When she alighted at the Inn at ¹Napoleon presented himself, pulld her by the ear and kissd her forehead.

Bonaparte's happiest days passd away when he dismissd from about him such men as Talleyrand and Fouché whose questions and objections compelld him to recur upon, modify and render practicable the grand plans which his ardent conception struck out at a heat. When he had Murat and such persons about him who marveld and obeyd, his schemes equally magnificent were not so well matured and ended in the projector's ruin.

I have hinted in these notes that I am not entirely free from a sort of gloomy fits with a fluttering of the heart and depression of spirits just as if I knew not what was going to befall me. I can sometimes resist this successfully but it is better to evade than to combat it. The Hangdog spirit may have originated in the confusion and chucking about of our old furniture, the stripping of walls of pictures and rooms of ornaments; the leaving a house we have so long calld our home is altogether melancholy enough. I am glad Lady S— does not mind yet and yet I wonder too – She insists on my remaining till Wednesday – not knowing what I suffer.² Meanwhile to make my recusant spirit do penance I have set to work to clear away papers and pack them for my journey. What a strange medley of thoughts such a task produces. There lie letters which made the heart throb when received now lifeless and uninteresting as are perhaps their owners – Riddles which time has read – Schemes which He has destroyd or brought to maturity – memorials of friendships and e[n]mities which are now alike faded. Thus does the ring of Saturn consume itself – Today annihilates yesterday as the old tyrant swallowd his children and the snake its tail – But I must say to my Gurnal as poor Byron did to Moore 'Damn it, Tom, don't be poetical.'³

Memorandm. I received some time since from Mr. Reddoch of Falkirk⁴ a sort of iron mallet said to have been found in the ruins of Graeme's Dike there. It was reclaimd about three months since by the Gentleman on whose lands it was found, a Doctor – by a very polite letter from his man of business.⁵ Having unluckily mislaid his letter and being totally unable either to recollect the name of the

1. Soissons.
2. They had lived at 39 Castle Street for twenty-four years.
3. For this story, see the Entry for 9 February 1826.
4. A slip for 'Halkirk' in Caithness.
5. James Burn, W. S., who had written on 16 December. Walpole.

proprietor or the professional gentleman I returnd this day the piece of antiquity from Mr. Reddoch who sent it to me. Wrote at the same time to Tom Grahame of Airth mentioning what I had done. 'Touch my honour touch my life – there is the Spoon' –[1]

14 TUESDAY J. B. calld this morning to take leave[2] and receive directions about proofs etc. Talks of the uproar about *Malachi* but I am tired of *Malachi* – the humour is off and I have said what I wanted to say and put the people of Scotland on their guard as well as Ministers if they like to be warnd. They are gradually destroying what remains of nationality and making the country *tabula rasa* for doctrines of bold innovation. Their lowering and grinding down all those peculiarities which distinguishd us as Scotsmen will throw the country into a state in which it will be universally turnd to democracy and instead of canny Saunders they will have a very dangerous North British neighbourhood.[3] Some [English] lawyer express[d] to Lord Elibank an opinion that at the union the English Law should have been extended all over Scotland. 'I cannot say how that might have answerd our purpose' said Lord Patrick who was never nonsuited for want of an answer 'but it would scarce have suited *yours* since by this time the *Aberdeen Advocates* would have possessd themselves of all the business in Westminster Hall.'

What a detestable feeling this fluttering of the heart is! I know it is nothing organick and that it is entirely nervous but the sickening effects of it are dispiriting to a degree. Is it the body brings it on the mind or the mind inflicts it upon the body? I cannot tell – but it is a severe price to pay for the *Fata Morgana* with which Fancy sometimes amuses men of warm imaginations. As to body and mind I fancy I might as well enquire whether the fiddle or fiddle-stick makes the tune. In youth this complaint used to throw [me] into involuntary passions of causeless tears. But I will drive it away in the country by exercise. I wish I had been a mechanic – a turning-lathe or a chest of tools would have been a Godsend – for thought makes the access of melancholy rather worse than better. I have it seldom thank God and I believe lightly in comparaison of others.

1. In his edition Douglas tells the story of the old lady suspected of pocketing a silver spoon at an auction sale who, when accused, refused to be searched and with these indignant words produced the spoon.
2. Scott was setting off for Abbotsford the next day.
3. The thought recurs in his letter to Croker a few days later: 'if you *unscotch* us you will find us damned mischievous Englishmen.' *Letters*, ix. 472.

It was the fiddle after all was out of order – not the fiddlestick – the body not the mind. I walkd out, met Mrs. Skene who took a turn with me in Princes Street – Bade Constable and Cadell farewell – and had a brisk walk home which enables me to face the desolation here with more spirit. News from Sophia. She has had the luck to get an anti druggist in a Dr. Gooch[1] who prescribes care for Johnnie instead of drugs and a little home brewd ale instead of wine and like a liberal phisician supplies the medicine he prescribes.

As for myself while I had scarce stird to take exercize for four or five days no wonder I had the mulligrubs. It is an awful sensation though and would have made an enthusiast of me had I indulged my imagination on devotional subjects. I have been always careful to place my mind in the most tranquil posture which it can assume during my private exercizes of devotion.

I have amused myself occasionally very pleasantly during the few last days by reading over Lady Morgan's novel of *O'Donnel*[2] which has some striking and beautiful passages of situation and description and in the comic part is very rich and entertaining. I do not remember being so much pleased with it at first – there is a want of story always fatal to a book the first reading and it is well if it gets the chance of a second – alas poor novel!

Also read again and for the third time at least Miss Austen's very finely written novel of *Pride and Prejudice*. That young lady had a talent for describing the involvements and feelings and characters of ordinary life which is to me the most wonderful I ever met with. The Big Bow wow strain I can do myself like any now going but the exquisite touch which renders ordinary common-place things and characters interesting from the truth of the description and the sentiment is denied to me. What a pity such a gifted creature died so early.[3]

1. Dr. Robert Gooch (1784–1830), an Edinburgh graduate with a special interest in gynaecology. In 1826 he became librarian to the King.

   Scott mistrusted Sophia's reliance on doctors. In a letter to Lockhart (dated 16 but by internal evidence 15 January 1826) he wrote: 'I thought it right to give Sophia a little paternal caution about engaging again with a pet docto[r] which next to a pet parson is an abomination. . . . I think this doctor-loving is Sophias most marked foible.' *Letters*, ix. 368. Such of Sophia's letters as survive are rather too full of the illnesses and ailments, actual and potential, of herself and her family.

2. It was published in 1814.

3. Scott's enthusiasm for Jane Austen is obvious in his review of *Emma* in the *Quarterly* for October 1815. Lockhart says that he used to read aloud from *Emma* and *Northanger Abbey* to the family circle. *Life*, vii. 5 n.

15 WEDNESDAY This morning I leave No 93[1] Castle Street for the last time. 'The cabbin was convenient'[2] and habit had made it agreeable to me. I never reckond upon a change in this particular so long as I held an office in the Court of Session. In all my former changes of residence it was from good to better – this is retrograding. I leave the house for sale and I cease to be an Edinburgh citizen in the sense of being a proprietor – which my father and I have been for sixty years at least. So farewell, poor 93, and may you never harbour worse people than those who now leave you. Not to desert the Lares all at once Lady S. and Anne remain till Sunday – As for me I go as aforesaid this morning.

Ha til mi tullidh.[3]

Abbotsford, 9 at night. The naturally unpleasant feelings which influenced me in my ejectment, for such it is virtually, readily evaporated in the course of the journey though I had no pleasanter companions than Mrs. Mackay the Housekeeper and one of the maids, and I have a shyness of disposition, which looks like pride but is not, which makes me awkward in speaking to my household domestics. With an out of doors labourer or an old woman gathering sticks I can talk for ever. I was wellcomed here on my arrival by the tumult great of men and dogs[4] all happy to see me. One of my old labourers killd by the fall of a stone working at Gattonside foot Bridge. Old Will Straiton, my man of wisdom and proverbs, also dead – he was entertaining from his importance and self conceit but really a sensible old man – When he heard of my misfortunes he went to bed and said he would not rise again and kept his word. He was very infirm when I last saw him. Tom Purdie in great glory being released from all farm duty and destined to attend the woods and be my special assistant. The Gardener Bogie is to take care of what small farm we have left which little would make me give up entirely.

16 THURSDAY Pleasant days make short journals and I have little to say to-day. I wrote in the morning at *Woodstock* – walkd from one till four. Was down at Huntly Burn and paid my respects to the ladies. The spring seems promising and everything in great order. Visited Will Straiton's widow who squezed out among many tears a petition

1. The slip here of '93' for '39' also occurs in letters to both his sons a week earlier. See *Letters,* ix. 451 and 455.
2. Jonson's *Every Man in his Humour,* i. 4.
3. 'I return no more', a Gaelic phrase.
4. Thomson's *Seasons,* 'Summer', l. 277.

for a house. I do not think I shall let her have one as she has a bad temper. But I will help her otherwise. She is greedy besides as was the defunct philosopher William. In a year or two I shall have on the Toft field[1] a gallant show of extensive woodland sweeping over [the] hill and its boundaries carefully conceald. In the evening after dinner read Mrs. Charlotte Smith's novel of *Desmond*,[2] decidedly the worst of her compositions.

17 FRIDAY Sent off a packet to J. B. – only 3 pages copy – so must work hard for a day or two. I wish I could wind up my bottom handsomely (an odd but acc[r]edited phrase) – the conclusion will not be luminous; we must try to make it dashing. Go spin, you jade, go spin. Have a good deal to do between hands in sorting up the newly arrived accession of books and furniture.

I need not have exulted so soon in having attaind ease and quiet. I am robbd of both with a vengeance – A letter from Lockhart with one enclosed from Sophia announces the medical people think the child is visibly losing strength, that its walking becomes more difficult, and in short that the spine seems visibly affected. They recommend tepid baths in Seawater so Sophia has gone down to Brighton leaving Lockhart in town who is to visit her once a week.[3] Here is my worst augury verified. See this Journal 2d. December last. The bitterness of this probably impending calamity is extreme. The child was almost too good for this world, beautiful in features and, though spoild by everyone, having one of the sweetest tempers as well as the quickest intellect I ever saw – a sense of humour quite extraordinary in a child, and owing to the general notice which was taken of him a great deal more information than suited his heirs.[4] He was born in the eighth month and such children are never strong, seldom long-lived – I look on this side and that and see nothing but protracted misery, a crippled frame and decayd constitution occupying the attention of his parents for years and dying at the end of that period when their hearts were turnd on him – Or the poor child may die before Sophia's

1. Part of the Abbotsford Estate.
2. *Desmond* appeared in 1792. For an article written by Scott on Charlotte Smith's novels, see *Misc. Prose Works*, vol. iv.
3. Mrs. Terry went with Sophia, along with two servants, David and Junor. They established themselves first at 60 Marine Parade, but within two days arranged to take lodgings at 25 Preston Street. Brighton was not a success. 'You have no idea how very very uncomfortable it is,' Sophia writes to Lockhart, 'how people can for pleasure come to such places I cannot think.' Sophia, 18, 20, 23 March, Abbots.
4. A slip for 'years'.

confinement and that may again be a dangerous and bad affair – Or she may by increase of attention to him injure her own health – in short to trace into how many branches such a misery may flow is impossible. The poor dear Love had so often a slow fever that when it pressed its little lips to mine I always foreboded to my own heart what all I fear are now aware of.[1]

Lockhart writes me that Croker is the author of the Letters in the *Courier* agt. *Malachi* and that Canning is to make another attack on me in House of Commons. These things would make a man proud. I will not answer because I must show up Sir William Rae[2] and even Lord Melville and I have done enough to draw public attention which is all I want. Let them call me ungrateful unkind and all sort of names so they keep their own fingers free of this most threatening measure. It is very curious that each of these angry friends, Melville, Canning, and Croker, have in former days appealed to me in confidence against each other.

While I smoked my cigar after dinner my mind has been running into four threads of bitter fancies or rather into three decidedly bitter and one that is indifferent – There is the distress incumbent on the country by these most untimely proceedings which I would stop with my life were that adequate to prevent them. 2 There is the unpleasant feeling of seeing a number of valued friends pass from me – that I cannot help – 3 There is the gnawing misery about that sweet child and its parents – 4 There is the necessity of pursuing my own labours for which perhaps I ought to be thankful since it always wrenches one's mind aside from what it must dwell on with pain. It is odd that the state of excitation with me rather increases I think than abates the power of labour. I must finish *Woodstock* well if I can, otherwise how the Philistines will rejoice.

18 SATURDAY Slept indifferently and under the influence of Queen Mab seldom auspicious to me – Dreamd of reading the tale of the Prince of the Black marble islands[3] to little Johnie extended on a paralytic chair and yet telling all his pretty stories about Ha-papa as he calls me and Chiefswood, and waked to think I should see the little darling no more – or see him as a thing that had better never have existed. Oh Misery misery that the best I can wish for him is early death with all the wretchedness to his parents that is like to ensue.

1. The calamity Scott feared was delayed, for Johnnie lived nearly six years more.
2. As Lord Advocate, Rae was the senior Scottish legal representative in Parliament and should, Scott thought, have led opposition to the measure in the House.
3. In *The Arabian Nights*.

I intended to have staid at home to-day but Tom[1] more wisely had resolved that I should walk and hung about the window with his axe and my own in his hand till I turnd out with him and helpd to cut some fine paling.

19 SUNDAY I have a most melancholy letter from Anne. Lady S— the faithful and true companion of my fortunes good and bad for so many years, has but with difficulty been prevaild on to see Dr. Abercromby and his opinion is far from favourable. Her astmhatic [sic] complaints are fast terminating in hydropsy as I have long suspected, yet the avowal of the truth and its probable consequences are overwhelming. They are to stay a little longer in town to try the effects of a new medicine. On Wednesday they propose to return hither. A new afliction where there was enough before. Yet her constitution is so good that if she will be guided by advice things may be yet ameliorated – God grant it, for really these misfortunes come too close upon each other.

A letter from Croker of a very friendly tone and tenor which I will answer accordingly, not failing however to let him know that if I do not reply it is not for fear of his arguments or raillery, far less from diffidence in my cause. I hope and trust it will do good.[2]

Maxpopple[3] and two of his boys arrived to take part of my poor dinner. I fear the little fellows had little more than the needful but they had all I had got to give them.

I wrote a good deal to-day notwithstanding heavy thoughts.

1. Tom Purdie.
2. Croker, whose article contained 'a few personal allusions that might as well have been spared' (*Life*, viii. 242), insisted that his attack on *Malachi* 'has nothing to do with our *private feelings*'. 16 March 1826, Walpole. For Scott's reply, see *Letters*, ix. 471.
3. William Scott of Maxpoffle (1773–1855), eldest son of Scott of Raeburn and Scott's Sheriff-Substitute. Scott described him elsewhere as 'a sort of original which exists here and there in Scotland a good gentleman-like honorable man in all his feelings, but beset with the two great national evils Pride and Poverty. He is a Scottish Hidalgo with a high sense of his own hereditary consequence . . . He has never been able exactly to understand how I came to be a baronet being only a cadet of his family. In short he is a great quizz. But then he has a wife and twelve children and what is worse an old papa who unnaturally persists in foxhunting though upwards of 80 and will not vacate possession of the family estate.' *Letters*, x. 138. No doubt he brought the Sheriff Court Processes on which Scott worked the following day.

20 MONDAY Despatchd proofs and copy this morning and Swanston [and] the carpenter coming in I made a sort of busy idle day of it with altering and hanging pictures and prints to find room for those which came from Edinburgh, and by dint of being on foot from ten to near four put all things into apple-pie order. What strange beings we are. The serious duties I have on hand cannot divert my mind from the most melancholy thoughts and yet the talking with these workmen and the trifling occupation which they give me serves to dissipate my attention. The truth is, I fancy, that a body under the impulse of violent motion cannot be stopd or forced back but may indirectly be urged into a different channel. In the evening I read and sent my sheriff court processes.

I have a sort of grudging to give reasons why Malachi does not reply to the answers which have been sent forth. I don't know – I am strongly tempted – but I won't – To drop the tone might seem mean and perhaps to maintain [it] would only exasperate the quarel without producing any beneficial results and might be considered as a fresh insult by my alienated friends. So on the whole I won't.

The thing has certainly had more effect than it deserves – And I suspect my Ministerial friends if they love me less will not hold me cheaper for the fight I have made. I am far from saying *Oderint dum metuerint*[1] but there is a great difference betwixt that and being a mere protegé – a poor broken-down man who was to be assisted when existing circumstances, that most convenient of all apologies and happiest of all phrases, would permit.

21 TUESDAY Perused an attack on myself with as much ability as truth by no less a man than Joseph Hume the Night-work man of the House of commons who lives upon petty abuses and is a very useful man by so doing. He has had the kindness to say that I am interested in keeping up the taxes. I wish I had any thing else to do with them than to pay them. But he lies and is an ass and not worth a man thinking about. Joseph Hume indeed, I say Joseph Hum and could add a Swiftian Ryhme but forbear.

Busy in unpacking and repacking the wine sent from Edin. It makes me a fine cellar-ful for many a day.

I wrote five pages of *Woodstock* which work begins

To appropinq' an end.[2]

1. Scott's variation of the tyrant's words in Accius: *Oderint dum metuant* – 'Let them hate, provided that they fear' – quoted by Cicero in *Philippics*, i. 14.
2. A favourite quotation of Scott's from Butler's *Hudibras*, pt. i, canto 3, l. 590.

22 WEDNESDAY A letter from Lord Downshire's man of business[1] about funds supposed to belong to my wife or to the estate of my late Brother in law. The possessor of the Secret wants some reward. If any is granted it should be a percentage on the neat sum recoverd, with the condition no cure no pay.[2]

I expect Lady S. and from Anne's last letter hope to find her better than the first anticipations led me to dread.

Sent off proofs and copy and shall indulge a little leisure to-day to collect my ideas and stretch my limbs. I am again far before the press.

23 THURSDAY Lady Scott arrived yesterday to dinner. She was better than I expected but Anne, poor soul, lookd very poorly and had been much worried with the fatigue and discomfort of the last week. Lady S. takes the digitalis and as she thinks with advantage though the medicine makes her very sick. Yet on the whole things are better than my gloom[y] apprehensions had anticipated.

I wrote to Lockhart and to Lady Downshire's Agent T. Handley Esqr., Pentonville, London.[3]

Took a good brushing walk: but not till I had done a good task.

24 FRIDAY Sent off copy, proofs etc. J. B. clamourous for a motto.

Go to.
D—n the mot-toe.[4]

It is foolish to encourage people to expect mottocs and such like Decoraments. You have no credit for success in finding them and there is a disgrace in wanting them. It is like being in the habit of shewing feats of strength which you at length gain no praise by accomplishing while there is some shame occurs in failure.

1. Thomas Handley of Gray's Inn.
2. Handley proposed to pay the 'rogue' 100 guineas, but was able to find the fund himself a week later. (Handley, 24 and 29 April 1826, Walpole). The origin of the fund is obscure. In 1778 a certain Wyrriott Owen mortgaged his estate, the money to be held in trust for Mme Charpentier, Lady Scott's mother, who apparently knew nothing of it. By the time it came to be paid to Lady Scott's children in 1833 it had accumulated to £6300. See Grierson, p. 49.
3. For these letters, apparently dated 21 and 22 March, see *Letters*, ix. 481 and 477. On the 30th Lockhart writes back to say that he has visited Handley as Scott had requested. Abbots.
4. *Woodstock*, unlike most of the earlier novels, has no motto on the title-page, although each chapter (except ch. 7) is headed, as usual, by a short quotation.

25 SATURDAY The end winds out well enough. I have almost finishd to-night – indeed I might have done so had I been inclined but I had a walk in a hurricane of snow for two hours and feel a little tired. Miss Margaret Fergusson came to dinner with us.

26 SUNDAY Here is a disagreeable morning, snowing and hailing with gleams of bright sunshine between and all the ground white and all the air frozen. I don't like this jumbling of weather. It is ungenial and gives chilblains. Besides with its whiteness and its coldness and its glister and its discomfort it resembles that most disagreeable of all things, a vain cold empty beautiful woman who has neither head nor heart but only features like a doll. I do not know but it is like this disagreeable day when the sun is so bright, and yet so uninfluential that

> One may gaze upon its beams
> Till he is starved with cold.[1]

No matter: it will serve as well as another day to finish *Woodstock*. Walkd ought[2] to the lake[3] and coquetted with this disagreeable weather whereby I catch chill-blains on my fingers and cold in my head. Fed the Swans.

Finishd *Woodstock* however *cum tota sequela* of title page introduction etc. and so as Dame Fortune says in Quevedo

> Go wheel and may the Devil drive thee.[4]

27 MONDAY Another bright cold day. I answerd two modest requests from widow Ladies – One whom I had already assisted on some law business on the footing of her having visited my mother requested me to write to Mr. Peele saying on her authority that her second son, a youth of infinite merit and accomplishment, was fit for any situation in a public office and that I requested he might be provided accordingly. Another widowd dame whose claim is having read *Marmion* and the *Lady of the Lake* besides a promise to read all my other works – Gad it is a rash engagement – demands that I shall either pay £200 to get her cub into some place or other or settle him in a seminary of education. Really this is very much after the fashion of the husbandman of Miguel Turra's requests of Sancho when

1. Unidentified.
2. A slip for 'out'.
3. Cauldshiels Loch, on the Abbotsford Estate.
4. *Fortune in her Wits*, iii. 107.

Governor. 'Have you any thing else to ask, honest Man?' quoth Sancho.[1] But what are the demands of an honest man to those of an honest woman and she a widow to boot? I do believe your destitute widow, especially if she hath a charge of children and one or two fit for patronage, is one of the most impudent animals living.

Went to Galashiels and settled the dispute about Sandie's Well. Lodged with George Craig[2] cash being the quarter's salary minus £20 advanced to Charles ————————————————— £230

               Deduced overdrawn replaced —— £150

Cash Lady Scott £20. Cash received and payable to Lady
               Scott ————————————— 20

                                     170
Remains balance   —————— £60

28 TUESDAY We have now been in solitude for some time – myself nearly totally so excepting at meals or on a call as yesterday from Henry and William Scotts of Harden. One is tempted to ask himself, knocking at the door of his own heart, Do you love this extreme loneliness? I can answer conscientiously *I do*. The love of Solitude was with me a passion of early youth when in my teens I used to fly from company to indulge visions and airy Castles of my own, the disposal of ideal wealth and the exercize of imaginary power. This feeling prevaild even till I was eighteen when Love and Ambition awaking with other passions threw me more into society, from which I have however at times withdrawn myself and have been always glad to do so. I have risen from a feast satiated and unless it be one or two persons of very strong intellect or whose spirits and goodhumour amuse me I wish neither to see the high the low nor the middling class of society. This is a feeling without the least tinge of misanthropy which I always consider as a kind of blasphemy of a shocking description. If God bears with the very worst of us we may surely endure each other. If thrown into society I always have and always will endeavour to bring pleasure with me, at least to shew willingness to please. But for all this 'I had rather live alone' and I wish my appointment so convenient otherwise did not require my going to Edinburgh. But this must be and in my little lodging I will be lonely enough.

Had a very kind letter from Croker disowning the least idea of personal attack in his answer to *Malachi*.

Reading at intervals a novel called *Grandby*[3] one of that very

1. *Don Quixote*, pt. ii, ch. 47.
2. George Craig, agent of the Leith Bank in Galashiels.
3. *Granby*, by T. H. Lister, 1826.

difficult class which aspires to describe the actual current of society; whose colours are so evanescent that it is difficult to fix them on the canvas. It is well written but over labourd – too much attempt to put the reader exactly up to the thoughts and sentiments of the parties – The women do this better – Edgeworth, Ferrier, Austen have all had their portraits of real society far superior to anything Man vain Man has produced of the like nature.

29 WEDNESDAY Workd in the morning – Had two visits from Colonels Russell and Fergusson. Walkd from one till half past four. A fine flashy disagreeable day, snow clouds sweeping past among sunshine, driving down the valley and whitening the country behind them.

Mr. Gibson came suddenly in after dinner. Brought very indifferent news from Constable's House. It is not now hoped that they will pay above 3/- or 4/- in the pound. Robinson supposed not to be much better [1]

Mr. G. goes to London immediately and is to sell *Woodstock* to Robinson if they can [pay] otherwise to those who will.[2] John Murray is [one such]. This work may fail perhaps though better than some of its predecessors. If so we must try some new manner. I think I could catch the dogs yet.

A beautiful and perfect lunar rainbow to-night.

30 THURSDAY Mr. Gibson looks unwell and complains of cold – Bitter bad weather for his travelling and he looks but frail.

These indifferent news he brought me affect me but to a little degree. It is being too confident to hope to ensure success in the long series of successive struggles which lies before me but somehow I do fully entertain the hope of doing a good deal.

31 FRIDAY

> He walk'd and wrote, poor soul, what then?
> Why then he wrote and walkd again.[3]

1. In the end Constable paid 2s. 9d. in the pound, and Hurst Robinson 1s. 3d.
2. The following evening 'Mr. Robinson arrived from London' and agreed to give £6500 for 7900 copies of *Woodstock*, 'the money to be payable in cash before delivery of the books'. Sederunt Book, i. 88. He was not, however, able to pay, and the novel was in the end published by Longman.
3. A parody of Prior's 'Epitaph' beginning 'Interr'd beneath this marble stone'.

But I am begun *Nap. Bon.* again which is always a change because it gives me a good deal of reading and research whereas *Woodstock* and such like being extempore from my mother wit is a sort of spinning of the brains of which a man tires. The weather seems milder to-day.

APRIL

1 SATURDAY *Ex uno die disce omnes.*[1] Rose at seven or soon[er], studied and wrote till breakfast with Anne about 1/2 before 10. Lady Scott seldom able to rise till 12 or one. Then I write and study again till one. At that hour to-day I drove to Huntly Burn and walkd home by one of the hundred and one pleasing paths which I have made through the woods I have planted, now chatting with Tom Purdie who carries my plaid and speaks when he pleases telling long stories of hits and misses in shooting twenty years back – sometimes chewing the cud of sweet and bitter fancy[2] – and sometimes attending to the humours of two curious little terriers of the Dandie Dinmont breed together with a noble wolf-hound puppy which Glengarry has given me to replace Maida. This brings me down to the very moment I do tell – the rest is prophetic. I will feel sleepy when this book is lockd and perhaps sleep untill Dalgleish brings the dinner summons. Then I will have a chat with Lady S. and Anne, some broth or soup, a slice of plain meat, and man's chief business in Dr. Johnson's estimation is briefly despatchd. Half an hour with my family and half an hour coquetting with a cigar, a tumbler of weak whisky and water, and a novel perhaps, lead on to tea which sometimes consumes another half hour of chat – then write and read in my own room till ten o'clock at night – a little bread and cheese, a glass of porter, and to bed.[3]

And this very rarely varied by a visit from some one is the tenor of my daily life, and a very pleasant one indeed were it not for apprehension about Lady S. and poor Johnie Hugh.[4] The former will I think do well – for the latter – I fear – I fear—

2 SUNDAY I am in a wayward humour this morning. I received yesterday the last proof Sheets of *Woodstock* and I ought to correct them. Now this *ought* sounds as like as possible to *must* and *must* I cannot abide. I would go to Prester John's country[5] of free good will

---

1. 'From this one day learn about them all' – a reminiscence of *Aeneid*, ii. 65.
2. *As You Like It*, iv. 3.
3. For another account of Scott's daily life at this time, written by his butler, see Note 5, p. 808.
4. His grandson Johnnie Lockhart.
5. Abyssinia or the Far East, depending upon which version of the legend Scott preferred.

sooner than I would *must* it to Edinburgh. Yet this is all folly and silly folly too and so Must shall be for once obeyd after I have thus written myself out of my aversion to its peremptory sound. – Corrected the said proofs till twelve o'clock when I think I will treat Resolution not to a dram as the drunken fellow said after he had passed the dram shop but to a walk, the rather that my eyesight is somwhat uncertain and wavering. I think it must be from the stomach; the whole page walzes before my eyes. J. B. writes gloomily about *Woodstock* – but commends the conclusion. I think he is right. Besides my manner is nearly caught and like Captain Bobadil I have taught nearly a hundred gentlemen to fence very nearly if not altogether as well as myself.[1] I will strike out something new.

3 MONDAY I have from Ballantyne and Gibson the extraordinary and gratifying news that *Woodstock* is sold for £8228 in all.

That is Hurst and Robinson ——————— £1728 ⎫[2]
Woodstock ——————————— 6500 ⎭

All for ready money – a matchless sale for less than three months' work. If *Napoln.* does as well or near it; it will put the Trust affairs in high flourish. Four or five years of leisure and industry would with success amply replace my losses and put me on a steadier footing than ever. I have a curious fancy. I will go set two or three acorns and judge by their success in growing whether I will succeed in clearing my way or not. I have a little tooth-ache keeps me from working much to-day, besides I se[n]t off per Blucher[3] copy for *Napoleon* as well as the damnd proofs –

1. *Every Man in his Humour*, iv. 5.
2. This is confused and meaningless. For 'Hurst and Robinson' read 'Cowan' (Constable's Trustee); for 'Woodstock' read 'Hurst, Robinson'. The bargain Gibson made with Robinson on his visit to Edinburgh, according to the letter to which Scott is referring, was as follows:

   'Mr Cowan is to pay in cash for his 1950 copies of
   Woodstock — £1728 ⎫ £8228 in all.'
   Hurst & Co — 6500 ⎭

   Gibson, 1 April 1826, Walpole.

   The cost of paper and printing had of course to be deducted from this sum. Gibson went to London to accept payment on 12 April, by which time Robinson had been forced to let Longman take up his share.
3. The coach which ran between Edinburgh and Jedburgh, via Melrose, thrice a week.

A blank forenoon but how could I help it, Madam Duty? – I was not lazy, on my soul I was not – I did not cry for half-holiday for the sale of *Woodstock*. But in came Colonel Fergusson with Mrs. Stewart of Blackhill or hall or something, and I must shew her the garden, pictures etc. This lasts till one, and just as they are at their lunch and obliged to go off, guard is relieved by the Laird and Lady Harden and Miss Eliza Scott; and my dear chief whom I love very much though [he] is a little obsidional or so remains till three. That same crown[1] composed of the grass which grew on the walls of besieged places should be offerd to visitors who stay above an hour in any decent person's house.

Wrote letters this evening.

4[2] TUESDAY Wrote two pages in the morning – then went to Ashestiel in the Sociable with Colonel Ferguson. Found my cousin Russell setled keenly to his gardening and his projects. He seems to have brought home with him the enviable talent of being interested and happy in his own place and projects. Ashestiel looks waste I think at this period of the year but is a beautiful place in summer where I passd nine happy years.[3] – Did I ever pass unhappy years any where? None that I remember save those at the High school which I thoroughly detested on account of the confinement – I disliked serving in my father's office too from the same hatred to restraint. In other respects I have had unhappy days, unhappy weeks – even on one or two occasions unhappy months – but Fortune's Finger[4] has never been able to play a dirge on me for a quarter of a year together.

I am sorry to see the Peel wood and other natural coppice decaying and abridged about Ashestiel.

> The horrid plough has razed the green
>   Where once my children plaid
> The axe has fell'd the haw[t]horn screen
>   The school-boy's summer shade.[5]

There was a very romantic pasturage called the Cow-park which I was particularly attachd to from its wild and sequestred character. Having

1. '*Corona obsidionalis*'. Tait.
2. '5' in the original.
3. Scott leased Ashestiel from his cousin James Russell from 1804 to 1811.
4. An allusion to *Hamlet*, iii. 2.
5. 'These lines slightly altered from Logan.' J. G. L. They occur in 'A Tale', st. 78.

been part of an old wood which had been cut down it was full of copse and hazel and oak and all sorts of young trees irregularly scatterd over fine pasturage and affording a hundred intricacies so delicious to the eye and the imagination. But some misjudging friend had cut down and cleard away without mercy and divided the varied and sylvan scene – which was divided by a little rivulet into the two most formal things in nature, a *thriving* plantation many-angled as usual and a park *laid down in grass* wanting therefore the rich graminivorous variety which nature gives it[s] carpet and having instead a beard of six days' growth, lean and hungry growth too – of rye-grass and clover – As for the rill it stagnates in a deep square ditch which silences its prattle and restrains its meanders with a witness. The original scene was of course imprinted deeper on Russell's mind than mine and I was glad to see he was intensely sorry for the change.

5 WEDNESDAY Rose late in the morning past eight – to give the cold and toothache time to make themselves scarce which they have obligingly done. Yesterday every tooth on the left [*deleted*] no – the right side of my head was absolutely walzing. I would have drawn by the half dozen but country dentists are not to be *lippend* to.[1] To-day all is quiet but a little swelling and stiffness in the jaw. Went to Chiefswood at one and markd with regret forty trees indispensably necessary for paling. Much like drawing a tooth – but they *are* wanted and will never be better but I am avaricious of grown trees having so few.

Workd a fair task – dined and read Clapperton's journey and Denman's into Bornou[2] – very entertaining and less botheration about mineralogy botany and so forth than usual. Pity Africa picks up so many brave men however.

Work in the evening.

6 THURSDAY Wrote in the morning – went at one to Huntley Burn where I had the great pleasure to hear through a letter from Sir Adam[3] that Sophia was in health and Johnie gaining strength. It is a fine exchange from deep and aching uncertainty on so interest[ing] a subject to the little Spitfire feeling of 'Well but they might have taken

---

1. '*Lippened*, i.e. relied upon.' J. G. L.
2. *Narrative of Travels in Northern and Central Africa in 1822, 1823 and 1824* by Major Denham, Captain Clapperton, and Doctor Oudney, 1826. Scott was much taken by these travels. On 10 June they were his chief topic of conversation with Captain Basil Hall, who had recently met Denham. *Life*, viii. 364.
3. Sir Adam Ferguson had been in Brighton.

the trouble to write'; but so wretched a correspondent as myself has not much to say so I will just grumble sufficiently to maintain the patriarchal dignity.

I returnd in time to work and to receive a shoal of things from J. B. Among others a letter from an Irish Lady who, for the *beaux yeux* which I shall never look upon, desires I will forthwith send her all the Waverley Novels which are publishd with an order to furnish her with all others in course as they appear which she assures me will be an aera in her life. She may find out some other epocha.

7 FRIDAY Made out my morning's task – At one drove to Chiefswood and walkd home by the Rymer's Glen, Mar's Lee and Haxellcleugh.[1] Took me three hours – the heath gets somewhat heavier for me every year – but never mind, I like it altogether as well as the day I could tread it best. My plantations are getting all into green leaf, especially the larches if theirs may be called leaves which are only a sort of hair. And from the number of birds drawn to these wastes I may congratulate myself on having litterally made the desert to sing. As I returnd there was in the phraseology of that prince of prigs in a white collarless coat and Chapeau-Bras Mister Commissary Ramsay 'a rather dense inspissation of rain.' Deil Care.

> Lord, who would live moiled in the Court
> That might enjoy such quiet walks as these?[2]

Yet misfortune comes our way too. Poor Laidlaw lost a fine prattling child of five years old yesterday.

It is odd enough. Iden the Kentish Esquire has just made the ejaculation which I adopted in the last page when he kills Cade and posts away up to court to get the price set upon his head. Here is a letter come from Lockhart full of Court news and all sort of news – best is his wife is well and thinks the child gains in health.

Lockhart erroneously supposes that I think of applying to Ministers about Charles and that notwithstanding Croker's terms of pacification I should find *Malachi* stick in my way. I would not make such an application for millions. I think if I were to ask patronage it would [not] be through them for some time at least, and I might have better access.[3]

1. Parts of the Abbotsford Estate.
2. *2 Henry VI*, iv. 10.
3. 'In a letter of the same day he says, "My interest, as you might have known, lies Windsor-way".' J. G. L.

8 SATURDAY We expect a *raid* of folks to visit us this morning whom we must have *dined* before our misfortunes. Save time wine and money these misfortunes and so far are convenient things. Besides there is a dignity about them when they come only like the Gout in its mildest shape to authorize the dignity of diet and retirement, the night gown and the velvet shoe. When the one comes to chalkstones and the other to prison though, there would be the devil. Or compare the effects of Surre Gout and absolute poverty upon the stomack – the necessity of a bottle of laudanum in the one case, the want of a morsel of meat in the other.

Laidlaw's infant died on Wednesday is buried to-day. The people coming to visit prevent my going and I am glad of it. I hate funerals – always did. There is such a mixture of mummery with real grief – the actual mourner perhaps heart broken and all the rest making solemn faces and whispering observations on the weather and public news and here and there a greedy fellow enjoying the cake and wine. To me it is a farce full of most tragical mirth[1] and I am not sorry (like Provost Coulter)[2] but glad that I shall not see my own. This is a most unfilial tendency of mine for my father absolutely loved a funeral and as he was a man of a fine presence and lookd the mourner well he was asked to every interment of distinction. He seemd to preserve the list of a whole bead roll of cousins merely for the pleasure of being at their funerals, which he was often asked to superintend and I suspect had sometimes to pay for. He carried [me] with him as often as he could to these mortuary ceremonies, but feeling I was not like him either useful or ornamental I escaped as often as I could.

I saw the poor child's funeral from a distance – Ah that Distance! what a magician for conjuring up scenes of joy or sorrow, smoothing all asperities, reconciling all incongruities, veiling all absurdness, softening every coar[se]ness, doubling every effect by the influence of the imagination. A Scottish wedding should be seen at a distance, the gay bound of the dancers just distinguishd amid the elderly groupe of the spectators – the glass held high and the distant cheers as it is swallowd should be only a sketch, not a finishd Dutch picture when it becomes brutal and boorish. Scottish psalmody too should [be] hea[r]d from a distance – The grunt and the snufle and the whine and the scream should be all blended in that deep and distant sound which rising and falling like the Eolian harp may have some title to be called the praise of our maker, – Even so the distant funeral, the few

---

1. *Midsummer Night's Dream*, v. 1.
2. A Lord Provost of Edinburgh who died in office, greatly
   consoled by the thought of the grand funeral that would follow.
   Life, iii. 217 n.

mourners on horseback, with their plaids wrapd around them. The father heading the procession as they enterd the river and pointing out the ford by which his darling was to be carried on the last long road – not [one] of the subordinate figures in discord with the general tone of the incident – the presence of the mourners seeming just accessories and no more to the general purpose of the procession, this is affecting – to be in the midst of the bustle is incongruous and unpleasant from the contradictions which it involves.

9 SUNDAY I workd at correcting proofs[1] in the morning and what harder is at correcting Manuscript which fags me excessively. I was dead sick of it by two o'clock the rather as my hand, O revered Gurnal, be it said between ourselves gets daily worse.

Have a letter from Mr. Handley which holds out some hope of Lady Scott's money being forth coming. It is a fund in Chancery and amounts or is stated to amount to about £4000 which would be a Godsend.

Lockhart's *Review* – Don't like his article of Sheridan's Life.[2] There is no breadth in it, no general views – the whole flung away in smart but party criticism. Now no man can take more general and liberal views of literature than J. G. L. But he lets himself too easily into that advocatism of stile which is that of a pleader not a judge or a critic and is particularly unsatisfactory to the reader. Lt. Colonel Fergusson dined here.

10 MONDAY Sent off proofs and copy galore before breakfast and might be able to give idleness a day if I liked. But it is as well reading for *Boney* as for any thing else and I have a humour to make my amusement useful. Then the day is changeable with gusts of wind and I believe a start to the garden will be my best out of doors exercize. No thorough hill expedition in this gusty weather.

11 TUESDAY Wrought out my task although I have been much affected this morning by the *Morbus* as I call it. Aching pain in the back rendering one posture intolerable, fluttering of the heart – idle fears gloomy thoughts and anxieties which if not unfounded are at least bootless. I have been out once or twice but am driven in by the rain. Mercy on us what poor devils we are! I shook this affection off

---

1. Since 'the last proof-sheets of *Woodstock*' were sent back corrected on 3 April, these must be proofs of the *Life of Napoleon.*
2. The review of Moore's *Life of Sheridan* in the *Quarterly*, no. 66, for which Scott sent some material on 29 December 1825.

however. Mr. Scrope and Colonel Fergusson came to dinner and we twaddled away the evening well enough.

12 WEDNESDAY I have finishd my task this morning at half past eleven, easily and early and I think not amiss. I hope J. B. will make some great points of admiration!!! Otherwise I will be disappointed. If this work answers – if it *but* answers it must set us on our legs. I am sure worse trumpery of mine has had a great run. Well I will console myself and do my best. But fashion changes and I am getting old and may become unpopular. But it [is] time to cry out when I am hurt. I remember with what great difficulty I was brought to think myself something better than common and now I will not in mere faintness of heart give up good hopes. So fortune protect the bold. I have finishd the whole introductory sketch of the Revolution[1] – too long for an introduction. But I think I may now go to my solitary walk.

13 THURSDAY On my return from my walk yesterday I learnd with great concern the death of my old friend Sir Alexr. Don which was shortly after confirmed. He cannot be above six or seven and forty. Without being much together we lived considering our different habits in much friendship together and I sincerely regret his death. His habits were those of a gay man much connected with the turf, but he possessd strong natural parts and in particular few men could speak better in public when he chose. He had tact, wit, power of sarcasm and that indescribable something which marks the gentleman. His manners in society were extremely pleasing and as he had a taste for literature and the fine arts there were few more pleasant companions, besides being a highly spirited, steady and honourable man. His indolence prevented his turning these good parts towards acquiring the distinction he might have attaind. He was among the *détenus* whom Bonaparte's iniquitous commands confind so long in France[2] and becoming there in possession of a large estate in right of his mother, the heiress of the Glencairn family, he had the means of

1. In other words he had finished the first two volumes of the *Life of Napoleon.*
2. Scott may have had Don in mind when he wrote: 'The mass of individual evil occasioned by this cruel measure was incalculably great. Twelve years, a large proportion of human life, were cut from that of each of these *Detenus*, as they were called, so far as regarded settled plan, or active exertion. Upon many, the interruption fell with fatal influence, blighting all their hopes and prospects; others learned to live only for the passing day, and were thus deterred from habitual study or useful industry.' *Life of Napoleon*, v. 78.

being very expensive and probably then acquired those gay habits which renderd him averse to serious business. Being our Member for Roxburgh Shire his death will make a stir amongst us. I prophesy Harden will be here to talk about starting his son Henry.

Accordingly the Laird and Lady calld. I exhorted him to write to Lord Montagu[1] instantly. I do not see what they can do better and unless some pick-thank intervene to insinuate certain irritating suspicions I suppose Lord M— will make no objection. There can be no objection to Henry Scott for birth, fortune or political principle, and I do not see where they can get a better representative.

14 FRIDAY Wrote to Lord M.[2] last night. I hope they will keep the peace in the County. I am sure it would be to me a most distressing thing if Buccleuch and Harden were to pull different ways being so intimate with both families.

I did not write much yesterday – not above two pages and a half – I have begun *Boney*[3] though and *c'est toujours quelque chose*. This morning I sent off proofs and manuscript. Had a letter from the famous Denis Davidoff, the Black Captain,[4] whose abilities as a partizan were so much distinguishd during the retreat from Moscow – If I can but wheedle him out of a few anecdotes it would be a great hawl.

A kind letter from Colin MacK—[5] he thinks the Ministry will not push the measure against Scotland.[6] I fear they will; there is usually an obstinacy in weakness – But I will think no more about it.

Time draws on. I have been here a month – Another month carries me to be a hermit in the city instead of the country. I could scarce think I had been here a week. I wish I was able even at great loss to retire from Edinburgh entirely. Here is no bile – no visits no routine – And yet on the whole things are as well perhaps as they are.

1. As the representative of the most powerful Tory family in the county, the Buccleuchs.
2. Lord Montagu. The letter is in Disc. i. 75.
3. This strange reference to a book he had begun the previous year is explained by this day's letter to Ballantyne: 'I am getting on with the actual life at last. The Introduction which it is a joke to call such will run I fear some way into the third volume.' *Letters*, ix. 508.
4. Delighted at his nephew's report that he is 'l'objet de l'interêt du premier genie de ce siecle.' 10 March 1826, Walpole.
5. Colin Mackenzie.
6. The measure against the banks which *Malachi* was designed to avert.

15 SATURDAY Received last night letters from Sir John Scott Douglas and from that daintiest of Dandies Sir William Elliot of Stobbs[1] canvassing for the County. Young Harry's[2] the lad for me. But will he be the lad for Lord Montagu? – there is the point. I should have given him a hint to attend to Edgerstane[3] – perhaps being at Minto and not there may give offence and a bad report from that quarter would play the D—l. It is rather too late to go down and tell them this and to say truth I don't like the air of making myself busy in the matter.

Poor Sir Alexander Don died not of a cramp in the stomach as was supposed but of a disease in the heart. The body was opened which was very right. Odd enough too to have a man, probably a friend two days before, slashing at one's heart as it were a bullock's.

I had a letter yesterday from John Gibson. The House of Longman and Coy guarantee the sale to Hurst and take the work if Hurst and Robinson (as is to be feard) can make no play.[4]

Also I made up what was due of my task both for thirteenth and fourteenth so hey for a Swiftianism.

> I loll in my chair
> And around me I stare
> With a critical air
> Like a calf at a fair
> And say I, Mistress Duty,
> Good-morrow to your beauty
> I kiss your sweet shoe-tie
> And hope I can suit ye.

Fair words butter no parsnips, says Duty; don't keep talking then but get to your work again. Here is a day's task before you, the Siege of Toulon.[5] Call you that a task? d— me I'll write it as fast as Boney carried it on.

1. 'I suppose he will have his own vote his factors & perhaps not certainly his brothers.' Buccleuch, 14 April 1826, Disc. i. 75.
2. Henry Scott of Harden.
3. John Rutherford of Edgerstone was Vice-lieutenant of the county.
4. 'It seems very doubtful whether Hurst & Co will be able to pay the money. If they are able to do it when the book arrives, Longman & Co will let them have it, for the latter have entered into the arrangement to accommodate Hurst & Co. If they are not able to pay the money, then Longman & Co dispose of the work themselves.' Gibson, 12 April 1826, Walpole.
5. *Life of Napoleon*, vol. iii, ch. 2.

16 SUNDAY I am now far ahead with *Nap*. I wrote a little this morning but this forenoon I must write letters, a task in which I am far behind.

Heaven sure sent letters for some witches plague.[1]

Lady Scott seems to make no way – yet can scarce be said to lose any – She suffers much occasionally, especially during the night – sleeps a great deal when at ease. All symptoms announce water upon the chest. A sad prospect.

In the evening a despatch from Lord Melville written with all the familiarity of former times desiring me to ride down and press Mr. Scott of Harden to let Henry stand and this in Lord Montagu's name as well as his own. So that the two propositions cross each other on the road and Henry is as much desired by the Buccleuch interest as he desires their support. I am very glad of it.

Sent off £10 to Mrs. Bohte bookseller's widow to pay an accompt due to her late husband.

Craig	£60
Draugh[t]	10
Ball.	£50

17 MONDAY Came over to Jedburgh this morning to breakfast with my good old friend Mr. Shortreed[2] and had my usual warm reception. Lord Gillies held the circuit court and there was no criminal trial for any offence whatsoever. I have attended these circuits with tolerable regularity since 1792 and though there is seldom much of importance to be done yet I never remember before the Porteous roll[3] being quite blank. The judge was presented with a pair of white gloves in consideration of its being a maiden circuit. Harden came over and talkd about his son's preferment naturally much pleased.

Received £100 from John Lockart for review of Pepyss[4] but this

1. Suggested by Pope's 'Eloisa to Abelard', l. 51.
2. Robert Shortreed (1762–1829), Sheriff-Substitute of Roxburghshire. Scott was introduced to him in 1792 and for seven successive years they raided Liddesdale together in search of ballads. Scott enjoyed his hospitality whenever he was in Jedburgh, and interested himself in settling a number of his sons.
3. The Porteous Roll: 'A roll of the names of offenders, which, by the old practice of the Justiciary Court, was prepared by the Justice-Clerk from the informations of crimes furnished to him or his deputies, by the local authorities, in the different districts comprehended within the circuits.' *Bell's Dictionary and Digest*. The name is thought to be derived from the practice of giving the names to the judge as he arrived at the town gate (*in portu*).
4. Published in the March *Quarterly*, no. 66.

is by far too much. £50 is plenty. Still I must impeticos the gratility¹ for the present for Whitsunday will find me only with £300 in hand unless Blackwood settles a few scores of pounds for *Malachi*.

Wrote a great many letters.² Dined with the Judge where I met the disappointed candidate Sir John Scott Douglas who took my excuse like a gentleman. Sir William Elliot on the other hand was, being a fine man, very much out of sorts that having got his own consent he could not get that of the County. He shewd none of this however to me.

18 TUESDAY This morning I go down to Kelso from Jedburgh to poor Don's funeral. It is I suppose forty years since I saw him first. I was staying at Sydenham,³ a lad of fourteen or by'r lady some sixteen⁴ and he, a boy of six or seven, was brought to visit me on a pony, a groom holding the leading rein – and now I, an old grey man, am going to lay him in his grave. Sad work – I detest funerals – there is always a want of consistency – it is a tragedy playd by strolling performers who are more likely to make you laugh than cry. No chance of my being made to laugh to-day. The very road I go is a road of grave recollections. Must write to Charles seriously on the choice of his profession and will do it now.⁵

19 WEDNESDAY Returnd last night from the House of death and mourning to my own, now the habitation of sickness and anxious apprehension. Found Lady S. had tried the fox glove in quantity till it made her so sick she was forced to desist. The result cannot yet be judged. Wrote to Mrs. Thos. Scott to beg her to let her daughter Anne an uncommonly sensible steady and sweet temperd girl come

1. *Twelfth Night*, ii. 3.
2. See *Letters*, x. i. for Scott's letter to Walter.
3. A house near Kelso.
4. *1 Henry IV*, ii. 4.
5. He offers him the choice of the English or Scottish Bar, or of the diplomatic service; the army is out of the question and he hopes he will not choose the Church. 'I have nothing to say against it but it is against my principles and feelings to recommend it.' *Letters*, x. 5. Charles did not much like the tone of this letter which accused him of lacking ambition and exertion, and he blamed Lockhart for reporting ill of him to his father. *Letters*, x. 28 n.

and stay with us a season in our distress.[1] Sent her £100 No 6567,[2] £50 to accompt of her Mrs. Thos Scott £100 allowance from me, the other £50 for travelling expences to Anne who I trust will come forthwith.

Two melancholy things – Last night I left my pallet in our family apartment to make way for a female attendant, and removed to a dressing-room adjoining. When to return or whether ever God only can tell. Also my servant cut my hair which used to be poor Charlotte's personal task. I hope she will not observe it.

The funeral yesterday was very mournful – About 50 persons present and all seemd affected. The domestics in particular were very much so. Sir Alexr. was a kind though an exact Master. It was melancholy to see those apartments where I have so often seen him play the graceful and kind landlord filld with those who were to carry him to his long home.

There was very little talk of the Election, at least till the funeral was over.

20 THURSDAY Lady Scott's health in the same harassing state of uncertainty yet on my side with more of hope than I had two days since.

Another death – Thos. Riddell younger of Camiston, Sergeant Major of the Edinburgh Troop in the merry days of our yeomanry[3] and a very good fellow.

The day was so tempting that I went out with Tom Purdie to cut some trees the rather that my task was very well advanced. He led me into the wood as the blind King of Bohemia was led by his four knights into the thick of the battle at Agincourt or Cressy and then like the old King 'I struck good strokes more than one'[4] which is manly exercize.

21 FRIDAY This day I entertaind more flattering hopes of Lady Scott's health than late events permitted. I went down to Mertoun with Colonel Fergusson, who returnd to dine here which consumed time so much that I made a short day's work.

1. For Scott's letter see *Letters*, x. 7. Anne arrived on 4 May and stayed until August. 'She is a very aimiable girl and very quiet which is very agreeable to me just now', writes Anne to Lockhart on 1 July 1826. 'If it had been Missie she would have talked and laughed so much I could not have borne it.' Abbots.
2. The two halves of the note were sent in separate letters. *Letters*, x. 7 and 10.
3. In 1797.
4. Froissart, bk. 1, ch. 129.

Had the grief to find Lady S. had insisted on coming downstairs and was the worse of it – Also a letter from Lockhart giving a poor account of the infant.[1] God help us – earth cannot.

22 SATURDAY Lady Scott continues very poorly. Better news of the child.[2]

Wrought a good deal to-day rather correcting sheets and acquiring information than actually composing which is the least toilsome of the three.

J. G. L. kindly points out some solecisms in my stile – as *amid* for *amidst, scarce* for *scarcely. Whose* he says is the proper genitive of *which* only at such times as *which* retains its quality of impersonification. Well! I will try to remember all this. But after all I write grammar as I speak, to make my meaning known, and a solecism in point of composition like a Scotch word in speaking is indifferent to me. I never learnd grammar and not only Sir Hugh Evans but even Mrs. Quickly might puzzle me about Jinnie's case and Horum harum horum.[3] I believe the Bailiff in *The Goodnatured Man* is not far wrong when he says 'One man has one way of expressing himself and another another – and that is all the difference between them.'[4]

23 SUNDAY Went to Huntley Burn to-day and lookd at the Colonel's projected approach. I am sure if the kind heart can please himself he will please me.[5]

A glorious day – bright and brilliant and I fancy mild.

Lady Scott is certainly better and has promised not to attempt quitting her room.

Henry Scott has been here and his canvas comes on like a moor-burning. I did the Assistants at Don's funeral too much honour when I recorded their abstaining from the affairs of the living even while shovelling the earth in upon the dead – One Gentleman, Mr. I. of H:[6] who had eat of poor Don's loaf and drunk of his cup almost daily – his toad-eater and bottle holder – just when the sod was clapd down with

---

1. Walter Scott Lockhart, born three weeks premature on the 16th.
2. Who, after an anxious day, 'began to pick up wonderfully'. Lockhart, 19 April 1826, Walpole.
3. *Merry Wives of Windsor*, iv. 1.
4. Goldsmith's *Good-natured Man*, Act iii.
5. As Scott owned Huntly Burn, any improvements suggested by the Fergusons would require his consent.
6. Probably George Burnet Innes, son of Gilbert Innes of Stow. Dr. Corson points out to me that the description of him in the Entry for 5 July 1830 would justify Scott's use of the term 'bottle holder'.

the spade took Henry Scott by the arm and with his foot on the grave of this friend who make[s] the vacancy which Henry wishes to fill said '*Now* I can wish you joy.' Henry shrunk from him with loathing. I wonder if there be any cause in nature for these hard hearts, as Lear says.[1]

24 MONDAY Good news from Brighton. Sophia and child both doing well and the child's name is announced to be Walter[2] a favourite name in our family, and I trust of no bad omen. Yet it is no charm for life; of my father's family I was the second Walter if not the third. I am glad the name came my way for it was born by my father, great grandfather and great great grandfather. Also by the grandsire of that last-named venerable person who was the first Laird of Raeburn.

Hurst and Robinson the Yorkshire tyke have faild after all their swaggering and Longman and Coy take *Woodstock*.[3] But if *Woodstock* and *Napoleon* take with the public I shall care little about their insolvency. And if they do not I don't think their solvency would have lasted long. Constable is sorely broken down.

> Poor fool and knave, I have one part in my heart
> That's sorry yet for thee –[4]

His conduct has not been what I deserved at his hand but I believe that walking blindfold himself he misled me without malice prepense. It is best to think so at least unless the contrary be demonstrated. To nourish angry passions against a man whom I really liked would be to lay a blister on my own heart.[5]

25 TUESDAY Having fallen behind on the 23d. I wrought pretty hard yesterday. But I had so much reading and so many proofs to correct that I did not get over the daily task so am still a little behind which I shall soon make up. I have got Nap: d——n him into Italy where with bad eyes and obscure maps I have a little difficulty in tracing out his victorious chess-play.

Lady Scott was better yesterday – certainly better – and was sound asleep when I lookd in this morning.

Walkd in the afternoon – I lookd at a hooded crow building near

---

1. *King Lear*, iii. 6.
2. It was usual in Scotland to name the first son after his father's father and the second after his mother's father.
3. The news came in a letter from Gibson. See *Letters*, x. 16.
4. *King Lear*, iii. 2.
5. For Constable as he used to be, see Scott's description in the Entry for 23 July 1827.

thicket with great pleasure. It is a shorter date than my neighbour Torwoodlee[1] thought of when he told me as I was bragging a little of my plantations that it would be long ere crows built in them.

26 WEDNESDAY Cheque on Galashiels £13. 0.0 £13.0.0 coals, to pay coals.

$£50$

Letters from Walter and Lockharts all well and doing well. Lady S. continues better so the clouds are break- Ball ing up. I made a good day's work yesterday and sent off proofs letters and copy this morn. So if this fine day holds good I will take a drive at one.

13
37

There is an operation calld Putting to Rights, *Scottice* Redding up, which puts me into a fever. I always leave any attempt at it half executed and so am worse off than before and have only embroild the fray.[2] Then my long back aches with stooping into the low drawers of old Cabinets and my neck is straind with staring up to their attics. Then you are sure never to get the thing you want. I am certain they creep about and hide themselves. Tom Moore gave us the Insurrection of the papers;[3] that was open war but this is system of privy plot and conspiracy by which those you seek creep out of the way and those you are not wanting perk themselves in your face again and again untill at last you throw them into some corner in a passion and then they are the objects of research in their turn. I have read in a French eastern tale[4] of an enchanted person calld *l'homme qui Cherche* – a sort of Sir Guy the Seeker always employd in collecting the beads of a chaplet which by dint of gramary always dispersed themselves when he was about to fix on the last upon the string. It was an awful doom – transmogrification into the Laidley worm of Spindlestaneheugh[5] woul[d] have been a blessing in compairaison. Now the explanation of all this is that I have been all this morning seeking a pa[r]cel of sticks of sealing wax which I brought from Edin: and the '*Weel Brandt and vast houd*'[6] has either

1. James Pringle of Torwoodlee, who had commanded the Selkirkshire yeomanry cavalry from the time it was raised, and was Convener and Vice-lieutenant of the county.
2. *Paradise Lost*, ii. 908.
3. See the poem of this name.
4. '*Trois princes de Sarendip*'. *Letters*, ix. 84.
5. A north-country legend and the subject of a ballad printed by Child in *English and Scottish Ballads*, i. 386. Scott used the legend in his presidential address to the Royal Society of Edinburgh in 1820: 'I spoke of the story of the Laidly worm to the Naturalists which made a great sensation. Dr Barclay says the horrid reptile produces the large brown butterfly.' *Letters*, vi. 305.
6. '*Fyn Segellak wel brand en vast houd*: old brand used by sealing-wax makers'. Douglas.

melted without the agency of fire or barricaded itself within the drawers of some cabin[e]t which has declared itself in a state of insurrection. A choice subject for a journal but what better have I! –

I did not quite finish my task to-day – nay I only did one third of it. It is so difficult to consult the maps after candles are lighted or to read the *Moniteur*[1] that I was obliged to adjourn – The task is three pages or leaves of my close writing per diem which corresponds to about a sheet (15 pages) of *Woodstock* and about twelves of *Bonaparte* which is a more comprehensive page. But I was not idle neither and wrote some Balaam[2] for Lockhart's *Review* – Then I was in hand a leaf above the tale so I am now only a leaf behind it.[3]

27 THURSDAY   This is one of those abominable April mornings which deserve the name of *Sans Cullotides* as being cold, beggarly, coarse, savage and intrusive. The earth lies an inch deep with snow to the confusion of the worshippers of Flora. By the way Bogie[4] attended his professional dinner and show of flowers at Jedburgh yesterday. Here is a beautiful sequence to their *floralia*. It is this uncertainty in April and the descent of snow and frost when one thinks themselves clear of them and that after fine encouraging weather that destroys our Scottish fruits and flowers. It is as imprudent to attach yourself to flowers in Scotland as to a caged bird. The cat sooner or later snaps up one and these d—d *Sanscullotides* annihilate the other. It was but yesterday I was admiring the glorious flourish of the pears and apricots and now hath come the killing frost.[5]

But let it freeze without we are comfortable within. Lady Scott continues better and we may hope has got the turn of her disease.

1. *Le Moniteur universal*, the official journal of the French government from 1789 to 1869, was Scott's source for many of the day-to-day events in the *Life of Napoleon*. In September 1825 Constable had sent him a set of the *Moniteur* commencing in June 1789 and continued to December 1823 in 77 volumes. *Letters*, ix. 206 n. and *A. L. C.*
2. '*Balaam* is the cant name in a newspaper office for Asinine paragraphs, about monstrous productions of nature and the like, kept standing in type to be used whenever the real news of the day leave an awkward space that must be filled up somehow.' J. G. L.
3. Scott also wrote to Ballantyne to say that he had an offer from Government to communicate the whole of the private correspondence from St. Helena but must study the papers in Downing Street. *Letters*, x. 20. This led to his London visit in October.
4. The Abbotsford gardener.
5. *Henry VIII*, iii. 2.

28 FRIDAY Beautiful morning but ice as thick as pasteboard too surely shew[in]g that the night has made good yesterday's threat. Dalgleish with his most melancholy face conveys the most doleful tidings from Bogie. But servants are fond of the woeful: it gives such consequence to the person who communicates bad news.

Wrote two leaves and read till twelve and then for a stout walk among the plantations till four. Found Lady Scott obviously better I think than I had left her in the morn. In walking I am like a spavind horse and heat as I get on. The flourishing plantations around me are a great argument for me to labour hard.

Barbarus has segetes –[1]

I will write my fingers' ends off first.

29 SATURDAY I was always afraid privately that *Woodstock* would not stand the test. In that case my fate would have been that of the unfortunate minstrel trumpeter Marine at the battle of Sheriff-Moor.

> By misfortune he chanced to fa', man,
>> And in saving his neck
>> His trumpet did brak
> And came off without musick at a', man.[2]

J. B. corroborated my doubts by his raven-like croaking and criticizing. But the good fellow writes me this morning that he is written down an ass[3] and that the approbation is unanimous. It is but Edinburgh to be sure – But Edinburgh has always been a harder critic than London. It is a great mercy and gives encouragement for future exertion. Having written two leaves this morning I think I will turn out to my walk though two hours earlier than usual. Egad, I could not persuade myself that it was such bad Balaam after all.

30 SUNDAY I corrected this morning a quantity of proofs and copy and dawdled about a little, the weather being of later becoming rather milder though not much of that. Methinks Duty looks as if she were but half pleased with me but would the pagan bitch have me work on the Sunday?[4]

---

1. '[Will] a stranger [reap] these crops?' Virgil's *Eclogues*, i. 71.
2. 'Sheriff-Muir', st. 20, ii. 3–6. Herd, i. 108.
3. *Much Ado about Nothing*, iv. 2.
4. A joke on Scott's part: a glance at the preceding entries shows that he worked harder on Sundays than on weekdays, especially when the Court was sitting.

MAY

1 MONDAY Cash in Excheqr. precepts received by Ballantyne – £170 which paid into Mr. Craig Leaves Ball. £207. If *Malachi* brings any thing

	£37.
	170.
	£207. Ball.

and £250 in June I will be quite well off. But I wish Walter's equipments and outfit (Nephew Walter) were paid back.[1]

I walkd to-day to the western corner of the Chiefswood plantation and marked out a large additional plantation[2] to be drawn along the face of the hill. It cost me some trouble to carry the boundaries out of the eye for nothing is so paltry as a plantation of almost any extent if its whole extent lies defined to the eye. By availing myself of the undulations of the ground I think I have avoided this for the present; only when seen from the Eildon hills the cranks and turns of the enclosure will seem fantastic at least untill the trees get high.

This cost Tom and me three or four hours. Lt. Colonel Fergusson joind us as we went home and dined at Abbotsford.

My cousin Barbara Scott of Raeburn came here to see Lady S. I think she was shockd with the melancholy change. She insisted upon walking back to Lessudden House, making her walk 16 or 18 miles, and though the carriage was orderd she would not enter it. The old caliban her father[3] will not even allow her a pony and I believe makes my Aunt lay out all the interest of her own fortune and Barbara's to keep the family and save his own wretched pelf.

2 TUESDAY Yesterday was a splendid May-day – to-day seems inclined to be *soft* as we call it but *tant mieux*. Yesterday had a twang of frost in it. I must get to work and finish Boaden's *Life of Kemble* and Kelly's *Reminiscences* for the *Quarterly*.[4]

I wrote and read for three hours and then walkd, the day being soft and delightful: but alas all my walks are lonely from the absence of my poor companion. She does not suffer thank God but strength must fail at last. Since Sunday there has been a gradual change – very gradual but alas to the worse – My hopes are almost gone. But I am determind to stand this grief as I have done others.

3 WEDNESDAY Another fine morning. I answerd a letter from Mr. Handley who has taken the pains to rummage the Chancery Records

1. Scott had borrowed £240 from John Gibson to equip nephew Walter for India. See the Entry for 6 February 1826.
2. Janeswood.
3. Walter Scott of Raeburn. For Scott's account of this relative and his quarrel with him, see the Entry for 23 May 1830.
4. Scott's article appeared in the June *Quarterly*, no. 67.

untill he has actually discoverd the fund due to Lady Scott's mother.[1] £1200 it seems have been invested in the estates of a Mr. Owen, as it appears, for Mde. Charpentier's benefit. But she dying the fund was lost sight of and got into chancery where I suppose it must have accumulated. But I cannot say I understand the matter; at a happier moment the news would have given poor Charlotte much pleasure. But now – it is a day too late –

4 THURSDAY On visiting Lady Scott's sick room this morning I found her suffering and I doubt if she knew me. Yet after breakfast she seemed serene and composed. The worst is she will not speak out about the symptoms under which she labours. Sad sad work! I am under the most melancholy apprehension for what constitution can hold out under these continued and wasting attacks?

My niece Anne Scott, a prudent, sensible and kind young woman, arrived to-day having come down to assist us in our distress from so far as Cheltenham.[2] This is a great consolation.

5 FRIDAY Haunted by gloomy thoughts but I corrected proofs from seven to ten and wrote from 1/2 past ten to one. My old friend Sir Adam[3] calld and took a long walk with me which was charity. His gaiety rubbd me up a little.

I had also a visit from the Laird and Lady of Harden. Henry Scott carries the County without opposition.

Drew on Craig for £20 to house expences.

£207
 20.
———
£187. Ball.

6 SATURDAY The same scene of hopeless (almost) and unavailing anxiety. Still wellcoming me with a smile and asserting she is better. I fear the fatal disease is too deeply entwined with the principles of life. Yet the increase of good weather, especially if it would turn more genial, might I think aid her excellent constitution.

Still labouring at this review[4] without heart or spirits to finish it – I am a tolerable Stoic but preach to myself in vain.

> – Since these things are necessities
> Then let us meet them like necessities –[5]

And so we will.

1. See the Entry for 22 March 1826.
2. See the Entry for 19 April 1826.
3. Sir Adam Ferguson.
4. Of the *Life of Kemble* and Kelly's *Reminiscences* for the *Quarterly*.
5. *2 Henry IV*, iii. 1.

7 SUNDAY Hammerd on at the Review till my back-bone ached. But I believe it was a nervous affection for a walk cured it. Sir Adam and the colonel dined here with my cousin Maxpopple so I spent the evening as pleasantly as I well could considering I am so soon to leave my own house, go like a stranger to the town of which I have been so long a citizen, and leave my wife lingering without prospect of recovery under the charge of two poor girls. *Talia cogit dura Necessitas.*[1]

8 MONDAY I went over to the Election at Jedburgh – carry Max-popple with me. There was a numerous meeting; the Whigs who did not bring ten men to the meeting of course took the whole matter under their patronage which was much of a piece with the Blue Bottle driving the carriage. I tried to pull [them] up once or twice but quietly having no desire to disturb the quiet of the Election. – To see the difference of modern times. We had a good Dinner and excellent wine and I had orderd my carriage at half past seven almost ashamed to start so early. Every body dispersed at so early an hour however that when Henry[2] had left the chair there was [no] carriage for me and Peter[3] proved his accuracy by shewing me it was but a quarter past seven. In the Days I remember they would have kept it up till daylight, nor do I think that poor Don would have left the chair before midnight. Well there is a medium. Without being a veteran Vice a Grey Iniquity[4] like Falstaff, I thank an occasional jolly bout if not carried to excess improved society. Men were put into good humour 'when the good wine did its good office';[5] the jest, the song, the speech had double effect; men were happy for the night and better friends ever after because they had been so.

9 TUESDAY My new Liverpool neighbour Mr. Bainbridge[6] breakfasts here to-day with some of his family; they wish to try the fishing in Cauldshields Loch and [there is] promise of a fine soft morning. But the season is too early.

1. 'Such things are forced on us by harsh necessity.'
2. Henry Scott of Harden, the new M. P. for Roxburghshire.
3. Peter Mathieson, the Abbotsford coachman.
4. *1 Henry IV*, ii. 4.
5. Southey's *Madoc*, ii. iv. 121–2.
6. George Bainbridge, a Liverpool banker, had taken Gattonside. 'He is a manly fellow', Scott wrote to Walter. 'He breakfasted and took a breakfast plate and admired it a good deal, saying as an apology he had begun the world in a china shop. He has two or three very dingy looking Misses and sons whom Dominie Thomson is to grind in consideration of 60 pounds a year.' *Letters*, x. 26. Bainbridge was the author of *The Fly-Fisher's Guide*.

They have had no sport accordingly after trying with trimmers. Mr. Bainbridge is a good cut of John Bull – plain sensible and downright, the maker of his own fortune and son of his own works.

10 WEDNESDAY To-morrow I leave my home; to what scene I may suddenly be recalld it wrings my heart to think. If she would but be guided by the medical people and attend rigidly to their orders some thing might be hoped but she is impatient with the protracted suffering and no wonder. Anne has a severe task to perform but the assistance of her cousin is a great comfort. Baron Weber the great *composer* wants me (through Lockhart[1]) to *compose* some thing to be set to music by him and sung [by] Miss Stephens – as if I cared who set or who sung any lines of mine. I have recommended instead Beaumont and Fletcher's unrivald song in the *Nice Valour*

> Hence all ye vain delights etc.[2]

11 THURSDAY

> Der abschi[e]d's tag ist da
> Schwer liegt er auf den herzen – schwer –[3]

Charlotte was unable to take leave of me being in a sound sleep after a very indifferent night. Perhaps it was as well – an adieu might have hurt her and nothing I could have expressd would have been worth the risk. I have forseen for two years and more that this menaced event could not be far distant. I have seen plainly within the last two months that recovery was hopeless – and yet to part with the companion of twenty nine years when so very ill – that I did not – could not forsee. It withers my heart to think of it and to recollect that I can hardly hope again to seek confidence and counsel from that ear to which all might be safely confided. But in her present lethargic state what would my attentions have availd? and Anne has promised close and constant intelligence. I must dine with James Ballantyne to-day *en famille*. I cannot help it but would rather be at home and alone. However I can go out too. I will not yield to the barren sense of hopelessness which struggles to invade me.

---

1. *Letters*, x. 29n.
2. Beaumont and Fletcher's *Nice Valour*, iii. 1.
3.   'The day of departure is come;
          Heavy lies it on the hearts – heavy.'
   This is the opening of the song which Scott translated for the
   use of the Royal Edinburgh Volunteer Light Dragoons in 1798.
   Life, ii. 13.

I drew upon Mr. Craig to-day the following sums

To my own account	——	£15	Ball. with Craig	£187	
To wages etc. for Anne	——	100	Deduct——	136	
To Dr. Clarkson	———	21		£51	
		£136	Ball. £ 51.0.0		

I passd a pleasant day with honest J.B. which was a great relief from the black dog which would have worried me at home. We were quite alone.

12 FRIDAY Well – Here I am in Arden[1] and I well say with Touchstone 'When I was at home I was in a better place'.[2] And yet this is not by any means to be complaind of – good apartments, the people civil and apparently attentive – no appearance of smoke and absolute warrandice against my dreaded enemies Bugs.[3]

I must when there is occasion draw to my own Baillie Nicol Jarvie's consolation, 'one cannot carry the comforts of the Saut Market about with one.' Were I well at ease in mind I think the body is very well cared for. I have two steady servants, a man and woman,[4] and they seem to set out sensibly and steadily enough. Only one lodger in the house, a Mr Shandy a clergyman, and despite his name said to be a quiet one.[5]

13 SATURDAY The projected measure against the Scottish bank notes has been abandond the resistance being general. Malachi might clap his wings upon this but alas! domestic anxiety has cut his comb.

I think very lightly generally of praise – it costs men nothing and is usually only lip-salve. They wish to please and most suppose that flattery is the ready to the good will of every professor of literature. Some praise however and from some people does at once delight and strengthen the mind and I record in this place the quotation with which Ld. C. Baron Shepherd concluded a letter concerning me to the Chief Commissioner. '*Magna enim illa laus et admirabilis videri*

1. No. 39 Castle Street having been put up for sale, and an offer of accommodation with the Skenes refused, Scott rented rooms from a Mrs. Brown at 6 North St. David Street.
2. *As You Like It*, ii. 4.
3. This warrandice proved illusory. The voracious bugs with which he shared Mrs. Brown's lodgings are referred to in the Entries for 13 June and 13 July 1826.
4. Dalgleish and Cissy. *Letters*, ix. 450.

*solet, subiisse casus sapienter adversos non fractum esse Fortuna, retinesse in
rebus asperis dignitatem.*[1] I record these words not as meriting the high
praise they imply but to remind me that such an opinion being
partially entertaind of me by a man of a character so eminent it
becomes me to make my conduct approach as much as possible to the
standard at which he rates it.

As I must pay back to Terry some cash in London, £170, together
with other matters here, I have borrowd from Mr. Alexr Ballantyne
the sum of £500 upon a promissory note for £512. 10. payable 15/18
of November to him or his order. If God should call me before that
time I request my son Walter will in reverence to my memory see that
Mr. Alexr. Ballantyne does not suffer for having obliged me in a sort
of exigency – He cannot afford it and God has given my son the
means to repay him.

14 SUNDAY A fair good morrow to you, Mr. Sun, who are shining so
brightly on these dull walls – methinks you look as if you were looking
as bright on the Banks of the Tweed but look where you will, Sir Sun,
you look upon sorrow and suffering. Hogg was here yesterday in
danger from having obtaind an accomodation of £100 from Mr.
Ballantyne, which he is now obliged to repay. I am unable to help the
poor fellow being obliged to borrow myself. But I long ago remon-
strated against the transaction at all and gave him £50 out of my
pocket to avoid granting the accomodation but it did no good.

I likewise received yesterday the unpleasing assurance that my
landlady had cribbed a piece of silk from the end of a packet
belonging to Mr. Allan[2] and been examined by the Magistrates
about it. But I find she had mentiond the thing to Dalgleish my
servant describing herself as a woman *much harassd*. Now in the first
place I think the poor woman may be innocent and were I to leave the
lodgings and make a noise it would ruin her. 2dly I have known ladies
of better rank perfectly capable of *nimming* as it were lace ribbands
and silk remnants who yet would not put forth their hands upon
men's apparel and linnen which with a few books is all I risque in her
custody. 3dly Her having spoke on the subject herself shews she

---

1. 'For it is usually thought a great and splendid commendation
   that he has endured adversity sensibly, has not been broken by
   Fortune, and has kept his dignity in hard times.' Cicero's *De
   Oratore*, ii. 346. Maria Edgeworth thought this stoicism 'a force
   of compression greater than all that even his strength of soul
   could afford.' See *Letters*, x. 31n.
2. George Allan, 'tailor, pelissemaker, & clothier, 33 Hanover st.'
   Edinburgh Post Office Directory.

intends like the fox to keep her own den clean, and I might go to another lodging where the Mistress was equally thievish but being still possessd of a fair character was more free to follow forth he[r] vocation. 4thly The Bureau, writing table, secretary's dispatch box etc., are my own as well as the cellaret and have capital keys. 5thly and lastly I have so little to lose that I would not be at the trouble to shift quarters for the risque. The woman is sensible she has a character to regain and I would not stand in her way and do not believe she would go to the Devil with such a dishclout as linnen of mine would make.

> So we'll stay with Mrs. Broon
> Though I fear she's but a loon –[1]

15 MONDAY   Received the melancholy intelligence that all is over at Abbotsford.

16 TUESDAY   She died at nine in the morning after being very ill for two days – easy at last.[2] I arrived here late last night. Anne is worn out and has had hystericks which returned on my arrival. Her broken accents were like those of a child, the language as well as the tones broken but in the most gentle voice of submission. 'Poor Mama – Never return again – gone for ever – a better place –' Then when she came to herself she spoke with sense freedom and strength of mind till her weakness returnd. It would have been inexpressibly moving to me as a stranger – what was it then to the father and the husband? For myself, I scarce know how, I feel sometimes as firm as the Bass rock sometimes as weak as the wave that breaks on it. I am as alert at thinking and deciding as I ever was in my life – yet when I contrast

1. For Dalgleish's account of life with Mrs. Brown, see note 6, p. 809.
2. Anne's letters describe her last days. On the 12th 'when the Doctor saw her he said she wd not out live the night' (to Lockhart, 13 May 1826, Abbots.) but she lingered on dosed with wine and laudanum. 'During the last dreadful night the Doctor was alas absent'; Lady Scott fell asleep at five; 'The Doctor came at light and said it was only sleep but I felt her pulse stop and called to him. He came to the bed and said she is gone. Mamma said in a soft sweet voice *No* and that breath was the last.' (To Sophia, ?21 May 1826, Abbots.) 'Poor Papa was obliged to leave her, to attend his duty in Edinburgh. Two days after his departure, she got much worse and suffered very great pain indeed; for the three last days it was so very terrible that I thank God that I was the only one of her family with her. Dr. Clarkson agreed with me in not sending for Papa till all was over, as it would have only hurt him, and poor Mamma was sensible to nothing but pain.' To Miss Millar, *Letters from Scott's Family*, pp. 118–19.

what this place now is with what it has been not long since I think my heart will break. Lonely – aged – deprived of my family all but poor Anne – impoverishd, an embarrassd man, I am deprived of the sharer of my thoughts and counsels who could always talk down my sense of the calamitous apprehensions which break the heart that must bear them alone. Even her foibles were of service to me by giving me things to think of beyond my weary self-reflections.

I have seen her – The figure I beheld is and is not my Charlotte – my thirty years' companion – There is the same symmetry of form though those limbs are rigid which were once so gracefully elastic – but that yellow masque with pinchd features which seems to mock life rather than emulate it, can it be the face that was once so full of lively expression? I will not look on it again. Anne thinks her little changed because the latest idea she had formed of her mother is as she appeard under circumstances of sickness and pain. Mine go back to a period of comparative health. If I write long in this way I shall write down my resolution which I should rather write up if I could. I wonder how I shall do with the large portion of thoughts which were hers for thirty years. I suspect they will be hers yet for a long time at least. But I will not blaze cambrick and crape in the publick eye like a disconsolate widower, that most affected of all characters.

17 WEDNESDAY Last night Anne after conversing with apparent ease dropd suddenly down as she rose from the supper table and lay six or seven minutes as if dead. Clarkson has no fear of the result of these affects.

Accompts stand as under.

To loan from Mr. Alexr. Ballantyne ————		£500
By sent to Terry ————————	£170	
By Dalgleish's wages £25 Cissy £5. 5–say—	30	
By Charles —————————	50	
By bill Mrs. Thos. Scott ————	25	
By Mr. Laidlaw for poor of Dryburgh — £3		
Do. Do. Melrose —— 5		
Balance ———————— 2		
Mournings Tom and Bogie ——— 10		
	— 25	
Ball. in desk. £135		
Mr. Craig's. 50 By Miss Fergussons interest ———75		
£185		
	—	£375
		125
Cash in purse—110		
Ball in purse 135		

18 THURSDAY Another day and a bright one to the external world again opens on us – the air soft and the flowers smiling and the leaves glittering. They cannot refresh her to whom mild weather was a natural enjoyment. Cearments of lead and of wood already hold her – cold earth must have her soon. But it is not my Charlotte, it is not the bride of my youth, the mother of my children, that will be laid among the ruins of Dryburgh which we have so often visited in gaiety and pastime – No no – She is sentient and conscious of my emotions some where – some how – *where* we cannot tell – *how* we cannot tell – yet would I not at this moment renounce the mysterious yet certain hope that I shall see her in a better world for all that this world can give me. – The necessity of this separation, that necessity which renderd it even a relief, that and patience must be my comfort. I do not experience those paroxysms of grief which others do on the same occasion – I can exert myself and speak even cheerfully with the poor girls. But alone or if any thing touches me, the choking sensation.

I have been to her room: there was no voice in it – no stirring – the pressure of the coffin was visible on the bed but it had been removed elsewhere – All was neat as she loved it but all was calm – calm as death. I rememberd the last sight of her – she raised herself in bed and tried to turn her eyes after me and said with a sort of smile 'You all have such melancholy faces.' They were the last words I ever heard her utter and I hurried away for she did not seem quite conscious of what she said – When I returnd immediatly [before] departing she was in a deep sleep. It is deeper now – This was but seven days since.

They are arranging the chamber of death, that which was long the apartment of connubial happiness, and of whose arrangements (better than in richer houses) She was so proud – They are treading fast and thick – For weeks you could have heard a foot-fall – Oh my God –

19 FRIDAY Anne, poor Love, is ill with her exertions and agitation, cannot walk – and is still hysterical though less so. I advised flesh-brush and tepid bath which I think will bring her about. We speak freely of Her whom we have lost and mix her name with our ordinary conversation. This is the rule of Nature. All primitive people speak of their dead and I think virtuously and wisely. The idea of blotting the name of those who are gone out of the language and familiar discourse of those to whom they were dearest is one of the rules of ultra civilisation which in so many instances strangle natural feeling by way of avoiding a painful sensation. The Highlanders speak of their dead children as freely as of their living and mention

how poor Colin or Robert would have acted in such or such a situation. It is a generous and manly tone of feeling – and so far as it may be adopted without affectation or contradicting the general habits of society I reckon on observing it.

20 SATURDAY To-night I trust will bring Charles or Lockhart one or both this evening – at least I must hear from them.[1] A letter from Violet[2] gave us the painful intelligence that she had not me[n]tionned to Sophia the dangerous state in which her mother was.[3] Most kindly meant but certainly not so well judged. I have always thought that truth even when painful is a great duty on such occasions and it is seldom that concealment is justifiable.

Sophia's baby was christend on sunday 14 May by [4] Brighton by the name of Walter Scott. May God give him life and health to wear it with credit to himself and those belonging to him. Melancholy to think that the next morning after this ceremony deprived him of so near a relation.

Sent £11. to Mr. Curle to remit Mrs. Bohte, York Street, Covent Garden, for books. I thought I had paid the poor woman before.[5]

Cash	£135
Off	11
	124
Craig	50
	£174

21 SUNDAY Our sad preparations for tomorrow continue. A letter from Lockhart doubtful if Sophia's health or his own state of business will let him be here. If they permit he comes to-night. From Charles not a word but I think I may expect him. I wish tomorrow were over – not that I fear it for my nerves are pretty good, but it will be a day of many recollections.

1. Scott had written to both on the 15th. *Letters*, x. 37. Lockhart, however, had no intention of coming. With mourning for the servants to pay for, 'I could scarcely afford this, which *must* be,' he writes to Sophia, '& also £40 for going to Scotland & back again.' Instead he joined her in Brighton. 19 May 1826, Abbots.
2. Lockhart's sister.
3. Lockhart, however, at Anne's request had warned her just in time. See Anne to Lockhart, 13 May 1826, and Lockhart to Sophia, 16 May 1826, Abbots.
4. Scott had written to Lockhart for the information needed to fill this blank: 'pray send me his day and hour of birth Christening Sponsors & Clergyman. I beg this particularly.' *Letters*, x. 33. Although Lockhart sent the names on 17 June (Walpole), Scott omitted to add them to the entry made in the family bible or to this page. The clergyman was an Oxford friend of Lockhart's, Mr. J. S. M. Anderson. Sophia, 10 May 1826, Abbots.
5. He had. See the Entry for 16 April.

22 MONDAY Charles arrived last night much affected of course. Anne had a return of her fainting fits on seeing him and again upon seeing Mr. Ramsay[1] the gentleman who performs the service. I heard him do so with the utmost propriety for my late friend Lady Alvanley, the arrangement of whose funeral devolved on me.[2] How little I could guess when where and with respect to whom I should next hear those solemn words. Well – I am not apt to shrink from that which is my duty merely because it is painful but I wish this day over. A kind of cloud of stupidity hangs about me as if all were unreal that men seem to be doing and talking about.

23 TUESDAY About one hour before the mournful ceremony of yesterday Walter arrived having travelld express from Ireland on receiving the news.[3] He was much affected, poor fellow, and no wonder. Poor Charlotte nursed him and perhaps for that reason She was ever partial to him – The whole scene floats as a sort of vision before me – the beautiful day, the grey ruins coverd and hidden among shreds of foliage and flourish where the grave even in the lap of beauty lay lurking and gaped for its prey. Then the grave looks, the hasty important bustle of men with spades and mattocks, the train of carriages – the coffin containing the creature that was so long the dearest on earth to me and which I was to consign to the very spot which in pleasure-parties we so frequently visited.[4] It seems still as if this could not be really so. But it is so – and Duty to God and to my children must teach me patience.

1. At Scott's request, John Gibson had arranged for Edward Ramsay (1793–1872), later Dean of Edinburgh, to perform the service. *Letters*, x. 40.
2. Lady Alvanley, whom Scott had known for twenty-five years, died in Edinburgh, where she had come for an operation, in January 1825.
3. Scott wrote to him on the 15th, as soon as he himself knew, but did not expect him at the funeral: 'Do not think of coming over for the last rites *cannot* be delayd till your arrival.' *Letters*, x. 36.
4. 'The friends assembled upon that occasion were very much surprised, when the procession reached the ground, to see Sir Walter step from his own carriage, which as usual had followed the hearse with the blinds drawn up. He assisted in bearing the coffin to the grave, stood beside it in silence till the ceremony was completed, then, solemnly bowing to the company assembled, again entered his carriage without uttering a word and drove home.' *Skene's Memories*, pp. 148–9.

Poor Anne has had longer fits since our arrival from Dryburgh than before but yesterday was the crisis. She desired to hear prayers read by Mr. Ramsay who performd the duty in a most solemn matter[1] – But her strength could not carry it through. She fainted before the service was concluded.

Ball.	£124. 0. 0
Clergmn—	15
	109
Craig—	50
	£159
By cash	11
	£170
Walter	5
	£165

24 WEDNESDAY Slept wretchedly or rather waked wretchedly all night and was very sick and bilious in consequence and scarce able to hold up my head with pain. A walk however with my sons did me a great deal of good: indeed their society is the greatest support the world can afford me. Their ideas of every thing are so just and honourable, kind towards their sisters and affectionate to me, that I must be grateful to God for sparing them to me and continue to battle with the world for their sake if not for my own.

25 THURSDAY I had sound sleep to-night and waked with little or nothing of the strange dreamy feeling which made [me] for some days feel like one bewilderd in a country where mist or snow has disguized those features of the landscape which are best known to him.

Walter leaves me to-day. He seems disposed to take interest in country affairs which will be an immense resource supposing him to tire of the army in a few years. Charles, He and I went up to Ashestiel to call upon the Misses Russells who have kindly promised to see Anne on Tuesday.

This evening Walter left us being anxious to return to his wife as well as to his regiment. We expect he will be here early in Autumn with his household.[2]

26 FRIDAY A rough morning and makes me think of St. George's Channel which Walter must cross to-night or tomorrow to get to Athlone. The wind is almost due east however and the channel at the narrowest point between Port Patrick and Donahadee. His absence is a great blank in our circle, especially I think to his sister Anne to whom he shows invariably much kindness. But indeed they do so without exception each towards the other and in weal or woe have shown themselves a family of love. No persuasion could force on

1. A slip for 'manner'.
2. Walter and Jane came for three weeks in August and September.

Walter any of his poor mother's ornaments[1] for his wife. He undid a reading glass from the gold chain to which it was suspended and agreed to give the glass to Jane but would [on] no account retain the chain. I will go to town on Monday and resume my labours. Being of a grave nature they cannot go against the general temper of my feelings and in other respects the exertion as I am convinced will do me good. Besides I must reestablish my fortune for the sake of the children and of my own character. I have not leisure to indulge the disabling and discouraging thoughts that press on me. Were an enemy coming upon my house would I not do my best to fight although oppressd in spirits and shall a similar despondency prevent me from mental exertion? It shall not by Heaven. This day and tomorrow I give to the currency of the ideas which have of late occupied my mind and with Monday they shall be mingled at least with other thoughts and cares. Last Night Charles and I walked late on the terrace at Kaeside[2] when the clouds seem[d] accumulating in the wildest masses both on the Eldon Hills and other mountains in the distance. This rough morning reads the riddle.

Dull, dropping, cheerless has the day been. I cared not to [be] carrying my own gloom to the girls and so sate in my own room dawdling with old papers which awaked as many stings as if they had been the nest of fifty scorpions. Then the solitude seemd so absolute – my poor Charlotte would have been in the [room] half a score of times to see if the fire burnd and to ask a hundred kind questions – Well – that is over – and if it cannot be forgotten must be rememberd with patience.

27 SATURDAY A sleepless night – It is time I should be up and be doing and a sleepless night sometimes furnishes good ideas. Alas! I have no companion now with whom I can communicate to relieve the loneliness of these watches of the night. But I must not fail myself and my family and the necessity of exertion becomes apparent. I must try a *hors d'œuvre*, something that can go on between the necessary intervals of *Nap*. Mrs. M. K's tale of the Deserter[3] with her interview with the lad's mother may be made most affecting but will hardly endure much expansion. The frame work may be a highland Tour

---

1. Anne fell heir to these, as Scott's letter to Sophia explains: 'After conversing on the subject with Walter and Charles who entirely agree with me I have desired Anne to select suitable memorials of the deceased for you and for Jane and to consider the rest as her own property.' *Letters*, x. 45.
2. Part of the Abbotsford Estate.
3. Mrs. Murray Keith's tale evolved into 'The Highland Widow', the first story in *Chronicles of the Canongate*, which was published the following year.

under the guardianship of the sort of postilion whom Mrs. M. K. described to me – a species of conductuer who regulated the motions of his company, made their halts and was their Cicerone.

28 SUNDAY I wrote a few pages yesterday and then   T. P. £25
walkd. I believe the description of the old Scottish lady[1] may do but the change has been unceasingly rung upon Scottish subjects of late and it strikes me that the introductory matter may be considerd as an imitation of Washington Irving. Yet not so neither – In short, I will go on to-day, make a dozen of close pages ready, and take J. B's advice. I intend the work as an *olla podrida* into which any species of narrative or discussion may be thrown. I wrote easily. I think the exertion has done me good. I slept sound last night and at waking as is usual with me I found I had some clear views and thoughts upon the subject of this trifling work. I wonder if others find so strongly as I do the truth of the Latin proverb *Aurora Musis amica*.[2] If I forget a thing over night I am sure to recollect it as my eyes open in the morning   the same if I want an idea or am encumberd by some difficulty – the moment of waking always supplies the deficiency, or gives me courage to endure the alternative.

29 MONDAY To-day I leave for Edinburgh this House of sorrow. In the midst of much distress I have the great pleasure to see Anne regaining her health and shewing both patience and steadiness of mind. God continue this for my own sake as well as hers. Much of my future comfort must depend upon her.

Expences

		Anne to various accots. and Cash in hand —	£40
Craig	£50	Tom purdie to Coals and to accot. ———	25
Anne drn.	20	Self to journey etc. ————————	5
Craig	30	Charles ————————————	10
Cash	40	Bogie —————————————	10
	70		£90
		Tom to further accot. ————	5
			95
		Cash ——————— £165	
		Deduce ——————— 95	
		Cash remaining ———— £70	

1. Mrs. Bethune Baliol in *Chronicles of the Canongate*.
2. 'Dawn a friend to the Muses'.

30 TUESDAY Returned to Edinburgh last night with Charles.[1]

This morning resume ordinary habits of waking in the morning, rising early and attending the Court. All will come easily round. But it is at first as if men lookd strange on me and bit their lip when they wrung my hand and indicated suppressd feelings. It is natural this should [be] – undoubtedly it has been so with me. Yet it is strange to find oneself resemble a cloud which darkens gaiety wherever it interposes its chilling shade. Will it be better when, left to my own feelings, I will see the whole world pipe and dance around me? I think it will – their sympathy intrudes on my private afliction.

I finishd correcting the proofs for the *Quarterly*.[2] It is but a flimsy article but then the circumstances were most untoward.

This has been a melancholy day – most melancholy – I am afraid poor Charles found me weeping – I do not know what other folks feel but with me the hysterical passion that compels tears is a terrible violence – a sort of throttling sensation – Then succeeded by a state of dreaming stupidity in which I ask if my poor Charlotte can actually be dead. I think I feel my loss more than at the first blow –

Poor Charles wishes to come back to study here when his term ends at Oxford. I can see the motive.

31 WEDNESDAY The melancholy hours of yesterday must not return – to encourage that dreamy state of incapacity is to resign all authority over the mind and I have been wont to say

My Mind to me a Kingdom is.[3]

I am rightful monarch and God to aid I will not be dethroned by any rebellious passion that may rear its standard against me. Such are morning thoughts, strong as carl-hemp says Burns,

> Come, firm Resolve, take thou the van,
> Thou stalk of *Carle-Hemp* in Man.[4]

Charles went by the Steam-boat this morning at six. We parted last night mournfully on both sides – poor boy – this is his first serious sorrow.

1. 'The cold east winds and the confinement of a town' made Edinburgh out of the question for Anne in her present state of health. Anne to Sophia, 28 May 1826, Abbots.
2. Of the review of Boaden's *Life of Kemble* and Kelly's *Reminiscences*.
3. The first line of a poem by Sir Edward Dyer in Percy's *Reliques*.
4. Burns's 'To Dr. Blacklock' ll. 36–7.

Cash   £40
        12
        ——
        £28

Settled with servants and gave them Cash in hand £12. Wrote this morning a Memorial on the claims which Constable's people prefer to *Woodstock* and *Napoleon*.[1]

JUNE

1 THURSDAY Yesterday I also finishd a few trifling Memoranda on a book called the *Omen*[2] at Blackwood's request. There is something in the work which pleases me and the stile is good though the story is not artfully conducted. I dined yesterday in family with Skene and had a visit from Lord Ch. Commissioner. We met as mourners under a common calamity[3] – there is something extremely kind in his disposition.

Sir R. D.[4] offers me three days of the country next week which tempt me strongly were it but the prospect of seeing Anne. But I think I must resist and say with Tilburina

Duty, I'm all thine own.[5]

If I do this I shall deserve a holiday about the 15th. June and I think it is best to wait till then.

2 FRIDAY A pleasant letter from Sophia poor girl – all doing well there for which God be praised.

I wrote a good task yesterday, five pages, which is nearly doubly the usual stint.[6]

I am settled that I will not go to Abbotsford till tomorrow fortnight.

I might have spared myself the trouble of my self denial for go I cannot, Hamilton[7] having a fit of gout.

Gibson seems in high spirits on the views I have given to him on the

1. The Memorial mentioned here is printed in Gibson's *Reminiscences*, pp. 23–6. For Constable's claim to these works, and the history of the arbitration, see Introduction, pp. xxxv–xxxvii.
2. *The Omen* by John Galt, which Scott had read on 23 February. His review appeared in the July *Blackwood's Magazine*, no. 114.
3. William Adam was still in mourning for his son, who had died while returning from India the previous September.
4. Sir Robert Dundas, his fellow Clerk of Session. He offers to do Scott's work for three days.
5. Sheridan's *Critic*, ii. 2: 'Duty, behold I am all over thine.'
6. This marks the resumption of the *Life of Napoleon*, laid aside since Lady Scott's death.
7. Robert Hamilton, another Clerk of Session.

nature of Constable and Company's claim. It amounts to this, that being no longer accountable as publishers they cannot claim the character of such, or plead upon any claim arising out of the contracts enterd into while they filld that capacity.

3 SATURDAY I was much disturbd this morning by bile and its consequences and lost so much sleep that I have been rather late in rising by way of indemnification. I must go to the map and study the Italian campaigns instead of scribbling.

4 SUNDAY I wrote a good task yesterday and to-day a great one, scarce stirring from the desk the whole day except a few minutes when Lady Rae calld. I was glad to see my wife's old friend with whom in early life we had so many *liaisons*. I am not sure it is right to work so hard. But a man must take himself as well as other people when he is in the humour. A man will do twice as much at one time and in half the time and twice as well that he will be able to do in another. People are always crying out about method and in some respects it is good and shows to great advantage among men of business. But I doubt if men of method who can lay aside or take up the pen just at the hour appointed will ever be better than poor creatures. L. L. S—t[1] used to tell me of Mr. Hoole the translator of Tasso and Ariosto, and in that capacity a noble transmuter of gold into lead, that he was a clerk in the India House with long rufles and a snuffcolourd suit of clothes who occasionally visited her father. She sometimes conversed with him and was amused to find that he *did* exactly so many couplets day by day neither more nor less and habit had made it light to him however heavy it might seem to the reader.

Well but if I lay down the pen as the pain in my breast hints that I should what am I to do? If I think – why I shall weep – and that's nonsense – and I have no friend now – none – to receive my tediousness for half an hour of the gloaming – Let me be grateful – I have good news from Abbotsford.[2]

5 MONDAY Though this be Monday[3] I am not able to *feague* it away as Bayes says.[4] Between correcting proofs and writing letters I have

1. Lady Louisa Stuart.
2. A fairly cheerful letter from Anne, reporting that Tom Purdie 'has peeled the larches' and that the dogs are well. ?3 June 1826, Walpole.
3. The Court of Session did not, and still does not, sit on Mondays.
4. In Buckingham's *Rehearsal*, iv. 2.

got as yet but two pages written and that with labour and a sensation of pain in the Chest. I may be bringing on some serious disease by working thus hard. If I had once justice done to other folks I do not much care, only I would not like to suffer long pain. Harden made me a visit. He agreed with me that Lord M.[1] affiché'd his own importance too much at the Election and says Henry is anxious about it. I hinted to him the necessity of counterbalancing it the next time which will be soon.

Thomson also calld about the Bannatyne club.[2]

These two interruptions did me good though I am still a poor wretch.

After all I have fagg'd through six pages and made poor Wurmser lay down his sword on the glacis of Mantua[3] – And my head aches – my eyes ache – my back aches – so does my breast – and I am sure my heart aches – And what can duty ask more?

6 TUESDAY I arose much better this morning having taken some medicine which has removed the strange and aching feeling in my back and breast. I believe it is from the diaphragm. It must be lookd to however. I have not yet breakfasted, yet have cleard half my day's work holding it at the ordinary stint.

Workd hard. John Swinton my kinsman[4] came to see me – very kind and affectionate in his manner. My heart always warms to that Swinton connection. So faithful to old Scottish feelings. Harden was also with me. I talkd with him about what Ld. M. did at the Election and find that he disapproves. I see these visits took place on the 5th.

7 WEDNESDAY Again a day of hard work – Only at half past eight I went to the Dean of Faculty's[5] to a consultation about Constable and

1. Lord Minto. 'It provoked me much to see how my freind Lord Minto labourd *s'afficher* as the patron of the affair.' To Lord Montagu, 8 May 1826, Disc. i. 81.
2. Of which he was Vice-president and Scott President. The Club, named after the sixteenth-century compiler of *Corpus poeticum Scotorum*, was founded by Scott in 1823 to print works illustrative of the history, antiquities and literature of Scotland. At this time it had thirty-one members, but it was shortly to increase its membership to 100.
3. *Life of Napoleon*, vol. iii, ch. 7.
4. John Swinton was the son of Scott's mother's cousin – a connection which only a Scot would think it worth while to keep in mind.
5. George Cranstoun's. He had been retained by Scott's Trustees as counsel in the arbitration between themselves and Constable's creditors.

met with said Dean and Mr. More and J. Gibson. I find they have as high hope of success as Lawyers ought to express and I think I know how our profession speak when sincere. I cannot interest myself deeply in it. When I had come home from such a business I used to carry the news to poor Charlotte who dressd her face in sadness or mirth as she saw the news affect me. This hangs bitterly about me – I had almost forgot the appointment if J. G.[1] had not sent me a card. I passd a piper in the street as I went to the Dean's and could not help giving him a shilling to play 'Pibroch a Donuil Dhu' for luck's sake.[2] What a child I am!

8 THURSDAY Bilious and head-ache this morning – A dog howld all night and left me little sleep – poor cur! I dare say he had his distresses as I have mine. I was obliged to make Dalgleish shut the windows when he appeard at ½ past six as usual and did not rise till nine when – *me voici* – I have often deserved a head ache in my younger days without having one and Nature is I suppose paying off old scores. Aye but then the want of the affectionate care that used to be ready with lowerd voice and stealthy pace to smooth the pillow and offer condoleance and assistance – gone – gone – for ever – ever – ever – Well there is another world and we'll meet free from the mortal sorrows and frailties which beset us here – Amen so be it – Let me change the topic with hand and head and the heart must follow.

I think that sitting so many days and working so hard may have brought on this head-ache. I must inflict a walk on my self to-day – Strange that what is my delight in the country is *here* a sort of penance – Well but now I think on it I will go to the Ch: Baron and try to get his Lordship's opinion about the question with Constable. If I carry it, as there is I trust much hope I shall, Mr. Gibson says there will be funds to divide 6/- in the pound without counting upon getting any thing from Constable or Hurst but sheer hard cash of my own. Such another pull is possible especially if *Boney* succeeds – and the rogue had a knack at his success – such another, I say, and we touch ground I believe. For surely Constable, Robinson, etc. must pay something. The struggle is worth waring[3] a headache upon.

I finishd five pages to-day, head-ache laziness and all.[4]

1. John Gibson.
2. The words of the song were Scott's.
3. 'Spending'.
4. This was also the date of a visit from a Miss Dalziel of uncertain age who wanted Scott to induce the King to appoint her his housekeeper at Holyrood. *Letters*, x. 55.

9 FRIDAY Corrected a stubborn proof this morning. These battles have been the death of many a man. I think they will be mine.[1] Well but it clears to windward so we will fag on.

Slept well las[t]night. By the way how intolerably selfish this journal makes one seem. So much attention to one's naturals and non naturals. Lord MacKenzie calld and we had much chat about parish business. The late regulations for preparing cases in the outer House does not work well, and thus our old machinery which was very indifferent is succeeded by a kind that will hardly move at all.[2] McKenzie says his business is trebled and that he cannot keep it up. I question whether the extreme strictness of rules of court be adviseable. In practice they are always evaded upon an equitable showing. I do not for instance lodge a paper *debito tempore*[3] and for an accident happening perhaps through the blunder of a writer's apprentice I am to lose my cause. The penalty is totally disproportiond to the delict and the consequence is that means are found out of evasion by legal fictions and the like – the judges listen to these – they become frequent and the rule of Court ends by being a scarecrow merely. Formerly delays of this kind were checkd by corresponding *amendes* – but the court relaxd these petty fines too often – Had they been more strict and levied the mulct on the agents with *no recourse* upon their clients the abuse might have been remedied. I fear the present rule is too severe to do much good.

One effect of running causes fast through the courts below is that they go by Scores to appeal and Lord Gifford has hitherto decided them with such judgement and so much rapidity as to give great satisfaction. The consequence will in time be that the Scottish Supreme court will be in effect situated in London. Then down fall – as national objects of respect and veneration – the Scottish bench – the Scottish Bar – the Scottish Law herself – And – And – there is an end of an auld Sang.[4] Were I as I have been I would fight

1. Ballantyne evidently objected about this time that Scott was dealing with the battles at unnecessary length. For Scott's defence, see *Letters*, x. 51: 'These Italian Campaigns are the ground of his reputation with military men and *must* be told in detail to be intelligible. Others may be greatly contracted. I am indeed afraid I may be too obscure from a desire to be short. We must show him as a soldier somewhere.'
2. See Introduction, pp. xxvi–xxvii.
3. 'At the due time'.
4. The words of James, 1st Earl of Seafield and Chancellor of Scotland, on the Union of the Scottish and English Parliaments, in 1707.

knee deep in blood ere it came to that – But it is a catastrophe which the great course of events brings daily nearer

And who can help it, Dick?[1]

I shall always be proud of *Malachi* as having headed back the Southron or helpd to do so in one instance at least.

10 SATURDAY This was an unusual teind day at Court.[2] In the morning and evening I corrected proofs – four sheets in number. And I wrote my task of three pages and a little more. Three pages a day will come at Constable's rate to about £12,000 to £15,000 per year. They have sent their claim. It does not frighten me a bit.

11 SUNDAY Bad dreams about poor Charlotte – woke thinking my old and inseparable friend beside me and it was only when I was fully awake that I could persuade myself that she was dark low and distant – and that my bed was widowd. I believe the phonomena of dreaming are in a great measure occasiond by the *double touch* which takes place when one hand is crossd in sleep upon another. Each gives and receives the impression of touch to and from the other and this complicated sensation our sleeping fancy ascribes to the agency of another being when it is in fact produced by our own limbs acting on each other. Well here goes – *incumbite remis*.[3]

12 MONDAY Finishd Vol. III of *Napoleon*. I resumed it on the 1st of June, the earliest period that I could bend my mind to it after my great loss. Since that time I have lived to be sure the life of a hermit except at attending the court five times in the week for about three hours on an average. Except at that time I have been reading or writing on the subject of Boney and have finish[d] last night and sent to printer this morning the last sheets of fifty two written since first June. It is an awful screed but grief makes me a house keeper and to labour is my only resource. Ballantyne thinks well of the work – very well – But I shall [expect] inaccuracies. An it were to do again I would get some one to look it over. But who could that some one be? Whom is there left of human race that I could hold such close intimacy with? No one. *Tanneguy du Chatel, ou es tu?*[4] Workd five pages.

House   £5   To House keeping. £5.

1. Suckling's 'Ballad upon a Wedding', st. 17.
2. The Teind Court usually met every second Wednesday. This extra sitting gave Scott a day at home.
3. 'Bend to the oars', *Aeneid*, v. 188.
4. Unidentified.

13 TUESDAY I took a walk out last evening after tea and calld on Ld. Commissioner and the Buchanan MacDonalds, that kind and friendly clan. The heat is very great and the wrath of the *bugs* in proportion. Two hours last night I was kept in an absolute fever. I must make some arrangement for winter. Great pity my old furniture was sold in such a hurry; the wiser way would have been to have let the House[1] furnishd. But it's all one in the Greek.

Peccavi – peccavi – Dies sine linea quidem.[2] I walkd to make calls – got cruelly hot – drank ginger beer – wrote letters. Then as I was going to dinner enter a big splay-footed, trifle-headed, old pottering minister who came to annoy me about a claim which one of [his] parishioners has to be Earl of Annandale and which he conceits to be establishd out of the *Border Minstrelsy.* He mentiond one curious thing, that three brothers of the Johnstone family, on whose descendants the male representation of these great Border chiefs devolved, were forcd to fly to the North in consequence of their feuds with the Maxwells and agreed to change their names. They sleepd on the side of the Soutra hills[3] and asking a shepherd the name of the place agreed in future to call themselves Sowtra or Sowter Johnstones. The old pudding headed man could not comprehend a word I either askd him or told him and maunderd till I wishd him in the Annandale Beef-Stand. Mr. Gibson Came in after tea and we talkd business.[4] The[n] I was lazy and stupid and dozed over a book instead of writing. So on the whole *Confiteor confiteor – culpa mea – culpa mea.*[5]

14 WEDNESDAY In the morning I began wt. a page and a half before breakfast – This is always the best way. You stand like a child going to be bathed shivering and shaking till the first pitcherfull is flung about your ears and then are as blythe as a water-wag-tail. I am just come home from P. House[6] and now, my friend Nap – have at you with a downright blow – Methinks I would fain [make] peace with my conscience by doing six pages to-night. Bought a little bit of Gruyere cheeze instead of our domestic choak-dog concern. When did I ever

1. 39 Castle Street.
2. 'I have sinned – I have sinned – a day without a single line!'
3. Eighteen miles to the south-east of Edinburgh.
4. The business discussed was whether or not to accept an offer of £1500 from Cadell for a continuation of the collective editions of the novels in 8vo, 12mo, and 18mo. *Letters*, x. 56. The Trustees were doubtful about the value of continuing the series, but finally decided to do so.
5. 'I confess, I confess – the blame is mine – the blame is mine.'
6. Parliament House, where the Court of Session sat.

purchase any thing for my own eating? – But I will say no more of that
6/- cheeze.   – and now to the tread Mill. Cheeze 6-/.

15 THURSDAY I labourd all the evening but made little way. There
were many books to consult and so all I could really do was to make
out my task of three pages. I will try to make up the deficit of tuesday
to-day and tomorrow. Letters from Walter all well. A visit yesterday
from Charles Sharpe.

16 FRIDAY Yesterday sate in the Court till near four. I had of course
only time for my task. I fear I will have little more to-day for I have
accepted to dine at Hector's.[1] I got yesterday a present of two
engravings from Sir Henry Raeburn's portrait of me[2] which, poor
fellow, was the last he ever painted and certainly not his worst. I had
the pleasure to give one to young Mr. Davidoff for his uncle the
celebrated Black Captain of the Campaign of 1812. Curious that he
should be interested in getting the resemblance of [a] person whose
mode of attaining some distinction has been very different. But I am
sensible that if there be any thing good about my poetry, or prose
either, it is a hurried frankness of composition which pleases soldiers
sailors and young people of bold and active disposition. I have been
no sigher in shades, no writer of

> Songs and sonnets and rustical roundelays
> Framed on fancies and whistled on reeds.[3]

17 SATURDAY Left Edinburgh to-day after Parlt House to come [to
Abbotsford].[4] My two girls met me at Torsonce which was a pleasant
surprize[5] and we returnd in the Sociable all together. Found every
thing right and well at Abbotsford under the new regime. I again
took possession of the family bedroom and my widowd couch. This
was a sore trial but it was necessary not to blink such a resolution –
Indeed I do not like to have it thought that there is any way in which
I can be beaten.

18 SUNDAY This morning wrote till $\frac{1}{2}$ twelve, good day's work at
Canongate Chronicle. Methinks I can make this work answer. Then

1. Hector Macdonald Buchanan's.
2. The engraver of Raeburn's 1823 portrait was William Walker.
3. From 'The Hunting of the Hare' in *The Convivial Songster*
   (1782), p. 324.
4. For the short holiday he had promised himself on 1 June.
5. The two Anne Scotts, his daughter and niece, who had written to
   say they would meet him there, where the coach changed horses.

drove to Huntley Burn and calld at Chiefswood.[1] Walkd home. The country crying for rain yet on the whole the weather delicious dry and warm with a fine air of wind. The young woods are rising in a kind of profusion I never saw else where. Let me once clear off these encumbrances and they shall wave broader and deeper yet. But to attain this I *must work*.

Wrought very fair accordingly till two then walkd and after dinner out again with the girls. Smoked two cygars first time these two months.

19 MONDAY Wrought very fair indeed and the day being scorching we dined al fresco in the hall among the armour and went out early in the evening. Walkd to the Lake and back again by the marle-pool. Very delightful evening.

20 TUESDAY This is also a hardworking day. Hot weather is favourable for application were it not that it makes the composer sleepy; pray God the reader may not partake the sensation. But days of hard work make short journals. To-day we again dine in the Hall and drive to Ashestiel in the evening *pour prendre le frais*.

21 WEDNESDAY We followd the same course we propose[d]. For a party of pleasure I have attended to business well. Twenty pages of Croftangry,[2] 5 printed pages each, attest my diligence and I have had a delightful variation by the company of the two Annes. Regulated my Little expences here.

		Anne	£5
	£	Tom	5
Cash. .	£28	Bogie . .	5
Dt. on Craig	10	These by cheque on Craig being	
	38	£10	
Laid out	38	Travelling expences	5
	0. 0. 0		
In Craig's hands £20.		Burn	£3
		Charles remitted	£10.0.0
			£38

22 THURSDAY Returnd to my Patmos. Heard good news from Lockhart. Wife well and John Hugh better. He mentions poor

1. A courtesy call on the new tenants of Lockhart's cottage, Captain and Mrs. Hamilton.
2. *Chronicles of the Canongate* (here named after the narrator, Chrystal Croftangry).

Southey testifying much interest for me even to tears. It is odd – Am I so hard-hearted a man? I could not have wept for him though in distress I would have gone any length to serve him. I sometimes think I do not deserve people's good opinion for certainly my feelings are rather guided by reflection than impulse. But every body has their own mode of expressing interest and mine is Stoical even in bitterest grief.

Agere atque pati Romanum est.[1]

I hope I am not the worse for wanting the tenderness that I see others possess and which is so amiable. I think it does not cool my wish to be of use where I can. But the truth is I am better at enduring or aiding than at consoling. From childhood's earliest hour my heart rebelld against the influence of external circumstances in myself and others. *Non est tanti!*[2]

To-day I was detaind in the court from ½ past ten till near four yet I finishd and sent off a packet to Cadell which will finish one third of the *Chronicle* vol. 1st.

Henry Scott came in while I was at dinner and sate while I eat my beefsteak. A Gourmand would think me much at a loss coming back to my ploughman's meal of boild beef or broild beef and Scotch broth from the rather recherché table at Abbotsford but I have no philosophy in my carelessness on that score. It is natural though I am no ascetic as my father was –

23 FRIDAY The heat tremendous and the drought threatening the hay and barley crop.[3] Got from the court at ½ 12 and walkd to the extremity of Harriot's row to see poor Lady Don: left my card as she does not receive any one. I am glad this painful meeting is adjournd.[4]

My cash is expended except £20 in Craig's hands – But I received to-day £10 from Blackwood for the article on the *Omen*. Time was I would not have taken these small Tithes of mint and cummin but scornful dogs will eat dirty puddings and I with many depending on me must do the best I can with my time, God help me.

---

1. 'To do and to suffer is Roman.'
2. 'It is not worth so much.'
3. The almanacks record 1826 as an exceptional summer, with the harvest begun all over Britain as early as July.
4. She had lost her husband, Scott his wife, since they last met.

By cash Blackwood £10 – Quarter's salary £250–£260
Discharge   To Miss Watson .   .   . £20
             To Oliphant and C. .   .   15
             To Mrs. Baxter .   .   .   5
             To Armstrong, Coppersmith   13
             To sundries and change.   .   2
                                        ———   55
                                    Ball £205

Craig .   . £24   Gad my braids[1] are walking the plank I think – Why
Remitted .   100   then to sea for more.
            ———
            124
In hand .   103
         ———   Antiquarian Society ——————   2
         £227   ———
                                              203
Whereof – to Mr. Craig £100.

24 SATURDAY Left Edinburgh yesterday after the Court, ½ past twelve, and came over here with the L. Ch. Baron and William Clerk to spend as usua[l] a day or two at Blair Adam.[2] In general this is a very gay affair. We hire a light coach and four and scour the country in every direction in quest of objects of curiosity. But the L.C.C.'s family misfortunes[3] and my own makes our holiday this year of a more quiet description and a sensible degree of melancholy hangs on the reunion of our party. It was wise however not to omit it for to slacken your hold on life in any agreeable point of connection is the sooner to reduce yourself to the indifference and passive vegetation of old age.

25 SUNDAY Another melting day. Thermometer at 78 degrees even here. 80 was the height yesterday at Edinburgh. If we attempt any active proceedings 'we dissolve ourselves into a dew'.[4] W. C.[5]

---

1. 'Broad-pieces'.
2. The home of William Adam in Kinross-shire. From 1817 until 1830 nine friends of antiquarian interests and social disposition spent a few days there at midsummer. Members of this 'Blair-Adam Club' were Sir William Adam, his son Captain Sir Charles Adam, Sir Adam Ferguson, Sir Samuel Shepherd, Scott, Will Clerk, Anstruther Thomson, Thomas Thomson, and the Revd. John Thomson.
3. The loss of his son John. See the Entry for 20 January 1826 and note.
4. *Hamlet*, i. 2.
5. Will Clerk.

mentiond to me last night a horrid circumstance about a very
particularly dear friend who lately retired suddenly and seemingly
causelessly from parliament.[1] He ascribed [it] to his having been
detected in unnatural practices – I hope there may be doubts of this
though he spoke very positively and the sudden and silent retreat
from a long wishd for seat look[s] too like truth. God, God whom
shall we trust! ! Here is learning, wit, gaiety of temper, high station in
society and compleat reception every where all at once debased and
lost by such a degrading bestiality. Our passions are wild beasts. God
grant us power to muzzle them.

We have lounged away the morning creeping about the place,
sitting a great deal and walking as little as might be on account of the
heat. Blair-Adam has been successively in possession of three
generations of persons attachd to and skilld in the art of embellishment and may be fairly taken as a place where Art and taste have done
a great deal to improve natur<ur>e. A long ridge of hilly and varied
ground sloping to the foot of the hill called Bennarty and which
originally was of a bare mossy boggy character has been clothed by
the son father and grandfather, while the undulations and hollows
which seventy or eighty years since mus[t] have lookd only like
wrinkles in the black morasses, being now draind and limed, are
skirted with deep woods, par[ti]cular[l]y of Spruce which thrives
wonderfully, and coverd with excellent grass.[2] We drove in the
Droskie and walkd in the evening.

26 MONDAY Another day of unmitigated heat; thermometer 82;
must be higher in Edinburgh where I return to-night when the
decline of the sun makes travelling practicable. It will be well for my
work to be there – not quite so well for me; there is a difference
between the clean nice arrangement of Blair Adam and Mrs.
Brown's accomodations though he who is ensured against worse
has no right to complain of them. But the studious neatness of
poor Charlotte has perhaps made me fastidious. She loved to see
things clean even to Oriental scrupulosity. So oddly do our deep

1. 'We understand that Mr. Heber's complaint, for which he has
   been recommended to travel upon the Continent, is an
   overattachment to *Hartshorn*', was *John Bull*'s version on 14 May.
   Richard Heber had been M.P. for Oxford University since 1821.
2. It was on this 'fine Sunday, lying on the grassy summit of
   Bennarty, above its craggy brow' that Scott suggested that Sir
   William Adam should write his account of the embellishment of
   the estate. It was privately printed in 1834. See *The Blair-Adam
   Estate*, Introduction, p. xxix.

recollections of other kinds correspond with the most petty occurrences of our life.

Lord Ch: Baron told us a story of the ruling passion strong in death. A Mr. Stevens, a Master in Chancery, was on his death bed – a very wealthy man – some occasion of great urgency occurd in which it was necessary to make an affidavit and the attorney missing one or two other Masters whom he enquired after ventured to ask if Mr. Stevens would be able to receive the deposition. The proposal seemd to give him momentary strength, his clerk was sent for and the oath taken in due form. The Master was lifted up in bed and with difficulty subscribed the paper – as he sank down again he made a signal to his clerk. 'Wallace' – 'Sir' – 'Your ear – lower – lower – Have you got the *half crown?*' He was dead before morning.

27 TUESDAY Returnd to Edinburgh late last night and had a most sweltering night of it. This day also cruel hot. However I made a task or nearly oo and read a good deal about the Egyptian expedition. Had comfortable accompts of Anne and through her of Sophia. Dr. Shaw[1] doubts if any thing is actually the matter with poor Johnie's back. I hope the dear child will escape deformity and the infirmities attending that helpless state. I have myself been able to fight up very well notwithstanding my lameness but it has cost great efforts and I am besides very strong.

Dined with Colin McKenzie, a fine family all growing up about him turning men and women and treading fast on our heels.

Some thunder and showers which I fear will be but partial. Hot – hot – hot –

28 WEDNESDAY Another hot morning – and something like an idle day though I have read a good deal. But I have slept also, corrected proofs and prepared for a great start by filling myself with facts and ideas.

	Household, Cissie £3 Dalgleish £3	.	.	£6
£103	Box of paints for my niece[2]	.	.	.	2
8				
£95				£8

29 THURSDAY I walkd out for an hour last night and made one or two calls; the evening was delightful.

1. John Shaw (1792–1827), surgeon to the Middlesex Hospital.
2. Niece Anne spent much of her time at Abbotsford on embroidery or painting flowers. See Anne to Lockhart, 1 July 1826, Abbots.

> Day its sultry fires had wasted
>   Calm and cool the moonbeam rose
> Even a captive's bosom tasted
>   Half oblivion of his woes.[1]

I wonder often how Tom Campbell with so much real genius has not maintaind a greater figure in the public eye than he has done of late. The *Magazine*[2] seems to have paralyzed him. The author not only of the *Pleasures of Hope* but of 'Hohen Linden' 'Lochiel' etc. should have been at the very top of the tree. Somehow he wants audacity – fears the public and, what is worse, fears the shadow of his own reputation. He is a great corrector too which succeeds as ill in composition as in education. Many a clever boy is floggd into a dunce and many an original composition corrected into mediocrity. Yet Tom Campbell ought to have done a great deal more: his youthful promise was great. John Leyden[3] introduced me to him. They afterwards quarrelld. When I repeated 'Hohenlinden' to Leyden he said 'Dash it, man, tell the fellow that I hate him but dash him he has written the finest verses that have been publishd these fifty years' – I did mine errand as faithfully as one of hermes messengers and had for answer 'Tell Leyden that I detest him but I know the value of his critical approbation'. This feud was therefore in the way of being taken up. 'When Leyden comes back from India' said Tom Campbell 'what cannibals he will have eaten and what tigers he will have torn to pieces'.

> paid board etc. for William.[4] See 1st July   £17
> A poor poetess .   .   .   . __1__
>   18

1. Thomas Campbell's 'The Turkish Lady', rather altered.
2. The *New Monthly Magazine*, which Campbell edited from 1820 to 1831.
3. The eccentric genius to whom Richard Heber introduced Scott in 1801. He assisted in the collection of ballads for the *Ministrelsy* before leaving for India in 1803. An oriental scholar of repute, he came to an untimely end in 1811 at the age of thirty-six 'dying as he lived, in the ardent pursuit of knowledge'. *Letters*, iii. 69. Scott's 'Life of Leyden' appears in *Misc. Prose Works*, vol. iv.
4. A nephew by the wrong side of the blanket, his brother Daniel's son. Scott apprenticed him to an Edinburgh clothier and then paid for him to go to London, but the boy ran off. Finally he was sent to Canada, where he made no mark and died in reduced circumstances in 1869. See also the entries for 13 April 1827 and 18 January 1831.

Gibson writes me that £2300 is offerd for the poor House. It is worth £300 more but I will not oppose my own opinion or convenience to good and well meant council, so farewell poor No 39. What a portion of my life has been spent there. It has shelterd me from the prime of life to its decline and now I must bid good bye to it – I have bid good bye to my poor wife, so long its courteous and kind mistress, and I need not care about the empty rooms. Yet it gives me a turn. I have been so long a citizen of Edinburgh, now an *indweller* only. Never mind – All in the days' work.

J. Ballantyne and R. Cadell dined with [me][1] and Pepys would say all was very handsome. Drank amongst us 1 bottle of Champagne, one of claret – a glass or two of port and each a tumble[r] of whisky toddy. J. B. had courage to drink his with *hot* water. Mine was iced.

30 FRIDAY Here is another dreadful warm day fit for nobody but the flies, and then one is confined to town

Yesterday I agreed to let Cadell have the new work[2] edit. 1500 – he paying all charges and paying also £500 – two hundred and fifty at Lambmas to pay J. Gibson money advanced on the passage of young Walter my nephew to India. It is like a thorn in one's eye this sort of debt and Gibson is young in business and somewhat involved in my affairs besides. Our plan is that this same Miscellany or Chronicle shall be committed quietly to the public and we hope it will attract attention – If it does not we must turn public attention to it ourselves. This latter issue of the business will resemble the old woman at Carlisle who not doubting that the highlanders when they took the place in 1745 were to violate all the women shut herself up in a bedroom to await her fate with decency. But after a little time [when] she saw no appearance of the expected violence she pop'd out her

1. This was a business dinner to discuss the publication of *Chronicles of the Canongate. Letters*, x. 64.
2. *Chronicles of the Canongate*. 'As the time employd was literally taken from the hours of sleep and exercize', Scott considered the work his own property, and made a private bargain with Cadell for £500 which would go towards paying off various debts of his own, not to the Trust. In October, when Cadell wished to raise the edition to 4000, Scott brought the transaction before the Trustees – as he should perhaps have done earlier – and they agreed to it. 'We . . . cordially approve of the arrangements you have made for its sale and publication. In the circumstances we think your retention of the £500 highly reasonable.' *Letters*, x. 114 and note. The first edition yielded £2228 to the Trust and £500 to Scott. Sederunt Book, ii. 88.

head and askd a Rorie who was passing 'Pray, Sir, is not the Ravishing going to begin?' –

Ravish or not, about one half of Vol. I. is written and there is worse abomination or I mistake the matter.

I was detaind in court till four – dreadfully close – and obliged to drink water for refreshment which formerly I used to scorn even on the Moors with a burning August sun, the heat of exercise, and a hundred springs gushing around me.

Corrected proofs etc. on my return. I think I have conquerd the Trustees' objections to carry on the small edition of Novels.[1]

Got Cadell's letter about the *Chronicle*.[2]

JULY

1 SATURDAY Another sunny day. This threatens absolutely Syrian drought.[3] As the Selkirk election comes on Monday I go out to-day to Abbotsford and carry young Davidoff and his Tu:[4] with me to see our quiet way of managing the Choice of a national Representative. Wrote to Gibson about the prose works.[5] Surely they could go on mean time.

1. Cadell had offered the Trust £1,500 for the right of taking over the printing and management of the 8vo, 12mo, and 18mo collected editions of the novels. Scott at first liked the proposal but finally agreed to carry on as before, printing the works with Ballantyne and then selling them to the highest bidder. Sederunt Book, i. 93 and 109 and *Letters*, x. 56.

2. Cadell's written acceptance of the bargain made about *Chronicles of the Canongate* at dinner the evening before. Cadell, 30 June 1826, Walpole. It was in reply to Scott's request: 'Will you put into the form of a letter what passed between us yesterday touching the book . . . My acceptance shall settle the matter between us.' *Letters*, x. 66. It was their invariable practice, it is evident from the Walpole Collection, to confirm their agreements in writing.

3. 'Every thing is burnt up – no flowers and no fruit. The cattle are dying in the fields for want of water.' Anne to Lockhart, 1 July 1826, Abbots.

4. His tutor, Mr. Collyar.

5. Four volumes – the *Life of Dryden*, *Life of Swift*, Introductions to Ballantyne's *Novelists' Library* and *Paul's Letters* – because of the arbitration were 'lying half printed, a dead burthen either on Constable's house or ours'. *Letters*, x. 71. Scott proposed to add two more volumes of miscellaneous writings and publish immediately, the profits to be applied as the arbiter should decide. The six volumes were accordingly

£95	To William Mitchel[1] (Nephw) ½ years board etc. £17	
21	Wine etc.	2
74 in hand	Antiqun. Society	2
Craig 120		
£194		£21

I wrote a page or two last night slumbrously.

2 SUNDAY Late at court, got to Abbotsford last nigh[t] with Mr. Davidoff or rather Count Davidoff about eight o'clock at night. I workd a little this morning then had a long and warm walk. Mr. and Mrs. Hamilton from Chiefswood, present inhabitants of Lockhart's cottage.

3 MONDAY At Selkirk, dined and spent the night with us which made the society pleasant. He is a fine soldierly looking man though affected with paralysis. His wife a fine good humourd little woman. He is supposed to be a writer in *Blackwood's* magazine. Since we were to lose the Lockharts we could scarce have had more agreeable folks.[2]

At Selkirk where Borthwickbrae[3] was elected with the usual unanimity of the Forest Freeholders. This was a sight to my young Muscovite. We walkd in the evening to the Lake.

4 TUESDAY Another warm and dry day. Why this passes.

Answer of a Russian peasant to Peter the Great who had askd his opinion of his new Capital Saint Petersburgh.

---

published, by Cadell, later in the year. Ultimately the proceeds were awarded to Constable's creditors, even though the bills with which Constable paid Scott had been returned dishonoured.

1. The husband of Carrie (or Currie) Lamb, mother of Daniel Scott's illegitimate son William. He had been apprenticed to David Bridges, an Edinburgh clothier, but after the death of Mrs. Bridges in October 1825 would have ceased to board in his house. This, as Dr. Corson pointed out to me, would account for the reference to '½ years board'.
2. Anne was already intimate with them. 'The Hamiltons and we meet almost every day. We generally meet either at Chiefswood or here in the evening and take long walks. They are famous walkers and they are people whom I like extremely. As she has no carriage I generally call for her to make visits.' Anne to Lockhart, 1 July 1826, Abbots. Both are pleasant, 'but I must own that I get on *much* better with Mr. Hamilton'. Anne to Sophia, 13 July 1826, Abbots.
3. William Eliot Lockhart of Borthwickbrae.

Before you lie the Ocean deeps
Behind you Grief in anguish weeps
On one side is the barren heath
On t'other is the groan of death.

Walkd in the evening.

5 WEDNESDAY Still very hot but with thunder-showers. Wrote till breakfast then walkd and signd the death warrant of a number of old firs at Abbotstown. I hope their deaths will prove useful; their lives are certainly not ornamental. Young Mr. Davidow enterd upon the cause of the late discontents in Russia which he imputes to a deep-seated Jacobin conspiracy to overthrow the state and Empire and establish a government by Consuls.

Craig	. £120	Cash. To Bogie £6
Anne £10		
Curle 50 .	60	Anne for house £20 Drat. £10 . . . 30
	60	Travelling 5
Cash in hand £74		Expences. 23 May to Mr Curl per Drat . 50
Deduce 31		
	43	
In purse and bank £103		£91

6 THURSDAY Returnd last night with my frozen Muscovites[1] to the Capital and sufferd as usual from the incursions of the black horse during the night. It was absolute fever. A bunch of letters but little interesting. Mr. Barry Cornwall writes to condole with me. I think our acquaintance scarce warranted this but it is well meant and modestly done. Myself I cannot conceive the idea of forcing myself on strangers in distress and I have half a mind to turn sharp round on some of my consolers.

Came home from court. R. P. Gillies calld. He is writing a satire. He has a singular talent of aping the measure and tone of Byron, and this poem goes to the tune of *Don Juan*. But [it] is the champagne after it has stood two days with the cork drawn.

Thereafter came Charles K. Sharpe and Will Clerk as Robinson[2] sayeth to my exceeding refreshment. And last not least Mr. Jollie, one of the triumvirs who manage my poor matters.[3] He consents to the going on with the small Edition of novels[4] which he did not before comprehend. All this has consumed the day but we will make up tideway presently. I must dress to go to Lord Medwyn to dinner and it is near time.

1. *Love's Labour's Lost*, v. 2.
2. Robinson Crusoe.
3. There were three Trustees: Gibson, Jollie, and Monypenny.
4. See the Entry for 30 June and note.

7 FRIDAY Coming home from Lord Medwyn's last night I fell in with Willie Clerk and went home to drink a little shrub and water over which we chatted of old stories untill half past eleven.

This morning I corrected two proofs of C—y[1] which is getting on. But there must be a little check with the throng business at the close of the Session D—n the Session. I wish it would close its eyes for a century. It is too bad [to] be kept broiling here. But on the other hand we must have the instinctive gratitude of the Laird of McIntosh who was for the King that gave McIntosh half a guinea the day and half a guinea the morn.[2] So I retract my malediction.

Received from Blackwood to accot. sales of *Malachi* – £72. 0. 0 with some odd Shillings.[3] This was for copies sold to Banks – The cash comes far from ill-timed having to clear all odds and ends before I leave Edinburgh. This will carry me on tidily enough till 25th. when precepts[4] become payable . . . Well – if Malachi did me some mischief he must also contribute *quodam modo* to my comfort.

8 SATURDAY Wrote a good task this morning – I may be mistaken but I do think the Tale of Elspat McTavish[5] in my bettermost manner but J. B. roars for chivalry; he does not quite understand that everything may be overdone in this world or sufficiently estimate the necessity of novelty. The highlanders have been off the field now for some time.

Returning from the court lookd into a fine Show of wild Beasts[6] and saw Nero the great lion whom they had the brutal cruelty to bait with bulldogs against whom the noble creature disdaind to exert his strength. He was lying like a prince in a large cage where you might be admitted if you [dared]. I had a month's mind – but was afraid of the Newspapers. I could be afraid of nothing else for never did a creature seem more gentle and yet majestic. I longed to caress him. Wallace the other lion, born in Scotland, seemd much less trustworthy. He handled the dogs as his namesake did the Southron.

In purse	£43		
Malachi minus		Paid Bridges' accompt———	31
Bridges–	41		
purse	£84		41
Craig	60		
	£144.		

1. Croftangry, i.e. *Chronicles of the Canongate*.
2. See *Waverley*, note 9.
3. Since he had already received £25 on 4 March, this payment, with the odd shillings, probably makes the total £100.
4. The quarterly payment of his salaries.
5. 'The Highland Widow', the first tale in *Chronicles of the Canongate*.
6. 'WOMBWELL'S IMMENSE MENAGERIE OF FOREIGN QUADRUPEDS AND BIRDS . . . including several animals entirely new (never having been before exhibited in Europe).' *Edinburgh Advertiser*, 7 July 1826. See note 7, p. 809.

Enter a confounded Dousterswivel[1] calld Burschal or some such name patronized by John Lockhart, Teacher of German and Learner of English.

He opend the trenches by making me a present of a German work calld *Der Bibelsche Orient* – then began to talk of literature at large and display his own pretensions – Askd my opinion of Gray as a poet – and wishd me to subscribe an attestation of his own mérits for the purpose of getting him scholars. As I hinted my want of acquaintance with his qualifications I found I had nearly landed myself in a proof for he was girding up his loins to repeated thundering translations by himself into German Hebrew until thinking it superfluous to stand on very much ceremony with one who used so little with me hinted at letters to write and got him to translate himself elsewhere.

Saw a house in Brunswick street which I liked. Below good kitchen and scullery and 3 rooms. Ground floor – good parlour and sitting room backward with small room.

Second floor Drawing-room and anti-room. One excellent bedroom or library – one small.

Four good rooms in the Attics. There are thus seven servants rooms and three good bedrooms supposing that one of the large rooms were occupied as a library.

The price is £1700 – very cheap for the premises. But there is £22 ground rent.

This evening supd wt. Thos. Thomson about the affairs of the Bannatyne – there were there the Dean,[2] Will Clerk, John Thomson, young Smythe of Methwyn – Very pleasant.

9 SUNDAY Rather slumbrous to-day from having sate up till twelve last night. We settled or seemd to settle on an election for the Bannatyne Club. There are people who would wish to confine it much to one party but those who were together last night saw it in the true and liberal point of view as a great national institution which may do much good in the way of publishing our old records providing we do not fall into the usual habit of antiquaries and neglect what is useful for things that are merely curious. Thomson is a host for such an undertaking.

I wrote a good day's work at the Canongate matter notwithstanding the intervention of two naps – I get sleepy oftener than usual – It is the weather I suppose. *Naboclish*.[3] I am near the end of the 1st. Volume: and every step is one out of difficulty.

1. The German villain in *The Antiquary*.
2. George Cranstoun, Dean of the Faculty of Advocates.
3. 'Don't mind it', an Irishism picked up the previous summer.

10 MONDAY Slept too long this morning; it was eight before I rose – half past eight ere I came into the parlour. Terry and J. Ballantyne dined with me yesterday and I suppose the wassail, though there was little enough of it, had stuck to my pillow.

This morning I was visited by a Mr. Lewis, a smart cockney, whose object is to amend the handwriting. He uses as a mechanical aid a sort of puzzle of wire and ivory which is put upon the fingers to keep them in the desired position like the puzzle on a dog's nose to make him bear himself right in the field. It is ingenious and may be useful. If the man come here as he proposes in winter I will take lessons. Bear witness, good reader, that if W. S. writes a cramp hand as you can bear witness is the case he is desirous to mend it.

Cash in purse £84
Lockhart   65   Rec[e]ived from Lockhart the money for the article[1]
               149   £70 minus £   advanced to Charles being in
Bank   60   cash – £65
               209

The frightful rumours about R. H—r[2] confirmd in their extent. His life was compromised but for the exertions of Hobhouse under Secy of State who detected a warrant for his trial passing through the office. These things, worse than loss of fortune or even loss of friends, make a man sick of this wordly [scene] where the fairest outsides so often cover the foulest vices. This then was the reason he seemd rather to shun his old friends and never came down to Scotland.

Dined with John Swinton *en famille*. He told me an odd circumstance. Coming from Berwick Shire in the Mail coach he met with a passenger who seemd more like a military man than any thing else. They talkd on all sort of subjects at length on politics. *Malachi's Letters* were mentiond when the stranger observed they were much more seditious than some expressions for which he had three or four years ago been nearly sent to Botany Bay. And perceiving John Swinton's surprize at this avowal He added 'I am Kinloch of Kinloch.'[3] This gentleman had got engaged in the Radical business (the only real gentleman by the way who did) and harangued the weavers of Dundee with such emphasis that he would have been tried and sent to Botany Bay had he not fled abroad. He was outlawd and only restored to his status on a composition with government. It seems to have escaped Mr. Kinloch that the conduct of a man who

1. The review of the *Life of Kemble* and Kelly's *Reminiscences*.
2. Richard Heber. See the Entry for 25 June.
3. After taking the chair at a Reform Meeting in Dundee he was indicted on a charge of sedition in January 1820, and outlawed when he failed to appear.

places a lighted coal in the middle of combustibles and upon the floor is a little different from him who places the same quantity of burning fuel in a fire grate.

11 TUESDAY The last day of the Session and as toilsome a one as I ever saw. There were about 100 or 120 cases on the roll and most of them of an incidental character which gives us Clerks the greatest trouble for it is the grashopper that is a burthen[1] to us. Came home about four tired and hungry. I wrought little or none, indeed I could not having books and things to pack: went in the evening to sup with John Murray where I met Will Clerk, Thomson—Henderland and Chas Stuart Blantyre, and had of course a pleasant party. I came late home though for me – and was not in bed till past midnight; it would not do for me to do this often.

12 WEDNESDAY I have the more reason to eschew evening parties that I slept two mornings till past eight. These vigils would soon tell on my utility as the divines call it. But this is the last day in town and the world shall be amended.

I have been trying to mediate between the unhappy R. P. G.[2] and his uncle Lord G.[3] The latter talks like a man of sense and a good relation and would I think do some thing for R. P. G. if he would renounce temporary expedients and bring his affairs to a distinct crisis. But this R. P. will not hear of but flatters himself with ideas which seemd to me quite visionary. I could make nothing of him but I conclude offended him by being of his uncle's opinion rather than his as to the mode of extricating his affairs.

Paid off Bills as follows

		Lodgings	£24	Of this sum £70
Cash	£149	Bill Iron-monger to acct.	20	was incurd last
Deduce	96	Stevenson Bookseller Do.	50	year so that I am
	53	Print of Lord Stair	1	only accountable
Paid	3	Dalgleish to Accot. . .	1	for £26 willfully
	£50		£96	expended.

My clumsy way of book-keeping answers very well. I find the balances come out accurate. I never bother myself with the silver. The Review money came well in and as it seems to do Lockhart service also we are [both satisfied].

1. Ecclesiastes 12: 5.
2. Robert Pierce Gillies.
3. Lord Gillies.

I am to dine out to-day – and I would fain shirk and stay at home – Never, Shylock like, had less will to supping forth but I must go or be thought sulky. Lord M.[1] and Lord Abercromby calld this morning and a world of people besides. Among others honest Mr. Wilson late of Wilsonton[2] who took so much care of me at London sending fresh eggs and all sort of good things. Well – I have dawdled and written letters sorely against the grain all day. Also I have been down to see Will: Allan's picture of the Landing of Queen Mary which he has begun in a great stile. Also I have put my letters and papers to rights which only happens when I am about to move and now having nothing left to do I *must* go and dress myself.

13 THURSDAY Dined yesterday with Lord Abercromby at a party he gave to Lord Melville and some old friends who formd the Contemporary club. Ld. M. and I met with considerable feeling on both sides and all our feuds were forgotten and forgiven. I conclude so at least because one or two people who I know to be sharp observers of the weather-glass on occasion of such squalls have been earnest with me to meet Lord M. at parties which I am well assured they would not have been (had I been Horace[3] come to life again) were they not sure the breeze was over.[4] For myself I am happy [th]at our usual state of friendship should be restored though I could not have *come down Proud Stomach* to make advances which is among friends always the duty of the richer and more powerful of the two.

To-day I leave Mrs. Brown's lodgings. Altogether I cannot complain but the insects were voracious even untill last night when the turtle soup and champagne ought to have me sleep like a top. But I have done a monstrous sight of work here notwithstanding the indolence of the last week, which must and shall be amended.

1. Lord Melville.
2. 'William Wilson, Esq. of Wandsworth Common, formerly of Wilsontown, in Lanarkshire.' J. G. L. (note to the Entry for 25 October 1826).
3. If Scott is Horace, Lord Melville is Maecenas, his patron. It is thought that there was at one time a coolness between Horace and Maecenas.
4. As early as 17 March Sir Robert Dundas had told Scott that Melville had written in a friendly fashion: 'Sir Walter shall find, that it [the *Malachi* affair] will not have diminished, even in the most trivial degree, the great regard I have ever felt towards him.' *Letters*, ix. 468 n.

So good bye, Mrs. Brown,
I am going out of town
Over Dale over down
Where bugs bite not
Where lodgers fight not
Where below you chairmen drink not
Where beside you gutters stink not
But all is fresh and clean and gay
And merry lambkins sport and play
And they toss with rakes uncommonly short hay
Which looks as if it had been sown only the other day
And where oats are at twenty five Shillings a boll they say
But all's one for that since I must and will away.

14 FRIDAY ABBOTSFORD – Arrived here yesterday before four
o'clock. Any body would think, from the Fal de ral tit conclusion
of my journal of yesterday that I left town in a very gay humour –
Cujus contrarium verum est.[1] But nature has given me a kind of
buoyancy – I know not what to call it – that mingled even with
my deepest aflictions and most gloomy hours. I have a secret pride – I
fancy it will be so most truly termd – which impels me to mix with my
distresses strange snatches of Mirth 'which have no mirth in them'.[2]
In fact the journey hither – the absence of the affectionate friend that
used to be my companion on the journey – and many mingled
thoughts of bitterness have given me a fit of the bile.

15 SATURDAY This day I did not attempt to work but spent my time
in the morning in making the necessary catalogue and distribution of
two or three chests of books which I have got home from the binder,
Niece Anne acting as my amanuensis. In the evening we drove to
Huntlyburn and took tea there. Returning home we escaped a
considerable danger. The iron screw bolts of the drivingseat suddenly giving way the servants were very nearly precipitated upon the
backs of the horses. Had it been down hill instead of bang on the level
the horses must have taken fright and the consequences might have
been fatal. Indeed they had almost taken fright as it was had not Peter
Mathieson, who in Mr. Fag's phrase I take to be 'the discreetest of
whips,'[3] kept his presence of mind when losing his equilibrium, so
that he managed to keep the horses in hand untill we all go[t] out. I
must say it is not the first imminent danger in which I have seen Peter
(my Automedon for near 25 years) behave with the utmost firmness.

1. 'Of which the contrary is true'.
2. Wordsworth's *Excursion*, i, 570.
3. Sheridan's *Rivals*, ii. 1.

16 SUNDAY Very unsatisfactory to-day. Sleepy, stupid, indolent – finishd arranging the books and after that was totally useless – unless it can be called study that I slumberd for three or four hours over a variorum edition of the Gill-Hill's tragedy.[1] Admirable recipe for low spirits – for not to mention the brutality of so extraordinary a murther it led John Bull into one of his most uncommon set of gambols untill at last he became so maudlin as to weep for the pitiless assassin Thurtell and treasure up the leaves and twigs of the hedge and shrubs in the fatal garden as valuable reliques, nay throngd the minor theatres to see the very roan horse and yellow Gigg in which the body was transported from one [place to another]. I have not stepd over the threshold to-day so very stupid have I been.

17 MONDAY *Desidiæ* longum valedixi.[2] Our time is like our money. When we change a guinea the shillings escape as things of small account. When we break a day by idleness in the morning the rest of the hours lose their importance in our eye. I set stoutly to work about 7 this morning to *Boney*

> And long ere dinner time I have
> Full eight close pages wrote
> What, Duty, hast thou now to crave?
> Well done, Sir Walter Scott.

18 TUESDAY This as yesterday has been a day of unremitting labour though I only got through half the quantity of manuscript owing to drowsiness, a most disarming annoyance. I walkd a little before dinner and after tea but was unable to go with the girls and Charles[3] to the top of Cauldshiels hill. I fear my walking powers

---

1. 'The murder of Weare by Thurtell and Co. at Gill's-Hill, in Hertfordshire. Sir Walter collected printed trials with great assiduity, and took care always to have the contemporary ballads and prints bound up with them. He admired particularly this verse of Mr. Hook's broadside –

   "They cut his throat from ear to ear,
      His brains they battered in;
   His name was Mr. William Weare,
      He dwelt in Lyon's Inn." ' J. G. L.

   For Scott's visit to Gill's Hill see the Entry for 28 May 1828.
2. 'I have said a long farewell to idleness.'
3. Who came to Abbotsford at the end of the Oxford term, ostensibly to study, actually to be near his widowed father. See the Entry for 30 May 1826.

are diminishing. But why not? they have been wonderfully long efficient all things considerd. Only I fear I shall get fat and fall into diseases. Well! things must be as they may.[1] Let us use the time and faculties which God has left us and trust futurity to his guidance. Amen!

Craig	£60	Paid Coals	£10
Paid in 13th.	48	Anne for house enterd before	10
	108	Travelling	2
Deduce Coals	10		22
In Bank	98		
In purse	£50		
To Bank	48		
	2		
Travels	2		
Purse	£0.0.0		

This is the day of Saint Boswell's[2] Fair. That watery Saint has for once had a dry festival.

19 WEDNESDAY Wrote a page this morning but no more. Corrected proofs however and went to Selkirk to hold Sheriff Court, Maxpopple being unwell.[3] This consumed the forenoon. Col. and Miss Fergusson with Mr. and Mrs. Laidlaw dined and occupied the Evening. The rain seemd to set in this night.

20 THURSDAY To-day rainy – A morning and forenoon of hard work – about five pages which makes up for yesterday's lee way. I am sadly tired however. But as I go to Mertoun[4] at 4 and spend the night there the exertion was necessary.

21 FRIDAY To Mertoun we went accordingly. Lord and Lady Minto were there with part of their family, David Haliburton, Muirhouselaw etc., besides their own large family. So my lodging was a little room which I had not occupied since I was a bachelor but often before in my frequent intercourse with this kind and hospitable family. Feeling myself returnd to that celibacy which renders many accomodations indifferent which but lately were indispensible, my imagination drew a melancholy contrast between the young man entering the world on fire

1. Corporal Nym's philosophy. *Henry V*, ii. 1.
2. The village of St. Boswell's four miles south-east of Melrose.
3. Scott's cousin, William Scott of Maxpoffle, as Sheriff-Substitute, conducted the weekly Courts. The Sheriff gave the verdict, but appeared in Court only for trials.
4. To visit the Scotts of Harden.

for fame and restless in imagining means of coming by it and the deprived and aged widower blazé on the point of literary reputation, deprived of the social comforts of a married state and looking back to regret instead of looking forward to Hope. This brought bad sleep and unpleasing dreams. But if I cannot hope to be what I have been I will not if I can help it suffer vain repining to make me worse than I may be.

We left Mertoun after breakfast and the two Annes and I visited Lady Raeburn at Lessudden. My Aunt is now in her ninetieth year – so clean, so nice, so well arranged in every respect, that it makes old age lovely. She talks both of late and former events with perfect possession of her faculties and has only faild in her limbs. A great deal of kind feeling has survived in spite of the frost of years.

Home to dinner and workd all the afternoon among the *Moniteurs* for a long time to little purpose for my principal acquisition was a head-ache. I wrote nothing to-day but part of a trifle for Blackwood.[1]

22 SATURDAY The same severe head-ache attends my poor pate. But I have workd a good deal this morning and will do more. I wish to have half the volume[2] sent into town on Monday if possible. It will be a royal effort and more than make up for the blanks of this week.

23 SUNDAY I wrote very hard this day and attaind page 40– 45 would be more than half the volume. Colonel Russell came about one and carried me out a walking which I was all the better of. In the evening we expected Terry and his wife but they did not come which makes me fear she may be unwell again.

24 MONDAY A great number of proof sheets to revise and send off and after that I took a fancy to give a more full account of the Constitution framed by Sieyes[3] – a complicated and ingenious web it is but far too fine and critical to be practically useful.

25 TUESDAY Terry and wife arrived yesterday both very well. At dinner time to-day came Dr. Jamieson of the Scottish Dictionary,[4] an

1. Blackwood's have no trace of any article written by Scott at this time except the review of Galt's *Omen*, for which he had been paid £10 on 23 June. See that day's Entry. 'The trifle' which he wrote can only be a reference to work on the proof-sheets.
2. Vol. iv of the *Life of Napoleon*.
3. See *Life of Napoleon*, vol. iv, ch. 5.
4. Dr. John Jamieson (?1759–1838), a Seceder minister, an antiquarian, and the author of the *Etymological Dictionary of the Scottish Language*, 1808–25. For Scott's first meeting with him in 1795, see *Letters*, i. 39.

excellent good man and full of auld Scottish cracks which amuse me well enough but are caviar to the young people. A little prolix and heavy is the good Dr., somewhat prosaic and accustomd to much attention on the Sunday from his congregation and I hope on the six other days from his family. So he *will* demand full attention from all and sundry before he begins a story and once begun there is no chance of his ending.

26 WEDNESDAY This day went to Selkirk and held a court. The Dr. and Terry chose to go with me. Capt. and Mrs. Hamilton came to dinner – desperate warm weather. Little done in the literary way except sending off proofs. Roup of standing corn etc. went off very indifferently.[1] Letter from Ballantyne wanting me to write about absentees. But I have enough to do without burning my fingers with politics. Paid Andw. Lang[2] by Cheque £21 received of county money. Got in some silver.

Craig	. .	£93
Drat	. .	21
		72

27 THURSDAY Up and at it this morning and finishd four pages. An unpleasant letter from London as if I might be troubled by some of the crers there when going to town to get materials for *Nap*. I have no wish to go – none at all – I would even like to put off my visit so far as John Lockhart and my daughter are concernd and see them when the meeting could be more pleasant – But then having an offer to see the correspondence from St. Helena I can make no doubt that I ought to go. However if it is to infer any danger to my personal freedom English wind will not blow on me. It is monstrous hard to prevent me doing what is certainly the best for all parties.[3]

1. The auction raised no more than £106. 16s. Sederunt Book, i. 150.
2. The Sheriff-Clerk for Selkirkshire, 'sensible steady and a good man of business'. *Letters*, viii. 504. Scott would have liked him to succeed Erskine as Sheriff-Substitute; instead Lang undertook to 'drynurse' Maxpoffle 'for a year or two'. *Letters*, viii. 506. He was the grandfather of Andrew Lang the man of letters, who wrote a life of Scott and edited the novels.
3. A certain Mr. Abud had bought up bills belonging to some of the London creditors and intended to insist on immediate payment in full. This might have obliged the Trustees to wind up the Trust and pay every creditor the few shillings in the pound that were available, but the Trust was saved by Sir William Forbes, who eventually bought Abud's bills from him at their face value.

    For Lord Bathurst's offer of the St. Helena papers see the Entry for 26 April 1826 and note. In the event Scott left for London on 13 October.

28 FRIDAY I am well nigh choked with the sulphurous heat of the
weather – or I am unwell for I perspire as if I had been walking hard
and my hand is as nervous as a paralytic's. Read through and
corrected *Saint Ronan's Well*.[1] I am no good judge but I think the
language of this piece rather good. Then I must allow the fashionable
portraits are not the true thing. I am too much out of the way to see
and remark the ridiculous in Society. The story is terribly contorted
and unnatural and the catastrophé is melancholy which should
always be avoided. No matter. I have corrected it for the press –

The worthy Lexicographer left us to-day. Somewhat ponderous he
is, poor soul – but there are excellent things about him – Action and
Reaction – Scots proverb – 'The unrest (i.e. pendulum) of a clock
goes aye as far the ae gait as the t'other.'[2]

Walter's account of his various quarters per last despatch. Query if
original.

> Loughrea is a blackguard place
> To Gort I give my curse
> Athlone itself is bad enough
> But Ballinrobe is worse.
> I cannot tell which is the worst
> They're all so very bad
> But of all towns I ever saw
> Bad luck to Kinnegad.[3]

Old Mr. Haliburton dined with us also Colonel Russell. What a
man for fourscore or thereby is old Haly, an Indian too. He came
home in 1785.

29 SATURDAY Yesterday I wrought little and light work almost
stifled by the smothering heat. To-day I wrought about half task

1. 'This Novel was passing through the press in 8vo, 12mo, and
   18mo, to complete collective editions in these sizes.'. J. G. L.
2. 'Goes always as far the one way as the other.'
3. A traditional rhyme with many local variants. Compare, for
   instance, this version sent by Dr. John Pym:
   > Galway is a blackguard place,
   > To Cork I give my curse,
   > Tralee itself is bad enough,
   > But Limerick is worse.
   > I cannot tell which is the worst,
   > They're all so very filthy,
   > But of all the towns I ever saw
   > Bad luck to Clonakilty.

in the morning and as a judgement on me I think for yesterday's sloth Mr. H. stayd unusually late in the forenoon. He is my friend, my father's friend, and an excellent sensible man besides and a man of eighty and upwards may be allowd to talk long because in the nature of things he cannot have long to talk.

		Gave Anne money for house —————	£25.0.0
Mr. Craig	£72	Gardener to accompt ———————	9.0.0
Drat	35	Closed up Edinr. accompts (total £2.3) from	
	37	Drat————	1
			35 0 0

If I do a task to-day I hope to send a good parcel on Monday and keep tryste pretty well.

30 SUNDAY I did better yesterday than I had hoped for – four instead of three pages which considering how my time was eat up by prolonged morning lounging with friend Hali was pretty fair.

I wrote a good task before eleven o'clock but then my good friends[1] twaddled and dawdled for near two hours before they set off. The time devoted to hospitality, especially to those whom I can reckon upon as sincere good friends, I never grudge but I like to –

Wellcome the coming speed the parting guest.[2]

By my will every guest should part at half past ten or arrange himself to stay for the day.

We had a long walk in a sweltering hot day – met Mr. Blackwood coming to call and walkd him on with us, so blinkd his visit – *gratias domine* ! ! – Askd him for breakfast tomorrow to make amends for staving him. I rather overwalkd myself – the heat considerd.

31 MONDAY I corrected six sheets and sent them off with eight leaves of copy so I keep forward pretty well – Blackwood the bookseller came over from Chiefswood[3] to breakfast and this kept me idle till eleven o'clock. At twelve I went out with the girls in the sociable and calld [on] the family at Bemerside,[4] on Dr. and Mrs. Brewster[5] and Mr. Bainbridge at Gattonside House. It was five e'er we got home so

---

1. Mr. and Mrs. Terry.
2. Pope's translation of Homer's *Odyssey*, xv. 84.
3. Blackwood was staying with Captain Hamilton, who was one of his authors.
4. The Haigs.
5. At Allerly, Melrose.

there was a day dishd unless the afternoon does something for us. I am keeping up pretty well however, and after all visitors will come and calls must be made.[1] I must not let Anne forgo the custom of well bred society.

AUGUST

1 TUESDAY Yesterday evening did nothing for the idlesse of the morning. I was hungry, eat and drank and became drowsy. Then I took to arranging the old plays of which Terry had brought me about a dozen and dipping into them scrambled through two – One calld *Michaelmas Term*[2] full of traits of manners and another a sort of bouncing tragedy called *The Hector of Germany* or *The Palsgrave*.[3] The last, worthless in the extreme, is like many of the plays in the beginning of the 17th. Century written to a good tune. The dramatic poets of that time seem to have possessd as joint stock a highly poetical and abstract tone of language so that the worst of them often remind you of the very best. The audience must have had a much stronger sense of poetry in those days than now since language was received and applauded at the Fortune or the Red Bull which could not now be understood by any general audience in Great Britain. This leads far.

This morning I wrote two leaves then out with Tom Purdie and gave directions about thinning all the plantations above Abbotsford properly so calld. Came in at one o'clock and now set to work.

> *Debout Debout, Lyciscas, debout.*[4]

Finishd four leaves. Received £150 Salary from Mr. Gibson.

2 WEDNESDAY Well and to-day I finishd before dinner five leaves more and I would crow a little about [it] but here comes Duty like an old housekeeper on an idle chamber maid. Hear her very words.

Duty Oh you crow do you? – pray can you deny that your sitting so quiet at work was owing to its raining heavily all the forenoon and indeed till dinner time so that nothing would have stird out that could help it save a duck or a goose? I trow if it had been a fine day by noon there

Cash paid into	
Bank	£150
Ballance	37
	£187

---

1. Scott's resolution after the financial crash to entertain no more company was becoming, as the entries for July have shown, more honoured in the breach than the observance.
2. By Middleton, 1607.
3. By Wentworth Smith, 1615.
4. Molière's *La Princesse d'Elide*, Prologue.

would have been aching of the head, throbbing shaking and so forth, to make an apology for going out.

Egomet Ipse And whose head ever throbbd to go out when it rained, Mrs. Duty?

Duty Answer not to me with a foolborn iest[1] as your poor friend Erskine used to say to you when you escaped from his good advice under the fire of some silly pun. You smoke a segar after dinner and I never check you – drink tea too which is loss of time and then instead of writing one other page or correcting those you have written out you rollock into the woods till you have not a dry thread about you and here you sit writing down my words in your foolish journal instead of minding my advice.

Ego Why, Mrs. Duty, I would as gladly be friends with [you] as Crabbe's tradesman fellow with his conscience[2] but you should have some consideration with human frailty.

Duty Reckon not on that – but however goodnight for the present. I would only recommend to you to think no thoughts in which I am not mingled – to read no books in which I have no concern – to write three sheets of botheration all the six days of the week *per diem* and on the seventh to send them to the printer. Thus advising I heartily bid you farewell –

Ego Farewell, Madam – (Exit Duty.) and be d—d to ye for an unreasonable bitch. 'The devil must be in this greedy gled' as the Earl of Angus said to his hawk; 'will she never be satisfied?'[3] I believe in my soul she is the very hag who haunted the merchant Abudah[4] – I'll have my great chest upstairs exorcized. But first I'll take a nap till supper which mus[t] take place within ten minutes.

3 THURSDAY Wrote half a task in the morning: from eleven till half past eight in Selkirk taking precognitions about a *row*[5] on Selkirk-hill-

---

1. *2 Henry IV*, v. 5.
2. Crabbe's *Struggles of Conscience*.
3. See *Tales of a Grandfather*, ch. 29.
4. In 'The Talisman of Oromanes' in Weber's *Tales of the East*, iii. 426–43.
5. To 'take precognitions' is to inquire into the facts connected with an offence to help the public prosecutor level his indictment. This particular row is described in the next day's letter to Maria Edgeworth: 'On the evening of last Monday a feud broke out at a Selkirk fair which has made some work for the Sheriff and very nearly for that other respectable office bearer to wit the Hangman. . . . One or two unfortunate civilians are much hurt their foemen having hammerd on their heads with stones which weapons were found coverd with blood and hair.' *Letters*, x. 84.

fair and came home famishd and tired. Now, Mrs. Duty, do you think there is no other Duty of the family but yourself or can the Sheriff Depute neglect his duty that the Author may mind *his*? – the thing cannot be; the people of Selkirk must have justice as well as the people of England books. So the two Duties may go pull caps about it. My conscience is clear.

4 FRIDAY Wrote to Miss Edgeworth on her sister's marriage which consumed the better part of the morning. I must read for Marengo[1] – item I must look at the pruning – Item at the otter hunt[2] – but my hope is constant to make up a good day's task notwithstanding. Faild in finding the otter and was tired and slept and did but a poor day's work.

		To pay for hay purchased	£41
Drat	£187	To Anne £10. repaid £1 to pocket—	31
In Bank	72		
	£115		£72

[There is no entry for Saturday, 5 August. Scott wrote on that day to Cadell asking him to pay £250 (half the money promised for *Chronicles of the Canongate*), and a longer letter to Gibson urging him to accept repayment of his loan which, as a trustee, he was reluctant to do (*Letters*, x. 86–8). Most of the day, it is reasonable to conjecture, would be spent on the *Life of Napoleon*, to make up for the 'poor day's work' mentioned in the previous entry.]

6 SUNDAY Wrote to-day a very good day's work. Walkd to Huntly Burn to Chiefswood and saw old Mrs. Tytler a friend when life was young. Her husband Lord Woodhouselee was a kind amiable and accomplishd man and when we lived at Laswade cottage soon after my marriage we saw a great deal of the family who were very kind to us as newly enterd on the world. Walkd home and workd in the evening. Four leaves finishd.

7 MONDAY My niece Anne leaves us this morning summond back from one scene of distress to another. Her uncle David Macculloch is extremely ill – a paralytic stroke I fancy – She is a charming girl,

1. *Life of Napoleon*, vol. iv, ch. 9.
2. The day before there had been 'a grand crusade against the otter with all the Harden boys and a pack of otter-hounds whose chidings are really the finest cry in the world'. The otter had escaped into a drain where he was blockaded for the night; they were now hoping to turn him out again. *Letters*, x. 85.

ladylike in thought and action and very pleasant in society. Gave her as above £20. We are to dine to-day with our neighbours at Gattonside.¹ Meantime I will avail myself of my disposition to labour and work instead of journalising.

Mr. H. Cranstoun lookd in – a morning call: He is become extremely deaf. He gave me a letter from the Countess Purgstall his sister which I have not the heart to open. So many reproachs I have deserved for not writing. It is a sad thing though [to] task eyes as hard wrought as mine to keep up correspondence. Dined at Gattonside.

8 TUESDAY Wrote my task this morning and now for walk. Dine to-day at Chiefswood, have company tomorrow. Why this is dissipation. But no matter, Mrs. Duty, if the task is done – 'Aye but' says she 'you ought to do some thing extra – provide against a rainy day –' 'Not I – I'll make a rainy day provide against a fair one, Mrs. Duty. I write twice as much in bad weather.' Seriously I write fully as much as I ought. I do not like this dull aching in the chest and the back and its giving way to exercise shews that it originates in remaining too long in a sitting posture. So I will take the field while the play is good.

9 WEDNESDAY I wrote only two leaves to-day but with as many additions as might rank for three. I had a long and warm walk. Mrs. Tytler of Woodhouselee, the Hamiltons and Colonel Fergusson dined here. How many early stories did the old lady's presence recall. She might almost be my mother yet there we sate like two people of another generation talking of things and people the rest knew nothing of. When a certain period of life is survived the difference of years between the survivors, even when considerable, becomes of much less consequence.

Besides my hot skin in the morning I drank iced porter and ginger beer and iced claret and was for my pains rewarded with a pretty little touch of Cholera Morbus in the night-time. Never mind. Such squalls cool the temperature.

10 THURSDAY Rose early and wrote hard so that [little] now remaining and workd hard till two when I went with Anne to Minto. The place being new to my companion gave her much amusement. We found the Scotts of Harden at Minto and had a very pleasant party I like Lady M.² particularly but missd my

1. The Bainbridges.
2. Lady Minto.

facetious and lively friend Lady A. M.[1] It is the fashion for women and silly men to abuse her as a blue-stocking – If to have wit, good sense and good humour, mixd with a strong power of observing and an equally strong one of expressing the result, be *blue*, she shall be as blue as they will. Such cant is the refuge of those who fear those who they [think] can turn them into ridicule – it is a common trick to revenge supposed raillery with good substantial calumny. Slept at Minto.

11 FRIDAY I was up as usual and wrote about two leaves meaning to finish my task at home but found Maxpopple here on my return which took up the evening.[2] But I shall finish the volume on Sunday, that is less than a month after beginning it. The same exertion would bring it out at Martinmas but December is a better time.[3]

12 SATURDAY Wrote a little in the morning then, Duty and I having settled that this is to be a kind of Holiday providing the volume be finishd tomorrow, I went to breakfast at Chiefswood and after that affair was happily transacted I wended me merrily to the Black Cock Stripe and there caused Tom Purdie and John Swanston cut out a quantity of firs. Got home about two o'clock and set to correct a set of proofs. James Ballantyne presages well of this work but is afraid of inaccuracies. So am I – but things must be as they may.[4] There is a kind of glamour about me which sometimes makes me read dates etc. in the proofsheets not as they actually do stand but as they ought to stand. I wonder if a pill of holy trefoil would dispell this fascination.

By the way John Swanston measured a young shoot that was growing remarkably and found that for three days successively it grew half an inch every day. Fine Ear used to hear the grass grow[5] – how far off would he have heard this extravagant rapidity of vegetation? The tree is a silver fir or spruce in the patch at the Greentongue Park.

13 SUNDAY Yesterday I was tired with labouring in the rough ground. Well! I must be content to feel my disabilities increase.

1. Lady Anna Maria Elliot, daughter of the first Lord Minto. See the Entry for 24 February 1826 and note.
2. Probably on Sheriff Court business.
3. Scott still assumes that the *Life of Napoleon* will be completed within six volumes; in fact it stretched to nine, and was not published until June 1827.
4. *Henry V*, ii.i.
5. In the fairy-tale of *Fortunio*, by the Countess d'Aulnoy.

One sure thing is that all wise men will soon contrive to lay aside inclination when performance grows toilsome. I have hobbled over many a rough heugh in my day; no wonder if I must sing at last

> Thus says the auld man to the Aik tree,
> Sair faild, hinny, since I kend thee.[1]

But here are many a mile of smooth walk just when I grow unable to face bent and brae and here is the garden when all fails. To a sailor the length of his quarter-deck is a good space of exercizing ground.

I wrote a good task to-day then walkd to the lake, then came back by three o'clock hungering and thirsting to finish the volume. I have seldom such fits of voluntary industry so Duty shall have the benefit.

Finishd Vol. IV this evening – *Deo Gratias*.

14 MONDAY

> This is a morning I have not seen many [a] day
> For it appears to set in for a rainy day.

It has not kept its word though. I was seized with a fit of the clevers and finishd my task by twelve o'clock and hope to add something in the evening. I was guilty however of some waywardness for I began Vol. V of *Bony* instead of carrying on the *Canongate* as I proposed. The reason however was that I might not forget the information I had acquired about the treaty of Amiens.

15 TUESDAY The weather seems decidedly broken. Yesterday indeed cleard up but this day seems to persevere in raining. Nabo-clish,[2] it's a rarity now a days. I wrote on though a little afflicted with the oppression on my chest. Sometimes I think it is something dangerous but as it always go[es] away on change of posture it cannot be speedily so. I want to finish my task – and then Good Night. I will never relax my labour in these affairs either for fear of pain or love of life. I will die a free man if hard working will do it. Accordingly to-day I cleared the ninth leaf, which is the tenth part of a volume in two days, $4\frac{1}{2}$ leaves a day. Walter and Jane with Mrs.

---

1. From *Rhymes of the Northern Bards*, edited by John Bell, 1812, p. 258.
2. 'Don't mind it.' See the Entry for 9 July 1826.

Jobson[1] are arrived to interrupt me. Paid five pounds to Mr. Laidlaw to purchase Lambs.

16 WEDNESDAY God be praised for restoring to me my dear children in good health which has made me happier than any thing which has happened these several months. Walter and Jane appear cordial and happy in each other, the greatest blessing Heaven can bestow on them or me who witness it. If we had Lockhart and Sophia there would be a meeting of the beings dearest to me in life.

		Expences Mr. Laidlaw as above for Lambs	£5
Cash	£115	Anne household expence	36
Drats.	52	Game Certificates	10
	£63		£52.0.0

Walkd down to Hun[t]ly Burn where I found a certain Lady[2] on a visit – so youthy – so beautiful – so strong in voice – with sense and learning – above all so fond of good conversation that in compassion to my eyes ears and understandg I bolted in middle of a tremendous shower of rain and rather chose to be wett to the skin than to be bethumpd with words at that rate. There seemd more than I of the same opinion for Colonel Fergusson chose the ducking rather than the conversation. Young Mr. Surtees came this evening.

17 THURSDAY Wrote half a leaf short of my task having proofs etc. to correct and being calld early to walk with the ladies. I have gaind three leaves on the two following[3] days so I cannot blame myself. *Sat cito si sat bene. Sat Boni* I am sure[4] I may say – a truly execrable pun that – hope no one will find it out.

In the evening we had Music from the girls and the voice of the harp and viol were heard in my halls once more which have been so long deprived of mirth. It is with a mixd sensation I hear these

---

1. Jane's mother came by Scott's invitation: 'I hope you will accomplish the kind promise you made me & meet them here so as to spend as much time with them as possible.' *Letters*, x. 82. Anne did not look forward to the visit: 'I dread to think of Mrs. Jobson and Jane but one cannot have Walter without them.' To Sophia, ?17 June 1826, Abbots.
2. 'The odious Miss Wells', as Walter describes her in a letter of 1 July 1827, Walpole.
3. Scott meant 'preceding'. He had written '4½ leaves a day' on the 14th and 15th instead of the usual three leaves.
4. 'Quickly enough if well enough. Enough of *Boney*, I am sure.'

sounds. I look on my children and am happy and yet every now and then a pang shoots across my heart. It seems so strange that my poor wife should not be there. But enough of this.

Colonel Fergusson dined.

18 FRIDAY Again I fell a half page behind, being summond out too early for my task,[1] but I am still two leaves before on the whole week. It is natural to see as much of these young people as I can. Walter talks of the Ionian Islands.[2] It is an awful distance. A long walk in very warm weather. Music in the evening.

19 SATURDAY This morning wrote none excepting extracts etc., being under the necessity of reading and collating a great deal which lasted till one o'clock or thereabouts when Dr. and Mrs. Brewster and their young people came to spend a day of happiness at the Lake. We were met there by Capt. and Mrs. Hamilton and a full party. Since the days of Seged Emperor of Ethiopia[3] these days of appointed sport and happiness have seldom answerd but we came off indifferently well. We did not indeed catch much fish but we lounged about in a delightful day, eat and drank, and the children, who are very fine infantry, were clamourously enjoying themselves. We sounded the Loch in two or three different places – the deepest may be 60 feet. I was accustomd to think it much more, but your deepest pools like your deepest politicians and philosophers often turn out more shallow than expected. The whole party dine with us.[4]

20 SUNDAY Wrote four leaves – the day wet and rainy though not uniformly so. No temptation however to play truant so this will make some amends for a blank day yesterday. I am in far advance on the press but it is but necessary if I go to Drumlanrig[5] on Wednesday as I

1. The early summons came as it did the day before from Anne and Jane. His sons were shooting over the Peel farm. *Letters*, x. 94.
2. Where he would be on the staff of the Governor, Sir Frederick Adam, the son of Scott's friend William Adam of Blair-Adam.
3. See Johnson's *Rambler*, nos. 204–5, for Seged's vain attempt to find happiness by pursuing it.
4. 'I gave a party to the sons of Dr. Brewster and some other little boys it consisted of about fifty old and young. We had the boat on the Lake and a sort of Djeune. It went off much better than I expected – none of the boys fell in to the Lake but on the contrary caught FOUR TROUT which they considered very *fine sprats*.' Anne to Sophia, 27 August 1826, Abbots.
5. To see the Duke of Buccleuch.

intend and to Lochore[1] next week which I also meditate. This will be no great interruption however if I can keep the *Canongate* moving for I shall be more than half a volume in advance[2] with *Napoleon*.

21 MONDAY Wrought out my task though much botherd with a cold in my head and face, how caught I know not.

Have sent over to Mr. Craig Bill for £250 and a drat. for £15 for my journey expenses. Mrs. Crampton, wife of the Surgeon Genl[3] in Ireland, sends to say she is hereabouts so we ask her. Hospitality must not be neglected and most hospitable are the Cramptons. All the cailliachs[4] from Huntly Burn are to be here and Anne wishes we may have enough of dinner. Naboclish! it is hoped there will be a *pièce de résistance*.

22 TUESDAY I have a note from Craig making my credit only £159. 4. By my accot. it is £313 – Some great mistake here. I think I have kept my entries regular and trust the error is on his side. Mrs. and Misses Cramptons departed. I was rather sorry to give them such brief entertainment for they were extremely kind. But going to Eldon Hall to-day and to Drumlanrig tomorrow there was nothing more could be done for them. It is raining now *successfully* as old Macfarlane of the Arroquhar [Inn][5] used to say. What is the odds we get a soaking before we cross the Birkendailly? – wet against dry ten to one –

23 WEDNESDAY Set off cheerily with Walter, Charles and Surtees[6] in the Sociable, to make our trip to Drumlangrig. We breakfasted at Mr. Boyd, Broadmeadows, and were received with Yarrow hospitality. From thence climbed the Yarrow and skirted Saint Mary's Lake and ascended the Birkhill path under the moist and misty influence of the Genius Loci. Never mind, my companions were

1. To visit Walter's estate in Fife.
2. In advance of the press. Ballantyne has been unable to keep up with the increased flow of copy.
3. Philip Crampton (1777–1858), Surgeon-General to the forces in Ireland, had befriended Walter and entertained Scott during the previous summer's Irish tour. *Life*, viii. 23.
4. 'Old women' in Gaelic, in this case the Ferguson sisters.
5. See *Letters*, iv. 265.
6. 'I am in a manner obliged to intrude on your grace's hospitality the further burthen of a college acquaintance of Charles's young Surtees whom I think you[r] Grace has seen at Abbotsford for which I must ask your Graces pardon. I cannot well leave him behind us.' *Letters*, x. 93.

merry and I cheerful. When old people can be with the young without
fatiguing them or themselves their tempers derive the same benefits
which some fantastic physicians of old supposed accrued to their
constitutions from the breath of the young and health[y]. You have
not – cannot again have, thier gaiety or pleasure in seeing sights but still it
reflects itself upon you, and you are cheerd and comforted. Our
luncheon eaten in the Herd's cottage but the poor woman saddend
me unawares by asking for poor Charlotte whom she had often seen there
alongst with me. She put me in mind that I had come twice over those
hills and bogs with a wheel-carriage before the road, now an excellent
[one], was made. I knew it was true but on my soul looking where we
must have gone I could hardly believe I had been such a fool – For riding,
pass if you will, but to put one's neck in such a venture with a wheel
carriage was too silly. Here we are however at Bitock's Inn for this night.

24 THURSDAY This morning lunchd at Parkgate under a very heavy
shower and then pushd on to Drumlanrig, where I was pleased to see
the old Castle and old servants solicitous and anxious to be civil. What
visions does not this magnificent old house bring back to me. The
exterior is much improved since I first knew it. It was then in the state
of dilapidation to which it had been abandond by the celebrated Old
Q.[1] and was indeed scarce wind and water tight. Then the whole wood
was felld and the outraged castle stood in the midst of waste and
desolation excepting a few scatterd old stumps not judged worth the
cutting. Now the whole has been ten or twelve years since completely
re-planted and the scatterd Seniors look as graceful as fathers surrounded by their children. The face of this immense estate has been
scarcely less wonderfully changed. The scrambling tenants who held a
precarious tenure of lease under the Duke of Queensberry at the risk
(as actually took place) of losing their possession at his death, have
given room to skillful and laborious men, working their farms regularly
and enjoying comfortable houses and their farms at a fair rent which is
enough to forbid idleness but not enough to overpower industry.

25 FRIDAY Here are Lord and Lady Home, Chas Douglas, Lord and
Lady Charlotte Stopford.[2] I grieve to say the last, though as beautiful
as ever, is extremely thin and looks delicate. The Duke[3] himself has
grown up into a graceful and apparently strong young man and

1. The fourth Duke of Queensberry.
2. A family party. Lady Home was a daughter of the third Duke of
   Buccleuch and Charles Douglas grandson of the second Duke.
   Lady Charlotte Stopford was a sister of the fifth Duke.
3. The fifth Duke of Buccleuch.

received us most kindly. I think he will be well qualified to sustain his difficult and important task. The heart is excellent, so are the talents, good sense and knowledge of the world, pickd up at one of the great English schools[1] (and it is one of their most important results) will prevent him from being deceived, and with perfect good nature he has a natural sense of his own situation which will keep him from associating with unworthy companions. God Bless him – his father and I loved each other well and his beautiful mother had as much of the angel in form face and disposition as is permitted to walk this earth. I see the balcony from which they wellcomd poor Charlotte and me long ere the ascent was surmounted streaming out their white handkerchiefs from the battlements. There were *four* merry people that day – now one sad individual is all that remains.

Singula praedantur anni.[2] I had a long walk to-day through the new plantations, the Duchesses Walk by the Nith etc. (formd by Prior's 'Kitty young and Gay'),[3] fell in with the ladies but their donkies out-walkd me – a flock of sheep afterwards outwalkd me and I begin to think on my conscience that a snail put on training might soon outwalk me. I must lay the old salve to the old sore and be thankful to be able to walk at all.

Nothing was written to-day my writing desk having been forgot at Parkgate but Tom Crichton kindly fetchd it up to-day so something more or less may be done tomorrow morning: And now to dress.

26 SATURDAY We took our departure from the friendly halls of Drumlanrig this morning after breakfast and leave-taking. I trust this young nobleman will be

> A hedge about his friends
> A hackle to his foes.[4]

I would [not] have him quite so soft natured as his grandfather whose kindness sometimes masterd his excellent understanding. His father had a temper which better jumpd with my humour.[5] Enough of ill nature to keep your good nature from being abused is no bad ingredient in their disposition who have favours to bestow.

1. Eton.
2. 'The years rob us of one thing after another,' Horace's *Epistles*, II. ii. 55.
3. Catherine Hyde, wife of the third Duke of Queensberry. The poem is Prior's 'Female Phaeton'.
4. 'Ballad on young Rob Roy's abduction of Jean Key, Cromek's *Collections*.' J. G. L. See also *Letters*, i. 119n.
5. *1 Henry IV*, i. 2.

In coming from Parkgate here (to Bitock's Bridge) I intended to accom[plish] a purpose which I have for some years entertaind of visiting Lochwood, the ancient seat of the Johnstones, of which King James said when he visited it that the man who built it must have been a thief in his heart. It is near to Mr. Johnstone Hope's mansion of Raehills. It raind heavily however which prevented my making this excursion and indeed I rather overwalkd myself yesterday and have occasion for rest.

> So sit down, Robin, and rest thee.[1]

27 SUNDAY To-day we journeyd through the hills and amongst the storms, the weather rather bullying than bad. We viewd the Grey Mare's Tail[2] and I still felt confident in crawling along the ghastly bank by which you approach the fall. I will certainly get some road of application to Mr. Johnstone Hope to pray him to make the place accessible. We got home to Abbotsford before ½ past five, having travelld 40 miles.

Found on our return Craig's letter explaining my accompt[3] agt. me alas – of which afterwards. It makes my Ball. as on margin. Mistake was in the amount of Ballance due at Christmas – £300 and upwards instead of £150 as I opined.

$$\frac{\begin{array}{r} £159 \\ 74 \end{array}}{£85}$$

28 MONDAY

Drew the following –

Anne	£30
Rent of Lochend to be repd. by Mr. Laidlaw	34
For travelling expenses	10
	£74

Set off with Walter and Jane[4] at seven o'clock and reachd Blair Adam in the midst of dinner time. By some of my not unusual

---

1. Untraced.
2. A waterfall on the road between St. Mary's Loch and Moffat.
3. See the Entry for 22 August.
4. Leaving the unfortunate Anne at Abbotsford. 'Walter and Jane have been here for about a fortnight with Mrs Jobson. Walter is in high spirits & quite well and I rather think Jane is improved but Heaven help us with Mrs Jobson. I had I thought expected all that was detestable but my expectations are far surpassed to say nothing of her vulgarity and bad manners they are nothing

blunders[1] we had come a day before we were expected. Luckily in this ceremonious generation there are still houses where such blunders only cause a little raillery and Blair Adm. is one of them. My excellent friend is in high health and spirits to which the presence of Sir Frederick[2] adds not a little. His Lady is here – a beautiful woman whose countenance realizes all the poetic dreams of Byron. There is certainly something of full maturity of beauty which seems framed to be adoring and adored and it is to be found in the full dark eye luxuriant tresses and rich complection of Greece and not among the pale unripend beauties of the North. What sort of a mind this exquisite casket contains is not so easily known. She is anxious to please and willing to be pleased and with her striking beauty cannot fail to succeed.

29 TUESDAY To-day we designed to go to Lochore – But
           Heigho the wind and the rain![3]

Besides Mrs and Admiral Adam, Mrs Loch, and Miss Adam, I find here Mr. Impey,[4] son of that Sir Elijah celebrated in Indian history. He has himself been in India but has, with a great deal of sense and observation, much better address than always falls to the share of the Eastern adventurer. The art of quiet and entertaining conversation which is always easy as well as entertaining is I think

---

but her temper is so very bad she is never pleased at any thing & it is one continued wrangle the whole *long day*. The gentlemen have been at Drumlanrig for five days they return today and tomorrow we meant to have all gone to pay a visit to the Chief Commissioner but Mrs Jobson was not inclined to be so easily moved out of her comfortable quarters so I had to save all dispute [to] give up going and remain at home quite alone other five days with the *old torment*. I am sure I would rather lose the pleasure of Walter's company than have that horrid woman.'
Anne to Sophia, 27 August 1826, Abbots.

1. For similar blunders, see the Entries for 22 November and 16 December 1825.
2. Sir Frederick Adam, fourth son of the Chief Commissioner. He was at this time Governor of the Ionian Islands, and his wife, Diamantina, as the Entry suggests, was Greek. He had fought at Waterloo and commanded the garrison at Brussels when Scott was there in 1815. When they met again during Scott's visit to Italy in 1832 Adam wanted Scott to go on to the Greek islands.
3. *Twelfth Night*, v. 1.
4. Edward Impey was acting Judge of the Provincial Court of Appeal at Moorshedebad. His father, Sir Elijah Impey (1732–1809), had been Chief Justice of Bengal and successfully defended himself when impeached by the House of Commons.

chiefly known in England. In Scotland we are pedantic and wrangle or we run away with the harrows on some topic we chance to be discursive upon – in Ireland they have too much vivacity and are too desirous to make a show to preserve the golden mean in conversing. They are the Gascons of Britain. George Ellis[1] was the best converser I ever knew; his patience and good breeding made me often ashamed of myself when I found my self going off at score upon some favourite topic. Richard Sharpe is so celebrated for this peculiar gift as to be generally calld Conversation *Sharpe*.[2] The worst of this talent is that it seems to lack sincerity. At least you never know what are the real sentiments of a good Converser, or at least it is very difficult to discover in [what] extent he entertains them. His politeness is inconsistent with energy.

Mrs. Impey, an intelligent person, likes music and particularly scotch airs which few people play better than Mrs. Loch and Miss Louisa Adam.

For forming a good converser, good taste and extensive information and accomplishment are the principal requisites to which must be added an easy and elegant delivery and a well-toned voice. I think the higher order of genius is not favourable to this talent.

Had a letter from Mr. William Upcott, Londn. Institution, proposing to me to edit an edition of Garrick's correspondence, which I declined by a letter of this day.

Thorough decided downfall of rain. Nothing for it but patience and proof-sheets.

30 WEDNESDAY Still at Blair Adam – the weather scarce permitted us more licence than yesterday. Yet we went down to Lochore and Walter and I perambulated the property and discussd the necessity of a new road from the South west.[3] Also that of planting some willows

1. George Ellis (1753–1815), whom Scott met in 1801 through Heber. Scott admired his *Specimens of the Early English Poets* and *Specimens of Early English Romances*, and their common interests drew them into close and friendly correspondence. Ellis introduced Scott to Canning, with whom he was associated in the *Anti-Jacobin*.

2. Richard Sharp (1759–1835), a Whig Member of Parliament and an original member of the Literary Society.

3. 'There is no doubt a good or even a decent approach would be of high consequence to the place. I never saw one which needed such an improvement more and I do not think Walter will hesitate at any reasonable expence to accomplish it', Scott had written a month earlier to Adam of Blair-Adam. *Letters*, x. 80. See also *Letters*, ix. 119, 133, 143–4.

along the ditches in the low grounds. Returnd to Blair adam to dinner.

31 THURSDAY Left Blair at seven in morning. Transacted business with Cadell and Ballantyne.[1] But our plans will I think be stopd or impeded by the operations before the Arbiter Mr. Irving who leans more to the side of the opposite than I expected.[2] I have a letter from Gibson, found on my arrival at Abbotsford, which give[s] rather a gloomy account of that matter. It seems strange that I am to be bound to write for men who have broken every bargain to me.

Arrived at Abbotsford at eight o'clock at night.

SEPTEMBER

1 FRIDAY Awaked with a head-ache which the reconsideration of Gibson's news did not improve. We save *Bonaparte* however and that is a great thing. I will not be downcast about it let the worst come that can but I wish I saw that worst. It is the devil to be struggling forward like a man in the mire and making not an inch by your exertion and such seems to be my fate. Well I have much to comfort me and I will take comfort. If there be further Wrath to come I shall be glad that I bear it alone. Poor Charlotte was too much softend by prosperity to look adverse circumstances courageously in the face. Anne is young and has Sophia and Jane to trust to for assistance.

2 SATURDAY Wrote this morning but only two pages or there abouts. At twelve o'clock set out with Anne and Walter to visit

1. The note arranging the meeting suggested 11 a.m. at Cadell's house, 134 George Street. *Letters*, x. 94.
2. Their plans were to sell *Woodstock* and the *Life of Napoleon* to Longman's. 'Mr Rees of the house of Longman & Co. has been here for some time', writes Gibson. 'I see very plainly he is anxious to have Napoleon.' This would be out of the question if Lord Newton (formerly Mr. Alexander Irving) decided that the works were Constable's, and Gibson was sure that *Woodstock* at least would be awarded to him. Sederunt Book, i. 121. 'As to Napoleon,' Scott reassured him, 'the only time price was ever spoken of betwixt us Constable said he would give me £10,000 for three volumes' (*Letters*, x. 94) and this could hardly be called a contract for the huge *Napoleon* that he was now writing.

at Makerston[1] but the road between Makerston and Merton being very bad we drove I dare say 30 miles in going and coming by a circuitous route and only got home at ½ past seven at night. Saw Lady Brisbane MacDougall but not Sir Thomas. Thought of old Sir Henry – and his older father Sir George[2] – Received a box of Australian seeds forwarded by Andrew Murray, now Head-Gardener to the governor, whom I detected a clever boy among my labourers in 1812 and did a little for him. It is pleasant to see men thrive and be grateful at the same time, so good luck to Andro Mora as we calld him.

3 SUNDAY Made up my missing task for yesterday and to-day also but not more, writing very heavily. Cousin Archie Swinton came to dinner; we had a dish of cousinred[3] of course and of auld lang syne.

4 MONDAY Archie Swinton left us this morning early. I wrote from 7 to half past two but partly that I had five proof sheets to correct partly that like old John Fraser 'I was not very *cleever* to-day' I made out but a page and a half.

£85

Drew for £10 on behalf of Tom.   10

Ball. 75

5 TUESDAY Wrote task and half a page more. Terry arrived and brought with him a Mr. Bruce from Persia with an introduction forsooth from Mr. Blackwood.[4] I will move a *quo waranto* against this species of introduction; and the good gentleman is to be here, he informs me, for two days. He is a dark foreign looking man of small stature and rather blunt manners which may be easily accounted for by his having been in the east for thirty years. He has a considerable share of information and made good play after dinner.

1. To see Sir Thomas Makdougall Brisbane (1773–1860), who had recently returned from New South Wales where he had been Governor from 1821 to 1825. He had served with distinction as a brigadier-general in the Peninsula; he was a noted astronomer, and succeeded Scott as President of the Royal Society of Edinburgh. Makerstoun was inherited from his wife's father, Sir Harry Makdougall, whose surname he added to his own in 1826.
2. Sir George Hay Makdougall, whom Scott remembered trying to induce him to crawl by 'dragging his watch along the carpet'. *Life*, i. 23.
3. 'A lot of talk about relatives'.
4. Scott was not intimate with Blackwood, whom in any case he considered a bore. See the Entry for 30 July 1826.

6 WEDNESDAY Walter being to return to Ireland for three weeks[1] sets off to-day and has taken Surtees and Charles alongst with him. I fear this is but a wild plan but the prospect seemd to make them so happy so that I could not find in my heart to say No sufficiently peremptorily. So away they all went this morning to be as happy as they can. Youth is a fine carver and gilder. Went down to Huntley Burn and dawdld about while waiting for the carriage to bring me back. Mr. Bruce and Colonel Fergusson potterd away about Persia and India and I fell asleep by the fireside. Here is a fine spot of work – a day diddled away and nothing to show for it. I must write letters now. There is nothing else for it.[2] But yaw – yaw – I must take a nap first. I had a letter from Jem Ballantyne, plague on him, full of remonstra[nc]e deep and solemn upon the carelessness of *Bonaparte*. The rogue is right too. But as to correcting my stile to the

Jemmy jemmy linkum feedle[3]

tune of what is calld fine writing – I'll be d— if I do.

Drew £12 in favour of Charles for his Irish jaunt. Same time exhorted him to make himself as expensive to Walter in the way of eating and drinking as he could. Mr. and Mrs. Impey[4] arrived to dinner.

£75
12
£63

7 THURSDAY Mr. Bruce left us this morning. From our joint observation he must be a half-cast, probably half an Arab. He told us of having been taken by pirates in the Arabian gulph and having received two thousand bastinadoes on the soles of his feet after which

1. 'He has had difficulty in getting leave,' Scott wrote to Jane's mother on 3 August, 'and that only for a short time but I hope to get it prolonged by using a little interest at the War Office or Horse Guards.' *Letters*, x. 82. He had been at Abbotsford for only three weeks and now returned to Ireland without Jane 'to some inspection or other'. *Letters*, x. 101. He was back within a month, however, with his leave prolonged until 16 January.
2. He wrote to Thomas Sharp of Coventry about Mystery Plays and to Abraham Cooper about a picture of a Border battle. See *Letters*, x. 95–9.
3. G. Colman's 'A Clerk I was in London gay', l. 2.
4. They had no doubt been invited to stay on their way south from Blair-Adam, where Scott had met them the week before. The visit was a success. 'I like Mr. Impey very much', Scott wrote to Morritt on the 8th. *Letters*, x. 101.

he was buried in a heap of dung by way of cure. Though the matter was certainly serious enough to the sufferer yet it excited our suppressd or scarce suppressd mirth. Alas let never traveller tell any distress which borders on the ludicrous if he desires to excite the sympathy of the audience.

Another thing he mentiond was the mode of seasoning timber for ship-building in the Arabian Gulph. They bury it in the sand within watermark and leave it exposed to the flux and reflux of the tide for six months at least but often for twelve or eighteen. The tendency to vegetation which produces the dry rot is thus prevented effectually and the ships built of this vessell[1] last for twenty years.

Mr. Bruce the bastinadoed – left us this morning promising wine from Shiraz[2] and arms from India.

We drove to Ashestiel in the morning after I had written a good task or nearly so (nay I lie – it wanted half a page) and passd a pleasant day. Terry read Bobadil[3] in the evening which he has I think improved.

8 FRIDAY I have rubd up by collation with Mr. Impey Sir Frederick Adam's idea of the Greeks. He deeply regrets the present war[4] as premature undertaken before knowledge and rational education had extended themselves sufficiently. The neighbourhood of the Ionian islands was fast producing civilisation and as knowlege is power it is clear that the example of Europeans and the opportunities of education afforded by the Ionian islands must soon give them an immense superiority over the Turk. This premature war has thrown all back into a state of barbarism. It was precipitated by the agents of Russia. In 20 or 30 years the superiority of the Greeks in intelligence and cultivated talent must have renderd them greatly superior to the Turk and it could not have happend that they should remain long in subjection. Sir Frederick spoke most highly of Byron, the soundness of his views, the respect in which he was held; his just ideas of the Grecian cause and character and the practical and rational wishes which he formd for them. Singular that a man whose conduct in his own personal affairs had been any thing but practical should be thus able to stand by the helm of a sinking state. Sir Frederick thinks he

---

1. A slip for 'wood'.
2. Three dozen bottles were duly sent. Bruce, 7 September 1826, Walpole.
3. Ben Jonson's *Everyman in his Humour*.
4. The War of Greek Independence, which had broken out in 1821 and was to continue until the independent kingdom of Greece was established in 1833.

might have done much for them if he had lived.[1] The rantipole
friends of liberty who go about freeing nations with the same success
which Don Quixote had in redressing wrongs have of course
blunderd every thing which they touched. – The Impeys left us
to-day and Captain Hugh Scott and his lady arrived. Task is bang up.

9 SATURDAY I begin to fear *Nap* will swell to seven volumes. I have a
long letter from James B. threatening me with eight but that is
impossible. The event of his becoming emperor is the central event
of his history. Now I have just attaind it and it is the centre of the third
volume.[2] Two volumes and a half may be necessary to complete the
whole.

Walkd with Hugh Scott up the Rhymer's glen and round by the
lake. Mr. Bainbridge of Gattonside house dined, also Colonel
Fergusson.

Was bang up to my task again this day.

10 SUNDAY Corrected proofsheets in the morning. Then immured
myself to write, the more willingly that the day seemd showery. But I
found myself obliged to read and study the map so much that I did
not get over half a sheet written. Walkd with Hugh Scott, through
Haxellcleuch. Great pleasure to show the young wood to any who
understands them well.

11 MONDAY Jane and her mother go into town this morning and
Anne with them to look out a lodging for us during the time we must
pass in town.[3] It seems strange to have this to-day, having had always
my father's house or my own to go to. But –

Sic transit gloria mundi[4]

To which rare and new adage our ancestors added by way of rhyme

Cabbage-kail are unco windy.

1. Byron had died of a fever at Missolonghi, while engaged in the
   cause, on 19 April 1824.
2. Scott is actually in the middle of vol. v, but as the first two
   volumes were an Introduction on the French Revolution, he
   counts this as the third volume of the *Life of Napoleon* proper. In
   the end the work stretched to nine volumes.
3. Scott was not anxious to renew acquaintance with the bugs and
   noise of 6 North St. David Street. He rented 3 Walker Street for
   the winter.
4. 'Thus does earthly glory pass away.' Thomas à Kempis's *Imitatio
   Christi*, I, iii. 6.

Drew on Craig as follows

	To Bogie for farm work garden etc. ————————	£20
£63	To Anne travelling expence ————————	10
40	To Jane (pocket money) ————————	10
£23		£40

This is going rather close – too little wind in the Bag. But the poor dears must have something in their pocket; and Quarter day comes in a week or ten days.

Well it is half past twelve o'clock and at length, having regulated all disappointments as to post-horses [and] sent three or four servants three or four miles of errands to remedy blunders which a little forethought might have prevented, my family and guests are separated

> Like youthful steers let loose, east north and south.[1]

Miss Millar[2] goes to Stirling, the Scotts to Lessudden, Anne and Jane to Edinburgh, and I am left alone. I must needs go up too to see some operations about the Spring which supplies us with water though I calculate my presence is not very necessary. So now – To work – to work –

But I reckond without my host or I should rather say without my *guest*. Just as I had drawn in my chair fitted a new Bramah on the stick and was preparing to feague it away I had a call from the oon of an old friend Mr. Waldie of Henderland.[3] As he left me enter young Whitebank and Mr. Auriol Hay of the Lion office[4] and we had a long armorial chat together which lasted for some time – then the library was to be lookd at etc. So when they went away I had little better to do than to walk up to the spring which they are digging and to go to my solitary dinner on my return.

12 TUESDAY Notwithstanding what is above said I made out my task yesterday or nearly so by working after dinner. After all these interruptions are not such bad things – they make a man keen of

1. *2 Henry IV*, iv. 2.
2. Formerly governess to his children. Anne wrote to Sophia: 'I had a long letter from Miss Millar who to my horror means to come here this August.' ?17 June 1826, Abbots.
3. A slip for Hendersyde.
4. Heraldry in Scotland is under the care of the Lord Lyon, King-of-Arms. Auriol Drummond Hay was Principal Clerk to the Lyon Court.

the work which he is withheld from and differ in that point much
from the indulgence of an indisposition to labour in your own mind
which increases by indulgence. *Les fâcheux* seldom interrupt your
purpose absolutely and entirely – you stick to it for contradiction's
sake.

Well – I visited the spring in the morning and completed my task
afterwards – As I slept for a few minutes in my chair, to which I am
more addicted than I could wish, I heard as I thought my poor wife
call me by the familiar name of fondness which she gave me. My
recollections on waking were melancholy enough. These be

The aery tongues that syllable men's names.[1]

All I believe have some natural desire to consider these unusual
impressions as bodements of good or evil[2] to come. But alas! this is a
prejudice of our own conceit. They are the empty echoes of what is
passd, not the foreboding voice of things to come.

I dined at the club[2] to-day at Selkirk and acted as croupier. There
were eighteen dined. Young men chiefly and of course young talk.
But so it has been will be and must be.

13 WEDNESDAY Wrote my task in the morning – and thereafter had a
letter from that Tupshead of a privy Councillor and booby of a baronet
Sir J. S.[4] This unutterable idiot proposes to me that I shall propose
to the D—ss D—r of R—[5] and offers his own Right Honourable
intervention to bring so beautiful a business to bear. I am struck dumb
with the assurance of his folly – absolutely mute and speechless – and
how to prevent him making me farther a fool is not easy for the wretch
has left me no time to answer him of the absurdity of what he proposes
– and if he should ever hint at such a piece of d—d impertinence what
must the Lady think of my conceit or of my feelings. Marry hang him,
brock![6] I will write to his present stye however that the Swine may if
possible have warning not to continue – this absurdity.[7]

1. Milton's *Comus*, l. 208.
2. *Macbeth*, iv. 1.
3. The Forest Club.
4. Sir John Sinclair.
5. Dowager Duchess of Roxburghe. Her husband, the fifth Duke,
   had died three years before.
6. *Twelfth Night*, ii. 5.
7. For Sinclair's impudent letter, which even suggests a plan for
   bringing them together at Fleurs when Sir John is there is
   October, see Partington p. 130. Scott's reply, politely angry, is

Dined at Major Scott[1] my cousin's where was old Lord Buchan.[2] He too is a prince of Bores. But age has tamed him a little and like the giant Pope in the *Pilgrim's Progress* he can only sit and grin at pilgrims as they go past and is not able to cast a fank[3] over them as formerly. A few quiet puns seem his most formidable infliction now-a-days.

14 THURSDAY I should not have forgotten among the memorabilia of yesterday that Mr. Naysmith the Dentist and his family calld and I shewd them the lions, for truly he that has rid a man of the tooth-ache is well entitled to command a part of his time. Item two young Frenchmen made their way to our sublime presence in guerdon of a laudatory copy of french verses sent up the evening before by way of Open Sesamum I suppose. I have not read them nor shall I. No man that ever wrote a line despised the *pap* of *praise* so heartily as I do. There is nothing I scorn more except those who think the ordinary sort of praise or censure is matter of the least consequence. People have almost always some private view of distinguishing themselves or of gratifying their curiosity – some point in short to carry with which you have no relation – when they take the trouble to praise you. In general it is their purpose to get the person praised to puff away in return. To me their rank praises no more make amends for their bad poetry than tainted butter would pass off stale fish.

15 FRIDAY Many proofs to correct and dates to compare – What signify dates in a true story? I was fidgetty after breakfast owing to perusing some advices from J. Gibson poor fellow.[4] I will not be

---

printed in *Letters*, x. 103: 'My dear Sir John – I am much
obliged to you for the good opinion your letter implies which I
must suppose serious because both my own feelings and the name
of the other person mentioned are matters which I am sure you
would not jest with. But besides that she should scarce make a
more imprudent choice than that which you think of for her I am
myself totally disinclind again to enter into the matrimonial state.
If at any future period I should change my mind on this subject
(which is most unlikely) I should endeavour to chuse a person of
my own condition and who would permit me to enjoy the
retirement and literary labour which constitute my principal
enjoyments and which would be much disturbd in the case
supposed.' The extent of Sir John Sinclair's sensitivity may be
gauged by the failure of this letter to put an end to the affair. He
writes again on 3 October regretting Scott's want of enterprise.
1. At Ravenswood, St. Boswell's.
2. See the Entry for 25 April 1829 and note.
3. A coil of rope.
4. The arbitration was thought to be going badly. See *Letters*, x. 104.

discouraged come of things what will. However I could not write continuously but went out by starts and amused myself by cutting trees in the avenue. Thus I dawdled till Anne and Jane came home with merry faces[1] and raised my spirits of course. After tea I e'en took heart of grace and finishd my task as I now do this day's journal.

I had an intimation from my sister-in-law that my niece Anne is about to be married to Mr. Allardyce, Surgeon at Cheltenham.[2] It is a second marriage on his part and he has a family, which is a disadvantage. But my excellent neighbour Dr. Scott of Darnlee gives him from knowlege a good character and I hope it will do well. No one can deserve domestic happiness better than Anne my niece.

16 SATURDAY Workd hard to-day and in morning and Evening made out five pages and a half, as much perhaps as one should attempt. Yet I was not over workd. On the contrary went out with Tom about one o'clock and cut trees etc. to clear the avenue and favour the growth of such trees as are designed for Standards. I received visits too – the Laird of Bemerside[3] who had been for nine years in Italy with his family. Also the Laird of Kippielaw[4] – Anne and Jane drove up and calld at the Haining.[5]

1. Anne was glad to be home, and away from Mrs. Jobson: 'I was tired to death with hunting for a house. I went through every one in Edinr. – and at last got a very pretty and uncommonly well furnished house in a Street called Walker Street . . . and it is only twenty-five guineas a month which is very cheap for this sort of house . . .
   'My sojourn in Edinr. was not very agreeable as I had the toothache the whole time and indeed with your friend the cramp in my stomach and to be ill at Mrs Jobson's is no joke. Thank heaven to my great joy Mrs Job did not return as she wished to be some time in Edinr.' Anne to Sophia, 17 September 1826, Abbots.
2. She had kept the secret of her engagement throughout her stay at Abbotsford, rather to the annoyance of Anne, who may perhaps be excused for triumphing a little when the marriage failed to take place because of the reappearance of the first Mrs. Allardyce: 'I do not believe in the story about *the Wife* and I even said when we first saw him that I was sure Anne wished to get off from the marriage but one is never quite sure of *any* of that family they have all a great deal of Mrs Scott about them.' Anne to Sophia, 26 March 1827, Abbots.
3. James Haig, who had been abroad not for nine years but since 1822. *Letters*, x. 187 n.
4. Andrew Seton Karr.
5. To visit John Pringle's family.

I expected James Ballantyne to dinner as he proposed but the worthy typographer appeard not. He is sometimes inaccurate in keeping such appointments which is not according to the Academy of compliments. But in the letter which announced his intended visit he talkd of having received himself a visit from the Cholera Morbus. I shall be very sorry if so unwellcome a guest be cause of the breach of his appointment.

17 SUNDAY Rather surprized with a letter from Lord Melville informing me that he and Mr. Peele had put me into the Commission for enquiring into the condition of the Colleges in Scotland.[1] I know little on the subject but I dare say as much as some of the official persons who are inserted of course. The want of efficient men is the reason alleged – I must of course do my best though I have little hope of being useful and the time it will occupy is half ruinous to me to whom time is everything. Besides I suppose the honour is partly meant as an act of Grace for *Malachi*. I shall never repent of that escapade although it offended persons for the time whose good opinion I value. J. B. continues ill at Teviot Grove[2] as they call it. I am a little anxious about him.

I finishd my task and an extra page – hope to do another before supper – Accomplishd the said diligent purpose.

18 MONDAY Rainy and gloomy – that small sifting rain driving on an eastern gale which intermits not. Wrote letters to Lord Melville etc. and agreed to act under the commission – settled to be at M. Castle Saturday 24th.[3] I fear this will interfere consumedly with business. I

1. After a dispute at Edinburgh between the Town Council and the Senatus Academicus about which had the power to alter the regulations governing degrees, the University petitioned Peel to set up a Royal Commission. In August it was announced that a Royal Commission had been issued for a Visitation of the Universities and Colleges of Scotland; its work continued until 1830, and many of its proposals were embodied in the Universities (Scotland) Act of 1858. Scott was among friends, for the Commission included Chief Commissioner Adam, Chief Baron Shepherd, David Boyle, Sir William Rae, George Cranstoun, and Lord Binning, as well as Lord Melville. See Sir Alexander Grant's *Story of the University of Edinburgh*, 1884, ii. 36–53.
2. George Hogarth's home in Jedburgh.
3. The usual approximate dating: Saturday was the 23rd not the 24th, and Scott's visit to Melville Castle actually took place on Monday the 25th.

corrected proof-sheets and wrote a good deal but intend to spend the rest of the day in reading and making notes. No bricks to be made without straw.

19 TUESDAY Circuit. Went to poor Mr. Shortreed's and regretted bitterly the distress of the family though they endeavourd to bear it bravely and to make my reception as comfortable and even cheerful as possible. My old friend R. S.[1] gave me a ring found in a grave at the Abbey to be kept in memory of his son.[2] I will certainly preserve it with especial care.

Many trifles at Circuit, chiefly owing to the cheap whiskey as they were almost all riots – One case of an assault on a deaf and dumb woman – She was herself the chief evidence. But being totally without education and having from her situation very imperfect notions of a Deity and a future state no oath could be administerd. Mr. Kinniburgh, Teacher of the Deaf and Dumb, was sworn interpreter together with another person, her neighbour, who knew the accidental or conventional signs which the poor thing had invented for herself as Mr. K. was supposed to understand the more general or natural signs common to people in such situation. He went through the task with much address and it was wonderful to see them make themselves intelligible by mere pantomime to each other. Still I did [not] consider such evidence as much to be trusted to in a criminal case. Several previous interviews had been necessary between the interpreter and the witness and this is very much like getting up a story. Some of the signs brief in themselves of which Mr. K. gave long interpretations put me in mind of Lord Burleigh in the *Critic*. 'Did he mean all this by the shake of the head?' 'Yes if he shook his head as I taught him.'[3] The man was found not guilty. Mr. K. told us of a pupil of his whom he restord as it may be said to humanity and who told him that his ideas of another world were that some great person in the skies lighted up the sun in the morning as he saw his mother light her fire and the stars in the evening as she kindled a lamp. He said the witness had ideas of truth and falsehood, which was I believe true, and that she had an idea of punishment in a future state, which I doubt. He confessd she could [not] give any guess at its duration whether temporary or eternal. I should like to know if Mr. K. is [in] that respect much wiser than his pupils.

Dined of course with Lord Mackenzie the Judge.

1. Robert Shortreed.
2. 'Mr. Thomas Shortreed, a young gentleman of elegant taste and attainments, devotedly attached to Sir Walter, and much beloved in return, had recently died.' J. G. L.
3. Sheridan's *Critic*, iii. 1.

20 WEDNESDAY Waked after a restless night in which I dreamd of poor Tom Shortreed. Breakfasted with the revd. Dr. Somerville.[1] This venerable old gentleman is one of the oldest of the literary brotherhood, I suppose about 87 and except, a little deafness quite entire. Living all his life in good society as a gentleman born, and having besides professional calls to make among the poor, he must know of course much that is curious concerning the momentous changes which have passd under his eyes. He talks of them accordingly and has written some thing on the subject, but has scarce the force necessary to seize on the most striking points – Palabras, neighbour Verges – gifts which God gives.[2] The bowl that rolls easiest along the green goes furthest and has least clay sticking to it. I have often noticed that a kindly placid goodhumour is the companion of longevity and I suspect frequently the leading cause of it. Quick keen sharp observation with the power of contrast and illustration disturbs this easy current of thought. My good friend the venerable Doctor will not I think die of that disease.

Called at Nisbit Mill on my cousin Charles[3] [as] we came [home]. His wife received me better than I deserved for I have been a sad neglectful visit[or]. She has a very pleasant countenance.

Some of the circuit lawyers dined here, namely R. Dundas, Borthwick, the facetious Peter Robertson, Mr. R. Adam Dundas, and with them Henry Scott of Harden.

21 THURSDAY Our party breakfasted late and I was heavy-headed and did not rise till eight – Had drank a little more wine than usual but as our friend Othello says 'that's not much.'[4] However we dawdled about till near noon ere all my guests left me. Then I walkd a little and cut some wood. Read afterwards. I can't get on without it. How did I get on before? – that's a secret – Mr. Thos. Tod and his wife came to dine. We talkd of old stories and got over a pleasant evening.

22 FRIDAY Still no writing. We have materials to collect – D—n you, Mother duty, hold your tongue. I tell you, you know nothing of the matter. Besides I corrected five sheets. I wish to God you had to do

1. 'The Revd. Dr. Thomas Somerville, minister of Jedburgh, author of the *History of Great Britain during the reign of Queen Anne*, and other works, died 14 May 1830 in the 90th year of his age, and 64th of his ministry.' J. G. L.
2. *Much Ado about Nothing*, iii. 5.
3. Charles Scott.
4. *Othello*, iii. 3.

with some other people just to teach you the difference. I grant that the day being exquisite I went and thin'd out the wood from the

£23
10
£13

North front of the house. Read and noted a great deal.

Drew for £10 for expences of travelling etc.

23 SATURDAY Wrought in the morning but at reading and proofs. That cursed battle of Jena is like to cost me more time than it did Bonaparte to gain it.[1] At Breakfast we had the Todds from Gala House bound on a fishing party to the Loch.[2] I met Colonel Ferguson about *one* to see his dogs run. It is a sport I have loved well but now, I know not why, I find it little interesting. To be sure I used to gallop and that I cannot now do. We had good sport however and killd four hares. I felt excited during the chace but the feeling was but momentary. My mind was immediatly turnd to other remembrances and to pondering upon the change which had taken place in my own feelings. The day was positively heavenly and the wild hill side with our little coursing party was beautiful to look at. Yet I felt like a man come from the dead looking with indifference on that which interested him while living. So it must be

When once life's day is near the gloaming.[3]

We dined at Huntley Burn kind and comfortable as usual.

24 SUNDAY I made a rally to-day and wrote four pages or nearly. Never stird abroad the whole day but was made happy after dinner by the return of Charles and Surtees full of their Irish jaunt and happy as young men are with the change of scene. Tomorrow I must go to Melville Castle. I wonder what I can do or say about these Universities. One thing occurs – the distribution of bursaries only *ex meritis*. That is I would have the presentations continue in the present patrons but exact that those presented should be qualified by success in their literary attainments and distinction acquired at school to hold these scholarships. This seems to be following out the idea of the founders of these scholarships who doubtless intended the furthering of good literature. To give education to dull mediocrity is a flinging of the children's bread to dogs – it is sharping a hatchet on a razor-strop, which renders the strop useless and does no good to the hatchet. – Well – something we will do –

1. See *Life of Napoleon*, vol. v, ch. 11.
2. Cauldshiels Loch on the Abbotsford estate.
3. Burns's 'Epistle to James Smith', l. 79.

25 MONDAY Morning spent in making up proofs and copy. Set out for Melville Castle with Jane who goes on to her mother at Edinburgh.[1]

Found Lord and Lady M. in great distress. Their son Robert is taken ill at a Russian town about 350 miles before Moscow – dangerously ill too and of a dysentery[2] – the distance increases the extreme distress of the parents, who however bore it like themselves. I was glad to spend a day upon the old terms with such old friends, and believe my being with them even in this moment of painful suspense, as it did not diminish the kindness of my reception, certainly rather seemd to divert them from the cruel subject.

Dr. Nicoll Principal of St. Andrews dined at M. Castle: a very gentlemanlike sensible man. We spoke of the visitation – of granting degrees – of publick examinations – of abolishing the election of Professors by the Senatus Academicus (a most pregnant source of jobs) – and much beside. But all desultory and Lord M. either had nothing particular to say to me or was too much engrossd with his family distress to enter upon it. He proposes to be here in the end of October.[3]

26 TUESDAY Returnd to Abbotsford after breakfast.[4]

Here is a cool thing of my friend J. W. C.[5] The Duke of Clarence dining at the Pavilion with the King happend by choice or circumstance to sit lower than usual at the table and being at that time on bad terms with the board of Admiralty took the opportunity to say that were he King he would do all that away and assume the office of Lord High Admiral. 'Your R.H. may act with great prudence' – said C—r. 'The last monarch who did so was James 2d. –' Presently after H.My. askd what they were talking of, 'It is, only his R.H. of C.' answerd C—r 'who is [so] condescending as to tell us what he will do when he is king.' A long letter from R. P. Gillies. I wonder how long

1. And thence to her uncle, Sir Adam Ferguson, for ten days, before returning to Abbotsford. See Anne to Sophia, 17 and 29 September 1826, Abbots.

2. Robert Dundas was accompanying the Duke of Devonshire to Moscow. See Anne to Sophia, 29 September 1826, Abbots. He recovered from this illness.

3. The visit could not be paid as Scott had set off for London and Paris. For his letter of apology, see *Letters*, x. 116.

4. He employed the time before breakfast, as he often did when away from home and his task, in correspondence. For the letters to Joanna Baillie and John Richardson written on this day, see *Letters*, x. 107–10.

5. J. W. Croker.

he could ask me to announce myself as the author of annotations on German novels which he is to write.

27 WEDNESDAY A day of honest labour – but having much to read, proofs to send off etc., I was only able to execute my task by 3 o'clock p.m.[1] Then I went to direct the cutting of wood along the road in front of the house. Dined at Chiefswood with Capt. and Mrs. Hamilton, Lady Lucy Whitmore[2] their guest, and neighbours from Gattonside and Huntlyburn.

28 THURSDAY Another hard brush and finishd four pages by twelve o'clock then drove out to Cowdenknows for a morning visit.[3] The house is ancient and curious though modernized by vile improvements of a modern roof and windows. The inhabited part has over the principal door the letters S. I. H. V. I. H. The first three indicate probably Sir John Hume but what are we to make of the rest? I will look at them more heedfully one day. There is a large room said to have been built for the reception of Queen Mary – if so it has been much modernized. The date on the door is 1576, which would bear out the tradition.[4] The last two letters probably signify lady Hume's name, but what are we to make of the V? Dr. Hume thinks it means *Uxor* but why should that word be in latin and the rest in Scotch?

Returnd to dinner, corrected proofs and hope still to finish another leaf, being in tight working humour – finishd the same accordingly.

29 FRIDAY A sort of zeal of working has seized me which I must avail myself of.[5] No dejection of mind and no tremor of nerves, for which God be humbly thankd. My spirits are neither low nor high – grave I think and quiet – a compleat twilight of the mind.

Good news of Johnie Lockhart from Lady Montagu who most kindly wrote on that interesting topic.[6]

1. Scott usually finished writing by 1 p.m.
2. Anne describes her as 'So terribly nervous that if the door is shut a little hard *she faints* in short she is *nerves all over*', and adds: 'Mrs Hamilton and Lady Lucy have sworn eternal friendship and embrace each other every five minutes.' Anne to Sophia, 29 September 1826, Abbots.
3. To Dr. James Hume.
4. In fact it would not. Mary fled to England in 1568 and did not return to Scotland.
5. 'Papa works so hard I never see him and look forward to a gloomy winter in Edinr.' Anne to Sophia, 29 September 1826, Abbots.
6. She had seen the children in Brighton. Lockhart and Sophia were on a short visit to France. Ibid.

I wrote five pages, nearly double task, yet wanderd for three hours axe in hand superintending the thinning of the home planting. That does good too. I feel it give steadiness to my mind which when abandond to thought without any personal and manual application [is prey to dejection]. Women it is said go mad much seldomer than men. I fancy if this be true it is in some degree owing to the little manual works in which they are constantly employd which regulate in some degree the current of ideas as the pendulum regulates the motion of the timepiece. I do not know if this is sense or nonsense but I am sensible that if I were in solitary confinement without either the power of taking exercise or employing myself in study six months would make me a madman or an idiot.

30 SATURDAY Wrote four pages. Honest James Ballantyne came about four. I had been cutting wood for two hours. He brought his child, a remarkably fine boy – well bred, quiet and amiable. James and [I] had a good comfortable chat, the boys[1] being at Gattonside House. I am glad to see him bear up against misfortune like a man. Bread we shall eat or white or brown,[2] that's the moral of it, Master Muggins.[3]

Quarter's Salary ———————		£250
Deduce		
Coachmaker to accompt ———	£50.0.0	
Anne to household expence ———	25	
		£180[4]

OCTOBER

I SUNDAY Wrote my task then walkd from one till half past four – Dogs took a hare. They always catch one on Sunday – a puritan would say the Devil was in them. I think I shall get more done this evening. I would fain conclude the volume at the treaty of Tilsit[5] which will make it a pretty long one by the bye. J. B. expressd himself much pleased with *Nap.* which gives me much courage. He is gloomy enough when things are not well. – And then I will try something at my *Canongate*. They talk about the pitcher going to the well but if it goes not to the well how shall

1. Charles and Surtees.
2. Prior's *Alma*, l. 1657.
3. Goldsmith's *She Stoops to Conquer*, i. 2.
4. The error made in subtracting is cancelled out by the similar mistake on 2 October.
5. See the *Life of Napoleon*. vol. v, ch. 13.

we get water? It will bring home none when it stands on the shelf I trow. In literature as in love courage is half the battle.

> The public borne to be control'd
> Stoops to the forward and the bold.[1]

2 MONDAY Wrote my task. Went out at one and wrought in the wood till four. I was made happy by a letter from my Nephew, Little Walter as we use[d] to call him from his age and size compared to those of his cousin. He has been kindly received at Bombay by the Governour Mountstuart Elphinstone and by Sir Thomas Bradford.[2] He is taking his ground I think prudently and is like to get on. Already First Lieutenant of Engineers – that is well to begin with.

In Bank   £180
Anne   15
          £160

Col. Ferguson, Miss Margaret and some ladies, friends of theirs, dine, also Mr. and Mrs. Laidlaw and James Laidlaw, and young Mr. N. Milne.[3]

3 TUESDAY I wrote my task as usual but strange to tell there is a want of paper. I expect some to-day. In the mean time to avoid all quarrel with Dame Duty I cut up some other leaves into the usual statutory size. They say of a fowl that if you draw a chalk line on a table and lay chick-a-diddle down with his bill laid upon it the poor Tony will imagine himself opposed by an insurmountable barrier which he will not attempt to cross. Such-like are one half of the obstacles which seem to interrupt our best resolves and such is my pretended want of paper. It is like Sterne's want of *sous* when he went to releive the pauvre Honteux.[4]

4 WEDNESDAY I ought to record with gratitude to God Almighty the continued health of body and mind which He has vouchsafed to grant me. I have had of late no accesses either of bile or of nervous affection and by mixing exercize with literary labour I have escaped the *Tremor*

1. Adapted from Edmund Waller's 'Of Love', ll. 13–14.
2. Scott knew them both, especially Sir Thomas, who had commanded the troops in Scotland from 1819 to 1825. By the next January 'little Walter . . . is in high feather being in close attendance on Governor Elphinstone lives in his family and talks of setting out for Poonah with his own *three* servants'. *Letters*, x. 154. He fulfilled Scott's prophecy of success, and became Chief Engineer of Sind.
3. A party of all his immediate neighbours – from Huntly Burn, Kaeside, and Faldonside
4. *Sentimental Journey*, 'Montriul'.

Cordis which on other occasions has annoyd me cruelly. I went to the Inspection of the Selkirkshire yeomanry by Colonel Thornhill, 7th. Hussars. The Colonel is a remarkably fine looking man and has a good address. His brow bears token of the fatigues of war. He is a great falconer and has promised to fly his hawks on friday for my amusement and to spend the day at Abbotsford. The young Duke of B.[1] was on the field looking at the Corps, most of whom are his tenants. They did very well and are fine smart young men and well mounted. Too few of them though which is pity. The exercize is a work which in my time [I] have loved well.[2]

Finishd my task at night.

5 THURSDAY I was thinking this morning that my time glided away in a singularly monotonous manner like one of those dark gray days which neither promises sunshine nor threatens rain, too melancholy for enjoyment, too tranquil for repining. But this day has brought a change which somewhat shakes my philosophy. I find by a letter from J. Gibson that I *may* go to London without danger and if I *may* I in a manner *must* to examine the papers in the Secy. of State's office about Bon. when at Saint Helena.[3] The opportunity having been offerd must be accepted and yet I had much rather stay at home. Even the prospect of seeing Sophia and Lockhart must be mingled with pain. Yet this is foolish too. Lady Hamilton[4] writes me that Pozzo di Borgo[5] the Russian Minister at Paris is willing to communicate to me some particulars of Bonaparte's early life. *Quaere* might I not go on there? In for a penny in for a pound. I intend to take Anne with me and the pleasure will be great to her who deserves much at my hand.

1. The Duke of Buccleuch.
2. Early in 1797 Scott had been instrumental in raising the Royal Edinburgh Volunteer Light Dragoons. He acted as quartermaster, and throughout the summer months of 1797 (when invasion from France was feared) joined in the regular exercises held before the days' work at 5 a.m. *Life*, i. 355.
3. See the Entries for 26 April and 27 July 1826 and notes.
4. Not Nelson's Lady Hamilton, but the wife of Sir Hew Dalrymple Hamilton of N. Berwick and daughter of Admiral Duncan. Her letter may have finally decided the issue, but he had thought of a visit to France since Constable had suggested that he go there after his Irish tour of the previous autumn. *Archibald Constable and his Literary Correspondents*, iii. 317.
5. The Corsican diplomat and royalist. He had come into his own after the accession of Louis XVIII but was less in favour under Charles X. Scott had met him in Paris in 1815.

Bank —— £160   **6 FRIDAY**

Ball. —— 75 / £85   Charles and his friend Surtees left us this morning. To his quarter £75.

Went to see Colonel Thornhill's hawks fly. Some part of the amusement is very beautiful particularly the first flight of the hawks when they sweep so beautifully round the company jangling their bells from time to time and throwing themselves into the most elegant positions as they gaze about for their prey. But I do not wonder that the impatience of modern times has renounced this expensive and precarious mode of sporting. The hawks are liable to various misfortunes and are besides addicted to fly away; one of ours was fairly lost for the day and one or two went off without permission but returnd. We killd a crow and frightend a snipe. There were however ladies and gentlemen enough to make a gallant show on the top of Whitlaw Kipps. The falconer made a fine figure, a handsome and active young fellow with the falcon on his wrist. The Colonel was most courteous and christend a hawk after me which was a compliment. The hawks are not christend till they have merited that distinction. I walkd about six miles and was not fatigued.

There dined with us Colonel Thornhill, Clifton, young Whitebank, Spencer Stanhope and his brother, with Miss Tod and my old friend Lockyer[1] secretary to Greenwich Hospital. We did not break up the party till one in the morning and were very well amused.

7 SATURDAY A weary day of rain. Lockyer and I chatted from time to time and I wrought not at *Boney* but upon the *Prose Works*[2] of which I will have a volume ready to send in on Monday. I got a letter from Jo: Gibson with an offer by Longman for *Napoleon* of ten thousand five hundred guineas which I have advised them to accept.[3] Also I hear there is some doubt of my getting to London from the indecision of these foolish Londoners.

I don't care whether I go or no and yet it is unpleasant to see how one's motions depend on scoundrels like these. Besides I would like

1. Edward Hawke Locker (1777–1849), Commissioner of Greenwich Hospital and formerly Secretary to Sir Edward Pellew. Scott used his notes about Napoleon on Elba in his *Life of Napoleon*.
2. See the Entry for 1 July 1826 and note.
3. 'In my opinion their offer amounting if I compute right to £11,025 or thereabout is very liberal and ought to be accepted. More *might* perhaps be squeezed out by hawking through the trade but besides this being discreditable in itself it is worth a large percentage to have honorable & substantial people to deal with.' *Letters*, x. 113.

to be there were it but to see how the cat jumps. One knows nothing of the world if you are absent from it so long as I have been.

8 SUNDAY Lockyer left me this morning. He is of opinion the ministry must soon assume another form but that the Whigs will not come in.[1] Lord Liverpool holds much by Lord Melville – well in point of judgement – and by the Duke of Wellington – still better – but then the Duke is a soldier, a bad education for a statesman in a free country. The Chancellor is also consulted by the Premier on all lawaffairs – Canning and Huskisson are at the head of the other party who may be said to have taken the cabinet by storm through sheer dint of talent. I should like to see how these ingredients are working but by the Grace of God I will take care of putting my finger into the cleft stick.

Lockyer has promised to get my young Cousin Walter Scott[2] on some Quarterdeck or other.

In my desk	Received from Mr. Cadell the 2d Instalment ad-
English Notes £50	vance of cash on *Canongate*. It is in English bills and
Bill $\frac{200}{£250}$	money in case of my going to town[3]——— £250.
	Mr. Laidlaw and George Skene dined.

9 MONDAY A gracious letter from Messrs. Abud and Son bill-brokers etc. assures Mr. Gibson that they will institute no legal proceedings against me for four or five weeks. And so I am permitted to spend my money and my leisure to improve the means of paying them their debts, for that is the only use of my present journey. They are Jews I suppose; the devil baste [them] for fools with a pork griskin. Were I not to exert myself I wonder where their money is to come from.

A letter from Gillies menacing the world with a Foreign miscellany.[4]

The plan is a good one but – he canna haud it as John Moodie[5]

1. For Cabinet changes at the time of the *Journal* see Appendix D, p. 826.
2. A son of William Scott of Maxpoffle, who later interfered in the arrangements. See the Entry for 9 December 1826.
3. Scott's expenses were refunded by the Trustees. See the Entry for 16 May 1827.
4. His first idea was to publish a complete novel or play in translation for each number; later he decided that the best plan was 'simply that of the "Quarterly" and "The Edinburgh" '. Gillies, 24 September 1826 and 31 March 1827, Walpole. The first number of the *Foreign Quarterly Review* made its appearance in this form in July 1827.
5. Vanburgh's *The Provoked Husband*, i. 1. 'Haud' means 'hold'.

says. He will think all is done when he has got a set of names and he will find the difficulty consists not in that but in getting articles. I wrote on the *Prose Works*.

Lord and Lady Minto dined and spent the night at Abbotsford.

10 TUESDAY Well – I must prepare for going to London and perhaps to Paris.

Bank —— £85	Paid Tom to accompt ———————— £10
Drat. —— 45	William Bogie Dt ———————————— 20
In Bank —— 40	Anne to house ——————————————— 15
In purse — 250	
£290	£45

The morning fritterd away. I slept till 8 o'clock – then our guests till twelve – then walkd out to direct some alterations on the quarry which I think may at little expense be renderd a pretty recess.[1] Wordsworth swears by an old quarry and is in some degree a supreme authority on such points. Rain came on; returnd completely wett. I had next the displeasure to find that I had lost the conclusion of Vol. V. of *Napoleon*, seven or eight pages at least, which I shall have to write over again unless I can find it.[2] Well – as Othello says, that's not much.[3] – My cousin James Scott came to dinner. I have great unwillingness to set out on this journey – I almost think it ominous. But

> They that look to freits, my master dear,
> Then freits will follow them.[4]

I will stick to my purpose. Answerd a letter from Gillies about establishing a Foreign Journal – a good plan – but I fear in sorry hands. Of those he names as his assistants those who can be useful will do little, and the labours of those who are willing to work will rather hold the publication [down] – down your dainty literature is. I fear it will not do.

I am downhearted about leaving all my things after I was quietly settled – it is a kind of disrooting that recalls a thousand painful

1. Scott was pleased with the results. See the Entry for 25 December 1826.
2. Scott found it and sent it to Ballantyne the next day. See *Letters*, x. 118.
3. *Othello*, iii. 3.
4. Herd, i. 38: 'Edom of Gordon' ll. 110–11. 'Freits' are omens or presages. *S. N. D.*

ideas of former happier journies. And to be at the mercy of these fellows –[1] God help – but rather God bless – man must help himself.

11 WEDNESDAY We are ingenious self tormentors. This journcy annoys me more than anything of the kind in my life. My wife's figure seems to stand before me and her voice is in my ears 'S—, do not go – ' It half frightens me. Strong throbbing at my heart and a disposition to be very sick. It is just the awakening of so many feelings which had been lulld asleep by the uniformity of my life but which awaken on any new subject of agitation – Poor poor Charlotte! ! I cannot daub it farther.[2] I get incapable of arranging my papers too. I will go out for half an hour. God relieve me –

I quelld this *hysterica passio*[3] by pushing a walk towards Kaeside and back again but when I returnd I still felt uncomfortable and all the papers I wanted were out of the way and all those I did not want seemd to place themselves under my fingers – my cash according to the Nature of riches in general made to itself wings and fled I veryly believe from one hiding place to another. To appease this insurrection of the papers I gave up putting my things in order till tomorrow morning.

Dined at Kippilaw with a party of neighbours. They had segars for me very politely. But I must break folks of this. I would [not] willingly be like old Dr. Parr[4] or any such quiz who has his tastes and whims forsooth that must be gratified. So no segars on the journey.

12 THURSDAY Reduced my rebellious papers to order. Remitted Andw. Lang £30 odd by cheque on Craig being County money received by me. Set out after breakfast and reachd Carlisle at eight o'clock at night.[5]

Bank	£40
Drt.	30
In Bank	10

13 FRIDAY We were off before seven and visiting Applebye Castle by the way (a most interesting and curious place by the way) we got to Morritt's about half past five where we had as warm a wellcome as

1. Creditors like Abud.
2. *King Lear*, iv. 1.
3. *King Lear*, ii. 4.
4. 'That model of pedants Dr. Philopatris Par', as Scott once called him (*Letters*, xii. 313) was Dr. Samuel Parr (1747–1825), a schoolmaster, book-collector and churchman, regarded by some as the Whig Johnson.
5. Apart from Scott and his daughter Anne, two servants were of the party – John Nicholson and Anne's maid, Aicheson. *Letters*, x. 119.

one of the warmest hearts in the world could give an old friend.[1] I saw
his Nephew's wife for the first time, a very pleasing young person. It
was great pleasure to me to see Morritt happy in the midst of his
family circle undisturbd as heretofore by the sickness of any that is
dear to him.

On recalling my own recollections during my journey I may note
that I found great pleasure in my companion's conversation as well as
in her mode of managing all her little concerns on the road. I am apt
to judge of character by good humour and alacrity in these petty
concerns.[2]

Quoad [*hoc*] I think that the inconveniences of a journey seem
greater to me than formerly while on the other hand the pleasures it
affords are rather less. The ascent of Stanemore seemd duller and
longer than usual and on the other hand Bowes which used to strike
me as a distinguishd feature in the [landscape] seemd an ill-formd
mass of rubbish a great deal lower in height than I had supposed. Yet
I have seen [it] twenty times at least. On the other hand what I lose in
my own personal feelings I gain in those of my companion who shows
an intelligent curiosity and interest in what she sees. I enjoy therefore
reflectively, *veluti in speculo*,[3] the sort of pleasure to which I am now
less accessible.

14 SATURDAY Strolld about in the morning with Morritt and saw his
new walk up the Tees which he is just concocting. Got a pamphlet he

1. Scott liked few men better than John Morritt of Rokeby (1772–
   1843). He approached very close to the ideal of the country
   gentleman of cultivated tastes. He had enough money to indulge
   his interests in antiquarianism and travel, and enough learning to
   write on the historical accuracy of Homer's Troy. Scott and he
   first met in 1808, introduced by Lady Louisa Stuart. They
   corresponded frequently, and Scott paid four visits to Rokeby,
   the last of them during his final journey south. *Rokeby* was
   dedicated, of course, to Morritt.
2. Scott's letters reflect his growing admiration for Anne: 'My great
   comfort is my daughter Anne,' he writes to Lady Abercorn,
   'who has shown in our distress a great deal more character than
   I had given her credit for but you know men are slow in
   perceiving the merit of woman which is hidden under so many
   flounces & furbelows.' *Letters*, x. 90. 'Anne in particular', he tells
   John Richardson, 'has proved a great treasure to me and I have
   had the satisfaction to find that under a manner which I have
   sometimes censured as having a little too much fashionable
   indifference she possesses a great deal of character and a high
   sense of duty.' *Letters*, x. 108.
3. 'As if in a mirror'.

has written on the Catholic question. In 1806 he had other views on that subject but live and learn as they say.[1] One of his squibs against Fox and Grenville['s] administration concludes

> Though they sleep with the Devil yet theirs is the hope
> On the ruin of England to rise with the Pope.

Set off at two and reachd Weatherby to supper and bed.

It was the Corporation of Leeds [that] by a subscription of £80,000 brought in the Anti-Catholic candidate. I remember their subscribing a similar sum to bring in Morritt if he would have stood.

Saw in Morritt's possession an original miniature of Milton by Cooper, a valuable thing indeed. The pedigree seemd authentic. It was painted for his favourite daughter – had come into possession of some of the Davenants – was then in the Devonshire collection from which it was stolen – Afterwards purchased by Sir Joshua Reynolds and at his sale by Morritt or his father.[2] The countenance handsome and dignified with a strong expression of genius. Probably the only portrait of Milton taken from the life excepting the drawing from which Faithorne's head is done.

15 SUNDAY Old England is no changeling. It is long since I travelld this road having come up to town chiefly by sea of late years. But things seem much the same. One race of rednosed innkeepers are gone and their widows, eldest sons and head waiters exercize hospitality in their room with the same bustle and importance. Other things seem externally at least much the same. The land however is much better ploughd, straight ridges every where adopted in place of the old circumflex of 20 years ago. Three horses however or even four are often seen in a plough yoked one before the other. Ill habits do not go out at once. We slept at Grantham w[h]ere we met with Captn. William Lockhart[3] and his Lady, bound for London like ourselves.

16 MONDAY Visited Burleigh this morning, the first [time] I ever saw this magnificent place where there are so many objects of interest and curiosity. The house is magnificent, in the stile of James Ist. reign and consequently in mixd Gothick. Of paintings I know nothing so

1. He was now 'a moderate proCatholic'. *Letters*, x. 227.
2. A note in the margin reads: 'No – it was left by Reynolds to Mason, by Mason to Burgh, and given to me by Mr. Burgh's widow. J. B. S. Morritt.'
3. John Lockhart's half-brother, M. P. for Lanarkshire.

shall attempt to say nothing. But whether to connoisseurs or to an ignorant admirer like myself the 'Salvator Mundi' by Carlo Dolce must seem worth a King's ransom – Lady Exeter, who was home, had the goodness or curiosity to wish to see us. She is a beauty after my own heart – a great deal of liveliness in the face – an absence alike of form and of affected ease and really courteous after a genuine and ladylike fashion.

We reachd Biggleswade to-night at six and paused here to wait for the Lockharts.[1] Spent the evening together.

17 TUESDAY *London*. Here am I in this capital once more after an April weather meeting with my daughter and Lockhart. Too much grief in our first meeting to be joyful[2] – too much pleasure to be distressing – a giddy sensation between the painful and the pleasurable. – I will call another subject.

Read over *Sir John Chiverton*[3] and *Brambletye House*,[4] novels in what I may surely claim as the stile

> Which I was born to introduce
> Refined it first and showd it's use.[5]

They are both clever books, one in imitation of the days of chivalry, the other by John[6] Smith one of the authors of the *Rejected Addresses*, dated in the time of the civil wars and introducing historical characters. I read both with great interest during the journey.

I am something like Captain Bobadil who traind up a hundred gentlemen to fight very nearly if not altogether as well as myself.[7] And so far I am convinced of this that I believe were I to publish *Canongate*

1. Captain and Mrs. William Lockhart.
2. This was their first meeting since Lady Scott's death.
3. *Sir John Chiverton*, by Harrison Ainsworth, was published anonymously in 1826.
4. As it dealt with the same period as *Woodstock* Scott had refused to read *Brambletye House* earlier. 'I look on it as one of the advantages attending the conclusion of *Woodstock* that the finishing of my own task will permit me to have the pleasure of reading BRAMBLETYE-HOUSE, from which I have hitherto conscientiously abstained.' Preface to *Woodstock*. Scott is a kinder critic than Lockhart, who thought Smith's book 'mere trash'. 27 April 1826, Walpole.
5. Swift's 'On the Death of Dr. Swift', ll. 57–8.
6. Lockhart noted in pencil in the margin that this should be 'Horace'.
7. Jonson's *Everyman in his Humour*, iv. 5.

Chronicles without my name (*nomme de guerre* I mean) the event would be a corollary to the fable of the peasant who made the real pig squeak against the imitator while the sapient audience hissd the poor grunter as if inferior to the biped in his own language. The peasant could indeed confute the longeared multitude by shewing piggy, but were I to fail as a knight with a white and maiden shield and then vindicate my claim to attention by putting 'by the Author of Waverley' in the title my good friend *Publicum* would defend itself by stating I had tilted so ill that my course had not the least resemblance to my former doings when indisputably I bore away the garland. Therefore I am as firmly and resolutely determined that I will tilt under my own cognizance.[1] The hazard indeed remains of being beaten. But there is a prejudice (not an undue one neither) in favour of the original patentee and Joe Manton's name has borne out many a sorry gun-barrell – More of this tomorrow –

Expence of journey	£41
Anne pocket money	5
Servants in journey	2
Cash in purse (silver not reckond).	2
	£50

This is like to be an expensive journey but if I can sell an early copy of the work to a French translator it should bring me home.

Thank God, little Johnie Hoo[2] as he calls himself is looking well though the poor dear child is kept always in a prostrate posture.

18 WEDNESDAY I take up again my remarks on imitations. I am sure I mean the gentlemen no wrong by calling them so and heartily wish they had followd a better model, but it serves to show me *veluti in speculo*[3] my own errors or if you will those of the *Stile*. One advantage I think I still have over all of them. They may do their fooling with

---

1. This was a change of heart. Originally the *Chronicles* was to be published in a small edition for Scott's own benefit, with no indication of the authorship. By 8 October, however, he tells Gibson he is less eager 'to let the work steal into the world . . . The last was my own idea but I have rather changed it'. *Letters*, x. 114–15. An edition of 8,000 acknowledged to be by the author of Waverley, will bring another £2,000 to the Trustees as well as £500 to himself. Sederunt Book, i. 185. See also the Entry for 30 June 1826 and note.
2. Johnnie Lockhart.
3. 'As in a mirror'.

better grace but I like Sir Andrew Aguecheek do it more natural.[1]
They have to read old books and consult antiquarian collections to
get their information – I write because I have long since read such
works and possess thanks to a strong memory the information which
they have to seek for. This leads to a dragging in historical details by
head and shoulders, so that the interest of the main piece is lost in
minute descriptions of events which do not affect its progress.
Perhaps I have sin'd in this way myself – indeed I am but too
conscious of having considerd the plot only as what Bayes calls
the means of bringing in fine things[2] so that in respect to the
descriptions it resembled the string of the Showman's box which
he pulls to show in succession Kings, Queens, the battle of Waterloo,
Bonaparte at Saint Helena, Newmarket races and White-headed Bob
floord by Jemmy from Town. All this I may have done, but I have
repented of it, and in my better efforts while I conducted my story
through the agency of historical personages and by connecting it with
historical incidents I have endeavourd to weave them pretty closely
together and in future I will study this more – Must not let the
background eclipse the principal figures – the frame overpower the
picture.

Another thing in my favour is that my contemporaries steal too
openly. Mr. Smith has inserted in *Brambletye House* whole pages from
De Foe's *Fire and Plague of London*.[3]

> Steal! foh! a fico for the phrase –
> Convey, the wise it call –[4]

When I *convey* an incident or so I am [at] as much pains to avoid
detection as if the offence could be indicted in literal fact at the Old
Bailey.[5]

But leaving this – hard pressd as I am by these imitators who must
put the thing out of fashion at last I consider like a fox at his last shifts
whether there be a way to dodge them – some new device to throw
them off and have a mile or two of free ground while I have legs and
wind left to use it. There is one way to give novelty – To depend for

1. *Twelfth Night*, ii. 3.
2. Buckingham's *Rehearsal*, iii. 1.
3. Defoe's *Journal of the Plague Year*, 1722.
4. Adapted from *Merry Wives of Windsor*, i. 3.
5. The sentence originally finished 'as if it made be [i.e. me] liable
   in literal fact at the Old Bailey'. As a second thought Scott
   added 'the offence could be indicted' in the margin, and failed
   to delete 'made' as well as 'it be liable'.

success on the interest of a well contrived story. But woe's me, that requires thought, consideration – the writing out a regular plan or plot – above all the adhering to [it] – which I never can do for the ideas rise as I write and bear such a disproportioned extent to that which each originally occupied at the first concoction, that cocksnowns ! I shall never be able to take the trouble. And yet to make the world stare – and gain a new march ahead of them all ! ! ! Well something we still will do.

> Liberty's in every blow
> Let us do or die.[1]

Poor Rob Burns, to tack thy fine strains of sublime patriotism – Better take Tristram Shandy's vein – Hand me my cap and bells there – so now I am equipd – I open my Raree Show with

> Ma'am, will you walk in and fal de ral diddle
> And, Sir, will you stalk in and fal de ral diddle
> And, Miss, will you pop in and fal de ral diddle
> And, Master, pray hop in and fal de ral diddle.[2]

Quaere. How long is it since I heard that strain of dulcet mood and where or how came I to pick it up? It is not mine though by your smile you seem to say so.[3] Here is a proper morning's work. But I am childish with seeing them all well and happy here and as I can neither whistle nor sing I must let the giddy humour run to waste on paper.

Sallied forth in the morning, bought a hat – Met S. W. K.[4] from whose discourse I guess that *Malachi* has done me no prejudice in a certain quarter,[5] with more indications of the times which I need not set down.

Sallied again after breakfast and visited the Piccadilly ladies.[6] Saw

1. 'Bruce's Address before Bannockburn', by Burns.
2. An allusion to *Tristram Shandy*, vol. vii. ch. 26.
3. *Hamlet*, ii. 2.
4. Sir William Knighton.
5. With the King.
6. Miss Antoinette Adelaide Dumergue (known as Sophia) and her housekeeper, Miss Sarah Ann Nicolson (usually given the courtesy title of Mrs.), Lady Scott's 'earliest and best friends'. *Letters*, xi. 399. 'Miss Dumergue appears to have grown shorter from her having got much larger all round and it makes me quite start to see the dreadful figure she makes of herself', writes Sophia to Anne on 17 December 1825. 'She wears a bright *pea* green stuff gown made very full in *front* a sort of Fly cap upon

Rogers[1] and Richd. Sharpe – Also good Dr. and Mrs. Hughes.[2] Saw also the Duchess of Buckingham and Lady Charlotte Bury with a most beautiful little girl.

Rees[3] breakfasted and agreed I should have what the Frenchman has offerd for the advantage of translating *Napoleon*[4] which being 100 guineas will help my expences to town and down again.

19 THURSDAY I rose at my usual time[5] but could not write so read Southey['s] *History of the Peninsular War*.[6] It is very good indeed, honest English good principle in every line, but there are many prejudices and there is a tendency to augment a work already too long by saying all that can be said of the history of ancient times appertaining to every place mentiond. What care we whether Iaen be the Aurigi Pringi or Onorigis of the ancient Spaniards or no – whether Saragossa be derived from Caesarea Augusta? Could he have proved it to be Numantium there would have been a concatenation accordingly.[7]

Breakfasted at Rogers' with Sir Thos. Lawrence, Luttrell[8] the

---

the top of her head under which her hair is dressed in the French form very full on each side.' She adds that Mrs. Nicky 'was not quite pleased at Lockhart hiring so good a house at least without consulting her'. Abbots. Writing to Sophia on 30 March 1826 Lockhart confesses to finding them 'if possible more disgusting than ever'. Abbots.

1. The wealthy banker Samuel Rogers (1763–1855), author of *The Pleasures of Memory* and *Italy*, patron of artists and writers, and a brilliant conversationalist. His breakfasts at St. James's Place were famous. Scott first met him during his visit to London in 1803.

2. Dr. Thomas Hughes was Vicar of Uffington, Canon of St. Paul's, and Clerk of the Closet to the King. His wife, 'good bothering Mrs. Hughes . . . one of those that wd rather have a sad tale to tell than none at all' (Lockhart, 30 January 1829, Walpole), first met Scott in 1806. *Mrs Hughes's Recollections*, p. 20. She was an assiduous correspondent and vain of her friendship with Scott. She was kind to Sophia in London, and Scott stood godfather to one of her grandchildren.

3. Owen Rees, a partner in Longman & Coy., who were to publish the *Life of Napoleon*.

4. The French translation was by François Licquet.

5. 7 a.m.

6. Gibson had procured the book for him before he left Edinburgh. *Letters*, x. 105 and 110. It was published over the period 1823–32.

7. Goldsmith's *She Stoops to Conquer*, i. 2.

8. Henry Luttrell (?1765–1851), wit, conversationalist, and versifier.

great London wit, Richard Sharpe etc. Sam made us merry with an account of some part of Rose's Ariosto,[1] proposed that the Italian should be printed on the other side for the sake of assisting the indolent reader to understand the English[2] and complaind of his using more than once the phrase of a lady having 'voided her saddle' which would certainly sound extraordinary at Apothecaries' hall. Well Will Rose carries a dirk too. The morning was too dark for Westminster Abbey which we had projected.

I went to the foreign office and am put by Mr. Horton Wilmot[3] into the hands of a confidential clerk, Mr. Smith, who promises access to everything. Then saw Croker who gave me a bundle of documents. Sir George Cockburn promises his despatches a[nd] journal.[4] In short I have ample prospect of materials.

Dined with Mrs. Coutts. Tragi-comic distress of my good friend on the marriage of her presumptive Heir with a daughter of Lucien Bonaparte.

20 FRIDAY Commanded down to pass a day at Windsor. This is very kind of His Majesty.

At Breakfast Crofton Croker,[5] author of the Irish fairy tales – Little as a dwarf, keen eyed as a hawk and of very prepossessing manners – Something like Tom Moore. There were also Terry – Allan Cunningham – Newton and others. Now I must go to work.

Went down to Windsor – or rather to the Royal Lodge in the Forest, which though ridiculed by connoisseurs seems to be no bad specimen of a royal retirement and is delightfully situated – a kind of cottage ornée, too large perhaps for the stile but yet so managed that in the walks you only see parts of it at once and these well composed and grouping with the immense trees. His Majesty received me with the same mixture of kindness and courtesy which has always distinguishd his conduct towards me. There were no company besides the royal retinue, Lady C.,[6] her daughter and two or three ladies. After we left table there was excellent Music by the Royal Band who lay ambushd in the greenhouse adjoining to the Apartment. The King made me sit beside him and talk a

---

1. William Rose's translation of *Orlando Furioso*, 1823–31.
2. 'Italian' in the original.
3. Robert John Wilmot Horton (1784–1841), Under-secretary for War and the Colonies.
4. Sir George conveyed Napoleon to St. Helena and remained there as Governor until 1816.
5. With whom Scott had been corresponding about fairy legends. See *Letters*, ix. 94 and 485.
6. Lady Conyngham, the King's mistress.

great deal – *too much* perhaps for He has the art of raising one's spirits and making you forget the *retenue* which is prudent everywhere especially at Court. But he converses himself with so much ease and elegance that you lose thoughts of the prince in admiring the well-bred and accomplishd gentleman. He is in many respects the model of a British monarch – has little inclination to try experiments on government otherwise than through his ministers, sincerely I believe desires the good of his subjects, is kind toward the distressd, and moves and speaks every inch a King.[1] I am sure such a character is fitter for us than a man who would long to head armies or be perpetually intermeddling with *La grande politique*. A sort of reserve which creeps on him daily and prevents his going to places of public resort is a disadvantage and prevents his being so generally popular [as] is earnestly to be desired. This I think was much increased by the behaviour of the rabble in the brutal insanity of the Queen's Trial[2] when John Bull, meaning the best in the world, made such a beastly figure.

21 SATURDAY Walkd in the morning with Sir William Knighton and received strong encouragement to hope H.M. would interest himself especially in Charles's being initiated in the diplomatic line when he shall have taken a degree at Oxford.

After breakfast went to Windsor Castle: met by appointment with my daughters and Lockhart and examined the improvements going on there under Mr. Wyattville who appears to possess a great deal of taste and feeling for the Gothick architecture.[3] The old apartments, splendid enough in extent and proportion, are paltry in finishing – instead of being lined with heart of oak the palace of the British Kings is hung with paper painted wainscoat colour. There are some fine paintings and some droll ones. Among the rest are those of divers princes of the House of Mecklenburg-Strelitz of which Queen Charlotte was descended – they are ill colourd ouran outang looking figures with black eyes and hook-noses in oldfashiond uniforms.

We returnd to a hasty dinner and then hurried away to see honest Dan Terry's house calld the Adelphi theatre,[4] where we saw *The Pilot* from the American novel of that name.[5] It is extremely popular, the

---

1. *King Lear*, iv. 6.
2. In August and September 1820.
3. So intense was his feeling for the Gothic that he had changed his name from Wyatt to Wyattville. For his work on Windsor Castle he was knighted in 1828.
4. Terry, in partnership with Frederick Yates, had managed the Adelphi since the previous year.
5. By Fenimore Cooper, 1824.

Dramatist having seized on the whole story and turnd the odious and ridiculous parts assigned by the original author to the British, against the Yankees themselves. There is a quiet effrontery in this that is of a rare and peculiar character. The Americans were so much displeased that they attempted a [row], which renderd the piece doubly attractive to the seamen at Wapping who came up and crowded the house night after night for support of the honour of the British flag. After all one must deprecate whatever keeps up ill will betwixt America and the Mother Country and we in particular should avoid awakening painful recollections. Our high situation enables [us] to contemn petty insults and to make advances towards cordiality.

I was however glad to see honest Dan's house as full seemingly as it could hold. The heat was dreadful and Anne was so very unwell that she was obliged to be carried into Terry's house, a curious dwelling no larger than a squirrel's cage which he has contrived to squeeze out of the vacant spaces of the theatre and which is accessible by a most complicated combination of staircases and small passages. Here we had rare good porter and oysters after the theatre and found Anne much better. She had attempted too much. Indeed I myself was much fatigued.

I had much confidential chat with Sir W. Knighton not fit to be here set down in case of accidents. He undertook most kindly to recommend Charles when he has taken his degree to be attachd to some of the Diplomatic missions which I think is best for the lad after all.[1]

22 SUNDAY This morning Drs. Gooch, Shaw and Yates breakfasted and had a consultation about wee Johnie. They give us great hopes that his health will be establishd but the seaside or the country seem indispensable. Mr. Wilmot Horton, Under Secy. of State, also breakfasted. He is *entêté* of some new plan of relieving the poors rates by encouraging emigration. But John Bull will think this savours of Botany Bay. The attempt to look the poor rates in the face is certainly meritorious.

Labourd in writing and marking extracts to be copied from Breakfast to dinner with the exception of an hour spent to telling Johnnie the history of his name sake Gilpin.[2]

Mr. William and Mrs. Lockhart dined with us. Tom Moore and Sir Thomas Lawrence came in the evening, which was a pleasant

---

1. The alternative was the Church, 'but it is', Scott wrote to Lockhart, '*entre nous* a sneaking line unless the adoption of it is dictated by a strong feeling of principle'. *Letters*, x. 28. Charles entered the Foreign Office in 1827, and died in the Service in 1841 on a mission to the Court of Persia. Scott's letter to Charles, retailing his conversation with Knighton, is printed in *Letters*, x. 120.

2. John Gilpin, in Cowper's poem.

soirée. Smoke my French – Egad it is time to air some of my vocabulary. It is I find cursedly musty.

23 MONDAY Sam. Rogers and Moore breakfasted here and we were very merry fellows. Moore seemd disposed to go to France with us.[1] I visited the Admiralty and got Sir George Cockburn's journal which is valuable. Also visited Lady Elizabeth and Sir Charles Stewart. My heart warmd to the former on account of the old Balcarras connection. Sir Charles and She were very kind and communicative. I forsee I will be embarrassd with more communications than I will use or trust to, colourd as they must be by the passions of those who make them. Thus I have a statement from the Duchesse d'Escars[2] to which the Bonapartists would I dare say give no credit. If Talleyrand for example could be communicative he must have ten thousand reasons for perverting the truth and yet a person receiving a direct communication from him would be almost barr'd from disputing it.

Sing Tantararara Rogues all.[3]

We dined at the Residentiary-House with good Dr. Hughes, Allan Cunningham, Sir Thos. Lawrence and young Mr. Hughes. Thomas Pringle is returnd from the Cape and Calld in my absence. He might have done well there could he have scourd his brains of politics but he must needs publish a whig journal at the Cape of Good Hope ! ![4] He is a worthy creature but conceited withal and *hinc illæ lachrymæ*.[5] He

1. 'Scott said, as I was coming away, "Now, my dear Moore, do think seriously of this; you would be of the greatest service to me, and we have a place for you in the carriage; only you must take care and not rumple Anne's frills."' The scheme was mentioned at their later meetings but, tempted as Moore was, he did not quite like to intrude himself or his politics on Scott. *Memoirs of Moore*, v. 122.
2. The wife of François, Comte d'Escars, who joined Charles X (as he became) in exile at Holyrood.
3. Fielding's *Grub-Street Opera*, iii. 14.
4. Thomas Pringle (1789–1834) was a young local farmer befriended by Scott in his early literary efforts. For a short time he edited *Blackwood's Magazine* before emigrating to South Africa with his father and brothers in 1820. He became public librarian in Cape Town and published *The South African Journal* and *The South African Commercial Advertizer*, both of which were suppressed by the government. After his return to Britain he became Secretary to the Anti-Slavery Society.
5. 'This is the cause of these tears.'

brought me some antlers and a skin in addition to others he had sent down to Abbotsford four years since.[1]

Crofton Croker made me a present of a small box of curious Irish antiquities containing a gold fibula etc. etc.

24 TUESDAY Labourd in the morning. At breakfast Dr. Holland[2] and Cohen whom they now call Palsgrave,[3] a mutation of names which confused my recollections. Item Moore. I workd at the Colonial office pretty hard. Dined with Mr. Wilmot Horton and his beautiful wife, the original

> She walks in Beauty etcaetera.

of poor Byron.

The conversation is seldom excellent among official people. So many topics are what Otaheiteans call *taboo*. We hunted down a pun or two which were turnd out as the stag at Empsom Races for the pursuit of all an[d] sundry. Came home early and was in bed by eleven.

25 WEDNESDAY As we move tomorrow for Paris I have listed my cash thus.

Cash in purse See Memorandm. of 17 curt.	£2	
Letter of credit on paris ————————	100	
	£102	

Cash from Mr. Barber making up		
ball. of bill on London ————	£100	
But deduce Barber's account — £18		
Also Acheson's wages paid to		
Anne	10	
Post horses while in London ——— 10		
Percy's *Reliques* for Johnnie ——— 2		

In purse   £160   —— 40

                                                              —— 60
                                                              £160

1. These were 'a most important and valued part of the decorations of an old Gothick entrance hall hung with armour antlers &c.' *Letters*, X. 120.
2. Henry Holland (1788–1873), an Edinburgh graduate, physician to Queen Caroline and later to Queen Victoria. He was married to Sydney Smith's daughter.
3. Francis Cohen (1788–1861) dropped his Jewish surname when he became a Christian in 1823. He was a noted medieval historian and Deputy Keeper of the Public Records.

Good Mr. Wilson and his wife at breakfast – also Sir Thomas Lawrence – Locker came in afterwards and made a proposal to me to give [up] his intended Life of George III in my favour on cause shown. I declined the proposal not being of opinion that my genius lies that way and not relishing hunting in couples – Afterwards went to the Colonial office and had Robt. Hay's[1] assistance in my inquiries – then to the French Ambassador for my passports – Pickd up Sotheby who endeavourd to saddle me for a review of his polyglott Virgil.[2] I fear I shall scarce convince him that I know nothing of the Latin Lingo. Sir R. H. Inglis,[3] Richd. Sharpe and other friends calld. We dine at Miss Dumergue's, and spend a part of our soiree at Lydia White's. Tomorrow

For France for France for it is more than need.[4]

26 THURSDAY Up at five and in the packet by six.[5] A fine passage save at the conclusion while we lay on and off the harbour of Calais. But the tossing made no impression on my companion or me; we eat and drank like dragons the whole way and were able to manage a good supper and best part of a bottle of Chablis at the classic Dessein's[6] who received us with much courtesy.

27 FRIDAY Custom House etc. detaind us till near ten o'clock so we had time to walk on the Boulevards and to see the fortifications which must be very strong, all the country round being flat and marshy. Lost as all know by the bloody papist bitch (one must be vernacular when on French ground) Queen Mary of red hot memory. I would rather she had burnd a score more of Bishops. If she had kept it her sister Bess would sooner have parted with her virginity – Charles I had no temptation to part with it – it might indeed have been shufled out of our hands during the civil wars but Noll would have as soon let Monsr. draw one of his grinders – then

1. The Secretary who had originally written to him the previous April.
2. Recently published – 'at his own expense of course'. Lockhart, 2 May 1826, Walpole.
3. Sir Robert Harry Inglis (1786–1855), President of the Literary Society. He shared Scott's antiquarian interests and his views on politics.
4. *King John*, i. 1.
5. The ship left from the Tower and so saved the coach journey to Dover.
6. The hotel in Calais patronized by most eminent English travellers abroad.

Charles II would hardly have dared to sell such an old possession as he did Dunkirk and after that the French had little chancet till the Revolution. Even then I think we could have held a place that could be supplied from our own element, the sea. *Cui bono?*[1] – None I think but to plague the rogues.

We dined at Cormont and being stopd by Mr. Canning having taken up all the post horses could only reach Montreuil[2] that night. I should have like[d] to have seen more of this place which is fortified, and as it stands on an elevated and rocky site must present some fine points. But as we came in late and left early I can only bear witness to good treatment, good supper, good *vin de Barsac* and excellent beds.

28 SATURDAY Breakfasted at Abbeville and saw a very handsome Gothic church and reachd Grandvilliers at night. The House is but secondrate though lauded by various English travellers for the moderation of its charges as was recorded in a book presented to us by the landlady. There is no great patriotism in publishing that a traveller thinks the bills moderate – it serves usually as an intimation to mine host or hostess that John Bull will bear a little more squeezing. I gave my attestation too however for the charges of the good Lady resembled those elsewhere and her anxiety to please was extreme. They must be harder hearted than I am to resist the *empressement* which may indeed be venal yet has in its expression a touch of cordiality.

29 SUNDAY Breakfasted at Beauvais and saw its magnificent Cathedral – unfinishd it has been left and unfinishd will remain of course, the fashion of Cathedrals being passd away. But even what exists is inimitable, the Choir particularly and the grand front. Beauvais is calld the *Pucelle* yet so far as I saw she wears no stays, I mean has no fortifications. On we run however. *Vogue la Galère et voilà nous à Paris*, Hotel de Winsor, where we are well lodged. France so far as I can see, which is very little, has not undergone many changes.[3] The sight of war has indeed passd away and we no longer see troops crossing the country in every direction, villages either ruind or hastily fortified – inhabitants shelterd in the woods and caves to escape the rapacity of the soldiers – all this has passd

1. 'For whose gain?' Cicero's *Pro Milone*, xii. xxxii.
2. Only forty-eight miles from Calais.
3. Scott's other visit to France was in the summer of 1815, in the aftermath of Waterloo. For an account of what he saw, see *Paul's Letters to his Kinsfolk*, 1816.

away. The inns are much amended. There is no occasion for that rascally practice of making a bargain – or *combien*-ing your landlady before you unharness your horses – which formerly was matter of necessity. The general taste of the English seems to regulate the travelling – naturally enough as the hotels of which there are two or three in each town chiefly subsist by them. We did not see one french equipage on the road. The natives seem to travell entirely in the diligence and doubtless *à bon marché*. But the road was throngd with English.

But in her great features France is the same as ever – An oppressive air of solitude seems to hover over these rich and extended plains while we are sensible that whatever is the motive of the desolation it cannot be sterility. The towns are small and have a poor appearance and more frequently exhibit signs of decayd splendour than of thriving and increasing prosperity. The *château*, the abode of the gentleman, and the *villa* the retreat of the thriving *negociant*, are rarely seen till you come to Beaumont.[1] At this place which well deserves its name of the fair-mount the prospect improves greatly and country seats are seen in abundance – Also woods sometimes deep and extensive at other times scatterd in groves and single trees. Amidst these the oak seldom or never is found. England, Lady of the Ocean, seems to claim it exclusively as her own. Neither are there any quantity of firs. Poplars in abundance give a formal air to the landscape. The forests chiefly consist of beeches with some birches and the roads are borderd by elms cruelly cropd, pollarded and switchd. The demand for firewood occasions these mutilations. If I could waft by a wish the thinnings of Abbotsford here it would make a little fortune of itself. But then to switch and mutilate my trees – not for a thousand francs – Aye – but Sour grapes quoth the fox.

30 MONDAY Finding ourselves snugly settled in Hotel de Windsor, Rue Rivoli, we determined to remain here at 15 francs per day. We are in the midst of what can be seen and are very comfortably fed and lodged.

This morning wet and surly. Sallied however by the assistance of a hired coach and Left cards for Count Pozzo di Borgo, Lord Granville our ambassador, and Monsr. Gallois,[2] author of the

1. About twenty miles from Paris.
2. To whom he carried a letter of introduction from Thomas Moore. *Memoirs of Moore*, v. 126. Douglas suggests that it was Jean-Antoine-Gauvain Gallois that Scott met and not the young Charles Gallois who translated a history of Naples.

History of Venice. Found no one at home, not even the old pirate Galignani[1] at whose den I ventured to call. Shewd my companion the Louvre (which was closed unluckily), the fronts of the palace with its courts, and all that splendid quarter which the fame of Paris rests upon in security. We can never do the like in Britain. Royal magnificence can be only displayd by despotic power. In England, were the most splendid street or public building to be erected the matter must be discussd in parliament or perhaps some sturdy cobler holds out and refuses to part with his stall and the whole plan is disconcerted. Long may such impediments exist. But then we should conform to circumstances and assume in our public works a certain sober simplicity of character which should point out that they were dictated by utility rather than show. The affectation of an expensive stile only places us at a disadvantageous contrast with other nations and our substitutes of brick and plaster for freestone resembles the mean ambition which displays Bristol stones in default of diamonds.

We went to theatre in the Evening – Comedie Française the place – *Rosemunde* the piece – It is the composition of a young man with a promising name, Emile de *Bonnechose* – the story that of fair Rosamond. There were some good situations and the Actors in the French taste seemd to me admirable particularly Mdell Bourgoin. It would be absurd to attempt to criticize what I only half understood but the piece was well received and produced a very strong effect. Two or three ladies were carried out in histerick – One next to our box was frightfully ill. A Monsieur *à belles moustaches* – the husband I trust, though it is likely they were *en partie fine* – was extremely and affectionately assiduous. She was well worthy of the trouble being very pretty indeed – the face beautiful even amidst the involuntary convulsions. The afterpiece was *Femme Juge et Partie,*[2] with which I was less amused than I had expected because I found I understood the language less than I did ten or eleven years since. Well well I am past the age of mending.

Some of our friends in London had pretended that at Paris I might stand some chance of being encounterd by the same sort of

---

1. The phrase was Lady Louisa Stuart's, in a letter of 4 September reporting that *The Lives of the Novelists* had been published by 'That French *pirate*, Galignani.' Walpole. The September *Quarterly* hoped that their notice of the pirated edition might 'induce those of whose property he has availed himself to imitate the shrewdness of his example'.
2. By Montfleury, 1669.

tumultuary reception which I met in Ireland;[1] but for this I see no ground.

It is a point on which I am totally indifferent – As a literary man I cannot affect to despize public applause – as a private gentleman I have always been embarassd and displeased with popular clamours even when in my favour. I know very well the breath of which such shouts are composed and am sensible those who applaud me to-day would be as ready to hiss me tomorrow and I would [not] have them think that I put such a value on their favour as would make [me] for an instant fear their displeasure. Now all this disclamation is sincere and yet it sounds affected. It puts me in mind of an old woman who when Carlisle was taken by the highlanders in 1745 chose to be particularly apprehensive of personal violence and shut herself up in the closet in order that she might escape ravishment. But no one came to disturb her solitude and she began to be sensible that poor Donald was looking out for victuals or seeking for some small plunder with[out] bestowing a thought on the fair sex. She pop'd her head out of her place of refuge with the petty question 'Good folks, can you tell when the ravishing is going to begin?'[2]

I am sure I will neither hide myself to avoid applause which probably no one will think of conferring nor have the meanness to do anything which can indicate I had any desire of ravishment. I have seen when the late Lord Erskine enterd the Edinburgh [theatre] papers distributed in the boxes to mendicate a round of applause, the natural reward of a poor player.

31 TUESDAY At breakfast visited by Monsr. Gallois, author of *The Decay and Fall of Venice*, an elderly French man (always the most agreeable class) full of information, courteous and communicative. He had seen nearly and remarkd deeply and spoke frankly; though with due caution.[3] He went with us to the Museum where I think the hall of Sculpture continues to be a fine thing, that of pictures but very tolerable when we reflect upon 1815. A number of great french daubs

1. Lockhart describes it as 'a terrible rushing and crushing to see the Baronet; Lord Wellington could not have excited a better rumpus. But the theatre in the evening completed the thing. I never heard such a row.' For an hour no word of *Much Ado about Nothing* could be heard until Scott at last rose and made a short speech to the audience. *Life*, viii. 21.
2. Scott has already told this story in the Entry for 30 June 1826.
3. To Moore Scott described him as 'by far the most intelligent clearheaded and unprejudiced man I met in Paris'. *Letters*, x. 132.

(comparatively) by David and Gerard cover the walls once occupied by the Italian *Chef-œuvres¹ – fiat Iustitia ruat caelum.²*

We then visited Notre Dame and the Palace of Justice. The latter is accompted the oldest building in Paris, being the work of Saint Louis. It is however in the interior adapted to the taste of Louis XIV. We drove over the Pont Neuf and visited the fine quais which was all we could make out to-day as I was afraid to fatigue Anne.

When we returnd home I found Count Pozzo di Borgo waiting for me. A personable man inclined to be rather corpulent, handsome features with all the Corsican fire in his eye.³ He was quite kind and communicative. Lord Granville had also calld and sent Mr. Jones⁴ to invite us to dinner tomorrow.

In the evening at the Odeon where we saw *Ivanhoe*. It was superbly got up, the norman soldiers wearing pointed helmets and what resembled much hauberks of mail which lookd very well. The number of the attendants and the skill with which they are moved and grouped on the stage is well worthy of notice. It was an opera and of course the story greatly mangled and the dialogue in a great part nonsense. Yet it was strange to hear anything like the words which I (then in an agony of pain with spasms in my stomach) dictated to William Laidlaw at Abbotsford now recited in a foreign tongue and for the amusement of a strange people. I little thought to have survived the completing of this novel.⁵

NOVEMBER

1 WEDNESDAY I suppose the Ravishing is going to begin for we have had the Dames des Halles with a bouquet like a Maypole and a speech full of honey and oil which cost me 10 francs. Also a small worshipper who would not leave his name but came *seulement pour avoir le plaisir la félicité* etc. etc. All this jargon I answer with corresponding *blarney* of my own for 'have I not lickd the black

1. The stolen treasures with which Napoleon filled the Musée Central des Arts in the Louvre had been returned to their owners.
2. 'Let justice be done though the heavens fall.' William Watson's *Quodlibets of Religion and State*, 1601.
3. They had met before, in 1815, but were reintroduced by a letter from Lady Dalrymple Hamilton. See the Entry for 5 October 1826 and Disc. i. 99.
4. Thomas Jones, a secretary at the British Embassy.
5. For the circumstances in which this novel was written, see *Life*, vi. 67–8.

stone of that ancient castle?'[1] As to french I speak it as it comes[2] and [like] Doeg in *Absalom and Achitophel* –

> – dash on through thick and thin
> Through sense and nonsense never out nor in[3] –

We went with Monsr Gallois to the Church of Ste. Genevieve and thence to the college Henri IV where I saw once more my old friend Chevalier.[4] He was unwell, swathed in a turban of nightcaps and a multiplicity of *robes de chambre* but he had all the heart and all the vivacity of former times. I was truly glad to see the kind old man – We were unlucky in our day for sights this being a high festival calld All Souls' day. We were not allowd to scale the steeple of Ste. Genevieve. Neither could we see the animals at the Jardin des plantes who, though they have no souls it is supposed and no interest of course in the devotions of the day, observe it in strict retreat like the nuns of Kilkenny.[5] I met however one lioness walking at large in the Jardin and was introduced. This was Made. de Souza, the authoress of some well known French romances of a very classical character I am told for I have never read them. She must have been beautiful and is still well lookd. She is the mother of the handsome Count de Flahault and had a very well looking daughter with her besides a son or two. She was very agreeable. We are to meet again. The day becoming decidedly rainy we returnd along the boulevards by the bridge of Austerlitz but the weather was so indifferent as to spoil the fine show.

We dined at the Ambassador's Lord Granville (formerly Lord Leveson Gower). He inhabits the same splendid [*hôtel*] which Lord Castlereagh had in 1815, namely Numero 30 Rue de fauxbourgh St. Honoré. It once belongd to Pauline Borghese and if its walls could speak they might tell us mighty curious stories. Without their having

1. On his Irish tour the previous summer.
2. Scott's French owed its greatest debt to Froissart. 'Sir Walter Scott speaks French so indifferently,' reported the *New Monthly Magazine* for January 1827, 'that he cannot maintain conversation in it, and the old ladies of the Faubourg St. Germain took advantage of this circumstance to overwhelm him with their compliments in bad English.'
3. Pt. ii, ll. 414–15.
4. Jean-Baptiste Le Chevalier (1752–1836), traveller, archaeologist, and writer on classical subjects. He showed Scott much kindness during his visit to France in 1815.
5. The nuns had amused Scott by their evident interest in the visitors, although they were supposed to be in strict retreat. See the Entry for 9 February 1826.

any tongue they spoke to my feelings 'with most miraculous organ'.[1] In these halls I had often seen and conversd familiarly with many of the great and powerful who won the world by its sword and divided it by their council.[2]

Here I saw very much of poor Lord Castlereagh, a man of sense, presence of mind, courage and fortitude, which carried him through many an affair of critical moment where finer talents might have stuck in the mire. He had been I think indifferently educated, and his mode of speaking being far from *precisely* logical or correct, he was sometimes in danger of becoming almost ridiculous in despite of his lofty presence which had all the grace of the Seymours and his determined courage. But then he was always up to the occasion and upon important matters was an orator to convince if not to delight his hearers. He is gone – and my friend Stanhope also whose kindness this town so strongly recalls. It is remarkable they were the only persons of sense and credibility who both attested on supernatural appearances on their own evidence, and both died in the same melancholy manner.[3] I shall always tremble when any friend of mine becomes visionary.

I have seen in these rooms the Emperor Alexr., Platoff, Schwarzenberg, old Blucher, Fouché, and many a *maréchal* whose truncheon had guided armies – All now at peace, without subjects, without dominion, and where their past life perhaps seems but the recollection of a feverish dream. What a group would this band have made in the gloomy regions described in the *Odessey*.[4] But to lesser things.

We were most kindly received by Lord and Lady Granville and met many friends, some of them having been guest[s] at Abbotsford – among these were Lords Ashley and Morpeth – There were also Charles Ellis (Lord Seaford now), his son *cum plurimis aliis*.[5] Anne saw for the first [time] an entertainment *à la mode de France* where the gentlemen left the parlour with the ladies. In diplomatic houses it is a good way of preventing political discussion which John Bull is always apt to introduce with the second bottle.

We left early and came home at ten at night much pleased at Lord and Lady Granville's kindness, though it was to be expected as our recommendations came from Windsor.

---

1. *Hamlet*, ii. 2.
2. When Scott visited Paris in the summer of 1815 his fame as a poet gave him the *entrée* to the society of the great, and he met there among others Wellington, Blücher, Platoff and the Emperor Alexander. See *Life*, v. 82–4.
3. By suicide.
4. Book xi, 'The Book of the Dead'.
5. 'With many others'.

2 THURSDAY Another gloomy day – a pize upon it and we have settled to go to Saint Cloud and dine if possible at the Drummonds at D'Auteuil. Besides, I expect poor R. W. S. to breakfast. There is another thought which depresses me.[1]

Well – but let us jot down a little politics as my book has a pretty firm lock.

The Whigs may say what they please but I think the Bourbons will stand. Gallois, no great Royalist, says that the Duke of Orleans lives in the best terms with the reigning family which is wise on his part for the golden fruit may ripen and fall of itself but it would be dangerous to

> lend the crowd his arm to shake the tree.[2]

The army, which was Bonaparte's strength, is now very much changed by the gradual influence of time which has removed many and made invalids of many more. The citizens are neutral and if the King will govern according to the Charte and what is still more according to the habits of the people he will sit firm enough and the constitution will gradually attain more and more reverence as age gives it authority and distinguishes it from those temporary and ephemeral governments which seemd only set up to be pulld down. The most dangerous point in the present state of France is that of religion. It is no doubt excellent in the Bourbons to desire to make France a religious country but they begin I think at the wrong end. To press the observances and ritual of religion on those who are not influenced by its doctrines is planting the young tree with its head downwards. Rites are sanctified by belief but belief can never arise out of an enforced observance of ceremonies; it only makes men detest what is imposed on them by compulsion. Then these Jesuits, who constitute emphatically an *imperium in imperio*,[3] labouring first for the benefit [of] their own order and next for that of the roman See, what is it but the introduction into France of a foreign influence whose interest may often run counter to the general wellfare of the kingdom?

We have enough of ravishment – Monsr. Meurice writes me that he is ready to hang himself that we did not find accomodation at his hotel and Made. Mirbel came almost on her knees to have permission

---

1. The Hon. W. R. Spencer, born wealthy and witty, had settled in Paris in 1825 because of his pecuniary difficulties; he died there in comparative poverty and obscurity in 1834.
2. Dryden's *Absalom and Achitophel*, pt. i, l. 203.
3. 'An empire within an empire'.

to take my portrait – I was cruel – but seeing her weeping ripe – consented she should come tomorrow and work while I wrote – A Russian princess Galitzin too demands to see me in the heroic vein. '*Elle vouloit traverser les mers pour aller voir S. W. S.*' and offers me a rendezvous at my hotel. This is precious tomfoolery – however it is better than being neglected like a fallen sky-rocket which seemd like to be my fate last year –[1]

We went to Saint Cloud with my old friend M. Drummond now at a pretty *maison de campagne* at Auteuil – Saint Cloud, besides i[t]'s unequalld views, is rich in remembrances.[2] I did not fail to revisit the Orangerie out of which Bon. expelld the Council of [the] younger. I thought I saw the scoundrels jumping [from] the windows with the bayonets at their backsides. What a pity the house was not two stories high. I askd the Swiss some questions on the locale which he answerd with becoming caution saying however that 'he was not present at the time'. There are also new remembrances, a separate garden laid out as a play-ground for the Royal children is calld il Trocadero from the siege of Calais.[3] But the Bourbons should not take military ground – it is firing a pop-gun in answer to a battery of cannon.

All within the house is changed – every trace of Nap. or his reign totally done away as if traced in sand over which the tide has passd. Moreau and Pichegru's portraits hang in the Royal Antechamber. The former has a mean look, the latter has been a strong and stern looking man. I lookd at him and thought of his death-struggles. In the guard room were the heroes of La Vendé – Charette with his white bonnet – the two La Roche Jacqueleins, L'Escure in an attitude of prayer, Stoflet the gamekeeper, with others.

We dined at Auteuil. Mrs. Drummond, formerly the beautiful Cecilia Telfer, has lost her looks but kept her kind heart. On our return went to The Italian opera and saw *Figaro*. Anne liked the music; to me it was all caviare.

A Mr. Creed dined with us – sensible – liberal in his politics but well informd and candid. He owes me – what – a drive from Auteuil to Paris.

Saasse whom I knew in Brussells calld upon slight right I think but let it pass.

1. By 'last year' Scott presumably means the time of the financial crash, January 1826.
2. Scott's poem, 'Saint Cloud' records happy summer evenings there in 1815 in the company of Lady Alvenley and her daughters. See *Poetical Works*, ix. 295.
3. i.e. Cadiz.

3 FRIDAY Sate to Made. Mirbel. Spencer at breakfast. Went out and had a long interview with the Marechal Macdonald the purport of which I have put down elsewhere.[1] Visited Princess Galitzin and also Cowper the americain Novellist. This man, who has shown so much genius, has a good deal of the manner or want of manner peculiar to his countrymen. He proposed to me a mode of publishing in America by entering the book as property of a citizen. I will think of this.[2] Every little helps, as the Tod says when etc. At night at the theatre de Madame where we saw two *petites piece*, *Le Mariage de Raison*, and *Le plus [beau] jour de ma vie*[3] both excellently playd. Afterwards at Lady Granville's route which was as splendid as any I ever saw and I have seen *beaucoup dans cet genre*. A great number of the ladies of the first rank were there and if honied words from pretty lips could surfeit I had enough of them. One can swallow a great deal of whipd cream to be sure and it does not hurt an old stomach.

4 SATURDAY Anne goes to sit to Made. de Mirbel. I calld after ten, Mr. Cowper and Gallois having breakfasted with me. The former seems quite serious in desiring the Ameracain attempt. I must however take care not to give such a monopoly as to prevent the American public from receiving the works at the prices they are accustomd to. I think I may as well try if the thing can be done.

After ten I went with Anne to the Thuilleries where we saw the Royal family pass through the glass gallery as they went to chapel. We were very much lookd at in our turn and the King en passant did me the honour to say a few civil words which produced a great sensation. Made. La Dauphine and Made. de Berri curtesied, smiled and look[d] extremely gracious, and smiles, bows and curtesies raind on us like odours from all the courtiers and court ladies of the train.

1. Presumably in his notes for the *Life of Napoleon*. Maréchal Macdonald, Duc de Tarente (1765–1840), had met Scott the previous year when he was visiting his kinsman Hector Macdonald Buchanan in Edinburgh. 'His appearance was far from military, much like some of these north country clergymen who come down to figure at the General Assembly; but he has a fine eye, and what is usually impressive, grey hair, with dark eye brows. The whole expression is plain and sagacious, and he seems very frank and communicative.' *Letters*, ix. 150.

2. Scott did explore Fenimore Cooper's idea (see *Letters*, x. 122) but in the end it proved impracticable. All Scott's novels had been pirated in America, where until the Chace Act of 1891 printers and publishers made free with the works of foreign authors.

3. By Eugène Scribe.

We were conducted by an officer of the Royal Gardes du Corps to a convenient place in chapel where we had the pleasure of hearing the Grand Mass performd with excellent music.

I had a perfect view of the King and royal family. The King is the same in age as I knew him in youth at Holyrood house.[1] Debonair and courteous in the highest degree. Made. Dauphine resembles very much the prints of Marie Antoinette in the profile especially. She is not however beautiful, her features being too strong, but they announce a great deal of character and the princess whom Bonaparte used to call the *Man* of the family. She seemd very attentive to her devotions. The Duchesse of Berry seemd less immersed in the ceremony and yawnd once or twice. She is a lively looking blonde, looks as if she were good humourd and happy, by no means pretty and has a cast with her eyes – splendidly adornd with diamonds however. After this gave Made. Mirbel a sitting where I encounter *Le General* her uncle[2] who was *Chef de l'État Major* to Bonaparte. He was very communicative and seemd an interesting person, by no means over much prepossessd in favour of his late Master whom he judged impartially though with affection.

We came home and dined in quiet having refused all temptations to go out in the evening; this on Anne's account as well as my own. It is not quite gospel though Solomon says it – The eye *can* be tired with seeing,[3] whatever he may alledge in the contrary. And then there are so many compliments. I wish for a little of the old Scotch cau[s]ticity. I am something like the bee that sips treacle.

5 SUNDAY I believe I must give up my journal till I leave Paris. The French are literally outrageous in their civilities – bounce in at all hours and drive one half mad with compliments – I am ungracious not to be so entirely thankful as I ought to this kind and merry people. We breakfasted *chez* Made. de Mirbel where were the Dukes of Fitz James, Cressieux I think, and Duras, goodly company, but all's one for that – I made rather an impatient sitter wishing much more to talk than was agreeable to Madame Mirbel. Afterwards we went to the

1. Charles X, formerly Comte d'Artois, was forced to live abroad until 1814. The British Government gave him apartments in Holyrood House – to which incidentally he returned in 1830 when he became once more an exile. The ducs de Berri and de Fitzjames, whom Scott mentions, were among the other French exiles whom he met at Holyrood.
2. General Monthion.
3. Possibly an allusion to Ecclesiastes 1: 8 'The eye is not satisfied with seeing, nor the ear filled with hearing.'

Champs Elysees where a balloon was let off and all sorts of fooleries performd for the benefit of the *bons gens de Paris* besides stuffing them with victuals. I wonder how such a civic festival would go off in London or Edinburgh or especially in Dublin. To be sure they would not introduce their shilelahs. But in the classic taste of the French there were no such gladiatorial doings. To be sure they have a natural goodhumour and gaiety which incl[in]es them to be pleased with themselves and everything about them.

We dined at the ambassador's where was a large party, Lord Morpeth, the Duke of Devonshire and others. All were very kind. Pozzo di Borgo there and disposed to be communicative. A large soirée in the evening where we had some music from Miss Wilkinson a relation of Mrs Siddons' friend and companion by mortal[s] hight Pat Wilkinson. Home at eleven. These hours are early however.

6 MONDAY Cowper came to breakfast but we were *obsédés partout*. A number of Frenchmen bounced in successively and exploded, I mean discharged their compliments, that I could hardly find an opportunity to speak a word or entertain Cowper at all. After we sate again for our portraits. Made. Mirbel took care not to have any one to divert my attention but I contrived to amuse myself with some masons finishing a façade opposite to me who placed their stones not like Inigo Jones but in the most lubberly way in [the] world with a help of a large wheel and the application of strength of hand. John Smith of Darnick and two of his men would have done more with a block and pully than the whole score of them. The French seem far behind in machinery. We are almost eaten up with kindness but that will have its end. I have had to parry several presents of busts and so forth. The funny thing was the airs of my little friend. We had a most affectionate parting wit[h] wet cheeks on the lady's side. The pebble-hearted cur shed as few tears as Crabbe of dogged memory.[1]

Went to Galignani's where the brothers after some palaver offerd me £105 for the transmission of *Napoleon* to be reprinted at Paris in English. I told them I would think of it. I suppose Treuttel and Wurtz had apprehended something of this kind for they write me that they had made a bargain with my publishers (Cadell I suppose) for the publishing my book in all sorts of ways. I must look into this.[2]

Dined with Marischal Macdonald and a splendid party. Amongst others Marischal Marmont – middle size, stout mad[e], dark complection and looks sensible – The French hate him much for his

1. In *Two Gentlemen of Verona*, ii. 3.
2. Treuttel and Wurtz published the French edition.

conduct in 1814 but it is only making him the scape goat.[1] Also I saw Monsr. Du Moller,[2] but especially Marquis de Lauriston who received me most kindly. He is personally like my cousin Colonel Russell. I learnd his brother Louis Law,[3] my old friend, was alive and the father of a large family. I was most kindly treated and had my vanity much flatterd by the men who had acted such important parts talking to me in the most frank manner.

In the evening to Princess Galitzin where were a whole covey of princesses of Russia arrayd in tartan with music and singing to boot. The person in whom I was most interested was Made. de Boufflers, upwards of eighty, very polite, very pleasant, and with all the *agremens* of a French court lady of the time of Made. Sévigné or of the correspondent rather of Horace Walpole.[4] Cowper was there so the Scotch and American lion took the field together. Home and settled our affairs to depart.

7 TUESDAY Off at seven and breakfasted Beaumain[5] and pushd on to Airennes.[6] This being a forced march[7] we had bad lodgings, wet wood, uncomfortable supper, damp beds and an extravagant charge. I was never colder in my life than when I waked with the sheets clinging round me like a shroud.

8 WEDNESDAY We started at six in the morning having no need to be calld twice so heartily was I weary of my comfortless couch. Breakfasted at Abbeville – then pushd on to Boulogne expecting to find the packet ready to start next morning and so to have had the advantage of the easterly tide. But lo ye! the packet was not to sail till next day so after shrugging our shoulders – being the solace *à la mode de France* – and recruited ourselves with a *poulet* and a bottle of Chablis *à la mode d' Angleterre*, we set off for Calais after supper and it was betwixt three and four in the morning before we got to Dessein's

1. A reference to Marmont's secret convention in 1814, by which he brought his *corps d'armée* over to the side of the Provisional Government. See *Life of Napoleon*, viii. 222–7.
2. Le Comte de Molé (1781–1855), statesman, author of *Essais de morale et de politique*, and friend of Napoleon.
3. Jacques Alexandre Bernard Law, Marquis de Lauriston, and his brother Charles Louis Law, of the family of the financier John Law, had been schoolfellows of Napoleon. Louis Law, when an *émigré*, had been a frequent guest of Scott's father.
4. Mme du Deffand.
5. A slip for 'Beaumont'.
6. i.e. Airaines.
7. They travelled over 200 miles in two days.

where the house was full or reported to be so. We could only get two wretched brick-paved garrets as cold and moist as [those] of Airennes instead of the comforts which we were received with at our arrival. But I was better prepared, stripd off the sheets and lay down in my dressing gown and so roughd it out *tant bien tant mal*.

9 THURSDAY At five in the morning we are calld – at six we got on board of the pacquet where I found a sensible and conversible man, a very pleasant circumstance. The day was raw and cold, the wind and tide surly and contrary, the passage slow, and Anne contrary to her wont excessively sick. We had little trouble at the Custom house thanks to the Secretary of the embassy Mr. Jones, who gave me a letter to Mr. Ward. Mr. Ward came with the Lieutenant Governor of the Castle and wishd us to visit that ancient fortress. I regretted much that our time was short and the weather did not admit of our seeing views. So we could only thank the gentlemen in declining their civility.

The castle, partly ruinous, seems to have been very fine – the cliff, to which Shakespeare gave his immortal name is as all the world knows a great deal lower than his description implies.[1] Our Dover friends, justly jealous of the reputation of their cliff, impute this diminution of its consequence to its having fallen in repeatedly since the poet's time. I confess I think it fully more likely that the imagination of Shakespeare, writing perhaps at a period long after he may have seen the rock, had described it such as he conceived it to have been. Besides Shakespeare was born in a flat country and Dover cliff is at least lofty enough to have suggested the exaggerated features to his fancy. At all events it has maintaind its reputation better than the Tarpeian rock – no man could leap from it and live.

Left Dover after a hot luncheon about four o'clock and reachd London at half past three in the morning.[2] So adieu to *la belle France* and wellcome Merry England.

10 FRIDAY Ere I leave *la belle France* however it is fit I should express my gratitude for the unwontedly kind reception which I met with at all hands. It would be an unworthy piece of affectation did I not allow that I have been pleased – highly pleased – to find a species of literature intended only for my own country has met such an extensive and favourable reception in a foreign land where there was so much *a priori* to oppose its progress.

For my work I think I have done a good deal but above all I have

1. See *King Lear*, iv. 6.
2. The distance was seventy-one miles.

been confirmd strongly in the impressions I had previously formd of the character of Nap. and may attempt to draw him with a firmer hand.

The effect of a succession of new people and unusual incidents has had a favourable effect [on my mind] which was becoming rutted like an ill kept highway. My thoughts have for some time flowd in another and pleasanter channel than the melancholy course into which my solitary and deprived state had long driven them and which gave often pain to be endured without complaint and without sympathy. 'Fors relief' as Marcellus says in *Hamlet* 'much thanks.'[1]

To-day I visited the public offices and prosecuted my enquiries. Left enquiries for the Duke of York who has recoverd from a most desperate state. His legs had been threatend with mortification but he was saved by a critical discharge – Also visited the D. of Wellington, Lord Melville and others, besides the ladies in Piccadilly.[2] Dined and spent the evening quietly in Pall Mall.[3]

11 SATURDAY Croker came to breakfast and we were soon after joind by Theodore Hooke alias John Bull:[4] he has got as fat as the actual monarch of the herd. Lockhart sate still with us and we had as Gil Blas [says] a delicious morning spent in abusing our neighbours, at which my three neighbours are no novices any more than I am myself though (like Puss in Boots who only caught mice for his amusement) I only am a chamber council in matters of scandal. The fact is I have refraind as much as humane frailty will permit from all satirical composition. There is an ample subject for a little black-balling in the case of Joseph Hume the great Oeconomist who has cheated the Greek loan so egregiously. I do not lack personal provocation (See 13 March last).[5] Yet I won't attack him at present at least. But *qui'l se garde de moi*.

1. *Hamlet*, i. 1. The speaker is Francisco, though, not Marcellus.
2. See the Entry for 18 October 1826 and note.
3. With the Lockharts, who lived at 25 Pall Mall.
4. Scott did not greatly like Hook nor his paper, *John Bull*. 'I do not look on Theodorus as fit company for ladies,' he warned Lockhart the previous year, 'and if you even haunt him much yourself you will find it tell against you. . . . He is *raffish* entre nous.' *Letters*, ix. 295. *John Bull* was a satirical Sunday newspaper, begun in 1820, which supported George IV and abused the Queen and her friends.
5. Hume, who had attacked Scott in the Commons (see the Entry for 21 March 1826 *not* 13 March), was himself under attack for jobbery in connection with the loan raised to help the Greek insurgents.

Ime not a King nor nae sic thing
My word it may not stand
And Joseph may a buffet bide
Come he beneath my brand.¹

At dinner we had a little blow-out on Sophia's part. Lord Dudley, Mr. Hay, Under Secretary of State,   .*Mistress*, as she calls herself, Joanna Baillie and her sister came in the evening. The whole went off pleasantly.

12 SUNDAY Breakfasted.

Went to sit to Sir T. L. to finish the picture for his majesty which every one says is a very fine one.² I think so myself and wonder how Sir Thomas made so much out of an old weather beaten block. But I believe the hard features of old Dons like myself are more within the compass of the Artist's skill than the lovely face and delicate complection of females. Came home after a heavy shower. I had a long conversation about D.³ with Lockhart – All that was whisperd is true – a sign how much better our domestics are acquainted with the private affairs of our neighbours than we are. A dreadful tale of incest and seduction and nearly of blood also – horrible beyond expression in its complications and events – 'And yet the end is not'⁴ – And this man was amiable and seemd the soul of honour – laughd too and was the soul of society. It is a mercy our thoughts are conceald from each other. O if at our social table we could see what passes in each bosom around we would seek dens and caverns to shun human society. To see the projector trembling for his falling speculations, the voluptuary ruing the event of his debauchery, the miser wearing out his soul for the loss of a guinea – all – all bent upon vain hopes and vainer regrets – we should not need to go to the hall of the Caliph Vathek to see men's hearts broiling under their black veils.⁵ Lord keep us from all temptation for we cannot be our own shepherd.

1. 'Auld Maitland', ll. 197–200 in Scott's *Border Minstrelsy*.
2. The portrait was commissioned from Lawrence by the King for his gallery at Windsor and the head had been painted as long ago as the winter of 1820–1. Lockhart considered that the finished picture was not a success, the head being small in proportion to the body. *Life*, vi. 201–2. See also Oliver Millar's comments in his *Later Georgian Pictures in the Collection of Her Majesty the Queen*, 1969, pp. 75–6.
3. Possibly Heber. See p. 186.
4. St. Matthew 24: 6.
5. In Beckford's *Vathek*, 1786.

We dined to-day at Lady Stafford's.[1] Lord S. looks very poorly but better than I expected. No company excepting Sam Rogers and Mr. Grenville;[2] the latter is better known by the name of Tom Grenville, a very amiable and accomplishd man whom I knew better about twenty years since. Age has touchd him as it has doubtless affected me. The great Lady received us with the most cordial kindness and expressd herself I am sure sincerely desirous to be of service to [the] Lockharts.

13 MONDAY I consider Charles's business as settled by a private intimation which I had to that effect from S. W. K.[3] So I need negotiate no further but wait the event. Breakfasted at home and somebody with us but the whirl of visits so great that I have already forgot the party. Lockhart and I dined at an official person's where there was a little too much of that sort of flippant wit, or rather smartness, which becomes the parochial Joe Miller of boards and offices. You must not be grave because it might lead to improper discussions and to laugh without a joke is a hard task. Your professd wags are treasures to this species of Company. Gil Blas was right in censuring the literary society of his friend Fabricio[4] but never the less one or two of the mess would greatly have improved the conversation of his *commis*. Went to poor Lydia White's[5] and found her extended on a couch, frightfully swelld, unable to stir, rouged, jesting, and dying. She has a good heart and is really a clever creature but unhappily or rather happily she has set up the whole staff of her rest in keeping literary society about her. The world has not neglected her. It is not always so bad as it is calld. She can always make up her soiree and generally has some people of real talent and distinction. She is wealthy to be sure and gives *petit diners* but not in a stile to carry the point *force d'argent*. In her case the world is goodnatured and perhaps it is more frequently so than is generally supposed.

1. The 'we' comprised Scott and Anne, Lockhart and Sophia. *Letters*, x. 126.
2. The Rt. Hon. Thomas Grenville (1755–1846) the statesman and bibliophile, who bequeathed his collection of books to the British Museum.
3. Charles would like a place in the public service, preferably in the Foreign Office, 'but should an employment in any of the offices be more easily attained than anything in the diplomatic line', Scott will be equally pleased, he tells Knighton. *Letters*, x. 126.
4. Le Sage's *Gil Blas*, bk. viii, chs. 9 and 13.
5. Scott met her when she spent some months in Scotland in 1808, 'a lioness of the first order, with stockings nineteen-times-nine dyed blue, very lively, very good-humoured, and extremely absurd'. *Letters*, ii. 5. She later helped him with material for his edition of Swift.

14 TUESDAY We breakfast at honest Allan Cunningham – honest allan – a leal true Scotsman of the old cast. A man of genius besides who only requires the tact of knowing when and where to stop to attain the universal praise which ought to follow it. I look upon the alteration of 'It's Hame and it's Hame' and 'A Wet Sheet and a Flowing Sea' as among the best songs going. His prose has often admirable passages but he is obscure and overlays his meaning, which will not do now a days when he who runs must read.

Dined at Croker's at Kensington with his family, the Speaker,¹ and the facetious Theodore Hook.

We came away rather early that Anne and I might visit Mrs. Arbuthnot² to meet the Duke of Wellington. In all my life I never saw him better. He has a dozen of campaigns in his body and tough ones. Anne was delighted with the frank manners of this unequald pride of British war and me he received with all his usual kindness. He talkd away about Bonaparte, Russia and France.

15 WEDNESDAY At Breakfast a conclave of medical men about poor little Johnie Lockhart. They give good words but I cannot help fearing the thing is very precarious and I feel a miserable anticipation of what the parents are to undergo. It is wrong however to despair. I was myself a very weak child and certainly am one of the strongest men of my age in point of constitution. Sophia and Anne went to the Tower – I to the Colonial office where I labourd hard.²

Dined with the Duke of Wellington. Anne with me who could not look enough at the *Vainqueur du Vainqueur de terre*.³ The party were Mr. and Mrs. Peele and Mr. and Mrs. Arbuthnot,⁴ Vesey Fitzgerald,⁵ Banks⁶ and Croker with Lady Bathurst⁷ and Lady Georgina.⁸ One

1. The Rt. Hon. Charles Manners-Sutton (1780–1845) who was Speaker from 1817 until 1835.
2. At the St. Helena papers.
3. Johnson's 'Letter to Lord Chesterfield'.
4. Charles Arbuthnot (1767–1850), the close friend of Wellington, was M. P. for St. Ives and Chancellor of the Duchy Court of Lancaster.
5. William Vesey Fitzgerald (1783–1843), recently appointed Paymaster-General. He became President of the Board of Trade in June 1828.
6. George Bankes (1788–1856), M. P. for Corfe Castle and a Baron of Exchequer. He was later a junior Lord of Treasury.
7. The wife of Henry, third Earl Bathurst who was later President of the Board of Trade, Secretary for War and Colonies, and Lord President of the Council in Wellington's administration.
8. Her elder daughter, Lady Louisa-Georgina.

gentleman took much of the conversation and gave us with unnecessary emphasis and at superfluous length his opinion of a late gambling transaction. This spoild the evening. I am sorry for the occurrence though for Lord Clanrickard is fetlock deep in it and it looks like a vile bog. This misfortune with the foolish incident at Dover will not be sufferd to fall to the ground but will be used as a counterpoise to the Greek loan. Peele askd me in private my opinion of three candidates for the Scotch gown and I gave it him candidly. We will see if it has weight.[1]

I begin to tire of my gaieties and the late hours and constant feasting disagree with me. I wish for a sheep's head and whisky-toddy against all the french cookery and Champagne in the world.

Well – I suppose I might have been a Judge of Session this term – attaind in short the grand goal proposed to the ambition of a Scottish lawyer.[2] It is better however as it is, while at least I can maintain my literary reputation.

I had some conversation to-day with Messrs. Longman and Co. They agreed to my deriving what advantage I could in America[3] and that very willingly. Also they cashd me a bill on Mr. Gibson to part payment of my Exchequer receipts for £50 Sterling.

16 THURSDAY Breakfasted with Rogers with my daughters and Lockhart. R. was exceedingly entertaining in his dry quiet sarcastic manner. At eleven to the Duke of Wellington's[4] who gave me a bundle of remarks on B's Russian Campaign, written in his carriage during his late mission to St. Petersburgh.[5] It is furiously scrawld and the Russian names hard to distinguish but it *shall* do me yeoman's service. Then went to Pentonville to old Mr. Handley, a solicitor of the old school and manager of the Downshire property.[6] Had an account of the claim arising on the estate

1. It had. Scott's early friend George Cranstoun was appointed later in the month.
2. After the financial crash his friends had offered to negotiate for him a seat upon the Bench (see the Entry for 7 February 1826), and had he accepted their proposal this vacancy might have been filled by himself instead of Cranstoun.
3. See the Entry for 3 November 1826 and note.
4. The 'visit for a few days' which Wellington invited him to make was prevented by the trip to France. This briefer meeting was arranged on his return. Wellington, 27 October and 12 November 1826, Walpole.
5. Later printed as 'Memorandum on the War in Russia in 1812' in *Despatches*, edited by Wellington's son, 1868.
6. See the Entry for 22 March 1826 and note.

of one Mrs. Owen due to the representatives of my poor wife's mother. He was desperately excursive and spoke almost for an hour but the prospect of £4000 to my children made me a patient auditor. Thence I passd to the Colonial office w[h]ere I concluded my extracts. Dined with Croker at the Admiralty *au grand couvert*. No less than five cabinet ministers were present, Canning, Huskisson, Melville, Duke Wellington, with sub secretaries by the bushell. The cheer was excellent but the presence of too many men of distinguishd rank and power always freezes the conversation. Each lamp shews brightest when placed by itself, when too close they neutralize each other.

17 FRIDAY My morning levee began with the arrival of Bahauder Jah[1] soon after Mr. Wright. Then I was calld out to James Scott the young painter. I greatly fear this modest and amiable creature is throwing away his time. Next came the Lithgow animal who is hunting out a fortune in Chancery which has lain *perdu* for thirty years. The fellow who is figure and manner the very essence of the creature called a sloth has attached himself to this pursuit with the steadiness of a well scented beagle. I believe he will actually get the prize. Eckford is his name.[2]

Sir John Malcolm acknowleges and recommends my Persian visitor Bruce.[3]

Saw the Duke of York. The change on H. R. H. is most wonderful. From a big, burly, stout man with a thick and sometimes an inarticulate mode of speaking, he has sunk into a thin faced, slender looking old man who seems diminishd in his very size. I could hardly believe I saw the same person though I was received with his usual kindness. He speaks much more distinctly than formerly; his complexion is clearer. In short H. R. H. seems on the whole more healthy after this crisis than when in the stall-fed state, for such it seemd to be, in which I remember [him]. God

1. Sir John Malcolm, just about to take up his new appointment as Governor of Bombay. He had been envoy to Persia and had held a number of important posts in India. He wrote the histories of both countries.
2. John Eckford was a hosier in Hawick, who laid claim in the name of his wife Helen to the estate of a certain Hector Lithgow. He was finally able to prove that Hector Lithgow was illegitimate, and that his property should therefore belong to Mrs. Eckford, who was aunt and next of kin to Hector's father, Alexander Lithgow. The case had already dragged out for nearly four years. Eckford, 20 March 1829, Walpole.
3. See the Entries for 5–7 September 1826.

grant it. His life is of infinite value to the King and Country – It is a *break water* behind the throne.

18 SATURDAY Was introduced by Rogers to Made. D'Arblay, the celebrated authoress of *Evelina* and *Cecilia*: an elderly lady with no remains of personal beauty but with a gentle manner and a pleasing expression of countenance. She told me she had wishd to see two persons – myself of course being one, the other Geo: Canning. This was really a compliment to be pleased with, a nice little handsome [pat] of butter made up by a neat-handed Phillis of a dairy maid instead of the grease fit only for cart-wheels which one is dozed with by the pound.

Made. D'Arblay told us the common story of Dr. Burney her father having brought home her own first work and recommended it to her perusal was erroneous – her father was in the secret of *Evelina* being printed. But the following circumstances may have given rise to the story. Dr. Burney was at Streatham soon after the publication where he found Mrs. Thrale recovering from her confinement, low at the moment and out of spirits. While they were talking together Johnson, who sate beside in a kind of reverie, suddenly broke out – 'You should read this new work, Madam – you should read *Evelina* – every one says it is excellent and they are right.' The delighted father obtain a commissi[on] from Mrs. Thrale to purchase his daughter's work and retired the happiest of men. Made. D'Arblay said she was wild with joy at this decisive evidence of her literary success and that she could only give vent to her rapture by dancing and skipping round a mulberry tree in the garden. She was very young at this time. I trust I shall see this lady again. She has simple and apparently amiable manners with quick feelings.

Dined at Mr. Peele's with Lord Liverpool, Duke of Wellington, Croker, Banks etc. The conversation very good, Peele taking the lead in his own house which he will not do elsewhere. We canvassd the memorable criminal case of Ashford.[1] Peele almost convinced me of the man's innocence. Should have been at the play but sate too late at Mr. Peele's.

So ends my campaign amongst these Magnificoes and potent Seigniors,[2] with whom I have found as usual the warmest acceptation. I wish I could turn a little of my popularity amongst them to

---

1. Abraham Thornton was tried for the murder of Mary Ashford in 1817 and acquitted. Her brother appealed against the acquittal and Thornton claimed the privilege of 'Wager of Battle' – for the last time before the law was abolished in 1819.
2. A reminiscence of *Othello*, i. 3.

Lockhart's advantage who cannot bustle for himself.[1] He is out of spirits just now and sees things *au noir*. I fear Johnie's precarious state is the cause.

I finishd my sitting to Lawrence and am heartily sorry there should be another picture of me except that which he has finishd. The person is remarkably like and conveys the idea of the stout blunt carle that cares for few things and fears nothing. He has represented the author as in the act of composition yet has effectually discharged all affectation from the manner and attitude. He seems pleased with it himself. He dined with us at Peele['s] yesterday, where by the way we saw the celebrated 'Chapeau de paille' which is not a *chapeau de paille* at all.[2]

19 SUNDAY Saw in the morning Duke of Wellington and Duke of York. The former so communicative that I regretted extremely the length of time but have agreed on a correspondence with him. *Trop d'honneur pour moi*. The Duke of Y. saw me by appointment. He seems still mending and spoke of state affairs as a high tory. Were his health good his spirit is as strong as ever. H.R.H. has a devout horror of the liberals – Having the Duke of Wellington, the Chancellor and (perhaps) a still greater person on his side, he might make a great fight when they split as split they will. But Canning, Huskisson, and a mitigated party of liberaux will probably beat them. Canning's witt and eloquence are almost irresistible. But then the Church, justly alarmd for their property which is plainly struck at, and the bulk of the landed interest, will scarce brook a mild infusion of Whiggery into the administration – Well time will show.

We visited our friends Peele, Lord Gwydyr, Arbuthnot etc. and left our tickets of adieu. In no instance during my former visits to London I never met with such general attention and respect on all sides.[3]

1. Scott believed it necessary to be known in society. He was pleased when Lockhart took a house in Pall Mall: 'It is better you have got a good house for there is scarce any thing in London so necessary to comfort and credit. You may *scrub* in your dinner as much as you please so you have a handsome front in a fashionable part of the town.' *Letters*, ix. 339. It worried him that Lockhart would not cultivate society assiduously enough: 'Lockhart will always be much liked by his intimates but an early scholarlike reserve prevents his making much figure in society.' *Letters*, ix. 417.

2. Peel had bought *The Spanish Hat* by Rubens in 1823. It is a beaver-hat, a *chapeau de poil*.

3. The confusion arises from an afterthought which prompted Scott to change 'all' to 'no instance during' without altering the rest of the sentence accordingly.

Lady Louisa Stuart dined with Wright and Mr. and Mrs. Christie.[1] Dr. and Mrs. Hughes came in the evening; so ended pleasantly our last night in London.

20 MONDAY Left London after a comfortable breakfast and an adieu to the Lockhart family. If I had had but comfortable hopes of that poor pale prostrate child, so clever and so interesting, I should have parted easily on this occasion but these misgivings overcloud the prospect. We reachd Oxford by six o'clock and found Charles and his friend young Surtees waiting for us with a good fire in the chimney and a good dinner ready to be placed on the table.[2] We had struggled through a cold sulky drizzly day which had deprived of all charms even the beautiful country near Henly. So we came from cold and darkness into light and warmth and society. N.B. we had neither daylight nor moonlight to see the view of Oxford from the Maudlin Bridge which I used to think one of the most beautiful in the world.

Upon finance I must note that after all *et caeteras* were paid I started from Pall Mall with something like £60 and upward, the principal part of which was £50 remitted by Gibson. The rest has been swallowd up in expence of travelling which has mounted high. I am too old to rough it and scrub it nor could I have saved fifty pounds by doing so. I have gaind however in health, in spirits, in a new stock of ideas, new combinations and new views. My self consequence is raised, I hope not unduly, by the many flattering circumstances attending my reception in the two capitals and I feel confident in proportion. In Scotland I shall find time for labour and for oeconomy.

21 TUESDAY Breakfasted with Charles in his Chambers[3] where he had every thing very neat – how pleasant it is for a father to sit at his child's board! It is like the aged man reclining under the shadow of the oak which he has planted – My poor plant has some storms to undergo but were this expedition conducive to no more than his entrance into life under suitable auspices I should [think] the toil and

1. Lockhart's old college friend Jonathan Henry Christie and his wife Mary. For an account of the duel between Christie and John Scott, who had abused Lockhart in *Baldwin's London Magazine*, see *Letters*, vi. 348 n.
2. 'We will write at what inn we are to take up our rest and hope you will order dinner and partake it with us. If Surtees is disengaged and will also dine with us it will do us a great favour.' *Letters*, x. 129.
3. At Brasenose.

the expence well bestowd – We then sallied out to see the lions. Guides being Charles, our friend Surtees, Mr. John Hughes,[1] young Mackenzie (fitz-Colin)[2] and a young companion or two of Charles's – Also Mr. Harrison of Maudlin college.[3] Remembering the extatic feelings with which I visited Oxford more than twenty five years since I was surprized at the comparative indifference with which I revisited the same scenes – My patron and conductor – the subject is too painful[4] – His brother then composing his prize poem and imping his wings for a long flight of honourable distinction is now dead in a foreign land[5] – Hodson[6] and other able men all entombed – The towers and halls remains but the voices which fill them are of modern days. Besides the eye becomes satiated with sights as the full soul loathes the honeycomb. I admired indeed but my admiration was void of the enthusiasm which I formerly felt. I remember particularly having felt while in the Bodleian like the Persian Magician who visited the enchanted library in the bowels of the mountain and willingly sufferd himself to be enclosed in its recesses while less eager sages retired in alarm.[7] Now I had some base thoughts concerning luncheon which was must munificently supplied by Surtees with the aid of the best ale I ever drank in my life – the real wine of Ceres and worth that of Bacchus.

Dr. Jenkins the Vice Chancellor did me the honour to call but I saw him not. I calld on Charles Douglas[8] at All Souls and had a chat of an hour with him.

Before three set out for Cheltenham, a long and uninteresting drive, which we achieved by nine o'clock. My sister in law and her daughter[9] instantly came to the hotel and seem in excellent health and spirits.

22 WEDNESDAY Breakfasted with Mrs. Scott and my nieces one of whom, Mrs. Huxley, I had not seen since a child. They were all well

1. Son of Dr. and Mrs. Hughes.
2. The son of Scott's friend Colin Mackenzie.
3. Probably John Butler Harrison (1790–1871).
4. He had been shown round by Richard Heber, now disgraced. See the Entries for 25 June, 10 July 1826 and 12 November 1826.
5. Reginald Heber, Bishop of Calcutta, who had died in India earlier in the year.
6. Dr. Frodsham Hodson, Master of Brasenose College, who died in 1822.
7. See Weber's *Tales of the East* (1812), ii. 452–7.
8. Second son of Archibald, first Baron Douglas, and stepson of Lady Frances Scott, sister to the third Duke of Buccleuch.
9. Mrs. Thomas Scott and Anne.

and happy. The death of Mrs. Scott's brother Mr. David Macculloch[1] has put them in possession of about £10,000, their mother
enjoying the interest, which renders them very independent from
having been very much otherwise. I saw Anne's Intended Dr.
Allardyce. He is middle aged, rather handsome than plain, professional in his manners but a man of business and of honour. He
proposes to settle her own fortune with £5000 more on her and her
children and as he has increasing practice no doubt they will be very
well off.[2] Dined with Mrs. Scott at four and leaving Cheltenham at
six or seven pushd on to Worcester to sleep.

23 THURSDAY Breakfasted at Birmingham and slept at Maccles-
field. As we came in between ten and eleven the people of the inn
expressd surprize at our travelling so late as the general distress of the
manufacturers has renderd many of the lower class desperately
outrageous. The inn was guarded by a special watchman who
alarmd us by giving his signal of turnout – But it proved to be a
poor deserter who had taken refuge among the carriages and who was
reclaimd by his Sergeant. The people talk gloomily of winter when
the distresses of the poor will be increased.

24 FRIDAY Breakfasted at Manchester. Ere we left the Senior
Church Warden Mr. Clegg came to offer us his services to show
us the town, principal manufactures etc. We declined his polite offer
pleading haste. I found his opinion about the state of the trade more
agreeable than I had ventured to expect. He said times were mending
gradually but steadily and that the poors rates were decreasing, of
which none can be so good a judge as the Church Warden. Some
months back the people had been in great discontent on account of
the Power-engines, which they conceived diminishd the demand for
operative labour. There was no politics in their discontent however
and at present it was diminishing. We again pressd on and by dint of

1. Anne had been summoned back from Abbotsford in August
   because of her uncle's stroke. See the Entry for 7 August 1826.
2. Scott felt responsible for his brother's widow and her daughter,
   and it was principally to satisfy himself about Dr. Allardyce that
   he had come. 'I must take Cheltenham on my way', he wrote to
   Ballantyne, 'to see matters suitably arranged for my nieces
   approaching marriage which is the least I can do after her
   kindness in our great affliction.' *Letters*, x. 125. The marriage did
   not in fact take place. His divorced first wife returned to the
   country prepared to be troublesome and Anne 'determined not
   to hazard her future peace and respectability by forming such a
   connexion'. See Grierson's note in *Letters*, x. 125.

exertion reachd Kendal to sleep thus getting out of the region of the stern sullen unwashd artificers[1] whom you see lounging sulkily along the streets of the towns in Lancashire, cursing it would seem by their looks the stop of trade which gives them leisure and the laws which prevent their employing their spare time in [the chase]. God's justice is requiting and will yet further Requite those who have blown up the country into a state of unsubstantial opulence at the expense of the health and morals of the lower classes.

25 SATURDAY Took two pair of horses over the Shap fells, which are coverd with snow, and by dint of exertion reachd Penrith to breakfast. Then rolld on till we found our own horses at Hawick and returnd to our own home at Abbotsford about three in the morning. It is well we made a forced march of about one hundred miles for I think the snow would have stoppd us had we lingerd.

26 SUNDAY Consulting my purse found my good £60 diminishd to

In purse £8.0.0.

Quarter less Ten – Naturally reflected how much expense has increased since I first traveld. My uncle's servant during the jaunts we made together while I was a boy used to have his option of a shilling per diem for board wages and usually preferd it to having his charges borne. A servant now a days to be comfortable on the road should have 4/- or 4/6 board wages, which before 1790 would have maintaind his master. But if this be pitiful, it is still more so to find the alteration in my own temper. When young and returning from such a trip as I have just had my mind would have loved to dwell on all I had seen that was rich and rare or have been placing perhaps in order the various additions with which I had supplied my stock of information, and now like a stupid boy blundering over an arithmetical question which is half obliterated on his slate I go stumbling on upon the audit of pounds shillings and pence. Why the increase of charge I complain of must continue so long as the value of the thing represented by cash continues to rise, or as the value of the thing representing continues to decrease – let the oeconomists settle which is the right way of expressing the process when groats turn plenty and eggs grow dear.

> And so twill be when I am gone
> The increasing charge will still go on
> And other bards shall climb these hills
> And curse your charge, *dear* evening bills.[2]

1. A phrase from Cowper's 'Table Talk', l. 512.
2. A parody of Thomas Moore's 'Those evening bells' in *Antional Airs* (1815).

Well – the skirmish has cost me £200 and upwards – I wishd to get information and have had to pay for it – the information is got, the money is spent, and so this is the only mode of accompting amongst friends.[1]

I have packd my books etc. to go by cart tomorrow to Edinburgh.

I idled away the rest of the day happy to find myself at home, which is home though never so homely, and mine is not so homely neither – on the contrary I have seen in my travels none I liked so well – fantastic in architecture and decoration if you please – but no real comfort sacrificed to fantasy. 'Ever gramercy my own purse' saith the Song.[2] 'Ever gramercy my own *house*' quoth I.

27 MONDAY Settled Bogie's accounts £50. But this corresponds with about £49. 12 lodged in the Galashiels bank proceeds of the farm so that I am little richer or poorer.

Cash in bank
price of wheat
about   £50
Drat. to Bogie   50
                 —————
                 £0.0.0

We set off after breakfast but on reaching Fushie Bridge at three found ourselves obliged to wait for horses, all being gone to the smithy to be rough-shod in this snowy weather. So we stayd dinner and Peter coming up with his horses bowled us into town about eight.[3] Walter[4] came and supd with us which diverted some heavy thoughts. It is impossible not to compare this return to Edinburgh with others in more happy times. But we should rather recollect under what distress of mind I took up my lodgings in Mrs. Brown's last summer and then the balance weighs deeply on the favourable side. This house is comfortable and convenient.

28 TUESDAY Went to Court and resumed old habits – Dined with Walter and Mrs. Jane at Jane's at Mrs. Jobson. When we returnd home were astounded with the news of Colonel Huxley's death and

1. Compare his letter to Cadell on the 30th: 'On reviewing my materials I do not grudge the time & money. They are capital.' *Letters*, x. 134.
2. By Dame Juliana Berners: 'Balade' at the end of 'Huntynge' in the *Book of St. Albans* (1496).
3. Scott was taking his carriage and horses to Edinburgh for the winter. At Torsonce, the first stage, he would leave his own horses to rest while he went on with a hired team. The lack of horses at Fushie Bridge allowed Peter Mathieson, who was bringing on Scott's horses, to catch up, and they finished the journey as they had begun it.
4. He and Jane were at Mrs. Jobson's, 6 Shandwick Place, very close to the house Scott had taken at 3 Walker Street.

the manner of it.[1] A quieter, more inoffensive, mild and staid mind I never knew. He was free from all those sinkings of the imagination which render those who are liable to them the victims of occasional low spirits. All belonging to this gifted as it is calld but often unhappy class must have felt at times that but for the dictates of religion or the natural recoil of the mind from the idea of dissolution there have been times when they would have been willing to throw away life as a child does a broken toy. I am sure I know one who has often felt so. But poor Huxley was none of these; he was happy in his domestic relations and on the very day on which the rash deed was committed was to have embarkd for rejoining his wife and child whom I so lately saw anxious to impart to him their improved prospects – O Lord, What are we? – Lords of Nature – why a tile drops from a house top which an elephant would not feel more than the fall of a sheet of paste-board and there lies his Lordship. Or something of inconceivably minute origin, the pressure of a bone or the inflammation of a particle of the brain, takes place and the emblem of the Deity destroys himself or some one else. We hold our health and our reason on terms slighter than one would desire were it in their choice to hold an Irish cabbin.

29 WEDNESDAY Awakd from horrid dreams to reconsideration of the sad reality – he was such a kind, obliging, assiduous creature. I thought he came to my bedside to expostulate with me how I could believe such a scandal – and I thought I detected that it was but a spirit who spoke by the paleness of his look and the blood flowing from his cravat. I had the night-mare in short, and no wonders.

I felt stupefied all this day but wrote the necessary letters notwithstanding. Walter, Jane and Mrs. Jobson dined with us – but I could not gather my spirits. But it is nonsense and contrary to my system which is of the Stoic school and I think pretty well maintaind. It is the only philosophy I know or can practise – but it cannot always keep the helm.

1. The news of the suicide in Halifax, Nova Scotia of his niece's husband came in two letters, one from Lockhart, the other from the captain of the ship on which Huxley was to have sailed home from Canada. *Letters*, x. 134 and 145. The evening before 'he seemd in very good spirits. . . . He had promised a brother officer some bottles of rum which he sent next day before breakfast with a note in the usual stile between friends perfectly distinctly written. When his servant returnd the deed was done. The man says his master had been *cross* as he calld it for two or three days before.' To Thomas. Huxley, 18 December 1826, Disc. i. 102.

30 THURSDAY I went to the Court and on my return set in order a sheet or two copy. We came back about two – the new form of hearing counsel makes our sederunt a long one.[1] Dined alone and workd in the evening.

DECEMBER

1 FRIDAY The Court again very long in its sitting and I obliged to remain till the last; this is the more troublesome as in winter with my worn out eyes I cannot write so well by Candle Light – Naboclish. When I am quite blind, *good night to you* as the one-eyed fellow said when a tennis ball knockd out his remaining luminary. My short residue of time before dinner was much cut up by calls – all old friends too and men whom I love but this makes the loss of time more galling that one cannot and dare not growl at those on whom it has been bestowd. However I made out two leaves better than I expected. I am now once more at my oar and I will row hard. –

2 SATURDAY Returnd early from court but made some calls by the way – Dined alone with Anne and meant to have workd but, I don't know how, this horrid story[2] stuck by me so I e'en read Boutourlin's account of the Moscow campaign[3] to eschew the foul fiend.

3 SUNDAY Wrote five pages before dinner. Walter ill with a neglected cold. Sir Thomas Brisbane and Sir William Arbuthnot calld, also John A. Murray. William dined with us, all vivid with his Italian ideas. Only Jane besides. Made out five pages I think or nearly.

4 MONDAY Much colded which is no usual complaint of mine – sniveling and sneezing in a most pitiful manner, but workd about five leaves. So I am quite up with my task work and better. But my books from Abbotsford have not arrived. Dined with the Royal Society club – about 30 members present – too many for company – after coffee the Society where like Mungo in *The Padlock*[4] I listend without understanding a single word to two scientific papers, one about the tail of a comet and the other about a chuckey stone. Besides hearing

---

1. Until the Judicature Act of 1825 business was conducted mainly by written depositions.
2. Huxley's suicide.
3. Boutourlin's *Histoire militaire de la campagne de Russie en 1812*, 1824.
4. Act i of Bickerstaffe's comic opera, first performed in 1768.

Basil Hall describe and seeing him exhibit a new Azimuth.[1] I have half a mind to cut the whole concern – and yet the situation is honourable and as Bob acres says one should think of their honour.[2] We took possession of our new rooms on the mound which are very handsome and gentlemanlike.[3]

5 TUESDAY Annoyd with the cold and its consequences all night and wish I could shirk the court this morning – But it must not be – Was kept late and my cold increased. I have had a regular attack of this for many years past whenever I return to the sedentary life and heated rooms of Edinburgh which are so different from the open air and constant exercize of the country. Odd enough that during cold weather and cold nocturnal journies the cold never touchd me yet I no sooner am settled in comfortable quarters and warm well aird couches but *la voilà*. I made a shift to finish my task however and even a leaf more so we are Bang up. We dined and supd alone and I went to bed early.

6 WEDNESDAY A bad and disturbd night with fever, headache and some touch of cholera morbus which greatly disturbd my slumbers. But I fancy Nature was scouring the gun after her own fashion. I slept little till morning and then lay a bed contrary to my wont untill half past nine o'clock when I came down to Breakfast. Went to Court and returnd time enough to write about five leaves. Dined at Skene's where we met Lord Elgin and Mr. Stuart, a son of Sir M. Shchaw Stewart whom I knew and liked, poor man. Among other things and persons we talkd of Sir John Campbell of Ardkinlas[4] who is now here.

1. The papers were 'Observations on one of the Comets of 1825 tending to establish a motion of rotation about its Axis – by Mr. James Dunlop, Paramatta – communicated by Sir Thomas Macdougall Brisbane K.C.B.', and 'A description of Sternbergite a new mineral species – by W. Haidinger Esq.' In addition 'Capt. Basil Hall R.N. exhibited and described a portable Azimuth & altitude Circle recently devised by Captain Kater'. Royal Society Minutes.
2. Sheridan's *Rivals*, iv. 1.
3. Scott's speech on this occasion is recorded in the Royal Society Minutes. At the end 'the thanks of the Society were unanimously voted to Mr. Playfair for the skill and taste he has displayed in the arrangement of their new premises'.
4. Sir James (not *John*) Campbell (1745–1832) was the eldest son of John Callander of Craigforth, but changed his surname when he inherited Ardkinglass from his cousin. In the course of a turbulent career he fought in the Seven Years War and the Ionian islands, was detained by Napoleon, and was married three times. His *Memoirs Written by Himself* appeared in 1832.

He is happy in escaping from his notorious title of Callander of Craig-forth. In my youth he was a blackleg and swindler of the first order and like Pistol did

> Somewhat lean to pick-purse quick of hand.[1]

He was obliged to give up his estate to his son Colonel Callander, a gentleman of Honour, and as Dad went to the continent in the midst of the French revolution he is understood to have gone through many scenes. At one time Lord Elgin assured us he seized upon the Island of Zante, as he pretended by direct authority from the English government, and reigned there very quietly for some months untill to appease the jealousy of the Turks Lord Elgin despatched a frigate to dethrone the new Sovereign. Afterwards he traversed India in dress of a faquir. He is now eighty and upwards. I should like to see what age and adventures have done upon him. I recollect him a very handsome plausible man. Of all good breeding that of a swindler (of good education be it understood) is the most perfect.

7 THURSDAY Again a very disturbd night scarce sleeping an hour yet well when I rose in the morning. I did not do above a leaf to-day because I had much to read. But I am up to one 4th. of the vol. of 400 pages which I began on the 1st. December current; the 31st. must and shall see the end of vol. VI. We dined alone. I had a book sent me by a very clever woman in defence of what she calls the rights of her sex among which she seems to claim the privilege of getting her husband with child. Clever though. I hope she will publish it.

We dined alone.

8 FRIDAY Another restless and deplorable knight – night I should say – faith either spelling will suit. I can tell my bowels that if they do not conduct themselves as bowels of compassion I will put the Doctor on them right or wrong.

Returnd early but much done up with my complaint and want of sleep last night. I wrought however, but with two or three long intermissions, my drowsiness being irresistible. Went to dine with John Murray where met his brother Henderland, Jeffrey, Harry Cockburn, Rutherfurd and others of that file.[2] Very pleasant – capital good cheer and excellent wine – much laugh and fun.

9 SATURDAY In gratitude I suppose for the good Burgundy and Champagne wt. which I treated them yesterday my bowels allowd me

1. *Henry V*, v. 1.
2. The Whig Party.

a good night's rest but began their old trade about seven in the morning. So that to keep promise with them I staid at home and sent for Doctor Ross who is to send some Doctor's stuff I suppose.

I do not know why it is that when I am with a party of my opposition friends the day is often merrier than when with our own set. Is it because they are cleverer? – Jeffrey and Harry Cockburn are to be sure very extraordinary men, yet it is not owing to that entirely. I believe both parties meet with the feeling of something like novelty – we have not worn out our jests in daily contact. There is also a disposition on such occasions to be courteous and of course to be pleased.

Wrought all day but rather dawdled being abominably drowzy. I fancy it is bile, a visitor I have no[t] felt this long time. Maxpopple's self conceited folly has given me the task of making up a foolish bevue about his son. I had got with great difficulty an appointment for the lad to be Midshipman on board the *Acorn* and his father by way of returning thanks and show[ing] his own consequence writes to Croker and Sir George Cockburn saying that he wishes the lad to go on board a Capt. Bathurst's ship etc. etc. They are indignant with him naturally enough for if he had interest to get his cub on board this same Captain Bathurst why did he trouble my friends or me?[1] This it is to serve fools.

10 SUNDAY An uncomfortable and sleepless night and the lime water assignd to cure me seems far less pleasant and about as inefficacious as lime punch would be in the circumstances. I felt main stupid the whole forenoon and though I wrote my task yet it was with great intervals of drowsiness and fatigue which made me, as we Scots say, *dover* away in my armchair. Walter and Jane came to dinner, also my Coz Col. Russell and above and attower James Ballantyne, poor fellow. We had a quiet and social evening I acting on prescription – Well – I have seen the day, but no matter.

11 MONDAY Slept indifferent well with a feverish halo about me. But no great return of my complaint – It paid it off this morning however but the difference was of such consequence that I made an ample day's work getting over six pages besides what I may do. On this, the 11th Decemr. I shall have more than one third of Vol VI finishd which was begun on the 1st. of this current month. Dind quiet and at home. I must take no more frisks till this fit is over.

---

1. For Scott's apologetic letter to Croker at the Admiralty, some of which is quoted in the note to the Entry for 19 March 1826, see *Letters*, x. 137.

When once life's day draws near the gloaming
Then farewell careless social roaming
And farewell jolly tankards foaming
            And frolic noise
And farewell dear deluding woman
            The joy of joys.[1]

Long life to thy fame and peace to thy soul, Rob Burns. When I want to express a sentiment which I feel strongly, I find the phrase in Shakespeare or thee. The blockheads talk of my being like Shakespeare – not fit to tie his brogues.

12 TUESDAY Did not go to the P. House;[2] but drove with Walter to Dalkeith where we missd the Duke[3] and found Mr. Blakeney.[4] One thing I saw there which pleased me much and that was [my] own picture painted twenty years ago by Raeburn[5] for Constable and which was to have been brought to sale among the rest of the wreck; hanging quietly up in the dining room at Dalkeith. I do not care much about these things yet it would have been annoying to have been knockd down to the best bidder even in effigy and I am obliged to the friendship and delicacy which placed the portrait where it now is. Dind at Archie Swinton's with all the cousins of that honest clan and met Lord Cringletie, his wife and others. Finishd my task this day.

13 WEDNESDAY Went to the Court this morning early and remaind till past three. Then attended a meeting of the Edinburgh Acady. Directors[6] on account of some discussion about flogging. I am an enemy to corporal punishment. But there are many boys who will not attend without it. It is an instant and irresistible motive, and I love boy's heads too much to spoil them at the expence of their opposite extremity. Then when children feel an emancipation on this point we may justly fear they will loosen the bonds of discipline altogether. The master I fear must be something of a despot at the risque of his

1. Burns's 'Epistle to James Smith', st. 14.
2. Parliament House.
3. The Duke of Buccleuch.
4. The Duke's tutor.
5. Not the well-known Raeburn, but his earlier portrait of Scott painted for Constable. When Constable became bankrupt it was bought by the Duke of Buccleuch and taken to Dalkeith. The portrait is the frontispiece to vol. iv of Lockhart's *Life*.
6. Scott was one of the founders of the Academy in 1824, and instrumental in having John Williams, the tutor of his son Charles, appointed Rector.

becoming something of a tyrant. He governs subjects whose keen sense of the present is not easily ruled by any considerations that are not pressing and immediate. I was indifferently well beaten at school but I am now quite certain that twice as much discipline would have been well bestowd.

Dined at home with Walter and Jane. They with Anne went out in the evening. I remaind but not I fear to work much – I feel sorely faggd. I am sadly faggd – My *bottom's* Lord (pardon, gentle Romeo) does not sit lightly on his throne:[1] – then I can not get — 's[2] fate out of my head – I see that kind social benignant face never turnd to me without respect and complacence – and I see it in the agonies of death. This is childish – I tell myself so and I hint the feeling to no one else. But here it goes down like the murderer who could not [help] painting the ideal vision of the man he had murderd and who he supposed haunted him. A thousand fearful images and dire suggestions glance along the mind when it is moody and discontented with itself. Command them to stand and shew themselves and you presently assert the power of reason over imagination. But if by any strange alterations in one's nervous system you lost for a moment the talisman which controuls these fiends? Would they not terrify into obedience with their mandates rather [than] we would dare longer to endure their presence?

14 THURSDAY Annoyd with this cursed complaint[3] though I live like a hermit on pulse and water. Botherd too with the court which leaves me little room for proof sheets and none for copy. They sate to-day till past two, so before I had walkd home and calld for half an hour on the Chief Commissioner[4] the work-part of the day was gone, and then my lassitude – I say lassitude – not indolence – is so great that it costs me an hour's nap after I come home. We dined to-day with R. Dundas, Arniston – Anne and I – There was a small cabal about Cheape's election for professor of Civil Law which it is thought we can carry for him. He deserves support having been very indifferently used in the affair of the *Beacon*[5] where certain high tories shewd a

---

1. *Romeo and Juliet*, v. 1, with *bottom's* substituted for 'bosom's'.
2. Huxley's.
3. The 'cholera morbus' from which he has been suffering since 6 December.
4. Charlotte Square, where the Rt. Hon. William Adam lived, was almost on his route home to Walker Street.
5. A slanderous Tory newspaper, started in January and hastily abandoned in September 1821 by a number of leading Edinburgh figures including Sir William Rae, John Hope, and

great desire to leave him to the mercy of the enemy. 'As Feeble says, I will never bear a base mind.'[1] We drank some 'victorious Burgundy' contrary to all prescription.

15 FRIDAY Egad I think I am rather better for my good cheer! I have passd one quiet night at least and that is something gaind. A glass of good wine is a gracious creature and reconciles poor mortality to itself, and that is what few things can do.

Our election went off very decently – no discussions or aggravating speeches. Sir John Jackass[2] seconded the Whigs' nominee: so much they will submit to to get a vote; the numbers stood Cheape 138 – Bell 132, Majority 6: mighty hard run. The Tory interest was weak among the old stage[r]s where I remember it so strong. But preferment, country residence etc. has thind them. Then it was strong in the younger classes. The new Dean, Henry Moncreiff,[3] presided with strict propriety and impartiality. Walter and Jane dined with us.

16 SATURDAY Another bad night. I remember I used to think a slight illness was a luxurious thing. My pillow was then softend by the hand of affection and all the little cares which were put in exercise to soothe the languor or pain were more flattering and pleasing than the consequences of the illness were disagreeable. It was a new sense to be watchd and attended and I used to think that the *Malade imaginaire* gaind something by his humour. It is different in the latter stages – the old post chaise gets more shatterd and out of order at every turn – Windows will not be pulld up, doors refuse to open or being open will not shut again (which last is rather my case). There is some new subject of complaint every moment. Your sicknesses come thicker and thicker, your comforting or sympathising friends fewer and fewer, for why should they sorrow for the course of nature? The recollection of youth, health and uninterrupted powers of activity neither improved nor enjoyd is a poor strain of comfort – The best is the long halt will arrive at last and cure all.

Scott. Cheape, a young advocate of two years' standing at the time, was one of the editors. The paper's attack on James Stuart of Dunearn, who thrashed the printer Stevenson for it in the street, was renewed by the *Glasgow Sentinel* after the *Beacon*'s demise and led to the duel on 22 March 1821 in which Sir Alexander Boswell was killed by Stuart.

1. *2 Henry IV*, iii. 2.
2. Sir John Sinclair.
3. James Moncrieff, Dean of the Faculty of Advocates in succession to George Cranstoun, now a judge.

We had a long businessday in the court. Came home through a cold easterly rain without a great coat and was well wet.

A goodly medicine for mine aching bones.[1]

Dined at Mr. Adam Wilson's[2] and had some good singing in the evening. Saw Dr. Stokoe who attended Boney in Saint Helena: a plain sensible sort of man.

17 SUNDAY This was a day of labour agreeably varied by a pain which renderd it scarce possible to sit upright. My journal is getting a vile chirurgical aspect. I begin to be afraid of the odd consequences complaints in the Port Esquiline are said to produce.

O learnd Adolphus Esculapion

Walter and Jane dined. Mrs. Skene came in in the evening.

18 MONDAY Almost sick with pain – and it stops everything. I shall tire of my journal if it is to contain nothing but biles and piles and plaisters and unguents. In my better days I had stories to tell but death has closed the long dark avenue upon loves and friendships and I can only look at them as through the grated door of a long burial place filld with monuments of those who were once dear to me and which I look at with no insincere wish that it may open for me at no distant period providing such be the will of God. My pains were then of the heart and had something flattering in their character – if in the head it was from the blow of a bludgeon gallantly received and well paid back. Still Colon has his rights. As Jeffrey said in a clever parody

> Whether we board a Berwick smack
> Or take the mail or mount a hack
> None leaves his a—e behind.[3]

The least honourd – the most indispensible part of our body corporate is sure to keep its place. I am always horrified to think of how the reverend Lord of the trouser may be treated by and by if this goes on.

1. *Troilus and Cressida*, v. 10.
2. One of the Depute Clerks of Session.
3. A free translation of Horace's *Odes*, iii. 2. 37 ff.: *post equitem sedet atra cura.*

> Ah dextrous Chirurgeons, mitigate your plan:
> Slice bullock's rumps – but spare the rump of man.

I went to the meeting of the Commissioners[1] – there was none to-day. The Carriage had set me down so I walked from the College. One of the sourest and most unsocial feeling days which I ever felt. Why should I have liked this? I do not know – it is my dogged humour to yield little to external circumstances. Sent an excuse to the Royal Society however.

19 TUESDAY Went to court – no I lie – I had business there. Wrote a task – no more – could not –

Went out to Dalkeith and Dined with the duke. It delights me to hear this hopeful young nobleman talk with sense and firmness about his plans for improving his estate and employing the poor. If God and the world spare him he will be far known as a true Scotts Lord.

20 WEDNESDAY This complaint still troublesome but being a Teind day I had a little repose. We dined at Hector Macdonald with William Clerk and some youngsters. Highland hospitality as usual. I got some work done to-day.

21 THURSDAY In the house till two o'clock nearly. Came home, corrected proof sheets etc. mechanically. All well would the machine but keep in order but 'The spinning wheel is auld and stiff.'[2] I think I shall not live to the usual verge of human existence. I shall never see the threescore and ten and shall be sumd up at a discount.[3] No help for it – and no matter either.

22 FRIDAY Poor old Honour and Glory dead – once Lord Moira more lately Lord Hastings. He was a man of very considerable talents but had an over-mastering degree of vanity of the grossest kind. It followd of course that he was gulleable. In fact the propensity was like a ring in his nose into which any rogue might put a string. He had a high reputation for war but it was after the pettifogging hostilities in America where he had done some clever things. He died having the credit, or rather having had the credit, to leave more debt than any man since Caesar's time. £1,200,000 is said to be the least. There was a time that I knew him well and regretted the foibles which mingled with his

---

1. i.e. the members of the Commission on the Scottish Universities.
2. See p. 11, note 1.
3. A true prophecy: Scott died aged sixty-one.

character so as to make his noble qualities sometimes questionable sometimes ridiculous. He was always kind to me[1] – poor Plantagenet.

Young Perceval[2] went out to dine at Dalkeith with me.

23[3] SATURDAY To add to my other grievances I have this day a proper fit of rheumatism in my best knee. I pushd to Abbotsford however after the court rose though compelld to howl for pain as they helpd me out of the carriage where [in] my chair I was a fixture. I suppose this is one consequence of my nocturnal disturbances.

24 SUNDAY By dint of abstinence and opodeldoc I passd a better night than I could have hoped for but took up my lodging in the chapel room as it is calld for going upstairs was impossible.

To-day I have been a mere wretch. I lay in bed till past eleven thinking to get rid of the rheumatism: then I walkd as far as Turnagain with much pain. And since that time I have just roasted myself like a potato by the fireside in my study, slumbering away my precious time and unable to keep my eyes open or my mind intent on anything if I would have given my life for it. I seemd to sleep tolerably too last night but I suppose Nature had not her dues properly paid. Neither has she for some time.

I saw the filling up of the quarry on the terras walk and was pleased.

25 MONDAY Anne and I dined at Mertoun[4] as has been my old wont and use as Christmas day comes about. We were late in setting out and I have rarely seen so dark a night: the mist rolld like volumes of smoke on the road before us.

26 TUESDAY Returnd to Abbotsford this morning. I hear it reported that Lord Buchan is very ill. If that be true it affords ground for hopes that Sir John Sinclair is not immortal. Both great bores but the Earl has something of wild cleverness far exceeding the ponderous stupidity of the Cavaliero Jackasso.

1. Scott had known Lord Moira during the stirring days of the Edinburgh Light Dragoons in 1805 when Moira was Commander-in-Chief in Scotland.
2. Dudley Montagu Perceval, son of Spencer Perceval (1762–1812), Prime Minister from 1809 until his assassination in 1812.
3. For the dating of this and the next two Entries see Appendix E, ii.
4. Where the guests included Jane and Mary Schetky, who found him 'a dear old man, for his hair is grey, and he looks old'. S. F. L. Schetky, Ninety Years of Work and Play, 1877, p. 146.

27 WEDNESDAY Still weak with this wasting illness but it is clearly going off. Time it should quoth Sancho. I began my work again which had slumberd betwixt pain and weakness. In fact I could not write or compose at all.

28[1] THURSDAY Stuck to my work. Mr Scrope came to dinner and remaind next day. We were expecting young Perceval and his wife, once my favourite and beautiful Nancy MacLeod and still a very fine woman, but they came not.

In bounced G. T.[2] alarmd by an anonymous letter which acquainted him that thirty tents full of Catholics were coming to celebrate High Mass in the Abbey Church: and to consult me on such a precious document he came prancing about seven at night. I hope to get him a kirk before he makes any extraordinary explosion of simplicity.

29 FRIDAY Mr. and Mrs. Perceval came to-day. He is son of the late lamented statesman equally distinguishd by talents and integrity. The son is a clever young man and has read a good deal, pleasant too in society but tampers with phrenology which is unworthy of his father's son. There is a certain kind of cleverish men either half educated or cock-braind by nature who are attached to that same turnipology.[3] I am sorry this gentleman should take such whims – sorry even for his name's sake. Walter and Jane arrived so our Christmas party thickens. Sir Adam and Colonel Ferguson dined.

30 SATURDAY Wrote and wrought hard then went out a drive with Mr. and Mrs. Perceval and went round by the lake. If my days of good fortune should ever return I will lay out some pretty rides at Abbotsford. Caution by a volunteer officer to his company: Gentlemen, when I says 'as you were' I means 'as you was'. My cousins Mary and James Scotts arrived – the latter[4] with his pipes which helpd the night away.

Last day of an eventful year, much evil and some good but especially the courage to endure what fortune sends without becoming a pipe for her finger.[5]

It is *not* the last day of the year but to-morrow being sunday we

---

1. 29 in the original.
2. The Revd. George Thomson.
3. It was much in vogue. Edinburgh had its own Phrenological Society at this time.
4. 'former' in the original.
5. *Hamlet*, iii. 2.

hold our festival of neighbours to-day instead. The Fergusons came in mass and we had all the usual appliances of mirth and good cheer. Yet our party like the Chariot wheels of Pharaoh when involved in the Red sea draggd heavily. Some of the party grow old and infirm; others thought of the absence of the hostess whose reception to her guests was always kind. We did as well as we could however.

> It's useless to murmur and pout
>   There's no good in making ado
> Tis well the old year is out
>   And time to beginn a new.[1]

31 SUNDAY It must be allowd that the regular recurrence of annual festivals among the same individuals has as life advances something in [it] that is melancholy. We meet on such occasions like the survivors of some perilous expedition, wounded and weakend ourselves and looking through the diminishd ranks of those who remain while we think of those who are no more. Or they are like the feasts of the Caribbs in which they held that the pale and speechless phantoms of the deceased appeard and mingled with the living. Yet where shall we fly from vain repining or why should we give up the comfort of seeing our friends because they can no longer be to us or we to them what we once were to each other?

1. Dryden's 'Secular Masque', ll. 94–7.

1827

1 MONDAY God make this a happy year to the King and country and to all honest men.

I went with all our family to-day to dine as usual at the kind House of Huntlyburn[1] but the same cloud which hung over us on Saturday still had its influence. The effect of grief upon [those] who like myself and S. A. F.[2] are highly susceptible of humour has I think been finely touchd by Wordsworth in the character of the merry village teacher Matthew – whom Jeffery profanely calls the hysterical schoolmaster.[3] But, with my friend Jeffery's pardon, I think he loves to see Imagination best when it is bitted and managed and ridden upon the *grand pas*. He does not make allowance for starts and sallies and bounds when Pegasus is beautiful to behold though sometimes perilous to his rider. Not that I think the amiable Bard of Rydale shows judgement in chusing such subjects as the popular mind cannot sympathise in.[4] It is unwise and unjust to himself. I do not compare myself in point of imagination with Wordsworth; far from it for [his] is naturally exquisite and highly cultivated by constant exercize. But I can see as many castles in the clouds as any man, as many genii in the curling smoke of a steam engine, as perfect a persepolis in the embers of a seacoal fire. My life has been spent in such day dreams. But I cry no roastmeat. There are times a man

1. It was Scott's habit to dine at Mertoun on Christmas Day, to entertain the Fergusons on New Year's Eve, and to dine with them at Huntly Burn on New Year's Day.
2. Sir Adam Ferguson.
3. 'A half-crazy sentimental person'. *Edinburgh Review*, no. 23.
4. Scott had a real regard for Wordsworth (see for instance *Letters*, x. 422) but could not understand his unwillingness to bow to the public taste. 'Wordsworth fails in receiving the universal suffrage he merits because his poetry is too subtle and metaphysical in the idea, & too blunt in the expression. He thinks like a profound philosopher often when he uses the language of common even vulgar life.' *Letters*, xi. 11.

should remember what Rousseau used to say. *Tais toi, Jean-Jacques. On ne t'endent pas!*[1]

2 TUESDAY I had resolved to mark down no more 'griefs and groans'. But I must needs briefly state that I am naild to my chair like the unhappy Theseus.[2] The rheumatism exasperated by my sortie of yesterday has seized on my only serviceable knee and I am, by Proserpine, motionless as an anvill. Leeches and embrocations are all I have for it. *Diable* there was a twinge – The Russells and Fergussons here but I was fairly driven off the pitt after dinner and compelld to retreat to my own bed, there to howl till morning like a dog in his solitary cabbin.

3 WEDNESDAY Mending slowly. Two things are comfortable – 1st. I lose no good weather out of doors for the ground is coverd with snow. 2d that by exerting a little stoicism I can make my illness promote the advance of *Nap*: As I can scarce stand however I am terribly awkward at consulting books, maps etc. The work grows under my hand however. Vol VI will be finishd this week I believe. Russells being still with us I was able by dint of handing and chairing to get to the dining room and the drawing room in the evening.

Talking of Wordsworth, he told Anne and I a story[3] the object of which was to show that Crabbe had not imagination. He, Sir George Beaumont and Wordsworth were sitting together in Murray the bookseller's back-room. Sir George after sealing a letter blew out the candle which had enabled him to do so and exchanging a look with Wordsworth began to admire in silence the undulating thread of smoke which slowly arose from the expiring wick when Crabbe put on the extinguisher. Anne laughd at the instance and enquired if the taper was wax, and being answerd in the negative seemd to think that there was no call on Mr. Crabbe to sacrifice his sense of smell to their admiration of beautiful and evanescent forms. In two other men I should have said 'this is affectations'[4] with Sir Hugh Evans. But Sir George is the man in the world most void of affectation and then he is an exquisite painter and no doubt saw where the *incident* would have succeeded in painting. The error is not in you yourself receiving deep impressions from slight hints but in supposing that precisely the same

1. Mme de Bouffler's words to Rousseau dissuading him from fruitless argument.
2. In Virgil's *Aeneid*, vi. 617. Scott quotes the passage in the Entry for 14 June 1830.
3. Probably in September 1825 when he accompanied Scott from Windermere to Lowther Castle during the return journey from Ireland.
4. *Merry Wives of Windsor*, i. 1.

sort of impression must arise in the mind of men otherwise of kindred feeling or that the commonplace folks of the world can derive such inductions at any time or under any circumstances.

4 THURSDAY My enemy gaind some strength during the watches of the night but has again succumbd under scalding fomentations of Camomile flowers. I still keep my State for my knee though it has ceased to pain me is very feeble. We began to fill the Ice House to-day. Dine alone – *en famille* that is – Jane and Anne, Walter and I – Why this makes up for *aiches* as poor John Kemble used to call them. After tea I broke off work and read my young folks the farce of *The Critic* and 'merry folks were we.'

5 FRIDAY I waked, or *aked* if you please, for five or six hours I think, then feverd a little. I am better though, God be thankd, and can now shufle about and help myself to what I want without ringing every quarter of an hour. It is a fine clear sunny day. I should like to go out but flannel and poultices cry Nay. So I drudge away with the assisting of Pellet[1] who has a real French head, believing all he desires should be true and affirming all which he wishes should be believed. Skenes (Mr. and Mrs. with Miss Jardine) arrived about six o'clock. Skene very rheumatic as well as I am.

6 SATURDAY Workd till dusk but not with much effect – my head seemd not clear somehow – W. Laidlaw at dinner – in the evening read Foote's farce of *The Commissary*, said to have been levelld at Sir Laurence Dundas. But Sir Laurence was a man of family. Walter and Jane dined at Mertoun.

7 SUNDAY Wrought till twelve then sallied and walkd with Skene for two miles – home and corrected proofs and to a large amount. Mr. Scrope and George Thompson dined.

8 MONDAY Slept well last night in consequence I think of my walk which I will god willing repeat to-day. I wrote some letters too long delayd and sent off my packets to J. B. Letter from C. Sharpe very pressing I should employ my interest at Windsor to oppose the alterations on the town of Edinburgh,[2] 'one word from you and all that.' I don't think I shall speak that word though. I hate the alterations that is certain. But then *ne accesseris in consilium nisi*

---

1. Pelet's *Mémoires sur la guerre de 1809*, 1824.
2. C. K. Sharpe was fighting to preserve Salisbury Crags, which were being used as a quarry, and the old houses near the Castle which were threatened by the would-be 'improvers' who were

vocatus[1] – what is the use of my volunteering an opinion? Again the value of many people's property may depend on this plan going forwards – have I a right from mere views of amenity to interfere with their serious interest? I something doubt it. Then I have always said that I never meddle in such work and ought I *sotto voce* now to begin it? By my faith I won't; there are enough to state the case besides me –

The young Duke of B.[2] came in to bid us God bye as he is going off to England. God bless him. He is a hawk of a good nest. Afterwards I walkd to the Welsh pool Skene declining to go for I

> – not over stout of limb
> Seem stronger of the two.[3]

Dined in family.

9 TUESDAY This morning received the long-expected news of the Duke of York's death. I am sorry both on public and private accounts. His R.H. was while he occupied the situation of next in the Royal succession a *Breakwater* behind the throne. I fear his brother of Clarence's opinions may be different and that he will hoist a standard under which will rendezvous men of desperate hopes and evil designs.[4] I am sorry too on my own account. The Duke of

---

rampant in this as in each succeeding age. Scott had supported him before almost against his better judgement: 'I fear the rabid disposition to demolish whatever looks ancient is a passion too strongly planted in the breast of all corporate bodies to be combated by any arguments of mine.' But on this occasion both the King and the Duke of Wellington declared against the improvers and Salisbury Crags at least were saved. See *The Correspondence of C. K. Sharpe.* ii. 355 ff.

1. 'Do not offer advice unless you are asked.'
2. The Duke of Buccleuch.
3. A free adaptation of Wordsworth's 'Simon Lee':

> For she, with scanty cause for pride,
> Is stouter of the two.

Scott may also have been thinking of the words 'so stout of limb' in 'Goody Blake and Harry Gill'.

4. A gossiping letter from Mrs. Hughes six months before had reported 'that the Duke of Clarence before he went abroad offered a bet of 100 guineas that he should be King in 6 months, adding "my brother the Duke of York is rotten, & my brother the King has the dropsy". To this abomination he adds that he shall restore the Slave Trade & make his daughters princesses in their own right.' 29 June 1826, Walpole.

York was uniformly kind to me and though I never taskd his friendship deeply yet I find a powerful friend is gone. His virtues were Honour, Goodsense, Integrity, and by exertion of these qualities he raised the discipline of the British army from a very low ebb to be the pride and dread of Europe. His errors were those of a sanguine and social temper – he could not resist the temptation of deep play which was fatally allied with a disposition to the bottle. This last is incident to his complaint which vinous influence soothes for the time while it insidiously increases it in the end.

Here blows a gale of Wind. I was to go to Galashiels to settle some foolish lawsuit and afterwards to have been with Mr. Karr of Kippilaw to treat about a march dike.[1] I shall content myself with the first duty for this day does not suit Bowden moor.

Went over to Galashiels like the Devil in a gale of wind, and found a writer[2] contesting with half a dozen unwashd artificers[3] the possession of a piece of ground the size and shape of a three cornerd pocket handkerchief – Tried to 'gar them gree'[4] and if I succeed I shall think I deserve something better than the touch of rheumatism which is like to be my only reward.

Scotts of Harden and John Pringle of Clifton dined and we got on very well.

10 WEDNESDAY Enter Rheumatism and takes me by the knee. So much for playing the peace-maker in a shower of rain. Nothing for it but patience, cataplasm of camomile, and labour in my own Room the whole day till dinner time – then company and reading in the evening.

11 THURSDAY Ditto repeated. I should have thought I would have made more of these solitary days than I find I can do. A morning or two or three hours before dinner have often done more efficient work than six or seven hours of these hours of languor, I cannot say of illness, can produce. A bow that is slackly strung will never send an arrow very far. Heavy snow. We are engaged to Mr. Scrope's but I think I shall not be able to go. I remaind at home accordingly and

1. A boundary wall.
2. A law agent.
3. Cowper's 'Table Talk', l. 52.
4. 'To make them agree'. The phrase was Lord Elchies's. Scott liked to tell the story of how when a case was likely to give him trouble he would appeal to the lawyers on both sides, 'Oh, Sirs, gar them gree – gar them gree – canna ye for God's sake gar them gree?' *Letters*, x. 195.

having nothing else to do workd hard and effectively. I believe my sluggish[ness] was partly owing to the gnawing rheumatic pain in my knee for after all I am of opinion pain is an evil let Stoics say what they will. Thank God it is an evil which is mending with me.

12 FRIDAY All this day occupied with cammomile poultices and pen and ink. It is now four o'clock and I have written yesterday and to-day ten of my pages, that is one tenth of one of these large volumes – moreover I have corrected three proof sheets. I wish it [may] not prove fool's haste. Yet I take as much pains to[o] as is in my nature.

13 SATURDAY The Fergussons with my neighbours Mr. Scrope and Mr. Baimbridge and young Hume eat a haunch of venison from Drummond Castle and seemd happy. We had music and a little dansing and enjoyd in others the buoyancy of spirit that we no longer possess ourselves. Yet I do not think the young people of this age so gav as we were. There is [a] turn for persiflage, a fear of ridicule among them, which stifles the honest emotions of gaiety and lightness of spirit, and people when they give [way] in the least to the expansion of their natural feel[ings]s, are always kept [in] order by the fear of becoming ludicrous. To restrain your feelings and check your enthusiasm in the cause even of pleasure is now a rule among people of fashion as much as it used to be among philosophers.

14 SUNDAY Well – my holidays are out – and I may count my gains and losses as honest Robinson Crusoe used to balance his accounts of good and evil.

I have not been able during three weeks to stir above once or twice from the house. But then I have executed a great deal of work which would be otherwise unfinishd.

Again I have sustaind long and sleepless nights and much pain. True – but no one is the worse of the thoughts which arise in the watches of the night, and for pain the complaint which brought on this rheumatic was not so painful perhaps but was infinitely more disagreeable and depressing.

Something there has been of dullness in our little reunions of society which did not use to cloud them. But I have seen all my own old and kind friends with my dear Children (Charles[1] alone excepted) and if we did not rejoice with perfect joy it was overshadowd from the same sense of regret.

1. He had stayed with his tutor over Christmas. Mrs. Hughes, 17 December 1826, Walpole. In fact Sophia was also absent from the family circle.

Again this new disorder seems a presage of the advance of age with its infirmities – But age is but the cypress avenue which terminates in the tomb where the weary are at rest. The distant sight of that haven ought to regulate our walk towards it, and on crutches or in a quadrille sinkpace there we must arrive.[1]

I have been putting my things to rights to go off tomorrow. Though I always wonder why it should be so I feel a dislike to order and to task work of all kinds a predominating foible in my disposition. I do not mean that it influences me in morals for even in youth I had a disgust at gross irregularities of every kind and such as I ran into were more from compliance with others and a sort of false shame than any pleasure I sought or found in dissipation. An intrigue of the heart carried me far, those of the senses had less effect on me. But what I mean is a detestation of precise order in petty matters – in reading or answering letters, in keeping my papers arranged and in order and so on. Weber and then Gordon used to keep my things in some order – now they are verging to utter confusion. And then I have let my cash run ahead since I came from the continent – I must slump the matter as I can.

15 MONDAY Off we came and despite of Rheumatism I got through the journey comfortably. Greeted on arrival by a number of small accompts whistling like grapeshot. They are of no great avail and incurd I see chiefly during the time of illness. But I believe it will take me some hard work till I pay them and how to get the time to work? It will be hard purchased if as I think not unlikely this bitch of a rheumatism should once more pin me to my chair. Coming through Galashiels we met the Laird of Torwoodlee, who on hearing how long I had been confined askd how I bore it, observing that he had once in [his] life, Torwoodlee must be between 60 and 70, [been] confined for five days to the house and was like to hang himself. I regret God's free air as much as any one but I could amuse myself were it in the Bastille.

16 TUESDAY Went to court and returnd through a curious atmosphere, half mist, half rain, famous for rheumatic joints. Yet I felt no increase of my plaguy malady but on the contrary am rather better. I had need, otherwise a pair of crutches for life were my prettiest help.

Walter dined with us to-day, Jane remaining with her mother. The good affectionate creatures leave us tomorrow;[2] god send them a

---

1. An allusion to *Much Ado about Nothing*, ii. 1.
2. 'Jane', wrote Anne to Sophia, 'seemed very glad to go away.' 26 January 1827, Abbots.

quiet passage through the Irish channel. They go to Gortz where Walter's troop is lying, a long journey for winter days.

17 WEDNESDAY Another proper day of mist sleet and rain through which I navigated homeward. I imagine the distance to be a mile and a half; it is a good thing to secure as much exercize.

I observed in the papers my old friend Gifford's funeral. He was a man of rare attainments and many excellent qualities. The translation of Juvenal is one of the best versions ever made of a classical author and his Satire of the *Baviad and Maeviad* squabashd at one blow a set of coxcombs who might have humbugd the world long enough. As a commentator he was capital could he but have suppressd his rancour against those who had preceded him in the task but a misconstruction or misinterpretation, nay the misplacing of a comma, was in Gifford's eyes a crime worthy of the most severe animadversions. The same fault of extreme severity went through his critical labours and in general he flagellated with so little pity that people lost their sense for the criminal's guilt in dislike of the savage pleasure which the executioner seemd to take in inflicting the punishment.

This lack of temper probably arose from indifferent health for he was very valetudinary and realized two verses where he says fortune assignd him

> —— One eye not over good
> Two sides that to their cost have stood
> A ten years' hectic cough
> Aches stitches all the various ills
> That swell the Devilish doctor's bills
> And sweep poor mortals off.

But he might also justly claim as her gift the moral qualities expressd in the next fine stanza

> ——— A soul
> That spurns the crowd's malign controul
> A firm contempt of wrong
> Spirits above afliction's power
> And skill to soothe the lingering hour
> With no inglorious song.[1]

18 THURSDAY To go on with my subject – Gifford was a little man dumpled up together and so illmade as to seem almost deformd but

1. 'Ode to the Rev. John Ireland', *The Maeviad*, by William Gifford.

with a singular expression of talent in his countenance. Though so little of an Athlete he nevertheless beat off the celebrated Dr. Woolcott when that celebrated person, the most unsparing calumniator of his time, chose to be offended with Gifford for satirizing him in his turn. Peter Pindar made a most vehement attack but Gifford had the best of the affray and remaind I think triumphant possessor of the field of action and of the assailant's cane. – G. had one singular custom. He used always to have a duenna of a housekeeper to sit in his study with him while he wrote. This female companion died when I was in London and his distress was extreme. I afterwards heard he got her place supplied. I believe there was no scandal in all this.

Here is another vile day of darkness and rain with a heavy yellow mist that might become Charing Cross, one of the benefits of our extended city; for that in our atmosphere [was] unknown till the extent of the buildings below Queens Street.[1] Macculloch of Ardwall calld.

Wrought chiefly on a critique of Mrs. Charlotte Smith's novels[2] and proofs.

19 FRIDAY Uncle Adam,[3] *Vide Inheritance,* who retired last year from an official situation at the age of 84, although subject to fits of giddiness and although carefully watchd by his accomplishd daughter is still in the habit of walking by himself if he can by possibility make an escape. The other day in one of these excursions he fell against a lamp post, cut himself much, bled a good deal and was carried home by two gentlemen. What said old Rugged and Tough? – Why that his fall against the post was the luckiest thing could have befallen him for that the bleeding was exactly the remedy for his disorder.

Lo! stout hearts of men![4]

Calld on said Uncle, also on David Hume, Lord Chief commissioner, Will Clerk, Mrs. Jobson and others. My knee made no allowance for my politeness but has begun to swell again and to burn like a scorpion's bite.

---

1. Between 1803 and 1823 the original New Town had been extended northwards as far as Royal Circus. See Youngson, p. 208.
2. Printed in *Misc. Prose Works,* vol. iv.
3. James Ferrier, formerly a Clerk of Session, the father of Susan Ferrier who wrote *Inheritance* and other novels.
4. Unidentified.

20 SATURDAY Scarce slept all night; scarce able to stand or move this morning – almost an absolute fixture.

> A sleepless knight
> A weary knight
> God be the Guide.[1]

This is at the Court a blank day being that of the poor Duke of York's funeral – I can sit at home luckily and fagg hard.

And so I have pretty well six leaves written and four or five proof sheets corrected. Cadell came to Breakfast, and proposes a[n] eighth volume for *Napoleon*. I told him he might write to Longman for their opinion. Seven is an awkward number and will extremely cramp the work. Eight too would go into six octavos should it ever be calld for in that shape. But it shall be as they list to serve it.[2]

21 SUNDAY A long day of some pain relieved by labour. Dr. Ross came in and recommended some stuff which did little good. I would like ill to lose the use of my precious limbs. Meanwhile patience, Cousin, and shufle the cards.[3]

Missie[4] dined with us to-day. An honest Scotch lass, ladylike and frank. I finishd about six leaves doing indeed little else.

22 MONDAY Work varied with camomile poultices – we get on though. A visit from Basil Hall with Mr. Audebon[5] the ornithologist who has followd that pursuit by many a long wandering in the American forests. He is an american by naturalization, a Frenchman by birth, but less of a Frenchman than I have ever seen – no dash or glimmer or shine about him but great simplicity of manners and behaviour – slight in person and plainly dressd, wears long hair which time has not yet tinged – his countenance acute, handsome and interesting, but still simplicity is the predominant character. I wish I had gone to see his drawings. But I had heard so much about that I resolved not to see them – a crazy way of mine, your honour! – five more leaves finishd.

1. Possibly, as Douglas suggests, a reminiscence of *A Midsummer Night's Dream*, iii. 2:
   'O weary night,
   O long and tedious night.'
2. It finally appeared in nine volumes.
3. A favourite tag of Scott's from *Don Quixote*, pt. ii, ch. 23.
4. Miss Macdonald Buchanan.
5. John James Audubon. During his visit to Edinburgh he read a paper to the Royal Society on 9 February; he was later elected a Foreign Member.

23 TUESDAY I have got a piece of armour, a knee-cape of Shamoy leather, which I think does my unlucky rheumatism some good. I begin too to sleep a nights which is a great comfort. Spent this day completely in labour; only betwixt dinner and tea while husbanding a tumbler of whisky and water I read the new novel *Elizabeth de Bruce*[1] – part of it that is –

24 WEDNESDAY Visit from Mr. Audubon who brings some of his birds. The drawings are of the first order, the attitudes of the birds of the most animated character and the situations appropriate – one of a snake attacking a bird's nest while the birds (the parents) peck at the reptile's eyes – They usually in the long run destroy him says the naturalist – The feathers of these gay little sylphs, most of them from the Southern states, are most brilliant, and are represented with what were it [not] connected with so much spirit in the attitude I would call a laborious degree of execution. This extreme correctness is of the utmost Consequence to the naturalist [but] as I think (having no knowlege of virtue) rather gives a stiffness to the drawings. This sojourner in the desert had been in the woods for months together. He preferd associating with the Indians to the company of the Back Settlers, very justly I daresay for a cilverlized[2] man of the lower order, that is the dregs of civilization, when thrust back on the savage state becomes worse than a saffage. They are Wordsworth's adventurer

> Deliberate and undeceived
> The wild men's vices who received
> And gave them back his own.[3]

The Indians he says are dying fast: they seem to pine and die whenever the white population approaches them. The Shawanese, who amounted Mr. Audubon says to some thousands within his memory, are almost extinct and so are various other tribes. Mr. Audubon could never hear any tradition about the mammoth though he made anxious enquiries. He gives no countenance to the idea that the red Indians were ever a more civilized people than at this day or that a more civilized people had preceded them in North America. He looks on the bricks etc. occasionally found and appeald to in support of this opinion to the earlier settlers, or where kettles and other utensils may have been found to the early trade between the Indians and the Spaniard.

1. By Christian Isobel Johnstone, 1827.
2. A slip for 'civilized'.
3. 'Ruth', ll. 48–50.

John Russell and Leonard Horner came to consult me about the propriety and possibility of retaining the Northern pronunciation of the latin in the new Edinburgh academy. I will think of it untill tomorrow, being no great judge. We had our solitary dinner; indeed it is only remarkable nowadays when we have a guest.[1]

25 THURSDAY Thought during the watches of the night and a part of the morning about the question of Latin pronunciation and came to the following conclusions – That the mode of pronunciation approved by Buchanan and by Milton and practiced by all nations excepting the English, assimilated in sound to[o] to the Spanish, Italian and other languages derived from the latin, is certainly the best and is likewise useful as facilitating the acquisition of sounds which the Englishman attempts in vain – Accordingly I wish the cocknified pedant who first disturbed it by reading *Emo* for *Amo* and *quy* for *qui* had choked in the attempt. But the question is whether youths who have been [taught] in a manner different from that used all over England will be heard if he presumes to use his latin at the bar or the senate and if he is to be unintelligible or ludicrous the question [is] whether his education is not imperfect under one important view. I am very unwilling to sacrifice our *Sumpsimus* to their old *Mumpsimus* – still more to humble ourselves before the Saxons while we can keep an inch of the Scottish flag flying – But this is a question which must be decided not on partialities or prejudices and as Mother Creswell[2] said to her customer – 'Nay then –'[3]

I got early from the court to-day and settled myself to work hard.

26 FRIDAY My rheumatism is almost gone. I can walk without Major Weir, which is the name Anne gives my cane because it is so often out of the way that it is suspected like the staff of that famous wizard to be capable of locomotion. Went to court and tarried till three o'clock after which transacted business with Mr. Gibson and Dr. Inglis as one of Miss Hume's trustees. Then was introduced to

1. Anne writes on this theme to Sophia on the 26th: 'He is working very hard, ten minutes at dinner is all I see of him. . . . I wish I was at Abbotsford where I might have somebody staying if it was only for the pleasure of *talking* for I am sure I will lose the use of my tongue. . . . I shall be glad when Buonaparte is done what a horrid long dose of History we will have to *read*.' Abbots.

2. Madam Cresswell, a noted courtesan and procuress who flourished in the late seventeenth century. See *Peveril of the Peak*, ch. 44.

3. Scott finally supported 'the plan of teaching the boys of the academy *both* the Scotch & English mode of pronouncing Latin'. Skene, 14 July 1827, Walpole.

young Mr. Rennie,[1] or he to me, by James Hall – a genteel looking young man and speaks well. He was calld into public notice by having many years before made a draught of a plan of his father[2] for London Bridge. It was sought for when the building was really about to take place and the assistance which young Mr. Rennie gave to render it useful raised his character so high that his brother[3] and he are now in first rate practice as civil engineers.

27 SATURDAY Read *Elizth. de Bruce* – it is very clever but does not show much originality: the characters though very entertaining are in the manner of other authors and the finishd and filldup portraits of which the sketches are to be found elsewhere. One is too apt to feel on such occasions the pettied resentment that you might entertain against one who had poachd on your manor. But the case is quite different, and a claim set up on having been the first who betook himself to the illustration of some particular class of characters or department of life is no more a right of monopoly than that asserted by the old buccaneers by setting up a wooden cross and killing an Indian or two on some new discoverd Island. If they can make anything of their first discovery the better luck theirs; if not, let others come, penetrate further into the country, write descriptions, make drawings or settlements at their pleasure.

We were kept in Parlt. House till three. Calld to return thanks to Mr. Menzies of Pitfoddells who lent some pamphlets about the unhappy Duke d'Enghien. Read in the evening Boutourlin[4] and Segur[5] to prepare for my Russian campaign.

28 SUNDAY Continued my reading with the commentary of D. of W.[6] If his broad shoulders cannot carry me threw the Devil must be in the dice. Longman and Coy agree to the VIIIth. Vol. It will make the value of the book more than £12,000. Wrought indifferent hard.

1. John Rennie (1794–1874), who was knighted in 1831 after completing London Bridge.
2. John Rennie (1761–1821), the designer of Waterloo Bridge, Southwark Bridge, and London Bridge.
3. George Rennie (1791–1866).
4. Boutourlin's *Histoire militaire de la campagne de Russie en 1812*, 1824.
5. Ségur's *Histoire de Napoléon et de la Grande Armée pendant 1812*, 1824.
6. The 'bundle of remarks on B's Russian Campaign, written in his carriage during his late mission to St. Petersburg' which the Duke had lent him on 16 November 1826.

29 MONDAY Mr. Gibson breakfasted with Dr. Marsh[m]an[1] the head of the Missionaries at Serampore, a great Oriental scholar. He is a thin dark-featured middle-sized man about fifty or upwards, his eye acute, his hair just beginning to have a touch of the grey. He spoke well and sensibly and seemd liberal in his ideas. He was clearly of opinion that general information must go hand in hand or even ought to precede religious instruction. Thinks the influence of European manners is gradually making changes in India. The Natives so far as their religion will allow are become fond of Europeans and invite them to their great festivals. He has a conceit that the Afghans are the remains of the ten tribes. I cannot find he has a better reason than their own tradition, which calls them Ben-Israel and says they are not Ben-judah. They have jewish rites and ceremonies but so have all Mahomedans – neither could I understand that their language has anything peculiar. The worship of Bhoodah he conceives to have [been] an original or rather the original of Hindhu religion untill the Bramins introduced the doctrines respecting Caste and other pecu liarities. But it would require strong proof to show that the super- stition of Caste could be introduced into a country which had been long peopled and where society had long existed without such restriction. It is more liker to be adopted in the early history of a tribe when there are but few individuals the descent of whom is accurately preservd. How could the castes be distinguishd or *told off* in a populous nation? Dr. Marshan was an old friend of poor John Leyden.[2]

30 TUESDAY Blank day in Court being the Martyrdom.[3] Wrought hard at Bon: all day though I had settled otherwise. I ought to have been at an article for John Lockhart[4] and one for poor Gillies[5] – but there is something irresistible in contradiction even when it consists in doing a thing equally labourious but not the thing you are especially calld upon to do. It is a kind of cheating the devil which a selfwilld monster like me is particularly addicted to. Not to make myself worse than I am though, I was full of information about the Russian campaign which might evaporate unless used like lime as

---

1. Dr. Joshua Marshman (1768–1837), the founder of Serampur College and translator of the Bible into Chinese.
2. See the Entry for 29 June 1826 and note.
3. Of Charles I.
4. His review of Mackenzie's *Life and Works of Home* which appeared in the June *Quarterly*.
5. For the projected *Foreign Quarterly Review*. See the Entry for 9 October 1827.

soon after it was wrought up as was possible. About three Pitfoddels calld – A bauld crack[1] that auld papist body and well informd. We got on religion. He is very angry with the Irish demagogues and a sound well thinking man. – I have made an ugly blot on the page somehow. Heard of Walter and Jane; all well God be praised.

By a letter from Gibson I see the gross proceeds of *Bonapart* at

eight volumes are –	£12,600
Discount five months	210
Net pounds	£12,390

I question if more was ever made by a single work or by a single author's labours in the same time. But whether it is deserved or not is the question.

31 WEDNESDAY Young Murray, son of Mr. M. in Albemarle street, breakfast[ed] with me. English boys have this advantage that they are well bred and can converse when ours are regular-built cubs – I am not sure if it is an advantage in the long run. It is a temptation to premature display.

Wet to the skin coming from the court. Calld on Skene to give him for the Antiquarian society[2] a heart, human apparently, stuck full of pins. It was found lying opposite to the threshold of an old tenement in   [3] a little below the surface – it is in perfect preservation. Dined at the Bannatyne club where I am chairman.[4] We admitted a batch of new members, chiefly noblemen and men connected with the public offices and records in London such as Palgrave, Petrie, etc. We drank to our old Scottish heroes, poets, historians, and printers, and were funny enough, though like Shylock I had no will to go abroad.[5] I was supported by Lord Minto and Lord Eldin.[6]

---

1. 'An entertaining talker, a gossip'. *S.N.D.*
2. Skene was Curator of the Society's Museum.
3. Dalkeith. See *Archaeological Scotica*, vol. iii.
4. The dinner should have taken place earlier in the month, but Scott's rheumatism postponed it until the same day as the election 'which will be convenient probably for many members'. *Letters*, x. 153. They had decided to raise the Club's membership from fifty to eighty. Bannatyne Club Minutes.
5. *Merchant of Venice*, ii. 5.
6. John Clerk (1757–1832), elder brother of Scott's friend Will Clerk, and son of the author of *Naval Tactics*. He was a judge. Helen Graham's mother thought him 'like a satyr, or a picture of Pan', and Miss Graham agreed: 'He is most uncouth, both in manners and appearance. He is sometimes, on account of his

FEBRUARY

1 THURSDAY I feel a return of the cursed rheumatism – how could it miss with my wettin[g]? Also feverish and a slight head ache. So much for claret and Champagne. I begin to be quite unfit for a good fellow – Like Mother Cole in the *Minor*[1] a thimblefull upsets me, I mean annoys my stomach for my brains do not suffer. Well – I have had my time of these merry doings.

> The haunch of the deer and the wines red dye
> Never bard loved them better than I.[2]

But it was for the sake of sociality never either for the flask or the venison. That must end – is ended – the evening sky of life does not reflect those brilliant flashes of light that shot across its morning and noon. Yet I thank God it is neither gloomy nor disconsolately lowering a sober twilight – that is all –

I am in great hopes that the Bannatyne club by the assistance of Thompson's wisdom industry and accuracy will be something far superior to the Dilletante model on which it started.[3] *The Historie of K. James VI, Melville's Memoirs,*[4] and other works executed or in hand, are decided boons to Scottish history and literature.

2 FRIDAY In confirmation of that which is above stated I see in Thorpe's sale Catalogue a set of the Bannatyne books lacking five priced at £25. Had a dry walk from the court by way of dainty and made it a long one. Anne went at night to Lady Minto's.

Hear of Miss White's death – poor Lydia. She had a party at dinner on the friday before and had written with her own hand invitations of another party. Twenty years ago she used to teaze me

---

name, mistaken for the Chancellor, but he says, 'It's all my "i"' – "i" alluding to the difference of spelling: "Eldin" is his name, "Eldon", the Chancellor's. He may say it's all in his "i" more ways than one, for one of his eyes look as if it was in pursuit of the other: that is a most hideous squint of a different species from any I ever saw before.' *Diaries of Helen Graham*, pp. 43–4.
1. A farce by Foote.
2. *Harold the Dauntless*, Canto II. viii. 11–12.
3. The model was the Roxburghe Club, founded in London in 1812.
4. *The Historie and Life of King James the Sext* appeared in 1825, and Melville's *Memoirs* in June 1827, both edited by Thomas Thomson.

with her youthful affectations, her dressing like the Queen of chimney Sweeps on may day morning and sometimes with rather a free turn in conversation when she let her wit run wild. But she was a woman of much wit and had a feeling and kind heart. She made her point good, a *Bas bleu* in London to a point not easily attaind, and contrived to have every evening a very good literary medlie and little dinners which were very entertaining. She had also the newest lions upon town. In a word she was not and would not be forgotten, even when the disease obliged [her] as it did for years to confine herself to her couch, and the world, much abused for hard-heartedness, was kind in her case, so she lived in the society she liked. No great expenditure was necessary for this. She had an easy fortune but not more. Poor Lydia – I saw the Duke of York and her in London when Death it seems was brandishing his dart over them.[1]

The view o't gave them little fright.[2]

Did not get quite a day's work finishd to-day thanks to my walk.

3 SATURDAY There is nought but care on every hand. James Hogg writes that he is to lose his farm on which he laid out or ra[ther] threw away the profit of all his publications.[3]

Then Terry has been pressd by Gibson for my debt[4] to him. That I may get managed.

I sometimes doubt if I am in what the good people call the right way. Not to sing my own praises, I have been willing always to do my friends what good was in my power and have not shund personal responsibility. But then that was in money matters to which I am naturally indifferent unless when the consequences press on me. But then I am a bad comforter in case of inevitable calamity and feeling proudly able to endure in my own case I cannot sympathise with those whose nerves are of a feebler texture.

Dined at Jeffrey's with Lord and Lady Minto, Jo: Murray and his lady, a Mr. Featherstone, an Americo-Yorkshire[man], and some

1. See the Entries for 13, 17, and 19 November 1826.
2. Burns's 'The Twa Dogs', l. 106.
3. The farm was Mount Benger, rented from the Duke of Buccleuch, and Hogg had been given until Whitsunday to pay his arrears. Hogg, 28 January 1827, Walpole. Scott interceded for him on more than one occasion. See the Index under Hogg.
4. Scott means 'my loan'. He had lent Terry £500 towards the purchase of the Adelphi Theatre.

others. Mrs. Murray is a very amiable person and seems highly accomplishd – plays most brilliantly.[1]

4 SUNDAY R.R. These two letters, you must understand, do not signify as in bibliomanic phrase a double degree of rarity, but chirurgically a double degree of rheumatism. The wine gets to weak places Ross says. I have a letter from no less a person than that pink of book-sellers, Sir Richard Philips, who it seems has been ruin[d] and as he sees me floating down the same dark tide sings out his *nos poma natamus*.[2] 'He be d—d' as old Wortley said to the Dancing Master.

5 MONDAY R. one R. will do to-day. If this cursed rheumatism gives way to February weather I will allow she has some right to be calld a spring month to which otherwise her pretensions are slender. I workd this morning till two o'clock and visited Mr. Grant's[3] pictures, who has them upon sale. They seem to my inexperienced eye genuine or at least good paintings. But I fear picture buying like horse jockeyship is a profession a gentleman cannot make much of without laying aside some of his attributes. The pictures are too high priced I should think for this market. There is a very knowing catalogue by Frank Grant himself. Next went to see a show of wild beasts. It was a fine one. I think they keep the[m] much cleaner than formerly when the strong smell generally gave me a headache for the day. The creatures are also much tamer which I impute to more knowlege of their habits and kind treatment. A lion and tigress went through their exercise like poodles, jumping, standing, and lying down at the word of command. This is rather degrading. I would have the Lord Chancellor of Beasts goodhumourd, not jocose. I treated the elephant, who was a noble fellow, to a shilling's worth of cakes. I wish I could have

1. Murray had married Miss Rigby of Lancashire only a month before. Scott's description of her to Lockhart has more of salt in it than the *Journal* entry: 'John Murray has brought down a lady a very pleasant woman well bred said to be learnd besides which she prudently keeps in the background. Item she hath £40,000. But then she has a *taste* in religion and is an Unitarian to the horror of our Saints and moreover she is none of the youngest besides.' *Letters*, x. 160.

2. A ball of new-dropp'd horse's dung,
      Mingling with apples in the throng,
      Said to the pippin plump and prim,
      'See, brother, how we apples swim'.
          Swift's 'Brother Protestants and Fellow Christians', ll. 11–14.

3. For Francis Grant, see the Entries for 24 and 26 March 1831 and note to the latter.

enlarged the space in which so much bulk and wisdom is confined. He kept swinging his head from side to side, looking as if he marvelld why all the fools that gaped at him were at liberty and he coopd up in the cage.

Dined at the Royal Society club – above 30 present.[1] Went to the Society in the evening and heard an essay by Peter Tytler on the first encourager of Greek learning in England.

6 TUESDAY Was at Court till two, afterwards wrote a good deal which has become a habit with me. Dined at Sir John Hay's where met the Advocate[2] and a pleasant part[y]. There had been a justiciary trial yesterday in which something curious had occurd. A woman of rather the better class, a farmer's wife, had been tried on the 5th. for poisoning her maid servant. There seems to have been little doubt of her guilt but the motive was peculiar. The unfortunate girl had an intrigue with her son, which this Mrs. Smith (I think that is the name)[3] was desirous to conceal from some ill advised puritanic notions and also for fear of her husband. She could find no better way of hiding the shame than giving the girl (with her own knowlege and consent I believe) potions to cause abortion, which she afterwards changed for arsenick as the more effectual silencing medicine. In the course of the trial one of the jury fell down in an epilectic fit and on his recovery was far too much disorderd to permit the trial to proceed. With only fourteen jurymen[4] it was impossible to go on. But the Advocate says she shall be tried anew since she had not tholed un assize. *Sic Paulus ait et recte quidem.*[5] But having been half tried I think she should have some benefit of it, as far as saving her life if convicted on the second indictment. The Advocate declares however she shall be hanged, as certainly she deserves. But it looks something like hanging up a man who has been recoverd by the surgeons, which has always been accounted harsh justice.

7 WEDNESDAY Wrote six leaves to-day[6] and am tired – that's all –

---

1. Audubon, Basil Hall's guest, sat opposite Scott and 'had a perfect view of the great man, and studied Nature from Nature's noblest work'. Audubon's *Journal*, under this date.
2. Sir William Rae, Lord Advocate.
3. She was Mary Elder or Smyth.
4. A Scottish jury consisted of fifteen jurors, not twelve as in England.
5. 'So said Paul – and rightly.'
6. As this was a Teind Court Wednesday Scott had the whole day for writing.

8 THURSDAY I lost much time to-day. I got from the Court about half past twelve, therefore might have reckond on four hours or three at least before dinner. But I had to call on Dr. Short[1] at two, which made me lounge till that hour came. Then I missd him and, too tired to return, went to see the exhibition where Skene was hanging up the pictures and would not let me in.[2] Then to the Oil Gas Coy. who propose to send up council to support their new bill.[3] As I thought the choice unadvisedly made I fairly opposed the mission, which I suppose will give much offence. But I have no notion of being shamefaced in doing my duty and I do not think I should permit forward persons to press into situations for which their vanity alone renders them competent.[4] Had many proof sheets to correct in the evening.

9 FRIDAY We had a long day of it at Court but I whipd you off half a dozen of letters, for as my cases stood last on the roll I could do what I liked in the interim. This carried me on till two o'clock. Calld on Baron Hume and found him as usual in high spirits notwithstanding his late illness. Then crept home – my Rheumatism much better though – Corrected lives of Lord Somerville and the King[5] for the prose works, which took a long time, but I had the whole evening to myself as Anne dined with the Swintons and went to a ball at the Justice Clerk's.[6] n.b. It is the first and only ball which has been given this season – a sign the times are pinching.

1. The army surgeon who attended Napoleon on St. Helena.
2. The Institution for the Encouragement of the Fine Arts, of which Skene was Secretary, began in 1819 with an exhibition of Old Masters lent by members, but from 1821 the annual exhibition was of contemporary work. See the Entry for 13 February 1826 and note.
3. A Bill to repeal the original Act which prevented their making gas from coal. See the note on the Oil Gas Coy. on pp. 805–6.
4. They proposed to send James Simpson, an advocate who dabbled in phrenology. 'I have tried to put a spoke in the wheel,' Scott writes to Lockhart, 'for to send to a business requiring some tact a sucking-turkey-like turnipologist would be melancholy indeed.' *Letters*, x. 159. Scott's efforts were successful; Mr. Hugh Bruce, advocate, went instead. To Henry Scott, 24 February, 1827, Disc. i. 123.
5. King George III.
6. It is to be hoped she enjoyed it, for a week later, 'Anne has a cold to which the one and only ball given in Edinburgh this season namely that of the Justice Clerk has contributed a reasonable share.' *Letters*, x. 160.

10 SATURDAY I got a present of Lord Frederick[1] Leveson Gower's printed but unpublishd 'Tale of the Mill'[2] – it is a fine tale of terror in itself and very happily brought out. He has certainly a true taste for poetry. I do not know why, but from my childhood I have seen something fearful or melancholy at least about a Mill. Whether I had been frightend at the machinery when very young, of which I think I have some shadowy recollection – whether I had heard the story of the Miller of Thirlestane and similar molendinar tragedies, I cannot tell. But not even recollection of the Lass of Peatie's mill, or the Miller of Mansfield or 'he who dwelt on the river Dee' have ever got over my inclination to connect gloom with a Mill, especially when sun is setting. So I enterd into the spirit of the terror with which Lord Frederick has invested his haunted spot. I dine with the Solicitor[3] to-day so *quoad* labour 'tis a blank. But then tomorrow is a new day.

> Tomorrow to fresh meads and pastures new.[4]

11 SUNDAY Wrought a good deal in the morning and landed Boney at Smolensk.[5] But I have him to bring off again and moreover I must collate the authorities on the movements of the secondary armies, Witgenstein's and the admiral with the break-tooth name.[6] Dined with Lord Minto where I met Thomson, Cranstoun and other gay folks. These dinner parties narrow my working hours yet they must sometimes be or one would fall out of the line of society and go to Leeward entirely, which is not right to venture. This is the High time for parties in Edinburgh. No wonder one cannot keep clear.

12 MONDAY I was obliged to read instead of writing, and the infernal Russian names which everybody spells *ad libitum* makes it difficult to trace the operations on a better map than mine. I calld to-day on Dr. Short, principal Surgeon at Saint Helena and who presided at the opening of Bonaparte's body. He mentions as certain the falsehood of a number of the assertions concerning his usage concerning the unhealthy state of the island and so forth. I have jotted down his evidence elsewhere. I could not write when I came home. Nervous a little, I think, and not yet up to the motions of Tchitchagoff as I must be before I can write. Will:[7] and Sir A. Fergusson dine here to-day –

1. Scott should have written 'Francis'.
2. It came from the author. 5 February 1827, Walpole. The poem was later published in *The Pilgrimage and other Poems*, 1856.
3. John Hope, the Solicitor-General.
4. Milton's *Lycidas*, l. 193.
5. See *Life of Napoleon*, vol. vii, ch. 9.
6. Tchitchagoff.
7. Will Clerk.

the first time any one has had that honour for long enough unless at Abbotsford. The good Lord chief Commissioner invited himself and I askd his son, Admiral Adam. Col. Fergusson is of the party.

13 THURSDAY The dining parties come thick and interfere with work extremely. I am however beforehand very far. Yet as James B. says, the tortoise comes up with the hare so puss[1] must make a new start. But not this week. Went to see the exhi[bi]tion. Certainly a good one for Scotland and less trash than I have seen at Somerset House, begging pardon of the Pock puddings. There is a beautiful thing by Landseer. A highlander and two staghounds engaged with a deer, very spirited indeed.[2] I forgot my rheumatism and could have wishd myself of the party – There were many fine folks and there was a collation, chocolate and so forth. We dine at Sir H. Jardine's with Lord Ch. Com., Lord Chief Baron etc.

14 WEDNESDAY 'Death's gi'en the art an unco devel '[3] Sir George Beaumont's dead. By far the most sensible and pleasing man I ever knew, kind too in his nature and generous – gentle in society and of those mild manners which tend to soften the causticity of the general London [tone] of persiflage and personal satire. As an amateur he was a painter of the very [highest rank]. Though I know nothing of the matter yet I should hold him a perfect critic on painting for he always made his criticisms intelligible and used no slang. I am very sorry, as much as is in my nature to be for one whom I could see but seldom. He was the great friend of Wordsworth and understood his poetry, which is a rare thing for it is more easy to see his peculiarities than to feel his great merit or follow his abstract ideas. I dined to-day at Lord Ch. Commissioner's. Lord Minto and Lord Ch. Baron, also Harden. Little done to-day.

15 THURSDAY Rheumatism returns with the snow. I had thoughts of going to Abbotsford on Saturday but if this lasts it will not do, and sooth to speak it ought not to do, though it would do me much pleasure if it would do.

I have a letter from Baron von Goethe[4] which I must have read to

1. To Scott, as to Burns, 'puss' was a hare, not a cat.
2. Landseer's *Taking a Buck*.
3. Burns's 'Tam Samson's Elegy', l. 17.
4. The letter was brought from Germany by a Mr. Henderson (possibly Alexander Henderson, a book-collector). Scott's reply is printed in *Letters*, x. 249. A year later Goethe wrote to Carlyle enclosing two medals for Scott.

me, for though I know German I have forgot their written hand. I make it a rule seldom to read and never to answer foreign letters from literary folks. It leads to nothing but the battledore and shuttlecock intercour[se] of compliments as light as cork and feathers. But Goethe is different and a wonderful fellow, the Ariosto at once, and almost the Voltaire of Germany. Who could have told me 30 years ago I should correspond and on something like an equal footing with the Author of *The Robbers* –?[1] Aye and who could have told me fifty things else that have befallen me? Dined at Lord   [2], John Forbes whileoms. Many English people and two foreigners from Mauritius to take the gown at our bar which I find gives them the right of practising in their courts.

16 FRIDAY R. Still snow: and alas no time for work, so hard am I faggd by the court and the good company of Edinburgh. I almost wish my rheumatics were bad enough to give me an apology for staying a week at home. But we have Sunday and Monday clear; if not better I will cribb off Tuesday, and Wednesday is Teind day. We dined to-day with Mr. Borthwick, younger of Crookstoun.

17 SATURDAY James Fergusson[3] ill of the Rheumatism in head and neck – and Hector B. Macdonald in neck and shoulders. I wonder, as Commodore Trunnion says,[4] what the blackguard hell's-baby has to say to the Clerks of Session. Went to the Second division to assist Hector. N.B. Don't like it half so well as my own for the speeches[5] are much longer and the speeches much longer. Home at dinner and wrought in the evening.

18 SUNDAY Very cold weather. I am rather glad I am not in the country. What says Dean Swift?

> When Frost and Snow come both together
> Then Sit by the fire and save shoe-leather.[6]

Wrought all the morning and finishd five pages. Missie dined with us.

1. Lockhart corrects to *Goetz* – the tragedy translated by Scott from the German in 1799.
2. Medwyn's. John Hay Forbes took the title of Lord Medwyn on his elevation to the Bench in 1825.
3. Two of Scott's fellow Clerks of Session.
4. In Smollett's *Peregrine Pickle*, ch. 13.
5. A slip for 'cases'.
6. Swift's *Journal to Stella*, Letter xiv.

19 MONDAY As well I gave up Abbotsford, for Hamilton is laid up with the gout.[1] The snow too continues with a hard frost. I have seen the day I would have liked it all the better. I read and wrote at the bitter account of the French retreat from Moscow in 1812 till the little room and snug fire seemd snug by comparaison. I felt cold in its rigour in my childhood and boyhood but not since. In youth and advanced life we get less sensible to it but I remember thinking it worse than hunger. Uninterrupted to-day and did eight leaves.[2]

20 TUESDAY At court, and waited to see the poisoning woman.[3] She is clearly guilty but as one or two witnesses said the poor wench hinted an intention to poison herself the jury gave that bastard verdict *Not proven*. I hate that Caledonian *Medium quid*.[4] One who is not *proved guilty* is innocent in the eye of law. It was a face to do or die, or perhaps to do to die.[5] Thin features which had been handsome, a flashing eye, an acute and aquiline nose, lips much markd, as arguing decision and I think bad temper – they were thin and habitually compressd, rather turnd down at the corners, as one of a rather Melancholy disposition. There was an awful crowd but sitting wtin the bar I had the pleasure of seeing much at my ease the Constables knocking the other folks about, which was of course very entertaining.

Lord Liverpool is ill of an apoplexy. I am sorry for it. He will be missd. Who will be got for premier? Not B.—[6] certainly he wants weight. If Peele would consent to be made a peer He would do better

1. Not for the first time. 'His gout attacks are apt to be so very convenient they come on during the Session & he recovers wonderfully during the recess.' Walter, 16 January 1826, Walpole.

2. This is the most yet achieved in a single day. Seventy leaves made 'a volume of the usual novel size'. Entry for 23 January 1826.

3. See the Entry for 6 February.

4. 'Compromise'.

5. 'Scott's description of the woman is very correct. She was like a vindictive masculine witch. I remember him sitting within the bar, looking at her. Lockhart should have been told that as we were moving out, Sir Walter's remark upon the acquittal was: "Well, sirs! all I can say is, that if that woman was my wife, I should take good care to be my own cook".' Henry Cockburn's *Circuit Journeys*, Entry for 12 April 1838.

6. 'B.' is Bathurst. The next Prime Minister, for the five months before his early death, was Scott's friend Canning. For the Cabinet changes involved see Appendix D, p. 826.

but I doubt his ambition will prefer the House of Commons.
Wrought a good deal.

21 WEDNESDAY Being the vacant Wednesday I wrought all the
morning. Had an answer from D. of W.[1] unsuccessful in getting
young Skene put upon the Engineer list; he is too old. Went out at
two with Anne and visited the exhibition. Also calld on the
Mansfield family and on Sidney Smith. Jeffrey unwell from pleading so long and late for the poisoning woman. He has saved her
throat and taken a quinsey in his own. Ad. Fergusson has had a fall
with his horse.

22 THURSDAY Was at court till two – then lounged till Will. Murray
came to speak about a dinner for the theatrical fund[2] in order to make
some arrangements. There are 300 tickets given out. I fear it will be
<in> uncomfortable and whatever the stoics may say a bad dinner
throws cold water on the charity. I have agreed to preside, a situation
in which I have been rather felicitous not by much superiority of wit
or wisdom far less of eloquence. But by two or three simple rules
which I put down here for the benefit of posterity.

1st. Always hurry the bottle round for five or six rounds without
pressing yourself or permitting others to propose. A slight fillip of
wine inclines people to be pleased and removes the nervousness
which prevents men from speaking – disposes them in short to be
amusing and to be amused.

2d. Push on, keep moving, as punch says – Do not think of say[ing]
fine things – nobody cares for them any more than for fine music,
which is often too liberally bestowd on such occasions. Speak at all
ventures and attempt the *mot pour rire*. You will find people satisfied
with wonderfully indifferent jokes if you can but hit the taste of the
company, which depends much on its character. Even a very high
part[y] primd with all the cold irony and *non est tanti*[3] feelings or no
feelings of fashionable folks may be stormd by a jovial rough round

1. The Duke of Wellington, to whom Scott had written on 15
   February. *Letters*, x. 156.
2. W. H. Murray, brother-in-law of Henry Siddons, was Manager
   of the Edinburgh theatre. According to Dibdin, 'Walter Scott
   was the person who aroused it from lethargy and stagnation . . .
   in setting the example of regularly patronizing the theatre, he
   was inevitably followed by the most intelligent of his time.' He
   had been a patron of the Fund 'for the relief and support of
   decayed performers' from its inception in 1819. Dibdin, pp. 257
   and 290–1.
3. 'It is not worth so much.'

and ready praeses. Choose your texts with discretion, the sermon may be as you like.

If a drunkard or an ass breaks [in] with any[thing] out of joint, if you can parry it with a jest, good and well; if not, do not exert your serious authority unless it is something very bad. The authority even of a chairman ought to be very cautiously exercized. With patience you will have the support of every one.

When you have drunk a few glasses to play the good fellow and banish modesty if you are unlucky enough to have such a trouble-some companion, then beware of the cup too much. Nothing is so ridiculous as a drunken praeses.

Lastly always speak short and *Skeoch doch na skial* – cut a tale with a drink.

> This is the purpose and intent
> Of gude Schir Walter's testament.[1]

We dine to-day at Mrs. Dundass of Arnistoun, Dowager.

———

[There is no Entry for 23 February, the date of the Theatrical Fund Dinner at which Scott publicly confessed to the authorship of the Waverley Novels.

With a reputation as poet, scholar, and lawyer to lose, Scott had cautiously published *Waverley* anonymously in 1814. The mystery of the authorship became such a subject of speculation, and sales were so gratifyingly large, that the novels which followed were also anonymous – or 'By the Author of *Waverley*' – and the mask was kept up so long that it became difficult to discard. No one, however, had much difficulty in guessing the author – *aut Walter Scott aut diabolus* – and the secret had already become public with his confession to the creditors after the financial disaster. Scott wrote as follows of the Dinner:

Besides the joke had lasted long enough and I was tired of it. I had not however the most distant intention of chusing the time and place where the thing actually took place for mounting the confessional. Ld. Meadowbank who is a kind and clever little fellow but somewhat bustling and forward said to me in the drawing room 'Do you care any thing about the mystery of the Waverley novels now' – 'Not I' I replied 'the secret is too

---

1. 'Sir Walter parodies the conclusion of King Robert the Bruce's "Maxims or Political Testament". See Hailes's Annals, A.D. 1311, or Fordun's Scoti-chronicon, xii. 10.' J. G. L.

generally known' – I was led to think from this that he meant to make some jocular allusion to Rob Roy . . . But when instead of skirmish of this kind he made a speech in which he seriously identified me with the Author of Waverley I had no opportunity of evasion and was bound either to confess or deny and it struck me while he was speaking it was as good and natural occasion as I could find for making my avowal.[1]

Lord Meadowbank's speech and Scott's reply are printed in Lockhart's *Life*, ix. 80–3.

'Sir Walter's demeanour is that of the greatest simplicity', wrote an Edinburgh accountant who was present at the Dinner. 'He stands very erect and without gesture, presenting, as an ingenious friend remarked to me, almost the appearance of a Statue. His style of speaking is conversational and not fluent, but full of that frankness and indescribable charm which impart ease and spirit to a company.'[2]]

———

24 SATURDAY I carried my own instructions into effect the best I could, and if our jests were not good our laugh was abundant. I think I will hardly take the chair again when the company is so miscellaneous; though they all behaved perfectly well. Meadowbank taxd me with the novels and to end that farce at once I pleaded guilty so that splore is ended. As to the collection it was much cry and little woo', as the Deil said when he shore the sow. Only £280 from 300 people but many were to send money tomorrow. They did not open books, which was impolitic, but circulated a box where people might put in what they pleased and some gave shillings, which gives but a poor idea of the company. Yet there were many respectable people and handsome donations. But this fashion of not letting your right hand see what your left hand doeth is no good mode of raising a round sum. Your penny-pig collections don't succeed. I got away at ten at night. The performers performed very like gentlemen, especiall[y] Will Murray. They attended as Stewards with white rods and never thought of sitting down till after dinner, taking care that the company was attended to.

25 SUNDAY Very bad reports of the speeches in the papers.[3] We dined at Jeffrey's with Sidney Smith, funny and good natured as

1. *Letters*, x. 173.
2. Mackersy's Diary, Nat. Lib. Scot. MS.
3. Scott was indignant at being misreported, in particular at being made to sound intolerant of those who disapproved of the theatre. See *Chronicles of the Canongate*, Appendix to Introduction.

usual. One of his daughters is very pretty indeed; both are well mannerd, agreeable and sing well. The party was pleasant.

26 MONDAY At home and settled to work – but I know not why I was out of spirits – quite the Laird of Humdudgeon and did all I could to shake it off and could not. James Ballantyne dined with me.

27 TUESDAY Humdudgeonish still, hang it, what fools we are. I workd but coldly and ill – yet something is done. I wonder if other people have these strange alternations of industry and incapacity. I am sure I do not indulge myself in fancies but it is accompanied with great drowsiness – bile I suppose and terribly jaded spirits – I received to-day Dr. Short and Major Crockat, who was orderly officer on Boney at the time of his death.

28 WEDNESDAY Sir Adam breakfasted, one of the few old friends left out' the number of my youthful companions. In youth we have many companions, few friends perhaps; in age companionship is ended except rarely and by appointment. Old men by a kind of instinct seek younger companion[s] who listen to their stories, honour their grey hairs while present and mimick and laugh at them when their backs are turn'd. At least that was the way in our day and I warrant our chicks of the present day crow to the same tune. Of all the friends that I have left I have none who has any decided attachment to literature. So either I must talk on that subject to young people, in other words turn proser, or I must turn tea table-talker and converse with ladies. I am too old and too proud for either character so I'll live alone and be contented. Lockhart's departure for London was a loss to me in this way. Came home late from the court. But workd tightly in the evening. I think discontinuing smoking as I have done for these two months passd leaves me less muzzy after dinner. At any rate it breaks a custom – I despise custom.

MARCH

1 THURSDAY At court untill two – Wrote letters under cover of the Lawyers' long speeches, so paid up some of my correspondents which I seldom do upon any other occasion. I sometimes let letters lie for days unopend as if that would postpone the necessity of answering them. Here I am at home and to work we go – not for the first time to-day for I wrought hard before breakfast. So glides away Thursday 1st. By the bye it is the anniversary of Bosworth field.

1. The omission of 'of' after 'left out' is common in spoken Scots.

In former days *Richd. IIId.* was always acted at London on this day. Now the custom, I fancy, is disused. Walpole's *Historic Doubts*[1] threw a mist about this Reign. It is very odd to see how his mind dwells upon [them] at first as the mere sport of imagination till at length they become such Dalilahs of his imagination that he deems it far worse than infidelity to doubt his Doubts. After all the popular tradition is so very strong and pointed concerning the character of Richard that it is I think in vain to doubt the general truth of the outline. Shakespeare we may be sure wrote his drama in the tone that was to suit the popular belief although where that did Richard wrong his powerful scene was sure to augment the impression. There was an action and a reaction.

2 FRIDAY Clerk walkd home with me from the Court. I was scarce able to keep up with him; could once have done it well enough. Funny thing at the theatre. Among the discourse in *High Life below Stairs* one of the Ladies' ladies asks who wrote Shakespeare. One says 'Ben Johnson' another 'Finis'.[2] 'No' said Will Murray 'it is Sir Walter Scott; he confessd it at a publick meeting the other day.'

3 SATURDAY Very severe weather, came home coverd with snow. White as a frosted plumb cake by jingo. No matter. I am not sorry to find I can stand a brush of weather yet. I like to see Arthur's Seat and the stern old castle with their white watch cloaks on. But as Byron said to Moore 'D—n me, Tom, don't be poetical.'[3] I settled to *Boney* and wrote right long and well.

4 SUNDAY

> When frost and snow come both together
> Then sit by the fire and spare shoe leather.[4]

So says Dean Swift and on that theme I sate in by the chimny nook with no chance of interruption and feagued it away as Bayes says.[5] Sir Adam came and had half an hour's chat and laugh. My jaws ought to be sore if the unwontedness of the motion could do it. But I have little to laugh at but myself and my own bizarreries are more like to make me cry. Wrought hard though – there's saving in that.

1. Horace Walpole's *Historic Doubts on Richard III*, 1768.
2. By Townley, Act ii.
3. For this story, see the Entry for 9 February 1826.
4. See p. 316, note 6.
5. Buckingham's *Rehearsal*, iv. 2.

5 MONDAY Our young men of first fashion in whom tranquility is the prime merit, a sort of quietism of foppery if one can use the expression, have one capital name for a fellow that outres and outroars the fashion, a sort of high buck as they were calld in my days. They hold him a vulgarian and call him a tiger. Mr. Gibson came in and we talkd over my affairs, very little to the purpose I doubt. Dined at home with Anne as usual and despatchd half a dozen Selkirk processes,[1] among others one which savours of hamesucken.[2] I think to-day I have finishd ¼ of vol. VIII and last. Shall I be happy when it is Done? Umph! – I think not – I will be like the old Frenchman who regretted his tape-worm.[3]

6 TUESDAY A long seat at court and an early dinner as we went to the play. John Kemble's brother acted Benedict. He is a fine-looking man and a good actor but not superior. He reminds you eternally that he is acting and he had got, as the Devil directed it, hold of my favourite Benedict for which he has no power. He had not the slightest idea of the part, particularly of the manner in which Benedict should conduct himself in the quarrelling scene with the Prince and Claudio in which his character rises almost to the dignity of tragedy. The laying aside his light and fantastic humour and showing himself the man of feeling and honour was finely markd of Yore by old Tom King. I remember particularly the high strain of grave moral feeling which he threw upon the words 'in a false quarrel there is no true valour –' which spoken as he did checkd the very brutal levity of the Prince and Claudio. There were two farces; one I wishd to see and that being the last was obliged to tarry for it. Perhaps the headache I contracted made me a severe critic on *Cramond Brigg*, a little piece ascribed to Lockhart.[4] Perhaps I am unjust but I cannot think it his; there are so few good things [in] it and so much prosing transferd [from] that mine of marrowless morality called the 'Miller of Mansfield'.[5] Yet it pleases –

---

1. Cases to be dealt with at Selkirk Sheriff Court.
2. 'The crime of feloniously beating or assaulting a person in his own house.' *Bell's Dictionary and Digest.*
3. 'Which supplied him with a certain degree of interesting employment in order to wind an inch of it up every day.' *Letters,* x. 211.
4. There is a marginal note by Lockhart: 'I never saw it – not mine. J. G. L.' *Cramond Brig* was first produced on 27 February. Douglas notes that it was 'said to have been written by Mr. W. H. Murray, the manager of the Theatre'.
5. A ballad in Percy's *Reliques.*

7 WEDNESDAY We are kept working hard during the expiring days of the Session but this being a blank day[1] I wrote hard till dressing time when I went to Will Clerk's to dinner. As a bachelor and keeping a small establishment he does not do these things often but they are proportionally pleasant when they come round. He had trusted Sir Adam to bespeak his dinner who did it *con amore* so we had excellent cheer and the wines were various and capital. As I before hinted it is not every day that McNab mounts on horseback[2] and so our landlord had a little of that solicitude that the party should go off well which is very flattering to the guests. We had a very pleasant Evening. The Chief Comr. was there, Admiral Adam, Jo: Murray and Thomson etc. etc., Sir Adam predominating at the head and dancing what he calls his merry Andrada in great stile. In short we really laughd and real laughter is a thing as rare as real tears. I must say too there was a *heart*, a kindly feeling prevaild over the party. Can London give such a dinner – it may but I never saw one – they are too cold and critical to be so easily pleased.[3] In the evening I went with some others to see the exhibition[4] lit up for a promenade where there were all the fashionable folks about town: the appearance of the rooms was very gay indeed.

8 THURSDAY It snowd all night which must render the roads impassable and will detain me here till Monday. Hard work at court as Hammie is done up with the gout. We dine with Lord Corehouse. That is not true by the bye for I have mistaken the day. It is tomorrow we dine there. Wrought but not too hard.

9 FRIDAY An idle morning, Dalgleish being set to pack my books. Wrote Notes upon a Mr. Kinloch's collection of Scottish ballads[5] which I communicated to the young author in the court this present morning: we were detaind till half past three o'clock in the Court so when I came home I was fatigued and slept. I walk slow, heavily, and with pain – but perhaps the good weather may banish the Fiend of the joints. At any rate impatience will 'do nae good at a', man'. Letter

1. A Teind Court Wednesday.
2. 'That singular personage, the late M'Nab of *that ilk*, spent his life almost entirely in a district where a boat was the usual conveyance.' J. G. L.
3. Lockhart, with justice, comments on the unfair comparison 'between the society of comparative strangers and that of old friends dear from boyhood'. *Life*, ix. 77.
4. The Institution's annual exhibition, in the rooms at the foot of the Mound.
5. George Kinloch's *Ancient Scottish Ballads*, 1827.

from Charles for £50.[1] Silver and gold have I none but that which I have I will give unto him.[2] We dined at the Cranstons, I beg his pardon, Lord Corehouse – Fergusson, Thomson, Will Clerk etc. were there, also the Smiths[3] and John Murray, so we had a pleasant evening.

10 SATURDAY The business at the Court was not so heavy as I have seen it the last day of the Session yet sharp enough. About three o'clock I got to a meeting of the Committee of the Bannatyne club.[4] I hope this institution will be really useful and creditable. Thomson is superintending a capital edition of Sir James Mellville's Memoirs. It is brave to see how he wags his Scots tongue and what a difference there is in the force and firmness of the language compared to the mincing English edition in which he has hitherto been alone known. Nothing to-day but correcting proofs. Anne went to the play. I remaind at home.

11 SUNDAY All my books packd this morning and this and tomorrow will be blank days or nearly such but I am far ahead of the printer who is not done with vol VII. while I am deep in volume VIII. I hate packing but my servants never pack books qui[te] to please me. James Ballantyne dined with us. He kept up my heart about *Bonaparte* which sometimes flags and he is such a grumbler that I think I may trust him when he is favourable. There must be sad inaccuracies, some which might certainly have been prevented by care, but as the Lazaroni used to say – 'Did you but know how Lazy I am'.

12 MONDAY Abbotsford. Away we set and came safely to Abbotsford amid all the dullness of a great thaw which has set the rivers a streaming in full tide. The wind is wintry but for my part

I like this rocking of the battlements.[5]

I was received by old Tom[6] and the dogs with the unsophisticated feelings of good will. I have been trying to read a new novel which I

---

1. 'Owing to my staying here during the vaccation my Battles have been higher [than] usual & much more so than I thought they would be. They amount to 43£ – how they come to so much the Fellows are the best judges.' Charles, 10 March 1827, Walpole.
2. Acts 3: 6.
3. The Sydney Smiths.
4. In the 'Antiquarian rooms' in the new Institution building. Laing, 8 March 1827, Disc. i. 128.
5. Edward Young's *Revenge*, i. 1.
6. Tom Purdie.

have heard praised. It is calld *Almacks*[1] an[d] the author has so well succeeded in describing the cold selfish fopperies of the time that the copy is almost as dull as the original. I think I will take up my bundle of Sheriff-court processes instead of *Almacks* as the more entertaining avocation of the two.

13 TUESDAY Before breakfast prepared and forwarded the processes to Selkirk.

accompt
Received of Mr Cadell – loan £   Paid Oil Gas Coy acct.– £[2]
Do. ——— 100   Charles ——————— 50
                Tom Purdie ———— 50

As I had loan of £250[3] at Michs from Cadell I am now verging on to the £500 which he promised to allow me in advance on 2nd. Series *Canongate Chronicles*. I do not like this but unless I review or write to some other purpose what else can I do? My own expenses are as limited as possible but my house expenses are considerable and every now and then starts up something of old scores which I cannot turn over to Mr. Gibson and his co-trustees. Well – time and the hour – money is the smalles[t] consideration.

Had a pleasant walk to the thicket though my ideas were olla-podrida-ish – curiously chequerd between pleasure and melancholy. I have cause enough for both humours, God knows. I expect this will not be a day of work but of idleness for my books are not come. Would to God I could make it light thoughtless idleness such as I used to have when the silly smart fancies rose in my brain like the bubbles in a glass of champagne, as brilliant to my thinking – as intoxicating as evanescent – But the wine is somewhat on the lees. Perhaps it was but indifferent cyder after all. Yet I am happy in this place where every thing looks friendly from old Tom to young Nym.[4]

1. Usually attributed to Marianne Spencer Stanhope. It was published in 1827.
2. In other words, Cadell settled the Oil Gas Company account on Scott's behalf.
3. Cadell's letter of 15 May shows that this was in fact an advance of only £200. Letters to Scott.
4. One of his dogs, better liked by himself than by his visitors, if Andrew Shortreed's account is accurate: 'I could not get my hat kept in my hand for Nimrod, the deerhound – he knocked it to the floor, I dare say half a dozen times. . . . [His dogs] follow him everywhere, whether to his study or to his dining room, and receive much of his attention. He frequently caressed and even kissed the large dog in particular.' 2–4 May 1827, Shortreed Papers.

After all he has little to complain of who has left so many things that like him.

14 WEDNESDAY All yesterday spent in putting to rights books and so forth. Not a word written except interlocutors.[1] But this won't do. I have tow on the rock and it must be spun off. Let us see our present undertakings. 1 Napoleon. 2 Review Hume, Cranbourne Chase and the mysteries.[2] 3 Something for that poor faineant G.[3] 4 Essay on ballad and song. 5 Something on the modern state of france. These two last for the prose works. But they may

> — do a little more
> And produce a little ore.[4]

Come, we must up and be doing. There is a rare scud without which says 'Go spin, you jade, go spin.'[5] — I loiterd on and might have answerd

> My spinning wheel is auld and stiff
> The rock o't winna stand, Sir.
> To keep the temper pin in tift
> Employs ower aft my hand, Sir.[6]

Smoked a brace of Segars after dinner as a sedative – this is the first time I have smoked these two months. I was afraid the custom would master me. Went to work in the afternoon and reviewd for Lockhart Mackenzie's edition of Home's works. Proceeded as far as the 8th. page.

15 THURSDAY Kept still at the Review till two o'clock, not that there is any hurry but because I should lose my ideas which are not worth preserving. Went on therefore. I drove over to Huntly Burn with Anne, then walkd through the plantations with Tom's help to pull me through the snow-wreaths. Returnd in a glow of heat and spirits. Corrected proof sheets in the evening.

1. The expression in proper legal terminology of the judgment given in Court, in this case the Sheriff Court.
2. Henry Mackenzie's *Life and Works of Home*, which Scott reviewed for the June *Quarterly*; Chafin's *Anecdotes of Cranbourne Chase*, 1818, and Thomas Sharp's Coventry Mysteries 1825.
3. Gillies.
4. Parody of the nursery rhyme, 'There was a little man', st. 2. ll. 4–6.
5. 'As the Earl of Pembroke said to the ejected Nun of Wilton.' Entry for 9 February 1826.
6. See p.11 note 1.

16 FRIDAY

> A trifling day we have had here,
> Begun with trifle and ended.[1]

But I hope no otherwise so ended than to meet the rubrick of the ballad: for it is but three o'clock. In the morning I was *l'homme qui cherche* –[2] every thing fell aside, the very pens absconded and crept in amon[g] a pack of letters and trumpery where I had the devil's work finding them. Thus the time before breakfast was idled or rather fidgetted away. Afterwards it was rather worse. I had settled to finish the Review when behold, as I am [apt] to do at a set task, I jibb'd and methought would rather have gone with Waterloo. So I dawdled as the women say with both, now writing a page or two of the Review, now reading a few pages of the battle of Waterloo by Capt. Pringle, a manuscript which is excellently written.[3] Well, I will find the advantage of it by and bye. So now I will try to finish this accursed Review for there is nothing to prevent me save the untractable character that hates to work on compulsion whether of individuals or circumstances.

17 SATURDAY I wrought away at the Review and nearly finishd it – was interrupted however by a note from Ballantyne demanding copy which brought me back from Home and Mackenzie to *Boney*. I had my walk as usual and workd nevertheless very fairly. Corrected proofs.

18 SUNDAY Took up *Boney* again. I am now at writing as I used to be at riding, slow heavy and awkward at mounting, but when I did get fixd [in] my saddle could screed away with any one. I have got a six pages ready for my learned Theban[4] tomorrow morning. William Laidlaw and his brother George dined with me. But I wrote in the evening all the same.

19 MONDAY Set about my labours but enter Capt. John Fergusson from the Spanish Main where he has been for three years. The honest tar sate about two hours and I was heartily glad to see him again. I had a general sketch of his adventures which we will hear more in detail

---

1. Farquhar's *Beaux Stratagem*, iii. 3: 'A trifling Song you shall hear'.
2. See p. 157, note 4.
3. It was printed as Appendix VIII to the *Life of Napoleon*.
4. *King Lear*, iii. 4.

when we can meet at Kaletime. Notwithstanding this interruption I have pushd far into the seventh page. Well done for one day. Twenty days should finish me at this rate and I read hard too. But allowance must be made for interruptions.

20 TUESDAY To-day workd till twelve o'clock then went with Anne on a visit of Condolence to Mrs. Pringle of Yair and her family.[1] Mr. Pringle was the friend both of my father and grandfather; the acquaintance of our families is at least a century old.

21 WEDNESDAY Wrote till twelve – Then out upon the heights though the day was stormy and faced the gale bravely. Tom Purdie was not with me. He would have obliged me to keep the shelterd ground. But I don't know.

> Even in our ashes live our wonted fires.[2]

There is a touch of the old spirit in me yet that bids me brave the tempest – the spirit that in spite of manifold infirmities made me a roaring boy in my youth, a desperate climber, a bold rider, a deep drinker and a stout player at single stick of all which valuable qualities there are now but slender remains. I workd hard when I came in and finishd five pages.

22 THURSDAY Yesterday I wrote to James Ballantyne acquiescing in his urgent request in extending the two last volumes to about 600 each. I believe it will be no more than necessary after all. But [it] makes one feel like a dog in a wheel always moving and never advancing. But I shall be as acquiescent as the drunken puritan when he made water under the spout – O Lord, if it is thy will etc. The first row of Joe Miller[3] will tell the rest. Here however comes Mrs Duty and I must to my task.

23 FRIDAY When I was a child, and indeed for some years after, my amusement was in supposing to myself a set of persons engaged in various scenes which contrasted them with each other and I remember to this day the accuracy with which my childish imagination [depicted them]. This might be the effect of a natural turn to fictitious

---

1. 'Papa was astonished at her total unconcern. She had *a crape apron on* which I could not keep my eyes off.' Anne to Sophia, ?23 March 1827, Abbots.
2. Gray's 'Elegy in a Country Churchyard' st. 23.
3. *Joe Miller's Jests*, by John Mottley, 1739.

narrative or it might be the cause of it or there might be an action and reaction – or it does not signify a pin's head how it is – But with a flash of this remaining spirit I imagine my Mother Duty to be a sort of old task mistress like the hag of the merchant Abudah in the *Tales of the Genii*[1] – not a hag though by any means; on the contrary my old woman wears a rich old fashiond gown of black silk with rufles of triple blonde lace and a coif as rich as that of pearling Jean.[2] A figure and countenance something like Lady D. S.'s[3] twenty years ago, a clear blue eye capable of great severity of expression and conforming in that with a wrinkled brow of which the ordinary expression is a serious approach to a frown – a cautionary and nervous shake of the head. In her witherd hand an ebony staff with a crutch head, a Tompion gold watch which annoys all who know her by striking the quarters as regularly as if one wishd to hear them – Occasionally she has a small scourge of nettles which I feel her lay across my fingers at this moment and so – *Tace* is latin for a candle.[4] I have 140 pages to write yet.

24 SATURDAY Does duty not wear a pair of round oldfashiond silver buckles? Buckles [s]he has but they are square ones. All belonging to duty is rectangular. Thus can we poor children of imagination play with the ideas we create like Children with soap bubbles. Pity that we pay for it at other times by starting at our shadows. Man but a rush against Othello's breast.[5]

The hard work still proceeds varied only by a short walk.

25 SUNDAY Hard work still but went to Huntleyburn on foot and returnd in the carriage. Walkd well and stoutly, god be praised, and prepared a whole bundle of proofs and copy for the Blucher tomorrow. That damnd work will certainly end some time or other. As it drips and driddles out on the paper I think of the old drunken presbyterian under the spout.

26 MONDAY Dispatchd packets. Colonel and Capt. Fergusson arrived to breakfast. I had previously determind to give myself a

1. See Weber's *Tales of the East*, 1812, iii. 420–43.
2. 'Pearling Jean' was the mistress of a seventeenth-century Stuart of Allanbank, killed by her lover's carriage as he drove away to desert her. Her ghost was reputed to haunt Allanbank in rustling silk and lace.
3. Lady Diana Scott, the mother of Hugh Scott of Harden.
4. 'A humorously veiled hint to a person to keep silent about something.' *O. E. D.* Douglas points out that Scott may have picked up the phrase from Swift's *Polite Conversation*.
5. *Othello*, v. 2.

day to write letters and as I expect John Thomson to dinner this day will do as well as another. I cannot keep up with the world without shying a letter now and then. It is true the greatest happiness I could think of would be [to] be rid of the world entirely excepting my own family. I have little pleasure in the world, less business in [it] and am heartily careless about all its concerns. Mr. Thomson came accordingly, not John Thomson of Duddingston whom the letter led me to expect but John Anstruther Thomson of Charlton, the son in law of Lord Ch: Commissioner.

27 TUESDAY Wrote two leaves this morning and gave the day after breakfast to my visitor who is a country gentleman of the best description. Knows the world having been a good deal attachd both to the turf and the field is extremely good humourd and a good deal of [a] local Antiquary. I shewd him the plantations, going first round the terrace, then to the Lake, then came down to Huntly Burn by the Rymer's glen, [and] took carriage at Huntly Burn. Almost the grand tour, only we did not walk from Huntly Burn. The Fergussons dined with us.

28 WEDNESDAY Mr. Thomson left us about twelve for Minto, parting a pleased guest I hope from a pleased landlord. When I see a ge'mman as *is* a gemman as the blackguards say, why I know how to be civil. After he left I set doggedly to work with *Bonaparte* who had fallen a little into arrear. I can clear the ground better now by mashing up my old work in the *Edinburgh Register*[1] with my new matter, a species of Colcannen where cold potatoes are mixd with hot cabbage. After all I think Ballantyne is right and that I have some talents for history writing after all. That same history in the *Register* reads prettily enough. *Coragio* cry Claymore. I finishd five pages but with addition from *Register* they will run to more than double I hope [and] like Puff in the *Critic* be luxuriant.[2]

Here is snow back again – a nasty comfortless stormy sort of a day.

> When frost and snow come both together
> Then sit by the fire and save shoe leather.[3]

Gad a mercy, Dean Swift, and so I will and will work off a day at *Boney* that shall know no interruption. What shall I do when

1. A week earlier Scott had asked Ballantyne to send the *Edinburgh Annual Register* for 1814, to which Scott had contributed the historical section. *Letters*, x. 177.
2. Sheridan's *Critic*, ii. 1.
3. See p. 316, note 6.

Bonaparte is done? He engrosses me morning noon and night. Never mind. *Komt zeit komt rath*[1] as the German says – I did not work longer than 12 however but went out in as rough weather as I have seen and stood out several snow blast[s].

29, 30 THURSDAY FRIDAY

> He walkd and wrought, poor soul, what then?
> Why then he walk'd and wrought again.[2]

31 SATURDAY Day varied by dining with Mr. Scroope where we found Mr. Williams and Mr. Simpson, both excellent artists. We had not too much of the pallet but made a very agreeable day out. I contrived to mislay the proof sheets sent me this morning so that I must have a revise. This frequent absence of mind becomes very exceeding troublesome. I have the distinct recollection of laying them carefully aside after I dressd to go to the Pavilion.[3] Well – I have a head[4] – the proverb is musty.

APRIL

1 SUNDAY The proofs are not to be found – Applications from R. P. G.[5] I must do something for him, yet have the melancholy conviction that nothing will do him any good. Then he writes letters and expects answers. Then they are bothering me about writing in behalf of the Oil Gas Light which is going to the Devil very fast. I cannot be going a begging for them or anybody – Please to look down with an eye of pity – a poor distressd creature – No, not for the last morsel of bread – a dry ditch and a speedy death is worth it all.

2 MONDAY Another letter from R. P. G. I shall begin to wish like S.[6] that he had been murtherd and robbd in his walks between Wimbledon[7] and London. John Murray and his young wife came to

1. 'With time comes counsel.' Proverb.
2. Adapted from Prior's 'Epitaph' beginning 'Interr'd beneath this marble stone'.
3. Scrope's house, rented from Lord Somerville.
4. 'And so has a pin'.
5. R. P. Gillies, wanting an article for his *Foreign Quarterly Review*.
6. Sophia.
7. The Lockharts had moved there 'for the winter months', thinking it better 'for John's health, to live in the country, and have only a lodging in town, where Mr Lockhart may have letters and papers sent'. *Letters from Scott's Family*, pp. 122-3.

dinner and in good time. I like her very much and think he has been very lucky. She is not in the vaward of youth but John is but two or three years my junior. She is pleasing in her manners and totally free from affectation – a beautiful musician and willingly exerts her talents in that way – is said to be very learnd but shows none of it. A large fortune is no bad addition to such a woman's society.[1] Maxpopple and his daughter dined with us. New proofs came to-day.

3 TUESDAY I had processes to decide and though I arose at my usual hour I could not get through above two of five proofs. After breakfast I walkd with John Murray and at twelve we went for Melrose where I had to show the lions; we came back by Huntlyburn where the carriage broke down and gave us a pretty long walk home. Mr. Scrope dined with his two artists and John. The last[2] is not only the best landscape painter of his age and country but is moreover one of the warmest-heart[ed] men living with a keen and unaffected feeling of poetry – Poor fellow – he has had many misfortunes in his family I drank a glass or two of wine more than usuall, got into good spirits and *Came from Tripoli* for the amusement of the good company. I was in good fooling.[3]

4 WEDNESDAY I think I have a little headache this morning; however, as Othello says, that's not much.[4] I saw our guests go off by seven in the morning but was not in time to give them Goodbye.

Mem. Fixd Saturday 14 Instant for Thomson's trial. Ten o'clock.

And now again, boys, to the oar![5]

I did not got to the oar though but walkd a good deal.

5 THURSDAY Heard from Lockhart the Duke of W.[6] and Croker are pleased with my historical labours – so far well – for the former, as a soldier said of him, 'I would rather have his long nose on my side as a whole brigade.' Well! something good may come of it and if it does it will be good luck for as you and I know, mother Duty, it has been a rumly written work. I wrought hard to-day.

1. For other descriptions of Mrs. Murray see the Entry for 3 February 1827 and note.
2. William Simson, Scrope's guest and a noted landscape painter, is meant.
3. *Twelfth Night*, i. 5.
4. *Othello*, iii. 3.
5. Swift's 'The Country Life', l. 44.
6. Wellington.

6 FRIDAY Ditto – ditto – I only took one turn about the thicket and have nothing to put down but to record my labours.

7 SATURDAY The same history occurs, my desk and my exercize. I am a perfect Automaton. *Bonaparte* runs in my head from 7 in the morning till ten at night without intermission. I wrote six leaves to-day and corrected four proofs.

8 SUNDAY Ginger, being in my room, was safely deliverd in own basket of four puppies – the mother and children all doing well – faith! that is as important an entry as my journal could desire. The day is so beautiful that I long to go out. I won't though till I have done something: a letter from Mr. Gibson about the trust affairs. If the infernal bargain[1] with Constable go on well there will be a pretty sop in the pan to the Creditors, £35,000 at least. If I could work as effectually for three years more I shall stand on my feet like a man. But who can assure success with the publick?

9 MONDAY I wrote as hard to-day as need be, finnish my neat eight pages and notwithstanding drove out and visited at Gattonside and Friar's hall. The devil must be in it if the matter drags out longer now.

I cleard eight pages to-day. Some change of hours about the Blucher prevents my getting proof-sheets.

10 TUESDAY But who cares?[2] Some incivility from the Leith Bank which I despise with my heels.[3] I have done for settling my affairs all that any man – much more – than most men could have done and they refuse a draught of £20 because in mistake it was eight pounds over-drawn. But what can be expected of a *Sow* but a *grumph*? Wrought hard – hard.[4]

1. The arbitration by Lord Newton about the profits from *Woodstock*, the *Life of Napoleon*, etc.
2. These three words should have been deleted along with the previous three sentences which ran as follows: 'The grass parks were rouped nearly £100 better than last year. Poor Abbotsford will come to good after all. In the mean time it is Sic vos non vobis –'. The confusion between this and the next entry suggests that Scott was in arrears and making up his journal for more than one day.
3. *Much Ado about Nothing*, iii. 4.
4. News came from Lockhart on this or the previous day that the Royal Society of Literature had deemed Scott 'worthy of one of their medals'. 5 April 1827, Walpole.

11 WEDNESDAY The Parks were rouped[1] for £100 a year more than they brought last year – *Sic vos non vobis*[2] – but who cares a farthing? If *Bony* succeeds we will give these affairs a blue eye and I will wrestle stoutly with them although 'My *Banks* they are covered with *bees*,'[3] or rather with *wasps*. A very tough day's work.

12 THURSDAY *Ha-a-lt* – as we used [to say]. My proof sheets being still behind – very unhandsome conduct on the part of the Blucher while I was lauding so profusely[4] – it is necessary to halt and close up our files – of correspondence I mean, so it is a chance if except for contradiction's sake or upon getting the proof sheets, I write a line to-day at *Boney*. – I did however correct five revised sheets, and one proof which took me up so much of the day that I had but one turn through the courtyard. Owing to this I had some of my flutterings, my trembling exies as the old people calld the ague. Wrote a great many letters – but no copy.

13 FRIDAY I have sometimes wonderd with what regularity, that is for a shrew of my impatient temper, I have been able to keep this journal with tolerable regularity. The use of the first person being of course the very essence of a diary I conceive it is chiefly vanity, the dear pleasure of writing about the best of good fellows, Myself, which gives me perseverance to continue this idle task. This morning I wrote till breakfast – then went out and markd trees to be cut for paling and am just returnd – and what does any one care? Aye but, Gad, I care myself though – William Scott my late brother Daniel's son seems to turn out ill. He was furnishd with money etc. by me to go to London his prenticeship being ended. But as I left Edinburgh at the time he chose to run away to his mother at Selkirk. I have done my duty by him in breeding him and maintaining. I will not do more.[5] We had at dinner to-day Mr. and Mrs. Cranstoun (Burn's Maria of Ballochmyle[6]), Mr. Bainbridge and daughters, and Colonel Russell to dinner.

1. 'Rented by auction.'
2. 'So you [strive] not for yourselves.'
3. Shenstone's 'Pastoral Ballad', pt. 2, l.1.
4. For Scott's praise of Marshal Blücher, see the *Life of Napoleon*, vol. viii, chs. 18 and 19.
5. In 1828, despite this resolution to do no more for him, Scott helped him to emigrate to Canada. See also the Entries for 29 June 1826 and 18 January 1831.
6. See 'The Braes of Ballochmyle', which laments her departure from the family estate.

14 SATURDAY Went to Selkirk to try a fellow[1] for an assault on Dr. Clarkson; fined him 7 guineas, which with his necessary expenses will amount to 10 guineas. It is rather too little but as his income does not amount to £30 a year it will pinch him severely enough and is better than sending him to an ill kept jail where he would be idle and drunk from morning till night. I had a dreadful head ache while sitting in the court – rheumatism in perfection. It did not last after I got warm by the fireside.

15 SUNDAY Delightful soft morning with mild rain. Walkd out and got wet as a Sovereign cure for the rheumatism. Was quite well though and scribbled away.

16 MONDAY A day of work and exercize. In the evening a letter from L.[2] with the wonderful news that the Ministry has broken up and apparently for no cause that any one can explain. The old grudge I suppose betwixt Peele and Canning which has gone on augmenting like a crack in the side of a house which enlarges from day to day till down goes the whole. Mr. Canning has declared himself fully satisfied with J. L. and sent Barrow to tell him so.[3] His suspicions were indeed most erroneous but they were repelld with no little spirit both by L. and myself and Canning has not been like another Great Man I knew to whom I shewd demonstrably that he had suspected an individual unjustly. 'It may be so' he said 'but his mode of defending himself was offensive.'

17 TUESDAY Went to dinner to-day to Mr. Bainbridge's Gattonside House and had fireworks in the evening made by Capt. Burchard, a

1. His name was Thomson. See the Entry for 4 April 1827.
2. Lockhart.
3. This refers to an incident not previously mentioned in the *Journal*. On 12 January Sophia wrote to her father about a post in the Excise which was about to fall vacant, and in a letter to Canning Scott duly recommended Lockhart to his consideration. Canning's reply was a shock to Scott and to his son-in-law: 'Mr. Lockhart has the reputation in London of being (and of having been invited from Scotland for the very purpose of being) at the head of that portion of the Press . . . which attacks, with a fury unknown, till lately, to modern political controversy, the measures, to which I am supposed to be favourable, and personally myself.' Scott's firm, polite reply apparently had its effect; Barrow's mission was to tell Lockhart that Canning had been misinformed and that he might therefore expect a kindness when the opportunity arose. *Letters*, x. 163, 192, and 194, and notes.

goodhumourd kind of Will Wimble. One nice little boy announced to us every thing that was going to be done with the importance of a prologue. Some of the country folks assembled and our party was enlivend by the squeaks of the wenches and the long protracted Eh Eh's by which a Teviotdale rup testifies his wonder.

18 WEDNESDAY I felt the impatience of news so much that I walkd up to Mr. Laidlaw surely for no other purpose than to talk politics. This interrupted *Bony* a little. After I return about 12 or one behold

'Tom Tack he comes from Buenos Ayres'[1]

with a parcel of little curiosities he had pickd up for me. As Tom Tack spins a *tough yarn* I lost the morning almost entirely[2] what with one thing what with t'other, as my friend the Laird of Raeburn says. Nor have I much to say for the evening, only I smoked a cigar more than usual to get the box ended and give up the custom for a little.

19 THURSDAY Another letter from Lockhart. I am sorry when I think of the goodly fellowship of vessells which are now scatterd on the ocean. There is the Duke of Wellington, the Lord Chancellor,[3] Lord Melville, Mr. Peele, and I wot not who besides, all turnd out of office or resigned.[4] I wonder what they can do in the House of Lords when all the great Tories are on the wrong side of the House. Canning seems quite serious in his views of helping Lockhart [which] I hope will come to something.

20 FRIDAY A surly sort of day. I walkd for two hours however and then returnd chiefly to *Nap*. Egad I believe it has an *End* at last, this blasted work. I have the fellow at Plymouth or near about it.[5] Well I

1. Charles Dibdin's 'Tom Tack's Ghost', st. 3.
2. Captain Ferguson's call is more vividly described in a letter to Lockhart: 'He put me to extremity by a dreadful long visit the other day which was employd in telling the most formidable stories. I have heard of people who began at the right [end] of a story & people who preferrd commencing at the wrong but I never heard any but J. F. who began in the middle & told backwards & forwards at the same time. He tells a story more in the manner of a terrier worrying a rat than anything else now he seems choaking upon [it] now he lets it go & has it to catch again.' *Letters*, x. 198.
3. Lord Eldon.
4. See Appendix D, p. 826, for the Cabinet changes at this time.
5. *Life of Napoleon*, vol. ix, ch. 2.

declare I thought the end of these beastly big eight volumes was like the end of the world, which is always talkd of and never comes.

21 SATURDAY Here is a vile day, downright rain, which disconcerts an inroad of bairns from Gattonside and of course annihilates a part of the stock of human happiness. But what says the proverb of your true rainy day?

> Tis good for book, tis good for work
> For cup and can or knife and fork.

22 SUNDAY Wrote till twelve o'clock then sallied forth and walkd to Huntly Burn with Tom and so, look you Sir, I drove home in the carriage with   [1]. Wrought in the afternoon and tried to read *De Vere*,[2] a sensible but heavy book written by an able[3] hand – but a great bore for all that – Wrote in the evening.

23 MONDAY Snowy morning. White as my shirt. The little Bainbridges came over invited to see the armoury etc.[4] which I stood showman to. It is odd how much less cubbish the English boys are than the Scotch. Well mannerd and sensible are the Southern boys. I suppose the sun brings them forwards. Here comes six o'clock at night and it is snowing as if it had not snowd these forty years before. Well I'll work away a couple of chapters – three at most will finish *Napoleon*.

24 TUESDAY Still deep snow – a foot thick in the Court yard I dare say. Severe wellcome to the poor lambs now coming into the world. But what signifies whether they die just now or a little while after to be united with sallad at luncheon time? It signifies a good deal too. There is a period, though a short one, when they dance among the gowans and seem happy. As for your aged sheep or weather, the sooner the[y] pass to the *norman* side of the vocabulary the better.[5] They are like some old dowager Ladies and gentlemen of my acquaintance; no one cares about them till they come to be *cut up*, and then we see how the tallow [lies] on the kidnies and the chine.

25 WEDNESDAY Snow yet and it prevents my walking and I grow bilious. I work hard though. I have now got Bony peggd up in the

---

1. Left blank in the original.
2. Robert Ward's *De Vere*, just published.
3. Scott originally wrote 'a dull'.
4. The armoury and hall at Abbotsford, hung with arms and other curiosities.
5. An allusion to the first chapter of *Ivanhoe*.

knotty entrails of Saint Helena[1] and may make a short pause. So I finishd the review of John Home's works which after all are poorer than I thought them. Good blank verse and stately sentiment but something lukewarmish excepting *Douglas*, which is certainly a masterpiece. Even that does not stand the closet. Its merit[s] are for the stage but it is certainly one of [the] best acting plays going. Perhaps a play to act well should not be too poetical.

There is a talk in London of bringing in the Marquis of Lansdowne, then Lauderdale will perhaps come in here. It is certain the old Tory party is down the wind not from political opinions but from personal aversion to Canning. Perhaps his satirical temper has partly occasiond this but I rather consider emulation as the source of, head and front of, the offending. Croker no longer rhimes to joker. He has made a good *coup* it is said by securing Lord Hertford for the new Administration. D— W—[2] calls him their *viper*. After all I cannot sympathise with that delicacy which throws up office because the most eloquent man in England and certainly the only man who can manage the House of Commons[3] is namd Minister.

26 THURSDAY The snow still profusely distributed and the surface as our hair used to be in youth after we had playd at some active game, half black, half white, all in large patches. I finishd the criticism on Home adding a string of Jacobite anecdotes like that which boys put to a kite's tail. Sent off the packet [to] Lockhart; at the same [time] sent Croker a volume of French tracts[4] con‑   Croker pamphlets. taining *La Portefeuille de Bonaparte* which he wishd to see. Received a great cargo of papers from Bernadotte,[5] some curious, and would have been inestimable two months back but now my siege is almost made. Still my feelings for poor Count Itterburg[6] the lineal and legitimate make me averse to have much to do with this child of the Revolution.

27 FRIDAY This hand of mine gets to be like a kitten's scratch and will require much decyphering or what may be as well for the writer,

1. *Life of Napoleon*, vol. ix, ch. 3. The allusion is to *Tempest*, i. 2.
2. The Duke of Wellington.
3. That is, Canning.
4. He had collected 'a pretty large set of things of the kind' by this time. *Letters*, x. 195.
5. Charles Bernadotte, a Marshal of France, who joined the Allies and in 1818 became King of Sweden.
6. The name assumed during his travels by Prince Gustavus Vasa, the son of Gustavus IV of Sweden. Scott saw much of him during his time in Scotland in 1819 and 1820, and found him 'a very pleasing young man'. *Letters*, vi. 23.

cannot be decypherd at all. I am sure I cannot read it myself. Weather better, which is well as I shall get a walk. I have been a little nervous as being confined to the House for three days. I was *l'homme qui cherche*[1] this morning. Well – I may be disabled from Duty but my tamed spirits and sense of dejection have quelld all that freakishness of humour which made me a voluntary idler. I present myself to the morning task as the hack horse patiently trudges to the pole of his chaise and backs however reluctantly to have the traces fixed. Such are the uses of adversity.[2]

28 SATURDAY Wrought at continuing the works with some criticism on Defoe.[3] I have great aversion, I cannot tell why, at stuffing in the *Border Antiquities*[4] into what they call the *Prose Works*. There is no encouragement to be sure for doing better for nobody seems to care. I cannot get an answer from J. Ballantyne whether he thinks the Review on the Highlands would be a better substitution.[5]

29 SUNDAY Col. and Capt. Fergusson dined here with Mr. Laidlaw. I wrote all the morning then cut some wood. I think the weather gets too warm for hard work with the axe or I get too stiff and easily tired.

30 MONDAY Went to Jedburgh to Circuit where found my old friend and schoolfellow D. Monypenny. Nothing to-day but a pack of riff-raff cases of petty larceny and trash. Dined as usual with the Judge[6] and slept at My old friend Mr. Shortreed's.

MAY

1 TUESDAY Brough[t] Andrew Shortreed[7] to copy some things I want. Maxpopple came with us as far as Lessudden and we stopd and

1. See p. 157, note 3.
2. *As You Like It*, ii. 1.
3. *Misc. Prose Works*, vol. iv.
4. Scott's Introduction to *Border Antiquities of England and Scotland*, 1814–17.
5. On 2 May Scott wrote again to Ballantyne, 'the *third* time of asking', to get his opinion of the article on the Culloden Papers which he had written for the *Quarterly* in January 1816. *Letters*, x. 199. It appears in vol. xx of the *Misc. Prose Works*.
6. That is, with David Monypenny, now Lord Pitmilly.
7. Scott had arranged by a letter of 27 April (Shortreed Papers) to take 'the young printer back to Abbotsford', where he intended him to transcribe either the 'Border Antiquities', or the 'Culloden Papers' for the *Misc. Prose Works*. 2 May 1827, Disc. i. 131. Shortreed had been trained by Ballantyne, but was unemployed for the moment. Scott later found him a place in London.

made a pilgrimage to Fair Maiden Lilliard's stone,[1] which has been restored lately to the credit of Mr. Walker of Muirhouselaw. Set my young clerk to work when we came home and did some laborious business. A Letter from Sir Thomas Lawrence informd me I am chosen Professor of Antiquities to the Royal Academy – A beautiful professor to be sure.

2 WEDNESDAY Did nothing but proofs this morning: at ten went to Selkirk to arrange about the new measures[2] which like all new things will throw us into confusion for a little at least. The weather was so exquisitely good that I walkd after tea to half past eight and enjoyd a sort of half lazy half sulky humour – like Caliban's – *There's wood enough within*.[3] Well I may be the Bear but I must mount the ragged[4] staff all the same. Got my quarter's salary in Exchequer and paid away great part. I set my myself to labour for R P G. The Germanic horrors are my theme and I think something may be yet made of them.[5]

Salaries	£149
Anne to mourning	£30
To House	25
To taxes to Mr Curle	36
	£91
Ball	£58
T. Purdie	20
	38

1. The stone marks the site of the Battle of Ancrum Moor, where Maiden Lilliard fell fighting to avenge the death of her lover in 1545. Shortreed describes their pilgrimage in a letter to his brother: 'As I had never seen Fair Maiden Lillyard's grave Sir Walter proposed that we shd leave the carriage and walk to it which was of course acceded to – He was pleased to find a large stone, tho' of uncouth shape and wretched sculpture erected since he had last visited the spot . . . he said he was glad to see the stone put up at all as it would mark a spot which many people would like to see and which few would otherwise be able soon to point out and besides it showed a spirit in the people to preserve the traces of former days which was very commendable. "I will speak to [Mr. Walker] (the farmer of the place) the first time I see him and thank him for having done it." . . . Standing here he described the Battle of Ancrum Moor to me pointing out the positions of the different troops – in what manner the two armies moved & pointing out the probable rising ground which concealed Buccleuch from the unsuspecting enemy.' 2–4 May 1827, Shortreed Papers.
2. The reorganization of the Sheriff Courts with a staff of properly qualified judges and officials was initiated by an Act of Parliament in 1825 (6 Geo. IV, cap. 23) and details would still remain to be settled in 1827.
3. *The Tempest*, i. 2.
4. *2 Henry Vi*, v. 1.
5. Scott's review of Hoffmann's novels, written to help Gillies, appeared in his *Foreign Quarterly Review* later this year.

3 THURSDAY An early visit from Mr. Thomas Stewart, Nephew of Duchess of Wellington, with a letter from his aunt. He seems a well behaved and pleasant young man. I walkd him through the Glen and returnd by the [lake]. Colonel Fergusson came to help us out at dinner and then we had our wine and wassail.

4 FRIDAY Corrected proofs in the morning. Mr. Stewart still here which prevented work; however I am far before hand with every thing. We walkd a good deal – Asked Mr. Alexr. Pringle, Whitebank, to dinner. This is rather losing time though.

5 SATURDAY Workd away upon these wild affairs of Hoffmann for Gillies. I think I have forgot my German very much, and then the stream of criticism does not come freely at all, I cannot tell why. I gave it up in despair at halfpast one and walkd out. Had a letter from R. P. G. He seems in spirits about his work. I wish it may answer. Under good management it certainly might. But – Maxpopple came to dinner[1] and Mr. Laidlaw after dinner so that broke up a day which I can ill spare. Mr. Stewart left us this day.

6 SUNDAY Wrought again at Hoffmann,[2] infructuously I fear, unwillingly I am certain, but how else can I do a little good in my generation? I will try a walk. I would fain catch myself in good humour with my task but that will not be easy.

	£38
Bogie	10
	28
Shillinglaw	12
	16
Sent Mr. Laidlaw	5
	£11

7 MONDAY Finishd Hoffman *talis qualis*.[3] I don't like it. But then I have been often displeased with things that have proved successful. Our own labours become disgusting in our eyes from the ideas having been turnd over and over in our own minds – to others to whom they are presented for

1. Shortreed has left his account of the conversation at dinner – riots in the London theatres in the 1790s, Scott's lack of success at the Bar, and border feuds, on which 'he gave a free swing to his prejudices and family pride'. Shortreed, 5–9 May 1827, Shortreed Papers.

2. A better alternative than 'the inaudibleness of old Mr. Thomson and the consequent inattentiveness of his congregation' suffered by the rest of the household. In the evening Shortreed hoped for the pleasure of 'hearing Sir Walter read a Sermon (which he is wont to do on Sundays). But I was disappointed for he retired to his study immediately after Tea and did not return till supper was announced.' Ibid.

3. 'Such as it is'.

the first time they have a show of novelty. God grant it may prove so. I would help the poor fellow if I could for I am poor myself.

8 TUESDAY Corrected Hoffmann with a view to send him off, which however I could not accomplish. I finishd a criticism on Defoe's writings. His great forte is his power of Vraisemblance.[1] This I have instanced in the story of Mrs. Veale's ghost. Ettrick Shepherd[2] arrived.

9 WEDNESDAY This day we went to dinner at Mr. Scroope's at the Pavilion where were the Haigs of Bemerside, Isaac Haig, Mr. and Mrs. Bainbridge etc. Warm dispute whether Parr are or are not salmon trout –

Fleas are not lobsters–d—n their souls.[3]

Mr. Scroope has made a painting of Tivoli which when mellowd a little by time will be a fine one. Letters from Lockhart with news concerning the beautiful mess they are making in London. Henry Scott will be threatend in Roxburghshire. This would be bad policy as it would drive the young Duke[4] to take up his ground, which unless pressd he may be in no hurry to do. Personally I do not like to [be] driven to a point as I think Canning may do much for the country providing he does not stand committed to his new Whig counsellors. But if the push does come I will not quit my old friends – *that* I am freely resolved and *dissolutely* as Slender says.[5]

10 THURSDAY We went to breakfast at Huntly Burn and I wanderd all the morning in the woods to avoid an English party who came to see the House. When I came home I found my Cousin Col. Russell and his Sister so I had no work to-day but my labour at proofs in the morning. To-day I dismiss my Aid-de-camp Shortreed, a fine lad but a little forward. The Boar of the forest left us after breakfast. Had a present of a medal[6] forming one of a series from Chantrey's busts.

1. This seems to be the first appearance of the word in English, four years before the Introduction to *Quentin Durward*, 1831, recorded by the *O. E. D.*
2. James Hogg. 'His friend Mr. Laidlaw was sent for but as he had already got dinner he came after ours.' Shortreed, 5–9 May 1827, Shortreed Papers.
3. 'Sir Joseph Banks and the boiled Fleas' in Peter Pindar's *Works*.
4. The Duke of Buccleuch.
5. *Merry Wives of Windsor*, i. 1.
6. Designed by T. Stothard, R. A.

But this is not for nothing: the donor wants a mottoe for the reverse of the King's Medal. I am a bad hand to apply to.

11 FRIDAY Hogg calld this morning to converse about trying to get him on the pecuniary list of the Royal Literary Society.[1] Certainly he deserves it if genius and necessity could do so. But I do not belong to the Society nor do I propose to enter it as a coadjutor. I don't like your Royal Academies of this kind; they almost always fall into jobs and the Members are seldom those which do credit to the literature of a country. It affected too to comprehend those men of Letters who are specially attachd to the crown and, though [I] love and honour my king as much as any of them can, yet I hold it best in this free country to preserve the exterior of independence that my loyalty may be the more impressive and tell more effectually. Yet I wish sincerely to help poor Hogg; and have written to Lockhart about it[2] – It may be my own desolate feelings, it may be the apprehension of evil from this political hocus pocus, but I have seldom felt more moody and uncomfortable than while writing these lines. I have walkd too but without effect. W. Laidlaw whose very ingenious mind is delighted with all novelties talkd nonsense about the new government in which men are to resign principle, I fear, on both sides.

12 SATURDAY Wrote Lockhart on what I think the upright and honest principle and am resolved to vex myself no more about it.[3] Walkd with my cousin Colonel Russell for three hours in the woods and enjoyd the sublime and delectable pleasure of being wise and listened to, on the subject of my favourite themes of laying out ground and plantation – Russell seems quite to follow such an excellent authority and my spirits mounted while I found I was haranguing to a willing and patient pupil. To be sure Ashestiel, planting the high knowes and drawing woodland through the pasture, could be made one of the most beautiful forest things in the world. I have often dreamd of putting it in high order and judging from what I

1. The Royal Society of Literature (founded in 1823) elected ten Associates to pensions of a hundred guineas. 'When such things are going,' writes Hogg, 'it is as good to put one's self in the way of them if practicable.' 28 January 1827, Walpole.

2. See *Letters*, x. 208. Scott was reluctant to approach the Society himself for fear that they would again ask him to join them.

3. Scott's advice is that Lockhart should accept any situation offered to him by Canning only after making his position clear: 'you must be understood before laying yourself under a personal obligation to reserve your right of withholding your support or expressing your disapprobation should your duty as a public journalist render this necessary'. *Letters*, x. 205.

have been able to do here I think I should have succeeded. At any rate
my Blue Devils are flown at the sense of entertaining some sort of
consequence – Lord, what fools We are –

13 SUNDAY A most idle and dissipated day, I did not rise till half past
eight o'clock. Col. and Capt. Fergusson came to breakfast. I walkd
half way home with them, then turnd back and spent the day, which
was delightful, wandering from place to place in the woods, sometimes reading the new and interesting volumes of *Cyril Thornton*,[1]
sometimes chewing the cud of sweet and bitter fancy[2] which
strangely alternated in my mind idly stirred by the succession of a
thousand vague thoughts and fears, the gay thoughts strangely
mingled with those of dismal melancholy tears which seemd ready
to flow unbidden, smiles which approachd to those of insanity, all
that wild variety of mood which solitude engenders. I scribbled some
verses or rather composed them in my memory. The contrast at
leaving Abbotsford to former departures is of an agitating and violent
description.

Assorting papers and so forth. I never could help admiring the
concatenation between Achitophel's setting his house in order and
hanging himself.[3] The one seems to me to follow the other as a matter
of course. I don't mind the trouble though my head swims with it. I
do not mind meeting accompts which unpaid remind you of your
distress or paid serve to show you you have been throwing away
money you would be glad to have back again. I do not mind the
strange contradictory mode of papers hiding themselves that you
wish to see and others thrusting themselves into your hand to confuse
and bewilder you. There is a clergyman's letter about the Scottish
pronunciation to which I had written an answer some weeks since
(the parson is an ass by the bye). But I had laid aside my answer,
being unable to find the letter which bore his address. And in the
course of this day both his letter with the address and my answer
which wanted the address fell into my hands half a dozen times but
separately always. This was the positive malice of some Hobgoblin
and I submit to it as such. But what frightens and disgusts me is those
fearful letters from those who have been long dead to those who

1. *The Youth and Manhood of Cyril Thornton* by Captain Thomas
   Hamilton (Scott's neighbour at Chiefswood), 1827.
2. *As You Like It*, iv. 3.
3. 'And when Ahithophel saw that his counsel was not followed, he
   saddled his ass, and arose, and gat him home to his house, to
   his city, and put his household in order, and hanged himself.'
   2 Samuel 17: 23.

linger on their wayfare through this Valley of tears. These fine lines of Spenser came into my head

> 'When Midnight o'er the pathless skies.'

Aye and can I forget the Author, the frightful moral of his own vision.[1] What is this world? – A dream within a dream – as we grow older each step is an awakening. The youth awakes as he thinks from childhood – the full grown man despises the pursuits of youth as a visionary – the old man looks on manhood as a feverish dream – The Grave the last sleep? – no it is the last and final awakening.

14 MONDAY To town per Blucher coach, well stewd and crushd, but saved cash, coming off for less than £2; posting costs nearly five and you don't get on so fast by one third. Arrived in my old lodgings[2] here with a stouter heart than I expected. Dined with Mr. and Mrs. Skene, and met Lord Medwyn and Lady.

Cash	£14
Anne	£5
Journey	2
Churches	1
Dalgleish	1
	9
	2
	15

15 TUESDAY Parliament House a queer sight. Lookd as if people were saying to each other the noble song of The Sky's falling Chickie diddle. Thinks I to myself, I'll keep a calm sough.

> Betwixt both sides I unconcerned stand by.
> Hurt can I laugh and honest need I cry?[3]

I wish the old government had kept together but their personal dislike to Canning seems to have renderd that impossible. I dined at a great dinner given by Sir George Clerk to his electors, the freeholders of Mid Lothian; a great attendance of Whig and Tory huzzaing each other's toasts. *If* is a good peace maker[4] but quarter-day is a better. I have a guess the best game-cocks would call a truce if a handful or two of oats were scatterd among them.

1. The quotation is from 'The Visionary' whose 'Visions of long-departed joys' Scott applies to W. R. Spencer's own case. The grandson of the Duke of Marlborough and a brilliant writer of *vers de societé*, he was now living the life of a miserable bankrupt abroad. Scott met him in Paris on 2 November 1826.
2. 3 Walker Street. Scott had taken the house only for the winter, intending to economize by going into lodgings or to the Albyn Club for the summer. This project went the way of many of his other economies, and Cadell (upon whom Scott increasingly relied) had taken a two-month lease of Walker Street for him. *Letters*, x. 186 and 193.
3. Prior's Democritus and Heraclitus, ll. 5–6.
4. *As You Like It*, v. 4.

16 WEDNESDAY Received from Mr. Cadell £123 in completion of the sum of £500 of second advance by him on the tales[1]

Inde	———————	£123
Cash in purse		2
		125

Remitted to Anne for wages—	£100[2]		
Subscription at the Club £7, 7s. say	8		
Cissy at leaving us ———————	1		
Mr. Alex Ballantyne's interest £12. 10s. say	12	£121	Ball. £4.0.
A new cane, dues at Parliamt House Sundries ———————		2	
			£2.

Mr. John Gibson says the trustees are to allow my expence in travelling, £300 with £50 taken in in Longman's bill; this will place me *rectus in curia*[3] and not much more, faith. There is a fellow bawling out a ditty in the Street, the burthen of which is

> There's nothing but poverty every where.

He shall not be a penny richer for telling me what I know but too well without him.

17 THURSDAY By cash from Mr. Gibson in part of my

Expences going to [Paris]		£230
Off contents of a bill accepted for me to Longmans		50
		180
To Tom Purdie[4] ———————	£100	
To Dalgleish's wages ———————	25	
	——	125
Ball ———————		55
Cash in purse		2
		£57

1. Cadell had advanced £200 the previous November, £76. 18s. in February and £100 in March. Letters to Scott, f. 30.
2. In the form of a receipt to be cashed in Selkirk. 'You will send a careful person for the money and give it to Tom.' *Letters*, x. 214.
3. 'Right in the eyes of the law', the phrase being used here to mean, simply, that he will break even. He had borrowed £250 from Cadell for the journey to London and Paris. See the Entry for 8 October 1826.
4. Not for wages but 'for other purposes'. *Letters*, x. 214.

Learnd with great distress the death of poor Richard Lockhart the youngest brother of my son in law. He had an exquisite talent for acquiring languages and was under the patronage of my kinsman George Swinton[1] who had taken him into his own family at Calcutta and now he is drownd in a foolish bathing party.

From Mr Caddel to accot. Tales of my grand-father. . . £85
Cash to pay Mr. Rudge recd. in Jany.   85

18 FRIDAY Heard from Abbotsford all well. Wrought to-day but awkwardly. Tom Campbell calld warm from his Glasgow Rectorship;[2] he is looking very well. He seemd surprized that I did not know any thing about the contentions of Tories Whigs and Radicals in the great commercial City. I have other eggs on the spit. He staid but a few minutes.[3]

19 SATURDAY Went out to-day to Sir John Dalrymple's at Oxenford, a pretty place. The Lady[4] a daughter of Lord Duncan. Will Clerk and Robt. Graeme[5] went with me. A good dinner and pleasant enough party but ten miles going and ten miles coming make twenty and that is something of a journey. Got a headache too by jolting about after dinner.

20 SUNDAY Wrote a good deal at Appendix[6] or perhaps I should say tried to write – Got myself into a fever when I had finishd four pages and went out at eight o'clock at night to cool myself if possible. Walkd with difficulty as far as Skene's,[7] and there sate and got out of my

Cash in purse £57
Sent to Bogle   45
                £12

1. Swinton's letter to his cousin, who passed the news to Scott, was written on 16 January 1827. Walpole.
2. Students at the Scottish universities elected, and still elect, their own representative to the University Court. Thomas Campbell had just been installed for the second time as Rector at Glasgow; in 1829 he was elected for a third term after a tie with Scott (who had not wished to stand). *Letters*, xi. 40 and n.
3. A soaking on the way home from Court brought on 'the rheumatism in head and shoulders' and prevented Scott from dining with the Skenes. *Letters*, x. 215.
4. A sister of Lady Hamilton who had written to introduce Scott to Pozzo de Borgo in Paris. Entry for 5 October 1826.
5. An Edinburgh advocate and a member of the Council of the Bannatyne Club.
6. The Appendix to the *Life of Napoleon*.
7. The bare half-mile from Walker Street to the West End of Princes Street.

fidgetty feeling. Learnd that the Princes Street people intend to present me with the key of their gardens[1] which will be a great treat as I am too tender hoof'd for the stones. We must now get to work in earnest.

21 MONDAY Accordingly this day I wrought tightly and though not in my very best mood I got on in a very business like manner. Was at the Gas council where I found things getting poorly on. The Treasury have remitted us to Exchequer. The Committee want me to make private interest with the L. C. Baron. That I won't do – But I will state their cause publickly any way they like.

22 TUESDAY At court – home by two walking through the Princes Street Gardens for the first time. Called on Mrs. Jobson. Workd two hours. Must dress to dine at Mr. John Borthwick with the *young folk*, now Mr. and Mrs. Dempster. Kindly and affectionately received by our good young friends who seem to have succeeded to their parents' regard for me.

23 WEDNESDAY Got some books etc. which I wanted to make up the St. Helena affair. Set about making up the Appendix but found I had mislaid a number of the said postliminary affair. Recollected sendin[g] it to the press but Ballantyne for some time denied the whole affair. At length made him understand what I wanted. Had Hogg's nephew here as a transcriber, a modest and well behaved young man – clever too I think.[2] Being Teind Wednesday I was not obliged to go to the court and am now *bang up* and shall soon finish Mr. Nappy – And how then? – Aye marry, sir, that's the question.

Cash in purse	£12
House	6
	£6
Charity	1
	£5 0. 0.

> Lord, what will all the people say,
> Mr. Mayor, Mr. Mayor.[3]

The fires of lowest hell fold in the people – as Coriolanus says – I live not in their report I hope.[4]

---

1. Scott was privileged: keys usually cost three guineas a year. For the Gardens and Skene's part in laying them out, see the Entry for 23 January 1826 and note.
2. Robert Hogg worked in Ballantyne's printing house. His recollections of Scott's fluent dictation and of his apparent ability to speak one sentence while composing the next are printed in *Life*, ix. 115.
3. Unidentified, but also quoted in *Letters*, vii. 335 and viii. 231.
4. *Coriolanus*, iii. 3.

24 THURSDAY Mr. Gibson paid me £70 more expences of my London journey. A good thought came in my head to write stories for little Johnie Lockhard from the History of Scotland[1] like those taken from the History of England. I will not write mine quite so simply as Croker has done.[2] I am persuaded both children and the lower class of readers hate books which are written *down* to their capacity and love those that are more composed for their elders and betters. I will make if possible a book that a child will understand yet a man will feel some temptation to peruse should he chance to take it up. It will require however a simplicity of stile not quite my own. The Grand and interesting consists in ideas not in words. A clever thing of this kind will have a run.

Cash	£70
Sent to Bogie —	45
	25
Cash in purse	5
	30
Dalgleish	2
	£28

25 FRIDAY

> Little to say
> But wrought away
> And went out to dine with the Skenes to-day.

Rather too many dinner engagements on my list. Must be hard hearted. I cannot say I like my solitary days the worst by any means. I dine when I like on soup or broth and drink a glass of porter or ginger beer – a single tumbler of Whisky and water concludes the debauch. This agrees with me charmingly. At ten o'clock bread and cheese, a single draught of small beer, porter or ginger beer, and to bed.

26 SATURDAY I went the same dull and weary round. Out to the Parlt. House which bothers one's brains for the day – nevertheless I get on, pages vanish from under my hand and find their way to J. Ballantyne who is grinding away with his presses. I think I may say now the dust raised about me by so many puzzling little facts I begin to get rid of, and then it is plain sailing to the [end]. Dined at Skene's with George Forbes and Lady but that was yesterday.

27 SUNDAY I got duckd in coming home from the court.[3] Naboclish. I thank thee, *pat*, for teaching me the word.[4] Made a hard day of it.

---

1. This is the genesis of *Tales of a Grandfather*, which was published before the end of the year.
2. J. W. Croker's *Stories from the History of England*, 1817.
3. This sentence must refer to the day before, as the Court did not of course sit on Sundays.
4. *Merchant of Venice*, iv. 1.

Scarce stird from one room to another but at bedtime finishd a handsome handful of Copy. I have quoted Gourgaud's evidence. I suppose he will be in a rare passion and may be addicted to vengeance like a long moustachoed son of a French bitch as he is.[1] Naboclish again for that

> Frenchman Devil or Don
> Damn him let him come on
> He shan't scare a son of the Island.[2]

28 MONDAY Another day of uninterrupted study; two such would finish the work with a murrain. I have several engagements next week. I wonder how I was such a fool as to take them. I think I shall be done however before Saturday.[3] What shall I have to think of when I lie down at night and awake in the morning? What will be my plague and my pastime? my curse and my blessing as ideas come and the pulse rises or as they flag and some thing like a snow haze covers my whole imagination. I have my highland tales[4] – and then – never mind, sufficient for the day is the evil thereof.[5]

29 TUESDAY Detaind at the house[6] till near three – made a call on Mrs. Jobson and others, also went down to the printing office. I hope James Ballantyne will do well. I think and believe he will. Wrought in the evening.

30 WEDNESDAY Having but a trifle on the roll to-day I set hard to work and brought myself in for a holyday or rather playd truant. At 2 o'clock went to a Mr. Mackenzie in my old house at Castle Street to have some touches given to Walker's print.[7] Afterwards having young Hogg with me as an amanuensis I took to the oar till near ten o'clock.

31 THURSDAY Being a court-day I was engaged very late. Then I calld at the Printing House but got not exact calculation how we

1. This prophecy proved true. For Gourgaud's wrath and the possibility of a duel with Scott see the Entries from 27 August to 17 September 1827 in particular.
2. 'The Snug Little Island', song by Thomas Dibdin.
3. *Napoleon* was not in fact finished until 7 June.
4. *Chronicles of the Canongate*.
5. St. Matthew 6: 34.
6. Parliament House.
7. The engraving from Raeburn's portrait mentioned in the Entry of 16 June 1826.

come on. Met Mr. Caddell who bids as the author's copy 1/- profit on each book of Hugh Littlejohn.[1] I thought this too little; my general calculation is on such profits that, supposing the book to sell to the public for 7/6, the price ought to go in three shares, on[e] to the Trade, one to the expence of print and paper, and one to the bookseller[2] and publisher between them, which of course would be 1/3 not 1/- to the author. But in stating this rule I omitted to observe that book[s] for young persons are half bound before the[y] go into the trade. This comes to about 9d per two volumes. The allowance[s] to the trade are also heavy so that 1/- per book is very well on great numbers. There may besides be a third volume. – Dined at James Ballantyne and heard his brother Sandie sing and play on the violin beautifully as usual. James himself sang the 'Reel of Tullochgorum' with hearty cheer and uplifted voice. When I came home I learnd that we had beat the Coal Gas Company which is a sort of triumph.[3]

JUNE

1 FRIDAY Settled my household book. Sophia does not set out till the middle of the week, which is unluck[y], our antiquarian skirmish beginning in Fife[4] just about the time she is to arrive. Letter from John touching public affairs; don't half like them and am afraid we shall have the Whig alliance turn out like the calling in of the Saxons. I told this to Jeffery who said they would convert us as the Saxons did the British. I shall die in my Paynimrie for one. I don't like a bone of them as a party. Ugly reports of the King's health – God pity this poor country

Cash to Clarkson £12	
To house	5
	17
Cash in purse	28
	11

should that be so but I think it a thing devised by the enemy. Anne arrived from Abbotsford. I dined at Sir Robert Dundas's with Mrs. Dundas, Arniston, and other friends. Workd a little, not much.

2 SATURDAY Do. Do – Dined at Baron Hume's – These dinners are cruelly in the way but *que faut il faire*? The business of the court must be done and it is impossible absolutely to break off all habit of visiting. Besides, the correcting of proof sheets in itself is now become

1. That is, *Tales of a Grandfather*.
2. A slip for 'author'.
3. A short-lived one, however. Although a committee had decided in their favour, the decision was reversed by Parliament itself a few days later. See the note on pp. 805–6.
4. The annual meeting of the Blair-Adam Club.

burthensome. Three or four a day is hard work. Met Baron Clerk etc. at dinner.

3 SUNDAY Wrought hard. I think I have but a trifle more to do but new things cast up; we get beyond the life however for I have killd him to-day.[1] The newspapers are very saucy; the *Sun* says I have got £4000 for suffering a frenchman to look over my manuscript. Here is a proper fellow for you. I wonder what he thinks Frenchmen are

Cash in purse £11.0.0   made of – walking money-bags doubtless. Now
Sent to Bogie   10.0.0   as Sir Fretful Plagiary says, another man would
         £1   be vexd at this[2] but I care not one brass farthing.

4 MONDAY The Birthday of our good old King. It was wrong not to keep up the thing as it was of yore with dinners and claret and squibs and crackers and Saturnalia. The thoughts of the subjects require sometimes to be turnd to the Sovereign were it but only that they may remember there is such a person. The Banatyne edition of Melville's *Memoirs* is out and beats all print. Gad, it is a fine institution that, a rare one by Jove, beats the Roxburgh.[3] Wrought very bobbishly to-day but went off at dinner time to Thomas Thomson[4] where we had good cheer and good fun. By the way we have lost our Coal Gas bill.[5] Sorry for it but I can't cry. Calld on John Swinton and Henderson of Eldonhall.

5 TUESDAY Proofs. Parliament House till two. Commenced the character of Bonape. To-morrow being a teindday I will hope to get it finishd – meantime I go out to-night to see *Frankenstein*[6] at the theatre.

6 WEDNESDAY *Frankenstein* is entertaining for once; considerable art in the man that plays the Monster to whom he gave great effect. Cooper is his name; played excellently in the farce too as a sailor – a more natural one I think than my old friend Jack Bannister though he has not quite Jack's richness of humour. I had seven proof sheets to correct this morning by Goles. So I did not get to composition till

---

1. i.e. Scott has reached the death of Napoleon. *Life of Napoleon*, vol. ix, ch. 8.
2. Sheridan's *Critic*, i. 1.
3. The Roxburghe Club.
4. To celebrate the publication of Melville's *Memoirs* which Thomson had edited.
5. See the note on the affairs of the Oil Gas Coy. on pp. 805–6.
6. Mary Shelley's novel appeared in 1818.

nine, work on with little interruption (save that Mr. Verplanck, an American, breakfasted with us) untill seven, and then walkd, for fear of the black dog or devil that worries me when I work too hard.

7 THURSDAY This morning finished *Bony*. And now, as Dame Fortune says in Quevedo's *Visions*, Go, Wheel, and the Devil drive thee. I arranged with Mr. Cadell for the property of *Tales of a Grandfather* 10,000 copies for £787. 10.[1] Payable as Below

In present cash including £85 advanced	£105.0.0
At Lammas —————————	82 10
At Martinmas —————————	300
At 1st January —————————	300
—————	787 10 0

Cash in purse £21   It was high time I brought up some reinforce-
Sundries —— 1   ments for my pound was come to halfcrowns and I
Anne to House 10   had nothing to keep house when the Lockharts
In purse £10   come. Credit enough to be sure but I have been
taught by experience to make short reckonings. Some great authors now will think [it] a degradation to write a child's book – I cannot say I feel it such. It is to be inscribed to my grandson and I will write it not only without a sense of its being *infra dig.* but with a grandfather's pleasure.

8 FRIDAY A Mr. Maywood, much protected by poor Alaster Dhu,[2] brought me a letter from the late Col. Huxley. His connection and

1. Scott intended this money for himself, although strictly it ought to have gone to the Trust. 'Remember I do not mean to give you this little Book, I must keep it for myself to pay my Current expenses, and for my family', he told Gibson 'in a jocular manner'. After anxious deliberation the Trustees recorded that 'taking into view how largely the creditors have drawn and were continuing to draw from the treasures of his genius since his embarrassments came upon him, and the *high moral feeling* from which his great and productive exertions on their behalf spring, and how indispensably necessary it was both for his health and his spirits that he should continue to live in the same easy and comfortable style to which he had long been accustomed, the Trustees did not see it to be their duty to interfere with him in reference to the Works in question.' Sederunt Book, ii. 214–15. See also *Letters* x. 86.
2. Alexander Campbell (1764–1824), musician and teacher of music in Edinburgh, whose *Albyn's Anthology* (1816) Scott had praised. He had taught Scott.

approach to me is through the grave but I will not be the less disposed to assist him if an opportunity offers. I made a long round to-day, going to David Laing's about the forwarding the books of the Bannatyne Club to Sir George Rose and Duke of Buckingham. Then I came round by the Printing office where the presses are groaning upon *Napoleon* and so home through the gardens. I have done little to-day save writing a letter or two[1] for I was fatigued and sleepy when I go[t] home and nodded, I think, over Sir James Mellville's *Memoirs*. I will do something though when I have dine[d]. By the way I corrected the proofs for Gillies.[2] They read better than I lookd for.

9 SATURDAY Corrected proofs in the morning. When I came home from court I found that John Lockhart and Sophia were arrived at Porto Bello where they have a small lodging[3] by the steam boat. I went down with a bottle of champagne and a flask of Maraschino and made buirdly cheer with them for the rest of the day. Had the great pleasure to find them all in high health. Poor Johnie is decidedly improved in his general health and the injury on the spine is got no worse. Walter is a very fine child.

10 SUNDAY Rose with the odd consciousness of being free of my daily task. I have heard that the fishwomen go to church of a sunday

1. Possibly the letter to the Duke of Buckingham (*Letters*, x. 219); the letter to Sir William Knighton accompanying the Bannatyne Club books destined for the King (*Letters*, x. 222); and the letter to Charles congratulating him on getting his degree (*Letters*, x. 221).
2. Of the article on Hoffmann's novels for the *Foreign Quarterly*.
3. The arrangement had caused some family strife. A London doctor had recommended sea-bathing for Johnnie; Sophia, therefore, insisted on the sea. Anne could not make her father agree to join them there: 'Nothing I can do will persuade Papa to *Live at* the sea. He says it is impossible for him to do that he wd. be wretched at the Sea side – in short he will *not do it*.' Anne to Sophia, 26 March 1827, Abbots. The compromise, suggested by Scott, of having Johnnie driven to the sea daily was rejected by Sophia, and the Lockharts took lodgings at 8 Melville Street in Portobello, which at that time was an independent town a few miles east of Edinburgh. Scott did not approve: 'The place is a stew pan in hot weather a watering pan in rainy weather and affords the accomodations of a piggery at all times when they might live at Abbotsford like a princess up to the ears in flowers and vegetables and as happy as a cow. There is no accounting for tastes.' *Letters*, x. 239.

with their creels new washd and a few stones in them for ballast just because they cannot walk steadily without their usual load. I feel some[what] like this and rather inclind to pick up some light task than to be altogether idle. I have my proof Sheets to be sure. But [what] are these to a whole day? Fortunately my thoughts are agreeable, cash difficulties etc. all provided for as far as I can see, so that we go on hooly and fairly.[1] Betwixt [now] and August 1st I should receive £750 and I cannot think I have more than the half of it to pay away. Cash to be sure seems to burn in my pockets.

> He wasna gien to great misguiding
> But coin his pouches wadna bide in.[2]

By goles this shall be corrected though –
   Lockhart gives a sad account of Gillies's imprudences.
   Lockhart dined with us[3] – day idle –

11 MONDAY The attendance on the committee and afterwards the Gnl Meeting of the Oil Gas Company took up my morning and the rest dribbled away in correcting proofs and trifling, reading among the rest an odd volume of *Vivian Grey*[4] – clever but not so much so as to make [me] in this sultry weather go up stairs to the drawing room to seek the other volumes. Ah villian, but you smoked when you read – Well, Madam, perhaps I think the better of the book for that reason. Made a blunder, went to Ravelstone[5] on the wrong day, this Anne's fault but I did not reproach her knowing it might as well have been my own.

12 TUESDAY At court a long hearing. Got home only about three. Corrected proofs etc. Dined with Baron Clerk and met several old friends. Will Clerk in particular.

13 WEDNESDAY Another long seat at Court. Almost overcome by the heat in walking home and renderd useless for the day. Let me be

---

1. 'Slowly and gently but steadily'. *S. N. D.*
2. Burns's 'On a Scotch Bard', ll. 43–4.
3. Not, however, a well-wined dinner. 'I was too late to get any save a single bottle which happend to be all in the House', Scott writes to Ballantyne inviting him to join them. 'Plenty of whiskey', he adds. *Letters*, x. 224.
4. By Disraeli, 1826–7.
5. To the Keiths.

thankful however: my lameness is much better and the nerves of my unfortunate ancle are so much strengthend that I walk with comparatively little pain. Dined at John Swinton's, a large party. These festive occasions consume much valuable time besides trying the stomach a little by late hours and some wine-shed – though that's not much.

14 THURSDAY Anne and Sophia dined – could not stay at home with them alone. We had the Skenes and Allan and amused ourselves till ten o'clock.

15 FRIDAY This being the day longsince appointed for our cruize to Fife, Thomas Thomson, Sir A. Fergusson, Willie Clerk, and I, set off with Miss Adam and made our journey successfully to Charlton[1] where were Ld. Chief Baron and Lord Ch. Commissioner all in the humour to be happy though time is telling with us all. Our good-natured host, Mr. A. Thompson, his wife and his goodlooking daughters, received us most kindly and the conversation took its old roll in spite of woes and infirmities. Charlton is a good house in the midst of highly cultivated land and immediatly surround[ed] with gar[d]ens and parterres together with plantations, partly in the old partly in the new taste. I like it very much though as a residence it is perhaps a little too much finishd. Not even a bit of bog to amuse one, as Mr. El[p]hinstone[2] said.

16 SATURDAY This day we went off in a body to St. Andrews, which Thomas Thomson had never seen. On the road beyond Charlton saw a small cottage said to have been the heritable appanage of a family called the King's [Cadger].[3] He had a right to feed his horse for a certain time on the adjoining pasturage. This functionary was sent to Falkland[4] with the fish for the royal table. The ruins[5] at St. Andrews have been lately cleard out. They had been chiefly magnificent from their size not their extent of ornament. I did not go up to Saint Rule's tower as on former occasions; this is a falling off for when before did I

1. This year, exceptionally, Anstruther Thomson of Charleton, William Adam's son-in-law, played host to the Blair-Adam Club.
2. Mountstuart Elphinstone the traveller, at this time Governor of Bombay.
3. 'James T. Davidson, in an article in the *Scots Magazine* for September 1939, shows convincingly that the word "Cadger" omitted by Scott, must be supplied.' Tait, p. 804.
4. Falkland Palace, Fife. For the Blair-Adam Club excursion there, see the Entry for 27 June 1829.
5. Of the cathedral.

remain sitting below when there was a steeple to be ascended? But the Rheumatism has begun to change that vein for some time past though I think this is the first decided sign of acquiescence in my lot. I sate down on a gravestone and recollected the first visit I made to St. Andrews now 34 years ago. What changes in my feeling and my fortune have since then taken place, some for the better, many for the worse. I rememberd the name[1] I then carved in runic characters on the turf beside the castle gate and I askd why it should still agitate my heart. But my friends came down from their tower and the foolish idea was chased away.

17 SUNDAY Lounged about while the good family went to Church. The day is rather cold and disposed to rain.

The papers say that the Corn bill is given up in consequence of the Duke of Wellington having carried the amendment[2] in the House of Lords. All the party here, Sir A. F. perhaps excepted, are Ministerialists on the present double bottom. They say the names of Whig and Tory are now to exist no longer – Why have they existed at all?

In the forenoon we morriced off to explore the environs; we visited two ancient Manor houses, those of Ely[3] and Balcaskie. Large roomy mansions with good apartments, two or three good portraits, and a collection of most extraordinary frights prodigiously like the mistresses of King George I. who came for all the goods and chattells of old England. There are at Ely House two most ferocious looking Ogresses of this cast. There are noble trees about the house. Balcasky put me in mind of poor Philip Anstruther, dead and gone many a long year since. He was a fine gallant lighthearted young sailor. I remember the story of his drawing on his father for some cash, which produced an angry letter from old Sir Robert to which Philip replied that if he did [not] know how to write like a gentleman he did not desire any more of his correspondence. Balcasky is much dilapidated but they are restoring the house in the good old stile with its terraces and yew hedges. The beastly fashion of bringing a bare ill sheard park up to your very door seems going down. We next visited with great pleasure the church of Saint Monans which is under a repair[4]

1. The name was that of Williamina Belsches, to whom Scott proposed in 1795. See the Entry for 18 December 1825.
2. The Bill was wrecked by the Duke's amendment that 'no foreign corn in bond should be taken out of bond until the average price of corn should have reached 66*s.*'
3. i.e. Elie.
4. The architect renovating St. Monance Church was Burn, and the cost (nearly £1400) was borne by the Anstruther family. *Blair-Adam Estate*, Introduction, p. xxiii.

designd to correspond strictly with the ancient plan which is the solid gloomy but impressive Gothic. It was built by David the 2d in the fullfilment of a vow made to St. Monans on the field of battle at Neville's Cross. One would have judged the king to be thankful for small mercies, for certainly Saint Monance proved but an ineffective patron.[1]

Mr. Hugh Cleghorn[2] dine[d] at Charlton and I saw him for the first time, having heard of him all my life. He is an able man, has seen much and speaks well, but Age has clawd him in his clutch[3] and he has become deaf. There is also Captain Black of the navy, Second Lieutenant of the Mars at Trafalgar. Villeneuve was brought on board that ship after the debate. He had no expectation that the British fleet would have fought till they had formd a regular line. Capt. Black disowns the idea of the French and Spaniards being drawn up chequer form for resisting the British attack and imputes the appearance of that array to sheer accident of weather.

18 MONDAY We visited Wemyss Castle on our return to Kinghorn. On the left before descending to the coast are considerable remains of a castle calld popularly the old Castle or MacDuff's Castle. That of the Thane was situated at Kennochquay at no great distance. The front of Wemyss castle to the land has been stripd entirely of its castellated appearance and narrowly escaped a new front. To the sea it has a noble situation overhanging the red rocks but even there the structure has been much modernized and tamed. Interior is a good old house with large oak staircases, family pictures, etc. We were received by Captn. Wemyss, a gallant sea Captain, who could talk against a Northwester – by his wife Lady Emma and her sister Lady Isabella – beautiful women of the House of Errol and vindicating its title to the '*handsome Hays*'.[4] We reachd the Pettycur about half past one, crossd to Edinburgh and so ended our little excursion. Of casualties we had only one – Triton the Housedog at Charlton threw down

Cash ———		£10
Paid carriage	£4	
Will Clerk	2	
Sundries	1	
		——
		7
		3

1. David II of Scotland was defeated in the battle, which took place in 1346, and was imprisoned in the Tower of London.
2. Hugh Cleghorn of Stravithie, now seventy-seven, the traveller and adventurer who annexed Ceylon to the British Empire and is thought to have been the original of Buchan's professor in *The Free Fishers*. See *The Cleghorn Papers*, 1827.
3. *Hamlet*, v. 1.
4. 'Lady Emma had provided an elegant repast for us on our return from the sea-shore. But time and tide, which waiteth for

Thomson and he had his wrist spraind. A restive horse threatend to demolish our Landau but we got off for the fright. Happily L. C. B.[1] was not in our carriage.

Dined at William McKenzie's to meet the Marquis and Marchioness of Stafford who are on their road to Dunrobin.[2] Found them both very well.

19 TUESDAY Lord Stafford desires to be a member of the Bannatyne club – also Colin M'Kenzie. Sent both names up accordingly.[3] The day furnishes a beggarly record of trumpery. From 8 o'Clock till 9 wrote letters – then Parliament House where I had to wait on without any thing to do till near two when rain forced me into the Antiquarian Musæum.[4] Lounged there till a meeting of the Oil Gas Committee at three o'clock. There remaind till near five. Home and smoked a cheroot after dinner. Calld on Thomson who is still disabled by his sprain. *Pereat inter hæc.*[5] We must do better tomorrow.

20 WEDNESDAY Kept my word, being Teind Wednesday. Two young Frenchmen, friends of Gallois, rather interrupted me. I had askd them to breakfast but they staid till twelve o'clock, which is scarce fair, and plagued me with Compliments. Their names are Remusat and Guizard,[6] pleasant goodhumourd young men. Notwithstanding this interruption I finishd near six pages, three being a good Session-day's work. *Allons vogue la galere.* Dined at the Solicitor's[7] with Lord Hopetoun and a parliament House party.

no man, compelled us to do what would have been rudeness in the extreme, if it had not been that necessity has no law, even in politeness; so we took a hasty leave of one of the most beauteous of her sex, and hurried off, unlunched, to Pettycur Harbour.' *Blair-Adam Estate*, Introduction, p. xxiv.

1. Lord Chief Baron Sir Samuel Shepherd.
2. Dunrobin Castle in Sutherlandshire.
3. They were elected the following February after the Club had decided to increase its membership to 100. Bannatyne Club Minutes.
4. In the rooms at the foot of the Mound.
5. Tait suggests that this is a reminiscence of Horace's *perditur haec inter misero lux*, 'this light is lost amidst misery', which Scott quotes in *Letters*, xii. 359.
6. Douglas identifies them as Charles de Rémusat, later Minister for Foreign Affairs, and M. de Guizard, later Director-General of the École des Beaux-Arts.
7. John Hope's.

21 THURSDAY Finishd five leaves[1] – that is betwixt morning and dinnertime. The Court detaind me till two o'clock. About nine leaves will make the volume quite large enough. I have not those damnd Spankers of *Napoleon* to furnish. By the way the booksellers have taken courage to print up 2000 more of the first edition which after the second volume they curtaild from 8000 to 6000.[2] This will be £1000 more in my way at least and that is a good help. We dine with the Skenes to-day, Lockhart being with us.

22 FRIDAY Wrought in the morning as usual. Receivd to breakfast Dr. Bishop, a brother of Bishop the Composer. He tells me his brother was very ill when he wrote 'The Chough and Crow' and other music for *Guy Mannering*. Singular, but I do think illness if not too painful unseals the mental – eye and renders the talents more acute – in the study of the fine arts at least.[3]

I find the difference on 2000 additional copies will be £3000 instead of £1000 in favour of the author My good friend Publicum is impatient. Heaven grant his expectations be not disappointed. *Coragio andiamos*! Such another year of labour and success would do much towards making me a free man of the forest. But I must to work since we have to dine with Lord and Lady Gray. By the way I forgot an engagement to my old friend Lord Justice clerk.[4] This is shockingly ill bred. But the invitation was a month old and that is some defence.

23 SATURDAY I corrected proofs and playd the grandfather in the morning. After Court saw Lady Wedderburn who askd my advice about printing some verses of Mrs. Heman[s] in honour of the late Lord James Murray who died in Greece. Also Lord Gray who wishes me to write some preliminary matter to his ancestor the Mr of Gray's correspondence.[5] I promised – But [his] ancestor was a

1. Of 'The Two Drovers', the last story in vol. i of *Chronicles of the Canongate*.
2. The decision to reduce the impression of the *Life of Napoleon* to 6000 was taken in April 1826 on the advice of Cadell and Ballantyne, who were anxious not to repeat old mistakes. 'In consequence of Constable's furious over-printing, not less than Fifty Thousand pounds worth of Waverly Novels, and Sir W. Scott's works, are at this good hour on hand!' wrote Ballantyne on 5 April 1826. Walpole.
3. Scott spoke from experience. *The Bride of Lammermoor, A Legend of Montrose,* and *Ivanhoe* were composed while he was in acute pain. See *Life*, vi. 87.
4. David Boyle.
5. *Letters and Papers relating to Patrick, Master of Gray* was published in 1835, edited not by Scott but by Thomas Thomson.

great rogue and if I am to write about him at all I must take my will of him. Anne and I dined at home. She went to the play and I had some mind to go too. But Miss Foote was the sole attraction and Miss Foote is only a very pretty woman and if she playd Rosalind better than I think she can it is a bore to see Touchstone and Jacques murderd. I have a particular respect for *As You Like It*. It was the first play I ever saw and that was at Bath in 1776 or 1777. That is not yesterday yet I remember the piece very well. So I remaind at home, smoked a segar, and workd leisurely upon the Review of the Cullodden papers which by dint of vamping and turning may make up the lacking copy for the works better, I think, than that lumbering Essay on Border Antiquities.

Received cash in part of salary		£150
Miss Fergusson's Interest	£73	
Tom Purdie	20	
Anne to household	25	
Sundries	1	
		124
		26
Cash in purse		2
		£28

Cash in purse £28

24 SUNDAY I don't care who knows it, I was lazy this morning. But I cheated my laziness capitally as you shall hear. My good friend Sir Watt, said I to my esteemd friend, it is hard you should be obliged to work when you are so disinclined to it. Were I you I would not be quite idle though. I would do something that you are not obliged to do, just as I [have] seen a cowardly dog willing to fight with any one save that which his master would have desired him to yoke with. So I went over the Review of the Culloden papers and went a great way to convert it into the Essay on Clanship etc. which I intend for the *Prose Works*. I wish I had thought of it before correcting that beastly border Essay. Naboclish!

25 MONDAY Wrote five pages of the *Chronicles* and hope to conquer one or two more ere night to fetch up the lee-way. Went and saw Allan's sketch of a picture for Abbotsford which is promising, a thing on the plan of Watteau. He intends to introduce some interesting characters and some I sus-pect who have little business there. Yesterday

Cash in purse	£28
from Mr Cadell	25
	£53
Bill to Charles	50
Ball.	3

I dined with the Lockharts at Porto Bello. To-day at home with Anne and Miss Erskine.[1] They are gone to walk. I have a mind to go to trifle. So I do not promise to write more to-night having begun the dedication (advertizement I mean) to the *Chronicles*. I have pleasant subjects of reflection. The fund in Gibson's hands will approach £40,000[2] I think.

Lord Melville writes desiring to be a candidate for the Bannatyne Club.[3]

I made a balance of my affairs and stuck it into my book. It should answer very well. But still

> I am not given to great misguiding
> But coin my pouches will na bide in
> With me it neer was under hiding
> I dealt it free. −[4]

I must however and will be independent.

26 TUESDAY

> Well if ever I saw such another thing since
> my mother bound up my head
> Here is nine of clock stricken and I am still
> fast asleep a bed.[5]

I have not done the like of this many a day. However it cannot be helpd. Went to court which detaind me till two o'clock. A walk home consumed the hour to three. I wrote in the court however to the Duke of Wellington[6] and Lord Bloomfield and that is a good job over.

I have a letter from Lord Melville desiring to be a member of the Bannatyne Club. Memorandm.

1. Lord Kinneddar's daughter was a close friend of Anne's. She had been staying at Abbotsford when Shortreed was there in early May. 5–9 May 1827, Shortreed Papers.
2. It was £36,000, nearly sufficient to pay 6s. 8d. in the pound. *Letters*, x. 266 n.
3. Scott wrote on this day to Cadell asking him to add Melville's name to the list of those to receive presents of the *Life of Napoleon*, his memory jogged perhaps by Melville's letter. *Letters*, x. 232. He was elected to the Club on 9 February 1828.
4. Burns's 'On a Scotch Bard gone to the West Indies', ll. 43–6.
5. A reminiscence of Swift's 'Mary the Cook-Maid's Letter'.
6. Probably a covering note for the *Life of Napoleon* which the Duke acknowledges having received on 2 July. Walpole.

A letter from a member of the Commission of the psalmody of the Kirk, zealous and pressing[1] – I shall answer him I think.

One from Sir James Stewart, on fire with Corfe Castle, with a drawing of King Edward occupying one page as he hurries down the steep mortally wounded by the assassin. Singular power of speaking at once to the eye and the ear. Dined at home. After dinner sorted papers – rather idle.

27 WEDNESDAY Corrected proofs and wrote till breakfast. Then the court. Calld on Skene and Chas. K. Sharpe and did not get home untill three o'clock and then so wet as to require a total change. We dine at Hector Buchanan Macdonald's where there is sometimes many people and little conversation. Sent a little chest of books by the carrier to Abbotsford.

A visit from a smart young man, Gustavus Schwab of Koenigsberg. He gives a flattering picture of Prussia, which is preparing for freedom. The King must keep his word though or the people may chance to tire of waiting.

Dined at Hector B. Macdonald's with rather a young party for Colin McKenzie and me.

28 THURSDAY Wrote a little and corrected proofs. How many things have I unfinishd at present?

Primo. *Chronicles* — 1st. volume not ended.

Do.——— Second vol. begun.

Introduction to Do.

Tales of my Grandfather.

Essay on Highlands,[2] this unfinishd owing to certain causes chiefly want of papers and books to fill up blanks which I will get at Abbotsford. Came home through rain about two and commissiond John Stevenson to call at three about binding some books. Dined with Sophia; visited on invitation a fine old little commodore Trunnion who, in reading a part of Napoleon's history with which he had himself been interested as commanding a flottilla,

1. The Revd. Charles McCombie, aged twenty-three, a member of the Church of Scotland Committee 'for the improving of the Psalmody', wanted Scott to rewrite all the Scottish metrical psalms. Despite the hopes of immortality which he held out – 'the melodies in which they rejoice on earth will not be forgotten – will be sung – in heaven' – Scott remained a traditionalist and declined to interfere. 2 June 1827, Walpole. See also the Entry for 29 May 1828.

2. Review of the 'Culloden Papers', rehandled for the *Prose Works*.

thought he had detected a mistake, but was luckily mistaken to my great delight.[1]

– I fear thee, ancient Mariner – [2]

To be crossexamined by those who have seen the true thing is the devil. And yet these eye witnesses are not all right in what they repeat neither – indeed cannot be so – since you will have dozens of contradictions in their statements.

29 FRIDAY A distressing letter from Haydon – imprudent probably, but who has not [been], and a man of rare genius. What a pity I gave that £10 to Craig. But I have plenty of ten pounds sure[3] and I may make it something better. I will get £100 at furthest when I come back from the country. Wrote at proofs but no copy – I fear I shall wax fat and kick[4] against Madam Duty but I augur better things.

Just as we were sitting down to dinner Cadell burst in, in high spirits with the sale of *Napoleon* the orders for which pour in and the public report is favourable. Detected two gross blunders though which I had orderd for cancel. *Supd* (for a wonder) with Colin Mackenzie and a bachelor party. Mr. Williams[5] was there whose extensive information, learning and lively talent makes him always pleasant company. Up till twelve, a debauch for me now adays.

30 SATURDAY *Redd up* my things for moving which will clear my hands a little on the next final flitting.[6] Corrected proof sheets.

1. Scott's letter to Walter suggests that he again tried to persuade Sophia to leave the place: 'Sophia is lying on a couch in a little lodging at Porto Bello the use of which I can scarce conceive for neither she nor either of the boys bathe in the sea. I suggested she might as well lie on the couch at Abbotsford and offerd to get one on purpose but did not prevail. We dined in her cage yesterday. She is quite well and the children very much so.' *Letters*, x. 235.
2. Coleridge's *Ancient Mariner*, pt. iv, l. 1.
3. Haydon was duly grateful. 'Thus ends another month, & I have painted in comparative blessedness! Thanks to Lord Gower & Lockhart & Sir Walter.' Haydon's *Diary* (31 August 1827), iii. 217.
4. Deuteronomy 32: 15.
5. The Rector of the Edinburgh Academy.
6. When the Court rises in mid July. The present visit is for four days only.

Williams told me an English bull last night. A fellow of a College, deeply learnd, sitting at a publick entertainment beside a foreigner tried every means to enter into conversation but the stranger could speak no dead language the Doctor no living one but his own. At last the scholar in great extremity was enlightened by a happy '*Nonne potes loquere cum digitis?*'[1] said as if the difficulty was solved at once.

Abbotsford. Reachd this about six o'clock.

JULY

1 SUNDAY A most delicious day in the course of which I have not done

> The least right thing.[2]

Before breakfast I employd myself in airing my old Bibliomaniacal hobby, entering all the books lately acquired into a temporary catalogue so as [to] have them shelved and markd. After breakfast I went out, the day being delicious – warm yet coold with a gentle breeze – all around delicious – the rich luxuriant green refreshing to the eye, soft to the tread and perfume to the smell. Wanderd about and lookd at my plantations – Came home and received a visit from Sir Adam. Loiterd in the Library till dinner time. – If there is any thing to be done at all today it must be in the evening. But I fear there will be nothing – One can't work always *nowther*

> – *Neque semper arcum*
> *Tendit Apollo.*[3]

There's warrant for it.

2 MONDAY Wrote in the morning correcting the Essay on the Highlands which is now nearly completed. Settled accompts with Tom and Bogie – Miss £10 strangely from my cash received on Saturday. I think I have only got £90 instead of £100. This is odd. I would rather lose twice the sum than suspect a servant. Went over to Huntley Burn at two

Salary balance due	£100
purse	3
	103
Mr Haydon	£10
Bogie	30
Tom	10
Post horses	3
	53
	£50

1. 'Can you not speak with your fingers?'
2. See the Entry for 31 March 1828 and note.
3. 'Nor does Apollo keep his bow always strung'. Horace's *Odes*, ii. 10. 19.

o'clock and reconnoitred the proposed plantation to be called Janeswood.[1] Dined with the Fergussons.

3 TUESDAY Workd in the morning upon the Introduction to the *Chronicles*: It may be thought egotistical [2] I earnd a bad accident had happend yesterday. A tinker (drunk I suppose) enterd the stream opposite to Faldonside with an ass bearing his children. The ass was carried down by the force of the stream and one of the little creatures was drownd. The other was brought out alive, poor innocent, clinging to the ass. It had floated as far down as Deadwater heugh. Poor thing – it is as well dead as to live a tinker. The Fergussons dine with us en masse, also Dr. Brewster. My stomach is something out of order.

4 WEDNESDAY Workd a little in the morning and took a walk after breakfast, the day so delicious as makes it heart-breaking to leave the country. Set out however about four o'clock and reachd Edin a little after nine. Slept part of the way. Read *De Vere*[3] the rest. It is well written in point of language and sentiment but has too little action in it to be termd a pleasing Novel. Every thing is brought out by dialogue, or worse, through the medium of the author's reflections, which is the clumsiest of all expedients.

5 THURSDAY This morning workd and sent off to J. B. the Introduction to the *Chronicles* containing my Confessions and did something but not fluently to the confessions themselves. Not happy however – the black dog worries me – bile I suppose.

In purse	£50
Anne ——	20
In purse	30
post horses	2
	£28

But I will rally and combat the ruiner.[4]

Ruiner it is, that wretched Malady of the mind.

Got quite well in the forenoon, went out to Porto Bello after dinner and chatted with little Johnie and told him the history of the Field of Preston-pans. Few remain who care about these stories.

1. Named in honour of his daughter-in-law.
2. As the first work to be published since his confession at the Theatrical Fund Dinner, it refers to his authorship of the novels and details his sources for a number of incidents and characters.
3. The novel by Robert Ward mentioned in the Entry for 22 April 1827.
4. Goldsmith. A song intended for *She Stoops to Conquer*.

6 FRIDAY   This morning wrought a good deal. But scarce a task. The court lasted till half past three, exhausting work in this hot weather. I returnd to dine alone, Anne going to Roslin with a party. Afternoon a Miss Bell[1] broke in upon me who bothered me some time since about a book of hers explaining and exposing the conduct of a methodist Tartuffe who had broken off (by anonymous letters) a match betwixt her and an accepted admirer. Tried in vain to make her comprehend how little the Edinburgh people would care about her wrongs since there was no knowlege of the parties to make the scandal acceptable. I believe she has sufferd great wrong.

Letter from Longman and Coy. to J. B. grumbling about bringing out the 2d Edit. because they have forsooth 700 Copies on hand out of 5000 five days after the first edition is out.[2] What would they have? It is uncomfortable though.

7 SATURDAY   Night dreadfully warm and bilious. I could not be fool enough surely to be anxious for these wise men of the east's prognostications. Letters from Lockhart give a very cheerful prospect – if there had been any thundering upsetting broadside he would have noticed it surely more or less. R. Cadell quite stout and determind to

Cash—	£28
Charles	£2
Sundries	1
	3
	£25

1. For her first visit and her story see the Entry for 2 February 1826.
2. Before publication on 27 June Cadell had already disposed of almost all his share of the 6000 copies printed. On the 22nd he arranged with Gibson that they would print an extra 2,000 copies, and by a letter of 25 June Longman's agreed. On 4 July, however, they wrote the letter referred to in the Entry, 'intimating that they had still a considerable number of the first impression of the work on hand, and that they wished the publication of the additional two thousand copies to be delayed'. Cadell, 'expressing his strong disapprobation of Messrs. Longman & Cos conduct', insisted that he had orders to meet immediately. 'He added that if there had been any error in printing the new impression, it had been entirely the fault of Messrs. Longman & Co. who not only had been the first to suggest the undertaking, but had kept him [Mr. Cadell] in perfect ignorance of what had been doing with the work in London, although he had repeatedly advised them of the progress of the sales in Edinburgh.' The Trustees could see no 'sufficient reason for opening up a concluded bargain' and Owen Rees, who came to meet them on the 16th, could not sway them. The final arrangement was that the Trustees would allow Longman & Coy. an additional discount of £174. Sederunt Book, i. 230–2.

go on with the second edition. Well I hope all's right – thinking won't help it.

Charles came down this morning[1] pennyless, poor fellow. But we will soon remedy that. Lockhart remits £100 for reviewing.[2] I hope the next will be for Sophia for each affairs loom well in the offing and if the trust funds go right I was never so easy. I will take care how I get into debt again. I do not like this croaking of these old owls of Saint Paul's[3] when all is done. The pitcher has gone often to the well. But – However I workd away at the *Chronicles*. I will take pains with them. I will by Jove.

8 SUNDAY I did little to-day but arrange papers and put bills, receipts etc. into Apple pye order. I believe the fair prospect I have of clearing off some encumbrances which are like thorns in my flesh, nay in my very eye, contribute much to this. I did not even correct proofsheets, nay could not, for I have cancelld two sheets *instante Jacobo*,[4] and I myself being somdele of his opinion, for as I said yesterday we must and will take pains. The fiddle faddle of arranging all the things was troublesome but they give a good account of my affairs. The money for the necessary payments is ready and therefore there is a sort of pleasure which does not arise out of any mean source since it has for its source the prospect of doing justice and achieving independence.

J. B. dined with me, poor fellow, and talkd of his views as hopeful and prosperous. God send honest industry a fine riddance.

9 MONDAY Wrote in the morning. At eleven went by appointment with Colin MacKenzie to the New Edinr. Academy. In the fifth class, Mr. Mitchell's, we heard Greek of which I am no otherwise a judge than that it was fluently read and explaind. In the Rector Mr. Williams's class we heard Virgil and Livy admirably translated *ad aperturan Libri*[5] and, what I though[t] remarkable, the Rector giving the English and the pupils returning with singular dext[e]rity the Latin not exactly as in the original but often by synonymes, which shewd that the exercize referd to the judgement and did not depend

---

1. 'By Wednesday's Steamboat i.e. the same Eternal Soho'. Lockhart to Sophia, 2 July 1827, Abbots.
2. For the review of Mackenzie's *Life and Works of Home* in the June *Quarterly*. Scott kept the proceeds of his reviews for his own use; they were not paid into the Trust.
3. Longman, Rees & Coy. of Paternoster Row, by St. Paul's.
4. 'At the urging of James'.
5. 'At the opening of the book', i.e. unprepared.

on the memory. I could not help saying with great truth that as we had all long known how much the pupils were fortunate in a Rector so we were now taught that the rector was equally lucky in his pupils. Of my young friends I saw a son of John Swinton, a son of Johnstone of Alva, and a son of Crawfurd Tait – Dined at John Murray's. Mr. and Mrs. Philips of Liverpool, General and Charles Stuarts of Blantyre, Lord Abercromby, Clerk and Thomson – pleasant evening.

10 TUESDAY Corrected proofs but wrote nothing. To court till two o'clock. I went to Caddel's by the Mound, a long roundabout,[1] transacted some business and left receipts for my salaries payable at 25th current £150. Arranged some business also as per margin. I met Baron Hume coming home and walkd with him in the gardens.[2] His remarkable account of his celebrated Uncle's last moments is in these words. Dr. Black calld on Mr. D. Hume on the morning in which he died. The patient complaind of having sufferd a great deal during the night and expressd a fear that his struggle might be prolonged to his great distress for days or weeks longer. 'No, sir' said Dr. Black with the remarkable calmness and sincerity which characterized him. 'I have examined the symptoms and observe several which oblige me to conclude that dissolution is rapidly approaching.' – 'Are you certain of that, Doctor?' 'Most assuredly so' answerd the physician. The dying philosopher extended his arm and shook hands with his medical friend. 'I thank you' he said 'for the news.' So little reason there were for the reports of his having been troubled in mind when on his deathbed.

Dined at Lord Abercrombie's to meet Lord Melville in private. We had an interview betwixt dinner and tea. I was sorry to see my very old friend this upright statesman and honourable gentleman deprived of his power and his official income which the number of his family must render a matter of importance. He was cheerful, not affectedly so, and bore his declension like a wise and brave man. I had nursed an idea that he had been hasty in his resignation. But from the letters which he shewd me confidentially which passd betwixt him and Canning it is clear his resignation was to be accomplishd not I

In purse	£25
Lockhart Revw.	100
	125

Allan to accot	£20
Household	25
Stable rent &c	6
Rent of House[3]	34
	£35
In purse	£40

1. Cadell's business premises were in St. Andrew Square. To go there down the Mound was not unreasonable, and the description of it as 'a long roundabout' reflects Scott's increasing lameness.
2. 3 Walker Street had been taken for two months at sixteen guineas a month. Letters, x. 193.
3. Princes Street Gardens.

suppose for personal considerations but because it renderd the admiralty vacant for the Duke of Clarence.[1] As his resignation was eagerly snapd at, it cannot be doubted but that if he had hesitated or hung back behind his friends, forcible means would [have] been used to compel to the measure which with more dignity he took of his own accord. At least so it seemd to me. The first intimation which Lord Melville received of his successor was through Mr. —— [2] who told him as great news there was to be a new Duke of York. Lord M— understood the allusion so little as to enquire whether his informer meant that the Duke of Cambridge had taken the Duke of York's situation when it was explaind to refer to the Duke of Clarence getting the Admiralty. There are some few words that speak volumes. Lord Melville said that none of them suspected Canning's negociations with the Whiggs but the Duke of Wellington who found it out through the ladies ten days before. I askd him how they came to be so unprepared and could not help saying I thought they had acted without consideration and that they might have shown a face even to Canning. He allowd the truth of what I said and seemd to blame Peele's want of courage. In his place, he said, he would have proposed to form a government disclaiming any personal views for himself as being Premier or the like – but upon the principle of supporting the measures of Lord Castlereagh and Lord Liverpool. I think this would have been acceptable to the King. Mr. Peele obviously feard his great antagonist Canning and perhaps threw the game up too soon. Canning said the office of Premier was his inheritance – he could not from constitution hold it above two years and then it would descend to Peele. Such is ambition! Old friends forsaken – old principles changed – every effort used to give the vessel of the state a new direction and all to be Palinurus for two years.[3]

11 WEDNESDAY Abbotsford. Workd at proofs in the morning – composed nothing – got off by one and to this place[4] between six and seven. My stomach disorderd with bile. Weather delicious.

1. The Duke of Clarence became Lord High Admiral, but did not sit in the Cabinet.
2. Blank in the original.
3. In fact Canning was Premier for less than six months.
4. Abbotsford. Sophia remained at Portobello where, as she writes to Lockhart the following day, there is 'absolutely nothing to say every day with me passing the same as the last betwixt my bed and sopha'. But she is better, so is Lockhart's sister Violet, and Johnnie's ear has stopped discharging. 'Nothing can be more attentive than David and the maids.' She goes to Abbotsford on the 27th. Abbots.

12 THURSDAY Unpacking and arranging; the urchins are stealing the cherries in the outer garden. But I can spare a thousand larch trees to put it in order with a good fence for next year. It is not right to leave fruit exposed for if Adam in the days of innocence fell by an apple how much may the little gossoon Jamie Moffat[1] be tempted by apples of gold in an age of iron. Anne and I walkd to Huntly Burn, a delicious excursion. That place is really become beautiful – the Miss Fergussons have displayd a great deal of taste. My stomach again discomposed – Take physic, pomp.[2] And so I will to-night.

Cash . . .	£40
Journey and Sundries	£3
Charity	1
Mr. Scrope Champag[n]e	16
Charless	1
Rail road	9
	— £30
In purse	£10

13 FRIDAY Two agreeable persons, Revd. Mr. Gilly one of the prebendaries of Durham with his wife, a pretty little woman, dined with us and met Mr. Scrope. I heard the whole history of the discovery of Saint Cuthbert's body at Durham Cathedral.[3] The Catholics will deny the identity of course but I think it is *constaté* by the dress and other circumstances. Made a pleasant day of it and with a good conscience for I had done my task this morning. Slept better to-night and less bilious.

14 SATURDAY Did task this morning and believe that I shall get on now very well –

Wrote about five leaves. I have been baking and fevering myself like a fool for these last two years in a room exposed to the south, comfortable in winter but broiling in the hot weather. Now I have removed myself into the large cool library, one of the most refreshing as well as handsomest rooms in Scotland, and will not use the study again till the heats are past. Here is an entry as solemn as if it respected the Vicar of Wakefield's removal from the yellow room to the brown. But I think my labours will advance greatly in consequence of this arrangement. Walkd in the Evening to the Lake.

15 SUNDAY Achieved six pages to-day and finishd vol I of *Chronicles*. It is rather long but I think the last story[4] interesting and it should not

1. The son, presumably, of the cottager of the same name who rented Broomlees on the Abbotsford estate, unless Scott is alluding to the notorious James Mackcoull, *alias* Moffat, who stole £20,000 from a Glasgow bank in 1811.
2. *King Lear*, iii. 4.
3. The discovery was made earlier this year. See Raine's *St. Cuthbert*, 1828.
4. 'The Two Drovers.'

be split up into parts. J. B. will I fear think it low; and if he thinks so others will. Yet – *Vamos* – Drove to Huntlyburn in the evening.

16 MONDAY Made a good morning's work of the *Tales.*[1] In the daytime corrected various proofs. J. B. thinks that in the propose[d] Introduction I contemn too much the occupation by which I have thriven so well and hints that I may easily lead other people to follow my opinion in vilipending my talents and the use I have made of them. I cannot tell. I do not like on the one hand to suppress my own opinion of the floccipaucinihilipilication with which I regard these things but yet in duty to others I cannot afford to break my own bow or befoul my own nest and there may be something like affectation and *nolo episcopari*[2] in seeming to under rate my own labours; so all things considerd I will eraze the passage. Truth should not be spoke at all times. In the evening we had a delightful drive to Ashestiel with Colonel and Miss Fergusson.

17 TUESDAY I wrote a laborious task, seven pages of *Tales*. Kept about the doors all day. Gave Bogie ten pounds to buy cattle tomorrow at Saint Boswell's fair. Here is a whimsical subject of afliction. Mr. Harper, a settler who went from this country to Botany Bay, thinking himself obliged to me for a recommendation to General McAllister and Sir Thomas Brisbane, has thought proper to bring me home a couple of Emusses. I wish his gratitude had either taken a different turn or remaind as quiescent as that of others whom I have obliged more materially. I at first accepted the creatures, conceiving them in my

In purse   £10   ignorance to be some sort of blue and green parrot
Bogie   10   which though I do not admire their noise migh[t]
      £0.0.0   scream and yell at their pleasure if hung up in the hall

among the armour. But your Emus it seems stands six feet high on his stocking soles and is little better than a kind of Kassowari or Ostrich. Hang them, they might [eat] up my collection of old arms for what I know. It reminds me of the story of the Adjutant birds in Theodore Hook's novel.[3] No – I'll no Emuses! –[4]

18 WEDNESDAY Enterd this morning on the history of Sir William Wallace.[5] I wish I may be able to find my way between what the child

---

1. i.e., *Tales of a Grandfather*.
2. 'I do not want to be a bishop.'
3. *Danvers*, in the first series of *Saying and Doings*, 1824.
4. It took Scott a fortnight to rid himself of them. See note 8, p. 811.
5. This means that *Tales of a Grandfather* had reached chapter 7.

can comprehend and what shall not yet be absolutely uninteresting to the grown reader. Uncommon facts I should think the best receipt. Learn that Mr. Owen Rees and John Gibson have amicably settled their difference about the last edition of *Napoleon*, the Trustees allowing the Publishers 9 months credit.[1] My nerves have for these two or three last days been susceptible of an acute excitement from the slightest causes, the beauty of the evening, the sighing of the summer breeze, brings the tears into my eyes not unpleasin[g]ly. But I must take exercize and caseharden myself. There is no use in encouraging these moods of the mind. It is not the Law we live on.

We had a little party with some luncheon at the Lake where Mr. Bembridge fishd without much success. Capt Hamilton and two Messrs. Stirlings, relation of my old friend Keir, were there and walkd with me a long round home. I walkd better than I have done for some days. Mr. Scrope dined with us. He was complaining of gout which is a bad companion for the stagshooting.

19 THURSDAY I pourd out my task this fornoon and a good deal more. Sent five or Six pages to James Ballantyne – i.e. I got them ready. And wrote till one afternoon. Then I drove over to Huntly Burn and walkd through the glens till dinner time. After dinner read and workd till bedtime. Yet I have written well, walkd well, talkd well and have nothing to regret.

20 FRIDAY Dispatchd my letters to J. B. with supply of copy and made up more than my task, about four leaves I think. Offerd my Emuses to the Duke of Buccleuch. I had an appointment with Captain Hamilton and his friends the Stirlings that they were to go up Yarrow to-day. But the weather seems to overcast.

My visitors came however and we went up to Newark. Here a little misfortune for Spice left me and we could not find her. As we had no servant with us on horseback I was compelld to leave her to her fate resolving to send in quest of her tomorrow morning. The keepers are my *bonos Socios*,[2] as the host says in the *Devil of Edmonton*[3] and would as soon shoot a child as a dog of mine. But there are tramps and traps and I am ashamd to say how reluctantly I left the poor little terrier to its fate. She came home to me however about an hour and a half after we were home to my great delectation. Our visitors dined with us and I found they were of the Drumpellier family.

1. See the Entry for 6 July 1827 and note.
2. 'Good companions'.
3. *The Merry Devil of Edmonton*, by 'T. B.'.

21 SATURDAY This morning wrote five pages of children's history. Went to Minto where we met, besides Lord M. and his delightful countess, Thomas Thomson, Kennedy of Dunure, Lord Carnarvon and his younger son and daughter in law. The dowager Lady Minto also whom I always delight to see, she is so full of spirit and intelligence. We rubbd up some recollections of twenty years ago when I was more intimate in the family till whig and tory separated us for a time. By the way no body talks whig or Tory just now and the fighting men on each side go about on each side muzzled and mute like dogs after a proclamation about canine madness – Am I sorry for this truce or not? – Half and half. It is all we have left to stir the blood – this little political brawling. But better too little of it than too much.

22 SUNDAY Rose a little later than usual and wrote a letter to Mrs. Joanna Baillie. She is writing a tragedy on witch craft.[1] I shall be curious to see it – Will it be real Witch craft – the *Ipsissimus Diabolus*[2] – or an impostor – or the half crazed being who believes herself an ally of condemnd spirits and desires to be so? That last is a sublime subject. We set out after breakfast and reachd this about two. Found Charles[3] much recoverd of his lumbago and thinking seriously of general study. I walkd from two till four, chatted a long time with Charles after dinner and thus went my day *sine linea*.[4] But we will make it up. James Ballantyne dislikes my drovers.[5] But it shall stand. I must have my own way sometimes.

I received news of two deaths at on[c]e. Lady Die Scott my very old friend, and Archd Constable the bookseller.

23 MONDAY Yes! They are both for very different reasons subjects of reflection. Lady Diana Scott, widow of Walter Scott of Harden, was the last person whom I recollect so much older than myself that she kept always at the same distance in point of years so that she scarce seemd older to me (relatively) two years ago when in her ninety second year than fifty years before. She was the daughter (alone

1. The play, suggested by a scene in *The Bride of Lammermoor*, was *Witchcraft, A Tragedy in Prose*. Scott read it the next year. Entry for 18 April 1828.
2. 'The very devil himself'.
3. He had spent a few days at Portobello with Sophia before joining his father at Abbotsford.
4. 'Without a line [written]'.
5. As expected. See the Entry for 15 July 1827. Scott's reply leaves no room for argument: 'I [am] not surprized at your opinion but as my own does not second it you will excuse my adhering to it once and away.' *Letters*, x. 263.

remaining) of Pope's Earl of Marchmount and like her father had an acute mind and an eager temper. She was always kind to me – remarkably so indeed when I was a boy.

Constable's death might have been a most important thing to me if it had happend some years ago and I should then have lamented it much. He has lived to do me some injury yet excepting the last £5000 I think most unintentionally. He was a Prince of Booksellers, his views sharp powerful and liberal, too sanguine however and like many bold and successful schemers never knowing when to stand or stop and not always calculating his means to his objects with mercantile accuracy. He was very vain, for which he had some reason, having raised himself to great commercial [eminence] as he might also have attaind great wealth with good management. He knew I think more of the business of a bookseller in planning and executing popular works than any man of his time. In books themselves he had much bibliographical information but none whatever that could be termd literary. He knew the rarer volumes of his library not only by the eye but by the touch when blindfolded. Thomas Thomson saw him make this experiment and that it might be complete placed in his hand an ordinary volume instead of one of these *libri rariores*;[1] he said he had over estimated his memory – he could not recollect that volume. Constable was a violent temperd man with those that he dared use freedom with. He was easily overawed by people of consequence but as usual took it out of those whom poverty made subservient to him. Yet he was generous and far from bad hearted. In person good looking but very corpulent latterly – a large feeder and deep drinker till his health became weak. He died of water in the chest which the natural strength of his constitution set long at defiance. I have no great reason to regret him yet I do – if he deceived me he also deceived himself.

Wrote five pages to-day and went to see Mr. Scrope, who is fast with the gout, a bad companion to attend him

> — To Athole Braes
> To shoot the dun deer down – down
> For to shoot the dun deer down.[2]

24 TUESDAY Finishd five pages before 11 o'clock at which time Mr. Deputy Register[3] arrived from Minto and we had an agreeable fornoon talking about the old days we have had together. I was

1. 'Rarer books'.
2. Untraced.
3. Thomas Thomson, who was Depute Clerk Register for Scotland.

Lent Thomson   £8
Borrd from Anne   5
£—

surprized to find that Thomson knew as little as I do myself how to advise Charles to a good course of Scottish history. Hailes and Pinkerton, Robertson and Laing,[1] there is nothing else for it, and Pinkerton is poor work. Laing besides his party spirit has a turn for generalizing which renders him rather dull, which was not the nature of the acute Orcadian.

25 WEDNESDAY Thomson left us this morning early. I finishd four pages and part of a fifth then drove to Huntly Burn and returnd through the glen. I certainly turn *heavy-footed*, not in the female sense however. I had one or two falls among the slippy heather not having Tom Purdie to give me his arm. I suppose I shall need a go-cart one of these days – And if it must be so – so let it be – *fiat voluntas tua* –[2]

A letter from John Gibson in the evening brought me word that Lord Newton had adjudged the profits of *Woodstock* and *Napoleon* to be my own.[3] This is a great matter and removes the most important part of my dispute with Constable's creditors. I waked in the middle of the night. Sure I am not such a feather-headed gull as not to be able to sleep for good news. I am thankful that it is as it is. Had it been other wise I could have stood it. The money realized will pay one third of all that I owe in the world – and what will pay the other two thirds? I am as well and as capable as when these misfortunes began, January was a year. The public favour may wane indeed but it has not yet faild as yet and I must not be too anxious about that possibility.

James B. is find[ing] fault with my tales[4] for being too historical; formerly it was for being too infantine. He calls out for starch and is afraid of his cravat being too stiff. Oh ye critics, will nothing melt ye?

1. Lord Hailes's *Annals of Scotland*, 1776–9; John Pinkerton's *Enquiry into the History of Scotland preceding the Reign of Malcolm III*, 1790, and his *History of Scotland 1371–1542*, 1797; William Robertson's *History of Scotland during the Reigns of Mary and James VI*, 1759; Malcolm Laing's *History of Scotland, from the Union of the Crowns to the Union of the Kingdoms*, 1800–4.
2. 'Thy will be done.'
3. On the argument that they 'clearly were never the subject of a completed bargain'. Gibson, Letters to Scott, f. 56. Cowan, however, lodged further objections, and it was not until December that the Trustees could pay the first dividend. See the Entry for 4 December 1827.
4. i.e., *Tales of a Grandfather*.

26 THURSDAY Wrote till one o'clock and finishd the 1st volume of *Tales*, about six leaves. Tomorrow I resume the *Chronicles*[1] tooth and nail. They must be good if possible. After all works of fiction, vzy Cursed Lies, are easier to write and much more popular than the best truths. Walkd over to the head of the Roman road coming round by Bauchland and the Abbot's walk. Wrote letters in the evening to Ballantyne, Gibson, Cadell, John Richardson, Colin MacKenzie and others.[2]

27 FRIDAY In the morning still busied with my correspondence. No great desire to take up the *Chronicles*. But it must be done. Deuce take the necessity and the folly and knavery that occasiond it. But this is no mister[3] now – Accordingly I set tightly to work and got on till two when I took a walk. Was made very happy by the arrival of Sophia and her babies all in good hea[l]th and spirits.

28 SATURDAY Workd hard in the morning. The two Ballantynes and Mr. Hogarth with them.[4] Owen Rees came early in the day. Fergussons came to dinner. Rees in great kindness and good humour but a little drumlie[5] I think about *Nap*. We heard Sandie's[6] violin after dinner

> — Whose touch harmonious can remove
> The pangs of guilty power and hopeless love.[7]

I do not understand or care about fine music but there is some thing in his violin which goes to the very heart. Sophia sung too and we were once more merry in hall.[8] The first time for this many a month and many a day.

1. The second volume of *Chronicles of the Canongate*, the story entitled 'The Surgeon's Daughter'.
2. The letters to Gibson and Cadell were about Lord Newton's arbitration, the letter to Richardson an invitation to Abbotsford (see *Letters*, x. 263–7), and the letter to Mackenzie about the Academy's Latin 'now in the hands of a very safe good humoured Committee to arrange with the Rector a plan of operations to teach both pronunciations'. Mackenzie, Letters to Scott, f. 63.
3. 'Any thing that is necessary'. Jamieson. Scott means that it is useless to cry over his situation now.
4. As arranged by Ballantyne. See 26 July 1827, *Walpole*.
5. 'Troubled, gloomy'. Jamieson.
6. Sandie Ballantyne's.
7. Dr. Johnson's 'Epitaph on Claudy Phillips, a Musician'.
8. Thomas Tusser's *Five Hundred Pointes of Good Husbandrie* (1573), 'August's absract', 26.

29 SUNDAY Could not do more than undertake my proofs to-day of
which J. B. has brought out a considerable quantity. Walkd at one
with Hogarth and Rees – the day sultry hot and we hot accordingly
but crept about notwithstanding. I am sorry to see my old and feal[1]
friend James rather unable to walk – once so stout and active – so was
I in my way *once*. Ah that vile word, what a world of loss it involves.

I had from Caddell an accompt of my precepts and payments on
my account as follows[2]

Dr.		Cr.	
Ballance of Allan's[3] accompt ——	£24	Precept ——	£150
To Haydon by £10 No 11745 —	10		
To J. Gibson annuities ——	20		
To paid for William Scott ——	9		

30 MONDAY One of the most peppering thunder storms which I
have heard for some time. Routed[4] and roard from six in the morning
till eight continuously.

The thunder ceased not nor the fire reposed.[5]

Well done, Old Botherby. Time wasted though very agreeably after
breakfast. At noon set out for Chiefswood in the carriage and walkd
home footing it over rough and smooth with the vigour of early days:
James Ballantyne marchd on too, somewhat meltingly but without

1. 'Loyal, faithful'. *S. N. D.*
2. From this time onwards Scott makes increasing use of Cadell as
   his banker and general man of business. Cadell, who saw the
   advantage of becoming indispensable to his author, was very
   accommodating. 'I would rather that you owed your publishers,
   who are making a penny siller by your works than others', he
   writes on the 28th. On 6 August he is dealing with 'the Small
   cash matters' entrusted to him, and will 'at all times be most
   happy to do any small matter of this kind'. On the 24th he
   writes again: 'May I take this opportunity of mentioning that
   there is a house to Let in Walker Street . . . which may be had
   for you for the coming winter . . . pray command my services if
   you wish anything done as to this'; and on the 28th: 'I hope you
   will not allow yourself to be "hard up" without letting me know
   . . . pray do not hesitate to say if you wish more money, it shall
   be instantly advanced.' Walpole.
3. Bell and Allan, Smiths. See Cadell, 28 July 1827, Walpole.
4. 'Bellowed.'
5. William Sotheby's 'Battle of the Nile' (1809), l. 76.

complaint. We again had beautiful music after dinner. The heart of age arose. I have often wonderd whether I have a taste for music or no. My ear appears to me as dull as my voice is incapable of musical expression and yet I feel the utmost pleasure in any such music as I can comprehend, learnd pieces always excepted. I believe I may be about the pitch of Jerry's connoisseurship and that 'I have a reasonable good ear for a jigg but your solos and sonatas give me the spleen.'[1]

31 TUESDAY Employd the morning in writing letters and correcting proofs. This is the second day and scarce a line written but circumstances are so much my apology that even duty does not murmur – at least not *much* – We had a drive up to Galashiels and sent J. B. off to Edinburgh in the Mail. Music in the evening as before. Guests.

AUGUST

1 WEDNESDAY My guests left me and I thought of turning to work again seriously. Finishd five pages. Dined alone excepting Huntly Gordon who is come on a visit, poor lad. I hope [he] is well fixd under Mr. Planta's patronage.[2] Smoked a cigar after dinner, laughd with my daughters and read them the review of Hoffmann's production out of Gillies's new Foreign review. The undertaking would do I am convinced in any other person's hands than those of the improvident editor. But I hear he is living as thoughtlessly as ever in London, has hired a large house and gives Burgundy to his guests.[3] This will hardly suit £500 a year.

Cash from Selkirk	£85
Anne house	£30
Dt. repaid	5
Tom	10
	45
In purse	£40

Cash in purse as above £40.

2 THURSDAY Got off my proofs. Went over to breakfast at Huntly Burn; the great object was to see my cascade in the glen suitably

---

1. Congreve's *Love for Love*, ii. 7.
2. Scott had helped to place Gordon in the Treasury under his friend Joseph Planta.
3. The information came from Lockhart: 'Mr Gillies has got a very pretty house (outside I mean) near Hyde park. I must see the inside in a day or two. He seems in high glee in a new surtout & continual invitations to come & take a soup o' Burgundy wi' him – the old idiot as usual.' 10 July 1827, Abbots. Scott's fears were justified. Gillies threw up the editorship of the *Foreign Quarterly* the following year and went bankrupt in 1829.

repaired. 'Cascade?' as Lord H.[1] said 'asking the ladies' pardon I could produce a more respectable waterfall from my own person!' Well but it is all I have got for one so I have had it put to rights by puddling and damming. What says the Frog in the fairy tale? –

> Stuff with moss and clagg with clay
> And that will weize the water away.[2]

Having seen the job pretty tightly done, walkd deliciously home through the woods. But no work all this while. Therefore 'up and at it.'[3] But in spite of good resolutions I trifled with my children after dinner and read to them in the evening and did just nothing at all.

3 FRIDAY Wrote five pages and upwards, some amends for passd laziness. Huntley Gordon lent me a volume of his father's Manuscript Memoirs. They are not without interest, for Pryce Gordon though a bit of a roué, is a clever fellow in his way. One thing struck me, being the story of an Irish swindler who calld himself Henry King Edgeworth, an impudent jawing fellow who deserted from Gordon's recruiting party, enlisted again and became so great a favourite with the Colonel of the regiment which he joind that he was made pay sergeant. Here he deserted to purpose with £200 or £300, escaped to France, got a commission in the corps sent to invade Ireland, was taken, recognised and hangd. What would Mr. Theobald Wolfe Tone[4] have said to such an associate in his regenerating expedition? – these are thy gods, o Israel. The other was the displeasure of the present Cameron of Lochiel on finding that the 40 Camerons with whom he joind the Duke of Gordon's Northern fencible regiment were to be dispersed. He had well nigh mutinied and marchd back with them. This would be a good anecdote for Garth.[5]

4 SATURDAY Spent the morning at Selkirk examining people about an assault, Max[6] being off to Seabathing. This comes of *manning one's*

1. Lord Hermand.
2. From a nursery tale, 'The Well of the World's End'. See *Letters*, vii. 311.
3. An allusion to Wellington's supposed command at Waterloo: 'Up, Guards, and at them!'
4. A founder of the United Irish Society, Tone allied himself with the French and made three attempts to invade Ireland to assist an Irish rebellion. He was captured in 1798 and condemned to death, but committed suicide in prison.
5. General David Stewart of Garth, author of *Sketches of the Highlanders of Scotland*, 1822.
6. William Scott of Maxpoffle.

self with his kin.[1] When I returnd I found Charlotte Kerr here with a clever little boy, Charles Scott, grandson of Charles of the Wool[2] and son of William and Grandnephew of John of Midgehope. He seems a smart boy and, considering that he is an only son with expectations, not *too* much spoild. General Yernolow calld with a letter from a Dr. Knox whom I do not know. If it be Vicesimus we met nearly 25 years ago and did not agree. But General Yernolow's name was luckily known to me. He is a man in the flower of life, about 30, handsome bold and enthusiastic, a great admirer of poetry and all that. He had been in the Moscow campaign and those which followd but must have been very young.[3] He made not the least doubt that Moscow was burnd by Rostopchin and said that there was a general rumour before the French enterd the town and while the inhabitants were leaving it that persons were left to destroy it. I askd him why the magazine of gunpowder had not been set fire to in the first instance. He answerd that he believed the explosion of that magazine would have endangerd the retreating Russians. This seemd unsatisfactory. The march of the Russians was too distant from Moscow to be annoyd by the circumstance. I pressd him as well as I could about the slowness of Koutousow's operations and he frankly ownd that the Russians were so much rejoiced and surprized to see the French in retreat that it was long ere they could credit the extent of the advantage which they had acquired. This has been but an idle day so far as composition is concernd but I was detaind late at Selkirk.

5 SUNDAY Wrote near six pages. General Yermolow left me with many expressions of enthusiastic regard as foreigners use to do. He is a kinsman of Princess Galitzin whom I saw at Paris. I walkd with Tom after one o'clock, dined *en famille* with Miss Todd,[4] a pretty girl, and wrote after dinner.

6 MONDAY This morning finishd proofs and was *bang up* with every thing. When I was about to sit down to write I have the agreeable

1. 'Employing one's relatives'. The note of acerbity may be excusable: it is the second year in succession that his cousin has had to go to the sea for his health at just this time. Anne to Sophia, 28 July 1826, Abbots.
2. Charles Scott of Woll.
3. He was twenty years older than Scott thought. At the time of the Moscow campaign he was second-in-command of the Russian armies and in favour of a more aggressive pursuit of Napoleon.
4. The family party included Morritt and his nieces. Miss Todd is probably the 'very handsome wild Irish girl who is residing with Mrs. Hamilton' mentioned in Scott's letter of the next day to C. K. Sharpe. *Disc.* i. 159.

Cash in purse	£40
Repd. by Mr. Thomson	5
Cash remitted by Mr. Cadell	82
	£127
Isaacks — £58	
Butcher old bill —— 35	
Charles —— 5	
—	98
	29
Bogie ——	20
	£9

tidings that Henderson, the fellow who committed the assault at Selkirk and who made his escape from the officers on Saturday, was retaken and that it became necessary that I should go up to examine him – Returnd at four and found Mrs. George Swinton from Calcutta, to whose husband I have been much obliged, with Archie and cousin Peggie Swinton, arrived. So the evening was done up.

7 TUESDAY Cousins still continuing we went to Melrose. I finishd however in the first place a pretty smart task, which is so far well as we expect the Skenes tomorrow. Lockhart arrived from London. His news are that Canning is dangerously ill. This is the bowl being broken at the cistern[1] with a vengeance. If he dies now it will be pity it was not four months ago. The time has been enough to do much evil but not to do any permanent good.

8 WEDNESDAY Huntly Gordon proposed to me this morning that I should give him my correspondence which we had begun to arrange last year. I resolved not to lose the opportunity and began to look out and arrange the letters from about 1810, throwing out letters of business and such as are private. They are of little consequence generally speaking yet will be one day curious. I propose to have them bound up to save trouble.[2] It is a sad task – how many dead, absent, estranged and alterd. I wrought till the Skenes came at four o'clock. I love them well, yet I wish their visit had been made last week; when other people were here. It kills time, or rather murders it, this company keeping. Yet what remains on earth that I like so well as a little society? I workd not a line to-day.

9 THURSDAY I finishd the arrangement of the letters so as to put them into Mr. Gordon's hands. It will be a great job done. But in the meanwhile it interrupts my work sadly for I kept busy till one o'clock to-day with this idle man's labour. Still however it might have been long enough e'er I got a confidential person like Gordon to arrange these confidential papers. They are all in his hands now. Walkd after one.

1. Ecclesiastes 12: 6.
2. The letter-books here referred to form a substantial part of the Walpole Collection in the National Library of Scotland.

10 FRIDAY This a morning of fidgetty nervous confusion. I Sought successively my box of Bramah pens, my proof sheets and last, not least anxiously, my spe[c]tacles. I am convinced I lost a full hour in these various chases. I collected all my insubordinate moveables at once but had scarce corrected the proof and written half a score of lines than enter Dalgleish declaring the Blucher hour is come.[1] The weather however is rainy and fitted for a pure day of work. I was able however only to finish my task of three pages.

The death of the Premier is announced. Late George Canning, the witty, the accomplishd, the ambitious – he who had toild 30 years and involved himself in the most harassing discussions to attain this dizzy height – he who had held it for three months of intrigue and obloquy – and now a heap of dust and that is all. He was an early and familiar friend of mine[2] through my intimacy with George Ellis. No man possessd a gayer and more playful wit in society – no one since Pitt's time had more commanding sarcasm in debate – in the House of Commons he was the terror of that species of orators calld the Yelpers. His lash fetch[ed] away both skin and flesh and would have penetrated the hide of a rhinoceros. In his conduct as a statesman he had a great fault – he lent himself too willingly to intrigue. Thus he got into his quarrel with Lord Castlereagh[3] and lost credit with the country for want of openness. Thus too he got involved with the Queen's party to such an extent that it fetterd

Cash		£9.0.0
Anne	£4	
Tom	5	
	—	9
		0.0.0

him upon that memorable quarrel and obliged him to butter Sir Robert Wilson with dear friend and gallant general and so forth. The last Composition with the Whigs was a sacrifice of principle on both sides. I have some reason to think they counted on getting rid of him in two or three years. To me Canning was always personally most kind. I saw with pain a great change in his health when I met him at Colonel Bolton's at Torrs[4] in 1825. In London I thought him looking better. Among my correspondence I have several letters from him.

11 SATURDAY Wrote nearly five pages then walkd. A visit from Henry Scott – nothing known as yet about politics. A high Tory

1. Proofs and copy passed between Scott and Ballantyne by the daily coach.
2. They first met, in London, in 1806, and their friendship grew from their common part in founding the *Quarterly* in 1808. See the Entry for 27 November 1825 and note.
3. They fought a duel, in which Canning was wounded, in September 1809.
4. A slip for Storrs, on Lake Windermere.

Administration would be a great evil at this time. There are repairs in the structure of our constitution which ought to be made at this season and without which the people will not long be silent. A pure Whig administration would probably play the devil by attempting a thorough repair. As to a compound or melo-dramatick Ministry, the parts out of which such a one could be organized just now are at a terrible discount in public estimation nor will they be at *par* in a hurry again. The publick were generally shockd at the complete lack of principle testified by public men on the late occasion and by some who till then had some credit to the public. The Duke of W.[1] has risen by his firmness on the one side, Earl Grey on the other.

12 SUNDAY Wrote my task and no more. Walkd with Lockhart from one o'clock to four. Took in our way the glen, which looks beautiful. I walkd with extreme pain and feebleness untill we began to turn homewards, when the relaxation of the ankle sinews seemd to be removed and I trode merrily home. This is strange, that exercize should restore the nerves from the chill or numbness which is allied to palsy I am well aware, but how it should restore elasticity to sinews that are too much relaxd I for one cannot comprehend. Colonel Russell came to dine with us and to consult me about some family matters. He has the spirit of a gentleman. That is certain.

13 MONDAY A letter from Booksellers at Brussells informs me of the pleasant tidings that *Napoleon* is a total failure, that they have lost much money on a version which they were at great expence in preparing, and modestly propose that I should write a novel to make them amends for loss on a speculation which I knew nothing about. 'Have you nothing else to ask?' as Sancho says to the farmer who asks him to stock a farm for his son, portion off his daughters, etc. etc. They state themselves to be young booksellers. Certes they must hold me to be a *very* young author.[2] *Napoleon* however has faild on the continent and perhaps in England also for from the mumbling, half grumbling tone of Longman and Coy dissatisfaction may be apprehended. Well! I can set my face to it boldly. I live not in the public opinion, not I. But egad I live *by* it and that is worse. *Tu ne cede malis sed contra*[3] etc.

1. The Duke of Wellington.
2. Scott told Gell 'he had returned for answer, that as soon as the translator would inform him how much he had intended to allow the original author in case the translation had sold well, he would consider the circumstance and the justice of the claim'. Gell, p. 12.
3. 'Do not give way to your troubles, but rather [go more courageously where your fortune allows you].' Virgil's *Aeneid*, vi. 95 f.

I corrected and transmitted sheets before breakfast; afterwards went and cut wood with Tom but returnd about twelve in rather a melancholy humour. I fear this failure may be followd by others and then what chance of extricating my affairs? But they that look to freats, freats will follow them.[1] *Hussards en avant* – Care killd a cat. I finishd three pages, that is a full task of the *Chronicles*, after I returnd. Mr. and Mrs. Phillips of Manchester came to dinner.

14 TUESDAY Finishd my task before Breakfast. A bad rainy day at which I should not have cared but for my guests. However, being good humourd persons and gifted with taste, we got on very well by dint of showing prints, curiosities, finally the House up stair and down, and at length by undertaking a pilgrimage to Melrose in the rain, which pilgrimage we accomplishd but never enterd the Abbey church, having just had wetting enough to induce us when we arrived at the gate to Turn again, Whittington.

15 WEDNESDAY Wrote in the morning. After breakfast walkd with Mr. Philips who is about to build and plan himself and therefore seemd to enter *con amore* into all I had been doing, askd questions and seemd really interested to learn what I thought myself not ill qualified to teach. The little feeling of superior information on such cases is extremely agreeable. On the contrary it is a great scrape to find you have been boring some one who did not care a damn about the matter so to speak and that you might have been as well employd in buttering a whin stone. Mr. and Mrs. Philips left us about twelve – day bad – I wrote nearly five pages of *Chronicles*.

16 THURSDAY A wet disagreeable sulky day but such things may be carried to account. I wrote upwards of seven pages and placed myself *Rectus in Curia*[2] with Madam Duty who was beginning to lift up her throat against me. Nothing remarkable except that Huntly Gordon left us.

17 FRIDAY Wrote my task in the morning. After breakfast went out and cut wood with Tom and John Swanston and hewd away with my own hand – remain on foot from eleven o'clock till past three doing in my opinion a great deal of good in plantations above the house where the firs had been permitted to predominate too much over the oack and hard wood. The day was rough and stormy – not the worse

---

1. 'Those that expect troubles will have troubles.' See p. 239, note 4.
2. 'Right in the eyes of the law'.

for working, and I could do it with a good conscience, all being well forward in the duty line. After tea I workd a little longer. On the whole finishd four leaves and upwards, about a printed sheet, which is enough for one day.

18 SATURDAY Finishd about five leaves and then out to the wood where I chopd away among the trees laying the foundation for future scenery. These woods will one day occupy a great number of hands. Four years hence they will employ ten stout woodsmen almost every day of the year. Henry and William Scott (Harden) came to dinner.

19 SUNDAY Wrote till about one, then walkd for an hour or two by myself entirely; finished five pages before dinner, when we had Capt. and Mrs. Hamilton and young Davidoff who is their guest. They remaind with us all night.

20 MONDAY I corrected proofs and wrote one leaf before breakfast. Then went up to Selkirk to try a fellow[1] for an assault. The people there get rather riotous. This is a turbulent fierce fellow. Some of his attitudes were good during the trial. This dissipated my attention for the day; although I was back by half-past two I did not work any more so am behind in my reckoning.

21 TUESDAY Wrote four pages – then set out to make a call at Sunderland hall and Yair but the old Sociable broke down before we had got past the thicket. So we trudged all back on foot and I wrote another page. This makes up the deficiency of yesterday.

22 WEDNESDAY I wrote four or five leaves but begin to get aground for want of India localities.[2] Colonel Fergusson's absence is unlucky. So is Maxpopple[3] and half a dozen Qui His besides, willing to write chitts, eat Tiffing and vent all their pagan jargon when one does not want to hear it and now that I want a touch of their slang, lo! there is not one near me. Mr. Adolphus (son of the celebrated council) and author of a work on the Waverly novels[4] came to make me a visit. He is a modest as well as an able man and I am obliged to him for the

1. The Henderson mentioned in the Entry for 6 August.
2. Needed for 'The Surgeon's Daughter'.
3. The Colonel was in Ireland and Maxpoffle seabathing. See the Entries for 22 September and 4 August 1827.
4. *Letters to Richard Heber, Esq., containing Critical Remarks on the Series of Novels beginning with Waverley, and an Attempt to ascertain their Author,* 1821.

delicacy with which he treated a matter in which I was personally so much concernd. Mr. and Mrs. Hamilton askd us to breakfast tomorrow.

23 THURSDAY Went to breakfast at Chiefswood which with a circuitous walk have consumed the day. Found in the first place my friend Allan the painter busy about a picture into which he intends introducing living characters, a kind of revel at Abbotsford. 2d a whimsical party consisting of John Stevenson the bookseller, Peter Buchan from Peterhead, a quiz of a poetical creature, and a Bookbinder, a friend of theirs. The plan was to consult me about publishing a great quantity of ballads which this Mr. Buchan has collected. I glanced them over. He has been very successful for they are obviously genuine and many of them very curious. Others are various editions of well known ballads. I could not make the man comprehend that these last were of little value, being generall[y] worse readings of what was already publishd. A small edition publishd by subscription may possibly succeed.[1] It is a great pity that few of these ballads are historical, almost all being of the romantic cast. They certainly ought to be preserved, after striking out one or two which have been sophisticated I suppose by Mr. Buchan himself which are easily distinguishable from the genuine ballads – no one but Burns ever succeeded in patching up old Scottish songs with any good effect.

24 FRIDAY Corrected proofs and wrote letters in the morning. Began a review upon Monteath's *Planter* for Lockhart.[2] Other matters at a stand. Took a drive down to Mertoun and engaged to dine there on Sunday first. This consumd the day.

25 SATURDAY Mr. Adolphus left us this morning after a very agreeable visit. We all dined at Dr. Brewster's – Met Sir John Wright, Miss Haig etc. etc. Slanderd our neighbours and were good company. Major John Scott there. I did a little more at the Review to-day. But I cannot go on with the tale without I could speak a little Hindhanee, a small seasoning of curry powder – Fergusson will do it if I can screw it out of him.

26 SUNDAY Encore Review – walk from twelve till three then down to Mertoun with Lockhart and Allan. Dined *en famille* and home by

---

1. Buchan's *Ancient Ballads and Songs* was published in 1828.
2. Scott's review of *The Forester's Guide and Profitable Planter* appeared in the October *Quarterly* no. 72.

half past ten. We thought of adding a third volume to the *Chronicles*
but Gibson is afraid it would give grounds for a pretext to seize this
work[1] on the part of Constable's Crers who seem determined to take
every advantage of me. But they can only show their teeth I trust;
though I wish the arbitration was ended

27 MONDAY Sent off proofs in morning, reviewed in afternoon.
Walkd from one till four – what a life of uniformity, yet I never wish to
change it. I even regret I must go to town to meet Lady Compton[2]
next week. A singular letter from a lady requesting I would favour a
novel of hers. That won't pass.

Cadell writes me transmitting a notice from the French papers that
Gourgaud has gone or is going to London to verify the facts alleged in
my *History of Napoleon,* and the bibliopolist is in a great funk. I lack
some part of his instinct.[3] I have done Gourgaud no wrong. Every
word imputed to him exists in the papers submitted to me as
historical documents and I should have been a shameful coward if
I had shund using them. At my years it is somewhat late for an affair
of Honour and as a reasonable man I would avoid such an arbitre-
ment. But will not plead privilege of literature. The country shall not
be degraded in my person, and having stated why I think I owe him
no satisfaction, I will at the same time most willingly give it to him.

> Il sera reçu
> Biribi
> A la façon de Barbaru
> Mon ami.[4]

I have written to Will Clerk to stand my friend if necessary.[5] He has
mettle in him and thinks of my honour as well as my safety.

1. On the argument, denied by Scott, that he had agreed with
   Constable to write him a new three-volume novel. Two volumes
   of short stories were clearly something different; three might
   have looked like the promised work.
2. See the Entry for 4 September 1827 and note.
3. *1 Henry IV,* ii. 4.
4. Le Sage's *Arlequin roy de Serendib,* ii. 2, in *Théâtre de la foire*
   (1721), tome I.
5. The documents which Scott had seen at the Colonial Office
   showed that General Gourgaud, who attended Napoleon on St.
   Helena, had assured the British Government that complaints of
   ill usage were unfounded while at the same time fanning French
   resentment against his rigorous confinement. For Scott's letter to
   Clerk, asking him to be his second, see *Letters,* x. 270.

28 TUESDAY Borrowd from Lockhart £5 note No. 5,533 which sent by post to Mr. William Laidlaw.[1] It goes tomorrow. I am still bothering with the review but gave Lockhart 15 leaves which is something. Learnd with regret that Williams leaves his situation of Rector of the New Accademy.[2] It is a shot in the wing of the institution for he is a heaven-born teacher. Walkd at two till four along the thicket and by the river side where I go seldom – I can't say why unless that the walk is less private than those more distant. Lockhart, Allan, and I, talk of an excursion to Kelso tomorrow. I have no friends there now – yet once how many.

29 WEDNESDAY Went on our little expedition, breakfasting at Mertoun – Calld at Fleurs where we found Sir John S— and his whole family.[3] The Great Lady receivd us well though we had been very remiss in our duty. From that we went to Kelso where I saw not a soul to acknowledge former acquain[tan]ce – How should I when my residence there was before 1783 I fancy?[4] The little cottage in which I lived with poor Aunt Jenny is still standing but the great garden is divided betwixt three proprietors. Its huge platanus tree witherd, I was told, in the same season which was fatal to so many of the species. It was cut down – The yew hedges, labyrinths, wildernesses, and other marks that it had once been the abode of one of the Millers connected with the Author of the *Gardener's Dictionary* (They were a quaker family) are all obliterated and the place as common and vulgar as may be. The lady the cottage belongs to was very civil. Allan as a man of taste was much delighted with what we saw. When we returnd we found our party at home in[creased] by Lady Anna Maria Elliot who had been shewing Melrose to two friends, Miss Drinkwaters. Lad[y] A.

1. Laidlaw, a casualty of retrenchment at Abbotsford, had written for money on the 24th. Scott, in a letter of this date, asks him to take it as a fee 'for rural advice' rather than a loan. 'Your leaving Kaeside', he adds, 'makes a most melancholy blank to us . . . I think loss of our walks plans discussions and debates does not make the greatest [i.e., least] privation that I experience from the loss of worlds gear.' Disc. i. 161 (partly printed in *Letters*, x. 273). He returned to Abbotsford when Tom Purdie's death made a factor indispensable.

2. His informant was Colin Mackenzie. 26 August 1827, Walpole. For the complications which followed see the Entry for 25 June 1828 and note.

3. An unlucky coincidence. It was Sir John who had written a year ago suggesting that Scott should come to Fleurs and propose to 'the Great Lady', the Dowager Duchess. See the Entry for 13 September 1826.

4. For Scott's early residence in Kelso for his health, see *Life*, i. 47 and 155–62.

M.'s wit and good humour made the evening go pleasantly off. There
were also two friends of Charles, by name Paley (a nephew of the Arch
Deacon) and Ashworth. They seem nice young men with modesty and
good breeding. I am glad, as my mother used to say, that his friends are
so produc[e]able. Moreover there came my old, right trusty and well
beloved friend John Richardson. So we were a full party. Lady Anna
Maria returnd in the evening – Francis Scott also dined with us.

30 THURSDAY Disposed of my party as I best might and workd at
my review. Walkd out at one and remaind till near five. Mr. Scott of
Harden and David Thomson, W.S. dined with us.

Received from Mr. Cadell to accot. cash from French and American publishers[1]			£200			
Hay for the season at 7d¼ 2000 stone and upward to Bogie	£61	1	4			
Coals	10	2	11			
Corn	13	13				
Rent of Lochbreist	34					
Work	4					
Bal. due Bogie	1	17	3			
				123	4	6
				76	15	6
Anne to a month house keeping	£45					
To a bill Laidlaw[2] Melrose	11					
Tom	5					
				61	0	0
Cash in purse				15		

Walkd with Mr. Allan through Haxell cleugh.

31 FRIDAY Went on with my review.[3] But I have got Sir Henry's
originall pamphlet which is very cleverly written. I find I cannot touch

1. It seems that Scott kept this, as he did money from articles for
   the *Quarterly*, for his own use. 'I think you told me some foreign
   cash would cast up in the course of this month', he writes to
   Cadell. 'I shall be *hard up* to settle my little harvest expences by
   & bye.' *Letters*, x. 273.
2. Nurseryman at Melrose.
3. Scott's first review (of Robert Monteath's *The Forester's Guide
   and Profitable Planter*) appeared in the October *Quarterly*, no. 72.
   The second article on 'Sir Henry's originall pamphlet' (Sir
   Henry Seton Steuart's 1824 report to the Highland Society) was
   delayed until the March *Quarterly*, no. 74.

on his mode of transplantation at all in this article; it involves many questions and some of importance. So I will make another article for January. Walked up the Rhymer's glen with John Richardson.

SEPTEMBER

1 SATURDAY Colonel Fergusson and Colonel Byres breakfasted, the latter from India, the Nephew of the old Antiquarian. But I had not an opportunity to speak to him about the eastern information required for the *Chronicles*. Besides my review is not finishd though I wrought hard to-day. Sir William Hamilton and his brother Capt. Hamilton calld also young Davidoff. I am somewhat sorry for my young friend. His friends permit him to remain too long in Britain to be happy in Russia. Yet this [is a] prejudice of those who suppose that when the institutions and habits by which they are governd come to be known to strangers they must become exclusively attachd to them. This is not so. The Hottentot returns from civilization to the wild manners of his Krawl and wherefore should not a russian resume his despotic ideas when restored to his country?

2 SUNDAY This was a very warm day. I remaind at home chiefly engaged in arranging papers as I go away tomorrow. It is lucky thes[e] starts happen from time to time as I should otherwise never get my table clear. At five o'clock the air became cooler and I sate out of doors and playd with the children. Anne who had been at Mertoun the day before brought up Anne and Elizabeth Scotts with her and Francis has been with us since yesterday. Richardson left us.

3 MONDAY Went on with my arranging of papers until twelve when I took chaise and arrived at Melville Castle. Found Lord and Lady M— and the two young Ladies – Dr. Hope, my old school fellow. James Hope and his son made up our party which was very pleasant. After they went away we had some private conversation about politics. The Whigs and tories of the Cabinet are strangely divided, the former desiring to have Mr. Herries for Chancellor of the Exchequer, the latter to have Lord Palmerston that Calcraft may be secretary at war. The King has declared firmly for Herries, on which Lord Goodriche with *tears* entreated Herries to remove the bone of contention by declining to accept. The King calld him a blubbering fool. That the King does not love or trust the Whigs is obvious from his passing over Lord Lansdowne, a man whom I should suppose is infinitely better fitted for a premier than Goodriche.[1] But he probably looks with no

1. For Goderich's Cabinet, see Appendix D, p. 826.

greater [favour] on the return of the High Tories. I fear he may wish to govern by the system of *Bascule* or balancing the two parties – a perilous game. The Advocate[1] also dined with us.

4 TUESDAY Came into town after breakfast and saw Gibson whose accompt of affairs is comfortable. Also William Clerk whom I found quite ready and willing to stand my friend if G—d[2] should come my road. He agrees with me that there is no reason why he should turn on me but that if he does, reason or none, it is best to stand buff to him. It is clear to me that what is least forgiven in a man of any mark or likelihood is want of that article blackguardly calld *pluck*. All the fine qualities of genius cannot make amends for it. We are told the genius of poets especially is irreconcileable with this species of grenadier accomplishment. If so *quel chien de genie!* – Saw Lady Compton. It does appear to me my good friend might have left me quiet at home for any advice I have to give her. But she has a perfect right to be *exigeante* even if it were so. I dine with her to-day and go to Glasgow with her tomorrow.[3]

5 WEDNESDAY Dined with Lady Compton yesterday and talkd over old stories until nine, our tete a tete being a very agreeable one. Then home to my good friend John Gibson's and talkd with him of sundries. I had an odd dream last night. It seemd to me that I was at a panorama where a vulgar little man behind me was making some very clever but impudent remarks on the picture and at the same time seemd desirous of information which no one would give him. I turnd round and saw a young fellow dressd like a common carter with a blue coat and red waistcoat and a whip tied across him. He was young with a hatchet face which was burnd to a brick colour by exposure to the weather, sharp eyes and in manner and voice not unlike John Leyden. I was so much struck with his countenance and talents that I askd him about his situation and expressd a wish to mend it. He followd me from the hopes which I excited and we had a dreadful walk among ruins and afterwards I found myself on

1. Sir William Rae, the Lord Advocate.
2. Gourgaud.
3. Lady Compton was Margaret, the daughter of his old friend Mrs. Maclean Clephane of Torloisk, who was shortly leaving for Italy in search of health. Mrs. Clephane wanted advice about her estate and about a legal dispute under arbitration, and only Scott would do: 'She wants much, if she goes, to see you first.' Lady Compton, 3 July 1827, Walpole. John Gibson was her man of business.

horseback and in front of a roaring torrent. I plunged in as I have formerly done in good sad earnest and got to the other side. Then I got home among my children and grandchildren and there also was my genius. Now this would defy Daniel and the soothsayers to boot nor do I know why I should now put it down except that I have seldom seen a portrait in life which was more strongly markd on my memory than that man's. Perhaps my genius was Mr. Dickinson, papermaker, who has undertaken that the London Crers who hold Constable's bills will be satisfied with ten shillings in the pounds. This would be turning a genius to purpose for 6/8 is provided and they can have no difficulty about 2/4.[1] These debts for which I am legally responsible though no party to their contraction amount to £30,000 odds.[2] Now if they can be cleared for £15,000 it is just so much gaind. This would be a giant's step to freedom – I see in my present comfortable quarters[3] some of my own old furniture in Castle Street, which gives me rather queer feelings. I remember poor Charlotte and I having so much thought about buying these things. Well – they are in kind and friendly hands.

6 THURSDAY Went with Lady Compton to Glasgow and had as pleasant a journey as the kindness, wit and accomplishment of my companion could make it. Lady C. gives an admirable account of Rome and the various strange characters whom she has met in foreign parts. I was much taken with some stories out a romance calld *Manucrit trouvé a Saragosse* by a certain Count John Potowsky,[4] a Pole. It seems betwixt the stile of Cazotte, Count Hamilton and Le Sage. The Count was a toiler after supernatural secrets – an adept

---

1. A slip for 3/4. Scott's arithmetic, like the dating of his letters, is that of a gentleman.
2. Scott's debts included '£13,800 being the amt. of several Bonds in which he is a joint obligant with Messrs. A Constable & Co. but the whole of which were the proper debts of the latter'. Sederunt Book, i. 260. A later calculation of the Trustees was that there were 'proper Debts of Archd. Constable & Co. ranking upon his Estate for the amount of – £50,000'. Sederunt Book, ii. 212. Had John Dickinson, of Longman and Dickinson the paper-makers, been able to do what is here stated, Scott would have speedily been able to clear himself.
3. John Gibson's house, 23 Lynedoch Place. 'On two several occasions he did me the kindness to reside two or three days in my house, and I need not say that we felt his visit to be an honour as well as a pleasure.' Gibson's *Reminiscences*, p. 39.
4. Count Jan Potocki, whose novel was published in St. Petersburg in 1805.

and understood the Cabala. He put himself to death with many odd circumstances inferring derangement. I am to get a sight of the book if it be possible. At Glasgow (Buck's Head) we met Mrs. Maclean Clephane and her two daughters and there was much joy. After the dinner the ladies sung, particularly Anna Jane who has more taste and talent of every kind than half the people going with great reputations on their backs.

A very pleasant day was paid for by a restless night. I was mauld by the bugs inhumanly.

7 FRIDAY This day had calls from Lord Provost[1] and from Mr. Rutherford (William) with invitations which I declined. Read in Manuscript a very clever play (comedy) by Miss A. J. Clephane in the old stile which was very happily imitated. The plot was confused – too much taking and retaking of prisoners but the dialogue was excellent.

Took leave of these dear friends, never perhaps to meet all together again for two of us are old. Went down by steam[2] to Col. Campbell's Blythswood House where I was most courteously received by him and his sisters. We are kinsfolk and very old acquaintance. His seat here is a fine one; the house built by Smirke is both grand and comfortable.

We walkd to Lawrence Lockhart's[3] of Inchinnan within a mile of Blythswood house. It is extremely nice and comfortable far beyond the stile of a Scotch clergyman but Lawrence is wealthy. I found John Lockhart and Sophia there returnd from Largs. We all dined at Col. Campbell's on turtle and all manner of good things. Miss A. and H. Walker were there. The sleep at night made amends for the Buck's Head.

8 SATURDAY Colonel Campbell carried me to breakfast in Glasgow and at ten I took chaise for Corehouse,[4] where I found my old friend George Cranstoun rejoiced to see me and glad when I told him what Lord Newton had determined in my affairs.[5] I should observe I saw the banks of the Clyde above Hamilton much denuded of its copse *untimely cut* and the stools ill cut and worse kept.

1. William Hamilton, a West India merchant.
2. Down the Clyde.
3. J. G. Lockhart's brother.
4. Near Lanark.
5. The matter was not yet finally settled, however. See the Entry for 25 July 1827 and note. Cranstoun's particular interest was that he had been retained as counsel by the Trustees at the beginning of the arbitration.

Cranstoun and I walkd before dinner. I never saw the Great fall of Corehouse from this side before and I think it the best point perhaps. At all events it is not that from which it is usually seen so Lord Corehouse[1] has the sight and escapes the tourists. Dined with him, his sister Mrs. Cunningham, and Corehouse.[2]

I omitted to mention in yesterday's note that within Blythswood's plantation near to the Bridge of Inchinnan the unfortunate Earl of Argyle was taken in 1685 at a stone calld Argyle's Stone.[3] Blythswood says the highland drovers break down his fences in order to pay a visit to the place. The Earl had passd the Cart river and was taken on the Renfrew side.

9 SUNDAY This is a superb place of Corehouse. Cranstoun has as much feeling about improvement as other things. Like all new improvers he is at more expence than is necessary, plants too thick and trenches where trenching is superfluous. But this is the eagerness of a young artist. Besides the grand lion, the Fall of Clyde, he has more than one lion's whelp – a fall of a brook in a cleugh calld Mill's Gill must be superb in rainy weather. The old Castle of Corehouse is much more Castle-like on this than from the other side. My old friend was very happy when I told him the opinion which Lord Newton had adopted in my affairs. To be sure if I come through it will be wonder to all and most to myself.

Left Corehouse at eight in the morning and reachd Lanark by half past nine. I was thus long in travelling three miles because the postilion chose to suppose I was bound for Biggar and was two miles ere I discoverd what he was doing. I thought he aimd at crossing the Clyde by some new bridge above Bonnington.

Breakfast at Lanark with the Lockharts and reachd Abbotsford this evening by nine o'clock.

Thus ends a pleasant expedition among the people I like most, Drawbacks only are It has cost me £15 including two gowns for Sophia and Anne – and I have lost six days' labour. Both may be soon made up.

N.B. – We lunchd (dined *videlicet*) with Professor Wilson at Inverleithen and met James Hog.

10 MONDAY Gourgaud's wrath has burst forth in a very distant clap of thunder in which he accuses me of combining with the ministry to

1. i.e. George Cranstoun, who had taken the title of Lord Corehouse on his elevation to the Bench.
2. A slip for '[Campbell of] Blythswood'.
3. At the end of his ill-starred expedition from Holland against James II and VII.

slander his rag of a reputation. He be d——d for a fool to make his case worse by stirring. I shall only revenge myself by publishing the whole extracts I made from the records of the Colonial Office in which he will find enough to make him bite his nails. I wonder he did not try to come over and try his manhood other wise. I would not have shund him nor any frenchman who ever kissd Bonaparte's breech.

Sick to-night of a disease very common at present affecting the stomach.

11 TUESDAY Went to Huntly burn and breakfasted with Colonel Fergusson, who has promised to have some Indian memoranda[1] ready for me. After breakfast went to clear the ground for a new plantation to be added next week to the end of Jane's wood. Came to dinner Lord Carnarvon and his son and daughter.[2] Also Lord Francis Leveson Gower the translator of the *Faust*. Mr. Herbert is unwell and keeps his bed. Anne has a swelld face and Charles is still afflicted with the rheumatics. However we shuffle off the evening.

12 WEDNESDAY Walk with Lord Francis. When we return, behold ye, Enter Lady Hamden and Lady Wedderburn – in the days of George's Square[3] Jane and Maria Browns, beauties and toasts. There was much pleasure on my side and some I suppose on theirs and there was a riding and a running and a chattering and an asking and a shewing, a real scene of confusion yet mirth and good spirits. Our guests quit us next day.

13 THURSDAY Find a man for an assault at Selkirk. He pleaded guilty which made short work. The beggarly appearance of the Jury in the new system is very worthy of note. One was a menial Servant.[4] When I returnd James Ballantyne and Mr. Cadell arrived.[5] They bring a good account of matters in general. Cadell explaind to me a plan for securing the copy right of the novels which has a very good

---

1. For use in 'The Surgeon's Daughter'.
2. His second son, the Hon. Edward Charles Hugh Herbert (1802–40), and his unmarried daughter, Lady Harriet Elizabeth (1797–1829).
3. Where Scott lived throughout his childhood and youth.
4. Scott distrusted the alteration which brought in jury trials to the Sheriff Courts. (See the Entry for 2 May 1827.) His objection to 'a menial Servant' was not mere snobbery, but a concern for fair play. In 1830 he tells Lockhart that 'a man who had got a citation as a juryman came under the idea he was himself to be a subject of trial for some unknown crime such was his accurate knowledge of the business in hand'. *Letters*, xi. 347.
5. By arrangement. See *Letters*, x. 275.

face. It appears they are going off fast and if the glut of the market is once reduced by sales the property will be excellent and may be increased by notes.[1] James B. brought his son. Robert Rutherford also here and Miss Russells.

14 FRIDAY In the morning wrote my answer to Gourgaud[2] – rather too keen perhaps but I owe him nothing and as for exciting his resentment I will neither seek nor avoid it.

Cadell's views seem fair and he is open and explicit. His brothers support him and he has no want of cash. He sells two or three copies of *Bonaparte* and one of the novels or two almost every day. He must soon he says apply to London for copies. Read a Refutation[3] as it calls itself of *Napoleon*'s history. It is so very polite and accomodating that every third word is a concession – the work of a man able to judge distinctly on specific facts but erroneous in his general results. He will say the same of me perhaps.

Ballantyne and Cadell leave us. Enter Miss Sinclairs, two in Number. Also a translator and a little Flemish woman his wife – very good-humourd, rather a little given to compliment, name Fauconpret. They are to return at night in a gigg as far as Kelso,[4] a bold undertaking. Russells leave us.

15 SATURDAY Anne and Charles are both indisposed, the weather I suppose unwholesome. We got on as we could.

		Cash from Cadell to accot of remitances		
In purse	£30	from [*illeg*]		£40
		To repaid Lockhart	£5.0.0	
		To Tweedside Charity club	5	
			—	10
		In purse		£30

1. This idea was put into practice in the Magnum Opus or collected, illustrated edition of the novels to which Scott added his notes.
2. The reply was to appear in the *Edinburgh Weekly Journal*. Scott sent it first to Clerk for an opinion. See *Letters*, x. 277–82, or *Life*, ix. 147.
3. Probably *Réfutation de la Vie de Napoléon de Sir Walter Scott*, by Jean François Caze, 1827.
4. Presumably they had set out before receiving Scott's second note to them: 'We can give you a comfortable bed and beg you will make your arrangements accordingly.' Disc. i. 112. De Fauconpret was the translator of Scott's novels into French.

16 SUNDAY The Ladies went to church. I God forgive me finishd the *Chronicles* with a good deal assistance from Colonel Fergusson's notes about Indian affairs. The patch is I suspect too glaring to be pleasing but the Colonel's sketches are capitally good. I understand too there are one or two East Indian novels which have lately appeard – Naboclish. *Vogue la galere.*

17 MONDAY The Miss Sinclairs left us in the morning victuald for a voyage over to Moffat to join their father. Receivd from James B. the proofs of my reply to Genl Gourgaud with some cautious Balaam from mine honest friend, alarmd by a highland Colonel who had described Gourgaud as a *Mauvais garçon*, famous fencer, marks man and so forth. I wrote in answer, which is true, that I would hope all my friends would trust to my acting with proper caution and advice. But that if I were capable in a moment of weakness of doing any [thing] short of what my honour demanded, I would die the death of a poisond rat in a hole out of mere sense of my own degradation. God knows that though life is placid enough with me I do not feel any thing to attach me to it so strongly as to occasion my avoiding any risque which the duty to my character may demand from me.

I set to work with the *Tales of a Grandfather* 2d Volume and finishd four pages.

18 TUESDAY Wrote five pages of the *Tales* – walkd from Huntly burn having gone there in the carriage. Charles is getting better of his rheumatism. Anne still poorly. Smoked my Segars with Lockhart after dinner[1] and then whiled away the evening over one of Miss Austen's Novels; there is a truth of painting in her writings which always delights me. They do not it is true get above the middle classes of Society. But there she is inimitable.

19 WEDNESDAY Wrote three pages but dawdled a good deal – yet the *Tales* get on although I feel bilious and vapourish, I believe I must call it. At such times my loneliness and the increasing inability to walk come dark over me. But surely these mulligrubs belong to the mind more than the body.

---

1. The remissness of Walter and the quarrel with Gourgaud were among the subjects discussed, judging by Lockhart's letter to Walter the next day: 'I am heartily sorry you & your wife have not made your appearance here as was promised and expected . . . The Peveril is obviously sulky at having missed the opportunity of a duello with one of Bony's Generals – *entre nous* he had all ready, even to his second.' Abbots.

20 THURSDAY A party to eat a haunch of venison. George Pringle of Torwoodlee, Whitebank and his brother Robert, Miss Pringles Whitebank, Mr. and Mrs. Scott Harden with Maria and Francis. Also Charles Dundas of Melville with a Mr. Loft, friend to Misses Russells, a stranger who must have been rather embarassd at finding himself plunged up to the ears amongst Scotts and Pringles. This gentleman's otherwise very handsome and intelligent face is defigured by want of an eye. He was civil to Miss Russells at Paris and even very [kind]. Such attention to two ladies neither young beautiful nor rich argues a genuine good disposition.

21 FRIDAY The Scotts of Harden, Laird and Lady, remaind with us but Frank and young Dundas go to Lockhart. Mr. Loft leaves us. So the party is in great measure broken up. I walkd a good deal with Mrs. Scott of Harden. Nevertheless I did not omit to write a little.

22 SATURDAY Mr. and Mrs. Scott leave us. Maria is to stay a day or two – Francis and Dundas return to dinner from Oakwood. Capt. and Colonel Fergusson – the last returned from Ireland – dined here. Prayer of the Minister of the Cumrays, two miserable islands in the mouth of the Clyde, 'O Lord, bless and be gracious to the Greater and the Lesser Cumrays and in thy mercy do not forget the adjacent islands of Great Britain and Ireland.' This is *Nos poma natamus*[1] with a vengeance.

23 SUNDAY Workd in the morning – then drove over to Huntly Burn chiefly to get from the good humourd Colonel the accurate spelling of certain Hindhu words[2] which I have been using under his instructions. By the way the sketches he gave me of Indian manners are highly picturesque. I have made up my journal which was three days in arrear. Also I wrought a little so that the 2 vol of *Grandfather's Tales* is nearly half finishd. Francis Scott left us after supper rather late for the Monk's ford.[3]

24 MONDAY Workd in the morning as usual and sent off the proofs and copy. Some things of the black dog still hanging about me but I will shake him off. I generally affect good spirits in company of my family whether I am enjoying them or not. It is too severe to sadden the harmless mirth of others by suffering your own causeless melancholy to be seen. And this species of exertion is like virtue

1. See the Entry for 4 February 1827 and note.
2. Having in effect his own printing-house, Scott was able to leave such details until the proof stage. See for instance *Letters*, x. 226.
3. The ford across the Tweed just below Abbotsford.

its own reward for the good spirits which are at first simulated become at length real.

25 TUESDAY Got into town by one o'clock, the purpose being to give my deposition before Lord Newton in a case betwixt me and Constable's crers. My oath seemd satisfactory but new reasons were alleged for additional discussion which is I trust to end this wearisome matter.[1] I dined with Mr. Gibson and slept there.[2] J.B. dined with us and we had thoughts how to save our copyrights by a bargain with Cadell. I hope it will turn to good as I could add notes to a future edition and give them some value.[3]

26 WEDNESDAY Set off in Mail coach and my horses met me at Yair Bridge. I travelld with rather a pleasant man, an agent I found on Lord Seaford's West Indian estates. Got home by twelve o'clock and might have been home earlier if the Tweed had not been too large for fording. I must note down my cash lest it gets out of my head. 'May the foul fa' the gear and the blaithrie o't.'[4] And yet there's no doing either with it or without it. I may record here an infernal rheumatick headache.

To Tom Purdie	£10		Cash in purse	£30
To Segars	3		Salary receved in	
To Mr. Bridges pr. Cadell for W. Scott	30		part by Cadell —	150
To expences into town and sundries	3			
Cash in purse £48 To Bogie harvest wages	40			
To Anne House	45			
Expences return	1			
	132			
Ball: in cash	48			
	£180			£180

1. The profits from *Woodstock* and the *Life of Napoleon* were still in dispute.
2. Gibson had written on 25 August: 'As most of your friends will be out of town next month, it would give me very great pleasure, & I should esteem it a great honor, if you would make my house your own when you come to town. My family will be at sea bathing quarters, so that you will not be annoyed with them.' Walpole.
3. Another allusion to what became the Magnum Opus.
4. 'Bagrie o't', l. 4. Herd, ii. 1.47. 'Blaithrie' means trumpery or foolishness.

27 THURSDAY The morning was damp dripping and unpleasant so I even made a work of necessity and set to the *Tales* like a dragon. I murderd Maclellan of Bomby at the Thrieve Castle – Stabbed the Black Douglas in the town of Stirling – astonishd King James before Roxburgh – and stifled the Earl of Mar in his bath in the Canongate.[1] A wild world, my Masters, this Scotland of ours must have been. No fear of want of interest; no lassitude in those days for want of work

> For treason d'ye see
> Was to them a dish of tea
> And murther bread and butter.[2]

We dined at Gattonside with Mr. Bembridge who kindly presented me with 6 bottles of super-excellent Jamaica Rum and with a manuscript collection of poetry said to be Swift's hand writing, which it resembles. It is I think poor Stella's. Nothing very new in it.[3]

28 FRIDAY Another dropping and briny day. I wrought hard at the *Historical Tales*[4] which get on fast. Anne and I drove to Haining and made a visit to the ladies of that mansion. Sophia went with us. On our return we found Mr. and Mrs. Sale Marten who spent the day with us quietly and took up their old quarters.

29 SATURDAY I went on with the little history which now (i.e. Vol II d) doth appropinque an end.[5] Received in the evening   [6] of the Roxburghe publications. They are very curious and genral[ly] speaking well selected. The following struck me. An Italian poem on the subject of Flodden field – the Legend of Saint Robert of Knares-borough. Two plays printed from Ms by Mr. Haslewood. It does not appear that Mr. H— fully appreciated the light which he was throwing on the theatrical History by this valuable communication. It appears that the change of place or of scene as we term it was intimated in the following manner.

1. In other words, he wrote chapters 21 and 22 of *Tales of a Grandfather*.
2. Shenstone's 'Rape of the Trap', st. 6.
3. Scott was, of course, the editor of Swift. The MS., which is late eighteenth century, is at Abbotsford.
4. i.e. *Tales of a Grandfather*.
5. Butler's *Hudibras*, pt. 1, canto 3.
6. Grierson suggests that Scott intended to insert 'Nos. 37 to 41' in the blank space. *Letters*, x. 285 n. The works referred to may be found under those numbers. Each member of the Club, instituted in 1812 to commemorate the sale of the great library of John, third Duke of Roxburghe, who died in 1804, was expected to print one book in an edition of not more than thirty-six copies.

In the middle of the stage was placed Colchester and the sign of Pigot's Tavern calld The Tarleton intimated what part of the town was represented. The name was painted above. On one side of the stage was in like manner painted a town which the name announced to be Maldon, on the other side A Ranger's lodge. The scene lay through the piece in one or other of these three places and the entrance of the characters determined where each scene lay. If they came in from Colchester then Colchester was for the time the scene of action. When that scene was shifted to Maldon it was intimated by the approach of the actors from the side where it was painted – a clumsy contrivance doubtless compared to changeable scenery yet sufficient to impress the audience with a sense of what was meant.

30 SUNDAY Wet drizzling dismal day. I finishd odds and ends, scarce stirring out of my room yet doing little to the purpose. Wrote to Sir Henry[1] about his queries concerning transplanted trees and to Mr. Freling concerning these Roxburghe club books. I have settled to print the Manuscript concerning the murder of the two Schaws by the Master of Sinclair.[2] I dallied with the precious time rather than used it. Read the two Roxburghe plays. They are by William Percy a son of the VIII Earl of Northumberland – worthless and very gross but abounding with matters concerning scenery and so forth highly interesting to the dramatic antiquary.

OCTOBER

1 MONDAY I sett about work for two hours and finishd three pages, then walkd for two hours – then home, adjusted Sheriff processes and cleard the table. I am to set off tomorrow for Ravensworth Castle to meet the Duke of Wellington[3] – a great Let off I suppose. Yet I would

1. Sir Henry Steuart.
2. Scott's edition of *Proceedings in the Court Martial held upon John, Master of Sinclair etc.*, was printed by the Club in 1828.
3. 'The Duke was then making a progress in the north of England, to which additional importance was given by the uncertain state of political arrangements; – the chance of Lord Goderich's being able to maintain himself as Canning's successor seeming very precarious – and the opinion that his Grace must soon be called to a higher station than that of Commander of the Forces, which he had accepted under the new Premier, gaining ground every day.' *Life*, ix. 156–7. Scott was invited by Lady Ravensworth who was 'naturally anxious to invite the Person to meet him, who would be most acceptable to the Hero of Waterloo'. 8 September 1827, Walpole.

almost rather stay and see two days more of Lockhart and my daughter who will be off before my return. Perhaps – But there is no end to perhaps. We must cut the rope and let the vessell drive down the tide of destiny.

Cash	£48
To pay an	
Accot. for Anne	5
	43

2 TUESDAY Set out in the morning at seven and reachd Kelso by a little past ten with my own horses. Then took the Wellington coach[1] to carry me to Wellington – smart that – Nobody inside but an old Lady who proved a toy woman in Edinburgh. Her head furnishd with as substantial ware as her shop but a good soul I'se warrant her. Heard all her debates with her Landlord about a new door to the cellar, etc. etc., propriety of paying rent on the 15th. or 25th. March. Landlords and tenants have different opinions on that subject. Danger of dirty sheets in inns. We dined at Wooler and I found out Doctor Douglas on the outside, son of my old acquaintance Dr. James Douglas of Kelso. This made us even lighter in hand till we came to Whittingham. Thence to NewCastle where an obstreperous horse retarded us for an hour at least to the great alarm of my friend the toywoman. N.B. She would have made a good featherbed if the carriage had happend to fall and her undermost. The heavy roads had retarded us near an hour more. So that I hesitated to go to Ravensworth so late. But my good woman's tales of dirty sheets and certain recollections of a Newcastle inn[2] induced me to go on. When I arrived the family had just retired. Lord Ravensworth and Mr. Liddell[3] came down however and real[ly] received me as kindly as possible.

3 WEDNESDAY Rose about eight or later. My morals begin to be corrupted by travel and fine company. Went to Durham with Lord Ravensworth betwixt one and two. Found the gentlemen of Durham county and town assembled to receive the Duke of Wellington. I saw several old friends and with difficulty sorted names to faces and faces to names. There was Headlam, Dr. Gilly and his wife, and a world of acquaintance beside. Sir Thomas Lawrence too with Lord Londonderry. I asked him to come on with me[4] but he could not. He is, from habit of coaxing his Subjects I suppose, a little too fair spoken

---

1. The Wellington ran between Edinburgh and London by way of Kelso, Newcastle, and York.
2. Moore too, on his way to Abbotsford in 1825 'got a wretched bed at Newcastle'. *Memoirs of Moore*, iv. 330.
3. Baron Ravensworth's son.
4. i.e. to Abbotsford.

otherwise very pleasant. The Duke arrived very late. There were bells and cannon and drums trumpets and banners besides a fine troop of yeomanry. The address was well expressd and as well answerd by the Duke. The enthusiasm of the ladies and the gentry was great – the common people were luke warm, The Duke has lost popularity in accepting political power. He will be more useful to his country it may be than ever but will scarce be so gracious in the people's eyes – And he will not care a curse for what outward show he has lost.

But I must not talk of curses for we are going to take our dinner with the Bishop of Durham, a man of amiable and courteous manners who becomes his station well but has traces of bad health on his countenance. We dined, about one hundred and forty or fifty men, a distinguishd company for rank and property. Marshal Beresford and Sir John[1] amongst others. Marquis of Lothian, Lord Duncombe, Marquis Londonderry and I know not who besides

> Lords and Dukes and noble princes
> All the pride and flower of Spain.[2]

We dind in the rude old Baronial hall, impressive from its rude antiquity and fortunately free from the plaster of former improvement as I trust it will [be] from the gingerbread tast[e] of Modern Gothicizers. The bright moon streaming in through the old Gothick windows made a light which contested strangely with the artificial lights within. Spears banners and armour were intermixd with the pictures of old and the whole had a singular mixture of Baronial pomp with the graver and more chastend dignity of prelacy. The conduct of our Reverend entertartainer suited the character remarkably well. Amid the wellcome of a Count Palatine he did not for an instant forget the gravity of the Church dignitary. All his toasts were gracefully given and his little speeches well made, and the more affecting that the failing voice sometimes reminded us that our aged Host labourd under the infirmities of advancd life. To me personally the Bishop was very civil and paid me his public compliments by proposing my health in the most gratifying manner.

The Bishop's lady received, a sort of drawing room, after we rose from table, at which a great many ladies attended. I ought no[t] to forget that the singers of the choir attended at dinner and sung the Anthem *Non nobis Domine*, as they said who understood them, very

1. Admiral Sir John Beresford, whom Scott had known when he commanded the Leith Station some years before.
2. 'Gentle River', l. 12, in Percy's *Reliques*.

well – and, as I think who did not understand the music, with an unusual degree of spirit and interest. It is odd how this can be distinguishd from the notes of fellows who use their throats with as little feeling of the notes they utter as if they were composed of the same metal with their bugle-horns.

After the drawing room we went to the Assembly rooms which were crowded with company. I saw some very pretty girls dancing merrily that old fashiond thing calld a country-dance which Old England has now thrown aside as she would do her creed if there were some foreign frippery offerd instead. We got away after midnight, a large party, and reachd Ravensworth Castle, Duke of Wellington, Lord Londonderry and about twenty besides, about half past one. Soda-water and to bed by two.

4 THURSDAY Slept till nigh ten fatigued by our toils of yesterday and the unwonted late hours. Still too early for this castle of Indolence for I found few of last night's party yet appearing. I had an opportunity of some talk with the Duke. He does not consider Foy's book[1] as written by himself but as a thing *got up* perhaps from notes. Says he knew Foy very well in Spain. Mentiond that he was like other French officers very desirous of seeing the English papers through which alone they could collect any idea of what was going on without their own cantonments for Napoleon permitted no communication of that kind with France. The Duke growing tired of this at length told Baron Tripp whose services he chiefly used in communication with the outpost that he was not to give them the newspapers – 'What reason shall I allege for withholding them?' said Baron Tripp. 'None –' replied the Duke. 'Let them allege some reason why they want them.' Foy was not at a loss to assign a reason. He said he had considerable sums of money in the English funds and wanted to see how stocks fell and rose. The excuse did not however go down – I remember Baron Tripp, a Dutch nobleman and a dandie of the first water and yet with an energy in his dandyism which made it respectable. He drove a gigg as far as Dunrobin Castle and back again *without a whip*. He lookd after his own horse for he had no servant and after all his little establishment of clothes and necessaries with all the accuracy of a *petit maitre*. He was one of the best dressd men and his horse was in equally fine condition as if he had had a dozen of grooms. I met him at Lord Somerville's and liked him much. But there was something exaggerated as appeard from the conclusion of his life. Baron Tripp shot himself in Italy for no assignable cause.

What is calld great society, of which I have seen a good deal in my

1. *Histoire de la guerre de la Péninsule sous Napoléon*, 1827.

day, is now amusing to me because from age and indifference I have lost the habit of conceiving myself as a part of it and have only the feelings of looking on, a spectator of the scene who can neither play his part well nor ill, instead of being one of the *dramatis personæ*, and, careless what is thought of myself, I have full time to attend to the motions of others.

Our party went to-day to Sunderland where the Duke was brilliantly received by an immense population chiefly of Seamen. The difficulty of getting into the rooms was dreadful for we chanced to march in the rear of an immense Gibraltar gun etc. all composed of glass which is here manufactured in great quantity. The disturbance created by this thing, which by the way I never saw afterwards, occasiond an ebbing and flowing of the crowd which nearly took me off my legs. I have seen the day I would have minded it little. The entertainment was handsome; about two hundred dined and appeard most hearty in the cause which had convend them – some indeed so much so that finding themselves so far on the way to perfect happiness they een threw discretion to the winds. After the dinner-party broke up there was a ball, numerously attended, where there was a prodigious anxiety discoverd for shaking of hands. The Duke had enough of it and I came in for my share for though as Jackall to the lion I got some part in whatever was going. We got home about half past two in the morning sufficiently tired. The Duke went to Seaham, a house of Lord Londonderry. After all, this Sunderland trip might have been spared.

5 FRIDAY A quiet day at Ravensworth Castle giggling and making giggle among the kind and frank hearted young people. Ravensworth castle is chiefly modern excepting always two towers of great antiquity. Lord Ravensworth manages his woods admirably well and with good taste. His castle is but half built; elections have come between.[1] In the evening plenty of fine music with heart as well as voice and instrument. Much of the music was the spontaneous effusions of Mrs. Arkwright[2] who had set 'Hohen Linden' and other pieces of poetry. The music was of a highly gifted character. She was the daughter of Stephen Kemble of corpulent memory. Her genius

1. Douglas, illustrating the cost of an election to the aristocracy, instances the £100,000 subscribed by the Duke of Northumberland in 1831.
2. Scott later learned that the tune he most admired had been composed not by Mrs. Arkwright but by Miss H. M. Browne, and he insisted on helping her to have her music published. See the Entry for 21 January 1828 and note.

she must have inherited from her mother who was a capital actress. Stephen was a stupid hulk. The Miss Liddells and Mrs. Barrington[1] sang the 'The Campbells are Coming' in a tone that might have waked the dead.

6 SATURDAY Left Ravensworth this morning and travelld as far as Whittingham with Marquis of Lothian. Arrived at Alnwick to dinner where I was very kindly received. The Duke[2] is a handsome man who will be corpulent if he does not continue to take hard exercize. The Duchess very pretty and lively but her liveliness is of that kind which shews at once it is connected with thorough principle and is not liable to be influenced by fashionable caprice. The habits of the family are early and regular. I conceive they may be termed formal and old fashiond by such visitors as claim to be the pink of the mode. The Castle is a fine old pile with various courts and towers and the entrance is magnificent. It wants however the splendid feature of a Keep which I recollect struck me at Alnwick.[3] The inside fitting up is an attempt at Gothick but the taste is meagre and poor and done over with too much gilding. It was done half a century ago when the kind of taste was ill understood. I found here the Bishop of Worcester;[4] Mr. and Mrs. Murray Ainslie of Elliston, a Mr. and Mrs. Raine, the former the duke's Chamberlain, and Capt and Mrs. Bowles.

7 SUNDAY This morning went to church and heard an excellent sermon from the Bishop of Worcester;[4] he has great dignity of manner and his accent and delivery was forcible. Drove out with the Duke and Mrs. Ainslie in a phaeton and saw part of the park which is a fine one lying along the Alne. But it has been ill planted. It was laid out by the celebrated Brown who substituted clumps of birch and Scottish firs for the beautiful oaks and copse which grows no where so freely as in Northumberland. To complete this the late Duke did not thin so the wood is in poor state. All that the Duke cuts down is so much waste for the people will not buy it where coals are so scarce.[5] Had they been oak wood the bark would have fetchd its value – had they been grown oak the sea ports would have found a market. Had they been [larch] the country demands for rustic purposes would have been innumerable. The D. does the best he

1. Their married sister.
2. The third Duke of Northumberland.
3. A slip for 'Warkworth'.
4. A slip for 'the Bishop of Gloucester', Dr. Bethell, who had formerly been tutor to the Duke.
5. Scott means 'plentiful'.

can to retrieve his woods but seems to despond more than a young man ought to do. It is refreshing to see a man in his situation give so much of his thoughts and time to the improvement of his estates and the wellfare of the people. The Duke tells me his people in Keeldar were all quite wild the first time his father went up to shoot there. The women had no other dress than a bedgown and petticoat. The men were savage and could hardly be brought to rise from the heath either from sullenness or fear. They sung a wild tune, the burden of which was *Ourina Ourina Ourina*. The females sung, the men danced round and at a certain part of the tune *Ourina* they drew their dirks which they always wore.

We came by the remains of the old Carmelite Monastery of Hulne which is a very fine object in the park. It was finishd by De Vesci. The gateway of Alnwick Abbey, also a fine speciment, is standing about a mile distant. The trees are much finer on the left side of the Alne where they have been let alone by the capability villain.[1] Visited the enceinte of the castle and peepd into the dungeon. There is also an armoury but damp and the arms in indifferent order. One odd petard looking thing struck me.[2] – Mem. to consult Grose.[3] I had the honour to sit in Hotspur's seat and to see the Bloody Gap, a place where the external wall must have been breachd. The Duchess gave me a book of etchings of the antiquities of Alnwick and Warkworth from her own drawings.[4] I had half a mind to stay to see Warkworth but Anne is alone. We had prayers in the Evening read by the Arch Deacon.[5]

The Marquis of Lothian on Saturday last told me a remarkable thing which he had from good authority. Just before Bonaparte's return from Elba there was much disunion at the Congress of Vienna. Russia and Prussia, conscious of their own merits, made great demands to which Austria, France and Britain were not disposed to accede. This went so far that war became probable and the very Prussian army which was so useful at Waterloo was held in readiness to attack the English. On the other hand England, Austria and France enterd into a private agreement to resist beyond a certain extent Prussia's demands of a barrier on the Rhine etc. and what is most singular of all it was from Bonaparte that the Emperor Alexander first

1. 'Capability' Brown.
2. A crude sketch follows in the original.
3. Francis Grose's *Military Antiquities etc. and Treatise on Ancient Armour, new. edit.*, 1801, is in the Abbotsford Library.
4. The privately printed volume of etchings by the Duchess, *Castles of Alnwick and Warkworth*, 1823, is in the Abbotsford Library.
5. 'Mr. Archdeacon Singleton'. J. G. L.

heard of this triple alliance. But the circumstance of finding Napoleon interesting himself so far in the affairs of Europe alarmd the Emperor more than the news he sent him. On same authority Gneisenau and most of Blücher's personal suite remaind behind a house at the battle of Ligny and sent out an officer from time to time but did not remain even in sight of the battle till Blucher put himself at the head of the cavalry with the zeal of an old hussar.

8 MONDAY Left Alnwick where I have experienced a very kind reception and took coach at Whittingham at eleven o'clock. I find there is a new road to be made between Alnwick and Wooler which will make the communication much easier and avoid Remside moor. Saw some fine young plantations about Wittingham suffering from neglect, which is not the case under his own eye. The Duke has made two neat cottages at Percy's Cross to preserve that ancient monument of the fatal battle of Hedgeley Moor.[1] The stones marking the adjacent spot calld Percy's Leap are 33 feet asunder – To shew the uncertainty of human testimony I measured the distance (many years since, it is true) and would have said and almost sworn that it was but eighteen feet.

Dined at Wooler and reachd home about 7 o'clock having left Alnwick half past nine. So it would be easy to go there to dinner from Abbotsford[2] starting at six in the morning, or seven would do very well.

9 TUESDAY After I came home last night my stomach was extremely disorderd – with bile I suppose from unwonted late hours and change of living – So much for turtle and venison every day. No proofs here which I think odd of Jas. B. But I am not sorry to have a day to write letters and besides I have a box of books to arrange. It is a bad mizzling day and might have been a good day for work but yet it is not quite uselessly spent. My indisposition is quite gone after an indifferent night.

10 WEDNESDAY Breakfasted at Huntley Burn with the merry knight Sir Adam Fergusson. When we returnd we found a whole parcel of proofs which had been forgot yesterday at the toll. So here ends play and begins work. Dr. Brewster and Mr. Thornhill. The latter gave me a box made of the real mulberry tree.[3] Very kind of him. I wrote better than task and yet took a good walk.

1. The Yorkists defeated the Lancastrians there in 1464.
2. The distance was fifty-five miles.
3. From Shakespeare's garden at New Place.

11 THURSDAY Being a base melancholy weeping day I een made the best of it and set in for work. Wrote ten leaves this day equivalent to forty pages. But then the theme was so familiar being Scottish history that my pen never rested. It is more than a triple task.

12 FRIDAY Sent off proofs and copy. Then proceeded with a full task of three pages. At one Anne drove me to Huntley Burn and I examined the earthen fence intended for the new planting[1] and alterd the line in some points. This employd me till near four, the time of my walking home being included.

13 SATURDAY Wrote in the forenoon. Lord Bessborough and Mr and Mrs. Ponsonby[2] calld to see the place. His lady[3] used to be civil to me in London. An accomplishd and pleasing woman, a *Chère Amie* of Sheridan's it was rumourd. This young Lady seems to have very indifferent health. They only staid one hour.

At dinner we had Lord and Lady Bathurst and my friend Lady Georgiana – Also Marquis of Lothian and Lord Castlereagh, plenty of fine folks. Expected also the Lord Register[4] and Mrs. Dundas but they could not come. Lord Bathurst told me that Gourgaud had negociated with the French government to the last moment of his leaving London, and that he had been told so by the French Embassador. Lord B. refused to see him because he understood he talkd disrespectfully of Napoleon.

I should have said we had the two miss Kerrs, Lord Robert's daughters, who sung beautifully.

14 SUNDAY I read prayers to the Company of yesterday and we took a drive round by Drygrange Bridge. Lord B. told me that the late King made it at one time a point of conscience to read every word of every Act of parliament before giving his assent to it. There was a mixture of principle and nonsense in this. Lord Lothian left us. I did a full task to-day, which is much considering I was a good deal occupied.

15 MONDAY My noble guests departed, pleased I believe with their visit. I have had to thank Lord Bathurst for former kindness. I respect

1. 'A new plantation to be added . . . to the end of Jane's wood'. Entry for 11 September 1827.
2. The third Earl of Bessborough, his son, and daughter-in-law.
3. Henrietta, wife to the third Earl.
4. The Rt. Hon. William Dundas, Principal Keeper of the Register of Sasines.

him too as one who being far from rich has on the late occasion preferd political consistency to a love of office and its emoluments.[1] He seems to expect no opposition of a formal kind this next Session. What is wonderful, no young man of talents seems to spring up in the house of Commons. I wonder what comes of all the clever lads whom we see at College. The fruit apparently does not ripen as formerly. Lord Castlereagh remaind with [us]. I bestowd a little advice on him. He is a warm hearted young fellow with some of the fashionable affectations of the age about him but with good feelings and an inclination to come forward. Henry Scott dined with us.

16 TUESDAY With all this racquetting the work advances fast. The third volume of the *Tales* is now half finishd and will I think be an useful work. Some drizzling days have been of great use to its progress. This visiting has made some dawdling but not much, perhaps not more than there ought to be for such a task.

I walkd from Huntley Burn up the little glen which was in all the melancholy beauty of Autumn – the little brook brawling and bickering in fine stile over its falls and currents.

17 WEDNESDAY Drove down to Mertoun and brought up Elizabeth Scott to be our guest for some day or so. Various chance guests arrived – One of the most wellcome was Captain McKenzie of the Celtic Society and the 72d Regiment. A picture of a highlander in his gigantic person and innocent and generous disposition. Poor fellow, he is going to retreat to Brittany to make his half pay support a wife and family. I did not dare to ask how many. God send I may have the means of serving him.

He told me a MacLean Story which was new to me. At the battle of Sheriffmoor[2] that Clan was commanded by a chief calld Hector. In the action as the Chief rushd forward he was frequently in situations of peril. His foster father followd him with seven sons whom he reserved as a bodyguard – whom he threw forward into the battle as he saw his chief pressd. The signal he gave was 'Another for Hector.' The youths replied 'Death for Hector' and were all successively killd. These words make the sign and counter sign at this day of the clan Gillian.[3]

Young Shortreed dined with us and the two Fergussons, Sir Adam and the Colonel. We had a pleasant evening.

---

1. He resigned when Canning became Prime Minister in April 1827.
2. A slip for the battle of Inverkeithing, 1651.
3. Scott made use of this story in *The Fair Maid of Perth* the following year.

18 THURSDAY I procured an interview between my gallant highland friend and young Clarkson. Mackenzie suffers cruelly as I believe under the same complaint of spasms by which I was so distressd[1] and was adopting the same ineffectual mode of relief. I made Clarkson give him the process of treatment by which I was cured as I believe radically. It consists in a bold use of calomel. He and young Shortreed left us. Well if I have not much power to help myself it is always lucky I can be of use to others.

19 FRIDAY Wrought out my task and better, as I have done for these several days past. Lady Anna Maria Elliot arrived unexpectedly to dinner and though she had a headache brought her usual wit and good humour to enliven us. She had met a Genl. Upton at Lord Mansfield's, one of the Fancy apparently, and was delighted with one or two slang stories which she had heard from him.

The grave expostulations of the insinuating Mr. Jackson and the replies of the no less celebrated Bill Gibbons gave her peculiar delight. 'How could the rascals be so cruel?' said Jackson to Bill, speaking of an old gentleman who being first beaten by footpads had been afterwards *done* by being flung into a well. 'Upon my word, Bill, this is greatly too bad. The robbery I can understand – but why [throw him into a] well?' – 'On my soul you take it up wrong, my dear fellow' said Will Gibbons. 'You see when an old gentleman is *lushy* it is quite common for them to walk into wells of their own accord – on my life nothing is more common, Mr. Jackson.'

Another time Jackson objected to some theft which had taken place on his own premises as being quite a breach of honour – 'I give you [my] word, Mr. Jackson, no thief would have thought of such a thing' said the apologist. 'Rely upon it, it must have been some of these dust men.'

20 SATURDAY Lady A. M. and Miss E. Scott left us. The day being basely muggy I had no walk which I was rather desirous to secure. I wrought however and two thirds of the last volume of *Tales of my Grandfather* are finishd. I received a large packet of proofs etc. which for some reason had been delayd. We had two of Dr. Brewster's boys to dinner – fine children they are, spirited, promising, and very well behaved.

21 SUNDAY Wrought till one o'clock – then walkd out for two hours though with little comfort the bushes being loaded with rain, but exercize is very necessary to me. I have no mind to die of my arm chair. A letter from Skene acquainting me that the Censors of the French press have prohibited the insertion of my answer to the man

---

1. The stomach cramps from which Scott suffered between 1817 and 1819. See *Life*, vi. 43.

Gourgaud.[1] This is their freedom of the press. The fact is there is an awkward composition between the government and the people of france that the latter will endure the former so long as they will allow them to lull themselves asleep with recollections of their past glory and neither the one nor the other sees that truth and honesty and freedom of discussion are the best policy. The knaves know there *is* an answer and that is all I care about.

Anne, Charles and I dined alone.

22 MONDAY Another vile damp drizzling day. I do not know any morning in my life so fit for work on which I nevertheless, while desirous of employing [it] to purpose, made less progress. A hang dog drowsy feeling wrought against me and I was obliged to lay down the pen and indulge myself in a *drumbly*[2] sleep. Bile I suppose.

The Haigs of Bemerside, Capt. Hamilton, Mr. Bainbridge and daughter, with young Nicol Milne and the Fergussons, dined here. Miss Haig sings Italian music[3] better than any person I ever heard out of the Opera House. But I am neither a judge nor admirer of the science – I do not know exactly what is aimd at and therefore cannot tell what is attaind. Had a letter from Colin MacKenzie who has proposed himself for the little situation in the Register House. I have written him begging him to use the best interest in his own behalf and neer mind me.[4]

23 TUESDAY Another sullen rainy day. Hazy weather, Mr. Noah, as Punch says in the Puppet Show. A headache too – I scarce drank an english pint of claret yesterday but as Mrs. Cole says in the farce 'Lackaday a thimbleful oversets me'[5] – not my head but my Stomach. Said headache was however washd away by a cup of tea. I workd slow however and untowardly and fell one leaf short of my task.

Went to Selkirk and dined with the Forest Club for the first time I

1. Written on 14 September and published in Ballantyne's
   Edinburgh Weekly Journal. See the Entry for that day. Skene was
   visiting Versailles at this time. *Letters*, x. 300.
2. 'Drumlie' means troubled or uneasy. Scott's underlining of the
   word suggests, however, that Tait is right in his conjecture that
   he is coining the word from 'drumble': to be sluggish.
3. The family had recently spent nearly five years in Italy.
4. Ferrier's office as Keeper of the Register of Entails was vacant,
   and Lord Register Dundas had recommended Scott. In a
   contest of generosity, Scott and Mackenzie each offered to
   withdraw in the other's favour (see *Letters*, x. 291, and
   Mackenzie, 25 October 1827, Walpole), but meanwhile the post,
   with its salary of £180 a year, was given to James Fergusson.
5. Foote's *The Minor*, Act i.

have been there this season. It was the collar day[1] but being extremely rainy I did not go to see them course. N.B. Of all things the greatest bore is to hear a dull and bashful man sing a facetious song.

24 WEDNESDAY Vilely low in spirits. I have written a page and a half and doubt whether I can write more to-day. A thick throbbing at my heart, and fancies thronging on me. A disposition to sleep, or to think on things melancholy and horrible while I wake. Strange that one's nerves should thus master them, for nervous the case is as I know too well. I am beginning to tire of my journal and no wonder, faith, if I have only such trash as this to record. But the best is a little exertion or a change of the current of thought relieves me.

God who subjects us to these strange maladies, whether of mind or body I cannot say, has placed the power within our own reach and we should be grateful. I wrestled myself so far out of the Slough of Despond as to take a good long walk and my mind is restored to its elasticity. I did not attempt to work especially as we were going down to Mertoun and set off at five o'clock.

25 THURSDAY We arrived at Mertoun yesterday and heard with some surprize that George[2] had gone up in an Air balloon and ascended two miles and a half above this sublunary earth. I should like to have a[n] account of his sensations but his letters said nothing serious about them. Honest George, I certainly did not suspect him of being so flighty.

I visited the new plantations on the river side with Mrs. Scott. I wish her Lord and Master had some of her taste for planting. When I came home I walkd through the Rhymer's glen and I thought how the little fall would look if it were heightend. When I came home a surprize amounting nearly to a shock reachd me in another letter from L. J. S.[3] Methinks this explains the gloom which hung about me yesterday. I own that the recurrence to these matters seems like a summons from the grave. It fascinates me. I ought perhaps to have

1. The hounds coursed annually for a silver collar.
2. Harden's fourth son, the Revd. George Scott, rector of Kentisbeare in Devon.
3. Lady Jane Stuart, the mother of Scott's first love, Williamina Belsches, had written on the 13th asking his permission to give some poems he once copied out to a young relative who 'has commenced bookseller'. Walpole. The surprise and shock of the second letter was the offer of Williamina's own commonplace-book – 'which I would with pleasure convey to you as a *secret* and *sacred* Treasure could I but know that you would take it as I gave it without a drawback or misconstruction of my intention'. 24 October 1827, Walpole. The correspondence continued and resulted in the meeting mentioned in the Entry for 6 November 1827.

stopd it at once but I have not heart to do so. Alas Alas – but why Alas? *Humana perpassi sumus.*[1]

26 FRIDAY Sent off copy to Ballantyne. Drove over to Huntley Burn at breakfast and walkd up to the dike they are building for the new plantation; returnd home. The Fergussons dined and we had the Kirn supper.[2] I never saw a set of finer lads and lasses and blithely did they ply their heels till five in the morning. It did me good to see them, poor things.

27 SATURDAY This morning went again to Huntley Burn to break-fast. There pickd up Sir Adam and the Colonel and drove down to Old Melrose to see the hounds cast off upon the Gateheugh, the high rockery amphitheatre which encloses the peninsula of Old Melrose, the Tweed pouring its dark and powerful current between them. The gallopping of the riders and hallooing of the huntsmen, the cry of the hounds and the sight of sly Reynard stealing away through the brakes waked something of the old spirit within me.

Even in our ashes glow their wonted fires.[3]

On return home I had despatches of consequence. John Gibson writes that Lord Newton has decided most of the grand question in our favour[4] – Good that – Revd. Mr. Turner writes that he is desirous by Lord Londonderry's consent to place in my hands a quantity of original papers concerning the public services of the late Lord Londonderry[5] with a view to drawing up [a] Memoir of his life. Now this task they desire to transfer to me. It is highly complimentary and there is this of temptation in it that I should be able to do justice to that ill requited Statesman in those material points which demand the eternal gratitude of his country. But then for me to take this matter up would lead me too much into the hackneyd politics of the House of Commons which *Odi et arceo*.[6] Besides I would have to

1. 'We have endured human things', a reminiscence of Horace's *Odes*, i. 3. 25.
2. The harvest festival, which Scott gave 'on the most approved model of former days, to all the peasantry on his estate, their friends and kindred, and as many poor neighbours besides as his barn could hold'. *Life*, vi. 252.
3. Gray's 'Elegy in a Country Churchyard' st. 23.
4. By this decision the profits of *Woodstock* and the *Life of Napoleon* were at last released to pay a first dividend to the creditors. Lord Newton had still to arbitrate on the ownership of the manuscripts of the novels and sundry lesser matters.
5. Viscount Castlereagh, who had committed suicide in 1822.
6. 'I hate and avoid', Horace's *Odes*, iii. 1.

study the Irish question and I detest study. Item I might arrive at conclusions different from those which my Lord of Londonderry [has reachd] and I have a taste for expressing that which I think. Fourthly and lastly[1] I think it is sinking myself into a party writer. Seventhly I should not [know] what to say to the disputes with Canning, and to conclude I think my Lord Londond. if he desired such a thing at my hands ought to have written to me. For all which reasons, good bad and indifferent, I will write declining the undertaking.

28 SUNDAY Wrote several letters and one to Mr. Turner declining the task of Lord Castlereagh's Memoirs with due acknowlegments.[2] Had his public and European politics alone been concerned I would have tried the task with pleasure. I wrote out my task and something more, corrected the proofsheets and made a handsome remittance of review copy to the press.

29 MONDAY I may as well square my accompts.

30 TUESDAY

By cash in purse ———————————		£43 0 0
To subscription to Canning Monument ——	£5 0 0	
To Bogie ———————————————	20 0 0	
Subscriptions to Forest Club —————	5 0 0	
Travelling expences —————————	12 0 0	
	———	£42 0 0
		£1 0 0
Cash for reviewing from Lockhart —————		100
Cash from Exchequer —————————		149
		£250 0 0
Cash to Charles[3] —————————		100
Balance —————		£150

Charles left us to take his degree.

31 WEDNESDAY Just as I was merrily cutting away amid my trees, arrives Mr. Gibson with a melancholy look and indeed the news he

1. Modelled on Dogberry's speech in *Much Ado about Nothing*, v. 1: 'sixth and lastly, they have belied a lady; thirdly, they have verified unjust things; and to conclude, they are lying knaves.'
2. For Scott's letter suggesting that Mr. Turner, who had visited Abbotsford in 1824, should himself write the biography, see *Letters*, x. 294.
3. Including the 'English Bill for £50 (fifty pounds) as Charles has to pay his fees for a degree' for which Scott wrote to Cadell. *Letters*, x. 294.

brought was shocking enough. It seems Mr. Abud, the same Jew broker who formerly was disposed to disturb me in London, has given the most positive orders to take out diligence against me for his debt of £1500.[1] This breaks all the measures we had resolved on and prevents the dividend from taking place, by which many poor persons will be great sufferers. For me the alternative will be more painful to my feelings than prejudicial to my interest. To take out a sequestration and allow the persons to take what they can get will be the inevitable consequence. This will cut short my labour by several years which I might spend and spend in vain in labouring to meet their demands. No doubt they may in the interim sell the life-rent of this place with the books and furniture. But perhaps it may be possible to achieve some composition which may save these articles as I would make many sacrifices for that purpose. Gibson strongly advises taking a sequestration at all events. But if the Creditors chuse to let Mr. Abud have his pound of flesh out of the first cut my mind will not be satisfied with the plan of deranging for the pleasure of disappointing him a plan of payment to which all the others had consented. We will know more on Saturday and not sooner. I went to Bowhill[2] with Sir Adam Fergusson to dinner and maintaind as good a countenance in the midst of my perplexities as a man need desire. It is not bravadoe. I literally feel myself firm and resolute.

NOVEMBER

I THURSDAY I waked in the night and lay two hours in feverish meditation. This is a tribute to natural feeling. But the air of a fine frosty morning gave me some elasticity of spirit. It is strange that about a week ago I was more dispirited for nothing at all than I am now for perplexities which set at defiance my conjectures concerning their issue. I suppose that I, the Chronicler of the Canongate, will have to take up my residence in the Sanctuary[3] for a week or so unless

1. For the previous threat from Abud, see the Entry for 27 July 1826 and note. If he had forced the Trust to break up by driving Scott to a sequestration, he would have harmed the creditors more than Scott himself, who would have lost nothing but his obligation to pay his debts in full. To avoid a sequestration which would have put an end to the Trust and given the creditors only a few shillings in the pound, Sir William Forbes bought up the bills held by Abud and added them to the debt due to his bank. Some account of the law of bankruptcy in Scott's time is given in the Introduction, pp. xxix–xxxiii.
2. The Selkirkshire seat of the Duke of Buccleuch.
3. The precincts of Holyrood remained a sanctuary until imprisonment for debt was abolished in 1880.

I prefer the more airy residence of the Calton jail or a trip to the Isle of Man. These furnish a pleasing choice of expedient. It is to no purpose being angry at Ehud or Ahab or whatever name he delights in. He is seeking his own and thinks by these harsh measures to render his road to it more speedy. And now I will trouble myself no more about the matter than I can possibly help which will be quite enough after all. Perhaps something may turn up better for me than I now look for.

Sir Adam Fergusson left Bowhill this morning for Dumfries-shire. I returnd to Abbotsford to Anne and told her this unpleasant news. She stood it remarkably well, poor body.

2 FRIDAY I was a little bilious to-night – no wonder; had sundry letters without any power of giving my mind to answer them – One about Gourgand with his nonsense. I shall not trouble my head more on that score. Well – it is a hard knock on the elbow. I knew I had a life of labour before me but I was resolved to work steadily – now they have treated me like a recusant turnspit and put in a red-hot cinder into the wheel alongst with ⌊me⌋. But of what use is philosophy, and I have always pretended to a little of a practical character, if it cannot teach us to do or suffer? The day is glorious – yet I have little will to enjoy it but sit here ruminating upon the difference and comparative merits of the Isle of Man and of the Abbey.[1] Hangd choice betwixt them. Yet were a twelvemonth over I should perhaps smile at what makes me now very serious – Smile – No – that can never be – my present feelings cannot be recollected with cheerfulness. But I may drop a tear of gratitude. I have finishd my *Tales* and have now nothing literary in hand.[2] It would be an evil time to begin any thing.

3 SATURDAY Slept ill and lay one hour longer than usual in the morning. I gaind an hour's quiet by it. That is much. I feel a little shaken at the result of to-day's post. Bad it must be whatsoever be the alternative. I am not able to go out. My poor workers wonder that I pass them without a word. I can imagine no alternative but either retreat to the Sanctuary or to the Isle of Man. Both shocking enough. But in Edinburgh I am always near the scene of action, freer from uncertainty and near my poor daughter. So I think I will prefer it. And thus I rest – in unrest – But I will not let this unman me; our hope heavenly and earthly is poorly anchord if the cable parts upon

1. The Isle of Man, as a refuge for debtors, had been used by Scott's friend Charles Kerr; Holyrood Abbey by Cadell earlier in this same year. Scott chose Holyrood and asked Cadell to arrange a lodging for him. *Letters*, x. 302.
2. *Tales of a Grandfather* was published early in December. 'My Aunt Margaret's Mirror' was begun six days after this Entry.

the strain. I believe in God who can change evil into good and I am confident that what befalls us is always ultimately for the best. I have a letter from Mr. Gibson purporting the opinion of the trustees and committee of creditors that I should come to town and interesting themselves warmly in the matter. They have intimated that the[y] will pay Mr. Abut a composition of six shillings pr. pound on his debt. This is handsome offer but I understand he is determined to have his pound of flesh. If I can prevent it he shall not take a shilling by his hardhearted conduct.

4 SUNDAY Put my papers in some order and prepared for my journey. It is in the stile of the Emperors of Abyssinia who proclaim 'Cut down the Kantuffa[1] in the four quarters of the world', for I know not where I am going. Yet were it not for poor Anne's doleful looks I would feel firm as a piece of granite. Even the poor dogs seem to fawn on me with anxious meaning as if there were some thing going on they could not comprehend. They probably notice the packing of the clothes and other symptoms of a journey.

Anne for household expences	£40
Ditto for sending to Cr. entrd.	100[2]
	140
Cash	150
Ball:	£10
Travellig.	£3
Jehu	1
	4
In cash	£6
Changed	1
In purse	£5

Set off at twelve firmly resolved in body and in mind. Dined at Fouchie – Ah good Mrs. Wilson,[3] you know not you are like to lose an old customer.

But when I arrived at Edinburgh at my faithful friend Mr. Gibson's – lo the scene had again changed and a new hare is started. Cadell whom I found with Mr. G. had learnd through the beautiful Mr. Robison of Hurst Robison and Coy. That there was some usurious transaction betwixt him and Abut about these bills and that the value given for them was gold ingots (the man is a gold refiner) rated to the discounter, considerably above the market price. This smacks of usury and explains Mr. Abut's great anxiety to push the matter to payment besides the hope of concussing me or some of my friends to pay the debt.

1. A thorn described by James Bruce in *Travels to discover the Source of the Nile*, etc., of which Scott owned the 1804 edition.
2. This money was to allow Anne to pay the wages if he had to take sanctuary. *Letters*, x. 302.
3. 'Mrs. Wilson, landlady of the inn at Fushie, one stage from Edinburgh –, an old dame of some humour, with whom Sir Walter always had a friendly colloquy in passing. I believe the charm was, that she had passed her childhood among the Gipsies of the Border. But her fiery Radicalism latterly was another source of high merriment.' J. G. L. On the first anniversary of Scott's death she visited Abbotsford.

5 MONDAY This morning was spent in meeting with Cadell, Gibson and the trustees in various times and places. Cadell's communications were clear and explicit. Robison told him that Mr. Abut had signd his certificate because he was under the necessity of stopping his mouth and dared not do otherwise. That he then told him the story of the gold bars being given to him at an over-value which he sold at a reduced value in the city.[1] Robison also said when the Banks refused to subscribe his certificate that he did not care – the time would come when he would be useful and then they would be glad to do it. Cadell himself offerd to set off instantly, find Robinson and bring him down to confirm this story. I have no doubt Cadell is serious in this desire and that he says the tale as it was said to him. But what made him keep Robinson's secret? – *Cela donne à penser*. The cutting down Robinson's bill would be as great a relief to his house as to us yet he does not seem to have told his own trustee. I suppose that he thought he had no great occasion to make enemies as Ahab probably would not sign his certificate if he stird. But when I came to be hard set at and the downfall of further literary enterprize seemd to be the consequence of Ahab's precipitation, he for his own sake and I believe sincerely for mine also resolved to bring out this secret. It would no doubt be a grand thing to turn the tables on Ahab and dock him entirely of the debt on which he uses such peremptory proceedings, but I must say my hopes are far beneath my fears. Robinson's word I have little reliance upon and I have great apprehension he spoke merely from the idea of gaining some personal importance at the time or that if there really be such a secret Ahab and Son have smotherd the evidence before they ventured to make such a peremptory demand upon the Debtor.

The Trustees were clearly of opinion that the matter should be probed to the very bottom; so Cadell sets off tomorrow in quest of Robinson whose haunts he knows. There was much talk concerning what should be done, how to protect my honour's person and to postpone commencing a defence which must make Ahab desperate

1. The Bill on which Abud & Coy. intended to arrest Scott had been the property of Hurst, Robinson who gave it to Abud, not for its face value in money but in exchange for gold. Abud put on this an inflated value of 90s. per oz. in order to make his profit on the transaction, and Robinson therefore had to sell it at 84s. per oz., so that he received 15 per cent less than the original Bill had been worth. The law allowed goods to be given for a discounted Bill, but only if they could be proved to represent full market value. Since the value of gold is easily established, Scott's Trustees now expected to be able to show that Abud & Coy. had acted illegally. *Letters*, x. 306 and 308.

before we can ascertain that the grounds are really tenable.[1] This much I think I can see that the Trustees will rather pay the debt than break off the Trust and go into a sequestration.

They are clearly right for them selves and I believe for me also. Whether it is in human possibility that I can clear off these obligations or not is very doubtful. But I would rather have it written on my monument that I died on the desk than live under the recollection of having neglected it. My conscience is free and happy and would be so if I were to be lodged in the Calton jail. Were I shirking from exertion I should lose heart under a sense of general contempt and so die like a poisond rat in a hole.

Dined with Gibson and John Home. His wife is a pretty ladylike woman.[2] Slept there at night.

6 TUESDAY The indefatigable Gibson saw Mr. Forman before breakfast. Mr. F is the person to whom Ahab entrusted the affair but who had written to reprobate his mode of proceeding. In consequence of his reproaches or from a doubt of our proceeding instantly to sequestration Ahab proposes now to take one 3d of the debt in present coin and two thirds at the distance of six and twelve months with security. It will take some time to discuss this proposal and therefore its being presented is most important. It enables us to gain time to enquire into the facts avouchd by Robinson. So all is suspended till we hear from Cadell which will decide us whether to adopt war or negotiation.

I took possession of No 6 Shandwick place, Mrs. Jobson's house.[3] Mr. Cadell had taken it for me, terms £100 for four months, cheap enough as it is a capital house. I offerd £5 for immediate entrance as I do not like to fly back to Abbotsford. So here we are establishd, i.e. John Nicolson and I, with good fires and all snug.

I waited on L. J. S. – an affecting meeting.[4]

1. The words 'We fear giving him time' are deleted after 'tenable'.
2. Scott may not have met her before this day as she had been at the sea with her children during his last visit. Gibson, 25 August 1827, Walpole.
3. Mrs. Jobson was spending the winter in Canterbury.
4. Lady Jane Stuart, mother of his first love, whose letters to Scott are mentioned in the Entry for 25 October 1827 and note. The tenor of this meeting may be guessed from her letter of 29 October: 'My age encourages me & I have long'd to tell you not the Mother who bore you (tho secretly) followed you more anxiously with her blessing than I! – Age has tales to tell & sorrows to unfold – Tho for 20 years I know not that I have met you, yet seen you often passing my windows & going into the house of my oposite neighbour – and do you think that then I saw you as nothing to me?' Walpole.

Sir William Forbes came in before dinner to me; highspirited noble fellow as ever; and true to his friend. Agrees with my feelings to a comma. He thinks Cadell's account must turn up trumps and is for going the vole.

7 WEDNESDAY Began to settle myself this morning after the hurry of mind and even of body which I have lately undergone. Commenced a review, that is an Essay on Ornamental Gardening for the *Quarterly*.[1] But I stuck fast for want of books. As I did not wish to leave the mind leisure to recoil on itself I immediately began the 2d Series of the *Chronicles of Canongate*,[2] the first having been well approved. I went to make another visit[3] and fairly softend myself like an old fool with recalling old stories till I was fit for nothing but shedding tears and repeating verses for the whole night. This is sad work. The very grave gives up its dead and time rolls back thirty years to add to my perplexities. – I don't care – I begin to grow over hardend and like a stag turning at bay my naturally good temper grows fierce and dangerous. Yet what a romance to tell and told I fear it will one day be. And then my three years of dreaming and my two years of wakening will be chronicled doubtless. But the dead will feel no pain.

8 THURSDAY *Domum mansi – lanam feci*[4] – I may borrow the old sepulchral mottoe of the Roman Matron. I staid at home and began the third volume of *Chronicles* or rather the 1st volume of the Second Series. This I pursued with little intermission from morning till night yet only finishd nine pages. Like the machinery of a steam engine the imagination does not work freely when first set upon a new task.

9 FRIDAY Finishd my task after breakfast, at least before 12. Then went to college to hear this most amusing good matter of the essay read.[5]

1. 'On Landscape Gardening', a review of Sir Henry Steuart's *Planter's Guide*, appeared in the *Quarterly* for March 1828, no. 74.
2. This was a false start. The second series, like the first, was to consist of short stories, and the tale begun on this day was 'My Aunt Margaret's Mirror'. Ballantyne's disapproval led Scott to publish it instead in *The Keepsake* and to write *The Fair Maid of Perth* as the second series of *Chronicles of the Canongate*.
3. To Lady Jane Stuart.
4. 'I stayed at home – I made wool.' An Epitaph of 150 B.C. with *mansi* for *servavi*.
5. In January 1827 the Universities Commission on which Scott was serving offered a prize of 100 guineas for an essay on 'The National Character of the Athenians'. It was won by J. Brown Patterson, whom Peel preferred to the parish of Falkirk in 1829 as a result. Sir Alexander Grant's *Story of the University of Edinburgh*, ii. 39 and 83–5.

Imprimus occurs a dispute whether the Magistrates as patrons of the University should march in procession before the Royal Visitors and it was proposed on our side that the provost, who is undoubtedly the first man in his own City, should go in attendance on the Principal with the Chairman of the Commission on the Principal's right hand and the whole commission following taking *pas* of the other Magistrates as well as of the Senatus Academicus – or whether we had not better waive all question of precedence and let the three bodies find their way separately as they best could. This last method was just adopted when we learnd that the question was not in what order of procession we should reach the place of exhibition but whether we were to get there at all which was presently after reported as an impossibility. The lads of the College had so effectually taken possession of the class room [in] which the Essay was to be read[1] that neither Learning or law, neither Magistrates nor Magisters, neither visitors nor visited, could make way to the scene of action. So we Grandees were obliged to adjourn the Sederunt till Saturday the 17th and so ended the Collie-Shangie – Calld at Ardwall's and Archie Swinton's.

Anne came home to dinner – well and happy.

10 SATURDAY Wrote out my task and little more. At twelve o'clock I went to poor Lady J. S. to talk over old stories. I am not clear that it is a right or healthful indulgence to be ripping up old sorrows but it seems to give her deepseated sorrow words and that is a mental blood-letting. To me these things are now matter of calm and solemn recollection, never to be forgotten yet scarce to be rememberd with pain.

We go out to Saint Catherine's[2] to-day. I am glad of it for I would not have these recollections haunt me and society will put them out of my head.

Met at Saint Catherine's Sir James Montgomery, his lady and a fine lively intelligent girl their Daughter, Miss Helen M. – Miss Skene, Mr. and Mrs. Durham Calderwood and others, and spent the evening pleasantly.

11 SUNDAY Sir William Rae read us prayers – Calderwoods left Saint Catherine's. Saunterd about the doors and talkd of old cavalry stories.[3] Then drove to Melville, and saw the Lord and Lady and

1. The chemistry classroom, the largest in Adam's building. Ibid.
2. Sir William Rae's house at Liberton, in those days outside Edinburgh.
3. Sir William Rae had been a major in the Yeomanry Cavalry thirty years before.

family. I think I never saw any thing more beautiful than the ridge of
Carnethy (Pentland)[1] against a clear frosty sky with its peaks and
varied slopes. The hills glowd like purple amethysts, the sky glowd
topaz and vermilion colours. I never saw a finer screen than Pentland
considering that it is neither rocky nor highly elevated. At dinner we
had Binning Monro's sons.

12 MONDAY I cannot say I lost a minute's sleep on accompt of what
the day might bring forth; though it was that on which we must settle
with Abut in his Jewish demand or stand to the consequence. I breakfasted with an excellent appetite, laughd in real genuine easy fun, and
went to Edin. resolved to do what should best become me. Calld on
Gibson and learnd with pleasure that Cadell had seen Robinson and
extracted from him a confession that the Bills were discounted for
gold bars stated to the discounters at a certain value while they were
sold at a less; this is less explicit than we could wish but it is sufficient
ground to go upon especially if said Robinson will come down to
Scotland and make oath as he seems willing to do. He is a rogue but
Cadell has a hank over him and a tight one – When I came home I
found Walter, poor fellow, who had come down on the spur[2] having
heard from John Lockhart how things stand. Gibson having taken out
a Suspension makes us all safe for the present. So we dined merrily.
He has good hope of his Majority and I must support his interest as
well as I can. Wrote letters to Lady Shelley, John L. and one or two
chance correspondents. One was singular. A gentleman writing
himself James Macturk tells me his friends have identified him with
Capt. Macturk of *Saint Ronan's Well* and finding himself much
inconvenienced by this identification he proposes I should apply
to the King to forward his restoration and advance in the service (he
writes himself late lieutenant 4th. Dragoon guards) as an atonement
for having occasiond him (though unintentionally no doubt) so great
an injury. This is one road to promotion to be sure. Lieut. Macturk is
I suppose tolerably mad.

We dined together, Anne, Walter, and I, and were happy at our
reunion when, as I was despatching my packet to London,

In started to heeze up our howp[3]

---

1. The Pentland Hills, of which Carnethy (1,898 ft.) is the highest,
   lie immediately to the south-west of Edinburgh.
2. From Canterbury, where he was stationed at this time.
3. 'Andro and his Cutty Gun', l. 15. Herd, ii. 153. 'To heeze up
   our howp' means 'to raise our hopes'.

John Gibson radiant with goodnatured joy. He had another letter from Cadell enclosing one from Robinson in which the latter pleges himself to make the most explicit affidavit to the usurious transaction in all the forms – nay Cadell's account bears that they not only sold the gold at an extravagant price but under cover of another house in the city bought the same gold at an under value – Robinson does not positively charge this last point but his declaration without it is quite explicit and full as need be and he offers to come off within twenty four hours. Some Chancery business and an arrest detains him in London. He expresses himself anxious to do justice to the Scotch creditors and to expose Abut. I wonder how the honest gentlemen will look when they hear the turn things have taken – will be happy to take a composition – But will you get it, Master Ahab? I hope a little sentiment of revenge is not very wrong. But certainly if they were driving me to utter extremity about a debt none of mine and iniquitously created by their usurious practices, why one may be glad to see the Whirligig of Time bring about his revenges.[1]

On these two last days I have written only three pages. But not from inaptitude or incapacity to labour. It is odd enough – I think it difficult to place me in a situation of danger or disagreeable circumstances purely personal which would shake my powers of mind yet they sink under mere lowness of spirit as this journal bears evidence in too many passages.

13 TUESDAY Wrote a little in the morning but not above a page, Went to the Court – About one returned and made several visits with Anne and Walter. Cadell came, glorious with success of his expedition, but a little allayd by the prospect of competition for the copyrights on which He and I have our eyes as joint purchasers.[2] We must have them if possible for I can give new value to an edition corrected with notes. *Nous verrons* – Capt. Musgrave of the House of Edenhall dined with us. After dinner while we were over our whisky and water and segars enter successively the merry Knight.[3] Misses Kerr came to tea and we had fun and singing in the evening.

1. *Twelfth Night*, v. 1.
2. He had 'found that the stock of the existing editions was so rapidly diminishing that several of the London houses had resolved to be bidders at the sale. He further ascertained that some of these houses were inclined to go as high as £8,000 for the property.' Sederunt Book, i. 338. The copyrights, which were being sold by Constable's creditors, were essential to plans for the Magnum Opus collected edition and to Scott's chances of ultimately paying off his debts.
3. Sir Adam Ferguson. Scott has omitted the remainder of the sentence.

14 WEDNESDAY A little work in the morning but no gathering to my tackle. Went to Court, remaind till nigh one. Then came through a pityless shower; dressd and went to the Christening of a boy of John Richardson who was baptized Henry Cockburn. Read the *Gazette* of the great battle of Navarrino[1] in which we have thumpd the Turks very well. But as to the justice of our interference, I will only suppose some Turkish plenipotentiary with an immense turban and long loose trousers comes to dictate to us the mode in which we should deal with our refractory liegemen the Catholics of Ireland – We hesitate to admit his in[ter]ference, on which the Moslem admiral runs into Cork Bay or Bantry Bay alongside of a British squadron and send[s] a boat to tow aside a fire-ship. A vessel fires on the boat and sinks her – Is there an aggression on the part of those who fired first or of those whose manœuvres occasiond the firing?

Dined at Henry Cockburn's with the Christening party.

15 THURSDAY Wrote a little in the morning. Detaind in court till two then returnd home wet enough. Met with Chambers and complimented him about his making a clever book of the 1745 for Constable's Miscellany.[2] It is really a lively work and must have a good sale. I suppose old Fraud and Suet[3] fop-doodled him out of the money, poor lad. Before dinner enter Cadell and we anxiously reviewd our plan for buyin[g] the copyrights on 19 Decemr. It is most essential that the whole of the Waverley novels should be kept under our management as it is calld. I may then give them a new impulse by a preface and notes and if an edition of say 30 volumes were to be publishd monthly to the tune of 5000, which may really be expected if the shops were once cleared of the over-glut, it would bring in £10,000 clear profit over all outlay; and so pay any sum of copymoney that might be ventured. I must urge these things to Gibson for except these copyrights be saved our plans will go to nothing.

Walter and Anne went to hear Madame Pasta sing after dinner. I remaind at home. Wrote to Sir William Knighton[4] and sundry other letters of importance, turning my attention to the fund in Chancery

1. Fought on 20 October 1827 between the Turks and a combined British, French, and Russian fleet under Admiral Codrington.
2. Robert Chambers's *History of the Rebellion 1745–6* had just appeared as vols. 15 and 16 of Constable's *Miscellany of Original and Selected Publications*.
3. Constable. Scott used the same phrase in 1817. See *Letters*, iv. 421.
4. About Charles, whom Scott was anxious to see settled in the Foreign Office. See *Letters*, x. 313.

which we have almost lost sight of. Walter and John Lockhart may
certainly manage it. I wrote an introduction to Miss Jane Nicolson
who knows most about the information which will be required in
Chancery.[1]

16 FRIDAY State of Cash affairs.

In purse		£5	0	0
By Mr. Cadell		300		
This in full of Cash payable at this time for the *Tales of my Grandfather*				
Do—Do—advanced to Mr. Jas.[2] Ballantyne by Do.		12	10	0
		£317	10	0

Outlay				
To wages – Anne	£100			
To wages Abbotsford	90			
To Charles	50			
To Lockhart's *Spanish Ballads*	1			
To paid Ballantynes interest	12	10		
		253	10	0
Balance in purse		£64	0	0

There was little to do in court to-day but one's time
is squanderd and their ideas broken strangely. At three we had
a select meeting of the O.Gas directors to consider what line we
were to take in the disastrous affairs of the Company. Agreed to go
to parliament a second time.[3] James Gibson and I to go up as our
solicitors – So curiously does interest couple up individuals though
I am sure I have no objection whatever to Mr. James Gibson Craig.

17 SATURDAY Returnd home in early time from the Court. Settled
on the review of ornamental gardening[4] for Lockhart and wrote hard.

---

1. Walter, during his short visit to Edinburgh, had agreed to call on
   Miss Jane Nicolson, his mother's old friend, and enlist her as a
   witness in the business of the money in Chancery. Lockhart was
   asked by a letter probably of this day (although dated the 14th)
   to 'take a trip down with him'. *Letters*, x. 310. In fact, her
   affidavit was not made until Scott's own visit to London in April
   and May of the next year.
2. Scott means 'Sandie', who had lent him £500 on 13 May 1826.
3. The company wanted an Act 'authorizing them to manufacture
   gas from coal'. See Note 1, pp. 805–6.
4. The article 'On Landscape Gardening' for the March *Quarterly*.

Want several quotations though – that is the bore of being totally without books. Anne and I dined quietly together and I wrote after tea – an industrious day.

18 SUNDAY This has been also a day of exertion. I was interrupted for a moment by a visit from young Davidoff with a present of a steel snuffbox, wrought and lined with gold, having my arms on the top and on the sides various scenes from the environs and principal public buildings of Saint Petersburgh – a *joli cadeau* – and I take it very kind of my young friend. I had a letter also from his uncle Dennis Davidoff, the Black Captain of the French retreat. The Russians are certainly losing ground and men in Persia and will not easily get out of the scrape of having engaged an active enemy in a difficult and unhealthy country. I am glad of it – it is an overgrown power and to have them kept quiet at least is well for the rest of Europe. I concluded the evening after writing a double task with the trial of Malcolm Gillespie, renownd as a most venturous excise officer but now like to lose his life for forgery.[1] A bold man in his vocation he seems to have been, but the law seems to have got round to the wrong side of him on the present occasion.

19 MONDAY Corrected the last proof of *Tales of my Grandfather*. Received Cadell at breakfast and conversed fully on the subject of the *Chronicles* and the application of the price of 2d Series, say £4000, to the purchase of the moiety[2] of the copy-rights now in the market and to be sold this day month. If I have the command of a new Edition and put it into an attractive shape with notes, introductions and illustrations that no one save I myself can give I am confident it will bring home the whole purchase money with something over and lead to the disposal of a series of the subsequent volumes of the following works[3] –

In purse	£64
Anne	£10.0.
Keith's Bishops and Sundries	2
—	12
Cash	52

---

1. He was tried at Aberdeen Circuit Court 'for the crime of forging certain bills'. See Shaw's *Decisions of the Court of Justiciary*, no. 164.
2. Cadell and the Trustees were to share the expense of buying the copyrights. Scott here proposes that their share should be financed from the price paid by Cadell for the second series of *Chronicles of the Canongate*.
3. The Trustees already owned the copyrights of the works listed here. Scott's point is that their value will be enhanced once they are part of a complete series.

St. Ronan's well ——————— 3 volumes
Redgauntlet —————————— 3
Tales of Crusaders ————— 4
Woodstock ————————————— 3
————
13 make a Series ⎫ 7 vols. 8vo.
of 7 volumes ⎭

The two series of the *Chronicles* and others will be ready about the same time. Helen Erskine dined with us.

20 TUESDAY Wrought in the morning at the Review which I fear will be lengthy. Calld on Hector[1] as I came home from the court and found him better and keeping a highland heart. There is something wrong about the kidnies which is an awkward business. I came home like a crow through the mist, half dead with a rheumatic headache caused by the beastly north east wind.

What am I now when every breeze appals me?[2] I dozed for half an hour in my chair for pain and stupidity. I omitted to say yesterday that I went out to Melville castle to enquire after my Lord Melville who had broke his collar bone by a fall from his horse in mounting. He is recovering well but much bruised. I came home with Lord Ch: Commissioner Adam. He told me a dictum of old Sir Gilbert Elliot speaking of his uncles – 'No chance of opulence' he said 'is worth the risk of a competence.' It was not the thought of a great man but perhaps that of a wise one. Wrought at my review and despatchd about half or better I should hope. I incline to longer extracts in the next sheets.

21 WEDNESDAY Wrought at the review.

At one o'clock I attended the general meeting of the Union Scottish assurance Coy.[3] There was a debate arose whether the ordinary acting directors should or should not have a small sum amounting to about a crown a piece allotted to them each day of their regular attendance. The proposal was rejected by many and upon grounds which sound very well. Such as the shabbiness of men being

1. Hector Macdonald Buchanan.
2. *Macbeth*, ii. 2.
3. The Scottish Union Fire and Life Insurance Coy., of which
   Scott was Governor. At the request of the Manager, Scott was in
   the chair: 'I think your presence will do much towards
   preventing any irregular discussions which are apt to arise in a
   large & popular assembly.' Sutherland Mackenzie, 26 October
   1827, Walpole.

influenced by a trifling consideration, like this and the absurdity of the Company volunteering a bounty to one set of men when there were others willing to act gratuitously and many gentlemen volunteerd their own services – though I cannot help suspecting that as in the case of ultroneous offers of service upon most occasions it was not likely to be acceptable. The motion miscarried however – impolitickly rejected as I think. The sound of five shillings sounds shabby but the fact is that it does in some sort reconcile the party to whom it is offerd to leave his own house and business at an exact hour. Whereas in the common case one man comes too late, another does not come at all, the attendance is given by different individuals upon different days so that no one acquires the due historical knowledge of the affairs of the company. Besides, the Directors by taking even this trifling sum of money [are] rendering themselves the paid servants of the company and are bound to use a certain degree of diligence much greater than if they continued to serve as hitherto gratuitously. The pay is like enlisting money which whether great or small subjects to engagement under the articles of war.

One Cockburn a china Merchant spoke – a picture of an orator with bandy legs, squinting eyes and a voice like an ungreased cart wheel. A liberty-boy I suppose. The meeting was somewhat stormy but I preserved order by listening with patience to each in turn: determined that they should weary out the patience of the meeting before I lost mine. An orator is like a top, let him alone and he must stop one time or another. Flog him and he may go on for ever.

Dined with directors of whom I only knew the Manager Sutherland Mackenzie, Sir David Milne and Wauchope, besides one or two old Oil Gas friends.[1] It went off well enough.

22 THURSDAY Wrought in the morning. Then made arrangements for a dinner to celebrate the Duke of Buccleuch coming of Age, that which was to have been held at Melville Castle being postpone[d] owing to Lord M's accident.[2] Sent copy of 2 Series of *Chronicles of Canongate*[3] to Ballantyne. The news from Ahab continues good. Their agent Mr Foreman shakes his head about the information he has received from London and talks of giving up their business. This looks ill for their £1500 which if they had been common civil and merciful would, or the greater part of it, have been paid without scruple. Miss Millar dined with Anne and me.

1. Colin Mackenzie and Dr. David Maclagan were Directors of both concerns.
2. His broken collar-bone. See the Entry for 20 November 1827.
3. The copy was of 'My Aunt Margaret's Mirror', which did not eventually appear in the *Chronicles*.

23 FRIDAY I bilkd the court to-day and workd at the Review. I wish it may not be too long yet know not how to shorten it. The post brought me a letter from the Duke of Buccleuch acquainting me with his Grandmother the Duchess Dowager's death.[1] She was a woman of unbounded beneficence to and even beyond the extent of her princely fortune. She had a masculine courage and great firmness in enduring afliction which pressd on her with continued and successive blows in her later years. She was about eighty four and nature was exhausted so Life departed like the extinction of a lamp for lack of oil. Our dinner on monday is put off. I am not superstitious but I wish this festival had not been twice delayd by such sinister accidents. First the injury sustaind by Lord Melville and then this event spreading crape like the shroud of Saladin[2] over our little festival. God avert bad omens.

Dined with Archie Swinton. Company Sir Alexr. and Lady Keith, Mr. and Mrs. Anderson, Clanronald etc.

Clanronald told us as an instance of highland credulity that a set of his highland kinsmen, Borradale and others, believing that the fabulous Water Cow inhabited a small lake near his house, resolved to drag the monster into day. With this view they bivouackd by the side of the lake in which they placed by way of night bait two small anchors such as belong to boats each baited with the carcase of a dog slain for the purpose. They expected the Water cow would gorge on this bait and were prepared to drag her ashore the next morning. When to their confusion of face the baits were found untouchd. It is something too late in the day for setting baits for Water Cows.

24 SATURDAY Wrote at review in the morning. I have made my revocation of the invitation for Monday. For myself it will give me time to work. I could not get home to-day till two o'clock and was quite tired and stupid. So I did little but sleep or doze till dressing time. Then went to Sir David Wedderburn's where I met three beauties of my own day, Margaret Brown, Maria Brown and Jane Wedderburn, now Lady Wedderburn, Lady Hampden and Mrs. Oliphant. We met the pleasant Irish family of Meath. The resemblance betwixt the Earl of Meath and the Duke of Wellington is something remarkably striking; it is not only the profile but the mode of bearing the person and the person itself – Lady Theodosia Brabazon, the Earl's daughter and a beautiful young Lady, told me that in Paris her father was often taken for Lord Wellington.

---

1. Lady Elizabeth Montagu, who had died on the 21st.
2. Used as a standard 'to admonish the East of the instability of human greatness' (Gibbon). Douglas.

25 SUNDAY This forenoon finishd the review and despatchd it to Lockhart before dinner. Will: Clerk, Tom Thomson and young Frank Scott dined with me. I have been vexd by Anne allowing Johnstone's bill to run up.[1] I hope this will not again happen as it may lead to unpleasant consequences. She is but a young house keeper but her situation should serve her instead of experience. We had a pleasant day. I have wrought pretty well to-day. But I must

> Do a little more
> And produce a little ore.[2]

26 MONDAY Corrected proofsheets of *Chronicles* and *Tales*,[3] advised Sheriff processes and was busy. Made some payments –

	Cash in purse		£52 0 0
Anne to pay Johnstone in part		£40	
Tom Allan to Royl. Society club and arrears of subscription		6	
Antiqn. Society		1	
Engineer for a plan of altering gas to coal Gas .		3	
			£50 0 0
Balance in purse			£2 0 0

Dined with Robert Dundas of Arniston – Lord Register – Bort[h]-wicks – etc. An agreeable evening.

27 TUESDAY Corrected proofs in the morning and attended the court till one or two o'clock, Mr. Hamilton being again ill. I visited Lady J. S.[4] on my return. Came home too faggd to do anything to purpose. Dined alone with Anne.

Anecdote from George Bell. In the days of Charles II or his brother flourishd an old Lady Elphinstone so old that she reachd the

1. She had begun with good intentions: 'You have no idea how regularly I keep house *no bills* every thing *paid* but I do hate to ask for money in these hard times.' Anne to Lockhart, 1 July 1826, Abbots. At the time of the crash Scott owed more than £186 to Robert Johnstone, his old schoolfellow, a leading grocer and a Bailie. Sederunt Book, i. 72.
2. Used on p. 327 and in *Letters*, iv. 533 and ix. 494.
3. 'My Aunt Margaret's Mirror' and *Tales of a Grandfather*, first series.
4. Lady Jane Stuart.

extraordinary period of 103. She was a keen Whig so did not relish Grahame of Clavers. At last, having a curiosity to see so aged a person, he obtaind or took permission to see her and askd her of the remarkable things she had seen. 'Indeed' said she 'I think one of the most remarkable is that when I enterd the world there was one Knox deaving us a' with his *Clavers*[1] and now that I am going out of it there is one Clavers deaving us with his *knocks*.'

28 WEDNESDAY Corrected proofs and went to court. Returnd about one and calld on the Lord Chief Baron. Charles arrived from Oxford[2] with good news of Sophia, Walter etc. Dined with the Duchess of Bedford at the Waterloo[3] and renewd as I may say an old acquaintance which began while her Grace was Lady Georgiana.[4] She has now a fine family, two young ladies silent just now, but they will find their tongues or they are not right Gordons. A very fine child, Alaster, who shouted, sung and spoke gaelic with much spirit. They are from a shooting place in the Highlands call[d] Invereshie in Badenoch which the Duke has taken to gratify the Duchesses passion for the heather.

29 THURSDAY My course of Composition is stopd foolishly enough. I have sent four leaves to London with Lockhart's Review. I am very sorry for this blunder and here is another. Forgetting I had been engaged for a long time to Lord Gillies – a first family visit too – and the Devil tempted me to accept of the office of President of the Antiquarian Society. And now they tell me people have come from the country to be present and so forth of which I may believe as much as I may. But I must positively take care of this absurd custom of confounding invitations. My conscience acquits me of doing so by Malice prepense. Yet one incurs the suspicion. At any rate it is uncivil

1. 'Annoying us all with his foolish talk'.
2. Where he had been dallying since taking his degree, to his father's annoyance: 'I cant think what is become of Charles. In my last letter I wishd him to come down here and not play the fool staying straggling where he has no longer any business. If he is within reach of you', Scott wrote to Lockhart, 'I will thank you to put him in mind that I wish him to learn something useful at this period of his life and not to wander about like a gentleman after his own desires.' *Letters*, x. 317.
3. The most splendid of Edinburgh's hotels, built in Waterloo Place in 1819. It met the need that had long been felt for 'a Tavern where more than fifty persons could be entertained with ease or comfort'. Youngson, p. 145.
4. Daughter of the fourth Duke of Gordon.

and must be amended.[1] Dined at Lord C. Commissioner's to meet the Duchess and her party. She can be extremely agreeable but I used to think Her Grace *journalière*. She may have [been] cured of that fault or I may have turnd less jealous of my dignity. At all events let a pleasant hour go by unquestiond and do not let us break ordinary gems to pieces because they are not diamonds. I forgot to say that Edwin Landseer was in the Duchesses train. He is in my mind one of the most striking masters of the modern school. His expression both in man and animals is capital. He shewd us many sketches of smugglers etc. taken in the Highlands, all capital.

> Some gaed there and some gaed here
> And a' the town was in a steer
> And Johnie on his brocket meare
>   He raid to fetch the howdie
> And turn him [*Illeg.*] and
> The bonnie Lads of Gowrie.[2]

30 FRIDAY Another idle morning, wrote letters however. Had the great pleasure of a letter from Lord Dudley acquainting me that he had received his Majesty's commands to put down the name of my son Charles for the first vacancy that should occur in the Foreign Office[3] and at the same time to acquaint me with his Gracious intentions which were signified in language the most gratifying to me. This makes me really feel light and happy and most grateful to the Kind and gracious Sovereign who has always shewn I may say so much friendship towards me. Would to God the *King's errand might lie in the Cadger's gait* that I might have some better way of showing my gratitude than merely by a letter of thanks or this private memorandum of my gratitude. The lad is a good boy and clever, somewhat indolent I fear yet with the capacity of exertion. Presuming his head is full enough of Greek and Latin he has now living languages to study. So I will set him to work on French, Italian and German that like the classic Cerberus he may speak a leash of languages at once. Dined with Gillies – very pleasant. Lord C. C., Will Clerk, Cranstoun and other old friends. I saw in the evening the celebrated Miss Grahame Stirling so remarkable for her power of

---

1. For a similar blunder and similar resolution, see the Entry for 16 December 1825.
2. The 'howdie' is the midwife. The song is unidentified.
3. Lord Dudley was Foreign Secretary from 1827 to 1828. The vacancy occurred within three months. See the Entry for 11 February 1827.

personifying a Scottish old lady. Unluckily she came late and I left early in the evening so I could not find out wherein her craft lay.[1] She lookd like a sensible woman.

I had a conference with my trustees about the purchase (in Coy with Cadell) of the copyrights of the Novels to be exposed to sale on 19th December and had the good luck to persuade them fully of the propriety of the project. I alone can by Notes and the like give these works a new value and in fact make a new edition. The price is to be made good from the 2d. Series *Chronicles of Canongate* sold to Cadell for £4000 and it may very well happen that we shall have little to pay as part of the Copyrights will probably be declared mine by the Arbiter and these I shall have without money and without price.[2] Cadell is most anxious on the subject. He thinks that two years hence £10,000 may be made of a new edition.

DECEMBER

1 SATURDAY This morning again I was idle. But I must work and so I will tomorrow whether the missing sheets arrive, aye or no, by goles. After Court I went with Lord Wriothesley Russell[3] to Dalkeith House to see the pictures. Charles K. Sharpe alongst with us. We satisfied ourselves that they have actually frames and that I think was all we could be sure of. Lord Wriothesley, who is a very pleasant young man, wellinformed and with some turn for humour, dined with us and Mr. Davidow met him. The Misses Kerrs also dined and spent the evening with us in that sort of society which I like best. Charles Sharpe came in and we laughd over oysters and Sherry

And a fig for your Sultan and Sophi.[4]

2 SUNDAY Labourd to make leeway and finishd nearly seven pages to eke on to the end of the missing sheets when returnd. I have yoked Charles to Monsr Surenne, an old soldier in Napoleon's italian army and I think a clever little fellow with good general ideas of

---

1. He saw her performance, however, at Lord Gillies's on 7 March 1828.
2. Although Scott had sold the copyrights to Constable for £12,000 in 1818, £7800 of the price had never been paid, and Scott therefore hoped (vainly as it turned out) that Lord Newton would declare a part of them to be still his property. *Life*, vi. 21, 420, and vii. 162; and Sederunt Book, i. 336.
3. The Duchess of Bedford's eldest son.
4. Congreve's *Way of the World*, iv. 11.

etymology.[1] Signor Bugnie is a good Italian teacher and for a German, why I must look about. It is not the least useful language of the leash.

Cash deficncy in last Fee fund now paid up — — —	£100	0 0
In purse — — — — — — — — —	2	0 0
	£102	0 0

Wine postages etc.	£20 0 0	
Housekeeper at Dalkeith Ho	1	
Anne to house keeping	30	
Subscription to Bannatyne club . . .	5 5	
		£56 5
		46 15 0
Subscription to prize Essay Royal Commission —	£5	
Sundries	1	
		6
In purse ——	£40 15	

3 MONDAY A day of petty business which killd a holiday – Finishd my tale of the Mirror:[2] Went with Tom Allan to see his building at Lauriston where he has displayd good taste; supporting instead of tearing down or destroying the old Chateau which once belongd to the famous Mississippi Law. The additions are in very good taste and will make a most comfortable house. Mr. Burn, architect, would fain have had the old house pulld down, which I wonder at in him though it would have been the practice of most of his brethren. When I came up to town I was just in time for the Bannatyne Club where things are going on reasonably well.[3] I hope we may get out some good historical documents in the course of the winter. Dined at the Royal Society Club which was full and frequent. Honble. Mr. Hutchison son of Lord Donoughmore and a Sir John Cayley of Yorkshire were guests. The former seems a sensible and pleasant man, the latter a Twaddle – a dashing talker saying an infinite deal of nothing. At the Society had some essays upon the specifick weight of the ore of Manganeze[4] which was

1. He was in Edinburgh, lodging at 12 George Street. Surenne, 31 October 1827, Walpole.
2. 'My Aunt Margaret's Mirror.'
3. This Annual General Meeting decided on a final extension of the membership to one hundred. The Club issued six new publications in the course of 1828.
4. The paper was read by Dr. Edward Turner, who became Professor of Chemistry at University College, London, the following year. Royal Society Minutes.

Caviare to the President and I think most of the members. But it seemd extremely accurate and I have little doubt was intelligible to those who had the requisite key. We supd at Mr. Russell's where the Conversation was as gay as usual. Lieut. Col. Fergusson was my guest at the dinner.

4 TUESDAY Had the agreeable intelligence that Lord Newton had finally issued his decree in my favour for all the money in the Bank, amounting to £32,000. This will make a dividend of six Shillings in the pound which is presently to be paid. A meeting of the Creditors was held to-day at which they gave unanimous approbation of all that has been done and seemd struck by the exertions which had produced £22,000 within so short a space. They all separated well pleased. So far so good. Heaven grant the talisman break not. I sent copy to Ballantyne this morning having got back the missing sheets from John Lockhart last night. I feel a little puzzled about the character and stile of the next tale. The world has had so much of chivalry. Yet scarce a good sum yet. Well! I will dine merrily and thank God and bid care rest till tomorrow. How suddenly things can overcast and how suddenly the sun can break out again. On the 31st October I was dreaming as little of such a thing as at present when behold there came tidings which threaten[d] a total interruption of the amicable settlement of my affairs and menaced my own personal liberty. In less than a month we are enabled to turn chase on my persecutors who seem in a fair way of losing their recourse upon us. *Non nobis Domine* –

I was at the Register Office with Thomson and visited Hay Drummond in his Lion's den.[1] He seems in a fine way of redeeming that office so long degraded.

Received this night the unexpected sum of £307. 10. as balance of cash gaind by Mr. Cadell's agreeing for the foreign editions of *Napoleon* and other matters. This is over and above the sum of £200 received 30 Aug. and two small sums of £ and £ advanced by Mr. Cadell. It came as they say in clipping time and will enable me to get clear of my debt to Mr. Gibson which should have been repaid long since.[2]

5 WEDNESDAY Applying the supply to the payment of debts the accompt will stand as follows.

1. He was Principal Clerk of the Lyon Court.
2. The money borrowed to equip Scott's nephew Walter for India on 6 February 1826.

By Cash in purse		£40 15 0
By Cadell's remittance		307 10
	Cash	348 5
per contra		
To Ballance due Johnstone	£52	
To Dill to Terry for books	32	
To Faulkner porter and spirits	69	
To ballance to Anne	2	
	—	155
		£193 5

I did a good deal in the way of preparing my new tale[1] and resolved
to make some thing out of the story of Harry Wynd. The North
Inch of Perth would be no bad name and it may be possible to take
a difference betwixt the old highlander and him of modern date.
The fellow that swam the Tay and escaped would be a good
ludicrous character. But I have a mind to try him in the serious
line of tragedy. Miss Baillie has made the Ethling[2] a coward by
temperament and a hero when touchd by filial affection. Suppose
a man's nerves supported by feelings of honour or say by the spur
of jealousy supporting him against constitutional timidity to a
certain point then suddenly giving way – I think some thing
tragic might be produced. James Ballantyne's criticism is too
much moulded upon the general tast[e] of novels to admit (I
fear) this species of reasoning. But what can one do? I am hard up
as far as imagination is concernd yet the world calls for Novelty.
Well – I'll try my brave coward or cowardly brave man. *Valeat
quantum.*[3]

Being a teind day remain at home till one adjusting my ideas on
this point untill one o'clock – then walkd as far as Mr. Cadell's.
Finally went to dine at Hawk-hill with Lord and Lady Binning. Party
were Lord Chief-Comr., Lord Chief Baron, Solicitor,[4] John Wilson,
Lord Corehouse. The night was so dark and stormy that I was glad
when we got upon the paved streets.

6 THURSDAY Corrected proofs and went to court. Bad news of
Abud's case. I hope the rogue won't beat us after all. It would be
mortifying to have these rascals paid in full as they must be while

1. The rest of the paragraph establishes that the 'new tale' was what
   became *The Fair Maid of Perth.*
2. In her play *Ethwald*, in *Plays of the Passions*, 1802.
3. 'For what it may be worth.'
4. i.e. William Adam, Sir Samuel Shepherd, and John Hope.

better men must lie bye. *Spero meliora.*[1] Went and paid the following
debts

	Cash in purse	—	£193	5
To Thos Purdie		£10 0 0		
To Mr. Mitchell[2] for Will. Scott		10 0 0		
To Coach Maker in part of bill		50 0 0		
To Tait Bookseller in full		24 0 0		
To John Stevenson in part		70 0 0		
To Beard's *Theatre of God's Judgements*[3]		1 10		
To Bill at Club		10		
			£166	0
	Cash in purse	£27 5 0		
	Circus[4] for a party . . .		2	5
			£25	0 0

I think that copy of Beard's *Judgements* is the first book which I have
voluntarily purchased for nearly two years. So I am cured of one folly
at least. Anne, Charles and I dined quietly at home.

7 FRIDAY Being a blank day in the rolls I staid at home and wrote
four leaves – not very freely or happily. I was not in the vein.[5] Plague
on it! Staid at home the whole day. There is one thing I believe
peculiar to me – I work, that is meditate for the purpose of working,
best when I have a *quasi* engagement with some other book for
example. When I find myself doing ill or like to come to a still stand in
writing I take up some slight book, a novel or the like, and usually
have not read far ere my difficulties are removed and I am ready to
write again. There must be two current[s] of ideas going on in my
mind at the same time, or perhaps the slighter occupation serves like
a woman's wheel or stocking to ballast the mind as it were by

1. 'I hope for better things', Cicero's *Epistulae ad Atticum*, 14. 16. 3.
2. Thomas Mitchell, who married William Scott's mother, wrote
   on the 4th to say that he had arranged a passage to Canada for
   William. Walpole.
3. The Revd. Thomas Beard's *Theatre of God's Judgements, Wherein
   is represented the admirable Justice of God against all notorious
   sinners, etc.* Scott owned a 2nd edition (1612) and a 4th edition.
   A. L. C.
4. 'DUCROW'S ROYAL AMPHITHEATRE . . . a choice Equestrian
   Spectacle' visited Edinburgh in November and December.
   Edinburgh Advertiser, 16 November 1827, etc.
5. *Richard III*, iv. 2.

preventing the thoughts from wandering and so give the deeper current the power to flow undisturbd. I always laugh when I hear people say do one thing at once. I have done a dozen things at once all my life. Dined with the family. After dinner Lockhart's proofs[1] came in and occupied me for the evening. I wish I have not made that article too long and Lockhart will not snip away.

8 SATURDAY Went to court and staid there a good while. Made some consultations in the advocates' library, not furiously to the purpose. Paid for Charles' teachers as under

			£25	0	0
Cash in purse ————————————					
French Italian riding ————————————			11	15	
			13	5	0
Balance due for Essay[2]	£5	0 }	1	5	0
	1	5 }			
	Cash in purse	£12	0	0	

Court in the morning – Sent off Lockhart's proof which I hope will do him some good. A precatory letter from Gillies. I must do Molière for him I suppose but it is wonderful that knowing the situation I am in the poor fellow presses so hard. Sure I am pulling for life and it is hard to ask me to pull another man's oar as well as my own. Yet if I can give a little help

> We'll get a blessing with the lave
> And never miss'd.[3]

Went to John Murray where was Sir John Dalrymple and Lady, Sir John Cayley, Mr. Hope Vere and Lady Elizabeth Vere, a sister of the Marquis of Tweddale and a pleasant sensible woman. Some turn for antiquity too she shows and spoke a good deal of the pictures at Yester. Henderland was there too. Mrs. John Murray made some very agreeable music.

9 SUNDAY I set hard to work and had a long day with my new tale. I did about twelve leaves. Cadell came in with notice that Robison had transmitted copies of Abut's own affidavits stating that they had given

1. Of the article on 'Ornamental Gardening'.
2. The balance of his subscription to the University Commissioners' Prize Essay fund, mentioned in the Entry for 9 November 1827. He had already paid £5 on 2 December.
3. Burns's 'To a Mouse', ll. 17–18.

gold bars for the notes which they discounted at a rate which he computes will bring the interest up to 10 per Cent. This is exactly in the teeth of their present affirmation that there were no gold bars but only ready money in question.[1] We will go marvellously cunningly to work with these honest gentlemen and get certified copies of their oaths to produce in contradiction of their present assertions. I hope there is no very great sin in feeling vindictive to the extent that I hope they may be caught in a trap of their own laying and baiting. Caddell and I also talkd upon the great project of buying in the Copyrights. He is disposed to finesse a little about it but I do not think it will do much good. All the fine arguments will fly off and people just bid or not bid as the report of the trade may represent the speculation as a good or bad one. I daresay they will reach £7000[2] but £8000 won't stop us, and that for books over printed so lately and to such an extent is a pro-di-gi-ous[3] price. Frank Scott came in this evening.

10 MONDAY I corrected proofs and forwarded copy. Went out for an hour to Lady J.S. Home and dozed a little half stupefied with a cold in my head, made up this journal however. Settled I would go to Abbotsford on the 24th from Arniston. – Before that time I trust the business of the Copyrights will be finally settled – if they can be had on any thing like fair terms they will give the greatest chance I can see of extricating my affairs. Cadell seems to be quite confident in the advantage of making the purchase upon almost any terms and truly I am of his opinion. If they get out of Scotland it will not be all I can do that will enable me to write myself a free man during the space I have to remain in this world.

I smoked a couple of segars for the first time since I came from the Country and as Anne and Charles went to the play I muddled away the evening over my Sheriff Court processes and despatchd a hugeous parcell to Will Scott at Selkirk. It is always something off hand. Coughing, sneezing and all the signs of a little naughty cold with stuffd head and a slight toasting of fever. *Margin*.

11 TUESDAY Wrote a little and seemd to myself to get on. I went also to court. On return had a formal communication from

---

1. See the Entry for 5 November 1827 and note, and the Entry for 12 November 1827.
2. They fetched over £8400. See the Entry for 20 December 1827.
3. An allusion to Dominie Sampson's favourite exclamation in *Guy Mannering*.

Ballantyne enclosing a letter from Caddel of an unpleasant tenor. It seems Mr. Cadell is dissatisfied with the moderate success of the 1st Series of *Chronicles* and disapproving of about half the volume already written of the second Series obviously ruing his engagement. I have replied that I was not fool enough to suppose that my favour with the public could last for ever and was neither shockd nor alarmd to find that it had ceased now as cease it must one day soon. It might be inconvenient for me in some respects but I would be quite contented to resign the bargain rather than that more loss should be incurd. I saw, I told them, no other receipt than lying lea for a little while taking a fallow-break to reli[e]ve my Imagination which may be esteemd nearly cropd out. I can make shift for myself amid this failure of prospects but I think both Cadell and J. B. will be probable sufferers. However they are very right to speak their mind and may be esteemd tolerable good representatives of the popular taste. So I really think their censure may be a good reason for laying aside this work though I may preserve some part of it till another day.[1]

Dined at Sir David Wedderburn's with Lady Hampden and others, all old friends and well arranged. A very pleasant party.

12 WEDNESDAY Reconsiderd the probable downfal[l] of my literary reputation. I am so constitutionally indifferent to the censure or praise of the world that never having abandond myself to the feelings of selfconceit which my great success was calculated to inspire I can look with the most unshaken firmness upon the event as far as my own feelings are concernd. If there be any great advantage in literary [fame] I have had it and I certainly do not care at losing it.

They cannot say but what I *had* the *crown*.

It is unhappily inconvenient for my affairs to lay bye my [work] just now and that is the only reason why I do not give up literary labour, but at least I will not push the losing game of novel writing. I will take back the sheets now objected to but it cannot be expected that I am to write upon return. I cannot but think that a little thought will open some plan of composition which may promise novelty at the least. I suppose I shall hear from or see these gentlemen to-day; if not, I must send for them tomorrow. How will this affect the plan of going shares

1. 'My Aunt Margaret's Mirror', the story to which Cadell objected, was published shortly afterwards in a yearly publication, Charles Heath's *Keepsake*. See the Entry for 13 April 1828.

with Cadell[1] in the Novels of earlier and happier debt?[2] Very much I doubt, seeing I cannot lay down the cash. But surely the trustees may find some mode of providing this, or else with cash to secure these copyrights. At any rate I will gain a little time for thought and discussion.

Went to the Court. At returning settled with Chief Commissioner that I should receive him on 26 December at Abbotsford.

After all may there not be in this failure to please some reliques of the very unfavourable matters in which I have been engaged of late, the threat of imprisonment, the resolution to become Insolvent? I cannot feel that there is – What I suffer bye is the difficulty of not setting my foot upon such ground as I have trode before and thus instead of attaining novelty I lose spirit and nature. On the other hand, who would thank me for 'repeated sheets'?[3] – Here is a good joke enough lost to all who have not known the Clerks' table before the Jurisdiction act.

My two learned Thebans[4] are arrived and departed after a long consultation. They deprecated a fallow-break as ruin. I set before them my own sense of the difficulties and risques in which I must be involved by persev[er]ance and shewd them I could occupy my own time as well for six months or a twelvemonth and let the public gather an appetite. They replied (and therein was some risk) that the expectation would in that case be so much augmented that it would be impossible for any mortal to gratify it. To this is to be added what they did not touch upon – the risque of being thrust aside altogether, which is the case with the horses that neglect keeping the lead when once they have got it: finally we resolved the present work should go on, leaving out some parts of the introduction which they object to. They are good specimens of the public taste in general and it is far best to indulge and yield to them unless I was very *very* certain that I

1. The plan of buying the copyrights jointly. The Trustees' share was to be financed from the purchase-money for the second series of *Chronicles*.
2. A slip for 'date' indicative of Scott's bórderer's accent.
3. Both Douglas and Tait printed 'repented', but the word is 'repeated'. A new novel on the old subjects might be said to be 'repeated sheets'. Before the Judicature Act of 1825 a device known as a 'repeated summons' was used in certain circumstances to avoid the raising of a cross-action, and 'repeated sheets' would be the interlocutors prepared by the Clerks of Session. I am indebted to the Lord President of the Court of Session, Lord Clyde, for the correct reading of 'repeated' and for his explanation of Scott's legal joke.
4. *King Lear*, iii. 4.

was right and they rank.[1] Besides I am not afraid of their being hypercritical in the circumstances, being both sensible men and not inclined to sacrifice Chance of solid profit to the vagaries of critical taste. So the word is 'As you were.'

13 THURSDAY A letter from Lockhart announcing that Murray of Albemarle Street would willingly give me my own terms for a volume on the subject of planting and Landscape gardening.[2] This will amuse me very much indeed. Another proposal invites me on the part of Colbourne to take charge of the Garrick papers. The papers are to be edited by Colman and then it is proposed to me to write a life of Garrick in quarto. Lockhart refused a thousand pounds which was offerd and carte blanche was then sent. But I will not boat. My book and Colman's would run each other down. It is an attempt to get more from the public out of the subject than they will endure. Besides my name would be only useful in the way of *puff* for I really know nothing of the subject. So I will refuse – that's flat.[3]

Having turnd over my thoughts with some anxiety about the important subject of yesterday I think we have done for the best. If I can rally this time as I did in the *Crusaders*,[4] why there is the old trade open yet. If not, retirement will come gracefully after my failure. I must get the return of the sales of the three or four last novels so as to judge what stile of composition has best answerd. Add to this, giving up just now loses £4000 to the trustees which they would not understand whatever may be my nice authorial feelings. And moreover it ensures the purchase of the copy-rights – i.e. almost ensures them.

14 FRIDAY Summond to pay up arrears of our unhappy Oil Gas concern, £140, which I performd by Drat on Mr. Cadell. This will pinch a little close but it is a debt of honour and must be paid. The publick will never bear a publick man who shuns either to draw his purse or his sword when there is an open and honest demand on him. I also settled with Mr. Gibson for £240 advanced to fit out and [equip] my nephew Walter for India on 6 November[5] 1826 in this

1. Perhaps a slip for 'wrong', easy to make if Scott pronounced it 'wrang'.
2. This was never written.
3. James Boaden's edition of *The Private Correspondence of David Garrick* appeared in 1831–2.
4. Where the failure of *The Betrothed* was followed by the success of *The Talisman*.
5. A slip for 'February'.

diary. This ought to go against the youngster out of his father's succession. Well – my funds stand thus –

In Cadell's hands last installment history		£300
By receipt to Mr. Marshall for Quarter's salary lodged with Mr. Gibson		250
		550
Draught to pay the Shares of Oil Gas Coy. and their installments on Mr. Cadell	£140	
By placed receipt for 4ter Salary in Mr. Gibson's hand to account of advances	250	
		390
In Mr. Cadell's hand	Ball.	£160
Cash in purse	£12	
Charles	3	
		9
		£169

There may be one or two accompts at Christmas but I expect few of any consequence except about £90 Melrose so that I will come on well enough as next month brings me in about £200 Salary etc. and probably £100 for reviewing, which with cash in hand will afford £360 to face all contingencies. I still owe £500 to Cadell and a like sum on note to John[1] Ballantyne. But I make as much out of a good garden and planting book as will pay up one of them if not both, besides affording a cool hundred or two to my proper pinch.

15 SATURDAY Workd in the morning on the sheets which are to be cancelld[2] and on the Tale of *Saint Valentine's Eve*, a good title by the way.[3] Had the usual *quantum sufficit* of the Court which if it did not dissipate one's attention so much is rather an amusement as otherwise. But the plague is to fix one's attention to the sticking point after it has been squanderd about for two or three hours in such a way. It keeps one however in the carreer and stream of actual life, which is a great advantage to a literary man.

I missd an appointment for which I am sorry. It was about our Advocates' Library which is to be rebuilt.[4] During all my life we have

1. A slip for 'Sandie'.
2. Parts of the Introduction to the second series of *Chronicles*.
3. The first edition appeared as *Chronicles of the Canongate*, the second as *St. Valentine's Day*.
4. See the Entry for 15 February 1826 and note.

mismanaged the large funds expended on the rooms of our library, totally mistaking the objects for which a library is built, and instead of taking a general and steady view of the subject, patching up disconnected and illsized rooms totally unequal to answer the accomodation demanded and bestowing an absurd degree of ornament and finery upon the internal finishing. All this should be reversed – the new Library should be calculated upon a plan which ought to suffice for all the 19th century at least and for that purpose should admit of being executed 'progressi[ve]ly' – then there should be no ornament other than that of strict architectural proportion and the rooms should be accessible one through another but divided with so many partitions as to give ample room for shelves. These small rooms would also facilitate the purposes of study. Something of a lounging room would not be amiss, which might serve for meeting of Faculty occasionally. I ought to take some interest in all this and I do. So I will attend the next meeting of committee. Dined at Baron Hume's and met General Campbell of Lochnell and his Lady.

16 SUNDAY Workd hard to-day and only took a half hour's walk with Hector MacDonald. Colin MacKenzie unwell. His astmha seems rather to increase not withstanding his foreign trip. Alas! long seated complaints defy Italian climate.[1] We had a small party to dinner. Capt and Mrs. Hamilton, Davidoff, Frank Scott Harden, and his Chum Charles Baillie second son of Mellerstain[2] who seems a clever young man, and two or three of the party staid to take wine and water.

17 MONDAY Sent off the beginning of the *Chronicles* to Ballantyne. I hate cancels; they are a double labour.

Mr. Cowan, Trustee for Constable's Crers, calld in the morning by appointment and we talkd about the upset price of the copyrights of *Waverley* etc. I frankly told him that I was so much concernd that they should remain more or less under my controul that I was willing with the advice of my Trustees to over[3] a larger upset than that of £4750 which had been fixd, and that I proposed the price sett up should be £250 for the poetry, Paul's letters etc. and £5250 for the novels, in all £5500. But that I made this proposal under the condition that in case no bidding should ensue then the copyrights should be mine so soon

1. An aphorism distressingly applicable to Scott's own experience four years after this.
2. George Baillie of Jerviswoode and Mellerstain.
3. Tait amended to over[bid]; Douglas printed 'offer', which is probably what Scott meant. 'Over' and 'offer' are nearly identical to a speaker with a border accent.

as the sale was adjournd without any one being permitted to bid after the sale. It is to be hoped this high upset price will

> – fright the fuds
> of the pock-puds – [1]

This speculation may be for good or for evil but it tends incalculably to increase the value of such copyrights as remain in my own person, and if a handsome and cheap edition of the whole with notes can be instituted in conformity with Cadell's plan it must prove a mine of wealth, three fourths of which will belong to me or my creditors.[2] It is possible no doubt that the works may lose their effect on the public mind but this must be risqued and I think the chances are greatly in our favour. Death (my own I mean) would improve the property since an edition with a Life would sell like wildfire. Perhaps those who read this prophesy may shake their heads and say 'Poor fellow! he little thought how he should see the publick interest in him and his extinguishd even during his natural existence.' It may be so – but I will hope better. This I know, that no literary speculation ever succeeded with me but where my own works were concernd[3] and that on the other hand these have rarely faild. And so – *Vogue la galère.*[4]

Dined with the Lord Chief Commissioner and met Lord and Lady Binning, Lord and Lady Abercromby, Sir Robert O'Callaghan etc. These dinners put off time well enough and I write so painfully by candle light that they do not greatly in[ter]fere with business.

18 TUESDAY I ought to have mentiond that yesterday I was at a meeting of the oil gas committee. In that unhappy concern we are now advised by James Simpson to commence making our own rosin by purchasing turpentine in a raw state and manufacturing it for sale. This does not resemble mending an old trade so much as it does setting up a new one. I wish I were free of this office of President. I don't half like it and yet it is shame to leave off when the ship is in danger.

1. 'Little Wat Ye', Herd, i. 118.
2. The other quarter would be Cadell's by virtue of his half-share in the early copyrights. For Cadell's efforts to increase his share in the copyrights, see the Entries for 20 December 1830 and 13 March 1831 and notes.
3. Scott is thinking of his unsuccessful and short-lived venture into publishing and book-selling in 1809 when, after a quarrel with Constable, he launched the firm of John Ballantyne & Coy. See Edgar Johnson, i. 306–20 and 412–25.
4. See p. 120, note 2.

Went to the meeting of Committee to-day and did not half like it. When things are unprosperous, irritation and animosity ensues, and of this there seem tokens amongst us which increase my desire to be off; as little good can be done without a determined spirit of union. Poor Huntly Gordon writes me in despair about £180 of debt which he has incurrd. He wishes to publish two Sermons which I wrote for him when he was taking orders but he would get little money for them without my name and that is at present out of the question.[1] People would cry out against the undesired and unwellcome zeal of him who stretchd his hand to help the ark even with the best intentions and cry Sacrilege. And yet they would do me gross injustice, for I would if calld upon die a martyr for the Christian religion, so completely is (in my poor opinion) its divine origin proved by its beneficial effects on the state of society. Were we but to name the abolition of slavery and of polygamy how much has in these two words been granted to mankind by the lessons of our saviour.

19 WEDNESDAY Wrought upon an introduction to the notices which have been recoverd of George Bannatyne, author or rather transcriber of the famous Repository of Scottish poetry generally known by the name of the Bannatyne Ms.[2] They are very jejune these same notices, a mere record of matters of business, putting forth and calling in of sums of money and such like. Yet it is a satisfaction to learn that this great benefactor to the literature of Scotland lived a prosperous life and enjoyd the pleasures of domestic society and in a time peculiarly perilous lived unmolested and died in quiet.

At 11 o'clock I had an appointment with a person unknown. A youth had written me demanding an audience. I excused myself by alleging the want of leisure and my dislike to communicate with a person perfectly unknown on unknown business. The application was renewd and with an ardour which left me no alternative so I named eleven this day. I am too much accustomed to the usual cant

1. A few days later Scott relented. 'As I have no money to spare at present,' he writes to Gordon on 28 December, 'I find it necessary to make a sacrifice of my own scruples, to relieve you from serious difficulties. . . . It is understood my name is not to be put on the title-page, or blazed at full length in the preface. You may trust that to the newspapers'. *Letters*, x. 350. Gordon extricated himself from his financial distresses by publishing them the following year under the title of *Religious Discourses by a Layman*.

2. This became no. 33 of the Bannatyne Club publications: *Memorials of George Bannatyne, 1545–1608, with Memoir by Sir Walter Scott*, 1829. The newly discovered manuscript belonged to Sir James Foulis of Woodhall.

of the followers of the muses who endeavour by flattery to make their bad stale butter make amends for their stinking fish. I am pretty well acquainted with that sort of thing. I have had madmen on my hand too[1] and once nearly was Kotzbued by a lad of the name of Sharpe.[2] All this gave me some curiosity but it was lost in attending to the task I was engaged in when the door opend and in walkd a young woman of middling rank and rather good address but something resembling our Secretary David Laing if dressd in female habiliments. There was the awkwardness of a moment in endeavouring to make me understand that she was the visitor to whom I had given the assignation. Then there were a few tears and sighs. 'I fear, madam, this relates to some tale of great distress.' 'By no means, Sir' and her countenance cleard up. Still there was a pause. At last she askd if it were possible for her to see the King. I apprehended then that she was a little mad and proceeded to assure her that the King's Secretary received all such applications as were made to his Majesty and disposed of them. Then came the mystery. She wishd to relieve herself from a state of bondage and to be renderd capable of maintaining herself by acquiring knowledge. I inquired what were her immediate circumstances and found she resided with an uncle and Aunt. Not thinking the case without hope I preachd the old doctrine of patience and resignation, I suppose with the usual effect.

Went to the Bannatyne club and on the way met Cadell out of breath coming to say he had bought the Copyrights after a smart contention.[3] Of this tomorrow. There was little to do at the Club.

Afterwards dined with Lord and Lady Abercromby where I met my old and kind friend Major Buchanan of Cambusmore. His father was one of those from whom I gaind most information about the old highlanders and at whose house I spent many merry days in my youth. The last time I saw old Camusmore was in [1809].[4] He sat up an hour later on the occasion though then eighty four. I shall never forget him, and was delighted to see the Major who comes seldom to town.

20 THURSDAY Anent the Copyrights – the pock puds were not frighted by our high price. They came on briskly four or five bidders abreast and

1. Notably his amanuensis Weber, who became insane in 1814 and attempted to force a duel on Scott. See *Life*, iv. 146.
2. See *Letters*, vi. 58.
3. In his eagerness to know the result of the sale, Scott had told Cadell to bring the news to the Bannatyne Club 'which has a meeting in the Antiquarian Societys rooms Mound you can send up your name'. *Letters*, x. 340.
4. The first of many visits was in 1793. Cambusmore is in the country described in *The Lady of the Lake*.

bid[s] went on till the lot was knockd down to Cadell at £8400 – a very large sum certainly yet he has been offerd profit on it already. For my part I think the loss would have been very great had we sufferd these copyrights to go from those which we possessd. They would have been instantly stereo-typed and forced on the market to bring home the price and by this means depreciated for ever, and all ours must have shared the same fate. Whereas husbanded and brought out with care they cannot fail to draw in the others in the same series and thus to be a sure and respectable source of profit. Considerd in this point of view, even if they were worth only the £8,400 to others they were worth ten thousand pounds to us. The largeness of the price arising from the activity of the contest only serves to shew the value of the property. Had at the same time the agreeable intelligence that the 8vo sets which were bought by Hurst and Coy at a depreciated rate are now rising in the market and that instead of 1500 sold they have sold upwards of two thousand copies. This mass will therefore in all probability be worn away in a few months and then our operations may commence. On the whole I am greatly pleased with the acquisition. If this first series be worth £8400 the remaining books must be worth £10,000, and then there is *Napoleon* which is gliding away daily for which I would not take the same sum, which would come to £24,200 in all for copyrights besides £20,000 payable by insurance. Add the value of my books and furniture, plate etc., there would be £50,000. So this may be considerd my present progress. There will still remain upwards of £35,000.

Heaven's arm strike with us – 'tis a fearful odds.[1]

Yet with health [and] continued popularity there are chances in my favour – Calld on the Ellises and lionized a little.

Dine at James Ballantyne[2] and happy man is he at the result of the sale; indeed it must have been the making or marring of him. Sir Henry Steuart there who 'foold me to the top of my bent.'[3]

21 FRIDAY A very sweet pretty looking young lady, the prima Donna of the Italian opera[4] now performing here, by name Miss Ayton, came to breakfast this morning with her father (a bore, after the

1. *Henry V*, iv. 3.
2. Cadell too was at this celebration dinner. See *Letters*, x. 340.
3. *Hamlet*, iii. 2.
4. Signor di Begni's Italian Opera Company opened in the Theatre Royal on 13 December with *Il barbiere di Siviglia*, in which Fanny Ayton sang Rosina. Dibdin, p. 322, and *Edinburgh Advertiser*, 14 December 1827.

manner of all fathers, mothers, aunts and other chaperones of pretty actresses). Miss Ayton talks very prettily and I dare say sings beautifully though too much in the Italian manner I fear to be a great favourite of mine. But I did not hear her, being calld away by the Clerks' coach.[1] I am like Jeremy in *Love for Love*. 'Have a reasonable good ear for a jig but your solos and sonatas give me the spleen.'[2]

Calld at Cadell's who is still enamourd of his bargain and with good reason as the London booksellers were offering him £1000 and £2000 to give up his bargain to them. He also ascertaind that all the copies with which Hurst and Robinson loaded the market would be off in a half year. Make us thankful the weather is clearing to windward. Cadell is cautious, steady and hears good counsel, and Gibson quite inclined, were I too confident, to keep a good look out ahead. Dined at home and in quiet. Wrote letters in the evening.

22 SATURDAY Publick affairs look awkward.[3] The present ministry[4] are neither whig nor tory and, divested of the support of either of the great parties of the state, stand supported by the will of the Sovereign alone. This is not constitutional and though it may be a temporary augmentation of the Sovereign's personal influence yet it cannot but prove hurtful to [the] Crown on the whole by tending to throw that responsibility on the Sovereign of which the Law has deprived him. I pray to God I may be wrong but an attempt to govern *par bascule* – by trimming betwixt the opposite parties – is equally unsafe for the crown and detrimental to the country and cannot do for a long time. The fact seems to be that Lord Goodriche, a well meaning and timid man, finds himself on a precipice – that his head is grown giddy and [he] endeavours to cling to the person next him. This person is Lord Lansdowne, who he hopes may support him in the House of Lords against Lord Grey, so he proposes to bring Lord Lansdowne into the Cabinet. The move I suspect was suggested by Huskisson, the Sitting part of poor Canning. But the King will not listen to the proposal. Lord G. resigns and his resignation is accepted. Lord Harrowby is then askd to place himself at the head of a new Administration –

1. The Clerks of Session shared a coach to Court in the morning. Scott enjoyed the 'ten minutes either of sense or fun' which the journey afforded. *Letters*, x. 358.
2. Congreve's *Love for Love*, ii. 7.
3. Like most of Scott's political Entries, this one coincides with receipt of a letter about public affairs from Lockhart. 19 December 1827, Walpole.
4. Lord Goderich's, which was in power from August 1827 to January 1828. See Appendix E, p. 827.

declines – the tried abilities of Marquis Wellesley are next applied
[to] – it seems he also declines and then Lord Goodriche comes back,
his point about Lord Lansdowne having faild, and his threatend
resignation goes for nothing. This must lower the Premier in the eyes
of every one. It is plain the K. will not accept the Whigs – it is equally
plain that he has not made a move towards the Tories and that with a
neutral administration this country, hard-ruled at any time, can be
long governd, I for one cannot believe. God send the good King to
whom I owe so much as safe and honourable extrication as the
circumstances render possible.

After Court Anne set out for Abbotsford with the Miss Kerrs. I
came off at three o'clock to Arnistoun where I found Lord Register[1]
and Lady, R. Dundas and Lady, Robt. Adam Dundas, Durham
Calderwood and lady, old and young friends. Charles came with me.

23 SUNDAY Went to church to Borthwick[2] with the family and heard
a well composed, well deliverd, sensible discourse from Mr. Wright
the clergyman, a different sort of person, I wot, from my old half
mad, half drunken little humpback acquaintance Clunie, renownd
for singing 'The Auld Mare's Dead'[3] and from the circumstance of
his being once interrupted in his minstrelsy by the information that
his own horse had died in the stable.

After sermon we lookd at the old castle,[4] which made me an old
man. The castle was not a bit older for the twenty five years which had
past away but the ruins of the visitor were very apparent – to climb up
ruind staircases, to creep through vaults and into dungeons, were not
the easy labours but the positive sports of my younger years, but that
time is gone by and I thought it convenient to attempt no more than
the access to the large and beautiful hall in which as it is somewhere
described an armed horseman might brandish his lance. The feeling
of growing and increasing inability is painful to one like me who
boasted in spite of my infirmity great boldness and dexterity in such
feats – the boldness remains but hand and foot, gripe and accuracy of
step, have altogether faild me – the spirit is willing but the flesh is
weak and so I must retreat into the invalided corps and tell stories of
my former exploits which may very likely pass for lies. We drove to

---

1. The Rt. Hon. William Dundas.
2. The parish of Borthwick is about twelve miles south-east of
   Edinburgh.
3. To whose singing Burns owed a version of 'Ca' the Yowes to the
   Knowes'. See *The Poems and Songs of Robert Burns*, ed. James
   Kingsley (1968), p. 1252.
4. Borthwick, which dates from the fifteenth century.

Dalhousie castle where the gallant Earl who has done so much to distinguish the British name in all and every quarter of the globe[1] is repairing the Castle of his ancestors which of yore stood a siege against John of Gaunt. I was Lord Dalhousie's companion at school where he was as much beloved by his companions as he has been ever respected by his companions in arms and the people over whom he has been deputed to exercise the authority of his Sovereign. He was always steady, wise and generous. His old Castle of Dalhousie – *potius* Dalwolsey – was mangled by a fellow calld I believe Douglas, who destroyed as far as in him lay its military and baronial character and roofd it after the fashion of a Poor's House. His architect, Burns, is now restoring and repairing in the old taste and I think creditably to his own feeling. God Bless the rooftree!

We returnd home through the Temple[2] banks by the side of the South Esk where I had the pleasure to see that Robert Dundas is laying out his woods with taste and managing them with care. His father and uncle took notice of me when I was 'a fellow of no mark or likelihood'[3] and I am always happy in finding myself in the old oak room at Arniston where I have drunk many a merry bottle and in the fields where I have seen many a hare killd.

24 MONDAY Left Arniston after breakfast and arrived to dinner at Abbotsford.

My reflections at entring my own gate were of a very different and more pleasing cast than those with which I left my house about six weeks ago. I was then in doubt whether I should fly my country or become avowedly bankrupt and surrender up my library and household furniture with the life rent of my estate to sale. A man of the world will say I had better done so. No doubt had I taken this course at once I might have employd the £25,000 which I made since the insolvency of Constable and Robinson's house in compounding my debts – But I could not have slept sound as I now can under the comfortable impression of receiving the thanks of my creditors[4] and the conscious feeling of discharging my duty like a man of honour and honesty. I see before me a long tedious and dark path but it leads to true Fame and stainless reputation. If I die in the harrows as is very

1. Particularly in the Peninsula and as Governor of Canada.
2. Temple is a village near Arniston.
3. *1 Henry IV*, iii. 2.
4. Scott would just have received the letter written by Donald Horne on behalf of the Committee of Creditors, which said: 'I beg to express to you their high sense of the Honorable, and meritorious exertions, which you have already made, and are still making for their benefit.' 22 December 1827, Walpole.

likely I shall die with honour; if I achieve my task I shall have the thanks of all concernd and the approbation of my own conscience. And so I think I can fairly face the return of Christmas day.

25 TUESDAY I drove over to Huntly Burn and saw the plantation which is to be called Janes wood in honour of my daughter in law.[1] All looking well and in order. Before dinner arrived Mrs. George Ellis and her nephew and niece, Mr. and Mrs. Charles Ellis, whom I was delighted to see as there are a thousand kind recollections of old days. Mrs. Geo Ellis is less changed in manner and appearance than anyone I know. The gay and light hearted have in that respect superiority over those who are of a deeper mould and a heavier. There is something even in the slightness and elasticity of person which outlasts the ponderous strength which is born down by its own weight. Col. Ellis is an enthusiastic soldier and though young served in Spain and at Waterloo.

> And so we held our Christmas-tide
> With mirth and burly cheer.[2]

26 WEDNESDAY Col. Ellis and I took a pretty long walk round by the glen[3] et caetera where I had an extraordinary escape by the breaking down of a foot-bridge as I put my foot upon it. I luckily escaped either breaking my leg by its passing through the bridge in so awkward a manner or tearing it by some one of the hundred rusty nails through which it fell. However I was not, thanks to Heaven, hurt in the slightest degree. Tom Purdie who had orders to repair the bridge long since was so scandalized at the consequence of his negligence that it passd and the bridge is repaird by the time I am writing this. But how the noiseless step of Fate dogs us in our most seeming safe and innocent sports.

On returning home we were joind by the Lord Ch: Commissioner, the Lord Chief Baron, and William Clerk of gentlemen, and of Ladies Miss Adam and young Miss Thomson of Charlton. Also the two Miss Kerrs, Lord Robert's daughters, and so behold us a gallant Christmas party full of mirth and harmony. Moreover Capt. John Fergusson came over from Huntley Burn. So we spent the day jocundly. I intend to take a holiday or two while these friends are about us – I have workd hard enough to merit it and

1. They were at this time 'planting busily'. *Letters*, x. 350.
2. 'The Boy and the Mantle', st. 2. Percy's *Reliques*.
3. The Rhymer's Glen.

– Maggie will not sleep
For that ere Summer.[1]

27 THURSDAY This morning we took a drive up the Yarrow in great force and perambulated the Duchesses walk with all the force of our company. The weather was delightful, the season being considerd, and Newark Castle amid its leafless trees resembled a dear old man who smiles upon the ruins which time has spread around him. It is looking more venerable than formerly for the repairs judiciously undertaken have now assumed colouring congenial with the old walls – formerly they had a raw and patchy appearance. I have seldom seen the scene look better even when summer smiled upon it.

I have a letter from James Hogg the Ettrick Shepherd asking me to intercede with the D. of Buccleuch about his farm. He took this burthen on himself without the advice of his best friends and certainly contrary to mine. From the badness of the times it would have been a poor speculation in any hands, especially in those of a man of letters whose occupations as well as the society in which it involves him [unfits him for such business.] But I hope this great family will be kind to them – if not, *cela ne tiendra pas a moi*. But I cannot and ought not to look for having the same interest with this gentleman which I exercized in the days of Duke Charles.[2]

28 FRIDAY A demand from Cadell to prepare a revised copy of the *Tales of my Grandfather* for the press. I received it with great pleasure for I always had private hopes of that work. If I have a knack for anything it is for selecting the striking and interesting points out of dull details, and hence I myself receive so much pleasure and instruction from volumes which are generally reputed dull and uninteresting. Give me facts I will find fancy for myself. The two first volumes of these little tales are shorter than the third by 70 or 80 pages. Cadell proposes to equalise them by adding part of Vol II to vol I and of vol III to vol II. But then vol I ends with the reign of Robert Bruce, vol II with the defeat of Flodden. Happy points of pause which I cannot think of disturbing; the first in particular for surely we ought to close one volume at least of Scottish history at a

---

1. Burns's 'Auld Farmer's New Year Salutation', ll. 77–8.
2. Scott's intercession was ultimately successful. On 7 January 1829 Lockhart writes to Sophia that the Duke, although 'turning out a stupid *scrub*', has 'given Hogg all his arrears'. Abbots. But by April 1830 he was so in arrears once more that Scott, as Sheriff, found himself subscribing 'a warrant of sale against poor James Hogg'. *Letters*, xi. 338.

point which leaves the Kingdom triumphant and happy, and alas! where do her annals present us with such an aera excepting after Bannockburn? So I will set about to fill up the volumes which are too short with some additional matter and so diminish at least if we cannot altogether remove the unsightly inequality in the size of volumes. The rest of the party went to Dryburgh, too painful a place of pilgrimage for me.[1] I walkd with the Lord Ch: Commissioner through our grounds at Huntly Burn and by taking the carriage now and then I succeeded in giving my excellent old friend[2] enough of exercise without any fatigue. We made our visit at Huntly Burn. Henry and Frank Scott of Harden dined.

30[3] SUNDAY Lord Chief Baron, Lord Chief Commissioner, Miss Adam, Miss Thomson Anstruther and William Clerk left us. We read prayers and afterwards walkd round the Terass. Laidlaw, Steel etc. I had also time to work hard on the additions to the *Tales of a Grandfather* volumes first and second. The day passd pleasantly over.

31 MONDAY Mrs. George Ellis is unwell, I hope not severely so, but the slightness of her figure must augur a delicacy of health and want of strength which expose her to sudden attacks. The Harden boys remaind with us. The Fergussons came over and we wellcomd in the new year with the usual forms of song and flaggon.

Looking back to the conclusion of 1826 I observe that the last year ended in trouble and sickness with pressures for the present and gloomy prospects for the past.[4] The sense of a great privation so lately sustaind, together with the very doubtful and clouded nature of my private affairs, pressd hard upon my mind. I am now perfectly well in constitution and though I am still in troubled waters yet I am rowing with the tide, and less than the continuation of my exertions of 1827 may with God's blessing carry me successfully through 1828, when we may gain a more open sea if not exactly a safe port. Above all, my Children are well – Sophia's situation excites some natural anxiety but it is only the accomplishment of the burthen imposed on her sex.[5] Walter is happy in the view of his Majority on which matter we have

1. Lady Scott had been buried there eighteen months before.
2. William Adam was Scott's senior by twenty years.
3. This and the following Entry are dated '29' and '30' by Scott. See Appendix E, iii.
4. A slip for 'future'.
5. She had been 'in daily expectation of her accouchement' for six weeks. Lockhart, 19 November 1827, Walpole.

favourable hopes from the Duke of Wellington.[1] Anne is well and happy and Charles's entry on life, under the highest patronage and in a line for which I hope [he] is qualified, is about to take place presently.[2]

For all these great blessings it becomes me well to be thankful to God who in his good time and good pleasure sends us good as well as evil.

State of Cash

In Mr. Cadell's hands as before leaving Edinburgh see 14th Current		£160
Cash in purse then		9
		169
To Anne to pay accompts before leaving town	£35 0 0	
To Charity	2	
To Charles pocket money	2	
To travelling to Abbotsford by two divisions with servants and sundries	5	
To short reckond on Oil Gas Coy call and be d—d to it	12	
		56
		£113
To Tom Purdie for cash to pay the Cottage guisards[3] their pence		2
Cash in Mr. Cadell's hand		£111

I may here remark that though the last year was a very expensive one and though

1. In his Christmas letter Scott urges Walter not to miss the Duke's levee on 19 January, nor the chance of meeting him at Lady Shelley's. *Letters*, x. 349. He was gazetted Major in February.
2. Lockhart's last letter had reported Lord Dudley as saying 'that Lord Wm. Harvey is very likely to go attaché to Vienna *immediately* in which case Charles will have his place at the Foreign office', 25 December 1827, Walpole. In the meantime he was 'refreshing his mind with french and his limbs with shooting – the last I believe most willingly'. To Lockhart, 7 January 1828, Disc. i. 189.
3. The term used of Scottish children when they dress up and go round singing for pennies. In Scott's time the guizards appeared at Hogmanay, not at Hallowe'en as they do now.

Vidimus 13 December

Cadell ———————————————————		£300
Salaries — £250 — £195 ———————		345
reviews ————————————————————		100
		———
		745

John Gibson about ————————	£300.0.0	
Oil Gas Coy —————————————	170	
Pringle Melrose ————————————	15	
Beaton Slater ————————————	10	
Sheep Usher and Land Cows ————	30	
Curle ———————————————————	32	
Ballance Bills ————————————	34	
	———	490
Ball —————————————————————		255
Applied to Gibson ————————————	£250	
Order etc. Cadell O.G. Coy —————	140	
		———
		390
Remains in Cadell's hand —————		£160
Melrose accompts —————————		87
		———
To living etc. ————————————		£73
Salary etc. ————————————————		£195
Review ———————————————————		100
		———
		295
5 Decr. Cash in purse ———————		£40
Dt. Cadell by J. B. ———————		307
		———
		£347
Johnstone Ballance ——————	£52	
Terry Ball. —————————————	32	
Faulkner ———————————————	69	
	———	
	153	
Anne to pay above £155 add.		
difference ———————————	2	
	———	
	155	
Tom Purdie —————————————	10	
William Scott ———————————	10	
	———	175
		172

13 Decemb.
Vidimus ——————

1828

1 TUESDAY

> As I walk by myself
> I talkd to myself
> And thus myself said to me.[1]

Since the 20 November 1825, for two months that is and two years, I have kept this custom of a diary. That it has made me wiser or better I dare not say but it shews by its progress that I am capable of keeping a resolution. Perhaps I should not congratulate myself on this – perhaps it only serves to show I am more a man of method and less a man of originality and have no longer that vivacity of fancy that is inconsistant with regular labour. Still, should this be the case, I should, having lost the one, be happy to find myself still possessd of the other.

We dined today at Huntly Burn, Miss Kerr going with us, Anne remaining with our guests at Home.

2 WEDNESDAY *Caecae mentes hominum!*[2] my last entry records my punctuality in keeping up my diary hitherto. My present labour, commenced notwithstanding the date upon the 9th January, is to make up my little record betwixt the second and that latter date. In a word I have been seven days in arrear without rhime or reason – days too when there was so little to write down that the least jotting would have done it. This must not be in future.

The Scotts of Harden were with us and we had a pleasant day.

3 THURSDAY Our friends begin to disperse. Mrs. Ellis, [who] has been indisposed for the last two days, will I hope bear her journey to

---

1. 'Old Song', quoted also on the title-page of the first volume of the *Journal*. See Herd, ii. 189. This entry is the first in the second volume of the manuscript.
2. 'Blind minds of men.' See Lucretius's *De Rerum Natura*, II. 14.

London well. She is the relict of my dear old friend George Ellis who had more wit, learning and knowlege of the world than would fit out twenty literati. The Hardens remaind to-day and I had a long walk with the Laird up the glen and so forth. He seemd a little tired and with all due devotion to my Chief I was not sorry to triumph over some one in point of activity at my time of day.

4 FRIDAY Visited by Mr. Stewart of Dalguize who came to collect materials for a description of Abbotsford to be given with a drawing in a large work, *Views of Gentlemen's Seats*. Mr. Stewart a well informd gentlemanlike young man, grave and quiet yet possessd of a sense of humour. I must take care he does not in civility over-puff my little assemblage of curiosities. Scarce any thing can be meaner than the vanity which details the contents of china closets – basins, ewers and Chamberpots. Horace Walpole with all his talents makes a silly figure when he gives an upholsterer's catalogue of his goods and chattles at Strawberry hill [1]

5 SATURDAY This day I began to review Taschereau's *Life of Molière* for Mr. Gillies who is crying help for God's sake.[2] Messrs. Treuttel and Wurtz offer guerdon. I shall accept because it is doing Gillies no good to let him have my labour for nothing and an article is about £100: in my pocket it may form a fund to help this poor gentleman or others at a pinch, in his I fear it would only encourage a neglect of sober oeconomy. When in his prosperity he askd me whether there was not in my opinion something interesting in a man of genius being in embarassd circumstances – God knows he has had enough of them since, poor fellow, and it should be rememberd that if he thus dallied with his good fortune his benevolence to others was boundless.

We had the agreeable intelligence of Sophia's being safely deliverd of a girl.[3] The mother and child Both well, that is doing well. Praised be God.

6 SUNDAY I have a letter from the Duke of Wellington making no promises but assuring me of a favourable consideration of Walter's

1. In his *Description of the Villa of Horace Walpole etc.*, 1774 and 1784.
2. '*The fate of our undertaking depends on this Number!*' Gillies, 24 December 1827, Walpole. Scott's review of Taschereau's *Life* and Auger's edition of the works appeared in the February number of the *Foreign Quarterly*.
3. There is a note in Sophia's handwriting pencilled in the margin: 'Charlotte born the 1st Jan.'

case should an opening occur for the Majority.[1] This same *step* is represented as the most important but so in their time were the Lieutenancy and the Troop. Each in its turn was the *Step* par excellence. It appears that these same steps are those of a Tread Mill, where the party is always ascending and never gains the top. But the same simile would suit most pursuits in life.

The Misses Kerr have left us on Friday – two charming young persons, well lookd, well mannerd and well born, above all well principled. They sing together in a very delightful manner and our evenings are the duller without them.

I am annoyd beyond measure with the idle intrusion of voluntary correspondents; each man who has a pen, ink, sheet of foolscap and an [hour] to spare flies a letter at me. I believe the postage costs me £100 besides innumerable franks; and all the letters regard the writer's own hopes or projects; or are filld with unaskd advice or extravagant requests. I think this evil increases rather than diminishes[2] On the other hand I must fairly own that I have receivd many communications in this way worth all the trouble and expence that the others cost me,[3] so I must lay the head of the sow to the tail of the grice[4] as the proverb elegantly expresses itself.

News again of Sophia and Baby. Mrs. Hughes thinks the infant a beauty – Johnie opines that it is not *very* pretty, and Grandpapa supposes it like other newborn children which are as like as a basket of oranges.

7 MONDAY Wrought at the review and finishd a good lot of it. Mr. Stewart left us, amply provided with the history of Abbotsford and its

1. 'Although I can make no promises of what shall be done in case certain expected events should occur, you may rely upon it that I shall not feel disposed to pass unnoticed the claims and Merits of Captain Scott only because he is Your Son. Believe me ever yours Most Sincerely – WELLINGTON.' *Letters*, x. 353 n. Walter paid for this 'step' himself by selling £2,780 worth of Jane's stock. Walter to Bayley, 22 April and 29 May 1829, Abbots.

2. Two had just arrived, one enclosing sheets of quotations from a work on Niagara Falls which the author hoped Scott would look into, another asking him if Brougham was the writer of a recent article in the *Edinburgh Review* (with which Scott had no connection). See Maude, and Philipeter, 3 January 1828, Walpole.

3. For instance, the story of Helen Walker which suggested the plot of *The Heart of Midlothian*, sent by a Mrs. Goldie, or the contributions of Joseph Train.

4. 'Balance gains against losses'. A grice is a young pig.

contents. It is a kind of Conundrum Castle to be sure and I have great
pleasure in it, for while it pleases a fantastic person in the stile and
manner of its architecture and decoration it has all the comforts of a
commodious habitation.

Besides the Review I have been for this week busily employd in
revising for the press the *Tales of a Grandfather*. Cadell rather wishd to
rush it out by employing three different presses but this *I repressd*
(smoke the pun). I will not have poor James Ballantyne driven off the
plank to which we are all three clinging. I have made great additions
to volume first and second of these *Tales* and I care not who knows it,
I think well of them. Nay – I will hash History with anybody, be he
who he will. I do not know but it would be wise to let romantic
composition rest and turn my mind to the History of England,
France and Ireland to be *da capo rota'd* as well as that of Scotland. They would laugh at me as an author for Mr. Newberry's shop
in Paul's Church Yard.[1] I should care little for that. *Virginibus
puerisque*[2] I would as soon compose histories for boys and girls
which may be useful, as fictions for Children of a larger growth which
can at best be only idle folk's entertainment. But write what I will or
to whom I will, I am doggedly determined to write myself out of the
present scrape by any labour that is fair and honest.

8 TUESDAY Despatchd my review (in part) and in the morning
walkd from Chiefswood all about the shearing flats and home by the
new walk which I have calld the Brideswalk because Jane was nearly
stuck fast in the bog there just after her marriage in the beginning of
1826.[3]

My post brings serious intelligence to-day and of a very pleasing
description. Longman and Coy, with a reserve which marks all their
proceedings, suddenly inform Mr. Gibson that they desire 1000 of
the 8vo. edition of *Saint Ronan's Well* and the subsequent series of
novels thereunto belonging for that they have only *seven* remaining,
and wish it to be sent to three printers and pushd out in three months.
Thus this great House without giving any previous notice of the state
of the sale expect all to be boot and saddle, horse and away, whenever
they give the signal. In the present case this may do because I will
make neither alteration nor addition till our *grande opus* the Improved
Edition goes to press. But ought we to go to press with this 1000
copies knowing that our project will supersede and render equivalent

1. The shop started by John Newberry (1713–67), publisher and
   originator of books for children.
2. 'For girls and boys.' Horace's *Odes*, iii. 1.
3. A slip for '1825'.

to waste paper such of them as may not reach the public before our plan is publickly known and begins to operate? I have I acknowlege doubt as to this. No doubt I feel perfectly justified in letting Longman and Coy look to their own interest since they have neither consulted me nor attended to mine, but the loss might extend to the retail booksellers and to hurt the men through whom my works are ultimately to find their way to the public would be both unjust and impolitic. On the contrary if the *Saint Ronan* series be hurried out immediately there is time enough perhaps to sell it off before the improved Edition appears. In the mean time it appears that the popularity of these works is increasing rather than diminishd, that the measure of securing the Copy rights was most judicious and that with proper management things will work themselves round. Successful first editions are good but they require exertion and imply fresh risque of reputation. But repeated editions tell only to the agreeable part of literature. Longman and Coy have also at length opend their oracular jaws on the subject of *Bonaparte* and acknowleged its rapid sale and the probable exhaustion of the present Edition.[1]

These tidings, with the success of the *Tales*, 'speak of Africa and golden joys.'[2] But the tidings arriving after dinner rather discomposed my digestion however simple and sober my fare had been. I cannot account for the connexion betwixt my feelings and my stomach but whatever agitates me puts the bile in motion and makes me sick.

I had not however leisure to be sick[3] beyond the moment that I needs must and in the Evening I wrote to Cadell[4] and Ballantyne at length, proposing a meeting at my house on tuesday first to hold privy council.

9 WEDNESDAY I had still a touch of bile this morning though very slight. My Christmas festivities had perhaps put [it] in motion.

My first reflexion was on *Napoleon*. I will not be hurried in my corrections of that work and that I may not be so I will begin them the instant that I have finishd the Review. It makes me tremble to think of the mass of letters I have to look through in order to select all those

---

1. The Entry of 11 January 1828 shows that Scott has misunderstood: the *Life of Napoleon* was not yet nearly sold out, and it was Cadell, not Longman, who wished to reprint *St. Ronan's Well* and the subsequent novels.
2. *2 Henry IV*, v. 3.
3. *1 Henry IV*, iv. 1.
4. For this letter, sent to Cadell through Ballantyne, see *Letters*, x. 355.

which affect the subject of Napoleon and which in spite of numerous excellent resolutions I have never separated from the common file from which they are now to be selected – Confound them, but they *are* confounded already. Indolence is a delightful indulgence but at what a rate we purchase it. To-day we go to Merton, and having spent some time in making up my journal to this length[1] and in a chat wt Captain John[2] who dropd in, I will presently set to the review – knock it off if possible before we start at four o'clock. Tomorrow when I return we will begin the disagreeable task of a thorough rummage of papers, books and documents. My character as a Man of Letters and as a Man of honour depends on my making that work as correct as possible. It has succeeded notwithstanding every effort here and in France to put it down and it shall not lose ground for want of backing.

We went to dine and pass the night at Mertoun, where we met Sir John Pringle, Mr. and Mrs. Baillie, Mellerstane, and their daughters.

10 THURSDAY When I rose this morning the weather was changed and the ground coverd with snow – I am sure it's winter fairly. We returnd after breakfast through an incipient snow storm coming on partially and in great flakes, the sun bursting at intervals through the interval of the clouds. At last *Die wolken laufen zusammen.*[3] We returnd from Mertoun after breakfast and made a slow journey of it through the swollen river and heavy roads. But here we are at last. I am rather sorry we expect friends to-day though these friends be the good Fergussons. I have a humour for work, to which the sober sad uniformity of a snowy day always particular[ly] disposes me, and I am sure I will get poor Gillies off my hand, at least if I had morning and evening. Then I would set to work with arranging every thing for these Second Editions of *Napoleon*, the Romances[4] etc. which must be soon got afloat. I must say 'the wark gangs bonnily on.'[5] Well I will ring for coals, mend my pen and try what can be done.

1. He has written eight days' entries on this date. See the Entry for 2 January 1828.
2. Captain John Ferguson.
3. 'The clouds are moving together', the German equivalent of 'Birds of a feather'.
4. The Magnum edition of the novels.
5. The words of David Dick, a Covenanter, as he watched the butchering of the prisoners taken after the defeat of Montrose at Philiphaugh.

I wrought accordingly on Gillies's review for the *Life of Molière*, a gallant subject. I am only sorry I have not time to do it justice. It would have required a complete re-perusal of his works, for which, alas, I have no leisure

> For long though pleasant is the way
> And Life, alas, allows but one ill winter's day.[1]

which is too literally my own case.

11 FRIDAY Resumd my labour, finishd the review *talis qualis*, and sent it off. Commenced then my infernal work of putting to rights. Much cry and little woo' – As the deil said when he shore the sow – But I have detected one or two things that had escaped me and may do more tomorrow.

I observe by a letter from Mr. Cadell that I had somewhat misunderstood his last. It is he not Longman that wish to publish the thousand copies of *Saint Ronan's* Series[2] and there is no immediate call for *Napoleon*. This makes [some] little difference in my computation. The pressing necessity of correction is put off for two or three months probably and I have time to turn myself to the *Chronicles*. I do not much like the task but when did I ever like labour of any kind? My hands were fully occupied to-day with writing letters and adjusting papers, both a great bore.

The news from London assure a change of Ministry. The Old Tories come in play but I hope they will compromise nothing. There is little danger since Wellington takes the lead.[3]

12 SATURDAY My expences have been considerably more than I expected, what with the Christmas carousing, the accumulation of bills of small amount, the expence of farm and the inexperience of poor Anne who learned her house keeping in an extravagant school.[4] It would require a total change in stile etc. to alter this much and I

1. Unidentified.
2. See the Entry for 8 January 1828.
3. Lord Goderich had resigned on the 8th; Wellington formed his Ministry on the 25th. Scott's trust in him was complete. 'As to the Duke of Wellington, my faith is constant, that there is no other man living who can work out the salvation of this country. I take some credit to myself for having foreseen his greatness, before many would believe him to be anything out of the ordinary line of clever officers. He is such a man as Europe has not seen since Julius Caesar'. *Letters*, xi. 29–30.
4. i.e. from her mother.

think that having the means of assisting myself and having done so
much I need not undergo the mortification of giving up
£100.   Abbotsford and parting with my old habits and servants. I borrowd a £100 from Cadell.

13 SUNDAY We had a slow and tiresome retreat from Abbotsford
through the worst of weather, half sleet half snow, dined with the
Royal Society Club and being an anniversary sate till nine o'clock
instead of ½ past seven.

14 MONDAY I read Cooper's new novel work, the *Red Rover*; the
current of the [novel] rolls entirely upon the Ocean. Something there
is too much of nautical language; in fact it overpowers every thing
else. But so people once take an interest in a description they will
swallow a great deal which they do not understand. The sweet word
Mesopotamia has its charm in other compositions as well as in
sermons. He has much genius, a powerful conception of character
and force of execution. The same ideas I see recur upon him that
haunt other folks. The graceful form of the spars and the tracery of
the ropes and cordage against the sky is too often dwelt upon.

15 TUESDAY This day the Court sate down. I missd my good friend
Colin Mackenzie who proposes to retire from indifferent health. A
better man never lived – eager to serve every one – a safeguard over all
public business which came through his hands. As Deputy Keeper of
the Signet he will be much missd. He had a patience in listening to
every one which is of the [first importance] in the management of a
publick body, for many men care less to gain their point than they do
to play the orator and be listend to for a certain time. This done and
due quantity of personal consideration being gaind, the individual
orator is usually satisfied with the reasons of the civil listener who has
sufferd [him] to enjoy his hour of consequence. I attended the Court
but there was very little for me to do.[1] The snowy weather has annoyd
my fingers with chillblains and I have a threatening of rheumatism
which Heaven avert.

James Ballantyne and Mr. Cadell dined with me to-day[2] and talkd

1. Scott may well have employed part of his time in writing the
   letter to Peel recommending Thomas Thomson as Colin
   Mackenzie's successor as Clerk of Session which is printed in
   Letters, x. 362.
2. Summoned by the letter of 8 January 'to take a quiet beefsteak
   . . . in Shandwick place on Tuesday at five o'clock'. *Letters*, x.
   356.

me into good humour with my present task[1] which I had laid aside in disgust. It must however be done though I am loth to begin to it again.

16 WEDNESDAY Again returnd early and found my way home with some difficulty, the weather a black frost powderd with snow, my fingers suffering much and my knee very stiff. When I came home I set to work but not to the *Chronicles*. I found a less harassing occupation in correcting a volume or two of *Napoleon* in a rough way. My indolence if I can call it so is of a capricious kind – it never makes me absolutely idle but very often inclines me, as it were from mere contradiction's sake, to exchange the task of the day for something which I am not obliged to do at the moment or perhaps not at all. This is too silly though and must be disused.

17 THURSDAY My knee so swelld and the weather so cold that I staid from the court. I nibbled for an hour or two at *Napoleon* then took handsomely to my gears and wrote with great ease and fluency six pages of the *Chronicles*. If they are but tolerable I shall be satisfied. In fact such as they are they must do, for I shall get warm as I work as has happend on former occasions. The fact is I scarce know what is to succeed or not, but this is the consequence of writing too much and too often. I must get some breathing space. But how is that to be managed? There is the rub.

18 FRIDAY Remaind still at home and wrought hard. The fountain
19 SATURDAY trickles free enough. But God knows whether the waters will be worth drinking. However I have finishd a good deal of hard work, that's the humour of it.[2] Sent an apology on 19 to Hector McDonald.[3]

20 SUNDAY Wrought hard in the forenoon. At dinner we had Helen Erskine whom circumstances lead to go to India in search of the domestic affection which she cannot find here[4] – Mrs. George Swinton

1. *The Fair Maid of Perth.*
2. Nym's phrase in *Henry V*, ii. 1.
3. An apology, no doubt, for his absence from work. Hector Macdonald Buchanan, as another Clerk of Session, would have to take on Scott's cases.
4. The daughter of Scott's late close friend William Erskine. The circumstances which drove her and her sister Jane to India were a quarrel with their aunt. *Letters*, x. 326–8.

and two young strangers, one a son of my old friend Dr. Stoddart of the *Times*, a well mannerd and intelligent youth; the other that unnatural character a tame Irishman resembling a formal Englishman.

21 MONDAY This morning I sent J. B. as far as page 43, being completely two thirds of the volume;[1] the rest I will drive on, trusting that contrary to the liberated post horse in John Gilpin the lumber of the wheels rattling behind me may put spirit in the poor brute who has to drag it.

Mr. and Mrs. Moschelles were here at breakfast. She a very pretty little Jewess. He one of the greatest performers on the pianoforte, of the day.[2] Certainly most surprizing and was [what] I rather did not expect, pleasing. Afterwards I went to the Oil Gas where we agreed to recommend a second application to parliament to be permitted to make gas from coal.[3] Without we get this the concern must be given up. For one I wish it were. I have been led to offer to go up to London to solicit for them but I hope they will be refractory and break up. Still I will not withdraw my plege.

1. The first volume of *The Fair Maid of Perth*.
2. Ignaz Moscheles, the teacher and friend of Mendelssohn, was now living in London. His diary records his visit to Scott: 'He opened the door himself, and welcomed us heartily; he was still suffering from gout, and walked with a stick. Before we had taken off our things we felt completely at home, and my wife's anticipated awe of the great man had entirely vanished. We sat down to breakfast forthwith, and a genuine good Scotch breakfast we had, served on handsome silver plate, by two servants in powder and livery.' Afterwards he played to the family. Scott, he adds, 'treated my wife like a pet daughter, kissed her on the cheek when we went away, and promised he would come and see the children, and bring them a book. This he did, and his gift was "Tales of a Grandfather".' *Life of Moscheles*, i. 202–4.

   Scott used the acquaintance to press forward his scheme of publishing the music of Miss H. M. Browne (Mrs Hemans' sister) which he had heard at Ravensworth Castle in October 1827. Moscheles writes on 17 March to say that he has arranged the publication with Mr. Willis and will himself look over the manuscript to 'discover any of those *little* errors which Ladies are apt to commit in musical composition'. On 18 June 1829 he writes again, 'happy to say that Miss Brown's publications have had great success in every respect'. Walpole.
3. See the note on the Oil Gas Coy. on pp. 805–6. Writing up his journal in arrears, Scott has mistaken the day. The report of his speech in the *Edinburgh Evening Courant* for 24 January indicates that the meeting was on Thursday 22 January.

I have this day the melancholy news of Glengarry's death[1] and was greatly shockd. The eccentric parts of his character, the pretensions which he supported with violence and assumption of rank and authority were obvious subjects of censure and ridicule which in some points was not undeserve[d]. He playd the part of a chieftain too nigh the life to be popular among an alterd race with whom he thought, felt and acted, I may say in right and wrong, as a chieftain of a hundred years since would have done, while his conduct was viewd entirely by modern eyes and tried by modern rules.

22 TUESDAY I am, I find, in serious danger of losing the habit of my journal and having carried it on so long that would be pity. But I am now on the 1st february fishing for the lost recollections of the days since the 21 January. Luckily there is not very much to remember or forget and perhaps the best way would be to skip and go on.

By missives dated this day I sold to Cadell and Coy ten thousand copies of Continuation of *Tales of a Grandfather* to include the reigns subsequent to the union for £800.[2]

Of which sum I received in the country £100 and in town £100.

In han[d]	£200
To receive at Whitsunday ————————————	200
Item Lambmas ———————————————————	200
Item Martinmas ———————————————————	200
	£800

The Cash I remitted to Mr Curle to pay advance for Forest's Bill[3] ———————————————	£32.16.9
Cash in purse £0.0.0 To Tom clears off all scores at Abbotsfd	67. 3.3
	£100. 0.0

23 WEDNESDAY Being a Teind day I had a good opportunity of work. I should have said I had given breakfast on the 21st to Mrs. and

1. He was bringing his daughters to Edinburgh for some gaiety, and died 'from a severe Concussion received on the head in the confusion when the Stirling Steam Boat struck on a rock about three miles West of Fort William'. Campbell, 22 January 1828, Walpole. For another account of his character, see the Entry for 14 February 1826.

2. The agreement was for an edition of 10,000, to be ready by Christmas and to be sold at 'ten shillings and sixpence for three volumes bound'. *Letters*, x. 365 and note.

3. Scott purchased guns for Walter and Charles later in the year from Forrest, the Jedburgh gunsmith.

Mr. Moschelles, he an excellent performer on the pianoforte, she a beautiful young creature 'and one that adores me' as Sir Toby says,[1] that is in my poetical capacity. In fact a frank and amiable young person. I liked Mr. Moschelles' playing better than I could have expected considering my own bad ear. But perhaps I flatter myself and think I understood it better than I did, perhaps I have not done myself justice and know more of musick than I thought I did. But it seems to me that his variations have a more decided stile of originality than those I have commonly heard which have all the signs of a *Da capo rota*.[2]

Dined at Sir Archd. Campbell's and drank rather more wine than usual in a sober way. To be sure it was excellent and some old acquaintances proved a good excuse for the glass.

24 THURSDAY I took a perverse fit to-day and went off to write notes etcaetera on *Guy Mannering*.[3] This was perverse enough but it was a composition between humour and duty and as such let it pass.

I renewd my engagement to the oil Gas Coy to go to London to enforce their bill. It will be chargeable besides being a cursed bore and an interruption of business. To be sure I have the pleasure of seeing Lockhart and Sophia and perhaps that of settling Charles. However I will not be surprized if the necessity should blow over.

25 FRIDAY

Drew my quarter precepts from Excheqr.

Contents	£150
To Anne house £25—Self £25	£50
Charles for accomps clothes teachers etc.	50
Ross physician	10
Charity	1
	111
Cash in purse	£39

I went on working sometimes at my legitimate labours sometimes at my bye jobs of Notes etc. but still working faithfully, in good spirits and contented.

Huntly Gordon has disposed of the two sermons to the bookseller Cobourne for £250, well sold I think and is to go forth as

1. *Twelfth Night*, ii. 3.
2. 'Going round from the beginning again'.
3. For the Magnum Opus.

immediately.[1] The man is a puffing quack but though I would rather the thing had not gone there and far rather that it had gone nowhere, yet, Hang it, if it makes the poor lad easy what needs I fret about it? After all there would be little grace in doing a kind thing if you did not suffer pain or inconvenience upon the score.

26 SATURDAY Being Saturday, attended Mr. Moschelles' concert and was amused, the more so that I had Mrs. M. herself to flirt a little with.[2] To have so much beauty as she really possesses and to be accomplishd and well-read, she is an unaffected and pleasant person. Mr. Moschelles gives lessons at two guineas by the hour and he has actually found scholars in this poor country. One of them at least (Mrs. John Murray) may derive advantage from his instructions for I observe his mode of fingering is very peculiar as he seems to me to employ the fingers of the same hand in playing the melody and managing the bass at the same time which is surely most uncommon.

I presided at the Celtic Society's dinner to-day and proposed Glengarry's memory, which, although there had been a rough dispute with the Celts and the poor Chief,[3] was very well received. I like to see men think and bear themselves like men. They were fewer in the tartan than usual, which was wrong.

27 SUNDAY Wrought manfully at the *Chronicles* all this day and have nothing to jot down – Only I forgot that I lost my lawsuit[4] some day last week or the week before. The usury was apparent but the Court did not think our statement such as ought to interrupt the currency of a bill of exchange and I daresay they were quite right. The rogue therefore gets his money, plack and bawbee. But it is always a

1. Gordon went to Colbourne on the advice of Lockhart, who thought the price offered 'a good deal too much – as they are so short'. Gordon, 24 January 1828, Walpole.
2. In honour of Scott's presence, Moscheles chose 'Pibroch of Donuil Dhu', which Scott had hummed to him at breakfast on the 21st, as the theme of his improvisations. 'My wife sat, as usual, in a remote corner of the room; Scott, however, found her out instantly, and sat down by her side, drawing upon her the envious eyes of many a fair beholder. His hearty bravoes and cheers, when I played, stimulated the audience to redouble their applause, which reached a climax when I gave them the Scotch airs.' *Life of Moscheles*, i. 205.
3. The '*row*' betwixt Glengarry and the Celtic Society which began about a *piper* shortly after the King's visit in 1822. *Letters*, vii. 237.
4. With Abud. See the Entry for 5 November 1827 and note.

troublesome claim settled and there can be no other of the same kind as every other Creditor has accepted the composition of 7/- in the pound which my exertions have enabled me to pay them. About £20,000 of the fund had been created by my own exertions since the bankruptcy took place and I had a letter from Donald Horne by commission of the Creditors to express their sense of my exertions in their behalf.[1] All this is consolatory.

28 MONDAY I am in the scrape of sitting to my picture and had to repair for two hours to-day to Mr. Colvin Smith, Lord Gillies's nephew. The Chief Baron had the kindness to sit with me great part of the time, as the Chief Commissioner had done on a late occasion. The picture is for the Chief Commissioner and the Chief Baron desires a copy.[2] I trust it will be a good one. At home in the evening and wrote. I am well on before the press notwithstanding late hours, lassitude and laziness.

I have read Cooper's *Prairie*, better I think than his *Red Rover* in which you never get foot on shore and to understand entirely the incidents of the story it requires too much nautical language. It is very clever though.

29 TUESDAY Tuesday at the court and wrote letters at home besides making a visit or two – rare things with me. I have an invitation from Messrs. Saunders and Ottley, Booksellers, offering me from £1500 to £2000 annually to conduct a Journal but I am their humble servant. I am too indolent to stand to that sort of work. And I must reserve the undisturbd use of my leisure and possess my soul in quiet. A large income is not my object. I must clear my debts and that is to be done by writing things of which I can retain the property. Made my excuses accordingly.

30 WEDNESDAY After Court hours I had a visit from Mr. Charles Heath[3] the engraver accompanied by a son of Reynolds the dramatist. His object was to engage me to take charge as Editor of a yearly publication calld the *Keepsake*, of which the plates are beyond

1. See the Entry for 24 December 1827 and note.
2. William Adam had asked Scott to sit for this portrait on the previous 23 October. Walpole. The copies made by the artist from his master-copy are listed in a note to the Entry for 22 January 1829.
3. Introduced by his publishers as 'the sole proprietor of that popular as well as splendid annual publication called "the Keepsake" '. Hurst Chance & Coy., 25 January 1828, Walpole.

comparaison beautiful. But the Letterpress indifferent enough. He proposed £800 a year if I would become Editor, and £400 if I would contribute from 70 to 100 pages. I declined both but told him I might give him some trifling thing or other and askd the young men to breakfast the next day. Workd away in the evening and completed 'in a way and in a manner' the notes on *Guy Mannering*. The 1st Volume of the *Chronicles* is now in Ballantyne's hands all but a leaf or two. Am I satisfied with my exertions? – So so – Will the public be pleased with them? – Umph. I doubt the bubble will burst. While it is current however it is clear I should stand by it. Each novel of three volumes brings £4000 and I remain proprietor of the mine when the first ore is cropd out. This promises a good harvest from what we have experienced. Now to become a stipendiary Editor of a Newsyear gift book is not to be thought of, nor could I agree to work for any quantity of supply to such a publication. Even the pecuniary view is not flattering though these gentlemen meant it should be so. But one hundred of their close printed pages, for which they offer £400, is not nearly equal to one volume of a novel for which I get £1300 and have the reversion of the copyright. No – I may give them a trifle for nothing or sell them an article for a round price but no permanent engagement will I make. Being the martyrdom there was no court. I wrought away with what appetite I could.

31 THURSDAY I received the young gentlemen to breakfast and expressd my resolution, which seemd to disappoint them as perhaps they expected I should have been glad of such an offer. However I have since thought there are these rejected parts of the *Chronicles* which Cadell and Ballantyne criticized so severely which might well enough make up a trifle of this kind[1] and settle the few accompts which, will I nill I, have crept in upon this new year, so I have kept the treaty open. If I give them one hundred pages I should expect £500. I was late at the court and had little time to write any till after dinner and then was not in the vein so commentated.

FEBRUARY

1 FRIDAY I had my two youths again to breakfast but I did not say more about my determination save that I would help them if I could make it convenient. The Chief Commissioner has agreed to let Heath have his pretty picture of 'A Study at Abbotsford' by Edwin

1. 'My Aunt Margaret's Mirror', 'The Tapestried Chamber' and 'The Death of the Laird's Jock' were accordingly published in *The Keepsake* for 1829.

Landseer, in which old Maida occurs. The youth Reynolds is what one would suppose his father's son to be, smart and forward and knows the world I suppose. I was too much faggd with sitting in the court to-day to write hard after dinner but I did work however.

2 SATURDAY Corrected proofs, which are now nearly up with me. This day was [an] idle one. For I remaind in court till one and sate for my picture till half past three to Mr. Smith Colvin,[1] a nephew of Lord Gillies and a cousin of R. P. G. He has all the steadiness and sense in appearance which his cousin lacks, whether he has genius or no I am no judge. My own portrait is like but I think too broad about the jowls, a fault which they all fall into as I suppose by placing their subject upon a high stage and looking upwards to them which must foreshorten the face. The Chieff Baron and Chief commissioner had the goodness to sit with me.

Dressd and went with Anne to dine at Pinkie House[2] where I met the president,[3] Lady Charlotte etc. – above all Mrs. Scott of Gala whom I had not seen for some time. We had much fun and I was as Sir Andrew Aguecheek says in good fooling.[4] A lively French girl, a governess I think but very pretty and animated, seemd much amused with the old gentleman. Home at eleven o'clock. Bye the bye Sir John Hope had found a Roman eagle on his estate at Fife with sundry of those pots and coffee-pots so to speak which are so common, but the eagle was mislaid so I did not see it.

3 SUNDAY I corrected proofs and wrote this morning but slowly, heavily, lazily. There was a mist on my mind which my exertions could not dispel. I did not get two pages finishd but I corrected proofs and commentated. We had a party at dinner, Jemima MacDonald, W. Clerk, Charles Sharpe, Davidoff and Francis Scott, with a good deal of fun and laughing.

4 MONDAY Wrote a little and was obliged to correct the *Molière* affair for R. P. G. I think his plan cannot go on much longer with so much weakness at the helm. A clever fellow would make it take the field with a vengeance but poor G. will run in debt with the booksellers and let all go to the devil. I sent a long letter to Lockhart received from Horace Smith, very gentlemanlike and well written, as complaining that Mr. Leigh Hunt had mixd him up in his *Life of*

1. A slip for 'Colvin Smith'.
2. The home of Sir John Hope.
3. The Rt. Hon. Charles Hope.
4. *Twelfth Night*, ii. 3.

Byron[1] with Shelley as if he had shared his irreligious opinion. Leigh Hunt afterwards at the request of Smith publishd a swaggering contradiction of the inference to be derived from the way in which he has named them together. Horatio Smith seems not to have relied upon his disclamation as he has requested me to mention the thing to John Lockhart and to some one influential about Ebony, which I have done accordingly.[2]

Lady Wedderburn came in with two Miss Kerrs and Frank Scott to supper; we had a tune adapted by Miss Brown to Lockhart's song of Zara's earrings[3] charmingly sung by the Miss Kerrs.

5 TUESDAY Concluded the first volume[4] before breakfast. I am but indifferently pleased. Either the kind of thing is worn out or I am worn out myself or, lastly, I am stupid for the time. The book must be finishd however. Cadell is greatly pleased with annotations intended for the new edition of the Waverley series. I believe that work must be soon sent to press which would put a powerful wheel in motion to clear the ship. I went to the Parlt. House and in return strolld into Cadell's[5] being rather anxious to prolong my walk for I fear the constant sitting for so many hours. When I returnd the Duke of Buccleuch came in. He is looking well and stout but melancholy about his sister Lady Charlotte Stopford. He is fitting up a part of Bowhill and intends to shoot there this year. God send him life and health for it is of immense consequence.

6 WEDNESDAY Court and visits wasted my time till past two and then I slept half an hour from mere exhaustion. Went in the Evening to the play and saw that good old thing an English tragedy well got up. It was *Venice Preserved*.[6] Mrs. H. Siddons who play[d] Belvidera with much truth feeling and tenderness, though short of her Mother in law's uncommon Majesty which is a thing never to be forgotten.

1. *Lord Byron and his Contemporaries*, 1828.
2. Scott showed the letter to Blackwood and he in turn passed it to Professor Wilson, who reviewed the book in March. Lockhart duly attacked Hunt and defended Smith in his review of Hunt's book in the March *Quarterly. Letters*, x. 368 and 373 and notes.
3. The song came from Lockhart's *Ancient Spanish Ballads, Historical and Romantic*. Miss Browne (for whom see the Entry for 21 January 1828) had dedicated the setting to Scott and sent it to him five days before. 31 January 1828, Walpole.
4. Of *The Fair Maid of Perth*.
5. In St. Andrew Square, which did not lie on the direct route to Walker Street.
6. By Otway, 1682.

Mr. Young playd Pierre very well – and a good Jaffier was supplied by a Mr. Vandenhoff. And so the day glided by, only three pages written, which however is a fear[1] task. It was a teind day so no court but very little work.

7 THURSDAY I wrote this morning till the boy[2] made his appearance for proofs then I had letters to write. Item at five o'clock I set out with Charles for Dalkeith to present him to the young Duke.[3] I think he looks melancholy; perhaps his sister Lady Charlotte Stopford's infirm state of health makes him anxious. I received a present to-day of a beautiful sketch of a hunter who had by accident shot his own dog and was mourning over him, the horse standing by in mute sympathy.[4] It was a very fine thing. I askd the Duke about poor Hogg. I think he has decided to take Mr. Riddell's opinion: it is unlucky the poor fellow having taken that large and dear farm.[5] Altogether Dalkeith was melancholy to-night and I could not raise my spirits at all.

8 FRIDAY I had a little work before dinner but we are only seven pages into Volume second. It is always a beginning, however perhaps not a good one. I cannot tell. I went out to call on Gala and Jack Rutherfurd of Edgerstane. Saw the former not the latter. Gala is getting much better. He talkd as if the increase of his village was like to drive him over the hill to Abbotsford side which would greatly beautify that side of the hill and certainly change his residence for the better, only that he must remain some time without any appearance of plantation. The view would be enchanting.

I was tempted to buy a picture of Nell Gwynn which I think has merit; at least it pleases me. Seven or eight years ago Graham of Gartmore bid for it against me and I gave it up at 25 guineas. I have now bought it for £18. 18.[6] Perhaps there was folly in this but I reckond it a token of good luck that I should succeed in a wish I had formerly harbourd in vain. I love marks of good luck even in trifles.

1. A slip for 'fair'.
2. From Ballantyne's printing-house.
3. The Duke of Buccleuch, who no doubt invited them when he called on the 5th.
4. The sketch came from the artist, Abraham Cooper, with a request for a few lines of poetry or prose. Scott sent him the poem 'The Death of Keeldar' in July, and it was published with the picture in *The Gem* for 1829. *Letters* x. 380, 394 and 457.
5. Mount Benger, which he took in 1820.
6. C. K. Sharpe, who also liked the picture, gave it house-room until Scott took it to Abbotsford in March. *Letters*, x. 381.

Wrote to Jane and Walter, anxious about the health of the latter who has a cough and takes no care of it.

Dined at Sir Robert Dundasses with Calderwood Durham,[1] his Lady, Captain Henry Dundas, R. Navy, and a pretty large party.

9 SATURDAY Sent off three leaves of copy; this is using the press like the famishd sailor who was fed by a comrade with shell fish by one at a time. But better anything than stop for the devil is to get set agoing again. I know no more than my old boots whether I am right or wrong but have no very favourable anticipations.

As I came home from the court about twelve I stepd into the Exhibition.[2] It makes a very good show: the portraits are better than last year; those of Colvin Smith and Watson Gordon especially improve. Landseer's 'Study at Abbotsford' is in a capital light and generally admired. I particularly distinguishd John Thompson's picture of Turnberry which is of the first rate of excellence. A picture by Scrope was also generally distinguishd. It is a view in the Calabrias. There is a rival exhibition[3] which does not hurt the earlier foundation but rather excites emulation. I am told there are good paintings there.

I came home with little good will to work but I will compell myself to do something; unluckily I have again to go out to dinner to-day being president of the Bannatyne.

The dinner was a pleasant one; about thirty members attended. I kept the chair till near eleven and the Company were very joyous.

10 SUNDAY I set myself doggedly to work and turnd off six leaves before dinner. Had to dinner Sir John Pringle, My dear Gala and his Lady, and young Mackenzie and Miss Jardine. I was quite pleased to see Gala so well recoverd of the consequences of his frightful fall which hung about him so long. He is one of the kindest and best informd men whom I know.

11 MONDAY I had Charles Young to breakfast with us who gave us some striking anecdotes of Talma during the reign of terror which may figure in *Napoleon* to great advantage.

---

1. A slip for 'Durham Calderwood'.
2. The annual exhibition of the Institution for the Encouragement of the Fine Arts.
3. The rival exhibition was mounted by a group of leading artists who were dissatisfied with the organization of the Institution. Under the presidency of George Watson they founded the Scottish Academy, which became the Royal Scottish Academy in 1838.

My son Charles left us this morning to take possession of his situation in the Foreign Office.[1] He has been very lucky. Correcting sheets etc. took up the morning hour.[2] I wrote three leaves before two o'clock and then went to the Oil Gas Coy. I was made a member with Mr. Gibson[3] and Mr. Cunninghame of a secret Committee which is to attempt a settlement of that affair.[4] I fear it will be attended with no small difficulty. Home at half past three. Day bitter cold with snow, a strong contrast to the mild weather we had last week.

Salutation of two old Scottish lairds, 'Yer maist obedient hummil servant Tannachy Tulloh.' – 'Your nain man Kilspindie' –

Finishd six pages. 25 pages of print that is or about the 13th part of a volume. That would be a volume in a fortnight with a holiday to boot. It would be possible enough for a little while.

12 TUESDAY I wrought hard this morning. Ballantyne blames the Ossianick monotony of my principal characters. Now they are not Ossianick. The language of the Ossianic poetry is highly figurative; that of the Knights of chivalry may be monotonous and probably is but it cannot be Ossianic. Sooth to say, this species of romance of chivalry is an exhaustible subject. It affords materials for splendid description for once or twice but they are too unnatural and formal to bear repetition. We must go on with our present work however *valeat quantum*.[5] Mr. Cadell, less critical than J. B., seems pleased. The world will soon decide if I get on at this rate for I have finishd four leaves to-day notwithstanding my attendance on the court.

13 WEDNESDAY Mr. McIntosh Mackay, Minister of Laggan, break-fasted with us this morning. This reverend Gentleman is completing the highland Dictionary[6] and seems very competent for the task. He left in my hands some papers of Cluny Macpherson concerning the affair of 1745 from which I have extracted an accompt of the battle of Clifton for

1. Charles was to lodge with Lockhart and Sophia, Scott paying them £150 a year in recompense. *Letters*, x. 384.
2. i.e. the time before breakfast.
3. Scott means James Gibson Craig (1765–1850) an Edinburgh W. S. and a Whig. He was born James Gibson and adopted his new surname in 1823 when he inherited the estate of Riccarton. He was created a baronet in 1831.
4. The Oil Gas Coy. were by now willing to amalgamate with the more successful Coal Gas Coy., if some such settlement could be achieved. See note 1, pp. 805–6.
5. 'For what it may be worth'.
6. The *Dictionarium Scoto Celticum: Dictionary of the Gaelic Language, etc.* 1828.

Waverley.[1] He has few prejudices (for a highlander) and is a mild well mannerd young man. We had much talk on highland matters.

Cash in purse ———————————————		£39
From Mr Cadell in advance ———————		100
		139.0.0
Anne for Bacon hams etc. —————	£10	
Charles to carry him to London ———	20	
Antiquarian Society ———————	1	
Sundries —————————————	8	
To a picture of Nell Gwyn £18.18. say—	19	
To Tom Purdie ——————— £20⎫		
To William Bogie ————— 16⎭	36	
	£94	
	£45.0.0	

The Children's Tales[2] continue in demand. Cadell expects a new edition of 10,000 about next year, which may be £750 or £800 in pouch, besides constituting a fine property.[3]

14 THURSDAY Mr. Edwards, a candidate for the situation of rector in the Edinburgh [Academy], a pleasant gentlemanlike man and recommended highly for experience and learning.[4] But he is himself afraid of wanting bodily strength for the work which requires all the nerve and muscle of Williams. I wish he had sat three inches taller and stout in proportion.

I had the whole of the cases on the Short roll.[5] Nevertheless I got out by two o'clock and went to the Waterloo Hotel by appointment where James Gibson Craig and Cunningham and [I] were to meet with Will Inglis, Mr. Munro, Mr. Trotter and Tom Burns upon a certain important transaction.[6] We debated a long time without

1. See the note to chapter 59 of *Waverley*.
2. *Tales of a Grandfather*.
3. Scott had written them for the benefit of himself and his family, not for the Trust.
4. The Revd. Joseph Edwards, of Hadleigh in Suffolk, the author of a Greek anthology, was recommended by letters from Sir James Mackintosh, Edmund Lodge and Drummond Hay. 22–25 January 1828, Walpole.
5. The list of cases depending before the Inner House of the Court of Session which were ready for hearing.
6. The proposed merger of the Oil Gas Coy. with the Coal Gas Coy. which was managed by the four men mentioned here, among others.

coming to a conclusion and adjournd till Saturday two o'clock – Mr. Craig did not come. We should have been the better of his assistance.

I went to Mr. John Russell's where there was an academical party at Dinner.[1] Home at nine, a Segar and to bed

15 FRIDAY Rose this morning about seven and wrought at the desk till breakfast; finishd about a page and a half – I was fagd at court till near two – then calld on Cadell and so home tired enough.

Of money matters I have to notice that I have in pouch				£45.0.0
Received from Exchequer £71.15 say	£71			
Paid to Mr. Langs account County money —	54			
	—			
	17			
Paid for dinner Bannatyne club ——	£2.8.0			
Sundries ————————————	12	3		
	—	—		
By Cash —		14		
		—		
		59 0 0		

16 SATURDAY There dined with me to-day Tom Thomson, Will Clerk, Mr. Edwards and my Celtick friend Mr. Mackay of Laggan. We resumed after the Court rose our conferences with the Coal Gas Company Committee, dodged and debated and stickled about our bargain for three hours with little effect except my getting a little insight into the mode of driving great bargains. We parted however *re infecta*. Yet as we approachd each other I think it will and must go on.

Dined at Lord Pitmilly's with Lord Justice Clerk, Lord Abercromby and his wife and daughter, Mr. Smyth Methven[2] etc.

17 SUNDAY A day of hard work, being I think eight pages before dinner. I cannot I am sure tell if it is worth marking down that yesterday at dinnertime I was strangely haunted by what I would call the sense of pre-existence, *videlicet* a confused idea that nothing that passd was said for the first time, that the same topics had been discussd and the same persons had stated the same opinions on the same subjects. It is true there might have been some ground for recollections considering that three at least of the company were old

1. A party of the Directors of the Academy, who had shortly to choose their new Rector.
2. George Smythe of Methven, a committee member of the Bannatyne Club.

friends and kept much company together, that is Justice Clerk, Abercromby and I. But the sensation was so strong as to resemble what is called a *mirage* in the desert or a calenture on board of ship when lakes are seen in the desert and sylvan landscapes in the sea. It was very distressing yesterday and brought to my mind the fancies of Bishop Berkeley about an ideal world. There was a vile sense of want of reality in all I did and said. It made me gloomy and out of spirits though I flatter myself it was not observd. The bodily feeling which most resembles this unpleasing hallucination is the giddy state which follows profuse bleeding when one feels as if they were walk[ing] on feather beds and could not find a secure footing. I think the stomach has something to do with it. I drank several glasses of wine but these only augmented the disorder. I did not find the *in vino veritas*[1] of the philosophers. Something of this insane feeling remains to-day but a trifle only.

18 MONDAY I had other work to do this day. In the morning corrected proofs. After breakfast met[2] a visit or two and met Sandie Buchanan whom it joys me to see. Then despatchd all my Sheriff processes save one which hitches for want of some papers. Lastly here I am before dinner with my journal. I sent all the County money to Andrew Lang. Wrote to Mr. Reynolds too; methinks I will let them have the Tales which Jem Ballantyne and Cadell quarrelld with[3] – I have askd £500 for them, pretty well that. I suppose they will be fools enough to give it me. In troth she'll no pe cheaper.

19 TUESDAY A day of hard and continued work, the result being eight pages. But then I hardly ever quitted the table save at meal time. So eight pages of my manuscript may be accounted the maximum of my literary labour. It is equal to forty printed pages of the Novels.[4] I had the whole of this day at my own disposal by the voluntary kindness of Sir Robert Dundas interfering[5] to take up my duty at the court. The proofs of my sermons is arrived but I have had no time saving to blot out some flummery which poor Gordon had put into the preface.

---

1. 'Truth in wine'.
2. A slip for 'made'.
3. The rejected parts of *Chronicles of the Canongate*, 'My Aunt Margaret's Mirror' and 'The Tapestried Chamber'.
4. For a similar achievement see the Entry for 11 October 1827.
5. Tait notes that Scott uses this word without any sense of 'meddling' or 'obstructing'.

20 WEDNESDAY Another day of labour but not so hard. I workd from eight till three with little intermission but only accomplishd four pages. Then I went out and made a visit or two and lookd in on Cadell. If I get two pages in the evening I will be satisfied for Vol. II may be concluded with the week or run over to Sunday at most – Will it tell, this work? I doubt it. But there is [no] standing still.

A certain Mr. Mackay from Ireland[1] calld on me, an active agent it would seem about the reform of prisons. He exclaims, justly I doubt not, about the state of our Lockup house. For myself I have some distrust of the fanaticism even of philanthropy. A good part of [it] arises in general of mere vanity and love of distinction gilded over to others and to themselves with some show of benevolent sentiment. The philanthropy of Howard mingled with his ill usage of his son seems to have risen to a pitch of insanity. Yet without such extraordinary men who call attention to the subject by their own peculiarities prisons would have remaind the same dungeons which they were forty or fifty years ago. I do not see the propriety of making them Dandy places of detention. They should be a place of punishment and that can hardly be if men are lodged better and fed better than when they are at large. The separation of ranks is an excellent distinction and is nominally provided for in all modern prisons. But the size of most of them is inadequate to the great increase of crime and so the pack is shufled together again for want of room to keep them separate. There are several prisons constructed on excellent principles, the oeconomy of which becomes deranged so soon as the death takes place of some keen philanthropist who had the business of a whole committee, which having lost him remaind like a carcase without a head. But I have never seen a plan for keeping in order these resorts of guilt and misery with[out] presupposing a superintendence of a kind which might perhaps be exercized could we turn out upon the watch a guard of angels. But alas, jailors and turnkeys are rather like angels of a different livery nor do I see how it is possible to render them otherwise. Superintendance is all you can

1. Dr. John Pym has been able to identify Scott's visitor for me. He was John McKay (1785–1848), a Dublin barrister who was Deputy Clerk of the Privy Council. No early records of the Association for the Improvement of Prisons and Prison Discipline in Ireland survive, but McKay must in all probability have been one of the founder-members in 1818; certainly he appears on the committee in *Watson's Almanac* for 1823. The Association, which was renamed the Howard Society in 1832, did much to end the horrors of the Irish prison system described in, for instance, Thomas Packenham's *Year of Liberty* (1969), pp. 278–9.

trust to and superintendance save in some rare cases is hard to come by where it is to be vigilantly and constantly exercized. *Quis custodiet ipsos custodes?*[1] As to reformation I have no great belief in it where the ordinary class of culprits who are vicious from ignorance or habit are the subjects of the experiment. 'A sliver from a broken loaf' is thought as little of by the male set of delinquents as by the fair frail charm[er]s who offer the public the use of their charms under such an allegory. The state of society now leads so much to great accumulations of humanity that we cannot wonder if it ferment and reek like a compost dunghill. Nature intended that population should be diffused over the soil in proportion to its extent. We have accumulated in huge cities and smothering manufactures the numbers which should be spread over the face of a country and what wonder that they should be corrupted? We have turnd healthful and pleasant brooks into morasses and pestiferous lakes; what wonder the soil should be unhealthy? A great deal I think might be done by executing the punishment of *death* without a chance of escape in all cases to which it should be found properly applicable, of course these occasions being diminishd to one out of twenty to which capital punishment is now assignd. Our ancestors brought the country to order by *kilting*[2] thieves and banditti with strings – So did the French when at Naples and bandits became for the time unheard of. When once the evil habit is alterd, when men are taught a crime of a certain character is connected inseparably with death, the moral habits of a population become alterd and you may in the next age remit the punishment which in this it has been necessary to inflict with stern severity. I think whoever pretends to reform a corrupted nation – or a disorderly regiment – or a ill orderd ship of war – must begin by severity and only resort to gentleness when he has acquired the complete mastery by terror – the terror being always attachd to the *law*; and, the impression once made, he can afford to govern with mildness and lay the iron rule aside.

Mr. Mackay talkd big of the excellent state of prisons in Ireland. *J'en doute un peu*. That the warm hearted and generous Irish would hurry eagerly into any scheme which had benevolence for its motive I readily believe, but that Pat should have been able to maintain that calm all-seeing all-enduring species of superintendence necessary to direct the working of the best plan of prison discipline I greatly hesitate to believe.

Well – leaving all this I wish Mr. Mackay good luck with some little

1. 'Who will guard the guards themselves?' Juvnal's *Satires*, vi. 347.
2. 'To kilt: to elevate or lift up anything quickly; then applied ludicrously to tucking up by a halter.' Jamieson.

doubt of his success but none of his intentions. I am come in work to that point where a lady who works a stocking must count by threads and bring [together] the various loose ends of my story. They are too many.

21 THURSDAY Last night after dinner I rested from my work and read third part of *Sayings and Doings*,[1] which shows great knowlege of life in a certain sphere and very considerable powers of wit which somewhat damages the effect of his tragic [scenes]. But he is an able writer and so much of his work is well said that it will carry through what is *manqué*. I hope the same good fortune for other folks.

I am watching and waiting till I hit on some quaint and clever mode of extricating[2] but do not see a glimpse of any one. James B. too discourages me a good deal by his silence, waiting I suppose to be invited to disgorge a full allowance of his critical bile. But he may wait long enough for I am discouraged enough. Now here is the advantage of Edinburgh. In the country if a sense of inability once seizes me it hangs on me from morning to night, but in Edinburgh the time is so occupied and fritterd away by official duties and chance occupation that you have not time to play Mr. Stevens[3] and be gentlemanlike and melancholy. On the other hand town; you never feel in town those spirit stirring influences – those glances of sunshine that make amends for clouds and mist. – The country is said to be quieter life – not to me I am sure. In the town the business I have to do hardly costs me more thought than just occupies my mind and I have as much of gossip and lady-like chat as consumes the time pleasantly enough. In the country I am thrown entirely on my own resources and there is no medium betwixt happiness and the reverse.

22 FRIDAY Went to court and remaind there untill one o'clock. Then to Mr. Colvin Smith's and sate to be stared at till three o'clock. This is a great bore even when you have a companion, sad when you are alone and can only disturb the painter by your chatter. After dinner I had proofs to the number of four. J. B. is outrageous about the death of Oliver Proudfute, one of the characters. But I have a humour to be cruel – [4]

His business 'tis to die.[5]

1. By Theodore Hook. The third series had just been published.
2. That is, of finding a convincing way forward for *The Fair Maid of Perth*.
3. Stephen in Jonson's *Every Man in his Humour*, i. 2.
4. Congreve's *Way of the World*, i. 9.
5. Besides, 'I cannot afford to be merciful . . . it would cost my cancelling half a volume.' *Letters*, xii. 458. The quotation comes from 'How Stands the Glass Around', *The Convivial Songster*, 1782, p. 329.

Received a present from a Mr. Dobie of Beith of a candlestick said to be that of the Revd. Mr. Guthrie, minister of Fenwick in the Seventeenth century – very civil of a gentleman unknown if there comes no request to look over poems or to get made a gauger or the like, for I have seen these king' of compliments made on the principle on which small balloons are sent up before a large one to see how the wind sits. After dinner proof sheets – my stomach something out of order.

23 SATURDAY Morning proof sheets galore. Then to parliamt. House – After that, at one, down to Sir William MacLeod Bannatyne who has made some discoveries concerning Bannatyne the collector of poetry and furnishd me with some notes to that purpose. He informs me that the MacLeod alias MacCruiskin who met Dr. Johnston on the isle of sky was Mr. Alexr. MacLeod, Advocate, a son of MacLeod of Muiravonside. He was subject to fits of insanity at times, very clever at others. Sir William mentioned the old Laird of Bernera who, summond by his Chief to join him with all the men he could make when the Chief was raising his men for Government, sent him a letter to this purpose. 'Dear Laird, No man would like better to be at Your back than I would. But on this occasion it cannot be – I send my men, who are at your service; for myself higher duties carry me elsewhere.' He went off according[ly] alone and joind Raasay as a volunteer.

I returnd by the Printinoffice and found J. B. in great feather. He tells me Cadell on squaring his books and making allowance for bad debts has made between £3000 and £4000 lodged in bank. He does nothing but with me. Thus we stand on velvet as to finance. Met Staffa[2] who walkd with me and gave me some gaelick words which I wanted.[3]

I may mention that I saw at the printing office a part of a review on Leigh Hunt's *Anecdotes of Byron* by Wilson.[4] It is written with power (apparently by Professor Wilson) but with a degree of passion which rather diminishes the effect, for nothing can more lessen the dignity of the satirist than being or seeming to be in a passion. I think it may

1. Possibly a slip for 'kind', although 'king' makes good sense.
2. Reginald Macdonald of Staffa (1778–1838), brother of Hector Macdonald Buchanan and son-in-law of Sir Henry Seton Steuart, whose surname he added to his own. He was Secretary to the Highland Society.
3. For *The Fair Maid of Perth*.
4. For Scott's interest in this review see the Entry for 4 February 1828 and note.

come to a bloody arbitrament for if L. H. should take it up as a gentleman Wilson is the last man to flinch. I hope Lockhart will not be draggd in as second or otherwise.

Went to Jeffrey's to dinner. There was Mrs. and Miss Sydney Smith, Lord Gillies, Corehouse etc. etc.

24 SUNDAY I fancy I had drunk a glass or two over much last night for I have the heart burning this morning. But a little Magnesia salves that sore. Meantime I have had an *inspiration* this morning which shows me my good angel has not left me. For this two or three days I have been at what the *Critic* calls a deadlock[1] – all my incidents and personages run into a gordian knot of confusion to which I could devize no possible extrication – I had thought on the subject several days with some[thing] like the despair which seized the fair princess commanded by her ugly step-mother to assort a whole garret full of tangled silk threads of every kind and colour when in comes prince Percinet with wand, whisks it over the miscellaneous mass, and lo! all the threads are as nicely arranged as in a seamstresses housewife. It has often happend to me that when I went to bed with my head as ignorant as my shoulders what I was to do next I have waked in the morning with a distinct and accurate conception of the mode, good or bad, in which the plot might be extricated. It seems to me that the action of the intellect on such occasions is rather accelerated by the little fever which an extra glass of wine produces in the system. Of course excess is out of the question – Now this may seem strange but it is quite true, and it is no less so that I have generally written to the middle of one of these novels without having the least idea how it was to [end], in short in the *Der donde diere* or *hab nab at a venture* stile of compositions.[2] So now this hitch bein[g] over I fold my paper, lock up my Journal and proceed to labour with good hope.

25 MONDAY This being Monday I carried on my work according to the new model, dind at home and in quiet. But I may notice that yesterday Mr. Williams, the learnd rector of our New Accademy who now leaves us, took his Dinner here; we had a long philological tete a tete. He is opinionative, as he has some title to be, but very learnd and with a juster view of his subject than is commonly entertaind, for he traces words to the same source not from sound but sense – He casts backwards thus to the root, while many compare the ends of the twigs without going further.

1. Sheridan's *Critic*, iii. 1.
2. Scott writes in similar terms in the Entry for 12 February 1826.

This night[1] I went to the funeral of Mr. Henderson late of Eildon hall, a kindhearted honest man who rose to great wealth by honest means and will be missd and regretted.[2] In the evening I went to the promenade in the Exhibition of pictures which was splendidly lighted up and filld with fashionable company. I think there was a want of beauty or perhaps the gas-lights were unfavourable to the ladies' looks.

26 TUESDAY Business filld up the day till one when I sate to Mr. Smith. Tiresome work even though Will Clerk chaperond me. We dined at Archd. Swinton's. Met Lord Lothian, Lord Cringletie etc. In this day I have wrought almost nothing. But I am nearly half a volume before the press. Lord Morton, married to a daughter of my friend Sir George Rose, is come to Edinburgh. He seems a very gentlemanlike man and she pleasing and willing to be pleased. I had the pleasure to be of some little use to him in his election as one of the Scottish peers. I owe Sir George Rose much for his attention to Walter when at Berlin.[3]

27 WEDNESDAY At court till half past two. Then to the Waterloo tavern where we had a final and totally infructuous meeting with the Committee of the Coal Gas people[4] – So now my journey to London is resolved on. I shall lose at least £500 by the job and get little thanks from those I make the sacrifice for. But the sacrifice shall be made. Any thing is better than to break one's word or desert a sinking vessell. Heartily do I wish these Colliers had seen the matter in the best light for their own interest. But there is no help. One thing is certain, that I shall see my whole family once more around me, and that is worth the £500. Anne too starts at the idea of the Sea.[5] I am horribly vexd however. Gibson always expected they would come in but there seemd to me little chance of it. Perhaps they thought we

1. Scott originally wrote: 'This night I went to a promenade' and when deleting 'a promenade' forgot to change the word 'night' to 'day'.
2. Beginning life as a clerk, he rose to be partner in a bank and made his fortune when he bought Craigleith quarry. *Life*, vii. 307–8. Much of the New Town was built of Craigleith stone.
3. Sir George Rose was Ambassador in Berlin when Walter went there to study tactics in 1822.
4. For the previous meetings see the Entries for 11 and 16 February 1828.
5. 'Indeed I wish to come by Sea. But Anne remembers my poor Glengarrys fate and supposes great men apt to go on a lee-shore.' *Letters*, x. 389.

were not serious in our proposal to push through the act. Wrought a little in the evening, not much.

28 THURSDAY At court till four. When I came home I did work a little. But as we expected company it was not to much purpose. Lord Chief Commissioner dined with us with Miss Adam. Mr. Hutchison a brother of Lord Donoughmore, and Miss Jones, Will Clerk and John Thomson made up the party and we had a pleasant party as such a handful always secures – Staid till wine and water time. Thus flew another day.

29 FRIDAY I had my proofsheets as usual in the morning and the Court as usual till two, then one or two visits and corrected the Discourses for Gordon.[1] This is really a foolish scrape but what could I do? It involved the poor lad's relief under something very like ruin.

I go[t] a letter from the young man Reynolds accepting on Heath's part my terms for article to the *Keepsake*, viz. £500, I to be at liberty to reprint the article in my works after three years. Mr. Heath to print it in the *Keepsake* as long and often as he pleases but not in any other form. I shall close with them. If I make my proposed Bargain with Murray[2] all pecuniary matters will be easy in an unusual degree.

Dined at Robert Hamilton with Lord and Lady Belhaven, Walter Campbell and a number of Westlanders.

MARCH

1 SATURDAY Wrought a little this morning, always creeping on. Looked at my cash affairs: oblige[d] to borrow £25 from Cadell.

	£59	
Cash 15 feby		£49
Borrowd from Cadell		25
		74
To Charles on leaving Edinr.	£25	
To Masters[3] etc.	10	
To House	25	
To divers accompts	7	
		67
Cash in purse		£7

We had a hard pull at the court and after it I walkd a little for exercize as I fear indigestion from dining out so often. Dined to-day with the

1. *Religious Discourses by a Layman.*
2. For a book on planting. See the Entry for 13 December 1827.
3. For Charles's Italian and French lessons.

Bankers who went as delegates to London in Malachi McGrowther's days. Sir John Hay, Kinnear and Tom Allan were my only acquaintances of the party; the rest seemd shrewd capable men. I particularly remarkd a Mr. Sandeman with a very intellectual head as I ever witnessd.

2 SUNDAY A day of hard work with little interruption and completed Vol. 2d.[1] I am not much pleased with it. It wants what I desire it to have, and that is passion. The two Ballantynes and Mr. Cadell dined with me quietly. Heard from them all in London, all well.[2]

3 MONDAY I set about clearing my desk of unanswerd letters which I had sufferd to accumulate to an Augean heap. I dare say I wrote twenty cards that might have been written at the time without half a minute being lost. To do every thing when it ought to be done is the soul of expedition. But then if you are interrupted eternally with these petty avocations the current of the mind is compelld to flow in shallows and you lose the deep intensity of thought which alone can float plans of depth and magnitude. I sometimes wish I were one of those formalists who can assign each hour of the day its spe[ci]al occupations not to be encroachd upon but it always returns upon my mind that I do better *à la débandade* than I could with rules of regular study. A work begun is with me a stone turnd over with the purpose of rolling it down hill; the first revolutions are made with difficulty but – *vires acquirit eundo*[3] – Now were the said stone arrested in its progress the whole labour would be to commence again. To take a less conceited simily, I am like a spavind horse who sets out lame and stiff but when he warms in his gear makes a pretty good trot of it, so that it is better to take a good stage of him while you can get it. Besides, after all, I have known most of those formalists who were not men of business or of office to whom hours are prescribed as a part of duty but who voluntarily make themselves

> Slaves to an hour and vassals to a bell[4]

To be what I call very poor creatures.

1. Of *The Fair Maid of Perth*.
2. The letter is from Sophia. The sum Scott intends to pay for Charles's board and lodging is 'far too much'; Walter 'is going to take a House at Hampton Court'; Johnnie, after reading *Tales of a Grandfather* is now 'mad about knights and bravery and war'. 27 February 1828, Walpole.
3. 'It acquires strength by going.' Virgil's *Aeneid*, iv. 175.
4. Oldham's 'Lines addressed to a Friend', l. 91, in *Poems and Translations*, 1683.

General Ainslie lookd in and saddend me by talking of poor Don. The General is a medallist and entertains an opinion that the Bonnet-piece piece of James V is the work of some Scottish artist who died young and never did any thing else. It is far superior to any thing which the mint produced since the roman denarii. He also told [me] that the name of Andria de Ferrara is famous in Italy as an armourer.

Dined at home and went to the Royal Society in the evening after sending off my processes for the sheriff court. Also went after the Society to Mr. James Russell's symposion.

4 TUESDAY A Letter from Italy signed J.S. with many acute remarks on inaccuracies in the *Life of Bonaparte*. His tone is hostile decidedly. But that shall not prevent my making use of all his corrections where just.

The wr[e]tched publication of Leigh Hunt on the subject of Byron[1] is to bring forward Tom Moore's life of that distinguishd poet[2] and I am honourd and flatterd by the information that he means to dedicate it to me.

A great deal of worry in the court to-day and I lost my spectacles and was a dark and perplexd man, found them again though. Wrote to Lockhart and to Charles and will do more if I can but am sadly done up. An old friend came and pressd unmercifully on some selfish request of his own to ask somebody to do something for his son. I shall be glad to be at Abbotsford to get rid of this town where I have not in the proper and social sense of the word a single friend whose company pleases me. In the country I have always Tom Purdie.

Cash in purse ————————————————		£7.0.0
received as a dividend on my father's share in		
Douglas Heron & Coy's hapless bank		47.0.0
Grey farrier's accot for the season		£7.0.0
remains in cash		£40.0.0
Ewart Sadlers accompt ————————	£12.0.0	
Gardners ————————————————	3	
Anne for sundries ——————————	5	
	———	20
remains		£20 0 0

Dined at Lord Chief Commissioner's where I met the first time for thirty years my old friend and boon-companion with whom I

---

1. *Lord Byron and his Contemporaries*, 1828.
2. *Byron's Letters and Journals. With Notices of his Life*, 1830.

shared the wars of Bacchus, Venus and sometimes of Mars. The past rushd on me like a flood and almost brought tears into my eyes. It is no very laudable exploit to record but I once drank three bottles of wine with this same rogue – Sir William Forbes and Sir Alexr. Wood being of the party. David Erskine of Cardross keeps his looks better than most of our contemporaries. I hope we shall meet for a longer time.

5 WEDNESDAY I corrected sheets and being a teind Wednesday began the second[1] volume and proceeded as far as page fourth. At three I went to a meeting of the Oil Gas to report the terms of composition. We agreed to reject them. But we are only negociating for better terms for we must strike flag for want of funds – This Mem[or]andum is only for myself.

We dined at Hector Macdonald's with several Highlanders most of whom were in their garb, intending to go to a great fancy ball[2] in the evening. There were young Cluny Macpherson, Campbell Airds, Campbell Saddell and others of the race of Diarmid. I went for an hour to the Ball where there were many gay and some grotesque figures. A dressd ball is for the first half hour a splendid spectacle; you see youth and beauty dressd in their gaiest attire, unlimited save by their own taste and enjoying the conscious power of charming which gives such life and alacrity to the features. But the charm ceases in this like every thing else. The want of masques takes away the audacity with which the disguized parties conduct themselves at a masquerade, and the sullen sheepishness which mingles makes them I suppose the worst maskers in Europe. At the only real masquerades which I have known in Edinburgh there were many, if not most of those who had determind to sustain characters who had more ill breeding than facetiousness. The jests were chiefly calculated to give pain and two or three quarrells were with difficulty prevented from ripening into duels – A fancy ball has no offence in it, therefore cannot be wreckd on this rock – but on the other hand it is horribly dull work when the first *coup d'oeuil* is family.[3]

There were some good figures and some grossly absurd. A very gay cavalier with a broad bright battle axe was pointed out to me as an eminent distiller and another Knight, as he desired [to be], armd in the black coarse armour of a cuirassier of the 17th century, stalkd about as if he thought himself the very mirror of chilvalry. He was the

---

1. A slip for 'third'.
2. Given by the Chief of the Macphersons.
3. Scott may have meant to write 'fairly over', or perhaps 'familiar'.

son of a celebrated upholsterer so might claim the broad axe from more titles than one.

There was some good dancing. Cluny Macpherson footed it gallantly.

6 THURSDAY Wrote two pages this morning before breakfast. Went to the court where I learnd that the Coalliers are in alarm at the determination shown by our committee and are willing to give better terms. I hope this is so – but *Cogan na Shie* – peace or war I care not – I never felt less anxiety about where I went and what I did – a feather just lighted on the ground can scarce be less concernd where the next blast may carry [it]. If I go I shall see my children – if I stay I shall mend my fortune. Dined at home and went to the play in the evening. Lady Torphichen had commanded the play and there were all my Swinton cousins young and old. The play was *A Bold Stroke for a Wife*,[1] Charles Kemble acting Feignall. The plot is extravagant enough, But with lively acting the ludicrousness of the situation bears it through and few comedies act better. After this came *Rob Roy* where the Baillie[2] playd with his usual excellence. The piece was not over until near one in the morning yet I did not feel tired, which is much.

7 FRIDAY To-day I wrought and corrected proof Sheets, went to the court and had a worry at the usual trashy small wares which are presented at the end of a Session. An official predecessor of mine, the facetious Robert Sinclair, was wont to say the three last days of the Session should be abolishd by act of Parliament. Came home late and was a good deal broken in upon by visitors. Amongst others John Swinton, now of Swinton, brought me the scull of his ancestor Sir Alan Swinton who flourishd five hundred years ago. I will get a cast made of the stout old Carle. It is rare to see a genuine relique of the mortal frame drawing so far back.

Went to My Lord Gillies's to dinner and witnessd a singular exhibition of personification.

Miss Stirling Grame, a lady of the Duntroon family from which Clavers was descended, looks like thirty years old and has a face of the Scottish cast with a good expression in point of good sense and good humour. Her conversation so far as I have had the advantage of hearing it is shrewd and sensible but noways brilliant. She dined with us – went off as to the play and returnd in the character of an old

1. By Mrs. Centlivre, 1718.
2. Charles Mackay, whom Scott nicknamed 'The Bailie' after his performances as Nicol Jarvie.

Scottish lady. Her dress and behaviour were admirable and the conversation unique. I was in the secret, of course did my best to keep up the ball, but She cut me out of all feather. The prosing account she gave me of her son the antiquary who found an auld wig in a slate quarry was extremely ludicrous and she puzzled the professor of agriculture with a merciless account of the succession of crops in the parks around her old mansion house. No person to whom the secret was not intrusted had the least guess of an imposture except one shrewd young lady present who observed the hand narrowly and saw it was plumper than the age of the lady seemd to warrant. This lady and Miss Bell of Coldstream have this gift of personification to a much higher degree than any person I ever saw.[1]

8 SATURDAY Wrote in the Morning – then to court where we had a Sederunt till nigh two o'clock. From thence to the Coal Gas committee with whom we held another and thank God a final meeting. Gibson went with me. They had Mr. Munro, Trotter, Tom Burns and Inglis – The scene put me in mind of Chichester Cheyne's story of a Shawanese India[n] and himself dodging each other from behind trees for six or seven hours each in hope of a successful shot. There was bullying on both sides but we bullied to best purpose for we must have surrenderd at discretion notwithstanding the bold face we put on it. On the other hand I am convinced they have got a capital bargain. They give 1000 shares of their stock to be divided amongst the stock holders of the Oil Gas company and take all our works off our hands. An advance of from 8/- to 10/- a share will clear off all our debts and leave us in possession of our shares of the Coal Gas which relieved from rivalry and competition will soon rise to a great percentage.[2] In short I think it a great thing for both parties. Dined at Lord Justice Clerk's[3] – nothing remarkable in the course of the evening.

9 SUNDAY I set about arranging my papers, a task which I always take up with the greatest possible ill will and which makes me cruelly nervous. I don't know why it should be so for I have nothing particularly disagreeable to look at – far from it, I am better than

---

1. Miss Graham tells us in her *Mystifications* (Edin., 1859) that Sir Walter, on leaving the room, whispered in her ear, 'Awa!, awa!, the deil's ower great wi' you.'
2. See note 1, p. 805–6.
3. David Boyle's.

I was at this time last year – my hopes firmer, my health stronger, my affairs betterd and bettering – Yet I feel an inexpressible nervousness in consequence of this employment. The memory though it retains all that has passd has closed sternly over it and this rummaging, like a bucket dropd suddenly into a well, deranges and confuses the ideas which slumberd on the mind. I am nervous and I am bilious and in a word I am unhappy – This is wrong – very wrong – and it [is] reasonably to be apprehended that some thing of serious misfortune will be the deserved punishment of this pusillanimous lowness of spirits – Strange! that one who in most things may be said to have enough of the 'care-na bye'[1] should be subject to such vile weakness – Well, having written myself down an ass I will daub it no farther[2] but e'en trifle till the humour of work comes.

Before the humour came I had two or three long visits – Drummond Hay the Antiquary and lion-herald[3] came in. I do not know any thing which relieves the mind so much from the sullens as trifling discussions about *antiquarian old-womanries* – It is like knitting a stocking, diverting the mind without occupying it, or it is like, by our lady, a mill dam which leads the attention gently and imperceptibly out of the channell in which they are chafing and boiling – to be sure it is only conducting them to turn a child's mill – What signifies that? – the diversion is a relief though the object is of little importance. I cannot tell what we talkd of but I remember we concluded with a lamentation on the unlikelihood that Government would give the Musaeum £2000 to purchase the bronze apollo lately discoverd in France[4] although the God of Delos stands six feet two in his stocking soles and is perfectly entire saving that on the right side he wants half a hip and the leg from the knee, and that on the left his heel is much damaged. Colonel Ferguson just come to town – dines with us. Miss Kerr came in in the evening.

10 MONDAY I had [a] world of trumpery to do this morning – cards to write and business to transact, visits to make etc. We made so bold

---

1. 'The sans souciant character', he calls it in the Entry for 10 March 1826.
2. A composite allusion to *Much Ado About Nothing*, iv. 2, and *King Lear*, iv. 1.
3. Auriol Drummond Hay was Secretary to the Antiquarian Society as well as Principal Clerk to the Lyon Court.
4. The gilt bronze Apollo of Lillebonne, found in 1823 and now in the Louvre. See E. Espérandieu and H. Rolland's *Bronzes antiques de la Seine Maritime*, 13th supplement (1959), pp. 24–5 and pls. III–V.

a fight with the Coal Gas Committee that though it was only gaining an honourable capitulation we have gaind honour and all seem rejoiced at having been able to save so much out of the fire in which they expected to lose every thing.

Received letters from the youth who is to conduct the *Keepsake*[1] with blarney an[d] a £200 Bank note. No Blarney in that. I must set about doing something for these worthies.

Anne is very ill of the earache and cannot stir tomorrow. I was obliged to go alone to dine at Mr Scott Gala's. Met the Sinclair family. Lady Sinclair told me a singular story of a decrepid man keeping a lonely toll at a place calld the Rowantree on the frontiers as I understood between Ayrshire and Dumfries shire.[2] It was a wild lonely spot and was formerly inhabited by robbers and assassins who murderd passengers. They were discoverd by a boy whom they had taken into the cottage as a menial. He had seen things which aroused his attention and was finally enlightend as to the trade of his masters by hearing one of them as he killd a goat remark that the cries of the creature resembled those of the last man they had dealt with. The boy fled from the house, lodged an information, and the whole household was seized and executed. The present inhabitants Lady Sinclair described as interesting. The man's feet and legs had been frost-bitten while herding the cattle and never recoverd the Strength of natural limbs. Yet he had acquired some education and was a country schoolmaster for some time till the distance and loneliness of the spot prevented pupils from attending. His daughter was a reader and begd for some old Magazins, Newspapers or any printed book that she might enjoy reading. They might have been better had they been allowd to keep a cow. But if they had been in comfortable circumstances they would have had visitors and lodgers who might have carried guns to destroy the gentleman's creation i.e. the game, and for this ri[s]que the wretches were kept in absolute and abject poverty. I would rather be Sir John[3] himself than this brutal Earl. The daughter shewd Lady Sinclair a well in the midst of a small bog of great depth into which like Thurtell and Probert they used to thrust the bodies of their victims till they had opportunity of burying them. Lady Sinclair stoopd to taste the water but the young woman said with a strong expression of horror 'You would not drink it?' Such an impression had the tale probably two centuries old made

1. Frederic Mansel Reynolds.
2. It is on the border between Ayrshire and Kirkcudbrightshire.
3. Sir John Sinclair, whom Scott derided as the prince of bores.

upon the present inhabitants of this melancholy spot. The whole legend is curious. I will try to get hold of it.[1]

II TUESDAY A long morning at court after which I walkd home and paid some things as under

In purse			£20.0.
Ballance of old accot John Stevenson vizt		£11	
Fees at the House and sundries		1	
Anne Charity		1	
Glasier and carpenter		1	
			14.0.0
	Ballance		£6
Ballance in cash			£6
In English Bank note			200
			£206

It was four ere I got home and I had a great deal to do though of a puddling kind of work. Another rector[2] started, recommended by Sir Francis Freling, Sir James Mackintosh and Dr. Maltby. I wish the place was filld with all my heart – so it were well filld.

I sent Reynolds a sketch of two Scottish stories for subjects of art for his *Keepsake*. The death of the Laird's jock the one, the other the adventure of Duncan Stuart with the stag.[3]

Mr. Drummond Hay breakfasted with me, a good fellow but a considerable bore. He brought me a beautiful bronze statue of hercules about ten inches or a foot in height, beautifully wrought. He bought it in France for 70 francs and refuse[d] £300 from Payne Knight. It is certainly a most beautiful piece of art. The lion's hide which hung over the shoulders had been of silver and to turn it to accompt the arm over which it hung was cut off; otherwise the statue was perfect and extremely well wrought. Allan Swinton's scull sent back to Archd Swinton.

Poor Anne was so ill of the earache as to put travelling out of the question whether today or tomorrow.

1. Douglas notes that the story appears, under the title of 'The Murder Hole', in *Blackwood's Magazine*, vol. xxv.
2. For the Edinburgh Academy.
3. The first of these was published and illustrated in *The Keepsake* for 1829. The other appeared as 'A Highland Anecdote' in *The Keepsake* for 1832.

12 WEDNESDAY   The Boy got four leaves of copy to-day and I wrote three more.

Cash—English Bank bill	£200
Cash	6
	206

To poor Nathaniel Gow[1] in memory of many a night of mirth and melody	£2	
Segars	1	
	—	£3
		£[20]3

Balanced with about £1 in silver.

When I had done writing I calld on Mr Gibson to request the Trustees would not sell the Coal Gas stock without consulting me which seems reasonable as I advanced £150 and upwards.

Received by Mr. Cadell from Treuttel and Wurtz for articles in *Foreign Review* £52. 10. which is at my credit with him. Poor Gillies has therefore kept his word so far but it is enough to have sacrificed £100 to him already in literary labour which I make him wellcome to. I cannot spare him more, which besides would do him no good.[2]

13 THURSDAY   I wrote a little in the morning and sent off some copy. We came off from Edinburgh at ten o'clock and got to Abbotsford by four where every thing looks unusually advanced, the birds singing and the hedges budding and all other prospects of spring too premature to be rejoiced in.

I found that like the foolish virgins the servants had omitted to get oil for my lamp so I was obliged to be idle all the evening. But though I had a diverting book, the *Tales of the Munster Festivals*,[3] yet an evening without writing hung heavy on my hand. The tales are admirable. But they have one fault, that the crisis is in more cases than one protracted after a keen interest has been excited, to explain and to resume parts of the story which should have been told before. Scenes of mere amusement are often introduced betwixt the crisis of the plot and the final catastrophe. This is impolitic. But the scenes and characters are traced by a firm, bold and true pencil and my very criticism shows that [the] catastrophé is interesting, otherwise who would care for its being interrupted?

1. The fiddler.
2. Scott had given Gillies the article on Hoffmann the previous May, but accepted fifty guineas for his article on Molière.
3. *Tales of the Munster Festivals* by Gerald Griffin, 1827.

14 FRIDAY Wrote from morning till one o'clock – then drove to Huntley Burn and walkd home from thence, going by the new plantations which seem well laid out and planted. I returnd by four. Dined and wrote after dinner so that it was an active an[d] useful day: five leaves were the produce.

15 SATURDAY Up and at work as usual. John Fergusson came to breakfast and stayed till eleven. After this I workd untill two o'clock when I made calls with Anne on Dr. Brewster who seems much satisfied with the composition between the rival Gas Companies[1] – then to Mr. Bainbridge and to honest Tom Bruce's who has just married a pretty, frank looking young woman. Askd them to dine on thursday.[2] This evening again there is nothing to say except that I sipt my whisky and water, smoakd my segars, and then went again to work for two hours – five leaves were again the produce of the day is five leaves.

16 SUNDAY The same record applies to these three days. From seven to half past nine writing – from half past nine to a quarter past ten a hearty breakfast. From eleven or thereby to one or two, write again, and from one or two ride, drive or walk till dinner time – for two or three hours – five till seven, dine and rest yourself – seven till nine, write two pages more. From nine to quarter past ten lounge, read the papers and then go to bed. If your story be tolerably formed you may I think keep at this rate for twelve days which would be a volume. But no brain could hold it out longer. Wrote two additional leaves in the evening.

17 MONDAY Sent away copy this morning to J. B. with proofs. I then wrote all the day till two o'clock, walkd round the thicket and by the water side and returning set to work again. So that I have finished five leaves before Dinner and may discuss two more if I can satisfy myself with the way of winding up the story. There are always at the end such a plaguy number of stitches to take up in the story which usually are never so well done but they make a botch. I will try if the segar will inspire me. Hitherto I have been pretty clear and I see my way well enough, only doubt of making others see it with sufficient simplicity. But it is near five and I am too hungry to write more.

Ego nunquam potui scribere jejunus.[3]

1. Dr. Brewster was a Director of the Oil Gas Coy.
2. The dinner-party actually takes place the following Friday.
3. 'I have never been able to write when dry.'

18 TUESDAY I was sorely worried by the black dog this morning, that vile palpitation of the heart – that *tremor cordis* – that histerical passion which forces unbidden sighs and tears and falls upon a contented life like a drop of ink on white paper which is not the less a stain because it conveys no meaning. I wrought three leaves however and the story goes on. I dined at the Club of the Selkirkshire yeomanry, now disbanded.

> The Eldridge knights gave up his arms
> With many a sorrowful sigh.[1]

The dissolution of the yeomanry was the act of the last ministry. The present did not alter the measure on account of the expense saved. I am one of the oldest if not the very eldest yeoman in Scotland and have seen the rise, progress, and now the fall of this very constitutional part of the national force. Its efficacy on occasions of insurrection was sufficiently proved in the radical time. But besides it kept up a spirit of harmony between the proprietors of land and the occupiers and made them known to and beloved by each other and it gave to the young men a sort of military and high-spirited character which always does honour to a country. The manufacturers are in great glee on this occasion. I wish Parliament as they have turnd the Yeomen adrift somewhat scornfully may not have occasion to roar them in again.[2]

19 WEDNESDAY I applied myself again to my labour, my mind flowing in a less gloomy current than yesterday. I labourd with little intermission excepting a walk as far as Faldonside with the dogs and at night I had not finishd more than three leaves. But indeed it is pretty fair. I must not work my brains too hard in case of provoking the hypochondria which extreme exertion or entire indolence are equally unfavourable to.

20 THURSDAY Thomson[3] breakfasted. I left him soon, being desirous to finish my labours. The volume is finishd, all but one fourth or somewhat shorter. Four days should despatch it easily but I have letters to write and things are getting into disorder. I took a drive with my daughter for exercize and calld at Huntly Burn. This evening went on with work as usual. There was not above four pages finishd but my Conscience is quiet on my exertions.

---

1. 'Sir Cauline', pt. 1, st. 32, in Percy's *Reliques*. Scott changed 'their' to 'his' in the first line, but forgot to delete the 's' on 'knights'.
2. *Coriolanus*, iv. 6.
3. The Revd. George Thomson.

21 FRIDAY I received young Whitebank¹ to breakfast and talkd genealogy which he understands well. I have not a head for it. I only value it as interspersed with anecdote. Whitebank's relationship and mine exists by the Shaws. A younger brother of Shaw of Sauchie, afterwards Greenock chief of the name, was minister of the kirk of Selkirk. My great Grandfather John Rutherfurd, Minister of the gospel at Yarrow, married one of this reverend gentleman's daughters and John Pringle, rector of Fogo, great grandfather of the present Whitebank, married another. It was Christian Shaw my grandmother who possessed the Manuscript respecting the murder of the Shaws by the Master of Sinclair.² She could not according to the reckoning of that age be a distant relation. Whitebank parted agreeing to return to dinner to meet the bride and bridegroom. I had little time to write for Colonel Russell my cousin calld between one and two and he also agreed to stay dinner. So I had a walk of three hours with him in the plantations. At dinner we had Mr. and Mrs. Bruce, Mr. Scrope, Mrs. and Dr. Brewster, Whitebank, Russell, and young Nicol Milne who will be a pleasant lad if he had a little polish. I was glad of the society as I had rather felt the *besoin de parler* which was perhaps one cause of my recent dumps. Scope and Colonel Russell staid all night. The rest went home.

22 SATURDAY Had a packet from James – Low about the novel but I had another from Cadell equall[y] uppish.³ He proposes for three novels in 18 months which would be £12,600. Well, I like the bookseller's predictions better than the printer's. Neither are bad judges but James who is the best is not sensible of historical descriptions and likes your novel stile out and out.

Cadell's letter also contain a state of cash matters, since much improved. I will arrange these a day or two hence. I wrote to-day and took a long walk. The thought more than once pressd on me, why go to London?⁴ I shall but throw away £150 or £200 which were better saved. Then on the other hand it is such a gratification to see all the

1. Alexander Pringle of Whytbank.
2. Which Scott edited for the Roxburghe Club. See the Entry for 30 September 1827. In fact Christian Shaw was Scott's great-grandmother, not his grandmother.
3. 'No sooner is one book done, than we receive orders for the next altho not named.' In Germany, he hears, 'they print 40,000 or 50,000 at a time!!!' 21 March 1828, Walpole.
4. The original reason for the journey had gone now that agreement had been reached with the Coal Gas Coy., but his family and his desire to alter a Road Bill which threatened his estate were still sufficient inducements.

children that I must be tempted. If I were alone I could scrub it but there is no doing that with Anne.

23 SUNDAY I wrought regularly till one and then took the wood and markd out to Tom the places I would have thind, particularly at the Carlin's hole which will require much thinning. I had a letter from Cadell stating that 3000 *Tales of a Grandfather* must go to press, hence a return to me of £240, the price being £80 per thousand.[1] This is snug enough and will prettily cover my London journey and I really think ought in fairness to silence my prudential remorse. With my usual delight in catching an apology for escaping the regular task of the day I threw by the novel of *Saint Valentine's Eve* and began to run through and correct the Grandfather's tales for the press. If I live to finish them,[2] they will be a good thing for my younger children. If I work to the amount of £10,000 a year for the Creditors I think I may gain a few hundreds for my own family at bye hours.

24 MONDAY Sent copy and proofs to J. B. I continued my revision of the *Tales of Grandfather* till half past one. Then went to Torwoodlee to wait on George Pringle and his bride. We did not see the young people but the old Laird and Miss Pringle gave us a warm reception and seemd very happy on the occasion – We had friends to dinner, Mr. and Mrs. Theobauld, Charles Ker and his wife, my old acquaintance Magdalen Hepburn whose whole [kin] was known to me and mine. I have now seen the fifth generation of the family in Mrs. Kerr's little girl who travels with them. Well – I partly wish we had been alone. Yet it is perhaps better. We made our day out tolerably well, having the advantage of Mr. Davidoff and his friend Mr. Colyar to assist us.

25 TUESDAY Mr. and Mrs. Kerr left us – Mr. Davidoff and Mr. Colyar also. Mr. Davidoff shewd himself a good [deal] affected. I hope well of this young nobleman and trust the result will justify my expectations. But it may be doubted if his happiness be well considerd by those who sent a young person destined to spend his life under a despotic government to receive the ideas and opinions of such a people so popular as we are

> ˙– Where ignorance is bliss
> Tis folly to be wise.[3]

1. A few days later Cadell raised this revised edition of the first series to 5000 and Scott was paid £400.
2. To finish, that is, the second and subsequent series of tales.
3. Gray's 'Ode on a Distant Prospect of Eton College' ll. 99–100.

We drove as far as Yair with Mr. and Mrs. Theobauld. The lady read after dinner and read well.

26 WEDNESDAY The Theobaulds left us, giving me time to work a little. A walk of two hours diversified my day. I received Cadell's scheme for the new Edition.[1] I fear the trustees will think Cadell's plan expensive in the execution. Yet he is right, for to ensure a return of speedy sale the new edition should [be] both handsome and cheap. He proposes size at Royal 12mo with a capital engraving to each volume from a design by the best artists in [the] land. This infers a monstrous expense but in the present humour of the public ensures the sale. Price will be 5/- per volume and the whole set, 32 volumes from *Waverley* to *Woodstock* included, will be eight pound.

27 THURSDAY This also was a day of labour affording only my usual interval of a walk. Five or six sheets was the result. We now appropinque an end.[2] My story has unhappily a divided interest. There are three distinct strands of the rope and they are not well twisted together – Ah Sirs, a foul fawt as Captain Jamy says.[3]

28 FRIDAY The days have little to distinguish each other – very little – The morning study, the noontide walk, all monotonous and inclined to be melancholy, God help me. But I have not had any nervous attack. Read *Tales of an Antiquary*,[4] one of the chime of bells which I have some hand in setting a ringing. He is really entitled to the name of an Antiquary. But he has too much description in proportion to the action. There is a capital wardrope of properties but the performers do not act up to their character.

29 SATURDAY Finishd Vol 3d. this morning. I have let no grass grow beneath my heels this bout. Mr. Cadell with J. and A. Ballantyne came to dinner.[5] Mr. and Mrs. George Pringle, new married, dined with us with old Torwoodlee. Sandie's musick made the evening go sweetly down.[6]

1. The Magnum Opus.
2. Butler's *Hudibras*, pt. 1, canto 3.
3. *Henry V*, iii. 2.
4. Sent to Scott by the author, James Thomson, who hoped he could arrange a review in *Blackwood's Magazine*. 12 March 1828, Walpole.
5. The beginning of a business visit proposed by Cadell. *Letters*, x. 404.
6. Alexander Ballantyne's 'powers as a player on the flageolet are something that partakes of fairy-land'. *Letters*, vii. 216. He also played the violin.

30 SUNDAY A long discourse with Cadell canvassing his scheme. He proposes I should go on immediatly with the new novel. This will furnish a fund from which may be supplied the advances necessary for the new work which are considerable and may reach from £4000 to £8000, the last sum quite improbable, before it makes returns. Thus we can face the expenditure necessary to set on foot our great work. I have written to recommend the plan to Jo: Gibson.[1] This theme renewd from Time to Time during the forenoon. Dr. Clarkson dined with us. We smoked and had whisky and water after.

31 MONDAY Settled with Mr. Cadell in the morning. Our accompt stood as under.

Mr. Cadell receivd from Treuttel and Wurz	£52.10
By receipt Salary	250
By profit on 5000 *Tales of My Grandfather*	400
	£702

Mr. Cadell has paid		
To Anne Housekeeping	£50	
To Taxes Jedburgh	33	
To Potts and Coy London[2]	34	
To my accompt Hay and Corn, Thompson ———	37	
Remitted to Mr. Lang ———————	147	
Stamps etc. —————————	1	302
		400
Cash in gold and notes for journey		50
Remains with Cadell at my Credit		350
Left receipts for Cash in Exchequer		150
Total Credit with Mr. Cadell		£500
Cash remitted to Mr. Lang as on opposite side		£147
Cash in purse		3
Total Cash		£150

1. The consent of the Trustees was required as by this plan the profits from *Anne of Geierstein* would not be immediately applied to paying off the creditors but would help to finance the Magnum Opus.
2. A MS 'Abstract of Bills for work executed in London', at Abbotsford, includes £35.17s to Potts and Collinson for drawing-room curtains.

Tom Purdie ————————————————		£25
Bogie		
To Lochend rent ——————————	£34.0.0	
On Coal account —————————	23.18	
On Corn account —————————	23.9	
Oil for Gas etc. —————————	14.7	
Wages ————————————————	9.9	
	105.3	£105
Again Clarkson's Accot —————		10
Miss Scott —————————————		5
Charity and incidents —————		2
		—— 147
Ballance		3
Cash for travelling from Cadell —————		50
English bank note ———————————		200
In Coutts by review ———————————		100
Total Cash		£353

Such being the state of my finance I left with Cadell orders to discharge about £300 of bills and remit £40 to Mrs. Macdonald the Housekeeper. So that his fund can only be reckond at £500 *minus* £340 or £160 ballance.

The Ballantynes and Cadell left us in high spirits, expecting much from the new undertaking, and I believe they are not wrong – As for me I became torpid after a great influx of morning visitors.

> I grew vapourish and odd
>> And would [not] do the least right thing
> Neither for goddess nor for god
>> Nor paint nor jest nor laugh nor sing.[1]

I was quite reluctant to write letters or do anything whatsoever. And yet I should surely write to Sir Cuthbert Sharpe[2] and Surtees. We dined alone. I was main stupid indeed and much disposed to sleep though my dinner was very moderate.

APRIL

1 TUESDAY All Fools' day, the only Saint that Keeps up some degree of credit in the world for fools we are with a vengeance. On this

1. Pope's 'On the Countess of Burlington cutting Paper', ll. 1–4.
2. Who had written on 10 February with corrections for the *Life of Napoleon*. Walpole.

memorable festival we playd the fool with great decorum at Col. Fergusson's, going to visit them in a cold morning. In the evening I had a distressing letter from Mrs. MacBarnet or some such name, the daughter of Captain Macpherson smotherd in a great snow storm. They are very angry at the *Review* for telling a rawhead and bloody bones story about him. I have given the right version of the Tale willingly but this does not satisfy.[1] I almost wish they would turn out a clansman to be free of the cumber. The vexation of having to do with ladies who on such a point must be unreasonable is very great. With a man it would be soon ended or mended. It really hurt my sleep.

2 WEDNESDAY I wrote the lady as civilly as I could explaining why I made no further apology, which may do some good. Then a cursed morning of putting to rights which drives me well nigh mad. At two or three I must go to a funeral, a happy and interesting relief from my employment. It is a man I am sorry for who married my old servant Bell Ormiston.[2] He was an excellent person in his way and a capital mason – a great curler.

3 THURSDAY Set off at 8 o'clock and fought forward[3] to Carlisle – a sad place in my domestic remembrances since here I married my poor Charlotte[4] – She is gone – and I am following faster perhaps than I wott of – It is something to have lived and loved and our poor children are so hopeful and affectionate that it chastens the sadness attending the thoughts of our separation. We slept at Carlisle. I have not forgiven them for destroying their quiet old walls and building two lumpy things like madhouses. The old gates had such a respectable appearances even

When Scotsmen's heads did guard the wall –

1. Scott illustrated his review of Hoffmann's works in the first number of the *Foreign Quarterly* with the tale (told him by the Revd. McIntosh Mackay) of a certain Captain Macpherson who was swept away by an avalanche along with five or six attendants and the entire shooting-lodge in which they were staying during a Christmas deer-hunt – a disaster attributed by the local people to diabolical agency. In her first very unreasonable letter, Mrs. MacBarnet hints that only her brother's absence saves Scott from an immediate challenge to a duel; the second professes to find the apology printed in the second number of the *Review* 'so far short of what I expected that my sister and myself are anything but satisfied with it'. Letters to Scott, ff. 83 and 85. See also Mackay's *Reminiscences*, pp. 7–9.
2. George Hamilton married Isobel Ormiston in 1812.
3. 'Fought forward' because 'Anne has a cold and I am paralyzed with rheumatism.' 3 April 1828, Disc. i. 208.
4. In Carlisle Cathedral on Christmas Eve 1797.

Come, I'll write down the whole stanza, which is all that was known to exist of David Hume's poetry and was written on a pane of glass in the Inn.

> Here chicks in eggs for breakfast sprawl
> Here godless boys God's Glories squall
> Here Scotsmen's heads do guard the wall
> But Corby's walks attone for all.

The poetical works of David Hume Esq. might as bookmakers know how be *driven out* to a hands[ome] quarto – Line 1st admits of a descant upon eggs roasted boild or poachd – Second, a history of the Carlisle cathedral with some reasons why the choir there has been proverbially execrable. Third, the whole history of 1745 with minute memoirs of such as mounted guard on the Scotch gate. I remember the spikes the heads stood upon. Lastly a description of Corby Castle with a plan and the genealogy of the Howards. Gad, the booksellers would give me five hundred for it – I have a mind to print it for the Bannatynians.

4 FRIDAY In our stage to Penrith I introduced Anne to the ancient Petreia, calld Old Penrith, and also to the grave of Sir Ewain Cæsarias, that knight with the puzzling name who has got more indistinct. We breakfasted at Buchanan's inn Penrith, one of the best on the road and a fine staunch fellow ownd it. He refused passage to some of [the] delegates who traversed the country during the Radical row and when the worthies threatend him with popular vengeance answered gallantly that he had not lived so long by the Crown to desert at a pinch. The *Crown* is the Sign of his inn. Slept at Garstang, an indifferent house. As a petty grievance my ink-holder broke loose in the case and spilt some of the ink on Anne's pelisse. Misfortunes seldom come single.

> Tis not alone the inky cloak, good daughter[1]

but I forgot at Garstang my two breastpins, one with Walter and Jane's hair,[2] another a harp of pure Irish gold, the gift of the Ladies of Llangollen.[3]

---

1. A parody of *Hamlet*, i. 2, line 77.
2. Given by them just after their marriage. *Letters*, ix. 16.
3. Lady Eleanor Butler and the Hon. Miss Ponsonby, whom Scott visited on his way back from Ireland. *Life*, viii. 47–50.

5 SATURDAY Breakfasted at Chorley and slept at Leek; we were in the neighbourhood of some fine rock scenery but the day was unfavourable; besides I did not come from Scotland to see rocks I trow –

6 SUNDAY Easter Sunday. We breakfasted at Ashbourne and went from thence to Derby and set off from thence to Draycot Hall (five miles) to visit Hugh Scott. But honest Hugh was like ourselves on the ramble. So we had nothing to do but to drive back to Derby and from thence to Tamworth, where we slept.

7 MONDAY We visited the castle in the morning. It is inhabited by a brother in law of the proprietor – And who is the proprietor? 'Why, Mr. Robins' said the fat housekeeper. This was not a name quite according with the fine chivalrous old hall in which there was no small quantity [of] armour and odds and ends which I would have been glad to possess. 'Well but, Madam, before Mr. Robins bought the place who was the proprietor?' 'Lord Charles Townshend, Sir' – This would not do neither – But a genealogy hanging above the chimneypiece informd me that the Ferrars were the ancient posessors of the mansion which indeed the horse shoes in the shield over the Castle gate might have intimated. Tamworth is a fine old place, neglected but therefore more like hoar antiquity. The keep is round. The apartments appear to have been modernized *tempore* Jaci Imi. There was a fine demipique saddle said to have been that of James 2d. The pommel rose and finishd off in the form of a swan's crest, capital for a bad horseman to hold on by.

To show Anne what was well worth seeing we visited Kenilworth. The relentless rain only allowd us a glimpse of these memorable ruins. Well! the last time I was here in 1815[1] these trophies of time were quite neglected. Now they approach so much nearer the splendour of Thunder ten-tronck as to have a door at least if not windows.[2] They are in short preserved and protected. So much for the Novels.[3] I observed decent children begging here, a thing uncommon in England, and I recollect the same unseemly practice formerly.

We went to Warwick Castle. The neighbourhood of Leamington, a watering place of some celebrity, has obliged the family to decline showing the Castle after ten o'clock. I tried the virtue of an old

1. During the return journey from France. *Life*, v. 88.
2. An allusion to *Candide*, ch. 1.
3. *Kenilworth*, in other words, had created the public interest which preserved the ruins of the castle.

acquaintance with Lord Warwick and wrote to him, he busy in the court house where the assizes were sitting. After some delay we were admitted and I found my old friend Mrs. Hume[1] in the most perfect preservation though as she tells me now 88. She went through her duty wonderfully though now and then she complaind of her memory. She has laid aside a mass of black plumes which she wore on her head and which resembled the casque in the *Castle of Otranto*. Warwick Castle is still the noblest sight in England. Lord and Lady Warwick came home from the court and received us most kindly. We lunchd with them but declined further hospitality. When I was last here and for many years before, the unfortunate circumstances of the late Lord W. threw an air of neglect about every thing. I believe the fine collection of pictures would have been sold by distress if Mrs. Hume my friend had not redeemd them at her own cost. I was pleased to see Lord Warwick show my old friend kindness and attention. We visited the monuments of the Nevilles and Beauchamps, names which make the heart thrill. The monuments are highly preserved.

We concluded the day at Stratford upon Avon.

8 TUESDAY We visited the tomb of the mighty wizzard. It is in the bad taste of James Ist's reign but what a magic does the locality possess. There are stately monuments of forgotten families but when you have seen Shakspeare what care we for the rest? All around is Shakspeare['s] exclusive property. I noticed the monument of his friend John a Combe immortalized as drawing forth a brief satirical notice of four lines.

After breakfast I askd after Mrs. Ormsby, the old Madwoman who was for some time tenant of Shakspeare's house and conceived herself to be descended from the immortal poet. I learnd she was dying. I thought to send her a Sovereign but this extension of our tour has left me no more than will carry me through my journey and I do not like to run short upon the road. So I take credit for my good intention and – keep my Sovereign – a cheap and not unusual mode of giving charity.

Learning from Washington Irving's description of Stratford[2] that the hall of Sir Thomas Lucy the Justice who renderd Warwickshire

---

1. Douglas quotes her obituary in the *Annual Register for 1834*:
   'Lately at Warwick Castle, aged ninety-three, Mrs. Home, for upwards of seventy years a servant of the Warwick family. She had the privilege of showing the Castle, by which she realised upwards of £30,000.'
2. In his *Sketch Book*, 1820.

too hot for Shakspeare and drove him to London was still extant, We went in quest of it.

Charlecote is in high preservation and inhabited by Mr. Lucy, descendant of the worshipful Sir Thomas. The Hall is about three hundred years old, an old brick structure with a gate-house in advance. It is surrounded by venerable oaks realizing the imagery which Shakspeare loved so well to dwell upon, rich verdant pastures extend on every side and numerous herds of deer were reposing in the shade. All showd that the Lucy family had retaind their 'land and beeves.'[1] While we were surveying the antlerd old hall with its painted glass and family pictures Mr. Lucy came to wellcome us in person and to show the house with the collection of paintings, which seems valuable and to which he has made many valuable additions.

He told me the park from which Shakspeare stole the buck was not that which surrounds Charlecote but belongd to a mansion at some distance where Sir Thomas Lucy resided at the time of the trespass. The tradition went that they hid the buck in a barn, part of which was standing a few years ago but now totally decayd. This park no longer belongs to the Lucys. The house bears no marks of decay but seems the abode of ease and opulence. There were some fine old books and I was told of many more which were not in order. How odd if a folio Shakspeare could be found among them. Our early breakfast did not prevent my taking advantage of an excellent repast offerd by the kindness of Mr. and Mrs. Lucy, the last a lively welsh woman. This visit gave me great pleasure; it really brought Justice Shallow freshly before my eyes – the *luces* in his arms which do become an old coat well[2] were not more lively plainly pourtrayd in his own armorials in the hall window than was his person in my mind's eye. There is a picture shown as that of the old Sir Thomas but Mr. Lucy conjectures it represents his son. There were three descents of the same name of Thomas. The party hath 'the eye sever and beard of formal cutt' which fills up with judicial austerity the otherwise social physiognomy of the worshipful presence with his fair round belly with fat capon lined.[3]

We resumed our journey. I may mention among the pictures at Charlecote one calld 'A Roman Knight' which seemd to me very fine – Teniers' 'Marriage' in which contrary to the painter's wont only persons of distinction are represented but much in the attitude in which he delights to present his boors – Two hawking pieces by Wouvermans – very fine specimens *cum aliis*.

1. Like Justice Shallow in *2 Henry IV*, iii. 2.
2. *Merry Wives of Windsor*, i. 1.
3. *As You Like It*, ii. 7.

We took our way by Edgehill and lookd over the splendid richness of the fine prospect from a sort of gazeebo or modern antique tower, the place of a Mr. Miller. It is not easy to conceive a richer and more peaceful scene than that which stretchd before us, and strife or the memory of strife seems to have nothing to do [there].

> But man records his own disgrace
> And Edgehill lives in history.[1]

We got on to Buckingham, an ugly though I suppose an ancient town. Thence to Aylesbury through the wealth of England in the scene of the old ballad

> Neither drunk nor sober but neighbour to both
> I met with a man in *Aylesbury* vale
> I saw by his face that he was in good case
> To speak no great harm of a pot of good ale.[2]

We slept at Aylesbury. The landlord, who seemd sensible, told me that the land round the town being the richest in England lets at £3. or £3. 10. and some so high as four pound per acre. *But* the poors rates are 13/- to the pound. Now my Whitehaugh at Huntly Burn yielded at last set £4 per acre.

9 WEDNESDAY We got to town about midday, and found Sophia, Lockhart and the babies quite well – delighted with their companion Walter[3] and he enchanted with his occupation in the foreign office – Johnie has a cold otherwise all are well and happy. I lookd into my cash and found £53 had diminishd on the journey down to about £3. In former days a journey to London cost about £30 or thirty guineas. It may now cost one fourth more. But I own I like to pay postilions and waiters rather more liberally than perhaps is right. I hate grumbling and sour faces and the whole saving will not exceed a guinea or two for being cursd and damnd from Dan to Beersheba. We had a joyful meeting I promise you.

10 THURSDAY I spent the morning in bringing up my journal interrupted by two of those most sedulous visitants who had objects of their own to serve and smelld out my arrival as the raven scents

---

1. Unidentified.
2. 'The Ex-ale-tation of Ale', st. 1. *A Collection of Old Ballads*, 1725, iii. 166.
3. A slip for 'Charles'.

carrion – a vile comparaison though what better is an old fellow mauld with rheumatism and other deplorables? Went out at two and saw Miss Dumergue and other old friends, Sotheby in particular less changed than any one I have seen. Lookd in at Murray's[1] and renewd old habits. This great city seems almost a waste to me, so many of my friends are gone. Walter and Jane coming up,[2] the whole family dined together and were very happy. The children joind in our festivity. My nameson,[3] a bright and blue eyed rogue with flaxen hair, screams and laughs like an April morning and the baby is that species of dough which is calld a fine baby. I care not for children till they care a little for me.

11 FRIDAY Cash matters in London

Cash in Coutts ———————————	£300	
But by cash given to Charles by Lockhart for club etc. ———————————	35	
Therefore cash ———————————		£265.0.0
By Cheque ———————————		£50.0.0
In Bank		£215.0.0
In purse ———————————	£3.0.0	
To John[4] Ballance of accot ———————	2.0.0	
	1	
By cheque on Coutts ———————————	50	
	——— In purse £50	

To Anne to accompt of £50 pocket money	£20	
To Charles	20	
To sundries ———————————	3	
	———	43
In purse ———————————		£7
May John balance due on his book	£5	
Dr. to Acct. ———————————	2	
	———	7
		£0.0.0[5]

---

1. The publisher's.
2. From Hampton Court, where Walter's regiment was stationed.
3. Walter, the Lockharts' second child.
4. His servant John Nicholson.
5. Four and a half blank pages follow.

Made calls, walkd myself tired. Saw Rogers, Sharpe, Sotheby and other old friends. Dined.[1]

12 SATURDAY Dinner at home, a little party of Sophia's in the evening. Sharpe told me that one evening being at Sheridan's house with a large party Tom S. came to him as the night drew late and said in a whisper 'I advise you to secure a wax light to go to bed with,' shewing him at the same time a morsel which he had stolen from a sconce. Sharpe followd his advice and had reason to be thankful for the hint. Tired and sleepy I make a bad night watcher.

13 SUNDAY Amused myself by converting the Tale of the Mysterious Mirror into 'Aunt Margaret's Mirror', designd for Heath's What dye call it.[2] Cadell will not like this but I cannot afford to have my goods thrown back upon my hands. The tale is a good one and is said actually to have happend to Lady Primrose, my great grandmother having attended her sister on the occasion. Dined with Miss Du-mergue. My proofs[3] from Edinburgh reachd to-day and occupied me all the morning.

14 MONDAY Labourd at proofs and got them sent off per Mr. Freeling's cover. So there's an end of the *Chronicles*. James rejoices in the conclusion where there is battle and homicide of all kinds. Always politick to keep a trot for the avenue like the Irish postillions. J. B. always calls to the boys to flog before the carriage gets out of the Inn yard. How we have driven the stage I know not and care not – except with a view to extricating my difficulties. I have lost no time in beginning the second series of *Grandfather's Tales* being determined to write as much as I can even here and deserve by industry the soft pillow I sleep on for the moment.

There is a good scene supposed to have happend between Sam Rogers and a Lady of fashion – the reporter Lord Dudley. Sam enters, takes a stool, creeps close to the lady's side who asks his opinion of the last new poem or novel – In a pathetic voice the spectre replies – 'My opinion? – I like it very much – But the world don't like it – But indeed I begin to think the world wrong in every

---

1. At the former Mrs. Coutts's, where he sat beside a German, Pückler-Muskau. 'Towards the end of dinner he and Sir Francis Burdett told ghost-stories, half-terrible, half-humorous, admirably, one against the other.' *A Regency Visitor*, ed. E. M. Butler, 1957, p. 312.
2. *The Keepsake*.
3. The last proofs of *The Fair Maid of Perth. Letters*, x. 404.

thing – except with regard [to] *you*.' Now Rogers either must have said this somewhere or he has it yet to say. We dined at Lord Melville's.

15 TUESDAY Got the lamentable news[1] that Terry is totally Bankrupt. This is a most unexpected blow though his carelessness about money matters was very great. Old debts it seems. God help the poor fellow. He has been ill advised to go abroad but now returns to stand the storm. Old debts it seems with principal and interest accumulated and all the items which load a falling man. And wife such a good and kind creature, and children. Alack alack. I sought out his solicitor.[2] There are £7000 or more to pay and the only fund his share in the Adelphi Theatre worth £5000 and upwards, and then so fine a chance of independence lost. That comes of not being explicit with his affairs.[3] The theatre was a most flourishing concern. I went down to his solicitors and lookd at the books and since have seen Yates.[4] The ruin is inevitable but I think they will not keep him in prison but let him earn his bread by his very considerable talents. I shall lose the whole or part of £500 which I lent him but that is the least of my concern. I hope the theatre is quite good for guaranteeing certain payments in 1829 and 1830. I judge they are in no danger.

I should have gone to the Club to-day but Sir James Mackintosh had mistaken the day. I was glad of it so staid at home and smoked with Lockhart.

It is written that nothing shall flourish under my shadow – the Ballantynes, Terry, Nelson, Weber, all came to distress.[5] Nature has written on my brow 'Your shade shall be broad but there shall be no protection derived from it to aught your favour.' Sate and smoked

1. In a letter from Terry who had fled to Boulogne and was already regretting it. 11 April 1828, Walpole.
2. 'Mr. Chisholme, No. 36 Lincolns Inn Fields a solicitor of the highest repute for character & ability.' Ibid.
3. Terry had not admitted to his backers (of whom Scott was one) that he was encumbered by old debts incurred before he took on the Adelphi. *Letters*, x. 417.
4. Terry's partner, the actor Frederick Henry Yates (1797–1842).
5. John Ballantyne's publishing house failed; James Ballantyne's printing business fell along with Constable and Scott in the crash of 1826; Nelson and Weber, whom Scott employed as amanuenses at different times, both came to untimely ends, the one in a Poors' Hospital, the other in an asylum.

and grumbled with Lockhart. I brought him to a point though on which I am to touch up S. W. Knighton.[1]

Another vexation. Lord Minto is disposed to quarrel with my tie with Sir William Scott about the contest between Oliver and young Elliot for the collectorship of the cess.[2] This is very illiberal for I had even refused to influence my own friends against Elliot. I will if this be adhered to do him as much harm as I can and I will go down to vote though I should travel day and night.

16 WEDNESDAY We dined at Dr. Young's; saw Captain Parry, a handsome and pleasant man. In the evening at Mrs. Cunliffe where I met sundry old friends – grown older –

17 THURSDAY Made up my gurnal which had fallen something behind. In this phantasmagorical place the objects of the day come and depart like shadows. Made calls: Gave Harper's Memorial[3] to Lord Leveson Gower. Went to Murray where I met a Mr. Jacob a great oeconomist. He is proposing a mode of supporting the poor by compelling them to labour by military force and under a species of military discipline. I see no objection to it, only it will make a rebellion to a certainty and the tribes of Jacob will certainly cut Jacob's throat.

Had an interesting interview with S. W. K. who is leaving the country on a secret Mission. He seems impressed with the

1. Scott duly touched up Sir William Knighton in a letter of the 17th. He was anxious to help the new Ministry led by his friends Wellington and Peel by giving them the support of the *Quarterly*. His idea was that Knighton should help Lockhart to find 'some confidential channel through which he may obtain a hint from time to time what he is to do & what forbear. . . . The whole daily press seems to me to have embraced democratical opinions without one exception. And it is worth while to secure and effectually direct this very important branch of the periodical literature.' *Letters*, x. 421.

2. The contest for the post of Collector of the Cess (i.e., of local taxes) was between Samuel Oliver and Gilbert Eliott. William Oliver, the Sheriff, the father of one of the candidates, had arranged a 'tie' between Scott and Sir William Scott of Ancrum who was in Aberdeen; Lord Minto's indignation arose from the mistaken idea that Scott had also tied with another gentlemen. Oliver, 19 April 1828, Walpole.

3. A protest drawn up by Mr. Harper of Darnick, about the proposed line of a new turnpike road. One purpose of Scott's visit was to use his influence in this matter, and he did so successfully. See the Entry for 24 April 1828.

importance of the facts I stated and refers me to Peele. His communication of the purpose respecting L. is perfectly reasonable and satisfactory. If my journey do no more, thus far has been well done.

Sir Frederick Watson.

Canning's conversion from popular opinions was strangely brought round. While he was studying at the Temple and rather en[ter]taining revolutionary opinions Godwin sent to say that he was coming to breakfast with him to speak on a subject of the highest importance. Canning knew little of him but received his visit and learnd to his astonishment that in expectation of a new order of things the English Jacobins desired to place him, Canning, at the head of their expected Revolution. He was much struck and askd time to think what course he should take – and having thought the matter over he went to Mr. Pitt and made the Antijacobin confession of faith in which he persevered until [his death.] Canning himself mentiond this to Sir W. upon occasion of giving a place in the Charte[r] House of some ten pound a year to Godwin's brother. He could scarce do less for one who had offerd him the dictator's curule chair.

Dined with Rogers with all my own family and met Sharpe, Lord John Russell, Jekyll and others. The conversation flaggd as usual and jokes were fired like minute guns producing an effect not much less melancholy. A wit should always have an atmosphere congenial to him otherwise he will not shine. Went to Lady Davy's where I saw the kind face and heard the no less friendly greeting of Lady Selkirk who introduced all her children to me.

18 FRIDAY Breakfast with Joanna Baillie and found that gifted person extremely well and in the display of all her native knowlege of character and benevolence. She looks more aged however. I would give as much to have a capital picture of her as for any portrait in the world. She gave me a Manuscript play to read upon Witchcraft.[1]

Dined with the Dean of Chester, Dr. Philpot,

> Where all above us was a solemn row
> Of priests and deacons, so were all below.[2]

There were the amiable Bishop of London (Howley), Coplestone whom I remember a first man at Oxford now bishop of Chester[3] and

---

1. For Scott's comments on *Witchcraft* (which he wished her to turn into blank verse) see *Letters*, x.425.
2. Crabbe's 'Tale of the Dumb Orators', ll. 346–7.
3. An error for 'Llandaff'.

Dean of saint Paul's, and other dignities of whom I knew less. It was a very pleasant day – the wiggs against the wits for a guinea in point of conversation. Anne lookd queer and much disposed to laugh at finding herself placed betwixt two prelates.

19 SATURDAY Breakfasted with Sir George Philips. Had his receipt against the blossoms being injured by frost. It consists in watering them plentifully before sunrise. This is like the mode of thawing beef. We had a pleasant morning, much the better that Morritt was with us. He has agreed to go to Hampton court with us tomorrow. Mr. Reynolds calld on me about the drawing of the Laird's Jock;[1] he is assiduous and attentive but a little forward:[2] poor Gillies also calld. Both askd me to dinner but I refused. I do not incline to make what is calld literary acquaintances and as for poor G. it is wild to talk about his giving dinner to others when he can hardly get credit for his own.

Dined with Sir Robert Henry Inglis[3] and met Sir Thomas Ackland my old and kind friend. I was happy to see him. He may be considerd now as the Head of the religious party in the House of Commons, a powerful body which Wilberforce long commanded. It is a difficult situation, for the adaptation of religious motives to earthly policy is apt – among the infinite delusions of the human heart – to be a snare – But I could confide much in Sir T. Ackland's honour and integrity. Bishop Bloomfield of   [4], one of the most learnd prelates of the Church, also dined.

Coming home an Irish coachman drove us into a Cul de Sac near Battersea Bridge. We were obliged to get out in the rain – The people admitted us into their houses where they were having their bit of supper, assisted with lights etc. and to the honour of London neither askd nor expected gratification.

1. Scott had suggested this as a subject for a picture in *The Keepsake* on 11 March 1828. See the Entry for that day.
2. His letters to Scott have more of impudence than wit: 'Owing to a mistake you made in the superscription, I did not receive your highly gratifying letter, until the afternoon of yesterday; indeed, I am inclined to think myself peculiarly lucky in receiving it at all; for unfortunately, I have not sufficient wealth to merit the distinction of giving my name to a street; and the Square most contiguous to my residence, is *Fitzroy*, not *Soho*.' He was sufficiently ill-bred to mention Scott's handwriting: 'As however, my stupidity, or want of eye sight, disable me from exactly decyphering every word, I am occasionally obliged to infer the sense from the context'. 24 February 1828, Walpole.
3. At Battersea Rise.
4. Chester.

I grieve to say poor little Johnie is very ill again. It will not perhaps be unlucky if we are obliged to return, to give Sophia an opportunity of going to Brighton.

20 SUNDAY We went to Walter's quarters in a body and saw Hampton Court with which I was more struck than when I saw it for the first time about 1806. The pictures are not very excellent but they are curious, which is as interesting except to connoisseurs. Two I particularly remarked, of James I and Charles I eating in public. The old part of the Palace built by Wolsey is extremely fine; two handsome halls are still preserved, one the ceiling of which is garnishd at the crossing and combining of the arches with the recurring heads of Henry VIII and Anne Boleyn – great stinginess in Henry for these ornaments must have been put up after Wolsey's fall. He could surely afford a diversity of this species of ornament if any man could. Formerly when the palace was complete a fishing house extended into or rather over the river. We had a good dinner from Walter and wended merrily home. Miss Dumergue was of the party and was well amused.

I had a private and satisfactory interview with Mr Peele.[1]

21 MONDAY Dining is the principal act of the day in London. We took ours at Kensington with Croker. There was Theodore Hooke and other witty men. He looks unhealthy and bloated. There was something, I know not what, awanting to the cheerfulness of the party

> And silence like a heavy cloud
> O'er all the warriors hung.[2]

If the general report of Croker's retiring be accurate it may account for this.

22 TUESDAY Sophia left this to take down poor Johnnie to Brighton. I fear – I fear – but we must hope the best. Anne went with her sister.[3]

Lockhart and I dined with Sotheby where we met a large dining party the orator of which was that extraordinary man Coleridge.

1. On the subject of opening a channel of communication between the government and the editor of the *Quarterly*. See p. 515, note 1.
2. 'Duncan', ll. 99–100. Herd.
3. Anne had to 'send back her tickets for Allmacks for the Caledonian Ball and all the fine affairs she had been asked to & quietly accompany her sister to help to nurse the sick boy'. *Letter*, x. 417.

After eating a hearty [dinner] during which he spoke not a word he began a most learnd harangue on the Samo-thracian misteries – which he considerd as affording the germ of all tales about fairies past, present and to come. He then diverged to Homer whose *Iliad* he considerd as a collection of poems by different authors at different times during a century. There was, he said, the individuality of an age but not of a country. Morritt, a zealous worshipper of the old bard, was incensed at a system which would turn him into a polytheist, gave battle with keenness and was joind by Sotheby our host. Mr. Coleridge behaved with the utmost complaisance and temper but relaxd not from his exertions. 'Zounds I was never so bethumped with words.'[1] Morritt's impatience must have cost him an extra sixpence worth of snuff.

We were to Lady Davy's in the evening where there was a fashionable party.

23 WEDNESDAY Dined at Lady Davy's with Lord and Lady Lansdowne an[d] several other fashionable folks – my keys were sent to Bramah's with my desk[2] so I have not had the means of putting down matters regularly for several days. But who cares for the whipd cream of London society? Our poor little Johnie is extremely ill and his mother has taken him down to Brighton – my fears have been uniform for this engaging child – we are in God's hands. But the comfortable and happy object of my journey is ended – Seged Emperor of Ethiopia was right after all.[3]

24 THURSDAY Spent the day in rectifying a road bill which drew a turnpike road through all the Darnickers' cottages and a good field of my own. I got it put to writes.[4] I was in some apprehension of being o[b]liged to address the Committee. I did not fear them for I suppose they are no wiser or better in their capacity of legislators than I find them every day at dinner. But I feard for my Reputation. They would

1. *King John*, ii. 1.
2. A bill from Bramah's, sent on 4 October 1831, is for 'Thoroughly cleaning and repairing a rosewood writing Desk, relining flaps with blue morrocco new portfolio in lid, & neat Gilt border.' Walpole.
3. Seged resolved to devote ten days to happiness, but was left instead 'to contemplate the innumerable casualties which lie in ambush on every side to intercept the happiness of man'. He wrote his story 'that no man hereafter may presume to say, "This day shall be a day of happiness." ' Dr. Johnson's *Rambler*, nos. 204–5.
4. A slip for 'rights'.

have expected something better than the occasion demanded or the individual could produce and there would have been a failure.

25 FRIDAY Threatend to be carried down to vote at the Election of a Collector of the Cess. Resolvd if I did go to carry my son with me which made me a double vote. Had some disagreeable correspondence about this with Lord Minto and the sheriff.[1]

We had one or two persons at home in great wretchedness to dinner. Lockhart's looks shewd the misery he felt – I was not able to make any fight and the evening went off as heavily as any I ever spent in the course of my life.

Finishd my turnpike business by getting the exceptionable clause omitted, which will be good news to Darnick. Put all the 'Mirror' in proof and corrected it. This is the contribution (part of it) to Mr. Reynolds' and Heath's *Keepsake*. I put my copies of the *Provincial Antiquities*[2] into Heath's hands to dispose of; they are twenty proofs and one copy plain, worth I should think about £100 – a fellow has offerd £80.

We dined at Richardson's with the two chief Barons of England and Scotland[3] – Odd enough the one being a Scottsman and the latter an Englishman – far the pleasantest day we have heard. I suppose I am partial but I think the lawyers beat the Bishops and the bishops beat the witts.

26 SATURDAY This morning I went to meet a remarkable man, Mr. Boyd of the House of Boyd Benfield and Company[4] which broke for a very large sum at the beginning of the war. Benfield went to the devil I believe. Boyd, a man of a very different stamp, went over to Paris to look after some large claims which his house had over the French Government. They were such as it seems they could not disavow however they might be disposed to do so. But they used every effort by foul means and fair to induce Mr. Boyd to depart. He was reduced to poverty, he was thrown into prison, and the most flattering prospects were on the other hand held out to him if he would compromise his claims. His answer was uniform. It was the property he said of his crers, and he would die ere he resignd it. His distresses were so great that a subscription was made among his Scottish friends to which I was a contributor through the request of

---

1. The Sheriff of Roxburghshire, William Oliver.
2. Scott's *Provincial Antiquities of Scotland* appeared between 1819 and 1826.
3. The Rt. Hon. Sir William Alexander and Sir Samuel Shepherd.
4. Walter Boyd (?1754–1837), M. P. for Lymington.

poor Will Erskine. After the peace of Paris the money was restored and, faithful to the last, Boyd laid the whole at his creditors' disposal, stating at the same time that he was pennyless unless they consented to allow him a moderate sum in name of per Centage in consideration of twenty years of danger, poverty and im[prisonment], all of which evils he might have escaped by surrendering their rights to the money. Will it be believed that a muck-worm was base enough to refuse his consent to this deduction, alleging he had promised to his father on his death bed never to compromise this debt? The wretch however was overpowerd by the execrations of all around him and concured with others in setting apart for Mr. Boyd a sum of £40,000 or £50,000 out of half a million of money. This is a man to whom statues should be erected and pilgrims should go to see him. He is good lookin[g] but old and infirm. Bright dark eyes and eyebrows contrast with his snowy hair and all his features mark vigour of principle and resolution.

My Morritt dined with us and we did as well as in the circumstances could be expected.

Released from the alarm of being summond down to the Election by a civil letter from Lord Minto.[1] I am glad both of the release and of the manner. I hate civil war amongst neighbours.

27 SUNDAY Breakfasted this day with Charles Dumergue on a *poulet à la tartare* and saw all his family, specially my godson. Calld on Lady Stafford and others and dined at Croker's in the Admiralty with the Duke of Wellington, Huskisson, Wilmot Horton and others, outs and inns – No politics of course and every man disguising serious thoughts with a light brow. The Duke alone seemd open though not letting out a word. He is one of the few whose lips are worth watching. I heard him say to-day that the best troops would run now and then. He thought nothing of men running, he said, providing they came back again. In war he had always his reserves. Poor Terry[2] was here when I returnd. He seems to see his matters in a delusive light.

28 MONDAY An attack this day or yesterday from poor Gillies boring me hard to apply to Menzies of Pitfoddels to entreat him to lend him money. I could not get him to understand that I was decidedly averse

1. 'I shall take care that our friends know the whole of this confusion as to ties to have arisen out of misunderstanding.' 25 April 1828, Walpole.
2. Scott had encouraged him to return and face his creditors. *Letters*, x. 408.

to write to another Gentleman with whom I was hardly acquainted to do that which I would not do myself.

Tom Campbell is in miserable distress – his son insane, his wife on the point of becoming so.

I nunc et versus tecum meditare canoros.[1]

We, i.e. Charles and I, dined at Sir Francis Freeling's with Colonel Harrison of the Board of Green Cloth, Dr. [Maltby] of Lincoln's Inn and other pleasant people. Doctor Dibdin too and Utterson, all old Roxburghe men. Pleasant party were it not for a bad cold which makes me bark like a dog.

29 TUESDAY Anne and Lockhart are off with the children this morning at seven and Charles and I left behind, and this is the promised meeting of my household. I went to Dr. Gilly's to-day to breakfast; met Sir Thomas Ackland who is the youngest man of his age I ever saw. I was so much annoyd with cough that on returning I took to my bed and had a siesta, to my considerable refreshment. Dr. Fergusson calld and advised caution in eating and drinking which I will attend to.

Dined accordingly. Duke of Sussex had cold and did not come. A Mr. or Dr. Pettigrewe[2] made me speeches on his account and invited me to see his Royal Highnesse's Library which I am told is a fine one. Sir Peter Laurie, late sheriff and in nomination to be Lord Mayor[3] of Lond beset me close and askd more questions than would have been thought warrantable at the west end of the Town. I learned from him two things concerning the Jews – First that they never even those of the lowest class get themselves drunk – Secondly that after marriage their wives are strictly correct in their conduct. I may add that to regale a Jew you must treat him with fish of different sorts. I bought some tincture of squills and antimonial wine, a tea spoonful of which will carry of[f] the botheration. I felt as if my throat had been flayed. I took a good dose of Antimonial wine mixd with squills, slept sound and waked well and hearty.

30 WEDNESDAY We had Mr. Adolphus and his father the celebrated lawyer to breakfast and I was greatly delighted with the information of

1. *deditary* is a slip for *meditare*. 'Go now and meditate to yourself melodious verses.' Horace's *Epistles*, ii. 2. 76.
2. Thomas Joseph Pettigrew (1791–1865), surgeon to the Duke of Sussex, who also employed him to catalogue the library at Kensington Palace.
3. A Haddington man who had made his fortune supplying saddles to the Indian Army. He was an alderman at this time, and became Lord Mayor in 1832.

the latter – A barrister of extended practice if he has any talents at all is the best companion in the world.

I went afterwards to Miss Nicolson and obtaind the full facts concerning the business of Owen and Morgan which seem nearly sufficient to recover that money for my children.[1]

Dined with Lord Alvanley and a fashionable party, Lord Fitzroy Somerset, Marquis and Marchss of Worcester etc. Lord Alvanley's wit made the party very pleasant as well as the kind reception of my friends the Misses Arden.

MAY

1 THURSDAY Breakfasted with Lord and Lady Leveson Gower and enjoyd the splendid treat of hearing Mrs. Arkwright sing her own music which is of the highest order – no forced vagaries of the voice, no caprices of tone, but all telling upon and increasing the feeling the words require.[2] This is

> Marrying Music to immortal verse.[3]

Most people place them on separate maintenance.

I met the Roxburghe Club and settled to dine with them on 15 current. Lord Spencer in the chair. We voted Lord Clive a member.

I dined to-day at Mr. Burney's on Clapham Common, a friend of Hugh Scott's, where I met Hugh and his wife.[4]

2 FRIDAY I breakfasted with a Mr. Belt, Great Ormond street, a lawyer, and narrowly escaped Mr. Irving the celebrated preacher.[5] The two ladies of the House seemd devoted to his opinions and quoted him at every word. Mr. Belt himself made some apologies for the Millennium. He is a smart little antiquary who thinks he ought to have been a man of letters and that his genius has been misdirected in turning towards the Law. I endeavour to combat this idea which his

1. The money in Chancery which had been due to Lady Scott. See the Entry for 22 March 1826 and note.
2. It was on this occasion that Scott whispered to Lockhart at the close of a song from his own novel *The Pirate*, 'Capital words – whose are they? Byron's I suppose, but I don't remember them.' *Life*, ix. 236.
3. Milton's *L'Allegro*, l. 137.
4. Scott had missed seeing them at Draycott on the journey to London. See the Entry for 6 April 1828.
5. Scott met him the following year, however. See the Entry for 23 May 1829.

handsome house and fine family should have checkd. Compare his dwelling – his comforts – with poor Tom Campbell's.[1]

I calld on Stephen Barber, went to the Bank and sold some stock belonging to poor Lady Scott which produced

by Barber's certificate ———————————————	£246.11. 4
Deduced expenses incurrd in Letters of Administration	13.19.10
	£232.11. 6

This is divisible amongst my four children
Also received 5½ years dividends due by the Bank. This
is my own as I had the life rent of this money	£21.12.11
Have given it to Mr. Chisholme for poor Terry's use—	21.12.11

I dined with the Literary Society, always rather heavy work, though some excellent men were there. I saw for the first time Arch deacon Nares, long conductor of the *British Critic*, a gentlemanlike and pleasing man. Sir Henry Robert Inglis presided.

3 SATURDAY Breakfasted at my old friend Gally Knight with whom in former days I used to make little parties to see poor Monk Lewis. After breakfast I drove to Lee and Kennedy's and commissiond seeds and flowers for about £10 including some specimens of the corsican and other pines. Their collection is very splendid but wants I think the neatness that I would <not> have expected in the first nursery garden in or near London. The essentials were admirably cared for. I saw one specimen of the Norfolk island pine, the only one young Lee said which has been reard from all the seed that was sent home. It is not treated conformably to its dignity for they cut the top off every year to prevent its growing out at the top of the conservatory. Sure it were worth while to raise the house alangst with the plant.

Lookd in at Murray's – wrote some letters etc. and walkd home with the Dean of Chester[2] who saw me to my own door. I had but a few minutes to dress and go to the Royal Academy to which I am attachd in capacity of Antiquities.[3] I was too late to see the paintings, but in perfect time to sit half an hour waiting for dinner as the President Sir Thos. Lawrence expected a prince of the blood[4] – He

1. See the Entry for 28 April 1828.
2. Dr. Phillpotts, who had visited Abbotsford the previous summer.
3. He had been their Professor of Antiquities for the past year. See the Entry for 1 May 1827.
4. The Duke of Clarence, 'who did not come, and never intended to come'. *Croker Papers*, i. 418.

came not but there [were] enough of grandees beside. Sir Thomas Lawrence did this very well and compliments flew about like sugar plums at an Italian carnival. I had my share and pleaded them immunities of a sinecure for declining to answer.[1]

After the dinner I went to Mrs. Scott of Harden to see and be seen by her nieces the Herbert ladies. I don't know how their part of the entertainment turnd out but I saw two or three pretty girls.

This day I paid Charles £55 to himself and the same sum to Lockhart so the money received from the Stocks stands thus

To the sum divisible——— £222.11.6			£222.11.6
To Lockhart's share paid to Charles	£55. 0.0		
To Charles' share do.	55		
	———		
	110. 0.0		
Balance in my hands £112.11.6			

4 SUNDAY I breakfasted this morning with Sir Coutts Trotter and had some Scottish talk. Visited Cowper after breakfast who kindly undertook to make my inquiries in Lyons.[2] I was at home afterward for three hours but too much tired to do the least right thing. The distances in London are so great that no exertion excepting those which a bird might make can contend with them. You return weary and exhausted fitter for a Siesta than any thing else. In the evening I dined with Mr. Peel, a great cabinet affair and too dignified to be very amusing though the Landlord and the pretty Landlady did all to make it easy.

5 MONDAY Breakfasted with Haydon and sate for my head.[3] I hope this artist is on his legs again: the King has given him a lift by buying

1. Croker says that Scott sat beside Herries, Davies Gilbert and the Speaker, and opposite Rogers, Croker, Sir A. Hume and Lords Farnborough and Cawdor. 'We had a good deal of talk and laugh in our circle.' Lawrence proposed Scott's health, and he in reply 'made a neat short speech'. *Croker Papers*, i., 418.
2. Fenimore Cooper succeeded in tracing the register entry of Lady Scott's baptism, required to help prove a title to the money in Chancery. *Letters*, x. 435 and 437.
3. Scott had called two days before and promised to return to have a sketch made of his head. 'Sir Walter came to breakfast according to promise – Talfourd, Eastlake, & a young Surgeon met him, and a very pleasant morning we had. He sat to me afterwards for an hour and ½, and a delightful sitting it was.' Haydon's *Diary*, iii. 273-4.

his clever picture of the election in the Fleet prison,[1] to which he is adding a second part representing the chairing of the Member at the moment when it was interrupted by the entry of the guards. Haydon was once a great admirer and companion of the champions of the Cockney School and is now disposed to renounce them and their opinions. To this kind of conversation I did not give much way. A painter should have nothing to do with politics. He is certainly a clever fellow but somewhat too enthusiastic which distress seems to have cured in some degree. His wife, a pretty woman, lookd happy to see me and that is something. Yet it was very little I could do to help them upon.

Dined at Lord Bathurst's in company with the Duke.[2] There are better accounts of Johnie. But alas –

6 TUESDAY Had a long and satisfactory discussion with Miss Nicolson. But I cannot get my hand upon Heath, Mrs. Carpenter's brother in law, with whom on the part of Mrs. Carpenter I wish to go hand in hand in this business.[3] Walter and Jane Dined with me in regent's park and we had a comfortable evening. They left town at eight o'clock for Hampton Court.

7 WEDNESDAY Breakfasted with Lord Francis Leveson Gower and again enjoyd the great pleasure of meeting Mrs. Arkwright and hearing her sing. She is I understand quite a heaven-born genius having scarce skill enough in music to write down the tunes she composes. I can easily believe this. There is a pedantry among great musicians that deprives their performances of much that is graceful and beautiful. It is the same in the other fine arts where fashion always preserves[4] cant and slang to nature and simplicity.

Dined at Mr. Watson Taylor's where plate etc. shone in great and somewhat ostentatious quantity. C. was there and very decisive and overbearing to a great degree.[5] Strange so clever a fellow should let his wit overrun his judgement. In genral the English understand conversation well. There is that ready deference for the claims of every one who wishes to speak time about and it is seldom now a days that '*A la stoccata*' carries it away thus.[6]

1. Haydon had recently been imprisoned for debt.
2. The Duke of Wellington.
3. Of the money in Chancery.
4. A slip for 'prefers'.
5. Croker. Douglas quotes the Duke of Wellington in Lord Mahon's *Notes of Conversations with Wellington* (1888), p. 100: 'He had observed on several occasions that Sir Walter was talked down by Croker and Bankes! who forgot that we might have them every day.'
6. *Romeo and Juliet*, iii. 1.

I should have gone to the Duchess of Northumberland's to hear musick to-night but I felt completely faggd and betook myself home to bed.

I learnd a curious thing from Emily Lady Londonderry, namely that in feeding all animals with your hand you should never wear a glove which always affronts them. She is good authority for this peculiarity.

8 THURSDAY Breakfasted at Somerset House with Davies Gilbert the new Praeses of the royal society.[1] Tea, coffee and bread and butter, which is poor work; certainly a slice of ham, a plate of shrimps, some broild fish or a mutton chop would have been becoming so learnd a body. I was most kindly received however by Mr. D. Gilbert and a number of the members. I saw Sir John Sebright[2] – a singular personage – he told me his uniform plan was to support ministers but he always found himself voting in opposition. I told him his deference to ministers was like that of the Frenchman to the enemy who being at his mercy askd for his life – 'Any thing in my power excepting that, Sir' said Monsr – Sir John has made progress in teaching animals without severity or beating. I should have liked to hear him on this topic.

I went to the city to see Mr. Heath, Mrs. Carpenter's brother in law, to apprize him how the Chancery business stood but missd him. Calld at Northumberland House and saw the Duke.[3] According to his report I lost much by not hearing the two rival nightingales Sontagg and Pasta last night but I care not for it. Calld on Miss Dumergue who kindly offers her *affidavit* in the Chancery case.

Met Sir W. K.[4] returnd from the continent. He gives me to understand I will be commanded for Sunday.[5] Sir W. K. askd me to sit for him to Northcote[6] and to meet him there at one tomorrow. I cannot refuse this but it is [a] great bore.

Dined with Mrs. Alexander of Ballochmyle, Lord and Lady Meath who were kind to us in Ireland, and a Scottish party – pleasant from

1. Davies Gilbert (1769–1839) was M. P. for Bodmin. He encouraged scientists and engineers, and himself wrote on Cornish history and literature. He was president of the Royal Society from 1827 to 1830.
2. M. P. for Herefordshire.
3. The Duke of Northumberland.
4. Sir William Knighton.
5. The royal command prevented Scott from visiting Walter at Hampton Court with Rogers and Fenimore Cooper as he had intended. *Letters*, x. 418 and 420. Instead he takes Rogers, Moore, and Wordsworth a fortnight later.
6. James Northcote, like Knighton, a Devon man.

hearing the broad acents and honest thoughts of my native land. A large party in the evening. A gentleman came up to me and askd 'if I [had] seen the *Casket*,[1] a curious work – the most beautiful, the most highly ornamented – and this the Editor or Editress – a female so interesting – Might he ask a very great favour' – and out he pulld a piece of this pic-nics – I was really angry – and said for a subscription he might command me, for a contribution No – that I had given to a great many of these things last year and finding the labour occupied some considerable portion of my time I had done a considerable article for a single collection this year, taken a valuable consideration for it and engaged not to support any other. This may be misrepresented but I care not – Suppose this patron of the muses gives five guineas to his distressd lady, he will think he does a great [deal] yet takes fifty from me with the calmest air in the world, for the communication is worth that if it be worth any thing. There is no equality in the proposal.

I saw to-day at Northumberland House Bridges the jeweller having and holding a George richly ornamented with diamonds, being that which Queen Anne gave to the Duke of Marlborough which his present representative paw[ne]d or sold and which the present King bought and presented to the duke of Wellington. His Grace seemd to think this interesting jewel was one of two which had been preserved since the first institution of that [order] – that, from the form and taste, I greatly doubt. Mr. Bridges put it again into his coat pocket and walkd through the street with £10,000 in his pocket. I wonder he is not hustled and robbd. I have sometimes envied rich citizens but it was a mean and erroneous feeling. This man B. who I suppose must be as rich as a Jew had a shabbly look in the D's presence, and though the latter was perfectly affable he plaid just a better sort of pedlar. Better be a poor gentleman after all.

9 FRIDAY   Grounds of Foote's farce of the *Cozeners*.[2] Lady L. Stuart – A certain Mrs. Phipps audaciously set up in fashionable quarter of London as a person through whose influence properly propitiated fine suits and situations of importance might certainly be obtaind, always for a consideration. She cheated many people and maintaind the trick for many months. One trick was to get the equipage of Lord North and other persons of importance to halt before her door as if their owners were within. With respect to most of them this was

1. *The Casket*, a miscellany of unpublished poems, many of them by poets of high repute, was edited by Mrs. Blencoe and published by Murray in 1828.
2. 1774.

effected by bribing the drivers – But a gentleman who watchd her closely observed that Charles J. Fox actually left his carriage and went into the house and this more than once. He was then it must be noticed in the ministry. When Mrs. Phipps was blown up this circumstance was recollected as deserving explanation, which Fox readily gave at Brooks and elsewhere. It seems Mrs. Phipps had the art to persuade him that she had the disposal of what was then calld a *hyæna*, that is an heiress – an immense Jamaica Heiress in whom she was willing to give or sell her interest to Charles Fox. Without having perfect confidence in the obliging proposer the great statesman though[t] the thing worth looking after and became so earnest on it that Mrs. Phipps was desirous to back out of it for fear of discovery. With this view she made confession one fine morning with many professions of the deepest feelings – that the hyæna had proved a frail monster and given birth to a girl or boy, no matter which – Even this did not make Charles quit chase of the hyæna. He intimated that if the cash was plenty and certain the circumstance might be overlookd. Mrs. Phipps had nothing for it but to double the disgusting dose – 'The poor child' she said 'was unfortunately of a mixd colour somewhat tinged with the blood of Africa – no doubt Mr. Fox was himself very dark and the circumstance might not draw attention' etc. etc. This singular anecdote was touchd upon by Foote and is the cause of introducing the negress into the *Cozeners* though no express allusion to Charles Fox was admitted. Lady L. tells me that in her youth the laugh was universal so soon as the black woman appeard. It is one of the numerous hits that will be lost to posterity. Jack Fuller, celebrated for his attempt on the speaker's wig, told me he was editing Foote but I think he has hardly tact enough. He told me Colman was to be his assistant.

Went down in the morning to Montagu House where I found the Duke[1] going out to suffer a recovery[2] – I had some fancy to see the ceremony but more to get my breakfast which I took at a coffee House at Charing Cross.

I sate to Northcote – who is to introduce himself in the same piece in the act of painting me like some pictures of the Venetian School. The artist is an old man low in stature and bent with years, fourscore at least. But the eye is quick and the countenance noble. A pleasant companion, familiar with recollections of Sir Joshua, Samuel Johnson, Burke, Goldsmith etc. His account of the last confirms all that we have heard of his oddities.

1. The Duke of Buccleuch.
2. 'A fictitious suit for the purpose of getting rid of an entail. Abolished by the Fines and Recoveries Act (1833).' Tait.

Dined with Mr. Arbuthnot where met Duke of Rutland, Lord and Lady Londonderry etc. etc. Went to hear Mrs. Arkwright at Lady Charlotte Greville's – Lockhart came home to-day.[1]

10 SATURDAY Another long sitting to the old wizzard Northcote. He really resembles an animated mummy. He has alterd my ideas of Sir Joshua Reynolds who from the expressions used by Goldsmith, Johnson, and others I used to think an amiable and benevolent character. But though not void of generosity he was cold, unfeeling and indifferent to his family. So much so that his sister Miss Reynolds after expressing her wonder at the general acceptance which Sir Joshua met with in society concluded with – 'For me, I only see in him a dark gloomy tyrant.' I own this view of his character hurt me by depriving me of a pleasing vision of the highest talents united with the kindest temper. But Northcote says his disagreeable points were rather negative than positive – more a want of feeling than any desire to hurt or tyrannize. They arose from his exclusive attachment to art.

Dined with a pleasant party at Lord Gower's – Lady Gower is a beautiful woman and extremely courteous. Mrs. Arkwright was of the party. I am getting well acquainted with [her] and think I can see a great deal of sense mixt with her accomplishment.

11 SUNDAY Breakfasted with Dr. Maltby, Preacher in Lincoln's Inn. He was to have been the next Bishop if the Whigs had held their ground. His person, manners and attainments would have suited the lawn sleeves well. I heard service in the chapel which is a very handsome place of worship. It is upstairs, which seems extraordinary, and the space beneath forms cloisters in which the ancient Benchers of the society of Lincoln's Inn are interd. I met my old friend Sir William Grant and had some conversation with him. Dr. Maltby gave us a good sermon upon the introduction of the Gospel. There was only one monument in the chaplet,[2] being an handsome tablet to the memory of Perceval. The circumstance that it was the only monument in the chapel of a society which had produced so many men of talents and distinction was striking – it was a tribute due to the suddenness of his strange catastrophe. There is nothing very particular in the hall of Lincoln's Inn nor its parlour which are like those of a college. Indeed the whole establishment has a monastic look.

Sate to Northcote, who only requires *deo gratias* another sitting. Dind with his Majesty in a very private party, five or six only being

1. From Brighton.
2. A slip for 'chapel'.

present. I was received most kindly as usual. It is impossible to conceive a more friendly manner than his Majesty used towards me.[1] I spoke to S. W. K.[2] about the dedication of the collected works and he says it will be highly well taken.[3]

I went after the party broke up to Mrs. Scott of Harden where I made acquaintance with her beautiful kinswom[an] Lady Sarah Ponsonby whose countenance is really seraphic and totally devoid of affectation.

12 MONDAY Old George II was as is well known extremely passionate. On these occasions his small stock of English totally faild him and he used to express his indignation in the following form 'G—d—n me who I am? Got d—n you who you be?' Lockhart and I visited a Mrs. Quillinan[4] with whom Wordsworth and his wife have pitchd their tent. I was glad to see my old friend whose conversation has so much that is fresh and manly in it. I do not at all acquiesce in his system of poetry and I think he has injured his own fame by adhering to it. But a better or more sensible man I do not know than W. W.

Afterwards Lockhart and [I] calld on Miss Nicolson and from thence I wanderd down into that immense hash of a city to see Heath[5] and fortunately caught hold on him. All this made me too late for Northcote, who was placable however.

Dined at Sir John Shelley's *à petit couvert* – Here were the Duke of Wellington, Duke of Rutland and only one or two more, particularly Mr. and Mrs. Arbuthnot. The evening was very pleasant and did not break up till 12 at night.

13 TUESDAY Breakfasted with Sir George Philips – there was Sidney Smith, full of fun and spirits, and his daughter who is a good humourd agreeable girl. We had a pleasant breakfast party.

The Catholics have carried their question[6] which I suppose will be thrown out in the Lords. I think they had better concede this oft disputed point and dissolved the league which binds so many people in opposition to government. It is a matter of great consequence that

1. The passage about the King is written with unusual care: Scott deleted 'most likely' before 'received'; 'kinder' before 'more friendly', and 'possesses towards' before 'used towards'.
2. Sir William Knighton.
3. The Magnum Opus was dedicated to George IV.
4. The mother of Edward Quillinan who later married Dora Wordsworth. They lived at 12 Bryanston Street, Portland Square.
5. About Lady Scott's money in Chancery.
6. For the Catholic Question, see Appendix D, p. 825.

men should not acquire the habit of opposing. No earthly advantage would arise to Ireland from ceding what is retaind where so much has been already yielded up. Indeed the Catholic gentry do not pretend that the granting the immunities they require would tranquilize the country but only that it would remove from men of honour all pretex for countenancing them. This is on the principle of the Solicitor of the unhappy Rajah Nundcomar who after extorting as much money as he could under pretence of bribing persons to procure his pardon, facilitate his escape etc., found himself pressd by his victim for a final answer. 'The preparations of death are ready' said the Rajah. 'I fear notwithstanding all you have told me their intention is to take my life.' 'By G—' replied the trusty Solicitor 'if they do I will never forgive them' – so if there are further disturbances after the Catholic claims are granted I suppose those by whom they are now advocated will never forgive their friends the Pats and that will be all John Bull will get for it. I dined with Lady Stafford for whom I have much regard. I recollect her ever since she stood at her aunt Lady Glenorchie's window in George's Square reviewing her regiment of Sutherland giants. She was as she ever is most attentive and kind.

14 WEDNESDAY I carried Lockhart to Lady Francis Gower to hear Mrs. Arkwright sing and I think he admired her as much as his nature permits him to love anything musical, for he certainly is not quickly moved by concord of sweet sounds[1] – I do not understand them better than him but the *voce del petto* always affects me and Mrs. A. has it in perfection. I have received as much pleasure from that lady's musick as sound could ever give me. Lockhart goes off for Brighton.[2]

I had a round of men in office. I waited on the Duke[3] at Downing Street and I think put L.[4] right there if he will look to himself.[5] But I can only *tee* the ball; he must strike the blow with the golf club himself. I saw Mr. Planta and he promises to look after Harper's business[6] favourably. Good gracious what a solicitor we are grown.

Dined with Lady Davy, a pleasant party but I was out of spirits, I think partly on Johnie's account partly from fatigue. There was Will He[n]ry Littleton amongst others – much of his oddity has rubbd off

1. *Merchant of Venice*, v. 1.
2. To rejoin Sophia and the children.
3. The Duke of Wellington.
4. Lockhart.
5. Lockhart tried, but was not admitted to the Duke, who told him, Lockhart complains, to 'write what I wish to communicate'. 18 June 1828, Walpole.
6. The question of the turnpike road through Darnick referred to on 17 and 24 April 1828.

and he is an honourd courtly gentleman with a great deal of wit and not one of the fine people who <do not> perplex you by shutting their mouths if you begin to speak. I never fear quizzing so am not afraid of this species of lying in wait. Lord have mercy on me if I were.

15 THURSDAY Dined at the Roxburgh Club. Lord Spencer presided but had a cold which limited his exertions. Lord Clive, beside whom I sate, was deaf though intelligent and goodhumourd, the Duke of Devonshire was still deafer. There were many little chirupping men who might have talkd but went into committee. There was little general conversation. I should have mentiond that I breakfasted with kind good Mrs. Hughes and met the Bishop of Llandaff – strongly intelligent – I do not understand his politicks about the Catholic question. He seems disposed to concede, yet is Toryissimus – perhaps they wish the question ended but the personal opinions of the Sovereign are too much interested to permit them to quit it.

In the midst of all this racket I have got Miss Jane Nicolson's affidavit respecting the money in chancery.[1] If I had done nothing else in this voyage it would have been worth taking.

16 FRIDAY Breakfasted with Mr. Reynolds, a miscellaneous party. Wordsworth right wellcome unto me was there. I had also a sight of Godwin the philosopher, grown old and thin – of Douglas Kinnaird whom I askd about Byron's statue,[2] which is going forward – of Luttrell and others whom I knew not. Went from breakfast down to Doctors Commons and consulted Mr. Slade about the chancery suit, then to Mr. Handley and reported progress.

I staid an instant at Pickering's, a young publisher, and bought some dramatic reprints. I love them very much but I would [not] advise a young man to undertake them. They are of course dear and as they have not the dignity of scarcity the bibliomaniacs pass them bye as if they were plated candlesticks. They may hold as good a light for all that as if they were real silver and therefore I buy them when I

1. Not without considerable trouble, however. A fortnight before, he wrote to Lockhart: 'I am getting Miss Nicolsons affidavit made and lodged in Chancery while she is in the humour & has the power of making it. I trust to get it finishd in the course of next week but I dare not quit town till it is finishd.' *Letters*, x. 413.

2. Scott had been asked by Hobhouse to be 'one of the members of the proposed committee' when the scheme was mooted in January 1826 (Hobhouse, 19 January 1826, Walpole), and he subscribed £25 to the memorial in June 1828. *Letters*, x. 433. The statue, which was intended for Westminster Abbey, was eventually erected in Trinity College Library, Cambridge.

can light on them. But here I am spending money when I have more need to make it. On Monday 26 it shall be Northward Ho!

Dined at Lady Georgiana and Mr. Agar Ellis. There were Lord and Lady Stafford there and others to whom I am sincerely attachd.

17 SATURDAY A day of busy idleness. Richardson came and breakfasted with me like a good fellow. Then I went to Mr. Chantrey and sate for an hour to finish the bust.[1] Thereafter about 12 o'clock I went to breakfast the second at Lady Shelley's where there was a great morning party. A young lady beggd a lock of my hair which was not worth refusing.[2] I stipulated for a kiss which I was permitted to take. From this I went to the Duke of Wellington who gave me some hints or rather details.[3] Afterwards I drove out to Chiswick where I had never been before. A numerous and gay party were assembled to walk and enjoy the beauties of that Palladian charm [and] made the place and highly ornamented gardens belonging to it resemble a picture of Watteau. There is some affectation in the picture but in the ensemble the original lookd very well. The Duke of Devonshire received every one with the best possible manners. The scene was dignified by the presence of an immense elephant who under charge of a groom wanderd up and down giving an air of Asiatick pageantry to the entertainment. I was never before sensible of the dignity which largeness of size and freedom of movement give to this otherwise very ugly animal. As I was to dine at Holland House I did not partake in the magnificent repast which was offerd to us and took myself off about five o'clock. I contrived to make a demi-toilette at Holland House rather than drive all the way to London. Rogers came to dinner which was very entertaining. The Duke of Manchester was there whom I remember having seen long ago. He had left a part of his brain in Jamaica by a terrible fracture yet notwithstanding

1. This was Chantrey's second bust of Scott. The original, done in 1820, had remained until now in the sculptor's possession. 'In the year 1828,' wrote Chantrey many years later, 'I proposed to the Poet to present the original marble as an Heirloom to Abbotsford, on condition that he would allow me sittings sufficient to finish another marble from the life for my own studio.' *Centenary Catalogue*, p. 48. Scott duly records the arrival of the original in the Entry for 2 July 1828.

2. 'When most of the people had gone, my daughter Fanny stole up to Walter Scott, and, while the great man was intent on his conversation, she cut off a lock of his hair!' *Lady Shelley's Diary*, ii. 314.

3. Probably about how the *Quarterly* could best serve the Government. See p. 515, note 1, and *Letters passim*.

accident and the bad climate was still a fine looking man. Lady Holland pressd me to stay all night which I did accordingly.

18 SUNDAY The freshness of the air, the singing of the birds, the beautiful aspect of nature, the size of the venerable trees, gave me all a delightful feeling this morning. It seemd there was pleasure even in living and breathing without any thing else. We (i.e. is Rogers and I) wanderd into a green lane borderd with fine trees which might have been twenty miles from a town. It will be a great pity when this ancient house must come down and give way to brick works and brick houses. It is not that Holland House is fine as a building; on the contrary it has a tumbledown look and although decorated with the bastard Gothick of James Ist's time the front is heavy. But it resembles many respectable matrons who having been absolutely ugly during youth acquire by age an air of dignity. But one is chiefly affected by the air of deep seclusion which is spread around the domain. I calld on Mr. Peele[1] as I returnd home and after that on Lord Melville. The latter undertook for Allan Cunningham's son's cadetship[2] for which I am right glad.

Dined at Mr. and Lady Sarah Ponsonby's who calld on us last year at abbotsford.[3] The party was very pleasant, having Lord and Lady Gower, whom I like, Mr. and Lady Georgiana Ellis and other persons of distinction. Saw Wordsworth too and learnd that Tom Moore was come to town.

19 MONDAY A morning of business – Breakfasted with Dumergue and one or two friends – then went into the city – Calld on Marshal and Simpkin[4] and heard a favourable report of the sale of the *Chronicles*.[5] Thence to Doctors Commons and then to Pentonville where I trust I have arranged the evidence as well as the case matter[6] will permit. It only hitches upon the death of Jean Charpentier which may be proved by a journey to France.

1. Also about the *Quarterly* and the Government. In Lockhart's absence in Brighton he had opened a letter to him from Peel, and now called at half-past one to 'carry Lockhart any commands with which you may please to entrust me'. 17 May 1828, Disc. i. 215.
2. See the Entry for 23 May 1828 and note.
3. See the Entry for 13 October 1827.
4. Simkin and Marshall, booksellers in Stationers Court, St. Paul's, Cadell's London associates.
5. That is, of *The Fair Maid of Perth*.
6. 'Case' is the last word on one page and 'matter' the first on the next. The case is of course the money in chancery.

Dined by command with the Duchess of Kent. I was very kindly recognised by Prince Leopold. I was presented to the little Princess Victoria, I hope they will change her name, the heir apparent to the crown as things now stand.[1] How strange that so large and fine a family as that of his late Majesty should have died off and decayd into old age with so few descendants. Prince George of Cumberland is they say a fine boy about nine years old – a bit of a pickle, swears and romps like a brat that has been bred in a barrack yard. This little lady is educated with much care and watchd so closely by the Duchess and the principal governess that no busy maid has a moment to whisper 'You are heir of England' – I suspect if we could dissect the little head we should find that some pigeon or other bird of the air had carried the matter. She is fair like the royal family but does not look as if she would be pretty. The Duchess herself is very pleasing and affable in her manners. I sate by Mr. Spring Rice, a very agreeable man. He is a great leader among the pro-Catholics. I saw also Charles Wynn and his lady, and the evening, for a court-evening, went agreeable off.

I am commanded for two days by Prince Leopold but will send excuses.

20 TUESDAY I set out for Brighton this morning in a light coach which performd the journey in six hours – otherwise the journey was uncomfortable. Three women the very specimens of womankind, I mean trumpery. A child who was sick but afterwards lookd and smiled and was the only thing like company. The road is pleasant enough till it gets into the Wealds of sussex, a huge succession of green downs which sweep along the seacoast for many miles. Brighton seems grown twice as large since 1815. It is a City of loiterers and invalids, a vanity fair for piping, dancing of bears and for the feats of Mr. Punch. I found all my family well excepting the poor pale Johnie and he is really a thing to break one's heart by looking at – Yet he is better – The rest are in high kelter.[2]

My old friend Will Rose dined with us, also a Doctor Yates and his wife, the Esculapius of Brighton, who seems a sensible man. I was entertaind with the empire he exerted over him as protector of his health. I was very happy to find myself at Sophia's quiet table and am only sorry that I must quit her so soon.

21 WEDNESDAY This being a fine day we made some visits in the morning in the course of which I waited on Mrs. Dorset, sister of Mrs. Charlotte Smith and herself the author of *The Peacock at Home*,[3]

1. On 22 August 1867, Queen Victoria marked her visit to Abbotsford by adding her signature to the fly-leaf of the Journal.
2. 'Cheer'. *S. N. D.*
3. Mrs. Dorset's *Peacock at Home and other Poems*, 1809, was in Scott's library.

one of the prettiest and liveliest *jeux d'esprit* in our language. She is a fine stately old lady – not a bit of a literary person, I mean having none of the affectation of it, but like a Lady of considerable rank. I am glad I have seen [her]. Renewd my acquaintance with Lady Charlotte Hamilton, née Lady Charlotte Hume, and talkd over some stories thirty years old at least.

We then took a fly as they call the light carriages and drove as far as the Devil's Ditch. A rampire it is of great strength and depth inclosing I presume the precincts of a British town that must have held 30,000 men at least. I could not discover where they got water.

We got home at four and dined at five and smoked segars till eight. Will Rose came in with his man Hinvaes[1] who is as much a piece of Rose as Trim was of Uncle Toby.[2] We laughd over tales 'both old and new' till ten o'clock came and then broke up.

22 THURSDAY Left Brighton this morning with a heavy heart. Poor Johnie looks so very poorly that I cannot but regard his case as desperate and then God help the child's parents. Amen!

We took the whole of one of the post coaches and so came rapidly to town, Sophia coming along with us about a new servant.

This enabled me to dine with Mr. Adolphus the celebrated barrister, father to my young friend who wrote so like a gentleman on my matters.[3] I met Mr. Gurney, Arch deacon Wrangham and a lawyer or two besides. I may be partial but the conversation of intelligent barristers amuses me more than that of other professional persons. There is more of real life in it with which in all its phases people of business get so well acquainted. Mr. Adolphus is a man of varied information and very amusing. He told me a gipsy told him of the success he should have in life and how it would be endangerd by his own heat of temper, alluding I believe to a quarrel betwixt him and a brother barrister.

1. David Hinves served Rose, who was paralysed, for forty years. He was a bookbinder, and a Methodist local preacher. Scott presented him with all his works. See *Life*, iv. 397–8, and *Letters*, vi. 225 and 479.
2. In Sterne's *Tristram Shandy*.
3. Scott had blundered by missing an earlier engagement with him. Anne had gone to Brighton, he explains in a letter of 15 May, and 'as she keeps the register of all my engagements I have been ever since like a Merchant deserted by his principal Clerk'. Disc. i. 218. The matter on which the younger Adolphus had written were his *Letters to Reginald Heber*, 1821, arguing that the unknown author of *Waverley* must be Scott.

23 FRIDAY I breakfasted with Chantrey and met the celebrated Coke of Norfolk,[1] a very pleasing man who gave me some accompt of his plantations. I understand from him that like every wise man he planted land that would not let for 5/- per acre but which now produces £3000 a year in wood. He talkd of the trees which he had planted as being so thick that a man could not fathom them. Withers, he said, was never employd save upon one or two small jobs of about twenty acres on which every expense was bestowd with a view to early growth. So much for Withers. I shall have a rod in pickle for him if it [is] worth while.[2] After sitting to Chantrey for the last time, I calld on Lady Shelley p.p.c.[3] and was sorry to find her worse than she had been.[4] Dined with Lady Stafford where I met the two Lochs, John and James – the former gave me his promise for a Cadetship to Allan Cunningham's son[5] I have a similar promise from Lord Melville[6] and thus I am in the situation in which I have been at Gladdies Wiel[7] when I have caught two trouts, one with the fly the other with the bobber. I have landed both and so I will now. Mr. Loch also promised me to get out Shortreed as a free mariner.[8] Tom Grenville was at dinner.

1. Thomas William Coke (1752–1842) of Holkham, agriculturalist and M. P. for Norfolk. He was created Earl of Leicester in 1837.
2. William Withers of Holt in Norfolk had just attacked Scott in his *Letter to Sir Walter Scott exposing certain fundamental errors in his late Essay on Planting.*
3. *Pour prendre congé* (to take leave).
4. She had been an invalid since an accident in 1825. *Lady Shelley's Diary*, ii. 310.
5. Cunningham had asked Scott's help the previous December. 'My eldest son Joseph is grown a tall stout active lad and will be 16 years old in June . . .' He has 'fixed his wish to be a soldier as firm nearly as predestination . . . A Cadetship in the British Artillery – or in the Indian army would be a benefit to him and a blessing to me. The former is in the gift of the Duke of Wellington, the latter in that of the East India Directors.' 17 December 1827, Walpole. Loch was a Director of the East India Company.
6. See the Entry for 18 May 1828.
7. A pool on the Tweed.
8. 'What I trust I may be able to procure you,' Scott writes to Andrew Shortreed, for whom he had already found employment as a printer with Spottiswood, 'is not any appointment under the company but merely the license of the Board of directors to go out to India as a free Mariner that is with permission to push your way in any line of trade which may suit you.' 10 June 1828, Shortreed Papers.

24 SATURDAY This day we dined at Richmond park with Lord Sidmouth. Before dinner his Lordship shewd me letters which passd between the great Lord Chatham and Dr. Addington, Lord Sidmouth's family.[1] There was much of that familiar friendship which arises and must arise between an invalid, the Head of an invalid family, and their medical adviser, supposing the last to be a wise and well bred man. The character of Lord Chatham's hand writing is strong and bold and his expressions short and manly. There are intimations of his partiality for William whose health seems to have been precarious during boyhood. He talks of William's imitating him in all he did and calling for ale because his father was recommended to drink it. 'If I should smoke' he said 'William would instantly call for a pipe' and he wisely infers 'I must take care what I do.' The letters of the late William Pitt are of great curiosity but as like all real letters of business they only *allude* to matters with which his correspondent is well acquainted and do not enter into details they would require an ample commentary. I hope Lord Sidmouth will supply this and have urged it as much as I can. I think, though I hate letters and abominate interference, I will write to him on this subject.

I have bought a certain quantity of reprints from a bookseller in Chancery Lane, Pickering by name. I urged him to print the Controversy between Greene and the Harveys[2] – He wishd me to write a third part to a fine edition of Cotton's *Angler*[3] for which I am quite incompetent.

I met at Richmond my old and much esteemd friend Lord Stowell looking very frail and even comatose – *Quantum mutatus*[4] – He was one of the pleasantest men I ever knew.

Respecting the letters, I pickd up from those of Pitt that he was always extremely desirous of peace with France and even reckond upon it at moment[s] when he ought to have despaird. I suspect this false view of the state of France (for such it was) which induced the British minister to look for peace when there was no chance of it damped his ardour in maintaining the war. He wanted the lofty ideas of his father – you read it in his handwriting, great Statesman as he was. I saw a letter or two of Burke's in which there is an *épanchement du cœur* not visible in those of Pitt who writes like a premier to his colleague. Burke was under the strange hallucination that his son who predeceased him was a man of greater talents than himself – On the contrary he had little talent and no resolution. On moving some

---

1. A slip for 'father'.
2. Gabriel Harvey's *Four Letters and Sonnets touching Robert Greene*, 1592.
3. 'This refers to the splendid edition of Walton and Cotton, edited by Nicolas.' Douglas. It appeared in 1836.
4. 'How much changed'. Virgil's *Aeneid*, ii. 274.

resolution in favour of the Catholics which were ill received by the House of Commons young Burke actually ran away, which an Orange man compared to a cross-reading in the newspapers. 'Yesterday the Catholic resolutions were moved etc. – But the pistol missing fire the villains ran off.'

25 SUNDAY After a morning of Letter writing, leavetaking, papers destroying and God knows what trumpery, Sophia and I set out for Hampton Court carrying with us the following lions and lionesses – Samuel Rogers, Tom Moore, Wordsworth with wife and daughter. We were very kindly and properly received by Walter and his wife[1] and a very pleasant party.

I learnd from Moore that Byron actually hung up portraits of Lady Oxford and Lady Caroline Lamb on each side of his chimney piece at his lodgings in Albany. Neither conquest was worth boasting but I wonder William Lamb did not resent it – From Lord Oxford nothing was to be expected. He is a poor Nincompoop.

26 MONDAY An awful confusion with paying of bills, writing of cards and all species of trumpery business. Southey who is just come to town breakfasted with us. He looks I think but poorly, but it may be owing to family misfortune. One is always tempted to compare Wordsworth and Southey – The latter is unquestionably the greater scholar, I mean possesses the most extensive stock of information, but there is a freshness, vivacity and spring about Wordsworth's mind which if we may compare two men of uncommon powers shows more originality. I say nothing of their poetry. Wordsworth has a system which disposes him to take the bull by the horns and offend public taste, which right or wrong will always be the taste of the public, yet he could be popular if he would, witness the feast at Brougham castle – 'Song of the Cliffords' I think is the name.

---

1. Scott had been doubtful enough of their reception to write mentioning that Wordsworth's wife and daughter were 'in all the senses of the word very plain persons', and to add, 'I have much regard for Wordsworth.' *Letters*, x. 422. 'On our arrival at Hampton (where we found the Wordsworths),' wrote Moore, 'walked about, the whole party, in the gay walk where the band plays, to the infinite delight of the Hampton *blues* who were all *eyes* after Scott, the other scribblers not coming in for a glance. The dinner odd, but being near Scott I found it agreeable, and was delighted to see him so happy with his tall son, the major, whom he evidently looks upon as a chevalier of romance.' *Memoirs of Moore*, v. 287.

I walkd down to call with Rogers on Mrs. D'Arblay. She shewd me some notes which she was making about her novels which she induced me to believe had been recollected and jotted down in compliance with my suggestions on a former occasion. It is curious how she contrived to get *Evelina* printed and published without her father's knowlege. Her brother placed it in the hands of one Lowndes who after its success bought it for £20!!! and had the magnan[im]ity to add £10, the price I think of *Paradise Lost*. One of her sister betrayd the secret to her father who then eagerly lent his ears to hear what was said of the new novel, and the first opinion which saluted his delighted ears was the voice of Johnson energetically recommending it to the perusal of Mrs Thrale.[1]

At parting Rogers gave me a gold mounted pair of glasses which I will not part with in a hurry. I really like Rogers and have always found him most friendly. After many petty delays we set off at last and reach Dushey Grove to dine with my kind and worthy family friend and relative David Haliburton. I am delighted to find him in all the enjoyment of life with the vivacity of youth in his sentiments and enjoyments. Mr. and Mrs. Campbell Marjoribanks are the only company here, with Miss Parker.

27 TUESDAY Well my retreat from London is now accomplishd and I may fairly balance the advantage and loss of this London trip. It has cost me a good deal of money and Johnie's illness has taken away much of the pleasure I had promised myself. But if I can judge from the reception I have met with I have the pleasure to know that I stand as fair with the public and as high with my personal friends as in any period of my life. And this has enabled me to forward the following object[s] to myself and others.

1st. I have been able to place Lockhart on the right footing in the right quarter, leaving the improvement of his place of vantage to himself as circumstances should occur.[2]

2d. I have put the Chancery suit in the right train which without me could not have been done.[3]

3d. I have pickd up some knowlege of the state of existing matter which is interesting and may be useful.

1. For another version of this story, see the Entry for 18 November 1826.
2. He had put him in touch with Wellington and Peel, and this might benefit him as well as the Government and the *Quarterly*.
3. See the Entries for 30 April and 6, 8, 15, 16, and 19 May 1828.

4th. I have succeeded in helping to get a commission for James Skene.[1]

5th. I have got two cadetships for the sons of Allan Cunningham.[2]

6. I have got leave to Andw. Shortreed to go out to India.

7. I have put John Eckford into correspondence with Mr. Loch who thinks he can do something for his claim on the estate of Lithgow.[3]

8thly. I have been of material assistance to poor Terry in his affairs.[4]

9thly. I have effectually protected my Darnick neighbours and myself against the new roadbill.[5]

Other advantages there are besides the great one of scouring up one's own mind a little and renewing intercourse with old friends, bringing oneself nearer in short to the currency of the time.

All this may way[6] against the expenditure of £200 or £250. when money is fortunately not very scarce with me.

We went out for a most agreeable drive through the Hertfordshire lanes – a strange intricate combination of narrow roads passing through this county winding and turning among oaks and other large timber just like pathways cut through a forest. They wind and turn in so singular a manner and resemble each other so much that a stranger would have difficulty to make way amongst them. We visited Moorpark (not the House of Sir William Temple) but that where the Duke and Duchess of Monmouth lived. Having rather a commanding situation you look down on the valley which being divided into small enclosures borderd with wood resembles a forest when so lookd down

1. Scott had earlier tried unsuccessfully to get Skene's son 'put upon the Engineer list'. See the Entry for 21 February 1827. When Scott reached Malta in 1831 he found him in the garrison there.

2. See the Entry for 23 May 1828 and notes.

3. See the Entry for 17 November 1826 and note. The letter of introduction was in these terms: 'In the person of John Eckford claimant of the estate of the deceased Lithgow I have the pleasure to introduce to you a genuine and accomplished *bore* of the most perfect species I have ever seen. Nevertheless in spite of his boring propensities or perhaps by means of them the man who with a slow voice and stupid manner is shrewd persevering and indefatigable has succeeded I think in proving Lithgows mother a whore . . . and of course her son a bastard.' 25 May 1828. Disc. i. 222.

4. Not only by sending him money and good advice but by attending the first meeting of his creditors. Terry, 10 June 1828, Walpole.

5. See the Entries for 12, 17, and 25 April and 14 May 1828.

6. A slip for 'weigh'.

on. The House has a handsome Entrance hall painted by Sir James Thornhill in a very french taste yet handsome. He was Hogarth's father in law and not easily reconciled to the match. Thornhill's paintings are certainly not of the first class yet the practice of painting the walls and roof of a dwelling house give[s] in years a warm and rich air to the apartments. Lord Grosvenor has now bought this fine place once Lord Anson's – hence the Moor park apricot is also called Ansoniana. After seeing Moor Park we went to the Grove, the Earl of Clarendon's country seat. The House looks small and of little consequence but contains many good portraits as I was told of the Hyde family. The park has fine views and magnificent trees.

We went to Cashiobury, belonging to the Earl of Essex – an old mansion apparently with a very fine park. The Colne runs through the grounds or rather creeps through them.

> For the Colne
> Is black and swoln
> > Snake-like he wind[s] his way
> Unlike the *Burns*
> From highland urns
> > That dance by crag and brae.

Borthwickbrae[1] came to dinner from town and we had a very pleasant evening.

My excellent old friend reminded me of the old and bitter feud between the Scotts and Haliburtons and observed it was curious I should have united the blood of two hostile clans.

28 WEDNESDAY We took leave of our kind old Host after breakfast and set out for our own land. Our elegant researches carried us out of the high road and through a labyrinth of intricate lanes which seem made on purpose to afford strangers the full benefit of a dark night and a drunk driver, in order to visit Gill's Hill famous for the murder of Mr. Weare.[2]

The place has the strongest title to the description of Wordsworth

> A merry spot 'tis said in days of yore
> But something ails it now – the place is cursed.[3]

1. W. Eliot Lockhart, M. P. for Selkirkshire.
2. William Weare was killed by John Thurtell and his accomplices in October 1823 in Gill's Hill lane. Scott owned five pamphlets connected with the murder and the trial of Thurtell and Hunt. *A. L. C.*, p. 296. See also the Entry for 16 July 1826.
3. 'Hart-leap Well', ll. 123–4.

The principal part of the house has been destroyd and only the kitchen remains standing. The garden has been dismantled though a few laurels and garden shrubs run wild continue to mark the spot. The fatal pond is now only a green swamp but so near the house that one cannot conceive how it was ever chosen as a place of temporary concealment of the murderd body. Indeed the whole history of the murder and the scenes which ensued are strange pictures of desperate and short-sighted wickedness. The feasting – the singing – the murderer with his hands still bloody hanging round the neck of one of the females the watchchain of the murderd man, argue the utmost apathy. Even Probert, the most frightend of the party, fled no further for relief than to the brandy bottle and is found in the very lane and at the spot of the murder seeking for the murderous weapon and exposing himself to the view of the passengers. Another singular mark of stupid audacity was their venturing to wear the clothes of their victim. There was a want of foresight in the whole arrangement of the deed and the attempts to conceal it which argued strange inconsideration which a professd robber would not have exhibited. There was just one single shade of a redeeming character about a business so brutal perpetrated by men above the very lowest rank of life – it was the mixture of revenge which afforded some relief to the circumstances of treachery and premeditation which accompanied [it]. But Weare was a cheat and had no doubt pillaged Thurtell who therefore deemd he might take greater liberties with him than with others.

The dirt of the present habitation equald its wretchd desolation and a truculent looking hag who shewd us the place and received half a crown lookd not unlike the natural inmate of such a mansion. She indicated as much herself, saying the landlord had dismantled the place because no respectable person would live there. She seems to live entirely alone and fears no ghosts she says.

One thing about this mysterious tragedy was never explaind. It is said that Weare as is the habit of such men always carried about his person and between his flannel waistcoat and shirt a sum of ready money equal to £1500 or £2000 – No such money was ever recoverd and as the sum divided by Thurtell among his accomplice was only about £20 he must, in slang phrase, have *bucketed his palls.*

We came on as far as Alconbury hill where we slept comfortably.

29 THURSDAY We travelld from Alconbury hill to Ferrybridge, upwards of a hundred miles amid all the beauties of flourish and verdure which Spring awakens at her first approach in the midland counties of England but without any variety save those of the season's making. I do believe this great North road is the dullest in the world

as well as the most convenient for the traveller. Nothing seems to me to have been alterd within twenty or thirty years save the noses of the landlords which have bloomd and given place to another set of proboscis's as germain as the old ones to the *very wellcome – please to light – Orses forward* and *ready out*. The skeleton at Barnby Moor has deserted his gibbet and that is the only change I recollect.

I have amused myself to-day with reading Lockhart's *Life of Burns*[1] which is very well written – in fact an admirable thing. He has judicious[ly] slurd over his vices and follies for although Currie,[2] I myself,[3] and others, have not said a word more on that subject than is true yet as the Dead corpse is straightend, swathd and made decent so ought the character of such an inimitable genius as Burns to be tenderly handled after the death. The knowlege of his various weaknesses or vices are only subjects of sorrow to the well disposed and of triumph to the profligate.

30 FRIDAY We left Ferrybridge at seven and turning westwards or rather northwestward at Boroughbridge we reach Rokeby at past three. A mile from the house we met Morritt looking for us. I had great pleasure in finding myself at Rokeby and recollecting a hundred passages of past time. Morritt looks well and easy in his mind which I am delighted to see. He is now one of my oldest and I believe one of my most sincere [friends]. A man unequald in the mixture of sound good sense, high literary cultivation and the kindest and sweetest temper that ever guided a human bosom. His nieces are much attachd [to] him and are deserving and elegant as well as beautiful young women. What there is in our partiality to female beauty that commands a species of temperate homage from the aged as well as extatic admiration from [the young] I cannot conceive but it is certain that a very large proportion of some other amiable quality is too little to counterbalance the absolute want of this advantage. I to whom beauty is and shall henceforward be a picture still look upon [it] with the quiet devotion of an old worshipper who no longer offers incense in the shrine but peaceably presents his inch of taper taking special care in doing so not to burn his own finger. Nothing in life can be more ludicrous or contemptible than an old man aping the passions of his youth.

Talking of youth there was a certain professor at Cambridge who

---

1. It had just been published as volume 23 of Constable's *Miscellany*.
2. Dr. Currie's *Burns' Works with Account of his Life*, 1800.
3. In his 'Reliques of Burns', an article for the *Quarterly* written in 1809.

use[d] to keep sketches of all the youths who from their conduct at College seemd to bid fair for distinction in life. He shewd these one day to an old shrewd sarcastic master of Arts, who lookd over the collection and then observed – 'A promising nest of eggs – what a pity the great part will turn out addle – ' And so they do – Looking round amongst the young men one sees to all appearances fine flourish – but it ripens not.

31 SATURDAY I have finishd Napier's *War in the Peninsula*.[1] It is written in the spirit of a Liberal but the narrative is distinct and clear and I should suppose accurate. He has however given a bad sample of accuracy in the case of Lord Strangford where his pointed affirmation has been as pointedly repelld. It is evident he would require probing. His defence of Moore is spirited and well argued though it is evident he defends the statesman as much as the general. As a *liberal* and a military man Colonel Napier finds it difficult to steer his course. The former character calls on him to plead for the insurgent Spaniard, the latter induces him to palliate the cruelties of the French. Good even to him untill next volume which I shall long to see. This was a day of pleasure and nothing else. After breakfast I walkd with Morritt in the new path he has made up the Tees. When last here his poor nephew[2] was of the party. It hugs on my mind, and perhaps on Morritt's. When we returnd we took a short drive as far as Barnard Castle and the old business of eating and drinking took up the remainder of the evening excepting a dip into the Greta walk.

JUNE

1 SUNDAY We took leave of our friends at Rokeby after breakfast and pursued our well known path over Stanmore to Brough, Appleby, Penrith and Carlisle. As I have this road by heart I have little amusement save the melancholy task of recalling the sensations with which I have traced [it] in former times all of which refer to decay of animal strength and abatement if not of mental powers at least of mental energy. The *Non est tanti*[3] grows fast at my time of life. We reachd Carlisle at seven o'clock and were housed for the night. My books being exhausted I lighted on an odd volume of the *Gentleman's Magazine*, a work in which as in a pawnbroker's shop much of real curiosity and value are stowd away and conceald amid

1. The first volume of Colonel W. F. P. Napier's *History of the War in the Peninsula* had just been published.
2. He had died late the previous year. *Letters*, x. 335.
3. That is, the feeling that all is worthless.

the frippery and trumpery of those reverend old gentlewomen who were the regular correspondents of the work.

2 MONDAY We intended a walk to the Castle but were bafled by rainy weather. I was obliged to wait for a certificate from the parish register.[1] *Hei mihi!!* I cannot have it till ten o'clock – or rather as it chancd till past eleven when I got the paper for which I waited. We lunchd at Hawick and concluded our pilgrimage at Abbotsford about nine at night where the joyful barking of the dogs with the sight of the kind familiar faces of our domestics gave us wellcome and I enjoyd a sound repose in my own bed. I remark that in this journey I have never once experienced depression of spirits or the *tremor cordis* of which I have sometimes such unpleasant visits. Dissipation and a succession of trifling engagements prevent the mind from throwing itself out in the manner calculated to exhaust the owner – and to entertain other people. There is a lesson in this.

3 TUESDAY This was a very idle day. I waked to walk about my beautiful young woods with old Tom and the dogs. The sun shone bright and the wind fand my cheek as if it were a welcoming. I did not do the least right thing except packing a few books necessary for writing the Continuation of the *Tales*.[2] In this merry mood I wanderd as far as Huntly Burn where I found the Miss Fergusons well and happy. Then I saunterd back to Abbotsford sitting on every bench by the way and thus

It grew to dinner in conclusion.[3]

A good appetite made my simple meal relish better than the magnificent cheer which I have lately partaken of. I smokd a segar, slept away an hour and read Mure of Auchendrayne's trial[4] and thus ended the day. I cannot afford to spend many such, nor would they seem so pleasant.

4 WEDNESDAY The former part of this day was employed much as yesterday but some packing was inevitable. Will. Laidlaw came to dinner of which we partook at three o'clock. Started at half past four and arrived at home if we must call it so at nine o'clock in the evening.

1. A certificate of his marriage, required in connection with Lady Scott's money in Chancery.
2. *Tales of a Grandfather*, second series.
3. A reminiscence of *King John*, i. 1: 'It draws toward supper in conclusion so.'
4. *Scotch Trials, containing Trial of Thomas Muir, Esq. etc.*, 1793.

I employd my leisure in the chaise to peruse Mure of Auchendrane's trial out of which something might be cooperd up for the publick. It is one of the wildest stories I ever read. Something might surely be twisted out of it.[1]

5 THURSDAY Cadell breakfasted in great spirits with the success of the *Fair Maid of Perth*. A disappointment being always to be apprehended I too am greatly pleased that the evil day is adjournd for the time must come, and yet I can spin a tough yarn still with any one now going.

I was much distressd to find that the last of the B.Ms,[2] a fine lad of about twentyone, is now decidedly infected by the same pulmonary complaint which carried off his four brothers in succession. This is indeed a cruel stroke and it is melancholy to witness the undaunted highland courage of the father.

I went to court and when I returnd did some work upon the *Tales*.

6 FRIDAY And now again, boys, to the oar.[3]

I have determined to work sans intermission for lost time and to make up at least my task every day. J. Gibson calld on me with good hopes that the Trustees will authorise the *grande opus* to be set afloat. They are scrupulous a little about the expens[e] of engraving but I fear the taste of the town will not be satisfied without them.[4] It is time the thing were settled. I wrought both before and after dinner and finishd five pages which is two above bargain.

---

1. *Auchindrane; or The Ayrshire Tragedy* was written late the following year.
2. James Grahame, the youngest son of Hector Macdonald Buchanan. His death is reported in the Entry for 10–14 June.
3. A reminiscence of Swift's 'The Country Life', l. 44.
4. Cadell had been busy while Scott was in London. On 10 May he reported 'a most agreeable meeting of two hour yesterday afternoon with Mr. Gibson, Mr. Jollie & Mr. Moneypenny' after which he did not 'in any way doubt their hearty assent to the whole plan'. Walpole. Gibson wrote the same day, however, doubtful about the proposed engravings and wondering 'whether something might not be saved on this head, & whether Mr. Cadell does not over-rate the necessity for splendid illustrations'. With lawyer's caution he would have them '*respectable* only, & not so *splendid* as Mr. Cadell contemplates'. Walpole. Cadell was determined, however, 'to have all the Engravings done in London, also Printed there – the superiority is so much beyond what we have in Edinburgh'. Sederunt Book, i. 384. The Trustees finally agreed to Cadell's plan a week later.

7 SATURDAY Saturday was another working day and Nothing occurd to disturb me.

8 SUNDAY I finishd five sheets this day. Will Clerk and Francis Scott of Harden came to dinner and we spent a pleasant evening.

9 MONDAY I labourd till about one and was then obliged to go to attend a meeting [of] the Oil Gas Coy, as I devoutly hope for the last time. After that I was obliged to go to sit to Colvin Smith[1] which is an atrocious bore but cannot be help[d].

Cadell renderd me report of accompts paid for me with vouchers which very nearly puts me out of all shop debts. God grant me grace to keep so. There remain in Mr. Cadell's hands of ballance £40.0.0
Add Cash payable at this term on the *Tales* ———— 200

		240.
Drew on him for ————		140.
In Cadell's hands		£100.
Add by Alex Ballantyne[2] ————		12.10
		£112
Disposed of Cash drawn as follows—Sum in purse—		£140.
Shares of Oil Gas – 7th. Installment	£75.0.0	
To Bogie at Abbotsford	20.	
To Scott plumber Kelso £9. 15 say	10.	
To Subscription to Jedburgh old church	10.	
		£115
		£25
To Anne ————	£5.0.0	
To Charity Mrs. Watson ————	5.	
To Subscription Bannatyne Club five guineas Say ————	6.	
To plans of Scottish burghs[3] ————	5.5	
To coach hire parliament House ————	2.7	
To sundries ————	8.	
		24.
	Ball.	1

1. To sit for the portrait which had been in abeyance since the end of February.
2. This is the interest on his loan to Scott and should have been subtracted not added.
3. Wood's *Town Atlas of Scotland*, 1828, listed in *A. L. C.*

10, 11, 12, 13, 14 TUESDAY TO SATURDAY During these five days almost nothing occurd to diversify the ordinary task of the day which I must own was dull enough. I rose to my task by seven, and less or more wrought it out in the course of the day, far exceeding the ordinneary average of three leaves per day. I have attended the parliament House with the most strict regularity and returnd to dine alone with Anne. Also I gave three sittings to Mr. Colvin Smith who I think has improved since I saw him.

Of important intelligence nothing occurs save the termination of all suspense on the subject of poor James Macdonald Buchanan. He died at Malta. The celebrated Dugald Stuart is also dead, famous for his intimate acquaintance with the history and philosophy of the human mind. There is much of water painting in all Metaphysics which consist rather of words than of ideas. But Stuart was most impressive and eloquent. In former days I was frequently with him[1] but not for many years. Latterly I am told he had lost not the power of thinking but the power of expressing his thoughts by speech. This is like the metamorphosis of Ovid, the bark binding in and hardening the living flesh.

15 SUNDAY W. Clerk, Francis Scott and Charles Sharpe dined with me but my task had been concluded before dinner.

16 MONDAY Dined at Dalmahoy [with] the young Earl and Countess of Morton. I like these young noble folks particularly well. Their manners and stile of living is easy and unaffected and I should like to see them often. Came home at night. The task finishd to-day. I should mention that the plan about the new edition of novels was considerd at a meeting of trustees and finally approved of. I trust it will answer. Yet, who can warrant the continuance of popularity? Old Corri,[2] who enterd into many projects and could never sett the sails of a windmill so as to catch the *aura popularis*,[3] used to say that he believed that were he to turn baker it would put bread out of fashion. I have had the better luck to dress my sails to every wind. And so blow on, God's wind, and spin round, whirlagig.

17 TUESDAY Violent rheumatic headaches all day – Wrought however but what addition[4] this troublesome addition may make to the

1. See *Life*, i. 59 and 235–6.
2. Natale Corri, who attempted to popularize Italian opera in his adopted town of Edinburgh.
3. 'The breeze of popular favour'. Horace's *Odes* iii, 2. 20.
4. A slip for 'difference'.

quality of the stuff produced, truly I do not know. I finished five leaves.

18 WEDNESDAY Some Italian gentlemen landed here under the conveyance of the Misses Haigs of Bemerside.[1] They were gentleman like men but as I did not dare to speak bad french I had not much to say to Foreigners. Gave them and their pretty guides a good breakfast however. The scene seemd to me to resemble Sheridan's scene in the *Critic*.[2] Here are a number of very civil gentlemen trying to make themselves understood and I do not know which is the interpreter. After all it is not my fault. They who wish to see me should be able to speak my language. I calld on Mrs. Stuart Mackenzie.[3] She received me with all the kindness of former days and I was delighted to see her. I sate about an hour with her. My head aches for all that and I have heavy fits of drowsiness. Well I have finishd my task and have a right to sleep if I have a mind. I dine to-day with Lord Mackenzie where I hope to meet Mrs. Stuart Mackenzie again for I love her warm heart and lively fancy. Accordingly I enjoyd this pleasure.

19 THURSDAY Scribbled away lustily – went to the P. H.[4] Wrote when I came home both before and after dinner – that's all I think. I am become a sort of writing Automaton and truly the joints of my knees especially the left are so stiff and painful in rising and sitting down that I can hardly help screaming – I that was so robust and active – I get into a carriage with great difficulty. My head too is botherd with rheumatic headaches. Why not? – I got headaches by my folly when I was young and now I am old they come uncalld – infirmity gives what indiscretion bought.

20 FRIDAY My course is still the same. But I have a painful letter from Lockhart which takes away the last hope of poor Johnie's recovery.[5] It is no surprize to me. The poor child so amiable in its disposition and so promising from its talents was not formed to be

1. The Haigs had spent some years in Italy.
2. Act i, scene 2.
3. Maria Elizabeth Frederica Stewart-Mackenzie (1783–1862), who succeeded her father Lord Seaforth as chief of the Clan Mackenzie. Three years after the death of her first husband, Sir Samuel Hood, she married James Stewart of Glasserton and changed her name to Stewart-Mackenzie.
4. Parliament House.
5. Johnnie Lockhart lived nonetheless for another three years.

long with us and I have long expected that it must needs come to us. I hope I shall not outlive my children in other cases and I think there is little chance of it. My father did not long survive the threescore and ten. It will be wonderful if I reach that goal of ordinary mortality. God send it may find me prepared, and whatever I may have been formerly high spirits are not now like to carry me away.

21 SATURDAY At court and calld on Ballantyne on my return. I was obliged to go to the Register Office at One where I wasted nearly an hour without meeting my brethren.[1] But I wrote a letter to Lockhart in the meantime. My niece Ann arrived to my great satisfaction. I am glad that Anne my daughter has such a sensible and clever companion.

I got in part of my Salary ———————————————		£150.0.0
Anne for the house ———————————————		50.
	Ballance	100.
In purse ———————————————		2.
Add cash with Mr. Cadell		112
In Mr. Marshalls [hands] to be paid this week		
balance of salary		100
		314

Dined at Baron Hume's.

22 SUNDAY Wrought ha[r]d. A note from Ballantyne complaining of my manuscript and requesting me to read it over. I would give £1000 I could but it would take me longer to read than to write. I cannot trace my *pieds de mouche* but with great labour and trouble. So e'en take your own share of the burden, my old friend, and since I cannot read be thankful I can write. I will look at his proof however and then be quiet and idle for the rest of the evening. I am come to Charles the first's trial[2] and though I have it by heart I must refresh myself with a reading of Clarendon.[3] Charles Sharpe and Francis Scott came in the evening.

1. His 'brethren' were probably the Committee of the Bannatyne Club. Thomas Thomson, the Vice-president, had his office in Register House.
2. See *Tales of a Grandfather*, ch. 45.
3. Edward, Earl of Clarendon's *History of the Rebellion and Civil War in England*, 1702-4.

23 MONDAY This morning the two Annes and I went to Sir Robert Liston at Liston Tower,[1] a beautiful retreat. The travels of the venerable Diplomatists are indicated by the various articles of curiosity which he has picked up in different corners of the world and put together with much taste. The conservatory and gardens are very fine and contain I suppose very curious plants, I am sure hard names enough. But then the little Gothick [towers], embowerd among trees and bushes, surrounded by these pleasant gardens, offering many a sunny walk for winter many a shade for summer, are inexpressibly pleasing. The good old Knight and his lady are worthy of it for they enjoy it. The artificial piece of water is a failure like most things of the kind. The offices without being on an extravagant scale are most substantial. The piggery in particular is quite a palace: and the animals clean and comfortable. I think I have caught from them a fit of piggish obstinacy. I came [home] at one, and cannot prevail upon myself to go to work. I answer the calls of duty as Caliban does those of Prospero, 'there's wood enough within.'[2] To be sure I have not got the Clarendon.

24 TUESDAY It was my father's own son, as John Hielandman said, who did little work both yesterday and to-day. I mean little in the way of literary work for as to positive work I have been writing letters about that Chancery business till I am sick of it. There was a long *hearing* and while Jeffrey exerted his Eloquence in the Inner House I plied my eloquence *de billet* in the Library.[3] So on the whole I am no bad boy. Besides the day is not yet over.

Cash in purse ———————————	£102.0.0	
To Mr. Gibson in full of his accot. ——	88.	
	14.	
With Mr. Cadell and Marshall ———	£212.	
£226 Ballance in cash as above ———————	£226	

25 WEDNESDAY I was surprized to hear that our Academy Rector Williams has renounced the Chair of Professor of Roman learning in

---

1. Scott should have written 'Milburn Tower'.
2. *The Tempest*, i. 2.
3. He wrote on this date to Fenimore Cooper in Paris asking him 'to employ an active agent' to search the records in Lyons for evidence of the birth of Lady Scott's brother and the death of her father. *Letters*, x. 438.

the new London university.[1] His alarm was excited by the interest taken by the prelates in opposing an High Church institution to that devised by Mr. Brougham. Both the Bishops and Williams have been unwise. The former have manœuvred ill. They should in the outset have taken the establishment out of the hands of the Whigs without suffering them to reinforce themselves by support from 'those who should have been their.'[2] And Williams was equally precipitate in joining an institution which a small degree of foresight might have assured him would be opposed by his spiritual Superiors. However there he stands, deprived of his professorship by his resignation and of his rectorship by our having engaged with a successor. I think it very doubtful whether the bishops will run him into their alliance. He has in that case offended both parties. But if they are wise they will be glad to pick up the best Schoolmaster in Europe though he comes for the present *Graia ex urbe*.[3] I accomplishd more than my task to-day.

26 THURSDAY Wrote a long letter to Lockhart about Williams' situation saying how by sitting betwixt two stools he

— had fallen with heavy thump
Upon his reverential rump.[4]

and how the Bishops should pick him up if they wanted their establishment to succeed. It is an awkward position in which Williams has placed himself. He loses the Whig chair, and has

1. John Williams had been Rector of the Edinburgh Academy since its inception in 1824. He resigned to take up the Chair of Latin in Brougham's new London University, but on finding the college unpopular among the High Church party to which he belonged took fright and withdrew. Although the Revd. Thomas Sheepshanks, who had been appointed only a week before, offered to stand down, the Directors of the Academy felt that they could not honourably allow him to do so, and Williams found himself without Chair or Rectorship. Scott, who was indefatigable in the service of his friends, then busied himself in pressing King's College, the High Church rival to Brougham's university, to make use of Williams as Professor of Latin. Not unnaturally they did not appoint him. Sheepshanks, however, resigned within a year, and Williams returned to the Academy, where he remained as Rector until 1847.
2. A reminiscence of *Macbeth*, v. 5.
3. 'From a Greek city', i.e., from the enemy camp.
4. Swift's epigram 'Friend Rundle fell'.

perhaps no chance of favour from High Church for having been willing to accept it. Even if they now give him promotion there will be a great outcry on his having left one institution to join another. He will be thickskind if he stands the clamour. Yet he has to all appearance rather sacrificed than advanced his interest. However, I say again the Bishops ought no[t] to omit securing him.

Mr. McIntosh Mackay breakfasted with me. Modest intelligent and gentle. I did my duty and more in the course of the day. John Forbes and his Lady came in for a call.

From Mr Cadell	———	£20.			
Cash in purse	———	14.			
		34			
Tom by basket	£15.		Cadell	———————	£112
Anne ———————	5.	20	To cash ————————		20
Cash in purse	£14		Ball. with Cadell		90

I am vexd about MacG[1] missing the church of Cupar in Angus. It is in the crown's gift and Peel, finding that two parties in the town recommended two opposite candidates, very wisely chose to disappoint them both and was desirous of bestowing the presentation on public grounds. I heard of this and applied to Mr. Peele[2] for Macintosh Mackay whose quite patience and learning are accompanied by a most excellent character as a preacher and a clergyman. But unhappily Mr. Peele had previously put himself into the hands of Sir George Murray who applied to Sir Peter his brother who naturally applied to certain leaders of the Church at Edinburgh and these reverend gentlemen have recommended that the Church which the minister desired to fill up on publick grounds should be bestowd on a boy,[3] the nephew of one of their number, of whom the best that can be said is that nothing is known since he has only been a few months in orders. This comes of kith kin and ally, but Peel shall know of it and may perhaps judge for himself another time.

27 FRIDAY I came out after court to Blair Adam with our excellent friend Revd. John Thomson of Duddingston, so modest and so accomplishd. Delightful drive and passage at the ferry. We found at

1. A slip for 'MacK', that is, 'Mackay'.
2. 'It would be a hundred pities if such literary talents and so much power of patient investigation should be lost in the remote solitude of a parish in the far highlands where he can neither have access to books or contact with literary society.' *Letters*, x. 434. For Peel's reply see Portington's *Letter-Books*, p. 42.
3. The Revd. Patrick James Stevenson.

Blair Adam the C. C.[1] and family, Admiral Adam and lady, Jo:
Thomson of Charlton and Miss T., Will Clerk, and last not least
Lord Chief Baron Shepherd, all in high spirits for our excursions.

Thomson described to me a fine dungeon in the old Tower at
Cassilis in Ayrshire. There is an outer and inner vaulted [chamber],
each secured with iron doors. At the upper end of the innermost are
two great stones or blocks to which the staples and chains used in
securing the prisoners are still attachd. Between these stone seats is
an opening like the mouth of a still deeper dungeon. The entrance
descends like the mouth of a draw well or shaft of a mine and deep
below is heard the sullen roar of the river Doon, one branch of which
passes through the bottom of [the] shaft and has probably swept away
the body of many [a] captive whose body after death may be they
summarily disposed of. I may find use for such a place – Story of
Kittle clarkie.

28 SATURDAY Off we goes to Castle Campbell[2] after breakfast, i.e.
Will Clerk, Admiral Adam, Jo Thomson and myself.[3] Tremendous
hot is the day and the steep ascent of the Castle which rises for two
miles up a rugged and broken path was fatiguing enough yet not so
much so as the streets in London. Castle Campbell is unalterd; the
window of which the disjointed stone <from> projects at an angle
from the wall and seems at the point of falling has still found power to
resist the laws of gravitation. Whoever built that tottering piece of
masonry has been long in a forgotten grave and yet what he has made
seems to survive in spite of nature itself. The curious cleft called
Kemp's Score which gave the garr[i]son access to the water in case of
Siege is obviously natural but had been improved by steps now
choked up. A girl who came with us recollected she had shewn
me the way down to the bottom of this terrible gulph seven years
ago.[4] I am not able for it now.

> Wont to do's awa frae me
> Frae silly auld John Ochiltree.[5]

1. Chief Commissioner William Adam.
2. Near Dollar in Clackmannanshire.
3. William Adam 'was not of this party, but partook of a returning
   jollification with those who were, at Rumbling Brig Inn'. *Blair-
   Adam Estate*, Introduction, p. xxvi.
4. During the second meeting of the Club in 1818, Scott,
   'appearing to possess all the activity of youth, went fearlessly
   down the yawning gulf into the dungeon'. Ibid., p. xiii.
5. Ramsay's *Tea-Table Miscellany*: 'John Ochiltree'.

29 SUNDAY Being Sunday we kept about the doors and after two took the drosky and drove over the hill and round by the Kiery Crags. I should have said Williams came out in the morning to ask my advice about staying another year in Edinburgh. I advised him if possible to gain a few days' time till I should hear from Lockhart. He has made a pretty mess for himself but if the Bishops are wise they may profit by it.[1] The sound practical advice of Williams at the first concoction would be of last consequence. I suspect the systems of eating-houses are the most objectionable part of the College discipline. When their attentions are to be given to the departments of the Cook and the butler all zeal in the nobler paths of education is apt to decay.

Well – to return to the woods – I think notwithstanding Lord Chief Commissioner's assiduity the[y] are in some places too thick. I saw a fine larch felld, 72 years old, value about five pounds.

Hereditary descent in the Highlands. A clergyman shewd J. T.[2] the island of Inch ma home in the Port of Monteith and pointed [out] the boat man as a remarkable person, the Representative of the heredi-tary gardeners of the Earls of Monteith while these earls existed. His son, a priggish boy, follows up the theme. 'Feyther, when Donald MacCorkindale dees will not the *family* be extinct?' Father after re[flection] 'No – I believe there is a man in Balquhidder who takes up the *Succession.*'

30 MONDAY We made our pleasant excursion to-day round the hill of Bennarty *par terre* and returnd *par mer*. Our route by land led us past Lochore where we made a pause for a few moments. Then proceeded to Ballingray or Bingray and so by Kirkness, where late ravages are supplied by the force of vegetation, down to the Shores of the Lochleven. We embarkd and went upon Saint Serf's island, supposed to have been anciently a cell of the Culdees. An ancient pin-fold or rather a modern pinfold constructed out of the ancient chapel is all that attests its former sanctity. We landed on Queen Mary's Island, a miserable scene, considering the purpose for which the castle was appointed. And yet the captivity and surrender of the Percy was even a worse tale since it was an eternal blight on the name of Douglas.[3] Well we got to Blair Adam in due time and our fine

1. By appointing him to the new King's College.
2. The Revd. John Thomson.
3. Mary Queen of Scots was imprisoned in the Castle in 1567–8.
   The 'worse tale' is that William Douglas, Keeper of the Castle, and James Douglas (the Regent Morton) were bribed in 1572 to hand over to execution Percy, seventh Earl of Northumberland, who had fled to Scotland after the Northern Insurrection of 1569.

company began to separate, Lord Chief Baron going off after dinner. We had wine and wassail and John Thomson's delightful flute to help us through the evening.

Thus end the delectations of the Blair Adam Club for this year. Mrs. Thomson of Charlton talks of Bethune's house and other fife wonders for the next year but who knows what one year may bring forth? Our Club has been hitherto fortunate. It has subsisted twelve years.

JULY

1 TUESDAY

> 'Up in the morning's no for me.'[1]

Yet here I am up at five, no horses come from the North Ferry yet.

> O Mr. Mitchell, Mitchell,
> Your promises and time keep stitch ill.

Got home however by nine and went to the Parliament House where we were detaind till four o'clock. Miss D—[2] dined with us, a professd lion huntress who travels the country to rouse the peaceful beasts out of their lair and insists on being hand and glove with all [the] leonine race. She is very plain besides frightfully red haird and out-Lydia-ing even my poor friend Lydia White. An awful visitation. I think I see her with javelin raised and buskind foot, a second Diana, rousing the hills of Westmoreland in quest of the lakers – Would to God she were there or anywhere but here – affectation is a painful thing to witness: and this poor woman has the bad taste to think direct flattery is the way to make her advances to friendship and intimacy.

2 WEDNESDAY I believe I was cross yesterday. I am at any rate very ill to-day with a rheumatic headache and a still more vile hypochondriachal affection which fill my head with pain, my heart with sadness and my eyes with tears. I do not wonder at the awful feelings which visited men less educated and less firm than I may call myself. It is a most hang dog cast of feeling but it may be chased away by study or by exercize. The last I have always found most successful but the first is most convenient. I wrought therefore and endured all this forenoon being a teind Wednesday. I am now in such a state that I would hardly be surprized at the worst

---

1. Burns's 'Up in the Morning'.
2. Miss Harriet Douglas, from America, later Mrs. Henry D. Cruger of New York.

news which could be brought to me. And all this without any rational cause why to-day should be sadder than yesterday.

Two things to lighten my spirits. 1st. Cadell comes to assure me that the stock of 12mos novels is diminishd from 3800, [which] was the quantity in the publisher's hands in March 1827, to 600 or 700. This argues gallant room for the publication of the new Series.' 2dly. Said Cadell is setting off straight for London to set affairs agoing. If I have success in this it will greatly assist in extricating my affairs.

		Cash from Mr Cadell ——	£22.	
		To sent Bogie ——	22.	
		Ball: remains with Cadell ——	£68.	
		To Cash in purse £ ——	14	
Marshal —	£100.	Grass for horses and straw for		
Cadell ——	68.	carriage	£5.	
Purse ——	1.	To John² to Blair Adam exp	3.	
——		To subscription to Horticultural		
£169.	Garden ——	3.	
		Bust carriage from London³ —	1.	
		Sundries ——	1.	
			—	13.
		In purse—£1.		

My aches of the heart terminated in a cruel aching of the head, rheumatic I suppose. But Sir Adam and Clerk came to dinner and laughd and talkd the sense of pain and oppression away. One cannot at times work themselves into a gay humour any more than we can tickle ourselves into a fit of laughter; foreign agency is necessary. My Huntress of Lions again dined with us. I have subscribed to her Album and done that was civil.

3 THURSDAY Corrected proofs in the morning and wrote a little. I was forct to crop Vol I⁴ as 30 pages too long – there is the less to write behind. We were kept late at the Court and when I came out I bethought me like Christian in the Castle of Giant Despair 'Wherefore should I walk along the broiling and stifling streets when I have a little key in my bosom which can open any lock in princes street walks and be thus on the castle banks, rocks and trees in a few minutes?' I

1. The Magnum Opus.
2. John Nicholson.
3. See the Entry for 17 May 1828 and note.
4. Of *Tales of a Grandfather*, second series.

made use of my key accordingly and walkd from the castle hill down to Wallace's Tower[1] and thence to the West end of Princes Street through a scene of grandeur and beauty perhaps unequald whether the foreground or distant view is considerd – All down hill too – foolish never to think of this before. I chatted with the girls a good while after dinner but wrote a trifle when we had tea.

4 FRIDAY The two Annes went off to Abbotsford[2] though the weather was somewhat louring for an open carriage but the day cleard up finely. Hamilton is unwell so we had a long hearing of his on our hands. It was four ere I got home but I had taken my newly discoverd path by rock, bush and ruin. I question if Europe has such another path. We owe this to the taste of James Skene.

But I must dress to go to Dr. Hope's who makes *chère exquise* and does not understand being kep[t] late.

5 SATURDAY Saturday, corrected proofs and wrought hard. Went out to dinner at Oxenford Castle and returnd in evengs in the company of Lord Alloway, Chief Baron, Clerk etc. and Mr. Bouverie, the English Commissioner or Solicitor.

6 SUNDAY A day of hard work. The second volume[3] is now well advanced well nigh one half. Dined alone and pursued my course after dinner. Seven pages were finishd. Solitude's a fine thing for work but then you must lie bye like a spider till you collect materials to continue your web. Began Simond's *Switzerland*[4] – clever and intelligent but rather conceited as the manner of an American Frenchman. I hope to knock something out of him though.

7 MONDAY Williams seems in uncertainty again and I can't guess what he will do. Surely it is a misery to be so indecisive. He will certainly gain the ill word of both parties and might have had the good word of all and indeed deserves it. We received his resignation to-day.[5] But if the King College are disposed to thrive they will keep eyes upon this very able man.

1. Otherwise known as Wellhouse Tower.
2. Escorted by Sir Adam Ferguson. *Letters*, x. 456. Anne Scott from Cheltenham had come north on 21 June. Scott was to join them at Abbotsford on 11 July.
3. Of *Tales of a Grandfather*, second series.
4. Louis Simond's *Journal of a Tour and Residence in Switzerland*, 1822. Scott is gathering material for *Anne of Geierstein*, which he began the following month.
5. At 'a tiresome meeting of the directors of the Academy'. 7 July 1828, Disc. i. 232.

8 TUESDAY Hard work in the Court. The Sederunts turn long and burthensome. I fear they will require some abridgement of vacation.

[In January Scott had twice allowed his *Journal* to lapse for a few days. In July it lapsed once more, and there are no further entries for 1828. The events of the missing months can, however, be traced from the letters he wrote and received.

The Courts rose on 11 July and Scott returned as usual to Abbotsford, where he had a succession of visitors. Morritt with his nieces, Dr. and Mrs. Hughes with their son, and the Misses Arden, were welcome guests in August, 'which', as Scott remarks, 'makes amends for some bores'.[1] Dr. Henry Phillpots, Dean of Chester, whom Scott had met in London, was unwell during his stay; Edward Pusey spent two days at Abbotsford in the course of his honeymoon in Scotland; and there was a trying visit from the Duc de Lévi, whom Scott described as 'the most complete French chatter box I ever met with'.[2] He was disappointed of visits from the people he most wanted to see. Walter intended to come with Jane in August; then, as Jane had to stay with her mother, he thought he would come in September instead, with Lockhart; finally, he could not get leave and did not come at all, nor did Lockhart. Charles was travelling in Germany: Scott had refused him the money to go further, on the score that 'Swiss German . . . is the worst possible and the Alps which are legitimate objects of curiosity will be found where they now are when you have leisure to go to seek them.'[3] Sophia was in Brighton with Johnnie, whose spinal complaint seemed unexpectedly less troublesome.

Scott's own health did not improve. In mid July he was 'half dead with rheumatism in the joints and loins',[4] and he needed the support of Tom Purdie, or, after Purdie had 'cut his foot with his axe (the ass)',[5] of John Swanston, to move around his plantations. His eyesight, too, was failing. 'I cannot write a word without glasses,' he complains, 'and even then make perpetual blunders.'[6] The death of two young neighbours – Maxpopple's eldest son lost at sea, and Dr. Brewster's thirteen-year-old son Charles drowned while bathing

1. *Letters*, x. 497.
2. *Letters*, x. 496.
3. *Letters*, x. 476–7.
4. *Letters*, x. 472.
5. *Letters*, x. 497.
6. *Letters*, x. 474.

in the Tweed – cast a shadow over the early part of the holiday. These losses were followed in mid September by the sudden decease of Scott's colleague Hector Macdonald Buchanan, and in October by the death of his aunt Jean Scott of Raeburn and of his old friend and rival Sir William Forbes.

During August Scott finished *Tales of a Grandfather*, second series (which by a late change of plan carried Scotland's history only as far as 1707, leaving the Jacobite risings for a third series). He read for *Anne of Geierstein*, which he began writing at the end of the month; and he reviewed *Hajji Baba in England* and (at Lady Davy's request) Sir Humphry's *Salmonia, or Days of Fly-Fishing* for the *Quarterly*. The closing months of the year saw steady progress on *Anne*, and on notes for the novels (as far as *A Legend of Montrose*) for the Magnum Opus.]

(Having omitted to carry on my diary for two or three days I lost heart to make it up and left it unfilld for many a month and day. During this period nothing has happend worth particular notice. The same occupations, the same amusements, the same occasional alternations of spirits gay or depressd, the same absence of all sensible or rational cause for the one or the other – I half grieve to take up my pen and doubt if it is worth while to record such an infinite quantity of nothing. But hang it! I hate to be beat so here goes for better behaviour.)

JANUARY

10 SATURDAY I resume my task at Abbotsford. We are here alone except Lockhart on a flying visit. Morritt, his Niece, Sir James Stewart, Skene, and an occasional friend or two, have been my guests since 31 December.[1] I cannot say I have been happy for the feeling of increasing weakness in my lame leg is a great offset – I walk now with pain and difficulty at all times and it sinks my soul to think how soon I may be altogether a disabled cripple. I am tedious to my friends and I doubt the sense of it makes me fretful.

Every thing else goes off well enough. My cash affairs are clearing and though last year was an expensive one I have been paying debt.

1. Lockhart gives a livelier account of the party in a letter to Sophia written on the 7th: 'Here are Skene & Sir Jamie Steuart who having got rid of his wife & his land is in prodigious spirits . . . 'Here are also Henry Scott (who indeed lives here as a rule all year) and two long boys of Colin Mackenzies. But how long any or all of these are to stay God knows . . . 'Sir Adam Lady F & the beastly old Toad Wells are all at Huntly Burn. Bell is vegetating very soberly. Mary invisible for headache – Margaret much as of yore only she has lost *all her teeth* & went out in convulsions here on Hogmanae at hearing yr papa expatiate, as is his custom, on the minutae of Duff James's Murder.' Abbots.

Yet I have a dull contest before me which will probably outlast my life. If well maintaind however, it will be an honourable one, and if the Magnum opus succeed it will afford me some repose.

11 SUNDAY I did not write above a page yesterday; most weary, stale and unprofitable[1] have been my labours – received a letter, I suppose from Made. T—,[2] proposing a string of historical subjects not proper for my purpose. People will not consider that a thing may already be so well told in history that Romance ought not in prudence to meddle with it. The ground coverd with snow which by slipperiness and the pain occasiond by my lameness renders walking unpleasant.

I settled cash matters thus

From Mr. Cadell to account ————————		£150.
Cash to Tom ————————————	£30	
— to Bogie for accompts ———————	100.	
— to Do. present ————————	5.	
— to Anne for letters (d—n them) ————	10	
— to Swanston for his cut hand ————	1.	
	———	146
		£4.

12 MONDAY This is the third day I have not walkd out, pain and lameness being the cause. This bodes very ill for my future life. I made a grearch[3] yesterday and to-day for letters of Lord Byron to send to Tom Moore[4] but I could only find two. I had several others and am shockd at missing them. The one which he sent me with a silver cup I regret particularly. It was stolen [out] of the Cup itself by some vile inhospitable scoundrel for a servant would not have thought such a theft worth while.

My spirits are low yet I wot not why. I have been writing to my sons. Walter's Majority was like to be reduced but is spared for the present.[5] Charles is going on well I trust at his foreign

1. *Hamlet*, i. 2.
2. Probably Madame Tussaud, for whom Scott had sat the previous year.
3. Probably a slip for 'great search', as Tait suggests.
4. For his *Byron's Letters and Journals etc.*, which was published in 1830.
5. 'I have a letter from Cap[t]ain Leech of Walters regiment acquainting me that there was to be no reduction this bout. I hope before one takes place he will be got first Major. The Duke seems to be retrenching on all hands.' *Letters*, xi. 89.

office.[1] So I hope all is well.

Loiterd out an useless day half arranging half disarranging books and papers and packing the things I shall want.

13 TUESDAY *Der abschied's tag ist da.*[2] The day of return to Edinburgh is come. I don't know why but I am more happy at the change than usual. I am not working hard and it is what I ought to do and must do. Every hour of laziness cries fie upon me. But there is a perplexing sinking of the heart which one cannot always overcome. At such times I have wishd myself a clerk quill driving for twopence per page; you have at least application and that is all that is necessary, whereas unless your lively faculties are awake and propitious your application will do you as little good as if you straind your sinews to lift Arthurs Seat.

14 WEDNESDAY Got home last night after a freezing journey. This morning I got back some of the last copy and tugd as hard as ever did sutor[3] to make ends meet. Then I will be reconciled to my task again which at present disgusts me. Visited Lady Jane[4] who tells me Sir W. Forbes[5] died with much less than could be expected and that the present Sir John is inconvenienced. I then calld on Mr. Robison and instructed him to call a meeting of the Council of the Royal Society as Mr. Knox proposes to read an essay on some dissections. A bold proposal truly from one who has had so lately the boldness of trading so deep in human flesh. I will oppose his reading in the present circumstances if I should stand alone but I hope he will be wrought upon to withdraw his essay or postpone it at least. It is very bad taste to push himself forward just now.[6] Lockhart dined with us

1. But there is the usual suspicion that he is not as earnest as his father would like. Short of money as ever, his first economy has been to give up his German lessons. *Letters,* xi. 67 n.
2. A line from the Troopers' song which he translated for the Edinburgh Light Dragoons. *Life,* ii. 13.
3. 'Shoemaker.'
4. Lady Jane Stuart, mother-in-law of Sir William Forbes.
5. Sir William Forbes, Scott's old friend and rival in love, had died on 24 October 1828.
6. Dr. Robert Knox, one of Edinburgh's best-known anatomists, had attracted his share of public odium in connection with the activities of Burke and Hare, who, beginning as body-snatchers, soon turned to the murder of vagrants and strangers as an easier means of supplying the anatomists with subjects at £7 to £10 a time. Knox's offer to read a paper was singularly ill-timed between the trial of Burke on 24 December and his execution on 28 January. See also the Entry for 28 January 1829 and note.

which made the evening a pleasant but idle one. Well! I must rouse myself

Awake arise or be for ever fallen! – [1]

15 THURSDAY Day began with beggars as usual and John Nicolson has not sense to keep them out. I never yield however to this importunity, thinking it wrong that what I can spare to meritorious poverty of which I hear and see too much should be diverted by impudent importunity. I was detaind at the parliament house till nearly three by the great case concerning prescription, Maule v. Maule. This was made up to me by hearing an excellent opinion from Lord Corehouse[2] with a curious discussion *in apicibus juris*.[3] I disappointed Grahame of a sitting for my picture.[4] I went to the Council of the Royal Society which was convened at my request to consider whether we ought to hear a paper on anatomical subjects read by Mr. Knox whose name has of late been deeply implicated in a criminal prosecution against certain wretches who had murderd many persons and sold their bodies to professors of the anatomical science. Some thought that our declining to receive the paper would be a declaration unfavourable to Dr. Knox. I think hearing it before Mr. Knox has made any defence (as he is stated to have in view) would be an intimation of our preference of the cause of Science to those of Morality and Common Humanity. Mr. Knox's friends undertook to deal with him about suffering the paper to be omitted for the present while *'adhuc coram judice lis est.'*[5]

16 FRIDAY Nothing on the roll to-day so I did not go to the Parliament House but faggd at my desk till two. Dr. Ross calld to relieve me of a corn which though my lameness needs no addition had tormented me vilely. I again met the Royal Society's council. Dr. Knox consents to withdraw his paper, or rather suffers the reading to be postponed. There is some great error in the law of the subject. If it was left to itself many bodies would be imported from France and

---

1. *Paradise Lost*, i. 330.
2. A complicated entail dispute between W. Maule and the Hon. W. R. Maule. Lord Corehouse's judgment runs to fifty-seven closely printed pages. Shaw's *Cases in the Court of Session*, vii. 527.
3. 'On the fine points of the law'.
4. Graham Gilbert's portrait was for the Royal Society of Edinburgh, in whose rooms it still hangs.
5. 'The case is still *sub judice*.' Horace's *Ars Poetics*, l. 78.

Ireland and doubtless many would be found in our hospitals for the service of the anatomical science. But the total and severe exclusion of foreign supplies of this kind raises the price of the Subjects as they are calld technically to such a height that wretches are found willing to break into 'the bloody house of life'[1] merely to supply the anatomists' table. The law which as a deeper sentence on the guilt of murder [enacts] that the body of the convi[c]ted criminal should be given up to anatomy is certainly not without effect for criminals have been known to shrink from that part of the sentence which seem[d] to aflict them more than the doom of death itself with all its terrors here and hereafter. On the other hand while this idea of the infamy attending the exposition of the person is thus recognized by the laws it is impossible to adopt regulations which would effectually prevent such horrid crimes as the murder of vagrant wretches who can be snatchd from society without their being missd as in the late conspiracy. For instance if it was now to be enacted, as seems reasonable, that persons dying in hospitals and almshouses who die without their friends claiming their remains should be given up to the men of science, this would be subjecting poverty to the penalty of these atrocious criminals whom Law distinguishes by the heaviest posthumous disgrace which it can inflict. Even cultivated minds revolt from the exposure on an anatomical table when the case is supposed to be that of one who is dear to them. I should, I am conscious, be willing that I myself should be dissected in publick if doing so could produce any advantage to Society but when I think on relations and friends being rent from the grave the case is very different and I would fight knee deep to prevent or punish such an exposure. So inconsistent we are all upon matters of this nature.

I dined quietly at home with the girls and wrote after dinner.

17 SATURDAY Nothing on the roll, corrected proofs and went off at 12 o'clock in the Hamilton stage[2] to William Lockhart's of Auchirait.[3] My companions, Mr. Livingstone a clergyman of Camnethan, a Baillie Hamilton, the King of trumps I am told in the Burgh of Hamilton, and a Mr. Davie Martin *qui gaudet equis et canibus.*[4] Got to Auchinrait by six and met Lord Douglas and his brother Captain Douglas R.N. John G. Lockhart also who had had a large communication from Duke of W.[5] upon the subject of the

---

1. *King John*, iv. 2.
2. 'The Rocket', which left from Princes Street daily at noon.
3. William Lockhart of Auchinraith, Lockhart's half-brother.
4. 'Who rejoices in horses and dogs'. Horace's *Ars Poetica*, 1. 162.
5. The Prime Minister, the Duke of Wellington.

bullion. The Duke scouts the oeconomists' ideas about paper credit after the leading proposition that all men shall be entitled to require gold.

18 SUNDAY We went, the two Lockharts and I, to William's new purchase of Milton.[1] We found on his ground a cottage where a man calld Greenshiels,[2] a sensible powerful mind[ed] person, had a[t] 28 (rather too late a week)[3] taken up the art of sculpture. He had disposed of the person of the King most admirably according to my poor thoughts and had attaind a wonderful [likeness] expressing ease and majesty at the same time. He was desirous of engaging on Burns' jolly beggars which I dissuaded. Caricature is not the object of Sculpture.[4]

We went to Milton on as fine a day as could consist with snow on the ground. The situation is eminently beautiful, a fine promontory round which the Clyde makes a magnificent bend. We fixd on a situation where the sitting room should command the upper view, and with an ornamental garden I think it may be made the prettiest place in Scotland.

1. William Lockhart had just bought the estate later known as Milton Lockhart and had asked Scott for advice on the house he was to build. *Letters*, xi. 94.
2. John Greenshields was a stonemason who taught himself sculpture. He was patronized by Sir James Stewart and Lord Elgin (from whom he had hurried back on this occasion especially to see Scott). Elgin was struck by 'the ardor and exquisite taste with which he examined a few fragments in my possession of Grecian Sculpture: & the critical discrimination with which he compared the apparent Simplicity of the labour in them, with the great beauty and effect produced'. 7 January 1829, Walpole. Scott replies to Lord Elgin that Greenshields seems to be 'one of those remarkable men who must be distinguished in one way or other'. He suggests that he should be encouraged to take important subjects, and to study for a time in London. *Letters*, xi. 97. The statue of Scott in Edinburgh's Parliament House and the statue of Glasgow's Scott Monument are by Greenshields.
3. *As You Like It*, ii. 3.
4. 'Upon the moment I did not like to mention to Mr. G. my objections against a scheme which was obviously a favourite one . . . I desired Mr. Lockhart of Milton to state to Mr. G. what I felt on the above subject.' *Letters*, xi. 100. Nonetheless *The Jolly Beggars* was completed, and applauded in Edinburgh the following winter.

19 MONDAY Posted[1] to Edinburgh with John Lockhart. We stopped [at] Allanton to see a tree transplanted which was performd with great ease.[2] Sir Henry is a sad coxcomb and lifted beyond the solid earth by the effect of his book's success. But the book well deserves it. He is in practice particularly anxious to keep the roots of the tree near the surface and only covers them with about a foot of earth.

Nota. Lime rubbish dug in among the roots of ivy encourages it much.

The operation delayd us three hours so it was seven o'clock before we reach our dinner and a good fire in shandwick place and we were well nigh frozen to death. During this excursion I walkd very ill – with more pain in fact than I ever remember to have felt and even leaning on John Lockhart could hardly get on – *Baad that* – *vara baad* – it might be the severe weather though and the numbing effect of the sitting in the carriage – Be what it will I can't help myself.

20 TUESDAY I had little to do at the court and returnd home soon. Honest old Mr. Ferriar is dead at extreme old age. I confess I should not wish to live so long. He was a man with strong passions and strong prejudices but with generous and manly sentiments at the same time. We used to call him Uncle Adam after that character in his gifted daughter's novel of the Heiress.[3]

I wrote a long letter after I came home to my Lord Elgin about Greenshields the sculptor.[4] I am afraid he is going into the burlesque lin[e] to which sculpture is peculiarly ill adapted. So I have expressd my veto to his patron. *Valeat quantum.*[5]

I also [answerd] a letter from Mrs. Professor Sandford at Glas[g]ow about reprinting MacAulay's history of Saint Kilda

1. This suggests that Lockhart had borrowed his father-in-law's vehicle for the visit to his family, Scott joining him two days later by stagecoach and then returning with him in his own carriage.
2. Scott was a member of the committee set up by the Highland Society to report on Steuart's methods. Steuart had been pestering Scott since 1827 to come and see a tree transplanted. The descriptions in his book (*The Planter's Guide,* 1828) 'fall much short of the reality, I mean in beauty and nicety of execution'. 8 September 1827, Walpole. See also 25, 28, 30 August, 25, 27 September 1827, Walpole.
3. Scott means *Inheritance,* by Susan Ferrier, 1824.
4. See *Letters,* xi. 96, and the Entry for 18 January 1829 and note.
5. 'For what it may be worth.'

advising them to insert the history of Lady Grange who was kidnapd and banishd thither.[1]

I corrected my proofs moreover and prepare to dine. After dinner we go to Euphemia Erskine's marriage.[2] Mr. Dallas came in and presented me with an old pedigree of the McIntoshes. The wedding took place with the usual April weather of smiles and tears. The bridegroom's name is Dawson. As he as well as the bride is very tall they have every chance of bringing up a family of giants. The bridegroom has an excellent character. He is only a captain but oeconomy does wonders in the army where there are many facilities for practizing it. I sincerely wish them happiness.

21 WEDNESDAY Anne has sufferd her accounts to get wrong again. It is hopeless to argue with her. She professes a purpose of amendment with the purpose I suppose of keeping her word but always fails. I must try to get her into better training. Went out to Dalkeith House to dine and stay all night. Found Marqs of Lothian and a family party. I liked the sense and spirit displayd by this young nobleman who reminds me so strongly of his parents whom I valued so highly.

22 THURSDAY Left Dalkeith after breakfast[3] and gaind the Parlt. House, where there was almost nothing to do, at eleven o'clock – Afterwards sate to Grahame who is making a good thing of it.[4] Mr. Colville Smith has made a better in one sense having sold ten or twelve copies of the portrait to different friends.[5] The Solicitor came

1. The book is the Revd. K. Macaulay's *History of St. Kilda*, 1764. The story of Lady Grange, who was kidnapped at the instigation of her husband and banished to St. Kilda, is told by Dr. Alexander Carlyle in his *Autobiography* (1760), pp. 10–13.
2. Euphemia was the daughter of Scott's old friend William Erskine. He met the young couple again in Malta. See the Entry for 22 November 1831.
3. 'A breakfast at half past eight that I may return in time for the court'. *Letters*, xi. 94.
4. 'With much skill and beauty of fin[i]shing he seems to me to have more of a certain rare quality calld *genius* than any one now going in Scotland', writes Scott, recommending Graham to the Duke of Buccleuch. *Letters*, xi. 95.
5. Colvin Smith's letter in the *Centenary Catalogue* states that the original was for William Adam and that copies were made for Sir Samuel Shepherd, Lord Gillies, Lord Jeffrey, Dr. Hughes, the Bishop of Llandaff, John Hope, Andrew Skene, Sir Frederick Adam, Mr. Blackburn, Mr. Campbell of Blythswood, Sir George Warrender, Mrs. Laing, Lord Minto, Taylor's Institute in Oxford, and Mr. Kay of London – as well as for two or three

to dine with me; we drank a bottle of Champagne and two bottles of claret which in former days I should have thought a very sober allowance since, Lockhart included, there were three persons to drink it. But I felt I had drunk too much and was uncomfortable. The young men stood it like young men. Skene and his wife and daughter lookd in in the evening. I suppose I am turning to my second childhood for not only am I filld drunk or made stupid at least with one bottle of wine but I am disabled from writing by chillblains on my fingers, a most babyish complaint. They say that the character is indicated by the hand writing. If so min[e] is crabbed enough.

23 FRIDAY Still severe frost annoying to sore fingers. Nothing on the roll. I sate at home and wrote letters to Wilkie, Landseer, Mrs. Hughes, Charles[1] etc. Went out to old Mr. Ferrier's funeral and saw the last duty rendered to my old friend whose age was

> — like a lusty winter
> Frosty but kindly[2]

I mean in a moral as well as physical sense.

I then went to Cadell's for some few minutes.

By the way Sir John Sinclair is provided with a substitute to continue the trade of *boring*. When he is calld to be a bore like some old classick amongst the heavenly constellations *haud deficiat alter*.[3] I saw with a sick and sorry heart his eldest son, tall and ungainly like the knight himself, with cheek as sleek as Oil and a wit as thick as mustard. Young hopeful's business with me was to invite me to be one of a committee who were to sit as Mr. Knox's friends in a Committee of enquiry on his late traffick with the West port. In other words to lend a hand to whitewash this much to be suspected individual. But he shall ride off on no back of mine and I feel no call to mix myself in the business at all. The rest of the committee are to be doctors and surgeons (ask my fellow etc.) and I suppose the

---

other people whom he could not recall. 'For seven of these,' he adds, 'Sir Walter gave me one sitting each.' *Centenary Catalogue*, p. 73.

1. The letters to Wilkie and Landseer were about illustrations for the Magnum Opus, the others replies to Mrs. Hughes (who had written to say that the Colvin Smith portrait and *Tales of a Grandfather* had arrived. 15 January 1829, Walpole), and to Charles, who had written at length about the avenues of promotion in the Foreign Office. 19 January 1829, Walpole.
2. *As You Like It*, ii. 3.
3. 'Another will not be lacking.'

doughty Sir John at the head of them all and this young boar pig to swell the cry. I will travell in no such boat.[1] I carri[e]d out Lockhart to Dalkeith wher[e] we dined, supd, and returnd through a clinking frost with snow on the ground. Lord Ramsay and the Miss Kerrs were at Dalkeith. The Duke[2] shews for [so] young a man a great deal of character and seems to have a proper feeling of the part he has to play. The evening was pleasant but the thought that I was now the visitor and friend of the family in the third generation lay somewhat heavy on me. Every thing around me seemd to say that Beauty, power, wealth, honour were but things of a day.

24 SATURDAY Heavy fall of snow. Lockhart is off in the mail.[3] I hope he will not be blockaded. The day bitter cold. I went to the court and with great difficulty returnd along the slippry street. I ought to have taken the carriage but I have a superstitious dread of giving up the habit of walking and would willingly stick to the last by my old hardy customs.[4] Little but trifles to do at the court. I wrote to Lord Register and Lord Melville about the situation of Keeper of Record of Entails. I suppose they will give it me as they proposed. It does not exceed £150. but that is always worth something.[5] My hands are so coverd with Chillblains that I can hardly use a pen. My feet *ditto*.

We bould away at 6 o'clock to Mr. Wardlaw Ramsay, found we were a week to[o] early and went back as if our noses had been bleeding.

25 SUNDAY Workd seriously all morning expecting the Fergussons to dinner. Alas instead of that I learn that my poor innocent friend Mary is no more. She was a person of some odd and peculiar habits, wore a singular dress and affected wild and solitary haunts, but she was at the same time a woman of talents and even genius. She used often to take long walks with me up through the glens and I believe her sincere good wishes attended me as I was always glad of an

1. For Knox's dealings with Burke and Hare see the Entries for 14 and 28 January 1829 and notes. The committee, which included Professor James Russell, Sir William Hamilton, and John Robison of the Royal Society, was set up in March. Its report, whitewashing Knox, is printed in Roughead's *Burke and Hare*, 1921, Appendix IX.

2. The Duke of Buccleuch.

3. The London Mail left Edinburgh at 7.30 a.m. and did the journey in forty-five hours.

4. Scott took the Clerks' Coach up to Court in the morning, but walked home after the day's business.

5. It went, however, to another Clerk of Session, James Ferguson. See the Entry for 22 October 1827 and note.

opportunity to shew her kindness. I shall long think of her when at Abbotsford. This sad event breaks up our little party. Will Clerk came however and his tete a tete was of course interesting and amusing in the highest degree. We drank some whisky and water and smoked a cigar or two till nine at night.

> No after friendship ere can raise
> The endearments of our early days.[1]

26 MONDAY I muzzd on, I can call it little better, with *Anne of Geierstein*. The materials are excellent but the power of using them is failing. Yet I wrote out about three pages sleeping at intervals. My cash affairs stand thus

To advanced by Mr. Caddel		£10
Expences of journey to Lanarkrkshire		6
	In cash	4.
Cash in purse		£4
received by Mr. Cadell at Exchcher		150.
Cash remitted by Miss Arden for expence of Lady Alvanley's monument[2]		42
		196

Cash to Mr. Lang by receipt	£100	
Of the above *Pub[li]ck* mony		
Pror fiscal	£42. 5.6	
Sheriff Clerk	34.11	
	76 16 6	
		76 16 6

To draw for T. Purdie and Bogie

Ball. 23. 3.6

	100
Altogether deduce	96
For Lady Alvanley's monument	38
	58
Four pounds of the balance lies to answer Braid's fees —	£4
therefore in cash	54

I have to receive the above £76. 16. 6. from government with my own appointments for circuit.

1. Logan's 'On the Death of a Young Lady', st. 9.
2. When Lady Alvanley died in Edinburgh in 1825 the funeral arrangements had fallen on Scott.

I will need to raise £200 or £300 to put by this Bill season. Anne has hardly used me kindly or fairly after declaiming so much against date.¹ It must be more closely lookd after.²

27 TUESDAY A great and gen[er]all thaw, the streets afloat, the snow descending on one's head from the roofs. Went to the Court. There was little to do. Left about twelve and took a sitting with Grahame who begs for another. Sir James Stewart stood bottle holder on this occasion. Had rather an unfavourable account of the pictures of James Stewart of Dunearn³ which are to be sold. I had promised to pick up one or two for the Duke of Buccleuch. Came home and wrote a leaf or two. I shall be soon done with the 2d Volume of *Anne of Geierstein*. I cannot persuade myself of the obvious risk of [not] satisfying the publick although I cannot so well satisfy myself. I am like Beaumont and Fletcher's Old Merryman who could not be persuaded that there was a chance of his wanting meat. 'I never came into my parlour' said he 'but I found the cloth laid and din[n]er ready. Surely it will be always thus. Use makes perfect.'⁴ My reflections are of the same kind and if they are unlogical they are perhaps not the less comfortable. Fretting and struggling does no good. Wrote to Miss Margaret Fergusson a letter of condoleance. Sent Tom an order for £23 found balance of £100 sent to Mr. Lang.

28 WEDNESDAY Breakfasted for a wonder abroad, with Hay Drummond whose wife appears a little pretty and agreeable woman. We worship his tutelar deity the Herculas and saw a good model of Hercules Bibax or the drunken Hercules. Grahame and Sir James Stewart were there. Home-baked bread an[d] soldier's coffee were the treat. I came home and Sir Robert Dundas having taken my duty at the court I wrote for some time but not much. Burke the Murderer hangd this morning. The mob which was immense demanded Knox and Hare but though greedy for more victims received with shouts

1. A slip for 'debt', a word which he probably pronounced in almost the same way.
2. A statement of accounts from Cadell on the 13th shows that Scott was living well beyond his means. Between 31 October 1828 and 10 January 1829 Cadell had paid out £1,954. 6s., which left Scott £554. 6s. in his debt. Cadell, 13 January 1829, Walpole. The *History of Scotland* written for Dr. Lardner was undertaken to clear off Anne's housekeeping debts. See the Entry for 16 April 1829.
3. The antagonist of Sir Alexander Boswell in the fatal duel of 1822. See the Entry for 14 December 1826 and note.
4. *The Knight of the Burning Pestle*, i. 3.

the solitary wretch who found his way to the gallows out of five or six who seem not less guilty than He. But the story begins to be stale insomuch that I believe a doggrel ballad upon it would be popular how brutal soever the wit. This is the progress of human passion. We ejaculate, exclaim, hold up to heaven our hand, like the rustic Phidele — next morning the mood changes and we dance a jig to the tune which moved us to tears.[1] Mr. Belt sends me a spec[i]ment of a Historical novel but he goes not the way to write it. He is too general and not sufficient[ly] minute. It is not easy to convey this to an author with the necessary attention to his feelings and yet in good faith and sincerity it must be done.

29 THURSDAY I had a vacant day once more by the kindness of Sir Robert,[2] unaskd but most kindly afforded. I have not employd it to much purpose. I wrote 6 pages to Croker who is busied with a new edition of Boswell's *Life of Johnson*[3] to which most entertaining book he hopes to make large additions from Mrs. Piozzi, Hawkins and other sources. I am bound by many obligations to do as much for him as I can, which can only respect the Scottish tour. I wrote only two or three pages of *Anne*. I am

> — as one who in a darksome way
> Doth walk with fear and dread.[4]

But walk I must and walk forward too [or] I shall be benighted with a vengeance. After dinner to compromise matters with my conscience I wrote letters to Bell, Mrs. Hughes[5] and so forth; thus I concluded the day with a sort of busy idl[e]ness. This will not do. By Cock and pye[6] it will not.

30 FRIDAY Mr. Stuart of   regiment[7] breakfasted with me, a grand nephew of Lady Louisa's and a very pleasing young gentleman. The coach[8] surprized me by not calling. *Will* it be for the

1. For Burke's execution see note 9, pp. 811–12.
2. Sir Robert Dundas.
3. *Boswell's Life of Dr. Samuel Johnson, including a Journal of a Tour to the Hebrides*, new edition with numerous additions and notes by J. W. Croker, LL.D., etc., 1831. For Scott's six pages of anecdotes about Johnson and Boswell see *Letters*, xi. 110.
4. Coleridge's 'Ancient Mariner'. ll. 446–7.
5. Thanking her for some engravings. *Letters*, xi. 107.
6. *Merry Wives of Windsor*, i. 1.
7. The 4th regiment of foot, stationed at Edinburgh Castle.
8. 'The Clerks' Coach.'

Ma[r]tyrdom? I trow it will, yet strange to say I cannot recollect if it is a regular holiday or not.[1]

> Uprouse you then, my merry merry men,
>   And use it as you may.[2]

I wrote in the morning and went at one o'clock to a meeting of Country gentlemen about bringing the direct road from London down by Jedburgh, said to be the nearest line by 50 miles. It is proposed the pleasant men of Teviotdale should pay not only their own share, that is the expence of making the road through our own county, but also the expence of making the road under the Ellsdon trust in Northumberland where the English would positively do nothing. I stated this to the meeting as an act of Quixotry. If it be an advantage, which unless to individuals may be doubted, it is equally one to Northumberland as to Roxburgh, therefor[e] I am clear that we should go æquals acquals. I think I have may be put a spoke in the wheel. The raising the statute labour of Roxburgh Shire to an oppressive extent to make roads in England is I think jimp legal and will be much complaind of by the poorer heritors.

Henry of Harden dine[d] with [me] tete a tete excepting the girls.

		In cash	£54
By paid Bland's fees ———————	£1		
By paid Cotton for Segars ———	5.		
To Anne ———————————	40.	49.	
	In purse Ball.	5.	

31 SATURDAY I though[t] I had opend a vein this morning and that it came freely but the demands of art have been more than I can bear. I corrected proofs before breakfast, went to court after that meal, was busy till near one o'clock, then I went to Cadell's where [I found] him preparing to circulate the prospectus of the magnum which will have all the effect of surprize on most people. I sate to Mr. Graham till I was quite tired, then went to Lady Jane,[3] who is getting better. Then here at four, fit for nothing but to bring up the silly Diary. The corpse of the Murderer Burke is now lying in state at the College in the

---

1. An indication of Scott's failing memory: 30 January has been a holiday in previous years.
2. Joanna Baillie's *Orra*, iii. 1.
3. Lady Jane Stuart.

anatomical class and all the world flock to see him.[1] Who is he says that we are not ill to please in our objects of curiosity? The strange means by which the wretch made money are scarce more disgusting than the eager curiosity with which the publick have lickd up all carrion details of this business.

I trifled with my work. I wonder how Johnson set himself dogged-ly[2] to it – to a work of imagination it seems quite impossible and one's brain is at times fairly addled and yet I have felt times when sudden and strong exertion throw off all this mistiness of mind as a north wind would disperse it.

Blow blow thou northern wind.[3]

Nothing more than about two or three pages. I went to the Parliament House to-day but had little to do.

I sate to Mr. Grahame, the last time Heaven be praised. If I be not known in another age it will not be for want of pictures. We dined with Mr. Ramsay Wardlaw[4] and Lady Anne – a fine family. There was little done in the way of work except correcting proofs. The bile affects me and makes me vilely drowsy when I should be most awake. Met at Mr. Wardlaw's several people I did not know. Lookd over *Cumnor Hall* by Mr. Usher Tighe of Oxford.[5] I see from the inscription on Tony Forster's tomb that he was a skillful planter amongst other fashionable accomplishments.

1. Burke's body was dissected by Dr. Alexander Monro on Thursday the 29th in the course of a lecture on the brain, and was put on general exhibition the next day to pacify the mob which had tried to force an entry. The scene is described in the diary of an Edinburgh accountant: 'Burke's body was lying stretched out on a table in a large sort of lumber or dissecting room, quite naked. The upper part of the skull had been sawn off and the brain extracted, but in other respects he was untouched, except, indeed, that the hair had been all shaven off his body.' 'The Edinburgh of Scott', in *The Scotsman* for 15 June 1907.
2. Boswell's *Life of Johnson*, v. 40.
3. *As You Like It*, ii. 7.
4. Scott means Wardlaw Ramsay. This was the engagement for which he had arrived a week early the previous Saturday.
5. H. U. Tighe's *Historical Account of Cumnor . . . illustrative of the Romance of Kenilworth*, 1821, sent him by Mrs. Hughes on the 15th, 'will afford some capital matter for notes to *Kenilworth*'. *Letters*, xi. 110.

FEBRUARY

1 SUNDAY *Domum mansi Lanam feci*[1] – Staid at home *videlicet* and labourd without interruption except from intolerable drowsiness; finishd eight leaves however, the best day's work I have made this long time. No interruption, and I got pleased with my work which ends the second Volume of *Anne of Geierstein*. After dinner had a letter from Lockhart with happy tidings about the probability of the Commission on the Stewart papers being dissolved. The Duke of W. says Commissions never either did or will do any good.[2] John will in that case be sole editor of these papers with an apartment at Saint James's *cum plurimis aliis*.[3] It will [be] a grand coup if it takes place –

2 MONDAY Sent off yesterday's work with proofs. Could I do as toughly for a week, and many a day I have done more, I should be soon out of the scrape. I wrote letters and put over the day till one when I went down with Sir James Stewart to see Stewart of Dunearn's pictures now on sale. I did not see much which my poor taste covets. A Hobbema much admired is I think as tame a piece of work as I ever saw. I promised to try to get a good picture or two for the young Duke –[4].

Dind with the old club instituted forty years ago. There were present Lord Justice Clerk,[5] Lord Advocate,[6] Sir Peter Murray, John Irving, William Clerk and I. It was a party such as the meeting of fellow scholars and fellow students alone could occasion. We told old stories, laughd and quaffd and resolved rashly perhaps that we would hold the club at least once a year, if possible twice. We will see how

1. 'I remained at home. I made wool.' See p. 375, note 5.
2. 'Dissolve the Commission by God – they have done nothing – no commission ever will do any good.' These were Wellington's words, according to Lockhart, whose news is that Lord Aberdeen is to propose to the Cabinet that Scott and he should be appointed editors of the Stewart Papers. 'In case the thing goes on the papers which are in a room in St. James's Palace will be given to my keeping & the room appropriated for my use. "It will be a great thing" said the Great Unseen [Sir William Knighton] "for you will be fairly on the perch – belong to us & have constant access." ' Lockhart, 30 January 1829, Walpole. However, the plan was scotched on financial grounds.
3. 'With very many other [benefits]'.
4. The Duke of Buccleuch.
5. David Boyle.
6. Sir William Rae.

this will fadge. Our mirth was more unexpected as Sir Adam, our first fiddle, was wanting owing to his family loss.[1]

3 TUESDAY Rose at eight – felt my revel a little in my head. The court business light – returnd by Cadell and made one or two calls. At Skene's especially where they have had the fever.[2] Fortunately the child has got what is cald the turn. Dinner and evening at home laboriously employed.

4 WEDNESDAY To-day I was free from duty and made good use of my leisure at home finishing the second volume of *Anne* and writing several letters. One to recommend Captain Pringle to Lord Beresford[3] which I send tomorrow through Morritt. My mother whips me and I whip the top. The girls went to the play.

Paid to Mr. Learmont to accot.	£100.
to Mr. Cockburn Do.	80.
Ross in full ————————	5.
Anne ————————	50.
Bill at Club ————————	2.
	237.

5 THURSDAY Attended the court as usuall, got dismissd about one. Finishd and sent off Vol 2d. of *Anne*.[4] Dined with robert Rutherford my cousin and the whole clan of Swinton.

Memdm. About Waterloo. When a heavy column of french infantry forced their way up to our first line and were about to crown the heights the heavy brigade was orderd to charge. The British horse being conceald from the enemy by the long scrambling hedge and a sudden dip of the ground on the outside of their charge had the complete effect of surprize. Dazzled with their own astonishing success, these regiments of horse having defeated at least four

1. Mary Ferguson's death is recorded in the Entry for 25 January 1829.
2. The typhus fever 'almost universal here chiefly amongst children of the higher ranks'. *Letters*, xi. 102. 'The deaths amongst us', Scott writes to Mrs. Hughes, 'continue fearfully frequent and all the mirth and festivity of the season are silent.' *Letters*, xi. 108.
3. Captain Pringle of the Royal Engineers, whose account of the battle of Waterloo Scott had made use of in the *Life of Napoleon* (see the Entry for 16 March 1827), wanted the Memoir he had written brought to the attention of Viscount Beresford, Master-General of the Ordnance. *Letters*, xi. 129–30.
4. 'Without great confidence that it will please'. *Letters*, xi. 129.

thousand french, they rushd on in disorder and receivd a charge on the left by a corps of lancers by which they sufferd much. The repulse of the light cavalry was occasiond by General the Marquis of Anglesea persisting in the rash attempt to charge a column of lancers formd in complete order having their flanks protected – Man and horse faulterd and faild when they came to lances points and as was to be expected about went our light cavalry. The desperate attempt was renewd three times – at each time with as little success as before. The lancers advancing to take advantage of the confusion their own flank became uncoverd and, a brigade of the British heavy Cavalry charging them at the same moment, they were over-throwown.

6 FRIDAY Corrected proofs in the morning – then to the Court, thence to Cadell's where I found some business cut out for me in the way of notes, which delayd me. Walkd home, the weary way giving my feet the ancient twinges of agony. Such a journey is a severe penance as [if I] had walkd the same length[1] with peas in my shoes to attone for some horrible crime by beating my toes into a jelly. I wrote some and corrected a good deal. We dined alone and I partly wrought partly slept in the Evening. It is now pretty clear that the Duke of W. intends to have a catholic bill.[2] He probably expects to neutralize and divide the catholic body by bringing a few into parliament where they will probably be tractable enough rather than a large proportion of them rioting in Ireland where they will be to a certain degree unanimous.

7 SATURDAY Up and wrought a little. I had at breakfast a son of Sir Thomas Lauder Dick, a very quick smart looking young fellow, who is on his way to the Continent with a tutor.[3] Dined at Mrs. George Swinton with the whole clan an[d] alliance.

8 SUNDAY I wrought the whole day and finishd about 6 pages of Manuscript of Vol. III. *Sat cito si sat bene.*[4] The Skenes came in to supper like the olden world.

1. From Cadell's to Shandwick Place was just a mile.
2. The Roman Catholic Relief Bill received the Royal Assent on 13 April 1829. See Appendix D, p. 825.
3. Sir Thomas Dick Lauder had asked for five minutes of Scott's time so that his son, who was going abroad with his tutor, Mr. Monkhouse of Queen's College, Oxford, could say 'he had had the supreme honor of seeing and conversing with Sir Walter Scott'. Lauder, 2 February 1829, Walpole.
4. 'Speedily enough if well enough.'

9 MONDAY Was up in good time (say half past seven) and employd the morning in correcting proofs. At twelve I went to Stuart of Dunearn's sale of pictures. This poor man fell like myself a victim to speculation and though I had no knowlege of him personally and disliked him as the Causer of poor Sir Alexander Boswell's death[1] yet 'had he been slaughterman to all my kin'[2] I could but pity the miserable sight of his splendid establishmen[t] broken up and his treasures of art exposed to public and unsparing sale. I wanted a picture of the Earl of Rothes for the Duke of Buccleuch, a fine Sir Joshua, but Balfour of Balbirnie fancied it also and having followd it to 160 Guineas [I let it go]. Charles Sharpe's account is that I may think myself in luck for the face has been reprinted. There is he says a print taken from the picture at Lesley House which has quite a different countenance from the present.

This job however took me up the whole morning to little purpose. Capt. and Mrs. Hall dined with us, also Sir James Stuart, Charles Sharpe, John Scott Gala etc. Miss Kerre came in the evening.

10 TUESDAY I was up at seven this morning and will continue the practize, but the shoal of proofs took up all my leisure. I will not I think go after these second rate pictures again to-day. If I could get a quiet day or two I would make a deep dint in the 3d. volume. But hashd and smashd as my time is who can make any thing of it? I read over Henry's *History of Henry VI and Edward IV.*[3] He is but a stupid historian after all. This took me up the whole day.

11 WEDNESDAY Up as usual and wrought at proofs. Mr. Hay Drummond and McIntosh Mackay dined. The last brought me his history of the *Blair Lleine* or white battle (battle of the Shirts). To the court and remaind there till two when we had some awkward business on the Counc[i]l of the Royal Society. A certain Mr. McV—[4] who is said formerly to have shewn great mathematical talent is a candidate for admission and it has pleased him to publish a pamphlet calld *An Apology for Astronomy* in which there are symptoms of insanity such [as] vague aspirations after the *perpetuum mobile* and

1. In the duel provoked by the attack on Stuart in the *Glasgow Sentinel*. See the Entry for 14 December 1826 and note.
2. *3 Henry VI*, i. 4.
3. The Revd. Dr. R. Henry's *History of Great Britain; from the invasion of Julius Caesar to the death of Henry VIII*, 12 vols. Scott owned the 4th edition, 1805–6.
4. The Revd. John MacVicar of Dundee, proposed by Dr. Graham the previous November. Royal Society Minutes.

certain other tropes of rhetoric in which Madness begins. I found out easily it was [not] sense though it might certainly have been science. But the puzzling thing is that his friends persevere in proposing him for election which the Council endeavour to prevent. Certainly the society wants enthusiasm but to bring actual insanity into it would hardly answer. We got the proposal adjournd however which is half the battle.

Wrote in the evening.

12 THURSDAY W. Lockhart came to breakfast, full of plans for his house[1] which will make a pretty and romantick habitation. After breakfast the Court claimd its vassal. As I came out Mr. Chambers introduced a pretty little romantic girl[2] to me who possessd a laudable zeal to know a live poet. I went with my fair admirer as far as the new rooms on the Mound where I lookd into the Royal society's rooms then into the Exhibition, in mere unwillingness to work and desire to dawdle away time. Learnd that Lord Haddington had bought the Sir Joshua.[3] I wrought hard to-day and made out five pages.

13 FRIDAY This morning Col. Hunter Blair breakfasted here with his wife, a very pretty woman with a good deal of pleasant conversation. She had been in India and had lookd about her to purpose. I wrote for several hours in the forenoon but was nervous and drumbly, also I botherd myself about geography; in short there was trouble, as miners say when the vein of metal is interrupted. Went out at two and walkd thank God better than in the winter which gives me hopes that the failure of the unfortunate limb is only temporary owing to severe weather. We dined at John Murray's with the Mansfield family. Lady Caroline Murray possesses I think the most pleasing taste for music and is the best singer I ever heard. No temptation to display a very brilliant voice ever leads her aside from truth and simplicity and besides she looks beautiful when she sings.

14 SATURDAY Wrote in the morning[4] which begins to be a regular act of duty. It was late ere I got home and I did not do much. The letters I receivd were numerous and craved answers.[5] Yet the 3d.

1. Milton Lockhart.
2. A Miss Inglis, 'a charming creature'. Chambers, 14 February 1829, Walpole.
3. At the sale described in the Entry for 9 February 1829.
4. i.e. before breakfast.
5. A letter to the Duke of Buccleuch, about paintings, is the only surviving letter written on this date. *Letters*, xi. 136.

volume is getting on Hooly and Fairly.[1] I am twenty leaves before the Printers but Ballantyne's wife is ill and it is his nature to indulge apprehensions of the worst, which incapacitates him for labour. I cannot help regarding this amiable weakness of the mind with something too nearly allied to contempt: I keep the press behind me at a good distance and I like the

> Post boy's horse am glad to miss
> The lumber of the wheels.[2]

I dined and finishd my post.

15 SUNDAY I wrought to-day but not much – rather dawdled and took to reading Chambers' *Beauties of Scotland*[3] which would be admirable if they were more accurate. He is a clever young fellow but hurts himself by too much haste. I am not making too much myself I know and I know too it is time I were making it – Unhappily there is such a thing as more haste and less speed. I can very seldom think to purpose by lying perfectly idle but when I take an idle book or a walk my mind strays back to its task out of contradiction as it were; the things I read become mingled with those I have been writing and something is concocted. I cannot compare this process of mind to any thing save that of a woman to whom the mechanical operation of spinning serves as a running base to the songs she sings or the course of ideas she pursues. The phrase *hoc age*[4] often quoted by my father does not jump with my humour.[5] I cannot nail my mind to one subject of contemplation and it is by nourishing two trains of ideas that I can bring one into order.

Colin Mackenzie came in to see me poor fellow. He looks well in his retirement. Partly I envy him – partly I am better pleased as it is.

16 MONDAY Stayd at home and labourd all the forenoon. Young Invernahyle calld to bid me interest myself about getting a lad of the House of Scott of Bavelaw a commission – how is this possible? The last I tried for there was about 3000 on the list – And they say the boy is too old being 24.[6] I scribbled three or four pages, forbore smoking

---

1. 'Slowly and gently but steadily.' *S. N. D.*
2. William Cowper's 'John Gilpin', ll. 231–2.
3. Robert Chambers's *Picture of Scotland*, sent by the author the day before. Walpole
4. 'Do this', i.e., concentrate on one thing at a time.
5. *1 Henry IV*, i. 2.
6. Scott none the less wrote on his behalf to Lord Montagu. See *Letters*, xi. 156.

and whisky and water, and went to the Royal Society. There Sir William Hamilton read an Essay, the result of some anatomical investigations, which containd a maskd battery against the phrenologists. It seems these worthies are agreed that the cerebellum is that part of the headpiece which influences the sexual organs and according to this hypothesis that same cerebellum should be stronger in men than in women, in adults than in children, in old men than in youths, in persons mutilated than in those who are in the natural state, and such the phrenologists aver <this> to be the case. But if Sir William's course of experiments are correct the very opposite is the truth.[1] I went to Dr. Russell's after all where I found General Dirom, Baron Clerk *et caetera*.

17 TUESDAY In the morning I sent off copy and proof. I receive the melancholy news that James Ballantyne has lost his wife. With his domestic habits the blow is irretrievable. What can he do, poor fellow, at the head of such a family of children? I should not be surprized if he were to give way to despair.

I was at the court where there was little to do but it diddled away my time till two. I went to the Library but not a book could I get to look at. It is I think a wrong system the lending books to private houses at all and leads to immense annual losses.[2] I calld at Skene and borowd a volume of his journal to get some information about Burgundy and Provence.[3] Something may be made out of King René but I wish I had thought of him sooner. Dined alone with the girls.

18 WEDNESDAY This being teind Wednesday I had holiday. Workd the whole day interrupted by calls from Dr. Ross, Sir Hugh Palliser, Sir David Hunter Blair and Colonel Blair. I made out about six pages before dinner and go to Lord Gillies's to dine with a good conscience. Hay Drummond came in and discharged a volley at me which Mons

1. The paper was 'On the size of the brain and the proportion of its parts, as affected by age, sex, or sexual mutilation'. Sir William Hamilton, who was Professor of Civil History at the university, had read a paper 'On Phrenology Considered in its Constitution' in April 1827. Royal Society Minutes.
2. When the National Library of Scotland came into being in 1925 by taking over from the Advocates' Library its collection of non-legal books, it discontinued the practice to which Scott objects, although an exception was made for those who were members of the Faculty of Advocates at that time.
3. For *Anne of Geierstein*. Skene's journals were in manuscript.

Meg could hardly have equald.[1] I will go set to work with Skene's journal. My head aches violently and has done so several days. It is cold I think.

At Lord Gillies's we found Sir John Dalrymple, Lady Dalrymple and Miss Fergusson, Mr. Hope Vere of Craigie hall, and Lady Elizabeth a sister of Lord Tweeddale, Sir Robert O'Callaghan, Captain Cathcart and others, a gay party.

19 THURSDAY An execrable day – half frost half fresh, half sleet half rain, and wholly abominable. Having made up my packet for the printing House and performd my duty at the court I had the firmness to walk round by the North Bridge and face the weather for two miles by way of exercise. Calld on Skene and saw some of his drawings of Aix.[2] It was near two before I got home and now I hear three strike. Part of this hour has been consumed in a sound sleep by the fireside after putting on dry things. I met Baron Hume and we praised each other's hardihood for daring to take exercize in such weather, agreeing that if a man relaxed the custom of his exercize in Scotland for a bad day he is not like to resume it in a hurry. The other moiety of the time was employd in looking over the *Mémoires de Fauche-Borel*.[3]

20 FRIDAY The court duty took me up from eleven till about three but left some time for labour which I employd to purpose, at least I hope so – I declined going to the Exhibition of paintings tonight – neither the beauties of art nor of nature have their former charms for [me]. I finishd however about seven pages of manuscript which is a fair half of volume third. I wish I could command a little more time and I would soon find you something or other. But the plague is that time is wanting when I feel an aptitude to work, and when time abounds the will, at least the real efficient power of the faculties, is awanting. Still however we make way by degrees. I glanced over some romances metrical publishd by Hartshorne[4] several of which have not seen the light. They are considerably curious but I was surprized to see them mingled with 'Blaunchflour' and 'Florice' and one or two others which might have been spared. There is no great display of notes or prolegomena and there is moreover no glossary. But the work is well edited.

1. The volley was *about* Mons Meg, whose restoration to the Castle Scott had been able to arrange. See the Entry for 9 March.
2. To assist him with the descriptions in *Anne of Geierstein*.
3. *Mémoires de Fauche-Borel (agent des Bourbons)*, 1829.
4. The Revd. C. H. Hartshorne's *Ancient Metrical Tales*, 1829.

21 SATURDAY Colonel Fergusson breakfasted with us. I was detaind at the parlt. House till the hour of poor Mrs. Ballantyne's funeral, then attended that melancholy ceremony. The husband was unable to appear; the sight of the poor children was piteous enough. James Ballantyne has taken his brother Sandy into the house, I mean the firm, about which there had formerly been some misunderstanding.

I attended the Bannatyne Club. We made a very good election bringing in Lord Dalhouise and the Lord Clerk Register.[1] Our dinner went pretty well off but I have seen it merrier. To be sure old Dr. J.[2] like an immense feather bed was *Burking*[3] me, as the phrase now goes, during the whole time. I am sure that word will stick in the language for an while.

22 SUNDAY Very rheumatick. I e'en turnd my table to the fire and feagued it away as Bayes says.[4] Neither did I so much as cast my eyes round to see what sort of a day it was. The splashing on the windows gave all information that was necessary. Yet with all my leisure during the whole day I finishd only four leaves of copy – somewhat of the least Mr. Matthew[5] – There was no interruption during the whole day though the above is a poor account of it. I reckon to have all completed before I leave town being more than half through volume 3.

23 MONDAY Up and at it. After Breakfast Mr. Hay Drummond came in enchanted about Mons Meg and roaring as loud as she could have done for her life when she was in perfect voice.

Paid Anne ———————	£30
Weighton Silversmith ———————	5
	35

James Ballantyne came in to my surprize about twelve o'clock. He was very serious and spoke as if he had some idea of sudden and speedy death. He mentiond that he had named Caddel, Cowan, young Hughes and his brother to be his trustees with myself and then add[ed] that in his letters to Mr. Cowan he had expressd himself unwilling that Alexander Ballantyne should be admitted as a partner

---

1. The Rt. Hon. William Dundas.
2. Dr. Robert Jamieson, lexicographer.
3. 'Smothering'. The word recurs in a more serious context in the Entry for 18 May 1831.
4. Scott's favourite phrase from Buckingham's *Rehearsal*, iv. 2.
5. Jonson's *Everyman in his Humour*, i. 4.

to the business but that the reasons of this arrangement had ceased – I understood them to have originated then with Mrs. Ballantyne – and it was his present wish that Sandie should enjoy one fourth of the business. I mark this down in case of need. He has settled to go to the country, poor fellow, to Timpandean as I think.

We dined at Skene's where we met Mr. and Mrs. George Forbes, Col. and mistress Blair, George Bell etc. The party was a pleasant one. Col. Blair said that during the battle of Waterloo there was at the commencement some trouble necessary to prevent the men from breaking their ranks. He expostulated with one man 'Why, my good fellow, you cannot propose to beat the French alone – better keep your ranks.' The man, who was one of the 71st, returnd to his ranks saying 'I believe you are very right, sir, but I am a man of a very *hot temper*.' There was much bonhommie in the reply.

24 TUESDAY Snowy miserable morning. I corrected my proofs but had no time to write any time. We, i.e. I myself and the two Annes, went to breakfast with Mr. Drummond Hay, where we again met Colonel and Mrs. Blair with Thomas Thompson. We lookd over some most beautiful drawings which Mrs. Blair had made in different parts of India[1] exhibiting a species of architecture so gorgeous and on a scale so extensive as to put to shame the magnificence of Europe. And yet in most cases as little is known of the people who wrought these wonders as of the Kings who built the periods.[2] Fame depends on literature not on architecture. We are more eager to see a broken column of Cicero's villa than all those mighty labours of barbarick power. Mrs. Blair is full of enthusiasm. She told me that when she workd with her pencil she was glad to have some one read to her as a sort of sedative, otherwise her excitement made her tremble and burst out a crying. I can understand this very well having often found the necessity of doing two things at once. She is a very pretty dark woman too and has been compared to Rebecca, daughter of the Jew Isaack of York.[3]

Detaind in the court till half past two bothering about Lady Essex Kerr's will witht. coming to a conclusion. I then got home too late to do any thing as I must prepare to go to Dalmahoy. Mr. Gibson came in for a little while. No news.

I went to Dalmahoy where we were most kindly received. It is a point of friendship however to go eight miles to dinner and return in

1. Douglas notes that some of these appeared in Colonel Tod's *Travels in Western India*.
2. Tait suggests that Scott meant 'pyramids'.
3. In *Ivanhoe*.

the evening[1] and my day has been cut up without a brush of work. Smoked a segar on my return being very cold.

25 WEDNESDAY This morning I corrected my proofs. *We get on* as John Fergusson said when they put him on a hunter. I fear their is too much historical detail and the catastrophe will be vilely huddled up. 'And who can help it, Dick?'[2] Visited James Ballantyne and found him bearing his distress sensibly and like a man. I calld also in at Cadell's and enquired after Lady Jane Stewart who is complaining. Three o'clock placed me at home and from that hour till ten, deduce two hours for dinner, I was feaguing it away.

26 THURSDAY Sent off ten pages this morning with a revise. We spy land but how to get my catastrophe packd into the compass allotted for it?

> It sticks like a pistol half out of its holster
> Or rather indeed like an obstinate bolster
> Which I think I have seen you attempting, my dear,
> In vain to cram into a small pillow-beer.[3]

There is no help for it, I must make a *tour de force* and annihilate both time and space.[4] Dined at home, nevertheless made small progress. But I must prepare my dough before I can light my oven. I would fain think I am in the right road.

27 FRIDAY The last post brought a letter from Mr. Heath proposing to set off his engravings for the magnum opus against my contributions for the *Keepsake*.[5] A pretty mode of accounting that would be – he be damnd – I wrote him declining his proposal and as he says I am still in his debt I will send him the old drama of the *House of Aspen* which I

1. After his last visit to the Earl and Countess of Morton Scott had commented, 'I should like to see them often.' Entry for 16 June 1828. But that was in summer weather.
2. Suckling's 'Ballad upon a Wedding,' l. 102.
3. Christopher Anstey's *An Election Ball*, Letter II.
4. Pope's 'Art of Sinking in Poetry', No. IV.
5. 'You are well aware that the whole of my house is so much occupied that I have not undertaken a Plate for any publisher the last three years – at the same time if possible I will exert myself to oblige you – there is however one condition which I trust you will not object to, namely that instead of money you pay me for any Plates I may Engrave by writing as many pages per Plate as may be agreed on.' Heath, 23 February 1829, Walpole.

wrote some thirty years [ago] and offerd to the stage.[1] This will make up my contribution and a good deal more if as I recollect there are five acts. Besides it will save me further trouble about Heath and his annual – 2dly. There are several manuscript copies of the play abroad and ~~some of them will be popping out one of these days in a contraband~~ manner. 3dly If I am right as to the length of the piece there [is] £100 extra work at least which will not be evil convenient at all.

Dined at Sir John Hay's with Ramsay of Barnton, his young lady, Sir David and Lady Hunter Blair etc.

I should mention that Cadell breakfasted with me[2] and entirely approved of my rejecting Heath's letter. There was one funny part of it in which he assured me that the success of the new Edition of the waverley novels depended entirely on the excellence of the illustrations[3] – *vous êtes jouallier Monsr. Josse.*[4] He touches a point which alarms me: he greatly undervalues the portrait which Wilkie has proposed to give me for this edition. If it is as little of a likeness as he ~~says it is a scrape – But a scrape be it. Wilkie behaved in the kindest~~ way considering his very bad health in agreeing to work for me at all and I will treat him with due delicacy and not wound his feelings by rejecting what he has given in such kindness.[5] And so farewell to Mr. Heath and [that] conceited vulgar Cockney his Editor.[6]

28 SATURDAY Finishd my proofs this morning and read part of a curious work calld *Memoirs of Vidocque,*[7] a fellow who was at the head

1. Scott has looked again at this free translation of Viet Weber's *Die heilig Vehme* when describing the Secret Tribunal in *Anne of Geierstein*. The play had been offered to Kemble in 1800, and was actually performed in Edinburgh on 17 December 1829.

2. 'At ¼ past nine' to discuss Heath's proposal. 'I cannot call at St. Andrew's Square having an appointment with Mr. Ross to cut a corn out of my foot which annoys me cruelly.' 26 February 1829, Disc. ii. 12.

3. 'You must not feel offended if I say that as they are not *new* works the *Plates* will be a great attraction, particularly now when the Arts are so appreciated – much of the extensiveness of the sale will depend on their *excellence* both as to design and Engraving.' Heath, 23 February 1829, Walpole.

4. Molière's *L'Amour médecin,* i. 1.

5. Heath says '*there is no resemblance*'. Heath, 23 February 1829, Walpole. Wilkie, agreeing to 'assist in the illustrations of the great work', has offered the portrait – begun when he was last at Abbotsford – as a gift. Wilkie, 30 January 1829, Walpole.

6. Reynolds. See the Entry for 19 April 1828 and note.

7. *Mémoires de Vidocque, Chef de la Police de Sûreté jusqu'en 1827,* 1828, was sent, at Scott's request, by the publisher of the *Foreign Quarterly*, where it had been reviewed. *Letters,* xi. 132.

of Bonaparte's police. It is a *picaresque* tale, in other words a romance of roguery. The whole seems much exaggerated and got up but I suppose there is truth *au fond*. I came home about two o'clock and wrought hard and fast till night.

I cannot get myself to feel at all anxious about this Catholic Question.[1] I cannot see the use of fighting about the platter when you have let them snatch the meat of[f] it. I hold popery to be such a mean and depriving superstition that I am not clear I could have found myself liberal enough for voting the repeal of them as they existed before 1780.[2] They must and would in course of time have smotherd popery and I confess I should have see[n] the old Lady of Babylon's mouth stopd with pleasure. But now you have taken the plaister off her mouth and given her free respiration I cannot see the sense of keeping up the irritation about their right to sit in parliament. Unopposed and the Catholic superstition may sink into dust with all its absurd ritual and solemnities. Still [it] is an awful risque. The world is in fact as silly as ever and a good competence of nonsense will always find believe[r]s. Animal magnetism, phrenology, have all had their believers and why not popery? Ecod if they begin to make smithfield broils I do not know where many an honest protestant can find courage enough to be carbonadoed. I should shrink from the thoughts of tar barrel and gibbet I am afraid and make a very pusillanimous martyr. So I hope the Duke of Wellington will keep the horned beast well in hand and not let her get her leg over the harrows.

MARCH

1 SUNDAY I labourd heard the whole day and between hands refreshd myself with Vidocque's *Memoires*. No one calld excepting Hay Drummond who had something to say about Mons Meg. So I wrote before and after dinner till no less than ten pages were finishd.

2 MONDAY I wrought but little to-day. I was not in the vein and felt sleepy. I thought to go out but disgust of the pavement kept me at

1. His Irish visit had moderated Scott's opinion on this question. He told Moore 'that he and Lockhart had gone there rather hostilely disposed towards the Catholic Emancipation, but that they had both returned converts to the necessity of conceding it'. *Memoirs of Moore*, iv. 333.
2. Presumably Scott is referring to the Relief Act of 1791, which removed many of the disabilities suffered until then by Roman Catholics.

home. *O Rus* etc.[1] It is pleasant to think that the 11 March sets us on the route for Abbotsford. I shall be done long before with this confounded novel.[2] I wish I were for I find trouble in bringing it to a conclusion. People compliment me sometimes on the extent of my labour but [if] I could employ to purpose the hours that indolence and lassitude steal from me they would have cause to wonder indeed. But day must have night, vigilance must have sleep, and labour bodily or mental must have rest. As Edgar says, I cannot fool it further.[3] Anne is gone to Hoptoun House for two days.

Dined at the Royal Society Club and went to the Society in the evening. There was a paper read by Mr. Bauld engineer upon the Subject of the miner's compass and the variations to which it is subject from magnetic and electrical qualities in the box of the compass itself or in different substances which approach the needle. On[e] thing struck me as curious, namely that the affection of the needle is not in proportion to the mass of the attractive substance [but] to its proximity to the implement. Thus an Iron buckle placed near to the compass will occasion a greater variation than a ship's cargo of iron bars stowd at a greater distance.

3 TUESDAY Began this day with labour as usual and made up my packet. Then to the Court where there is a deal of business. Hamilton having now a serious fit of the gout is not expected to aid any more than reason. I wrote a little both before and after dinner. Niece Anne and I dined alone. Three poets calld each bauling louder than the other *subscribe subscribe*. I generally do if the work be under 10/- but the wares were every one so much worse than another that I declined in the three instances before me. I got cross at the repeated demands and could have used Richard's appology.

Thou troublest me I am not in the vein.[4]

4 WEDNESDAY Being Teind Wednesday I settle myself at my desk and labourd the whole forenoon; got on to p. 72 so there cannot be

1. 'O countryside, [when am I to see you?]'. Horace's *Satires*, ii. vi. 60.
2. In fact *Anne of Geierstein* was not finished until the end of April. The political unrest created by Catholic Emancipation made immediate publication undesirable, and Scott laid it aside in the hope that at Abotsford he might 'strike out something better by the braes and burn sides'. Entry for 14 April 1829.
3. *King Lear*, iv. 1, with 'fool' in place of 'daub'.
4. *Richard III*, iv. 2.

more than twenty pages wanted. Mr. Drummond Hay who has an alertness in making business out of nothing came to call once more about Mons Meg – He is a good humourd gentlemanlike man but I would Meg were in his belly or he in hers.

William Laidlaw also calld, whom I askd to dinner.

At four o'clock arrives Mr. Cadell with his horn charged with good news – The prospectus of the magnum already issued only a week has produced such a demand among the trade that he thinks he must add a large number of copies that the present edition of 7000 may be increased to the demand – he talks of raising it to ten or 12,000. If so I shall have a powerful and constant income to bear on my unfortunate debts to a large amount yearly and may fairly hope to put my debts in a secure way of payment even if I should be cut off in life or in health and the power of labour. I hope to be able in a year or two to make proposals for eating with my own spoons and using my own books, which if I can give value for them can hardly I think be refused to me.[1] In the mean time I have enough and something to bequeath to my poor children. This is a great mercy but I must prepare for disappointment and I will not be elated.

Laidlaw dined with me and poor fellow was as much elated with the news as I am for it is not of a nature to keep it secret. I hope I shall have him once more at Kayside to debate as we use[d] to do on religion and politics.[2] Meanwhile, Patience cousin and shufle the cards.[3]

I must do what I can to get Cadell's discharge from his creditors.[4] This I have always done and so far effectually. But it would be most inconvenient to be at the mercy of creditors who may at any moment make an enquiry into his affairs and so stop his operations. The Old Bank of Scotland are the only parties whose consent has not been obtaind to his discharge and they must see their interest in consenting

1. In fact the creditors made him a gift of his furniture and library after the second dividend in December 1830.
2. The chance for Laidlaw to return to Kaeside came in 1830 when Tom Purdie's death left the estate without a manager.
3. A favourite phrase of Scott's from *Don Quixote*, pt. ii, ch. 23.
4. As a partner in Constable and Coy. Cadell had gone bankrupt in January 1826 along with the others. As an undischarged bankrupt he could officially be employed only as Head Clerk in the publishing house which in fact he ran, and Scott was anxious to see him released from this inconvenient situation. The Royal Bank of Scotland, pressed by Scott in December, had concurred. *Letters*, xi. 76. The Bank of Scotland had not yet agreed (see *Letters*, xi. 135 and note) but the discharge was effected a few months later.

to if for the expediting of my affairs, since to what purpose oppose it for they have not the least chance of mending their own by refusing it.

5 THURSDAY Proofs arranged in the morning. Sir Patrick Walker, that Solomon the Second, came to propose to me that some benefit society which he patronizes should attend upon Mons Megg.[1] But hav[ing] the Celts[2] at my disposal I have every reason to think they would be affronted at being musterd along with Sir Peter and his tail of trade's lads. I went to the court which detaind me till two, then to poor old Lady Seaforth's funeral which was numerously attended. It was near four ere I got home bringing Skene with me. We calld at Cadell's; the edition of the Magnum is raised from 7000 to 10,000. There will really be a clearance in a year or two if R. C. is not too sanguine. I never saw so much reason for indulging hope. By the bye I am admitted a Member of the Maitland club,[3] a Society on the principle of the Roxburghe and Bannatyne. What a tail of the Alphabet I should draw after me were I to sign with the indications of the different societies I belong to, beginning with President of the Royal society of Edinburgh and ended with Umpire of the Six foot high Club.[4] Dined at home and quiet with the girls.

6 FRIDAY Made some considerable additions to the Appendix to General preface.[5] I am in the sentiments towards the publick that the buffoon player expresses towards his patron.

> Go tell my young Lord, said this modest young man,
>   I[f] he will but invite me to dinner
> I'll be as diverting as ever I can
>   I will on the faith of a sinner.[6]

1. At her restoration to the Castle on 9 March. Sir Patrick was Secretary of the Scottish Naval and Military Academy, and it was no doubt the boys being trained there that he intended to bring.
2. The Celtic Society.
3. For the letter announcing the formation of this new club in Glasgow, see Nicolas, 28 February 1829, Walpole.
4. Apart from the five societies mentioned in this Entry, Scott was a Professor of the Royal Academy; a member of the Royal Society (London), the Celtic Society, the Royal Institution for the Encouragement of the Fine Arts in Scotland, the Society of Antiquaries of Scotland, the Royal Company of Archers, the Pitt Club and more than a dozen others.
5. Of the Magnum Opus.
6. Untraced.

I will mul[t]iply the notes therefore where there is a chance of giving pleasure and variety. There is a strange gleam of hope on my affairs than has yet touchd on them. It is not steady or certain but it is bright and conspicuous. Ten years may last with me though I have little chance of it. At the end of this time these works will have operated a clearance of debt – Especially as Cadell offers to accommodate with such money as their House can save to pay off what presses. I hope to save rather than other wise and if I leave my literary property to my children it will make a very good thing for them and Abbotsford must in any event go to my family. So on the whole I have only to pray for quiet times for how can men mind their serious business, that is according to Cadell's views buying Waverley novels, when they are going mad about the Catholic question? Dined at Mr. Nairne's where there was a great meeting of Bannatynians, rather too numerous, being on the part of our host an Election dinner.[1]

7 SATURDAY Sent away proofs – This extrication of my affairs, though only a Pisgah prospect, occupies my mind more than is fitting but with[out] some such hope I must have felt like one of thee victims of the wretch Burke struggling against a smothering weight on my bosom till nature could endure it no longer. No – I will not be sport of circumstances. Come of it what will *I'll bend my brows/ Like highland truis* and make a bold fight of it –

> The best o't the warst o't
> Is only just to die.[2]

And die I think I shall though I am not such a coward as *mortem conscire me ipso*.[3] But I 'gin to grow a weary of the Sun[4] and when the plant no longer receives nourishment from light and air there is a speedy prospect of its withering.

Dined with the Banking club of Scotland in virtue of Sir Malachi Malagrowther;[5] splendid entertainment of cours[e]. Sir John Hay in the chair.

1. He had been elected on 28 January.
2. Burns's 'Epistle to Davie,' ll. 27–8.
3. '*Mortem consciscere mihi ipsi* ("to commit suicide") is meant.' Tait.
4. *Macbeth*, v. 5.
5. Whose *Letters* had 'headed back the southron' from the Scottish banks in 1826. Scott took this opportunity of speaking to Kinnear, a Director of the Bank of Scotland, about Cadell's discharge. *Letters*, xi. 147–8.

8 SUNDAY Spent the morning in reading proofs on additions to Magnum.[1] I got a note from Cadell in which Ballantyne by a letter inclosed totally condemns *Anne of Geierstein* 3 volumes nearly finishd – a pretty thing truly for I will be expected [to begin] all over again. Great dishonour in this, as Trinculo says, besides an infinite loss;[2] sent for Cadell to attend me next morning[3] that we may consult about this business. Peel has made his motion on the Catholic question with a speech of three hours. It is almost a complete surrender to the Catholics and so it should be for half measures do but linger out the feud. This will or rather ought to satisfy all men who sincerely love peace and therefore all men of property. But will this satisfy Pat, who with all his virtues is not the most sensible person in the world? – Perhaps not and if not it is but fighting them at last. I smoked away and thought of ticklish politics and bad novels – Skenes supd with us.

9 MONDAY Cadell came to breakfast. We resolved in privy council to refer the question whether *Anne of G—n* be sea worthy or not to further consideration; which as the book cannot be publishd at any rate during the full rage of the Catholic question may be easily managed. After breakfast I went to Sir William Arbuthnot's and met there a select party of Tories to decide whether we should act with the Whigs by owning their petition in favour of the Catholics. I was not free from apprehension that the petition might be put into such general[4] language as I at least was unwilling to authenticate by my subscription. The solicitor[5] was voucher that they would keep the terms quite general. Whereupon we subscribed the requisition for meeting with a slight alteration affirming that it was our desire not to have intermeddled had not the Anti Catholics pursued that course. And so the Whigs and we are embarkd in the same boat. *Vogue la galère.*[6]

1. *Old Mortality* was now in hand. *Letters*, xi. 147.
2. Stephano in *The Tempest*, iv. 1.
3. 'If possible . . . before nine'. *Letters*, xi. 147.
4. The sense of what follows suggests that this is a slip for 'particular'.
5. The Solicitor-General, John Hope.
6. Scott was only reluctantly pro-Catholic. 'God knows if I thought the old Lady of Babylon were *in extremis* I should be little disposed to play Edmund Burke and assist her with cordials & restoratives but could find in my head to play his namesake William and catch *t'ould woman* by the nose and throat a la mode of the Grassmarket. But that is not now the question. She is on her feet and active and what good is to be got by

Went about one o'clock to the Castle where we saw the Auld Murderess Mons Meg brought up there in solemn procession to re-occupy her ancient place on the Argyle Battery.[1] Lady Hopeton was my belle. The day was cold but serene and I think the Ladies must have been cold enough, not to mention the Celts who turnd out upon the occasion under the leading of Cluny-Macpherson, a fine spirited lad. Some rockets were thrown up, one of which fell on my daughter's head and nearly set her on fire. We had luncheon from the mess of the 73d. Mons Meg is a monument of our pride and poverty. The size is immense but six smaller guns would have been made at the same expence and done six times as much execution as she could have done. There was immense interest taken in the Show by the people of the town and the numbers who crowded the Castle hill had a magnificent appearance. About 30 of our Celts attended in costume and <as> there was a highland regiment on duty, with dragoons and artillerymen who made a splendid show. The dexterity with which the last man'd and wrought the windlace which raised Old Megg weighing seven or eight tons from her temporary carriage to that which has been her basis for many years was singularly beautiful as a combined exhibition of skill and strength. My daughter had what [might] have proved a frightful accident. Some rockets were let off one of which lighted upon her head and set her bonnet on fire. She neither screamed nor ran but quietly permitted Charles K. Sharpe to extinguish the fire which he did with great coolness and dexterity. All who saw her, especially the friendly Celts, gave her merit for her steadiness and said she came of good blood. I was very glad and proud of her presence of mind. My own was not put to the trial. We lunch'd with the Regimt. now in the Castle. My own courage was not tried, for being at some distance escorting the beautiful and lively Countess of Hopeton I did not hear of the accident till it was over. The little entertainment gave me an opportunity of observing what I have often before remarkd, the improvement in the character of our <the> young and subaltern officers in the army which in the course of a long and bloody war had been in point of rank and manners something deteriorated. The number of persons now applying for

---

withholding a small addition when you have given them the means of consolidating their strength is I fear considering the divided state of parliament only to be answerd with a submissive shrug.' *Letters*, xi. 144–5.

1. The massive fifteenth-century cannon was removed to the Tower of London in 1754. Its restoration to Edinburgh Castle was a result of King George IV's 1822 visit to Scotland and the promises extracted from him and the Duke of Wellington by Scott.

commissions (3000 being now on the lists) gives an opportunity of selection and officers should certainly be *gentlemen* with a complete opening to all who can rise by merit. The stile in which duty and the knowlege of their profession is enforced prevents *fainéants* from long remaining in the profession.

In the evening I presided at the Celtick Club which received me with their usual partiality. I like this Society and willingly give myself to be excited by the sight of handsome young men with plaids and claymores and all the alertness and spirit of highlanders in their native garb. There was the usual degree of excitation, excellent dancing, capital songs, a general inclination to please and be pleased. A severe cold caught on the battlements of the castle prevented me from playing first fiddle so well as usual but what I could do was received with the usual partiality of the Celts. I got home fatigued and *vino ciboque gravatus*,[1] about eleven o'clock. We had many guests some of whom, English officers, seemed both amazed and surprized at our wild ways, especially at the dancing without ladies and the mode of drinking favourite toasts by springing up with one foot on the bench and one on the table, and the peculiar shriek of applause so unlike English Cheering.

10 TUESDAY This may be a short day in the diary though a busy one to me. I arranged books and papers in the morning and went to court after breakfast where, as Sir Robert Dundas and I had the whole business to discharge, I remain till two or three. Then visited Cadell and transacted some pecuni[ary] matters as follows

Deposited with Mr. C. my receipt for next quarter's salary due 21 current			£250
On which Mr. Cadell advance me in the following man[n]er		£100	
To domestic expences	£40		
To Mr. Sinclair russian warehouse his account paid by Mr. Cadell	29		
To Thomson for hay and corn Do	30		
To Ewart sad[d]ler	5		
	———		95
	£95		———

£5 odds in
purse omitting shillings.

1. 'Weighed down with wine and food'.

II WEDNESDAY I had as usual a sort of levée the day I was to leave town, all petty bills and petty business being reserved to the last by those who might as well have applied any one day of the present month.

But I need [not] complain of what happens to my betters for on the last day of the Session there pours into the court a succession of trifles which give the Court and especially the clerks much trouble, in so much that a ci-devant brother of mine proposed that the last day of the Session should be abolishd by statute. We got out of court at ¼ past one and got to Abbotsford at ½ past seven, cold and hungry enough to make Scots broth, English roast-beef and a large fire very acceptable.

12 THURSDAY I set apart this day of trifles and dawdling yet I meditate doing something on the popish and protestant affray. I think I could do some good and I have the sincere wish to do it. I heard the merry birds sing, reviewd my dogs and was chee[r]ful. I also unpackd books. Deuce take arrangement. I think it the most complete bore in the world but I will try a little of it – I afterwards went out and walkd till dinner time. I read Reginald Heber's journal[1] after dinner. I spent some merry days with him at Oxford when he was writing his prize-poem. He was then a gay young fellow, a wit and a satirist and burning for literary fame. My laurels were beginning to bloom and we were both mad-caps – Who would have fortold our future lot?

> Oh little did my mither ken
> The day she cradled me
> The land I was to travel in
> Or the death I was to dee.[2]

13 FRIDAY Wrought at a review of Fraser Tytler's *History of Scotland*.[3] It is somewhat saucy towards Lord Hailes.[4] I had almost stuck

1. Dr. Reginald Heber's *Narrative of a Journey through the Upper Provinces of India*, 3rd edition, 1828, is in the Abbotsford library.
2. 'The Queen's Marie', ll. 101–4: *Border Minstrelsy*.
3. P. F. Tytler's *History of Scotland*, Edinburgh, 1828. The references to this review are confusing without more knowledge than the *Journal* entries afford. The review of Tytler was to be prefaced 'with an introductory Essay on the twilight period' based on Ritson's *Annals of the Caledonians, Picts, and Scots, etc.*, 1828. This introduction, however, 'swelld into a separate article'. *Letters*, xi. 155. Between 13 and 30 March Scott is writing about Ritson's *Annals*; thereafter on Tytler's *History of Scotland*.
4. Lord Hailes's *Annals of Scotland*, 1776.

myself into the controversy slough of Despond, the controversy that is between the Gothick and Celtic system, but cast myself like C[h]ristian with a strong struggle or two to the farther side of the slough; and now will I walk on my days rejoicing, not on my article however but to the fields. Came home and rejoiced at dinner. After tea I wroted a little more. I begin to warm in my gears and am about to awake the whole controversy of Goth and Celt. I wish I may not make some careless blunders.

14 SATURDAY Up at eight, rather of the latest – then faggd at my Review both before and after breakfast. I walkd from one o'clock till near three. I make it out I think rather better than of late I have been able to do in the streets of Edinburgh where I am ashamed to walk so slow as would suit me. Indeed nothing but a certain suspicion that once drawn up on the beach I would soon break up prevents my renounced pedestrian exercize altogether, for it is positive suffering and of an acute kind to[o].

15 SUNDAY Altogether like yesterday. Wrote in the morning – breakfasted – Wrote again till one – Out and walkd about two hours – to the quills once more – Dinner – smoked a brace of segars and lookd on the fire, a page of writing and so to bed.

16 MONDAY Day sullen and bitter cold. I fear it brings chillblains on its wings. A dusting of snow in thin flakes wandering from the horizon and threating a serious fall. As the murderer says to Banquo 'Let it come down';[1] we shall have the better chance of fair weather hereafter. It cleard up however and I walkd from one or thereabout till within a quarter of four an[d] then returnd somewhat thirsting and sickish having overeat myself I suppose even at the wholesome meal of breakfast this morning. A card from Mr. Dempster of Skibo whose uncle George Dempster I knew many years since, a friend of Johnson, Sir Joshua Reynolds and all that set; a fine goodhumourd old gentleman. Young Mrs. Dempster is a daughter of my early friend and patron Robt. Dundas of Arnistoun, Lord Advocate, and I like her for his sake. Mr. Dempster is hunting and I should have liked to have given his wife and sister refuge during the time he must spend over moss and moor. But the two Annes going to Edinr. to a fancy ball makes it impossible till they return on friday night.

17 TUESDAY The Annes went off at eight morning – After breakfast I drove down to Melrose and waited on Mrs. and Miss Dempster and

1. *Macbeth*, iii. 3.

engaged them for Saturday. Weather bitter cold, yea atrociously so. Naboclish – the better for work. Ladies whose husbands love foxhunting are in a poor way. Here are two pleasant and pretty women peggd up the whole day

> In the worst inn's worst room[1]

for the whole 24 hours without interruption. They manage the matter otherwise in france where Ladies are the Lords of the Ascendant. I returnd from my visit to my solitary work and solitary mealing. I eked out the last to two hours' length by dint of smoking which I find a sedative without being a stimulant.

18 WEDNESDAY I like the hermit life indifferent well nor would, I sometimes think, break my heart were I to be in that magick mountain[2] where food was regularly supplied by ministering genii and plenty of books were accessible without the least intervention of human society. But this is thinking like a fool. Solitude is only agreeable when the power of having society is removed to a short space and can be commanded at pleasure. It is not good for man to be alone. It blunts our faculties and freezes our active virtues. And now my watch pointing to noon I think after four hours' work I may indulge myself with a walk. The dogs see me about to shut my desk and intimate their happiness by caresses and whining. By your leave Messrs. Genii of the mountain library, if I come to your retreat I'll bring my dogs with me –

The day was showry but not unpleasant – soft dripping rains attended by a mild atmosp[h]ere that spoke of flowers in their seasons and a chirping of bird[s] that had a touch of spring in it. I had the patience to get fully wet and the grace to be thankful for it –

Come, a leetle flourish on the trumpet – Let us raise the Genius of this same red mountain so calld because it is all the year coverd with roses. There can be no difficulty in finding it for it lies towards the Caspian and is quoted in the Persian Tales. Well I open my ephemerides, form my scheme under the suitable planet and the Genie obeys the invocation and appears. Genie is a misshapen dwarf with a huge jolterhead like that of Boerhave on the bridge,[3] his limbs and body marvellously shrunk and disproportiond. 'Sir Dwarf' said I undauntedly 'thy head is very

---

1. Pope's *Moral Essays*, Epistle iii. l. 299.
2. See Weber's *Tales of the East*, 1812, ii. 452–7.
3. 'This head may still be seen over a laboratory at no. 100 of the South Bridge, Edinburgh.' J. G. L.

large and thy feet an[d] limbs somewhat small in proportion.' 'I have cramd my head even to the overflowing with Knowlege and I have starved my limbs by disuse of exercize and denial of sustenance.' 'Can I acquire wisdom in thy solitary library?' 'Thou mayst.' 'On what conditions?' – 'Renounce all gross and fleshly pleasures – eat pulse and drink water, converse with none but the wise and learnd, alive and dead.' – 'Why, this were to die in the cause of wisdom' – 'If you desireth to draw from our library only the advantage of seeming wise you may have it consistent with all your favourite enjoyment.' 'How much sleep?' 'A Lapland night – eight months out of the 12.' 'Enough for a dormouse, most generous genius. – A bottle of wine?' 'Two if you please but you must not seem to care for them. Segars in loads. Whiskey in lashings; but they must be taken with an air of contempt, a floccipaucinihilipilification of all that can gratify the outward man.'[1] 'I am about to ask you a serious question. When you have stuffd your stomach, drunk your bottle, smoked your segar, how is he to keep himself [awake]?' – 'Either by Cephalic snuff or ca[s]tle building.' 'Do you approve of Castle building as a frequent exercise?' – Genie – 'Life were not life without it.

> Give me the joy that sickens not the heart
> Give me the wealth that has no wings to fly'[2]

Author. 'I reckon myself one of the best aerial architects now living and *Nil me penitet hujus ausi*'[3] – Genie. '*Nec est cur peniteat*[4]; most of your novels have previously been subject for airy castles' – 'You have me – and moreover a man of imagination derives experience from such imaginary situations. There are few situations in which I have not in fa[n]cy figured and there are few of course which I am not previously prepared to take some part in.' Genie. 'True but [I] am afraid your having fa[n]cied yourself victorious in many a fight would be of little [use] were you suddenly calld to the field and your personal infirmities and nervous capaticities both rushing upon and incapacitating you.' 'My nervous agitations – aw[a]y with thee.

Down down to Limbo and the burning Lake
False fiend, avoid –'[5]

1. Scott turned over two pages at this point, so that there is a sheet left blank.
2. 'Castle-building', Scott's *English Minstrelsy* (1810), i. 242.
3. 'I do not repent of this flight.'
4. 'Nor is there any reason for you to repent.'
5. *2 Henry VI*, i. 4.

> So there ends the tale
> > With a hey with a hey
> So there ends the tale
> > With a ho.
> There's a moral if you fail
> To seize it by the tail
> Its import will exhale
> > You must know.

19 THURSDAY The above was written yesterday before dinner though appearances are to the contrary. I only meant that the studious solitude I have sometimes dreamd of unless practized with rare stoicism and privation was apt to degenerate into secret sensual indulgences of coarser appetites which, when the cares and restraints of social life are removed, are apt to make us think with Doctor Johnson our dinner the most important event of the day. So much in the way of explanation, a humour which I love not. Go to – My girls return from Edinburgh with full news of their *bal paré*.

20 FRIDAY We spent this day on the same terms as formerly. I wrought walkd dine[d] drank and smoked upon the same pattern.

21 SATURDAY Tomorrow brought Mrs. Dempster and her sister in law Miss Dempster. To dinner came Robert Dundas of Arniston from the hunting field and with him Mr. Dempster of Skibo, both favourites of mine. Mr. Stewart,[1] the grand nephew of my dear friend Lady Louisa, also dine[d] with [us] together with the Lyons from Gattonsid[e], and the day passd over in hospitality and social happiness.

recvd from Caddell ————			£110.0.0
Of which to Bogie ————	£52		
to Tom ————	35		
to Ballantyne, Writer ———	9		
	——	96	
		14.0.0	
Add cash in purse ————		2	
Total Ballance in purse ————		£16	

22 SUNDAY Being Sunday I read prayers to our guests then went a long walk by the lake to Huntleyburn. It is somewhat uncomfortable

---

1. 'An amiable & promising young man modest and well informd.' *Letters*, xi. 160.

to feeling difficulties increase and the strength to conq[uer] diminish but why should man fret when iron is dissolved by rust and brass corroded, and can our dreams be of flesh and blood enduring? But I will not dwell on this depressing subject. My liking to my two young guests is founded on 'things that are long enough ago.'[1] The first stateman of celebrity whom I personally was [acquainted with was] Mr. Dempster's Grand Uncle George Dempster of Dunnichen celebrated in his time, and Dundas's father was when Lord Advocate the first man of influence who took [a] kindness for me.

23 MONDAY Arrived to breakfast one of the Courland nobility, Baron A. von Meyersdorff, a fine lively spirited young man fond of his country and incensed at its degradation under Russia. He talkd much of the Orders of Chivalry who had been feudal Lords of Livonia especially the order of Porte Glaive to which his own ancestors had belongd. If he report correctly there is a deep principle of action at work in Germany, Poland, Russia etc. which if it does 'not die in thinking'[2] will one day make an explosion. The Germans are a nation however apt to exhaust themselves in speculation. The Baron has enthusiasm and is well read in English and foreign literature. I kept my state till one and wrote notes for Croker upon Boswell's scottish [tour].[3] It was an act of friendship for time is some thing a scarce article with me. But Croker has been at all times personally kind and actively serviceable to me and he must always command my best assistance. Then I walkd with the Baron as far as the lake. Our sports men came in good time to dinner and our afternoon was pleasant.

24 TUESDAY This morning our Sportsmen took leave and their *Ladykind* (to *renchérir* on Anthony A Wood and Mr. Oldbuck[4]) followd after breakfast and I went to my work till one and at that hour treated the Baron to another long walk with which he seemd highly delighted. He tells me that my old friend the Princess Galitzin is dead. After dinner I had a passing visit of Kinnear to bid me

1. 'Schulagaroo', an Irish song of which a MS. is at Abbotsford.
2. Dryden's *Absalom and Achitophel*, l. 552.
3. For his edition of Boswell's *Life of Johnson*, mentioned in the Entry for 29 January 1829. Croker had written requesting help: 'I hope you may find time to read the Hebridean journey, pencil in hand, so as to let me know *who* is *who*. There are many personal allusions which Boswell left in designed obscurity, for reasons which can no longer exist. If not explained *now*, they will be dark for ever.' 10 March 1829, Walpole.
4. Jonathan Oldbuck, in *The Antiquary*, refers frequently to his 'womankind'.

farewell. This very able and intelligent young [man], so able to throw a grace over commercial pursuits by uniting them with literature, is going with his family to settle in London. I do not wonder at it. His parts are of a kind superior to the confined sphere in which he moves in Scotland. In London he says there is a rapid increase of business and its opportunities.[1] Thus London licks the butter of[f] our bread by opening a better market for ambition. Were it not for the difference of the religion and laws poor Scotland could hardly keep a man that is worth having and yet men will not see this. I took leave of Kinnear with hopes for his happiness and fortune but yet with some regret for the sake of the Country which loses him. The Baron agreed to go with Kinnear to Kelso and exit with the usual demonstrations of German enthusiasm.

25 WEDNESDAY I workd in the morning, and think I have sent Croker a packet which may be useful and to Lockhart a critick on rather a dry topick, vizt the Ancient Scottish history. I remember R. Ainslie, commonly calld the Plain Man, who piqued himself on his powers of conversation, striving to strike fire from some old flinty wretch whom he found in corner of a publick coach, at length addressd him 'Friend, I have tried you on politics, literary matters, religion, fashionable news etc. etc. and all to no purpose.' The dry old rogue twisting his muzzle into an infernal grin replied 'Can you [say] ony[thing] clever about bend leather?' The man be it understood was a leather merchant. The early history of Caledonia is almost as hopeless a subject. But off it goes and with it a parcel of Notes for Croker's edition of Boswell.

I walkd up the Glen with Tom for my companion. Dined. Heard Anne reading a paper of anecdotes about Cluny Macpherson and so to bed.

26 THURSDAY As I have been so lately John[s]onizing I should derive if possible some personal use. Johnson advises Boswell to keep a diary but to omit registers of the weather and like trumpery. I am resolved in future not to register what is yet more futile – my gleams of bright and clouded temper. Boswell, whose nervous [ailments] were one half madness one half affectation, has thrumd upon this topick till it [is] threadbare. I have at this moment forty things to do and a great inclination to do none of them. I ended by working till two, walking till five, writing letters and so to bed.

1. Thomas Kinnear left Edinburgh with £60,000 in his pocket to try to become a second Thomas Coutts. He died eighteen months later. See *Letters*, xi. 415 n.

27 FRIDAY Letters again. Let me see. I have wrote to Lord Montagu about Scott of Bavelaw's commission in which Invernahyle interests himself[1] – item to a Lady who is pestering me about a Miss Campbell sentenced to transportation for stealing a silver spoon – item to John Eckford about the measures to be observed for realizing the Lithgow succession[2] – item James Loch to get an appointment for Sandie Ballantyne's son[3] – Not one, as Dangle says, about any business of my own.[4] My correspondence is on a most disinterested footing. This lasts till past eleven, then enters my cousin R.[5] and remains for two hours till politics, family news, talk of the neighbourhood are all exhausted and two or three reputations torn to pieces in the scouring of them. At length I walk him out about a mile and come back from that *empêchement*. But it is only to find Mr. C—n[6] my neighbour in the parlour with the girls and there is another sederunt of an hour – Well such things must be and our friends mean them as civility and we must take and give the currency of the country. But I am *diddled* out of a day all the same. The ladies come from Huntlyburn and cut off the evening. Misses Erskine of Vanelaw were included among the invaders.

28 SATURDAY In spite of the temptation of a fine morning I toild manfully at the review[7] till two o'clock commencing at seven. I fear it will be uninteresting but I like the muddling work of antiquities and besides wish to record my sentiments with regard to the Gothick question. No one that has not labourd as I have done on imaginary topics can judge of the comfort afforded by walking on all fours and being grave and dull. I dare say when the clown of the pantomime escapes from his nightly task of vivacity it is his especial com[fort] to smoke a pipe and be prosy with some goodnatured fellow the dullest of his acquaintance. I have seen such a tendency in Sir Adam Fergusson the gayest man I ever knew, and poor Tom Sheridan has complaind to me on the fatigue of supporting the character of an agreeable companion.

Mr. Anderson, son of my old friend Samuel Anderson, arrived

1. See *Letters*, xi. 156 and the Entry for 16 February 1829.
2. Eckford, who now had all the necessary affidavits, had written for advice. See 20 March 1829, Walpole, and the Entries for 17 November 1826 and 27 May 1828.
3. Probably James Robert Ballantyne, later distinguished for his work in India as an educationalist and oriental scholar.
4. Sheridan's *Critic*, i. 1.
5. Robert Rutherford.
6. Henry Cranstoun.
7. See the Entry for 13 March 1829 and note.

here at two o'clock on his way to London and dined and spent the day with us but after tea I stubbornly retired to work – I am tired and stupefied with segars and their regular menstruum – *vino ciboque gravatus*[1] – though not a bit hazy and so Good Night.

29 SUNDAY Mr. Anderson left us this morning. I wrote, read and walkd with the most stoical regularity. This muddling among old books has the quality of a sedative and saves the tear and wear of an overwrought brain. I wanderd on the hills pleasantly enough and concluded a pleasant an[d] labourious day.

30 MONDAY I finishd the remainder of the criticism and sent it off. Pray heaven it break not the mail coach down. Lord and Lady Dalhousie and their relation Miss Hawthorn came to dinner to meet whom we had Dr. and Mrs. Brewster. Lord Dalhousie has more of the Caledonian *prisca fides*[2] than any man I know now alive. He has served his country in every quarter of the world and in every climate yet though my contemporary looks ten years my junior. He laughd at the idea of rigid temperance and held an occasional skirmish no bad thing even in the west Indies, thinking perhaps with Armstrong of

– the rare debauch.[3]

In all incidents of life he has been the same steady, honest, true hearted Lord Dalhousie tha[t] Lordie Ramsay promised to be when at the High School.[4] How few such can I remem[ber]. And how poorly have honesty and valour been rewarded. Here at the time when most men think of repose he is trundled off to command in India. Would it had been the Chief Governorship. But to a command without war sounds like bare livelihood and that is all.[5] I askd him what he thought of strangling a Nabob and rifling his jewel closet and he answe[re]d 'No no, an honest man!' I fear we must add, a poor one. Lad[y] Dalhousie, formerly Miss Brown of Coulston, is an amiable, intelligent and lively woman who does not permitt society to 'cream and mantle like a standing pool.'[6]

1. 'Weighed down with wine and food'.
2. 'Old-world faith'.
3. Armstrong's *Art of Preserving Health*, ii. l. 465.
4. In other words he has fulfilled the promise shown when he was only Lord Ramsay, son of the eighth Earl.
5. Lord Dalhousie was going out to India as Commander-in-Chief. Fortunes were made from the prize money of a successful campaign, but no war was likely at this time.
6. *The Merchant of Venice*, i. i.

31 TUESDAY The weather, drifting and surly, does not permit us to
think of Melrose and I could only fight round the thicket with Dr.
Brewster and Lord [Dalhousie]. Lord Dalhousie gave me some
inter[est]ing accounts of the American Indians. They are according
to his Lordship decaying fast in numbers and in principal. Lord
Selkirk's property now makes large returns from the Stock of the
North West Company and Hudson's bay Companies having united.
I learnd from Lord Dalhousie that he had been keeping a diary since
the year 1800. Should his narrative ever see the light what a contrast
will it form to the flourishing vapouring accounts of most of the
French Marchals. Mr. and Mrs. Skene with their daughter Kittey
who has been indisposed came to dinner and the party was a well
assorted one.

APRIL

1 WEDNESDAY A pretty first of April truly – the hills white with
snow, I myself as bilious as a dog. My noble guests left about noon. I
wrote letters as if I had not bile enough in my bosom already; and did
not go out to face the snow wr[e]aths till half past two when I am
resolved to make a brush for exer[c]ize. There will be fine howling
among the dogs for I am about to shut my desk. Found Mrs. Skene
disposed to walk so I had the advantage of her company. The snow
lay three inches thick on the ground. But we had the better appetite
for dinner after which we talkd and read without my lifting a pen.

2 THURSDAY Begins with same brilliant prospect of snow and sun
shine dazzling to the eyes and chilling to the fingers, a beastly
disagreeable coldness in the air. I stuck by the pen till one then
took a drive with the ladies as far as Chiefswood and walkd home.
Young William Forbes came and alongst with him a Southern, Mr.
Cleasby. I hope I shall not call him Mr. Chiesley[1] which there is some
temptation to do and some reasons against doing.

3 FRIDAY Still the same party. I faggd at writing letters – to Lockhart[2] – to Charles – to John Gibson – to Mr. Cadell – Croker, Lord

---

1. Scott had recently written a note for the Society of Antiquaries
   on Chiesley of Dalry, who murdered Sir George Lockhart in
   1689. *Letters*, xi. 95.
2. Approving his refusal to meddle with the daily press. In a letter of
   30 March Lockhart describes the interview with Croker mentioned
   in this Entry: 'The Duke of Wn. finds himself without one
   newspaper *he* can depend on. He wishes to buy up some evening

Haddington[1] and others. Lockhart has had an overture through Croker requesting him to communicate with some newspaper on the part of the government which he has wisely declined. Nothing but a through-going Blackguard ought to attempt the daily press unless it is some quiet country Diurnal. Lockhart has also a wicked wit which would [make] an office of this kind more dangerous to him than to downright dulness. I am heartily glad he has refused it. Sir James MacIntosh and Lord Haddington have spoken very handsomely[2] of my accession to the Catholic petition and I think it has done some good. Yet I am not confident that the measure will disarm the Catholic spleen. And I was not entirely easy at finding myself allied to the Whigs even in this instance where I agree with them. This is witless prejudice however. My walk today was up the Rhymer's Glen with Skene. Col. Ferguson dined with us.

4 SATURDAY Mr. Cleasby left this morning. He has travelled much and is a young man of copious conversation and ready language aiming I suppose at parliament.[3] William Forbes is singing like [an] angel in the next room but he sings only Italian music which says nought to me – I have a letter from one David Paterson, a fellow who was Dr. Knox's jackall for buying murderd bodies, suggesting that I should write on the subject of Burke and Hare and offering me his invaluable collection of anecdotes.[4] 'Curse him's imperance and

---

print, such as the *dull* Star; and could I do anything for it? I said I was as well inclined to serve the Duke as he could be – but it must be in other fashion. He then said *he agreed* wt me – but there was a 2d question: could I find them an Editor & undertake to communicate between them & him – in short save the Treasury the inconvenience of maintaining immediate & avowed intercourse w the Newspaper press? . . . I have considered the matter at leisure, & resolve to have nothing to do w it.' Walpole.

1. In reply to a letter apologizing for what *The Times* misreported him as saying about Scott and the Catholic Question. Haddington, 30 March 1829, Walpole.
2. In the Commons and Lords respectively. Lockhart, 30 March 1829, Walpole.
3. Anthony Cleasby (1804–79) was at this time a Fellow of Trinity College, Cambridge. He did stand for Parliament but was not elected; he became a judge and was knighted in 1868.
4. 'I am led to think your pen and abilitys will be imployed in collecting metereals for the ground work of a piece wherin to exebit to other ages the awfull tragedy of burke and hare . . . if such be your pleasure I can give you sketches of one or two persons who I dair say will be promenent characters in the above.' 3 April 1829, Walpole.

him's damn insurance' as Mungo says in the farce[1] – 'Did ever one hear the like?' The scoundrel has been the companion and patron of such atrocious murderers and kidnappers and he has the impudence to write to any decent man. Corrected proof sheets and dedication of the Magnum and sent them off.

5 SUNDAY Read prayers to what remains of our party, being Anne, my niece Anne, the four Skenes and William Forbes. We then walkd and I returnd time enough to work a little at the criticism.[2] Thus it drew towards dinner in conclusion.[3] After which we smokd, told stories and drank tea.

6 MONDAY Workd at the Review[4] for three or four hours yet, hang it, I can't get on. I wonder if I am turning dunny in other matters. Certainly I cannot write against time as I used to do. My thoughts will not be duly regulated. My pen declares for itself, will neither write nor spell and goes under independant colours. I went out with the child Kitty Skene on her poney. I don't much love Children, I suppose from want of habit, but this is a fine merry little girl. William Forbes sang in the evening with a feeling and taste indescribably fine but as he had no Scottish or English songs my ears were not much gratified. I have no sense beyond Mungo. 'What signify me hear if me no understand?'[5]

William Forbes leaves us. As to the rest the old story. Scribble till two then walkd for exercise till four. Deil ha'et else for company eats up the afternoon so nothing can be done that is not achieved in the forenoon.

7 TUESDAY We had a gay scene this morning, the foxhounds and merry hunters in my little base-court which rang with trampling steeds and rejoiced in Scarlet jackets and ringing horns. I have seen the day worlds would not have bribed me to stay behind them. But that is over and I walked a sober pace up to the Abbot's knowes from which [I] saw them draw my woods but without finding a fox. I watchd them with that mixture of interest affection and compassion which old men feel at looking on the amusements of the young. I was so far interested in the chace itself as to be sorry they did not find. I had so far the advantage of the visit that it gave me an object for the morning exercise which I would otherwise only have been prompted

1. Bickerstaffe's *Padlock*, Act 1.
2. Of Tytler. See note to the Entry for 13 March 1829.
3. A reminiscence of *King John*, i. 1. See p. 547, note 3.
4. See note 2.
5. See note 1.

to by health and habit. It is pleasant to have one's walk, as heralds say, with a difference.

Skene sketching with his son to see Holidean.[1] By the way the fox hounds hunted the cover far too fast. When they found a path they ran through it pele-mele without beating at all. They had hardly left the Hare hole cover when a fox whom they had over run stole away. This is the consequence of breeding dogs too speedy.

8 WEDNESDAY We have the news[2] of the Catholic question being carried in the House of Lords by a majority of 105 upon the second reading. This is decisive and the balsam of Fierabras[3] must be swallowd – It remains to see how it will work. Since it was indubitably necessary I am glad the d[ec]ision on the case has been complete. On these las[t] three days I have finishd my review of Tytler for Lockhart and sent it off by this post. I may have offended Peter by censuring him for a sort of petulance towards his predecessor Lord Hailes.[4] This day visited by Mr. Carr of   [5] who is a sensible, clever young man and by his two sisters, beautiful singer the youngest and to my taste and English music.

9 THURSDAY Labourd correcting proofs and revising; the day infinitely bad, word till three o'clock then tried a late walk and a wet one. I hear bad news of James Ballantyne. Hypocondriack I am afraid and religiously distressd in mind.[6]

I got a book from the Duke de Léviz, the same gentleman with whom I had an awkward meeting at Abbotsford owing to his having forgot his credentials which left me at an unpleasant doubt as to his

---

1. The attraction to the artist was the ruined cell formerly belonging to the monks of Melrose Abbey.
2. In a letter of the 5th from Lockhart. Walpole.
3. *Don Quixote*, pt. i, ch. 17.
4. 'Too eager to display that Lord Hailes had left him something to do, it seems to us that this young gentleman had committed an error of taste in pointing out the errors of the venerable annalist.' *Quarterly*, no. 82.
5. Morton Carr, of the Excise, was a Hampstead neighbour of Joanna Baillie, who introduced him as 'One of my young favorites. . . . He is with all his other good qualities a modest man, and will not presume.' Undated, Walpole. See also Baillie, 13 February 1829, Walpole.
6. Cadell had written on the 2nd: 'Ballantyne is not getting better. I think he is worse than he was, he has got among the Henry Grey enthusiasts in religion, which is doing him no good.' *Letters*, xi. 168 n.

character and identity.[1] His book is inscribed to me with hyperbolical praises. Now I don't like to have, like the Persian poets who have the luck to please the Sun of the univers[e], to have my mouth cramd with sugar-candy[2] which politeness will not permit me to spit out and my stomach is indisposed to swallow. The book is better than would be expected from the exaggerated nonsense of the dedication.

10 FRIDAY Left Abbotsford at seven to attend the Circuit.[3] *Nota Bene* half past six is the better hour. Waters are extremely flooded. Lord Meadowbank at the circuit. Nothing tried but a few trumpery assaults. Meadowbank announces he will breakfast with me tomorrow so I shall return tonight. Promised to my cousin Charles Scott to interest myself about his getting the farm of Milsington upon Borthwick water and mentiond him to Colonel Riddell as a proposed offerer. The tender was well received. I saw James the piper and my cousin Anne. Sent to James Veitch the Spyglass of professor Fergusson to be repaird. Dined with the judge and returnd in the evening.

11 SATURDAY Meadowbank breakfasted with us and then went on to Edinr. Pressd by bad news of his family. His wife (daughter of my early patron President Blair) is very ill, indeed I fear fatally so. I am sorry to think it is so. When the King was here[4] She was the finest woman I saw at Holyrood. My proofs kept me working till two then I had a fatiguing and watery walk. After dinner we smoked and I talkd with Mr. Carr over criminal jurisprudence, the choicest of conversation to an old lawyer, and the delightful musick of Miss Isabella Carr closed the day. Still I don't get to my task. But I will tomorrow or next day.

1. His book was *The Carbonaro, A Piedmontese Tale*, 1829. The 'awkward meeting' took place the previous August. Douglas comments: 'This must have been an unusual experience for the head of a family that considered itself to be the oldest in Christendom. Their château contained, it was said, two pictures: one of the Deluge, in which Noah is represented going into the Ark, carrying under his arm a small trunk, on which was written "*Papiers de la maison de Lévis*"; the other a portrait of the founder of the house bowing reverently to the Virgin, who is made to say, "*Couvrez-vous, mon cousin.*" '.
2. James Marioer, *The Adventures of Hajji Baba of Ispahan*, ch. 28.
3. At Jedburgh.
4. In 1822.

12 SUNDAY Read prayers. Put my books in order and made some progress in putting papers in order which have been multiplying on my table. I have a letter from that impudent lad Reynolds[1] about my contribution to the *Keepsake*. Sent to him the *House of Aspen* as I had previously determined.[2] This will Give them a lumping pennyworth in point of extent but that is the side I would have the bargain rest upon. It shall be a warning after this to keep out of such a scrape.

13 MONDAY In the morning before Breakfast I corrected the proof of the critique on the life of Lord Pitsligo in *Blackwood's Magaz.*[3] At breakfast to increase the confusion at the departure of Skene and his lady and family and of Mr. Carr and his sisters.[4] Time was dawdled away till near twelve o'clock and then I could not work much. I finishd however a painful letter to J. Ballantyne which I hope will have effect upon the painful nervous disorder he complains of. He must 'awake arise or be forever fallen'[5] – I walked happily and pleasantly till from two o'clock till four. And now I must look to *Anne of Geierstein*. Hang it – it is not so bad after all though I fear it will not be popular. In fact I am almost expended. But while I exhort others to exertion I will not fail to exert myself. I have a letter from R. P. G. proposing to subscribe to assist him from £25 to £50 pounds.[6] It will do no good but yet I cannot help giving him something.

> A Daimen icker in a thrave
> Is small request.
> I'll get a blessing wi' the lave
> And never miss it.[7]

I will try a Review for the *Foreign* and he shall have the proceeds.[8]

1. It begins, impudently enough, 'I have had the pleasure of receiving your letter; I must own that I regret its delay.' Reynolds, 7 April 1829, Walpole.
2. On 27 February.
3. See *Blackwood's Magazine*, no. 152.
4. They 'came to Abbotsford for a day and staid a week, so I suppose they liked us as well as we did them.' *Letters*, xi. 175.
5. *Paradise Lost*, i. 330.
6. Gillies's proposal was that his friends should subscribe to avoid 'the irretrievable ruin of my family and all my prospects' and that he would insure his life in their favour. Gillies, 10 April 1829, Walpole.
7. Burns's 'To a Mouse' st. 3.
8. Scott's generosity gets the better of the resolution made on 12 March 1828 not to help Gillies further. The review which he wrote was of Pastoret's *Le Duc de Guise à Naples*.

14 TUESDAY I sent off proofs of the review of Ritson for John Lockhart. Then set a stout heart to a stay brae[1] and took up *Anne of Geierstein*. I had five sheets standing by me which I read with care and Satisfied myself that worse had succeeded but it was while the fashion of the thing was new. I retrenchd a good deal about the Troubadours which was really *hors de place*. As to King René I retaind him as a historical character.[2] In short I will let the sheets go nearly as they are for though J. B. be an excellent judge of this species of composition he is not infallible and has been in circumstances which may biass his mind. I might have taken this determination a month since and I wish I had. But I thought I might strike out something better by the braes and burn sides. Alas! I walk along them with painful and feeble steps and invoke their influence in vain. But my health is excellent and it were ungrateful to complain either of mental or bodily decay.

We calld at Ellieston to-day and made up for some ill bred delay. In the evening I corrected two sheets of the Magnum as we call it.

15 WEDNESDAY I took up *Anne* and wrote with interruption of a nap (in which my readers may do well to imitate me) till two o'clock. I wrote with ease having digested Comines.[3] Whether I succeed or not it would be dastardly to give in. A bold countenance often carries of[f] an indifferent cause but no one will defend him who shows the white feather. At two I walkd till near four – Dined with the girls, smoked two cigars, and to work again till supper, then slept like a top, amount of the day's work 3 pages, a round task.

16 THURSDAY I wanted to go out with Bogie to plant some shrubs in front of the old quarry but it rains cats and dogs as they say. A rare day for grinding away at the old mill of imagination yet somehow I have no great will to the task. After all however the morning proved a true

1. 'A steep hill'. The phrase is proverbial in Scotland.
2. The Entry for 8 March 1829 notes that Ballantyne 'totally condemns *Anne of Geierstein*'. In effect Scott now takes the advice given by Cadell a month before: 'Agreeing with him in a great degree about the episode, if I may so call it, on the Troubadours, but not agreeing with him about what you have done after that, allow me to suggest to you to cancel that part about the Troubadours and no more, and finish the story in your own way.' He adds, thriftily: 'The Troubadours for all this must not be lost, it will make a capital note to the collected edition.' 19 March 1829, Walpole.
3. *Mémoires de Philippe de Commines, sur les faicts et gestes de Loys XI et Charles VIII*, 1524.

april one, sunshine and shower, and I both workd to some purpose and moreover walkd and directed about planting the quarry. The post brought matter for a may or april morning[1] – a letter from Sir James McIntosh telling me that Moore and he were engaged as contributors to Longman's Encyclopedia and asking me to do a volume at £1000, the subject to be the history of Scotland in one volume.[2] This would be very easy work. I have the whole stuff in my head and could write *currente calamo*.[3] The size is as I compute it about one 3d. longer than the *Tales of my Grandfather*. There is much to be said on both sides. Let me balance Pros and Cons after the fashion of honest Robinson Crusoe.

Pro. It is the sum I have been wishing for, sufficient to enable [me] to break the invisible but magic circle which petty debts of myself and others have traced round me.[4] With common prudence I need no longer go frand to mouth or what is worse anti[ci]pate my means. I may also pay off some small shop debts etc. belonging to the trust, clear off all Anne's embarassment and even make some foundation of a provision for her. *N. Bene*. I think this whacking reason is like to prove the gallon of Coniac Brandy which a lady recommended as the foundation of a liqueur – 'Stop ther[e], Madam, if you please' said my Grandfather Dr. Rutherford 'you can [add] nothing to that; it is flanconade with a thousand pounds and a capital hit by Gad.'[5]

Contra. It is terribly like a hack-author to make an abridgement of what I have written so lately.

Pro. But a difference may be taken, a history may be written of the same country on a different plan, general where the other is detaild and philosophical where it is popular. I think I can do this and do it with unwashd hands too.[6] For being hackd what is it but another word for being an author. I will take care of my name doubtless but the five lett[er]s which form it must take care of me in turn. I never [knew] name or fame burn brighter by over chary keeping of it. Besides there are two gallant hacks to pull with me.

Contra. I have a monstrous deal on hand. Let me see. Life of Argyle

1. *Twelfth Night*, iii. 4.
2. Sir James was to write the History of England and Moore the History of Ireland for Dr. Lardner's *Cabinet Cyclopaedia*. From Scott he wanted 'little more than an Abridgement of what you have told to your Grandchild.' Mackintosh, 14 April 1829, Walpole.
3. 'With flowing pen'.
4. The debts of which Scott complains in the Entry for 26 January 1829.
5. Sheridan's *Critic*, ii. 2.
6. *1 Henry IV*, iii. 3.

and Life of Peterborough[1] for Lockhart. 3d. Series *Tales of my Grandfather* – Review for Gillies[2] – New Novel[3] – End of *Anne of Geierstein*.

Pro. But I have just finishd two long reviews for Lockhart[4] – the third series is soon discussd. The review may be finish[d] in three or four days and the Novel is within a week and less of conclusion. For the rest we must first see how this goes off. In fine, within six weeks I am sure I can do the work and secure the independence I sigh for – Must I not make hay while the sun shines? Who can tell what leisure, health and life may be destined to me?

Adjournd the debate till tomorrow morning.

17 FRIDAY I resumed the discussion of the bargain about the History. The ayes to the right, the Noes to the left. The ayes have it – So I will write to Sir James of this date. But I will take a walk first, that I will. A little shaken with the conflict for after all were [I] as I have been —

> My poverty but not my will consents.[5]

I have been out in a most delicious real spring day. I returnd with my nerves strung and my mind determined. I will make this plunge and with little doubt of coming off no loser in character. What is given in detail may be suppressd, general views may be enlarged upon and a bird's eye prospect given not the less interesting that we have seen its prominent points nearer and in detail. I have been of late in a great degree free from waferd letters, sums to make up, notes of hand wanted and all the worry of an embarassd man's life. This last struggle will free me entirely and so help me heaven It shall be made. I have written to Sir James stating what I apprehended the terms to be, £1000 namely for one volume containing about one 3d more than one of the volumes of *Tales of my Grandfather*, and agreeing to do so.[6] Certes few men can win £1000 so readily. We dine with the Fergusons to-day at four. So off [we] went and safely returnd.

1. Lockhart had proposed these as possible contributions to Murray's Family Library (which he edited), but they were never written.
2. Of Pastoret's *Le Duc de Guise à Naples*.
3. *Count Robert of Paris*, not begun in fact until September 1830.
4. Of Ritson's *Annals of the Caledonian* and Tytler's *History of Scotland*.
5. *Romeo and Juliet*, v. 1.
6. The work finally grew to two volumes, however, for which Scott was paid £1500. *Life*, ix. 321.

18 SATURDAY Corrected proofs. I find J. B. has not returnd to his business though I wrote him how necessary it was. My pity begins to give way to anger. Must he sit there and squander his thoughts and senses upon cloudy metaphysicks and abstruse theology till he addles his brains entirely and ruins his business? I have written to him again, letter third and I am determined last.[1]

Wrote also to the fop Reynolds with preface to the *House of Aspen*.

Then to honest Joseph Train desiring he would give me some notion how to serve him with Mr. Carr[2] and to take care to make his ambition moderate and feasible. My neighbour Mr. Karr of Kippilaw struck with a palsy while he was looking at the hounds, his pony remaind standing by his side. A sudden call if a final one. That strange desire to leave a prescribed task and set about something else seized me irresistibly. I yielded to it and sit down to try at what speed and in what manner I could execute this job of Sir James McIntosh and I wrote three leaves before rising, well enough I think. The girls made a round with me. We drove to Chiefswood, went from that to Jane's wood up the Rhymer's glen and so home. This occupied from one to four. In the evening I heard Anne read Mr. Peel's excellent bill on the police of the Metropolis which goes to disband the whole generation of Dogberry and Verges. Wrote after tea.

Kippilaw is recovering; fortunately he was found by a medica[l] man.

19 SUNDAY I made this a busy day. I wrote on at the history till two o'clock. Then took a gallant walk. Then began reading for Gillies's article. James Ferguson dined with us. We smoked and I became woundy sleepy. Now I have taken collar to this arrangement I find an open sea before me which I could not have anticipated, for though I should get through well enough with my expectations during the year yet it is a great thing to have a certainty to be clear as a new pin of every penny of debt – There is no being obliged or asking favours or getting loan[s] from some grudging friend who can never look at you after but with fear of losing his cash or you at him without a humiliating sense of having

1. In reply Scott receives 'a manly sensible letter from J. B. He admits the unreasonableness of his conduct and promises amendment'. *Letters*, xi. 172. He returns to work on the 20th.

2. Train was an Excise officer, and Carr had come to Scotland as Supervisor of Excise. Scott had commended Train to him during his visit and Carr had promised to help if possible. For the letter to Train see *Letters*, xi. 173.

extorted an obligation. Beside my large debts I have paid since I was in trouble at least £2000 of personal incumbrances. So no wonder my nose is still under water. I really believe the sense of this apparently unending struggle, schemes for retrenchment in which I was unseconded,[1] made me lowspirited, for the Sun seems to shine brighter upon me as a free man.

Nevertheless Devil take the necessity which makes me drudge like a very hack of Grub-street.

> May the foul fa' the gear and the blathrie o't.[2]

I walkd out with Tom's assistance, came home, went through the weary work of cramming and so forth. Wrought after tea and then to bed.

20 MONDAY As yesterday till two – 16 pages of the history written, not worth less than one fifth of the whole book. What if they should be off? I were finely holpd for throwing my time away A toy! they dare not – [3]

Lord Buchan is dead, a person whose immense vanity bordering upon insanity obscured or rather eclipsed very considerable talents. His imagination was so fertile that he seemd really to believe the extraordinary fictions which he delighted in telling. His oeconomy, most laudable in the early part of his life when it enabled him from a small income to pay his father's debts, became a miserable habit and led him to do mean things. He had a desire to be a great man and a Mecoenas *à bon marché*. The two celebrated lawyers his brother[s] were not more gifted by nature than I think he was but the restraints of a profession kept the eccentricity of the family in order. Henry Erskine was the best-natured man I ever knew, thouroughly a gentleman and with but one fault. He could not say *no* and thus sometimes misled those who trusted him. Tom Erskine was positively mad. I have heard him tell a cock and a bull story of having seen the ghost of his father's servant John Burnet with as much sincerity as if he believed every word he was saying. Both Henry and Thomas were saving[4] men yet both died very poor. The one at one time

---

1. First by his wife; latterly by Anne who had 'learned her house keeping in an extravagant school'. Entry for 12 January 1828.
2. See the Entry for 26 September 1827 and note.
3. Scott was writing the *History* before the terms had been finally agreed. The Entry for 23 April 1829 shows that he had no cause for worry.
4. What follows suggests that Scott meant to write 'getting' not 'saving'.

618 *The Journal of Sir Walter Scott*

possessd £200,000, the other had a considerable fortune. The Earl alone has [died] wealthy. It is saving not getting that is the mother of Richess. They all had wit. The Earl's was crack braind and sometimes caustic – Henry's was of the very kindest, best humourd and gayest kind that ever cheerd Society – that of Lord Erskine was moody and maddish. But I never saw him in his best days.

Went to Haining – Time has at last touchd the beautiful Mrs. Pringle. I wonder he was not ashamed of himself for spoiling so fine a form. But what cares he? Corrected proofs after dinner. James B. is at last at work again.

21 TUESDAY Spend the whole morning at writing – Still the *History* such is my willful whim. Twenty pages now finishd. I suppose the clear 4th part of a volume. I went out but the day being sulky I sate in the Conservatory after trying a walk. I have been glancing over the works for Gillies's review[1] and I think on them between hand while I compose the history. An odd habit of doing two things at once but it has always answerd with me well enough.

22 WEDNESDAY Another hard day's work at the *History*, now increasd to the Bruce and Baliol period and threatening to be too lengthy for the *Cyclopedia*. But I will make short work with wars and battles. I wrote till two o'clock and strolld with old Tom and my dogs till half past four, hours of pleasure and healthful exercize and today taken with ease. A letter from J. B. stating an alarm that he may lose the printing of a part of the Magnum.[2] But I shall write him he must

1. Probably Modena's *Memoirs* and Aloff's *Memoirs*, both concerned with the revolution at Naples. Cochrane of Treuttel and Wurtz had sent them on the 4th. Walpole.
2. 'Mr. Cadell', he writes, 'is now taking in estimates from other printers.' This is unfair for two reasons: 'One is, that I have purchased a large stock of types, which are greatly injured by being exposed to the operation of Stereotyping; whereas my competitors would print from the plates. The other is, that I pay a man 30/- p. week, for the exclusive purpose of attending to the Magnum; whereas my competitors will have the advantage of those labours without paying a penny of the expense; as they are to be employed only to cast off the impression.' 22 April 1829, Walpole.
   There is more trouble in September, when Cadell threatens to take away the printing from Ballantyne, who has laid out £4000 to equip himself for it, unless he will do it for less than the estimates he accepted. 'From 14/- p. ream, he has got us down to 12/- and now meditates, by compelling us to hot-press for

be his own friend, set shoulder to the wheel and remain at the head of his business and so I will to my proofs – And of that I must make him aware. And so I set to my proofs.

Better to work, says the inscription on Hogarth's Bridewell, than to stand thus.

23 THURSDAY A cold blustering day – bad wellcome for the poor lambs. I made my walk short and my task long, my work turning entirely on the history, all on speculation. But the post brought me a letter from Dr. Lardner the manager of the *Cyclopedia* agreeing to my terms so all is right there and no labour thrown away. The volum[e] is to run to 400 pages. So much the better. I love elbow room and will have space to do something to purpose. I replied agreeing to his terms and will send him copy so soon as I have corrected it. The Colonel and Miss Ferguson dined with us. I think I drank rather a cheerful glass with my good friend. Smoked an extra cigar so no more at present.

25 SATURDAY After writing to Mr. Cochrane,[1] to Cadell and J. B.,[2] also to Mr. Pitcairn:[3] it was time to set out for Lord Buchan's funeral. The funeral letters were signd by Mr. H. David Erskine, his Lordship['s] natural son. His nephew the young Earl was present but neither of them took the head of the coffin. His Lordship's funeral took place in a chapell amongst the ruins. His body was in the grave with its feet pointing westward. My cousin Maxpopple was for taking notice of it but I assured him that a man who had been wrong in the head all his life would scarce become right headed after death.[4] I felt

---

nothing, to lower that last charge to 10/6d.; or 20 p.cent below the original estimate.' Ballantyne, 4 September 1829, Walpole. Scott supports Ballantyne in a letter to Cadell. To take his printing elsewhere 'would be morally wrong and good cannot come of it'. *Letters*, xi. 326.

1. Of Treuttel and Wurtz who published the *Foreign Quarterly*.
2. Probably the undated note in *Letters*, xi. 175: 'I heartily congratulate you on your return to the duties of this world . . . I confess I was very rough but it was only in proportion to the interest I took in your motions and you are very good natured to forgive it.'
3. Robert Pitcairn, a young antiquary and assistant to Thomas Thomson, who corresponded frequently with Scott about the book he was writing on Scottish criminal trials.
4. Four years before, Moore had been surprised to find in the ruins 'Lord Buchan's own tombstone ready placed, with a Latin inscription by himself on it, and a cast from his face let into the stone'. *Memoirs of Moore*, iv. 330.

something at parting with this old man though but a trumpery body. He gave me the first approbation I ever obtaind from a stranger. His caprice had led him to examine Dr. Adams's class[1] where [I], a boy twelve years old and then in disgrace for some aggravated case of negligence, was calld up from a low bench and recited my lesson with some spirit and appearance of feeling the poetry (it was the apparition of Hector's ghost in the *Æneid*) and [earnd] the noble earl's applause. I was very proud of this at the time. I was sad from another account – it was the first time I had been among these ruins[2] since I left a very valued plege there. My next visit may be involuntary. Even God's will be done. At least I have not the mortification of thinking what a deal of patronage and fuss Lord Buchan would bestow on my funeral.[3] Maxpopple dined and slept here with four of his family much amused with what they heard and saw. By good fortune a ventriloquist and partial juggler came in and we had him in the library after dinner. He was a half starved, wretched looking creature who seemd to have eat more fire than bread. So I caused him to [be] well stuffd and gave him a guinea rather to his poverty than to skill, and now to finish *Anne of Geierstein*.

26 SUNDAY But not a finger did I lay on the jacket of *Anne*. Looking for something I fell in with the Little drama long amissing calld the *Doom of Devorgoil*. I believe it was out of mere contradiction that I sate down to read and correct it merely because I would not be bound to do aught that seemd compulsory. So I scribbled at [the] piece of nonsense till two o'clock and then walkd to the lake. At night I flung helve after hatchet and spent the evening in reading the *Doom of Devorgoil* to the girls who seemd considerably interested. Anne objects to the mingling the comick goblinry which is comic with the serious which is tragic. After all I could greatly improve [it] and it would [not] be a bad composition of that odd kind to some pick-nick receptacle of all things.[4]

27 MONDAY This day must not be wasted. I breakfast with the Fergusons and dine with the Brewsters. But by heave[n] I will finish

1. The Rector's class at the High School.
2. The ruined Abbey of Dryburgh, where Scott had buried his wife in 1826.
3. During Scott's illness of 1819 Buchan called to assure him that he would personally take charge of the funeral. *Life*, vi. 90–2.
4. *The Doom of Devorgoil* was written in 1817. *Life*, v. 197. It was published, along with *Auchindrane*, in an octavo volume, early in 1830.

Anne of Geierstein this day betwixt the two engagements. I don't know why nor wherefore but I hate Anne. I mean Anne of Geierstein; the other two Annes are good girls.

Accordingly I well nigh accomplishd my work but about three o'clock my story fell into a slough and in getting it out I lost my way and was forced to pos[t]pone the conclusion till tomorrow. Wrote a good day's work notwithstanding.

At Dr. Brewster's we found Mr. and Mrs. Wyburgh, the latter a daughter of Archie Tod of Drygrange, Mrs. Clerk and her son Captain Clerk and I know no[t] who dined beside.

28 TUESDAY I have slept upon my puzzle and will now finish it. Jove bless my Pia Mater[1] as I see not further impediment before me – The story will end and shall end because it must end and so here goes – After this doughty resolution I went doggedly to work and finishd five leaves by the time when they should meet the coach. But the misfortune of writing fast is that one cannot at the same time write concisely.[2] I wrote two pages more in the evening. Stayd at home all day. Indeed the weather, sleety rainy stormy, forms no tempting prospect. Bogie[3] too who sees his flourish going to wreck is looking as spiteful [as] an angry fiend towards the unpro[pi]tious heavens. So I made a day of work of it

And yet the end was not.[4]

29 WEDNESDAY This morning I finishd and sent off three pages more and still there is something to write but I will take the broad axe to it and have it ended before noon. – This has proved impossible and the task lasted me till nine when it was finishd *tant bien que mal*. Now will people say this expresses very little respect for the public? In fact I have very little respect for that dear *Publicum* whom I am doomd to amuse, like Goody Trash in *Bartholomew Fair*, with rattles and gingerbread, and I should deal very uncandidly with those [who] may read my confessions were I to say I knew a publick worth caring for or capable of distinguishing the nicer beauties of composition. They weigh good and evil qualities by the pound. Get a good name and you may write trash. Get a bad one and you may write like Homer without pleasing a single reader. I am perhaps *l'enfant gâté de succès* but I am brought to the stake perforce and must stand the course.[5]

1. *Twelfth Night*, i. 5.
2. Cf. Pascal's *Lettres Provinciales* (1657), xvi.
3. The gardener at Abbotsford.
4. St. Matthew 24: 6.
5. *Macbeth*, v. 7.

Having finishd *Anne* I began and revised 15 leaves of the History and sent them to Dr. Lardner. I think they read more trashy than I expected. But when could I ever please myself even when I have most pleased others? Then I walkd about two hours by the thicket and riverside watching the appearance of Spring which as Coleridge says

> Comes slowly up this way.[1]

After dinner and tea I resumed the task of correction[2] which is an odious one but must be attempted, aye and accomplishd too.

30 THURSDAY Dr. Johnson enjoins Bozzy to leave out of his diary all notices of the weather as insignificant. It may be so to an inhabitant of Bolt Court in Fleet Street who need care little whether it rains or snows except the Shilling which it may cost him for a Jarvie.[3] But when I wake and find a snow shower sweeping along destroying hundreds perhaps of young lambs and famishing their mothers I must consider it as worth noting. For my own poor share I am as indifferent as any Grubstreeter of them all

> — and since tis a bad day
> Rise up rise up, my merry men,
> And use it as you may.[4]

I have accordingly been busy. The weather did not permit to go beyond the Courtyard for it continued cold and rainy. I have employed the day in correcting the history for *Cyclopoedia* as far as page 35 exclusive and have sent it off or shall tomorrow. I wish I knew how it would run out. Dr. Lardner's measure is a large one. But so much the better. I like to have ample verge and space enough and a mere abridgement would be discreditable. Well Nobody can say I eat the bread of idleness. Why should I? Those who do not work from necessity take violent labour from choice and were necessity out of [the] question I would take the same sort of literary [labour] from choice – something more leisurely though.

1. Coleridge's 'Christabel', pt. i, l. 22.
2. Of proofs of the Introduction to *Rob Roy*. See *Letters*, xi. 177.
3. A hackney coach.
4. Joanna Baillie's *Orra*, iii. 1.

MAY

1 FRIDAY Weather more tolerable. I commenced my review on the Duke of Guise's expedition for my poor correspondent Gill –.[1] Wrote six leaves. What a curious tale is that of Massaniello.[2] I went to Huntly Burn in the Sociable and returnd on foot to my great refreshment. Evening as usual. Eat, drank, smoked and wrote. Cash stands thus

8 April—In purse. £16—8 By bill on Cadell			£30
„ Bil			
9th April—Bill on Cadell			30
In purse			16
			45
Anne at turn		£30	
Sundries at Circuit		3	
To a juggler[3]		1	
Sundries		5	39
	Balance		6
1 May—Cash from Exchequer			149
			155
2 Tom		£40	
3 Bogie		50	
4 Anne		60	150
	Remains		£5

2 SATURDAY A pitiful day of rain and wind, labourd the whole morning at Gillies's review. It is a fine subject – the Duke of Guise at Naples and I think not very much known though the story of Massaniello is. I have a letter from Dr. Lardner proposing to me to publish the history in June but I dare not undertake it in so short a space, proof sheets and all considerd. It must be October[4] no help for it – Wrote after dinner as usual.

3 SUNDAY The very same diary might serve this day as the last. I sent off to Gillies half his review and I wish the other half at old Nick.

1. Gillies.
2. F. Midon's *History of the Rise and Fall of Masaniello, the Fisherman of Naples*, etc., 1729.
3. See the Entry for 25 April.
4. From July to September was considered a dead time by the booksellers.

4 MONDAY A poor young woman came here this morning, well dress[d] and well behaved with a strong northern accent. She talkd incoherently; long story of a brother and lover both dead. I would have kept her here till I wrote to her friends, particularly to Mr. Sutherland (an Aberdeen bookseller) to inform them where she is. But my daughter and her maidens were frightend as indeed there might be room for it and so I sent her in one of Davidson's chaises[1] to the Castle at Jedburgh and wrought[2] to Mr. Shortreed to see she is humanely treated.[3] I have written also to her brother.

> Long shall I see these things forlorn
> And long again their sorrows feel.[4]

The rest was write walk eat smoke – smoke and write again.

5 TUESDAY A moist rainy day, mild however and promising good weather. I sat at my desk the whole day and workd at Gillies's review. So was the day expended.

6 WEDNESDAY I sent off the review[5] – Received the sheets of the Secret Tribunal[6] from Master Reynolds – Keith Scott, a grandson of James Scott my father's cousin german, came here, a fine lively boy with good spirits and amiable manners. Just when I had sent off the rest of Gillieses manuscript W. Laidlaw came so I had him for my companion in a walk which the late weather has prevented for one or two days. Col: and Misses Fergusson and Margaret Fergusson came to dinner and so passd the evening.

7 THURSDAY Captain Percy,[7] brother of Lord Louvaine and son of Lord Beverley, came out to dinner. Dr. and Mrs. Brewster met him. He is like his brother Lord Louvaine an amiable, easy and accomplishd man who has seen a great deal of service an[d] roamd about with tribes of western Indians. He is very agreeable and I like him much. He reminds me of his brother Lord Louvaine. Keith Scott a grandson of James Scott is also here.

1. Davidson kept the inn at Melrose.
2. A slip for 'wrote'.
3. Jedburgh Castle was the county jail, and Robert Shortreed the Sheriff-Substitute for Roxburghshire.
4. Crabbe's 'Sir Eustace Grey', ll. 3–4.
5. It was published in the *Foreign Quarterly Review* for June 1829.
6. *The House of Aspen* (in which the Secret Tribunal is described).
7. 'Who is just beginning his residence at Edinr. for the next year – as Commissioner of the Excise.' Stuart Dundas, 28 March 1829, Walpole.

8 FRIDAY Went up Yarrow with Captain Percy which made a complete day's idleness for which I have little apology to offer. I heard at the same time from the President[1] that Sir Robert Dundas is very unwell. So I must be in Edinburgh on Monday 11th. Very disagreeable now the weather is becoming pleasant.

9 SATURDAY Captain Percy left us at one o'clock. He has a sense of humour and aptness of comprehension which renders him an agreeable companion. I am sorry his visit has made me a little idle but there is no help for it. I have every thing to-day previous to my going away but *que faut il faire*? One must see society now and then and this is really an agreeable man. And so *transeat ille*.[2] I have walkd and was so fatigued as to sleep and now I will attack John Lockhart's proof Sheets[3] of which he has sent me a revise. In the evening I corrected proofs for the Review.

10 SUNDAY This must be a day of preparation which I hate.[4] Yet it is but laying a side of few books and arranging a few papers – And yet my nerves are flutterd and I make blunders and mislay my pen and my keys and make more confusion than I can repair. After all I will try for once to do it steadily. – Well! I have toild through it. It is like a ground swell in the sea that brings up all that is disgusting from the bottom – admonitory letters – unpaid bills – few of these thank my modern stars – all that one would wish to forget perks itself up in your face at a thorough Redding up – Devil take it – I will get out and cool the fever that this turmoil has made in my veins. The delightful Spring weather conjured down the evil spirit. I sate a long time with my nerves shaking like a frightend child and then laughd at it all and [walkd] by the side of the river coming back by the thicket.

11 MONDAY We passd the morning in the little arrangements previous to our departure and then returnd at night to Edinburgh bringing Keith Scott along. This boy's Grandfather was a cousin German of my father, James Scott by name, very clever and particularly well acquainted with Indian customs and manners. He was one of the first settlers in P. of Wales Island. He was an active-minded man, and thought and wrote a great deal. I have seen a

1. The Lord President of the Court of Session, the Rt. Hon. Charles Hope.
2. 'Let him pass'.
3. Of Ritson's *Caledonian Annals. Letters*, xi. 177.
4. 'There is an operation calld Putting to Rights, *Scottice* Redding up, which puts me into a fever.' Entry for 26 April 1826.

trunk full of his Mss. Unhappily instead of writing upon some subject on which he might have conveyd information he took to writing on metaphysics and lost both his candles and his labour. I was consulted about publishing some part of his works but could not recommend [them]. They were shallow essays with a good deal of infidelity exhibited. Yet James Scott was a very clever man. He only fell into the common mistake of supposing that arguments new to him were new to all others.

His son when I knew him long since in this country was an ordinary man enough. This boy seems smart and clever.

We reachd the House[1] in the evening; it was comfortable enough considering it had been shut up for two months. I found a letter from Cadell asserting his continued hope in the success of the Magnum. I began to be jealous[2] on the subject but I will know tomorrow.

12 TUESDAY Went to Parlt. House – Sir Robert Dundas very unwell. Poor Hamilton on his back with the gout – So was obliged to have the assistance of Roland from the second Division – Saw Cadell on the way home – I was right – He had been disappointed in his expectations from Glasgow and other mercantile places where Trade is low at present. But

> Tidings did he bring of Africa and golden joys.[3]

The Magnum has taken extremely in Ireland which was little counted on and elsewhere. Hence he proposes a new Edition of *Tales of my G.* first series. Also an enlargement of the 3d. Series. All this drives poverty and pinch which is so like poverty from the door.

I visited Lady J. S.[4] and had the pleasure to find her well.

I wrote a little and got over a place that botherd me.

Cadell has apprehensions of *A. of G.*,[5] so have I – Well the worst of it is we must do something better.

13 WEDNESDAY Attended the court which took up a good deal of time. In my return saw Sir Robert Dundas who is better and expects to be out on tuesday. I went to the Highland Society to present Miss Grahame Stirling's book being a translation of Gelieu's work on

1. 6 Shandwick Place.
2. 'Apprehensive.' *S. N. D.*
3. *2 Henry IV*, v. 3.
4. Lady Jane Stuart.
5. *Anne of Geierstein*.

bees[1] which was well received. Went with the girls to dine at Dalhousie Castle where we were very kindly received. I saw the Edgewell tree,[2] fatal says Allan Ramsay to the family from which he was himself descended. I also saw the fatal Coalston pear, said to have [been] preserved many hundred years <and certainly a p[e]ar changed in>. It is certainly a pear either petrified or turnd into wood with a bit out of one side of it.[3] It is a pity to see my old school companion, this fine true hearted nobleman of such an ancient and noble descent, after having followd the British flag through all quarters of the world again obliged to resume his wanderings[4] at a time of life equal I suppose to my own. He has not however a grey hair in his head.

14 THURSDAY Left Dalhousie at eight to return here to Breakfast where we received cold tidings. Walter has had an inflammatory attack and I fear it will be necessary to him to return without delay to the continent.[5] I have letters from Sophia and Sir Andrew Haliday. The last, a vulgar forward man, has been of the utmost service by bleeding and advising active measures. How little one knows to whom they are to be obliged. I wrote to him and to Jane recommending the Ionian Islands where Sir Frederick Adam would I am sure give Walter a post on his staff.[6] The kind old chief Commissioner at once interested himself in the matter. It makes me inexpressibly anxious yet I have kept up my determination not to let the chances of

1. Jonas de Gelieu's *Bee Preserver: or Practical Directions for the management and preservation of Hives.* From the French, 1829.
2. 'An oak tree which grows by the side of a fine spring near the Castle of Dalhousie; very much observed by the country people, who give out that before any of the family died a branch fell from the Edgewell Tree.' Allan Ramsay's *Works*, i. 329.
3. Lady Dalhousie was Miss Brown of Coulston before her marriage.
4. Lord Dalhousie was about to become Commander-in-Chief in India.
5. His persistent cough had been giving concern and he had spent March and April on a tour through France, northern Italy, and Switzerland. Walter, 2 April 1829, Walpole.
6. Walter had talked of this possibility before. See the Entry for 18 August 1826. 'It would obtain for him the necessary residence in a favourable climate and enable him at the same time to retain his regimental rank', Scott writes to Jane. 'Otherwise I see nothing for it but going on half pay for a little while.' The Chief Commissioner, Sir Frederick's father, 'is certain that Sir Frederick will do everything in his power to receive Walter into his military establishment'. *Letters*, xi. 183.

fate come over me like a summer cloud.[1] I wrote four or five pages of the history to-day notwithstanding the agitation of my feelings.

15 FRIDAY Attended the court where Mr. Roland and I had the duty of the first division,[2] Sir Robert and Hamilton being both laid up. Spoke with the Solicitor[3] on the subject of Skene's succeeding to the Clerkship of Session in case of a vacancy[4] but did not make any impression. Dined at Granton[5] and met Lord and Lady Dalhousie, Sir John Hope, etc. I have spelld out some work this day though I have been rather knockd about.

16 SATURDAY After the court this day I went to vote at the Archers' hall where some of the members had become restive. They were outvoted two to one. There had been no division in the Royal Body Guard[6] since its commencement but these times make divisions every where. A letter from Lockhart brings better news of Walter but my heart is heavy on the subject. I went on with my history however for the point in this world is to do what we ought and bear what we must. Dined at home and wrote in the Evening.

17 SUNDAY I never stirrd from my seat all this day. My reflections as suggested by Walter's illness were highly uncomfortable and to divert it I wrought the whole day save when I was obliged to stop and lean my head on my hand. Real afliction however has something in it by which it is sanctified. It is a weight which, however oppressive, may [like] a bar of iron be conveniently disposed on the sufferer's person. But the unsubstantiality of hypochondriac affections is one of its greatest torments. You have a huge feather-bed on your shoulders which rather encumbers and oppresses you than calls forth strength

1. *Macbeth*, iii. 4.
2. Adam Rolland was a Principal Clerk in the Second Division of the Court of Session.
3. John Hope, the Solicitor-General.
4. Writing to Lockhart the previous August (and suggesting that he might think of becoming a Clerk of Session) Scott calculated that four vacancies were soon likely: 'Hector MacDonalds health and spirits . . . will incline him to retire so soon as he can . . . Ferriar is considerably upwards of 80 and poor Colin Mackenzies health is very precarious. . . . Bob Hamiltons very precarious hold of existence should be considerd.' *Letters*, x. 480–1.
5. With the Lord President, the Rt. Hon. Charles Hope.
6. The Royal Company of Archers, still the Sovereign's bodyguard in Scotland, of which Scott was a Brigadier-General.

and exertion to bear it. There is something like madness in that opinion and yet it has a touch of reality. Heave[n] help me.

18 MONDAY I resolved to take exercise to-day so only wrought till twelve. I sent off some sheets and copy to Dr. Lardner. I find my written page goes as better than <two> one to two of his print so a little more than a 190 of my writing will make up the sum wanted.

I sent him off as far as p. 62. Went to Mr. Colvin Smith at one and sate for my picture to three, there must be an end of this sitting. It devours my time.

Sent some remittances to the country. My cash affairs stand thus[1]

Cash from Mr. Cadell			£300.
Anne for House and wages		£125.0.0	
Tom—Book and £3 borrowd	£85.		
Bogie for book	48.		
Pringle postages	25	158	
Ballantyne Int. and Bannatyne club together about		18	
		301	
Cash in purse and borrowd from Tom			8
			308
			301
Cash in purse			7
Deduce expence coming to town and sundries			4
			£3.

I wrote in the evening to Walter, James MacCulloch, to Dr. Lardner and others and settled some other correspondence.

I am now in Mr. Cadell's debt on immediate advances no less than	£973
But there are sums coming in from various quarters to the amount of	800
So the unprovided Ballance is only	£173
Besides the sums credited to me by Mr. Cadell abridging the ballance as above I ought to have from reviewing work already done and to be done	£150
The Salaries etc. due June July September October	800
History due in August	1000
altogether	£1950

1. Cadell had sent a statement of Scott's account on the 15th. Walpole.

beyond which there are [no] debts and living not very considerable I will certainly become a saving man[1] at last. Walter's wants are to be taken into consideration.[2]

19 TUESDAY I went to the Court and abode there till about one and in the Library from one to two when I was forced to attend a publick meeting about the King's Statue.[3] I have no turn for these committees and yet I get always jamd into them. They take up a cruel deal of time in a way very unsatisfactory. Dined at home and wrought hard. I shall be through the Bruce's reign. It is lengthy but hang it it was our only Halcyon period. I shall be soon done with one half of the thousand pounds worth.

20 WEDNESDAY Mr. Cadell breakfasts with me with a youngster for whom he wants a letter to Sir Commander or Governor of Bombay.[4] After breakfast C. and I had some talk of business. His tidings like those of Ancient Pistol are of Africa and Golden joys. He is sure of selling at the starting 8000 copies of the Magnum at a profit of £70. per 1000, that is per month. This seems certain. But he thinks the sale will rise to 12,000[5] which will be £280 more or £840 in all.

£560
280
———
840

This will tell out a gross divisible profit of upwards of £25,000. This is not unlikely but after this comes a series of twenty volumes at least which produce only half that quantity indeed but then the whole profits save commission are the author's.[6] That will come to as much as the former, say £50,000 in all. This supposes I carry on the works of fiction for two or three novels more. But besides all this Cadell entertains a plan of selling a cheaper edition by numbers and number men[7] on

1. An allusion to the Entry for 20 April 1829: 'It is saving not getting that is the mother of Richess.'
2. He is thinking of Walter's possible need of 'A years care and abstinence', perhaps abroad on half-pay. He promises him 'in June £100 and another soon after'. *Letters*, xi. 188–9.
3. By Chantrey. George IV suggested the Castle battery as a site, but the statue was finally placed in George Street.
4. Sir Thomas Bradford (Commander-in-Chief) or Sir John Malcolm (Governor).
5. Lockhart says that the monthly sale actually reached as high as 35,000. See *Life*, ix. 326.
6. Whereas Cadell held a half-share of the early copyrights which they had bought back on 20 December 1827, the later copyrights belonged entirely to the Trust.
7. 'I am so much assailed by the *number men* that I have serious thoughts of a re-issue on 1 January next on a less expensive paper – less costly printing – indeed all departments at less cost.' Cadell, 27 March 1829, Walpole.

which he gives half the selling price. One man, Mr. Ireland,[1] offers to take 10,000 copies of the Magnum and talks of 25,000. This allows a profit of £50 per thousand copies, not much worse than the larger copy, and Cadell thinks we [may] carry on both. I doubt this. I have grea[t] apprehension that thes[e] interlopers would disgust the regular trade with whom we are already deeply engaged. I also fear a friend's selling the worse copies at the higher price. All this must be thought and cared for. In the mean time I see a fund from which large payments may be made to the Trustees, capable of extintinguishing the debt large as it is in ten years or earlier, and leaving a reversi[o]n to my family of the copy rights. Sweet bodements – good[2] – But we must not reckon our chickens before they are hatchd though they are chipping the shell now. We will see how the stream takes.

Dined at a public dinner given to the excellent Lord Dalhousie before his departure for India. An odd way of testifying respect to publick characters by eating drinking and roaring. The names however will make a good shew in the papers. Home at ten.

Good news from Sophia and Walter. The latter[3] has had some internal revolution and is relieved and Walter's cough is almost gone. Still I am zealous for the Mediterranean when the season comes which may be the beginning of September.

21 THURSDAY This is only the 23 on which I write yet I have forgotten any thing that has passd on the 21st. worthy of [note]. I wrote a good deal I know and dined at home. The step of time is noiseless as it passes over an old man. The *non est tanti*[4] mingles itself with every thing.

22 FRIDAY I was detaind long in the Court though Ham.[5] had returnd to his labour. We dined with Capt. Basil Hall and met a Mr. Codman or some such name with his lady from Boston – the last a pleasant and well mannerd woman, the husband Bostonian enough. We had Sir William Arbuthnot besides and his lady.

By the bye I should have rememberd that I calld on my old friend Lady Charlotte Campbell and found her in her usual good humour though *miffd* a little I suspect at the history of Gillespie Grumoch in

---

1. Alexander Ireland, a Manchester bookseller and an early apostle of cheap literature for the masses.
2. *Macbeth*, iv. 1.
3. A slip for 'former'.
4. That is, the feeling that all is worthless.
5. Robert Hamilton.

the *Legend of Montrose*.[1] I saw Haining[2] also looking thin and pale. These should have gone to the memorandum of yesterday.

23 SATURDAY Went to day to call on the commissioner[3] and saw at His Grace's Levee the celebrated Divine and soi disant prophet Irving.[4] He is a fine lookg. man (bating a diabolical squint) with talent on his brow and madness in his eye. His dress and the arrangement of his hair indicated that much attention had been bestowd on his externals and led me to suspect a degree of self conceit consistent both with genius and insanity.

Came home by Cadell who persists in his visions of El Dorado. He insistances I will probably bring £60,000 within six years to rub off all Constable's debts which that sum will do with a vengeance. Cadell talks of offering for the poetry to Longman.[5] I fear they will not listen to him. The *Napoleon* he can command when he likes by purchasing their stock on hand. The lives of the novelists may also be had.[6] Pleasing schemes all these but dangerous to build upon. Yet in looking at the powerful machine which we have put in motion it must be ownd 'as broken ships have come to land.'

Waited on the Comr. at five o'clock and had the pleasure to remain till eight when the debate of the Assembly was over. The question

1. Gillespie Grumach, Marquis of Argyll and chief of the Campbells, leads the opposition to Montrose in the novel. Lady Charlotte would not much like the description of the battle of Inverlochy in chapter 19 where her ancestor watched from a safe distance while his followers were routed by Montrose.

2. John Pringle of Haining.

3. Lord Forbes, the year's Lord High Commissioner to the General Assembly of the Church of Scotland, which met and still meets in Edinburgh in the latter part of May.

4. The Revd. Edward Irving. founder of the 'Holy Apostolic Catholic Church' and prophet of the second coming, whom Scott 'narrowly escaped' in London on 2 May 1828. In 1832 he was forced to retire from his London church after claiming that the unknown tongues with which members of his congregation had begun to speak were of divine origin, and in 1833 he was convicted of heretical views.

5. Longman owned the copyrights of *The Lay of the Last Minstrel* and of some shorter poems, so that the poetry could not be added to the Magnum Opus unless they were willing to sell. At the crash they had also bought, for £1214, 583 copies of Scott's *Poetical Works*, 351 of *The Lady of the Lake*, and 273 of *Marmion* – the entire stock lying in Ballantyne's printing-house. Sederunt Book, i. 155.

6. Scott had retained the copyrights of these works.

which employd their eloquence was whether the celebrated Mr. Irving could sit there as a ruling elder.[1] It was settled, I think justly, that a divine being of a different order of officers in the Kirk cannot assume the character of a Ruling Elder seeing he cannot discharge its duties.

Mr. Irving dined with us. I could hardly keep my eyes off him while we were at table. He put me in mind of the Devil disguised [as] an angel of light so ill did that horrible obliquity of vision harmonize with the dark tranquil features of [a] face resembling that of our Saviour in Italian pictures with the hair carefully arranged in the same manner. There was much real or affected simplicity in the manner in which he spoke. He rather *made play* and spoke much across the table [to] the solicitor and seem[d] to be good humourd. But he spoke with that kind of unction which is nearly [allied] to cajolerie. He boasted much of the tens of thousands that attended his ministry at the town of Annan, his native place, till he well nigh provoked me to say he was a distinguishd exception to the rule that a prophet was not esteemd in his own country. But time and place were not fitting.

24 SUNDAY I wrote or *wrought* all the morning yea even to dinner time. Miss Ker and Mrs. Skene and Will Clerk dined. Skene came from the Commissioner's[2] at seven o'clock. We had a merry evening. Clerk exults in the miscarriage of the Bill for the augmentation of the Judges' salaries. He and the other clerks in the Jury Court had hoped to have had a share in the proposed measure but the Court had considerd it as being *Nos poma natamus*.[3] I kept our own pippins quiet by declining to move in a matter which was to expose us to insult of a certain refusal. Clerk with his usual felicity of quotation said they should have rememberd the clown's exhortation to Lear 'good nuncle, tarry and take the fool with you.'[4]

25 MONDAY Wrote in the morning. Dr. MacIntosh MacKay came to breakfast and brought with him to show me the young Chevalier's target purse and snuff box, the property of Cluny MacPherson. The pistol[s] are for holsters and no way remarkable, a good serviceable pair of weapons silver-mounted. The Targe is very handsome indeed, studded with ornaments of silver, chiefly emblematic, chosen with much taste of device and happily executed. There is a contrast

1. That is, as a lay member. The Assembly is composed of Ministers and Elders, ordained and lay members.
2. Lord Forbes.
3. See the Entry for 4 February 1827 and note.
4. *King Lear*, i. 4.

betwixt the shield and purse, the targe being large and heavy, the purse though very handsome unusually small and light.[1] After one o'clock I saw the Duke and Duchess of Gordon. Then went to Mr. Smith's to finish a painting for the last time.[2] The Duchess calld with a Swiss lady to introduce me to her friend while I was doing penance. I was heartily glad to see her Grace once more. Calld in at Cadell's – His orders continue so thick that he must postpone the delivery for several days to get new engravings thrown off etc. *Vogue la Galère!* From all that now appears I shall be much better off in two or three years than if my misfortunes had never taken place. *Periissem ni periissem.*[3]

Dined at a dinner given by the Antiquarian Society to Mr. Hay Drummond, Secretary to the society, now going Consul to Tangiers. It was an excellent dinner, turtle, Champagne and all the *agrémens* of a capital meal for £1. 6. a head. How Barry[4] managed I can't say. The object of this compliment spoke and drank wine incessant[l]y, good-naturedly delighted with the compliment, which he repeatedly assured me he value[d] more than a hundred pounds. I take it that after my departure, which was early, it would be nec[e]ssary to 'carry Mr. Silence to bed.'[5]

26 TUESDAY The business at the court heavy – Dined at Gala's and had the pleasure to see him in amended health. Sir John and Lady Hope were there and the evening was lively and pleasant. George's Square is always a melancholy place for me. I was dining next door to my father's former house.[6]

27 WEDNESDAY Another dinner day. But I got up the additional notes for the Waverley novels. They seem to be setting sale[7] with a

1. Scott turned the phrase to good use in the evening when he showed the relics to the Antiquarian Society. 'His introductory remarks were brief, but of course, appropriate, and with his own significant and emphatic tone, he added: 'but I find the *shield* to be very *heavy*, and the purse to be very light!' The expressions, terse and brief as they were, carried the whole gist of the Royal owner's unhappy history.' Mackay's *Reminiscences*, p. 15.
2. Probably the Colvin Smith portrait bought by Sir John Hope, who had written on the 14th to thank Scott for agreeing to an additional sitting 'to perfect a copy for me'. Walpole.
3. 'I would have perished had I not persevered', the punning motto of the Anstruthers.
4. Barry's Hotel was at 6, 7, and 8 Princes Street.
5. *2 Henry IV*, v. 3.
6. No. 25, in which Scott lived until his marriage.
7. An interesting slip for 'sail'.

favourable wind. I had to-day a most kind and friendly letter from the Duke of Wellington, which is a thing to be vain of. He is a most wonderful man to have climbd to such a height without ever slipping his foot. Who would have said in 1815 that the Duke would stand still higher in 1829. And yet it indubitably is so. We dined with Lady Charlotte Campbell, now Lady Charlotte Bury, and her husband who is an egregious fop but a fine draughtsman.[1] Here is another day gone without work in the evening.

28 THURSDAY The court as usual till one o'clock. But I forgot to say Mr. MacIntosh Mackay breakfasted and inspected my curious Irish Ms which Dr. Brindley[2] gave me. Mr. Mackay, I should say Doctor who well deserved the name, reads it with tolerable [ease] so I hope to knock the marrow out of the bone with his assistance. I came home and dispatchd proof Sheets and revises for Dr. Lardner. I saw kind John Gibson and made him happy with the fair prospects of the Magnum. He quite agrees in my views A young clergyman named McCombich from Aberdeen Shire also calld to-day. I have had some consideration about the renewal or retranslation of the Psalmody.[3]

I had peculiar views adverse to such an undertaking. In the first place it would be highly unpopular with the lower and more ignorant rank many of whom have no idea of the change which those spiritual poems have sufferd in translation but consider their old translations as the very songs which David composed. At any rate the wiser class think that our fathers [were] holier and better men than we and that to abandon their old hymns of devotion in order to grace them with newer and more modish expression would be a kind of sacrilege. Even the best informd who think on the subject must be of opinion that even the somewhat bald and rude language and versification of the psalmody gives them an antique and venerable air and their want of the popular graces of modish poetry shows they belong to a stile

1. The Revd. Edward Bury, whom Lady Charlotte Campbell married after the death of her first husband, had been tutor to her son.

2. The Revd. Dr. John Brinkley, Bishop of Cloyne, Astronomer Royal for Ireland, President of the Royal Irish Academy and an Honorary Member of the Royal Society of Edinburgh. Scott made his acquaintance during his Irish tour in 1825. The manuscript was 'The Book of Rights', edited in 1962 for the Irish Texts Society by Professor Myles Dillon.

3. The metrical version of the psalms traditionally used by the Scottish Churches in preference to any other songs of praise, and still much used today. For McCombich's proposal see the Entry for 26 June 1827 and note.

where ornaments are not required. They contain, besides, the very words which were spoken and sung by the fathers of the reformation, sometimes in the wilderness, sometimes in fetters, sometimes at the stake. If a Church possessd the vessells out of which the original reformers partake of the Eucharist it would be surely bad taste to melt them down and exchange them for more modern. No no. Let them write hymns and paraphrases if they will but let us have still

All people on the earth that dwell.[1]

Law and Devotion must loose some of their dignity as often as they adopt new fashions.

29[2] FRIDAY The Skenes came in to Supper last night – Dr. Scott of Haslaar Hospital[3] came to breakfast. He is a Nephew of Scott of Scalloway who is one of the largest proprietors in Shetland. I have a warm recollection of the kindness and hospitality of these remote isles[4] and of this gentleman's connections in particular, who well-comed me both as a stranger and Scott, being duly tenacious of their Clan. This young gentleman is high in the medical department of the Navy. He tells me that the Ultima Thule is improving rapidly. The old clumsy plough is laid aside. They have built several stout sloops to go to the deep sea fishing instead of going thither in open boats which consumed so much time between the shore and the Haf or fishing spot. Pity but they would use a steam boat to tow them out. I have a real wish to hear of Ze[t]-land's advantage. I often think of its long isles, its towering precipices, its capes covered with seafowl of every class and description that Ornithology can find names for, its deep caves, its smoked geeze and its sour sillocks.[5] I would like to see it again. After the court I came round by Cadell who is like Jemmy[6] Taylor

full of mirth and full of glee.

1. The first line of Psalm 100, 'The Old Hundredth', in the Scottish metrical version.
2. For the dating of this and the next eight Entries see Appendix E, v, p. 828.
3. The naval hospital at Portsmouth.
4. Scott visited the Shetlands in the summer of 1814 on the yacht of the Commissioners of the Northern Lights. *Life*, iv. 180 ff.
5. 'This name is given in Orkney . . . to fry of different kinds.' Jamieson.
6. A slip for Billie Taylor in the ballad of that name.

For which he has good reason having raised the impression of the Magnum to 12,000 copies and yet the end is not[1] for the only puzzle now is how to satisfy the delivery fast enough.

30 SATURDAY We dined at Craig Crook with Jeffrey. It is a most beautiful place tastefully planted with shrubs and trees and so sequesterd that after turning into the little avenue all symptoms of the town is left behind you. He positively gives up the *Edinburgh Review*.[2] A very pleasant evening. Rather a glass of wine too much, for I was heated during the night. Very good news of walter. If the lad will but be considerate, he may do well enough[3] and he is so for the present.

31 SUNDAY Being Sunday I remaind to work the whole day and finishd half of the proposed volume of history. – I was not disturbd the whole day, a thing rather unusual.

JUNE

1 MONDAY A little startled this morning at passing a quantity of blood. It may be an awkward symptom and it may not. Either way I am firmly resolved. Received Mr. Rees of London and Col. Ferguson to breakfast. Mr. Rees is clear of opinion our scheme (the magnum) must answer. I got to letter writing after breakfast and cleard off old scores in some degree. Dr. Ross calld and would hardly hear of my going out. I was obliged however to attend the meeting of the trustees for the Theatre. The question to be decided was whether we should have decided on embracing an option left to us of taking the old theatre at a valuation, or whether we should leave it to Mrs. Siddons

1. Matthew 24: 6.
2. He was to be Dean of the Faculty of Advocates from July, and thought it 'not quite fitting that the official head of a great law corporation should continue to be the conductor of what might be fairly enough represented as in many respects a party journal'. Lord Cockburn's *Life of Jeffrey* (1852), i. 284.
3. Scott was sure Walter neglected himself. 'This disorder has hung about you for years for want of medical care', he wrote a few days before this. 'You would hardly see Ross or treat him even civilly. You would [not] take medicines which if you had done like any person of common sense would probably have rid you of a disease which has shown itself too deeply seated.' *Letters*, xi. 190. 'One would think', he complains to Lockhart, 'he has a mind to kill himself in order to spite the Doctors.' *Letters*, xi. 192.

and Mr. Murray to make the best of it.[1] There were present Sir Patrick Murray, Baron Hume, Lord Provost, Sir John Hay, Mr. Gilbert Innes and myself. We were all of opinion that personally we ought to have nothing to do with it. But I thought as trustees for the public we were bound to let the publick know how the matter stood and that they might if they pleased have the theatrical property for £16,000 which is dog cheap. They were all clear to give it up (the right of reversion) to Mrs. Siddons. I am glad she should have it, for she is an excellent person and so is her brother. But I think it has been a little jobbd. There is a clause providing the new patentees may redeem. I desired that the circumstances should notice that we were only exercizing our own judgement leaving the future trustee[s] to exercise theirs. I rather insisted there should be some saving clause of this kind, even for the sake of our honour. But I could not prevail upon my colleagues to put such a saving clause on the minutes though they agreed the possibility of the new patentees redeeming on behalf of the publick. I do not think we have done right.

I calld on Mr. Cadell whose reports of the Magnum might fill up the dreams of Alnashar should he sleep as long as the Seven sleepers. The rest was labour and letters till bed time.

2 TUESDAY The ugly symptom still continues. Mr. Ross does not mak[e] much of it and I think he is apt to look grave. I wrote in the morning. Dr. Mackintosh Mackay came to breakfast and brought a gaelick book which he has publishd, the poetry of Rob Don,[2] some of which seems pretty as he explaind it. The court kept me till near two and then home comes me I. Our noon and evening was spent as usual. In the evening Dr. Ross orderd me to be cupd, an operation which I only know from its being practized by that eminent medical practitioner the Barber of Bagdat. It is not painful and I think resembles a giant twisting about your flesh between his finger and thumb.

1. The patent originally granted to Henry Siddons was due to expire a year later, and the Trustees had to decide whether to exercise their option of buying the buildings in Shakespeare Square for which Mrs. Siddons had now paid the full purchase price of £42,000. As the Entry shows, they allowed her to retain the property, although they could have bought it for only £16,000, its real value. The new patent was granted to her brother, W. H. Murray. Dibdin, p. 349, and Home, 15 June 1830, Walpole.

2. *Songs and Poems in the Gaelic Language*, 1829. Rob Donn, or Robert the Brown, was the nickname of Robert Mackay (1714–78), a herdsman-poet from Sutherland.

3¹ WEDNESDAY I was obliged to absent myself from the court on Dr. Ross's positive instance and what is worse I was compelld to send an apology from Hopetoun House where I expected to see Made. Carodori who was to sing 'Jock of Hazeldean'. I wrote the song for Sophia and I find my friends here still prefer her to the foreign syren.

> However, Madame Caradori,
> To miss you I am very sorry.
> I should have taken it for glory
> To have heard you sing my border story.

I workd at the *Tales of my Grandfather*² but leisurely. My awkward symptom has entirely disappear[d] I suppose by the cupping for drugs seldom have much effect on me unless they are of an active character. But I remain listless drowsy and my back is as sore as that of a galld horse.

Cadell came to dine with me *tête à tête* for the girls are gone to Hopetoun House. We had ample matter to converse upon for his horn was full of good news. While we were at dinner he had letters from London and Ireland which decided him to raise the impression of *Waverly* to 15,000. This with 10,000 on the Number line which Ireland³ is willing to take will make £18,000 a year of divisible profit. This leads us to a further speculation.

This leads us to a further speculation as I said of great importance – Longman and Coy have agreed to sell their stock on hand of the poetry in which they have certain shares, their shares included, for £8000.⁴ Cadell thinks he could by selling off at cheap rates, sorting, making waste etc. get rid of the Stock for about £5000 leaving £3000 for the purchase of the copy rights and proposes to close the bargain as much cheaper as he cares but at all events to close it. Whatever shall fall short of the price returnd by the stock, the sale of which shall be entirely at his risque, shall be reckond as the price of the copy right

---

1. The first paragraph is dated '4' and the second '5' in the original. See Appendix E, v, p. 828.
2. The second series.
3. The Mr. Ireland of the Entry for 20 May 1829.
4. Longman's stock was considerable. It included nearly 3000 unsold copies of the 180 *Poetical Works*, more than 1000 foolscap copies of *The Lay*, 1300 8vo copies of *The Lord of the Isles* and hundreds of copies of the other poetical works. The important factor, though, was that they were willing to sell their interest in the copyright along with their old stock. The final price, thanks to Mr. Dickinson who helped the Trustees with the negotiation, was £7000. Sederunt Book, ii. 51–4.

and we shall pay half of that balance. I had no hesitation to authorize him to proceed in his bargain with Owen Rees of Longman's house upon that principle. For supposing according to Cadell's present idea the loss on the stock shall amount to £2000 or three thousand pounds the possession of the entire and undivided [copyright] will enable us calculating upon similar success as that of the novels to be at least 500 per Cent.

Longman and Coy have indeed an excellent bargain but then so will we – We pay dear indeed for what the ostensible subject of sale is but if it sets free almost the whole of our copy rights and places them in our own hands we get a most valuable *quid pro quo*. There is only one fourth I think of *Marmion* in Mr. Murray's hand and it must be the deuce if that cannot be [acquired].[1] Mr. Cadell proposed that [as] he took the whole books on his risk he ought to have compensation and proposed that it should consist in the sum to be given to me for arranging and making additions to the volumes of poetry thus to be republishd. I objected to this. For the first place he may suffer no loss, for the books may go off more rapidly and better than he thinks for or expects. In the second place I do not know what my labours in the poetry may be. In either case it is a blind bargain. But [if] he shou[l]d be a sufferer beyond the clear half of the loss which we agree to share with him I agreed to make him some compensation and he is willing to take what I shall think just. And so stands our bargain.

4 THURSDAY Still remain quit[e] free from that ugly complaint. The Cupping I suppose removed it. Remaind at home and wrote about four pages of *Tales*. I should have done more, but my head as Squire Sullen says achd consumedly.[2] Rees has given Cadell a written offer[3] to be binding till the 12th. Meantime I have written to Lockhart to ask John Murray if He will treat for the fourth Share of *Marmion* which he possesses. It can be worth but little to him and gives us all the copyrights.

I have a letter from Sir Thomas Dick Lauder touching[g] a Manuscript of Messrs. Hay Allen calld the *Vestiarium Scotiæ* by a Sir Richard Forester. If it is an imposition it is cleverly done but I doubt the quarter it comes from. These Hay Allans are men of warm imaginations. It makes the strange averment that all the low Country gentlemen and Border clans wore tartan and gives Setts of them all. I must see the Ms before I believe in it. The Allans are singular men of

1. Murray presented it to Scott a few days later. See the Entry for 11 June 1829.
2. Farquhar's *The Beaux Stratagem*, ii. 1.
3. About the stock and copyrights of the poetry.

much accomplishment but little probity, that is in antiquarian matters.[1]

Maxpopple who is in town came in to supper.

£10.   Caddell lent me £10, funny enough after all our grand expectations for Croesus to want such a gratility.

5 FRIDAY I rose at seven and wrote Sir Thomas Lauder a long warning on the subject of these Allans and their Manuscript. Proceeded to write but found myself pulld up by the necessity of reading a little. This occupied my whole morning. The Lord President calld very kindly to desire me to keep at home tomorrow. I thought of being out but it may be as well not. I am some how or other either listless or lazy. My head aches cruel. I made a fight at working and reading till eleven and then came sleep with a particoloured [mantle] of fantastic hues and wrapt me into an imaginary world.

6 SATURDAY I wrote the whole morning till two o'clock. Then I went into the gardens of Princ[e]'s street to my great exhilaration. I never felt better for a walk; also it is the first I have taken this whole week and more. I visited some remote garden grounds where I had not been since I walkd there with the good Samaritan Skene sadly enough at the time of my misfortunes.[2] The shrubs and young trees which were then invisible are now of good size and gay with leaf and blossom. I too – old trunk as I am – have put out tender buds of hope which seemd checkd for ever. I may now look with fair hope to freeing myself of obligation from all men and spending the rest of my life in ease and quiet. God make me thankful to so cheering a prospect.

———

[There is no Entry for 7 June, of which day nothing is known except that 'the heat at the chapel' gave Anne 'a fainting fit.'[3]]

———

1. The *Vestiarium Scoticum* was published in 1842 by John Sobieski Stuart (the title adopted by one of the Hay Allans), but posterity has shared Scott's doubts about the authenticity of the manuscript. For his letter to Sir Thomas Lauder, see *Letters*, xi. 198.
2. See the Entries for 23 January and 12 February 1826.
3. *Letters*, xi. 204.

8 MONDAY I wrote in the morning, set out for a walk at twelve o'clock
as far as Mr. Cadell's. I found him hesitating about his views and
undecided about the number plan.[1] He thinks the first plan answers so
much beyond expectation it is pity to interfere with it and talks of re-
engraving the plates. This will be touchy. But nothing is resolved on.

9 TUESDAY Anne had a little party where Lady Charlotte Bury, Lady
Hopeton and others met the Carodori who sang to us very kindly.
She sang 'Jock of Hazeldean' very well and with a peculiar expression
of humour. Sandie Ballantyne kindly came and helpd us with fiddle
and flageolet. Willie Clerk was also here. We had a lunch and [were]
very very gay. Not the less so for the want of Mr. Bury who is – a
thorough paced coxcomb – with some accomplishments however. I
drank two glasses of Champaigne which have muddied my brains for
the day. Will Clerk promise[d] to come back and dine on the wreck of
the Turkey and tongue, pigeon pye etc. He came accordingly and
staid till nine so no time for work. It was not a lost day however.

10 WEDNESDAY *Nota Bene* my complaint quite gone. I attended the
Court and sat there till late. Evening had its lot of labour which is I think
a second nature to me. It is astonishing to me how little I look into a book
of entertainment. I have been reading over the *Five Days of St. Albans*,[2]
very much *extra mœnia flammantia mundi*[3] and possessd of considerable
merit though the author loves to play at Cherry pit with Satan.[4]

11 THURSDAY I was kept at court by a hearing till near three then
sate to Mr. Grahame for an hour and a half. When I came [home]
behold a letter from Mr. Murray very handsomely yieldin[g u]p the
fourth share of *Marmion* which he possessd.[5] After we went to the
theater, w[h]ere *St. Ronan's Well* was capitally acted by Murray and
the Bailie[6] – The part of Clara Mowbray hung heavey for want of

1. The cheaper edition of the Magnum Opus. See the Entry for 20
   May.
2. William Mudford's *The Five Nights of St. Albans*, 1829.
3. 'Beyond the flaming walls of the universe.' Lucretius' *De rerum
   natura*, i. 72.
4. *Twelfth Night*, iii. 4.
5. 'This share has been profitable to me Fifty-fold beyond what
   either its publishers or author could have anticipated and
   therefore my returning it, on such an occasion, you will, I trust,
   do me the favour to consider in no other light than as a mere act
   of grateful acknowledgement for benefits already received.'
   Letters, xi. 198 n.
6. Charles Mackay, who always acted Bailie Jarvie in *Rob Roy*.

Mrs. Siddons. Poor old Mrs. Renaud, once the celebrated Mrs. Powel, took leave of the stage. As I was going to bed at twelve at night in came R. P. Gillies like a tobacco cask (well crackd of me). I shook him off with some difficulty pleading my having been lately ill but he is to call tomorrow morning.

12 FRIDAY Gillies made his appearance.[1] I told him frankly I thought he conducted his affairs too irregularly for any one to assist him and I could [not] in charity advise anyone to encourage subscriptions but that I should subscribe myself. So I made over to him about £50 which the *Foreign Review* owes me[2] and I will grow hard-hearted and do no more. I was not long in the court but I had to look at the controversy about the descent of the Douglas family.[3] Then I went to Cadell and found him still Cock a hoop. He has raised the Edition to 17,000, a monstrous number, yet he thinks it will clear the 20,000, but we must be quiet in case people *jealouse*[4] the failure of the plates. I calld on Lady J S[5] When I came home I was sleepy and overwalkd. By the way I sate till Grahame finishd my picture. I fell fast asleep before dinner and slept for an hour. After dinner I wrote to Walter, Charles, Lockhart and John Murray and took a screed of my novel[6] so concluded the evening idly enough.

Received from Mr. Cadell		£100.0.0
Cash in purse		3.
		103.0.0
To Anne	£20.	
In purse £12. To Bogie	20.	
To Tom purdie	30.	
To Mr Grahame annes portrait —	20.	
To a new bar gown	1.	
	—	£91.0.0
		12.0.0

1. He had been arrested for debt, released again, and had come north to raise money 'by appeals personal – the letters not having answered'. Lockhart, 3 and 6 June 1829, Walpole. 'The Lord forgive you for letting Gillies loose on us', replies Scott in this day's letter to Lockhart. *Letters*, xi. 205.
2. For his review of Pastoret's *Duc de Guise à Naples*.
3. For the *History of Scotland*.
4. 'Suspect.' Jamieson.
5. Lady Jane Stuart.
6. *The Five Nights of St. Albans*.

13 SATURDAY We hear of Sophia's mottions. She is to set sail by steam boat on the 16, Tuesday, and Charlie is to make a run down with her. But alas my poor Johnie is I fear come to lay his bones in his native land. Sophia can no longer disguize it from herself that as his strength weakens the disease increases. The poor child is so much bent on coming to see Abbotsford and Grandpapa that it would be cruel not to comply with his wish and if Afliction comes we will bear it best together.

> Not more the schoolboy who expires
> Far from his native home desires
> To see some friend's familiar face
> Or meet a parent's last embrace.[1]

It must be all as God wills it. Perhaps the native air may be of service.

More news from Cadel. He deems it necessary to carry up the edition to 20,000.

This day was fixed for a start to Abbotsford[2] where we arrived about six o'clock, evening. To my thinking I never saw a prettier place and even the trees and flowers seemd to say to me, we are your own again.[3] But I must not let imagination jade me thus.[4] It would be to make disappointment doubly bitter and God knows I have in my child's family matter enough to check any exuberant joy.

14 SUNDAY A delicious day threatening rain but [in] the languid and affecting manner in which Beauty demands sympathy when about to weep. I wanderd about the banks and braes all morning and got home about three and saw every thing in tolerable order excepting that there was a good number of branches left in the walks. There is a great number of trees cut and bark collected. Colonnel Ferguson dined and spent the afternoon with us.

15 MONDAY Another charming day. Up and dispatchd packets to Ballantyne[5] and Cadell; neither of them was furiously to the purpose

1. Shenstone's 'Song IX', st. 5, *Songs and Ballads*, 1743
2. 'We take a sniff of Abbotsford Air from Saturday to Wednesday when we come back in hopes to have Sophia and the babies on thursday or friday.' *Letters*, xi. 206.
3. That is, free from debt, thanks to the success envisaged for the Magnum Opus. Scott's letters at this time are full of this hope, and the old dream of buying the neighbouring estate of Faldonside from Nicol Milne revives. *Letters*, xi. 196.
4. *Twelfth Night*, ii. 5.
5. The Appendix to *Rob Roy* for the Magnum Opus. *Letters*, xi. 209.

but I had a Humour to be alert. I walkd over to Huntly Burn and round by Chiefswood and Jane's wood when I saw Capt. Hamilton. He is busy finishing his peninsular campaigns.[1] He will not be cut out by Napier whose work[2] has a strong party cast and being besides purely abstract and professional to the publick seem[s] very dull. I read Genl. Miller's account of the South American War.[3] I liked it the better that Basil Hall brought the author to breakfast with [me] in Edinr., a fin[e] tall military figure, his left hand witherd like the prophet's gourd and plenty of scars on him. There have been rare doings in that vast continent but the strife is too distant, the country too unknown, to have the effect upon the imagination which European wars produce.

This evening I indulged in the *far niente*, a rare event with me but which I enjoy proportionall[y].

16 TUESDAY Made up parcels for Dr. Lardner and now I propose to set forth my Memoranda of Byron for Moore's acceptance[4] which ought in civility to have been done long since. I will have a walk however in the first place.

I did not get on with Byron so far as I expected – began it though and that is always something. I went to see the woods at Huntly Burn, mars lea etc. Met Captain Hamilton who tells me a shocking thing. Two Messrs. Stirling of Drumpellar came here and dined one day[5] and seemd spirited young men. The younger is murderd by pirates. An Indian vessell in which he saild was boarded by these miscreants who behaved most brutally and he offering resistance I suppose was shockingly mangled and flung in the sea. He was afterwards taken up alive but died soon after. Such horrid accidents lie in wait for those whom we see all joyous and unthinking

1. Thomas Hamilton's *Annals of the Peninsular Campaigns*, 1829.
2. Colonel W. F. P. Napier's *History of the War in the Peninsula, etc.*, 1828.
3. He came on 9 June and inscribed with that date a copy of the 2nd edition (1829) of his *Memoirs of General Miller, in the Service of the Republic of Peru*, 1827. Abbots. Library, D.2. 25–60.
4. For Moore's *Life of Byron*, which was to be dedicated to Scott and for which he had been looking out letters in January. See the Entries for 4 March 1828 and 12 January 1829. His memory has been jogged by Lockhart's letter of the 6th: 'Moore is at my elbow & says he has not the face to bother you but he is come exactly to that point where your additional reminiscences of Lord Byron wd come in – So he is waiting for a week or so in case they shd be forthcoming.' Walpole.
5. See the Entry for 18 July 1827.

sweeping along the course of life, and what end may be waiting ourselves – Who can tell?

17 WEDNESDAY Must take my leave of sweet Abbotsford and my leisure hour, my eve of repose. To go to town will take up the morning.

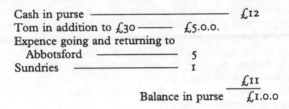

Cash in purse	——————————	£12
Tom in addition to £30	————	£5.0.0.
Expence going and returning to		
Abbotsford	——————	5
Sundries	—————	1
		£11
	Balance in purse	£1.0.0

We set out about 11 o'clock, got to Edinburgh about five where I dined with Baron Clerk and a few Exchequer friends. Lord Chief Baron, Sir Patrick Murray, Sir Henry Jardine etc. etc.

18 THURSDAY Corrected proofs for Dr. Dionysius Lardner. Cadell came to breakfast. Poor fellow, he looks like one who had been overworkd and the difficulty of keeping paper makers up to printers, print[er]s up to draughtsmen, artists to engravers and the whole party to time, requires the utmost exertions. He has actually orderd new plates[1] although the steel ones which we employ are supposed to throw off 30,000 without injury. But I doubt some thing of this. Well since they will buckle fortune on our back we must bear it scholarly and wisely.[2] I went to court, calld on my return on J. B. and Cadell. At home I set to correct *Ivanhoe*. I had twenty other things more pressing but after all these novels deserve a preference. Poor Terry is totally prostrated by a paralitick affection. Continuance of existence not to be wish[d] for.

Tomorrow I expect Sophia and her family by Steam.

19 FRIDAY Sophia and Charles who acted as her escort arr[i]ved at nine o'clock morning fresh from the Steam boat. They were in excellent health, also the little boy and girl, but poor Johnie seems very much changed indeed and I should not be surprized if the scene shortly closes. There is obviously a great alteration in strength and features. At dinner we had our family chat on a scale that I had not enjoyd for many years. The Skenes supd with us.

---

1. For another edition, aimed at those who regretted not subscribing for the first.
2. *Merry Wives of Windsor*, i. 3.

20 SATURDAY Corrected prove sheets in the morning for Dr. Lardner. Then I had the duty of the Court to perform. As I came home I recommended young Shortreed to Mr. Cadell for a printing Job now and then when Ballantyne is overloaded which Mr. Cadell promised accordingly

Lady Anna Maria Elliot's[1] company at dinner helpd on our family party and passd the evening pleasantly enough, my anxiety considering.

21 SUNDAY A very wet sunday. I employd it to good purpose, bestowing much labour on the *History*[2] ten pages of which are now finishd. Were it not for the precarious health of poor Johnie I would be most happy in this reunion with my family but, poor child, this is a terrible drawback.

£10.   Borrowd from Mr. Cadell and paid to Anne £10.

22 MONDAY I keep working though interruptedly but the heat in the midst of the day makes me flag and grow irresistably drowsy. Mr. and Mrs. Skene came to supper this evening. Skene has engaged himself in drawing illustrations to be etched by himself for *Waverley*.[3] I wish it may do.

23 TUESDAY I was detaind in the court till half past [three]. Captain William Lockhart dind with Skene. The Captain's kind nature had brought him to Edinburgh to meet his Sister in law.

24 WEDNESDAY I was detaind late in the court but still had time to go with Adam Wilson and call upon a gentlemanlike East Indian officer calld Colonel Franklin who appears an intelligent and respectable man. He writes the History of Capt. Thomas, a person of the condition of a common sea-man who raised himself to the rank of a native prince and for some time waged a successful war with the powers around him. The work must be entertaining.[4]

1. She had travelled with Sophia on the boat and been 'the greatest possible comfort'. Sophia to Lockhart, 20 June 1829, Abbots.
2. *Tales of a Grandfather*, third series.
3. Skene's *Sketches of the existing Localities alluded to in the Waverley Novels, drawn and etched by himself*, 1829–31, came out in twenty-one numbers 'simultaneously with each volume of the new series of the novels'. *Skene's Memories*, p. 159.
4. Scott acquired two editions of Francklin's *Military Memoirs of George Thomas etc.*, 1803.

25 THURSDAY Finishd correcting proofs for *Tales* third series; the
court was over soon but I was much exhausted on the return home,
quite sleepy and past work. I lookd in on Cadell whose hand is in his
housewifcap[1] – driving and pushing to get all the work forward in due
order and cursing the delays of artists and engravers. I own I wish he
had not hamperd ourselves with such causes of delay.

Got from Mr. Cadell		£150
Anne	£75	
Sophia	10	
Charles	15	
Anne my niece *en Cadeau*	25	
	—	125
		£25
Anne		20
		£5

26 FRIDAY Mr. Ellis[2] missionary from the South Sea Islands
breakfasted, introduced by Mr. Fletcher Minister of the parish of
Stepney, also two Mr. Halls sons of an old acquaintance Mr. Hall of
Donahadee.[3] Mr. Ellis's account of the progress of civilization as
connected with religion is very interesting. Knowlege of every kind is
diffused, reading writing printing abundantly common. Polygamy
abolishd. Idolatry is put down, the priests, won over by the Ch[i]efs,
dividing among them the consecrated lands which belong to their
temples. Great part of the population are still without religion but
willing to be instructed. Wars are become infrequent and there is in
each state a sort of representative body or senate who [are] a check on
the Despotism of the Chief. All this has come hand in hand with
religion.

Mr. Ellis tells me that the Missionaries of different sects avoided
carefully letting the natives know that there were points of
[dis]union between them. Not so som[e] Jesuits who had lately
arrived and who taught their own ritual as the only true one. They
brought all their mechanical assistances along with them and a

1. That is 'business'. The allusion is to the ballad 'Get up and bar
   the door'.
2. William Ellis (1794–1872), later Assistant Foreign Secretary to
   the Church Missionary Society. The publishers had presented
   Scott with his *Tour through Hawaii*, 4th ed., 1828. *A. L. C.*
3. Edward Hull, the leading citizen and magistrate as well as
   Harbour Official of Donaghadee, Co. Down, the main port for
   the crossing from Scotland to Ireland.

Galvanick battery for working miracles. But they will find the natives acquainted with the electrical process, the Missionaries having instructed them in several branches of civil science. Where knowlege is diffused priest-craft must retreat. Mr. Ellis describe[d] their poetry to me and gave some examples. It had an Ossianick character and was composed of metaphor. He gave me a small collection of hymns printed in the Island. If this gentleman is sincere, which I have no doubt of, he is an illustrious character. He was just about to return to the Friendly Islands having come here for his wife's health.

After the court we set off (the Two Thomsons and I) for Blair Adam where we held our MacDuff-Club or the twelfth anniversary. We met the Chief Baron, Lord Sydney Osborne, Will Clerk, the merry Knight Sir Adam Ferguson, with our venerable Host the Lord Chief Commissioner, and merry men were we.

2/ SATURDAY I ought not where merry men convene to omit our jovial so[n] of Neptune Admiral Adam. The morning proving delightful We set out for the object of the day which was Falkland. We passd throu[gh] Lochore but without stopping and saw on the road eastward two or three places, as Balbedie Strathhenry Pitlochie and some others known to me by name. Also we went through the town of Leslie and saw what remains of the celebrated rendezvous of rustick gallantry calld Christ's Kirk on the green. It is now cut up with house[s], one of the most hideous of which is a new church having the very worst and most offensive kind of Venetian windows. This I am told has replaced a quiet lowly little gothick build[ing] coeval perhaps with the royal Poet who celebrated the spot.[1] Next we went to Falkland where we found Mr. Howden, factor of Mr. Tindal Bruce, waiting to show us the palace.

Falkland has most interesting remains. A double entrance tower and a side building running east from it is roofd and in some degree habitable, a corresponding building running Northward from the eastern corner is totally ruinous, having been destroyd by fire. The architecture is highly ornament[ed] in the stile of the palace at Stirling. Niches with statues, with projections, cornices etc., are lavishd through out. Many curious medallions exhibited such heads as those preserved from the King's Room at Stirling, the originals perhaps being the same. The repeated cypher of James V and Mary of Guise attest the builders of this part of the place. When complete it had been a quadrang[l]e. There is as much of it as remaind when

1. King James I of Scotland, who wrote the poem 'Christ's Kirk on the Green'.

Slezer publishd his drawings.[1] Some part of the interior has been made what is calld habitable, that is a half dozen of bad rooms have been gotten out of it. Am clear in my own mind a ruin should be protected but never repaird. The proprietor has a beautiful place call[d] Nuthill within ten minutes' walk of Falkland and commanding some fine views of it and of the Lomond Hill. This should be the residence. But Mr. Bruce and his predecessor, my old professor John Bruce,[2] deserve great merit for their attention to prevent Dilapidation which was doing its work fast upon the ancient palace. The only remarkable apartment was a large and well proportiond gallery with a painted roof *tempore Jacobi Sexti* and built after his succession to the throne of England. I noticed a curious thing, a hollow column conceald the rope which rung the castle Bell keeping it safe from injury and interrup[ti]on.

The Town of Falkland is old with very narrow streets. The arrival of two carriages and a gigg was an event important enough to turn out the whole population. They are said to [be] less industrious, more dissipated and readier to become soldiers than their neighbours, so long a court retains its influence.

We dined at Wellfield with my friend George Cheape with whom I rode in the cavalry some 30 years ago. Much mirth and good wine made us return in capital tune.[3] The Chief Baron and Admiral Adam did not go on this trip. When we returnd it was time to go to bed by a candle.

28 SUNDAY Being Sunday we lounged about in the neighbourhood of the Crags call[d] the Keiry Craigs etc. The sheriff substitute of Kinross came to dinner and brought a gold signet which had been found in that town.[4] It was very neatly work[d], about the size of a shilling. It bore in a shield the Arms of Scotland and Eng[land] party per pale those of Scotland occupying the dexter side. The shield is of the heater or triangular shape. There is no crown nor legend of any kind; a slip of gold folds upwards on the back of the hinge and makes the handle neatly enough. It is too well wrought for David IId's time

---

1. John Slezer's *Theatrum Scotiae, containing Prospects of their Majesties' Castles and Palaces, etc.*, 1693.
2. Professor of Logic at the University of Edinburgh.
3. 'We had great amusement in exhausting Mr. Cheape's calculated allowance of claret, and forcing him, under a roar of laughter and applause, to send to the cellar for more.' *Blair-Adam Estate*, Introduction. p. xxv.
4. The seal, thought to be that of Joan of Beaufort, wife to James I of Scotland, had been found in April. *Archaeologia Scotica*, iv. 420.

and James the IV is the only monarch of the Scottish line who, marrying a daughter of England, may carry the arms of both countries party per pale. Mr. Skelton is the name of the present possessor.

Two reported discoveries. One that the Blaeberry shrub contains the tanning quality as four to one compard to the oak – which may be of great importance as it grows so commonly on our moors.

The other that the cutting of an apple tree or other fruit tree may be preserved by sticking it into a potatoe and planting both together. Curious if true.

29 MONDAY We dined together at Blair Adam having walkd in the woods in the morning and seen a beautiful new walk made through the woody hill behind the house. In a fine evening after an early dinner our party returnd to Edinburgh and there each dispersed to his several home and resting place. I had the pleasure to find my family all well except Johnie who is no worse however than usual [1]

30 TUESDAY After my short sniff of country air here am I again at the receipt of Custom. The sale with Longman and Coy for stock and copy rights of my works is completed for £7000 at dates from 12 to 36 months.[2] There are many sets out of which we may be able to clear the money and then we shall make some thing to clear the copyright. I am sure this may be done and that the bargain will prove a good one in the long run. Dined at home with my family, whom as they disperse tomorrow I have dedicated the evening to.

JULY

1 WEDNESDAY This morning wrote letters and sent them off by Charles. It was teind Wednesday so I was at home to witness the Departure of my family which was depressing.[3] My two daughters

1. His state can be judged from Anne and Sophia's letters to Lockhart. Anne writes that he 'is certainly weaker. He is still able to go out in the open air for an hour every day the rest he is on the sofa in the Drawing-Room and appears quite happy.' 27 June 1829, Abbots. He is so annoyed by 'the fatigue of dressing' that they have been obliged, Sophia reports, 'to cut all his clothes in front to get them on'. 26 June 1829, Abbots.
2. See the Entry for 3 June 1829 and note.
3. And noisy. 'The flapping of doors squalling of maids and creaking of trunks becomes intolerable and I have no recourse save in the conversation of the carter who has brought in two carts of wood from Abbotsford.' *Letters*, xi. 364.

with the poor boy Johnie went off at ten o'clock, my son Charles with
my niece about twelve.[1] The house filld with [the] little bustle
attendant on such a removal then became silent as the grave. The
voices of the children which had lately been so clamourous with their
joyous shouts are now hushd and still. A blank of this kind is
somewhat depressing and I find it impossible to resume my general
tone of spirits. A lethargy has crep[t] on me which no efforts can
dispell and as the day is rainy I cannot take exercize. I have read
therefor[e] the whole morning and have endeavourd to collect ideas
instead of expending them. I have not been very successful. In short
Diem Perdidi.[2]

From Mr. Cadell ————————	£25.	
Anne ————————————	£10.	
Sophia —————————————	10.	
Charles lodgings ———————	1.	21.
		£4.

Localities at Blair Adam

> Lochournie and Lochournie moss
> The Louting stane and Dodgel's cross
> Craig i Cat and Craig i Cro
> Craig-averal the King's cross and Drumglow.

2 THURSDAY I mad[e] up for my deficiencies yesterday and besides
attending the Court wrote five close pages which I think is very near
double task. I was alone the whole day and without interruption. I
have little doubt I will make my solitude tell upon my labours
especially since they promise to prove so efficient. I was so languid
yesterday that I did not record that J. Ballantyne, his brother Sandie,
and Mr. Cadell dined here on a beef steak and smoked a segar and
took a view of our Eldorado which will be rich enough unless it *sham
good likely*.

1. Anne and Sophia were taking the children to Abbotsford, where
   Scott was to join them on the 11th. Charles was escorting his
   cousin Anne (who had spent the past year in Scott's household)
   as far as London. After 'a very long & uncomfortable passage –
   near 4 days' by the steamboat *City of Edinburgh*, he left her 'at
   that Yankee Miss Douglas's' and went himself to Lockhart's.
   Lockhart to Sophia, 6 July 1829, Abbots.
2. 'I have lost a day.'

3 FRIDAY Labourd at court where I was kept late and wrought on my return home finishing about five pages. I had the great pleasure to learn that the party with the infantry got safe to Abbotsford and Johnie was not worse than usual.[1]

4 SATURDAY After the court I came home and set to work still on the *Tales*. When I had finishd my bit of dinner and was in a quiet way smoking my segar over a glass of negus Adam Fergusson comes with a summons to attend him to the Justice Clerk's[2] where it seems I was engaged. I was totally out of case to attend his summons, redolent as I was of tobacco, but I am vexd at the circumstance. It looks careless and which is worse affected, and the Justice is an old friend moreover. I rather think I have been guilty towards him in this respect before.[3] Devil take my stupidity. I will call on Monday and say here is my sabre and here is my head.

5 SUNDAY Sir Adam came to breakfast and with him Mr. and Mrs. Johnstone of Bourdeaux, the lady his cousin by Dr. Black. I could not give them a right Scottish Breakfast being on a Sunday morning.[4] Labord on the *Tales* the whole morning. The post brought two letters of unequal importance, one from a person calling himself Haral announcing to me the terrifick circumstance that he had written against the Waverley novels in a publication calld *La Belle Assemblée*[5] at which doubtless he supposes I must be much annoyd. He be damd and that's plain speaking. The other from Lord Aberdeen announcing that Lockhart, Dr. Gooch and myself are invested with the power of examining the papers of the Cardinal Duke of York and reporting what is fit for publication.[6] This makes it plain that the Invisible[7] neither slumbers nor sleeps.[8] The toil and remuneration

1. The journey had required two carriages and some anxious forethought. 'The only way we can do it', Sophia had written to Lockhart on 23 June, 'will be to give Johny my carriage to himself to lie at length on the seat with Anne and I time about sitting on a stool by his side. Anne's carriage will take the rest of the party.' Abbots.
2. David Boyle's.
3. See the Entry for 22 June 1827.
4. When the servants were not expected to cook. The 'right Scottish Breakfast' is reminiscent of Dr. Johnson's approval of this meal in Scotland.
5. See Harral, 30 June 1829, Walpole.
6. See the Entry for 1 February 1829 and note.
7. Sir William Knighton.
8. An allusion to Psalm 121, verse 4.

must be Lockhart's and to any person understanding that sort of work the degree of trust reposed holds out hope of advantage. At any rate [it] is a most honourable trust and I have written in suitable terms to Lord Aberdeen to express my acceptance of it, adverting to my necessary occupations here and expressing my willingness to visit London occasionally to superintend the progress of my work. Treated myself, being considerably faggd, with a glass of poor Glengarry's super excellent whiskey and a segar, made up my journal, wrote to the girls, and so to roost upon a crust of bread and a glass of small beer, my usual supper.

6 MONDAY I labourd all the morning without any thing [un]usual save a call from my cousin Mary Scott of Jedburgh whom I persuaded to take part of my chaise to Abbotsford on Saturday. At two o'clock I walkd to Cadell's and afterwards to a committee of the Bannatyne Club. Thereafter I went to Leith where we had fixd a meeting of The Club[1] now of forty one years' standing. I was in Chair and Sir Adam Croupier. We had the Justice Clerk, Lord Abercromby, Lord Pitmilly, Lord Advocate, James Fergusson, John Irving and William Clerk, and passd a merry day for old fellows. It is a curious thing that only *three* have died of this club since its formation. These were the Earl of Selkirk, James Clerk[2] Lieutenant in the Navy, and Archibald Millar, W.S.[3] Sir Patrick Murray was an [un]willing absentee. There were absent Professor Davidson of Glasgow besides Glassford who has cut our society and poor James Edmondstoune whose state of health precludes his ever joining society again. We took a fair but moderate allowance of wine, sung our old songs and were much refreshd with a hundred old stories which would have seemd insignificant to any stranger. The most important of these were old College adventurers of love and battle.

7 TUESDAY I was rather apprehensive that I might have felt my unusual dissipation this morning but no[t] a whit. I rose as cool as a cucumber and set about to my work till breakfast time. I am to dine with Ballantyne to-day. To morrow with John Murray. This sounds sadly like idleness except what may be done either in the morning before breakfast or in the broken portion of the day between attendance on the court and my dinner meal, a vile drowsy yawning fagged portion of existence which resembles one's day as a portion of

1. This is a reunion of college friends. See the Entry for 2 February 1829.
2. A slip for James Bruce.
3. Scott forgets Lord Reston, who died in 1819.

the shirt escaping betwixt one's waistcoat and breeches indi[c]ates his linen.

Dined with James Ballantyne who gave us a very pleasant party. There was a great musician. Mr. Neucom, a German, a pupil of Haydn, a sensible pleasant man.[1]

8 WEDNESDAY This morning I had an ample doze of proofs and could do nothing but read them. The court kept me till two. I was then half tempted to go to hear Mr. Neucom perform on the organ which is said to be a most masterly exhibition. But I reflected how much time I should lose by giving way to temptation and how little such ears as mine would be benefited by the exhibition and so I resolved to return to my proofs having not a little to do. I was so unlucky as to meet my foreigner along with Mr. Lainé the French Consul and his lady who all invited me to go with them. But I pleaded business and was sate[2] down doubtless for a Goth as I deserved. However I got my proofs settled before dinner time and began to pack up books etc.

I dined at John Murray's and met amongst others Mr. Schutze the brother in law of poor George Ellis. We conversed about our mutual friend and about the life Canning was to have written about him and which he would have done *con amore*. He gave me two instances of poor George's neatness of expression and acuteness of discrimination. Having met for the first time 'one Perceval a young lawyer' he records him as a person who with the advantage of life and opportunity would assuredly rise to the head of affairs. Another gentleman is briefly characterized as a 'man of few words and fewer ideas.' Schuze himself is a clever man with something dry in his manner, owing perhaps to an imp[e]r[f]ection of hearing. Murray's parties are always agreeable and well chosen.

9 THURSDAY I began an immense arrangement of my papers but was obliged to desist by the approach of Five o'clock[3] having been enabled to shirk the court. I had the whole day to do what I wishd and as I made some progress I hope I will be strengthend to resume the task when at Abbotsford.

Heard of the death of poor Bob Shortreed the companion of many a long ride among the hills in quest of old ballads. He was a merry

1. Sigismund Ritter von Neukomm (1778–1858), Austrian pianist and composer. He was a friend of Mendelssohn and of Scott's acquaintance Moscheles.
2. A slip for 'set', which Scott would pronounce as 'sate'.
3. The dinner hour.

companion, a good singer and mimick and full of Scottish drollery. In his company and under his guidance I was able to see much of rural society in the mountains which I could not otherwise have attaind and which I have made my use of. He was in addition a man of worth and character. I always burthend his hospitality while at Jedburgh on the Circuit and have been useful to some of his family.[1] Poor fellow, he died at a most interesting period for his family when his eldest daughter was about to make an advantageous marriage.[2] So glide our friends from us *haec poena diu viventibus*.[3] Many recollections die with him and with poor Terry.[4] I dined with the Skenes in a family way.

10 FRIDAY Had a hard day's work at the court till about two and then came home to prepare for the country. I made a *talis qualis* arrangement of my papers which I trust I shall be able to complete at Abbotsford for it will do much good. I wish I had a smart Boy like red Robin the Tinker. Wrote also a pack of letters.

Cash from Mr. Cadell ————————	£60	
In purse ————————	4	64
Club at Leith ————————	1. 4	
Coach hire ————————	.10	
Gown keeps ————————	6	
Sundries ————————	2.	
	4.	
Coals to John ————————	32.	
Do. for Small accots. postage etc.	3	
	39	
	25	
Journy about ————————	3	
	£22	

1. Scott had been instrumental in having Thomas, the eldest son, appointed Procurator Fiscal of Roxburghshire, in getting a cadetship for Pringle, and employment as a compositor for Andrew.
2. John Shortreed's letter about his father's death adds that 'Margaret's marriage with Mr. Brown of Rawflat was to have taken place so immediately as Tuesday next'. 8 July 1829, Walpole. The bridegroom was a widower and 'a crack farmer'. *Letters*, xi. 245.
3. 'This is the penalty of living a long time.'
4. Terry had died on 22 June.

11 SATURDAY I was detaind in the court till nearly one o'clock, then set out and reachd Abbotsford in five or six hours. Found all well and Johnie rather better. He sleeps by virtue of being in the open air a good deal.[1]

13ᵃ MONDAY The day excessive rainy, or, as we call it, Soft. I e'en unpackd my books and did a great deal to put them in order. But I was sick of the labour by two o'clock and left several of my books and all my papers at sixes and sevens. Sir Adam and the Colonel dined with [us]. A spanish gentleman with his wife, whom I had seen at the French Consul's, also dropd in. He was a handsome, intelligent and sensible man. His name I have forgot. We had a pleasant evening.

14 TUESDAY This day I wrote till one, resuming the *History* and making out a day's task. Then went to Chiefswood and had the pleasure of a long walk with a lady well known in the world of poetry, Mrs. Hemans. She is young and pretty though the mother of five children as she tells me. There is taste and spirit in her conversation. My daughters are critical and call her *blue* but I think they are hypercritical.[3] I will know better when we meet again. I was home at four. Had an evening walk with little Walter who held me by the

1. The letters written every other day by Sophia to Lockhart preserve a vivid picture of the previous ten days at Abbotsford. 'The rain has been incessant' and Johnnie, who spends most of the day 'upon the sopha' sleeps badly at night. Lockhart is to bring Sophia her '*Flannel dressing gown*' which she needs 'for sitting up at night with Johny'. However, they have been able to take the children out. They have been to Melrose in the sociable on the 7th, and to Galashiels (probably to meet Scott coming from Edinburgh) on the 11th – an expedition which proved 'most unlucky' as they were caught in the rain and 'had to take shelter with John and all the children at Ladhope for an hour'. And there are expeditions within the grounds too: 'After the childrens dinner Anne and I mean to join the procession in a walk to see the poultry – Johny in his carriage drawn by Ludlow – Johny holding Marian's bridle in his hand upon which Wa and Baby are seated time about Nurse and Letitia bringing up the rear.' Sophia to Lockhart, 2, 4, 6, 8, and 12 July 1829, Abbots.
2. One Entry is missed between 12 and 21 July, probably the Entry for 12 July. See Appendix E, vi, p. 829.
3. Sophia describes her to Lockhart as a 'vulgar looking woman with a veil pinned in the mantilla fashion on her head'. Although this 'vulgar blue woman' has only a slight acquaintance with the Hamiltons, she does not think 'they will get rid of her till they leave Chiefswood'. 12 and 16 July 1829, Abbots.

finger, gabbling eternally much that I did and more that I did not understand. Then I had to write a long letter to Lockhart, collect and read and dispa[t]ch proofs etc.; and to bed heartily tired though with no great exertion.

15 WEDNESDAY A rainy forenoon broke the promise of a delightful morning. I wrote $4\frac{1}{2}$ pages[1] to make the best of a bad bargain. If I can double the daily task I will be something in hand. But I am resolved to stick to my three pages a day at least. The 12th. of August will then complete my labours.

16 THURSDAY This day two very pretty and well bred boys[2] came over to breakfast with us. I finished my task of three pages and better and went to walk with the little fellows round the farm, by the lake etc. etc. They were very good companions. Thom has been busy thinning the terrace this day or two and is to go on.

Cash in purse ————	£22.	
Tom ————	20	
Cash in purse	£2	

17 FRIDAY I made out my task work and betook myself to walk about twelve. I feel the pen turn heavey after breakfast; perhaps my solemn morning meal is too much for my intellectual powers but I wont abridge a single crumb for all that. I eat very little at dinner and can't abide to be confined in my hearty breakfast. The work goes on as task-work must, slow, sure, and I trust not drowsy though the author is. I sent of[f] to Dionysius Lardner (Goodness be with us what a name) as far as page 38 inclusive but I will wait to add tomorrow's quota. I had a long walk with Tom. I am walking with more pleasure and comfort to myself than I have done for many a day. May heaven continue this great mercy which I have so much reason to be thankful for.

18 SATURDAY We calld at Chiefswood and askd Capt. Hamilton and Mrs. H. and Mrs. Hemans to dinner on Monday. She is a clever person and has been pretty. I had a long walk with her tete-a-tete. She told me of the peculiar melancholy attachd to the word no more. I could [not] help telling as a diff[e]rent application of the word [how] an old dame riding home along Cocke[n]zie sands pretty bowsy fell off the pillion and her husband, being in good order also, did not miss

1. Of the *History of Scotland*.
2. Charles and Henry Hemans. *Memoirs of Mrs. Hemans*, p. 180.

[her] till he came to Preston-pans. He instantly returnd with some neighbours and found the good woman seated amidst the advancing tide which began to rise with her lips ejaculating to her cummers[1] who she supposed were still pressing her to another cup 'Not ae drap mair I thank you kindly.' We dined in family and all well.

19 SUNDAY A sunday with alternate showers and sun-shine. Wrote double task which brings me to page forty six inclusive. I read the *Spaewife* of Galt.[2] There is something good in it and the language is occasionally very forcible but he has made his story difficult to understand by adopting a region of history little known and having many heroes of the same name whom it is not easy to keep separate in his memory. Some of the traits of the Spaewife who conceits herself to be a Changeling or Ta'en away is very good indeed. His highland Chief is a kind of Caliban and speaks like Caliban a jargon never spoken on earth but full of effect for all that.

20 MONDAY I finishd two leaves this morning and rec[e]ived the Hamiltons and Mrs. Hemans to breakfast; afterwards we[3] drove to Yarrow and shewd Mrs. Hemans the lions. The party dined with us and staid till evening.[4] Of course no more work.

1. 'Gossips.' Jamieson.
2. John Galt's *Spaewife* was published in 1823.
3. Sophia was of the party, Anne staying at Abbotsford with the children. Anne to Lockhart, 20 July 1829, Abbots.
4. This is Mrs. Hemans' account of the day: 'I went with him in an open carriage. We forded Ettrick river, passed Carterhaugh (the scene of the wild fairy legend of "Tam o' Linn"), and many a cairn and field of old combat, the heroes of which seemed to start up before me, in answer to the "mighty master's" voice, which related their deeds as we went by. . . . But Yarrow! beautiful Yarrow! we wound along its banks, through some stately grounds belonging to the Duke of Buccleuch; and was it not like a dream to be walking there with Sir Walter Scott by my side, reciting, every now and then, some verse of the fine old ballad? We visited Newark Tower, and returned to Abbotsford through the Tweed. The rest of the day was passed at that glorious place, the hall of which, in particular, is a scene to dream of, with the rich, purple light streaming in through its coloured windows, and mantling its stately suits of armour and heraldic emblazonries. We had a great deal of music in the evening – Sir Walter is particularly fond of national airs – and I played many of my waltzes, and mazurkas, and Spanish melodies, for which I wish you could have heard how kindly and gracefully he thanked me.' *Memoirs of Mrs. Hemans*, pp. 178–9.

21 TUESDAY A rainy day and I am very drowsy and would give the world to [sleep]. I wrote four leaves however and then my industry dropd me. I have made up for yesterday's short task.

———

[There are no further entries until the following May. Scott spent the summer at Abbotsford as usual, in the company of Anne, Sophia, and the children. The letters of this summer paint a charming picture of Scott and his grandchildren. 'I never saw Papa take to a child so much as he has done to Watt who to say truth makes himself most engaging to him', writes Sophia to Lockhart early in July; 'he climbs up upon his knee kisses his hand brings him his stick and now I find out makes his morning visits for *pater* in his study.'[1] 'Baby improves every day', Anne tells Lockhart later in the month. 'Walter has been teaching her to say Devil which was taught him by Johnny who says he was taught by Papa.'[2] Sophia was confined to bed for several weeks by a severe attack of rheumatism in one knee, and she was unable to return to London with Lockhart and Johnnie at the end of September. Baby, it seems, joined in the morning visits to the study. 'She goes in Papas room in the morning,' Sophia reports to Lockhart with barely concealed pride, 'and draws upon his books and papers and when he scolds her she climbs up his knee kisses him and says dear dear Grandpa.'[3]

Charles, who made his visit in September, 'came down loaded with rheumatism',[4] and Scott finally succeeded in arranging to have him posted as an unpaid attaché to the Embassy at Naples for the sake of his health. Walter was expected, but had to postpone his visit because he was required for duty at a court martial.

There was the usual stream of visitors. They included Lady Shelley, Susan Ferrier, Mrs. Hemans, Henry and Arthur Hallam, David Wilkie, Archdeacon Wrangham, and the Sotheby family. 'Here is my old acquaintance Sotheby (not Southey) with his wife and two daughters sate down upon [me] like a Coroners jury upon a smotherd man', Scott writes to Walter. 'How I long to say to him as poor Sir Harry Englefield did in his dying moments "Sotheby – GO –".'[5]

At the beginning of November Scott returned to Edinburgh more willingly than usual, shaken by the death of Tom Purdie. 'He

1. 2 July 1829, Abbots.
2. 20 July 1829, Abbots.
3. 20 October 1829, Abbots.
4. *Letters*, xi. 239.
5. *Letters*, xi. 228.

was found dead yesterday morning by his daughters,' Sophia writes to Lockhart on 1 November, 'sitting quite upright by the fire in his own house. He had been supping in the kitchen here and was drunk as Nicolson walked home with him and left him sitting where he was found at five in the morning . . . I never saw Papa so affected he wont go out and says for the first time in his life he wishes the day was come to take him to Edinr.'[1] John Swanston, who took over as his attendant out-of-doors, never quite replaced Purdie. The single compensation was that the Trustees had to install Laidlaw at Kaeside once more to take charge of the plantations. Lady Jane Stuart and Sir Thomas Lawrence died the same autumn, and retirement deprived Scott of Sir Samuel Shepherd, who returned to England.

On 15 February 1830 Scott himself had a stroke. 'Anne would tell you of an awkward sort of fit I had on Monday last', he writes to Lockhart on the 22nd. 'It lasted about five minutes during which I lost the power of articulation or rather of speaking what I wishd to say . . . I feel thank God no mental injury which is most of all to be deprecated.'[2] It is the beginning of the end. None the less the 'cloudiness both of words and arrangement'[3] which Lockhart finds in the works of the year that follows is not yet noticeable in the *Journal*, and Scott drives himself on with ever greater urgency. 'They say do not work,' he tells Lockhart, 'but my habits are such that [it] is not easily managed for I would be driven mad with idleness.'[4]

His chief concern was to finish the notes for the Magnum Opus. As early as December 1829 he had seen 'a signal of breaking up' in the passage of more blood. 'Waverley & its companions go on like whip and spur', he writes to Lockhart. 'I am busied finishing the edition so that you whom I naturally look to as my substitute may have as little trouble as possible.'[5] By April, hurried on by the thought that 'that fit of giddiness was rather an awkward warning',[6] he had finished the notes to thirty-five volumes of the Magnum, whose huge sales – 20,000 copies of *Waverley* by August – seemed to justify his hopes of clearing his debts within five or six years.

The *History of Scotland* for Lardner's *Cyclopaedia* was published on 1 November 1829, followed immediately by the Third Series of *Tales of a Grandfather*. Just before Christmas *The House of Aspen* was

1. 2 November 1829, Abbots.
2. *Letters*, xi. 297–8.
3. *Life*, ix. 337.
4. *Letters*, xi. 298.
5. *Letters*, xi. 275.
6. *Letters*, xi. 317

performed at the Edinburgh Theatre; *Auchindrane* was published along with *The Doom of Devorgoil* early in 1830. After his illness Scott began a fourth series of *Tales of a Grandfather*, on the history of France, and took up Murray's offer of £700 for a volume of *Letters on Demonology and Witchcraft* for the Family Library.]

MAY

23 SUNDAY About a year ago I took the pet at my diary chiefly becaus[e] I thought it made me abominably selfish and that by recording my gloomy fits I encouraged their recurrenc[e] whereas out of sight out of mind is the best way to get out of them. And now I hardly know why I take it up again but here goes. I came here to attend Raeburn's funeral.[1] I am near of his kin, my great grandfather Walter Scott being the second son or first Cadet of this small family. My late kinsman was also married to my aunt, a most amiable old lady. He was never kind to me and at last utterly ungracious. Of course I never liked him and we kept no terms. He had forgot though an infantine cause of quarrell which I always rememberd. When I was four or five years old I was stayin[g] at Lessudden house, an old mansion, the abode of this raeburn. A large pigeon house was almost destroyd with Starlings, then a common bird though now seldom seen. They were seized in their nests and put in a bag and I think drownd or thre[s]hd to death or put to some such end. The servants gave one to me which I in some degree tamed and the brute of a laird seized and wrung its [neck]. I flew at his throat like a wild cat and was torn from him with no little difficulty. Long afterwards I did him the mortal offence to recall some superiority which my father had lent to the Laird to make up a qualification which he meant to exercize by voting for Lord Minto's interest against poor Don. This made a total breach between t[w]o relations who had never been friends and though I was afterwards of consid[e]rable service to his family[2] he kept his illhumour alleging justly enough that I did these kind actions for the services of his wife and family not his benefit. I now saw him at the age of eighty two or

1. 'I shall go to his funeral', Scott wrote to Charles, 'for as we were not on very good terms there is the more reason for observing the bien seance.' 20 May 1830, Disc. i. 72 'Raeburn' is of course Walter Scott of Raeburn.
2. Notably in appointing his son William (Maxpoffle) his Sheriff-Substitute.

three deposited in the ancestral grave, dined with my cousins and returnd to Abbotsford about eight o'clock.

24 MONDAY Calld on my neighbour Nic[o]l Milne of Faldonside to settle something about the road to Selkirk, afterwards wen[t] to Huntly burn and made my compliments to the family. Lunched at half past two and drove to town, calling in George's Square on Gala. The proposal is to give up the present road to Selkirk in favour of another on the North side of the river to be completed by two bridges. This is an object for Abbotsford.[1] In the evening came in to town. Letter from Mr. H— soliciting £20.[2] Wait till Lockhart comes.

25 TUESDAY Get into the old mill this morning and grind aw[a]y. Walkd in very bad day to George's [Square] from the parliament House through paths once familiar but not trod for twenty years, met Scott of Wool and Scott of Gala and consulted about the new road between Galashiels and Selkirk. I am in hope to rid myself of the road to Selkirk which goes too near me at Abbotsford. Dined at Lord Chief Commissioner's where we met the New Chief Baron Abercromby[3] and his lady. I thought it was the first time we had met for above forty years but he put me in mind we had dined one day at John Richardson's.

26 WEDNESDAY Wrought with proofs etc. at Lockhart's *Demonology*[4] which is a cursed business to do neatly. I must finish it though for I need money. I went to the court; from that came home and scrambled on with half writing, half reading, half idleness till evening. I have laid aside smoking much and now unless tempted by company rarely take a segar. I was frightend by a species of fit which I had in March[5] which took from me my power of speaking. I am told it is from the stomach. It lookd woundy like palsy or apople[x]y. Well be it what it will, I can stand it.

1. The road on which Abbotsford stands was at this time the main road. The present-day road follows the line proposed here.
2. Haydon was once again in the King's Bench for debt. Haydon, 22 May 1830, Walpole.
3. Sir Samuel Shepherd had retired in February from the Court of Exchequer and was succeeded by the Rt. Hon. James Abercromby, the brother of Scott's friend George Abercromby. He was elected M. P. for Edinburgh in 1832 and became Speaker of the House of Commons in 1835.
4. *Letters on Demonology and Witchcraft addressed to J. G. Lockhart, Esq.*, for which Murray had offered £600.
5. It was actually on 15 February 1830. See p. 661.

27 THURSDAY Court as usual. I am agitating a proposed retirement from the court. As they are only to have four instead of Six clerks of Session in Scotland it will be their interest to let me retire on a superannuation. Probably I shall make a bad bargain and only get ⅔do of the salary instead of ⅘tho. This would be hard but I could save between two or three hundred pounds by giving up town residence and surely I could do enough with my time in Reviews and other ways as to make myself comfortable at Abbotsford. At any rate *Jacta est Alea*.[1] Sir Robert Peel and the Advocate seem to acquiesce in the arrangement and Sir Robert Dundas retires alongst with me.[2] I think the difference will be infinite in point of health and happiness.

28 FRIDAY Wrought in the morning, then the court – then Cadell's.[3] My affairs go on up to calculation and the magnum keeps its ground. If this can last for five or six years longer we may clear our hands of debt but perhaps I shall have paid that of nature before that time come. They will have the books and Cadell to manage them who is a faithful pilot. The poetry which we purchased for   [4]payable in two years is melting off our hand and we will feed our magnum in that way when we have sold the present stock by which we hope to pay the purchase money and so go on velvet with the continuation of the Magnum.[5] So my gen[e]ral affairs look well. But there has been mis[ma]nagement in the household department.[6] I expect Lockhart

1. 'The die is cast.'
2. The Lord Advocate's Bill was the Scottish Judicature Act (1 Will. IV, cap. 69), which altered the number of Judges from fifteen to thirteen. It also provided for reducing the Clerks of Session from six to four in number by appointing no successors when the next two vacancies occurred. Scott wrote to Peel and Knighton offering to go at once if he might do so on a reduced salary. *Letters*, xi. 332 and 335. Sir William Rae, the Lord Advocate, had written on the 18th to say that Peel and he saw no difficulty 'as soon as the Bill is passed'. Walpole. Scott finally retired in November on a salary reduced from £1300 to £866.
3. After a talk in the shop they went together 'to see Lauder the Painter and his Picture from the Bride of Lammermoor'. Cadell's Diary.
4. £7000. For the bargain with Longman's, see the Entry for 3 June 1829 and note.
5. Scott means that when they have cleared the present stock of the poems they will add a new edition of the poems to the Magnum Opus, and in this way recoup the price paid to Longman's for the copyrights.
6. Anne does not learn. See the Entries for 25 November 1827, 12 January 1828, and 21 January 1829.

and Sophia to arrive this evening in the roads,[1] and breakfast with us tomorrow. This is very reviving.

29 SATURDAY The Lockharts were to appear at nine o'clock but it is past four and they come not. There has been easterly wind and a swell of the sea at the mouth of the firth but nevertheless I wish they would come. The mach[i]nery is liable to accidents and they may be delayd thus.[2]

Mr. Piper the Great Contractor for the Mail coaches, one of the sharpest men in his line, calld here to-day to give his consent to our line of road. He pays me the [compliment] of saying he wishes my views on the subject. That is perhaps fudge but at least I know enough to chuse the line that is most for my own advantage. I have written to make Gala acquainted that my subscription depends on their taking the Gala foot road; no other would suit me. After dinner I began to teaze myself about the children and their parents and night went down on our uncertainty.

30 SUNDAY Our travellers appeard early in the morning *cum tota sequela*[3] – Right happy were we all. Poor Johnie looks well. His deformity is confirmd, poor fellow, but he may be a clever lad for all that. An imposthume in his neck seems to be the crisis of his complaint. He is a gentle placid creature. Walter is remarkably handsome and so is little W[h]ippety stourie[4] as I call her. After breakfast I had a chat with Lockhart about affairs in gen[e]ral, which, as far as our little interests are concernd, are doing very well. Lockhart is now established in his reputation and literary prospects.[5] I wrote some more in his *Demonology*, which is a scrape I think. About one Skene and I walkd round and across the castle Hill; it is strange how easily this circuitous pass carries us over so great a height. The day went off as usual.

1. Leith Roads. They were coming 'in the steam boat setting sail on the 26'. *Letters*, xi. 351.
2. 'They had broken a crank & drove up the Humber to be repair[d].' *Letters*, xi. 362.
3. 'With all their following'.
4. Charlotte, who 'will be the smartest of the party if they do not take care of themselves'. *Letters*, xi. 298. The nickname comes from a Scottish fairy-tale.
5. 'You will be glad to hear', he has written to Scott on the 17th, 'that I have begun at last to make a little money. During the last twelvemonths I have one way & another cleared upwards of £5,000; and do not perceive any reason that it shd be otherwise next.' Walpole. 'He has his Review so well in hand that he can afford three months in Scotland' (*Letters*, xi 368) and he is thinking of standing for Parliament. *Letters*, xi. 346-7 and note.

31 MONDAY Set to work early and did a good day's work without much puffing and blowing. Had Lockhart at dinner and a tete a tete out over our segar. He has got the right ideas for getting to the very head of the literary world and now stands very high as well for taste and judgement as for genius. I think there is no fear now of his letting a love of fun run away with him. At home the whole day except a walk to Cadell's who is enlarging his sale. As he comes upon heavey months and is come now to the *Abbot* the *Monastery* and the less profitable or popular of the novels this is a fortunate circumstance. The management seems very judicious.

JUNE

1 TUESDAY Proofs and court the inevitable employments of the day. Louisa Kerr dined with us and Williams lookd in. We talkd a good deal on Celtick witchery and fairy lore. I was glad to renew my acquaintance with this able and learnd man.[1]

2 WEDNESDAY The Lockharts lef[t] us again this morning and although three masons are clanking at their work to clean a well the noise is mitigated now the poor babies' clang of tongues is removed. I set with myself to write, determining to avoid reasoning and bring on as many stories as possible.[2] Being a Teind Wesnday I may work undisturbd and I will try to get so far ahead as may permit a journey to Abbotsford on Saturday. At Nine o'clock was as far ahead as p. 57. It runs out well and 150 pages will do.

3 THURSDAY Finishd my proofs and sent them off with copy. I saw Mr. Dickinson[3] on Tuesday, a right plain sensible man. He is so confident in my matters that, being a large creditor himself, he offers to come down with the support of all the London crers to carry through any measure that can be devised for my behoof. Mr. Cadell shewd him that we are five Years forward in matter prepared for press. Got Heath's illustrations which I dare say are finally engraved but common-place enough in point of Art.[4]

1. See the Entry for 25 June 1828 and note.
2. That is, to string together anecdotes of demonology rather than discuss the subject in general terms.
3. John Dickinson, of Longman and Dickinson the stationers, who had been helpful before. See the Entries for 5 September 1827, and 3 June 1829 and note. Scott had met him in Cadell's shop two days before. Cadell's Diary.
4. He told Cadell that he thought the faces 'not Scotch'. Cadell's Diary.

4 FRIDAY Court as usual and not long detaind – visited Cadell. All right and his reports favourable, it being the Launch of our annual volume now traversing a year with unblemishd reputation and success uninter[r]upted.[1] I should have said I overhauld proofs and furnish[d] copy in the morning betwixt 7 and ten o'clock.

After coming from the Court I met Wool and Gala and agreed upon the measures to be attempted at Selkirk on the 8th. at the meeting of trustees.[2] The evening smoked an extra cigar (none since tuesday) and dedicated the rest to putting up papers etc. for Abbotsford. Anne wants me to go to hear the Tyrolese minstrels,[3] but though no one mor[e] esteems that bold and highspirited people I cannot but think their *udalling*, if this be the word, is a variation or set of variations upon the tones of a Jack ass. So I remain to dribble and scribble at home.

5 SATURDAY I rose at seven as usual and to say truth dawdld away my time in putting things to rights, which is a vile amusement, and writing letters to people who write to ask my opinion of their books,[4] which is as much as to say Tom come Tickle me. This is worse than the other pastime but either may serve for a broken day and both must be done sometimes.

After the court started for Abbotsford at half past twelve at noon and her[e] we are at half past five *impransi*.[5] The country looks beautiful though the foliage, Larches in particular, have had a blight. Yet they can hardly be said [to] lose foliage since they have but a sort of Brushers at best.

6 SUNDAY Went through a good deal of duty as to proofs and the like. At two set out and reach by four Chiefswood where I had the happiness to find the Lockharts[6] all in high spirits, well and happy. Johnie must be all his life a weakly child but he may have good health and possesses an admirable temper. We dined with the Lockharts and were all very happy.

1. In other words, it is the first anniversary of the publication of the first volume of the Magnum Opus.
2. About the new road between Galashiels and Selkirk.
3. This was the final concert of 'THE TYROLESE MINSTRELS THE RAINER FAMILY'. *The Scotsman*, 2 June 1830.
4. The letters were probably to James Thomson, Edmund Temple, and General Ainslie, all of whom had just sent copies of their books. See 25, 27, 29 May 1830, Walpole.
5. 'Undined'.
6. Captain and Mrs. Hamilton had left Chiefswood for Italy the previous autumn. *Memoirs of Mrs. Hemans*, p. 177.

7 MONDAY Same duty carefully performed. I continued working till about one o'clock when Lockhart came to walk. We took our course round by the Lake. I was a good deal faggd and must have tired my companion by walking slow. The Fergussons came over, Sir Adam in all his glory, and the night drave on wi' sangs and clatter.[1]

8 TUESDAY Had not time to do more than correct a sheet or two. About 11 set off for Selkirk where there was a considerable meeting of road trustees. The consideration of the new road was intrusted to a committee which in some measure blinks the question. Yet I think it must do in the end. I dined with [the] club,[2] young Chesters president. It is but bad fun but I might be father of most of them and must have patience. At length

> Hame cam our Gudeman at e'en
> And hame cam He.[3]

9 WEDNESDAY In the morning I advised sheriff court processes, carried on the *Dæmonology* till twelve, then put books etc. in some order to leave behind me. Will it be orderd that I come back not stranger like a sojourner But to inhabit here?[4] I do not know. I shall be happy either way. It is perhaps a violent change in the end of life to quit the walk one has trod so long and the cursed sp[l]enetic temper which besets all men makes you value opportunities and circum-stances <which> when one enjoys them no longer. Well! things must be as they may, as says that great philosopher corporal Nym.[5]

I had my walk and on my return found the Lockharts come to take luncheon and leave of us. Reachd Edinburgh at 9 o'clock. Found among less interesting letters two from Lord Northampton on the death of the poor Marchioness[6] and from Anna Jane Clephane on the same melancholy topic. *Hei mihi!*

10 THURSDAY Corrected proofs, prepared some copy and did all that was right. *Nota Bene* the Coach calld not so I hobled up to the

---

1. Burns's 'Tam o' Shanter', l. 45.
2. The Forest Club.
3. 'Our Gudeman cam hame at E'en', Herd, ii. 74.
4. If his retirement can be arranged he will return in July never to leave again. The phrase comes from Psalm 39 in the Scottish metrical version.
5. *Henry V*, ii. 1.
6. The daughter of Mrs. Maclean Clephane. She had died in Italy. *Letters*, xi. 359.

Court and found my services unnecessary. Walkd round by Caddell's; all is well only I have lost two or three hours. Dined and wrought in the evening – yet I did not make much way after all.

11 FRIDAY In the morning the usual labour of two hours. God bless that habit of being up at seven. I could do nothing without it but it keeps me up to the Scratch as they say. I had a letter this morning with deep mo[u]rning paper and seal; the mention of my nephew in the first line made me sick fearing it had related to Walter. It was from poor Sir Thomas Bradford who has lost his Lady but was indeed an account of Walter and a good one.[1]

12 SATURDAY A day of general labour and much weariness.

13 SUNDAY The same may be said of this day.

14 MONDAY And of this, only I went out for an hour and a half to Mr. Colville Smith to conclude a picture for Lord Gillies.[2] This is a sad relief from labour.

> Scdct æternumque sedebit
> infel[i]x Theseus.[3]

But Lord Gillies has been so kind and civil that I must have his picture as like as possible.

15 TUESDAY I had at Breakfast the son of Mr. Fellenbug of Hofwylle of Switzerland, a modest young man. I used to think his father something of a quack in proposing to dis[c]over how a boy's natural genius lies with a view to his education.[4] How would they have made *me* a scholar is a curious question. Whatever was forced on me as a task I should have detested. There was also a gentlemanlike little man Le Chevalier de Demgarten. Silent and speaks no English.

1. 'He proves himself in every way worthy of the name he bears & possesses that true soldierlike feeling & talent, which if a more extensive field was open to him, could not fail to render him distinguished in the highest branches of his profession.' 3 June 1830, Walpole.
2. This was yet another copy of the Colvin Smith portrait. See the Entry for 22 January 1829 and note.
3. 'Unfortunate Theseus sits and will sit for eternity'. Virgil's *Aeneid*, vi. 617.
4. Scott adds in a letter to Lockhart: 'I hate educations sur un grande systeme. All men who have turnd out worth any thing have had the chief hand in their own education.' *Letters*, xi, 365.

Poor George Scott Harden is dead of the typhous fever. Poor dear boy! I am sorry for him and yet more for his parents. I have a letter from Henry on the subject.

16 WEDNESDAY I wrote this fornoon till I completed the 100 pages, which is well done. I had a call from Colin MacKenzie whom I had not seen for nearly two years. He has not been so well and looks ghastly but I think not worse than I have seen him of late years. We are very old acquaintances. I remember he was one of a small party at College that formd ourselves in a club calld the Poetical Society; the other members were Charles Kerr of Abbotrule[1] (a singular being), Colin MacLarine (insane), Colin and I, who have luckily kept our wits. I also saw this morning a Mr. Lowe, a youth of great learning who has written a good deal on the early history of Scotland.[2] He is a goodlooking frank gentleman like lad. With these good gifts only a parish school Master in Aberdeenshire. Having won a fair holiday I go to see Miss Kemble for the first time. It is two or three years since I have been in a threatre[3] once my delight.

17 THURSDAY Went last night to theatre and saw Mrs Fanny Kemble's Isabella[4] which was a most creditable performance. It has much of the genius of Mrs. Siddons her Aunt. She wants her

1. Charles Kerr of Abbotrule was four years older than Scott. He became a Writer to the Signet in 1789, without acquiring any of the sober or industrious habits of his brethren. Later that year he fled to the Isle of Man and married the seventeen-year-old daughter of a merchant there; his father disinherited him, and he was packed off to the West Indies. In 1791, however, his father died, and with Scott's help he contrived to win back the ancestral estate of Abbotrule in Roxburghshire. By 1818 his spendthrift habits had forced him to sell it (thus fulfilling Walter Scott senior's prophecy that 'his plans . . . will end in his ruin') and he died in 1821. His letters to Scott have enough close parallels with the early pages of *Redgauntlet* to establish that he was, as Partington was the first to notice, the real original of Darsie Latimer. See Nat. Lib. Scot. MS. 871, and Wilfred Partington's *Sir Walter Scott's Postbag* (1932), pp. 312–36.
2. The Revd. Alexander Low's *History of Scotland from the Earliest Period to the middle of the Ninth Century*, 1826.
3. Scott had forgotten that he saw *St. Ronan's Well* the previous year. See the Entry for 11 June 1829.
4. The play was Southerne's *The Fatal Marriage*. Lockhart had seen the eighteen-year-old Fanny Kemble as Juliet the previous October and been impressed although 'a play-hater'. Lockhart to Sophia, 13 October 1829, Abbots.

beautiful countenance, her fine form and her matchless dignity of step and manner. On the other hand Mrs. Fanny Kemble has very expressive though not regular features, and what is worth it all, great ene[r]gy mingled with and chastized by correct taste. I sufferd by the heat lights and exertion and will not go back to-night for it has purchased me a sore headache this theatrical excursion. Besides the play is Mrs. Beverly[1] and I hat[e] to be made miserable about domestic distress. So I keep my gracious presence at home to-night though I love and respect Miss Kemble for giving her active support to her father in his need and preventing Covent Garden from coming down about their ears. I corrected proofs before Breakfast, attended court, but was idle in the forenoon the headache annoying me much. Dinner will make me better. And so it did. I wrote in the evening three pages and tolerably well, though I may say with the Emperor Titus (Not Titus Oates) that I have lost a day.

18 FRIDAY Young John Colquhoun of Killermont and his wife breakfasted with us, a neat custom that and saves wine and was-sail. Thence to Court and arranged for our departure for Blair Adam, it being near midsummer when the club meets. Anne with me and Sir Adam Ferguson. The day was execrable. Our meeting at Blair Adam was cordial but our numbers diminishd; the good and very clever Lord Chief Baron is returnd to his own country[2] with more regrets than in Scotland usually attend a stranger. Will Clerk has a bad cold, John Thomson[3] is detaind. But the Chief commissioner, Admiral Adam, Sir Adam, John Thomson and [I] make a[n] excellent concert. I only hope our venerable host will not fatigue himself for he has had cold and fatigue. Tomorrow we go to Culross which Sir Robert Preston is repairing and the wise are asking for whose future enjoyment. He is upward of ninety but still may enjoy the bustle of life.

19 SATURDAY Arose and expected to work a little but a friend's house is not favourourable; you are sure to want the book you have not brought, and are in short out of sorts like the Minister who could not preach out of his own pulpit. There is some thing fanciful in this and something real too and I have forgot my watch and left half my gloves at home.

Off we set at halff past eight o'clock, Lord Chief Commissioner

---

1. *The Gamester*, by Edward Moore.
2. Sir Samuel Shepherd had retired to England.
3. A slip for 'Thomas Thomson'.

being lef[t] at home owing to a cold. We breakfasted at Luscar, a place belonging to Adam Roland, but the gout had arrested him at Edinburgh so we were hospitably received by his family. The weather most unpropitious, very cold and rainy. After breakfast to Culross where the veteran Sir Robert Preston shewd us his curiosities. Life has done as much for him as most people. In his ninety Second year he has an ample fortune, a sound understanding, not the least decay of eyes ears or taste, is as big as two men and eats like three. Yet he too experiences the *Singula præntdantur anni*[1] and has lost something since I last saw him. If his appearance renders old age tolerable it does not make it desirable. But I fear when Death comes we shall be unwilling for all that to part with our bundle of sticks. Sir Robert amuses himself with repairing the old House of Culross built by the Lord Bruce of Kinloss. What the use of it is destined to be is not very evident. It is too near his own comfortable mansion of Valleyfield to be useful as a residence if indeed it could be formd into a comfortable modern house. But it is rather like a banquetting house. Well he follows his own fancy. We had a sumptuous cold dinner. Adam grum[bled] it was not hot, so little can war and want break a man to circumstances.[2] We return to Blair Adam in the eveni[n]g through 'the wind but and the rain.'[3] For June weather it is the most ungenial I have seen. The beauty of Culross consists in magnificent terraces rising on the sea beach and commanding the opposite shore of Lothian; the House is repairing in the stile of James VI. The windows have pediments like Herriot's work.[4] There are some fine Reliques of the old Monastery with large Saxon arches. At Luscar I saw with pleasure the painting by Raeburn of my old friend Samuel Roland[5] Esq. who was in the external circumstances but not in frolick or fancy my prototype for Paul Pleydell.[6]

20 SUNDAY We settled this morning to go to Church at Lochore – that is at Ballingray[7] – but when we came to the earthly paradise so calld we were let off for a card for there was no sermon for which I could not for my heart be sorry. So after looking at Lochore back we came to lounge and loiter about till dinner time. The rest of the day

1. 'One by one the years rob us.' Horace's *Epistles*, ii. ii. 55.
2. Sir Adam had gone through the Peninsular Campaign and been a prisoner of war.
3. *Twelfth Night* v. i.
4. George Heriot's Hospital (now George Heriot's School) in Edinburgh.
5. A slip for 'Adam Rolland'.
6. In *Guy Mannering*.
7. Instead of to Cleish Kirk as usual.

was good company, good cheer and good conversation. Yet to be idle here is not the thing and to be busy is impossible so I wish myself home again in spite of good entertainment. We leave to[morrow] night after an early dinner and I will get to work again.

21 MONDAY Wrote to Walter a long letter. The day continued dropping occasionally but Sir Adam was in high foolling and we had an amazing deal of laughing. We stole a look at the Kierie Crags between showers. In the mean time George Cheap and his son came in. We dined at half past three but it was seven we set off and did not reach the house in Shandwick place till eleven at night. Thus ended our club for the year 1830 its 13th. anniversary. Its number[s] were diminishd by absence and indisposition but its spirit was unabated.

22 TUESDAY Finishd proofs and some copy in the morning. Returnd at noon and might have labourd a good day's work but was dull drowsy and indolent and could not, at leas[t] did not, write above half a page. It was a day lost and indeed it is always with me the consequence of mental indolence for a day or two. So I had a succession of eating and dozing which I am ashamed of for there was nothing to hinder me but 'thick coming fancies'[1] – Pshaw rabbit un!

23 WEDNESDAY Workd well this morning and then to court. At two calld on Mr. Gibson and find him disposed for an installment.[2] Cadell has £10,000 and Gibson thinks £12,000 will pay 2/6. I wish it could be made 3/- which would be fifteen thousand.

Presided at a meeting of the Bannatyne Club. The Whigs made a strong party to admit Kennedy of Dalquharran[3] which set aside Lord Medwyn who had been longer on the roll of Candidates. If politics get into this club it will ruin the literary purpose of the meeting and the General good humour with which it has gone. I think it better to take the thing goodhumouredly and several of them volunteerd to say that Medwyn must be the next which will finish all *à l'aimable* which will be desireable. If it come to party-work I will cut and run. Confound it my eyes are closing now even *now* at half past four.

Dined with Lord Medwyn a pleasant party. The guest of importance

1. *Macbeth*, v. 3.
2. The second dividend to the creditors, declared on 17 December 1830.
3. A slip for 'Dunure'.

Mrs. Peter Latouche[1] from Dublin, a fine old dame who must have been beautiful when young being pleasant and comely at seventy. Saintly it appears.

24 THURSDAY Hard work with Ballantyne's proofs and revises but got them accomplishd. I am at the twelfth hour but think I shall finish this silly book before the tenth of July.[2]

Notwithstanding this sage resolution I did not write half a page of the said *Dæmonology* this day. I went to the Court, calld on Mr. Cadell, returnd dog tired, and trifled of my time with reading the trial of Corder.[3] What seemd most singular was his love to talk of the young woman he had murderd in such a manner as to insinuate the circumstances of his own crime which is a kind of necessity which seems to haunt conscience-struck men. Charles Sharpe came in at night and supd with us.

25 FRIDAY Slept [a] little later than I should. The proofs educated the morning. The court and walk home detaind me till two. When I return, set to work and reach p. 210 of copy. There is little or nothing else to say. Skene was with me for a few minutes. I calld at Cadell also who thinks a dividend of 3 per pound will be made out. This will be one half of the whole debts and leave a sinking fund for the rest about £10,000 a year if the beast live and the branks[4] bide hail.

26 SATURDAY Miss Kemble and her father breakfasted here with Sir Adam and Lady Fergusson. I like the young Lady very much respecting both her talents and the use she has made of them. She seems merry unaffected and good humourd. She said she did not like the apathy of the Scottish audiences who are certainly not [inclined] to give applause upon credit. I went to the court but soon returnd. A bad cold in my head makes me cough and sneeze like the Dragon of Wantley.[5] The Advocates' bill[6] is read a third time. I

---

1. Elizabeth, the second wife of the Dublin financier and banker who had been Walter's landlord during his stay at St. Stephen's Green. Sir Thomas Acland had written to introduce her to Scott (22 May 1830, Walpole) and she duly visited Abbotsford on 15 July 1830.
2. The last day of the Session.
3. William Corder, he murderer of Maria Marten, executed in 1828.
4. 'A sort of bridle, often used by country people.' Jamieson. The phrase comes from Burns's letter to Nicol, 1 July 1787.
5. In Percy's *Reliques*.
6. Proposing the reduction of the Clerks of Session from six to four. See the Entry for 27 May 1830 and note.

hardly know whether to wish it passd or no and am therefore *in utrumqu[e paratus]*.[1]

28[2] MONDAY In the morning workd as usual at proofs and copy of my Infernal *Demonology*, a task to which my poverty and not my will consents.[3] About twelve o'clock I went to the country to take a day's relaxation. We, i.e. Mr. Cadell, Mr. James Ballantyne and I, went to Preston pans and getting there about one surveyd the little village where my aunt and I were lodgers for the sake of sea bathing in 1778[4] I believe. I knew the house of Mr. Warroch where we lived a poor cottage of which the owners and their family are extinct. I recollected my juvenile ideas of dignity attendant on the large gate – a black arch which lets out upon the sea. I saw the church where I yawnd under the inflictions of a Doctor McCormick, a name in which dullness seems to have been hereditary. I saw the links where I arrangd my shells upon the turf and swam my little skiffs in the pools – Many comparaisons betwe[e]n the man and the recollections of my kind aunt, of old George Constable[5] who I think dangled after her, of Delgaty a veteran half pay Lieu[t]enant who swaggerd his solitary walk on the Parade as he calld a little open space before the same pool. We went to P[r]eston and took refuge from a thunder plump in the old tower. I rememberd the little garde[n] where I was cramd with goose berries and the fear I had of Blind Harry['s][6] spectre of Fawdoun shewing his headless trunk at one of the windows. I rememberd also a very good natured pretty girl (my Mary Duff[7]) whom I laughd and rompd with and loved as children love. She was a Miss Dalrymple, daughter of Lord Westhall a Lord of Session, was afterwards married to Anderson of Winterfield, and her daught[er] is now [the wife] of my colleague Robert Hamilton. So strangely are our cards shufled. I was a mere child and could feel none of the Passion which Byron alleges, yet the recollection of this good humourd companion of my childhood is like that [of] a morning dream nor should I now greatly like to dispell it by seeing the original who must now be sufficiently time honourd.

1. '[Prepared] for either eventuality.'
2. '27' in the original. Cadell's Diary proves, however, that the excursion took place on Monday the 28th.
3. *Romeo and Juliet*, v. 1.
4. For Scott's reminiscences of these early days with his aunt Janet, see *Life*, i. 32–5.
5. In a letter to Basil Hall, Scott names him as the original of Jonathan Oldbuck in *The Antiquary. Letters*, xii. 36.
6. The author of the fifteenth-century poem *The Wallace*.
7. An early love of Byron's.

Well – we walkd over the field of battle, saw the Prince's park, Cope's loan markd by slaughter in his disastrous retreat, the Thorn tree which marks the centre of the battle and all besides that was to be seen or supposed. We saw two broad swords found on the field of battle, one a highlander's, an Andr[e]w Ferrara, another the drag oon's sword of that day. Lastly we came to Cockenzie where Mr. Francis Caddell my publisher's brother gave us a kind reception. I was especiall[y] glad to see the mother of the family, a fine old Lady who was civil to my aunt and me and I recollect well used to have us to tea at Cockenzie. Curious that I should long afterward have an opportunity to pay back this attention to her son Robert. Once more what a kind of shufling of the hand dealt us at our nativity. There was [illegible] Mr. F. Cadell and one or two young ladies and some fine fat children. I should be a bastard to the Time[1] did I not tell our fare. We had a *Tiled* whiting,[2] a dish unknown elsewhere so there is a bone for the gastronomes to pick. Honest John Wood my old friend dined with us. I only regret I cannot understand him[3] as he has a very powerful [memory] and much curious information. The whole day of pleasure was dampd by the news of [the] King's death. It was fully expected, however, and the termination of long illness. But he was very kind to me personally and a kind Sovereign. The common people and gentry join in their sorrows. Much is owing to Kindly reccollection of his visit to this country[4] which gave all men an interest in him.[5]

29 TUESDAY The business of the court was suspended so back I came without stop or stay and to work went I. As I had arisen early I was sadly drowsy. However I fought and faggd during [the] day. I am still in hope to send my whole Manuscript to Ballantyne before the 10 July. Well I must devote some thing to myself. I must do some thing better than these Dæmonological trash. It is nine o'clog and I am weary, yea my very spirit's tired.[6] After ten o'clock Mr. Davis,[7] an American bar[r]ister of eminence deputed to represent the American

1. *King John*, i. 1.
2. A whiting dried in the sun. Only two days before Scott had told Cadell about 'the nice dinner of whitings' he remembered enjoying at Mrs. Warroch's house at Prestonpans in his youth. Cadell's Diary.
3. Wood, the editor of Douglas's *Peerage of Scotland*, was deaf and dumb.
4. The visit of 1822, which Scott had organized.
5. See note 10, pp. 813–15, for Cadell's account of the day's events.
6. *Coriolanus*, i. 9: 'Yea, my memory is tir'd.'
7. Charles S. Daveis of Portland.

States in a dispute concerning the boundaries of Nova Scotia and New England, with an [in]troduction to me from Mr. Ticknor, calld. I was unable to see him and put him off till tomorrow morning at Breakfast.

30 WEDNESDAY The new King was proclaimed and the College of Justice took the oaths. I assisted Mr. Daveis, who is a pleasant well informed man, to see the ceremony which probably he would hardly witness in his own country. A day of noise and bustle. We dined at Mr. and Mrs. Strange. *Chère exquise* I suppose. Many friends of the Arniston family. I thought there was some belief of Lord Melville losing his place. That he may exchange it for another is very likely but I think the Duke[1] will not desert him who adhered to him so truly.

JULY

1 THURSDAY Mr. Davis breakfasted with me. On nearer acquaintance I was more galld by some portion of continental manners than I had been at first, so difficult is it for an American to correct their ideas of our ideas of perfect good breeding. I did all that was right however and askd Miss Ferriar whom he admires prodigiously to meet him at dinner. Hither came also a young friend, Mr. Pusey,[2] a good natured young man. So I have done the polite thing every way. Thompson also dined with us. After dinner I gave my strangers an airing round the Corstorpin hills and returnd by the Cramond road.[3] I sent to Mr. Gibson Cadell's proje[c]t for Lambmas which raises £15,00[0] for a Dividend of 3/- to be then made. I think the trustees should listen to this which is paying one half of my debt. The project runs thus

Cash for Magnum presently due	£7000
Do to be advancd on quarter from Lambmas to Christmas	2500
New Novel gainst Christmas	2500
	12,000
Funds with the Trustees	3000
	£15,000

1. The Duke of Wellington.
2. Edward Pusey (1800–82) the theologian, later celebrated for his part in the Oxford Movement. He had been introduced by Morritt two years earlier. 18 June 1828, Walpole.
3. Corstorphine and Cramond, now parts of the city, lay a few miles outside Edinburgh to the west and north-west.

By this means we should pay half of the debts at once and with the addition of £20,000 I think arising in insurances[1] I clear off £30,000 without much exertion, which would reduce the rest to about £20,000 which may be managed one way or other.

2 FRIDAY Have assurances from James Gibson[2] that £15,000 should be applied as I proposed. If this can be repeated yearly up to 1835 the matter is ended and well ended. Yet woe's me the public change their taste and their favourites get old. Yet if I was born in 1771 I shall only be sixty in 1831 and by the same reasoning 64 in 1835, so I may rough it out yet be no Sir Charles Preston.[3] At any rate it is all I have to trust to.

I did a morning task – and was detaind late at the Court. Came home, eat a hearty dinner and s[l]umberd after it in spite of my teeth, and made a poor night's work of it. One's mind gets so dissipated by the fagging yet insignificant business of the offices. My release comes soon but I fear for a term only for I doubt if the[y] will carry through the court-Bill.[4]

3 SATURDAY My day began at Seven as usual. Sir Adam came to breakfast. I read Southey's *Pilgrim's Progress*[5] and think of reviewing the same. I would I had books at hand. To the court and remaind till two. Then went to look at the drawings for repairing Murthlie, the house of Sir John or James Stewart now building by Gillespie Grahame and which he has pland after the fashion of James VIth's reign, a kind of bastard Grecian,[6] very fanciful and pretty though. Read Hone's *Every day Book*[7] and with a better opinion of him than I

1. The Trustees had bought Constable's policy on Scott's life (which would realize £15,000), continued Ballantyne's (worth £5000) and taken out a further policy of their own for £2000. Sederunt Book, i. 35.
2. A slip for 'John Gibson'.
3. Sir Robert Preston, whom he had visited on 19 June 1830, was ninety-one.
4. The Bill which, by reducing the number of Clerks of Session, would offer Scott the chance to retire, nonetheless became law shortly afterwards.
5. The Abbotsford Library contains Robert Southey's *John Bunyan's Pilgrim's Progress, With Life of the Author*, etc., Proof Prints, 1830.
6. F. H. Groome's *Ordnance Gazetteer of Scotland*, 1884, describes it as 'a splendid Elizabethan structure . . . left unfinished at the death of the sixth baronet in 1838'.
7. William Hone's *Every-Day Book and Table Book: or Everlasting Calendar of Popular Amusements, Sports, Pastimes, Ceremonies, Manners, Customs, and Events, etc.*, 1830.

expected from his anti-religious frenzy. We are to dine with the Skenes today. Which we did accordingly, meeting Mr. and Mrs. Strange, Lord Forbes and other friends.

4 SUNDAY Was a complete and serious day of work only interrupted in the evening by Yankee Davis who with all the freedom and ease of continental manners gratified me with his gratuitous presence. Yet it might have been worse for his conversation is well enough, but it is strange want of tact to suppose one must be alike wellcome to a stranger at all hours of the day. But I have stuffd the port folio so do not grudge half an hour.

5 MONDAY I was up before seven and resumed my labours and by breakfast time I had reachd p. 133 of my labours which may reach to 160 or 170 as I find space and matter. Buchanan[1] came and wrote about 15 of his pages, equal to mine in proportion of three to one. We are therefore about p. 138 and [in] sight of land. At two o'clock went to bury poor George Burnet the son of Gilbert Innes in as direct a rain as I ever saw, was in S[h]andwick [place] again by four and made these entries. If Blessed is the corps[e] that the rain rains on poor George Burnet's obsequies have been as *wet* as he himself used to be a nights though with less generous liquor. I dine to-day with the Club, grant heaven it fair before six o'clock.

We met at Barry's[2] and had a gallant dinner but only five of our number was present. Alas, sixty does not rally to such meetings with [the] alacrity of sixteen and our Club has seen the space between these terms. I was home and abed when Charles arrived and waked me, poor fellow. He is doing very [well] with his rheumatick limbs.[3]

6 TUESDAY I did little this morning but correct some sheets and was at the Court all morning: about two I calld at Mr. Cadell's and I learnd the Dividend was arranged. Sir Adam fell in with us and laid anchors to windward to get an invitation to Cockenzie for next year,

1. John Buchanan, who worked under Thomas Thomson in Register House and acted occasionally as an amanuensis for Scott.
2. Barry's Hotel in Princes Street.
3. The severity of his rheumatism can be gauged by a letter from Lockhart to Sophia the previous July which tells how Charles, after a soaking in the street, 'is chained up w his old rheumatism so bad that he can't walk accross his room – indeed that I have been obliged to undress him & put him into his bed like a child these two nights'. 11 July 1829, Abbots.

being struck with my lifelike description of a tiled haddock.[1] I came home much faggd, slept for half an [hour] (I don't like this lethargy) read *Gli promessi sposi*[2] and was idle. Miss Kerr dined and gave us musick.

7 WEDNESDAY This morning corrected proofs with which J. B. proceeds lazily enough and alleges printing reasons of which he has plenty at hand. Though it was the Teind Wednesday the Devil would have it that this was a court of Session day also for a cause of mine. So there I sate hearing a dozen cases of augmentation of Stipend pleaded and wondering within myself whether any thing can be predicated of a Scottish parish, in which there cannot be discoverd a reason for enlarging the endowments of the Minister. I returnd after two with a sousing shower for companion. I got very wet and very warm. But shall we go mourn for that, my dear?[3] I rather like a flaw of weather – It shews something of the old man is left. I had Mr. Buchanan to help pack my papers and things and got thorough part of that unpleasant business.

8 THURSDAY I had my letters as usual but no proofs till I was just going out – Paid Anne £100 of cash for current expences – Returning from the Court met Skene who brought me news that our visit was at an end on Saturday, poor Colin[4] having come to town very unwell. I calld to see him and found him suffering under a degree of slow palsy, his spirits depressed and his looks miserable, worse a great deal than when I last saw [him]. His wife and daughter were in the room dreadfully distressd. We spoke but a few words referring to recovery and better days which I suspect neither of us hoped for. I lookd only on the ghost of my friend of many a long day and he, while he said to see me did him good, must have had little thought of our ever meeting under better auspices. We shall of course go straight to Abbotsford instead of travelling by Harcass as we intended.

9 FRIDAY Two distressd damsells on my hands, one, a friend of Harriet Swinton, translates from the Italian a work on the plan of *Gli*

1. Sir Adam was 'in good fooling' as usual. It was a whiting, though, not a haddock, that Scott had eaten. See the Entry for 28 June 1830.
2. Manzoni's *I promessi sposi*, 1827, of which Scott owned the 1829 edition.
3. *Winter's Tale*, iv. 3.
4. Colin Mackenzie, now living in retirement at Harcass, where his brother-in-law Skene, along with Scott, had intended to visit him. He died in September.

promessi Sposi but I fear she must not expect much from the trade. A translation is with them a mere translation, that is a thing which can be made their own at a guinea per sheet and they will not have an excellent one at a higher rate. Second is Miss Young[1] daughter of the excellent Dr. Young of Hawick. If she can from her father's letters and memoranda extract materials for a fair simple account of his life I would give my name as editor and I think it might do, but for a large publication – palabras, Neighbour Dogberry,[2] the time is bye. Dined with the Bannatyne where we had a lively party.[3] Touching the songs an old roué must own an improvement in the times when all paw-paw words are omitted and naughty inuendos *gazés* – One is apt to say

> Swear me, Kate, like a Lady as thou art
> A good mouth filling oath and leave forsooth
> And such protests of petty gingerbread.[4]

I think there is more affectation than improvement in the new mode.

10 SATURDAY Rose rather late, the Champagne and turtle I suppose for our reform inclu[d]es no fasting. Then poor Ardwall[5] came to breakfast; then Dr. Young's daughter. I have perfected with Cadell a plan of her father's life to be edited by me.[6] If she does but tolerably

1. It was during her first visit, on the same business, that Scott had his stroke. See p. 661 and the Entry for 20 December 1830.
2. *Much Ado about Nothing*, iii. 5.
3. The meeting was at the Waterloo Tavern and 'chiefly for convivial purposes'. Bannatyne Club Minutes. It was the last meeting of the Club that Scott attended.
4. *1 Henry IV*, iii. 1.
5. McCulloch of Ardwall, brother of Mrs. Thomas Scott, had gone bankrupt. At the end of the month, when his country creditors refused to accept an immediate payment of 6s. 8d. with the promise of a similar payment in four or five years, he fled to England. Scott sent him £30. In October he returned to commence a Cessio. Nairne, 28 July, and 3 and 19 August 1831, Walpole.
6. The work was never published, however. 'When I found, by taking some pains with the manuscripts that there was no possibility of giving them the fashion of the day or ensuring a sale necessary to defray expenses and produce her some emolument, I looked through her father's works with a view to some selection such as might be republished with advantage. But unhappily the times are daily more unfavourable for success, and I have no hopes of success either to Miss Young, or advantage to the publick from the works of her father, just, true and well-expressed as they are.' Mrs. Scott Moncrieff, 17 December 1830, Disc. ii. 157. Instead Scott sent Miss Young £10.

she may have a fine thing of it. Next came the court where sixty judgements were pronounced and written by the Clerks, I hope all corr[e]ctly though an error might well happen in such a crowd and Carmichael, one of [the] best men possible, is beastly stupid.

Be that as it may off came Anne Charles and I for Abbotsford; we started about two and the water being too deep did not arrive till past seven. Dinner etc. filld up the rest of the day.

11 SUNDAY Corrected my proofs and the lave of it till about one o'clock. Then started for a walk to Chiefswood which I will take from Station to station¹ with a book in my pouch. I have begun *Lawrie Todd*² which ought considering the author's indisputed talents to have been better. He might have laid Cowper³ aboard but he follows far behind. No wonder. Galt, poor fellow, was in the King's Bench when he wrote it; no whetter of genius is necessity though said to be the mother of invention.

12 MONDAY Another wet day but I walkd twice up and down the terrace and also wrote a handsome scrap of copy though mistified by the want of my books⁴ and so forth. Dr. and Mrs. Lockhart and Violet⁵ came to luncheon and left us to drive on to Peebles. I read and loiterd and longed to get my things in order. Got to work however at seven in the morning.

13 TUESDAY Now what a thing it is to be an ass.⁶
I have a letter from a certain young man of a sapient family announcing that his sister had so far mistaken my attentions as to suppose I was only prevented by modesty from stating certain wishes and hopes etc. The party is a woman of rank, so far my vanity may be satisfied. But to think I would wish to appropriate a grim grenadier

1. Scott had placed seats at convenient distances between Abbotsford and Chiefswood. On this day he would no doubt call at Kaeside where the Laidlaws had been installed once again on 22 June.
2. By Galt, 1830. It was among the 'one or two books of light reading for the journey to Abbotsford' that he had selected from Cadell's on the 9th. Cadell's Diary.
3. Fenimore Cooper.
4. Notably the Abbé de Vertot's *History of the Knights of Malta*, 1728, which he required for *Count Robert of Paris. Letters*, xi. 373.
5. J. G. Lockhart's father, mother, and sister. The Revd. John Lockhart is described in *Letters*, ix. 139 as 'that best & dullest of all possible doctors'.
6. *Titus Andronicus*, iv. 2.

made to mount guard at St. James – The Lord de[i]ver me. I excused myself with little picking upon the terms and there was no occasion for much delicacy in repelling such an attack.[1]

14 WEDNESDAY The court of Session Bill[2] is now committed in the House of Lords so it fairly goes on this season this season, and I have I suppose to look for my congé.

15 THURSDAY I can hardly form a notion of the possibility that I am not to return to Edinburgh. My clerk Buchanan come[s] here and assists me to finish the *Dæmonology* and be d—d to them. But it is done to their hand. Two Ladies, Mrs. La Touche of Dublin[3] and her niece Miss Boyle, came to spend a day or two. The aunt is a fine old Lady, the conversation that of a serious person frighted out of her wits by the violence and sup[e]rstitions of our workers of miracles in the west.[4] Miss Boyle is a pretty young woman rather quiet for an Irish lass.

16 FRIDAY We visited at Lessudden yesterday and took Mrs. Latouche thither. To-day as they had left us we went alone to Major John's[5] house of Ravenswood and engage[d] a large party of cousins to dine tomorrow. In the evening a party of foreigners came around the door and going out I found Le Compte Wladislaus de Potocki, a great name in Poland, with his Lady and brother in law, so offerd wine coffee tea etc. The Lady is strikin[g]ly pretty. If such a woman as she had taken an affection for a lame Baronet nigh sixty

1. It seems from the Revd. John Sinclair's letter that he had intercepted a love-letter from his eldest sister to Scott and wanted 'a few lines which happily may open her eyes, and prevent all further uneasiness'. Partington's *Letter-Books*, p. 132. Scott's reply unfortunately does not survive. According to Helen Graham's *Diaries*, the six daughters of Sir John were known as 'The Great Sinclairs' and the part of George Street where they crossed over 'The Giants' Causeway'. 'And d'ye know they say all the gentlemen are afraid to make up to one of them, for fear if he married one he would be, they say, married to them all? And there's another name they call them themselves, d'ye know, "Plague," "Pestilence" and "Famine," "Battle," "Murder" and "Sudden Death".' *Diaries of Helen Graham*, p. 33.
2. See the Entry for 27 May 1830 and note.
3. See the Entry for 23 June 1830 and note.
4. These 'miracles' are described in *Peace in Believing, a Memoir of Isabella Campbell*, 1829.
5. Major John Scott's.

years old it would be worth speaking about. I have finishd the *Dæmonology* and have a mind to say D—n it, but the subject is damnd to my hand.

17 SATURDAY Another bad day, wet past all efforts to walk and threatens a very bad harvest. Persecuted with begging letters. An author's Pegasus is like a post chaise leaving the door of the inn, the number of beggars is uncountable. The language they hold of my character for charity makes my good reputation as troublesome as that of Joseph Surface.[1] A dinner of cousins, the young Laird of Raeburn[2] – so he must be calld though nearly as old as I am – at the head. His brother Robert who has been in India for forty years excepting one short visit. A fine manly fellow who has belld the cat with fortune and held her at bay as a man of mould may. Being all kinsmen and friends we made a merry day of our reunion. All left at night.

18 SUNDAY 'Time runs I know [not] how away' – here am I beginning the second week of my vacation – though what needs me note that; vacation and Session will probably be the same to me in future. The long remove must then be lookd to for the final signal to break up and that is a serious thought. I have corrected two sets of proofs, one for the mail another for the Blucher tomorrow.

[This summer, for the last time, Scott enjoyed the company of all his family at Abbotsford. The Lockharts were at Chiefswood, and Scott and Anne were joined first by Charles (who left late in August to take up his post at Naples) and then on 15 August by Walter.]

SEPTEMBER

5 SUNDAY In spite of resolution I have left my diary for seven weeks, I cannot well tell why. We have had the usual number of travelling counts and Countesses, Yankees male and female and a Yankee Doodle-*Dandy* into the bargain, a smart young Virginia man. We have had friends of our own also, the Miss Ardens, young Mrs.

1. In Sheridan's *School for Scandal*. See Act ii. scene 2.
2. William Scott of Maxpoffle, Laird of Raeburn since his father's death in May.

Morritt and Anne Morritt, most agre[e]able visitors.[1] Cadell came out here yesterday with his horn filld with good news.[2]

He calculates that in October the debt will be reduce[d] to the sum of – £60,000, half of its original amount –

He computes sales and advance of a sum of money for copyrights which he proposes to purchase will produce against October 1832 – £15,000

That between October 1833–4 the same sum may be produced by the conclusion of the periodical issue sale of poetry   15,000

These two sums will [clear] —————————   30,000

                                                    30,000

He proposes to [borrow] on £22,000
    Life insurances ————————————   15,000
     Interest at 4 per Cent £600 per ann
He himself to advance on copyright ———   15,000

                                               ——— £30,000

This will in effect put an end to the trust, only the sales and produce must be pleged to answer the last £1500[0] and the annuity interest of £600.

In this way Mr. Cadell will become half partner in the remaining volumes of the books following *Saint Ronans*; with all my heart but he must pay well for it, for it is good property.[3] Neither is any value stated for literary profits. Yet four years should have four novels[4] betwixt 1830 and 1834. This at £2500 per volumum might be £8000 which would diminish Mr. Cadell's advance considerably. All this seems feasible enough so my fits of sullen alarm are ill placed. It makes me care less about the terms I retire upon. The efforts by

1. 'This autumn he was far more troubled with the invasions of strangers, than he had ever been since his calamities of 1826.' *Life*, ix. 355.
2. *Merchant of Venice*, v. 1.
3. Cadell was so sure of the profits to be made that he was willing to advance almost any sum to acquire a half-share of the copyrights. Scott held out until July 1831 when he finally sold the half interest in the novels after *Quentin Durward* for £10,000. Sederunt Book, ii. 232–3. After Scott's death Cadell advanced the money to buy up the remaining debts in exchange for the half of the copyrights which he did not already hold. This was a bad bargain for Scott's children, but it made Cadell's fortune. He died worth more than £100,000.
4. Only two were written: *Count Robert of Paris* and *Castle Dangerous*.

which we have advanced thus far are new in literature and what is gaind is secure.

———

[The autumn was marred by rain and visitors. 'Our weather here has been terrible constant storms of thunder wind and tempest floods which threatened to take away Sophia and her cottage', he writes to Walter. 'She . . . was found flitting her children best china & carpets into the garret.'[1] Inevitably she had another bout of rheumatism before the family returned to London by steam-packet at the beginning of October. 'The cursed tide of visitors does not end,' Scott writes to her later in the month, 'only the weather is like to keep them within doors which makes the plague greater.'[2]

In September Scott spent a week at Glenlee and Drumlanrig visiting Sir Adam Ferguson and the Duke of Buccleuch. In October a second dividend of 3s. in the £ was paid to the creditors, with the help of four or five thousand pounds advanced by Cadell to make up the necessary sum. The death of Colin Mackenzie, his colleague of the Clerks' Table, who 'tarried so long that retirement could do little for him',[3] strengthened Scott's resolve to retire; and the passing of a new Act of Parliament enabled him to do so on 12 November, on a salary reduced from £1,300 to £866.

National and local affairs took up much time and energy in the last months of the year. The King's death meant a general election, and Scott took his usual part. The younger Adolphus, who visited Abbotsford in October, has left a description of the meeting at Jedburgh, where Scott seconded Henry Scott of Harden, and at the election dinner made a speech 'rich in humour and feeling, and graced by that engaging manner of which he had so peculiar a command'.[4] On 15 November, however, Wellington resigned, after the ultra-Tories (offended by his liberal attitude to Catholic Emancipation) had voted with the Whigs; Lord Grey formed an administration which Scott deeply mistrusted; there were riots in many large towns. To Walter, whose troop had been hurried from Sheffield to Birmingham, Scott writes, 'I wish I could see appearance of opposing efficient measures to these insane rioters & I fear we have parted with old Waterloo just when the country needed him most. The fiends of reform have it their own way now.'[5]

1. *Letters*, xi. 396.
2. *Letters*, xi. 399.
3. *Letters*, xi. 391.
4. *Life*, ix. 359. But see also p. 691.
5. *Letters*, xi. 420.

Locally 'the new disease to which all country gentlemen are subject by contagion to wit the Roadmania'[1] was raging. Scott favoured the scheme proposed for a new road to Selkirk, for the good reason that 'the adoption of that line must be followed by the alteration of the road which passes Abbotsford to a private one.'[1] There was a sharp contest with those who opposed the change, and it was not until December that Scott's party was victorious.

Throughout this time Scott continued to write. *Tales of a Grandfather*, fourth series, and *Letters on Demonology and Witchcraft* were published before Christmas. He reviewed Southey's edition of *Pilgrim's Progress* for the September *Quarterly*, and wrote an article for the December number on 'Ancient Criminal Trials', to whet public interest in Robert Pitcairn's forthcoming book. Against the advice of his doctors, he began in September a new novel, *Count Robert of Paris*, whose early chapters dismayed Ballantyne and Cadell – for the deterioration of Scott's powers, not yet evident in his letters, was only too obvious in a work of fiction.

The most important event of these months, briefly alluded to in the Entry for 20 December 1830, was Scott's second stroke in November. The Entries which follow, full of omissions and mis-spellings, muddled and almost illegible, are clear about one thing only: this second warning must soon be succeeded by incapacity and death.]

DECEMBER

20 MONDAY From September 5 to Decemr 20 is a long gap and I have seen plenty of thingks worth recollecting had I markd them down when they were gliding past. But the time has gone bye. What I feel capable of taking up I will.

Little self will jostle out every thing else and my affairs, which in some respects are excellent, in others like the way of the world [are] far from being pleasant.

Of good I have the pleasure of saying I have seen my children well and in good health and know these are [blessings]. The dividend of 3/- in the pound has been made to the Creditors and the Creditors have testified their sense of my labours by surrendering my books, furniture, plate and curiosities.[2] I see some friends of mine think this is not handsomely done. In my

1. *Letters*, xi. 416.
2. The creditors unanimously adopted on 17 December Gibson Craig's resolution "That Sir Walter Scott be requested to accept of his furniture, plate, linens, paintings, library, and curiosities of

opinion it is extremely so. There is few things so [easy] as to criticize the good things one does and to show that we ourselves would have done handsomely. But those who know the world and their own nature are always better pleased with one kind action carried through and executed than with twenty that only glide through their imagination, while perhaps they tickle the imagination of the Benevolent Barmecide who supposes both the entertainment and the eater. These articles do not amount to less than £10,000 at least and without dispersing them entirely might furnish me a fund for my younger children;[1] now suppose these Creditors had not seriously carried their purpose into execution the transaction might have been afterward challenged and the ease of mind which it produced to me must have been uncertain in comparaison. Well! one half of this claims are cleard off, furnishd in a great measure by one half issue of the present edidition of the Waverly novels which had reachd 20th of the Series.

It cannot be enpected that 20 more will run off so fast; the later volumes are less favourite and are really less interesting. Yet when I read them over again since the composition I own I found them considerably better than I expected and I think if other circumstances do not crush them and blight their popularity they will make their way. Mr. Cadell is still desirous to acquire one half of the property of this part of the work which is chiefly my own. He proposes by assembling all my detachd works of fiction [and] Articles in annuals so that the whole, supposing I write as is proposed Six new volumes, will run the Collection to fifty when it is time to close it. Between cash advanced on this property and a profit on the sale of this second part Mr. Cadell thinks, having taken a year or two years' time to gather a little wind into the bag, I will be able to pay on my part a further sum of £30,000 or the moiety remaining of the whole debts, amounting now to less than £60,000.

Should this happy period arrive in or about the year 1832, this heavy work will be well nigh finishd. For although £30,000 will still

---

every description, as the best means the creditors have of expressing their very high sense of his most honourable conduct, and in grateful acknowledgement for the unparalleled and most successful exertions he had made, and continues to make, for them.' *Life*, x. 19. 'The feeling of the Creditors', wrote Gibson, 'was that they were only doing an act of justice.' 18 December 1830. Walpole.

1. Walter agreed, in January, to pay £2000 to Anne and Charles, and £1000 to Sophia, in return for sole possession of the library – 'not', as Scott says, 'a jews bargain'. *Letters*, xi. 457.

remain yet ther[e] is £20,000 actually secured upon my life and the remaining £10,000 is set against the sale of Waverly which shall have been issued.[1] Besides which the[re] is the who[le] poetry, *Bonaparte* and sev[e]ral other articles, equal in a short time to pay up the balance and afford a very large reversion.

This view cannot be absolutely certain but it is highly probable and is calculatented in the manner in which [one] builds schemes and not visions. The year 1833 may probably see me again in possession of my estate.

A circumstance of great consequence to my habits and comforts was my being released from the Court of Session on November 1830 (18th day). My Salary which was £1300 was reduced to £840.[2] My friends were just then leaving office,[3] were desirous to patch up the deficiency with a pension. I do not see well how they could do this without being charged with Obloquy which they shall not be on my account. Besides, though £500 a year is a round sum yet I would rather be independent than I would have it.

My kind friend the lord Ch. Com. offerd to interfere to have me named a P. Councillor. But besides that when [one] is poor one ould to avoid taking rank I would be much happier if I though any act of kindness was done to help forward Charles and, having said so much I made my bow and declined[4] my purpose of remaining satisfied with the article of my knighthood.[5] And here I am for the rest of my life I suppose with a competent income which I can make [easy by my literary efforts].

All this is rather pleasing nor had I the least doubt that I could make myself easy by literary labour. But much of it looks like winding up my bottom for the rest of my life. But there is a worse symptom of settling accompts of which I have felt some signs.

Last summer[6] Miss Young, the daughter of Dr. Young, had occasion to call on me on some business in which I had hopes of

1. i.e., the last £10,000 has to be set against future sales of the Magnum edition of the Waverley Novels whose publication will by then be complete.
2. The figures are inaccurate. Scott retired on the 12th, and his salary was reduced to two-thirds.
3. Wellington's administration left office on 15 November.
4. A slip for 'declared'.
5. For Scott's letters to William Adam see *Letters*, xi. 418 and 422. Adam used his influence, as Scott had suggested, to ensure that the new King did not forget Charles. See the Entry for 3 January 1831.
6. This visit and Scott's first stroke actually took place on 15 February. See p. 661.

serving her. As I endeavourd to explain to her what I had had to say I had the horror to find I could not make Myself understood. I stammerd, s[t]utterd, said one word [in place] of another – did all but speak – Miss Young went away frightend enough, poor thing, and Anne and Violet Lockhart were much alarmd. I was bled with cupping glasses, took medicine, and lived on panada, but in two or three days I was well again. The physicians throught or said at least that the evil was from the stomach. They might be very right for I had just discussed a large plate of muffins and other very indi-gestibl[e] things as eggs and hung beef. It is very sertain that I have seemd to speak with an impedimend and I was or it might be fancied myself troubled with a mispronouncing and hesitation. I felt this particularly at the Election[1] and sometimes in society. This went on till this last November when Lord came out to make me a visit. I had for a long time taken only one tumble[r] of whiskey and water without the slightest reinforcement. This night I took a very little drop, not so much as a bumper glass of whisky altogether. I[t] made no difference in my head that I could discern. But when I went to the dressingroom I sank stupefied on the floor. I lay a minute or two, was not found luckily, gatherd, and got to my bed. I was alarmed at this second warning. Consulted Abercromby an[d] Ross and got a few restrictive orders as to diet.[2] I am fain attend to them for as Mrs. Cole says 'Lackaday a thimble full over sets me.'[3]

To add to these feelings I have the constant increase of my lameness. The thigh joint knee joint and ancle joint.

21 TUESDAY I walk with great pain in the whole limb and am at every minute during an hour's walk remind[ed] of my mortality. I should not care for all this if I was sure of dying handsomely. Cadell's calculation would be sufficiently firm though the author of Waverlyey had pulled on his last nightcap. Nay they might be even more trust worthy if remains and memoirs and such like were to give a zest to the

1. The election meeting at Jedburgh, where he had seconded Henry Scott of Harden. Adolphus, who was present, was 'a little disappointed' with the speech but does not seem to have realized that Scott was in difficulties. *Life*, ix. 357–60.
2. The diet affected his good spirits, according to Skene. 'His bodily energies were much relaxed, and he became heavy and dull, and was never again roused to the hilarity which was natural to his disposition.' *Skene's Reminiscences*, p. 182.
3. Foote's *The Minor*, Act 1.

posthumous.[1] But the fear is the blow be not sufficient to destroy life and that I should linger on 'an idiot and a show'.[2]

Setting this apart howowevr I have to mention other circumstances which have led to important consequ[en]ces which I shall briefly mentiont. The time was now come when I found it necessary to commence a new volume of fiction. The name was *Count Robert of Paris*, the scen[e] opend at the gates of Constantinople, the scene was at the golden Gate of Byzantium. I had askd James Ballantyne who is extremely candid. He returnd for answer that he thought the work altogether a failure. Mr. Caddell expressd him[self] less positively.[3]

I was never fond of my own efforts; a[t] present I had the reason to be very doubtful of them in the present case. I caught the alarm of my criticks and announced my purpose of going to a warmer climate to ward of[f] the blow of fate.[4] My two friends came out on the next saturday and expressd much concern. Some of it might be selfish regret but I think, I am certain, both my friends thought as much on me as themselves.[5] After all I considerd that [I] might be stupid and yet not strike[6] with a paralsy and that I nought not to throw up the game. It was agreed after long pros and con; it was settled to trie the tale once more and only bring it forward or not as it would be found to succeed.

22 WEDNESDAY But in the mean while a step which I had taken at first almost by accident turnd out a deeper subject of dispute than the rejecting or committing the novel.

1. 'For you have Lockharts tried talents to write some sort of life or biographical sketch', he wrote to Walter a few days later. *Letters*, xi. 450.
2. 'And *Swift* expires a Drivler and a Show': Johnson's *Vanity of Human Wishes*, l. 318. 'I am not afraid to die', Scott told Gibson, 'but I dread the death of the mind before the body: that happened to my father.' Gibson's *Reminiscences*, p. 42.
3. Cadell objected only to the outlandish proper names. See *Letters*, xi. 431–40, for the correspondence between Scott, Cadell, and Ballantyne on the subject.
4. 'My present idea is to go abroad for a few months if I hold together as long. So ended the fathers of the Novel Fielding & Smollet and it would be no unprofessional finish.' *Letters*, xi. 432.
5. Cadell at least saw it from the business point of view: 'There are so many points requiring your presence in this Country, the Notes to the Novels, – not to mention those several at press – the many views connected with your work which at all times require your opinion and sanction.' Cadell, 10 December 1830, Walpole.
6. Tait emended unnecessarily to 'stricken', but 'strike' in the sense of 'give in' seems to be Scott's meaning.

The succession of the Whig administration,[1] the disturbances in the country and the probable consequence of the Reforme of parliament were a natural temptation to me for ascertaining the state of my seven witts. As I got on I became interested. My two friends listend and appllauded and I myself thought I had worded my argument in strong terms. Mr. Cadell began to think it a pity that I did no[t] throw my lucubrations into a pamphlet. But my friend Caddell is a Whig and finding the doctrines I advocated still [more] and more diverging from those he heard in his own back shop he became alarmd for the fate of his author, prognosticated annihilation by the vengeful Whigs and plainly let me know that he did not think it so safe to adventure. On this point I was it may be believed inflexible for as they [say] my family is proverbially obstinate, I am; when I take up a subject with a consciousness of being right no interest or selfish motive shall ever make me abandon my purpose. At length finding me inexerable Mr. Cadell was pacified on considereration that the Newspapers should be the means of enlighten[ing] the publick and and we parted on good terms and hopes.[2] But fall back fall Edge nothing shall induce me to publish what I do not think advantageous to the community or suppress what is –

To add for the day to the Evil there of, I am obliged this day to hold a black fishing court at Selkirkshire. This is always a very unpopular matter in on[e] of our countries as the salmon never do get up to the heads of the waters in whol[e]som[e] season and are there in numbers in spawning time. So that for several years during late the late period the gentry, finding no advantage from preserving the spawning fish, neglected the matter altogether in a kind of dudgeon and the peasantry laid them waste at their will. As the property is very valuable the proprietors down the country agreed to afford some additional passage for fish when the river is open providing they will protect the spawning fish during close time. A new act has been passd with heavey penalties and summary powers of recovery. Some persons are cited under it today and a peculiar licence of poaching having always distinguishd the district of late years we shall be likely

1. Under Lord Grey.
2. Cadell's objections were firstly that Scott was using arguments already discredited, and secondly that his proclamation of high Tory views at this time might affect the popularity of his works. Scott wanted to publish a pamphlet, a fourth *Epistle of Malachi*; Cadell and Ballantyne, after an unpleasant scene, at length compromised on anonymous publication in the *Edinburgh Weekly Journal*. 'This was the understanding when the conference broke up; but the unfortunate manuscript was soon afterwards committed to the flames.' *Life*, x. 23.

to have some disturbance. They have been holding a meeting for reform in Selkirk and it will be difficult to teach them that this consists in any thing else save [the] privilege of obeying only such laws as please them – Whe shall see but I would have counselld the matter to have been delayd for a little season. I shall do my duty however. Do what is right come what will –

23[1] THURSDAY Six black fishers were tried, four were condemnd. All went very quietly untill the conclusion when one of the criminals attempted to break out. I stopd him for the time with my own hand. But after removing him from the Court house to the Jail he broke from the officers who are poor feeble old men, the very caricature of peace-officers.[2]

24 FRIDAY This morning my old acqua[i]ntance and good friend Miss Bel Fergusson died, after a short illness. An old friend and a woman of the most excellen[t] condition. The last two or almost three years were very sickly.

A bitter cold day. Anne drove me over to Huntlyburn to see the aflicted family. I found Colonel Fergusson and Capt. John R.N. in deep afliction expecting Sir Adam hourly. Anne sets of[f] to Mertoun and I remain alone.[3] I write to Walter about the project of making my succession in moveables.[4] J. B. send[s] me praises of the work I am

---

1. Previous editors, following Scott, have started the Entry for the 23rd at the beginning of the previous paragraph, which must, however, be a continuation of the previous day's entry, wrongly dated, since the Court was held on Wednesday the 22nd, not on Thursday the 23rd. The likely explanation is that Scott did not date the Entry at the time of writing and put '23' in later at the wrong place.

2. For a full account of this incident and its aftermath see note 11, pp. 815–16.

3. 'Anne goes to Mertoun to go with Mrs. Scott to chapel tomorrow at Kelso. I go down for my Christmas goose & stay there Sunday.' *Letters*, xi. 449.

4. The suggestion was made by Cadell, who more and more becomes Scott's adviser, banker, and man of business: 'Allow me, now that the Library, Furniture, &c &c are all at your disposal, to recommend you to provide for Miss Scott by a burden on these moveables – that is, that your successor should pay a sum for them, which sum ought to be settled on Miss Scott . . . it is of the last importance to an unprotected female to be as independent . . . as possible'. *Letters*, xi. 450 n. For the arrangement finally arrived at see the Entry for 7 January 1831 and note.

busy with. But I suspect a little supercherie though he protests not.[1] He is going to the country without send[ing] me the political article. But he shall either set up or return it. I won't be tutord by any one in what I do or forbear.

25 SATURDAY Have sketchd a political article on a union of Tories and an income tax. It would do good I am sure. But then shall I give myself up to this irritating temptation again after I have resolved against it so often? My pride strongly tempts me for the match wants but blowing and I would fain not appear the helpless Creature which perhaps I really am. J. B. but particularly R. C. argue strongly against it – a great deal for a Bookseller to argue against any thing that is sure to sell. But this startles me as much as an attempt to catch a shy horse suddenly by the bridle. This is obstinacy. There is vanity in the resolution besides. But yet one quarrels with so many friends and has so many heart burnings. I remember my escapade about the currency.[2] Above all I fear that whoreson touch of the Apoplexy – My mind I conceive is as strong as ever but there is a wavering in my composition sadly visible. I am not the man that I was and must keep in the background. I will correct my effusion however and keep a copy. But I will not shew my teeth if I find I cannot bite. Arrived at Mertoun and found with the family Sir John Pringle, Major Pringle and Charles Baillie. Very pleasant Musick by the Miss Pringles.

26 SUNDAY Prayers after breakfast, being sunday. Afterwards I shut myself up in Mr. Scott's room. He has lately become purchaser of his Grandfather's valuable Library which was collected by Pope's Lord Marchmount.[3] Part of it is a very valuable collection of Tracts during the great Civill war. I spent several hours in turning them over but I could not look them through with any accuracy. I passd my time very pleasantly and made some extracts however, and will resume my research another day.

Major Pringle repeated some pretty verses of his own composing.

1. The praise of Ballantyne and Cadell, according to Lockhart, was dictated, as Scott suspected, by kindness not sincerity. 'If we did wrong', says Cadell, 'we did it for the best: we felt that to have spoken out as fairly on this as we had done on the other subject, would have been to make ourselves the bearers of a death-warrant.' *Life*, x. 25.
2. The success of the *Letters of Malachi Malagrowther* in 1826.
3. John Richardson and Henry Scott had bought the Marchmont Library, which was about to be scattered, the previous May. Richardson, 20 May 1830. Walpole.

I had never more decided inclination to go loose yet I know I had better keep quiet.[1]

27 MONDAY Commences snow and extremely bitter cold. When I returnd from Mertoun half frozen I took up the Magnum and began to notify the Romance calld *Woodstock* in which I got some assistance from Harden's ancient tracts. I ought rathe[r] to get on with *Robert of Paris*. But I have had all my life a longing to do some thing else when I am calld to particular labour – a vile contradictory humour which I cannot get rid of. Well I can work at something so at the Magnum work I. The day was indeed broken, great part having been employd in return from Mertoun.

28 TUESDAY Drove dow[n] to Huntly Burn. Sir Adam very melancholy the death of his sister having come with a particular and shocking surprize upon him. After half an hour's visit I returnd and resumed the Magnum.

29 WEDNESDAY Attended poor Miss Bell Fergusson's funeral. I sate by revd. Mr. Thompson.[2] Though ten years younger than me I found the barrier between him and me much broken down. We rememberd though with more or less accuracy, we took the same old persons for subjects of correspondence of feeling and sentiment. The difference of ten years is little after sixty has passed. In a cold day I saw poor Bell laid in her cold bed. Life never parted with a less effort. Letter from Cadell offering to advanc[e] on second Series French *Tales*.[3] This will come in good time and keep me easy. He proposes *views* for the Magnum. I fear politics may disappoint them. Tomorrow is our road meeting.

30 THURSDAY Meeting at Selkirk to-day about the new road to Galashiels where was the largest meeting I ever saw in Selkirkshire. We gain the victory by no less than 14 to 4.[4]

1. Another reference to his political article.
2. Not 'Dominie Sampson' but his father, the minister of Melrose, who was actually thirteen years older than Scott.
3. This, the fifth series of *Tales of a Grandfather*, was never completed nor likely to be. Cadell is lending Scott money as tactfully as he can.
4. The vote was expected to be as close as 13 to 9 if all those who were against the scheme attended the meeting. Opposition to the line of the road came from Lord Napier, 'who has I think a wild idea of getting a road over to Etterick by the Hartleap through as solitary a country as is to be found in Scotland' (to Henry Scott, 19 November

I was named one of the committee to carry the matter on so in gaining my victory I think I have caught a Tartar for I have take[n] on trouble enough. Some company, Lord Napier, Scotts of Har[d]en, Johnstone of Alva, Major Pringle, in the evening. Had some private conversation with H. F. S. and R. J.[1] and think there is life in a Mussell. More of this hereafter.

31 FRIDAY My two young friends left this morning but not without reviving our conversation of last night. We carried on the little amusements of the day and spent our Hogmanae pleasantly enough in spite of very bad auguries.

1830, Disc. ii. 142), and from Alexander Pringle, who was conveniently served at Whitebank by the old road. Many others had doubts on financial grounds. The interest to subscribers was to be only 2½ per cent, and to encourage users the pontage was to be one-half of the former tolls. Scott himself was to subscribe £400. The *Journal* gives little idea of the energy Scott expended at this time on the business of the new road; a better indication is the Abbotsford Collection which preserves two dozen letters on the subject written to Scott between 27 October 1830 and 11 January 1831.

1. 'H. F. S.' is Henry Scott of Harden, the Member for Roxburghshire. 'R. J.' is James Johnstone, who had just inherited Alva from his father ('J. R. J.'). Both young men were Tories of the stamp which Scott approved and it is not hard to guess at the subject of conversation. Johnstone's letters at this time show him to be one of the Reformers' bitterest opponents, and Henry Scott is urged by Sir Walter a few days later to make a stand against Reform by gathering round him in effect a nationalist party. *Letters*, xi. 455.

1831

1 SATURDAY I cannot say the world opens pleasantly with me this new year. I will strike the balance. There are many things for which I have reason to be thankfull.

1st Cadell's plans seem to have succeeded and he augurs that next two years will well nigh [clear the remaining debt] reckoning £30,000 on the stuff now in hand and £20,000 on the insurance money and £10,000 to be borrowd somehow. This would bring us wonderfully home.

2dly Cadell is of opinion if I meddle in politicks, and I am strong[ly] tempted to do so, I shall break the milkpaily, and threatens mè with the fate of Basil Hall who as he says destroyd his reputation by writing impol[it]ick politicks.[1] Well it would be my risque and if I can do some good, which I rather think, is it right or man[l]y to keep myself back?

3dly. I feel myself Decidedly weaker in point of health and am now confirmd I have had a paralitic touch. I speak and read with embarassment and even my handwriting seems to stammer.[2] This general failur[e]

> With mortal crisis doth portend
> My days to appropinque an end.[3]

I am not solicitous about this, only if I were worthy I wou[l]d pray God for a sudden death and no in[ter]regnum between I cease to exercize reason and cease to exist.

1. Basil Hall was a Whig. His address to the Dunbar Mechanics Institution had been published in 1828.
2. In the original it is painfully obvious that from this point onwards Scott's handwriting is much deteriorated. The firm and evenly spaced lines of the early Entries have given way to a spidery hand which wavers over the paper.
3. Butler's *Hudibras*, pt. 1, canto 3.

The Scotts of Harden, Pringles of Stitchill and Russells of ashestiel are all here. I am scarce fit for company though.

2 SUNDAY Held a great palaver with the Scotts etc. I find my tongue apt to fail me but this is very like to be fancy and I must be cautious of giving way to it. This cautions me against publick exertion much more than Cadell's prognostications which my blood rises against, which are ill calculated to keep me in restraint. We dozed through a gloomy day being the dullest of all possible thaws.

3 MONDAY I had a letter from L. C. C. mention[ing] the Kg's intention to take care of Charles's interest and promotion in the Foreign office,[1] an additional reason why I would not plunge rashly into politics yet not one which I can understand as putting a padlock on my lips neither. I must[t] write to L. C. C. that I may be calld on to express an opinion on the impending changes, that I have an opinion and a strong, and that I hope this fresh favour [is not seen] as padlocking my lips in a time when it would otherwise be proper to me to speak or write. I am shockd to find that I have not the faculty of delivering myself with facility, an embarassment which may be fanciful but is altogether as annoying as if real.

4 TUESDAY A base gloomy day and dispiriting in proportion. I walk out with Swanston[2] for about an hour, everything gloomy as the back of the chimney when there is no fire in it. My walk was a melancholy one, feeling myself weaker at every step and not very able to speak. This surely cannot be fancy yet it looks some thing like it. If I knew but the extent at which my inability was like to stop, but every day is worse than another. I have trifled much time, too much. I must try to get afloat tomorrow; perhaps getting an amanuensis might spur me on for one half is nerves. It is a sad business though.

5 WEDNESDAY Very indifferent with more awkward feelings than I can well bear up against. My voice sunk and my head strangely confused. When I begin to form my ideas for conversation expressions fail me even in private conversation and yet in solitude they are sufficiently arranged. I incline to hold that these ugly symptoms are the work of imagination. But as Dr. Adam Fergusson, a firm man if ever there was one in the world, said on such an occasion was wont to

1. See Adam, 31 December 1830, Walpole, and the Entry for 20 December 1830.
2. John Swanston, the Abbotsford forester who became Scott's attendant out of doors after Tom Purdie's death.

say, what is worse than imagination? As Anne was vexd and frightend I allowd her to send for young Clarkson. Of course he could tell me little save what I knew before.

6 THURSDAY A letter from Henry Scott about the taking ground for keeping the Reform in Scotland upon the Scottish principles.¹ I will write him my private sentiments but avoid being a *Boute feu*. Go this day to Selkirk where I found about 120 and more persons of that Burgh and Galashiels who were sworn in as Special Constables, enough to maintain the peace. What shockd me particularly was the weakness of my voic[e] and the confusion of my head attempting to address them which was really a poor affair. On my return I found Revd Mr. Milne of Quebeck a friend of my sister in law. Another time would have been better for compagny but Captain John Fergusson and Mr. Laidlaw coming in to dinner we got over the day well enough.

7 FRIDAY A fine frosty day and my spirits lighter. I have a letter of great comfort from Walter who in a manly, handsome and dutifull manner expressd his desire to possess the Library and moveables of every kind at Abbots. with such a valuation laid upon them as I chuse to impose.² This removes the only delay to making my will. Supposing the Literary property to clear the debts by aid of insurances and other things, about 1835 it will come into my person and I will appoint the whole to work off the heritable debt of £10,000 pounds, then the whole that is remaining. If the literary property can produce that sum besides what <it> has been already done, I wou[l]d Convey it to the three younger children.³

1. Henry Scott's news is that the Government intends '*To give votes to land holders of the rent value of £10 per an* Thus at once putting an end to our whole system.' [4 January] 1831, Walpole. Scott's reply is '*Principiis obsta*: Oppose anything that can in principle innovate on the Constitution.' *Life*, x. 30.
2. 'I should be very sorry indeed to see the Library broken up, or Abbotsford in any way altered from its present state, and therefore if you chuse, I would rather that a valuation was put upon the Books, pictures, Cabinets, arms, curiosities &c so as to enable me by paying down the sum at which the valuation is made to retain them.' Walter, 1 January 1831, Walpole. Scott asked his son to pay only £5000 in all, although the value was nearer £10,000.
3. The arrangement proposed in these two sentences is this: when Scott's works have cleared the main debt for the Trustees they will become his property again and he will apply the first £10,000 of future profits to paying off the debt with which Abbotsford is encumbered (his only remaining debt), then divide the literary property between Sophia, Charles, and Anne. Walter, of course, will have Abbotsford.

8 SATURDAY Spent much time in writing instruction for trying[1] will an[d] testament. Sent off my parcel by Dr. Milne who leaves to-day. Have up two boys for shop lifting. Remain at Galashiels till four o'clock and return starved. Could work none and was idle all evening; try tomorrow for a work day, so loiter on

9 SUNDAY Went over to Galashiels and was busied the whole time till 3 o'clock about a petty thieving affair and had before me a pair of gallows birds to whom I could say nothing for total want of proof except like the sapient Elbow, thou shalt continue, thou knave thou, thou shalt continue.[2] A little gallow brood they were and their fate will catch it. Sleepy idle and exhausted in the [evening]. Wrought little or none in the evening.

10 MONDAY Wrote a long letter to Henry[3] who is a fine fellow and what I call a Heart of gold. He has sound peart[s], good sense, and [is] a true man. Also I wrote to my excellent friend the Lord Chief.[4] – I thought it right to say that I accepted with gratitude his majesty's goodness but trusted it was not to bind me to keep my fingers from pen and ink should a notion impress me that I could help the country – I walked a little to my exceeding refreshment.[5] That I am using that family ungratefully. But I will not for a punctilio avoid binding if I can a strong party together for the King and country, and if I see I can do any thing or have a chance of it I will not fear for the skin-cutting. It is the selfishness of this generation that drives me mad.

> A hundred pounds?
> Ha thou hast touchd me nearly.[6]

I will get a parcel copy tomorrow. Wrote several letters at night.

11 TUESDAY Wrote and sent off about 3 of my own pages tomorrow then walked with Swanston. Anne confined to her bedroom by a blister. I tried to write before dinner but with drowsiness and pain in

1. Probably 'drawing' is intended. Cadell received Scott's instructions on the 11th and transmitted 'the Draft of the deed' drawn up by Mr. Wood; W. S., on the 20th. Cadell, 20 January 1831, Walpole.
2. *Measure for Measure*, ii. 1.
3. Henry Scott of Harden. See the Entry for 6 January and note.
4. William Adam. See the Entries for 20 December 1830, 3 January 1831, and notes.
5. Robinson Crusoe's phrase, of which Scott was fond.
6. Sheridan's *Critic*, ii. 2.

my ha[n]ds made little way. My friend Will Laidlaw came in to dinner and after dinner kindly offerd his services as amanuensis. Too happy was I and I immediatly plunged him into the depth of *Count Robert* so we got on 3 or 4 pages, worth perhaps double the number of print. I hope it did not take him too short but after all to keep the press going without an amanuensis is impossible and the publishers may well pay a sponsible person.[1] He comes back tomorrow. It eases many of my anxieties and I will stick to it tomorrow before riding. I really think Mr. Laidlaw is pleased with the engagement for the time. Sent off six close pages.

12 WEDNESDAY I have a visit from Mr. MacDonald[2] the Sculptor who wishes to model a head of me. He is a gentleman like man and pleasant as most sculptors and artists of reputation are, yet it is an awful tax upon time. I must manage to dictate while he models which will do well enough.

So there we sate for thre[e] hours or four, I sitting on a stool mounted on a packing box for the greater advantage, McDonald modelling and plastering away and I dictating without interim to good natured Will Laidlaw who wrought withou[t] remission. It is natural to ask do I progress but this is too feverish a question. A man carries no scales about him to ascertain his own value. I always remember the prayer of virgil's sailor in extremity

> Non jam prima peto Mnestheus neque vincere certo.
> Quamquam O! sed superent quibus hoc, Neptune, dedisti.
> Extremos pudeat rediisse. Hoc vincite, cives,
> Et prohibete nefas. –[3]

We must to our oar, but I think this and another are all that even success would prompt me to write and surely those that have been my defenders

> Have they so long held out with me untired
> And stop they now for breath – Well. Be it so –[4]

1. He was paid '£10 or £10 10/- p Vol.'. Cadell's Diary.
2. Lawrence MacDonald, one of the founders of the British Academy of Arts in Rome, noted for his portrait busts.
3. 'I, Mnestheus, no longer seek first place, nor do I struggle to win; Although . . .! – but may they win, Neptune, to whom you have granted this prize. Let us be ashamed of coming in last. Do better than that, my friends, and avoid disgrace.' The prayer of Mnestheus when lying last in the boat race: *Aeneid*, v. 194–7.
4. *Richard III*, iv. 2.

13 THURSDAY Went to Selkirk on the business of the new High road. I perceive Whitebank and my cousin Col. Russell of Ashestiel are disposed to peep into the expences of our next year's outlay which must be provided by loan. This will probably breed strife. Wrote a hint of this to Charles Balfour Scott. Agreed with Smith[1] so far as contracting for the bridges[2] at the estimate of £1200 each. I suspect we are something like the good manager who distressd herself with buying barga[i]ns. Anne unwell and forced to keep her room which [is] ill timed as Mr. and Mrs. James are our guests.

15 SATURDAY Gave the morning from ten till near *two* to Mr. Macdonald who is proceeding admirably with his bust. It is bloody cold work but he is an enthusiast and much interest[ed]; besides I can sit and dictate away to Mr. Laidlaw and so get forward while I am advancing Lorenzo di Guasca which is his travelling name. I wrote several letters too and got through some business. Walked and took some exercize between one and three and visited Anne who is not so well as I could wish her. I have Mr. MacDonald and the James's male and female for the evening.

16 SUNDAY Being sunday read prayers. Mr. and Mrs. James go to look for a house which they desire to take in this country.[3] As Ann is still ill the presence of strangers though these are pleasant is rather annoying. MacDonald the sculptor continues working to form a new bust out of my old scalp. I think it will be the last sitting which I will be enticed to. I am made to sit on an old packing case in extreme cold. But in mitigation I am allowd to dictate to Mr. Laidlaw. Thank heaven the work finishes tomorrow.

17 MONDAY This morning when I came downstairs I found Mr. Macdonald or as the Italians calld him Lorenzo di Guasca slabbering away at the model. He has certainly great enthusiasm about his profession which is a *sine qua non*. It was [not] till 12 that a post-chaise carried off my three friends. I had wrote two hours when Dr. Turner, Mrs. Scott of Harden's [physician] came in and I had to take him to see my [daughter] and unfold my own complaints. I was sick of these interruptions and di[s]missd Mr. Laidlaw, having no hope of

1. John Smith of Darnick, who had built the second portion of Abbotsford.
2. The new road required bridges over the rivers Tweed and Ettrick about two miles above Abbotsford.
3. William Scott having now taken possession of Lessudden, they were able to rent Maxpoffle from him.

resuming my theme with spirit. God send me more leisure and fewer friends to pick it away by tea spoonfulls.

Another fool sends to [entreat] an autograph which he should be ashamed in civility to ask as I am to deny. I got notice of poor Henry Mackenzie's death. He has long maintaind a niche in Scottish literature, gayest of the gay though most sensitive of the sentimental.

18[1] TUESDAY Came down from my bedroom at eight and took a rummage in the way of putting things to rights. Receivd a letter from William Scott, a natural son of my brother Daniel's.[2] Living poor enough from his not having advised any friend where he was. He is a dour temperd boy (He did not borrow that quality) but I think well principled. I will write to Dr. Milne in his favour. The foolish lad might have been well enough off by this time had he been pleased to let any one know where he is. Lord Dalhousie at my request wrote in his favour to Sir Thomas Kemp.[3] But I fear the letter is lost.

Dictated to Laidlaw till about one o'clock during which time it was rainy. Afterwards I walkd sliding about in the mud and very uncomfortable. In fact there is no mistaking the three sufficients[4] and fate is now straitening its circumvallat[io]ns and [I] am little likely to be better than I am. I am heart whole as a biscuit[5] and may last on as now for eight or ten years; the thing is not uncommon considering I am only in my sixtieth year. I cannot walk but the intense cold weather may be to blame in this. My riding is but a squire scramble but it may do well enough for exercise and though it is unpleasant to find one's enjoyment of hill and vale so much abridged yet still while I enjoy my books and am without acute pain I have but little to complain of considering the life I have led.

So hap what may
Time and the hour run through the roughest day.[6]

18 TUESDAY Mr. Laidlaw came down at ten and we wro[u]ght till one. This should be a good thing for an excellent man and is an

1. Two Entries are dated '18'. See Appendix E, vii, p. 829 for a possible explanation.
2. See the Entry for 29 June 1826 and note.
3. Lt.-Gen. Sir James Kempt, Governor of Nova Scotia until 1828.
4. Lockhart traced the allusion to Mrs. Piozzi's poem 'The Three Warnings'.
5. Commodore Trunnion's phrase, a favourite of Scott's, from Smollett's *Peregrine Pickle*.
6. *Macbeth*, i. 3.

important one to me as it saves both my eyesight and nerves, which last are cruelly affect[ed] by finding those who look out of the windows grow gradually darker and dark[er].[1] Rode out or more properly was carried out into the woods to see the course of a new road which may serve to carry off the thin[n]ings of the trees and for rides. It is very well lined and will serve both for beauty and convenience. Mr. Laidlaw engages to come back to dinne[r] and finish two or three more pages. Met my agreeable and lady-like neighbour Mrs. Brewster on my pony and I was actually ashame[d] to be seen by her.

Sir dennis Brand and on so poor a steed![2]

I believe detestable folly of this kind is the very last that leaves us. One would have thought I ought to have little vanity at this time o' day. But it is an abiding appurtenance of the old Adam and I write for penance what like a fool I actually felt.

19 WEDNESDAY Wrote on by Mr. Laidlaw's assistance. Things go bobbishly enough; we have a good deal finishd before dinner. Henry Scott comes to dine with me *vis à vis* and we have a grand dish of politics. The friends of Old Scotland want but a signal. A certain great lawyer says that if Sir W. S. wrote another *Malachi* it would set more men on fire than a dozen associations. This almost tempts me. But the canny lad says moreover that to appeal to national partiality, i.e. that you should call on Scotsmen to act like Scotsmen, is unfair and he would be sorry it was known he, late and future place man, should encourage such paw paw doings. Yet if Sir W. S. could be got to stand forlorn Hope,[3] the legal gentleman would suggest etc. etc. Suggest and be damnd? Sir W. S. k[n]ows when to [doff] his bonnet and when to cock [it] in the face of all and sundry. Moreover he will not be made a catspaw of, look you now.[4]

20 THURSDAY Wrought all morning; a monstrous packet of letters at mid day. Borrow honest Laidlaw's fingers in the evening. I hope his pay will recompense him. It is better than grieving[5] or playing

1. An allusion to Ecclesiastes 12: 3.
2. Crabbe's *Borough*, Letter xiii, l. 199.
3. The capital letter suggests that 'A certain great lawyer' can be identified as the former Solicitor-General and future Justice-Clerk, John Hope.
4. A reminiscence of Fluellen or Sir Hugh Evans.
5. i.e., being a grieve or estate-manager.

Triptolemus.[1] Should be if I am hardworking 100 guineas, which with his house, cow and hive rent would save I believe some painful thoughts to him and his amiable wife and children. We will see how the matter fadges. Almost finishd the 1st volume.

21 FRIDAY James Ballantyne in extacies at our plan of an amanuensis. I myself am sensible that my fingers began to stammer, that is to write one word instead of another very often. I impute this to fancy, the terrible agency of which is too visible in my illness, and it encourages me to hope the fatal warning is yet deferrd. I feel lighter by a million ton since I made this discovery. If I can dictate fre[e]ly and without hesitation my fear to speak at the meeting about the road was vain terror and so *Andiamos Caracco!* Wrote some letters this afternoon.

22 SATURDAY Mr. Laidlaw rather late of coming: One of his daughters has been ill and he is an approved physician. Pity when one so gifted employs his skill on himself and family for all patients. We got on however to p. 46.

23 SUNDAY I wrought a little to-day. Walkd to Chiefswood or rather from it as far only as Habbie's How. Came home cold indeed but hearty, slept after dinner. I think the peep real or imaginary at the gates of death has given me firmness not to mind little aflictions. I have jumbled this and the preceding day strangely when I went to Chiefswood and Huntley Burn. I thought this a workday.[2]

24 MONDAY Workd with Mr. Laidlaw and as the snow was on the ground did so without intermission which must be sinking to the spirits. Held on however.

25 TUESDAY Same dazzling waste rendering my footing insecure and leaving me no refuge but in sitting at home and working till one o'clock. The[n] retired upon the Sheriff court processes. Poor Bran,[3] poor fellow, lies yawning at my feet and cannot think what is become of the daily scamper which is all his master's inabi[li]ty affords him. This grieves me by calling back the days of old. But I may call them as I may

Youth winna return nor the days of Lang Syne.[4]

1. The rural economist in *The Pirate*.
2. Scott did not ask Laidlaw to work for him on Sunday. See the Entries for 12 and 27 February 1831.
3. The deerhound given him by Cluny Macpherson.
4. 'The Days o' Lang Syne', perhaps by Susanna Blamire, *Caledonian Musical Repository*, 1806, p. 210.

26 WEDNESDAY Mr. Macculloch of Ardwall came here on the melancholy business of surrender of his effects to his Crers in a *cessio bonorum.*[1] I have now Skene[2] and him to the relief of my spirits and the diminishing of my time. Mr. Laidlaw joind us at dinner. At night I took some stronger medicine than I had been used to which continued its effects on me almost the whole night – Bitter cold.

27 THURSDAY So fagd by my frozen vigils that I slept till after ten. When I lose the first two hours in the morning I can seldom catch them again during the whole day. A friendly visit from Ebenezer Clarkson of Selkirk, a medical gentleman in whose experience and ingenuity I have much confidence as well as his personal regard to myself. He is quite sensible of the hesitation of speech of which I complain and thinks it arises from the stomach. Recommends the wild mustard as an aperient. But the brightest ray of hope is the chance that I may get some mechanical aid made by Fortune at Broughton Street[3] which may enable me to mount a pony with ease and to walk without torture. This would indeed be almost a restoration of my youth, at least of a green old age full of enjoyment – the shutting one out from the face of living nature is almost worse than sudden death.

28 FRIDAY I wrote with Laidlaw. It does not work clear, I do [not] know why. The plot is nevertheless a good plot and full of expectation.[4] But there is a cloud over me I think and interruptions are frequent. I creep on however.

29 SATURDAY Much in the same way as yesterday rather feeling than making way. Mr. Williams and his brother came in after dinner, wellcome both. Yet the day was not happy; it consumed me an afternoon which though well employd and pleasantly had the disagreeable office of being kept from useful work.

1. See the Entry for 10 July 1830 and note. He had just spent a month in the Canongate Jail and was now about to declare himself bankrupt. Scott admired 'the practical philosophical [manner] with which he bore his misfortun[e]s'. *Letters*, xi. 480. For the procedures concerning bankrupts at this time, see Introduction, p. xxxii.
2. Skene had been alarmed into a quick visit by the gloomy tone of Scott's letter to him about his will. Skene, 18 January 1831, Walpole.
3. 'Fortune, James, spine-machine, truss, and bandage-maker, artificial legs, &c. 29 Broughton Street.' *Edinburgh Post Office Directory.*
4. *1 Henry IV*, ii. 3.

30 SUNDAY Snow deep which makes me alter my purpose of going to town tomorrow – for to-day my friends must amuse themselves as the[y] can do to till.

31 MONDAY Retain my purpose however and set out for Edinburgh alone, that is no one but my servant.[1] The snow became impassable and in Edinburgh I remain immoveably fixd for ten days, that is till Wednesday, never once getting out of doors save to dinner when I went and returnd in a sedan chair.[2] I commenced my quarantine in Mackenzie's hotel[3] where I was deadly cold and tolerably noisy. The second day Mr. Cadell made a point of his coming to his excellent house where I had no less excellent an apartment and the most kind treatment, that is no making a show of me for which I was but in bad tune.[4] The physical folks Abercrombie and Ross bled me with cuppy glass, purged in conformity, and restricted me of all creature comforts.[5] But they did me good as I am sure they meant to do sincerely and I got rid of a giddy feeling which I have been plagued with and have certainly returned much better. I did not neglect my testamentary affairs. I executed my last will,[6] leaving Walter burdend by his own choice with £1000 to Sophia and another received at her marriage and £2000 to Anne and the same to Charles.[7] He is to advance them money if they want it, if not to pay them interest, which is his own choice otherwiser I would have sold the books and rattletraps. I have made provisions for clearing my estate by my

1. John Nicholson.
2. Sedan chairs lingered on in Edinburgh until after 1850. The stand at the junction of Castle Street and George Street was conveniently close to Mackenzie's Hotel.
3. Nos. 1 and 3 Castle Street.
4. Scott dined with Cadell on 1 February, and the following day was invited to stay at 16 Atholl Crescent. *Letters*, xi. 466. 'His host perceived that he was unfit for any company but the quietest, and had sometimes one old friend, Mr. Thomson, Mr. Clerk, or Mr. Skene, to dinner – but no more. He seemed glad to see them – but they all observed him with pain. He never took the lead in conversation, and often remained altogether silent.' *Life*, x. 36–7. Scott was grateful for Cadell's hospitality. 'Some German cases of liqueurs' (which he was now forbidden by his doctors) accompanied his letter of thanks. *Letters*, xi. 467.
5. All, that is, 'excepting two glasses of wine which I have barterd for half a weak glass of spirits and water as more natural to the animal'. *Letters*, xi. 471.
6. On 4 February, witnessed by Nicholson and deposited with Cadell. *Life*, x. 37.
7. For these provisions see the Entry for 7 January 1831 and note.

publications should it be possibl[e], and should that prove possible, from the time of such clearance being effected to be a fund available to all my childrey who shall be alive or leave representatives. My bequests must many of them seem hypothetical but the thing being uncertain must be so stated.

Besides during the unexpected stay in town I employd Mr. Fortune, an ingenious artist, to make a machine to assist my lame leg. An odd enough purchase to be made at this time of day. Yet who would not purchase ease? – I dined with Lord Chief Comr., with the Skenes twice, with Lord Medwyne, and was as happy as anxiety about my daughter would permit me.

The appearance of the streets was most desolate, the hackny coaches strolling about like ghosts with four horns, foot passengers few but the lowest of the people.

I wrote a good deal of *Count Robert*, yet I cannot tell why my pen stammers egregiously and I write horridly incorrcorect. I long to have friend Laidlaw's assistance.[1]

FEBRUARY

9 WEDNESDAY A heavey and most effective thaw coming on I got home about five at night here. I find the haugh coverd with water; dogs, pigs, cows, to say nothing [of] human beings, all who slept at the offices in danger of being drownd. They came up to the mansion house about midnight with such various clamour that Anne thought the House was attackd by Capt. Swing and all the Radicals.[2]

10 THURSDAY I set to work with Mr. Laidlaw and had after that a capital ride; my poney, little used, was [some] what frisky, but I rode on to Huntlyburn. Began my diet on my new regime and like it well, especially porridge to suppen.[3] It is wonderful how old tastes rise.

1. For Cadell's account of these days in Edinburgh, see note 12, p. 816.
2. Anne, 'having first lockd herself in her own room began ringing the bell to enquire who had possessd themselves of the rest of the premises.' *Letters*, xi. 473. 'Capt. Swing' was the name adopted by the authors of threatening letters during this period of riot and unrest.
3. The diet allowed him to eat 'broth & pudding three days in the week – fish or a bit of meat, one glass of wine, and see nobody at dinner on any accompt'. *Letters*, xi. 466. 'I . . . sup on porridge and milk', he tells Lockhart, 'which I got them to allow me instead of sago or some such slop.' *Letters*, xi. 471.

11 FRIDAY Wrought again to day and John Swanston walkd with me,[1] wrote many letters and s[e]nt copy to Ballantyne, rode as usual. It is well enough to ride every day but confounded tiresome to write it down.

12 SATURDAY[2] I did not ask down Mr. Laidlaw thinking it fair to spare his Sunday. I had a day of putting to rights, a disagreeable work which must be done. We agreed too that Anne should go to Edinburgh about her throat. I took the occasion to tell Mr. Cadell that Malachi will break forth again but I will not make a point of it with him.

13 SUNDAY I do not fear there will be as many to strike up as to strike Down and I have a strong notion we may gain the day.[3] I have a letter from the Duchess of Wellington asking a copy of Mellville's *Memoirs*. She shall have it if it is my last.[4]

14 MONDAY I had hardly begun my letter to Mr. Cadell than I began also to 'pull in resolution'.[5] I considerd that I had no means of retreat and that in all my sober moments, meaning my unpassionate ones for the Doctors have taken from me the means of producing Dutch courage, I have lookd on political writing as a false step and especially now when I have a good deal at Stake. So upon the whole I took the parcel from Anne and cancelld the letter announcing the publication. If this was actually meanness it is a foible nobody knows of.

Anne set off for Edinburgh after breakfast. Poor girl, She is very nervous. I wrote with Mr. L— till one, then had a walk till three, then wrote this diary till four.

Must try to get some thing for Mr. Laidlaw for I am afraid I am twaddling. I do not think that my head is weakend but a strang[e] vacillation makes me suspect. Is it not thus that men begin to fail, becoming as it were infirm of purpose?[6]

1. 'I contrive to get hoisted on a quiet pony and for greater security have John Swanston to attend me on foot.' *Letters*, xi. 472.
2. If Scott's date, the 12th, is correct, this is the Entry for Saturday. See Appendix E, viii, p. 829.
3. Scott is thinking again of the Second Reform Bill, introduced by Lord John Russell on 1 March.
4. It was. He could not lay hands on a copy and to her delight sent her his own. She acquired another in London and sent him that in exchange. Duchess of Wellington 23 February and 1 April 1831, Walpole.
5. *Macbeth*, v. 5.
6. ibid.

> – that way madness lies let me shun that
> No more of that –[1]

Yet why be a child about it? What must be will be.

15 TUESDAY I wrote and corrected thorough the long day till one o'clock then rode out as far as Dr. Scott's and calld on him. Got a fresh doze of proofs at Matheson's and returnd home. At nine o'clock at night had a Card from Miss Bell wishing to speak to me about some highland music. Wrought for answer I knew nothing of the matter but would be happy to see Mrs. and Miss Bell to breakfast. I had a letter of introduction by Robert Chambers which I declined being then unwell.[2] But as Trotter of Braid said 'The Ladies maun come.'

16 WEDNESDAY Mrs. Bell and Miss Bell Maclachlane of the west highlands, mother and daughter, made their way to me to breakfast. I did not wish to see them being strangers but she was very pretty, that is the daughter, and enthusiastic and that is always flattering to an old gentleman. She wishes to have word to Celtick melodies and I have promised her some to the Air of 'Crochallan' and incline to do her good perhaps to the extent of getting her words from Lord Francis Leveson gower, Lockhart and one or two others.[3] We parted, she pleased with my willing patronage and I with [the] uncommon handsome countenance she Shewd me.

This detaind Mr. Laidlaw *re infecta*[4] and before I had written a page the poney came to the door but wrote some thing after dinner.

17 THURSDAY We had the usual course of study exercise and food in the forenoon, was extremely sleepy in the afternoon which made I fear but bad work; we progress however.

1. *King Lear*, iii. 4.
2. Miss Bell McLauchlan of Lochgilphead had sent a copy of her *Celtic Melodies* the previous June. Purdie, 5 June 1830, Disc. ii. 76. Chambers had written on 7 February and Scott's letter deferring the visit came too late. 'I regret much', Chambers writes on 1 March, 'that, like the duckling which quacked as the Irishman swallowed it under the impression that it was an egg, you were "a little too long a-spaking", and so Miss Maclauchlan had taken silence for an invitation, and gone to inflict a visit upon you.' Walpole.
3. Scott promised her an English version of the Gaelic 'Argyll's Fold or Colin's Cattle' (MacLauchlan, 10 March 1831, Walpole) and he did ask Lockhart for assistance: 'I like pretty admirers and always endeavour to help.' *Letters*, xi. 472.
4. 'With nothing done'.

18 FRIDAY In riding met Sir Adam Fergusson and askd him and his brother the Colonel to dinner tomorrow. Wrote in mean time as usual.

19 SATURDAY Plagued by the stay for leg starting a screw bolt which is very inconvenient.[1] Sent off this morning proofs as far as end of 1s[t] Volume and twenty manuscript pages equal to about a quarter of the second. Is it good or not? I cannot say. I think it betterns as it goes on and so far so good. I am certain I have written worse abomination, as John Ballantyne, poor fellow, used to say. I had a demand from Sa[n]die of a balance of £300 owing to him which he must have at Whitsunday. Mr. Cadell must help me, that is flat.[2] If the Count goes forward well he will not hesitate and I do not think he flags.

20 SUNDAY Wrote five pages this morning then road out to the Hill and lookd at some new planted, rather transplanted, trees. Mr. Laidlaw gone for the day. I trust I shall have proofs to correct. In the mean time I may suck my paws and prepare some copy or rather assemble the raw material.

21 MONDAY A letter from Anne postponing her return till tuesday and saying she thinks it for the best; pray God it may. Sent on a parcel this morning by coach and r[e]ceive answer from Mr. Lang, Sheriff Clerk. All right. I was somewhat afraid that a Bank receipt with £50 subscription to the Bridges[3] might have miscarried. But all is right. I made up parcels for Edinburgh by Mailcoach and by Blucher to go tomorrow 2d volume *Redgauntlet*.[4] At one fetched a walk through wet and dry looking at the ravages of the late flood. After I came in till two hours after teatime busied with the Sheriff court processes which I have nearly finishd. After this I will lounge one with annotating. The *Tales of the Crusades* come next.

22 TUESDAY Wrought with Mr. L. from ten to three then took the pony carriage with the purpose of going to Chiefswood, but a heavy squall came on with snow so we put about ship and returnd. Read Littelton's *History of England*[5] to get some notes for *Crusaders* vol. I. After dinner Mr. Laidlaw from six to eight: sent off six pages.

1. The stay turned out to be 'what Wordsworth calls somewhat between a hindrance and a help'. *Letters*, xi. 472.
2. Of course he did. Scott's letter of thanks is in *Letters*, xi. 475.
3. To help pay for the bridges over the Tweed and Ettrick required for the new road.
4. That is, notes on *Redgauntlet* for the Magnum.
5. George, first Baron Lyttleton's *History of the Life of Henry the Second*, 1767–71.

23 WEDNESDAY, 24 THURSDAY, 25 FRIDAY These three days I can hardly be said to have varied from my ordinary for Action. Rose at 7, dressed before 8, wrote letters or did any little business till ¼ past nine. Then breakfast. Mr. Laidlaw comes from ten till one. Then take the pony and ride *quantum mutatus*[1] two or three miles, John Swanston walking by my bridle rein least I fall off. Come home about three or four. Then to dinner on a single plain dish and half a tumbler, or byr lady three fourths of a tumbler, of w[h]isky and water. Then sit till 6 o'clock when enter Mr. Laidlaw again and works commonly till eight; after this work usually alone till half past nine then work till half past nine, sup on porridge and milk and so to bed. The work is half done. If any asks what time I take to think on the composition I might say in one point of view it was seldom five minutes out of my head the whole day. In another light it was never the serious subject of consideration at all for it never occupied my thoughts entirely for five minutes together except when I was dictating to Mr. Laidlaw.

26 SATURDAY Went through the same routine, only being Saturday Mr. L. does not come in the evening. I think there is truth in the well known phrase *Aurora musis Amica*.[2] I always have a visit of Invention between six and seve[n], that is if any thing has been plaguing in the way of explanation I find it in my head when I wake between six and seven. I have need of it tonight.

27 SUNDAY Being Saturday no Mr. Laidlaw came yesterday evening nor to-day being sunday. Truth is I began to fear I was working too hard and gave myself to putting things in order and working at the magnum and reading stupid German novels in hopes a thought will strike me when I am half occupied with other things. In fact I am like the servante in the *Clandestine Marriage* who assures her mistress She always watches best with her eyes shut.[3]

28 MONDAY Past ten and Mr. Laidlaw, the model of [a] Clerk in other respects, is not come yet. He has never known the value of time so is not quite accurate in punctualality but that I hope will come if I can drill him to it without hurting him.[4] I think I hear him coming. I

1. 'How changed'. Virgil's *Aeneid*, ii. 274.
2. 'Dawn, friend to the Muses'.
3. Colman and Garrick's *Clandestine Marriage*, v. 1.
4. Scott did not succeed. On 23 August 1831 he writes to Cadell, 'I begin to find Mr. Laidlaw has too little the habits of exactness and punctuality for an amanuensis. He leaves me whole mornings alone which may do once or twice but is a cruel drag on my proceedings.' Cadell Letters.

am like the poor wizzard who is first puzzled how to raise the Devil and then how to employ him. But *vogue la galère*. Worked till one then walkd with great difficulty and pain till half past two. I think I can hardly stir without my poney which is a sad job. Mr. Laidlaw dines here.

MARCH

1 TUESDAY, 2 WEDNESDAY, 3 THURSDAY All these thre[e] days I wrote afternoon and faggd forenoon. Kept up the ball indifferent well but began to tire on the third and suspected that I was flat – a dreary suspicion not easily chase[d] away when once it takes root.

4 FRIDAY Laid aside the novel and began with vigour a review of Robson['s] sad *State of Heraldry*.[1] But I missd some quotations which I could not get on without. I gave up and took such a ride [as I can] now adays, returnd home and found Colonel Russell there on a visit. Then we had dinner and afterwards the making up this miserable journal – Resolved for Bowhill this morning next coming.

5 SATURDAY I have a letter from our Member Whitebank[2] adjuring me to assist the gentlemen of the County with an address against the Reform Bill which menaces them with being blended with Peebles Shire and losing of consequence one half of their franchise. Mr. Pringle conjures me not to be very nice in chusing my epithets. Mr. Pringle, Torwoodlee, comes over and speaks to the same purpose adding it will be the greatest service I can do the county, etc. This in a manner drives me out of a resolution to keep Myself clear of politics and let them fight dog fight bear. But I am too easy to be persuaded to bear a hand. The young Duke of Buccleuch comes to visit me also. So I promise to shake my duds and give them a cast of my calling, fall back fall edge.

7 MONDAY, 8 TUESDAY, 9 WEDNESDAY, 10 THURSDAY In these four days I drew with anxiety an Address exprobatory of the bill both with respect to Selkirkshire and in its general purport. I was not mealy mouth[d] and those who heard the beginning could hardly avoid listening to the end. It was certainly in my best stile and would have

---

1. Thomas Robson's *The British Herald*, 1830, which was dedicated to Scott. The review was never published, although there is a galley-proof in the National Library of Scotland.
2. Alexander Pringle of Whytbank who had succeeded W. Elliot-Lockhart of Borthwickbrae as M. P. for Selkirkshire.

made a deal of noise. From the uncompromising stile it would have attracted attention. Mr. Laidlaw, though he is Master t'other side on the subject, thinks it the best thing I ever wrote and I myself am happy to find that it cannot be said to smell of the apoplexy; the pointed passages were on the contrary clever and well put. But it was too declamatory, too much like a pamp[h]let, and went far too generally into opposition to please the country gentlemen who are timidly inclin[ed] to dwell on their own grievances rather [than] the publick wrongs.

11 FRIDAY This day we had our meeting at Selkirk. I found Borthwickbrae (late member) had sent the form of an address which was finishd by Mr. Andrew Lang. It was the reverse of mine in every respect. It was short and to the point. It only containd a rem-onst[r]ance against the incorporation with Selkirkshire[1] and left it to be inferd that they approved the Bill in other respects. As I saw that it made[2] the ideas of the meeting (six in number) better by far than such an address as mine I instantly put it in my pocket. But I endeavourd to add to their complaint of a private wrong a general clause stating their sense of the hazard of passing a bill full of such violent innovations at once on the public. But though Harden, Alva and Torwoodlee voted for this measure it was refused by the rest of the meeting to my disappointment, since in its present state [it] will not be attended to and is in fact too milk and water to attract notice. I am however personally out of the scrape unless some gentle [men of the press lay hold of this].

I was a fool to stir such a mess of skimd milk with so honourable an action.[3] If some of [the] gentlemen of the press whose livelihood is lying had hold of this story what would they make of it? And how little would I care. One thing is clear. It gives me a right to disclaim future interference and let the world wag, Sessa.[4]

12 SATURDAY Wrote the history of my four days' Labour in vain to Sandie Pringle, Whitebank, and so *transeat* with *cæteris erroribus*.[5] I only gave way to one jest. A ratcatcher was desirous to come to complet[e] his labours in my house and I who thought he only talkd and laughed with the servants recommended to him to go to the head courts and meetings of freeholders where he would find rats in plenty.

1. A slip for 'Peeblesshire'.
2. Probably a slip for 'met'.
3. *1 Henry IV*, ii. 3.
4. *Taming of the Shrew*, Induction.
5. 'Let it pass with the rest of my mistakes.'

13 SUNDAY I have finally arranged a thorny transaction. Mr. Cadell has an interest<ing> amounting to an half. But after these there come the ffollowing set of novels which are entirely my own

Saint Ronan's well	3 volumes
Tales of Crusaders	4 volumes
1st *Chronicles* ————	2
Anne of Geiersn.	3
Red Gauntlet	3
Woodstock————————3	
2 *Chronicles*————————3	
Count Robert	3

In all 24 volumes which begin printing which will begin printing after *Quentin Durward* which concludes the year 1831. For half the property he proposes to pay six thousand guineas on 2d february 1831.[1] I think that with this sum and others coming in I may reduce the debt to £45,000.

But I do not see clearly enough through this affair to accept this offer. I. I cannot see that there is wisdom in engaging Mr. Cadell in deep speculations <which> unless they served him very much. I am in this respect a burnd child and I have not forgotten the fire or rather the furnace. II. I think the property worth more if publickly sold. III I cannot see any reasons which should render it advantageous for me to sell one half of this property it being admitted at the same [time] highly judicious to keep the other half, this does not fadge. IV us to the immediate command of the money I am not pressd for it nor having any advantage by paying it a year or two sooner or lat<t>er. The actual proceeds of the sales will come in about 1834 and I dare say will not be far behind in amount the sum of £6000.

In short I will not sell on a rainy day as our proverb says. I have communicated my resolution to Cadell to whom no doubt it will be a disappointment, for which I am sorry but cannot help it.

14 MONDAY Had a very sensible and goodhumourd answer from Mr. Cadell readily submitting to my decision. He mentions what I am conscious of, the great ease of accompting if the whole is divided into two halves. But this not an advantage to me but to them who keep the books and therefore I cannot be moved by it. It is the great advantage of uniformity of which Malachi Malagrowther tells so much. I do not fear that Mr. Cadell will neglect the concern because he has not the large share in it which he had in the other. He is I think

1. A slip for 1832.

too honest a man. He has always shown himself every way willing and ready to help me and verily he hath his reward, and I can afford him on that property a handsome percentage for the management. But if his fate was to lose considerably by this transaction I must necessarily be a sufferer, if he be a great gainer it is at my expence, so it is like the children['s] game of Oddo I win Evens you lose. So will say no more about it.[1] I think I will keep my ground nearly so these cursed politicks do not ruin the country. I am unable to sit at good men's boards and Anne has gone to Mertoun to-day without me. I cannot walk or ride but for a mile or two. Naboclish! never mind. I am satisfied that I am heart whole as a biscuit and may live to see the end of these affairs yet. I am driving on the *Count of Paris* right mer[r]ily. I have plenty of leisure and *vive la plume*. I have arranged [the] matter as I think for the best so will think no more about it.

15[2] TUESDAY The affair with Mr. Cadell being settled I have only to arrange a set of regular emploolyement for my time without over fatiguing myself. What I at present practice seems active enough for my capacity and even if I should reach the threescore and ten from which I am thrice three years distant or nearer ten, the tim[e] may pass honorably usefully and profitably both to myself and other people. My ordinary for Action runs thus. Rise at a quarter before seven. At quarter after nine breakfast, with eggs, or in the singular number, at least. Before breakfast private letters etc. After breakfast Mr. Laidlaw comes at ten and we write together till one. I am greatly helpd up by this excellen[t] man who takes pains to write a good hand and supplies the want of my own fingers as far as another person's can. We work seriously at the task of the day till one o'clock when I sometimes walk, not often however, having faild in strength and suffering great pain even from a very short walk. Oftener I take the pony for an hour or two and ride about the doors. The exercize is humbling enough for I require to [be] lifted on horseback by two servants and one goes [with] me to take care I do not fall off and break

1. Scott's reasoning is perfectly sound. Nonetheless when Cadell raised his offer from £6300 to £10,000 in July, Scott agreed to sell him a half-share in the novels listed in the Entry for 13 March. Sederunt Book, ii. 232–3. Although ultimately Cadell benefited, he was taking a considerable risk by offering a lump sum at an early date in return for profits which were uncertain and spread over many years. For Cadell's earlier attempt to buy this share of the copyrights, see the Entry for 5 September 1830.
2. Scott dated this '16' instead of '15' and was one day out for the next five Entries also. They have been redated here. See Appendix E, ix, p. 830.

my bones, a catastrophé very like to happen. My proud promenade, *à pied or à cheval* as it happens, concludes by three o'clock. An hour intervenes for making up my journal and such light work. At four comes dinner, a plate of broth or soup much condemnd by the doctors, a bit of plain meat, no liquor stronger than small beer, and so I sitt quiet till six o'clock when Mr. Laidlaw returns and remains with me till nine or three Quarters past, as it happens. Then I have a bowl of porridge and milk which I eat with [the] appetite of a child. I forgot to say that after dinner I am allowd half a glass of whisky or gin made into weak grog. I never wish for any more. Nor do [I] in my secret soul long for a cigar though once so fond of them. About six hours per day is good working if I can keep at it.

16 WEDNESDAY Little of this day but that it was so [un]commonly windy that I was almost blown off my poney and was glad to grasp the mane to prevent it's actually happen[ing]. Rode round by Briggends. I began the 3 volume of *Count Robert of Paris* which has been on the anvil during all these vexatious circumstances of politics and health. But the blue heaven bends over all. It may be ended in a fortnight if I keep my scheme. But I will take time enough. This would be on Thursday. I would like it much.

17 THURSDAY We get well on. *Count Robert* is finishd so far as the second goes and some twenty of the third. *Blackwood's Magazine* after long bedaubing me with compliment has begun to bedaub Lockhart for my sake or perhaps me for Lockhart's sake with abuse; for two or three numbers he has opend his fire or rather leveld his long gun with a *posse tirare* supposing that [I] should deprecate further hostilities – he be damnd. He is by inclination and habits what others are by education and necessity, a thorough going gen[t]leman of the press without shame or ju[d]gement. As a politici[a]n he puts one in mind of Barm Jock of other days, a kind of blustering idiot whom a mob carried upon their shoulders during a riot rather as their banner than banner-man. But Barm Jock proved before judge and Jury that he was mortal drunk the whole time. Notwithstanding his low propensities John Wilson is a clever feller or more he is a man of genius or rather

A hare braind Hotspur guided by a whim[1]

only it is not always an honorable one. Lockhart's chiefs offence seems to have been explaining the humbug of shewing up Hogg as a fool and

1. *1 Henry IV*, v. 2.

blackguard in what the[y] call the *Noctes*.[1] For me I care wonderfully little eith[er] for his flattery or his abuse. I have tried to be of use to him which piece of folly may be a very good reason for attacking me.

18 FRIDAY I made a hard working day almost equal to twenty pages. But there was some reason for it for Ballantyne writes me that the copy sent will not exceed 265 pages when the end of vol II is markd so 45 more pages must be furnishd to run it out to pages 329. This is an awful cast back. So the gap is to be made up.

19 SATURDAY I thought I was done with politics but it is easy getting into the mess and difficult and sometimes di[s]graceful to get out. I have a letter from Sheriff Oliver desiring me to go on Monday[2] (tomorrow) and shew countenance by adhering to a set of propositions being a resolution. Tho' not well drawn they are un-comprom[i]zing enough so I will not part company. Had a letter too from Henry Scott. He still expects to refuse the Bill. I wrote him that would but postpone the evil day unless they could bring forward a strong administration and what is most essential a system of financence, otherwise it won't do. Henry has also applied to me for the rejected address.[3] But this I shall decline.

21 MONDAY Went over to-day at nine o'clock to the meeting;[4] a great number present with a tribune full of Reformers who shewd their sense of propri[e]ty by hissing hooting and making all sort of noises. And these unwashd artificers are from henceforth are to select our legislators. What can be expected from [them] except such a thick headed plebian [as] will be a hare-braind Hotspur guided by a whim. There was some speaking but not good. I said something[5] for I could not sit quiet.

1. The *Noctes Ambrosianae* were conversation-pieces in Scots between Christopher North and the Ettrick Shepherd (Professor John Wilson and James Hogg) and they were not devoid of personal satire. The article to which Scott objects, however, analyses his *Demonology* and quite legitimately finds fault with it for its self-contradictions and the repetitious clumsiness of its style. Lockhart's offence was to have described Hogg as a 'boozing buffoon'. See *Blackwood's Magazine*, nos. 175 and 178.
2. To Jedburgh, to a meeting at 1 p.m. Oliver, 18 March 1831, Walpole.
3. See the Entries for 10 and 11 March 1831.
4. The meeting was held on 21 March, which dates this Entry.
5. For this speech – 'delivered in a tone so low, and with such hesitation in utterance, that only a few detached passages were intelligible to the bulk of the audience' – see *Life*, x. 46.

We did not get home till about nine; have fasted the whole time. James,[1] the blockhead, lost my poor Spice a favourite terrier. The fool shut her in a stable and some body he says opend the door and let her out. I suspect she is lost for aye for she was carried to Jedburgh in a post chaise.[2]

25 FRIDAY[3] The measure[4] carried by a single vote. In other circumstances one would hope for the interference of the House of Lords but it is all Hab Nab at a venture, *De Donde Diere* as Cervantes says. The worst is that there is a popular party who want personal power and are highly unfitted to enjoy [it]. It has fallen easily the old Constitution, no bullying Mirabeau to assail, no eloquent Maury to defend. It has been thrown away like a child's broken Toy. Well *transeat*;[5] the good sense of the people is much trusted to; we will see what it will do for us.

The curse of Cromwell on those whose conceit brought us to this pass. *Sed transeat*. It is vain to mourn what cannot be mended.

24 THURSDAY Frank Grant and his Lady came here. Frank Grant and his wife. Charles[6] will I believe and if he attends to his profession be one of the celebrated men of the age. He [is] well known to me as the companion of my sons and the partner of my daughters. In youth, that is extreme youth, he was passionately fond of fox hunting and other sports but not of any species of gambling. He had also a strong passion for painting and made a little collection. As he had sense enough to feel that a younger brother's fortune would not last long under the expences of a good stud and a rare collection of Chef d'Oeuvres, he used to avow his intention to spend his patrimony, about £10,000, and then again to make his fortune by the law. The first he soon accomplishd. But the Law is not a profession so easily acquired nor did Frank's talents lie in that direction. His passion for paintings turnd out better. Nature had given him the rare power of judging soundly of painting and in a remarkable degree the power of imitating it. Connoisseurs approved of his sketches both in pencil and oils but not without the sort of criticisms made on these occasions,

1. Dr. Corson suggests that this is his servant James Jameson, who shoed the horses.
2. A letter of the 24th, however, reports 'that she is recoverd'. *Letters*, xi. 494.
3. For the dating of this Entry see Appendix E, ix, p. 736.
4. The Second Reform Bill.
5. 'Let it go.'
6. A slip for 'Frank'.

that they were admirable as an amateur but it could not be expected that he should submit to the technical drudgery absolutely necessary for a profession, and all that species of criticism which gives way before natural genius and energy of character.

Mean time Frank Grant who was remarkably handsome and very much the man of fashion married a young lady with many possibilities as Sir Hugh Evans says.[1] She was eldest sister of Farq[u]h[a]rson of Invercau[l]d chief of that Clan, and the young man himself having been almost paralyzed by the Malaria in Italy Frank's little boy by this match becomes Heir to the estate and Chieftainship. In[2] the mean time fate had another chance for him in the matrimonial line. At Melton Mowbray during the hunting season he had become acquainted (even before his first marriage) with a niece of the Duke of Rutland, a beautiful and fashionable young woman[3] with whom he was now thrown into company once more. It was a natural consequence that they should marry. The lady had not much wealth but excellent connections in society to whom Grant's good looks and good breeding made him very acceptable.

In the mean time Frank saw the necessity of doing something to keep himself independent, having I think too much spirit to become a Stulko drinking out the last glass of the bottle, riding the horses which the Laird wishes to sell and drawing sketches to amuse my lady and the children, besides a prospect on Invercauld elevating him when realized to the rank of the Laird's father.

26 SATURDAY Grant was above all this and honorably and manfully resolved to cultivate<d> his taste for painting and become a prof[ess]ional artist. I am no judge of painting but I am conscious that Francis Grant possesses, with much taste, a sense of beauty derived from the best source, that of really good society, while in many modern artists the total disgusting want of that species of feeling is so great [as] to be revolting. His former acquaintances render his immediate entrance into business completely secure and it will rest with himself to carry on his success. He has I think that degree of ener[g]y and force of character which will make him keep

---

1. *Merry Wives of Windsor*, i. 1.
2. Previous editors started a new Entry with this word, dating it '25 March'. In fact the paragraph runs straight on and Scott's 'March 25' in the margin is accounted for by his usual practice of redating when he turns the page. If he was making up this Entry on the 25th, as seems likely (see Appendix E, ix), the mistake is easily accounted for.
3. Miss Norman, daughter of the Duke's elder sister.

and enlarge any character which he may inquire. He has confidence too in his own powers, always a requisite for a young painter whose aristocratic pretensions will be envied, must be envied, by the half bred mass who would fain see the field exclusivel[y] filld by such raff as they themselves.[1]

27 SUNDAY Frank Grant is still with me and is well pleased, I think very deservedly so, with a cabinet picture of myself, armour and so forth, together with my two noble Staghounds of the greyhound race. I wish Cadell had got it; [it] is far better than Watson[2] though his is well too. The dogs sate charmingly but the picture took up some time.

28 MONDAY We went out a little ride, the weather most tempting, the day beautiful. We rode and walkd a little.

29 TUESDAY We had an hour's sitting of the dogs and a good deal of success. I cannot compose my mind on this publick measure. I trust it will not please those whom it is the object to please.

30 WEDNESDAY Bob Dundas[3] and his wife Miss Durham that was came to spend a day or two. I was hear[t]ily glad to see him being my earliest an[d] best friend's [son]. John Swinton came by Blucher on the part of an anti reform meeting in Edinburnr who exhorted me to take up the pen, but I declined and pleaded health which God knows I have a right to urge. I might have urged almost the chance of my breaking down but that would be a cry of those kind which might very well prove real.

31 THURSDAY Swinton returnd in the forenoon yesterday after luncheon. He took denial qui[e]tly and ownd it would be wrong to press me. I have shared any thing that came fair on me but I do not see the sense of standing forth a champion. It is said that the Duke of Bukcleugh has been offerd the title of Monmouth if he would cease to oppose. He said there were two objections. They would not give it

1. Scott's high Tory views become more pronounced as he gets older and more ill. He still had the restraint, however, to delete the last sentence of the Entry: 'Most likely it will come to a civil war one day.'
2. Scott had sat to John Watson Gordon for Cadell the previous May. Grant's portrait was for Lady Ruthven. 26 March 1831, Disc. ii, 244.
3. The son of the Rt. Hon. Robert Dundas.

him if he seriously thought of it, and [he] would not take it if they did. The Dundasses went off to-day. I was glad I had seen them although visitors rather interrupt work.

APRIL

2 SATURDAY Mr. Henry Liddell, eldest son of Lord Ravensworth, arrivd here. I like him and his brother Tom very much although [they] are what may be termd fine men. Young McKenzie of Cromarty came with him, who is a fine lad and sings very beautifully. I knew his father and mother and was very glad to see him. They had been at Mertoun fishing salmon with little sport.

3 SUNDAY A letter from the Lord Chief Commissioner reporting Lor[d] Palmerston's and Sir Herbert Taylor['s] favourable letters in Charles' favour.[1] Wrote a grateful answer and resolved that as I have made my opinion publick at every place where I could be calld on or expected to appear I will not thrust myself forward when I have nothing to say. May [the] Lord have mercy on us and incline our hearts to keep this vow.

4 MONDAY Mr. Liddell and Hay Mackenzie left us this morning. Liddell shewd me yesterday a very good old fashiond poem worthy of Pope or Churchill in old fashiond hexameters, calld 'The Savoyard'. He has promised me a copy for it is still being printed. There are some characters very well drawn. The force of it belies the author's character of a Dandie too hastily ascribed to the author. He is accomplishd as an artist and musician and certainly has a fine taste for poetry though he may never cultivate [it]. He promises to bring his lady, who is very clever but pretty high they say in the temper, to spend a day or two with us after as she has been confined in Edinburgh.

5 TUESDAY This fift[h] day of April is the March fair at Selkirk. Almost every one of the family goes there, Mr. Laidlaw among others. I have a hideous paralytick custom of *stuttering* with my pen and cannot write without strange blunders yet I cannot find any failure in my intellect. Being unable to w[r]ite to purpose with my own hand This forenoon is a sort of holiday to me. The third volume of *Count Robert* is fairly begun but I fear I shall want stuff to fill it for I would not willingly bombast it with things inappropriate. If [only] I

---

1. Adam had offered to use his influence on behalf of Charles. See the Entries for 20 December 1830 and 3 January 1831.

could fix my mind to the task to-day. My temper notwithstanding my oath sets strong towards politics, where I would be sure of making a figure and feel I could carry with me a great part of the middling class who wait for a shot between wind and water, half comic half serious, which is a better argument than most which are going. The regard of my health is what chiefly keeps [me] in check; the provoking odium I should mind much less, for there will always be as many for as against me, but it would be a foolish thing to take flight to the next world in a political gale of wind. I[f] Cadell gave me the least encouragement I would give way to the temptation. Meantime I am tugging at the chain for very eagerness. I have done enough to in[c]ence people against me without perhaps doing so much as I could, would or should have done.

6 WEDNESDAY I have written to Alva and Lord Elgin explaining why I cannot as they encourage me to do take upon me the cause of the publick and bell the cat with the Reformers. I think I have done enough for an individual. I have more than half dictated the third volume to Mr. Laidlaw. But I feel the subject wants action and that a little repose will be very necessary. Resolve tomorrow shall be a resting day. I have not had one this long time. I had a letter from Croker advising a literary adventure – the personal history of Charles Edward.[1] I think it will do:

7 THURSDAY Methough[t] it will answer will answer will answer well. Croker thinks thinks it will answer well. Rode to Melrose and brought hom[e] the letters from the post office.

8 FRIDAY I sent Swanston last night to Melrose to purchase from Wat Ormston[2] if he can a break of transp[l]anted oaks, very fine seedlings, the Duke[3] not having sent me the acorns he promised. This is so fine and so dropping that if possible I will have them transplanted this morning which will be a great point gaind for Jane's wood and for the park planting next year. Also I took leave of poor Major John Scott who being aflicted with a distressing astmha has resolved upon selling his house of Ravenswood which he had dressd

---

1. 'I am in possession of five or six Manuscripts copies or large extracts taken under my own eyes. Croker thinks and I am of his opinion that if there was room for a personal narrative of the Chevalier it would answer admirably.' *Letters*, xii. 9.
2. Walter Ormiston, the nurseryman in Melrose, had died in 1818, but the business was still carried on by the family.
3. 'The Duke', in a local context, is usually the Duke of Buccleuch.

up with much neatness and going abroad to Jamaica. Without having been intimate friends we were always affectionate relations and now we part probably never to meet in this world. He has a good deal of the character said to belong to the family. Our parting with mutual feeling may be easily supposed.

9 SATURDAY This being Saturday I expect the Bibliopololist and typographer about two o'clock, I suppose, when I shall have much to journalize. Failuures among the trade are alarming yet not if we act with prudence. *Nous verrons.* Mr. Cadell and J. Ballantyne with the son of the latter. Their courage is much stouter than I apprehended. Cadell says he has lost £1000 by bad debts which is less than he expected by bad times coming on at this time [when] we have been obliged to publish the less popular part of the Waverley novels. At present I incline to draw a period after fo[r]ty eight volumes and to closing the publication. About nine or ten volumes will then conclude our Magnum opus so calld, an[d] Mr Cadell thinks we shall then beglin the Poetical works in twelve volumes with illustrations by Turner which he expects to rise as far as 12,000. The size is to be that of the Waverley novels.[1]

10 SUNDAY I had a letter from Mr. Cowan, trustee for Constable's creditors, telling that the manuscript[s] of the Wavely novels had been adjudged to him[2] and offering them to me or rather asking my advice about the disposal of them. Answerd that I considerd myself as swindled out of my property and therefore will give no consequent[3] to any sale of the pillage. Cadell says he is determined to get the Mss from Cowan. I told him I would give him the *rest* of the Mss, which are in my own hand, for Mr. Caddell has been very friendly to me in not suffering me to want money in difficult times. We are not pushd by our debtors[4] so can take our own time an[d] as our plans pro[s]per we can pay off debt. About two o'clock enter two gen[t]lemen in an open carragiage, both from Makerstoun and both captains in the

1. These plans were carried out. *The Waverley Novels*, new edition, *with the Author's Introductions and Notes*, 48 vols., 1829–33, was followed by *Poetical Works*, new edition, *with Introductions by the Author, and Additional Notes by the Editor*, 12 vols., 1833–4.
2. Lord Newton decided that the manuscripts were a *gift* to Constable 'in some measure of a remunatory nature', and that the condition attached (that the secret of the authorship should not be revealed) lapsed with Scott's own avowal. Gibson, 11 April 1831, Walpole.
3. Presumably 'consent' is intended.
4. A slip for 'creditors'.

navy.[1] Capt. Blair, a son of the Member for Ayrshire my old friend the laird of Blair. Resisting their courteous invitation or rather Sir Thomas Brisbane's who [was] their backing. Just as they retreate Mr. Pontey[2] is announced. I was glad to meet this great forestester. He is a little man and got along with an air of talent something like Gifford the famous Editor of the *Quarterly*. As in his case mental acuteness gave animation to that species of countenance which attends personal deformity. The whole of his face was bizarre and and odd yet singularly impressive. He Walkd round, I with great pain, by the hooded corbies' seat and this great Lord of the woodland gave the plantation great approbation. He seems rather systematic in pruning yet he is in a great measure right. I see he has been opposed tolerarably obstinate in his opinions.[3] He dined, and took leave, leaving me flatterd with his applause and pleased with having seen him.

11 MONDAY   This day I went with Anne and Miss Jane Erskine to see the laying of the stones of foundation of two bridges in my neighbourhood over Tweed and the Ettrick.[4] There were a great many people assembled. The day was beautiful, the scene was romantic, and the people in good spirits and good humour. Mr. Paterson of Galashiels made a most excellent prayer, Mr. Smith[5] gave a proper repast to the workmen, and we subscribed Sovereigns a piece to provide for any casualty or divide if there providentially be none. I laid the foun[d]ation stone of the bridge over Tweed and Mr. C. B. Scott of Wool <that> the foundation stone of that of Ettrick. The general spirit of good humour made the scene though without parade extremely interesting.

12 TUESDAY   We breakfasted with the Fergussons after which Anne and Miss Erskine walkd up the Rhymer's Glen. I could have as easily made a pilgrimage to Rome with pease in my shoes unboild. I drove home and began to work about ten o'clock. At one o'clock I rode and

1. Captain Blair was the son of William Blair of Blair, M. P., and his friend was a Captain Robertson. Brisbane, April 1831, Walpole.
2. William Pontey, author of *The Forest Pruner*, 1808, and *The Profitable Planter*, 1808.
3. This was probably intended to read: 'I see he is, being opposed, tolerably obstinate in his opinions.'
4. These bridges carried the new road along the west side of the Tweed where the old road had kept to the east side past Abbotsford.
5. The builder.

sent off what I had finishd. Mr. Laidlaw dined with met. In he afternoon we wrote five or six pages more. I am I fear sinking a little from having too much space to fill and a want of the usual inspiration. Which makes me, like the chariot wheels of Pharaoh in sands of the Red Sea, drive heavily. It is the less matter if this prove as I suspect the last of this fruitful family.[1]

13 WEDNESDAY Corrected a proof in the morning. At ten o'clock began where I had left off at my romance. Mr. Laidlaw agrees as to the portion of what we are presently busy [with's] worth. Laidlaw begins to smite the rock for not giving forth the water in quantity sufficient. I remarkd to him that this would not profit much. Doing perhaps twelve pages a day will easily finish up us: and if it prove dull why dull it must be. I shall perhaps have half a dozen to make up this night.

I have against me the disadvantage of being calld the Just and every one of course is willing to worry me. But they have been long at it. And even those works which have been worst received at their appearance now keep their ground fairly enough. So we'll try our old luck another voyage. It is a close thick rain and I cannot ride and I am too dead lame to walk in the house. So feeling really exhausted I will try to sleep a little.

My nap was a very short one and was agreeably replaced by Basil Hall's *Fragments of Voyages*.[2] Every thing about the i[n]side of a vessell is interesting and my friend has the great sense to know this is the case. I remember when my eldest brother took the humour of going to sea, James Watson[3] used to be invited to George's Square to tell him of such tales of hardships as might disgust him with their service. Such were my poor mother's instructions. But Captain Watson could not either render a sea life disgusting to the young Midshipman or to his brother who lookd on and listend. The account of assistance given to the Spaniards at Cape Finisterre and the absurd behaviour of the Junta a[re] highly interesting; a more inefficient yet a more resolved class of men than the Spaniar[d]s were never conceived.

14 THURSDAY Advised by Mr. Cadell that he has agreed with Mr. Turner, the first draughtsman of the period, to furnish to the poetical works two decorations to each of the proposed twelve volumes, to wit

1. In fact *Castle Dangerous*, begun in July 1831, was still to come.
2. Captain Basil Hall's *Fragments of Voyages and Travels*, 1831–3.
3. The father of Watson Gordon the artist and a distant relative of Scott's mother.

an print and a vignette to each at the rate of £25 for each which is cheap enough considering these are the finest speciments of art going. The difficulty is to make him come here to take drawings. I have written to the man of art inviting him to my house, though if I remember he is not very agreeable[1] and offerd to transport him to the places where he is to exercise his pencil. This may do some thing. Cadell may give him some money; this will more mitigate. Lastly, his mode of Drawing is to take various drawings of remarkable corners and towns and stick them all together. He can therefore derive his subjects from good accurate drawings so with Skene's assistance we can equip him. We can put him at home in all the subjects.

Lord Fincastle came to dinner. Lord Meadowbank and his son, Skene and his son, Col. Russell and his sisters dined with us.

15 FRIDAY Lord Meadowbank etc. went to Newark with me and returnd to dine with the foregoing. Charming day.

16 SATURDAY Lord Meadowbank to the circuit[2] and our party to their various homes. By the bye John Pringle and his brother of Haining dined with us yesterday. Skene walks with me and undertakes readily to supply Turner with subjects. Weather enchanting. About one hundred leaves will now complete *Robert of Paris. Quaere* if the last? Answ[e]r, not knowing, can't say. I think it will.

17–24 SUNDAY 16[3] APRIL TO SUNDAY 24 of the same month unpleasantly occupied by ill[ness] and its consequences. A distinct stroke of paralysis affecting both my nerves and speech though beginning only on Monday with a very bad cold.[4]

1. Scott wrote at Cadell's prompting: 'Your kindly promised invitation to Abbotsford might come in *at this moment.*' 13 April 1831, Walpole. Turner did prove a difficult guest, as Scott expected, and Cadell wrote on 19 September regretting 'that M. Turner should have annoyed you all so much'. Walpole.
2. The Circuit Court at Jedburgh.
3. A slip for '17'.
4. The first signs of distress were noted by Skene's son in his Diary. Scott did not come to breakfast on the Sunday. He appeared later in the day and took no notice of any of his guests. He told the story of a pauper lunatic who believed that the asylum in which he lived was his private house, but complained that everything he ate tasted of porridge. After an interval he told the same story over again and a third time. See Douglas's note.

'On the Monday night', Anne writes to Sophia, 'he was in great danger, for three hours, and Dr. Clarkson has since told

24 SUNDAY Doctor was brought out by the friendly care of Cadell but young Clarkson had already done the needful, that is had bled and blisterd severely and placed me on a very restricted diet. Whe[ther] these precautions have been taken in time I cannot tell. I think they have though severe in themselves beat the disease but I am alike prepared

> *Seu versare dolos seu certæ incumbere¹ morti.*[1]

I only know that to live as I am just now is a gift little worth having. I think I will be in the Secret next week unless I recruit greatly.

27 WEDNESDAY They have cut me off from animal food and fermented liquor of every kind and would press upon me such trash as panada macaroni and the like which affects my stomach. This I will none of but quietly wait till my ordinary diet is permitted and thank God I can fast with any one. I walkd out and found the day delightfull; the woods too looking charming just bursting forth to the tune of the birds. I have been whistling on my wits like so many chickens and cannot miss any of them. I feel on the whole better than I have yet done. I believe I have fined and recoverd[2] and so may be thankful.

28 THURSDAY, 29 FRIDAY Walter made his appearance, well curd, stout and completely recoverd of his stomach complaints by

---

me it was to his great surprise he got through'. She sent for Dr. Abercrombie from Edinburgh and for Walter: 'When Papa was so ill on the Monday I wrote to him to come immediately but my letter was directed to Birmingham instead of Sheffield.' 25 April 1831, Abbots. As a result she bore the brunt on her own as she so often had to do. 'I am vexed, none of my family have yet come down', she writes to Susan Ferrier on the 29th. 'They treat his last attack too lightly . . . Jane Erskine was here during his illness for four days, but was obliged to leave me on account of the illness of a relation.' *Memoir of Susan Ferrier*, pp. 250–1.

Although Scott recovered surprisingly well, 'his face for many days *was* quite distorted' and still, on the 25th, 'he is unstable to a degree that is dreadful'. Anne to Sophia, 25 April 1831, Abbots.

1. 'Either to resort to trickery or to submit to certain death.' Virgil's *Aeneid*, ii. 62.
2. 'Fining' and 'suffering a recovery' are devices for getting rid of an entail. Scott's stroke seems to have rid him of his other ailments.

abstinent. He has youth on his side and I in age must submit to be a lazar. The medical men persist in recommending a seton. I am no friend to these nasty remedies and will be sure of the necessity before I yield consent.[1] The dying like an Indian under tortures is no joke, and as Commodore Trunnion says I feel heart whole as a biscuit. My mind turns to politics. I feel [a] little [better] just now and so I am. I will wait till Lockhart comes but that may be too late.

30 SATURDAY, MAY 1 SUNDAY To meet Sandy Pringle tomorrow to settle the day of election[2] on Monday. Go on with *Count Robert* half a dozen leaves per day. I am not much pleased with my handy work. The Chancery money seems like to be paid.[3] This will relieve me of poor Charles who is at present my ch[i]ef burthen. The task of pumping my brains becomes inevitably harder when

Both chain pumps are choked below.[4]

And though this may not be the case literally yet the apprehension is wel[l] nigh as bad.

2 MONDAY The day passd as usual in dictating (too little) and noting a good deal. I must get finishd with *Count Robert* who is progressing, as the transatlantic say, at a very slow pace indeed. By the bye I have a letter from Nathan T. Rossiter, New York City, Williamstown, offering me a collection of poems by Byron which are said to have been found in Italy some years since by a friend of Mr. Rossiter.[5] I don't see I can at all be entitled to these so shall write to decline them. If Mr. Rossiter chuses to publish them in Italy or America he may, but publishd here they must be the property of Lord Byron's Executor.

1. The seton was finally put in on 30 May. Sophia to Lockhart, 31 May 1831, Abbots.
2. Parliament had been dissolved on 23 April.
3. The case was decided on 21 March 1832 and the money paid the following year.
4. George Alexander Stevens's 'The Storm', stanza 7.
5. Rossiter's letter speaks of 'a number of fugitive poems – Among them I should think the conclusion of this celebrated piece of Giaour'. 25 March 1831, Walpole.

3¹ TUESDAY Sophia arrives with all the children looking well and beautifull except poor Johnie who looks very pale² – But it is no wonder, poor thing.

4 WEDNESDAY I have a letter from Lockhart promising to be down by next wednesday, that is to-day.³ I will consult him about Byron's exors and as to these poems said to be his Lordship's. They are very probably first copies thrown aside or may not be genuine at all. I will be glad to see Lockhart. My pronunciation is a good deal improved. My time glides away ill employd.⁴ But I am afraid of the palsy. I should not like to be pind to my chair. But I believe even that kind of life is more endurable than we could suppose. Your wishes are limited to your little circle, yet the *idea* is terrible to a man who has been active. My own circle in bodily matters is daily narr[o]wing. Not so in intellectual matters, but I am perhaps a worse judge. The plough is coming to the end of the furrow. So it is likely I shall not reach the common goal of mortal life by a few years. I am now in my sixtieth year only, and threescore and ten years do sum up.⁵

1. On this day Anne writes to her former governess that 'after *mature deliberation I rejected my little* — , but he has got over it, and is going to be married, which I am glad of, to a lady with a great deal of money, which I found *afterwards* would be *very* necessary'. *Letters from Scott's Family*, p. 135. This may be 'the little Couper' about whom she writes to Missie the previous July (Nat. Lib. Scot. MS. 1752, f. 93.) but I cannot identify him with certainty.

2. 'After the roughest passage Capt. Bain says he has ever made except when the wind was high', during which Sophia never left her berth, they reached Abbotsford at half past eight in the evening. Sophia describes Scott's state to Lockhart in a letter of the next morning: 'At first I was quite surprised at him looking so very well his head has been shaved & he wears a greek red cap that Walter had given him & which improves rather than otherwise his appearance his spirits seemed quite good but dear Lockhart his speech is FAR from being quite recovered.' 3 and 4 May 1831, Abbots.

3. In his confusion of mind Scott has misread the letter, which refers to the following Wednesday. Lockhart, 1 May 1831, Walpole.

4. He continued, however, to rise at 6; he worked until 1, when he went out on the pony or in the carriage; he dined at 3.30, took tea with his family at 6, and went to bed at 8.30. Sophia to Lockhart, 4 May 1831, Abbots.

5. Psalm 110, in the Scottish metrical version.

5 THURSDAY A fleece of letters which must be answerd I suppose, all from persons my zealous admirer[s] of cours[e] and expecting a degree of gen[e]rosity which will put to rights all their maladies physical and mental, and expecting that I can put to rights whatever losses have been their lot, raise them to a desireable rank and [be] their protector and patron. I must, they take it for granted, be astonishd at having an address from a stranger; on the country[1] I would be astonishd if one of these extravagant epistles were from any one who had the least title to enter into correspondence with me. I have all the plague of answering these teazing people.[2] Mr. Burns the architect came in, struck by the appearance of my house from the road. He approved my architecture greatly. He tells me the ædifice for Jeanie Deans, that is her prototype, is nigh finishd so I must get the inscription ready.[3] Mr. Burns came to meet with Pringle of Haining but alas, it is two nights since, this poor young man driving in from his own lake where he had been fishing <and> an ill broken horse ran away with [him] and at his own stable door overturnd the vehicle and fractured poor Pringle's scull. He died yesterday morning, a bad business, so Young a man, the proprietor of a good estate and a well disposed youth. His politics were I think mistaken, being the reverse of his father's, but that is nothing at such a time. Burns went on to Richardson's place of Kirklands[4] where he is to meet the proprietor, whom I too would wish to see. But I can hardly make it out. Here is a world of arrangements. I think we will soon hit upon some thing. My son Walter takes leave of me to-day to return to Sheffield. At his entreaty I have agreed to put in a seton which they seem all to recommend. My own opinion is this addition to my tortures will do me no good but I cannot hold out against every one.

1. Scott means 'contrary'.
2. They probably included a man with four children under ten, and unfortunate in business, who wanted an opinion on the manuscript of his book, and a lady from America requesting a copy of Scott's *History of Scotland* which she apparently intended to publish in America, devoting the profits to a scheme for teaching negroes to read the Bible. Neilson, 21 April 1831, and Kinnear, 23 February 1831, Walpole.
3. Mrs. Goldie, who sent Scott the story which suggested Jeanie Deans's walk to London, had wished 'that Helen Walkers grave should be marked by a tomb stone'. Scott paid and Burn drew the plan. *Letters*, xi. 303. The stone stands in Irongray churchyard.
4. For Scott's advice to Richardson when he was negotiating for the estate, near Ancrum, in 1829, see *Letters*, xi. 234, 237, 244, 248.

So when the present blister is well over let them try their seton as they call it.

6 FRIDAY, 7 SATURDAY Here is a precious job. I have a formal remonstrance from these critical persons Ballantyne and Cadell remonstrating against the last volume of *Count Robert*[1] which is within a sheet of being finishd. I suspect their opinion will be found to coincide with that of the publick; at least it is not very different from my own. The blow is a stunning one I suppose for I scarcely feel it. It is singular but it comes with as little surprize as if I had a remedy ready. Yet God knows I am at sea in the dark and the vessell leaky, I think, into the barga[i]n. I cannot conceive that I should have tied a knot with my tongue which my teeth cannot untie. We will see. I am determined to write a political pamphlet *coute que coute*. Aye should it cost my life.[2] I will right and left on those unlucky proof sheets and alter at least what I cannot mend.

8 SUNDAY I learn by a letter from a certain Ostler of Birminghng- ham that Mr. Hamper of that town to whom I was obliged for various antiquarian communications had terminated his existence, worn out by struggling against the disgrace of being a member of a struggling firm and the prospect of three impoverishd daughters. I am truly sorry for it. He appeard an obliging, reading and attentive man and must have sufferd much in the fatal transit.[3] But fear implanted in every one's nature acts as a centinel to assure us that rash actions will not become too frequent. They were not so even among the Ancients who honourd and applauded those who committed them. I am sure it is mere fear keeps half the world, especially if they have been blisterd bled and criticized. I have sufferd terribly, that is the truth, rather in body than in mind, and I often wish I could lie down and sleep without waking. But I will fight it out if I can. It will argue too great an attachment of consequence to my literary labours to sink under [so]

1. 'I confess the combat and what follows have cast a gloom over me . . . The composition appears to my poor wits, excellent, better you never wrote, but it is the incidents that are damning.' Cadell, 6 May 1831, Walpole.
2. 'I think I will try a political pamphlet after all', he writes to Cadell. 'Good cannot come of leaving our friends and I am determined to shew that I am not dead if I am dying.' 8 May 1831, Disc. ii. 284.
3. He had been 'found (suspended) cold, and stiff, from one of the bed-posts!' Thomas Osler, 5 May 1831, Walpole. Hamper had sent Scott an inventory of the furniture at Kenilworth Castle. *Letters*, xi. 295 and *Kenilworth*, note viii.

searching a time. Did I know how to begin I would begin this very day although I knew I should sink at the end. After all this is but fear and faintness of heart though of another kind from that which trembles at a loaded pistol. My bodily strength is terribly gone, perhaps my mental too.

9 MONDAY The weather uncommonly beautiful and I am very eager to get on thinning woods while the peeling season lasts. We made about £200 off wood last season and times render the sum worth looking at.

10 TUESDAY Some repairs on the mill dam still keep the people employed and we cannot get to the thinning. Yet I have been urging them for a month. It is a great faultt of Scottish servants that they cannot be taught to time their turns.[1]

11 WEDNESDAY By old practice I should be going into town to-day, the Session sitting tomorrow. Am I happier that I [am] free from this charge? Poorer I am, that is certain, and times begin to render my literary [earnings] more precarious than usual. Very weak, scarce able to crawl about without the pony, lifted on and off, and unable to walk half a mile save with great pain.

12 THURSDAY Resolved to lay by *Robert of Paris* and take it up when I can work. Thinking on it really makes my head swim and that is not safe. Miss Ferrlar comes out to us. This gifted personage besides having great talents has conversation the least exigent of any author, female at least, whom I have ev[e]r seen among the 'long list I have encounterd with', simple, full of humour, and exceedingly ready at repartee, and all this without the least affectation of the blue stocking.[2]

1. On this day Lockhart arrived. 'The most painful sight I had ever then seen' is his description of Scott. 'All his garments hung loose about him; his countenance was thin and haggard, and there was an obvious distortion in the muscles of one cheek.' *Life*, x. 66.
2. Susan Ferrier had been invited in the hope that her visit would tempt Scott into working less. *Life*, x. 68–9. Since the *Journal* itself scarcely gives an adequate idea of Scott's declining powers, Susan Ferrier's recollections of her visit to Abbotsford (printed in the Edinburgh Edition of *Marriage*, 1881) are valuable for their description of the man who was rewriting *Count Robert of Paris* and running the gauntlet of the Jedburgh mob:
   'His figure was unwieldy, not so much from increased bulk as

13 FRIDAY Mr. or more properly Dr. Mac Intosh Mackay comes out to see me, a simple learnd man and a highlander who weighs his own nation justly, a modest and estimable person. I was beat up at midnight to sign a warrant against some delinquents. I afterwards heard that the Officers were pursued by a mob from Galashiels with purpose of deforcing them as far as Saint Boswel's Green but the men were lodged in Jedburgh Castle.

Merry doings, good Madam, as the Sandwich islander wrote to his patroness in England. Reports of mobs at all the Elections which I fore[1] will prove true. They have much to answer for who in gaiety of heart have brought a peaceful and virtuous population to such a pass.

14[2] SATURDAY, 15 SUNDAY Rode with Lockhart and Mr. Mackay through the plantations and spent a pleasanter day than of late years. Story of a haunted glen in Laggan. The story a very cruel one. A chieftain's daughter or cousin loved a man of low degree. Her kindred discovered the intrigue and punishd the lover['s] presumption by binding the unhappy man and laying him naked in one of the large ants' nests common in a highland forest.

He died in agony of course and his mistress became distracted, roamd wildly in the glen till she died, and her phantom finding no repose haunted it after her death to such a degree that the people shund the road by day as well as night. Mrs. Grant of Laggan tells the story with the addition that Mr. Grant her husband, then minister of Laggan, fixd a religious meeting in the place and by the exercize of publick worship there overcame the popular terror of the Red woman. Dr. Mackay seems to think that she was rather banishd

---

from diminished life and energy; his face was swollen and puffy, his complexion mottled and discoloured, his eyes heavy and dim; his head had been shaved, and he wore a small black silk cap, which was extremely unbecoming . . . [At dinner] Sir Walter did not join us till the dessert, when he entered, assisted by his servant, and took his place at the foot of the table. His grandchildren were then brought in, and his favourite, Johnie Lockhart, was seated by his side. I must have forgot most things before I can cease to recall that most striking and impressive spectacle, each day repeated, as it seemed, with deepening gloom. The first transient glow of cheerfulness which had welcomed my arrival had passed away, and been succeeded by an air of languor and dejection which sank to deepest sadness when his eye rested for a moment on his once darling grandson.'

1. 'I fear' or 'I foresee' must be intended.
2. See Appendix E, x, p. 830.

by a branch of the parliamentary road[1] being up the glen than by the prayers of his predecessor's preaching. Dr. Mackay, it being sunday, favourd us with an excellent discourse on the Socinian controversy which I wish my friend Mr. Laidlaw had heard.

16 MONDAY Dr. Mac Ky left us early this morning and I rode and studied as usual working at the *Tailes of my Grandfather*.[2] Our good and learned Dr. wishes to go down the Tweed by Berwick. It is a laudable curiosity and I hope will be agreeably satisfied.

17 TUESDAY I wrote and rode as usual and had the pleasure of Miss Ferriar's company in my family hours which was a great satisfaction; she has certainly less affec[ta]tion than any female I have known [who] has stood so high, even Joanna Baillie hardly excepted. By the way She has enterd on the Socinian controversy [for] which I am very sorry. She has publishd a number of texts[3] on which she conceives the controversy to rest but it escapes her that she can only quote them through a translation. I am sorry this gifted woman is hardly doing herself justice and doing what is not required at her hands. Mr. Laidlaw of course thinks it the finest thing in the world.

18 WEDNESDAY Went [to] Jedburgh to the election greatly against the wishes of my daughters.

The mob were exceedingly vociferous and brutal as they usually are nowadays. But the Sheriff[4] had two troops of dragoons at Ancrum bridge and all went off quietly. The populace gatherd in formidable numbers, a thousand from Hawick also. They were most blackguard and abusive; the day passd with much clamour and no mischief. Henry Scott was reelected for the last time I suppose. *Troja fuit*.[5] I left the Burgh in the midst of Abuse and the gentle hint of Burke Sir Walter. Much obliged to the bra lads of Jeddart. Upwards of forty freeholders voted for Henry Scott and only fourteen [for] the puppy that opposed him.[6] Even of this party

1. One of the Wade roads built during the pacification of the Highlands after 1745
2. The fifth series, continuing the history of France, never completed.
3. *View of the General Tenour of the New Testament regarding the nature and dignity of Jesus Christ*, 1831.
4. William Oliver, Sheriff of Roxburghshire.
5. 'Troy has been', i.e., 'this is the end of Troy', an allusion to Virgil's *Aeneid*, ii. 325.
6. Sir William Francis Eliott of Stobs and Wells.

he gaind far the greater number by the very awkward Coalition with Sir William Scott of Ancrum. I came home tired enough at seven at night.

19 THURSDAY Wrote and read till one o'clock fool myself still tird and my neck sore. The blister rising again I suppose. Rode out and found the mill pond finishd. At my post got a letter from Mr. Cadell agreeing like a wor[t]hy bibliopole to stand Tom Callender for £300 or £400 this uncommercial year.[1] I will go on and work like a tiger at the *Tales of my Grandfather* etc. If I recover I have no fear of doing well enough and if I die I shall leave enough of literary remains to clear Cadell, so we are safe any way.

20 FRIDAY This is the Selkirk Election which I supposed would be as tumultuous as the Jedburgh one. But the Sutors[2] of Selkirk had got a new light and saw in the proposed Reform Bill nothing but a mode of disfranchising their ancient Burgh. Although the crowd was great yet there was a sufficient body of special constables[3] hearty in their useful office and the election pass[d] as quietly as I ever witnessd one. I came home before dinner very quiet. I am afraid there is something serious in Galashiels. Jeffrey is fairly funkd about it and has written letters to the authorities of Roxburghshire and Selkirk shire to caution us against the making the precognitions publick, which looks ill.[4] Yet I think he would have made arrests when the soldiers were in the country. The time which I settled at Abbotsford, 1811 Whitsunday, I broke up a conspiracy of the weavers. I[t] will look like signalizing my removal if another takes place just now. Incendiary letters have been sent and the householders are in a general state of alarm. The men at Jedburgh Castle are said to be disposed to make a clean breast; if so we shall soon know more of the matter.

Lord William Graham[5] has been nearly murderd at Dunbarton.

1. 'The sum you require you must have,' writes Cadell on the 18th. Walpole. In his letter of this date to Cadell Scott used the same phrase, 'to stand Tom Callender', meaning apparently to pay someone else's expenses. Cadell Letters.
2. The generic nickname of Selkirk men.
3. The Special Constables in Selkirk were of Scott's creation. See the Entries for 23 December 1830 and 6 January 1831 and note 10, p. 813.
4. Jeffrey feared a riot if the preliminary investigation of the men arrested a week before (see the Entry for 13 May) were not held behind closed doors.
5. The M. P. for Dunbartonshire.

Why should he not have brought down fifty or an hundred 'lads with the kilts' each with a good kent in his hands fit to call the soul out of the body of three weavers?[1] They would have kept order I warrant ye.

21 SATURDAY Little more than my usual work and my usual exercize. I rode out through the pla[n]tations and saw the woodmen getting down what was to fall; it seems there will be as much for sale as last year of bark. I think about £40 pounds worth. A very nice additional pond to the saw mill has been contrived and executed. As for my *Tales* they go on well and are amusing to myself at least. The history of France is very entertaining.

22 SUNDAY I have a letter from my friend John Thomson of Duddingston. I had transmitted him an order for the Duke of Buccleuch for his best picture at his best price leaving the choice of the subject and every thing else to himself. He expresses the wish to do at an ordinary price a picture of common size. The declining to put himself first will I fear be thought like shrinking from his own reputation – which nobody has less need to do. The Duke may wish a large picture for a large price for furnishing a large apartment; even the Artist should not shrink from it. I have written him my opinion.

The feeling is no doubt an amiable though a false one. He is modest in proportion to his talent. But what brother of the fine arts ever approached man to please himself?

23–5 MONDAY–WEDNESDAY Workd and exercized regularly. I do not feel that I care twopence about the change of diet as to taste but I feel my strength much decayd. On horseback my spine feels remarkabbly sore and tired with a five miles ride. We expect Walter coming down for the Fife election which he is expected to gain.[2]

[By the 18th of July Scott was sufficiently recovered to spend a few days in the west with Lockhart, revisiting Douglas Castle and refreshing his memories of the scenes he needed for *Castle Dangerous*, which he had just begun. He then settled to *Count Robert of Paris* and the new novel, and completed both, after a fashion, by the end of August.

1. *Twelfth Night*, ii. 3.
2. He comes to Abbotsford on the 28th after assisting Colonel Lindsay of Balcarres, the anti-Reform candidate, to beat Captain Wemyss by 16 votes. Walter, 29 May 1831, Abbots.

The principal visitors of the summer and autumn (apart from the Lockharts, who were at Chiefswood, and Walter, who came whenever he could be spared from duty) were Turner, while working on his illustrations of the *Poetical Works*, the younger Adolphus, Captain James Glencairn Burns (a son of the poet), and, just before Scott's departure for London, Wordsworth. The Preface to *Yarrow Revisited* gives some account of these last days:

'But to return to Abbotsford, the inmates and guests we found there were Sir Walter, Major Scott, Anne Scott, and Mr. and Mrs. Lockhart, Mr. Liddell, his Lady and Brother, and Mr. Allan the painter, and Mr. Laidlow, a very old friend of Sir Walter's . . . In the evening, Mr. and Mrs. Liddell sang, and Mrs. Lockhart chanted old ballads to her harp; and Mr. Allan, hanging over the back of a chair, told and acted odd stories in a humorous way. With this exhibition and his daughter's singing, Sir Walter was much amused, as indeed were we all as far as circumstances would allow. But what is most worthy of mention is the admirable demeanour of Major Scott during the following evening, when the Liddells were gone and only ourselves and Mr. Allan were present. He had much to suffer from the sight of his father's infirmities and from the great change that was about to take place at the residence he had built, and where he had long lived in so much prosperity and happiness. But what struck me most was the patient kindness with which he supported himself under the many fretful expressions that his sister Anne addressed to him or uttered in his hearing. She, poor thing, as mistress of that house, had been subject, after her mother's death, to a heavier load of care and responsibility and greater sacrifices of time than one of such a constitution of body and mind was able to bear. Of this, Dora and I were made so sensible, that, as soon as we had crossed the Tweed on our departure, we gave vent at the same moment to our apprehensions that her brain would fail and she would go out of her mind, or that she would sink under the trials she had passed and those which awaited her. On Tuesday morning Sir Walter Scott accompanied us and most of the party to Newark Castle on the Yarrow. When we alighted from the carriages he walked pretty stoutly, and had great pleasure in revisiting those his favourite haunts. Of that excursion the verses 'Yarrow revisited' are a memorial.'

Scott had reluctantly agreed in July 'to do the only thing that will really do him good going abroad and trying a complete change of climate',[1] and on 23 September he left Scotland to winter in the Mediterranean. His original intention had been to go by a steam-boat

1. Sophia to Charles, 17 July 1831, Abbots.

to Rotterdam, up the Rhine to Mayenz, and then to post over the Simplon Pass. However, at Cadell's suggestion, Basil Hall asked Sir James Graham at the Admiralty if Scott could not be given a passage in a man-of-war. Graham at once suggested the *Barham*, and the King a few days later made Scott's passage a Royal Command.[1]

With Lockhart and Anne in attendance, he reached London on the 28th, pausing to spend a last day with Morritt. It was not an easy journey. They battled with gales as far as Rokeby. Anne was in no state to travel, 'being visited with several attacks of blood spitting and great pain.'[2] Scott himself 'would not pass any object to which he had ever attached special interest, without getting out of the carriage to revisit it'.[3]

In London everyone found Scott sadly different from the man they had known. 'When he entered the hall, which he seemed hardly able to crawl across, he held out his hand to my husband,' says Mrs. Hughes, 'exclaiming, "You see a broken down man in every sense, my dear Doctor!" – but he was chearful during the breakfast and eat heartily, being particularly pleased with some Yarmouth bloaters which were at table.'[4] Sir William Knighton 'observed him much changed. He was considerably thinner; his countenance expressed doubt and dejection'.[5] Thomas Moore 'was rather shocked at seeing and hearing Scott; both his looks and utterance, but particularly the latter, showing strongly the effects of paralysis'.[6]]

INTERVAL

I have been very ill and if not quite unable to write I have been unfit to do. I have wrought however at two Waverly things but not well and what is worse past mending. A total prostration of bodily strength is my chief complaint. I cannot walk half a mile. There is beside some mental confusion with the extent of which I am not perhaps fully acquainainted. I am perhaps setting. I am myself inclined to think so and like a day that has been admired as a fine one the light of it sets down amid mists and storms. I neither regret nor fear the approach of death if it is

1. Hall's *Fragments*, iii, Ch. 27; and Cadell, 19 September 1831, Walpole.
2. Scott to Laidlaw, Disc. ii. 397.
3. *Life*, x. 107
4. *Mrs. Hughes's Recollections*, p. 334.
5. *Memoirs of Knighton*, ii. 230.
6. *Memoirs of Moore*, vi. 226.

coming. I would compound for a little pain instead of this heartless muddiness of mind which renders me incapable of any thing rationional. The expence of my journey will be some thing considerable which I can fence against by borrowing £500 from Mr. Gibson. To Mr. Cadell I owe already with the cancels on these apoplectic books about £200 and must run it up to £500 more at least.[1] Yet this heavy burthens would be easily borne if I were to be the Walter Scott I once was, but the change is great. This would be nothing providing that I could count upon these two books having a sale equal to their predecessors. But as they do not deserve the same countenance they will not and cannot have such a share of fav[ou]r and I have only to hope that they will not involve the Waverley[2] which are now settling[3] 30,000 volumes a month, in their displeasure. Something of a *journal* and the *Reliquiae Trotcosienses*[4] will probably be moving articles and I have in short no fears on pecuniary matters. Well said Colin Mackenzie [of] the Ruin which I fear involves that of my King and Country

> Shall this Desolation strike thy towers alone?
> No, sad Ellan Donan, such ruin 'twill bring
> That the storm shall have force to unsettle the throne
> And thy fate shall be mixd with the fate of thy King.[5]

This I for[e]see that the great part of the memorialists are bartering away the dignity of their rank by seeking to advance themselves by a job, which is a melancholy sight. The ties between democrat and aristocrat and democrat are sullen discontent with each other. The former are regarded as a Housedog which has manifested signs of incipient canine madness and is not to be trusted. Walter came down

1. *Count Robert of Paris* and *Castle Dangerous*, written after his 'apoplexy', had to be extensively revised – an expensive business when all corrections were made in proof. His debts were greater than he realized. According to Cadell's letter of 13 September he owed him £2630, of which £1950 was advanced against works to be written. Walpole.
2. The Magnum Opus.
3. A slip for 'selling'.
4. 'Cadell undertakes for expences suppose £1000 or £1500 on condition of my keeping a journal that may be visible one day.' *Letters*, xii. 28. The *Reliquiae*, suggested by Cadell as light work after Scott's first stroke and intended at that time for the relief of Terry's widow, was a descriptive catalogue of the curiosities he owned. See *Life*, ix. 356, and *Letters*, xi. 292.
5. Colin Mackenzie's 'Ellandonan Castle' in Scott's *Border Minstrelsy*, pt. 3.

to-day to join our party; yesterday Wordsworth, his son[1] and daughter, came to see us and we went up to yarrow yesterday. The eldest son of Lord Ravenswood[2] also came to see us with his accomplished Lady. We had a pleasa[n]t party, and to-day were left by the Liddells. *Manent* the three Wordsworth *cum cæteris*. A German or Hungarian Count Erdödy or some such name also retires.

We arrived in London after a long and painful journey. The weakness of my limbs palpably increasing and the physick prescribed making me weaker every day.[3] Lockhart, poor fellow, is as attentive as possible and I have thank God no pain whatever, but the decay can [not] be so easy at last – it would be too happy and I fancy the instances of Euthanasia are not in very serious cases very common. Instances there certainly [are] among the learnd and unlearnd. Dr. Black,[4] Tom Purdie. I should [wish] if it pleased God to sleep off in such a quiet way. But we mus[t] take what fate sends. I have not warm hopes of being myself again.

Wordsworth and his daughter, a fine girl, were with us on the last day. I tried to write in her Diary and made an ill favoured botch.[5] No help for it; sti[t]ches will wear and elbows will out, as the tailor says.

The King has locald me on board the *Barham* with my suite consisting of my eldest son, youngest daughter, and perhaps my daughter in law,[6] which with poor Charles will make a goodly tail. I fancy the head of this tail cuts a poor figure scarce able to stir about.

1. His nephew, Charles Wordsworth, a student of Christ Church, is meant.
2. A slip for 'Ravensworth'. Henry Liddell had promised on 4 April 1831 to bring his wife to see Scott.
3. Scott blamed the doctors rather than the disease for his state. 'In fact without any any visible complaint but a suddenly reduced diet and a regular quantity of drastic medicine I have been gradually reduced from a state of health in which I walkd easily to Chiefswood to one in which I can scarce crawl from one chair to another and [e]very day my remainder of strength slowly declines.' To Laidlaw, 1 October 1831, Disc. ii. 397.
4. Adam Ferguson's relative, Prof. Joseph Black, set down his cup and 'expired without spilling a drop'. *D. N. B.* For Purdie's death, see p. 661.
5. 'While putting the book into her hand, in his own study, standing by his desk, he said to her in my presence – 'I should not have done anything of this kind but for your father's sake: they are probably the last verses I shall ever write.'' ' Preface to *Yarrow Revisited*.
6. Walter and Anne sailed with Scott, but Jane took fright and preferred 'remaining with her mother in single blessedness'. To Cadell, 18 October 1831, Disc. ii. 415.

The town is afoam with politics. The report is that the Lords will throw out the bill.[1]

And now, morning of 8th October, I learn it is quoited down stairs like a shovel board shil[l]ing with a plague to it as the most uncalld for attack upon a free constitution under which men lived happily which ever was ventured in my day.

Well it would have been pleasing to have had some share in so great a victory, yet even now I am glad I have been quiet. I believe I should only have made a bad figure. Well I will have time enough to think of all this.

OCTOBER

9 SUNDAY The report to-day is that the Chancellor will unite with the Duke of Wellington and Sir Report Peel [to] bring in a bill of his own cocting modified to the taste of the other two, with which some think the other two will be satisfied. This is not very unlikely for Lord Brougham has been displeased with not having been admitted to Lord John Russell's task of bill drawing; he is a man of unbounded ambition as well a[s] unbounded talent and unhesitating temper.[2] Here have been hosts of people, particularly the Duke of Buccleuch, to ask me to the Christening of his son and Heir when the King stands godfather.[3] I am askd as an ally and friend of the family which makes the compliment greater. Singular that I should [have] stood good gather[4] to this duke himself representing some great man. Painful suspicions about Mr. Murray which God avert. Lockhart and Sophia might be ruind by a failure there. If trade would revive this course I should hope might be avoided. If the public be again occupied by a sea of restless politicks I fear they will sink. Lord Louvain calls.

10 MONDAY[5] Yesterday we dined alone so I had an opportunity of speaking seriously to John but I fear procrastination. It is the crisis of

1. The Second Reform Bill. See Appendix D, p. 825.
2. 'Well! one lives to see strange things' Scott told Shortreed, 'Brougham Chancellor of England! I remember, Mr. Shortreed, of his being as mad as a march hare at a Jedburgh Circuit. . . . And to think that that outré being is now Lord Chancellor of England – Good God!' Shortreed Papers.
3. Anne tells Cadell on 3 October that 'They seem annoyed about the King's offering to stand God-father to the child, as both King and Queen and all the Royal family must be at the christening.' Cadell Letters.
4. A slip for 'godfather'.
5. In this and six of the next seven date headings Scott wrote 'November' instead of 'October'.

Friar Bacon's Brazen head,[1] *Time is Time was* but the tim[e] may soon come *Time shall be no more.* The Whigs are not very bold. Not much above 100 met to support Lord Grey to the last. Their resolutions are moderate probably because they could not have carried stronger. I went to breakfast at Sir Robert Henry Inglis and coming home about twelve found the mob rising in the Regent's park and roaring for reform as rationally as such a party of Angusshire cattle would have done. Sophia seemd to adopt [the attitude] the jolly host does in the play. 'These are my windows' said shutting the shutters. 'Let them batter. I care not serving the good Duke of Norfolk.' After a time they passd out of our sight and wearying doubtless to seek a more active scene of reformation. As the night closed the citizens who had hitherto contented themselves with shouting became more active and when it grew dark set forth to make work for the glasiers.

11 TUESDAY Tuesday we set out in the morning to breakfast with Lady Gifford.[2] We passd sev[e]ral glorious specimens of the last night's feats of the reformers. The Duke of New Castle's and Lord Dudley's house was very sufficiently broken. The maidens however had resisted from the top of the house with coals which had greatly embarassd the assailants. Surely if the people are determined on using a right so questionable, and the government resolved to consider it as too sacred to be resisted, some modes of resistance might be resorted to of a character more ludicrous than fire arms – coals for example, scalding oil, boiling water, or some other mode of defence against a sudden attack. We breakfaced with a very pleasant party at Lady Giffard. I was particularly happy to meet Lord Sidmouth, at seventy five he tells me as mu[ch] in health and spirits as at sixty. I also met Captain Basil[3] to whom I owe so much for promoting my retreat in so easy manner. I found my appointment to the *Barham* had been pointed out by Captain Henry Duncan R.N. as being a measure which would be particularly agre[e]abl[e] to the officers of the service. This is too high a compliment.

In returning I calld to see the repairs at Lambeth which are proceeding under the able direction of Blore who met me there. They are in the best gothick taste and executed at the expence of a large sum to be securd by way of mortgage payable in fifty years, each

---

1. In Greene's *Frier Bacon and Frier Bongay*, first acted in 1594.
2. At Roehampton.
3. Captain Basil Hall, described by Scott as 'that curious fellow who takes charge of every one's business without neglecting his own'. *Life*, x. 110.

Incumbent within the time paying a proportion of about £4000 a year. I was pleased to see this splendour of Church Architecture returning again.

At home we found Mrs. Thomas Scott with her three daughters and little Tom Huxley all comely and clever girls and apparently entertaining a warm regard for their uncle. I paid Mrs. Scott £150 (one hundred and fifty pounds) of my Mother's legacy which was pledged in my hands as a security for my my poor brother's intromissions with the pay of the regiment.[1] I imagine there will be £600 or £700 of balance remaining which I should be glad to pay to my Nephew Walter. Government have repeatedly renewd and departed from their claim on Mr. Robert MacCulloch of the navy pay office, the claim fluctuating from £2000 or £3000 to £500 and falling at the last report considerably within the latter sum which is nothing surely to be afraid of. Mr. MacCulloch thinks there is not a penny due and that the claim will not again be brought forward by the government.

My relations come to breakfast tomorrow. Lord Mahon, a very amiable as well as clever young man, comes to dinner with Mr. Croker. Lady Louisa Stuart in the afternoon or more properly at night.

12 WEDNESDAY Misty morning looks like a yellow fog which is the curse of London. I would har[d]ly take my share of it for a share of its wealth and its curiosity, a vile double distilld fog of the most intolerable kind. Children scarce stirrining yet but Baby and the Macao beginning their Macao notes. Among other feats of the mob on Monday a gentleman who saw the onslaught told me two men got on the Lord Londonderry's carriage and struck him. The high chief Constable came to the rescue and belabourd the rascals who ran and roard. I should have liked to have seen the onslaught. Dry beating and plenty of it is a great operator of a Reform among these gentry. At the same time Lord Londonderry is a brainsick man very unlike his brother. He horsewhippd a centinel under arms at Vienna for obeying

1. When Scott's brother Tom, paymaster of the 70th Regiment, died in Canada in 1823, some discrepancy in the accounts of the regiment while in Ireland had not been satisfactorily explained and a pension was at first refused to his widow. No question of dishonesty was involved, and the claim made by the Government seems to have been a mistake. In April 1827 Mrs. Scott was placed on the Pension List, Scott and her own brother Robert MacCulloch standing surety in case the Government's claim should be allowed. E. H. Fairbrother's 'Scott Records at the War Office', *Notes and Queries*, vol. 12.

his consigne which was madness. On the other side all seems to be prepared. Strong bodies of the Police are station'd in all the squares and places supporting each other regularly; the men themselves say that their numbers amount to 3000 and that they are supported by troops in still greater numbers so that the conservative force is sufficiently strong.

four o'clock.

A letter from the Duke saying the party[1] is put off by command of the King and probably the day will be put off untill the Duke's return from Scotland. So our hopes of seeing the fine ceremony is all ended.

13 THURSDAY *Nocte pluit tota*,[2] an excellent recipe for a mob, so they have been quiet accordingly as we are inform'd. Two or three other wet nights would do much to weary them out with inactivity. Millman, whom I remember a fine gentleman like young man, dined here yesterday and is turn'd much coarser. He says the fires have never ceased in his country but that the sufferings and oppressions occasioned by the Poors Rate are very great and there is no persuading the English farmer than an amended system is comfortable both to rich and Poor.

The plan of ministers is to keep their places maugre Peers and Commons both while they have the countenance of the crown. But if a prince shelters by authority of the prerogative ministers against the will of the other authority of the state Quaere does he not quit the Defence which supposes he can do [no] wrong? This doctrine would make a curious change of parties – Will they attempt to legitimate the Fitz Clarences?[3] God forbid, yet it may end in that. It would be Paris all over. The family is said to have popular qualities. Then what would be the remedy? Marry! seize on the Person of the Princess Vittoria, carrying her North and setting up the banner of England with the Duke of W— as Dictator – A brave *brave et demi*! Well I am too old to fight and therefore should keep the windy side of the Law; besides, I shall be burn'd out before times come to a decision. In the mean time the King dare not go to stand godfather to the son of one of his most powerful peers – a party of his own making – lest his loving

---

1. The Buccleuch christening. 'The ladies were much disappointed in the postponement of the fete. I am very happy having no taste for a bouquet of stones.' To Laidlaw, 17 October 1831, Disc.ii. 412.
2. 'It rains all night.'
3. See the Entry for 9 January 1827 and note.

subjects pull the house about the ears of his noble host and the company invited to meet him. Their loyalty has a pleasant way of displaying itself. I will go to Westminster after breakfast and see what people are saying and whether the *Barham* is like to sail or whether its course is not alterd to the coast of the Low Countries[1] instead of the Mediterranean.

14 FRIDAY Tried to walk to Lady Louisa Stuart's but took a little vertigo and came back. Much distrest by a letter from Walter.[2] He is like to be sent on an obn[o]xious service with very inadeq[u]ate force, little prospect of thanks if he does his duty and much of blame if he is unable to accomplish it. I have little doubt he will ware his mother's calf skin on them. The manufacturing districts are in great danger. London seems pretty secure.

Sent off the R[e]vise of Introduction[3] to Mr. Cadell.

15 SATURDAY A letter from Walter with better news. He has been at hardhead[s] with the rogues and come off with advantage, in short practized with success the art of drawing two souls out of one weaver.[5] All seems quiet now and I suppose the Major will get his leave as proposed. Two ladies, Byron's Mary Chaworth [one], have been frightend to death while the mob tore the dying creatures from their beds and proposed to throw them in to the flames, drank the wine, destroyd the furniture, and committed other excesses of a Jacquerie. They have been put down however, by a strong force of yeomanry and Regulars. Walter says the soldiers fired over the people's heads whereas if they had levelld low the bullets must have told wider among the multitude. I can't approve this for in such cases severity is ultimate mercy. However if they have made a sufficient impression to be striking, why enough is as good as a feast.

16 SUNDAY There is a strange story about town of ghost seeing vouchd by Lord Prudhoe, a near relation of the Duke of Northumberland and whom I know as an honourable man, and Colonel [Felix] described as a cool-headed sensible man of worth and honour. Palsgrave who dined with us yesterday told us twice over

1. To encourage the Belgians and Dutch to settle their differences.
2. At Sheffield.
3. The Introduction to the final series of *Tales of My Landlord* in which Scott takes farewell of his readers.
4. This Entry is actually dated '16 October' by Scott, and the next one '16 Novemr.'
5. *Twelfth Night*, ii.3.

the story as vouchd by Lord Prudhoe, and Lockhart gave us Colonel Felixes edition which coincided exactly. I will endeavour to extract the Essence of both.

While at Grand Cairo they were attracted by the report of a physician who could do the most singular magical feats and was in the habit not only of relieving the living but calling up the dead. This sage was the member of a tribe of the interior part of Africa. They were some time (two years) in finding him out, for he by no means pressd himself on the curious only[1] nor did he on the other hand avoid them but when he came to Grand Cairo readily agreed to gratify them by a sight of his wonders. The scenes exhibited were not visible to the operator himself nor to the person for whose satisfaction they were calld up, but as in the case of Dr. Dee and other Adepts by means of a Viewer, an ignorant Nubian boy whom to prevent imposture the English gentlemen selected for the purpose and as they though[t] without any risque of imposture by confederacy betwixt him and the physician. The process was as follows. A black square was drawn on the palm of the boy's hand or rather a kind of pentacle with an arabic character inscribed at each angle. The figures evoked were seen through this space as if the substance of the hand had been removed. Magic rites and particularly perfumes were liberally resorted to. After some suffumigation the Magician declared that they could not proceed untill the Seven flags should become visible. The boy declared he saw nothing, then said he saw a flag, then two, often hesitated at that number for a certain time, and on several occasions the spell did not work and the operation wen[t] no further. But in gen[e]ral the boy saw the seven flags through the aperture in his hand. The Magician then said 'We must call the sultaun' and the Boy said he saw a splendid tent fixd surrounded by immense hosts, E[b]lis no doubt and his angels. The person evoked was then named and appeard accordingly. The only indispensibl[e] requisite was that he was named speedily for the Sultaun did not like to be kept waiting. Accordingly, William Shakespeare being named the boy declared that he saw a Frank in a dress which he described as that of the reign of Elizabeth or her successor having a singular countenance, a high forehead and a very little beard. Another time a brother of [the] Colonel was named. The boy said he saw a Frank in his uniform dress and a black groom behind him leading a superb horse. The dress was a red jacket and white pantaloons and the principal figure turning round the boy announced that he wanted his arm as was the case with Felix's brother. The ceremony was repeated fourteen times, respectfully in twelve instances, and in two it faild from nonappearance of the twelve banners in the first instance.

1. These two words are almost illegible.

The apparent frankness of the operator was not the least surpr[i]zing part of the affair. He made no mystery, said that he possessd this power by inheritance as a family gift, yet that he could teach it and was willing to do for no enormous sum, nay one which seemd very moderate. I think two gentlemen embraced the offer; one of them is dead and the other still abroad. The Sage also took a price for exhibition of his skill but it was a moderate one being regulated on the expence of the perfumes consumed in the ceremony. There remains much more to ask but I understood the witnesses do not like to bother about, which is very natural.

One would like to know a little more of the Sultaun, of the care taken to secure the fidelity of the boy who was the viewer and on whom so much dependend?

Whether another sage practizing the same feat, as it was said to be hereditary, was ever known to practize in the city? The truth of a story so irreconciliable with the common course of nature must depend on cross examination. If one should find while at Malta that they had an opportunity of expiscating this matter though at the expence of a voyage to Alexandria it would hardly deter me.[1]

The girls go to the Chapel Royal this morning at Saint James's. A visit from the Honble John forbes, son of my old and early friend Lord Forbes, who is our fellow passenger. The ship expects presently to go to sea. I was very glad to see this young officer and to hear his news. Drummond and I have been friends from our infancy.

17 MONDAY The morning beautiful to-day. I go to look after the transcrip[t] in the Museum[2] and Leave a card on a set of chess men

1. In Malta Scott learned that Sir John Stoddart's son, 'an excellent arabian scholar', had seen three of the exhibitions and was able to explain the mystery. To Lockhart, 24 November 1831, Disc.ii. 430. Douglas refers the reader to the *Quarterly*, no. 117, which also has some account of the matter.

2. He had already been twice to the British Museum to read 'The Woodstock Scuffle' and 'The just Devil of Woodstock', which are printed as appendices to the Magnum edition of *Woodstock*. He was now collecting them from the copier. To Cadell, 7, 14 and 18 October 1831, Disc.ii. 401–6 and 415. The Journal of Sir Frederic Madden (Bodleian Library MS. Eng. hist. c. f. 57) gives an interesting description of Scott at this time: 'His appearance & manner struck me much, I shd. instantly have known him, from the portraits of him, but it is impossible to convey by the pencil, an idea of the uncouthness of his appearance and figure. His hair almost white, large grey

thrown up by the sea on the C[o]ast of Scotland which were offerd to sale for £100.[1] The King Queen Knights etc. were in the costume of the 14th Century, the substance ivory or rather the horn of the mors[2] somewhat injured by the salt water in which they had been immersd for som[e] times. Sir John Malcolm told us a story about Garrick and his wife. The Lady admired her husband greatly but blamed him for a taste for low life and insisted that he loved better to play Scrub to a lowlifd Audience than one of his superior characters before an Audience of taste. On one particular occasion She was at her box in the theatre. *Richard IIId* was the performance and Garick's acting, especially in the night scene, drew down universal applause. After the play was over Mrs. G— proposed going home which Garick declined alleging he had some business in the green room which must detain him. In short the Lady was obliged to acquiescence and [to] wait the beginning of a new entertainment in which was introduced a farmer giving his neighbours an account of the wonders se[e]n on a visit to London. This character was received with such peals of applause that Mrs. Garick began to think it rivald those which had been so lately lavished on Richard the third. At least she observed her little spaniel dog was making efforts to get towards the balcony which separated him from the facetious farmer. She became at [that] aware of the truth. 'How strange' he said 'that a dog should know his master and a woman in the same circumstances should not recognize her husband.'

18 TUESDAY Sophia had a small but lively party last night, as indeed she has had every night since we were here.[3] Ladies – Lady Louisa Stuart, Viscountess Mountagu, Miss Fanny Mountagu, Lady Macleod and two or three others. Gentl[e]men – Lord Montagu,

---

unexpressive eyes – a red-sandy complexion and straggling whiskers – slow and thick manner of speaking – and broad Scotch accent. – His figure equally gauche – square built – limping very much, so as to elevate the right shoulder above the left, and using for support an immense thick stick; dressed in checkered black & white trousers and dark square cut coat.'

1. According to Madden (ibid., f. 61) eighty-two pieces, belonging to four or five sets, had been brought to the Museum only that morning by a dealer from Edinburgh named Forrest. Some of them may be seen in the Museum of Antiquities in Edinburgh; and there are replicas in the British Museum.

2. i.e. tusk of the walrus.

3. 'We *never* dine out but have two or three friends at breakfast and never more than two at dinner, and he seems to enjoy it so much.' Anne to Cadell, 3 October 1831, Cadell Letters.

Macleod, Lord Du<n>dley, Rodgers. A good deal of singing. Binning Monro.¹ If Sophia keeps to early hours and small parties she may pick London for small parties as poor Miss White did and without much expence. A little address is all that is necessary. Sir John² insists on my meeting this Rammahoun Roy.³ I am no believer in his wandering knight so fair.⁴ The time is gone of sages who traveld to collect wisdom as well as heroes to reap honour. Men think and fight for money. I won't see the man if I can help it. Flatterers are difficult enough to keep at a distance though they be no renegades. I hate a fellow who begins with throwing away his own religion and then affects a prodigious respect for another.

Captain H. Duncan calld with Captn Pigot, a smart looking gentleman like man, and announces his purpose of sailing on monday. I have made my preparations for being on board on monday which is the day appointed.

19 WEDNESDAY Capt. Duncan told me jocularly never to hark a naval Captain's word on shore and quoteded Sir William Scott who used to say waggishly that there was nothing so accomodating as a naval captain on shore but when on board he became a per[e]mptory lion. Henry Duncan has behaved very kindly and says he only discharges the wishes of his service in making me as easy as possible, which is very handsome. No danger of feud, except about politics which would be impolite on my part, and though it bars out one great subject of discourse it leaves enough besides. That I might have nothing doubtful Walter arrives with his wife, both ready to sail.⁵ so what little remains must be done without loss of time.

20 THURSDAY This is our last morning so I have money to draw for and pay away, to see dear Lord Montagu too. The Duchess came yesterday. I suppose £50 will clear me with some balance for Gibraltar.

I leave this country uncertain if it has got a total pardon or only a reprieve.⁶ I won't think of it as I cann do no good. It seems to be in one of those crises by which Providence reduces nations to their original Elements. If I had my health I should take the world for me to

---

1. i.e., Monro Binning, an Edinburgh advocate.
2. Sir John Malcolm.
3. A Brahmin philosopher from Bengal who was a fashionable curiosity at the time. He died in England two years later.
4. *1 Henry IV*, i. 2.
5. Jane had come to see them off, not to sail with them. The mistake indicates Scott's confused state.
6. From Reform.

bustle in but I am weak as water and shall be glad when I have put the Mediterranean between the island and me.

21 FRIDAY, 22 SATURDAY Spent in takings of Farewell and adieus which had been put off till now, a melancholy ceremonial, with some a useless one. Yet there [are] friends whom it sincerely touches one to part with. It is the cement of life giving way in a moment. Another unpleasant circumstance is one is calld upon to recollect those whom Death or estrangement have severed as must fall after starting merrily together in the voyage of life.

23 SUNDAY Portsmouth. Arrived here in the evening.[1] Found the *Barham* will not sail till the 26 October, that is Wednesday next. The Girls break loose, made with the craze of seeing sights, and ran the risque of our losing some of our things and deranging the Naval officers who offer their services with their natura[l] gallantry. Capt. Pigot came to Breakfast wt several other officials. The Girls contrived to secure a sight of the Block harness and manufactury[2] together with that of the Biscuit also invented by Brunel. I think that I have seen the first of these wonderful [inventions] in 1816 or about that time. Sir John Foley gives an entertainment to the Admiralty[3] and sends to invite [me] but I pleaded health and remaind at home. Neither will I go out a sight-seeing, which madness seems to have seized my women kind.

This ancient town is one of the few in England which is fortified and which gives it a peculiar appearance. It is much surrounded with heaths or thin poo[r] muirs coverd with heather, very barren in that aspect ye[t] capable of being converted into rich arable and pasturage. I would [not] desire a better estate than to have 2000 acres which would be worth 40 shillings an acre.

24 MONDAY My womankind are gone out with Walter and Captain Hall. I wish they would be moderate in their demands on people's complaisance; they little know how inconvenient are such seizures. A

---

1. 'After a pelting day of rain of which my daughters & son being outside the former in spite of entreaty got a large share'. To Cadell, 24 October 1831, Disc.ii. 421.
2. These were among the earlier examples of production by mechanical rather than manual processes. Scott had spent a day in the dock-yard in 1807. *Life*, iii. 10.
3. 'The Lords of the Admiralty happened to be at Portsmouth on a tour of inspection.' Hall's *Fragments*, ch. 27. Sir Thomas Foley (not Sir *John*) was Port Admiral of Portsmouth.

sailor is in particular a bad refuser and before he can turn three times round he is bound with a triple knot to all kinds of [engagements]. The wind is west, that is to say contrary, so our sailing on the day after tomorrow is highly doubtfull.

25 TUESDAY A gloomy October day, the wind inflexibly constant in the west which is fatal. Sir James Graham proposes to wait upon us after breakfast. A trouble occurs about my taking a oath before a Master Extraordinary in chancery[1] but such cannot easily be found as they reside in chambers in town and rusticate after business so they are difficult to catch as an eel. At ten my children set off to the Dock yard which is a most proditious effort of machinery and they are promised the sight of an anchor in the act of being forged, a most Cyclopean sight. Walter is to call upon the Solicitor and appoint him to be with [me] by twelve. About the reign of Henry VIII the French took the pile, as it was calld, of Tondray but were beat off. About the end of the American war an individual named John Aiken or John the Painter[2] undertook to set the dockyards on fire and in some degree accomplishd his purpose. He had no accomplice and to support himself committed solitary robberies. Being discov[e]rd he long hung in chains near the outward fortifications. Last Night a deputation of the literary and Philosophical Society of Dublin[3] came to present me with the honorary freedom of their body which I accepted with becoming gratitude. There is little credit in gathering the name of a disabled invalid.

Here I am going a long and curious tour without ability to walk a quarter of a mile. *Quaere* what hope of recovery? I think and think in vain when attempting to trace the progress of this disease, and so gradually has my health declined that I believe it has been acting upon me for ten years gradually diminishing my strength. My mental faculties may perhaps recover; my bodily stren[g]th cannot return unless climate has an effect on the human frame which I cannot

1. In connection with Lady Scott's Chancery money.
2. James Aitken, an Edinburgh painter who had taken first to highway robbery and then to the American cause.
3. 'Dublin' is, of course, a slip for 'Portsmouth'. They arrived, inconveniently, in the middle of dinner, but Scott saw them immediately. Hall's *Fragments*, ch. 27. 'The interview lasted upwards of an hour; and although Sir Walter was evidently labouring under severe indisposition, the deputation were highly gratified by the recital of various interesting anecdotes, in which the slumbering energies of his mind broke through the trammels which appeared to hold it in temporary subjection.' *The Annual Register 1831*, Chronicle, p. 169.

possibly believe or comprehend. The safe resolution is to try no foolish experiments but make myself as easy as I can – without suffering myself to be vexd about what I cannot help. If I sit on the deck and look at Vesuvius it will be all I ought to think of.

Having mentiond John the Painter I may add that it was in this town of Portsmouth that the Duke of Buckingham was stabbd to death by Felton,[1] a fanatic of the same kind with the Incendiary though perpetrator of a more manly crime. This monster-breeding age can afford both Feltons and John Aikens in abundance. Every villag[e] supplies them while in fact a deep feeling of the coarsest selfishness furnishes the ruling motive instead of an affectation of publick spirit, that hackneyed affectation of patriotism as like the reality as a Birmingham hal[f]penny to a guinea.

The girls I regret to see have got a senseless custom of talking politics at all weathers and in all sort of company.[2] This can do no good and may give much offence. Silence can offend no one and there are pleasanter or less irritating subjects to talk of. I gave them both a hint of this and bid them both remember they were among ordinary strangers who had no [connection with us]. How little young people reflect what they may win or lose by a smart reflection imprudently fired off at a venture. Mr. Barrow of the Admiralty came in and told us the whole fleet, *Barham* excepted, were orderd to the North Sea to help to bully the King of Holland[3] and that Capt. Pigot, whose motions are of more importance to us than those of the whole British navy, sails as certainly as these things can be prophesied on Thursday 27th October.

26 WEDNESDAY Here we still are fixd by the inexorable wind. Yesterday we askd a few old friends, Mr. and Mrs. Obournes and a two or three others, to tea and talk for I think they had little more. I engaged in a new novel by Mr. Smith calld *New Forest*. It is written in an old stile calculated to meet the popular ideas, somewhat like *Man as He is Not*[4] and that class. The author's opinions seem rather to sit loose upon [him] and to be adopted for the nonce and not very well

1. In 1628.
2. Captain Hall was a Whig, and so probably were Duncan and Pigot. Anne had learned her politics from her father.
3. 'An idea at that time prevailed that an armament was about to be fitted out against Holland . . . I had detected a lurking sort of hope on Sir Walter's part, that the frigate prepared for his reception would be one of those ordered away, and that he might thus have an excuse for not leaving the country.' Hall's *Fragments*, ch. 27.
4. *Hermsprong or Man as he is not* (1796), by Robert Bage.

brought out. His idea of a heroe is an American philosopher with all the affected virtues of a republican which no man believes in. This is very tiresome not to be able to walk abroad for an instant but to be kept in this old house which they call the Fountain,[1] a mansion made of wood in imitation of a ship. The timbers were well trieid last night during the squall. The thermometer has sunk an inch very suddenly which seems to argue a change and probably a deliverance from Port.

Sir Michael Seymour, Mr. Harris, Captain Lawrence came to greet us after breakfast, also Sir James Graham.[2] They were all learnd on the change of weather which seems to be generally expected. I had a good mess of Tory chat with Mr. Harris; we hope to see his daughters in the evening. He keeps his courage amid the despair of too many of his party.

About one o'clock our Kofle, as Mungo Park words it, set out, self excluded, set out to witness the fleet sailing from the ramparts.

27 THURSDAY The weather is more moderate and there is chance of our sailing. We whiled away our time as we could relieved by several kind visits. We realized the scene of hopeless expectation described by fielding in his *Voyage to Lisbon*,[3] which identical tract Capt. Hall, who in his eagerness to be kind seems in possession of the wishing cap of Fortunatus, was able to provide for us. Tomorrow is spoke of as certainly a day to move.

28 FRIDAY But the wind is as unfavourable as ever and I take a hobbling morning walk upon the rampart where I am edified by a good natured officer who shews me the place markd by a buoy where the *Royal George* went down 'with 1500 men'.[4] Its hull still forms a shoal which is still in existence, a neglect scarcely reconcileable with the splendour of our proceedings where our navy is concerned. Saw a battle on the rampart between two sailor boys who fought like game cocks. Return to the Fountain to a voluminous breakfast. Capt. Pigot

1. The Fountain Inn, at which they lodged because the George was full. Hall's *Fragments*, ch. 27.
2. This was a naval party. Graham was an admiral and Harris a captain; Seymour was Resident Commissioner at Portsmouth and Lawrence ran the Naval Academy.
3. Fielding's *Journal of a Voyage to Lisbon*, which describes his departure from England in 1754 in a vain quest for health. Basil Hall found a copy in 'Mr. Harrison the bookseller's'. Hall's *Fragments*, ch. 27.
4. His companion in this seven o'clock walk was Captain Hall, to whom he quoted part of Cowper's 'Loss of the Royal George'. Hall's *Fragments*, ch. 27.

calls with little hope of sailing to-day. I make my civil affidavit yesterday by Mr. Minchin, a Master extraordinary in Chancery, which I gave to Sophia last night.[1]

29 SATURDAY The weather is changed and I think we shall sail. Capt Forbes comes with offer of the Admiral's Sir Michael Seymour's barge but we must pause on our answer. I have had a very disturbdd night.

Capt Pigot's summons is at length brought by his own announcement and the same time the Admiral's barge attends for our accomodation and puts us and our luggage on board of the *Barham*, a beautiful ship, a seventy four cut down to a fifty[2] and well deserving all the commendations bestowd on her. The weather a calm which is almost equal to a favourable wind so we glide beautifully along by the Isle of Wight and the outside of the island. We landsfolk feel that queerish sensation when withouout being in the least sick we are not quite well. We dine enormously and take my cot at nine o'clock where we sleep undisturbd till seven.

30 SUNDAY Find the Bill of Portland in sight having run about forty miles during the night. About the middle of the day turn sea sick and retire to my berth for the rest of the evening.

31 MONDAY A sleepless night and a bilious morning yet not so very uncomfortable as the phrase may imply. The bolts clashd and made me dream of poor Bran. The wind being nearly comple[te]ly contrary we have by ten o'clock gaind Plymouth and of course will stand westward for cape Finisterre. Terrible tossing and much sea sickness beating our passage against the turn. I may as well say we had a parting visit from Lady Graham, who came off in a steamer, saluted us *à la distance* and gave us by signal her *bonne voyage*.

On Sunday we had prayers and sermon from Mr. Marshal our Chaplain, a Trinity College youth who made a very respectable figure.

Sailing less ro[u]gh.

NOVEMBER

1 TUESDAY The night was less dismal than yesterday and we hold our course though with an unfavourable wind, and make it is said

---

1. To take back to London. Thomas and William Minchin of Portsea were well-known local attorneys.
2. Ships were rated by the number of guns they carried. The reduced number gave added speed.

about forty miles progress. After all this sort of navigation recommends the steamer which forces its way whether the breeze will or no.

2 WEDNESDAY Wind as cross as two sticks with nasty squal[ls] of wind and rain. We keep dodging about the Lizard and Land's End without ever getting out of sight of those interesting terminations of old England. Keep the deck on the whole day though bitter cold. Betake myself to my *berth* at nine though it is liker to my coffin.

3 THURSDAY The Sea sickness has pretty much left us but the nights are far from voluptuous, as Lord Stowell says. After breakfast I establish myself in the after cabbin to read and write as well as I can, whereof this is a bad specimen.

4 FRIDAY The current unfavorable and the ship pitching a great deal. Yet the vessel on the whole keeps her course and we get on our way with hope of reaching Cape Finisterre when it shall please God.[1]

5 SATURDAY We still creep on this petty space from day to day[2] without being able to make way but also without losing any. Mean while *frolich!* we become freed from the nausea and disgust of the sea sickness and are chirrupping merrily. Spend the daylight chiefly on deck where the sailors are traind in exercizing the great guns on a new sort of carriage call'd from the inventor Marshall's which seems ingenious.

6 SUNDAY No prongress to-day – the Ship begins to lay her course but makes no great way. Appetite of the passengers excellent which we amuse at the expence of the sea stock, cold beef and biscuit. I feel myself very helpless on board but every body is ready to assist me.

7 MONDAY The wind still holds fair though far from blowing steadily but by fits and variably. No object to look at

> One wide way water all around us
> All about us one '*grey*' sky.[3]

---

1. 'Here we *are driven* back by contrary wind and squalls and all sort of disagreable things to Sidmouth. It is very provoking as we sailed last Saturday morning and have done nothing. We are again going to sail just now *hoping for a fair wind.*' Anne to Cadell, 4 November 1831, Cadell Letters.
2. *Macbeth*, v. 5.
3. Stevens's 'The Storm', st. 5, with '*grey*' for 'black'

There are neither birds in the air, fish in the sea, nor object on face of the waters. It is odd that though once so great a smoker I now never think on a segar. So much the better.

8 TUESDAY As we began to get southward we began to feel a milder and more pleasing temperature and the wind becomes decidedly favourable when we have nearly traversed the famous bay of Biscay. The [wind] now got into a sort of trade wind blowing from the east.

9 WEDNESDAY This morning run seventy miles from twelve at night. This is something like going; till now bating the rolling and pitching we lay as

> – idle as a painting ship
> Upon a painted ocean.[1]

10 THURSDAY Wind changes and is both mild and favourable. We pass Cape Ortugal. See a wild cluster of skerries or naked rocks calld Berlinguas rising out of the sea like MacLeod's Maidens on the isle of skye.

11 FRIDAY Wind still more moderate and fair yet it is about 11 knots an hour; we pass Oporto and Lisbon in the night. See the coast of Portugal. A bare wild Country with here and there a church or convent. If it keeps fair this evening [we] see Gibraltar which would be very desirable. Our sailors have been exercized at a species of sword exercize which recalls many recollections.

12 SATURDAY The favourable wind gets back to its quarters in the South west and becomes what the Italians call the Sirocco, abominated for its debilitating qualities. I cannot say I feel them but I dreamt obscure dreams all night which are probably to be credited to the Sirocco. After all it is not an uncomfortable wind to a Caledonian wild and stern. Ink won't serve.[2]

13 SUNDAY The wind continues unaccomodating all night and we see nothing although we promised ourselves to have seen Gibraltar or at least Tangiers this morning. But we are disappointed of both. Tangiers reminds me of my old antiquarian friend Auriol Hay Drummond who is Consul there. Certainly if a human voice could have made its hail heard through a league or two of contending wind

---

1. Coleridge's 'Ancient Mariner', pt. ii, ll. 117–18.
2. This Entry is blotched and scratchy.

and wave it must have been Auriol Drummond. I remember him at a dinner given by some of his friends when he left Edinburgh where he discharged a noble part 'self pulling like Capt Crowe for dear life for dear life against the whole boat's crew'[1], speaking that is against thirty members of a drunken company and maintaining the predominance.[2] Mons Meg was at that time his idol. He had a sort of avarice of proper names and besides half a dozen which were his legitimately he had a desire to be calld *garvadh*, which uncouth appellative he claimd on no very good authority to be the ancient name of the Hays – a tale. I loved him dearly. He had high spirits, a zealous faith, good humour, and enthusiasm, and it grieves me that I must pass within ten miles of him and leave him unsaluted for, Mercy a ged, what a yell of gratulation would there be. I would put up with a good rough gale which would force us [into] Tangiers and keep us there for a week but the wind is only in gentle opposition like a well drilld spouse.

Gibraltar we shall see this evening. Tangiers becomes out of the question. Captain says we will lie bye during the night rather, sooner than darkness shall devour such an object of curiosity, so we must look sharp for the old rock.

14 MONDAY The horizon is this morning full of remembrances. Cape Saint Vincent, Cape Spartell, Tarifa, Trafalgar, all spirit stirring sounds, are within our ken and recognized with enthusiasm both by the old sailors whose memory can reinvest them with their terrors and by the naval neophytes who hope to emulate the deeds of their fathers. Even a non combattant like myself feels his heart beats faster and fuller though it is only with the feeling of the unworthy boast of the substance in the fable. *Nos poma natamus.*[3] I begin to ask myself Do I feel any symptoms of getting better from the climate which is delicious and I cannot reply with the least consciousness of certainty. I cannot in reason expect it should be otherwise. The failure of my limbs has been gradual and it cannot be expected that an infirmity which at least a year's bad weather graduall[y] brought on should diminish before a few mild and serene days. But I think there is some change to the better. I certainly write easier and my spirits are better. The officers compliment me on this and I think justly. The difficulty will be to abstain from working hard but we wil[l] try.

I wrote to Mr. Cadell to-day and will send my letter ashore to be put into Gibraltar with the officer who leaves us at that garris[o]nce.

1. In Smollett's novel *Sir Launcelot Greaves*, 1762.
2. See the Entry for 25 May 1829.
3. See the Entry for 4 February 1827 and note.

In the evening we saw the celebrated fortress that we had heard of all our lives and which there is no possibility of describing well in words, though the idea I had formd of it from prints, panoramas and so forth proved not very inaccurate. Gibraltar then is a peninsula having a tremendous precipice on the Spanish side, that is upon the North, where it is united to the main land by a low slip of land calld the neutral ground. The fortifications which rise on the rock are innumerable and support each other in a manner accounted a model of modern art. The northern face of the rock itself is hewn into tremendous subterranean batteries calld the Hall of Saint George and so forth mounted with guns of a large calibre. But I have heard it would be difficult to use them from the effect of the report on the artillery men. The east side of the fortress is not so precipitous as the north and it is on this it has been usually assaild; it bristles with guns and batteries and has at its Northern extremity the town of Gibraltar which seems from the sea a thriving place, and from thence declines gradually to Cape Europa where there is a great number of remains of old caverns and towers formerly the habitation or refuge of the Moors. At a distance and curving into a bay lies Algeziras and the little Spanish town of Saint Roque where the Spanish lines were planted during the siege.[1] From Europa point the eastern frontier of Gibraltar runs pretty close to the sea which arises in a perpendicular face and is calld the back of the rock. No thoughts can be entertaind of attacking it although every means was used to make the assault <in> as general as possible. The effort sustaind by such extraordinary means as the Floating Batteries were entirely directed against the defences on the west side which if it could have been continued for a few days with the same fury with which it commenced must have worn out the force of the garrison. The assault had continued for several houres without success on either side when a private man of the artillery, his eye on the Floating Batteries, suddenly calld with extacy 'She Burns by God' and first that vessell and then others were visibly discerned to be on fire and the Besiegers' game was decidedly up.

We stood into the bay of Gibraltar and approachd the harbour

1. Scott is referring to the great Siege of Gibraltar by the French and Spanish between 1779 and 1783. In 1782 ten heavily armoured vessels (Scott's 'Floating Batteries'), proof against ordinary shot, were sent close in to the rock in what was intended to be a final assault. The garrison, which had been experimenting with new artillery methods, destroyed them utterly by using red-hot shot. See John Drinkwater's *History of the Siege of Gibraltar*, 1785.

firing a gun and hoisting a signal for a boat – One according[ly] came off, a man of war's boat, but refused to have any communication with us on account of the Quarantine. So we can send no letters ashore and after some pourparler Mr. [*illegible*] instead of joining his regiment must remain on board. We learn an unpleasant piece of news. There has been a tumult at Bristol and some rioters shot, it is said fifty or sixty.[1] I would flatter myself that this is rather good news since it seems to be no part of a formd insurrection but an accidental scufle in which the mob have had the worst and which, like Tranent, Manchester and Bonnymoor,[2] have always had the effect of quieting the people and alarming men of property. The Whigs will find it impossible to persuade men to be plunderd by a few blackguards by them calld the people, and education and property will recover an ascendence which they have only lost by faintheartedness. We backd out the Bay by means of a current to the eastward which always runs there, admiring in our retreat the lighting up the windows in the town and the various barracks or country seats visible on the Rock. The far as we are from home the general lighting of windows in the evening reminds us we are still in merry old England where in reverse of its ancient Law of the Curfew almost every individual however humble his station takes as of right a part of the evening for enlarging the scope of his industry or of his little pleasures. He trims his lamp to finish at leisure some part of his task which seems in such circumstances almost voluntary while his wife prepares the little meal which is to be its legitimate reward. But this happy privilege of freemen English have ceased.[3] One happiness it is they will soon learn their error.

15 TUESDAY I had so much to say about Gibraltar that I omitted all mention of the Straight or more distant shores of Spain and Barbary which form the extreme of our present horizon. They are highly interesting; a chain of distant mountains sweep round Gibraltar, bold, peakd, well fined and deeply indented, the most distinguishe[d] points occasionally garnishd with an old watch tower to afford protection agains[t] a corsair. The mountains seemd to be like those

1. On 29 and 30 October the Bishop's Palace, the Mansion House, the Customs House and other buildings were burnt down by rioters.
2. The East Lothian, Stirlingshire, and Manchester disturbances took place in 1797, 1820, and 1826 respectively.
3. A confused sentence, alluding presumably to the smashing of windows by Radicals. See, for instance, the Entries for 10 and 11 October 1831.

of the first formation, liker in other words to the highlands than thos[e] of the South of Scotland. The chain of hills in Barbary are of the same character but more lofty and much more distant, being I conceive a part of the celebrated ridge of Atlas.

Gibraltar is one of the pillars of Hercules, Ceuta on the Moorish side is well known to be the other: to the westward of a small fortress garrisond by the Spaniards is the Hill of Apes, the corresponding pillar to Gibraltar. There is an extravagant tradition that there was once a passage under the sea from the one fortress to the other and that an adventurous Governor who puzzled his way to Ceuta and back again left his gold watch a prize to him who had the courage to go to seek it.

We are soon carried by the joind influence of breeze and current to the Africain side of the Straits and coast near by along a wild shore formd of mountains, like those of spain of varied form and outline. No churches, no villages, no marks of human hand are seen. The chain of hills show a mockery of cultivation but it is only wild heath intermingled with patches of bar[r]en sand. I look in vain for cattle or flocks of sheep and aunt Anne as vainly entertains hopes of seeing lions and tigers on a walk to the sea shore. The land of this wild country seems to have hardly a name. The Cape which we are doubling has a one however, the Cape of the Three points.

That we might not be totally disappointed we saw one or two men engaged apparently in ploughing distinguishd by their turbans and the long pikes which the[y] carried. Dr. Liddell says that on former occasions he has seen flocks and shepherds but the war with France[1] has probably laid the country waste.

16 WEDNESDAY When I wakend about seven found that we had the town of Oran twelve or fourteen mile off astern. It is a large place on the Sea beach near the bottom of a bay, built close and packd together as Moorish [towns] from Fez to Timbuctoo usually are; a considerable hill rises behind the town which seem[s] capable of holding ten thousand inhabitants. The hill up to its eastern summit is secured by three distick lines of fortification made probably by the Spanish when Oran was in their possession. Latterly it belongd to the state of Algiers but whether it has yielded to the French or not we have no means of

1. Algeria had been ruled by Turkey until 1830. In 1827 a dispute between the Dey and the French consul led to a three-year blockade by the French fleet. An army under the command of General de Bourmont landed in June 1830, and on 5 July Algiers capitulated. The countryside, however, was not finally subdued until 1848.

knowin[g]. A french schooner of 18 guns seems to blockade the harbour. We show our colours and she displays hers and then resumes her cruise looking as if she resumed her blockade. This would infer that the place is not yet in French hands. However we have in any events no business with Oran, whether African or French. Bristol is a more important subject of consideration but I cannot learn there are papers on board.

One or two other towns we saw on this dreary coast, otherwise nothing but a hilly coast cover[d] with shingles and Gum cistus which attracted us to [look] for a short while. The night sets in calm but with no small degree of rolling.

17 THURSDAY In the morning we are off Algiers of which Captain Pigot's complaisance affords a very satisfactory sight. It is built on a sloping hill running down to the sea and on the waterside is ext[r]emely strong. A very strong mole or causeway enlarges the harbour by enabling them to include a little rocky island and mount immense batteries with guns of great number and size. It is a wonder in the opinion of all judges that Lord Exmouth's fleet was not altogether cut to pieces.[1] The place is of little streng[t]h to the Land; a high turreted wall of the old fashion is its best defence. When Charles V[2] attackd algiers he landed in the bay to the west of the town and marchd behind it. He afterwards reachd what is still calld the emperor's fort, a building more highly situated than any part of the town and commanding the wall which surrounds it. The Moors did not destroy this when Bourmont landed with the French. Unlike Charles V that general disembarkd to the eastward of Algiers and at the mouth of a small river, he then marchd into the interior and fetching a circuit presented himself on the northern side of the town. Here the Moors had laid a simple stratagem for the destruction of the invading army. The Natives had conceived they would rush at once to the fort of the Emperor which they there fore mined and expected to destroy a number of the enemy by its explosion. This obvious device of war was easily avoided and the Moor and General Bourmont, in possession of the heights from which Algiers is commanded, had no difficulty in making himself master of the place. The french are said now to hold their conquest with difficulty owing to a general commotion among the Moorish

---

1. In 1816 Admiral Sir Edward Pellew bombarded the town when the Dey refused to abolish Christian slavery, and was created Viscount Exmouth in recognition of the exploit.
2. Charles V of Spain (1500–58), during his war against Suliman the Magnificent.

chiefs of whom the Bey was the nominal sovereign. To make war on these wild tribes would be to incur the disaster of the Emperor Julian.[1] To neglect their aggressions is scarcely possible.

Algiers has at first an air of diminutiveness inferior to its fame in ancient and modern times. It runs up from the shore like a wedge, composed of a large mass of close packd white houses piled as thick to each other as they can stannd with terraced roof and without windows. So the number of its inhabitants must be immense in comparaison to the ground the buildings occupy – not less perhaps than 30,000 men. Even from the distance we view it the place has a singular Oriental look very dear to the imagination. The country around Algiers is the same hilly description with the ground on which the town is situated, a bold hilly beach. The shores of the bay are stud[d]ed with villas and ex[h]ibit enclosures, some used for agriculture, some for gardens, one for a mosque with a cemetery around it. It is said they are extremely fertile, the first example we have seen of the exuberance of the African soil. The villas we are told belong to the Consular establishment. We saw our own who, if at home, had no remembrance upon us. Like the Cambridge professor and the Elephant 'we were a paltry beast and he would not see us' for though we drew wtin cannon [range] our fifty 36 pounders might have attracted some attention. The Moors shewd their old cruelty on the late occasion. The crew of two foreign vessells having fallen into their hands by ship wreck were murderd two thirds of them in cold blood. There are reports of a large body of french cavalry having shewn itself without the town. It is also reported by Lieutenant Walker that the Consul hoisted *comme de raison* a british flag at his country house so our vanity is safe.

We leave Algiers and run along the same kind of heathy, cliffy, barren reach of hills terminated into high lines of ser[r]ated ridges and scarce shewing an atom of cultivation but where the mouth of a river or a sheltering bay has encouraged the Moors to some species of fortification.

18 FRIDAY Still we are gliding along the c[o]ast of Africa with a steady and unrufled gale, the weather delicious. Talk of an island of wild goats by name Galita; this species of deer park is free to every one for shooting upon. Belongs probably to the A[l]gerines or Tunisians whom circumstances do not permit to be very scrupulous in asserting their right of dominion. But Dr. Liddle has himself been present at a grand *Chasse* of the goats so the thing is true.

1. The Emperor Julian was cut to pieces by the Persians in similar hot, desert country in the year 363.

The wild sinuosities of the land make us each moment look to see a body of Arabian cavalry wheel at full gallop out of one of these valleys, gallop, scour along the beach and disappear up some other recess of the hills. In fact we see a few herds but a red cow is the most formidable monture that we have seen.

A gen[e]ral day of exercize on board, as well great guns as small arms. It was very entertaining to see the men take to the quarters with the unanimity of an individual. The Marines shot a target to pieces. The boarders scoured away to take their position on the yards with cutlass and pistol. The exhibition continued two hours and was loud enough to have alarmd the shores where the Algerines might if they had thought fit have imputed the firing to an opportune quarrel between the french and British and have shouted 'Allah Kerim! God is mercifull'. This was the Dey's remark when he heard that Charles X was dethroned by the Parisians.[1]

We are near an African Cape calld Bugaroni where in the last war the Toulon fleet used to trade for cattle.

19 SATURDAY Wind favourable during night, dies away in the morning, and blows in flurries rather contrary. The steamboat packet which left Portsmouth at the same time with us passes us about seven o'clock and will reach a day or two before us. We are now off the coast of Tun[i]s, not so high and rocky as that of Algiers and apparently much more richly cultivated. A space of considerable length along shore between a conical hill calld Mount Balatz and Cape Bon which we past last night is occupied by the French as a Coral fishery.

They drop heavy shot by lines on the coral reeves and break off fragments which they fill up with nets. The algerines seizing on about two hundred Neapolitans thus employd gave rise to the bombardment of their town by Lord Exmouths. All this coast picturesquely covered with inclosures and buildings is now clothed with squally weather; one hill has a smoky umbrella displayed over its peak which is very like an volcanoe; m[a]ny islets and rocks being the Italian names of Sisters, brother[s], dogs, and suchlike epithets. T[he] view is very striking with varying rays of light and portions of shade mingling and changing as the wind rises and falls.

About one o'clock we pass the situation of Ancient Carthage but saw no ruins though such are said to exist; a good deal of talk about two ancient lakes called Bardo.[2] I knew the name but little more. We pass

1. In July 1830.
2. The two lakes near Carthage are the Lake of Tunis and Lake of Manuba. Bardo was a residence near the Lake of Manuba.

in the evening two rocky islets or skerries rising straight out of the water calld *gli frateli* or *the brothers*. Wind rather comes about again.

20 SUNDAY A fair wind all night, running at the merry rate of nine knots an hour; in morning we are in sight of the highest island of Pantelleria which the Sicilians use as a state prison a Species of Botany Bay. We are about thirty Miles from the Burning island – I mean Graham's – but neither that nor Ætna make their terrors visible.

At noon Graham's island appears, greatly diminishd since last accounts. We got out the boats and surveyed this new production of the earth with great interest. Think I have got enough to make a letter to our Royal Society and friends at Edinb.[1] 37.10½ Latitude 12.44..40 15″.2do or 12.44 had lying North and south by compass by Mr. Bokely the Captn clerk. Returnd on Board at Dinner time.

21 MONDAY Indifferent night. In the morning we are running off Goza, a subordinate island to Malta, int[e]rsected with innumerable inclosures of dry stone dikes similar to those used in Selkirk shire, and this likeness is increasd by the appearance of sundry square towers of Ancient days. In former times this was believed to be Calypso's island and the Cave of the Enchantress is still shewn: we saw the entrance from the deck, as rude a cavern as ever opend out of a granite rock. The place of Saint Paul's shipwreck is also shewn, no doubt on similarly respectable authority.

At last we opend Malta, an island or rather a city like no other in the world. The sea port, formerly the famous valetta, comes down to the sea shore. On the one side lay [the Knights], on the outer side lay the Turks and finally got entire possession of it while the other branch remaind in the power of the Christians. Mutual Cruelties were exercized: the Turks seizing on the remains of the knights who had so long defended Saint Elmo cut the Malteze cross on the bodies of the slain and tying them to planks let them drift with the receding tide into the other branch of the harbour still defended by the Christians. The Grand Master in resentment of this cruelty

1. Graham's Island, produced by a submarine volcano a few months before, was on the point of disintegrating. Scott insisted on landing and was carried over it on a seaman's back. Anne also landed: 'I am quite considered here a heroine for so daring', she writes to Sophia on the 25th. 'I burnt my shoes quite through.' Abbots. For Scott's letter, dictated to the captain's clerk, see *Life*, x. 126. Skene writes on 28 December to say that he read it 'to a most numerous assemblage of the Royal Society' the day after its arrival. Letters to and from Scott, f. 212.

Caused his Turkish prisoners to be decapitated and their heads thrown from mortars into the camp of the Infidels.[1]

22 TUESDAY To-day we enterd Malta harbour and to Quarantine which is here very strict; we are condemnd by the board of Quarantine to ten days' imprisonment or sequestration and go in the *Barham*'s boat to our place of confinement built by a Grand Master named Manuel for a palace for himself and his retinue.[2] It is spacious and splendid but not comfortable, the rooms connected out of one into the other by an arcade into which they all open and which forms a delightful walk. If I was to live here a sufficient tim[e] I think I could fit the apartments up so as [to] be handsome and even imposing but at present they are only kept as barracks for the infirmary or Lazaretto. A great numbers of friends[3] come to [see us] who are not allowd to approach nearer than a yard.[4] This, as the whole affair is a farce, is ridiculous enough. We are guarded by the officers of health in a peculiar oo[rt] of livroy or uniform with yollow necks who skip up and down with every man that stirs and to mend the matter.

My friends Captn and Mrs. Dawson,[5] the daughter and son in law of the late Lord Kinneder, occupying as military quarters one end of the Man[o]el Palace have chosed to remain though therebye subjected to Quarantine and so become our fellows in captivity. Our

1. The siege of Malta to which Scott refers here and in subsequent Entries took place between May and September 1565 when the Knights of St. John under their Grand Master, La Valette, beat off a much larger Turkish force under Mustapha and Dragut. After a most heroic defence, the fort of St. Elmo fell; but Dragut was killed and the Turkish losses were so immense that Mustapha decided to abandon the siege.

2. These precautions were on account of the cholera, but as they had left England before the first outbreak on 26 October their quarantine was shortened from thirty days to only nine. Susan Frere. Fort Manoel, built by Manoel de Vilhena in the eighteenth century was much preferable to the ordinary lazaretto.

3. Lockhart mentions Colonel Bathurst, Sir William Alexander, James Hookham Frere, and Dr. and Mrs. Davy. *Life*, x. 130–1. John Stoddart, 'the oldest friend you have at Malta' he calls himself in a letter of the 21st, also visited on the 22nd. Letters to and from Scott, f. 207.

4. 'Between Mr. Frere's habitual absence of mind, and Sir Walter's natural Scotch desire to shake hands with him at every meeting, it required all the vigilance of the attendant genii of the place, to prevent Mr. F. from being put into quarantine along with him'. *Life*, x. 134.

5. Scott had attended their wedding on 20 January 1829.

good friend Capt Pigot, hearing some exaggerated report of our being uncomfortably situated, comes himself in his barge with the purpose of reclaiming his passengers rather than we should be subjected to the least inconvenience. We returnd our cordial thanks but felt we had already troubled him sufficiently. We dine with Mrs. and Captn Dawson. Sleep in our new quarters and notwithstand[ing] Mosquito curtains and iron bedsteads are severely annoyd by vermin, the only real hardship we have to complain of since the tossing on the Bay of Biscay and which nothing could save us from.

Les Maltois ne se mariaent jamais dans le mois de Mai. Ils espérèrent si mal des ouvrages de tout genre commencé durant son cours qu'ils ne se faisaient pas couper d'habits pendant cet mois.[1] The same superstition prevails in Scotland.

23 WEDNESDAY This is a splendid town; the sea penetrates it in sev[e]ral places with Creeks formd into formd harbours surrounded by buildings and these aga[i]n coverd with fortifications. The streets are of very unequal heights and as there has been no attempt at lowering them the greatest variety takes place between them, and the singula[ri]ty of the various buildings leaning on each other in such a bold, picturesque and uncommon manner suggests some ideas for finishing Abbotsford by a screen on the west side of the old Barn with a fanciful wall decorated with towers to inclose the Bleaching Green ornamented with watch tower[s] such as these, of which I can get drawings while I am here. Employd the forenoon in writing to Lockhart. I am a little at a loss what account to give of myself. Better I am decidely in spirit but rather hamp[e]rd by my companions who neither are desirous to follow my amusements nor anxious that I should adopt theirs. I am getting on well with this *Siege of Malta*[2] very well. I think if I continue it will be ready in a very short time and I will

1. 'The Maltese never marry in the month of May. They expect enterprises of all kinds to go so badly during its course that they will not cut out clothes during that month.'
2. The first mention of this new novel is in a letter to Cadell from Portsmouth on 24 October: 'My eyes and power of writing are better since I left Scotland which has put an idea in my head which is worth entertaining. It is a novel calld the Knight of Malta which I will *finish* before I print a page and so avoid the errors of last season & try to do it *as well as I can* and unless I grow worse it shall be one of the best which I have written & will have much description & some real history.' Disc, ii. 421. By 18 December it is 'about one fourth finishd'; a month later it is half-written, and by 26 January 'near done'; but on 6 March he writes again to say that he has burned half of it by mistake.

then get the opinion of others and if my charms hold I will be able to get home through Italy – and take up my own trade again.

24 THURSDAY We took the Quarantine boat and visited the outer harbour or great port in which the ships repose when free from their captivity; all the British ships of war ar[e] three ships at least of fifty of these reduced first rates, a formidable spectacle as they all carry fifty guns of great weigh[t]. If they go up the Levant as reported they are a formidable weight in the bucket. I was sensible while looking at them of the truth of Cowper's description of the beauty of their build, their tapering rigging and masts,[1] and how magnificent it looks as

> *Hulky and vast the gallant war ship rides.*[2]

We had some pride in looking at the *Barham* in particular, once in a particular manner our own abode. Captn Pigot and some of his officers dined with us at our house of captivity. By a special grace our abode here is to be shortend one day. So we leave on Monday first which is an indulgence. To-day we again visit Dragut's point. The Guardians who attend to take care that we Qua[ra]ntiners do not kill the people whom we meet tell some stories of this famous corsair but I scarce can follow their arabic. I must learn it though for the Death of Dragut would be a fine subject for a poem. But in the meantime I will prooceed with my Knights.

28[3] MONDAY by permission of the Quara[n]tine board we were set at liberty and lost no time in quitting the Dreary Fort of Don Manuel with all its mosquitoes and its thousands of Lizards which shook shaking their heads at you like their brother in the New Arabian tale of Daft Jock. My son an[d] daughter were already much tired of the imprisonment. I myself cared less about it. But it is unpleasant to be thought so very unclean and capable of poisoning a whole city. We took our G[u]ardians' boat and again made a round of the harbour, were met by Lady Frances Bathurst's[4] car[r]iage and carried to very excellent Apartment[s] at Beverley's hotel. In passing I saw something of the city and very comical it was, but more of that hereafter. At

---

To Cadell, Disc. ii. 437, 455, 457, and 497. See also Donald Sultana, *The Siege of Malta Rediscovered*, Edinburgh, 1977.

1. See the Entry for 14 January 1828.
2. Unidentified.
3. For the dating of this and subsequent Entries, see Appendix E, xi, pp. 830–1.
4. A slip for Lady Frances Hotham, wife of Vice-Admiral Sir Henry Hotham, the Commander-in-Chief in the Mediterranean.

or about four o'clock we went to our old habitation the *Barham*, having again to dine in the ward room, where we had a most handsome dinner and were dismissd at half past six. After having the pleasure to receive and give a couple hours of satisfaction. I took the boat from the chair and was a little afraid of the activity of my assistants but it all went off capitally, and so to Beverley's[1] and bed in quiet.

29 TUESDAY At two o'clock Mrs. Colonel Bathurst[2] transported me to see the Metropolitan church of Saint John, by the far most manificend place I ever saw in my life. Its huge and ample vaults are of the Gothick or[der], the floor is of marble, each stone containing the inscription of some ancient Knight adornd with some patent of mortality and an inscription recording his name and family. For instance one knight I believe had died in the infidels' prison. To mark his fate one stone amid the many colourd pavement represented a door composed of grates (iron grates I mean) displaying behind them an interior which a skeleton is in vain attempting to escape from by bursting the bars. If you conceive he has pined in his fetters there for centuries till dried in the ghastly image of death himself it is a ghastly imagination. The roof which bends over this scene of death is splendid[ly] ornamented and gilded, is splendidly adornd with carving and gilding while the varied colours and tinctures both above and beneath, free from the tinselly effect which might have been apprehended, [appear] with greatest taste and solemnity in the dim religious light which they probably owe to the time which the colouring has remain[d].

Besides this main Aisle which occupies the centre there is added a chapter house in which the Knights were wont to hold their meetings. At the upper end of this Chapter house is the fine Martyrdom of Saint John the Baptist, by a Caravaggio though this has been disputed. On the left hand of the body of the church lie a series of Subordinate aisles or chapels built by the devotion of the different tongues and where some of the worthies inhabit the vaults beneath; the other side of the church is occupied in the same manner. One chapel in which the communion was imparted was sp[l]endid[ly] adorned by a silver row of silver pillars which divided the worshippers from the priest. Immense riches had been taken from this chapel of the Holy Sacrament by the french:[3] a golden lamp of immense size and ornaments to the value of 50,000 crowns more are mentiond in

1. The plaque on the site of Beverley's hotel wrongly states that Scott lodged there from 21 November.
2. The wife of Colonel Thomas Bathurst, who was acting as Governor in the absence on leave of General Ponsonby.
3. During Napoleon's occupation of the island in 1798.

particular. The rich railing had not escaped but to escape the soldiers' rapacity it was painted to resemble wood and escaped detection.

I must visit this magnificent Church another time; today I have done it at the im[m]in[en]t risque of a bad fall.

30 WEDNESDAY We drove out to se[e] a Malteze village highly ornamented in the usual tast[e]. Mrs. Bathurst was so good [as] to take me there in her carriage. We dined with Colonel Bathurst and her.

DECEMBER

1 THURSDAY I visited my old and much respected friend Mr. John Hookham Frere[1] and was much gratified to see him the same man I had always known him, become perhaps a little indolent: but that's not much. A good Tory as ever when the love of many is waxed cold.

At night a Grand Ball in honour of your humble Servant,[2] about 400 gentlemen and Ladies. The former British of the Army, navy or civil service. Of the ladies the Island furnishd a fair proportion. I mean viewd in either way.

I was introducd to a mad Italian Improvis[a]tory who with difficulty [was] prevented from rendering a poem in praise of the

1. Frere – diplomat, wit and poet, schoolfellow of Canning, and one of the moving spirits of the *Anti-Jacobin* in 1797–8 – met Scott through their mutual friendship with George Ellis. In 1818 he retired to Malta for the sake of his wife's health and she died there ten months before Scott's visit. When he heard that Scott thought of wintering in the Mediterranean he wrote on 6 October urging him to make his goal Malta – 'the true climate for a sexagenerian' – rather than Naples. Letters to and from Scott, f. 187. Anne was amused at the warmth of Scott's attachment to Frere, 'with whom he swears eternal friendship', she writes to Sophia on 4 December. Abbots. Frere was living in General Ponsonby's house at San Antonio, while his own was being repaired.
2. The Ball was given in his honour by the Garrison. 'The decorations were laboriously appropriate. Sir Walter entered (having been received at the door by a deputation of the dignitaries of the island) to the sound of Scotch music; and as it was held in the great room of the Auberge de Provence, formerly one of the festal halls of the Knights of Malta, it was not a bad scene – if such a gaiety was to be inflicted at all.' Mrs. Davy in *Life*, x. 136. 'He had the good nature to stay three hours, and leave a general persuasion that he was very much amused.' Susan Frere.

King and imposing a Crown on my head *volens nolens* – Some of the officers easily conceiving how disagreeable this must have been to a quiet man got me out of this scrape and I got home uncrown[d] about midnight, uncrown[d], unpoetized and unspeechd.

2 FRIDAY I have made some minutes, some observations, and toild some thing at my *Siege*. But I do not find my health gaining ground. I visit Frere at San antonio, a beautiful place with a splendid garden which Mr. Frere will never tire of unless some of his family come to carry him home by force.

3 SATURDAY, 4 SUNDAY Lady Hotham was kind enough to take me a drive and we dined with them, a very pleasant party. I pick up some anecdotes of the latter siege. Make another pilgrimage escorted by Captain Pigot and several of his officers. We took a more accurate views of this splendid structure.[1] They now pray for the King etc. since the Catholic Bill. I went down into the vaults and made a visiting acquaintance with La Valette whom greatly to my joy I found most splendid[ly] provided with a superb sepulchre of Bronze on which he reclines in the full armour of a Knight of chivalrie.

5 MONDAY There are two good libraries on a different plan and for different purpose. A moder[n] subscription library that lends its own books and an ancient foreign library which belonged to the Knights but does not lend books out.[2] Its value is considerable but the funds unfortunately are shamefully small. I may do this last some good. I have got in a present from Frere the p[r]ints of the Siege of Malta very difficult to under stand, and on loan from Mr.Murray agent of the navy Office the loan of the original of Boiardo,[3] to be returnd though Mr. Murray is very good natured about it. He is the brother of Murray of Albemarle street.

6 TUESDAY–8 THURSDAY My chief occupation has been driving with Frere. Dr. Liddal declines a handsome fee[4] – I will want to send

1. The Church of St. John.
2. The first was the garrison library; the second what is now the Royal Malta Library.
3. Malteo Maria Boiardo's *Orlando inamorato* was an early favourite of Scott's. *Life*, .64.
4. He had a difficult patient. Anne writes to Sophia that Mr. Liddell 'has done what he can to regulate his diet but that is impossible & like all the medical men Papa has seen he has given it up in dispair at the same time though I am vexed about

some oranges to the children. I am to go with Colonel Bathurst to-day as far as to wait on the Bishop.[1] My old friend Sir John Stoddart's[2] daughter to be married to a Captain Atkinson.

9 FRIDAY Ride with Frere, much recitation.

10 SATURDAY–12 MONDAY Obliged to draw upon Messrs. Coutts in London by the medium of my friend Sir John Stoddart for £60 and afterwards still more reluctantly by the complaisance of Mr. Beverly of our Hotel two Bills per   [3] each which Walter signs. I fear this is £20 or £30 over my boundary and otherwise irregularly but I do not think my old friends in the Strand will be apt to refuse my bills. I have written to them and to Caddell telling my present situation which is like to be bad enough unless I hear from him.

Captain Pigot inclines to take me on with him to Naples[4] after

---

Papa taking so little care of himself which since we have been on shore he has certainly done'. There was a danger too of Scott's becoming over-excited by too much company:

'What I dread is his going out to dinner which he will do. His arrival has caused such a sensation here, and we have so many visitors, I thought we saw, and heard, every Lady at Malta through the Barriers but I find I am mistaken and there is such lots of people we must still see.'

After a few days, though, Anne succeeded in cutting down the dinner-parties and in persuading Scott that he was 'better *without champagne*'. 25 November–4 December 1831, Abbots.

1. See the Entry for 13–17 December.

2. Sir John Stoddart, at this time Chief Justice in Malta, and formerly Editor of the *New Times*, had known Scott since 1800. To him Scott owed his first meeting with Wordsworth. *Life*, ii.160.

3. £70. Disc.ii.450.

4. Anne makes it clear that it was not Captain Pigot but Walter, anxious to return to duty in England, who persuaded Scott to leave Malta so soon, 'though Dr. Liddell & Dr. Davy were most anxious he should remain', and though in doing so they missed their letters from home. Anne to Sophia, 22 December 1831, Abbots. Walter was not an ideal travelling companion: 'I cant say my dear Soph I found *Walter* any comfort to me. I believe I wrote to you that Papa had given up all dinner Parties. Of course I never left him but Walter was out all day long & *all night* dining at Messes & the swearing at *waiters* & bills in the morning was too much for ones patience . . . you can have *no idea* what it is to travel with him. Street & Nicolson have both nearly given up their places.' Anne to Sophia, 22 December

which he goes to Tunis on government service. This is an offer not to be despised though at the expence of protracting the news from Scotland which I engage to provide for in case of the Worst by offering Mr. Cadell a new romance to be calld the *Siege of Malta*, which if times be as they were when I came off [he] should be thankful [to take] at a round sum, paying back not only what is over drawn but supplying finances during the winter. But the post is so uncertain that I do not know what to think and must take some strong measure if I am dishonourd.

> The devil take order now I'll to the throng.
> Let Life be short else shame will be too long.[1]

13 TUESDAY–17 SATURDAY I feel well and alert though meditating a sad purpose in case of my being disgraced. I ought to say that before leaving Malta I went to wait on the Archbishop. A fine old gentleman, very handsome, and one of the priests who commanded the malteze in their insurrection against the French when they began to pillage the Churches durring the war.[2] I took the freedom to hint that as he had possessd a journal of this blockade it was but due to his country and himself to give it to the publick and offerd my assistance. He listend to my suggestion and seemd pleased with the proposal which I repeated more than once and apparently with success. Next day the Bishop returnd my visit in full state attendant by the individuals among his clergy and superbly drest in costume, the perils[3] being very fine.

The last night we were at Malta we experienced a rude shock of an earth quake which alarmd me though I did not know what it was. It

---

1831, Abbots. Anne may perhaps be excused for her moment of triumph on the voyage: 'Walter was sick yesterday which rather pleased me.' Ibid. Although Scott told him 'he must alter his way of life at Naples' things seem to have gone on there at first much as before. 'Walter & Charles except eating *dinner* sometimes are never at home day or night and it really is hard upon me to have all to do.' Anne to Sophia, 22–30 December 1831, Abbots.

1. *Henry V*, iv. 5.
2. Caruana, at that time a canon, took command when the Maltese rebelled in September 1798 after the French attempted to loot valuables from the church at Notabile. The British and Portuguese allies assisted by blockading the island.
3. A slip for 'pearls' which reproduces the 'Berwickshire burr' of Scott's speech.

was said to foretell that the Ocean which had given birth to Graham's island had like Pelops devourd its own offspring and we are told it is not now visible, and will be perhaps hid from those who risk the main but as we did not come near its latitude we cannot say from our own knowledge that the news are true.

I found my old friend John Hookham Frere at Malta as fond as ever of old ballads. He took me out almost every day and favourd me with recitations both of the translations of the *Cid* and the continuation of *Whistlecraft*.¹ He also acquainted me that he had made up to Mr. Coleridge the pension of £200 from the board of literature out of his own fortune.²

13 Decembr 1831. We left Malta on this day and after a most picturesque voyage between the coast of Sicily and Malta arrived here on the 17 where we were detaind for quarantine, whence we were not dismissd till the day before Christmas.³ I saw Charles,⁴ to my great joy, and agreed to dine with his mast[e]r Right Honble Mr. Hill,⁵ resolving it should be my first and last engagement at Nables.

Next morning Much struck with the beauty of the Bay of Naples. It is insisted that my arrival has been a signal for the greatest eruption from Vesuvius which that mountain has favoured us with for many a day.⁶ I can only say as the Frenchman said of the commet supposed

1. Frere's *ottava rima* poem, *Prospectus and Specimen of an intended National Work, by William and Robert Whistlecraft, etc.*, 1817–18.
2. William IV discontinued the pension of a hundred guineas a year which George IV paid to ten associates of the Royal Society of Literature.

   Scott told Mrs. Davy, in a passage omitted by Lockhart, that Frere overestimated Coleridge: ' "Frere's own quickness", he said, "often makes sense out of Coleridge's nonsense, for really I am profane enough to think that great part of his prose-writing is very little better." ' Mrs. Davy's Journal.
3. They put up first at the Hotel de la Grande Bretagna, then in the Palazzo Caramanico. The weather was 'horrid cold', Anne tells Sophia, and Scott so 'restless and unhappy' that Anne wondered if he should have left home. 22–30 December 1831, Abbots.
4. 'He looks very well' with his newly grown moustaches, Anne tells Sophia, but 'on account of Quarantine can only come & speak along side of the ship.' Ibid.
5. The British Ambassador in Naples.
6. A few days later some of the party had a closer view. 'On Xmas night when returning from San Carlo with my Brother & Capt. Pigot of HMS "Barham" we observed the lava running in considerable quantity down the side of the mountain. Altho' it

to foretell his own death '*Ah, Messieurs, la Comète me fait trop d'honneur*.' Of letters I can hear nothing. There are many English here of most of whom I have some knowlege and w Whom I am connected. I never go out in the evening but take airings in the day time almost daily. The day after Christmas I went to see some old parts of the town amongst the rest a tower calld torre del Carmi[ne] which figured during the Duke of Guise's adventure[1] and the gallery of as old a church w[h]ere Thoma Anelliana was shott at the conclusion of his carreer. I markd down the epithet of a former emperor Conradidino[2] which is striking and affecting. It would furnish matter for my Tour if I wanted them.

> Naples, thour't a gallant City
> But thou hast been dearly bough[t].[3]

So is King alphonso made to sum up the praises of this princely town with the losses which he had sustaind in making himself master of it. I lookd on it with something of the same feelings. I may adopt the same train of thought when I recollect Lady Northampton, Lad[y] Abercorn[4] and other friends much beloved who have met their death in or near this city.

---

was then past eleven we lost no time in getting a carriage & about 1 in the morning found ourselves on the path which leads to the Hospice.

'The spectacle was magnificent . . . The labour of climbing thro' the ashes was very severe and about the middle of the hill proved too much for Capt. Pigot who descended and waited for us at the bottom of the stream.'

The brothers went on, however, and finally, refreshed by 'ham and wine' at the hermitage, 'descended to Resina & from thence to Pompeii'. Charles Scott's Journal.

1. Scott had reviewed *Le Duc de Guise à Naples* for the *Foreign Quarterly* in 1829.
2. Conradin (1252–68), whose father had been Emperor of Germany. He was executed after a vain attempt to reconquer Naples, and lies in the Church of Santa Maria del Carmine.
3. Douglas suggests that this is an imperfect reminiscence of 'The King of Aragon' in Lockhart's *Spanish Ballads*:
   'O city', saith the King, 'how great hath been thy cost,
   For thee I twenty years – my fairest years – have lost'.
   Alfonso the Magnanimous, King of Aragon and Sicily, ruled Naples from 1443 to 1458.
4. For Lady Northampton's death see the Entry for 9 June 1830; Lady Abercorn, to whose husband Scott's father had been man of business, died in Naples in 1827.

25 SUNDAY Bay of Naples. The name of this fine old dignitary of the Romish church is Don Francis Caruana, Bishopop of Malta.

We are once more fairly put into quarantine with a boat of quar[antine]. Captain Pigot does not I think quite understand the freedom his flag is treated with and could he find law for so doing would try his long 36 pounders on the town of naples and its castles, not to mention a sloop of ten guns which has ostentatiously enterd the bay to assist them. Lord knows we would make Ducks and drakes of the whole party with the *Barham*'s terrible battery. There is a new year like to begin and no news from Britain. By and Bye I will be in the condition of those who are <in> sick and in prison and entitled to visits and consolation on principles of Christianity.

26 MONDAY Villeria Strada Nova. Went ashore, admitted to prattique and were received here. Walter has some money left, which we must [resort] to or try a begging box. for I see no other resource since they seem to have abandond me so particular[ly].[1] Got a coach by the week[2] and go ashore each day to sight seeing. Have the pleasure to meet Mr. and Mrs. Laing Meason of Lindertis[3] and have their advice and assista[n]ce and company in our wanderings almost every day. Mr. Meason has made some valuable remarks on the baiæ where the villas of the middle ages are founded, the lower stories at least, upon the ancient maritime villas of the Romans, so the boot of the moderns gall the kybe[4] of the age preceding them. The reason seems to be the very great durability with which the Romans finishd their domestic

1. Before leaving Malta Scott had spent more than the £750 which he had drawn in London; no letter came because of their unexpectedly quick departure from Malta, and he became excessively agitated as is evident from the numerous letters he sent to Cadell. See Disc. ii and Cadell Letters, *passim*. Walter, however, had a credit of £200 in Malta, and Scott's worries were over when Cadell arranged a further credit of £800 with Coutts's correspondents, Messrs. Falconer & Coy. of Naples. Letters to and from Scott, ff. 203, 128, and 130.
2. The original has 'coach' but 'week' can be supplied from a deletion.
3. The pleasure was Scott's rather than Anne's. She wrote to Sophia on 2 January that 'The worst amongst the English is that horrid Mrs. Laing Meason.' Abbots. She later discovered that 'She has an Italian Prince *attached* to her.' To Sophia, 17 February 1832, Abbots. Scott knew Laing Meason as a Bannatynian, a Director of the Scottish Union Insurance Coy., and a brother of Malcolm Laing the historian.
4. *Hamlet* v. 1.

architecture of maritime arches with which they admitted the sea into their lower houses.

We have seen the Strada Nuova, a new access of extreme beauty which the Italians owe to Murat.[1] We were run away with into the grotto very nearly but luckily stopd before we enterd it and so saved our lives.[2] The bay of Baiae Naples is one of the finest things I ever saw. Vesuvius controuls it on the opposite side to the town.

1. Napoleon appointed Joachim Murat King of Naples in 1808. His splendid Via Nuova runs from the gates of the Capodimonte palace.
2. This may be the incident referred to by Gell: 'Mr. Laing Meason and Miss Scott leapt out, at great risk to themselves, in the hope of arresting them. Sir Walter seemed to have little fear of such accidents.' Gell, p. 10.

JANUARY

5[1] THURSDAY Went by invitation to wait upon a priest who almost rivals my fighting Bishop of Malta. He is the old Bishop of Tarentum and notwithstanding his age, eighty and upwards,[2] is still a most interesting man, a face formd to express an interest in whatever passes, caressing manners and a total absence of that rigid stiffness which hardens the heart of the old and converts them like trees into a sort of petrifaction. Apparently his foible was a fondness for cats, one of them, a superb brinded persian cat, seem'd a great beauty and a particular favourite. I think we would have got on well together if I could have spoken English or French or Latin[3] but Helas! I once saw Lord Yarmouth have a persia[n] cat but not quite so fine as that of the Bishop. He gave me a latin d[e]votional poem and an engraving of himself and I came off about two o'clock.

6–12 FRIDAY-THURSDAY We reach the 12 January amusing ourselves as we can, generally seeing company and taking airings in the forenoons in this fine country.[4] Sir William Gell, a very pleasant

1. '5 January 1834' in the original.
2. The Archbishop of Tarentum, Giuseppe Capecelatro, was in his eighty-ninth year.
3. Corson quotes a letter from Gell in Madden's *Literary Life of the Countess of Blessington*. ii. 71: 'I observed Walter Scott and Monsignore did not make it out very well together, for the Archbishop will not take the trouble to talk much or long together in French.' Gell, p. 43.
4. To this can be added Scott's own account of the days in Naples in a letter to Cadell written about 7 January: 'My life is pretty much this. Rise at seven and write three or four hours if I have the humour which I generally have. Then eat a good breakfast at twelve which is chiefly bread and butter and a bunch of grapes, never take butcher meat. Then I go out for amusement or instruction with some friends to see some object in this country of many remembrances, an[d] home in time as to dine at seven, some friends male & female; always break up at eight or nine at

man,[1] one of my chief chicerone[s]. Lord Hertford[2] for Lady Strahan's health comes to Naples. I am glad to keep up an old acquaintance mad[e] up in the days of George the fourth. He has got a breed from Maida of which I gave him a puppy and of which I gave him a puppy.

There was a great crowd at the Palazzo which all persons attended, being the King's[3] Birthday; the apartments are magnificent and the various kinds of persons who came to pay court were splendid. I went with the boys and in my old Brigadier general of the archers' guard wore a very decent green uniform laced at the cuffs and pantaloons and look[d] as well as sixty could make it out when sworded and featherd *comme il fault.* I passd well enough. Very much afraid of a fall on the slippy floor but escaped that disgrazia. The ceremony was very long. I was introducd to many distinguish[d] persons and but for the want of language got on well enough. The King spoke to me about five minutes of which I hardly understood five words. I answerd him in a speech of the same length and all [I'll] be bound equally unintelligible and we made the generall key [s]tone of the harangue *la belle langue et le beau ciel* of *sa majesté.* Very fine dresses, very many diamonds brooches there soever. A pretty spanish Ambassadress Comptess da Costa, pretty and her husband. Saw the Countess de Lubzeltern who has mad[e] an acquaintance and seems to be very clever. I will endeavour to see her again. Introduced to another Russian countess of the Diplomacy.[4] Got from court about two o'clock.

---

night and think themselves well used with a dish of coffee with which they are quite well entertained. In this way we see some of the most distinguished persons both for rank and interest in this celebrated city.' Disc. ii. 450.

1. Gell, author of *The Topography of Troy,* had met Scott at Lord Abercorn's, probably in 1807. Since 1820 he had lived in Italy. He was paralysed and used a wheelchair. Cole, who saw them in Naples, thought 'No two men could otherwise be more dissimilar than the knight and baronet. Sir William Gell, the polished courtier, classical topographer and foreign habitué, with features moulded as from Parian marble, seemed Eurystheus by the side of Hercules.' Cole's 'Memorial of a Tour'.

2. 'Lord Hertford, who was said to resemble George IV, was rubicund, with white forehead and an expression of good humour. He was guardian to the Miss Strahans, they were his "wards"; their almost equally beautiful mother, who was in her autumnal bloom, was his "re-ward".' Cole's 'Memorial of a Tour'.

3. Ferdinand II, King of Naples from 1830 to 1859.

4. She spoke of *Count Robert.* 'Don't read *Count Robert of Paris;* it's not worth reading' was Scott's reply. Cole's 'Memorials of a Tour'.

I should have mentiond that I had a letter from Skene and one from Cadell as far back as 2 December, a mo[n]strous time ago, yet puts a period to my anxiety. I have written to Cadell for particulars and suppl[i]es and besides have written a great many pages of the *Siege of Malta* which I think will succeed. I think £200 a month or thereby will do very well and it is no great advance.

16 MONDAY Another piece of intelligence was certainly to be expected but now it has come afflicts us much – poor Johnny Lockhart. The boy is gone whom we have made so much of.[1]

I[t] could not have been latter better and might have been much worse. I went in evening to the Opera to see that amusement in its birth Place which is now so widely receivd over Europe. The Opera House[2] is suprerd but can seldom be quite full; on this night however it was. The Guards, Citizens, and all persons dependent on the court or having any thing to win or lose by it are expected to take places liberally and applaud with spirit.

The King bowd much on entrance and was receivd in a popular manner which he has no doubt deserved having relaxed many of his father's violent persecutions against the Liberals, mad[e] in some degree an amnesty, and employd many of thes[e] characters. He has made efforts to lessen his expences. But then he deals in military affairs and that swallows up his savings, and Heaven only knows whether he will bring [them] to fight, which the Martinet syst[em] alone will never do. His health is undermined by epileptic fits which with his great corpulence makes men throw their thoughts on his brother prince Charles.[3] It is a pity. The King is only two and twenty years old.

The Opera bustled off wtout any remarkable music and so far as I understand the language no poetry, and except the *Coup d'œil* which [was] magnificent it was poor work. It was on the subject of Constantine and Croesus, marvellous good matter I assure you. I came home at half pas[t] nine without waiting the ballet, but I was dog sick of the whole of it.

Went to the Studio[4] to-day and had no answer to my memorial

1. He had died on 15 December.
2. The San Carlo opera house, one of the largest in Europe, had been rebuilt in 1816.
3. Anne found him 'rather handsome & very civil to the English flirting with all the young ladies'. Anne to Sophia, 17 February 1832, Abbots.
4. 'The National Studio Library that is.' To Cadell, 18 January 1832, Disc. ii. 455.

to Monsr. Reiper, the Minister of the interior,[1] which it seems is necessary to make any copies from the old romances. I find it is an affair of state and Monsr can only hope it will be grantd in two or three days to a man that may leave Naples tomorrow. He offers me a loan of what books I need, Boyer's annals[2] includeded, but this is also a delay of two or three days. I think really the Italian men of letters do no[t] know the use of time made by those of other places but I must have patience. In the course of my return home I calld by advice of my *valet de place* at a Bookseller's where he said all the great Messieurs went for booksellers. It had very little the air of a place of such resort, being kept in a gar[r]et above a Coach house which seemd to contribut[e] to the ease of the horses as well as that of the coach men and stable grooms. Here some twenty or thirty odd volumes were produced by an old woman but nothing that was mercantile so I left them for Lorenzo's learnd friends and yet I was sorry too for the Lady who shewd them to me was very [civil], and understanding that I was the famous Chevalier carried her kindness as far as I could desire. The Italians understand nothing of being in a hurry but perhaps it is their way. If it be done to make the favour the greater why D—n these *Posse tirare* –

24 TUESDAY The King grants the favour askd. To be perfect I should have the books [out] of the room but this seems to hurt Monsr Delicteriis[3] as he, kind and civil as he is, would hardly [allow me] to take my labours out of the Studio where there are hosts of idlers and echoes and askers and no understanders of askers. I progress however as the Americans say. I have found that Sir William Gell's amanuensis is at present disengaged and that he is quite the man for copying the romances, which is a plain black letter of 1377, at the cheap and easy rate of 3 quattrins a day.[4] I am ashamed of the lowness of the remuneration but it will dine him capital[ly] with a share of a bottle of wine or by our Lady a whole one if he likes it, and thrice the sum would hardly do that in England. But we dawdle and that there is no avoiding. I have found another object in the Studio, the language of Naples; one

1. The Marchese Nicola Santangelo was in fact Minister of the Interior. I cannot trace M. Reiper.
2. Abel Boyer's yearly *Register*, 1703–13, which Scott probably wanted for his *Private Letters of the Seventeenth Century*. See p. 785, note 1.
3. The Chevalier de Licteriis.
4. Sticchini's transcript of 'Sir Bevis of Hampton' is in the Abbotsford Library.

work in this dialect, for such it is, was describe[d] to me as a history of ancient Neapolitan legends *quite in my way* and it proves to be a dumpy fat 12mo edition of Mother Goose's tales wt. my old friends puss and boots, Blue beard, an[d] almost the whole stock of this v[e]ry collection. If this be the original of that charming book it is very curious for it shows the right of Naples to the authorship. But there are French editions very early also. For there are two, whether French or Italian, I am uncertain, of different dates both having claim to [be] the original edition each omitting some tales which this has; to what common original we are to refer them the Lord knows. I will look into [it] very closely and if this sam[e] copiator is worth his ears he can help me. My friend Mr. D— will aid me but I doubt he hardly likes my familiar[it]y with the department of letters in which he has such an extensive and valuable charge. Yet he is very kind and civil and promises me the loan of a Neapolitan vocablulary which will set me up for the attack upon Mother Goose. Spirit of Tom Thumb assist me! I could I think make a neat thing of this, obnoxious to ridicule perhaps – what then! The author of *Ma Sœur Anne* was a cleve[r] man and his tale will remain popular in spite of all gibes and flouts soever. So *vamos! Caracci.* If it was not for the trifling and dawdling peculiar to this country I should have tim[e] enough but their trifling with time is the devil.

I will try to engage Mr. Gell in two researches in his way and more in mine, viz. the Andrea Ferrara and the Bonnet piece.[1] Mr. Keppel Craven[2] says Andrea de Feraras are frequent in Italy; plenty to do if we had alert assistants.

But Gell and Laing Meason have both their own investi[ga]tions to puzzle out and why should they mind these affairs?

The weather is very cold and I am the reverse of 'The idiot boy'

> 'for as my body's growing worse,
> My mind is growing better.'[3]

Of this I am distinctly sensible and thank God that the mist attending this whoreson apoplexy is wearing off.

---

1. Respectively a sword blade, and a gold coin issued by James V.
2. The Rt. Hon. Keppel Craven, Sir William Gell's friend, had lived in Naples since 1805.
3. Wordsworth's poem says of Susan Gale:

> 'And, as her mind grew worse and worse,
> Her body – it grew better.'

I went to the Studio and copied Bevis of Hampton, about two pages for a pattern, from thence to Sir William Gell and made an appointment at the studio with his writer tomorrow at ten when I trust I shall find Dedectrius (Delecterus)[1] there. But the gentleman with the classical name is rather kind and friendly in his neighbour's behalf.

26[2] THURSDAY This day arrived, for the first time indeed, answer to last post end of December, arrived an epistle from Caddell full of good tidings. *Castl[e] Dangerous* and *Sir Robert of Paris*, neither of whom I deemd sea worthy have performd 2 voyages, that is each sold off about £3400 and the same of the curr[e]nt year.[3] It proves what I have thought almost impossible, that I might write myself [clear]. But as yet my spell holds fast. I have besides two or three good things in which I may advance with spirit. And with palmy hopes on the part of Caddel and myself. He thinks he will so[o]n cry victoria on the bet about the bet on his hat. He was to get a new one when I had paid off all my debts. And I, uncorrected by misfortune, supposed our who[le] plan had gone to the Devil and seriously thought of thinking[4] from the affair of my own exertions. Yet even when I was meditating all this I had sure enough to remark that it was a base cowardly think and that I should lose all the insurances which must come to £20,000 if I die without self Agency. I can hardly, now that I am assured all is well again, form an idea to myself that I could think it was otherwise.

And yet I think it is the publick that are mad<e> for passing this two volumes. But I will not be the first to cry them down in the market for I have others in hand which judged with equal favour will make fortunes of themselves. Let me see what I have on the stocks.

1. That is, the Chevalier de Licteriis.
2. '16' in the original.
3. Scott has muddled Cadell's news which was, first, that
   '*Count Robert & Castle Dangerous* – appeared about a month ago, & were received by the public most kindly, so much so, that deil ane remains to tell any dolorous tale, they are all gone', and secondly that the profit from sales of the Magnum for the half-year was £3600, an improvement of £400 on the previous six months. Letters to and from Scott, f. 124.
4. Possibly 'shrinking' is intended.

Cas[t]le Dangerous suppose future Editions ——	1000
Robert of Paris Do. Do. ——	1000
Lady Louisa Stuart[1] ——	500
Knight of Malta ——	2500
~~*Trotcosiana Reliquia*~~ ——	~~2500~~

I have returned to my old hopes and think of giving Milne an offer for his estate[2]	£10,000
Letters or tour of Paul[3] in three volumes ——	3000
Reprint of *Bevys of Hampton* for the Roxburghe Club —	
Essay on the napolitan dialect[4] ——	
	£0000

FEBRUARY

9[5] THURSDAY We went to Pompeii to-day, a large party all disposed to enjoy the sight the fine weathe[r]. We had Sir Frederick and Lady Adams, Sir William Gell, the Coryphæus of our party who playd his

1. This was a 'little Quiz . . . meant to run to about 100 pages or thereby'. It was a supposed transcript from an old library, written partly by Lady Louisa Stuart, partly by Scott, and intended as a 'Humbugg on the publick'. It was sent to Cadell on 5 March. To Cadell, *Disc.* ii. 437, 469, 495. It was published as *Private Letters of the Seventeenth Century*, ed. Douglas Grant, 1947.

2. The delusion that he was already clear of his debts and in a position to spend money again gained an increasing hold in the months that followed. In April Cadell reports to Walter, who is concerned about his father's affairs, that Scott has drawn '£2,000 in six months!! . . . he writes to me to buy up debts, to buy carriage horses, to buy ponies – *I pay no attention* to these instructions – they are wholly out of the question at present.' Cadell to Walter, 30 April 1832, Abbots.

   A few days later Gibson, in response to a similar approach from Walter, sets out the state of Scott's debts. Of the original £120,912, only £54,768 still remains; the Trustees have £1500 in cash and Life Insurance will ultimately account for £22,000, but this leaves a debt still of £31,268. 'Your father', he concludes, 'must have taken too sanguine a view of his affairs.' 7 May 1832, Abbots.

3. The diary of his journey to Italy.

4. By 23 March he had added to this list a poem 'of 300 pages to be calld A midsummer Night's dream or a vision of Rhodes'. To Cadell, *Disc.* ii. 520.

5. '10' in the original. Gell says they went on the 9th, however.

part very well.[1] Miss Feronnai. Daughters of Monsr Le Duc de la Feronnai,[2] the head I believe of the Constitu[ti]onal royallists, very popular in France and like to be calld back to the ministry

[3] with two or three other ladies particularly Mrs. Ashley, Born Miss Baillie, very pretty indeed and lives in the same house.[4] The Countess de la Ferron have a great deal of talent both musical and dramatic.

16 THURSDAY Sir William Gell calld and took me out to sights, one a Bookseller at the Port di Capua whose stock is worth looking over.[5] We saw among the old buildings of the city an ancient palace cald the Vicaria which is changed into a prison. Then a new palace[6] which was honord with Royal residence instead of the old Dungeon. I saw allso a gate termd the Capuan where there is a fine arch and tower calld the Capuan Gate, formerly one of the City towers and a very pretty one. We advanced to see the ruins of a palace[7] said to be a habitation of Queen Joan and w[h]ere she put her lovers to death chiefly by potioning, thence into a well smothering them, and other little tenderly trifling matters of gallantry.

MARCH

Embarkd on an excursion to Paestum with Sir William Gell and Mr. Laing Meason in order to see the fine ruins at Paestum. We went out

1. He was an expert on Pompeii. His *Pompeiana* was published 1817–19.
2. La Ferronays (1777–1842), a French diplomat.
3. Blank in the original.
4. She had the added virtue of keeping Walter at home. 'Having so very pretty a person as Mrs. Ashley all day in the house keeps him in *good humour* and as the Italians do not admire her & no english worth while flirting with & being accustomed to a great deal of attention she has no objection to his devotion to her.' Anne to Sophia, 17 February 1832, Abbots. Her brother, Henry James Baillie, proposed to Anne and was accepted, although either Scott's death or his father's opposition prevented the marriage. Cadell's Diary.
5. 'I have packd some good Italian books they have not cost me above £60 or £70', Scott writes to Cadell on 23 March. Disc. ii. 515. Some of them are listed in *A. L. C.*, pp. 339–40.
6. The Palazzo Reale.
7. Poggio Reale, a mile from Naples, used by Queen Joan in the fourteenth century. See Gell, p. 9.

by Pompei wh[i]ch we had visited before and which fully maintains its character as one most striking piece of antiquities where the furniture, treasure and household is preserved in the excavacated houses just as found when excavacated by the labourers appointed by Government. The inside of the apartments are adornd with curious painting if I may call them such in Mosaick. A meeting between Darius and Alexander is one of the most remarkable; the drawing is remarkably fine. A street calld the street of *tombs* begins and reaches a considerable way out of the City, having been flank[d] by tombs on each side as the law directed. The entrance into the town affords an interesting picture of the private life of the Romans. We came next to the vestiges of Herculaneum which is destroyd like Pompeii, but by the Lava or molten stone which cannot be removed whereas the tufa or volcanic ashes can be with ease removed from Pompeia which it has filld up lightly and can be with ease removed if care is used. After having refreshd in a cottage in the desolate town[1] we proceed on [our] journey proceding eastward flanked by one set of heights stretching from vesuvius and forming a prolongation of that famous mountain. Another chain of mountains seems to intersect our course in an opposite direction and descends upon the town of Casteamara. Different from the range of heights which is prolonged from Vesuvius, this second which runs to Castella mare is entirely <of> composed of granite and as is always the case with mountains of this formation betrays no trace of volcanick agency. Its range was indeed broken and split up into specimens of rock of most romantic appearance and great variety, displaying granite rock as the principal part of its composition. The country on which these hills border is remarkable for its powers of vegetation and produces vast groves of vine, elm, ches[t]nut and similar trees which grow when stuck in by cuttings and produce lacrymae christi in great quant[i]ties – not a bad wine though the stranger requires to be used to it. The sea shore of the bay of Naples forms the boundary on the right of the country through which our journey lies and we continue to approach to the granite chain of eminence which stretch before us as if to bar our passage.

---

1. Gell was amused at Scott's lavish hospitality, 'for after we had finished, not only the servants were fed with the provisions Sir Walter had brought, but the whole remainder was distributed among the poor people who had been driven into the tavern by the rain.

   'This liberality occasioned a deficit on the following day when the party started without provision for the solitudes of Paestum'. Gell, p. 17.

As we advanced to meet the great barrier of cliffs a feature becomes opposed to us of a very pronounced character quich seems qualified to interrupt our progress. A road leading straight across the branch of hills is carried up the steepest part of the mountain, ascending by a succession of zigzags which the french la[i]d by scale strai[gh]t up the hill; this I learnd there was an improvement which led by a path con[n]ect[ed] with the tower to which it ascended. The tower is situated upon an artificial eminence, worked to a point and placed in a defensible position between two summits, hills about nearly the same height the accession of the defenders of the which the defenders of the pass could effectually prohibit. Sir William Gell, whose knowledge of the antiquities of this country are extremely remarkable, acquainted me with the history. In the middle ages the pasturages on the slope of these hills, especially on the other side of these hills, belonged to the rich republic of Amalphi who built this Tower as an exploratory Gazabo from which they could watch the motions of the Saracens who were wont to annoy them with plundering excursions, but after this fastness [was built] the people of Amalphi usually defeated and chastized them. The ride over the opposite side of the mountain was described as so uncommonly pleasant as made me long to ride it with assistance of a pony. That however was impossible. We arrived at a country house occupying in a confused sort of a manner a large town situated in a ravine in a hollow and which was calld Lacava from some concavitys which it exhibited. We received the most warm hospitality from Miss Whyte, an english Lady who has settled at la Cava, and she afford[ed] us the warmest hospitality that is consistent with a sadly cold dwelling house. They may say what they like of the fine climate of Naples, unquestionably they cannot say too much in its favour. But yet when a day or two of gold[1] weather does come the inhabitants are without the means of parrying the temporary inclemency which even a scotsman would scorn to submit to. However warm or cold to bed we went, and rising next morning by seven at 7 seven we left La Cavas and making some thing like a sharp turn back wards but keeping nearer to the gulph of Missian, we kept nearer to its shores than in yesterday's journey. We kep[t] a good road towards Paestum, and in defiance of a cold drizzling day wen[t] on at a round paice. The country through which we travelled was wooded and stockd with wild animals towards the fall of the hills and we saw at a nearer distance a large swampy plain, pasturd by a singularly bizar[r]e looking fierce looking buffaloe though it might maintain a much preferable stock. This palace of Persano was anciently kept up for the

1. A slip for 'cold'.

king's Sport. But any young man having a certain degree of interest is allowd to shew it in the chase which it is no longer an object to preserve.[1] The guest however if he shoots a deer or a buffalo or wild boar must pay the Keeper at a certain price fixd not much above its ~~price in the market, which a sportsman would hardly think above its~~ worth for game of his own killing.

The town of Sarentum[2] is a beautiful seaport town and it is as it were wrapt in an Italian Cloak hanging round the limbs, or to speak common sense the new streets which they are rebuilding. We made no stop at Sarentum but continued to traverse the great plain of that name within sight of the sea which is chiefly pastured by that queer looking brute the Buffaloe concerning which they have a notion that it returns its value sooner and with less expence of feeding than any other animal.

At length we came to two streams which join their forces, it would seem to flow across the plain to the bottom of the hills. One however flows so flat as almost scarcely to move, and sinking into a kind of stagnant pool is swallowd up by the earth without proceeding any further untill after remaining buried for two or three years[3] under ground it again bursts forth to the light and resumes its course. When we crossd this stream by a bridge which they are now repairing we en[t]ered a second plain very like that which we had [left] and displaying a similar rough and savage cultivation. There savage herds were under the guardianship of shepherds as wild as they were themselves, clothed in a species of sheep skins and carried a sharp spear with which they herd and sometimes kill their buffaloes. Their farm houses are in very poor order and with every mark of poverty, and they have the character of being moved to dishonesty by anny thing like opportunity.

Of this there was a fatal instance but so well avenged that it is not like to be repeated till it has long faded out of memory. The story I am assured happened exactly as follows.

A certain Mr. Hunt, lately married to a Lady of his own age and seeming to have had what is too often the Englishman's characteristic of More Money than wit, arrived at naples a year or two ago *en famille*[4] and were desirous of seeing all the sights in the vicinity of this celebrated place. Among others Paestum was not forgot. At one of

1. This was one of the first economies made by Ferdinand II on his accession.
2. i.e., Sorrento.
3. A slip for 'miles'.
4. In 1824, apparently during a honeymoon tour. See Corson's note in Gell, p. 47.

the poor farm houses where they stoppd the inhabitant set her eyes on a toilet apparatus which was composed of silver and had the ap[p]earance of great value. The woman who spread this report addressd herself to a youth who had born[e] arms and undoubtedly he fainted[1] no more hesitation in [calling] on his companions than the person with whom the idea had originated. Five fellows not known before this time for any particular evil must however [have] agreed to rob the English gentleman of the Treasure of which he had made such an imprudent display. They were attackd by the banditti in several parties but the principal attack was given to Mr. Hunt's carriage and a servant of that gentleman being as well as himself puld out of the carr[r]iage and watchd by those who had undertaken to conduct this bad deed. The man who had been the soldier, probably to keep up his courage began to bully, talk violently, and strike the *valet de place*, who screamd out in a plaintiff manner 'Do not injure me'. His master, hoping to make some impression, said 'Do not hurt my servant' to which the principal Brigand replyied 'If he dares to act shoot him.' The man who stood over Mr. Hunt unfortunately took his Captain at the word and his unfortunate shot mortally wounded the unfortunate gentlema[n] and his wife who both died next day at our landlady Miss White's who had the charity to receive him that they might hear their ow[n] language on their death bed.[2] The Neapolitan government made the most uncommon exertions. The whole of the assassins were taken within a fortnight and executed within a week afterwards.

In this wild spot renderd unpleasing by the sad remembrance of so inhuman an accident and the cottages which serve for refuge for so wretched and wild a people exist the celebrated ruins of Paestum, and being without arms of any kind the situation was a dreary one, and though I can scarce expect now to defend myself effectually yet the presence of my pistol would have been an infinite cordial. The ruins are of very great antiquity which for a very long time has not been suspected as it was never suppose[d] that the sybarrites, a luxurious people, were early possessd of a stile of architecture simple, chaste and inconconceivably grand which was lost before the time of augustus who is said by Suetonius to have undertaken a journey on purpose to visit these remains of an architecture, the most simple and massive of which Italy at least has any other specimen. The

1. Perhaps a slip for 'feigned'.
2. Gell's version is that finding no surgeon who would risk his life
   she ventured alone to the spot 'well provided with lint,
   medicines and all that could be useful to the wounded persons'.
   Gell, p. 16.

Greeks have specimens of the same kind but it is composed not of stone like Paestum but of marble. All this has been a discovery of recent date.

The ruins which exist without exhibiting much demolition are three in numbers. The first is a temple of immense size having a portico of the largest columns of the most awful species of classick architecture. The rooff which was composed of immense stones was destroyd, but there are remains of the Cella contrived for the sacrifices to which the priests and persons of high office were alone [admitted]. A piece of architecture more massive without being cumbrous or heavy was never invented by a mason.

A second temple in the same stile was dedicated to Ceres as the large one was to Neptune, on whose dominion they lookd and who was the tutelar Deity of Paestum and so calld from one of his Greek names. The fane of Ceres is finishd with the greatest accuracy and beauty of proportion and taste and in looking upon it I forgot all the unpleasant and oppressive feelings which at first oppressd me.

The third was not a temple but a Basilike or species of town-house as it was calld, having a third row of pillars running up the middle bet[w]een the two which surrounded the sides and were common to the Basilike and temple both. These surprizing publick edifices have therefore all a resemblance to each other though also points of distinction. If Sir William Gell makes clear his theory he will throw a most precious light on the origin of civilization proving that the sciences have not sprung at once into light and life but rose gradually into extreme purity and continued to be best practized best by those who first invented them. Full of these reflections we returnd to our hospitable Miss Whyte in a drizzling evening, but unassassinated and our hearts completely filld with the magnificence of what we had seen.

18 THURSDAY Miss Whyte had in the mean[while] by her interest at La Trinita[1] with the Abbot <had> obtaind us permission to pay a visit to him and in invitation indeed to dinner which only the weather and the health of Sir William Gel[l] and myself prevented our accepting. After breakfast therefore on the 18th of march we set out for the convent, situated about two or thre[e] miles from the town in a very large ravine not unlike the bed of the Roslin river[2] and traverersed by

1. 'The splendid Benedictine Monastery of La Trinità della Cava'. Gell, p. 18.
2. 'The scenery recalled to his mind something of the kind which he had seen in Scotland, on which he repeated the whole of the ballad of Jock of Hazeldean . . . with great emphasis and in a clear voice.' Gell, p. 18.

roads which from their steepness and precipitance are not att all laudable. But the views were beautifull and changing incessant[ly] while the Spring advancing was spreading her green mantle over rock and tree and making that beautiful which was lately a blighted and sterile thicket. The convent of trinita itself holds a most superb situation on the projection of an ample rock. It is a large edifice but not a handsome on[e], the Monks reserving their magnificence for their Churches, but was surrounded by a circuit of fortifications which when there was need were mand by the vassalls of the convent in the true stile of the feudal system. This was in some degree the case at the present day. The Abbot, a gentlemanlike and respectable looking man attended by several of his monks, received us with the greatest politeness[1] And conducted us to the building where we saw two grea[t] sculptured vases or more properly sa[r]cofagi of mar[ble] well carved in the antique stile and adornd with the story of Meleager. They were in the shape of a large bath and found I think at Paestum. The old church had passd to decay about a hundred years ago when the present fabrick was built which is a modern fabrick but very beautifully arranged and worthy of the place which is eminently beautiful, and of the Community who are Benedictines, the most gentlemanlike order in the Roman Church.

We wer[e] conducted to the private repos[i]tory of the Chapel which contains a number of interesting deeds granted by Sov[e]reigns of the Grecian, Norman and even Saracen descent. One from Roger King of Sicily extend[s] his Majestie's protection to some half dozen men of consequence whose names attested their sarac[en]ism. In all the Society I have been since I commenced this tour I chiefly regretted on the present occasion the not having refreshd my Italian for the purpose of conversation. I should like to have conversed with the churchmen very much and they seemd to have the same inclination. But it is too late to be thought of though I could rea[d] Italian well once.

The Church might boast of a grand organ with fifty seven stops all which we heard pla[y]ing by the ingen[i]ous Organist.

We then returnd to Miss Whyte's for the evening, ate a mighty dinner, and battled cold weather as we might.

In further remarks on paestum I may say there is a city wall in wonderful preservation, one of the gates of which is partly entire and

---

1. 'The Abbot was of a princes family no less than a descendant or collateral connection at least of Thomaus Aquinaus . . . We were treated with every politeness and the Monks shewd their superior pretensions over other ecclesiastics to birth & good breeding', wrote Scott to Lockhart on 13 March. Disc. ii. 507.

displays the figure of a syren and under the architrave, but the antiquity of the sculpture is doubted though not that of the inner part of the gate, so at least thinks Sir William, our best authority on such matters. Many antiquities have been and many more probably will be discoverd. Paestum is a place which adds dignity to the peddling trade of the ordinary antiquarian.

19 FRIDAY This morning we set off at seven in the morning for naples. We observed remains of an aqueduct in a narrow, apparen[t]ly designd for the purpose of lead[ing] water to La Cava, but had no time to conjecture on the subject and took our road back to pompei and passd through two towns of the same name, Nocera de ¹and Nocera de Paganis. In the latter village the Saracens obtain a place of Refuge from which it takes the name. It is also said that the circumstanc[e] is kept in memory by the complexion and features of this second Nocera which are peculiarly of the African cast and tincture. After we passd Pompeii where the continued severity of the weather did not permit us according to our purpose to take another survey, we saw in the adjacent village between us and Portici the scene of two assassinations still kept in remembrance. The one I believe was from the motive of plunder. The head of the Assassin was set up after his execution upon a pillar which still exists, and it remaind till the scull rotted to pieces.

The other was a story less in the common stile and of a more interesting character. A farmer of an easy fortune and who might be suppose[d] to leave to his daughter, a very pretty girl and an only child, a fortune thought in the village very considerable, she was, under the hope of sharing such a prize, made up to by a young man in the neighbourhood, handsome, active, and of a very good general character. He was of that sort of person who are generally successful among women and the girl was supposed to have encouraged his addresses but her father on being applied to gave him a direct and positive refusal. The gallant resolved to continue his addresses in hopes of overcoming this obstacle by his perseverance but the father's opposition seemd only to increase by the lover's pertinacity. At length as the father walkd one evening smoking his pipe upon the Terrace before his door the lover unhappily passd by and struck with the instant thought that the obstacle to the happiness of his life was now entirely in his own power he rushd upon the father, pierced him with three mortal stabs of his knife and killd him dead on the spot, and made his escape to the mountains.

What was most remarkable was that he was protected against the

1. Blank in the original. The missing word is 'Cristiani'.

police, who went as was their duty in quest of him, by the inhabitants of the neighbourhood who afforded him both shelter and such food as he required, looking on him less as a willful crim[i]nal than an unfortunate man who had been surprized by a strong and almost irresistible temptation, so congenial at this moment is the Love of vengeance to an Italian bosom and though chastized in general by severe punishment so much are criminals sympathised with by the community.

20[1] SATURDAY I went with Miss Talbott[2] and Mr. Lushington and his sister to the great and celebrated church of Saint Domenico del Maggiore which is the most august of the Dominican churches who once possessd eighteen shrines in this part of naples. It contains the tomb of Saint Thomas of Aquinas and also the tombs of the royal family which remain in the vestry. There are some large boxes coverd with yellow velvet which contain their remains which stand ranged on a spec[i]es of shelve formd by the heads of a set of oaken presses which contain the vestment of the monks. The pictures of the Kings are hung above their rexiv[3] boxes containing their boxes without any other means of preserving them. At the bottom of the lofty and nar[r]ow room is the celebrated marqs di Lantrech,[4] one of Charles Vth's most renownd generals who commanded at the Battle of Pavia. There are celebrated small portrairts over his tomb: In one apartment is copied a skeleton as moralizing the universal pow[e]r of death engaged in destroying remains with their mattoc[k]. The church itself is very large and extremely handsome with many handsome marble tombs in a very good stile of Arch[i]tecture. The time being now nearly the second week in Lent the church was full of worship[p]ers.

———

[There are no Entries for the next few weeks, but a letter of 19 March from Charles[5] to Lockhart gives a glimpse of their domestic life at this time:

We are going on fairly here but the Bart has not made up his mind as to his proceedings at the end of this month. He talks of going to Rome and Ann seems to have set her mind upon it but for my own part I should be rejoiced if they would stay at Naples. Moving about seems always to make him nervous and unwell . . .

1. '18' in the original.
2. Scott gave her an inscribed copy of Heber's *Hymns* in Naples.
3. 'Respective' is probably meant.
4. Scott means the Marquis of Pescara (1489–1525).
5. Abbots.

We have had an inundation of horrid people who I hope will be the first victims of the Cholera should it visit us e.g. Miss Skene who is travelling with a rich old fool (as she said herself) a Mrs. Russel; & Miss Douglas the American. Ann has picked up some very decent friends & guardian Angels and seems to like the place which were it not for the beastly 'society' as it is called is a perfect paradise.

A postscript adds that they are going to Rome in three weeks' time.]

_____

NAPLES 15 APRIL 1832

15 SATURDAY I am on the Eve of leaving Naples after a residence of three or four months, my strength strongly returning[1] though the weather has been very uncertain. What with the interruption occasiond by the Colora[2] and other inconvenilenence I have not done much. I have sent home only the Letters by L. L. Stuart and three volumes of the *Siege of Malta*. I sent them by Lord Cowper's son,[3] Mr. Cowper returning his leave being out. I [sent] two chests of books by the Messrs. turner, Malta, who are to put them on board a vessell to be forwarded to Mr. Cadell through Whitaker. I have hopes they will come to hand safe. I have bought a small closing carriage warra[n]ted new and English, cost me £200, for the convenience of returning home. It carries Anne, Charles and the two servants,[4] and we start tomorrow morning for Rome after which we shall be home ward steering for the greek skeeme[5] is blown up as Sir Frederick Adam is said to be going to Madras so he will be unable to send a frigate as a promised. I have spent on the expences of medical persons and books etc. etc. about 20,000 Dollars, which is a large sum yet not excessive considering I have remittd about Dollallrs 1000 to which I will have perhaps had to add about £1000 more. Meantime we have

1. This was a delusion shared by no one who saw him at this time.
2. i.e., the periods spent in quarantine.
3. Probably the Hon. W. F. Cowper (1811–88) of the Royal Horse Guards.
4. Walter had returned to his regiment on 5 March. To Cadell, 6 March 1832, Disc. ii. 497.
5. 'Sir F. Adam has offered his steam boat to take us to Corfu', Anne tells Sophia on 17 February. Abbots. Scott's letters to Cadell in Disc. ii show that he had every intention of visiting the Greek islands, until Sir Frederick was appointed Governor of Madras.

to add a curious journey of it. The Brigands of whom there are so many strories, a half dozen are afloat once more and many carriages stopd. A curious and popular work for a work would be a history of these ruffians. Washington Irving has attempted something of the thing.[1] But the person attempting this should be an Italian perfe[c]tly acquainted with his country, character and manners. Mr. Raxhealy, an apothecary, told me a singularly [horrible story] which happend in Calabria about six years ago, and which I may set down just now as coming from a respectable authority though I do not [vouch for it].

DEATH OF EL BIZARRO[2]

The man was calld from his wily inexarolable temper Il Bizarro i.e. the Bizar; he was captain of a gang of Banditti whom he governd by his own authority till he increasd them to 1000 men both on foot and horseback, whom he maintaind in the mountains of Calabria between the French and Neapolitan both of which he defied and pillaged the country. High rewards were set upon his head, to very little purpose as he took care to guard himself against being betrayd by his own gang, the common fate of those banditti who become great in their vocation. A French Colonel whose name I have forgot occupied the count[r]y of Bizarro with such success that he formd a cordon around him and his party and in[c]luded him between the folds of a military column. Well nigh driven to submit himself, the robber with his wife, a very handsome woman, and a child of a few months old, took a possession beneath the arch of an old bridge which crosst ther[e] and by an escape almost miraculous were not perceivd by a french strong party whom the french maintaind on the top of the arch. Night at length without a discovery which every moment might have made. When it became quite dark the Brigand, enjoining strictest silence on the female and child, resolve[d] to steal from his place of shelter and as the[y] issued forth kept his hand on the child's throat. But as when they began to be moved the child naturally cried its father in a rage stiffened his gripe so relentlessly that the poor infant never offended more in the same manner.

This horrid [s]in [du]ly led to the con[c]lusion of the Robber's life. His wife had never been very fond of him though he trusted her more than any who approach'd him. She had been originally the wife of another man murderd by her second husba[nd], which second marriage she was compelled to undergo and to affect at least the

---

1. In *Tales of a Traveller*, pt. 3: 'The Italian Banditti.'
2. Scott wrote this story up at greater length but it was never published.

conduct of an affectionate wife. In their wanderings she alone knew where he slept for the night. He left his men in a body upon the top of an open hill round which they set watches. He then went apart into the woods with his wife and having chusen a glen or obscure and deep thicket of the woods there took up his residence for the night. A large Calabrian sheep dog, his constant attendant, was then tied to a tree at some distance to secure his slumbers, and having place[d] his carabine within reach of his lair he consignd himself to such sleep as belongs to his calling. By such precautions he had secured his rest for many years.

But after the death of the child the measure of his offence towards the unhappy mother was full to the brim and her thoughts became determined on revenge. One evening he took up his quarters for the night with the Precautions, but without the usual success. He had laid his carabine near him as usual and betaked himself to rest as usual when his partner arose from his side and ere he became sensible she had done so she seized [his weapon] and discharging [it] in his booom ended at once his life and crimes. She finishd her work by cutting of[f] the Brigand's head and carrying it to the princ[i]pal town of the province where she deliverd it to the police and claimd and obtaind the reward attachd to his head which was paid accordingly. This female still lives, a stately, dangerous looking woman yet scarce ill thought of considering the provocation.

The dog struggled extremely to get loose on hearing the shot. Some say the female shot it, others that in i[t]s rage it very near gnawd through the stout young tree to which it was tied. He was worthy of a better master.

The distant encampment of the band was disturbd by the firing of the Bizarro's carabine at midnight. They waked and ran through the woods to seek the Captain. But finding him headless and lifeless they became so much surprize[d] that many of them surrenderd to the government and relinquishd their trade, and the band of Bizarro as it lived by his ingenuity broke up by his death.

A story is told even nearly as horrible as the above respecting the cruelty of this Bandit which seems to enti[t]le him to the title of one of the most odious wretches of his name. A French officer who had been active in pursuit of him fell into his hands and was made to die [the death] of Marsyas or Saint Polycarp, that is, the period being the middle of summer, he was flayd alive and being smeard with honey was exposed to all the intolerable insects of a southern Sky. The corps was also informd where the[y] might find their officer if they thought proper to send for [him]. As more than two days elapsed before the wretched man was found nothing save his miserable reliques could be found. I do not warrant this stories but such are told currently.

Tour from Naples to Rome
14th April 14th 1432

Having remaind several months at Naples we resolved to take a tower to Rome during the Holy Week and view the Ecclesiastical shows which take place [which] although diminshd in splendour were expected to take place but diminishd by the Pope's poverty, even to see his diminish[d] rites so on the 15[1] we set from Naples. We embarkd on the famed Appian way which runs pre   . We set out according to agreement, my children unwell, one with a pain in the stomach the other with the rhe[u]matism, both in very bad temper and my own not excellent. We started from Naples throu[gh] the reviewing Ground call[d] Champ du Mars[2] and so on through the *terra di lavoro*, a rich and fertile country, and breakfasted at St. Agatha – a wretched place. But we had a *disgrazi[a]* as I had purchased a travelling carriage assured that it was English build and all that. However were we half a mile on our journey, a bush she[e]rd, a wheel came of[f], and by dint of contrivances we got fought our way back to Agata where we had a miserable lodging and wretched dinner.[3] The people were civil however and no bandits abroad, being kept in awe by the escort of the King of Westphalians[4] who was on his road to Naples. The wheel was so effectually repaird by commencing the task at seven in the morning when we started with some apprehention of suffering from crossing the very moist Marshes calld the Pontine Bogs which lie between Naples and Rome. This is not the time when their exhalations are most

---

1. They started on the 16th, according to the letter from Charles quoted below.
2. The Paese dei Marsi.
3. 'We started from Naples on the 16th in our new carriage which the Lord confound. At Capua while I was one moment away from the voiture to attend to Ann who was unwell out comes a soldier rides against the pole and breaks it short off. In about an hour it was cobbled and all proceeded smoothly till 2 miles out of St. Agata where as I had foreseen John declared that the hind wheel was parting company with the carriage. Before they came to the cut direct we were fortunately able to pull up and I sent the Postillion back for men to drag us up. After having sat an hour in the dark we were put sufficiently to rights to return to the Inn and sleep with the bugs etc. Started next morning after 4 hours work on the wheel.' Charles to Sophia, 24 April 1832, Cadell Letters.
4. Jérôme Bonaparte, Napoleon's brother, King of Westphalia between 1807 and 1813.

dangerous though [they] seem to be safe at no time. We remarkd the celebrated Capua which is distinguishd into the new and old. The New Capua is on the banks of the river Volturno which conducts its waters into the moats. It is still a place of some strength in modern war. The approach to the old Capua is obstructed by an ancient bridge of a singular construction and consists of a number of massive towers half ruind. We did not pass very near to these but the site seems very strong. We passd all singuessa or Sessa, an ancient greek town sitituated not far from shore.

The road from Naples to Capua resembles an orchyard on both sides but alas! it runs through these infernal marshes which there is no shunning and which the example of many of my friends proves to be exceeding dangerous. The road though it has the appearance of winding among hills is in fact on the left side near limited by the Sea coast running northward. It comes into its more proper line at a celebrated sea marsh calld Camerina concerning which the Oracle said *Ne moveas Camerinam*[1] and the transgression of which preecept brought on a pestilence. The road here composes a wild pass borderd by a procky prespis, on one hand coverd with wild shrubs, flowers, and plants, and on the other by the sea. After this we came to [a] military posilition where Murat used to quarter a body of troops and cannonade the English Gun boats, which were not slow in returning the compliment. The English then garrison[d] Italy [and] Sicily under Sir Thom Moore.[2] We supt at this place half fitted up as a barrack half as an Inn. We supd there (the name of the Distric[t] and is now calld Teracina) we suppupd there torablily comfortarbly.

Near Itri a ruind tower is shewn termd the tomb of Cicero, which may be doubted. I ought, before quitting Teracina to have mentiond the view of the town and castle of Gaeta from the pass I have mentiond and from the inn. It is a castle of great stren[g]th. I should have mentiond Aversa remarkable for a house for insane persons on the humane plan of not agitating their passions.

After a long pilgrimage on this beas[t]ly road we all fell asleep in spite of warnings to the connty[3] and before we beat the *reveillez* were within twenty mile which provd forty of the City of Rome. I think I felt the effects of the bad air and damp in a very bad headache. After a steep climb up a slippry ill pave[d] road Velletri[1] receivd us like an

1. 'You should not move Camarina'. Virgil's *Aeneid*, iii. 700. In fact this Camarina was in Sicily.
2. A slip for Sir John Stuart, who defeated the French in Calabria in 1806.
3. 'Contrary' is meant.

answer and accomodated us in an ancient villa and château which is the original habitation of an old Noble. I would like<d> much to have taken a look at it but I am tired by my ride.[2] I fear my time for such researches is now gone. Mont Albano, a pleasant place, should also be mentiond; especially a forest or avenue of grand oaks which leads y[o]u pretty directly into the vicinity of Rome.

My son Charles had requested the favour of our friend Sir William Gell to bespeak a lodging for [us], which considering his bad health was scarcely fair; my daughter had imposed the same favour but they had omitted to give precise direction how to correspond with their friends concerning the execution of their commission. So there we were as we had reason to think possessd of two apartments and not knowing the [way] to any of them. We enterd Rome by a gate surmounted by one of the Old Pontiffs,[3] but which I forgot, And so paraded the streets by moonlight to discover if possible some appearance of the learnd Sir William Gell or the pretty Mistress Astly.

At leng[t]h we found our old servant who guided us to the lodgings taken by Sir William Gell where all was comfortable, a good fire included which our fatigue and the chilliness of the night required. We dispersed as soon as we had taken some food and wine and water.

We slept reason[a]bly but on the next morning[4]

━━━━━━━

[Sir William Gell's *Reminiscences* and Lockhart's *Life of Scott* give some account of his stay in Rome, of his social life there, and his visits to Bracciano, Frascati, and the tombs of the Stewarts in St. Peter's. On Easter Day he was seen by Owen Blayney Cole, who had met him at Naples, at one of the 'Ecclesiastical shows' which had drawn him to Rome:

He was seated on the roof of one of the twin colonnades in the Piazza di San Pietro to receive the Papal blessing – *Urbi et Orbi*. Amid the crowds of heads ranged along the portico on the right

1. Their movements are made clear by Charles Scott's Entry for 17 April: 'Slept at Terracina dined at Valetii [i.e., Velletri] and reached Rome at about 7 p.m. on the 18th.'
2. 'Papa was a good deal the worse for this journey and Ann also has not been so well but at present the former has quite recovered and I hope the young lady will soon be right again.' Charles to Sophia, 24 April 1832, Cadell Letters.
3. Porta S. Giovanni.
4. These are the last words of the *Journal* apart from some jottings at the back of the volume belonging apparently to 1828. They are printed in Appendix G, p. 841.

as you face the Basilica, that of the bard-baronet was most conspicuous from below. His visage, now altered by time or rather by suffering, showed to greater advantage at a distance; and his countenance like the sun beamed forth, when, after a short period of expectation, Gregory XVI came forward to a window or arched recess in front of St. Peter's with his hands full of indulgences, which were eagerly scrambled for by the populace below.[1]

Scott started for home on 11 May 1832. The pocket journal kept by his son Charles is disappointingly brief, and informative only about dates, places, and the names of the inns at which they put up; but although it tells us nothing about Scott himself it at least allows us to trace the slow homeward story stage by stage. They went by way of Perugia, Florence, and Bologna to Venice, where they arrived on the 19th and stayed four days. 'We took rooms at the "Leone Bianco" a very good Hotel,' Charles noted in his journal, 'and altho every room was occupied we found the master & servants very civil and attentive & the charges moderate.' Cole and his travelling companion saw Scott setting off by gondola with Anne to visit Byron's Palazzo Mocenigo, and at Vicenza on the 23rd were invited to Scott's tea-table, and heard him talk of the postponed Buccleuch christening, of Scottish music, and the threatened duel with Gourgaud. Scott's party travelled on the next day through Verona to Ala, and reached the 'Kaiser's Krone' at Bozen on the 25th. They crossed the Brenner Pass and pushed on to Innsbruck and Munich by the 30th. After two days at Ulm, where they were detained by the sickness of a servant, they reached Mainz on June the 7th and took the steamer for Cologne the next morning. Charles's diary is then huddled to its conclusion:

9th From Cöln – my poor father taken ill about 1 post from Nimeguen where we arrived at 5.

10 Miserable day at Nimeguen.

11 Sailed for Rotterdam 12th in small steamer to Helvioitslazo man dead of the Cholera had been just removed when we went board the Queen of the Nethds.

13th June – arrived in London about 7 p.m.

In London Lockhart was at hand, and he is the best witness of Scott's three weeks at the St. James's Hotel in Jermyn Street, of the journey north, and of the last days at Abbotsford. They travelled north by steam-boat, and on Wednesday, 11 July, left Edinburgh for

1. Cole's 'Memorial of a Tour', p. 260.

Abbotsford. Throughout the journey Scott had been barely conscious of his surroundings, but as they descended the vale of Gala

> he began to gaze about him, and by degrees it was obvious that he was recognising the features of that familiar landscape. Presently he murmured a name or two – 'Gala Water, surely – Buckholm – Torwoodlee'. As we rounded the hill at Ladhope, and the outline of the Eildons burst on him, he became greatly excited, and when turning himself on the couch his eye caught at length his own towers, at the distance of a mile, he sprang up with a cry of delight.[1]

There followed a few summery days on which he was well enough to enjoy his house and garden once more. On the 17th he was wheeled into his study at his earnest request and set in front of his desk:

> 'Now give me for my pen, and leave me for a little to myself.' Sophia put the pen into his hand, and he endeavoured to close his fingers upon it, but they refused their office – it dropped on the paper. He sank back among his pillows, silent tears rolling down his cheeks.[2]

It was the end, as Lockhart says, of the final glimpse of daylight. He went to bed and scarcely rose from it again, although he kept a lingering hold on life for two months more. His death is best described in Lockhart's words:

> About half-past one P.M., on the 21st of September, Sir Walter breathed his last, in the presence of all his children. It was a beautiful day – so warm that every window was wide open – and so perfectly still, that the sound of all others most delicious to his ear, the gentle ripple of the Tweed over its pebbles, was distinctly audible as we knelt around the bed, and his eldest son kissed and closed his eyes.[3]

Within five weeks the Trust for which Scott had laboured so manfully was in a position to pay off the remainder of his debts. Robert Cadell had long seen the advantage of putting an end to the

---

1. *Life*, x. 207. Dr. Corson points out to me that Lockhart is romancing. The towers of Abbotsford are not visible until one is within a few yards of the house.
2. *Life*, x. 212.
3. *Life*, x. 218.

Trust before the creditors demanded interest as well as principal. He was himself willing to buy up the debts which were still outstanding, but his first attempt to do so had failed. He now convinced Walter, Charles, and Lockhart that this was their best course of action, and offered them the money that was needed: £24,500 in all. In return he received from the family the copyrights which reverted to them on the expiry of the Trust, and thereby became sole possessor of the copyrights in Scott's works. In the long term it was a bad bargain for Scott's family; but at the time it offered them the chance to put a speedy end to the Trust. On 1 October they wrote to the Trustees with their proposal. The fund created since the commencement of the Trust they calculated at £51,127. 19s. 11d.; the money in hand (including £22,000 in life insurances) was £34,178. 18s., 'or somewhat under 6/- per pound'. The sum required to make this up to 9s. in the £[1] they offered to make available at once. 'It is obvious', their letter concluded, 'that we venture on a heavy responsibility which may eventually bring personal embarrassment to ourselves. To do this we have felt it our duty; and we shall be consoled whatever may be the result, with the reflection that we have done our utmost towards executing the purposes which our venerated Parent had in view.' The proposal was put to the creditors at their final meeting on 29 October, and was 'carried unanimously and by acclamation'.[2]

---

1. 9s. in the £ had already been paid, and the gift to Scott of his library and furniture was held to equal a further 2s. By contrast, Constable & Coy. paid 2s. 9d., Hurst, Robinson 1s. 3d.
2. Sederunt Book, iii. 85–9.

Additional Notes

1. The Edinburgh Oil Gas Light Coy., p. 7.

The Company, of which Scott was chairman, was formed at a meeting held on 27 November 1823 and incorporated by Act of Parliament (5 Geo. IV, cap. lxxvi) in May of the following year. The Act made it clear that it was to be an Oil Gas company, 'nor shall it be lawful for the said company to manufacture or produce gas or inflammable air, or the products obtained in the process of making gas or inflammable air, from pit coal, cannal coal, or coal of any other species, description, or denomination'.

There were constant difficulties. Complaints about the insufficiency of the gas fittings were remedied by setting up a new department to make these themselves. Funds ran short, and two calls of 10 per cent each had to be made on the Proprietors in December 1825 and January 1826. Then in June 1826 'a considerable leakage and defalcation of gas' was discovered. At this point a committee was appointed to examine the future prospects of the Company:

> The result of the inquiries of this committee, after a most anxious and careful investigation, in which they were assisted by persons of great scientific acquirements, was not favourable to the probability of ultimate success in the manufacture of oil gas, and their report having been laid before a General Meeting of Directors, held on the 24th of October 1826, a new committee was appointed, with instructions to consider the expediency of attempting to convert the Company into an establishment for the manufacture of coal gas.

A Bill was duly introduced in the summer of 1827 for the repeal of the prohibition against making coal gas contained in the original Act, and the committee of Parliament to which it was referred reported in favour. However, 'it was lost in the House, in consequence of the active and combined opposition of the Edinburgh and English Coal Gas Companies'.

The Oil Gas Coy. then investigated the possibility of manufacturing gas from rosin or other substances, but were driven to the conclusion that only coal held out any hope of profit. On 22 January 1828 they resolved, therefore, to introduce another Bill into Parliament, and appointed a committee, which included Scott, to push the matter on. In fact no Bill was necessary, as the Coal Gas Coy. proved willing to negotiate a merger. After the hard bargaining recorded in the *Journal*, agreement was reached on 8 March 1828; the conditions were approved by the Oil Gas Directors on the 10th, and ratified by the Proprietors on the 27th. The Oil Gas Proprietors saved something from the wreck, and the Coal Gas Company, now renamed the Edinburgh Gas Light Company, was freed from competition. (See *Edinburgh Oil Gas Light Coy. v. Clyne*, 10 Shaw's *Court of Session Reports*, p. 723, and 2 Shaw and M'Lean's *House of Lords Reports*, p. 243.)

2. An evening with Mathews, p. 68.

While Mathews was acting sume of his black art tricks there was no respect of persons. All assembled in the drawing-room unless one who looked after the under part of the house. Mr. Mathews came to me and ast me what character I would take. I said I did not understand what was to be done, therefore I could not take any character.

'Sir Walter, what do you say Dalgleish is to be?'

'I think just what he is. He makes a very good butler.'

'Well, Dalgleish, I will let you. Here, how do you draw Sir Walter's corks?'

In one moment there is one gone, which makes me jump off my feet, and sume of the onlookers screeched out aloude. He drew two more and with a vengeance too. 'That is your character and trade.'

[Then followed imitations of Peter Matheson the coachman, and of an argument between the voices of John Nicholson the footman and Lady Scott.]

It is too tedisum to go through all the characters, but there was not a night during his stay but he was at work, which keepet the house in an uproar of laffter. (Dalgleish, ii. 88–9.)

3. The days following the crash, pp. 72–5.

At the failure of Sir Walter I did not hear of it until the afternoon, but I see that all was not right with them, for they were sitting with millincoly countinances. Dinner was taken up the same as usual. I, taking off the cover of the tureen, Sir Walter says: 'Dalgleish, just leave us and I will ring the bell when we want you.'

In about ten minutes the bell rings, 'Take away dinner', nothing touched.

As soon as dinner was down, I went out, and passing down South Castle Street, I meets a friend of Sir Walter's, he stopping me ast how the family was. I said I could scarcely answer his question with satisfaction.

'How is Sir Walter in spirits?'

'I cannot say that any of them is in good spirits.'

'No wonder', says the gentleman.

'Pray Sir, do you know anything that has taken place?'.

'Have you not heard of it? Sir Walter has lost seventy thousand pound.'

I turned back and went into the house.

Tea being taken up at the usual hour. In a quarter of an our the bell rings.

'Take away tea.' No soiled cups.

Taking up supper at ten o'clock it was ordered away.

'No porter to-night, Dalgleish.' This Sir Walter always had instead of supper.

Off to bed they goes. Nothing said.

I called Sir Walter at seven. 'Verrey well, I hear you.'

No word of Sir Walter until nine o'clock. Thinks I, this is not your ordinary way, however it is excusable.

They assembled in the dining-room to breakfast. In the course of an hour the bell rings, 'Take away the things.' The same way, nothing touched.

About twelve o'clock hir Ladyship called me upstairs. We went into the diningroom. 'Dalgleish, I suppose you have heard what has happened with Sir Walter?'

'Yes, my Lady.'

'Well, you will have to look out for a situation as we will be obliged to part with all our servants and the carrage and horses.'

'I am very sorry to hear it, but I shall not leave you.'

'Oh, you know we will have nothing, so we cannot pay your wages.'

'I don't care. I will not go.'

So in six weeks after this hir Ladyship told me to let the servants know, to keep their minds easy, they would be the same as ever.

But I return back to where they had tasted nothing. I was determined if possible to get them to taste something, so about one o'clock I took in a few mutton chops and placing them upon the table Lady Scott ast what this was.

'What a fine chop, do have one papa, since Dalgleish has been so kind', (said Miss Scott).

Sir Walter, giving me a look, went forward and partook, Miss following the example. After they had satisfied themselves so far they thanked me kindly. So after things was brought to an understanding they came wonderful round, but still something always preyed upon their minds, although they did not show anything before strangers, yet I knew how they were feeling; they were not the same people. (Dalgleish, iii. 228–9.)

4.   Removing the wine, p. 125.
At the time we was removing the wine out of the seller in the town house to be sent to Abbotsford, Sir Walter cumes down to see how I was getting on.

'Have you any notion what quantity of wine there will be?'

'I cannot answer your question just now, Sir Walter, but I am keeping a correct account of the dozens as I pack them up.'

'Verrey good, but you must not taste ower often, or then you will be apt to forget.'

'Well, Sir Walter, I have packet up a good many dozens already, and I have not tasted yet, but as you are here, if you have no objections, we will have a tasting.'

'No, no, I have no objections.'

So drawing a bottle of white wine, and offering him the furst of it, he just put it to his lips and said 'it would be a very poor cellar if it could not afford a little to support you when you was working so hard.'

I packet up three hundred and fifty dozens of wine, and thirty-six dozens of spirits, and never tasted untill we was putting it past into Abbotsford cellars. (Dalgleish, iii. 225.)

5.   Scott's daily life, p. 142.
I give a small sketch of Sir Walter's habits. In the first place he was called at six o'clock morning in the summer, and seven in the winter. He occupied his studdy untill breakfast time. No sooner breakfast over than to his studdy. If the day proved fine a short walk about twelve o'clock; if not, he was in his studdy untill dinner was announced to him. As soon as dinner was removed here was spirits and warm water put down with three seegars. After he had enjoyed himself with this, off to his studdy. No more of Sir Walter until ten o'clock. As there was always sumething in the form of a supper he made his appearance, but not for supper, for this he never partook of. A tumbler of porter was his favourite. Off to bed half-past ten or eleven at latest. When there was cumpany I have known him to sit till twelve, but even then verrey seldom. When there was ladies and gentlemen came to Abbotsford who never had been there before, Sir Walter was sure to have them off upon sume excurshen to let them see sume old rewen, and the different cenerys round about. He was verrey attentive to strangers, I may well say to everybody. All the

seven years I was in his service I never seed him the least the worse of licure. A most happy gentleman when all his family was around him (Dalgleish, iii. 224–5.)

6. Life with Mrs. Brown, p. 166.

We was not longe in our new apartments untill the landlady thought propper to remove the furniture that was in Sir Walter's sitting-room, and beginning about the hour of twelve, night, and carrying on until three the morning. So Sir Walter gote out of all patience, and as his sleeping room and mines was almost opposite, he calls out, 'Dalgleish, are you sleeping or waking?'

'Waking, Sir Walter.'

'They are surely turning the house out of the window. I wish you would slip down and see if they are fashing anything in my sitting-room.'

I did, and told Sir Walter there was not a bit of furniture left into it.

'Oh, the divell take your lodgings! Stop them emediatly,' and he on with his cloathes and down stairs he cumes.

'Well, Mrs B. What is the meaning of all this noise at this time in the morning? And whare is the furniture that you have taken out of this room?'

'I have taken it to another lodging house, which I took yesterday.'

'Well, you will cause it to be brought back to this lodging, and if not I will send the beegels after you, for you have no right to touch a bit of furniture that is in the rooms I have taken, without asking my liberty, and you and Dalgleish will go imediately to whare you have caused it to be conveyed and let him have access.'

This was to bring his papers.

I brought the papers, but they were all overlaid with ink. I did not know how to face him. I thinks to myself, 'it is not my fault.' I went upstairs and presented them. As soon as he looked upon them, 'Oh, the divell take these flittings! She has thrown me a week back, before I can replace them. I think all is goine against me together'. (Dalgleish, iii, 223–4.)

7. Nero, p. 193.

Saturday 8th July. We went this morning to see the wild beasts, exhibiting on the Mound, an immense terrace 30 feet high, formed by the earth taken out excavations, under the adjoining new streets, and running across and along the kind of chasm, or gap, called the North Loch, that separates the old and new towns. There was at this menagerie the usual display of wolves, bears, hyenas, tigers, monkeys etc. etc . . .

But the great attraction of the show was the far famed Nero, the lion, born in the mound 6 years ago. He was extended couchant, in a large cage, 3 sides of which projected into the menagerie. His size surpassed any ideal dimensions I had ever assigned to this noble animal; and I understand he is the largest yet seen in England. This may be owing to the certain, well regulated supply of food he gets, with the small exhaustion to which he is subject, when compared with these particulars in a state of nature, in which the one is precarious, the other excessive. He lay in an attitude of perfect composure, bearing in his countenance an air of conscious power and dignity, mingled with a benevolent expression, bespeaking him the King of Beasts. Near the cage stood an elderly gentleman in deep mourning, leaning on a staff, in silent contemplation, aloof from the crowd that was following the keeper in his hackneyed zoological notices of the different animals. Waiting his conclusion with that batch, we were whiling away the time in a close examination of the sublime Nero. A nearer approach shewed us that we were not only in the vicinity of the shaggy monarch of the woods, but in close contact with the master spirit of the age . . . *Sir Walter Scott, Bart.* We were introduced in due form, and exchanged a few words, but there was evidently a painful depression of his mind. The recent loss of his wife, great pecuniary embarrassment; with a *mauvais resultat* to certain letters from one Malachi Malagrowther,- all are obviously preying upon him. His countenance shews no one indication of genius, it is heavy without being, as in Johnson, grave and authoritative.- -Sir Walter's has a youthful, without a playful expression; there is no quickness, fire, or even observation in the eye; yet, how much pleasantry, taste, wit, imagination, and sublimity exist, in that wonderful mind! His dress was neglected, almost shabby, with a long hat band, and weepers; and he walked with more difficulty than even his constitutional lameness seemed to cause. He very soon went away, having apparently dedicated his visit to Nero; whom I should not be surprised by and bye to see figure in some future work by the Great Unknown. After going the rounds with the keeper, and hearing how "these here hanimals inhabits Hasia, and them there Americay", we returned to the attractive Nero. The keeper going into his cage was followed by several children, who patted and sat down upon him; a thing the more remarkable; as tho' but just awakened from a sound sleep, he bore the intrusion with his wonted impassibility. For us, we were satisfied with stroking his back thro' the bars. "Wallace", the brother of this lion, is much smaller, and more savage, having speedily disposed of the bulldogs that were set upon him, while the mild Nero declined all but defensive measures. (Unpublished Diary of Lady Strange, wife of Sir Thomas Strange, Chief Recorder of Madras.)

8. The emus, p. 373.
Scott turned in desperation to Cadell:

> My dear Sir, – I am in a great & rather uncommon scrape out of which you must help me. One Mr Harper who went as a settler (not at government expence) to New South Wales thinking himself more obliged to me than perhaps he really was has brought over two Emusses for my special use and acceptance. Now I knew [no] more what an Emuss was like than what a phoenix was like but supposed them some sort of large parrots & thought they would hang well enough in the hall amongst the armour. But they prove to be six feet high and being as I take it akin to your ostrich may be cursedly mischievous besides expense & trouble. In this dilemma & not willing to affront a good & kind man I have written to Mr Somerville Writer Edinr. (Mr Harpers friend) to get him permission to transfer the birds to the King and [if] Mr Harper will give his consent I would wish them sent with every due precaution by the next steamboat to the Royal Menagerie at the tower. Do for gods sake seek out Mr Somerville without loss of time and try to get me free of the Emusses; the matter is pressing for I expect every moment to see the Emusses arrive here followed by the whole mob of Melrose and Darnick. (*Letters*, x. 255.)

But the King, it seemed, was already provided with emus. Harper himself called on Cadell and assured him 'that his Emus are as inoffensive as Turkies – feed on the natural grapes, and follow him in the quietest manner' (Nat. Lib. Scot., Cadell, MS. 869, f. 52), but Scott remained adamant. His next thought was that the Duke of Buccleuch might like them, and on 1 August he told Cadell he had 'written to John Gibson praying him to give them hospitality at Dalkieth where they will be in care.' (Disc. i. 157.)

9. The execution of Burke, pp. 574–5.
A letter to C. K. Sharpe shows that Scott watched the execution of Burke from the window of a bookbinder who lived at 423 Lawnmarket:

> Respected Sir – I respectfully beg leave to mention that I will be happy to give you a share of one Window on the morning of the Execution of Burke.
>
> Mr. Stevenson Bookseller wishes one Window for Sir Walter Scott and yourself but on account of the number that has applied, that will be out of my power. But I shall be happy to

accomodate Sir Walter & yourself with a share of one.

I am respected Sir Your most obed. & humble Servant – Robert Seton. (Nat. Lib. Scot., MS. 1791.)

Scott described what he had seen, in a letter to Mrs. Hughes written on 29 January 1829: 'Burke was executed yesterday morning. He died with firmness though overwhelmed with the hooting cursing and execrations of an immense mob which they hardly suspended during the prayer & psalm.' (*Letters*, xi. 108.)
Hare and his wife had escaped by turning King's evidence, and the case against M'Dougal was 'not proven'. Scott's letters at this time show that he blamed the anatomists, in particular Dr. Knox, as well as the murderers:

> I cannot imagine [he wrote to Walter] that this same Doctor who paid a high price to the most wretched & desperate of men for the bodies of his fellow creatures with marks of violence on them which intimated the manner of their death can be exculpated though it may be difficult to bring proof home to them.
>
> Certainly it will be no excuse to them at a different tribunal that they did not direct any one murther though they held out a bait which led to commission of many. (*Letters*, xi. 93–4.)

The 'doggrel ballads' which Scott mentions in the *Journal* were, of course, shortly on sale. A favourite subject was Daft Jamie, one of the victims, who inspired, for instance, 'A Laconic Narrative of the Life & Death of James Wilson, Known by the Name of Daft Jamie, PRICE THRIP PENCE' and 'Lines supposed to have been written by Mrs. Wilson, Daft Jamie's Mother' (which might be had for a penny). Other ballads included 'Confessions, Lamentations & Reflections of William Burke – A New Song' which begins

> Come all you resurrection men, I pray you now beware,
> You see what has happened William Burke, and likewise
> William Hare,

and concludes with an appeal for vengeance against M'Dougal and the Hares:

> Now Hare should follow after, if right it does take place,
> For these women they should be burnt alive for such a
> murdering case.
> (Nat. Lib. Scot., MS. 1791.)

10.   The visit to Prestonpans, pp. 676–7.

We reached Preston Pans precisely at 2 o'clock. Francis was in waiting at the Distillery. we alighted at the east end of the Distillery nearly opposite to a house possessed by Mr and Mrs Warroch when Sir Walter came to Preston Pans for Sea bathing some 53 years ago – we adjourned to the sea side below a kind of arch or pend and stood on the bullwork for some time. there was thunder at this moment, when some of us proposed to take shelter from the impending rain but Sir Walter objected to any other shelter than a cotters house by the road – after cracking for some time at this spot & looking over a plan of the battle of Preston Pans which Francis had in his pocket we set out for our visit to the field. Sir Walter agreeing to go by the Village of Preston, Bankton &c – I forgot to mention, that on alighting from the carriage I introduced Francis to Sir Walter, strange to say they had not met before – I introduced Francis as Sir Walters veiled publisher for three years – Sir Walter was very pleasing in his reply & said he expected to meet to day a very old friend in my mother –

We all trudged up Preston loan – the rain becoming heavy. Sir Walter mentioned a thunder storm which broke almost over his head one day this last spring when walking out at Abbotsford. it was so near as to make him start – it did some damage at Melrose – Sir Walter stated that his dogs which were with him ran off home –

The rain becoming heavier, Francis got the gate of Preston Tower garden opened where we retreated under cover of the ruin, which Sir Walter admired very much, as well as the old cross at Preston. on mentioning the annual meeting of packmen, he stated that for many years Scotch packmen travelled all over the continent of Europe and were more esteemed than those of any other country on account of the probity & resolution. While Francis showed Ballantyne up the Tower, Sir Walter and I had a confab on business matters, principally about the proposed dividend on his affairs in autumn. I could not help saying that these gentlemen might get over their difficulties if I as the Publisher was so willing to stretch a point to meet whatever call they chose to make on me. Francis & Ballantyne joined us after this when we walked up the narrow road to Bankton gate – at this spot Sir Walter repeated to Francis the entire Ballad of Johny Cope – on Francis telling a story of Skirving the author of the song and the Lieutenant Smith who is named in it Sir Walter told one where Skirving was going to be challenged by Smith – 'Skirving was threshing corn when he received the message. he replied that he should like to see this Smith for if he thought he could fight him he would do it, if not he would follow Mr Smiths example and run away'. Francis's story was that Smith being quartered at Haddington had Skirving pointed out to him on market day with straw ropes round his leg & on going up to him and asking if he Skirving was the author of the song Skirving replied – 'Yes my name is Adam Skirving and if what I said was na true you wad na care sae muckel about it'. Ballantyne was very obtuse in understanding the locale of the ground where the battle was fought. it was some time before he could be made to understand it. Francis tried it, I tried it, and then Sir Walter – we journeyed cracking and talking to the east end of the Meadow Mill, Sir Walter repeating with great glee another humerous ballad about Sir John Hope at the concluding stanza of which we all had a hearty laugh. Sir Walter told the story of Dr Carlisle and his friends joining the Kings Army before the battle. on this we turned down the coal road & had a crack about the Seton family and their large possessions where we were walking on my mentioning their extensive coal operations, Francis took out of his pocket and read an extract from one of the Bannatyne club books about the coal. on which Sir Walter said that he had a duplicate of the Volume and as he (Francis) liked such matters, he would have much pleasure in sending it to him, on which I added that the addition of inscribing the Volume would enhance the gift, which he promised to do most willingly. we journeyed on towards Cockenzie till we were made up to by a Mr Steele, the resident constable in Tranent, who seeing us walking near the Thorn tree came to Francis and offered to bring two swords which he knew were at Preston, and which were found on the field of battle – when Francis said they could be procured I said 'that I trapped one of them for the Armoury at Abbotsford, that all such relics were better in a great collection than single.' Sir Walter replied 'I do most cordially accede to that doctrine' after this we moved on to Cockenzie, which we reached a little after 4 – my Mother, Janet, Georgina Cathcart & Mr Wood were in the Drawing-room (we passed Mr Wood at Ravenshaugh on our way out) Sir Walter was uncommonly pleasing in his address to my mother, he acknowledged her as the 'fifty years acquaintance of a lame boy who had been made very happy with her attentions long ago' I was particularly struck at the ease and urbanity of his manner – he shook hands cordially with Mr Wood as another old friend. Sir Walter had told us that he recollected his visit to P. Pans for the benefit of bathing was after Burgognes surrender in the American war. he well remembered Mr George Constable (the Monkbarns of the Antiquary) and Lieutenant Dalgetty discussing the military movement and tracing them on a map. the boy then remarked his fears 'that they would lose themselves among the lakes' – which Dalgetty dispelled by saying 'they would take care of that' –

We all retired to purify for dinner Sir Walter to the yellow (now Blue room) – we had just returned when the repast was announced. Sir Walter took Janet, Mr Wood my Mother. the dinner was excellent – the first course was almost all fish – tiled whitings being at the foot – they were excellent fresh out of the sea that morning & had a most delicious taste of salt – the conversation during dinner was very amusing & pleasing in every way. Sir Walter did say one or two good things during dinner but I forget them. one in particular which I regret much. Mr Wood alluded again and again to his acquaintance with Sir Walters old friends particularly old Mr Keith of Ravelston and a Mr Wm Keith. to Sir Walters father living in Carrubers Close then at the head of the Horse Wynd, when Sir Walter was born, but the house is now pulled down. the whole time during dinner and after dinner was one stream of amusing and pleasing conversation. Sir Walter was very attentive to the children – and discussed Franks accident on his nose. Whiskey was introduced after the ladies retired. there was a good deal of talk of the Yeomanry and their doings at Musselburgh when in quarters.

About ½ p 7 there was a sign of movement – we reached the drawing room a short time after this on our way up I asked a seat for Mr Wood to town, and in the drawing room I asked leave for Francis & Janet to see Abbotsford on their way to Crailing to Mary Patons marriage – Sir Walter asked how long they intended to stay, for he would soon be there in person. Martha was handing tea when he said to her 'Martha you are like Martha of old troubled with many things' – at 8 the horses were ordered, when Sir Walter took leave he was particularly polite to my mother & Janet – to Janet he said at parting 'Your father was a very old friend of mine. dear me how often I have to talk of other peoples fathers now' we all left about 8 – seated as before, the evening was very fine. (Cadell's Diary.)

11. The prisoner's escape, p. 694.
Scott's part, as described by Peter Rodger, the Procurator Fiscal of Selkirkshire, was as follows. 'The prisoner, thinking it a good chance to escape, made a movement in the direction of the door. This Sir Walter detected in time to descend from the bench and place himself in the desperate man's path. "Never," said he, "if you do, it will be over the body of an old man".' (Craig-Brown's *Selkirkshire*, ii. 140.) The prisoner was 'a strong savage fellow very much incenced and disposed to be violent', Scott tells Charles. 'He broke from the poor old miserable officers sprang over the benc[h]es and would have got away altogether if I had not stopd him. I sent for irons but the officers put them on so ill that though he left the court quietly enough he got free from them in the middle of the street where I left them making no very [heroic] figure.' (*Letters*, xi. 444.)
Nor was this all. 'Not ten minutes after you left this on Wednesday', writes Maxpoffle, 'we had precious riots in which Mr. Thomson & the Water Bailiff Graham were obliged to run for their lives amongst volleys of Stones, one of which struck Mr. T. a most violent blow on

the back near the Tail.' (W. Scott, 25 December 1830, Walpole.)

The officers were too old, as Andrew Lang the Sheriff Clerk testifies: 'Ingles and Tait are the only ones who have even the semblance of efficiency, and Ingles who has been a very active man is now too old to be what he has been, while Tait wants size and strength.' (Nat. Lib. Scot., MS. 869, f. 141.) He suggested appointing three or four active young Constables and swearing in a hundred Special Constables for service in emergencies. The idea was put into effect at once. (See the Entry for 6 January 1831.)

12.　The visit to Edinburgh early in 1831, pp. 708–9.
Cadell's Diary makes it possible to trace the events of these days in Edinburgh with some accuracy. Scott visited Cadell's shop, along with McCulloch of Ardwall, shortly after his arrival on Monday, 13 January. He had hoped to lodge with the Skenes, but their house was full and they had taken rooms for him in Mackenzie's Hotel. There Scott was visited the next morning by Cadell, followed by Dr. Abercrombie and Dr. Ross, who advised him to adopt a strict diet. He dined at Cadell's along with Skene, James and Sandy Ballantyne, Cochrane of Treuttel and Wurtz, and George Moir.

On Wednesday 2 February, after dining at Skene's with Will Clerk, Scott went to stay with Cadell at 16 Atholl Crescent. The days that followed were spent quietly in the house. There were calls on the Thursday from the two doctors and from Skene; Ballantyne came to dinner. During the night the household was 'alarmed by the violent ringing of Sir Walters bed room bell, his servant Nicholson after some time answered it. On asking Sir Walter when at breakfast on the morning if he had been unwell – he said "no I got over the wrong side of the bed, and could not find my way in again. I fortunately however got my hand on a bell".'

On the 4th John Wood brought the will for Scott to sign. John Nicholson was asked to witness it, as Cadell was 'more than once mentioned in the Deed'. Scott dined at Lord Medwyn's on this day, and on the next at the Lord Chief Commissioner's, where he met Mrs. Stewart Mackenzie. On Sunday the 6th Will Allan the painter came to dinner and talked of Constantinople, which Scott was anxious to hear about, 'so as to help his description in Count Robert'. On Monday Thomas Thomson came to dinner, and in the evening Mr. Fortune arrived with 'the prop to his right leg'. On Tuesday the 8th Scott dined once more at the Skenes', and on his return had a business talk with Cadell, whose house he left the next morning at a quarter to ten to return to Abbotsford.

Chronology of the Life of Sir Walter Scott

1771   Walter Scott, son of Walter Scott, W.S., and his wife Anne Rutherford, is born in the College Wynd on 15 August.

1772 or 3   Is left lame in his left leg by an attack of polio.

1773–5   Lives at Sandy-Knowe near Kelso for the sake of his health.

     Family removes to George Square, Edinburgh.

1775–6   Visits London and Bath with his aunt, Miss Janet Scott.

1778   Spends the summer at Prestonpans for sea-bathing.

1779–83   Attends the High School in Edinburgh.

1783   Returns for some months to Kelso, where he attends the Grammar School and meets John and James Ballantyne.

1783–6   Attends classes at Edinburgh University.

1786   Is apprenticed to his father.

1787–8   Is ill, and convalesces at Kelso.

1789–92   Attends classes, mainly in Law, at the University.

1792   Is admitted to the Faculty of Advocates on 11 July. Falls in love with Williamina Belsches. Visits Liddesdale in search of ballads, Northumberland, and the Highlands.

1795   Declares himself to Williamina by letter.

1796   Loses her to William Forbes. Becomes a Curator of the Advocates' Library. Publishes some translations from Bürger.

1797   Becomes Quartermaster in the Edinburgh Volunteer Dragoons.

     Meets Charlotte Carpenter at Gilsland in the summer, and marries her at Carlisle on 24 December.

1798   Rents a cottage at Lasswade.

1799	Is appointed Sheriff Depute of Selkirkshire.
	Translates Goethe's *Goetz* and writes 'Glenfinlas'.
1801	Buys 39 Castle Street.
1802	Publishes *Minstrelsy of the Scottish Border*, vols. i and ii.
1803	Publishes vol. iii of the same.
1804	Rents Ashestiel from his cousin James Russell.
1805	Goes into partnership with James Ballantyne, printer.
	Begins, and lays aside, *Waverley*.
	Publishes *The Lay of the Last Minstrel*.
1806	Is appointed a Principal Clerk of Session.
1808	Assists in the founding of *The Quarterly Review*.
	Publishes *Marmion* and his edition of Dryden.
1809	Quarrels with Constable, and starts his own publishing-house in partnership with John Ballantyne.
1810	Visits the Hebrides.
	Resumes, and again lays aside, *Waverley*.
	Publishes *The Lady of the Lake*.
1811	For £4000 buys the farm of Cartley Hole, and renames it Abbotsford.
1812	Removes from Ashestiel to Abbotsford, begins to enlarge the house and plant the estate.
1813	Is forced to let Constable rescue John Ballantyne & Coy.
	Refuses the Prince Regent's offer of the Laureateship.
	Buys more land at Abbotsford.
	Publishes *Rokeby*.
1814	Visits Orkney, Shetland, and the Hebrides on a tour of the Northern Lights.
	Publishes his edition of Swift and, anonymously, his first novel, *Waverley*.
1815	Dines with the Prince Regent in London.
	Visits the field of Waterloo.
	Meets Wellington, Tsar Alexander, and others in Paris.
	Publishes *The Lord of the Isles*, and *Guy Mannering*.
1816	Publishes *Paul's Letters*, *The Antiquary*, *The Black Dwarf*, and *Old Mortality*.
1817	Suffers from gallstones.
	Fails to become a Baron of Exchequer.
	Buys Toftfield, adjoining Abbotsford.
	Publishes *Rob Roy*.
1818	Brings to light the Regalia of Scotland.
	Continues to enlarge and embellish Abbotsford.
	Is offered a Baronetcy by the Prince Regent.
	Sells his copyrights to Constable for £12,000.
	Attends the first full Blair-Adam Club meeting.

Publishes *The Heart of Midlothian.*

1819   Suffers severely from gallstones.

Buys a commission for his son Walter.

Receives Prince Leopold at Abbotsford.

Publishes *The Bride of Lammermoor, A Legend of Montrose,* and *Ivanhoe.*

1820   Visits London, and sits to Lawrence and Chantrey.

Is gazetted Baronet in April.

His elder daughter, Sophia, married to John Gibson Lockhart.

Is elected President of the Royal Society of Edinburgh.

Publishes *The Monastery* and *The Abbot.*

1821   Attends the Coronation of George IV.

Embarks on further building schemes at Abbotsford.

Supports *The Beacon.*

Sells more copyrights to Constable for £5500.

Publishes *Kenilworth* and *The Pirate.*

1822   Arranges the visit of George IV to Edinburgh.

Asks for the return to Scotland of Mons Meg.

Publishes *The Fortunes of Nigel* and *Peveril of the Peak.*

1823   Suffers his first stroke.

Becomes Founder-President of the Bannatyne Club, a member of the Roxburghe Club, and Chairman of the Edinburgh Oil Gas Coy. Sells yet more copyrights to Constable for £5500.

Publishes *Quentin Durward.*

1824   Speaks at the opening of the Edinburgh Academy.

Publishes *St. Ronan's Well* and *Redgauntlet.*

1825   Settles Abbotsford on Walter at his marriage to Jane Jobson.

Begins *The Life of Napoleon.*

Visits Ireland, and on his return renews friendships with Canning, Wordsworth, and Southey.

Publishes *The Betrothed* and *The Talisman.*

1826   Is financially ruined in January.

His wife dies in May.

Visits London and Paris to gather material for *Napoleon.*

Publishes *Woodstock.*

1827   Publicly confesses that he is the author of *Waverley.*

Buys back the copyrights of the novels.

Pays a first dividend to his creditors.

Publishes *The Life of Napoleon* and *Chronicles of the Canongate.*

1828   Visits London.

Begins the notes for the Magnum edition of his works.

Publishes *The Fair Maid of Perth* and *Tales of a Grand-father*, first series.

1829   Publishes *Anne of Geierstein; The History of Scotland*, vol. i; *Tales of a Grandfather*, second series; and the first volumes of the Magnum.

1830   Suffers strokes in February and November.

Resigns his Clerkship of Session.

Pays a second dividend to his creditors, and is presented by them with his library.

Publishes *Tales of a Grandfather*, third series; *The History of Scotland*, vol. ii: and *Letters on Demonology and Witchcraft*.

1831   Suffers another stroke in May.

Sails on H. M. S. *Barham* to Malta and Naples, accompanied by Anne and Walter.

Publishes *Tales of a Grandfather*, fourth series; *Count Robert of Paris*; and *Castle Dangerous*.

1832   Leaves Rome for Scotland in May.

Has another stroke at Nijmegen.

Reaches Abbotsford in July.

Dies there on 21 September.

(See Lockhart's *Life*; the *Journal*; Melville Clark's *Sir Walter Scott: the Formative Years*, 1969, and Edgar Johnson's *Sir Walter Scott: The Great Unknown*, 1970.)

Country Houses of the Journal and their Owners

Abbotsford	Sir Walter Scott
Allanton	Sir Henry Seton Steuart
Allerly, Melrose	Dr. Brewster
Alva	James Johnstone
Ancrum	Sir William Scott
*Arniston	Robert Dundas
Ashestiel	Col. James Russell
Auchinraith	William Lockhart
Bemerside	James Haig
Blair-Adam	Rt. Hon. William Adam
Blythswood	Col. Archibald Campbell
Borthwickbrae	William Eliott Lockhart
Bowhill	The Duke of Buccleuch
Charleton	Anstruther Thomson
Chiefswood	John Gibson Lockhart; Capt. Thomas Hamilton
Clifton	John Pringle
Corehouse	George Cranstoun, Lord Corehouse
Cowdenknowes	Dr. James Hume
*Craigcrook	Francis Jeffrey
*Dalhousie Castle	The Earl of Dalhousie
*Dalkeith	The Duke of Buccleuch
*Dalmahoy	The Earl of Morton
Drumlanrig	The Duke of Buccleuch
Drygrange	Thomas Tod

Edgerstone	John Rutherfurd
Eildon Hall	Alexander Henderson
Faldonside	Nicol Milne
Fleurs	The Dowager Duchess of Roxburghe
Gala House	John Scott
Gattonside	George Bainbridge
*Granton	The Rt. Hon. Charles Hope
Haining	John Pringle; later Robert Pringle
Huntly Burn	The Misses Ferguson
Kippilaw	Andrew Seton Karr
Lessudden	Walter Scott of Raeburn; later William Scott
Lochore	Walter Scott, Scott's son
Makerstoun	Sir Thomas Brisbane Makdougall
Maxpoffle	William Scott; later G. P. R. James
Mellerstain	George Baillie
*Melville Castle	Viscount Melville
Mertoun	Hugh Scott of Harden
Milton-Lockhart	William Lockhart
Minto	The Earl of Minto
Newton Don	Sir Alexander Don
*Oxenfoord	Sir John Dalrymple
The Pavilion	William Scrope
*Pinkie	Sir John Hope
*Ravelston	Sir Alexander Keith
*St. Catherine's	Sir William Rae
Sunderland Hall	J. Scott of Woll
Torwoodlee	James Pringle
Whytbank	Alexander Pringle
Yair	Alexander Pringle

Near Edinburgh.

Edinburgh Addresses

Abercrombie, Dr. John	19 York Place
Adam, Rt. Hon. William, of Blair-Adam	31 Charlotte Square
Ballantyne, James	18 Albany Street
Ballantyne, James, & Coy.	Paul's-work, Canongate
Boyle, Rt. Hon. David	28 Charlotte Square
Buchanan, Hector Macdonald	129 George Street
Cadell, Robert	16 Atholl Crescent (home)
	41 St. Andrew Square (shop)
Clerk, William	1 Rose Court
Constable, Archibald, & Coy.	10 Princes Street
Cranstoun, George (Lord Corehouse)	12 Ainslie Place
Cringletie, Lord (J. W. Murray)	17 Charlotte Square
Dundas, Sir Robert	32 Heriot Row
Ferrier, James, and Susan	25 George Street
Forbes, John Hay (Lord Medwyn)	4 Shandwick Place
Forbes, Sir William	86 George Street
Forbes, Hunter & Coy., bankers	Parliament Square
Gibson, John, jun., W. S.	23 Lynedoch Place (home)
	10 Charlotte Street (business)
Gillies, Lord (Adam Gillies)	16 York Place

Jobson, Mrs. Rachel	6 Shandwick Place
Kerr, Lord Robert, and the Misses Kerr	36 Albany Street
Mackenzie, Colin	12 Shandwick Place
Meadowbank, Lord (Alexander Maconochie)	13 Royal Circus
Medwyn, Lord (John Hay Forbes)	4 Shandwick Place
Monypenny, David (Lord Pitmilly)	15 Charlotte Square
Murray, John Archibald	122 George Street
Murray, James Wolfe (Lord Cringletie)	17 Charlotte Square
Pitmilly, Lord (David Monypenny)	15 Charlotte Square
Ross, Dr. Adolphus	10 Abercromby Place
Russell, Prof. James	30 Abercromby Place
Rutherford, Robert, W. S.	64 Great King Street
Scott, Sir Walter	39 Castle Street (1825)
	6 North St. David Street (May–July 1826)
Scott, Sir Walter	3 Walker Street (November 1826–July 1827)
	6 Shandwick Place (November 1827–July 1830)
Sharpe, Charles Kirkpatrick	93 Princes Street
Shepherd, Sir Samuel	16 Coates Crescent
Shortt, Dr. Thomas	10 Castle Street
Skene, James, of Rubislaw	126 Princes Street
	46 Moray Place
Smith, Colvin	32 York Place
Stuart, Lady Jane	12 Maitland Street
Swinton, Archibald	9 Shandwick Place
Swinton, John	16 Inverleith Place
Thomson, Thomas	42 Charlotte Square

(Source: *Edinburgh Post Office Directory*.)

Politics in the Journal

CATHOLIC EMANCIPATION

The Act referred to in the *Journal* is the Catholic Emancipation Act of 1829 (10 Geo. IV, cap. 7). It threw open to Roman Catholics most civil and military offices, and removed the obligation to take a declaration against transubstantiation.

THE TIMETABLE OF REFORM

First Reform Bill

1 March 1831	Lord John Russell explains Government plans.
22 March	Second Reading passes the Commons by one vote.
28 March	A general illumination in Edinburgh. Unlighted windows smashed by the mob.
22 April	Parliament dissolved after a wrecking amendment carried on the 19th.

Second Reform Bill

21 September 1831	Bill passes Commons with a huge majority.
23 September	The Scottish measures passed.
8 October	The Bill thrown out by the Lords. Disturbances throughout the country.

Third Reform Bill

17 July 1832	Receives the Royal Assent.

THE CABINET

	In 1825	Apr. 1827	Sept. 1827	Jan. 1828	Nov. 1830
Prime Minister	Liverpool	Canning	Goderich	Wellington	Grey
Lord Chancellor	Eldon	Lyndhurst	Lyndhurst	Lyndhurst	Brougham
Chancellor of the Exchequer	Robinson[1]	Canning	Herries	Goulburn	Althorp
Home Secretary	Peel	Sturges Bourne[2]	Lansdowne	Peel	Melbourne
Foreign Secretary	Canning	Dudley	Dudley	Dudley[3]	Palmerston
Secretary for War and Colonies	Bathurst	Goderich[1]	Huskisson	Huskisson[3]	Goderich
President of the Board of Trade	Huskisson	Huskisson	Grant	Grant[3]	—
President of the Board of Control	Wynn	Wynn	Wynn	Melville	Grant
Master of the Mint	Maryborough	Tiernay	Tiernay	Herries	—
Master General of the Ordnance	Wellington	Anglesey	Anglesey	—	—
First Lord of the Admiralty	Melville	(Duke of Clarence, Lord High Admiral)			Graham
Secretary at War	—	Palmerston	Palmerston	Palmerston[4]	—
Chancellor of the Duchy of Lancaster	Bexley	Bexley	Bexley	Aberdeen	Holland

(Source: Sir Llewellyn Woodward's *Age of Reform*, 1938.)

1. Robinson was created Viscount Goderich in 1827.
2. Succeeded in July 1827 by Lansdowne.
3. In June 1828 Dudley, Huskisson, Grant, and Palmerston were
   replaced by Aberdeen, Murray, Vesey-Fitzgerald, and Hardinge
   respectively.

Dating

Dates, like grammar and the drier parts of genealogy, were details for which Scott showed a fine disregard. It is no surprise, therefore, to discover that a number of Entries bear the wrong date in the original. In this edition I have departed from the practice of previous editors, who copied Scott's dating even where it was incorrect, and have made the necessary alterations wherever there was sufficient evidence to establish the right date with reasonable certainty.

When Scott turned a page it was his custom to write the date again in the margin of the new leaf. Sometimes he would add a paragraph to an Entry later in the day. Frequently he was a day or two behind and wrote a number of Entries retrospectively. In these circumstances it is easy to see the kind of mistakes that could occur, and the wonder is only that a man who cared so little for dates should make as few errors as he did.

The principal Entries which have been redated in this edition are these:

(i) *The Entry for 7 January 1826*

The 7th was actually a Saturday, not a Sunday. Although it is usually easier to mistake a date rather than a day of the week, the Entries which follow confirm that Scott has written the wrong day but the correct date in this instance. We know that Mathews was expected 'on Monday' (*Letters*, ix. 365), and his arrival is duly noted on the 9th, which was a Monday. The Entry for the 8th therefore refers to Sunday, and that for the 7th to Saturday. The error is easily explained if Scott was making up his *Journal* a day later.

(ii) *The Entries for 5, 6, and 7 April 1826*

In the original (although not in previous editions of the *Journal*) the Entry for the 5th is misdated '4', because Scott, when writing the last date (from the page before) at the top of his new page, copied down '3' instead of '4' April. As the Entry for that date began only on the bottom line of the previous page, its date might well be covered by his finger as he turned the leaf. This mistake resulted in the wrong dating of three Entries. On the 8th he seems to have realized that there was an error somewhere, and he wrote in '7th' opposite the last paragraph of the previous day's Entry.

(iii) *The Entries for 23, 24, and 25 December 1826*

Scott dated the first of these Entries '24' and included both the other Entries in his account of the 25th. The date of what is here assigned to the 23rd is proved by the reference to the Court, which rose for its vacation on that Saturday. The next paragraph clearly refers to the first night at Abbotsford (the night of 23–4 December), which helps to date this and the following paragraph as the 24th. The next paragraph (where a change of ink is apparent) refers to Christmas Day and must therefore be the Entry for the 25th.

(iv) *The Entries for 30 and 31 December 1827*

Scott dates the last two Entries for the year '29' and '30', but since the first alludes to Sunday prayers and the second to welcoming in the New Year, there can be no doubt that they belong to the 30th and 31st.

(v) *The Entries between 29 May and 8 June 1829*

The dates assigned to these Entries in this edition follow neither the manuscript nor the dating of previous editors, but are based on internal evidence. What seems to have happened is this.

On turning the page after writing the first paragraph of the Entry for 28 May, Scott wrote the date in the margin at the top of the new page, as was his custom, but made the understandable error of writing the next date in the sequence instead of repeating '28'. As he did not notice his mistake, but continued to date each new Entry from the previous day's, all the Entries as far as 3 June are wrong by one day. On the 3rd (by Scott's dating, the 4th) he made a second mistake, writing '5' opposite the paragraph beginning 'Cadell came to dine', which actually seems to be an addition to his account of the day rather than a new Entry. The next two Entries are therefore wrong by two days. Scott dates them '6' and '7' but they actually belong to the 4th and 5th. The letters to Lockhart and Sir Thomas Lauder, which Scott said he wrote on these days, survive, and they are correctly dated '4 June' and '5 June'. There is further confirmation in the visit of the Lord President, who tells Scott not to come to Court the next day: this does not make sense if the next day is Monday (a blank day in the Court), but it is perfectly appropriate to the 5th. The next day's Entry is dated '8' by Scott, following his previous mistakes, but almost certainly refers to Saturday the 6th as it is dated in this edition. There is no Entry for Sunday the 7th. On the Monday he realizes that he has gone wrong, and without attempting to correct past mistakes writes '8' in the margin again, the correct date for that day.

(vi) *The Entries between 12 and 21 July 1829*

At some point Scott missed a day's Entry without noticing that this threw his dating into confusion. From internal evidence it seems that every Entry between 12 and 21 July is one day wrong in the manu-script, and in this edition the dates have been altered accordingly.

The fixed points are these. The 11th must be correct, as it is a Saturday, and the Court rose that day for the summer vacation. The Entry which Scott dated '18' must belong to the 19th, because its first words are 'A Sunday' and Sunday was the 19th. Similarly, the next Entry, which Scott dated '19', clearly refers to Monday the 20th, since the Hamiltons and Mrs. Hemans, who were invited 'to dinner on Monday', duly come to dinner. Between the 12th and the 18th, therefore, one day's Entry has been omitted. The strong presumption is that it is the Entry for the 12th. The Entry given in this edition under the 13th is dated '12' by Scott, but the 12th was a Sunday, and this does not look like the Entry typical of Sundays at Abbotsford: even Spanish visitors were unlikely to depart so far from the custom of the country as to 'drop in' on the day of rest. On the assumption that it belongs to Monday the 13th, it has been so dated in this edition, and the succeeding dates altered accordingly.

(vii) *The Entry for 18 January 1831*

Two successive Entries are dated '18' by Scott. The obvious solution – that he was making up the day missed on the 14th – cannot be correct, since the two Sundays on either side of the 18th are correctly dated '16' and '23'. There is simply one Entry too many for this week. Scott's state was such that on the 23rd he confessed that he had 'jumbled this and the preceding day strangely'. Something of the same sort may have happened here, and the two Entries for the 18th may merely be different versions of the same day's events.

(viii) *The Entry for 12 February 1831*

The evidence of Scott's letters at this time is that the Entries between 9 and 14 February are correctly dated. He did return to

Abbotsford on Wednesday the 9th (see *Letters*, xi. 467) and Anne did
leave for Edinburgh on Monday the 14th. The 12th, therefore, cannot
be Sunday as Scott says it is. Probably he was making up his *Journal*
on Sunday the 13th, and once more 'jumbled this and the preceding
day strangely', as he had done on 23 January.

(ix) *The Entries between 15 and 26 March 1831*

After the Entry for the 14th Scott skipped a date, and was one day
in advance (as have been previous editors of the *Journal*) for all the
Entries between 15 and 21 March. The correct dating is proved by the
references to the Reform meeting (dated '22' by Scott), which is
known to have taken place on Monday 21 March.

The next Entry ('The measure carried by a single vote') is dated
'23' by Scott, but certainly belongs to the 25th (as dated by Lockhart
in the *Life*). The vote on the Reform Bill was not taken until 4 a.m. on
the 23rd, and Alexander Pringle's letter announcing the defeat 'by a
majority of *one* – 302 to 301' (23 March 1831, Walpole) would arrive
at the earliest on the 25th. Scott probably made up his *Journal*
retrospectively, and put down the important news of the day first,
before turning his thoughts to Frank Grant's arrival the day before.
He had leisure to do so on the 25th, as Laidlaw 'was not able to come
down this morning' (25 January 1831, Cadell Letters).

(x) *The Entries between 14 and 17 May 1831*

Scott dated these Entries '14', '15', and '16–17'. The 13th is
certainly correctly dated, as a note from Dr. Mackay from Melrose
is dated 'Friday', but the reference to Sunday in the next Entry shows
that it must refer, at least in part, to the 15th. It seems probable that
this is a composite Entry covering both Saturday and Sunday.

(xi) *The Entries between 28 November and 25 December 1831*

The dating of these Entries is editorial, Scott's dates bearing no
relation either to the letter in the Abbotsford Collection written by
Anne to Sophia between 29 November[1] and 4 December, or to Mrs.
John Davy's Malta Journal, most of which is printed in *Life*, x. 132–
45. The matter is further complicated by Mrs. Davy's misdating of all
her Entries (the 5th for the 4th and so on).

The dates given here are conjectural, but are based on allusions in

---

1. She misdates it 'Tuesday 30 Decr.', but the 'Tuesday', and
   references to their very recent escape from quarantine, establish
   the 29th as the probable date.

the *Journal* Entries to events known to us, from other sources. The fixed points are:

that Scott was released from quarantine on 28 November, and dined that evening on board the *Barham* (Anne's letter);

that on the next Wednesday, that is, on the 30th, they were invited to dine with the Bathursts (ibid.);

that on Thursday, 1 December, a Ball was given in Scott's honour (ibid.);

that on the 3rd Dr. and Mrs. Davy, in company with some officers from the *Barham*, dined with Scott at Beverley's Hotel (Mrs. Davy's Journal);

that Sunday the 4th 'Sir Walter spent chiefly in St. John's Church, the beautiful temple and burial place of the knights, and there he was much pleased and interested' (ibid.);

that on the 5th he dined with the Stoddarts, where he may have heard of Sir John's daughter's approaching marriage (ibid.);

that on the 6th he was unwell (ibid.);

and that on the 9th he drove with Frere to Cittavecchia, and met Mrs. Davy and a friend at the church there (ibid.).

Silent Corrections

DATE OF ENTRY	CORRECTION	ORIGINAL
1825		
23 November	my previous	by previous
25	learn	learnd
	but a poor	put a poor
	Dined	Dind
30	though till	thought till
	twenty or thirty	twenty or twenty
1 December	number of burnings is	numbers of burnings is
	reasonably	reasonable
5	at present	at presence
7	from Sir John	for Sir John
10	his works	their works
	soul	sould
	and of perfect	of and perfect
14	whether it is	why it is
22	Can't say	Can't said
1826		
13 January	company	companion
19	see	seek
26	their *heaven*	his *heaven*
29	correspond	corresponds
6 February	repaid	repaind
13	by amateurs	be amateurs
	creature when	creature who
19	talk of	take of
2 March	change	changed

DATE OF ENTRY	CORRECTION	ORIGINAL
3 March	go out	got out
	give us	given us
	to break	to breaking
4	with it	without it
14	took a turn	took a turnd
21	appropinque	appropinquy
28	canvas	canval
4 April	As for	At for
7	gains	gainst
12	set	sets
26	pa[r]cel	pacels
	cabin[e]t	cabints
27	admiring	admired
29	earlier	early
2 May	hopes are	hopes is
7	ever after	every after
16	I am deprived	I may deprived
23	manner	matter
14 June	home from	home for
24	in quest of	in question of
8 July	brutal	brutally
13	happy that	happy at
	I leave	I leaves
	complain	complaint
15	have taken	having taken
28	and my hand	any my hand
1 August	than now	and now
22	departed	department
23	skirted	skirkted
28	Greece	Greeces
19 September	her neighbour	his neighbour
	trusted to	trusted too
	Yes	Yet
26	talking of	talking off
29	myself of	myself off
5 October	repining	repinind
16	objects of interest	objects of interesting
19	the English	the Italian
20	is fitter	it fitter
30	have them think	have think them
	their displeasure	my displeasure
4 November	many	manner

DATE OF ENTRY	CORRECTION	ORIGINAL
8 November	till next day	to next day
9	passage slow	passage slowly
16	my extracts	by extracts
18	[pat] of butter	of putter
1 December	Candle Light	Candle Night
11	Dined	Dind
	thy fame	the fame
12	Dined	Dind
15	went off	went of
17	labour	labourd
19	true	truet
30	whose	was
1827		
8 January	my interest	by interest
9	writer	writing
20	absolute	absolutely
24	never hear	never here
25	too	to
31	below	belong
3 February	lose	loss
5	much of	much off
6	consent	consend
8	made me	made be
15	though	thought
16	cribb off	crib of
20	crowd	crowded
3 March	sorry	sorrow
16	Afterwards it	Afterwards in
14 April	while	which
16	down	downs
13 May	I had written	a had written
18	any thing	any think
26	may say	say may
31	too little	two little
28 June	mistake	mistaken
18 July	reader	ready
19	I got	is got
8 August	company keeping	company keepind
10 September	ever	every
26	too large	two large
2 October	retarded	retarding

DATE OF ENTRY	CORRECTION	ORIGINAL
3 October	light which	light with
4	considerable	considerably
	gun	guns
7	by de Vesci	be de Vesci
27	away through	awake through
20 November	north east wind	north east what
10 December	to the Country	from the Country
20	sum	some
	forced	forces
28	succeeded	succeeding
1828		
11 January	said	say
16	makes me	makes be
23	than	that
30	70	£70
	100	£100
7 February	mute	mude
13	expects	excepts
17	resemble	resemblage
18	made a visit	met a visit
19	prisons would have	prisoners would have
	so the pack	to the pack
	class	clause
	ferment reek and	ferment and reek
21	hangs on me	hands on me
27	job and get	job ang get
29	It involved	In involved
5 March	if not most	if not post
	armour	armourd
9	most things	most thinks
18	sorely	solely
22	packet from	packet for
8 April	when you have seen	which you have seen
	than that	that that
	as four pound	at four pound
20	complete	completely
24	better than	better that
25	resolvd	reslovd
	we have had	we have heard
26	moderate sum	moderate some
3 May	would have expected	would not have expected

DATE OF ENTRY	CORRECTION	ORIGINAL
4 May	easy	ease
8	like to hear	like to heard
	asks me	asks be
	then the Editor	this the Editor
	is worth that	is not worth that
11	an handsome	and handsome
13	acquire	acquiring
14	any thing	any think
	who perplex	who do not perplex
19	name	mame
28	spot of the murder	spot of the murderer
17 June	stuff	stuffd
23	among trees	amond trees
27	passes	passing
29	the systems of	they systems of
	eating-houses are	eating-houses and
1829		
22 January	portrait	protrait
31	little done	littled done
6 February	tractable	tractably
13	ever heard	every heard
27	young lady	young lade
8 March	by a	bia
9	desire	desirous
	so well as usual	so well asual
13	is between	it between
18	misshapen	misshaken
	if you please	if you pleasing
	but they must	by they must
21	sister in law	sister in life
	purse	purpose
22	when iron	with iron
25	remember	remain
27	pestering me	pestering be
	observed	observing
	things	thinks
28	especial	especially
9 April	thing	think
15	seized me	seized be
17	huge	huse
22	little	litter
29	particular	particularly

DATE OF ENTRY	CORRECTION	ORIGINAL
13 June	strength	strengthen
	God	Gods
27	now cut up	not cut up
8 July	invited me	invited my
19	difficult	different
	kind of	king of
1830		
23 May	out of sight	ought of sight
14 June	possible	possibly
17	preventing	preventind
	ears	years
19	destined to be	destined to me
	too near	two near
	residence	resident
20	of mine	of mean
	interesting	interested
	ought to avoid	ould to avoid
	be much happier	me much happier
	declared	declined
22	safe	fafe
25	remember	remain
26	through	throuth
29	saw	say
1831		
6 January	burgh	burch
	tell me little	tell be little
7	remaining	retaining
26	medicine than	medicine that
30	me	be
31	is till Wednesday	it till Wednesday
	an apartment	at apartment
19 February	bolt	bold
7–10 March	general	generally
	stile	smile
	thinks	things
14	his fate	this fate
15	the pony	they pony
	a child	I child
17	supposing	suppose
19	letter too	letter two

DATE OF ENTRY	CORRECTION	ORIGINAL
25 March	amuse my lady	amuse by lady
	marry	memory
26	judge of painting	judging of painting
31	give it him	give at him
3 April	nothing to say	nothing to day
5	others	otherwise
6	more than half	more that half
10	of talent	off talent
	took leave	took leaving
12	too much space	two much space
19 May	leave enough	lead enough
Interval	help	helf
20 October	world	worldly
23	that is	that it
24	demands	depalnds
25	possibly	possible
26	too many	two many
11 November	If it	It it
12	probably	probable
14	gradual	dradual
	by them calld	by calld them
17	with terraced	which terraced
18	imputed	imputing
29	free from	from from
13–17 December	superbly	suprebly
13	old parts	old parst
1832		
6–12 January	I'll be bound	all be bound
16	answer	answerd
24	if this sam[e]	it this sam
	kind	King
March	defensible	defensibly
	with which	with with
	throw a most precious	through a most precious
15 April	bespeak	bespear

Memoranda

(These appear on the last two leaves of the second volume of the manuscript after two hundred and sixty-three blank leaves, and refer to 1828)

Memdm. to send Mrs. Fullarton a copy of 'Auld Robin Gray'. To send Drummond Hay a copy *Memorials of Haliburtons*.

1st April	Memordum Credit with Cadell		£500
	Draw on him for	£40	
	Sent him accounts for	300	
		———	340
		£ in cash 160 with Cadell	
	In English Notes & gold	250	
	Cash at Coutts	100	
	Don for Terry	50	
	Total Cash in hand	£560	
	Heath in London	300	
	Review probable	100	
		£960	
	Journey must be £200		
	Soph ——————— 100		
	Hutchinson & Lear		
	month ————— 200		
	Charge on Gas —— 100		
		650	
		£310	

Memorandum. Assessd Taxes in two months of £33. 3. 9 each are payable at 5 April and 10 October to George Scott without further intimation.[1]

Lee an[d] Coy to flowers £11. 7. 6.

1. A letter from Samuel Oliver, the Collector of Cess in
   Roxburghshire, proves that Scott paid taxes amounting to £33.
   4s. 9d. a half-year (6 April 1831, Walpole).

Index

Entries are alphabetical except that wives immediately follow their husbands.

A Scottish judge in the Court of Session takes the courtesy title of Lord. His wife, in Scott's day, remained Mrs.

Works by Scott appear under their individual titles.